HANDBOOK OF SPORTS AND MEDIA

LEA'S COMMUNICATION SERIES
Jennings Bryant/Dolf Zillmann, General Editors

HANDBOOK OF SPORTS AND MEDIA

Edited by

Arthur A. Raney
College of Communication
Florida State University

Jennings Bryant
College of Communication & Information Sciences
The University of Alabama

Routledge
Taylor & Francis Group
New York   London

Senior Acquisitions Editor: Linda Bathgate
Assistant Editor: Karin Wittig Bates
Cover Design: Tomai Maridou
Photo Credit: Mike Conway © 2006

This book was typeset in 10/12 pt. Cheltenham, Italic, Bold, and Bold Italic.
The heads were typeset in GillSans, Bold, Italics, and Bold Italics.

Routledge
Taylor & Francis Group
270 Madison Avenue
New York, NY 10016

Routledge
Taylor & Francis Group
2 Park Square
Milton Park, Abingdon
Oxon OX14 4RN

Library of Congress Cataloging-in-Publication Data
Handbook of sports and media / edited by Arthur A. Raney, Jennings Bryant.
    p. cm. – (LEA's communication series)
    Includes bibliographical references and index.
    ISBN 0-8058-5188-7 (casebound : alk. paper) — ISBN 0-8058-5189-5 (pbk. : alk. paper)
    1. Mass media and sports–Handbooks, manuals, etc. I. Raney, Arthur A.
II. Bryant, Jennings. III. Series.
    GV742.H35   2006
    070.4′49796—dc22   2006000395

Contents

Dedication

To our fathers:

Art dedicates this volume to Donald C. Raney, who shared his love of Caywood Ledford's voice over AM radio, his marvel at Ted Williams' vision, his tickets to see Bear Bryant's 315th victory, and his undying love, support, and encouragement. Thanks, Coach.

Jennings dedicates this volume to Jennings F. Bryant, Sr., who spent untold hours with his less athletically gifted son, trying to teach me to master the basic skills of almost any sport or game that can be played with a ball. Although you never managed to teach me your 90-mph fastball, your awesome 3-point shot, your 300-yard drive, or any other facet of your incredible athletic repertoire, what you did teach me in those thousands of hours of loving tutelage has made me a much better person and father. Thank you.

Preface

On Friday, June 7, 2002, London stood still. England's industrial sector screeched to a halt earlier in the day as nearly 20% of the workforce—about 6 million workers—called in sick. No doubt, many had visited the special Web site providing excuses to offer employers for just this occasion ("England grinds to a halt," 2002). Just after noon, the eyes of the nation turned to the thousands of large-screen televisions that had been placed in pubs, theaters, city squares, offices, factories, supermarkets, and churches. No, this was not another Windsor wedding, though the participants were treated like royalty: England's national team was facing rival Argentina in the first round of the 2002 FIFA World Cup. The anxious throngs were not to be disappointed as England's David ("Bend it Like") Beckham's penalty shot in the 44th minute found the back of the net for the game's only score.

Soccer (or *football* to our friends outside the United States) may be the world's most popular sport, but it definitely is not the only one that draws television viewers. Four of the ten most watched shows in U.S. television history have been Super Bowls; a fifth was the 1994 showdown on Olympic ice between Nancy Kerrigan and Tonya Harding. It is hardly breaking news that sporting events draw spectators, viewers, listeners, and readers by the billions. The importance of sports on the contemporary global entertainment landscape is undeniable. This importance is in large part due to the ever-evolving relationship between sports and media—a relationship appropriately characterized as win-win-win for media outlets, sports leagues, and fans alike.

It probably comes as little surprise that the formal study of sports and media boasts a rich and intellectually diverse tradition. However, despite two noteworthy exceptions—Larry Wenner's seminal anthology *Media, Sports, and Society* (1989) and his follow-up *MediaSport* (2002)—few have attempted to fashion a sports–media collage using the full pallet of colors offered in the extant eclectic literature, perhaps out of fear that the various intellectual traditions represented therein might clash. Yet with the recent advances in media technology ushering in an Entertainment Society saturated with sports offerings, the time for such a project is now. *Handbook of Sports and Media* represents our best effort to provide such a picture.

From the outset of the project, the two of us committed to drawing together the leading lights from disciplines such as communication, media studies, sports management and studies, kinesiology, psychology, sociology, and history. Our goal was to identify and synthesize the research into the numerous facets of the sports–media relationship. We sought to privilege no single perspective: present, past, and future; U.S. and international; mainstream and alternative press; team and individual sports; print and electronic media; empirical and critical scholarship. They are all here. While we do not claim to offer the reader a *comprehensive* volume, we hope that you will agree that we have come pretty close.

THE DEVELOPMENT OF SPORTS MEDIA

We have organized *Handbook of Sports and Media* around four major themes: history, industry, audiences, and critical issues. The first section, "The Development of Sports Media," contains three outstanding chapters. In the first, "Sports and Media in the Ancient Mediterranean," classicist Thomas Scanlon details the earliest representations of sports in the "media" forms of the early Egyptian, Greek, and Roman (to name a few) civilizations.

Jennings Bryant and Andrea Holt detail the rise and development of sports media in the United States from colonial America to today. In "A Historical Overview of Sports and Media in the United States," the authors—examining media forms (e.g., newspapers, magazines, television), content providers and vehicles (e.g., ESPN, *The Sporting News,The Wild World of Sports*), and pioneering figures (e.g., Grantland Rice, Roone Arledge, Frank Deford)—chronicle the evolution of the sports–media relationship in the country where many of the preeminent sports communication developments have occurred.

Lawrence Wenner, in his chapter "Sports and Media Through the Super Glass Mirror: Placing Blame, Breast-Beating, and a Gaze to the Future," cleverly views Janet Jackson's Super Bowl halftime show scandal through the interpretive lens he has shaped during the past 20 years of examining sports and media. The result is a detailed elucidation of the key issues sure to confront sports media scholars in the future.

THE COVERAGE AND BUSINESS OF SPORTS MEDIA

The 15-chapter second section begins with an overview of the current business of mediated sports coverage. In "Sports Media: A Modern Institution," Rob Bellamy explores the essential characteristics of mediated sports that have made the industry the cultural and institutional force that it is today. Dan Brown and Jennings Bryant's chapter titled "Sports Content on U.S. Television" serves as a cogent companion piece, providing myriad examples (both general and specific) of those characteristics from across the sports television landscape in the United States.

Television, of course, is not the only place one finds sports and sports-related programming. Newspapers and magazines boast a rich history of sports coverage; Wayne Wanta explores the quantity and quality of current print coverage in his chapter "The Coverage of Sports in Print Media." Similarly, sport's relationship with radio dates back to the earliest days of commercial broadcasting. John Owens' "The Coverage of Sports on Radio" offers both a narrative of sports radio's history—from KDKA's airing of prize fights in the 1920s to XM Satellite's latest MLB deal—and an updated overview of the scholarly investigations into that history.

"Broadcast Television and the Game of Packaging Sports," authored by David Sullivan, investigates the ways in which the medium has expanded spectator access to events and athletes, strengthened the reach of leagues, magnified the perceived importance of sports across the globe, and elevated the modern athlete to the level of international celebrity and star. Chris Wood and Vince Benigni illuminate the role of cable television in this process as well, demonstrating the impact of the latter on the former. In their chapter "The Coverage of Sports on Cable TV," the authors investigate the past and speculate on the future of cable networks such as ESPN and Fox Sports Net as they transform what and how sports are covered around the world.

Also transforming the sports–media relationship are the internet and World Wide Web, which offer around-the-clock webcasts, online gambling sites, and sports blogs. Michael Real offers in "Sports Online: The Newest Player in Mediasport" a comprehensive analysis of the impact of these new media technologies on the sports media industry and its fans.

Three specific "cases" of sports media coverage are next explored. Glenn Cummins examines the various ways that sports have been used as the vehicle for other forms of narrative entertainment in his chapter "Sports Fiction." Helen Jefferson Lenskyj investigates the at-times contentious relationship between the mainstream and alternative media during the 2000 Olympic Games in Sydney, Australia, in her chapter "Alternative Media versus The Olympic Industry." And Andrew Tudor, in "World Cup Worlds: Media Coverage of the Soccer World Cup 1974 to 2002," offers insight into the systems of discourse used to (often stereotypically) represent nations, athletes, teams, and citizens during the past three decades of World Cup media coverage.

Much has been previously written about the ways that women and men are differentially covered and represented in sports media. Margaret Duncan plumbs the depths of this topic in her chapter titled "Gender Warriors in Sport: Women and the Media," examining issues of gender, class, race, and sexuality in the production, coverage, and reporting of sports by various print and electronic media outlets.

The final four chapters in the section explore various business aspects of the sports–media relationship. First, in "Utilizing Televised Sports to Benefit Prime-Time Lineups: Examining the Effectiveness of Sports Promotion," Andrew Billings summarizes the importance of sports in the overall promotional efforts of television networks, providing evidence of this importance from a host of scholarly studies into sports promotion effectiveness. Marc Krein and Sheree Martin open the doors of the television production truck and describe the current state of the art of sports production in their chapter "60 Seconds to Air: Television Sports Production Basics and Research Review." The authors also provide an overview of the existing scholarly literature on sports production effects. Next, in his chapter "Sports Economics and the Media," Mike Mondello offers assistance in navigating the multibillion dollar world of television licensing rights with the NFL, MLB, NBA, and NHL, along with examining the role that other professional sports leagues, intercollegiate athletics, and various international sporting events play in the sports–media economy. On center stage in Mondello's analysis is the financial marriage between sports and television. Finally, the corporate sponsorship of sports and sporting events adds another layer of complexity to the sports–media industry. Lance Kinney, in the chapter "Sports Sponsorship," describes this practice (and its pitfalls) and reviews the current literature on the potential impacts of sports sponsorship on audience members.

SPORTS MEDIA AUDIENCES

The third section of the volume is dedicated to all of us who help elevate and illustrate the power of sports in modern media culture: the fans. Seven chapters are included in the section "Sports Media Audiences," all of which are dedicated to an essential feature of or experience within sports fan culture. In the first chapter, Art Raney investigates "Why We Watch and Enjoy Mediated Sports." He uses a media-entertainment theory perspective to explore the motivations for, as well as the cognitive, emotional, and social reactions to, consuming sports in the media.

As Raney illustrates in his chapter, fan allegiance to teams and athletes drives the enjoyment of mediated sports. Psychologist Daniel Wann explores this relationship in much more detail in his chapter "The Causes and Consequences of Sport Team Identification." Specifically, Wann explicates the concept known as team identification, as well as explores the potential behavioral, affective, and psychological consequences of team identification.

For decades questions concerning the negative impacts of media violence have dominated social conversations about media effects. Sports in the media have not escaped this line of questioning. Barrie Gunter provides a detailed and updated glimpse into this complex area of study and debate in his chapter "Sports, Violence, and the Media." Specific to the sports media–violence debate has been the charge that sports viewing leads to problems within the family, in particular that sports can foster an environment that is more conducive to domestic violence. Walter Gantz, Samuel D. Bradley, and Zheng Wang, in their chapter "Televised NFL Games, the Family, and Domestic Violence," shed further light on this issue by presenting original research from a season's worth of televised NFL games in 15 U.S. cities.

In chapter 10, Michael Real identifies various ways that new media technologies have changed the sports–media relationship from the standpoint of the media. The final three chapters of this section are dedicated to exploring ways that these new technologies are transforming the relationships audiences have with the sports they love and with the media outlets that bring the games to them. First, Richard Lomax introduces the reader to the world of fantasy sports. In his chapter "Fantasy Sports: History, Game Types, and Research," Lomax illuminates the surprisingly long and rich history of these activities, as well as examines how this multimillion dollar cottage industry is impacting the ways that audiences relate to sports.

Another booming new tech industry is, of course, video games, and as author David Leonard reports, "The sports gaming industry is the crown jewel of the video games world...account[ing] for more than 30% of all video game sales." In "An Untapped Field: Exploring the World of Virtual Sports Gaming," Leonard investigates the social, cultural, and economic meaning of these heretofore mostly ignored set of games. Finally, Joe Mahan and Steve McDaniel discuss the ways that internet technologies have radically changed the mediated sports production complex as described previously by Wenner (1989). Specifically, in "The New Online Arena: Sport, Marketing, and Media Converge in Cyberspace," the authors explore the cyberbranding practices of professional and amateur sports leagues, teams, and athletes, along with the ways that sports fans are using new technologies to enhance their fan experiences.

CRITICAL PERSPECTIVES ON SPORTS MEDIA: CASES AND ISSUES

The final section of *Handbook of Sports and Media* contains nine chapters that summarize and critically engage some of the most controversial and important topics in the field. The first essay in the section is Joseph Maguire's "Sport and

Globalization: Key Issues, Phases, and Trends." While grappling with issues of both globalization and sports, Maguire illuminates various structured processes that characterize the development, flow, and experience of global sports and provides a sobering analysis of the nexus of transnational corporations involved in the sports–media complex, environmental exploitation, and the vanishing of local cultures.

In "Sport, the Media, and the Construction of Race," Andrew Grainger, Joshua Newman, and David Andrews offer one of the most comprehensive examinations to date of the complicated interactions between sport, media, and race. Focusing primarily on the ways that African-American male athletes have been represented in print and electronic media, the authors deftly discuss the myths of racial meritocracy, natural physicality, and transcendence that are perpetuated by media stereotyping in sports coverage, as well as issues of the commodification and marginalization of Blackness. As somewhat of a companion piece, Davis Houck chronicles the media-representation narrative of PGA megastar Tiger Woods in "Crouching Tiger, Hidden Blackness: Tiger Woods and the Disappearance of Race." The essay weaves autobiography with critical analysis to illustrate the personal and global dimensions of the phenomenon that is Tiger (and Earl) Woods.

Whereas Duncan in chapter 14 provides an overview of the broad issues wrapped up in the media representations of gender in sports coverage, Daniela Baroffio-Bota and Sarah Banet-Weiser take up the specific case of gender (and race) representations in mediated team sports. In "Women, Team Sports, and the WNBA: Playing Like a Girl," the authors primarily use WNBA coverage to illustrate the ways that media provide a framework of meaning around the biological difference between females and males, but in doing so seem to accentuate particular differences as important and in support of racist and sexist ideologies.

In "Thinking Through Power in Sport and Sport Media Scholarship," Mary McDonald provides an extensive summary of the major ways that issues of power have been imagined with the realm of sports and media. In doing so, she articulates both the strength and the limitations of envisioning these relationships strictly from a Foucauldian perspective (as has much of the existing literature), pointing to the promise of recent postcolonial writings by Perez, Jamieson, and Abded-Shehid in further understanding issues of power, sports, and media.

In his second *Handbook* chapter, "A World of Criminals or Media Construction?: Race, Gender, Celebrity, and the Athlete/Criminal Discourse," David Leonard examines the complex relationships between the representation of race, celebrity, and crime in sports coverage. "Sporting Bodies" is Davis Houck's second essay as well. In it, Houck explores the various ways that sport is bound up in the body, including sexuality, physicality, race, muscularity, and mortality.

Four scholars—C. Richard King, Laurel Davis-Delano, Ellen Staurowsky, and Lawrence Baca—collaborate to examine the relationship between media coverage of Native American sports mascots and public opinion. In "Sports Mascots and the Media," the authors explore issues of media production, texts, consumption, and social context as they discuss this perpetually controversial issue.

In the final chapter in the volume, Marie Hardin introduces the reader to the often overlooked issues surrounding media coverage of events featuring disabled athletes. "Disability and Sport: (Non)Coverage of an Athletic Paradox" challenges prevailing cultural hegemonic forces within the media industries to engage, embrace, and promote the legitimacy of disabled athletes and the sports they play.

FINAL THOUGHTS

Adopting the sports adage—There is no I in TEAM—we readily admit the role of so many others in the compilation of this volume. We thank each of our talented collaborators whose collected contributions to the area of sports and media over the years have been tremendous. We are honored that you have joined us in this effort. We are also grateful to the universities that provide the support and freedom for all of us to participate in the larger academic conversations.

While Jennings has worked with the wonderful people at Lawrence Erlbaum Associates, Publishers, for a number of years, this was Art's first direct experience with them. The chance to collaborate with you (again) has been a pleasure. To Linda Bathgate, your guidance, encouragement, and support in this venture were invaluable. To the other members of the Erlbaum team, like Karin Wittig Bates, who have been involved in the various aspects of the project, we say "Thank you." Also, thanks to Art's research assistant Lindsay Carlson for her keen editorial eye on early drafts of all 34 of the chapters.

To all of the students of sports and media, we celebrate and encourage your intellectual pursuits. Our hope is that this volume can help serve as a block upon which you build the future of the field.

Art also wishes to thank his children, Austin and Reed, for their spirits of play and wonder that help him feel young and bring him endless joy, and, most of all, he thanks his wife and life-companion, Laura, whose love, patience, support, and encouragement make his life abundantly and undeservingly rich. Jennings wants to thank his offspring team of Alison, Todd, and Adrienne for allowing him to pitch whenever we play baseball or softball. And to Sara, his wife and best friend of 37 years, thanks for so willingly suspending disbelief and allowing me to joyously watch all those many hours of televised sports in the at-least-partially false name of scholarship.

Again, it has been our great pleasure to work with and learn from our generous collaborators who represent many universities, countries, and intellectual perspectives. It is with considerable pride that we offer this collection of their genius to you.

—Arthur A. Raney
—Jennings Bryant

REFERENCES

England grinds to a halt [Electronic version]. (2002, June 7). *The Gazette (Montreal)*, p. F2. Retrieved April 21, 2005, from http://web.lexis-nexis.com

Wenner, L. A. (Ed.). (1989). *Media, sports, and society*. Newbury Park, CA: Sage.

Wenner, L. A. (Ed.). (2002). *MediaSport*. London: Routledge.

HANDBOOK OF SPORTS
AND MEDIA

THE DEVELOPMENT
OF SPORTS MEDIA

1

Sports and Media
in the Ancient Mediterranean

Thomas F. Scanlon
University of California, Riverside

Media (plural of medium) can be understood in the dictionary sense of "a means of mass communication, such as newspapers, magazines, or television." Of course, the ancient Mediterranean world had none of these modern media. How can one translate modern mass communication forms of media, and the industry, institutions, and audience around them, into equivalent ancient social and cultural forms?

The ancient equivalent of our media were any broad public forms of communication, including the publicly performed Homeric epics or odes of Pindar, the published writings of Plato, monumental inscriptions and statues honoring victors, graffiti by gladiator fans, and countless showy gimmicks like elaborate starting gates designed to promote the popularity of events. Arguably all media are forms of rhetoric, that ancient science of civic conversation, normally limited to the art or science of effective speech and writing to inform or persuade. Homer, Pindar, and Plato are included in the ancient sense. By extension into modern cultural analysis, the rhetoric of mass media can apply to nonverbal communication, arguably also comprising visual and performing arts, which would include monuments and sideshow events for sports. Thus understood, the area of study becomes so broad and inclusive that a discrete study is impossible. All outward appearances of sports, for instance, can be called "media" in the semiotic sense of means of communicating by symbolic referents in the costume and accoutrements of athletes, in the architecture of the sports venues, in the non-sporting aspects of sports festivals such as cultural or religious sideshows, etc. Where can one draw the line?

Here we limit the question by locating the ancient equivalent of modern media in the following two areas:

- sports-associated written texts including literature (Homer, Pindar, et al.) and inscriptions (victor inscriptions, rules relating to gymnasia, etc.)

- sports-related art and architecture, primarily vase painting and sculpture and the actual sporting structures

We will discuss what the media are, as defined above, and briefly how these media were supported by social institutions and how they communicated to their contemporary audience. We will proceed chronologically, from about 2600 B.C. to A.D. 400, starting with Egyptian and Near Eastern civilizations, then Minoan Greece, Mycenaean Greece, Homer, the sixth century B.C. revolution in sports with gymnasia and new festivals, Pindar and Plato, the fourth century expansion of stadia size, Roman spectacles and chariot races, the spread of Roman amphitheaters, and Roman art and sports.

Almost every society has adopted or created a number of leisure activities, playful competitions that are most commonly today assigned the name "sports," with appropriate linguistic variants in other languages (Guttmann, 1978; Sansone, 1988). Yet the cross-cultural term obscures or obliterates many important distinctions between the ways in which these activities function within their own cultural context. The precise events and rules vary; even phenomena that bear a formal resemblance to one another may function in radically different ways from culture to culture. In short, each society invests its sporting activities with a particular set of cultural values that are preserved in and transmitted by those practices. While the modern term *sport* gives a false sense of the fixed categorization of certain kinds of activity, it also forestalls the better understanding of those activities free of anachronistic prejudice. The *sport* of any one society can be understood only to the extent that the values, implicit or explicit, of such activity can be understood in their own proper and total historical and social context.

So the concept shifts within each culture, often represented by one or several words comparable with our term for sports: In Greece there are *agōnes* and *aethla* (contests); in Rome there are *ludi* and *munera* (games, shows); the Sumerians had *lirùm* (athletics); and Egyptians had the term *swtwt* (sports). Each culture's own concepts and to some extent each people's own nomenclature for their competitive physical leisure activities aid in our selection of what to include in this overview. Our boundaries must be flexible from culture to culture and sensitive to each culture's own definitions so as to understand the diverse phenomena in their context.

The present object is to explain how in each time and place the sports of that era were publicly represented over the millennia. The exact form of media used, the expense given to the media presentation, the nature of the target audience for the media, the breadth of the 'broadcast,' and other information will indicate the role that sports played in that culture, be it entertainment, political power, social status, religious authority, etc. In the end, the co-existence of sports with public media for thousands of years is not in itself remarkable. A public contest must be announced and the victors given their honor. Rather, what is remarkable is the rich variety across ancient cultures and the continuity of social and political aims. Media are used as a tool that is a direct reflection of socio-political realities in the culture in question. To understand the relation of sport to media, one must, for any culture, read backwards from the greater historical context into the specific instance of public representation. In the case of sports and media, the appreciation of cultural context will, in turn, illustrate how the use of media changes from a reinforcement of social hierarchy to a force to democratize to a tool for repressing competitors of lowly stature, such as gladiators. Media are not the message, but they are fundamental aspects of the message.

EGYPTIAN AND NEAR EASTERN SPORTS

Ancient Egyptian civilization spanned three millennia, from about 2950 B.C. to 30 B.C., namely from the Archaic Period, to the Old, Middle, and New Kingdoms and the Later Period, after which it fell under Roman rule. It is a cliché, though essentially accurate, that the pharaoh was synonymous with order, prosperity, and power within the ancient Egyptian world. His welfare was, as with many ancient kingships, synonymous with that of the state, and it would be unthinkable to allow him to suffer defeat in a sporting competition. The king must have no rivals.

It comes then as no surprise that the power of the pharaoh was demonstrated for three millennia in the public performance of a run performed solo during the jubilee celebration. The celebration, also known as the Festival of Sed, the Festival of Renewal, and the Ritual of Renewal, in Egyptian *hb-sd*, took place on the thirtieth anniversary of the ruler's reign and effected his regeneration and renewal, despite the advancement of years. The deities, accouterments, and contextual inscriptions for the festival vary with different rulers. The run itself, oriented exactly on a north-south axis in its one extant track at the site of Saqqara (ca. 2640–2475 B.C.), is perhaps more a symbolic striding the length of the north-south oriented Land of the Nile, and the two sets of semicircular turning posts may symbolize the hemispheres of the earth (Decker, 1992). Several inscriptions and relief sculptures depict the running king in an event that is properly a ritual, not sport, because it was a bald demonstration of physical strength. The royal run may be taken as a prominent instance of the political appropriation of sports, but it is in itself not sports. The iconography bears out this interpretation in consideration of the position of the legs and of the supposed racetrack.

Allegedly incredible displays of strength and skill in archery were another medium by which the pharaoh demonstrated to the people his natural superiority. These were also depicted in public monuments with hieroglyphic inscriptions and relief depictions of the ruler shooting through copper plates of several inches thickness. Once again, the images of strength are exploited to reinforce pharaonic omnipotence.

We move now to the realm of more properly competitive Egyptian sports in which the non-elite participated, most prominently that of wrestling. The visual representations of wrestlers span two thousand years, from the early third millennium until the late second millennium B.C. They are done as relief sculptures, statuettes, temple decorations, tomb paintings, and crude sketches on potshards. Not surprisingly, the peaks of popularity of the images coincide with the economic prosperity of the Middle and New Kingdoms, presumably because the economy allowed more stability. Some relief sculptures illustrate wrestlers performing before the king, a show that underlines the king's patronage and ultimate social authority (Decker & Herb, 1994).

Sumerian civilization had its beginnings in the southern Mesopotamian plain in the fifth millennium B.C. It was later conquered and ruled by Sargon of Agade (2371–2316 B.C.), the first recorded emperor in history and founder of the "first Empire" of Sumer. Sumer lasted as a significant power until the end of the Third Dynasty of Ur (2212–2004 B.C.), a cultural and administrative high point whose achievements included brilliant temple architecture and the earliest version of the *Epic of Gilgamesh*. Shulgi, one of this dynasty's kings, boasted of his own athletic skills, including wrestling, and may have actually promoted the writing of epics about Gilgamesh in part to underline his divine ancestral ties (Kovaks, 1989, p. xxiii).

Gilgamesh's legend includes a famous scene in which Enkidu, the "man of nature" sent by the gods to curb Gilgamesh's tyranny, stands in the path of the hero and wrestles him.

The high culture of Sumer's Third Dynasty was the most important period of Sumerian sports and arguably the historical genesis for sports highlighted with civic importance. At this time wrestling, boxing, and the footrace are first evidenced in the contexts of formal public occasions (Rollinger, 1994). Shulgi was the second emperor of the Neo-Sumerian empire of the Ur-III period (2112–2004 B.C.) and a self-proclaimed successful sportsman (Vermaak, 1993). Most famously Shulgi claims to have run from Nippur to Ur and back in one day. The "King of the Road" boasts of his cross-country achievements in an extensive hymn: "I stretched my legs, crossing along the roads of the land." By implication, his course is co-extensive with his kingdom, and mention of the roads underlines the order and prosperity of the realm. Significantly, the run is not a race, but part of the leading procession of the festival celebrations, much like the Egyptian pharaoh's run at Saqqara. Hence Shulgi's achievement is a ritual and symbolic act asserting the monarch's primacy.

Gilgamesh and Shulgi therefore illustrate how the royal hierarchy of Sumerian civilization is validated and upheld by the use of media. The publicly recited text of the culture's major heroic epic ennobles wrestling as a royal sport. Shulgi's promotion of the epic and his special adoption of sporting skills shrewdly tie the king to the hero through athletic prowess. But this instance of a kingly sportsman is, so far as we know, the only one in ancient Sumeria, and we must assume that only here were sports promoted as the validation for rule.

In the second millennium, Mesopotamia was dominated no longer by the earlier Sumerian and Akkadian powers, but alternately by Assyrians in the North and Babylonians in the South. Most famously, Hammurapi (ruled ca. 1792–1750 B.C.) consolidated Mesopotamian rule in an empire administered from his capital in Babylon. Though this empire soon diminished under Hamurrapi's successors, the Babylonians excelled in cultural and intellectual achievements, including literature, astronomy, and mathematics between 1800 and 1600 B.C. The cylinders, which seem to have been worn as magical amulets, depict wrestling, armed combat with daggers or swords, and boxing. Despite the lack of written texts that so enlighten the Sumerian case of the late third millennium, the cylinder stones provide a tantalizing glimpse into sports in the Yamhad kingdom of ancient Syria in the 1600s B.C. Near Eastern sports were far from homogenous among near neighbors over this span of time. We know of no single political figure like the Sumerian King Shulgi, who exploited sports to the fullest for Ur. The relative size of the Syrian wrestling images suggests that the performances did not have the central importance that they had in the Third Dynasty of Sumer. On the other hand, the Syrians, like the Sumerians and the Egyptians, evidence a few instances of boxing, though none of those cultures were boxing fanatics. The contexts of the Sumerian images give hints that the sports took place at least sometimes in cult festivals, and on occasion with royal on-lookers. It may be the fault of a paucity of evidence, but the Syrian contests and their participants appear not to have enjoyed the same high political and religious honor as did their Sumerian counterparts. The 1600s B.C. constituted a Dark Age in the entire Near East after the collapse of the First Dynasty of Babylon engineered by Hamurrapi and the raid of the Hittite ruler Murshili (ca. 1620–1595 B.C.) (Rollinger, 1994).

From Sumer and Syria we move a bit later and northward to the civilization of the Hittites. The Hittite peoples spoke a form of Indo-European language and flourished in Asia Minor regions of central Anatolia and northern Syria from about 1800 to 1200 B.C. During these six centuries, the government was centralized around a series of monarchs from about 1650 B.C. on; and their capital was at Hattusas, near modern Boghazkoy in central Turkey. From the fifteenth to mid-fourteenth centuries B.C., they had particular conflicts with the neighboring Hurrians and may have come into contact with Mycenaean Greeks, whom they refer to as the Ahhijawa (Achaeans?). The Hittites and Egyptians stood as the two dominant powers of the Near East during the thirteenth century.

The Hittite texts from the second millennium B.C. document virtually all of the athletic contests described in Homer: footraces, archery, armed combat, weight throwing, boxing, and wrestling. Hittite chariot racing and javelin throwing are not attested as competitive events, though the culture widely used spears and chariots, particularly in military contexts. A footrace described as the "earliest mention of an *agon* in cuneiform literature" is staged before the Hittite king during a spring ritual called the Antahsum festival in Hattusas (Puhvel, 2004, p. 27). The king's bodyguards are the runners, and the victor is given a traditionally honorific title, "he of the ass-bridle." The king watches the event from the platform of his royal chariot. The presence of the king as a VIP spectator and the designation of his bodyguards as the sole contestants put sports again in the royal orbit, but unlike the Sumerian Shulgi, the Hittite king did not exploit the sporting associations for political capital (Puhvel, 1988).

The Hittite texts, like those of other Near Eastern cultures, are in the form of clay tablets and are meant to memorialize and preserve activities and events with special religious, political, or commercial importance. The circulation of these texts was probably limited, more for the perusal of high officials, priests, and wealthy traders than for the public display of the king's patronage of festivals. In our discussion of sports and media, the Hittite tablets reveal that the rulers were apparently not eager to portray themselves as sportsmen; rather, the festivals themselves, as described in the tablets, were a performance medium of splendid ritual in which the king stood as patron of his people and host of the games. The propaganda value of those festivals is the most noteworthy aspect of media.

MINOAN AND MYCENAEAN GREECE

The odd sport of bull leaping may have originated in the Near East (perhaps as acrobatic display or religious ritual) and spread to Minoan Crete, to judge from Near Eastern decorative cylinder stones showing bull leaping and dating as early as the earliest Cretan bull-leaping depictions (Sipahi, 2001). This fact reminds us of the commonality of bull sports in the eastern Mediterranean in the Bronze Age. There are also large bull-leaping frescoes in the palace at Knossos. But the lack of monumental civic media publicizing the sport also suggests that these events never sought or obtained the popularity that Greek and Roman sports did in later centuries.

Minoan civilization reached its cultural and political zenith during the second palace period, circa 1600 to 1450 B.C., and Cretan artistic representations of bull leaping fall mostly within that period. Based upon the study by John Younger (1976), current chronology suggests that the earliest Cretan seals are not later than 1700 to 1600 B.C. (Middle Minoan III) and the latest is circa 1300 B.C. (Late Minoan III B:1). Younger concludes that "bull leaping discontinued perhaps at the close of

Late Bronze Age III A or early in the Late Bronze Age III B period after which the leapers are depicted in the floating pose which is not directly copied from the sport". Minoan art of that period also tells us that women, distinguished by their white skin in the frescoes, were among the participants in the bull-leaping events. This was, so far as we know, the only "sport" in which Minoan women participated; boxing and possibly wrestling and armed combat were practiced, but only by Minoan men. Bull leaping can more probably be described as an athletic event and not merely entertaining acrobatics since it is represented together with scenes of other competitive athletics on the famous Hagia Triada rhyton vase (Stone rhyton from Hagia Triada, now in National Museum, Herakleion, Inv. no. 342.498.676, dated 1550–1500 B.C.). The rhyton itself may have been used in later Greek culture as a vessel for pouring libations. So the medium here appears to be a sacred vessel, perhaps used in festivals or funerals. The events themselves may have been rites of passage for native Cretan youths, and the religious aspect is reinforced by the medium of the vase (Scanlon, 1999).

The Mycenaean or "Late Helladic" Period of Greek History, about 1600 to 1100 B.C., shows few surviving remnants of sports contests publicized as we have seen in the Near East in texts or art (Mouratidis, 1989). One exception is a ceramic *larnax* or sarcophagus from about 1200 B.C. found in Tanagra, Central Greece, on which are painted scenes of bull leaping on one side, and men in an armed duel on the other (Decker, 1982–83). The common scholarly assumption, and the best guess to date, is that these represent funeral games performed for the person buried in the larnax. This is the fullest sports narrative from the Mycenaean period, and it tells us that the Minoan and Near Eastern bull sports were probably still practiced centuries later on the Greek mainland. The larnax also tells us that bull games happened in the context of another contest strange to later Greece, namely the armed duel of contemporary warriors. The Tanagra piece is a rare but telling piece. It suggests that the local Greek elite from this period appropriated the traditions of the Near Eastern and Minoan kings in order to evoke their regal splendor, even though the Greek lords' power and domain were much more limited. The Mycenaeans probably adapted bull contests to their own practice of funeral games, including other athletic contests known from historical times. The larnax is also a virtual missing link, archeologically, between the earlier Bronze Age regal sports and, after a historical gap in our records, the later Archaic Age (about 800 to 500 B.C.) when Homeric epics allude to legendary funeral games played by the Greek heroes of the Trojan War.

HOMERIC SPORTS AND THE EARLY OLYMPICS

During the so-called Dark Ages of Greece, from about 1100 B.C. to 750 B.C., culture receded, writing systems vanished, art was virtually absent, and the economy went into evident collapse. Many kings ruled small regions of the mainland and islands while their citizens subsisted on modest farming, husbandry, and fishing. Thus "media" were at a minimum, until the advent of an economic and cultural renaissance marking the Archaic Period, 800 to 500 B.C.

Did Homeric and heroic poetry in some sense create the ancient Olympics? Did those well-known media validate and fuel a broader popularity of the festival? Homeric epics are of course the earliest literary testimony for any Greek sports, most prominently the funeral games for Patroclus in *Iliad* 23 and the "after-dinner games" at Phaeacia in *Odyssey* 8. The most widely used traditional date for the founding of the first Olympics is 776 B.C., the date given in the Olympic victor list of Hippias of Elis composed about 400 B.C. The 776 foundation has long been disputed, but here we accept that the games likely began in or about 776 B.C., mainly for reasons of archeological evidence (Lee, 2004). This date falls just before the traditional dates of 750 to 725 for the composition of the two great Homeric epics. Again, with Homer's texts, the dates of inception are disputed. Undoubtedly, parts of the *Iliad* and *Odyssey* retain passages that reflect historical Bronze Age society and poetry, and oral versions with some greater poetic synthesis of extant myths existed since at least the eighth century. This study follows in general the evolutionary model of the Harvard scholar Gregory Nagy for the formative stage of diffusion in the second half of the eighth century and a more definitive stage in the middle of the sixth, when Panathenaic recitations began under the regime of the Peisistratids (Nagy, 1996). The text as we have it is the product of centuries of fluidity, with some orthodoxy of general episodes during the performances in Athens during their Panathenaic festival, standardizing the text from the late fourth to mid-second century B.C., then relative rigidity from that point on.

In sum, then, the traditional Olympic founding date of 776 precedes the possession of an authoritative and canonical text of the Homeric epics. The two epics do not, moreover, explicitly mention the Olympics, nor do the Olympics foundation stories in turn evidence explicit connections with heroic narratives of the eighth or seventh centuries B.C. Despite these difficulties and the apparent fluidity of the epic media, the broader heroic ethos incorporated in eighth to sixth century Greek culture was a crucial and arguably essential catalyst for establishment of the Olympics and the other Panhellenic games. Although the Olympics and the Homeric epics were both probably roughly contemporaneously "invented" or at least "repackaged" from pre-existing customs in the eighth century, both experienced centuries of fluidity in form and content, and, in my view, the two phenomena did not have immediately widespread Panhellenic prestige and canonical status. Rather, both gradually rose in visibility during the course of the seventh century, with the Olympics fueled by civic enthusiasm for the contests in the heroic legends, and with three rival Panhellenic games, namely, the Pythia, the Nemea, and the Isthmia, reorganized between 586 and 573 B.C., as a result of this movement. The model for the heroic myth serving as a catalyst is the allusion to or appropriation of mythical foundations seen in the sports of other cultures (Scanlon, 2004). The Greek use of heroic epic as a mythic foundation for the games is arguably the most famous manifestation of sports given meaning by a dominant media presentation of the ultimate champions, Homeric heroes who competed as toughly as they fought in battle.

MEDIA AND GREEK SPORTS IN THE CLASSICAL, HELLENISTIC, AND ROMAN ERAS

The next most famous literary media of sports in Greece were the victory odes, *epinikia*, written from the mid-500s B.C. to the late 400s B.C. These songs were sung either at the victory site or at the victor's home and were commissioned by the victor's family to be written by the best poet they could afford. Ibykos was the earliest, Pindar the best known today, flourishing in the early fifth century. Even the tragedian Euripides tried his hand at the genre with the last known hymn in 416 for the notorious politician and general Alcibiades' chariot victory at the Olympics. The poet arranged the staging and the performance of the ode, possibly including choral song, individual song, dance, and lyre- and flute-playing. The *epinikia* were meant to reflect the fame of the poem's patron through enduring memory for all time, with ample allusions to one's family lineage and comparisons to heroic ancestors and divine favor for the victor. The victor effectively became a new-age hero, greater than most mortals, and was given enhanced status (and frequently huge valuable prizes from the locals) upon return to his community. Leslie Kurke (1991) sees the *epinikia* as systems of exchange of symbolic capital, between victor and his homeland, victor and a society of noble gift exchange, and victor and city-state (polis). Pindar does not represent the old noble ethic, nor does he operate in an aesthetic vacuum, but his odes reflect the new social situation into which the individual has arrived through sociopolitical changes in consequence of the rise of the polis. Interestingly, the rise of the victory ode coincides with the beginning of a mania for sports festivals in the mid-sixth century B.C., and ends with the turmoil and identity crisis among Greek states during the traumatic Peloponnesian War. The war was a political, economic, and cultural earthquake that shook the idea of a unified Greek Panhellenic unity. After the Persian War, 490 to 479 B.C., the Greeks saw themselves as a people rejecting tyranny and domination and sharing a common religion and culture in opposition to the barbarian Persians. When the Athenian and Spartan superpowers of their day fell into all-out war, both sides were seriously debilitated and demoralized by the effort. The splendid hymns celebrating aristocratic values and Panhellenic vision seemed suddenly outmoded.

A more prosaic verbal medium publicizing the earliest games were the sacred envoys (*theoroi*) or truce-bearers (*spondophoroi*) sent forth by the organizers of the Olympics and other major festivals to invite all Greeks to the festivities. For the Olympics, word went out prior to the games announcing the sacred truce, the month-long period during which participants and spectators were to be allowed safe passage to the games under the protection of the gods (wars did not cease altogether). Groups of such envoys were dispatched to all sections of Greece, each likely assigned specific villages to visit and specific envoy-receivers (*theorodokoi*), local contacts to facilitate the job of the envoy in getting out the message. In short, it was a very sophisticated public relations machine that we know was in place for Delphi and Nemea at least by the Hellenistic era, possibly earlier, and probably was in place at Olympia and Isthmia for their events as well (Miller, 2004). These were the ancient prototypes of modern publicity via print and broadcast media, with the real difference that a strong religious sanction enforced the solemnity of the games and even of the announcements throughout the Greek world.

Between the visual and verbal media of Greek athletics stand the so-called agonistic inscriptions, documents inscribed in stone recording everything from the simplest notice of an individual's victory in such-and-such a contest of a given festival, sometimes with a note about distinctions ("first," "only"), to a full set of regulations of training or the complete list of victors in a given year of the festival (Crowther, 1989; Young, 1996). These inscriptions begin slowly in the sixth century B.C., then appear in proliferation from the fifth century B.C. to the third century A.D., with certain ebbs and flows according to the prosperity of the era and the community (inscriptions being expensive!) (Farrington, 1997). As a medium, the inscription ensured permanence unmatched until the cyber texts of today, without, of course, the transportability of modern media. Yet for the village or site where the inscription was placed, it stood both as text and quasi-sculpture, to be admired when residents passed it every day, even if they could not read it – their literate neighbors told of the great feats of the names thereon. This medium was again in the direction of the democratization of sports, enshrining the talented but lowborn individual on a level with heroes, noble ancestors, victorious generals, city leaders, and gods.

Turning now to the visual media and their relation to Greek sports, we see that victor monuments were set up to honor Olympic and other victors, as Pausanias most famously describes the statues in eighteen chapters of Books Five and Six of his work. He describes about two hundred such monuments at the Olympic site. The benefactor was the city-state of the victor, or at times his trainer (Mann, 2001). The earliest statues of athletic victors at Olympia, according to Pausanias, were wooden ones for Praxidamas and Rhexibios, victors respectively in 544 and 536 B.C. Later victory statues were of stone or bronze. The statues appear in the mid-sixth century period when the victory ode began. The period was also thirty or so years after the establishment of Panhellenic super-games at Delphi, Nemea, and Isthmia roughly after the Olympic model. So the statues were part of the sports craze of the day, and, unlike the odes, the statues were retained as a custom into the Roman era. But what was the message of victor monuments set up in the sanctuary of the god who was patron of the festival? Were the statues votive or honorific, were they to pay homage to the god or to honor the athlete himself? All chariot statues are said to be votives to the gods, but athlete statues are neither consistently honorific nor votive. It may well be that they functioned simultaneously as both. The base on which almost all statues stood had an inscription, which normally identified the victor, his home city-state, the games and event of the victory, and the source of the dedication (Hyde, 1921; Lattimore, 1988).

Statues, often with identifying inscriptions, were from about 500 B.C. to the Roman era the common medium for Greek rulers, generals, politicians, philosophers, and prominent citizens to memorialize themselves publicly. Athletes' statues must be understood in that context of raising up the individual. But unlike those famous or wealthy from normal civic activities, the athletic victors had a sudden and irreversible projection from obscurity into fame. It was no accident that the rise of athletic victor statues coincided with the rise of more democratic or egalitarian forms of rule in Greece in the sixth century, culminating in the Kleisthenic democratic reforms in Athens in 508/507 B.C. The Greek statuary practices in particular contrast sharply with Egyptian, Near Eastern, and even earlier Minoan or Greek uses of artistic media to highlight sports as the gift of the elite ruler to his people. Through the proliferation of statues and in other media, sports in Greece reflected directly the new broader rule of law over the older elite hierarchies. We cannot claim, as some do, that by dropping their clothes and competing in the nude, Greek athletes may have been the main impetus for an ethos of egalitarian value of all men whatever their birth, and looked more at actual merits than clothing (Miller, 2000). This goes too far and puts too much weight on one factor. Whatever the complex origins of Greek egalitarian rule, the sixth century athletic revolution certainly reinforced and reflected the tide of the times toward greater individual liberty and an emphasis on merit over birth.

Plato (ca. 429–347 B.C.) certainly echoed this message of self-empowerment through the balance of care for the mind and the body, notably in his *Republic*. His "school," the Academy, was of course a gymnasium and grove for a hero that existed as a training space on the edge of Athens long before the philosopher taught there. Platonic writings went far in their insistence on physical upbringing for the "guardians," the promising leaders of the state, measured by intellectual acumen, physical strength, and a finely honed sense of justice. Plato has clearly co-opted sports into the domain of social and political reform. It matters less that his idealistic vision was never fully adopted or implemented than that the Greek world was exposed to ideas which shifted the appreciation of how physical, intellectual, and moral education were interrelated and equally in need of cultivation in the gymnasia that were the schools and universities of the day. We cannot underestimate the crucial importance of Plato's teachings in the history of sports and media. Plato's *Republic*, and to some extent his *Laws*, gave less inspired civic leaders a rough model against which to measure their own social constructions. Aristotle's Lyceum, Zeno's Stoa, and other philosophical venues were also training spots for physical sports. Gymnasia sprang up in the fourth century B.C. across the Greek-speaking world, including Asia Minor, the Near East, and in Italy and Sicily in the Greek West.

The fourth century began the Hellenistic Era and marked a second boom period in Greek sports, with the further democratization of the phenomenon. Athletic guilds arose during the rule of Alexander the Great (336–323 B.C.), and they proliferated along with more unions and clubs for present and ex-athletes thereafter. Alexander himself backed athletics and chariot racing, and hastened the export of these events to the wider Eastern Mediterranean, Persia, and as far as India (Miller, 2004). So the spread of athletics in the Hellenistic period led slowly to a popularization of the games for spectators. Even before Alexander in the fourth century, large sums were spent on transforming stadia and gymnasia into luxury facilities.

For Americans in the later twentieth and early twenty-first century, the ready parallel is the transformation of U.S. sports into a spectators' heaven with mega-arenas and stadiums, "Jumbotron" scoreboards, music, visual displays during the competition, and the highly lucrative industry of broadcast sports. All of these items as a package constitute the media of sports as we know them today. We know well how the Athens games sought to rival or better those of Sydney, Atlanta, Barcelona, Seoul, and Los Angeles: flashier competition sites, more high-tech facilities for media and visitors, more impressive opening and closing ceremonies, and so on. Off the field of play, there are high-stakes competitions for the boast of the best games ever. The honor of winning the best staging not only ensures tourist and business revenues, it gives a city lasting fame in the history of the Games.

So it was for Hellenistic Greeks: bigger stadia, more amenities like running water at the stadium site, tunnels with dramatic entrances for athletes, and ever more impressive technology in the starting gates for runners. Today, we share with the ancients a collective weakness for the spectacular, theatrical elements of sports generally and the Olympics in particular. Both then and now are prized those aspects that are staged or architected to emphasize maximum drama and involve the audience in the contests. The Hellenistic era was the start in recorded history of competition for popularity contests in the best packaging of sports.

Ancient Olympia had a modicum of high spectacle from the start. The ritual sacrifice of 100 oxen to the patron god, Zeus, took place on the middle day of the games. The roasted meat was doled out for the victory celebration. In the animal sacrifice and the final big party, the ancients had their counterpart of the modern opening and closing ceremonies. Pheidias' statue of Zeus in the temple at Olympia, completed by about 430 B.C., was itself a major tourist attraction at the site and stood for almost 800 years as one of the Seven Wonders of the Ancient World. But in the Hellenistic period, an Olympic tunnel was built from 340 to 330 B.C., likely under Macedonian influence (Miller, 2004). The tunneled entrance for players is a stroke of architectural genius for the medium of sports, a refinement of drama carried over from the ancient Greek stadiums and Roman arenas. It was first adopted in

U.S. stadiums in the early twentieth century, mainly in college stadium architecture. Now it is so standard that we consider it a requirement, not a refinement.

Mechanized starting gates called *hyspleges* (singular, *hysplex*) were built from the fourth century B.C. onwards in Greek stadia (Valavanis, 1999). A fifth century prototype at Isthmia was short-lived, but in the mid- to late-300s stadia at Nemea, Isthmia, Epidauros, and Corinth evidence a system of horizontal cords across all runners' lanes; the cords were tied to vertical posts or arms that were set into a torsion mechanism of twisted rope, like the arm of a catapult device. The twisted rope provided torsion to throw the arm forward to the ground, and the cord barrier fell with it, allowing the runners to sprint forward. A fair start was ensured for all. The spectacular aspect was that the dropping wooden bar made a slapping noise against the ground, effectively a crack like that of the modern starting pistol that signals the instant of the start to the spectators. At Olympia evidence of such devices is found at the western and eastern starting lines dating at least to 340 B.C. At Nemea the hysplex dates to about 280 B.C. Military technology of torsion was reapplied to competitive running, to get an objectively administered standard start. Just as important is the motive of adding more impressive theatrics in the less showy running events (Miller, 2004).

In the second century B.C., architectural media moved to even greater showmanship. More complex and monumental models of *hyspleges* were engineered, again in the interests of one-upmanship in staging of the games. These were built with stone pillars framing the starting lanes, sometimes with ornately fluted columns, capitals, and even lintel blocks. The runners took off almost as if from between the columns in a colonnaded stoa. The mechanisms for the dropping gate barriers became even more sophisticated with pulleys and metal springs to release the bars. These luxury-model structures appeared not at the established Panhellenic games, which needed no crowd-drawing gimmicks, but at the well-funded second tier of competitions at Epidauros (Games for Asklepios), Kos (Games for Apollo), and Priene (Panathenaia?). Kos was the medical center of Hellenistic Greece because of associations with Hippocrates and Apollo, which meant that it also had the most complex and showy of all starting gates of the Hellenistic period (built in the second c. B.C.), seemingly in competition with the devices at Epidauros and Priene. Runners at Kos were partly hidden by the gates themselves. A spectacular start was marked by the sudden explosion of the runners and the noise of the tightly cocked metal-spring starting bolt. The refined architecture of limestone half columns and finely carved capitals set a stage that combined spontaneous reality with a theatrical performance. On the coast of Asia Minor, Priene's hysplex (ca. 130 B.C.) also boasted two systems for introducing torsion and release. Later still, in the Roman period, the island of Rhodes, sponsor of various sports festivals, boasted a very high-tech hysplex in its stadium, (re)built possibly for the visit of Hadrian in A.D. 123. This mechanism of the Roman era was in effect an attempt to restore and even top the achievements of past Greek sites like the nearby Priene and Kos (Valavanis, 1999).

ROMAN SPECTACLES AND CHARIOT RACES

On the Italian peninsula, the Etruscan peoples held sway, even ruling Rome, from about 600 to 500 B.C. The Etruscans loved Greek sports and incorporated athletics and chariot races into their funeral games. The clearest evidence of this Hellenophilia is the tomb painting of Etruscan elite, which includes scenes of boxing, footraces, discus and javelin throwing, and chariot racing (with some variations on Greek practice). It is noteworthy that Greek sports flourished in Etruscan lands during the sixth century when there was an athletic boom period in Greece itself. But unlike Greece, the Etruscan monarchs and the local nobles apparently sponsored the games as a gift to their people rather than an opportunity for the talented young men to prove their mettle and be awarded great fame. The Etruscan use of media compared to Greek shows this change: depictions were confined to tomb paintings to honor those already rich and powerful; there were no inscriptions, victor odes, or other monuments or performances, so far as we know, to honor the individual victors in the games. Individuality was subsumed in the name of athletics and chariot races as entertainment.

The Romans overthrew their Etruscan masters in 509 B.C., virtually at the same time that democratic reforms were first enacted in Athens. But the enthusiastic democratization of athletics in Greece at this juncture contrasts sharply with its being made suddenly peripheral in Italy. For the most part, the Romans did not share Hellenomania with the Etruscans. Athletics were a frivolous distraction from the business of war, trade, and development of a solid infrastructure in Italy's cities and regions. Rome was focused firmly on military might from the 400s to the 100s B.C. It controlled most of Italy below the Po River by 272 B.C. and in 146 B.C. had annexed Greece (Macedonia) as a province, which it remained for the duration of the Roman Republic and Empire. Greek sports were occasionally staged in Rome, mainly as part of grander festivals sponsored by politicians to solidify popular support (Crowther, 1983).

Sports at Rome took mainly two forms, that of games (*ludi*) including primarily gladiatorial contests and beast games in arenas or amphitheaters, and circuses (*circenses*), chariot races. Games of gladiators are recorded from as early as 264 B.C. but really became a cultural function in the first century B.C. and flourished until the fourth century A.D. Chariot races may have been held occasionally in Rome as early as the fourth century B.C., judging from the establishment of the Circus Maximus then, but serious chariot-mania began in the first century B.C. Both types of contests were presented from the start as benefactions by the wealthy elite for the people, and as such they were also officially called gifts (*munera*). Though there were religious aspects to both games and circuses, and though gladiators and charioteers gained individual fame, the function of these public contests was entirely different from those of the Greeks. For some reason (expense? popularity?), circuses traditionally had stronger ties to the "imperial cult" than did other games. This cult devotion functioned something like the playing of the national anthem at the beginning of sports events today. Attendance is virtually a patriotic act. The gladiators and the chariot drivers were, with few exceptions, noncitizens drafted from the talent pool of slaves, ex-slaves, prisoners, or criminals. The contests were not open to skilled entrants from all over the Roman world, and the fame that an individual competitor obtained was not that of an honored citizen who enhanced the status of his family and city.

The big business of entertainment for the masses was at the heart of the organizations of both games and circuses. Gladiators were managed by the director (*lanista*) of their school or family (*familia*) who let them out for sponsors, often political candidates. Charioteers belonged to teams called factions directed by corporate bosses called masters (*domini*). In the provinces outside of Rome, the organizational systems were likely more fluid. Chariot teams must have gone on "road tours" to local circus venues. Wherever the games or circuses took place, the primary duty for funding went to wealthy magistrate-politicians. So in this context, the media or communication machines for publicizing games and circuses were different in aim and kind from the media of Greek athletics. Arguably every aspect of the Roman games and circuses was a medium aimed to capture the attention and favor of the audience.

Literary media are less our concern here than pragmatic publicity or visual arts. There were no Roman Homers or Pindars or Platos whose literary works elevated the role of public sporting competitions in Roman culture. Ennobling the role of these contests in their society to entice citizens to participate, as was done in Greece, was not the point in Rome. We omit here mention of certain allusions in literary texts: the qualified praise in passing from Cicero and Pliny the Younger for gladiators' bravery, the utter disdain for the shows by the philosopher Seneca, the epigrammatist Martial's series of poems appreciating the grotesque scenes in competition during the dedication of the Colosseum, the gossipy musings of the poets Ovid and Juvenal about the sex appeal of the contests, and the dinner-party banter about the recent games in Petronius' parodic *Satyricon*. None of these is more than a trifling reference appropriating for the author's purposes scenes from the realia of life in Rome. Though Cicero does attempt to philosophize gladiatorial endurance while condemning the practice overall, generally the sources do not claim that the contests fulfill a socially redeeming function. Still, there were public-relations efforts by the contests' sponsors before the events to draw a crowd and afterwards to generate gratitude from the masses for the money spent for their amusement. Augustus, the first emperor, for instance, set up inscriptions after his death reminding Romans of his "Achievements" (*Res gestae*), giving prominence to the numerous gladiatorial games he sponsored, involving tens of thousands of combatants, hunt-the-beast games, mock naval battles, and a few displays of Greek athletics for good measure (Brunt & Moore, 1967). Graffiti uncovered in Pompeii document the painted notices of games, much like modern posters and billboards. And some gladiators themselves could have funerary monuments set up by family or supporters (Koehne & Ewigleben, 2000). But all in all, the written and literary media related to games and circuses fall far short of the Greek masterpieces lauding athletics, and we can attribute that absence to the obvious difference in function of sport in each culture.

The visual media market for Roman competitions is only a bit more fruitful source. A whole tourist-and-fan art industry accompanied the events. Hundreds of small clay oil lamps must have been sold at the arena site as souvenirs. Pottery, mirrors, knives, and similar items were sold to the masses of less wealthy admirers of the contestants. Small but well-sculpted statues of gladiators and charioteers were common, both in terracotta and in bronze. These were presumably the keep-sakes of wealthier fans. The wealthiest supporters of games and circuses were likely themselves also the financial sponsors of the actual events. Many sponsors must have built into their budget the funds for commissioning a mosaic to be placed in the floors of their villas, where the beast games, gladiator battles, and other spon-sored events were vividly depicted. On rare occasion the sponsor himself would even be portrayed in the scene, as was done on a mosaic showing the host holding the bags of prize money (Museum of Sousse, Tunisia; Blanchard-Lemée, Ennaïfer, Slim, & Slim, 1995; Koehne & Ewigleben, 2000). Very few of the Roman visual media, we note, are monuments of civic pride like the Greek victor statues. The Roman objects are either trivial souvenirs or the private memorials of the elites to recall their benefactions to visitors to the mansion.

The most visible media promoting sports in the Roman era were, of course, the amphitheater and circus structures themselves. The Roman sites competed for architectural praise and audience approval, as did the Greek stadia, by adding elaborate audience-pleasing fixtures. The circus chariot courses were common throughout the Roman Empire, with the Circus Maximus at Rome being the oldest and most elaborate structure, its first phase in 329 B.C. Almost all later circuses copied the full features of the structure renovation by the Emperor Trajan by A.D. 103. Starting gates were in a curve with finely sculptured facades. The central barrier was ornamented with pools, sculptures, cone-shaped turning posts, Egyptian obelisks, and lap-counting devices. These ornaments became standard for almost all later monumental circuses throughout the empire. The people loved the features and would have been happy with no less.

Italy and Sicily themselves had five circuses attested at Rome and at least ten throughout the rest of the area. Nine circuses are attested for North Africa, mostly built in the first and second centuries A.D. The Iberian peninsula (Spain and Portugal; ancient Lusitania and Baetica) had twenty-two known circuses, the earliest in the first century A.D. at the major towns of Merida, Tarragona, and Toledo, with Merida influencing others in the province. There are only five securely identified circuses, dating from the first to third centuries A.D., in the Northwest (mostly Gallic) Provinces covered by modern France, the Benelux countries, Britain, and the western region of Germany, but there are doubtless many more not yet excavated, many made of wooden stands which have vanished. The demand for permanent stone fixtures found in the climatically milder, horse-breeding regions of Spain, Italy, and North Africa was not evident in Northern Europe. Twenty-one circuses are known from the Eastern Provinces of the Empire, comprising modern Greece, Turkey, Syria, Israel, Egypt, and Libya. All but three of these eastern fixtures were likely built in the second century A.D. or later, where philhellenic emperors showered attention and at times direct benefactions. Many of the eastern circuses likely served double duty as the locus for Greek athletics games in the region. Interestingly, the Greek mainland, Aegean islands, and Asia Minor coast (Ionia) evidence no Roman circuses except for the Romanized urban centers of Gortyn (Crete), Constantinople, Thessaloniki, and Nicomedia. The circus craze seems therefore not to have been absent anywhere in the Roman Empire, but it was muted or adapted to local demand and pragmatic concerns (Humphrey, 1986).

The amphitheater was a Roman invention, first made of wood in 53 B.C. by Gaius Scribonius Curio, who joined two theater buildings to enclose the space. The effect was to isolate and give greater esprit de corps to the crowd, who could look at each other as well as the contests. In later buildings made of stone, colorful awnings furnished shade. The ornamental building façade was impressive with attached columns and multiple stories. Audience walkways and seating areas were logically organized. Special imperial or VIP box-seat sections and hierarchically assigned seats distinguished the classes attending. After Augustus, the amphitheater was frequently tied to the cult or the emperor, with an altar connected to the site. Amphitheaters were as widespread as circuses and equally impressive for the sake of pleasing the people. The amphitheaters were in sum badges of local pride and emblems of the power and authority of imperial oversight. They were structures at once a token of elite patronage welcoming to the less empowered and an imposing reminder of the imperial hierarchy of power.

As with circus structure, local sites competed for the best facility, but none outdid the Roman Colosseum, technically the Flavian Amphitheater, which was the standard from A.D. 80 onward. Prior to the amphitheater, gladiator games had been held in the circuses, but after construction of the Colosseum, every Roman city worth the name had an amphitheater. Italy and Sicily has seventeen preserved amphitheaters, from the first century B.C. to the fourth A.D. The Iberian Peninsula has eleven certainly identified, Britain two, and the Northeast provinces from Belgian and Germany to Austria, Serbia, Croatia, and Macedonia have twenty-seven. Gauls may not have been the best chariot fans, but they did love their theatrical and gladiatorial performances, to judge from their seventy-one attested pure or mixed-use amphitheaters and over seventy theaters. The Gauls notably mixed the amphitheater uses by including stages on some venues for performing local Gallic rituals alongside their devotion to the emperor (Futrell, 1997; Humphrey, 1986). In Greece, Asia Minor, the Near East, and Egypt, gladiator and beast games were held, sometimes in traditional theaters (as at Athens' Theater of Dionysus) and sometimes in amphitheaters (as at Corinth). Greeks seem to have backed gladiator games given in their region beginning with the imperial cult in the first century A.D., even while they continued to hold their own athletics and their own chariot races apart from Roman customs. Greece has five such preserved structures where gladiator games were held, Asia Minor has ten, and North Africa (Morocco, Algeria, Tunisia, Libya) has ten (Golvin & Landes, 1990; Welch, 1999).

CONCLUSIONS

The relation of visual and verbal media to sports in the ancient Mediterranean has brought us full circle over an arc of about 3000 years. As we have described them, media are a tool of society, a means of transmitting a message, primarily one from the rulers to the ruled. In strictly hierarchical powers under the strong rule of a central monarch or elite, sports are represented as a benevolent benefaction from the rich, noble, and empowered to those marginalized. When the rule of law allows more egalitarian sharing of authority, sports reflects the higher valuation of the individual and his merits. Among Egyptians, Mesopotamians, Hittites, and Minoans, contests were put on at the expense of the elite nobility as a display of power. The contestants were largely unknown and without special honor, in written or visual media. Instead the media reflect the glory of the game's sponsor, and the sponsor in effect basks in the glory of the success of whomever wins. The heroic noble athletes of Homeric and Archaic Greece shift this picture somewhat, seen in the vivid narratives of Homer and Pindar, so that individuals who compete are the ones honored above the sponsor himself. Then Greek city-states admit more egalitarian rule of law in the sixth century B.C., notably at Athens with Solon's laws of the early 500s and Cleisthenes' reforms of the late 500s. In that political and social context, two things happen. In the fifth century and later, the participants in sports begin to emerge from the non-elite on the basis of merit and skill, and the media of sports aim to please larger masses of fans. The Greek victor ode goes out of style as too stuffy, and the competition sites become more spectator-friendly (bigger stadia, proper seats in place of hillsides, and water facilities). The sites also become more concerned with showmanship (tunnels and starting gates), again as a concession to the populace.

Rome's use of media in sports is most complex over the nearly thousand-year history of that state. Romans declined to adopt Greek sports as it had their other cultural areas, and indeed did not highlight any leisure sports for their own citizens to gain public honor. Instead military skill was the exclusive path to honor for the male Roman citizen. Sporting contests functioned mainly for entertainment and were financed by the elite to entertain the masses. Gladiator contests emerged probably from local Italian duels held at the funerals of prominent men, but they were transformed into events that simultaneously brought esteem to the sponsor and intentional death to many criminal or slave competitors. Though the Roman structure of government did allow participation and representation in the pre-imperial Republican period, by the time of the empire, the first three centuries A.D., individual liberties were diminished to meaninglessness, and the emperor held sway much in the manner of other monarchs. Roman literature was almost mute on the virtues of Roman games, and their arts were also minimal compared with the Greeks'. So the most powerful media of the games and circuses were in fact the architecture of the facilities themselves. The amphitheaters and racetracks, along with the events inside them, were monumental works meant to provoke awe, admiration, and obedience in the citizens. The Roman relation of media to sports in a sense comes full circle where the audience of those ruled are meant to be impressed by the patronage of the rulers, as had been the case in Egypt and the Near East.

Media of the modern world borrow selectively from the past, from the mass-audience attractions of the Romans and Hellenistic Greeks, from the early Greek custom of honoring individual merits with public honors, and from the widespread custom of making the games into a medium of power for the sponsors.

REFERENCES

Blanchard-Lemée, M., Ennaïfer, M., Slim, H., & Slim, L. (1995). *Mosaics of Roman Africa. Floor mosaics from Tunisia.* New York: George Brazzillier.

Brunt, P. A., & Moore, J. M. (1967). *Res Gestae Divi Augusti. The achievements of the Divine Augustus.* Oxford, U.K.: Oxford University Press.

Crowther, N. (1983). Greek games in Republican Rome. *L'Antiquite Classique, 52,* 268–273.

Crowther, N. (1989). The Sebastan games in Naples (IvOl. 56). *Zeitschrift für Papyrologie und Epigraphik, 79,* 100–102.

Decker, W. (1982–83). Die mykenische Herkunft des griechischen Totenagons. *Stadion, 8–9,* 1–24.

Decker, W. (1992). *Sports and games of Ancient Egypt.* New Haven, CT: Yale University Press.

Decker, W., & Herb, M. (1994). *Bildatlas zum sport im Alten Aegypten* (Vol. 1). Leiden, Netherlands: Brill.

Farrington, A. (1997). Olympic victors and the popularity of the Olympic Games in the Imperial Period. *Tyche, 12,* 15–46.

Futrell, A. (1997). *Blood in the arena: The spectacle of Roman power.* Austin: University of Texas.

Golvin, J., & Landes, C. (1990). *Amphitheatres et Gladiateurs.* Paris: CNRS.

Guttmann, A. (1978). *From ritual to record: The nature of modern sports.* New York: Columbia University Press.

Humphrey, J. H. (1986). *Roman circuses: Arenas for chariot racing.* Berkeley: University of California Press.

Hyde, W. W. (1921). *Olympic victor monuments and Greek athletic art.* Washington: Carnegie Institution.

Koehne, E., & Ewigleben, C. (2000). *Gladiators and Caesars. The power of spectacle in ancient Rome.* Berkeley: University of California.

Kovacs, M. G. (Trans.) (1989). *The Epic of Gilgamesh.* Stanford, CA: Stanford University Press.

Kurke, L. (1991). *The traffic in praise: Pindar and the poetics of social economy.* Ithaca, NY: Cornell University Press.

Lattimore, S. (1988). The nature of early Greek victor statues. In S. Bandy (Ed.), *Coroebus triumphs: The alliance of sport and the arts* (pp. 245–256). San Diego, CA: San Diego State University Press.

Lee, H. M. (2004). The 'first' Olympic games of 776 B.C. In W. Raschke (Ed.), *The archeology of the Olympics* (pp. 110–118). Madison: University of Wisconsin.

Mann, C. (2001). *Athlet und Polis im archaischen und frühklassischen Griechenland.* Göttingen, Germany.

Miller, S. (2000). Naked democracy. In P. Flensted-Jensen, et al. (Eds.), *Polis & politics* (pp. 277–296). Copenhagen, Denmark.

Miller, S. (2004). *Ancient Greek athletics.* New Haven, CT: Yale University Press.

Mouratidis, J. (1989). Are there Minoan influences on Mycenaean sports. *Nikephoros, 2,* 43–63.

Nagy, G. (1996). *Homeric questions.* Austin: University of Texas.

Puhvel, J. (2004). Hittite athletics as prefigurations of ancient Greek games. In W. J. Raschke (Ed.), *The archaeology of the Olympics: The Olympics and other festivals in antiquity* (pp. 26–31). Madison: University of Wisconsin Press.

Rollinger, R. (1994). Aspekte des Sports im Alten Sumer. Sportliche Betätigung und Herrschaftsidiologie im Wechselspiel. *Nikephoros, 7,* 7–64.

Sansone, D. (1988). *Greek athletics and the genesis of sport.* Berkeley: University of California Press.

Scanlon, T. (1999). Bull sports, cults, and women's status in Minoan crete. *Nikephoros, 12,* 33–70.

Scanlon, T. (2004). Homer, the Olympics, and the heroic ethos. In M. Kaila, et al. (Eds.), *The Olympic games in antiquity: Bring forth rain and bear fruit (Hue Kue)* (pp. 61–94). Athens, Greece: Atrapos Press.

Sipahi, T. (2001). New evidence from Anatolia regarding bull-leaping scenes in the art of the Aegean and the near east. *Anatolica, 27,* 107–126.

Valavanis, P. (1999). *HYSPLEX: The starting mechanism in ancient stadia. A contribution to ancient Greek technology.* Los Angeles: University of California.

Vermaak, P. S. (1993). Sulgi as sportsman in the Sumerian self-laudatory royal hymns. *Nikephoros, 6,* 7–21.

Welch, K. (1999). Negotiating Roman spectacle architecture in the Greek world: Athens and Corinth. In B. Bergmann & C. Kondoleon (Eds.), *The art of ancient spectacle* (pp. 125–146). London: National Gallery of Art.

Young, D. C. (1996). First with the most: Greek athletic records and 'specialization.' *Nikephoros, 9,* 175–197.

Younger, J. (1976). Bronze age representations of Aegean bull-leaping. *American Journal of Archaeology, 80,* 125–137.

2

A Historical Overview of Sports and Media in the United States

Jennings Bryant
Andrea M. Holt
University of Alabama

Although the United States is a relatively young country, it has spawned many of the world's preeminent developments in sports communication, several of which epitomize modern sports–media relationships. In fact, the idiosyncratic nature of U.S. culture has greatly facilitated this close-knit, even symbiotic, association. As McChesney (1989) noted:

> The nature of the sport–mass media relationship has been distinctly shaped by the emerging contours of American capitalism since the 1830s. On one hand, much of sport and virtually all of the mass media have been organized as commercial enterprises throughout this history. Many of the specific developments in the sport–mass media relationship can be fathomed only through the continual recognition that each of these institutions has been constituted of individual units first and foremost striving for economic profit in some level of competition with each other. On the other hand, sport emerges as an institution especially well suited culturally and ideologically, first, to the emerging capitalism of the century, and, second—and indeed, far more so—to the mature corporate capitalistic society of the twentieth century. (pp. 49–50)

We have no disagreement with the thrust of McChesney's (1989) assertion. However, for the sake of completeness and veridicality, we think the claim is overly narrow in two ways. First, we would argue that many cultural forces and social movements other than capitalism helped shape the complex, mutually interdependent relationship between sports and media in the United States Second, it is important to recognize that some of the essential elements of the sports–media union in the United States, capitalistic or otherwise, were derived long before the

1830s. In fact, some of the most important formative roots of the relationships between sports and media in America were developed during the colonial era.

Looked at somewhat differently, during the more than two and a quarter centuries of America's existence, as the country made its transition from an agricultural society, through an industrial society, and finally into the early phases of an information society (Rogers, 1986), each epoch of social evolution has witnessed important sports–media developments that were affected by the evolving sociocultural environment. In this chapter we attempt to highlight some of the most important developments in sports and media in each of these historical epochs, and we attempt to identify key motivational factors for these effects. Taken together, these developments have helped create a society whose citizens are voracious consumers of mediated sports, and media systems that are highly dependent on sports for their manifest content as well as their economic well being.

SPORTS AND MEDIA DURING THE AGRICULTURAL AGE

The type of society that most early settlers of the American colonies experienced, and that is experienced by many citizens in developing countries around the globe today, is what is often called an agricultural society or an agrarian society (cf. Black & Bryant, 1995; Rogers, 1986). Typically life in agricultural societies is a struggle for survival, a series of challenges that must be met to garner one's daily bread. According to classical formulations of agricultural societies, neither sports nor media typically play dominant roles or fill essential social functions because leisure time is a rare commodity and so-called discretionary income is largely nonexistent. Despite these odds, some vital taproots of the sports–media interface were established in America during the agricultural age.

Undoubtedly the first and most important sports–media development during this era was the inclusion of sports reports in newspapers. "One of the earliest known sports stories appeared in the *Boston Gazette* on March 5, 1733. It was a description of a prize fight held in England, and it was copied from a London newspaper—a practice typical of the day" (Enriquez, 2002, p. 198). It is noteworthy that this event was covered as general news, as a matter of surveillance of the general environment, albeit long after the event took place. Also noteworthy is the fact that this earliest development in sports and media was imported from Europe. As we will see, most future innovations in sports and media were to come from America.

Because most colonial newspapers were written for the relatively small number of wealthy, better educated, elite potential readers—an orientation that lingered until the *Penny Press* era of the 1830s (Thompson, 2004)—and because many colonial sports events were grassroots in origin, newspaper coverage of sports occurred particularly when the sporting event was relevant within some larger social context. For example, newspapers might well cover a horse race, but only when a Northern horse raced against a Southern horse (i.e., regionalism), or they might cover a boxing match, but primarily when an American boxed against a Brit (i.e., nationalism; Enriquez, 2002). The sports covered most commonly were horse racing, which was the most popular sport of the day, and boxing, a sport that in those days was popular among the common folk and elite alike.

To functionally address this void in sports coverage by newspapers, the sports magazine, an early specialized medium, emerged and became quite popular. Seven sports magazines came into existence between the mid-1820s and mid-1830s, although some of them died soon after birth. These magazines, which constitute the second sports–media innovation of the agricultural era, only remotely resembled their modern heirs, and their journalistic standards typically were quite rudimentary. "In general, the editor-publisher was the sole owner, manager, and primary author for his or her particular magazine" (McChesney, 1989, p. 50). The most popular and influential of such magazines were John Stuart Skinner's *American Turf Register and Sporting Magazine* (1829) and William T. Porter's *Spirit of the Times* (1821). Not only did these two magazines help popularize horse racing, they also did much to standardize thoroughbred racing nationwide, by reporting in substantial detail rules, betting standards, weights, times, and the like. In 1839, Porter purchased the *Turf Register* and folded it into the *Spirit of the Times* (Enriquez, 2002), thereby foreshadowing a trend that would come to typify the media institutions of the modern era. This forerunner of modern corporate media mergers provided a third major sports-communication innovation of agriculture-age America.

By the end of the 1840s, interest in sports and sports journalism had increased substantially. Porter's *Spirit of the Times* became quite successful, reaching 100,000 readers. It also expanded its coverage to include boxing and began to promote other less popular sports. Its most concerted effort to stimulate the American appetite for sports and to increase readership was a failed attempt to establish cricket as the national game (Nugent, 1929), so even the market leader of sports media during the agrarian era had one notable failure.

The 1830s and 1840s also witnessed a marked change in newspapers and their readership. The most remarkable change was the birth of the Penny Press, which made newspapers extremely profitable by expanding circulation through offering and promoting popular content; by targeting and attracting a new audience of middle-class, urban readers; and by shifting the burden of the costs of readership from circulation to advertising (Thompson, 2004). As might be anticipated from such shifts in markets and content, sports coverage increased in the Penny Press. Many of the innovations in sports journalism in this era came from James Gordon Bennett's *New York Herald*, although Bennett sometimes expressed regret about the increasing prominence of sports in society. Despite his own misgivings about his paper's sports coverage, "Bennett was one of the first exponents of 'sensationalism' as a means of generating circulation, and sport fit comfortably within this rubric" (McChesney, 1989, p. 51), so cover sports he did. Other prominent Penny Press newspapers that included sports content were Horace Greeley's *New York Tribune* and Henry Raymond's *New York Times*. However, coverage was more occasional than regular, and nothing that approximated a daily sports page or sports column emerged in America during the agricultural age (Betts, 1974).

SPORTS AND MEDIA DURING THE INDUSTRIAL AGE

The Industrial Revolution began in Britain in the late 1700s with the invention and widespread adoption and adaptation of the steam engine, which augmented human potential exponentially in the service of manufacturing and transportation. Although other countries such as France, Belgium, and the United States witnessed

Britain's success with considerable envy and began to gear up for industrial development, three fourths of the U.S. labor force was still engaged in agricultural pursuits in the 1790s. In fact, it was the middle of the nineteenth century before the United States fully entered the industrial age. However, by the end of the nineteenth century, the United States had become the global industrial leader in manufacturing and transportation, beginning what has become known as the Second Industrial Revolution. This second period of intense industrialization facilitated the development of numerous communication technologies, such as the telegraph, telephone, radio, and television, as well as major improvements in printing and composition technologies, along with the invention or refinement of many other industrial goods ("Industrial Revolution," 2005).

As the United States began its industrial revolution, sports were becoming increasingly popular, as well as becoming better organized and more commercialized. In fact, the industrial age seemingly provided a most hospitable climate for the development of sports. "As it did with many other aspects of society, the industrial revolution dramatically changed things as far as sports spectatorship was concerned" (Bryant, Zillmann, & Raney, 1998, p. 257). Or, as Zillmann and Paulus (1993) suggested,

> Lending some degree of support to the orthodox Marxist view that spectatorship, as a significant form of recreation, is an outgrowth of the monotony of machine-dictated labor, sports events became the weekend love affair of all those whose workday was strictly regulated by production schedules. (p. 601)

As important as industrialization was to the development of sports communication during this period, the dominant social development of the time was regional divisiveness in the developing nation. During the devastating mid-nineteenth century Civil War, some new developments in sports took place. "The Civil War introduced baseball to an entire generation of Americans, as the troops on both sides played the game when time permitted. Indeed, baseball emerged as the preeminent national team sport during this period" (McChesney, 1989, p. 52). Shortly after the war, the first professional baseball league, the National League, was formed. Newspaper sportswriters were very influential in the development, advancement, and legitimization of the league. Much like the impact of sports magazines on horse racing during the prior century, a new generation of sportswriters and advocates, most of them newspaper-based this time, helped standardize and make more sophisticated the rules of and techniques for reporting about baseball, developing format innovations like box scores and detailed statistical analyses of pitching and hitting, which helped draw new fans to the new league. As Enriquez (2002) concluded,

> Baseball was a solidly middle class sport with considerable appeal to the working man, a perfect sport for newspapers trying to expand downward across class lines to reach the middle and working classes. One such newspaper was James Gordon Bennett's *New York Herald.* Bennett's strategy for creating a broad-based truly popular newspaper centered on the use of news features, including sports news, to attract a wider audience. (p. 199)

With these breakthroughs came several "firsts," including (1) the first specialized sports reporters: "Earliest specialization in sports news is represented by the 'turf men' who on some papers covered races in addition to other duties" (Mott, p. 443); (2) even more specialized baseball reporters: "Probably the first baseball reporter was Henry Chadwick, who had written about cricket matches for the *Times* and later the *Tribune*, but who went to work with the *Herald* as a sports reporter in 1862" (Mott, p. 443); (3) the first woman sports reporter: "A 'wild Irish girl' of robust stature named 'Middie' Morgan covered races and cattle shows for the *New York Times*, beginning in 1870" (Mott, p. 443); (4) the first newspaper sports pages (Stephens, 1987) and sports department: "Sports news increased in the seventies, and when Pulitzer bought the *World* he organized a separate sports department" (Mott, p. 443); and (5) the first sports editors: "By the end of the period, virtually all the great papers in the leading cities had 'sporting editors'" (Mott, p. 443)—all important innovations of the early stages of America's industrial age.

Sporting magazines continued to play an important role in sports development, including the advancement of baseball. Two new magazines—*Sporting Life* (1883) and *The Sporting News* (1886)—focused on baseball, and both were located outside of the New York media center (in Philadelphia and St. Louis, respectively). These magazines helped further legitimize baseball and fueled the fervor associated with this new, relatively egalitarian, national pastime.

This regular, routine reporting of sports in newspapers and specialized magazines helped shift the cultural attitude towards sports in general, and during the 1870s through the 1890s, America's love affair with sports began. The antisports attitudes of the Puritan era quickly dissipated and were replaced with a new "progressive" credo that sports were important for the development of mind, body, and society.

A second major contributory factor that aided the development of sports journalism was the adoption of compulsory education laws by several states, beginning with Massachusetts in 1851. The compulsory-education movement had the desired effect of upgrading the literacy of the common citizen, at least to the extent that readership of newspaper sports pages and sports magazines became much more widespread.

A third critical dimension of the social and economic development of sports was the infusion of new waves of immigrants into the American cultural milieu. These immigrants helped energize the new American industrial expansion, and because many of them lived in cities, they contributed importantly to the urbanization required to provide the critical mass needed to support professional sports teams. Moreover, because different ethnic groups tended to choose different cities—and even relatively homogeneous neighborhoods within a city—in which to live, this helped develop cultural distinctiveness in the fan bases in different cities, which helped create very distinct team "personalities," which, in turn, enhanced competition. These team identities led to the increased use of human interest elements in writing about sports contests and in myriad other ways facilitated the expansion of baseball and other team sports, as well as sports fans' interests in the coverage of those sports by the emerging mass media. Moreover, many of the immigrant groups brought with them interests in sports that had previously not been popular in the United States, which were covered by the specialized newspaper serving these groups, adding further diversity to the sports–media profile in America.

With these several developments, the symbiotic relationship between sports and media grew closer and closer. As Michener (1976) observed, "one of the happiest relationships in American society is between sports and the media. . . . In the early years of this century baseball prospered mainly because it received at no cost reams of publicity in daily and Sunday newspapers" (p. 355). Seymour (1960) commented on this interconnectivity even more directly in discussing the development of a national association of baseball writers in 1887:

> All sides now recognize that their interests are identical. The reporters have found in the game a thing of beauty and a source of actual employment. The game has found in the reporters its best ally and most powerful supporter. Hence the good feelings all along the line. (p. 351)

Several shifts in emphasis in sports coverage occurred during the late nineteenth century, and not all of the important changes in sports journalism were initially directed towards the new mass audience.

> Middle-class newspapers also created a middle-class identity for the elite sport of intercollegiate football. Since colleges enrolled the sons of the well-to-do, intercollegiate matches became elite social events. Most newspapers covered football games with relatively little emphasis on the game itself and significant emphasis on the spectators. In a story on the Yale–Princeton match in 1897, the *New York Times* wrote, "A list of the well-known men and women who went to the football game from this city yesterday would be simply made up of the rolls of the Princeton and Yale Universities, the New York Athletic Club, and the Social Register." (Enriquez, 2002, p. 200)

Naturally, middle-class readers who desired upward mobility became very interested in this collegiate football phenomenon, which increased the demand for football tickets and for coverage of college football games in mass-audience newspapers. Once again, sports journalists help codify the rules of the game and the techniques for covering football contests as they explained details of the games to these new sports fans.

Not all sports coverage of the era was of team sports, of course. Some of the individual sports of the day that received extensive newspaper coverage might even seem a bit esoteric by contemporary criteria, such as newspapers' love affair with wheeled sports long before NASCAR came on the scene. Mott (1950) reported, "Throughout the bicycle craze of the nineties, many of the leading newspapers maintained special departments for wheelmen, sometimes edited by authorities in the field, giving news of cycle racers, of the activities of wheelmen's clubs, and of manufacturers' new models" (p. 579).

During the period bridging the nineteenth and twentieth centuries, sports reporting gradually became a regular feature of daily newspapers. Major events, such as championship prizefights and leading horse races, drew substantial attention from most papers. When the first baseball World Series was played in 1903, even the stodgiest major newspapers developed an interest in sports, and sports gradually ascended the national stage. As Mott (1950) put it, "Emphasis on sports was characteristic of the yellow press, which developed for that department a slangy and facetious style. This exploitation did much to promote national interest in league baseball and in prizefighting" (p. 579). McChesney (1989) added, "The 'nationalization' of sport was greatly encouraged by improvements in transportation, communication, and social mobility" (p. 54). With nationalization and increased public interest, "News of sports had a remarkable development during the period. It came to be segregated on special pages, with special make-up, pictures, and news-writing style" (Mott, p. 579).

A concomitant development during this period was the emergence of star sportswriters, who fused their journalistic fervor with a love of sports and of colorful language, the combination of which made sports journalism a recognized and celebrated form of communication and entertainment:

> Joe Vila, of the New York *Sun*, who invented play-by-play reports of football games; Damon Runyon, of the Denver *Post* and the New York *American*; W. O. McGeehan, who began a distinguished career on San Francisco papers and finished it on the New York *Herald Tribune*; Charles E. Van Loan, of various California and New York papers, and many others. (Mott, 1950, p. 579)

World War I contributed to the nationalization of sports and to the centrality of sports to American culture because military leaders thought that keeping their soldiers, sailors, and pilots who were posted overseas abreast of sporting events back home was good for the morale of the troops. Therefore, sports were covered by military publications, and military personnel from all areas of the United States discussed and cussed each other's teams. This focus seemingly primed the returning military personnel's interest in sports when the fighting ended and the troops returned stateside to family and home.

When U.S. military personnel returned from Europe, they found newspapers with increasingly sophisticated sports coverage. Moreover, they found a generation of gifted sportswriters who left their imprint on sports journalism and the American psyche in the post-World War I period. Charley Dryden in San Francisco and Grantland Rice in Nashville, Atlanta, Washington, D.C., and New York City made their popular sports columns some of the most widely read and entertaining features of newspapers of the day. Rice, in particular, seemed to be a person for the times.

> Grant came into the world at a fortunate time for us all. . . . Life still meant, to the great majority of Americans, only work—hard work, long hours—the harder and longer the more commendable. Play was for boys and for fools. It was the function and duty of men to work.
>
> This austere tradition Grant helped mightily to break down. He was the evangelist of fun, the bringer of good news about games. He was forever seeking out young men of athletic talent, lending them a hand and building them up, and sharing them with the rest of us as our heroes. He made the playing fields respectable. Never by preaching or propaganda, but by the sheer contagion of his joy in living, he made us want to play. And in so doing he made us a people of better health and happiness in peace: of greater strength in adversity. This was his gift to his country; few men have made a greater. (Rice, 1954, unnumbered prologue)

Rice's lead paragraph in the *New York Tribune* on October 19, 1924, describing a Notre Dame–Army football game, is one of the most quoted newspaper leads ever, and we feel obligated to add to its total count in order to share his gift and a feel for the eloquent if overstated writing of the time:

> Outlined against a blue-gray October sky, the Four Horsemen rode again. In dramatic lore they are known as Famine, Pestilence, Destruction and Death. These are only aliases. Their real names are Stuhldreher, Miller, Crowley and Layden. They formed the crest of the South Bend cyclone before which another fighting Army football team was swept over the precipice at the polo Grounds yesterday afternoon as 55,000 spectators peered down on the bewildering panorama spread on the green plain below. (p. 1)

Novak (1976) called this opening "stanza" "the statue made of words" (p. 243), because the column led to the creation of an actual statue of the football version of the Four Horsemen. Enriquez (2002) reflected, "Rice's style was lush, romantic, lyrical, full of classical and historical allusion, often written in verse. His voice was often imitated and satirized but, as with Dryden before him, never with his skill" (p. 201).

Writing that approached this level of insight or eloquence earned bylines for preeminent sportswriters, a very rare occurrence in journalism in this period, and their sports columns often graced the front pages of newspapers as circulation builders. Clearly sports journalism and sports commentary had come of age.

As Betts (1952) observed, "sport swept over the nation in the 1920s, and, at times, seemed to be the most engrossing of public interests" (pp. 422–423). Susman (1975) added, "It was in the '20s that the American infatuation with professional athletics began, giving a virtual coup de grace to religion as the non-economic and non-sexual preoccupation of millions of middle-class Americans" (pp. 191–192). Clearly the 1920s—often referred to as the *Golden Age of Sports*—saw media coverage of sports reach new heights in American culture, and the sports pages became a central, widely read, and indispensable section of the daily paper. Schlesinger (1933) reported that whereas the average newspaper devoted .04% of its editorial content to sports in 1880, and 4.0% in 1900, by the 1920s the average paper devoted between 12% and 20% of its editorial space to sports coverage.

One of the considerable challenges for journalists during the late nineteenth and early twentieth centuries was knowing how and where to draw the line between journalism and public relations, between sports news and sports publicity. The emerging sports teams and sports leagues witnessed firsthand the power of the press to build and sustain audiences for their games (and dollars for their coffers) and, knowing that sports journalists were poorly paid, rolled out the red carpet and put on the feedbag to make reporters act like cheerleaders with media megaphones. The teams, especially major league baseball teams, plied journalists with free food at the ballpark and free transportation, food, and lodging if they accompanied the team on the road (Enriquez, 2002). In return, they expected the sportswriters to serve as publicists for their team and their sport (another innovation that lingers as a curse of modern times).

A worthy case study of the extent to which such publicity resulted in competition between newspapers, albeit with boxing rather than baseball, is Stephens' (1983) examination of newspaper coverage of "The Fight of the Century" (a boxing match between "Gentleman Jim" Corbett versus "Ruby Rob" Fitzsimmons that was held on Saint Patrick's Day in 1897) by the Chicago *Tribune* and the San Francisco *Examiner*. As journalism historian Mott (1950) suggested, "No sports story had ever been played up so prominently as was the Corbett–Fitzsimmons bout in Nevada City in

1897" (p. 578). According to Stephens (1983), both the *Tribune* and the *Examiner* featured numerous stories and illustrations about the fight for several days leading up to it, with some of the sensationalized stories commanding the front page of the papers, and with both papers running specials or extras to cover the fight even more extensively. "Stories set in larger than average type, huge and prominent illustrations and novelty style headlines were used" (Stephens, 1983, p. 11). On the actual day of the fight, the Chicago *Tribune* ran 15 articles on the fight, including a front-page article. Not to be outdone, the San Francisco *Examiner* ran 16 articles and 8 illustrations on the fight on March 17, and on March 18 ran 21 articles and 16 illustrations. That's sensationalism!

Speaking of the *Tribune*, Arch Ward, the sports editor of the *Chicago Tribune*, was probably the most blatant publicist among the prominent journalists of the early twentieth century. Among Ward's public relations activities for various sports were founding the major league baseball All-Star Game, an annual football game between the National Football League (NFL) champions against a team of college all-stars, the Golden Gloves amateur boxing tournament, and the All-America Football Conference (a rival to the fledgling NFL). Ward actively curried the favor of the sports leagues and teams, but in return he expected access to sources that others did not receive and information well before it was released to other newspapers. It is anyone's guess how intimate Ward and kindred sports–media bedfellows would have become had it not been for the development of alternative celluloid and electronic media, which soon vied successfully for favors of their own, reducing the grip that sports seemed to be developing over newspapers (Enriquez, 2002).

The incursion of the newer media of the early industrial age into sports journalism is foreshadowed by a note in Stephens' (1983) aforementioned case study of "The Fight of the Century." On the day of the fight (March 17, 1897), the following note appeared in the Chicago *Tribune*: "The *Tribune* will display bulletins today on the prize fight. It has secured a telegraph wire to the ring in Carson City and a competent man will describe the progress of the fight, blow by blow, until the contest is decided. The bulletins will be posted thirty seconds after they are written in the far Western city" (Stephens, 1983, pp. 10–11). "Media historians have devoted a substantial amount of attention to the effects of the telegraph on newspapers" (Smethers & Jolliffe, 1992, p. 83). One of the noteworthy features of their reports is who first utilized the telegraph for sports reporting—none other than "the father of wireless": "Wireless was first used for news reporting in connection with the international yacht races of 1899. Guglielmo Marconi, a young man of 25, handled the transmission of this report for the Associated Press" (Mott, 1950, p. 579). Although some of the changes wrought by the telegraph have been evaluated negatively (e.g., standardization of content and format), others have suggested that the telegraph helped build the enormous power of the press, adding increased timeliness to the content of newspapers (e.g., Tebbel, 1974). For certain, the telegraph helped impart timeliness to sports communication and furthered the nationalization of sports.

A second newer technology that helped publicize sports and add to the stature of athletes was the newsreel. Film began to develop as a mass medium during the late nineteenth century, and when movie houses became popular in the 1920s and 1930s, newsreels became a standard part of America's new Saturday pastime of going to the movies. Pathé News and Fox Movietone News produced hundreds of these celluloid news magazines. Among the most popular newsreel features were clips from sporting events, and sportsreels helped nationalize sports by visualizing major sports heroes who had never before been seen by sports fans outside of the cities where they played.

However, it was with the emerging electronic medium of radio that sports really caught fire. The commercial birth of radio is typically dated 1920. "The entrepreneurs of early radio were quick to see the value of sports coverage, especially live play-by-play" (Smethers & Jolliffe, 1992, p. 83).

> The first broadcast of a major league baseball game was heard on August 5, 1921, over station KDKA in Pittsburgh, the nation's first radio station. In 1923 the World Series was broadcast to an ad hoc network of stations across the country. The first program aired on the NBC radio network was a sporting event, the heavyweight championship fight between Jack Dempsey and Gene Tunney on September 23, 1926. Radio broadcasts of sporting events allowed millions of fans to experience events with an immediacy that newspapers could not match. (Enriquez, 2002, p. 202)

Despite considerable early resistance to radio by team owners and managers, who feared that radio coverage would erode game attendance, loyal listeners soon regularly crowded round the family radio set to listen to sportscasts of all kinds. Bittner and Bittner (1977) suggested that radio was the first "personal medium" (p. 3), and they noted that it was sports that brought the nation together on radio— virtually, at least: "By January of 1927, NBC had two networks in operation, the Red Network and the Blue Network. NBC utilized them to cover the 1927 Rose Bowl Game, which became America's first transcontinental network broadcast" (p. 3).

Radio had the capability of infusing the immediacy of live sports coverage with gratuitous drama in ways heretofore impossible. The inimitable James Michener (1976) shared this story in his book *Sports in America*:

> Let me explain how I became a connoisseur of radio and television broadcasters. I was working in Colorado back in 1936, and on a blustery Saturday afternoon I was driving home with my car radio on. It was a football game between two western universities, late in the final quarter. It was obviously a game of heroic proportions, with players from the home team—I forget its name—performing miracles. They must have been playing over their heads, because although I didn't catch the score, they were socking it to their opponents, and the announcer was breathless in his excitement over the performance of his heroes. Then the game ended and he revealed the score. His miracle players had lost, something like 42-0, and I realized for the first time that the announcer's job was to create suspense, sustain tension, and give the listener the feeling that he had participated in a game which had been decided only in the final seconds. (pp. 383–384)

Like newspapers and magazines before them, radio sportscasting was soon to develop its own stars. The preeminent sportscaster of the 1920s was Graham McNamee, who was not particularly knowledgeable about sports but had a great voice and a flair for the dramatic. When the Jack Dempsey–Gene Tunney heavyweight boxing matches were broadcast on makeshift national radio networks in 1926 and 1927, more than 100 radio listeners purportedly dropped dead from listening to McNamee's blow-by-blow tense calling of the fight (Evensen, 1996; Rader, 1984). Evensen (1996) examined these Dempsey–Tunney fights not only in terms of important social and media developments, but also as sports events that contained or were imbued with many of the ingredients of great drama, which, in turn, helped create a new generation of media celebrities:

> The first [of two parallel struggles] is the story of two fighters of very different temperament and background whose personal drama was staged in a squared ring through the promotional genius of the era's greatest showman. The other contest was fought between star sportswriters and senior editors of different dispositions and values, whose struggle over tall-tale telling in the nation's sports pages, and eventually in radio, reflected journalism's uncertain complicity in the manufacture of celebrity in an era of personal publicity. Each battle sheds light on the role of sport, celebrity, and mass-mediated civic spectacle in defining and stylizing competing values of urban America during the nation's interwar era. (p. x)

The stories that could be told about the firsts and foibles of early radio sportscasting are legion, but we will offer only one more example of the electronic frontier mentality of the era, which also illustrates the fusion of radio sportscasting with another fledgling medium, with the resultant product seasoned with drama— a convergence that has characterized the sports–media relationship ever since. Coverage of home games by radio flourished in the 1920s, but because AT&T and its patent alliance charged exorbitant rates for long-distance telephone lines, covering away games was prohibitively expensive for radio stations. So the radio entrepreneurs of the day utilized dramatic "re-creations" to fill the void.

> Like live game broadcasts, re-creations were colorful, lively, up-to-the-minute broadcasts of ongoing sports contests—provided by announcers who were nowhere near the games. . . . Instead these announcers broadcast from their home studios, re-creating the games using Morse code play-by-play coming in from distant ballfields via Western Union. This technique made continuous coverage of sports teams possible. Continuous coverage, in turn, helped develop a following among fans and a highly salable programming schedule for radio stations. (Smethers & Jolliffe, 1992, p. 84)

Re-creations remained popular until 1955, when the courts ruled that broadcasters had to pay teams a royalty for re-creating their games, which brought that practice to a screeching halt (Rader, 1984). Given the success of re-creations, is there any wonder that play-by-play and color commentators today feel free to add drama and illusion to their sportscasts and to our games?

As might be expected, radio's success with sportscasts left newspapers scrambling. One adjustment newspaper editors and writers made was to focus on areas not covered very well in radio play-by-play—strategy and analysis, sports personalities, off-the-field events, misdeeds of athletes, and so forth. In other words, they adjusted their focus and provided informational and functional alternatives, the way older media have responded to newer media through the years. This helped maintain newspapers' place in the media market among readers and advertisers alike.

A new and very different sports magazine also emerged to provide what radio could not. Simply called *Sport*, it was first published in 1946. "It was the first general-circulation magazine devoted entirely to sports. Its main distinction was its full-page color photographs, usually in heroic action poses or in strong close-ups and well suited to being cut out and tacked to a boy's bedroom wall" (Enriquez, 2002, p. 202).

Again, the idea was to find a market niche to provide what radio could not, and because *Sport* hired a superlative slate of sportswriters, it succeeded admirably.

Newspapers also were to find two eloquent sports journalists in the post-World War II period. Red Smith, who did most of his best writing for the *New York Herald Tribune*, was the heir apparent to Grantland Rice, and he was the most widely syndicated sports columnist of the day. Like Rice, he offered a literate, witty style, although Smith was much more understated in delivery than was Rice. Jimmy Cannon, who also wrote for New York newspapers, primarily the *Post* and the *Journal American*, also provided a poignant voice for sports. "His style was romantic, world-weary, witty, and passionate" (Enriquez, 2002, p. 202). Smith and Cannon helped bring sports to life for a new generation of sports enthusiasts and chronicled the best sports stories of their time in their memorable manners.

But the biggest sports story of the post-World War II American industrial age was television. Like radio, television allowed sports fans to experience their games with immediacy and with more detail than newspapers or sports magazines would ever care to provide. Additionally, unlike any other medium to date, television provided moving pictures to accompany the sounds that radio offered, and with the addition of color commentators, cutaways, crowd shots, close-ups of emotional displays, and a wide range of special effects, television was to create a new sport of every sport it covered. Inevitably television was transformative—sometimes it transformed sports for the better, sometimes for the worse, sometimes it even created new sports of its own (e.g., Michener, 1976; Rader, 1984). As Enriquez (2002) reported, "Television broadcasting affected different sports in different ways. It devastated boxing, had mixed effects on baseball, and proved a boon to college and professional football" (p. 202).

Lest we get ahead of our story, we should examine the roots of sports television:

> Television came into the sports world on May 17, 1939 as the RCA mobile TV unit showed a Columbia–Princeton baseball game from Baker Field. A single camera stood near the third-base line, sweeping back and forth. By the time the unit went to Ebbets Field for a Brooklyn Dodgers and Cincinnati Reds game, they had added a second camera. (Hitchcock, 1989, p. 1)

Initially television was not to be the darling of team sports because the primitive video technologies and fledgling camera operators and editors were to make somewhat of a mockery of the complex games and play of team sports.

> Indeed, two of the leading sports on television were professional wrestling and Roller Derby. They were often broadcast during prime time, since they were ideally suited for low-budget television; a single camera could focus on one or two people at a time....At its high point, wrestling was broadcast by over 200 stations on a weekly basis, but it was quickly relegated to the fringes of television, along with Roller Derby, as television turned to baseball and football and more expensive nonsports prime-time fare by the mid-1950s. (McChesney, 1989, p. 60)

However, it was not until the early 1960s that television was to truly wrest control from its sibling broadcast medium, radio, and begin an ascendancy in sports coverage that was to last through the portals of the information age to the present era. Videotape technology had emerged in the 1950s, in part developed by Bing Cosby Enterprises (Nmungwun, 1989), and this was to prove to be an essential technological development for advancements in television sportscasting. Relying heavily on videotape, ABC-TV created a sports anthology show called the *Wide World of Sports*, which launched in 1961 (Hitchcock, 1989).

> Through the use of videotape and commercial jet travel, events from around the world (such as the world championships of track and field) could be recorded, returned and edited into a tight, exciting package. The use of videotape gave the game of football a whole new image. Videotape was used to create the "instant replay." It was first used during the 1963 New Year's Eve Army–Navy game. During 1964, it was a standard sportscasting technique. The instant replay changed football from brutal, quick collisions into graceful leaps, tumbles and falls. It gave football an aura of art in movement. It made football attractive to entirely new segments of the audience. (Hitchcock, 1989, p. 2)

McChesney (1989) has argued cogently that in addition to its audiovisual superiority, five major developments led to the supremacy of television in sports coverage. First was its skyrocketing penetration rate, as it rapidly entered the vast majority of American homes. Second was the radically improving technology of television, including the development of color technology. Third was the Sports Broadcasting Act of 1961, "which permitted professional sports teams in a league to negotiate as one unit with broadcasters" (p. 61), and which prior to that time had been considered an infringement of antitrust laws. Fourth was a trend by networks and stations to purchase broadcast rights directly from the teams and leagues, which allowed the media to then sell time on their sportscasts to advertisers, which proved to be immensely profitable. Fifth, and most importantly, was simply that certain big-ticket advertisers, like manufacturers of automobiles, trucks, and business equipment, discovered that televised sports gave them an ideal entry into the living rooms—and thereby the eyes and ears—of the highly desirable male audience.

The importance of a single individual to the success of sports television also should be mentioned. Roone Arledge, a producer for ABC Sports, was one of the most influential change agents in all of television. As Sugar (1978) noted, "In a field devoted to fashioning halos for personalities, Roone Arledge wears a special nimbus. He is that rarity in American television, a behind-the-scenes superstar" (pp. 61–62). Or,

> His stature rests not so much on being a one-man laboratory for the discovery of new forms, as in being a master of theory and techniques who has made important contributions to the development of both.... However you look at it, he has made ABC Sports the biggest jock on the broadcast block and has had a fertilizing effect on all of television sports. (p. 62)

What did Arledge do that was so different from his predecessors or competitors? Many things, but perhaps most important was that he presented all televised sports from the perspective of what the typical fan would see if he or she attended the game live.

He prepared a mammoth loose-leaf notebook, still legendary in the corridors of ABC, which said that covering a televised game should be just like being a spectator at the game; you not only looked at the game in front of you, but at other people in the stands, the players on the sidelines, and the action around you, whether that be cheerleaders or marching bands or personalities in the stands. (Sugar, 1978, p. 77)

In addition to bringing the viewers to the game—as well as bringing the whole game to viewers—Arledge revolutionized the production components of the game. He placed microphones on the field; he first doubled and then tripled the standard number of cameras used to cover the game; he accentuated the personalities of players and coaches; he oversaw the development and implementation of the instant replay; he allowed the play-by-play and color commentators much more freedom to dramatize and personalize the event, as well as to use replay and graphics to underscore analysis; and he made *Monday Night Football* (*MNF*) de rigueur viewing in sports bars and homes throughout America, thereby extending the weekend one more day for avid football fans. Enriquez (2002) summarized Roone Arledge's contributions quite well: "Under Arledge, television assumed every role previously played by print media: it served as the primary medium for experiencing events, it provided detailed analysis, and it gave human faces to the participants" (p. 205).

Perhaps because ABC trailed CBS and NBC in overall program ratings, the network attempted numerous sports innovations during the 1960s and early 1970s. In addition to launching *Wide World of Sports* in 1961 and *Monday Night Football* in 1970, it also pioneered coverage of the Olympic Games, taking the games "from relative anonymity to the premier sporting event telecast every four years" (McChesney, 1989, p. 63). ABC also made the Olympic coverage lucrative, and rights payments for Summer Olympics broadcasts jumped from $5 million in 1968 to hundreds of millions in the 1980s.

While ABC sports was developing its innovative sports department, which would ultimately result in Roone Arledge becoming Vice President for Sports (and later, of news), CBS was staking much of its sports future on the fledgling National Football League (NFL), which also proved to be a sage move. Prior to the late 1950s, professional football had been a relatively minor attraction in the sports world, although it certainly had a loyal nucleus of hardcore fans. However, as television developed into a national medium and television's production values and professional announcing teams rapidly became more sophisticated, the NFL began to capture the imagination of fans nationwide. This was a sport that seemed ideally suited for television. Football's periodized action allowed sportscaster commentary and special effects like instant replay to complement and dramatize play, and its violence and mayhem and its relatively slow ball movement and highly visible ball were easy for viewers to see. Season these and other favorable ingredients with the wise guidance of the NFL's television-savvy early commissioners Bert Bell and Pete Rozelle, two of the most gifted architects of televised sports in the history of the sports–media tradition, and CBS had a recipe for great success. Indeed, within a decade of its regular coverage by national television, the NFL had become America's leading spectator sport. In 1962, CBS agreed to pay the NFL the then unheard-of amount of $4.5 million per year for broadcast rights. Two years later, with rising visibility and concomitantly spiraling Nielsen ratings, Rozelle negotiated a rights fee of $14 million per year (McChesney, 1989), and the stage was set for the ascendancy of the NFL to become America's sport—at least its most beloved televised sport.

Despite its successes and innovations, the NFL was relatively conservative in its expansion policies throughout the 1950s and early 1960s. Entrepreneurs in major cities without NFL teams wanted in on the action at a much faster pace than the NFL commissioners thought was beneficial to the league. Therefore, in 1960, team owners in heretofore-unserved cities formed a competitive professional football league—the American Football League (AFL)—and the AFL negotiated a contract with ABC Sports prior to its initial kickoff. This set a new precedent in terms of sports–media relationships because for the first time a new sports product and brand was created with the hope that new audiences and advertisers would make the venture financially feasible largely through television revenues. This was a model that would become quite common in the information age.

The next major development in NFL–media relationships occurred in 1965, when NBC entered into a bidding war with CBS for NFL coverage rights and lost. Then NBC turned its attentions to the AFL, with which it negotiated a $42-million rights contract over a five-year period, which gave the AFL near parity with the NFL in terms of coverage and compensation. "In effect, the network had become a copromoter of the AFL. The plan worked. The AFL began to sign top NFL players and the NFL, once it realized that the NBC contract guaranteed the AFL's existence" (McChesney, 1989, pp. 62–63), realized that change was inevitable. In 1966, Congress passed legislation that permitted the AFL to merge with the NFL. "As part of the deal, NBC was permitted to telecast half of the merged league's games along with CBS" (McChesney, p. 63).

The two parts of the merged league agreed to play a championship game after the regular season ended. The first game was played on January 15, 1967. It was technically called "The AFL–NFL World Championship Game of Professional Football"; fortunately, it soon became known as the Super Bowl—the Goliath of media–sports collaborations. The first Super Bowl was telecast by both NBC and CBS and was the first dual-network, color-coverage simulcast of a sports event. It also attracted the largest audience ever to see a sporting event at that time—73 million viewers. This, of course, proved to be par for the course. The Super Bowl is routinely the top-rated telecast of the television season, and 37 of the top 50 sports telecasts of all time are Super Bowl Games ("TV Basics," 2005). Moreover, Super Bowl Weekend has achieved the status of a national holiday, created not by Hallmark but by television and the NFL.

Eying the success of the NFL's television coverage, the commissioners of professional baseball, basketball, and hockey, as well as collegiate football and basketball, all negotiated lucrative network broadcast contracts during the 1960s. Building on the success of these affiliations, during the 1970s and 1980s the networks programmed more and more sports as they discovered the immense popularity that sports programming offered. The advertisers loved sports programming because it enabled them to reach the affluent male audience that was otherwise difficult to get en masse. By the mid-80s, the three major networks were all selling more than $1 billion dollars in advertising on their sports programming (Powers, 1984; Rader, 1984), and the era of Big Sports–Big TV had definitely arrived. Viewing of sports television was to become the prototypical leisure activity of the industrial age—symbolizing the way the working man celebrated his free time.

As might be anticipated, Big Sports–Big TV was to create a new celebrity class—the big-time television sportscaster. Many names could be found on a list of sportscaster celebrities of the industrial age, including Curt Gowdy, Jim McKay,

John Madden, Pat Summerall, Al Michaels, Dick Stockton, Keith Jackson, Don Meredith, Frank Gifford, Brent Musburger, and Dick Vitale—many of whom survived or even thrived in the information age—but the archetype sportscaster of the industrial age was Howard Cosell. Howard Cosell was a sportscasting-lightening rod; for many years he was simultaneously voted the "most loved" and "most hated" sportscaster in America. "He had neither a pleasant voice nor a pleasant face, but he worked hard, never flinched from asking tough questions, and utilized his prodigious memory and prodigious vocabulary to great advantage" (Enriquez, 2002, p. 205). Cosell was a protégé of Roone Arledge. Cosell's early reputation was made as a highly competent fight announcer, and Arledge had supported Cosell's unflinching endorsement of boxer Muhammad Ali through a string of controversies (i.e., Ali's religious conversion, name change, political stances, refusal to be inducted into the Army). Cosell paid Arledge back for his loyalty with his much-heralded reporting for ABC at the 1972 Olympic Games in Munich, where he covered the Palestinian terrorists' capture and execution of Israeli athletes, as well as the games themselves, with considerable sophistication and aplomb.

But it was for his controversial, opinionated announcing on *Monday Night Football* that Cosell is best known. As Cosell repeatedly claimed, "We make sports entertaining." He was indeed a consummate showperson, and *MNF* provided a worthy stage.

> He was intelligent, insightful, and provocative, utterly unlike the smooth, portentous commentators working NFL games on other networks. He was teamed with Don Meredith, a former quarterback for the Dallas Cowboys. Cosell's sesquipedalian, provocative persona contrasted nicely with Meredith's folksy, regular-guy style. Keith Jackson, a veteran of ABC's college football crew, provided play-by-play, but the main focus was the by-play between Cosell and Meredith. (Enriquez, 2002, p. 205)

When Keith Jackson left the *MNF* team after one year with Cosell, Frank Gifford replaced him, and the Cosell–Meredith–Gifford trio flourished for several years. However, "much of the show's popularity derived from viewers' loathing of Cosell. Viewers were angered when he told them that a player wasn't particularly good or even that the player had made mistakes. Hating Cosell became a national pastime" (Enriquez, 2002, p. 205).

Two new sports media founded in the industrial age have also flourished in the information age. The first is an update of an innovation of the agriculture age: a new sports magazine. In many ways, *Sports Illustrated* offers a classic example of an old medium responding to a new one—in this case, the incursion of television into the world of sports. *Sports Illustrated*, or *SI*, was first published in 1954. Magazines were looking for sports that television was not covering, so *SI* first covered upper-class sports like yachting and golf. However, under the leadership of managing editor Andre Laguere from 1960 to 1974, the magazine shifted its focus toward mainstream sports, developed a distinctive style, and "became the dominant national news medium for middle-class spectator sports" (Enriquez, 2002, p. 204). *SI*'s niche was explaining the nuances of popular spectator sports, like college and pro football, baseball, basketball, and hockey, to the armchair spectator long before the metaphor of the couch potato became popular. It also became the locus for innovative sports action photography and was noteworthy for constantly seeking new photographic and printing technologies and techniques. But the magazine was best known for its excellent writing (and, much later, for its swimsuit issue; see Curtis, 2005, for an historical overview). Writers like Dan Jenkins and Frank Deford set the tone for the magazine, offering surprisingly sophisticated psychological and socio cultural insights as well as lucid prose. Not only did *Sports Illustrated* tackle traditional sports stories, it also wrote about and editorialized about the complex and pertinent sports issues of the day. It worked hard to become a complementary sports medium with television, and thereby became an important institution in its own right.

Another important sports–media innovation of the industrial age began on September 7, 1979. Father and son Bill and Scott Rasmussen began a bold and extremely successful new chapter in the history of sports and media in the United States that day, by launching the Entertainment and Sports Programming Network, better known as ESPN. The new 24-hours-per-day cable network began as an alternative to the sports section of daily newspapers and originally featured short sports segments in standard television news-type broadcasts. It also featured coverage of relatively unorthodox sporting events, such as tractor pulls, games of the short-lived United States Football League (USFL), college soccer, and hydroplane and auto racing, which sometimes seemed to be covered to fill time as much as to attract viewers ("ESPN," 2005). Its signature program from the day of the launch was a highlight program originally called *Sports Recap* but soon renamed the more familiar *SportsCenter.* Featuring an engaging cast of smart-mouth, quipping, clever anchors like Chris Berman (hired one month after ESPN's inception; see "Chris Berman," 2003), Dan Patrick, and Keith Olbermann and managed behind the scenes by the brilliant John Walsh, *SportsCenter* become obligatory viewing for several generations of sports enthusiasts. Or, as Enriquez (2002) indicated, "*SportsCenter* inspired fanatical loyalty in viewers and became the standard for television coverage of sports news" (p. 206). ESPN ascended even more lofty heights in 1987, when the network landed a contract to cover National Football League games on Sunday evenings, an event that helped turn ESPN from just another cable television network "to a marketing empire and a cornerstone to the enthusiastic 'sports culture' it largely helped to create" ("ESPN," 2005, pp. 2–3).

Newspapers did not stand still with the ascendancy of television journalism. "The level of sports coverage remained in the 12–20% of editorial content range that had been established in the 1920s until the 1970s, when it tended to move upward for the very reasons it was so high in the first place: Sports coverage was very popular, relatively inexpensive, and noncontroversial" (McChesney, 1989, p. 66). A newcomer to the newspaper scene devoted even more of its editorial content to sports coverage. The national newspaper *USA Today* devoted fully 25% of its editorial space to sports, and many subscribed to this paper because of its excellent and timely sports coverage. *Sports Illustrated*'s "Frank Deford described it as 'a daily *Sporting News* wrapped in color weather maps'" (McChesney, 1989, p. 66).

All in all, by the conclusion of the industrial age in the United States, four of the conventional mass media—newspapers, magazines, television, and radio—had made sufficient adjustments that all of them were providing substantial sports content and making considerable income from the coverage of sports. Film, too, was doing quite well with its coverage of sports, albeit largely in the form of fictionalized sports drama (see chaps. 5 and 11, this volume). The sports–media relationships of the industrial age ended this era having achieved the level of a complex but well-integrated social system, complete with abundant interdependencies and occasional tensions and out-and-out conflicts.

SPORTS AND MEDIA DURING
THE INFORMATION AGE

Considerable disagreement exists over when the information age began. Some have claimed it began in the 1440s with the invention of the printing press (e.g., Southon, 2001), although few scholars would agree. Others have argued that the key line of demarcation was the development of the Internet and the introduction of digital communication in the 1960s, at least in the United States. But our preference is to delimit the information age in the United States from the period of the 1990s to the foreseeable future. Why? This is the period in which more than 50% of the workforce in the United States has been made up of information workers (currently at 55%), and this is the era of the World Wide Web, which made digital communication a practical reality for the average citizen (Black, Bryant, & Thompson, 1998).

More important than when the information age began is how life in information societies is different from life in agricultural and industrial ages. Rogers (1986) delineated five key differences in life in these three epochs, of which we will mention only two: In terms of the most essential *technology*, in the agriculture age, manual labor ruled the day; in the industrial age, it was the steam engine; and in the information age, computers and electronics became the technologies of choice. Regarding the predominant type of *communication medium*, for the agriculture age, it was one-way print media (e.g., newspapers, magazines); for the industrial age, one-way electronic media (e.g., radio, television, film) predominated; for the information age, interactive media that allow one-to-one as well as many-to-many communication (e.g., Internet) have become the main communication source.

Another key characteristic of the information age is that the *rate of change* is constantly increasing. As Dionne (1987) has said, "The Industrial Revolution changed the way we work in two centuries. The Information Revolution has done as much in two decades" (p. 2). Major information-age media developments also include a trend toward *specialization* of programming in order to meet the needs and interests of an increasingly *fragmented* audience. And a final characteristic that we would note is that media have engaged in so-called *convergence* in myriad ways. In discussing convergence, we follow the lead of Gordon (2003), who explicated that term to include convergence of ownership (e.g., merger of media conglomerates), convergence of tactics (e.g., partnerships between media entities), convergence in structure (e.g., shared space and resources by two or more media entities), convergence in information gathering (e.g., covering a story using multiple media), and convergence in presentation (e.g., new forms of storytelling across multiple media platforms). As we examine the evolution of sports and media in the information age, we will see that this is exactly what is happening in the sports–media world.

Our coverage of sports and media developments during the information age will, of necessity, be qualitatively and quantitatively different from our historical overview of sports–media in the agriculture and industrial age, for two reasons: First, we are still in the early stages of the information age; therefore, it is impossible to gain the sort of distanced historical perspective that such scholarship entails. Second, and more practically, many of the other chapters of this volume cover these developments in great detail. For example, the chapters by Brown and Bryant on "Sports Content on U.S. Television" and by Krein and Martin on "60 Seconds to Air: Key Developments and Production Basics of a National Television Sports Broadcast" examine a vast array of major new developments in television coverage of sports. Therefore, although we will point out major trends and daily developments in sports and media relationships in the information age, we will do so primarily in a macroanalytic manner.

A New Broadcast Network Heavily Invested in Sports

Ironically, one of the most important sports-communication developments of the information age is an extension of one of the main thrusts of the industrial age—the addition of a new broadcast network that has excelled in sports programming. A recent release from Fox Sports trumpets "FOX Completes 10th Anniversary Year as Top-Rated Network for Sports" and adds: "It is the eighth consecutive year the network has been number one" ("FOX completes," 2005, p. 1). Through clever negotiating and positioning, and because of the financial commitment of owner Rupert Murdock (through his News Corporation), Fox has managed to acquire the broadcast rights to "television's most formidable audience-producing programming lineup, led by the NFL, MLB and NASCAR.... Five of the top-10 rated sports programs on television in 2004 were broadcast on FOX" ("FOX completes," 2005, p. 1).

Fragmentation and Specialization of Programming

It is now quite common for broadcast networks to cover several different games of the same sport at the same time, distributing their telecasts of the different games to affiliate stations within the geographic regions of interest. Often cutaways from a game will provide studio-based updates of various games that are common to all of the regional telecasts, which are presented by sports anchors, or if a game in one region gets sufficiently lop-sided to reduce its entertainment value, coverage may shift to a more tightly contested game outside of the geographic region of interest (much to the consternation of loyal sports fans who tuned in to see a particular game, for which coverage is now limited to occasional updates).

Sports coverage by cable networks has become even more specialized, with the News Corporations' 2005 Cable Sports Division divided into Fox College Sports, Fox Sports Enterprises, Fox Sports in Español, Fox Sports Net, Fox Sports World, and the Speed Channel. Fox Sports Net includes more than two dozen regional sports channels or networks, all owned by the News Corporation. Via its regional cable networks, Fox offers numerous regional sports news programs (e.g., *Southern Sports Report*) in addition to coverage of regional games of all sorts. ESPN has become extremely specialized also. In addition to ESPN per se, the ESPN family of cable sports networks includes ESPN2 (typically more of the same), ESPN-NEWS (providing 24-hours-per-day highlights, scores, and breaking stories from the sports world), ESPN Classic (documentaries and replays of great games in sports history), ESPN Deportes (a Spanish-language sports network), ESPNHD (presents normal ESPN programming in high definition), and ESPNU (a college athletics channel).

For the truly hardcore sports fan, satellite networks like Dish Network and Direct TV offer an amazing array of premium sports programming, such as *NFL Sunday Ticket, MLB Extra Innings, NBA League Pass, NHL Center Ice, ESPN Full Court: College Basketball, WNBA Season Pass, MLS Direct Kick, English Premier League*, and the like, in addition to numerous boxing and wrestling events that are available on a periodic pay-per-view basis. With these specialized packages, which in 2005 were available from between $49 and $299 per package, the avid fan can essentially choose any game in any sport he or she wants to watch from practically anywhere around the world ("Dish or Direct," 2005).

Another initiative in specialization to seek a hardcore sports audience was the move to all-sports radio. Historically radio's important role in sports communication was to present games to national audiences, with play-by-play provided by legendary announcers like Red Barber, Mel Allen, and Dizzy Dean. When such coverage was usurped by television and the Internet, one of the new ways radio found to serve sports fans and survive was to supplement play-by-play coverage with sports talk and other sports information 24 hours per day, especially on the AM dial. Although sports discussion shows date from the 1950s and were quite popular, especially immediately before and after important games in major cities, it was the advent of interactive caller-based sports programs that ultimately led to the success of all-sports radio. Some of the programming of such niche radio is local, but many of the most popular sports talk shows are national and are provided by syndicates, or they are found on the all-sports networks, like ESPN radio. Some of the most successful examples of such sports-talk programming is abrasive and often is inflammatory if not incendiary, but it has become a staple for sports fans in major radio markets (Munson, 1993; Norman, 1990). With the increased popularity of satellite radio, specialized sports packages such as NFL or NBA radiocasts can be the constant mobile companion to the most avid sports fans, adding to the richness, variability, and customization of sports radio.

Related Business Ventures

In the industrial age, sports networks basically presented sports coverage, news, and the like. In the information age, collateral sports-related business ventures have ruled the day. For example,

> ESPN launched the ESPN Radio network on January 1, 1992, *ESPN The Magazine* on March 11, 1998, and its ESPN Zone franchise of restaurant/entertainment complexes in Baltimore, Maryland on July 11, 1998. . . . The ESPY Awards are also administered by ESPN, which it initiated in 1993. . . . Starting with their 2004 lineup of sports games, Sega acquired the ESPN license to integrate the "TV show look & feel" into its franchise of video games covering America's major professional sports leagues and college basketball. The deal will end after the 2005–2006 sports season. After the 2005–2006 season, Electronic Arts will acquire the ESPN license to use for 15-years on their video games. ("ESPN," 2005, p. 3)

Other sports entities are expanding their media-related enterprises in similar manners. Such entrepreneurial ventures greatly facilitate convergence as discussed by Gordon (2003).

Sports Dot.coms

One of the hallmarks of the information age is the extensive use of computers and networks. Many of the giants of sports communication have employed or contracted with web designers and programmers to create exceptionally fine Web sites, including some of the most popular ones on the Internet today. "ESPN launched their own website known as ESPN SportsZone in 1995. After 1998, the site was renamed to ESPN.com. In 2001, ESPN.com created a new website called *Page 2*, which includes sports opinion columns from several writers" ("ESPN," 2005, p. 3). ESPN has been a leader in using their Web sites as portals via which the fans can interact with games presented on ESPN or its sister network ABC (both owned by Disney), creating more active, engaged viewers of sportscasts. But not all has been rosy for the interactive division of ESPN. One of the hot stories of 2004 was MSN (Microsoft Network) switching from ESPN.com to FOX.com as its online provider of sports information, with Fox stories featured on—and the Fox site linked to—the MSN home page. It is obvious that many companies will increasingly join the competition for the dot.com sports fan.

In fact, an amazing array of Web sites is already available for information-age sports fans. In addition to classic Web sites associated with the cable sports networks are the Web sites associated with magazines (e.g., SI.com), networks (e.g., CBS.sportline.com), sports associations (e.g., NCAA.com), leagues (NBA.com), teams (e.g., HarlemAllStars.com), tournaments (e.g., NIT.org), camps (e.g., quarterbackschool.com), specialized news (e.g., collegefootballnews.com), specialized talk (e.g., chicksonfootball.com), and blogs of every persuasion. Moreover, it seems that every player, coach, team—and even every youth league star athlete and team—now has a Web site devoted to its coverage. In fact, many have many more than one Web site, with major college and university athletic departments having a vast array of commercial as well as public-access Web sites devoted to their various teams. Offering what may be the ultimate in sports fan convenience, nowadays Web sites exist to help sports fans search for the best Web sites for each sport, team, and so forth (e.g., BestSearchers.com).

Crossover as Convergence

An additional sign of the times is crossover representation between media, a form of convergence (Gordon, 2003). For example, *Sports Illustrated*'s columnists regularly appear on ESPN as well as CNN, *Sports Illustrated*'s Frank Defore does a popular weekly segment on National Public Radio, pro football stars show up on *Wheel of Fortune* for NFL Players Week, the sports stars de jour appear regularly on early morning and late night television and radio talk shows—and these examples are just the tip of the proverbial iceberg.

If Howard Cosell typified the industrial-age sportscaster, John Madden must be the information-age sports-and-media personality archetype. Madden, a Super Bowl winning coach, was paid $7.5 million in 2002 to call NFL games for FOX, making him the highest-paid sportscaster in the world, and his four-year, $32-million deal with FOX in 1994 provided him with a more lucrative contract than any NFL player at the time ("John Madden," 2005). Madden turned down a three-year $15-million extension with FOX and the last year of his $7.5-million-per-year salary to sign with ABC to provide color commentary for the network's venerable *Monday Night Football* for a mere $5 million per year (Helfand, 2005). Not everything about John Madden is *IA* (i.e., information-age-like); in fact, in some ways Madden definitely is old school, with his refusal to fly and his "All Madden" team of bruisers and overachievers. On the other hand, because he is all over the tube and the Net doing commercials, endorsements, cross-program plugs, interviews, and the like, and because he is one of the most successful names in electronic gaming, he is a wonderful icon for the information age's fusion of sports and media.

The Future of Sports and Media

Where do we go from here? What will the next phase of the information age bring? Some things are almost certain to get bigger and bigger. For example, "the world-wide television audience for the Athens 2004 Olympic Games was 3.9 billion people compared to the 3.6 billion for the Sydney 2000 games. The FIFA World Cup media rights value rose to $879 million for the 2006 tournament, a 15% increase since 2002" ("Sport and the media," 2005). And it is highly likely that the cost for commercials during the Super Bowl will continue to rise; for example, the average 2005 Super Bowl commercial sold for $2.4 million, whereas in 2004 it cost $2.3 million, up from $2.1 million in 2003.

However, the converse of all this gigantism—specialization and segmentation—undoubtedly will continue as a major trend as well. With the proliferation in coverage of women's sports, youth sports, and new sports, audience niches will be widely sought by media providers and advertisers alike, so long as a critical mass of viewers can be reached. With the movement of streaming video onto the Internet, not only can the mother of Ute All-American Andrew Bogurt stay at home in Australia and watch via computer and the Web her son play basketball in real time during the "Sweet 16" NCAA contest between Kentucky and Utah, but "EveryMom" can watch her youth league soccer son or daughter play in real time during a local match. In addition to providing T-shirts and soft drinks, tomorrow's team sponsor will be expected to provide sponsorship support for the Web site and maybe even a few bucks for the camcorder operator and Web sysop.

A recent Harris Interactive poll revealed some insightful information about the future of sports, sports participation, and sports and media. In a report entitled "Youth Trends and the Impact on Sportainment's Future," the following conclusions were drawn: "If today's youth are tomorrow's consumers, the future looks strong for sports" (HarrisInteractive, 2001, p. 1). Not only were today's youth found to be more interested in more different sports than were their parents, they were more likely to attend and watch sporting events than were their elders. The report concluded with diverse ways for "sponsors to learn how to effectively reach the diverse and 'fickle' youth market" through sports and sports programming (HarrisInteractive, 2001, p. 1). The more things change, the more they seem to remain the same.

REFERENCES

Betts, J. R. (1952). *Organized sport in industrialized America*. New York: Columbia University Press.

Betts, J. R. (1974). *America's sporting heritage: 1850–1950*. Reading, MA: Addison-Wesley.

Bittner, J. R., & Bittner, D. A. (1977). *Radio journalism*. Englewood Cliffs, NJ: Prentice-Hall.

Black, J., & Bryant, J. (1995). *Introduction to media communication* (4th ed.). Madison, WI: Brown & Benchmark.

Black, J., Bryant, J., & Thompson, S. (1998). *Introduction to media communication* (5th ed.). New York: McGraw-Hill.

Bryant, J., Zillmann, D., & Raney, A. A. (1998). Violence and the enjoyment of media sports. In L. A. Wenner (Ed.), *MediaSport* (pp. 252–265). London: Routledge.

Chris Berman—Pre-game, halftime, post-game host. (2003, April 18). *ABC Sports*. Retrieved March 21, 2005, from http://espn.go.com/abcsports/bios/s/chrisberman.html

Curtis, B. (2005, Feb. 16). The *Sports Illustrated* Swimsuit Issue: An intellectual history. *Slate*. Retrieved March 13, 2005, from http://slate.msn.com/id/2113612/

Dionne, J. L. (1987). *The information revolution*. New York: McGraw-Hill.

Dish or Direct: Seasonal sports on satellite TV. (n.d.). Retrieved March 24, 2005, from Dish or Direct Web site http://www.dishordirect.com/sat/sports_seasonal.php

Enriquez, J. (2002). Coverage of sports. In W. D. Sloan & L. M. Parcell (Eds.), *American journalism: History, principles, practices* (pp. 198–208). Jefferson, NC: McFarland.

ESPN. (n.d.). *Wikipedia*. Retrieved March 22, 2005, from http://www.answers.com/topic/espn

Evensen, B. J. (1996). *When Dempsey fought Tunney: Heroes, hokum, and storytelling in the Jazz Age*. Knoxville: University of Tennessee Press.

FOX completes 10th anniversary year as top-rated network for sports. (2005, January). *FOXSports.com*. Retrieved March 22, 2005, from http://msn.foxsports.com/other/story/3293362

Gordon, R. (2003). The meanings and implications of convergence. In K. Kawamoto (Ed.), *Digital journalism: Emerging media and the changing horizons of journalism* (pp. 57–74). Lanham, MD: Rowman & Littlefield.

HarrisInteractive (2001, June 29). Youth trends and the impact on Sportainment's future. *News Room*. Retrieved March 23, 2005, from http://www.harrisinteractive.com/news/allnewsbydate.asp?NewsID=324

Helfand, L. (2005). Sportscaster salaries. *AskMen.com*. Retrieved March 23, 2005, from http://www.askmen.com/sports/business_100/114_sports_business.html

Hitchcock, J. R. (1989). *Sports & media*. Terre Haute, IN: ML Express.

Industrial Revolution. *Microsoft Encarta Online Encyclopedia 2005*. Retrieved March 11, 2005, from http://encarta.msn.com/encyclopedia_761577952_3/Industrial_Revolution.html

John Madden. (2005). *Infoplease*. Retrieved March 23, 2005, from http://infoplease.com/ipsa/A0109416.html

McChesney, R. W. (1989). Media made sport: A history of sports coverage in the United States. In L. A. Wenner (Ed.), *Media, sports, & society* (pp. 49–69). Newbury Park, CA: Sage.

Michener, J. A. (1976). *Sports in America*. New York: Random House.

Mott, F. L. (1950). *American journalism: A history of newspapers in the United States through 260 years: 1690 to 1950* (Rev. ed.). New York: Macmillan.

Munson, W. (1993). *All talk: The talkshow in media culture*. Philadelphia: Temple University Press.

Nmungwun, A. F. (1989). *Video recording technology: Its impact on media and home entertainment*. Hillsdale, NJ: Lawrence Erlbaum Associates.

Norman, G. (1990, October 8). Yak attack. *Sports Illustrated*, pp. 108–121.

Novak, M. (1976). *The joy of sports*. New York: Basic Books.

Nugent, W. H. (1929, March). The sports section. *American Mercury, 16*, 329–338.

Powers, R. (1984). *Supertube: The rise of television sports*. New York: Coward-McCann.

Rader, B. (1984). *In its own image: How television has transformed sports*. New York: Free Press.

Rice, G. (1954). *The tumult and the shouting: My life in sport*. New York: Dell.

Rogers, E. M. (1986). *Communication technology: The new media in society*. New York: Free Press.

Schlesinger, A. M. (1933). *The rise of the city*. New York: Macmillan.

Seymour, H. (1960). *Baseball, the early years*. New York: Oxford University Press.

Smethers, J. S., & Jolliffe, L. (1992). The partnership of telegraphy and radio in "re-creating" events for broadcast. *Journal of Radio Studies, 1*, 83–96.

Southon, M. (2001, March). Who will become wealthy in the information age? *Netculture Forum*. Retrieved March 11, 2005, from http://www.netculture.greng/showdocwars.asp?view=75

Sport and the media. (2005). Retrieved Mach 10, 2005, from http://www.the-infoshop.com/study/mt26636_sport.htm

Stephens, G. B. (1983). Fight of the century. The media buildup: "Gentleman Jim" vs. "Ruby Rob." *Media History Digest, 3*, 6–14, 45, 64.

Stephens, J. (1987). The rise of the sports page. *Gannett Center Journal, 1*, 1–11.

Sugar, B. R. (1978). *"The thrill of victory": The inside story of ABC sports*. New York: Hawthorn Books.

Susman, W. (1975). Piety, profits, and play: The 1920's. In H. H. Quint & M. Cantor (Eds.), *Men, women, and issues in American history* (pp. 187–201). Homewood, IL: Dorsey.

Tebbel, J. (1974). *The media in America*. New York: Thomas Crowell.

Thompson, S. (2004). *The penny press: The origins of the modern news media, 1833–1861*. Northport, AL: Vision Press.

TV Basics: Top 50 sports telecasts of all time. (n.d.) *Media Trends Track*. Retrieved March 23, 2005, from http://www.tvb.org/rcentral/mediatrendstrack/tvbasics/17_Top50SportsTelecasts.asp

Zillmann, D., & Paulus, P. B. (1993). Spectators: Reactions to sports events and effects on athletic performance. In R. N. Singer, M. Murphey, & L. K. Tennant (Eds.), *Handbook of research on sports psychology* (pp. 600–619). New York: Macmillan.

3

Sports and Media Through the Super Glass Mirror: Placing Blame, Breast-Beating, and a Gaze to the Future

Lawrence A. Wenner
Loyola Marymount University

"This is another fine mess you've gotten me into" was the way Oliver Hardy put it to Stan Laurel on many occasions. Like Hardy, I would like to (unfairly) place blame where it is due. I may not be Stan Laurel wimpering to the most classic of Oliver Hardy's signature lines, but I have Michael Real to blame for this "fine mess" of media and sports that he has "gotten me into." If I hadn't, as a graduate student, read Real's 1975 *Journal of Communication* article "The Super Bowl: Mythic Spectacle" as required reading in one of Sam Becker's media and society classes, my role (and that of many others) in what is really the wonderfully "fine mess" of studying media and sport would not have been possible. So let's place the blame where it is due, with Real. It is worth reflecting a bit on Real and one road to the present that is suggested by his work before considering the road ahead.

THE ROAD TO GETTING REAL ABOUT SPORTS AND MEDIA

In 12 pages, Real took sport and its mediation seriously, critically engaged that connection, and made linkages to the core cultural values and political sensibilities that formed the contours of national ideology in a commodified and globalized context. To my mind and to many others, Real had thrown a long forward pass. And, in an era where media scholarship had come to be aligned with an ascendant communication science, he did it without testing a hypothesis or counting anything apart from the ludicrously small amount of time the ball was actually in play during this super spectacle. Real's larger point—that the game of mediated sport was much more than the game—stuck. That point, however obvious it may seem today, marked an important tipping point, a critical event (c.f. Kraus & Davis, 1975) for the study of media and sport. Before Real's "Super Bowl" the mediation of sports was not part of the disciplinary conversations in either media studies or sports studies; afterwards the door had been opened and such consideration had standing, if not much immediate traction.

Looking back, what was most puzzling was how long it took for many, including myself, to catch Real's long bomb. There were exceptions, of course (and Bryant and his colleagues were notable repeat offenders). Yet, as I have observed elsewhere (Wenner, 1989b, 1998b), the late 1970s and early 1980s saw remarkably few published studies that considered media and sport. In the academic culture of the time, the topic of sports media carried risks to undermine the credibility of the untenured. To put it another way, the "popular" was not yet popular, and there was a fear factor in approaching sport. Sport in media studies and the media in sport studies both faced disciplinary discrimination. These areas were often viewed as "not ready for prime time" and their legitimacy needed proving. The disciplinary biases paralleled the common perception in journalism that the sports pages were the toy department of the metropolitan daily newspaper, a place where "real" journalism was not done. Similarly, in communication studies, sports were seen by many as deserving of a place at the margins as they were more "frivolous" than the discernably "serious" social effects agenda of an increasingly scientized discipline's own quest for place in the social science community. Undoubtedly, conflated fears of scholarship infused with fanship lurked beneath the surface. While sports could be put in the toy department of media studies, media played that role in sports studies. Sport studies had its own disciplinary issues that conspired against media inquiry. Its quest for legitimacy moved from being a sidelight in the often academically maligned physical education to a similar position in the area's scientized recasting as kinesiology. In the first instance, adding media to the mix would be adding insult to injury (in terms of a seriousness to bolster disciplinary credibility), and in the second instance, media inquiry drifted further away from the core science aimed at understanding the body in movement and exercise.

As has been nicely chronicled by Trujillo (2003), there was a self-reflexive awareness amongst the early settlers (and the many want-a-bes in the closet) of sports communication. To be sure, there was an excitement amongst those gathered for a brew or two after early-in-the-game sessions on media and sport in the early and mid-1980s at meetings of the Speech Communication Association and the North American Society for the Sociology of Sport. But the joking about the prospects for a Sports Communication Division in one of the major communication organizations recognized that much would have to take place for sport to be taken seriously in the context of communication study. Most of us in the field of communication knew that, for the time being, the reaction we'd get back in our home academic departments would be chilly bemusement that would demand explanation.

Fortunately, it was not cold for long. Once the ice was broken, much melted quickly. In hindsight, I think it helped that a distinguished group of scholars with credentials established in other areas of communication research were willing to join with me in a maiden voyage (Wenner, 1989a) that went under the title *Media, Sports, and Society*. With books taking so long to actually get to press, that volume's contributors joined me on a barnstorming tour of major meetings that included the National Communication Association, the International Communication Association, the International Association for Mass Communication Research, the Western States Communication Association, the North American Society for the Sociology of Sport, the North American Society for Sport Management, and the American Alliance for Health, Physical Education, Recreation, and Dance. The strategy was to go from nowhere to everywhere. While at times many came out of the closets to attend the mediated sports sessions at the major communication meetings, there were handfuls in the audience for a number of these early panels.

The reactions, however, were far different at the sports meetings. Here meeting rooms were jammed and communication scholars were welcomed with open arms and the hopes that they could advance sport studies. This kind of reaction continues to this day. The study of mediated sport, while tolerated and accepted in the mainstream communication organizations, has, with an ascendant role for cultural studies, become a core line of inquiry in sports studies. As a result, there was shifting tilt of balance to sports sociologists, as opposed to communication scholars, in my attempt to update the terrain of the field in *MediaSport* (Wenner, 1998a) in the late 1990s. Quite simply, at that time, there was more there. The authorship pattern in this *Handbook* shows that the core contributions of scholars from outside the field of communication continue to play an integral role. It remains that the role of "sports" in "comm" has had less impact than vice versa. While I do not believe it has been the case that any communication journal has done a special issue on sports, sports journals have welcomed communication scholars into their fold, with Toby Miller following me as editor of the *Journal of Sport and Social Issues* and my being asked to edit a late 2004 special issue of the *Journal of Sport Management* on "Issues in Sports Media."

In considering my comments on the future of studying the media and sport relationship for this *Handbook of Sports and Media*, it is clear that much has changed. The "popular" has long been popular and no longer is seen at odds with the legitimate. Cultural studies has made its mark and the study of media and sport has become truly interdisciplinary. As a result, sportscomm now comprises a widely recognized academic area, one with a vibrant present and a discernable past. And thanks again to Mike Real, and a forward looking international organization, the International Association for Mass Communication Research, there is now a media and sports division in one of communication's academic societies, and the institutionalization of sportscomm for the National Communication Association and the International Communication Association cannot be far behind. However, while it is certain, to quote the Virginia Slims tagline in sponsoring the women's tennis tour in the 1980s, that the academic enterprise of studying media and sport has "come a long way, baby," it is less clear that the object of our inquiry has made similar social progress.

We are in many ways in regressive social times, and sport and its mediation play a role here. The games we play and the public stories we weave about them tell tales about social priorities, actions, and distractions. In telling ways, stories of sport and the character of their mediation inform answers to the question of what follows postmodernism in the saga of late capitalism. The door that is cracked gives us many hints. While the possibilities for sport itself are of course far ranging, the more truncated space for sport that is "ready for prime time" and featured in a role on the mediascape remains leaning to core sensibilities of a hypermasculinity that might far better be vestigial. Women's place in sport that is mediated remains too often secondary and reflective of the male standard. Race and ethnicity continue to play centrally on the canvas of mediated sport in distorted ways that are often at odds with other cultural formations. Sport continues to play a pivotal role in the identities that form nationalism even as mediated sport attempts to port itself as globalized product. In that quest, sport, like many other cultural products, has been hypercommercialized and more and more becomes a media product first, and more telling, a media strategy. As a result, mediated sport has played a fundamental part of the machinery that helped blur the hero with the celebrity and meld the two as marketing tool. That these issues, and the many more that are considered in this volume, are only the tip of the media and sport iceberg tell us that the future of media and sport inquiry will be an expansive one.

LEARNING FROM A BUMP (AND A BREAST) IN THE ROAD

Because the landscape of media and sport inquiry is so vast, my attempt to gather hold of some strategies for the future is inspired by Real's original case study. In this instance, I suggest that we gaze ahead through a more limited set of issues raised by one of sport's most notable recent critical events, one that has been characterized as "Super Bowl 38D" (Costello & Moos, 2004). Led by an all-time high of nearly a million complaints to the FCC and breaking the record for the number of Internet hits (Lewczak & Lapidus, 2004; Steenberg, 2004), the fallout over the fallout of Janet Jackson's breast in the 2004 Super Bowl halftime show broadcast has been considerable (Wenner, 2004). There is some patent absurdity to the case, but this undergirds rather than belies its importance as a barometer of key issues before media and sports scholars. And while the 2004 Super Bowl broadcast certainly does not raise the specter of issues considered in this *Handbook*, it suggests some overarching concerns that can help guide future inquiry.

In hindsight, this incident reminds us that timing is everything. On the face of it, a pratfall such as Jackson's "wardrobe malfunction" that led to an exposed breast could have been easily excused as an honest mistake. But during the dinner hour, with families viewing together, in the most watched of television programs, in the context of an already raunchy halftime show, amidst advertising that crossed the line too many times towards the vulgar, in a spectacle that many believed featured privileged and steroid-enhanced athletes who had learned to skirt not only drug testing but broader social rules including those of sex and excess, Jackson's briefly bared breast was a molehill that easily became a mountain. Indeed, Janet Jackson's breast was not the only thing that took a beating after all was said and done about the CBS broadcast of Super Bowl XXXVIII. As a result of Jackson's breast-baring, there was a good deal of breast-beating in the corporate suites of CBS and the National Football League over their roles and garbled explanations. The fallout of the breast spun out as a public relations disaster for both the media and sports industries. The results were chilling for the media more broadly and showcased an increasing distaste for the monster that many thought big-time sport had become. In trying to make sense of the cultural import of the Jackson incident, I have argued that it is best understood as a case study in organizational action and media strategy gone ethically awry (for more extensive analysis, see Wenner, 2004). In a way, it provides a not so surprise ending to the story that Mike Real began to tell in 1975. Let me briefly background the case and then reflect on the intersection of some of the issues that come together.

Super Shock and Bra

The 2004 Super Bowl broadcast that featured Jackson closing the halftime show was, like most sports broadcasts, an exercise in mutual beneficence and the building of corporate synergy. It had long since been supersized. The ever-growing hyping of the game and its broadcast had led to a state of affairs that announcer Dick Enberg once maladroitly but accurately called "an unannounced American holiday" (Wenner, 1989c, p. 166). Coming in the collective doldrums of winter, deadly mid-season lulls in the basketball and hockey seasons, and the film industry's pre-Oscar meaningful new-release moratorium, there was a void for this kind of cultural event to fill. As a result, ratings for Super Bowl broadcasts have long lead the top-rated television programs lists, and its advertising holes and sponsorships have long been the most desirable and expensive. Thus, when what was to go wrong went wrong, the logic of the entire enterprise was more prone to dissection. This, of course, goes contrary to the corporate goals of naturalizing these processes so that they fly comfortably under the cultural radar. When we got a look under the hood of this event, what was largely seen was a mediaworld and a sportsworld out of touch and out of control.

Jackson's breast came out as a coda on a halftime show that was a corporate partnership between the NFL and CBS and the synergy that Viacom was nurturing between its graying CBS brand and its more youthful MTV sibling. At the urging of the broadcast rights-holder CBS, the NFL hired MTV to produce its halftime show, as it had three years earlier (a show that had featured instances of crotch grabbing and many near misses of mammary exposure) (Rich, 2004). In going to that well again, the program featured three icons with the contemporary edginess of rap and hip-hop—P. Diddy, Kid Rock, and Nelly—and Jackson, a less of-the-moment pop star, who had never been bashful in using sex towards self-promotion. The NFL and CBS, as older juggernauts long in the corporate mainstream, were struggling to show they were hip and use that to advantage in attracting desirable and elusive youthful consumers into their tents. This was a classic "Joe Camel" strategy and not without risks. One risk was that this manufactured edginess would be too easily spotted as corporate artifice in the service of invigorating their brands. The other was that this edginess would alienate the core older audiences for the NFL and CBS. Both risks materialized, for the effective organizational control that was critical to the success of the media strategy turned out to be both elusive and ineffective. The NFL and CBS had ample opportunity to exercise their oversight powers. Given their experiences with the tone of the show three years prior, they not only approved the talent and material for the halftime show, but "signed off" after seeing the performances and choreography from "every camera angle" (see Attner, 2004; Drudge, 2004; Rybak, 2004).

The halftime show that emerged was edgy. There were few surprises. True to form, P. Diddy's raps glorified violence and his choreography simulated sex. With the nickname "Pimp of the Nation," Kid Rock sealed his reputation as potty mouthed with lyrics that paid homage to hookers and druggies as heroes, all the while costumed in a shredded American flag poncho that struck many as defilement and an insult to U.S. forces overseas. Nelly followed the form of his performance in the halftime show three years earlier by adding some crotch grabbing not seen in the rehearsals to amplify the "bodacious ass" and "take off all your clothes" aspects of his song "Hot in Herre" (Nason, 2004). With the stage thusly set, Jackson closed the show by teaming in a duet of "Rock My Body" with Justin Timberlake, who as a member of 'NSYNC had matched Nelly in crotch grabbing during a performance in the aforementioned earlier show. The finale featured Jackson in sexy black dominatrix garb dirty dancing—bumping and grinding—with Timberlake. All tracked with the rehearsal, until, as one observer (Rybak, 2004, p. 1A) noted, "Right after Timberlake sang the lyric "I'm going to have you naked by the end of this song," he reached across Jackson's gladiator-type bustier and pulled off the fabric covering her right breast, which sported a sun-shaped metal stud."

This flash of naked breast made this Super Bowl broadcast "the first bowl game to become the subject of both congressional hearings and a federal investigation on indecency" (Kelly, Clark, & Kulman, 2004, p. 49) and brought the words *nipple shield* to many a family dinner conversation.

The reconstruction by the players and the stakeholders shortly after the event was telling. Out of the chaos came a pattern. Everyone apologized but much of it was either unconvincing or shifted blame. The principals cast the incident as an accident, but undercut that notion's plausibility by admitting to some undisclosed planning for a more G-rated version of the stunt. Timberlake opened the door first by contritely apologizing and blaming a "wardrobe malfunction" that he pitched as unintentional and regrettable. Unfortunately, Timberlake undercut his sincerity and stoked the fire when further hounded on the matter by laughing and saying "we love giving you something to talk about" (Rosenthal, 2004, p. 12). Jackson lagged in response until the following day. She too cast the incident as an accident but admitted a "surprise" had been planned after rehearsals that required a "costume reveal." For the mishap, she apologized to all—the public, MTV, CBS, and the NFL. Still, her response fueled questions about intentionality. With the nipple shield in place, the breast seemed suspiciously ready for prime time, and the explanation that a red lace bra beneath the bustier was supposed to be revealed lost credibility. This was enhanced later by two other indicants. One was that a Jackson assistant had gone shopping in the days prior to the show and had come back with selections for consideration. Second, reports that "top executives" at CBS had approved the reveal reeked of complicity in the corporate suites, especially when paired with promises of "something shocking" seen on the MTV Web site in the rollup to the event (Nevius, 2004, p. A1). Regardless, many felt that "two microns of red lace over Jackson's areola wouldn't have made [it] any better" (Poniewozik, 2004, p. 73), given the rape fantasy context of the song and the explicitness of the choreography.

The way that the "suits" expressed disappointment with the incident and engaged in an endless circle of finger pointing did not help matters. Corporate executives at CBS and the NFL were comfortable letting the performers and the edgy MTV culture take the fall. That the initial CBS response attempted to show they were clueless that something like this would happen worked against them. They expressed disappointment with the performance like a parent with shock and dismay over a child's drug use when there were telltale signs of problems. Further, the initial CBS apology was only for "[t]he moment [that] did not conform to CBS broadcast standards" (Shales, 2004, p. C1), and their "surprise" belied their oversight of rehearsals and approval of what they otherwise characterized as a "superb broadcast" (Carter & Sandomir, 2004, p. D1). The heights of the "cluelessness defense" came in Viacom's then-President Mel Karmazin's congressional inquiry admission that he was "told that that's the way adults are dancing these days" and that he "wouldn't have picked these songs," he would have "had Andy Williams" (Meek, 2004, p. 18). With this, even *Advertising Age* was aghast over the lack of control and willingness to take responsibility ("Credibility malfunction", 2004).

The NFL response was far less clueless than CBS and far more angry. Their breadth of their disappointment broke with CBS's continued efforts to limit the offense to the breast. Moving beyond being duped by wayward artists, they attacked, feeling burnt by and holding MTV responsible for the whole halftime- show fiasco. Unfortunately for the NFL, MTV mounted the "Viacom defense" on the matter. They cried foul, noting that an "in-charge" NFL had reviewed material, dancing, and garb during the rehearsals and further had experience with MTV producing similar acts and material, including crotch grabbing, in the halftime show three years earlier, and none of that had fallen "under [the NFL's] microscope" (Poniewozik, 2004, p. 70). For MTV, the NFL was being stodgy and there really was only need to apologize for that "one moment." For the other parts of the program, MTV was unapologetic with its chairman making the case that hip-hop had been "the most dynamic force in pop music for the past two decades" and suggesting for anyone under 40 that the rest of the show was "old hat" (Carter, 2004, p. E1). About the best the NFL could do was stomp off, claiming that they had had a "communication problem" with and difficulty controlling MTV, and in the future they would take the reigns of managerial control, something that they had all along in this instance but had bungled. This public spatting over blame and cultural sensibilities caused *Time* magazine to announce, "Let the bogus outrage and culture wars begin!" (Poniewozik, 2004, p. 70).

The bogus and not so bogus outrage was seen in a broader and lingering deconstruction of the event. At first glance, the implausibility and shifting of blame seen in the reconstruction of the incident was what caused this story to have remarkable legs. But, when examined more carefully, the tipping-point character of the event relative to the moral landscape drove consideration of structural forces little explored in media discourse. As I have noted in more detail elsewhere (Wenner, 2004, p. 329),

> In a sound-bite media economy where the media are largely populated by conglomerates willing to reward the creative community for pushing the cultural bounds in order to break through increasing noise and clutter, the public airing and raising of questions about the structural pressures that lead to media and corporate excess become unusual. Unfortunately for the NFL and CBS, the stars aligned in this instance.

That so many voices were not willing to let Jackson and Timberlake take the fall alone drove this. Right-wing media pressure groups, as Thompson put it, had hit the "mother lode" (Carter, 2004, p. E1). Technology amplified by blogging and the batch e-mailing strategies stirred the drink of the FCC's then-Chairman Michael Powell, who recently had been upping the ante for media indecency infractions. While Powell weighed in on the whole of the halftime show as "onstage copulation" and the FCC eventually levied a $550,000 fine to the CBS stations for the offense, Congress grabbed what was an incendiary political opportunity to grandstand in hearings that dressed down both CBS and the NFL (Ahrens & de Moraes, 2004; de Moraes, 2004). The chill that the media felt was palpable, and the year that followed was to feature numerous examples of the media reigning themselves in as they approached moral flashpoints.

That the multidirectional bungling of the corporate spin was cast as tiresome "don't-blame-me's" ("Credibility malfunction," 2004) opened the door for a larger scrutiny of life in the fast lane of big-time sport, a world where marketing excess and moral pratfalls were wearing thin. Ultimately, it was the NFL that took it hardest on the chin for being disingenuous in attempting to shift blame in the matter. Under the microscope came its double standards with a broad array of problematic practices that ranged from trash talking in its licensed video games to glorification of violence to scantily clad cheerleaders to its use of faux militarism and nationalism in promotional themes to unfair labor practices that included racial discrimination in hiring minorities in management (Bondy, 2004). The particular coarseness in the 2004 Super Bowl commercials were seen as being on the NFL's watch. That the NFL was embarrassed by the halftime show when the broadcast's much-touted commercials featured flatulence, crotch jokes, crude double entendres, and warnings for products should an erection linger beyond four hours struck many as the height of hypocrisy (Elliott, 2004).

SUPER THEMES

The media dissection and political outfall that came on the heels of the 2004 Super Bowl broadcast shows the central role that media and sports can play in the larger public discourse about mass culture, its foibles, and how to control and police it. Mediated sports, and even one event, can be a lens through which to better understand broad cultural dynamics. This case, while limited, suggests a number of conceptual pairings, some binaries and some not, that are worthy of attention in future media and sport inquiry.

Pop and Hip-Hop

This case reminds us that sport and its mediation are always on a continuum of hipness, perched at a delicate balance between mass popularity and the edgy knowingness of the next cool thing that will differentiate youthful audiences from the mainstream. This connection of mediated sport to the popular is deserving of our attention as we attempt to understand sport in the context of broader social forces. While pop's place on the moral axis can be more easily discounted, its juxtaposition with its oppositional derivatives can be particularly instructive. A good case in point for us to follow will be the emergence of "extreme" sports that aim to corral fragmented audience in compelling ways by positioning deviance as a major selling point.

Sex and Gender

That a sexual offense in this case stoked such significant cultural reaction is telling. On one hand, it tells us that sex and sports don't mix, which Miller's (2001) treatment has demonstrated is patently absurd, and on the other, it tells us much about the peculiarities of American culture in this reaction in contrast to other sensitivities, particularly those about the routinization of gratuitous violence in the games we play and elsewhere. While our understandings of the media's vastly different treatment of men and women is considerable, the imbalances continue to be more so. Title IX, in a sense, has never been a meaningful part of prime time for mediated sport. Sport, especially in the forms that dominate the mediascape, remains as a select and powerful bastion of vestigial hypermasculinity and, as such, we should use this lens to understand our identities. Sexual offenses at the perimeter of sport should also continue to garner attention. We need to begin to interrogate these irregularities as well as others that are seen as they tell us much about cultural assumptions of heterosexuality and its prowess in sport and life.

Race and Ethnicity

While unspoken in my analysis and in much of the press reaction to the Jackson case, it is clear that reactions to this incident are conflated with understandings about race and ethnicity. That the halftime show was dominated by African-American artists and that the offense was ostensibly the playing of rape fantasy by a White man upon an African-American woman was not missed by many. Yet sport and its mediation regularly miss stories about racial and ethnic portrayals and relations that matter. An easy case-in-point here remains the structural bias of Whites in sport management positions and minorities on the field or court. Media regularly glosses over that story because of the need to sell an unblemished mediated sport product. Of particular interest to scholars should be understanding the cultural dynamic that comes about with White audiences watching sports dominated by minority players. This is a cultural anomaly for which understanding may be prescient to understanding shifts of cultural power.

Young and Old

We often miss the obvious in studying media and sport. This case reminds us that sport itself is youth on parade and that it is increasingly being pitched to a youthful audience. Especially as many nation's populations are both aging and living longer, we need to turn some attention in media and sport inquiry to lifecycle dynamics. We need to better understand the relationship between sports spectatorship and sports activity, and media scholars in particular will need to be informed more broadly about the sociology of sporting activity relative to other forces.

Celebrity and Hero

At the core, the Jackson case is really a bellyflop of the interaction between mediated sport and celebrity culture. There have been many fine works recently (c.f. Andrews & Jackson, 2001; Whannel, 2002) that have looked at the far-reaching impacts of the sporting celebrity. Because the sports star is perhaps the most easily identified hero in the contemporary era, this dynamic will continue to deserve our attention. Stories of the rise of heroes and others about their downfall are among the most compelling moral stories that culture tells and retells. We need to continue to interrogate these lessons and make connections between celebrity and its use in sports culture to its counterparts in other spheres of popular and political life.

Mass and Fragments

Because the Super Bowl is so unusual, this case reminds us of the death of the truly mass audience. And its programming strategy for its halftime show reminds us of the market's preference for certain segments over others. Presently, sport is being used as a way to hold larger audience fragments together in an era of increasing fragmentation. While sport may continue in its role of providing the broadest ground for shared cultural experience, it seems unlikely that it will be able hold a firm line against the trend of a media more and more attuned to niches. We should watch the playing out of this with interest. As well, in our work we should monitor which of the niches are given primacy, how this comes about, and what is the role for the grassroots and the authentic.

Technology and Activity

That replays of Janet Jackson's exposed breast received an all-time high of Internet hits tells us that social infractions, in sport and elsewhere, can far more easily be subjected to lasting moral interrogations. The shaping of public opinion was changed by the blogging and political response that was enabled through communities that would not have had coherence without newer technologies. The whole experience reminds us that the changing nature of audience activity, for sports and media content, has structurally altered the way events come to be understood. In the future, our inquiries into audience experience and mediated sport will have to better interface with understandings of how experiencing media is now a multistream phenomenon.

National and Global

The Super Bowl reminds how when the megaevents of sport and media mix they are most likely to command the powers of nationalism while, at the same time, benefiting the global interests of transnational corporations. That there have been so many sporting events in the United States recently that help fuel a nationalism that is in aid of an ideological position that has come with a most tenuous ascent to executive political power is worthy of more reflection. Why is it that organized sport and its mediated formations are so likely to align with the powers that be, even on issues where there is clear evidence of considerable dissent? We need to trace this with better understanding to the social structures of sport and its historical roles in culture and look ahead for ways for mediated sport to play to broaden its interface with political discourse. This notion may strike many as contrary to the idea that the political does not have a place in sport, but I think this is wishful thinking. Politics has always had a place in sport, and in a mediated age, we need to bring it out of the shadows and broaden its scope.

Super and Ordinary

The Super Bowl generally, and the 2004's "breast bowl" in particular, reinforce how important it is for us to study "media events" (see Dayan & Katz, 1992; Scannell, 1995) for clues to social and cultural shifts. Many media events may be planned and largely play out according to script, while others, far more important, such as the fireworks that followed the planned halftime show in the Jackson case, may be far more "critical" (Kraus & Davis, 1975) and deserving of our attention. However, in our focus on the big, we risk overlooking the ordinary and its constancy of drip in the social mix. It is clear that media researchers have long been drawn to questions, such as violence and stereotyping, where there are hopes of demonstrating dramatic effects and often come away disappointed. It is the "drip, drip, drip" rather than the "big bang" that really matters in assessing media effects, and media and sport inquiries need to dig in more clearly both for long haul and to understand the everyday.

Frame and Game

A number of years ago, when doing a more extensive analysis on a Super Bowl pregame show (Wenner, 1989c), I made an argument that was in essence "the frame is more important than the game." That understandings of both frame and game are needed in getting the big picture about the mediation of sport is very much showcased in this volume. Dissecting mediated sport content for overt or covert prejudice or for sense-making logics that are deserving of more scrutiny is an important element of the research agenda. However, from the perspective of the communication discipline in particular, the broader cultural sense making that comes with the mediation of sport is where much of the compelling action promises to be. The newer frames—cyberspace, gaming, disability, fiction, and fantasy sports among them—will add important perspectives on that sense making.

Selling and Distraction

Mediated super sport and its more regular counterpart are, as much as anything, about the big sell. The case of the Super Bowl reminds us of the present state of affairs in advertising. Getting commercial messages out of the clutter and getting the undistracted attention of the audience have become primary challenges. Both the ubiquity of advertising and the "run the other way" technologies like TiVo make an event like the Super Bowl aberrant in that people actually look forward to the commercials. But that will not be business as usual, and the march of product placement, cross-marketing strategies, and the like will continue to assault the landscape of media and sport. Here, there are many questions to answer for audience researchers, policy analysts, and media ethicists.

Control and Denial

One of the most interesting issues highlighted by the "nipplegate" saga of 2004's Super Bowl are those having to do with organizational control and the taking of responsibility. That those most in control were those in most denial over their power presents a conundrum arranged along a spectrum of deception and spin. In that light, it is satisfying to see the extensive attention given in this volume to institutional perspectives. We need to look under the hood of mediated sports more carefully. Critical studies of production context and reporting, and marketing, sponsorship, and promotion in their socioeconomic context, need far greater attention.

Deviance and Distaste

The premier lesson that came with the fallout of Janet Jackson's breast was that mediated sport is very much perched on a moral landscape. Moral action and mediated sport interact with each traffic stop of a wayward athlete, with revelations over performance-enhancing drugs, with each instance of sexual misconduct or domestic abuse, and with every fight in a sporting contest that becomes more than that. Each consideration of issues such as these, especially when considered with the backdrop of exorbitant salaries and the cultural worth of big-time sport and its largesse, become an opportunity to reexamine not only our cultural values and priorities but the ethics of the marketplace. As the Jackson incident portends, public distaste over sport may occasion broader moral fissures. As such, they are sites of both political opportunity and policy action that can have far-reaching consequences.

THE ROAD AHEAD

The host of issues that are raised by the Janet Jackson incident and the increasingly hypercommercialized backdrop for mediated sport suggests that there is much work to be done, in these and other areas, as inquiry moves ahead. While even the partial and highly selected pairings presented above may be daunting in taking in the whole of the media and sport mix, they are indicative of what we might see should we step back from the more highly demarcated areas of inquiry hinted at in this volume's treatment. The individual areas within media and sport inquiry, and the relations that media and sport have with other areas of communication and social inquiry, are necessarily "blurred genres" (Geertz, 1973). As such, they demand big questions, messy ones, that tend to see forests rather than trees. Towards that end, let me siphon further to four lines of concern that I think deserve attention as we gaze to the future of inquiry about sports and media.

Sports, Media, and Dirt

There is little doubt that one of the chief reasons that the scholarly community has finally blessed the study of mediated sport has been the recognition of the powerful role that sports plays in culture. We have widely turned the corner that sport is merely a toy store and that its mediated form is just entertainment. Mediated sport and all of its appendages (its commercial space, its marketing strategies, its manufactured synergies) all gain power from the cultural meanings and logic of sport itself. The way this works and the propriety of it raises questions that are far more complex than at first glance. Towards a more focused interrogation of this, I have earlier suggested (Wenner, 1991, 1994) a reliance on Leach's (1976, p. 62) arguments "that *power is located in dirt.*" I have taken Leach's notion of "dirt" to mean the "cultural borrowing that allows one cultural entity to adopt the logic of another" (Wenner, 1991, p. 392). As such, there are no necessary negative connotations to "dirt"; in fact, "dirty uses" may be logical, deemed appropriate, and fully enjoyed. But they are by definition "parasitic" in that, as Hartley (1984) has argued, there is a "cultural leak" from one place to another and texts are necessarily "contaminated by seepages from other parts of culture, including media" (Wenner, 1991, p. 392). "Cultural dirt" such as "sports dirt," like its organic counterpart, is something that lands where it did not originally belong. Dirt, even when its importation has been mechanized or routinized, is, in a way, out of place. In the mediated sports context, sports dirt is at the core of what makes it powerful. For the fan in particular, sports dirt is compelling. I have argued elsewhere that "the sports fan has long enjoyed rolling around in this dirt" and goes to "great lengths to unearth this dirt many times over in watching television sports programming, in reading the sports pages in the daily newspaper, and in conversations with friends and acquaintances about sports" (Wenner, 1991, p. 404). We know, for example, that it is the "essential dirtiness" of many sports-themed beer commercials that contribute to their success by giving "the fan one more opportunity to turn that soil and revel in its richness" (Wenner, 1991, p. 404). A key element, discomforting for some, is that the notion of dirt and using it as an analytic tool requires making judgments about what is dirt, the propriety of a "dirty" use, and the way that positively infused "dirty logics" overcome associations that we have with that to which it is appended. The upside, however, for "dirty" interrogations are considerable, and this notion will help us tremendously in understanding how "interpretive communities" (Fish, 1980) make sense of media that have been touched by sport.

Sports, Media, and Organizational Action

Done originally for the *Journal of Sport Management*, my look at the dynamics behind and cultural reaction to the baring of Janet Jackson's breast centers on organizational action and the ethos of managerial decision making. My study, however, was necessarily reliant on reconstruction at a distance. My strategy, and the foci of the vast proportion of the agenda of media and sport scholarship, reminds us that sometimes we do the easy things first. Consequently, we see that the vast bulk of scholarship has focused on either examinations of mediated sport content (both critical and "count-em" studies) or those of the mediated sport audience (surveys, experiments, and small scale ethnographies). All of these studies are important to our understandings. But what they share in common is relatively easy access to data. In the future, we will need to prioritize getting access to sport organizations and to media organizations as they fashion their sport-centered product. To be sure, this will be no easy task, but I think it will help us to understandings about professional life that will inform our content studies and enrich our understandings of how the audience has been conceptualized. Such a focus means thinking more in terms of the traditions of occupational sociology and the tensions of "creativity and constraint" that confront media workers (c.f. Ettema & Whitney, 1982). Revisiting that tradition a bit more may also cause some reflection on the framing of our area of inquiry beyond mediated sport to a broader sportscomm where the traditions of organizational, group, and interpersonal communication inform our understandings about the dynamics of sport.

Sports, Media, and the Moral Order

As I have suggested in my pairing of deviance and distaste above, the Jackson case reminds us that mediated sport very much interacts with moral sensibilities. If ever there was an example of a mediated moral panic button, the Jackson case was it. Sport, and our cultural understanding of it, very much plays out along a moral spectrum. Its mediation tells us regularly how good sportsmanship is linked to ethical health and should be praised. The stories of athletes gone awry, on and off the field, provide regular moral fodder. And with the constant pushing of bounds in a cluttered and competitive marketplace, the routine practices of media entities will more and more push the tolerances of propriety. Given this, media and sport inquiry needs to ponder how its own ethical interrogations might best proceed. One avenue might be to follow some of the leads seen in sport-centered inquiry (c.f. McNamee & Parry, 1998; Morgan, Meier, & Schneider, 2001; Tomlinson & Fleming, 1997). Another approach would to to build on the emerging traditions of ethical criticism (c.f. Booth, 1988; Carroll, 2000; Gregory, 1998). In any case, media and sport researchers should not be afraid to bite the ethical bullet. Taking an ethical stand, whether making clearer the liabilities that are suggested out of social scientific findings or questioning the propriety of sense making in studies of media workers or their audience, can only help get our work more into the public dialogue.

Sports, Media, and Citizenship

This last concern really should be the big picture, but I'm not so sure its been in the picture much at all. When we think about mediated sports, we very often think about its consumption and thereby are thinking about consumers. But sport and its mediation plays out on a far greater field than the consumption economy. Consumers of mediated sport are foremost citizens. To the degree that their citizenship is formed by and influenced by mediated sport, we should be paying particular attention. It is notable the topic of mediated sports and politics is absent from the mix in this volume. For this, I don't hold the editors responsible. Rather, we may have gotten out of the practice of looking through this lens. This is notable in that sports metaphor is often used in politics, that we see politicians make media opportunities to bask in the reflected glory of sports success, and the sport system's logic has long been bolstered by the notion that sports builds character. There are many important opportunities ahead for researchers to visit the intersection where media and sports meet politics and citizenship. While there are many clues to where to start on this agenda, Miller (1998) articulated a particularly compelling set of arguments about the contours of "cultural citizenship" as a way to think about how the popular interacts with everyday political life. In the realm of sport, there is no better place to start to trigger thinking than Gruneau's (1983) classic work on the dynamics of sport and class. Finally, given the vastly greater "mediasport" (Wenner, 1998a) world we have before us today, with multiple sports networks, sports talk radio, and the prospects of cyberspace and gaming, it may be an appropriate time to revisit the "sport as opiate" hypothesis afresh and without the constrictions of more formal Marxist logic (Hoch, 1972). There is little question that mediated sport has garnered a good deal of our attention, and the political significance of this distraction is certainly worthy of our consideration.

A POSTGAME COMMENT

My efforts to put a limited set of big issues on the agenda of inquiry about sports and media come on the heels of a vastly greater set of issues addressed and suggested by the authors in this *Handbook*. At the beginning of my essay, I spoke to the difficulties facing scholars of media and sport to gain academic traction. While much in the cultural climate has changed in terms of taking sport and its mediation seriously in academic and other spheres, there remain strong voices and much public sentiment for us to look the other way, to let the masses have a little fun. A good encapsulation of that sentiment was voiced by Gregg Easterbrook (2005, p. D7) in a Super Bowl Sunday critique in the *New York Times*:

> The Super Bowl is outsized, preposterous, excessive—which is the good thing about it. This is also why attempts to find hidden meaning are doomed to futility. The game has no vast social significance. The Super Bowl is just a big, overdone party. Every year, news organizations labor to supply ultraserious analyses of the Super Bowl buildup. They quote sociologists on the philosophy of mass culture, economists on the class structure of sports, media theorists on the fine points of sports symbolism. Last year 144 million Americans watched the Super Bowl, joined by an estimated one billion more around the world. Surely an event watched by such an incredible number of people must ooze significance! But somber analyses of the Super Bowl look for import that is not there. It is essential to bear in mind that professional sports are, foremost, entertainment....Neither year's ads denote any larger development. They're just a bunch of ads, dreamed up to cause laughs and sell Tabasco sauce. Don't try to analyze whether the cheerleaders represent objectification

or empowerment. It's simply entertainment. . . . Just don't try to find any larger significance, because there isn't any.

Easterbrook's comments are important and should remind us that sports fans and marketers are not looking for us to rain on or reign in their parade. However, when we hear comments like this, we shouldn't be disgruntled. It indicates that we've gotten their attention. We should continue to have fun making sense of the social power of the media and sport mix while we show that it is far more than mere entertainment. We need to keep working and engage in public discussion to show how the mediated sports carnival relates to capital—economic capital, cultural capital, and political capital. The work in this volume shows that we are on the right track and, to Mr. Easterbrook and to those with like sentiments, it should indicate in no uncertain terms that we respectfully disagree.

REFERENCES

Ahrens, F., & de Moraes, L. (2004, February 3). FCC is investigating Super Bowl show: Halftime performance faces indecency standard. *Washington Post*, p. A1.

Andrews, D. L., & Jackson, S. J. (Eds.).(2001). *Sport stars: The cultural politics of sporting celebrity*. London: Routledge.

Attner, P. (2004, February 16). To know list 3: The NFL had it coming. *Sporting News*, p. 4.

Bondy, F. (2004, February 4). NFL has more pressing flesh. *New York Daily News*, p. 50.

Booth, W. C. (1988). *The company we keep: An ethics of fiction*. Berkeley: University of California Press.

Carroll, N. (2000). Art and ethical criticism: An overview of recent directions in research. *Ethics, 110*, 350–387.

Carter, B. (2004, February 5). Bracing for fallout for super indignation. *New York Times*, p. E1.

Carter, B., & Sandomir, R. (2004, February 3). Pro football: Halftime-show fallout includes F.C.C. inquiry. *New York Times*, p. D1.

Costello, C., & Moos, J. (2004, February 10). Puns generated from Super Bowl controversy. *CNN Daybreak*. [Television Broadcast: Transcript #021012CN.V73]. Atlanta, GA: CNN.

Credibility malfunction. (2004, February 9). *Advertising Age*, p. 14.

Dayan, D., & Katz, E. (1992). *Media events: The live broadcasting of history*. Cambridge, MA: Harvard University Press.

de Moraes, L. (2004, February 26). It's congressional chew-out-the-networks time, episode 2. *Washington Post*, p. C7.

Drudge, M. (2004, February 1). Outrage at CBS after Janet bares breast during dinner hour; Super Bowl show pushes limits. Retrieved August 11, 2004, from http://www.drudgereportarchives.com/data/2004/02/03/20040203_003406_mattjj.htm.

Easterbrook, G. (2005, February 6). Don't analyze that: A day of excess won't kill us. *New York Times*, p. D7.

Elliott, S. (2004, February 3). Class and taste take a beating as the Adbowl dissolves into the "stupidity sweepstakes." *New York Times*, p. C5.

Ettema, J. S., & Whitney, D. C. (Eds.). (1982). *Individuals in mass media organizations: Creativity and constraint*. Beverly Hills, CA: Sage.

Fish, S. (1980). *Is there a text in this class? The authority of interpretive communities*. Cambridge, MA: Harvard University Press.

Geertz, C. (1973). Thick description: Toward an interpretive theory of culture. In *The interpretation of cultures* (pp. 3–30). New York: Basic Books.

Gregory, M. (1998). Ethical criticism: What it is and why it matters. *Style, 32*, 194–220.

Gruneau, R. (1983). *Class, sports, and social development*. Amherst: University of Massachusetts Press.

Hartley, J. (1984). Encouraging signs: TV and the power of dirt, speech, and scandalous categories. In W. Rowland & B. Watkins (Eds.), *Interpreting television: Current research perspectives* (pp. 119–141). Beverly Hills, CA: Sage.

Hoch, P. (1972). *Rip off the big game*. Garden City, NY: Doubleday.

Kelly, K., Clark, K., & Kulman, M. (2004, February 16). Trash TV. *U.S. News & World Report*, pp. 48–52.

Kraus, S., & Davis, D. (1975). Critical events analysis. In S. Chaffee (Ed.), *Political communication*. Beverly Hills, CA: Sage.

Leach, E. (1976). *Culture and communication*. Cambridge, England: Cambridge University Press.

Lewczak, J., & Lapidus. M. (2004, May). The impact of the Janet Jackson "incident" on advertising: How the costume malfunction is likely to raise the standards and decency on network television. *Metropolitan Corporate Counsel*, p. 6.

McNamee, M. J., & Parry, S. J. (Eds.).(1998). *Ethics and sport*. London: E & F.N. Spon.

Meek, J. G. (2004, February 12). Execs call nipplegate unbearable. *New York Daily News*, p. 18.

Miller, T. (1998). *Technologies of truth: Cultural citizenship and the popular media*. Minneapolis: University of Minnesota Press.

Miller, T. (2001). *Sportsex*. Philadelphia: Temple University Press.

Morgan, W. J., Meier, K. V., & Schneider, A. J. (Eds.). (2001). *Ethics in sport*. Champaign, IL: Human Kinetics.

Nason, P. (2004, February 3). Analysis: Janet Jackson's surprise. *United Press International*. Retrieved August 11, 2004, from LexisNexis Academic Universe.

Nevius, C. W. (2004, February 3). FCC inquiry, uproar over Super Bowl halftime peepshow. *San Francisco Chronicle*, p. A1.

Poniewozik, J. (2004, February 6). The hypocrisy bowl. *Time*, pp. 70–74.

Real, M. R. (1975). The Super Bowl: Mythic spectacle. *Journal of Communication, 25*(1), 31–43.

Rich, F. (2004, February 16). My hero, Janet Jackson. *New York Times*, p. B1.

Rosenthal, P. (2004, February 3). Cover story so bad, even FCC sees through it. *Chicago Sun-Times* [special edition], p. 12.

Rybak, D. C. (2004, February 3). Halftime exposure starts a blame game. *Minneapolis Star Tribune*, p. 1A.

Scannell, P. (1995). Media events. *Media, Culture, & Society, 17*, 151–157.

Shales, T. (2004, February 2). Incomplete! *Washington Post*, p. C1.

Steenberg, A. (2004, February 5). Janet tops on Internet; boob hits record number searches. *Toronto Sun*, p. 2.

Tomlinson, A., & Fleming, S. (Eds.). (1997). *Ethics, sport, and leisure: Crises and critiques*. Aachen, Germany: Meyer and Meyer Verlag.

Trujillo, N. (2003). Introduction. In R. S. Brown & D. J. O'Rouke, III (Eds.), *Case studies in sport communication* (pp. xi–xv). Westport, CT: Praeger.

Wenner, L. A. (Ed.).(1989a). *Media, sports, and society*. Newbury Park, CA: Sage.

Wenner, L. A. (1989b). Media, sports, and society: The research agenda. In L. A. Wenner (Ed.), *Media, sports, and society* (pp. 13–48). Newbury Park, CA: Sage.

Wenner, L. A. (1989c). The Super Bowl pregame show: Cultural fantasies and political subtext. In L. A. Wenner (Ed.), *Media, sports, and society* (pp. 157–179). Newbury Park, CA: Sage.

Wenner, L. A. (1991). One part alcohol, one part sport, one part dirt, stir gently: Beer commercials and television sports. In L. R. Vande Berg & L. A. Wenner (Eds.), *Television criticism: Approaches and applications* (pp. 388–407). New York: Longman.

Wenner, L. A. (1994). The Dream Team, communicative dirt, and the marketing of synergy: USA basketball and cross-merchandizing in television commercials. *Journal of Sport and Social Issues, 18*(1), 27–47.

Wenner, L. A. (Ed.). (1998a). *MediaSport*. London: Routledge.

Wenner, L. A. (1998b). Playing the MediaSport game. In L. A. Wenner (Ed.), *MediaSport* (pp. 3–13. London: Routledge.

Wenner, L. A. (2004). Recovering (from) Janet Jackson's breast: Ethics and the nexus of media, sports, and management. *Journal of Sport Management, 18*, 315–334.

Whannel, G. (2002). *Media sport stars: Masculinities and moralities*. London: Routledge.

THE COVERAGE AND
BUSINESS OF SPORTS MEDIA

4

Sports Media: A Modern Institution

Robert V. Bellamy, Jr.
Duquesne University

The contribution of sports to media is difficult to overstate. In terms of content, hundreds of television and radio programs and networks, magazines, videogames, and newspapers focus on sport, as do hundreds of thousands of Internet sites. The seemingly insatiable appetite for sports content long ago extended from game or event coverage to reviews, previews, and "inside" information. The consistently growing importance of sports also is demonstrated by the expanding amount of fantasy sports information, lifestyle content, and even fictional content related to sports.

The importance of sports as media content programming and software is further demonstrated by its key role in the diffusion of the newer media technologies. Just as sports broadcasts (primarily baseball and boxing) were used to market television sets in the 1950s, media sports are today a major selling point for digital and high-definition television (HDTV) receivers, as well as videogames (see Lomax, chap. 23) and broadband Internet service (see Real, chap. 10; Mahan & McDaniel, chap. 25; Lomax, chap. 23, this volume; and King, 2005).

Even nonfans can not help but notice how much media attention sports receive. Sports coverage consistently and increasingly appears both in its own specialized all-sports media (ESPN, *Sports Illustrated*, CBS Sportsline, et al.) and as an integral part of the news of the day. Unlike most other industries, sports capture the attention of the public on an ongoing basis.

At a macrolevel, sports and media have long been considered to be separate institutions in a symbiotic, if somewhat dysfunctional, relationship. Sports content allowed media to reach desirable and otherwise difficult-to-reach audiences, while the publicity and money from media helped sports to become consistently more profitable and culturally important (Bellamy, 1998; McChesney, 1989; Rowe, 1999). While this relationship endures, the importance of sports content to media has reached the point where it makes less and less sense to discuss sports and media as separate institutions.

This chapter is about the evolution and present relationship of the sports and media industries but, more importantly, about the increasingly powerful media entertainment industry, and the importance of sports to that power and influence. Following Wenner (1998), I argue that "MediaSport" is now an institution of its own (although obviously with a variety of permutations), worthy of the scholarly pursuit. In addition to intrinsic MediaSport content, another area worthy of consideration is the influence of sport on nonsports media content. Television examples include the increasing value of live programming, *zap-proof* advertising, reality programs based on competition, and content that can be repurposed for other media outlets both domestically and globally. Newspapers devote more space to sports because sports and entertainment news, which often and increasingly overlap, are perceived in the industry as one of the key ways of attracting younger readers, a demographic segment that is increasingly difficult for newspapers to attract.

Magazines devoted to sports are increasingly common for the same reasons. Magazines, one of the better barometers of popular culture due to their ubiquity and diversity, have taken a lead role in promoting the intersection of sports and entertainment with such sports-as-entertainment titles as *ESPN, the Magazine*, as well as the many features on sports personalities in such nonsports celebrity titles as *People* and *Us*. Sports radio has been one of the most successful radio formats of the last 15 years and has joined conservative talk radio in leading to somewhat of a revival in the fortunes of AM radio. Both of the formats have thrived in large part on "guy talk," a format with topics said to be of interest to men. In short, there is now a nexus of sport and entertainment similar to that of popular music and movie and television performers that is an important part of media business and culture.

While both older and newer media inform much of the content of this chapter, the emphasis is on television. While recognizing the crucial role of earlier print and electronic mass media in the rising importance of sports, television's advent in the mid-twentieth century was, and remains, key to our understanding of MediaSport. The full blooming of the intersection and symbiosis of sports and media occurred with the development of television. Television continued and expanded the nationalization of sports begun by radio. Television was the major component of the "circuits of promotion" that made sporting events and personalities "newsworthy" (Whitson, 1998, pp. 57–72).

The centrality of television's role is not likely to radically change with the new technologies. Broadband Internet, for example, is offering an increasing amount of television content. Streaming or downloading video files from the Internet is becoming as common as downloading audio or print files. Mobile/cell telephones with live video capability are beginning to diffuse throughout the globe, which will expand television's already ubiquitous presence.

Play, games, and competitions have been part of the human experience virtually since the beginning of recorded history (see Scanlon, chap. 1, this volume). Long before the development of mass media, sports were an integral part in the lives of people and social groups all over the globe in this premodern era. In addition, the psychological hold of sports on humans is a very complex set of issues that have kept many scholars in sociology, kinesiology, psychology, and now leisure studies, business, and communication occupied for years (Coakley, 2003; Eitzen, 2001; Wann, Melnick, Russell, & Pease, 2001). However, sports as most individuals conceive them today are defined as something that you watch, listen to, read about, and talk about rather than something you do. My intent here is not to disregard the hundreds of millions of people who participate in athletics of one sort or another. Rather, it is to argue that the position of *spectator* has long defined big time sports and is the essential linkage of media studies to sport.

RISE OF "BIG TIME" SPECTATOR SPORT

Big time sports are organized, professional (even in terms of amateur sports management), and content for media. They grew from relatively disorganized amateur roots parallel to and a component part of industrialization from the early to mid-nineteenth century. There obviously are far too many social effects of industrialization to discuss here. Suffice it to say that urbanization, the resultant dislocation and alienation of many people, the rapid movement to a cash economy, the spread of systemized education, and the shift in time perspective to one bound by defined work, sleep, and leisure/personal time were all essential elements in the rise of both mass media and spectator sports. Sports provided the new Penny Press with content that was interesting to readers at a time when larger circulation and advertising support were essential to the development of the modern newspaper.

A key side benefit of the increase in newspaper sports coverage, as McChesney (1989) explained, is that sports coverage is almost always much less controversial than coverage of political economic issues. Over time, sports became even more important in the consolidation of the industry and the consequent development of the concept of newspapers as a nonpartisan "objective" source of news. Sports and other entertainment and amusements (theatre, vaudeville, amusement parks, et al.) gained untold amounts of free publicity from the papers affirming and promoting their importance. The symbiosis between big time sports and the mass media was established from the very beginning of both institutions (see Wanta, chap. 6, this volume, for more on the present state of print coverage of sports). However, it would take the rise of electronic media to make spectator sports an important component of popular culture throughout the nation.

Broadcasting and Sport

The relationship of sports and radio goes back to the earliest days of commercial radio service with Pirates games on Pittsburgh's pioneering KDKA-AM in the early 1920s. Soon after, baseball, college football, and boxing became among the most popular radio events (see Bryant, chap. 2, and Owens, chap. 7, this volume, for more on the history and present status of radio sports). Sports were found to be a major factor in the selling of radio receivers, an attribute still relevant today in television and broadband. Major sponsors soon became heavily involved with sports sponsorships. In many local markets, a local brewery exploited the close relationship between the consumption of beer and the enjoyment of sports. As in the case of most other radio programming, mentions of the sponsor (e.g., "Ballantine Blasts") were commonly sprinkled throughout the radio broadcast.

At first, the marriage of television and big time sports was almost perfect. At a time when the major motion picture studios considered the new medium an adversary, sports events provided television networks and stations with some of its most successful programming. Although episodic series eventually replaced most sports from the prime time hours, sports filled an ever-increasing amount of weekend airtime. Sports were ideal because of the action they provided, the male audience they attracted, the beer and razors that they sold, and their relatively low cost for the amount of programming they provided.

Big time sports and the Big 3 networks that dominated television for years were both oligopolies and cartels (Alexander, Owers, Carveth, Hollifield, & Greco, 2003; Bellamy, 1998). The barriers to entry were very high, innovation was limited, and collusive behavior was common. Both had legal protections and obligations as "special" types of businesses—sports leagues and organizations through court decisions that defined them as not "in commerce," and broadcasters through their federal licensing in "the public interest." However, by the 1960s there was little doubt but that television was the dominant partner in the marriage. A growing course of criticism about how television had or was destroying sport was often heard from the print media. The clout of sports, a result of years of cumulative media exposure, was such that legal action was taken to protect certain sports from the "alleged" dangers of television. The most important remains the *Sports Broadcasting Act of 1961* or SBA (P.L. 87-331, 75 Stat. 732). The SBA granted professional sports leagues an exemption from antitrust laws to pool their league members' broadcast rights for sale to television and radio. This was the culmination of the nationalization of sport that had been set in motion years earlier and led to the enormous and almost ever-increasing rights fees for big time sports telecasts.

Obviously, the 40-plus years since the SBA have seen enormous change in the television and other media industries. Sports leagues and organizations have not changed as radically as television in structure, although the changes they have undergone are almost all in reaction to the changes in television.

Attributes of MediaSport

A review of the attributes of sports to media (and particularly television) should do two things. First, it must reflect the inherent aspects of sporting events that make them such important and ubiquitous media content and programming. Second, the ongoing changes and challenges in the media industries must also be considered. Any number of scholars in a wide variety of disciplines have argued that we are now in a postmodern period in which traditional definitions and assumptions are now being contested (Kellner, 1995; Real, 1998; Schimmel, 2001). Certainly an argument can be made that the changes in the media industries of the last generation that now afford the user much more control (at a price), while countering the new user power with the development of a new and even more powerful oligopolistic industrial structure, is evidence of the postmodern condition (Bellamy & Walker, 1996).

Whatever the label we wish to place on the changes occurring within and between the media and sports industries, there is little doubt that there has been a large increase on the importance media entities place on sports or sports-influenced content. In many ways, sports are a *key exemplar* of the programming perceived as necessary to the continuing growth of television both domestically and around the world. Television's unparalleled ability to create interest for, popularize, and normalize whatever it emphasizes means that sports' importance to other media and to the public at large is certain to similarly increase.

The primary reasons for the sports as *key television exemplar* argument are these:

1. Sporting events typically are presented live with the attendant element of real-time suspense.
2. Unlike other "live" events, sports are regularly scheduled and continuing like other entertainment series, which makes them cost effective compared to many other forms of programming.
3. There are minimal barriers of language and literacy for sports viewers.
4. Even those who are not fans have a generally benign attitude toward sport. Very few people are sports haters/evaders, especially when viewing in groups.
5. Sports are so culturally ingrained that they can have direct and powerful media effects, such as civic or even national celebration, that most programming cannot. The connection to such celebration and emotion is highly desired by advertisers and programming outlets.
6. Sports telecasts offer many opportunities for zap-proof advertising.
7. Sports telecasts are widely regarded as an excellent forum for effective promotion of other television promotions.
8. The long-term marriage of television and sports is so wellestablished that the industries are increasingly integrated in effect or in fact. Vertical integration (control of programming by the program outlet) is a key desire and strategy of the major media firms (Bellamy & Walker, 2005).

Media Differences and Sports Attributes

Before elaborating on the eight factors that make sports a key programming exemplar to television and, to some degree, other media, some of the differences between media need to be briefly considered. For example, broadcast television will have an increasingly problematic relationship with sports coverage. The dilution of network viewers coupled with the high cost of major sports rights fees and the increasing amounts of revenue realized from moving sports to cable/satellite channels all work against major sports remaining a network staple. The most recent NBA television contract, for example, de-emphasizes regular season network television broadcasts in favor of cable channels that can both give the league more prime time exposure ("Hoops TV," 2004). Only the NFL gets any substantive amount of regular season prime time coverage on broadcast television.

Already the major broadcast networks are starting to make up for their loss of big time sports by entering into low- or no-cost deals with new leagues and events. Examples of this include NBC's unsuccessful co-ownership of the XFL and the present deal (with no network ownership stake) with the Arena Football League and "extreme" action sports (Bellamy, 1998; Bellamy & Walker, 2005).

Of course, the cultural value of sports continues to prevent or at least delay the diversion of some major sport product to cable/satellite television. Such events as the NFL Conference Championship Games and Super Bowl, MLB's World Series, and major Olympic events are likely to remain on U.S. broadcast television for the next generation due to the serious political fallout and negative public relations reaction to any attempt to move them to a pay system. However, with approximately 85% of U.S. television households now paying for multichannel television via cable or satellite, the idea of paying for television is increasingly normalized in the population.

There are significant differences among big time sports that also need to be considered in any discussion of the sports and media. The NFL, for example, has long been regarded as both the most television friendly and television savvy of sports leagues. Like its collegiate farm system, the NFL has the advantage of playing at a time when household viewing levels are increasing as fall replaces summer, and of playing on a field that is easy to cover with television equipment and that works with standard television's aspect ratio (and even better with wide-screen HDTV). The NFL also has the decided advantage of producing a limited amount of product (32 teams playing 16 game schedules) that enhances the value of each game. Although noted but usually ignored, NFL games are a major source of illegal gambling action, further enhancing its value as television programming. While other North American-based sports leagues and associations share some of the attributes of the NFL, none have all of them (Bellamy, 1998).

SPORTS AS EXEMPLAR

Despite the differences among sports and television distribution outlets, there are the attributes that most all sports share that have made them such a key programming software and content element. While I have already explained why the emphasis in the following discussion is on television, this should be taken by the reader to mean *all* forms of television. After all, whether delivered by an analog or digital broadcast signal, received via a wired or wireless broadband connection, or viewed from a stored disc (such as a DVD or videogame cartridge), the audience member is watching or using television. In addition, the reception level of television should not be limited to the traditional view of an individual or small group watching a relatively nonmobile and mainly noninteractive machine. Television refers to multiple modes of reception ranging from the person watching live game action via streaming video on her computer monitor to another person watching specifically archived highlights of a favorite player on his cell phone to the group watching a championship game on a large flat-screen HDTV monitor in a sports bar.

The Reality Factor

Most popular sports events on television, radio, or, increasingly, the Internet are live. Technical requirements and the difficulty of production and content control have relegated most other live programming to niche status. Note, however, that such exceptions as the Academy Awards consistently are among the highest-rated programs. Clearly, the audience likes live television and regards it as something "special."

In live television, the outcome can not be predicted with certainty or given away by another person or the media. Sport fulfills the public's desire for unpredictable excitement very nicely. Unlike news, which is often avoided except when there is a major breaking story, sports, even to the casual fans, are something new (i.e., no repeats except on ESPN Classic) and exciting.

Another important value of live presentation is that live television programming is well suited to the integration of promotional and advertising messages. Such messages are not only normalized in such live programming as sports (see "The Zap-Proof Factor," discussed later), but can be inserted, deleted, or altered during the telecast. In addition, live programming is less subject to time shifting than other programming forms. After all, after an event is over the value of seeing a repeat of it is much reduced as the in-the-moment excitement has passed. The economic importance of this is that spot advertisements are much more likely to be seen in their entirety than is the case with time-shifted programs, where spots are commonly avoided (Bellamy & Walker, 1996; J. B. Chabin, personal communication, February 7, 2005; M. Danielski, personal communication, March 11, 2005).

The Regularly-Scheduled and Cost-Effective Factors

The many television award programs are further evidence of the popularity of live programming. The problem is that, no matter how many award shows are created and televised, they cannot be regularly scheduled in the same way as sports. Although the culmination of sports competition typically is a huge once-a-year or more infrequent event such as the Master's, the Olympic medal events, the Daytona 500, the Super Bowl, or the World Cup, sports provide television with hours and hours of regularly scheduled live programming. This is a vital part of sports appeal to television programmers for two major reasons.

First, television has the most costly and voracious appetite of any medium. With most every outlet now on a 24/7 schedule, the need for programming to fill so much time is an ever-present consideration. A regular season of the games of a league or a specific team or a season (such as NASCAR and the PGA) fills a lot of time that would otherwise have to be filled with other programming.

Second, sports, unlike many other types of programming, is cost efficient for television outlets. One example is the rise of multichannel cable- and satellite-delivered television and its early innovation of channels devoted to nothing but sports, including ESPN on the national level and the many regional sports networks [RSNs] that developed in most all the major metropolitan areas of the United States (Bellamy, 1993b). Although the popular press often features laments about the high cost of rights fees, television outlets consider the fees to be economically effective or they would not keep paying the ever-escalating cost.

Cost effectiveness relates at a more macrolevel with network prestige and legitimacy among the advertising and investment communities. A good example of this was CBS' loss of NFL rights to Fox in the early 1990s. Although there were other factors at work, including a national business slump, the loss of the rights was a proximate cause in CBS losing many major affiliates to Fox and in piling up losses in its stock value (Bellamy, 1998). Therefore, sports may indeed be worth the cost even if a profit can not be generated from the rights fees. Of course, the all-sports cable networks such as ESPN and its spin-offs and the various RSNs *must* have sports to have any marketplace credibility.

Sports on television are also cost effective because they are better than most any other programming genre at attracting a consistent audience of hard-to-reach (primarily young male) viewers that many advertisers covet. This is why advertisers are willing to pay increasing amounts of money at a time when the average ratings for most all television programming are decreasing (Bellamy, 1998).

The International Literacy Factor

Sports easily cross international and intercultural boundaries despite differences in language and both written and visual literacy. Even if one does not understand all the rules, strategy, and subtleties of ice hockey, for example, most everyone can understand the basic point of the game from a telecast regardless of the language in which it is presented. Most sports have simple objectives that can be grasped easily because the sports, game and competition culture essentially is universal, and many "foreign" games have similarities to indigenous games. The globalization of sports and television is a way to enhance the value of the product already purchased for domestic distribution with little added cost.

Another media factor is the increasing influence of the Olympics and the World Cup in spreading an interest in particular sports to the rest of the world. The result is obvious when we see professional baseball in Asia, basketball and soccer in much of the world, and ice hockey in central and eastern Europe. This does not even include the continuing influence of the individual sports such as tennis, golf, and auto racing that have long been international and now can reach international media audiences.

Because many sports are already globalized and because others have the potential to become so, is it any surprise that the increasingly international media entertainment industry sees them as a key element in the extension of power and influence (Bellamy, 1993a; Bellamy & Chabin, 1999; M. Danielski, personal communication, March 11, 2005)? For example, the presence of Yao Ming has allowed the NBA to make inroads into the vast Chinese media market, while MLB has an increasing presence in both Central and South America and Asia due to the success of such stars as Sammy Sosa, Ichiro Suzuki, Edgar Renteria, and others ("Global NBA," 2004; "MLB International," 2004).

One of the few rivals to sports telecasts in the ability to cross global boundaries of language and literacy are action adventure programs and movies. The global popularity of Jackie Chan, Vin Diesel, and others, and such television series as *Xena*, *Hercules*, and so forth, is certainly not based on complex narratives. The appeal is more visceral and universally understood— good versus evil, right versus wrong, often violent conflict and action, and a lack of moral ambiguity. These values, of course, are part and parcel of the narratives found in sports coverage.

The Benign Viewer Factor

Can you think of anyone who hates mediated sports? I do not mean the people who criticize the announcers or the coverage, but someone who literally will leave the room during a telecast? While we may know people who dislike a certain type of sports or sports entertainment (boxing, professional wrestling, and cricket come to mind), rarely do we encounter a sports or a sports television hater.

Part of the reason is who we associate with, but another very important factor is the constant media attention that sports receive, which makes them not only acceptable but also expectable that one will know something about sports even if he or she is not a "die hard" fan. Sports are such an ingrained part of our daily lives and popular culture that to be ignorant of them is to be uncool or out of the loop. Consider for a moment how much of our day-to-day communication revolves around a sports star, a team, or events. Some knowledge of sport is one of the important currencies of interpersonal communication.

An example of this is the continuing popularity of sports bars (which in regard to health is an oxymoronic term at best) as a conduit for group interaction that presupposes and supports at least some level of interest in sports. Combine this with the vast availability of sports information available through media and it is easy to see why sports, at least in an abstract way, have become a relatively benign cultural force even to nonfans and, obviously, something much more than that to many.

This "benign neglect at best" attitude translates into value for sports as television product. In a time when most all television viewers are armed with RCDs and many viewing options as well as myriad other entertainment options, programming that viewers strongly dislike is to be avoided at almost all costs. Sports as integrated into the larger world of entertainment have become an important part, rather than just a niche, of popular culture. They are difficult to avoid and even more difficult to completely ignore if one wants to fit in with society (Kellner, 1995; Whitson, 1998).

The concept of sports as popular culture is in many ways more relevant to the general mass entertainment broadcasters and cablecasters than the specialized niche or subniche cable and satellite networks. A football game is more profitable for CBS and its affiliates than, for example, a program on politics or international news because in part the much larger and more desirable audience that football attracts is a product of the fact that many people will watch a football or other sporting event even if their interest is relatively low because it is the "in" thing to do. On the other hand, a niche channel such as CNN, MSNBC, or Fox News Channel caters specifically to the relatively small audience that has a ravenous appetite for political and other news. Similarly, one of the ESPN networks or FOX Sports Net appeals to the more hardcore sports fan.

The Loyalty and Effects Factors

In current programming vocabulary, loyal viewers are referred to as *appointment viewers*. Such viewers are brand loyal and have increasing value in the increasingly diffuse television environment. As mentioned, sports telecasts have the ability to aggregate a consistent and highly valued audience out of groups that are not particularly attracted to other types of programming. Many sports fans, therefore, are appointment viewers with ever-increasing value.

In addition, sports telecasts can have strong audience effects that reinforce their popularity and strength as a television product. While the effects are not necessarily caused by television, extensive media coverage enhances them. Sometimes, as in the case of the disturbances that too often break out after the local team's championship victory, the effects are destructive. More common, however, are the celebrations of victory or even laments of defeat that result in increased media consumption to get the most information possible. These have increased the value of both pre, post, and review sports programs, Web sites, and publications.

The loyalty and celebratory effects factor also manifests itself in consumerism and the transference of loyalty from sports to sponsor (King, 2005; Schimmel, 2001). Sports fans are ready and willing consumers of team-licensed apparel, videos, and a seemingly never-ending slew of souvenirs and paraphernalia—a consumption pattern that spikes with televised and otherwise media-saturated events. Although there is some of this with other television programs, there is a large degree of difference between fans of *Friends* and fans of the Boston Red Sox. The former watch the program in syndicated repeats and on DVDS, may talk about the latest romantic situations of the characters or the actors who appear in the series, and may even buy a sweatshirt or a Central Perk coffee mug or get a Jennifer Aniston-inspired hair style. However, adults who did much more than this (i.e., decorating her or his apartments like Monica's, placing posters of the cast all over her or his homes) would be considered odd or, at least, juvenile. Contrast this with the many adults who own and display sports memorabilia and spend enormous amounts of time and money in celebrating the Red Sox or another favorite team. While one could and should argue that the Red Sox are real and *Friends* is not, the fact remains that for most people at most times their favorite sports team or athlete is also in large part a creation and product of the media. After all, most of the fans that celebrated the Red Sox World Series victory of 2004 rarely, if ever, have met any of the players or have been to games regularly if at all.

One of the very few cultural products that can come close to the loyalty that sports engender in its fans is the attraction that adolescents have for their music idols. There are indeed many, many young people (primarily females) who decorate with and own any number of Avril Lavigne, Beck, and Kanye West products. For many other young people (primarily male), the equivalent is sports. The difference, of course, is that the appeal of sports is often not outgrown and is, in fact, not only tolerated but also encouraged and celebrated in adult society and in the media.

The Zap-Proof Factor

Perhaps the key importance of sports as television product are the opportunities provided for sponsors to reach their intended targets. Once again, this is an increasingly difficult task in a television world made up of millions of restless viewers armed with RCDs and other navigation devices such as personal or digital video recorders (PVRs/DVRs) or media-center computers. An increasing number of individuals now have the ability to design individual menus of programming. Any advertising message integrated with program content is *zap-proof* (Bellamy, 1998; Bellamy & Walker, 1996). The key concept is that it is impossible for the viewer to avoid advertising messages without missing part of the sports event.

Sports telecasts are, of course, loaded with such advertising and sponsorship opportunities. McAllister (1998) detailed the vast number of product mentions in a Tostitos Fiesta Bowl telecast. His point was that the integration of advertising into the telecast leads to both multiple audio sponsor mentions (virtually every time the bowl was mentioned) as well as video (the sponsor's logo on the playing field). This form of audience creation and targeting is common in most every sport telecast.

Consider the many advertising messages embedded in most any sports contest: the name of the venue, electronic and changeable billboards on or near the scoreboard and throughout the stadium or arena (including the playing surface), virtual advertising that appears on television but not at the venue, the on-air sponsor billboards (i.e., "this telecast is brought to you by . . . "), in-game features (review of the action/scoring recaps), after-game features ("Star of the Game"), uniform logos, Gatorade on the bench, and so forth. Although sports are not the only television programs with content/advertising integration (e.g., *Survivor, American Idol, The Apprentice,* and other "reality" programs that, like sports, are based on competition and a live element), they are *the* most common forum for the practice.

The practice of advertising integration is part of sports history and has long been accepted by sports viewers. We likely would be startled to watch (or even listen to) a sports event without nearly constant commercial exposure. Although the practice of advertising/content integration goes back to the very beginnings of commercial broadcasting, zap-proof advertising is critical to the present television industry. The increasingly restless audience can easily zap undesirable content. With research indicating that commercials are one of the major causes of zapping, integrating advertising into the program content, as has long been the case with sports, is seen as critical to the long-term health of television advertising (Bellamy & Walker, 1996).

The Promotion Factor

Conventional wisdom about sports on television is that they are superb promotional platforms for other programs. Sports telecasts constantly promote other programs on the channel or network both aurally and visually. The virtual billboards behind home plate in World Series promoting the new fall season, the appearance of network celebrities in the broadcast booth promoting their series or movie, and the hype leading up to the Super Bowl are examples.

Conventional wisdom is often incorrect, and there is some evidence to suggest that this is the case here. Eastman and Otteson (1994), for example, found that sports are no more effective as a promotional platform than other programs. Although not conclusive, this calls into question one of the major justifications for escalating sports rights fees.

However, as long as sports continue to have the many attributes discussed in this chapter, there is little chance that the conventional wisdom will change. Sports telecasts, despite declining ratings on many television outlets, continue to attract a desirable and zap-proof advertising that may not be exposed to promotion in other ways. In addition, the value of sports to some television outlets is more than just their immediate ability to reap profitable advertising sales or even to be successful near-term promotional platforms. Brand identity is particularly important in a cluttered television environment in order to stand out from competing television and other media outlets. Being able to brand itself as "The Network of the Olympics" is seen as a way for NBC to distinguish itself from rivals at the same time it has abandoned many other major league sports. Fox, as mentioned previously, was able to brand itself as a legitimate "Big 4" network by leveraging its acquisition of the NFL, MLB, and, more recently, NASCAR (Bellamy, 1998; Bellamy & Traudt, 2000).

The Integration Factor

In the last decade there has been a shift in the way that the sports business and media business talk about one another for public consumption. Today, the symbiosis of the two industries is recognized and even celebrated as fact with all the talk of "partners" (Bellamy, 1998; Bellamy & Walker, 2005). In addition, sports leagues now refer to themselves as being in the media business via their partnerships and their own Web sites, publications, and even television channels (e.g., NBA-TV, the NFL Channel). The most celebrated sports executive today (NBA Commissioner David Stern) and perhaps of all time (the late NFL Commissioner Pete Rozelle) are both regarded as media geniuses.

As I have attempted to demonstrate throughout this chapter, sports are an integral part of the media entertainment and leisure time industries. However, symbiosis works in various ways. Media corporations are also sports owners and, in the latest development, sports owners are now explicitly in the media business.

There are many reasons for large media firms to own professional sports teams. Vertical integration of media and sports guarantees programming with no costs outside the external exchange of rights fees. Thus, ownership integration of two cartels appears to be a "win-win" for the team and the media company. A good example of how ownership of sports teams can benefit media outlets is Ted Turner's leveraging of his Atlanta Braves ("America's Team") as a key element of building his cable empire (now a unit of Time Warner). Sports made his weak UHF station attractive to cable systems around the country and gave him a steady and large (several hundred hours a year) source of programming he did not have to produce or pay rights fees to obtain. News Corporation's (i.e., Rupert Murdoch's) ownership of the Los Angeles Dodgers; AOL Time Warner's ownership of the Atlanta Braves, Hawks, and Thrashers; Disney's ownership of Anaheim's Angels and Mighty Ducks; and several other media/team co-ownerships were all unsuccessful attempts to replicate Turner's success (Bellamy & Walker, 2005).

The recent divestiture of sports team ownership from large media firms is not evidence of a decline in the importance of sports to media and media to sports. In fact, there appears to be a movement back to a traditional form of vertical integration where teams (producers) control the distribution and exhibition of their own product. New York's YES network is the exemplar of this trend. YES feeds millions of dollars of revenue into the coffers of the Yankees, Nets, and Devils. These teams do not have to share revenue with another company such as FOX (the dominant owner/operator of RSNs). Team owned RSNs presently are one of the major trends in the sports television business (Bellamy & Walker, 2005).

Team-owned television operations were originally created in the early days of multichannel television (late 1970s and early 1980s) and are based on models developed in the 1950s for some of the early pay-television schemes (Bellamy, 1993b; Bellamy & Walker, 2005). What is different now is that the technological infrastructure of satellites, cable, Internet, and, increasingly, broadband and digital transmission has now developed to offer realistic ways for sports teams to become their own producers, distributors, and exhibitors. This infrastructure makes it possible for teams to offer game coverage targeted to different types of viewers at different prices. Coverage can be in high or standard definition, with or without digital enhancements, in packages focusing on only one team or offering all the league games. With these pay enhancements, even a relatively small core of fans can generate huge amounts of new money for popular teams even as most fans continue to get their coverage through existing broadcast and cable channels.

CONCLUSIONS

Space obviously does not allow an analysis of all the components of the media/communication and sports nexus. One important component that does need to be mentioned is the public relations (PR) and marketing value of big time sports in civic culture. There are no generally accepted metrics to measure the monetary value of the publicity or brand equity that comes with being a "major league" city (Aaker, 1995). In fact, Noll and Zimbalist (1997) and Shropshire (1995) are among the economists who have argued that cities typically do not benefit from subsidizing sports franchises or major events. However, in an age of increasingly cluttered messages, having a city's name in the media from the exploits of sports teams must be regarded as having substantial value. In terms of wide circulation (i.e., the city name in most all sports media on a consistent and ongoing basis) and brand identity of cities (Kotler, 2002), there are few if any businesses that come close to generating the PR value of a professional major league sports franchise.

The ongoing integration of the once disparate media forms of television, radio, newspapers, and the Internet is another dynamic in the media sports nexus. New forms of value-added coverage (i.e., HDTV, interactive games, gambling, fantasy sports, inside info) have been developed and implemented to make the sports business–media outlet–consumer connection stronger.

One of the present mantras in the entertainment and information industries is "on hand and on demand" (J. B. Chabin, personal communication, February 7, 2005). This means that the consumer expects to have whatever content she or he wants whenever she wants and wherever he is located. To many people this means television on portable carry-along devices in addition to audio, phone services, and PDA functions. Content that reflects and defines popular culture is the most important content for such personal media devices. Sports increasingly is an integral part of our popular and mediated culture (King, 2005).

Sports have evolved from a business that had a series of highly beneficial relationships with the media business to one of the central components of the increasingly global media entertainment industry. This is due to the combination of attributes that sports offer media, and particularly television. A consistent, loyal, and lucrative audience less able to avoid advertising and promotional messages and tied into an emerging global popular cultural and consumer mainstream is one of enormous value to media. When that audience also consists of niches that can be aggregated into valuable commodities for advertisers and marketers throughout the globe, there is an even increased value to sports that most other media content cannot match.

REFERENCES

Aaker, D. A. (1995). *Building strong brands*. New York: Free Press.

Alexander, A., Owers, J., Carveth, R., Hollifield, C. A., & Greco, A. N. (Eds.). (2003). *Media economics: Theory and practice* (3rd ed.). Mahwah, NJ: Lawrence Erlbaum Associates.

Bellamy, R. V., Jr. (1993a). Issues in the internationalization of U.S. sports media: The emerging European marketplace. *Journal of Sport and Social Issues, 17*(3), 168–80.

Bellamy, R. V., Jr. (1993b). Regional sports networks: Prime network and SportsChannel America. In R. G. Picard (Ed.), *The cable networks: The rise of nonbroadcast video programmers* (pp. 163–73). Riverside, CA: Carpelan.

Bellamy, R. V., Jr. (1998). The evolving television sports marketplace. In L. A. Wenner (Ed.), *MediaSport: Cultural sensibilities and sport in the media age* (pp. 73–89). London: Routledge.

Bellamy, R. V., Jr., & Chabin, J. B. (1999). Global promotion and marketing of television. In S. T. Eastman, D. A. Ferguson, & R. A. Klein (Eds.), *Promotion and marketing for broadcasting and cable* (pp. 211–232). Boston: Focal.

Bellamy, R. V., Jr., & Traudt, P. J. (2000). Television branding as promotion. In S. T. Eastman (Ed.), *Research in media promotion* (pp. 127–59). Mahwah, NJ: Lawrence Erlbaum Associates.

Bellamy, R. V., Jr., & Walker, J. R. (1996). *Television and the remote control: Grazing on a vast wasteland*. New York: Guilford.

Bellamy, R. V., Jr., & Walker, J. R. (2005). Whatever happened to synergy? MLB as media product. *NINE: A Journal of Baseball History and Culture, 13*(2), 19–30.

Coakley, J. (Ed.). (2003). *Sports in society* (8th ed.). New York: McGraw-Hill.

Eastman. S. T., & Otteson, J. L. (1994). Promotion increases ratings, doesn't it? The impact of program promotion in the 1992 Olympics. *Journal of Broadcasting and Electronic Media, 38*(3), 307–322.

Eitzen, D. S. (Ed.). (2001). *Sports in contemporary society: An anthology*. New York: Worth.

Global NBA programming. (2004). Retrieved on March 11, 2005, from http://www.nba.com/schedules/international_nba_tv_schedule.html

Hoops TV. (2004). Retrieved on March 11, 2005, from http://www.insidehoops.com/hoopstv.shtml

Kellner, D. (1995). *Media culture: Cultural studies, identity and politics between the modern and the postmodern*. London: Routledge.

King, B. (2005, March 7–13). The 24/7 fan. *Street & Smith's SportsBusiness Journal*, pp. 23–37.

Kotler, P. (2002). *Marketing places*. New York: Free Press.

McAllister, M. P. (1998). College bowl sponsorship and the increased commercialization of amateur sports. *Critical Studies in Mass Communication, 15*(4), 357–381.

McChesney, R. W. (1989). Media made sport: A history of sports coverage in the U.S. In L. A. Wenner (Ed.), *Media, Sports, & Society* (pp. 49–69). Newbury Park, CA: Sage.

MLB International. (2004). Retrieved on March 11, 2005, from http://mlb.mlb.com/NASApp/mlb/mlb/international/index.jsp?feature=mli

Noll, R. G., & Zimbalist, A. (Eds.). (1997). *Sports, jobs, and taxes: The economic impact of sports teams and stadiums*. New York: Brookings Institution.

Real, M. R. (1998). MediaSport: Technology and the commodification of postmodern sport. In L. A. Wenner (Ed.), *MediaSport: Cultural sensibilities and sport in the media age* (pp. 14–26). London: Routledge.

Rowe, D. (1999). *Sport, culture and the media: The unruly trinity*. Philadelphia: Open University Press.

Schimmel, K. S. (2001). Take me out to the ballgame: The transformation of production-consumption relations in professional team sport. In C. L. Harrington & D. D. Bielby (Eds.), *Popular culture: Production and consumption* (pp. 36–52). Malden, MA: Blackwell.

Shropshire, K. L. (1995). *The sports franchise game: Cities in pursuit of sports franchises, events, stadiums, and arenas*. Philadelphia: University of Pennsylvania Press.

Sports Broadcasting Act. (1961). P.L. 87-331. 75 Stat. 732.

Wann, D. L., Melnick, M. J., Russell, G. W., & Pease, D. G. (2001). *Sports fans: The psychology and social impact of spectators*. New York: Routledge.

Wenner, L. A. (Ed.). (1998). Playing the MediaSport game. In L. A. Wenner (Ed.), *MediaSport: Cultural sensibilities and sport in the media age* (pp. 3–13). London: Routledge.

Whitson, D. (1998). Circuits of promotion: Media, marketing, and the globalization of sport. In L. A. Wenner (Ed.), *MediaSport: Cultural sensibilities and sport in the media age* (pp. 57–72). London: Routledge.

5

Sports Content on U.S. Television

Dan Brown
East Tennessee State University

Jennings Bryant
University of Alabama

"What's on television?" In the current media environment, if your answer is "sports," you will always be entirely correct, no matter when the question is asked. Sports programming has become ubiquitous on American television—a message system universal.

NORMATIVE DATA ON WHAT'S ON: AN OVERVIEW

An analysis of a week of broadcast and basic cable programming during June 2004 using *TV Guide* magazine for the 35th largest television market in the United States (Greenville, Spartanburg, Anderson, SC; Asheville, NC) illustrates the volume of sports on television (Bryant, Brown, & Cummins, 2004). Although the publication underreports daytime programming, 532 sports programs were listed, serving up 38,675 minutes, or nearly 645 hours, of content. Given that a week has only 168 hours, not only are sports on 24/7, sports aficionados typically have several viewing choices at any given time. Table 5.1 displays a breakdown of the content types available during this sample week. Table 5.2 shows these types by parts of the programming day.

Event Programming

When most people think of sports programming, they probably think of event coverage—live telecasts of sporting events, ranging in scale from the Super Bowl or the World Cup on major broadcast networks to live local coverage of a small-college women's volleyball match on a low-power television station. Indeed, as can be seen by combining across columns in Table 5.1, Bryant et al.'s (2004) analysis revealed

TABLE 5.1

Frequency and Cumulative Duration of Sports Programming Presented in a Single Market During One Week by Type of Network and Program Type

| | Network Type | | | | | |
| | Broadcast | | Cable | | Cable Sports | |
Program Type	# shows	Cum. dur.	# shows	Cum. dur.	# shows	Cum. dur.
Discussion	4	150	1	30	49	2,195
Documentary	—	—	2	120	—	—
Event coverage	14	1,920	27	3,140	113	13,290
Instruction	—	—	—	—	9	300
Journalism	7	210	6	110	148	7,245
Magazine	10	330	17	660	64	2,550
Past Event	—	—	—	—	6	390
Reality	—	—	—	—	1	60
Special	—	—	—	—	1	60
Sports fiction	1	120	50	5,555	2	240
Program-type combined	36	2,730	103	9,615	393	26,330

Note: Cumulative duration (Cum. dur.) is reported in minutes.

that 154 of the sports shows (28.9%), amounting to 18,350 minutes of available sports programming (47.4%), was coverage of sporting events.

This event-centered sports coverage is illustrated by listings from the CBS SportsLine Web site ("National Listings," 2004) for Saturday, June 26, 2004. Nationally televised golf events that day included coverage of the LPGA, the PGA Tour, the Nationwide Tour, and the Champions Tour. Thirteen Major League Baseball games appeared on television that day. The Fox Network carried four games nationally, and local stations in Baltimore, Denver, St. Louis, and San Diego carried games. Regional networks carried the remaining games. A San Antonio station carried a WNBA basketball game, and ESPN2 televised a professional soccer match.

Sports Journalism

However, in addition to televised events, many other kinds of sports programming have become commonplace, especially on cable networks or cable sports networks. For example, sports journalism programs, such as ESPN's *SportsCenter* or Fox Sports Network's (FSN) *NASCAR This Morning*, account for a larger number and percentage of sports programming (161 programs, 30.3%) than does event coverage, although event coverage accounts for considerably greater cumulative duration of programming than does sports journalism (7,565 minutes, 19.6%) because of the greater length of most event coverage.

Sports Fiction and Magazines

One remarkably large source of regular sports programming is sports fiction (e.g., movies like *The Natural* and series like ESPN's *Playmakers*), which contributed

TABLE 5.2
Frequency and Cumulative Duration of Sports Programming Presented in a Single Market During One
Week by Daypart and Program Type

Daypart Duration	Program Type	# of Programs	Cumulative
Daytime	Discussion	8	240
	Documentary	1	60
	Event coverage	55	7,835
	Journalism	29	1,420
	Magazine	28	960
	Past event	1	60
	Sports fiction	16	1,761
	Program combined	138	12,336
Early prime	Discussion	17	540
	Event coverage	29	3,540
	Journalism	29	1,215
	Magazine	13	510
	Past event	1	60
	Special	1	60
	Sports fiction	4	450
	Program combined	94	6,375
Late prime	Discussion	9	605
	Event coverage	3	255
	Journalism	8	390
	Magazine	1	30
	Sports fiction	1	95
	Program combined	22	1,375
Morning	Discussion	2	60
	Documentary	1	60
	Event coverage	12	2,130
	Journalism	30	1,800
	Magazine	1	30
	Sports fiction	13	1,366
	Program combined	59	5,446
Night	Discussion	2	60
	Event coverage	25	1,500
	Journalism	33	1,545
	Magazine	11	600
	Sports fiction	9	1,000
	Program combined	80	4,705
Prime	Discussion	16	870
	Event coverage	30	3,090
	Instruction	9	300
	Journalism	32	1,195
	Magazine	37	1,410
	Past event	4	270
	Reality	1	60
	Sports fiction	10	1,243
	Program combined	139	8,438
Daypart Combined	Program combined	532	38,675

Note: Cumulative duration is reported in minutes.

53 shows (10.2%) for a total of 5,915 hours (15.3%) to the profile by Bryant et al. (2004). Other major contributing genres of sports programming include sports magazine shows (e.g., FSN's *Sportsman's Adventure* or Spike's *MotoWorld*), which contributed 91 programs (17.1%) and 3,540 telecast minutes (9.2%); and sports discussion shows (e.g., FSN's *Best Damn Sports Show Period* or ESPN's *Outside the Lines*), which contributed 54 programs (10.2%) for 2,375 minutes cumulative duration of sports programming (6.1%).

Less Common Sports Programming

As Tables 5.1 and 5.2 reveal, other less-common forms of sports programming are also available, including sports instruction (e.g., Golf Channel's *Golf Academy*), replays of past sporting events (e.g., Golf Channel's *Booz Allen Classic*), sports documentaries (e.g., HBO's *When It Was A Game*), sports reality programs (e.g., Speed's *I Wanna Date a Race Car Driver*), and sports specials (e.g., ESPN's *ESPY Nomination Show*). Such less-frequently occurring formats combined accounted for 19 programs (3.5%) and 930 cumulative minutes of telecast time (2.4%) in Bryant et al.'s (2004) sample.

In some respects, the sports-programming profile presented by Bryant et al. (2004) is merely the proverbial tip of the iceberg. That profile was for basic cable telecasts in a single television market, which happened not to include a number of available sports networks (e.g., ESPN Classics, CSS). How much more sports programming is available when these and other missing networks are added? Or when premium sports channels or other specialty sports channels available via digital cable packages are assessed? Or when the specialized packages available via satellite networks are considered? Sports programming truly is a ubiquitous component of the media fare of the information age.

WHAT'S ON AND WHAT'S WATCHED

Discussing the content of sports on television now means talking about the most popular programs on cable television, which has surpassed over-the-air broadcast television in audience attention (Federal Communications Comission, 2004). Nielsen Media Research reported that, as of the end of October 2003, ESPN led all basic cable programming with an average rating of 2.4 in prime time, the period from 8:00 p.m. through 11 p.m. Eastern time (ET) each evening. The rating refers to the proportion of homes tuned to a given channel, and this rating reflected an average of 2.8 million American households tuned to ESPN on a typical evening, up by 41% from the previous year (Romano, 2003h).

"Sporting events reigned as cable's biggest attractions early in the year (2003). TNT's NBA All-Star Game and the network's NASCAR Budweiser Shootout and ESPN's NFL Pro Bowl and Holiday Bowl telecasts ranked as the most watched programs" (Romano, 2004e, p. 18). Cable's top 16 shows in 2003 among adults 18 to 49 included 8 sports shows, including the top 3. Among adults 25 to 54, 10 of the top 20 programs displayed sports content, including 3 of the top 4 shows. Considering all viewers together, 8 of the top 14 shows featured sports content, including the top 5 shows.

What kind of content generates such popularity on cable television? Just how popular are sports television programs? How pervasive is the sports genre in cable and broadcast television programming? For openers, 13 of the 30 top-rated television programs in 2003 conveyed sports content ("Top 100 television programs," 2004). The sports programming day begins with ESPN's *SportsCenter* as early as 5:00 a.m. and extends around the clock, giving sports networks negotiating power with cable systems, as exemplified by ESPN's habit of raising rates charged to cable systems every year (Higgins, 2003a).

Beyond the attention paid to ESPN shows and revenues, the influence of even the network's promotional campaigns is shocking. When ESPN included in a series of on-air promotions about what life might be like without sports three spots about a largely unknown community on the upper Michigan peninsula, the community catapulted to instant fame and fortune. The spots featured fans of the Watersmeet High School Nimrods showing their school spirit. Within seven weeks after the first spot appeared on January 26, 2004, Watersmeet sold $40,000 worth of sports clothing from mail orders and hits on the high school Web site. The campaign was followed by increased ratings (e.g., February 2004 was the most watched February ever for both ESPN and ESPN2). The month was "the eighth consecutive month of ratings growth for ESPN" (Thomaselli, 2004, p. 6).

Types of Sports Content on Television

Method

Systematically examining any aspect of the popularity of television content presents an economic problem because reports of the audience ratings of programming are proprietary information. The prime source is Nielsen Media Research, which provides the television and advertising industries with data about television audiences. These data are reported in a variety of daily and weekly publications, and this section of this chapter includes frequent references to data from weekly reports from *Broadcasting and Cable* (*B&C*) magazine about sports programs airing in 2003. Although this chapter includes many normative data and anecdotal citations from 2004 publications, emphasis on the 2003 time frame provides a baseline for interpreting the content, frequency, and popularity of sports on television.

B&C reports provide listings of the top 10 broadcasting and cable shows of each week, the top shows among audience members of ages 18 to 49, and a complete listing of shows airing on major networks in prime time. Daytime listings and audience size estimates for programs rated lower than the top 10 are available from Nielsen for substantial fees that are prohibitively high for noncommercial users.

One of the limitations of this data source is that much of the daily sports telecasts air outside the framework of the Nielsen reporting base. For example, many sports events that appear on cable television attract audiences but fail to reach the top 10 cable shows of the week; sports events appear in prime time on individual broadcast stations but not on major networks; and many sports events appear on both cable and broadcast outlets during daytime hours and draw comparatively small audiences, often failing to reach a rating of 1.0. All of these circumstances preclude the events being reported in the *B&C* listings on which much of the information from this chapter is based. Therefore, this chapter does not claim to offer a comprehensive listing of all sports that appear on television. However, the chapter does summarize the most popular sports events that appear on cable television and the broadcast sports events seen by the largest audiences.

Sports News and Talk

Dozens of sports news and talk shows appear on television daily. An exhaustive list would be pointless, so this section will provide detailed examples from ESPN and Fox, the two largest providers of such programs.

Since its debut in 1979, ESPN has become a fixture in cable television households, reaching them all. The network regularly presents news, talk, and discussion shows that air on both ESPN and ESPN2, including *Around the Horn, Outside the Lines, Pardon the Interruption, Sports Reporters*, and *The Hook Up*. Other specialty discussion shows include *NBA Matchup, NFL Matchup*, and *Baseball Tonight*. A variety of shows appear during specific times of the year, featuring pending events or events in progress, such as *U.S. Open Preview* for golf and *Today at Wimbledon* for tennis.

SportsCenter

These shows air at multiple times during the week. ESPN's *SportsCenter* is the king of sports news and discussion, presenting at least 23 hours of live weekly programming with daily shows at 6:00 p.m., 11:00 p.m., and 1:00 a.m. ET. The live editions are taped and re-aired with live updates throughout the week. "In an average week, 28 million people check out *SportsCenter* during the week, and 22 million watch the show on weekends" ("Media Insight: ESPN SportsCenter," 2003, para 2).

SportsCenter has become a part of the larger sports culture, transcending the mundane updates of sports scores and news to become a daily ritual for millions of people. The nightly 11:00 p.m. show averages more than 78% male, compared with 45.3% of viewers throughout the day. The show "directly inspired the creation of at least two other programs, including *Dream Job*, a reality show in which the prize was an anchor slot on *SportsCenter*, and *Sports Night*, a short-lived sitcom" (Callahan, 2004, p. 23). *SportsCenter* began airing in high definition in June 2004, part of the benefit from the network's having built a new 120,000-square-foot production facility at its home in Bristol, Connecticut (The team player, 2004). The show uses research by its own staff members and that of commissioned others. Senior Coordinating Producer Craig Lazarus "is interested in stories that highlight sports and crossover into popular culture and societal issues. He looks outside traditional venues and stretches his people to show the human side of a story" ("Media Insight: ESPN SportsCenter," 2003, para 4).

Fox Competitors to SportsCenter

Fox Networks offer regionally specific versions of ESPN's *SportsCenter*, such as *Southern Sports Report,* and regionally focused specialty news shows, such as *Braves Report*, which target viewers in the southeastern states. Also similar to ESPN's array of sports news and talk shows, Fox presents such shows as *AFL Weekly; Around the Track; Big 12 Showcase* and other conference-specific counterparts; *Fox Sports Net Across America; NASCAR This Morning; NBA Action; Totally NASCAR; I, Max;* and *The Tim McCarver Show*. Fox brought the rowdy macho atmosphere of its Sunday NFL pregame shows to a nightly format in *Best Damn Sports Show Period*. The *Business Wire* described the show as "sports conversation from the fans' and players' points of view. Blending sports, comedy and an irreverent tone, *BDSSP* takes a humorous look at the sports happenings of the day, and features special guests" ("Rudi Johnson," 2004, p. 6238).

Morning Talk

ESPN's *Cold Pizza* began in late 2003, coinciding with the tenth anniversary of ESPN2, following the patterns seen in early morning news magazine shows each weekday. In fact, the consulting producer worked at the *Today* show on NBC during the 1980s, and the show stressed entertainment designed to attract casual fans who might not find the highly structured *SportsCenter* shows attractive (Romano, 2003e).

Football

Football is big on television, even in syndicated game shows. *Wheel of Fortune* aired an NFL Players Week during January 2003. Pro football players competed on the show to win money for charities ("Wheel of Fortune loves football," 2003). "National Football League games are consistently the biggest draw in cable, regularly scoring an 8 or 9 household rating for ESPN's Sunday-night game" ("What's hot in cable," 2003, p. 14).

Super Bowl

The Super Bowl is annually one of the most watched events in television. Mark LaNeve, general manager at the Cadillac division of General Motors in Detroit described the Super Bowl as "one of the few properties that exist today where people are still actually watching the commercials" (Elliott, 2004a, para 11). *Advertising Age* reported that when the spending is adjusted for inflation, the $42,000 price of a 30-second spot for Super Bowl I reaches $239,167 in today's dollars.

The average 2004 Super Bowl commercial sold for $2.3 million, up from $2.1 million in 2003. Because people watch the commercials in the game in large numbers, pressure to present outstanding ads runs high. "You're very thoughtful about the commercial you run because there are two games going on, the football game and the commercial game," said Abby F. Kohnstamm, senior vice president for marketing at International Business Machines (Eggerton, 2004, p. 30).

Commercials in the 2004 game introduced competition among the standard kinds of products, such as automobiles, movies, and credit cards. However, controversy erupted from the inclusion of competing ads for drugs designed to treat erectile dysfunction, as well as the lack of taste in many of the commercials. The 2004 Super Bowl ads included "a dog trained to bite crotches, a flatulent horse, a monkey pitching woo to a woman, a man tortured with a bikini waxing and an elderly couple fighting over a bag of potato chips" (Elliott, 2004b, para 1).

Halftime entertainment at the Super Bowl has changed dramatically over the years. In the 1960s and 1970s, the early days of the annual contest, the shows featured marching bands and performers like Woody Herman and Al Hirt. Michael Jackson and a crowd of children at halftime in 1993 drew higher ratings than the game itself. Rocker band Aerosmith performed in Super Bowl XXXV, and U2 in 2002 upped the noise level of the halftime show. The huge audience for the Super Bowl has always attracted people who want to perform on the world's stage (Sandomir, 2004b).

The 2004 halftime show competed with a pay-per-view lingerie bowl featuring female models playing football while dressed in underwear. Meanwhile, back at the stadium, the second of two MTV halftime productions in four years featured rapper P. Diddy, followed by the duo of Janet Jackson and Justin Timberlake. When Timberlake accidentally (?) revealed one of Ms. Jackson's breasts for less than two seconds, a national debate followed about whether the incident was planned and the extent of its impact. The claim of accident was somewhat muted by the presence of an object to hide the nipple, and the Federal Communications Commission launched an investigation of CBS after the baring. The fallout from the furor intimidated other broadcasters from airing anything that might be considered controversial. Less than a week after the game, Janet Jackson was cut from the Grammy Awards telecast, and "NBC announced that it would pull a scene from (an) episode of its hit drama *E.R.* because an 80-year-old woman's breast was briefly exposed" (Carter, 2004a, para 2). "In its desire to produce something bigger than a football game, the N.F.L. lost control of its product. Lie down with dogs, you get up with fleas. The N.F.L. is scratching itself today" (Vecsey, 2004, para 16).

Observers might wonder about all the fuss. The sex card was hardly new to either the Super Bowl or to the NFL. When the Dallas Cowboys introduced their sexy cheerleaders more than a quarter century before, CBS sports producer Chuck Milton commented, "The audience deserves a little sex with its violence" (Rich, 2004, para 8).

The 2003 Super Bowl telecast of the game between the Tampa Bay Bucaneers and Oakland Raiders attracted 43.4 million households, a rating of 40.7, and a share of 61. The previous two Super Bowls earned average ratings of 40.4 and shares of 61, about 1% less than the 2003 contest (McClellan, 2003a). Not surprisingly, it was the highest-rated sports program of the year. Nielsen Media Research reported that the game, the 37th Super Bowl, ranked as the second most watched Super Bowl ever, with more than 137.6 million viewers tuning in for at least part of the game. The top-rated game pitted the Pittsburgh Steelers and Dallas Cowboys in 1996. The average audience throughout the 2003 game reached 88.6 million viewers.

"CBS and its co-owned Viacom networks [planned] more game-related coverage then [sic] ever before" (McClellan, 2003b, p. 16). Jim Nantz, CBS announcer, devised the idea for an opening ceremony, called *Super Bowl XXXVII: A Houston Salute*, on the previous Monday, similar to the opening of the Olympic Games. The program represented the first such opening for the game. Including the pregame show that began at 11:00 a.m. ET, Super Bowl Sunday became such an event that the network generated approximately $170 million worth of advertising.

Additionally, the Viacom cable networks ran special programming related to the Super Bowl. The night before Super Bowl Sunday, CBS kicked off with the *Super Bowl's Greatest Commercials*. On Sunday, Nickelodeon aired live reports from a child reporter on *Nick Games and Sports*. The pregame show began with a 60-minute *Nickelodeon Takes Over the Super Bowl*. MTV produced the second hour, modeled after *Total Request Live*. MTV also produced halftime entertainment for the game, a project that generated months of publicity, both positive and negative, from the exposed breast of Janet Jackson that emerged during the number with Justin Timberlake. At 1:00 p.m., CBS ran the *Phil Simms All-Iron Team*, leading into the four-hour *NFL Today* actual pregame program.

CMT ran a live top-20 countdown at the game. Spike TV conducted a sweepstakes awarding a ticket to the game with a commitment to document the day for a show called *Ten Things Every Guy Should Experience*. Other Super Bowl-related programming appeared on TV Land and BET.

Other NFL Football

Another football showcase, *Monday Night Football* on ABC, attracted an average of 12.1 million households on 17 dates during 2003, generating average ratings of 11.3 and shares of 18.9. These figures showed about the same levels as 2002 games. The top 8 highest rated broadcast sports programs of 2003 were football telecasts, as were 16 of the top 18 highest rated sports broadcasts of the year. The only non-football games in the top 18 were 2 seventh games (Red Sox–Yankees and Marlins–Cubs) in the Major League Baseball playoffs. The top six football telecasts involved NFL games.

Twenty NFL games appeared on ESPN and earned top-10 cable program status during 2003, averaging an audience of 6.4 million households. Fourteen episodes of *NFL Primetime*, an ESPN show recapping NFL games, showing extensive highlights, placed in the top-10 cable shows of 2003. These 14 shows attracted an average audience of 3.5 million. Combined, these 34 professional football shows produced an average audience of 5.2 million households.

ESPN football games "earned the highest ratings among all advertising-supported cable programs during the football season. The average cable ratings reached 7.8 and the average audience included 9.3 million viewers" (Romano, 2004b).

Broadcast Sunday NFL games on Fox in 2003 averaged a 10.4 rating and 15.9 million viewers, like the figures for *Monday Night Football*, about the same as a year earlier. CBS averaged a 9.7 rating and 14.8 million viewers in 2003, slight increases over the previous year (Romano, 2004b, p. 16).

Football watching in cities with NFL teams qualifies as fanatical. For example, the top-ranked market in America in watching sports on TV is the Green Bay–Appleton, Wisconsin area ("Packers pervasive," 2003). Although the city of Green Bay is home to only about 100,000 people, the market of more than a million includes other cities, such as Oshkosh and Appleton. Nevertheless, the market is small by the standards of most cities with professional sports teams. When the beloved Packers play, Fox affiliate WLUK-TV earns an average rating of 54 and share of 80.

NFL Game Elements

When fans tune in to professional football, what do they see? NFL games in 2003 averaged 3 hours, 15 seconds. In a December 2003 playoff game between the Indianapolis Colts and Denver Broncos, the CBS telecast included "133 replays, 141 graphics, 222 changes to the corner score box, ... 107 shots of the coaches and 80 fan shots ... 29 (commercial breaks) showing 78 advertisements, and ... 34 promotions for ... other programming" (Sandomir, 2004a).

In another NFL playoff game televised by ABC, the Tennessee Titans versus the Baltimore Ravens, 16 minutes and 48 seconds of game action occurred, averaging 6.9 seconds per play. The telecast included 108 replays, 56 shots of coaches, 67 commercials, and 29 promotional spots touting other programming on the network (Sandomir, 2004a).

Content Innovations

When Fox lured the NFL away from its commitment to CBS in 1993, Fox began spending an average of $395 million per year to televise National Football Conference games. "Fox's pre-emptive maneuver helped raise television sports rights fees while revolutionizing sports broadcasts with innovations that included the Fox Box, pregame comics and ultra-slow-motion replays" (Sandomir, 2003, para 5).

The Fox Box sprang from a 1992 device used for soccer on Sky Sports, the News Corporation satellite company in England. It offered game information, including the continuously updated game clock, in a corner of the screen. David Hill, chairman of the Fox Sports Television Group, developed it after being frustrated by tuning in late to a soccer match on television and being unable to find out the score. After an ESPN official saw it and brought it to World Cup soccer telecasts in 1994, Hill spread the innovation to other sports, and all the major American networks joined in.

Fox also introduced a miniature football field in its pregame show set and sound effects accompanying the start of instant replays. *Fox NFL Sunday*, the pregame show, also introduced raucous bantering among its football experts, a comedian, and a sexy female weathercaster. After Jimmy Kimmel broke the comedian barrier on Fox football shows in 1999, ABC followed suit by hiring Dennis Miller in 2000 for its *Monday Night Football* broadcast team.

Telecasts of other sports participated in such innovations, too; Catchercam, microphones on bases and outfield walls, and the glowing hockey puck came from Fox. "In cooperation with NBC and TNT, [Fox] inaugurated the satellite-based NASCAR driver identification system" (Sandomir, 2003, para 8).

NCAA Football

College football also commands great popularity. The highest rated NCAA game involved the Ohio State victory over Miami in the 2003 Fiesta Bowl on January 3, 2003. The game attracted 18.4 million households, with a rating of 17.2 and a share of 29. Considering only the 15 prime-time network broadcasts of NCAA games, an average of 9.5 million households tuned in, with an average rating of 8.8 and average share of 15.1. The nine NCAA football telecasts that earned top-10 cable status in a week of 2003, all appearing on ESPN, reached an average of 3.1 million households, less than a third of the audience size of the prime-time broadcasts of NCAA games.

All broadcast football shows in prime time during 2003 numbered 69 programs and attracted an average audience of 12.1 million households, with a rating of 11.6 and share of 19.5. Televised college football games often tend to run longer than NFL games, perhaps because of different rules regarding clock stoppages and different lengths of halftime breaks. In the 2004 Sugar Bowl, pitting Louisiana State against Oklahoma, the ABC telecast included "111 replays, 163 informational graphics, 262 changes in the corner score box (down and yardage, statistics), 86 crowd or marching band shots, 120 cuts to the coaches, 28 shots of cheerleaders and 20 sideline reports" (Sandomir, 2004a, para 1). Only 16 minutes and 28 seconds of action, 7.3% of the 3-hour and 43-minute contest, occurred in the game. The typical play of the 161 plays (offensive run, pass, kick, or kickoff) consumed only 8.1 seconds. The game was punctuated with 79 commercials that appeared in 25 breaks from this action. This Sugar Bowl ran slightly longer than the average Bowl Championship Series football game, which lasted 3 hours, 39 minutes and ranged from 3 hours, 14 minutes (Rose Bowl) to 4 hours, 1 minute (Fiesta Bowl).

Baseball

Major League Baseball on television reveals how much of sports television falls outside the parameters of the *B&C* reporting structure that underscored the tracking in this chapter of audience popularity of sports. In 2003, 3,942 games featured local television coverage, 84 more games than the previous record high for one season in 2002. Major League teams in 2003 averaged broadcasting 41.3 of their regular season games and cablecasting 90.1, a total of 131.4 of the 162-game season. The number of games being carried by broadcasting stations dropped by 10.2% in 2003 from the previous year, as the trend toward cable emphasis continued the fall in appeal of broadcast coverage every year since 1996. Five Major League teams (Pittsburgh, Toronto, Montreal, Cleveland, and Cincinnati) offer no over-the-air television broadcast coverage of their games.

Fox Sports Net has tended to dominate the rights for local game telecasts until recently, when some teams began to negotiate new rights deals to independent stations. In 2003, Major League Baseball earned $692.2 million in rights charges from local television ("Baseball seeks key," 2003), but Fox declared losses of $909 million in 2002 for its baseball rights deals (Higgins, 2003a). Fox has deals with 19 Major League Baseball teams for televising games.

In 2002, the New York Yankees started the Yankees Entertainment and Sports Network (YES), kicking off excitement among teams that want to profit from increased revenues from television affiliate stations on their networks and advertising revenue that goes along with the games (Cable catches baseball fever, 2003). An arbitration board ruled that Cablevision must include YES on its basic group of channels, those available for the lowest subscription price. Cablevision is a Multiple System Operator (MSOs own more multiple cable systems) serving the New York area, among others, and the company wanted to place YES on a special tier requiring viewers to pay extra, above the amount that they pay to receive basic channels ("Yanks top Cablevision," 2004). This ruling constituted a victory for the Yankees in getting their channel in front of more viewers.

In 2003, the Kansas City Royals began their own Royals Sports Television Network, striking an agreement with Time Warner to provide their games to "400,000 homes in Kansas, Missouri, Nebraska, Iowa, Arkansas, and Oklahoma" ("Cable catches baseball fever," 2003, p. 31). The team planned to expand that coverage.

WTBS, channel 17 in Atlanta, is also carried by a huge number of cable systems to audiences around the world. In 2003, 90 regular season games played by the Atlanta Braves were carried by the station, which was owned by AOL–Time Warner. Fox Sports Net, a regional network, carried 25 Braves games, and Turner South carried 36 Braves games.

Similarly, Chicago television station WGN carried 70 of the Cubs games, and Fox Sports Net carried 72 regular season games. WGN also included 29 White Sox games, of which Fox Sports Net carried 100 games. The ratings for these games tend to fall short of those achieved by the top-10 cable programs reported weekly in the *B&C* coverage.

The same is true of television stations other than these superstations, whose coverage is extended beyond their local markets by being included in many cable operators' channel offerings. KTVK carried 75 of the Arizona Diamondbacks games, and Fox Sports Net included 60 such games. KSTC carried 26 regular season games of the Minnesota Twins, while Fox Sports Net carried 105 games. Every Major League Baseball team has some sort of television contract for regular season game coverage ("Cable catches baseball fever," 2003).

Baseball's highlight of the year, of course, is the World Series. The first four games of the 2003 Series between the New York Yankees and Florida Marlins outdrew the Series of the previous year between the San Francisco Giants and California Angels by 15%, averaging 19.5 million viewers, a 12.4 rating, and a 24 share. However, the Giants–Angels Series attracted a record low audience, averaging a rating of 11 and share of 20 ("World Series outpacing '02," 2003). Baseball cannot support its claim to be the national pastime on the basis of television ratings.

Basketball

NCAA Men's Basketball

"For CBS, March Madness is nothing but net.... The Tiffany network...netted a record $380 million for the three-week (National Collegiate Athletic Association) basketball classic..." held in 2004 (McClellan, 2004, p. 15). Earlier, CBS purchased $6.2 billion worth of rights to televise NCAA events in 22 sports. Local television station affiliates of CBS agreed to pay $8 million toward the costs of the deal in exchange for a promise by CBS not to ask for affiliates to pay for future programming rights (Eggerton, 2003).

Expanding its television coverage of the NCAA men's basketball tournament, CBS Sportsline.com teamed with AOL Broadband and The FeedRoom on the Internet to provide games to fans of teams whose games were not broadcast in their area. The FeedRoom handled the technical details of this coverage. "We think of broadband as an MSO that has 50 million subs" (i.e., subscribers), said FeedRoom CEO Jon Klein ("Rim shots," 2004, p. 19).

NCAA Women's Basketball

Women's basketball has demonstrated drawing power on television, too. The 2004 NCAA championship game between Connecticut and Tennessee captured a 4.3 overnight rating, the highest rating for that event since ESPN began carrying the game in 1996. That figure represented a 23% increase over the 3.5 rating in the 2003 women's championship game. The overnight rating measures audiences in the 55 largest television markets in America, covering 70% of the entire audience. Attracting an audience approaching four million households, "the Huskies' 70–61 win was the most-watched basketball game, collegiate or pro, in the network's 25-year history...UConn became the first Division I school to win both the men's and women's championships in the same year" (Associated Press, 2004).

National Basketball Association

Although women's college basketball did not generate equivalent ratings to those of professional men's basketball, ratings for the National Basketball Association games did not generate quite as much enthusiasm. Despite a quantum leap in high-definition television technology for the 2003 NBA finals, the opening game of the series between the San Antonio Spurs and New Jersey Nets attracted a record low rating (8.1) in the overnight measurements by Nielsen Media Research, by far the lowest since the People Meters came into use in 1987 (Martzke, 2004). Granted, the San Antonio team represented a relatively small market, but the New Jersey team seemed to be a New York area team. Expectations ran high for the 2004 finals when the powerful Los Angeles Lakers reigned as heavy favorites over the Detroit Pistons. The 2004 finals ratings for that opening game increased by 43% over the previous year's game to 11.6.

Larry Novenstern, who worked for an agency representing advertisers on the telecasts of the NBA finals, found the relatively low ratings of little concern. "People are watching as much television as two years ago, but there are many more viewing choices.... Not matching the rating of two years ago is consistent with erosion on national TV" (Martzke, 2004).

NASCAR Motor Racing

Although football draws the most fans to televised sports, no sports fans are likely to show more passion for their sport than motor racing fans, especially NASCAR fans. "Lots of TV executives and analysts get agitated over the surging costs of sports rights. But one thing even critics agree on: NASCAR is worth it" (Higgins, 2003b). NASCAR events are ratings hits on NBC, Fox, TNT, and FX, with ratings routinely "generating 4.0-plus Nielsen household ratings for networks whose daytime ratings average well under 1.0" (Higgins, 2003b, p. 16).

Two major NASCAR events were televised in prime time by major networks during 2003: the Daytona 400 on July 5 and the Budweiser Shootout on February 8. The Daytona race ranked as the number 10 prime-time show of the week, and its postrace show ranked as the number 46 prime-time show of the week. The same race July 3, 2004, renamed the Daytona Pepsi 400, ranked as the number 20 show in prime time that week, earning a rating of 5.2 and a share of 12, and reaching 5.6 million households (Nielsen Media Research, 2004).

The 2003 Coca-Cola 600 ran over its planned time into the prime-time period and attained a 4.7 rating and an 11 share. Its postrace show on May 25 ranked 53rd among all prime-time shows of the week. The three 2003 races appearing on prime-time television averaged a 5 rating and an 11.3 share.

Between May 3 and September 14, 2003, seven NASCAR races placed in the top 10 cable shows of the week, reaching an average of 3.7 million households each. Two of those races, the New England 300 and the Pennsylvania 500, ranked as the number-one most viewed cable programs in weeks in which they occurred. Both races were seen on TNT in July.

Even so, the losses estimated by analyst Richard Bilotti for NASCAR programming for TNT and FX in 2002 reached $50 million and $19 million, respectively. However, even Bilotti "expect[ed] FX to start making profit simply on ad sales— nearly unheard of in the money-losing TV sports game, where networks bet that they can promote the rest of their schedules during races and games" (Higgins, 2003b, p. 16).

Perhaps that popularity explains why NASCAR has developed a significant television presence. *Autoweek* magazine summarized a weekend of automobile racing on television beginning Friday, September 19, 2003 ("Television," 2003). *The Speed Channel* programming on Friday included qualifying for the weekend NASCAR Busch and Winston (now Nextel) Cup Series races in Dover, Delaware, at 1:30 p.m. and 2:30 p.m., respectively. At 4:00 p.m., the same channel carried the USAC Racing Series from Tulsa, Oklahoma. NASCAR Past Champions ran at 6:00 p.m. *Totally NASCAR* ran at 6:30 p.m., with *Trackside* at Dover, Delaware, at 7:00 p.m. At 11:00 p.m., the SCCA ProRally aired from Bemidji, Minnesota. On the same day, *Inside Drag Racing* aired at 6:00 p.m. on ESPN2. *Totally NASCAR* appeared on Fox Sports Net at 6:00 p.m.

Speed Channel programming for the next day, Saturday, September 20, 2003 included *Trackside* at Watkins Glen at 11:00 a.m.; *Speed Touring Car Championship* from Monterey, California, at 2:00 p.m.; *Speed GT Championship* from Monterey, California, at 3:00 p.m.; *NASCAR Craftsman Truck Series* from Fontana, California, at 4:00 p.m.; *My Classic Car* at 6:30 p.m.; *Speed News Saturday* at 7:00 p.m.; *Legends of Motorsport* at 7:30 p.m.; *IHRA Drag Racing* from Cleveland, Ohio, at 8:00 p.m.; and *ASA Racing Series* from Schererville, Indiana, at 9:00 p.m.

Other channels airing racing shows on that day include TNT's coverage of the *NASCAR Busch Series* from Dover, Delaware, at 1:00 p.m. ESPN2 carried NHRA qualifying trials from Memphis, Tennessee, at 3:30 p.m.

NASCAR has traditionally been popular in the South. For example, Roanoke–Lynchburg, Virginia, is the Nielsen Media Research television market number 66, and sports fans there like NASCAR. Among television viewers surveyed by Scarborough Research 2003 Release 1 Multi-Market (February 2002–March 2003), 37% of the respondents described themselves as NASCAR fans, giving them an index of 196 on a scale in which the average is 100 ("Blue Ridge boom," 2004).

However, NASCAR would like to expand its popularity to other regions. To that end, a Labor Day race entered the programming mix in 2004 in California, where audience ratings before then tended to be low. This strategy helped appease program sponsors who wanted more national exposure for their ad spending. NASCAR also scheduled more races in prime time to attract larger audiences (Higgins, 2003b).

Table 5.3 presents an alphabetized list of 29 motor sports shows airing during a week, many appearing multiple times, in June 2004. Televised event coverage is excluded from the list, and NASCAR plays a prominent role.

Professional Wrestling

Professional wrestling began sometime around 1900 in carnivals around the country, and the participants fixed the matches to prevent serious injuries ("From carney to primetime," 2003). By 1948, the sport achieved a national presence that was punctuated by regional operations, which staged matches for local television. Between 1948 and 1955, the three major networks of the time (CBS, NBC, and Dumont) carried professional wrestling programming. Although network telecasts soon abandoned wrestling, it remained popular among local stations because of cheap production costs. In 1983, Vince McMahon, with 13 years of experience as a wrestling promoter, purchased the rights to his father's company and built the popular World Wrestling Federation. The name changed in 2002 to resolve a copyright dispute with the World Wildlife Fund. In 1984, McMahon began editing footage from matches for a prime-time cable show on the USA Network. In 1993, he started *Raw*, a live production that became a genuine television phenomenon, and the organization reportedly earned about $42.5 million on $385 million in revenues for 2003 (Haley, 2003).

By 2003, *WWE Raw* was practically a staple in the top 10 cable shows each week. The average rank in the top-10 weekly cable programs of the 10 p.m. show for 2003 was 3.3, reaching an average of 3.4 million households weekly. The show was the top-ranked cable program of the week 14 times in 2003. The 10 p.m. edition slightly outdrew the earlier show on average by 3.2 to 3.0. Airing twice each week, the two cable shows combined placed 82 shows in the top-10 category during the year, averaging a 3.1 rating and an audience of 3.3 million households.

In addition to the steady weekly cable audience performance of *WWE Raw*, the broadcast show, *WWE Smackdown!*, averaged a rank of 81 among all prime-time shows during 2003. The show generated an average rating of 3.3 and an average share of 5.3, reaching a weekly average of nearly 3.5 million households.

TABLE 5.3
Motor Sports Programs by Network Listed in One Week
of *TV Guide* Magazine

Program Name	Network
Around the Track	FSN
Auto Racing	ESPN2
Auto Racing	FX
Auto Racing	Speed
Behind the Headlights	Speed
Cannonball!	Speed
Dangerous Curves	Spike
Dirtrider Adventure	OLN
Drag Racing	ESPN
I Wanna Date a Race Car Driver	Speed
Motorcross: AMA 125cc Competition	ESPN2
Motorweek	Speed
MotoWorld	Spike
NASCAR Drivers: 360	FX
NASCAR Edition Speed News	Speed
NASCAR Prerace	FX
NASCAR This Morning	FSN
NASCAR Victory Lane	Speed
NBS 24-7	Speed
Raceline	Channel 13, 18, 21
Ride with Funkmaster Flex	Spike
SpeedNews Sunday	Speed
Stock Car Nation	Spike
Top Dead Center	Spike
Totally NASCAR	FSN
Trackside	Speed
Truck Racing	Speed
Wind Tunnel	Speed

Source: Bryant, Brown, & Cummins (2004).

In all, WWE airs eight shows weekly, including three highlight shows and a magazine show, all of which promote WWE pay-per-view events that sold 7.1 million purchases in 2002 (Haley, 2003). The television shows were seen by 24 million viewers each week in 2003.

In 2003, Viacom, owner of UPN and Spike TV, paid $300,000 per week for the rights to *WWE Smackdown!* and $600,000 per week for the rights to air the shows, but not everything was coming up roses for the wrestling shows. The UPN *WWE Smackdown!* show that aired every Thursday peaked in the 2000–2001 season and afterward lost more than half of its teenage male audience (Albiniak, 2003). During fall 2003, the losses eased, but male teenage viewers were down by 8% from the previous season, and male viewing between ages 18 and 34 declined by 19%, although the show remained one of the highest rated programs on UPN. The show on occasion drew as well as NBC among male teens, ranking as high as third among the six major broadcast networks in all of the important young adult demographic groups, including all adults between ages 18 and 49.

Similar drops occurred for the Monday night edition of *WWE Raw*, but the show remained among Spike TV's best. Regarding fall 2003, "*Raw's* 3.0 average rating in men 18–34 and 3.6 in male teens is far higher than Spike's overall prime-time averages 0.6 and 0.7 in both demos, and wrestling consistently remains among the top ten shows on basic cable" (Albiniak, 2003, p. 44).

Regional Sports Channels

By the end of 2003, regional channels typically recorded a 10% to 14% gain in ad revenue over the previous year (Breznick, 2003). Fox Sports Net includes 20 regional sports channels that are owned by the News Corp., and the company represents four others in selling advertising. A News Corp. report from November 2003 attributed its 24% revenue growth to escalating ad sales, affiliate fees, and numbers of subscribers to satellite television distribution systems.

Baseball drives profitability for many regional sports channels. The largest gains among regional sports networks occurred at the affiliates in Miami, Chicago, and San Francisco, cities that all enjoyed great success in baseball during the 2003 season, leading a national baseball rating of 3.8 for the entire season. This surge overcame a huge ratings drop during the spring following the American invasion of Iraq.

Rainbow Sports Networks is another prominent regional sports company, operating six major sports networks in "New York, Chicago, Ohio, San Francisco, New England, and Florida. (Although most are called Fox Sports Net, Rainbow stills (sic) controls them.)" (Breznick, 2003, p. 28). In San Francisco, interest in Giants' slugger Barry Bonds probably fueled the popularity of watching the team on television, and the promises to advertisers of ratings of 4.5 were exceeded by the achievement of an average 2003 rating of 6. Interest was strong enough to attract national advertisers, such as Bank of America, to telecasts on regional Rainbow networks.

In early 2003, Kroenke Sports Entertainment, owner of the NHL Colorado Avalanche and the NBA Denver Nuggets, rejected renewal of a seven-year contract with Fox Sports Net reportedly worth more than $100 million (Romano, 2003a). Kroenke's strategy involved starting its own sports network, based on its team properties.

Starting such an enterprise involves programming a channel, setting up distribution to reach viewers, and selling advertising. Most regional sports channels can attract fees from cable operators of $1 to $2 per subscriber, unless the channels become part of a tier of sports channels. Because of these business requirements, not all regional networks succeed. For example, efforts to start regional networks failed for ESPN in 1997 in Denver for all teams, for Southwest Sports in 1999 in Dallas for the Rangers (MLB) and Stars (NHL), for Ackerly in 2000 in Seattle for the Mariners (MLB) and SuperSonics (NBA), and for Paul Allen in 2001 in Portland for the Trailblazers (NBA) (Romano, 2003a).

The Kroenke break from Fox in an effort to start a new regional network in Denver resembles efforts by Chicago's Cubs, White Sox, Blackhawks, and Bulls to form their own regional channel with Comcast. However, Kroenke lacked the Colorado Rockies Major League Baseball team. Fox protects itself against such threats of losing its regional contracts by staggering agreement expiration dates. Protecting Fox in the Kroenke case are contracts to televise the Rockies' games through 2007 on Fox Sports Rocky Mountain. Despite some contract losses, with millions of dollars and vital content for regional sports networks at stake, in 2003 Fox retained rights to 69 of 80 professional teams in hockey, basketball, and baseball.

Other regional sports channels that were planning in 2003 to launch include Victory Sports One, targeting fans of the University of Minnesota and the Minnesota Twins. Houston Regional Sports Net proposed a 2005 beginning featuring games of the Houston's MLB Astros and NBA Rockets.

Some regional sports networks other than Fox Sports Net have operated for years. Since 1997, Cox has televised games via Cox and Time Warner cable systems of the San Diego Padres and San Diego State Aztecs. Also since 1997, Comcast has delivered games on its own cable systems and those of several cable operators of the Philadelphia Phillies (MLB), Flyers (NHL), and 76ers (NBA).

Comcast began serving the Washington and Baltimore areas in 2000 with games of the Orioles (MLB), Wizards (NBA), and Capitals (NHL). These games reached viewers not only via Comcast and various other cable systems, but also via the satellite television providers DirecTV and EchoStar.

In 2002, the New York Yankees (MLB) and New Jersey Nets (NBA) began offering games in the New York area. The games were made available via special tiers on several cable operators' systems and via DirecTV.

New Sports Channels

In the 1990s, expanding cable and satellite systems were desperate for new content and new channels. By the early twenty-first century, these systems had plenty of channels, and no one channel or no new channel seemed likely to powerfully affect the number of subscribers, dictating a change in strategy of starting new networks (Romano, 2003i). In the early 1990s, startups such as the Golf Channel and Outdoor Life Network required about $100 million to break even.

New channels are attempting to begin with smaller amounts of money. Among a dozen new channels launched in 2003, at least eight offered sports content. Those eight channels include CSTV (college sports), NFL Network, The Football Network (not NFL), Fuel (Fox action sports), NBATV, The Tennis Channel, and the Sportsman Channel.

The Sportsman Channel functions as a cooperative of producers who own the rights to their respective programs. CSTV CEO Brian Bedol once founded Classic Sports by selling the channel to cable MSOs that own several cable operations. Later, Bedol pitched his channel to the corporate companies, such as Time Warner and Adelphia. "Now nothing happens until the corporate ink is dry" (Romano, 2003i, p. 52).

The NFL Network, which debuted on November 4, 2003, features a variety of football content, including news, features, and classic games. NFL Films provided the production operation for the channel. The network carried no live NFL games because the league sold the rights to its games to Fox, CBS, ABC, and ESPN in "the most lucrative sports rights deal" of them all, a $16 billion package that ran through 2005 (Romano, 2003d, p. 8). With a choice channel number placement next to ESPN on the satellite service, the NFL Network had about 11 million subscribers on DirecTV's basic package at start-up, an unusually hefty audience for a fledgling channel.

The new channel emerged in an exclusive arrangement with the satellite service because of the desire among cable operators to have out-of-market NFL games, but getting carriage on cable systems was not easily assured. The network was not able to command high subscriber fees, but digital programming was in demand during 2003, and the NFL Network offered programs both in high-definition and as video-on-demand. Cable operators questioned the demand for year-round football, and ESPN felt that it had nothing to fear from fans who would get their football news first from ESPN, and only "the extreme football nut who doesn't get enough NFL will turn over [to the NFL Network]" (Romano, 2003d, p. 8). "What cable operators really want[ed was] a piece of the NFL's coveted out-of-market package, which gave, say, an ex-Chicagoan living in New York a chance to see every Bears game" (Romano, 2003f, p. 9).

The NFL Network shut down in December 2003, unable to pay its bills. Although the network continued seeking investors to keep it alive, the quest seemed doubtful (Sandomir, 2004d).

Although the National Hockey League has had a digital channel in Canada for more than two years, no such channel is available in the United States (Romano, 2003g). The NHL would like to change that by offering a niche channel for its die-hard fans, simultaneously providing a means for promoting the league all year. Stability in television contracts has been merely a dream for the NHL, which left Fox in 1999 for a five-year contract with ESPN and ABC for $600 million per year.

ESPN moved the hockey nights from Wednesdays to Thursdays in 2002 when a new deal brought NBA games to the channel. In 2003 to 2004, shooting for larger audiences, "the NHL [made] 20 ESPN games exclusive. Fans [got] to pick about seven ESPN2 games through online voting, and more than 300 games [were] produced in high definition to air on HDNet, ESPN HD, ABC or regional sports nets" (Romano, 2003g, p. 13).

Even while attempting to form a hockey channel, the NHL continued to negotiate with cable television. Natural links supporting those negotiations include Comcast, the largest cable MSO and owner of the NHL Philadelphia Flyers; and Cablevision, which serves three million subscribers in the New York area while owning the New York Rangers.

If the hockey channel were to come to fruition, the NHL could follow the model of the NBA by reserving a set of games for its own channel. Alternatively, the league might follow the lead of the NFL Network and the Canadian NHL Network by leaving its regular season and playoff games for the other broadcast and cable television groups, airing preseason games and games from outside the NHL on its own network (Romano, 2003g).

Other Sports

Olympics

The Olympic Games constitute one of the biggest television events in sports. For the August 2004 Olympics in Athens, Greece, NBC Universal Sports planned to televise 1,210 hours of events, more than triple the amount of coverage of the 2000 Olympics. Of that coverage,

> NBC [scheduled] 226 hours in prime-time, afternoon and late night; MSNBC...133 hours; CNBC...111 hours; Bravo...122 hours; USA Network...49 hours; and 124 NBC affiliates...[offered] a digital cable channel showing 399 hours of HDTV coverage (eight hours live, repeated twice daily)...The Olympics [telecast ran] virtually nonstop. For example, MSNBC [carried] events from 2 to 7 a.m. Eastern on weekdays, with Bravo covering from 5 a.m. to noon and USA from 7 to 10 a.m. MSNBC...broadcast again from

10 a.m. to 4 p.m., and NBC [coverage ran] from 12:30 to 4 p.m. NBC... broadcast the Games again from 8 p.m. to midnight, with a replay of the prime-time coverage from 2 to 5 a.m. Coverage in the afternoons [was] provided by Telemundo, between 1 and 8 p.m., and by Bravo and CNBC, from 5 to 8 p.m. (Sandomir, 2004h, para 3–7)

Leading to the Olympics come the Olympic trials, events in which competitors vie for spots on the teams that represent their countries in the Olympics. The 2004 trials were surrounded by allegations of use of performance-enhancing drugs. Perhaps that cloud reduced the audience response to the telecasts of the trials on NBC. The track and field trials achieved only a 3.2 audience rating in July 2004 on a Saturday night, down by 20% from the 2000 events. However, the combination of track and field with swimming events on the following Sunday evening rose by 10% over the 2000 ratings to 4.4 (Sandomir, 2004j).

College Sports

The College Sports Television Network began in 2003 just after the end of the NCAA men's basketball tournament. The network began with widest availability through satellite distributor DirecTV, which offered the programming to its subscribers as part of a special sports package. It has cut "programming deals with more than 1,200 universities and scores of athletic conferences. Some men's basketball and football games are on the schedule, but most programming will be less-covered sports, such as lacrosse, hockey, baseball, volleyball, golf, track and gymnastics" (Romano, 2003c, p. 13).

Tennis

Tennis in 2003 was highlighted by CBS coverage of the U.S. Open. Ratings rose over the three-day weekend of Labor Day by 6% over the previous year to a 1.7 rating and 5 share. The USA Network carried preliminary matches in the tournament from August 25 through September 4, earning only a 1.0 rating, off by 38% from 2002 (Larson & Consoli, 2003).

Star Factor

LeBron James

Also fueling the growth in sports viewing, "the LeBron factor" (Breznick, 2003, p. 28) illustrated the penchant of sports programmers to use the power of stars in attracting audiences to both local and national programming. High school phenom LeBron James signed a four-year contract with the NBA Cleveland Cavaliers, a chronically weak team. Soon thereafter, UPN affiliate WUAB-TV signed a four-year contract, with a fifth-year option, to televise games of the Cavs, starting in fall 2003. Diluting the local station's audience, ESPN joined WUAB in carrying James' first game, but the station still managed a 7.3 rating and 16 share. Taking both ESPN and WUAB together, the combined audience for the game in the Cleveland market reached a 12.2 rating and 27 share. Among WUAB viewers in the coveted 25 to 52 age bracket, the ratings doubled. After 37 games, only 11 of which the Cavaliers won, the wisdom of that four-year deal for WUAB became clear as the station carried 20 of the games. After having earned a 1.7 rating and 3 share for the same amount of coverage in 2002, WUAB soared to average a 6.2 rating and 11 share (Eggerton, 2004).

The success extended to regional audiences. For the first 15 Cleveland games, Fox Sports Ohio earned a 4.3 average rating, up from 1.3 in 2002 for the same period, an increase of 229%. The national gains did not duplicate the spectacular increase in the local and regional markets. Cable station TNT carried three of the Cavaliers' games, earning an average rating of 1.7, up 6% over the 1.6 average for the other games that season. Average ratings for TNT in 2003 at that point were up by 32% over 2002 (Eggerton, 2004).

Tiger Woods

Golfer Tiger Woods is another major star whose aura is powerful enough to dictate television content decisions. ABC televised the 2004 Buick Open, a PGA men's golf tournament that featured a programmer's dream, a three-way sudden death playoff. However, the players involved included Sergio García, Padraig Harrington, and Rory Sabbatini. The ABC officer in charge explained why the network left the match at 7:00 p.m. for a 90-minute show containing reruns of *America's Funniest Home Videos,* abandoning the playoff dueling on the course: "García has some ratings zip, but the others do not. But if Tiger Woods, Goofy and Sneezy were on the course, ABC would have deep-sixed *America's Funniest*" (Sandomir, 2004i, para 5).

Although Phil Mickelson shed his burdensome label as the best golfer never to have won a major by edging Ernie Els by a single stroke in the 2004 Masters golf tournament in Augusta, Georgia, the Nielsen Media Research audience data support that claim about Tiger power. With Tiger Woods out of contention, the Masters ratings fell by 12% from the previous year to 7.3 (Sandomir, 2004e).

Lance Armstrong

Cycler Lance Armstrong carried enough star power to entice the Outdoor Life Network to carry the Tour de France bicycle race. For example, the race aired in early July 2004 beginning at 9:00 a.m. The network also offered companion programs to the telecasts of the race, such as *The Lance Saga: The Real Life Saga of Armstrong's Quest for Six* (8:30 p.m. ET on Thursdays) and *The Road to the Tour* (9:00 p.m. ET on Thursdays).

Smarty Jones

Stars need not be human to engender extraordinary attention from television. During the spring months of 2004, thoroughbred horse racing saw the emergence of a major star in Smarty Jones, winner of both the Kentucky Derby and the Preakness Stakes. The ESPN prerace Kentucky Derby Special earned the highest ratings for any Derby prerace program since 1990 for the network at 1.4. The counterpart Preakness Stakes Special set a record for ratings for that show at 1.0. Smarty Jones was the odds-on favorite to complete the coveted Triple Crown, a feat performed by only 11 horses in more than a century of racing. For the final leg of the prize, the Belmont Stakes, ESPN added 5.5 hours of programming to its plans. On the day before the big race, June 5, 2004, ESPN carried two preliminary races from Belmont Park. On race day, June 5, ESPN and its sister networks under the Disney ownership umbrella carried 7.5 hours of Belmont Stakes coverage ("ESPN extends Belmont," 2004). Nielsen Media Research reported that NBC's coverage of the race produced the highest Belmont Stakes audience ratings since 1981, with a rating of 11.3 and a share of 16 ("Smarty helps NBC," 2004).

Kobe Bryant

Reminiscent of the O. J. Simpson case, sometimes sports figures dominate news outside their sporting environs. Jessell (2003) criticized the media for overemphasizing the rape trial of basketball star Kobe Bryant because the story lacked meaning for people not directly connected to the case, writing that "the media has a role in this as it does all trials: to bear witness and make sure that justice is done. That's it. Anything else is pandering and sensationalism" (p. 33).

Non-Event Sports or Fictional Sports Programming

Sport in fictional entertainment is a popular commodity. Table 5.4 lists 35 sports fiction programs, many of which appeared first as theatrical motion pictures, that appeared in one week of *TV Guide* magazine during June 2004 (Bryant, et al., 2004).

ESPN programming also exemplifies how interest in sports goes well beyond the viewing of live events through an ambitious schedule of original dramatic portrayals set in the world of sports. Innovating with made-for-sports television movies about Bob Knight (*Season on the Brink*) and Bear Bryant (*The Junction Boys*), ESPN planned several movies about noted sports figures. *Hustle* portrayed baseball star Pete Rose, who was banned from his sport for gambling. NASCAR fans were the target audience of *3: The Dale Earnhardt Story*. In addition to movies, the network planned for shows about college gambling (*The Fix*) and high school basketball, the latter based on a book by Spike Lee.

Playmakers perhaps won the prize as the most controversial of the programs in this genre. The ESPN dramatic series about a fictional football team aroused the ire of the NFL because of provocative stories that included drugs, sex, and homosexuality. The show never mentioned the NFL but engendered a wide range of reactions. NFL Commissioner Paul Tagliabue called it a "gross mischaracterization of our sport" (Sandomir, 2004c, para 8), but former star player and CBS commentator Deion Sanders agreed that the show accurately portrayed the league.

Although the network denied that pressure from the league led to the cancellation of the series, the show was successful, and the network did not renew it, despite its success. ESPN claimed not to have sought approval from sports leagues for its originals and promised continued controversial story lines (Romano, 2004d).

Reality (?) Shows

Two sports shows appeared among the programs that received promotion at the January 2004 meeting of the Television Critics Association meeting. One was *Dream Job*, a competition for an ESPN announcing job, and in the other "Outdoor Life pitched *Samurai Sportsman*, an unscripted show in which actual samurai attempt such sports as bass fishing" (Romano, 2004a, p. 16).

In the spring of 2004, 12 of the top-20 prime-time network television shows were classified as "reality" shows. Perhaps "unscripted" more accurately describes these shows, and *American Idol* on Fox became the standard setter for the genre. "The Fox network, for example, has basically announced that because it has two pillars for its programming—baseball in the fall and *American Idol* in the winter—it no longer has

TABLE 5.4
Sport Fiction Network Listed in One Week of *TV Guide* Magazine

Program Name	Network/Channel
Love & Basketball	ABC
Into Character	AMC
Bend It Like Beckham	Cinemax
Swimfan	Cinemax
Hoosiers	CMT
Heaven Can Wait	Encore
The Color of Money	Encore
The Scout	ESPN Classics
The Sandlot	Family Channel
The Natural	Family Channel
Air Bud	Family Channel
The Slugger's Wife	Flix
Heaven Can Wait	Flix
Unholy Rollers	Flix
The Cutting Edge	Flix
The Games	Fox Movie Channel
Like Mike	HBO
Necessary Roughness	HBO
Everybody's All American	HBO
Ice Castles	HBO
Juwanna Mann	HBO2
Eight Men Out	Showtime
RollerBall	Showtime2
Cannonball!	Speed
Rocky V	Spike
BASEketball	Starz
Major League	Starz
The Rookie	Starz
The Sixth Man	Starz
Undisputed	Starz
Caddyshack	TBS
The Champ	Turner Classic Movies
City for Conquest	Turner Classic Movies
Grand Prix	Turner Classic Movies
Happy Gilmore	USA

Source: Bryant, Brown, & Cummins (2004).

a fall television season" (Carter, 2004b, para 1). Although the Fox strategy would seem to cast sports as the counterpart to reality programming, the sports genre also includes reality entries. The *American Idol* model seemed to have an imitator in ESPN's *Dream Job*, which pitted aspiring announcers competing for an ESPN position. "However, ESPN claimed to have had the show in development before *American Idol* debuted and became a hit, but the ESPN delayed its show to avoid seeming too much like a copy" (Romano, 2004a, p. 16).

NBC's *The Contender* and Fox's *The Next Great Champ* were both announced in spring 2004 as planned reality boxing television shows. The premises of the programs were the same, following the model of *American Idol* but having contestants box instead of sing. NBC accused Fox of stealing its idea (Carter, 2004c).

Not Merely English

More than 11 million Hispanic households in America are available to sports programmers, especially for soccer and boxing that is not shown on pay-per-view. (Clarke, 2003). After experimenting with Sunday evening programming in Spanish, ESPN began a Spanish channel in 2003 called ESPN Deportes. ESPN planned to offer Spanish programming of games from Major League Baseball, the NBA, and the NFL on Deportes.

Fox Sports en Espa nol, which began offering 24-hour programming in 1996, serves about 5 million subscribers (Romano, 2003b). The network previously tapped the Hispanic market for sports in addition to soccer, the most popular sport for that audience group. Fox included Spanish coverage of Latin American soccer and boxing, as well as two seasons of CART open-wheel auto racing.

International competition faces both the sports participants in these events and the new American networks. Univision and Telemundo, for example, already were carrying FIFA World Cup soccer, the most popular sporting event in the world. Telemundo includes NBA and Olympics coverage, courtesy of parent company NBC.

Popularity of Sports Violence

For 2003, *B&C* listed 196 broadcast sports events that appeared on prime-time broadcast network television, and 170 sports events qualified as top-10 cable shows. Table 5.5 shows the types of sports shows and frequencies that the respective types of sports earned top-10 cable status during 2003. Notably, professional wrestling shows accounted for 48.8% and football for 25.3% of the sports shows with top-10 cable appearances during the year. All of the 26 basketball shows that placed in the top-10 category feature National Basketball Association (NBA) games. Therefore, nearly three quarters of the sports shows earning top-10 rankings during 2003 featured violent physical contact of wrestling and football, and another 15.3% of the programs featured the extremely rough play of the NBA.

Many fans have noticed how the character of play in the NBA has changed over the years, perhaps becoming more suited to the television audience. A once graceful and obviously athletic game "is now one primarily of power and aggression: players

TABLE 5.5
Frequency of Top-10 Cable Sports Shows by Sport in 2003

Sport	Number of Appearances in B&C Top-10 Cable Lists
Wrestling	83
Football	43
Basketball	26
Baseball	7
NASCAR	7
Sports News	3
Dog Show	1

gravitate to the same space and try to go over or through one another" (Sokolove, 2004, para 23).

Similarly, prime-time broadcast network sports shows also focus on professional wrestling and football, at least in terms of frequency of airing. Football accounted for 68 of 196 such shows, or 34.7% of the total. Wrestling aired 50 times during the year on UPN's regular Thursday night show, *WWE Smackdown*, reaching 25.5% of the total number of such broadcast sports shows. Among the 32 basketball telecasts in the data set, 15 featured NBA games, raising the total for these three sports to 133 or 67.9% of the total number of 2003 prime-time broadcast events.

TRENDS AND CONCLUSIONS

The obvious route from examining sports content on television considers how the process of televising sport has affected the medium, as other chapters in this volume do. For this chapter, however, let us make the point that no doubt exists that televised sports have influenced sports and fans of sports through daily presence. For example, consider how the presence of daily highlight shows influenced not only how games are viewed but also how they are played. Richard Sandomir, writing for the *New York Times*, reviewed a special ESPN program looking back over the network's first 25 years:

> ESPN is the V. I. Lenin of the highlight revolution. No other force approaches it for making fans view games as slivers of digitized video divided into home runs, brawls, touchdown dances, blocked shots, 3-pointers and great catches for the pleasure of the anchors' richly hyped descriptions. In assessing the impact of highlights on viewers, athletes and anchors, ESPN soft-pedals itself, amid an otherwise compelling segment that finds Shaquille O'Neal confessing that the highlight culture has "taken over basketball." There is no reflection on how "SportsCenter" sired and perpetuated a culture where video clips defined sports as never before. Or how ESPN created a rhythm and structure to its highlights that enslaved fans to "SportsCenter," which airs 27 times daily. (Sandomir, 2004g, para 7)

Sports on television remain popular with fans for a variety of reasons. Clearly, fans want to enjoy the action and escape from mundane affairs. Sometimes, however, reality encroaches on the hallowed ground of televised competition, and sports announcers find themselves in the middle of news stories, such as reports of athletes and drugs that surfaced in 2004. "In the absence of news, repeating what has been reported is an unproductive exercise for an audience that prefers to watch games, which are cluttered by too many commercials and sponsored enhancements" (Sandomir, 2004f, para 17).

High-Definition Television

The content of sports highlights and sports news is also related to the manner in which sports programming is presented to viewers. High-definition television (HDTV) offers viewers new on-screen perspectives that exceed the capabilities of mere analog and digital television signals. HDTV delivers a picture with the 16:9

aspect ratio and 5.1-channel audio for a more realistic viewing experience that is stunning for audiences accustomed to other forms of television that offer a 4:3 aspect ratio and typically only a single channel of audio.

ABC presented the 2000 Super Bowl by high-definition (HD) telecast, but subsequently stopped using it for NFL games. The network resumed high definition for Monday Night Football games and the Super Bowl in 2003 (Kerschbaumer, 2003a). For fall 2004, the Fox Network planned HD telecasts of six NFL games each week. The games will be available to NFL Sunday Ticket subscribers (Kerschbaumer, 2004c).

NBC telecast the 2004 Daytona 500 in high definition (Kerschbaumer, 2004a). The National Basketball Association finals in June 2003 were broadcast by ABC in high-definition television. NBA TV, owned by the league, began offering 24 hours of daily high-definition programming in May 2003 to cable audiences of Cablevision, Cox Communications, and Time Warner Cable as well as to subscribers of satellite services DirecTV and EchoStar (Kerschbaumer, 2003b; Romano, 2003f). TNT HD debuted its high-definition channel service with the NBA Western Conference finals in 2004 (Romano, 2004c). Comcast SportsNet began producing games in high definition in fall 2003, not merely for the Philadelphia 76ers; the cable giant also produced HD telecasts for the hometown Flyers (NHL) and Phillies (MLB) (Clarke, 2004). A 2004 deal involving Cox Communications, Sony, and the San Diego Padres of Major League Baseball presented high-definition MLB telecasts in the stadium and on cable TV, featuring specials and contests for baseball fans, cable users, and buyers of Sony high-definition sets (Belson, 2004).

High-definition telecasts mean much more than merely viewing events on bigger screens. HDTV could have profound implications for attendance at live sporting events. Perhaps the most reluctant entrant to the HDTV dance, the Fox Network planned for 2004 to "begin broadcasting major sporting events in HDTV... There is no denying the power of HD sports: Sharper images neatly transplant the viewer out of the living room and into the stadium, minus the obnoxious drunks" (Kerschbaumer, 2004b, p. 18).

The future holds exciting changes in how fans view sports on television. Plans for interactive viewing were being implemented by Charter Cable during 2004. Fans using the system will see a screen containing four panels with four different angles of viewing. They will have a choice of audio feeds and screen information with on-the-spot statistical updates and information about competitors. Fans participating in a variety of fantasy leagues in which fans succeed on the basis of actual player performances will enjoy current data delivered in the telecast ("Click your pick," 2004).

The Future

The complexity of the viewing experience for sports on television long ago exceeded that available to ticket holders who attend events. Fans at stadiums now expect big screens on hand to replay the action that just occurred in front of them. Will the realism of high-definition television coverage and surround-sound realism at home reduce the desire among fans to fight their way through throngs to get to the games at increasing ticket prices? Or will the growing expense to television networks and stations for the rights to events drive more networks to follow the lead of NBC, disdaining the opportunity to cover sports events in hopes of recovering losses from higher audience ratings among nonsports programming? Stay tuned.

REFERENCES

Albiniak, P. (2003, November 17). WWE feels the pain. *Broadcasting & Cable, 133*(46), 1, 44.

Associated Press. (2004, April 8). Overnight 4.3 rating is up 23 percent. *ESPN.* Retrieved April 8, 2004, from http://sports.espn.go.com/ncw/ncaatourney04/news/story?id=1777819&partnersite=espn

Baseball seeks key to the Fox TV lock. (2003, March 31). *Broadcasting & Cable, 133*(14), 31–33.

Belson, K. (2004, July 6). Ball club drives an HDTV bandwagon. *New York Times.* Retrieved July 6, 2004, from http://www.nytimes.com/2004/07/06/business/06hdtv.html?ex=1090123366&ei=1&en=23fe0e06299e75f8.

Blue Ridge boom. (2004, May 17). *Broadcasting & Cable, 134*(19), 17.

Breznick, A. (2003, November 24). Sports nets score big. *Broadcasting & Cable, 133*(46), 26, 28.

Bryant, J., Brown, D., & Cummins, G. (2004). [A comprehensive profile of one week's sports programming in a Top-50 DMA]. Unpublished raw data.

Cable catches baseball fever. (2003, March 31). *Broadcasting & Cable, 133*(14), 31.

Callahan, S. (2004, May 3). ESPN's *SportsCenter*; Network's flagship continues to draw the elusive male viewer. *B to B, 89*(5), 23.

Carter, B. (2004a, February 5). After furor, Janet Jackson to be cut from Grammy Awards. *New York Times.* Retrieved February 5, 2004, from http://www.nytimes.com/2004/02/05/business/media/05tube.html?ex=1076992194&ei=1&en=3664f4bf4891c6f0

Carter, B. (2004b, April 19). Reality intrudes on a spring rite of network TV. *New York Times.* Retrieved April 19, 2004, from http://www.nytimes.com/2004/04/19/business/media/19network.html?ex=1083569635&ei=1&en=01b072274f027016

Carter, B. (2004c, May 10). Reality TV hits (further) below the belt. *New York Times.* Retrieved May 10, 2004, from http://www.nytimes.com/2004/05/10/business/media/10tube.html?ex=1085194176&ei=1&en=f4a87c3688ff71b3

Clarke, M. M. (2003, March 22). A fiesta of games. *Broadcasting & Cable, 133*(13), 33.

Clarke, M. M. (2004, March 15). Team spirit. *Broadcasting & Cable, 134*(11), 32.

Click your pick. (2004, May 3). *Broadcasting & Cable, 134*(18), 86.

Eggerton, J. (2003, December 8). CBS, affils deal on NCAA. *Broadcasting & Cable, 133*(49), 10.

Eggerton, J. (2004, January 19). LeBron lifts ratings in Ohio. *Broadcasting & Cable, 134*(3), 30.

Elliott, S. (2004a, January 29). Advertising: Super Bowl retains status as must-buy television. *New York Times.* Retrieved January 29, 2004, from http://www.nytimes.com/2004/01/29/business/29adcol.html?ex=1076385506&ei=1&en=02ccc697d7ad1946

Elliott, S. (2004b, February 3). Advertising: The Super Bowl of stupidity? *New York Times.* Retrieved February 3, 2004, from http://www.nytimes.com/2004/02/03/business/media/03adco.html?ex=076839801&ei=1&en=aeeac35aaf0e9d03

ESPN extends Belmont Stakes coverage. (2004). *ThoroughbredTimes.Com.* Retrieved June 8, 2004, from http://www.thoroughbredtimes.com/todaysnews/newsview.asp?recno=45293&subsec=1

Federal Communications Commission. (2004). In the Matter of Annual Assessment of the Status of Competition in the Market for the Delivery of Video Programming (Tenth Annual Report), CS Docket No. 03-172. Retrieved February 26, 2004, from http://www.fcc.gov/mb/

From carney to primetime. (2003, February 24). *Broadcasting & Cable, 133*(8), 8A.

Haley, K. (2003, February 24). Inside a revolution. *Broadcasting & Cable, 133*(8), 3A–11A.

Higgins, J. M. (2003a, April 24). ESPN, MSOs face off. *Broadcasting & Cable, 134*(17), 51–52.

Higgins, J. M. (2003b, November 27). Get your motor runnin'. *Broadcasting & Cable, 133*(47), 16.

Jessell, H. A. (2003, August 4). TV's big assist. *Broadcasting & Cable, 133*(31), 33.

Kerschbaumer, K. (2003a, January 20). ABC Sports turns to an old friend. *Broadcasting & Cable, 133*(3), 58.

Kerschbaumer, K. (2003b, May 5). NBA commits to games in high-definition. *Broadcasting & Cable, 133*(18), 20.

Kerschbaumer, K. (2004a, February 2). NASCAR revs up HD. *Broadcasting & Cable, 134*(5), 33.

Kerschbaumer, K. (2004b, February 2). High-def ticket. *Broadcasting & Cable, 134*(12), 18.

Kerschbaumer, K. (2004c, May 3). Fox Sports high on Grass (Valley). *Broadcasting & Cable, 134*(18), 94.

Larson, M., & Consoli, J. (2003, September 8). USA offers makegoods for rain-soaked U.S. Open. *Mediaweek, 13*(32), 6.

Martzke, R. (2004, June 7). Lakers–Pistons ratings send mixed signals. *USAToday.Com.* Retrieved June 8, 2003, from http://www.usatoday.com/sports/basketball/playoffs/2004-06-07-game1-ratings_x.htm

McClellan, S. (2003a, March 3). Game is good for ABC, advertisers. *Broadcasting & Cable, 133*(5), 22.

McClellan, S. (2003b, November 3). CBS eyes a $170 million Sunday. *Broadcasting & Cable, 133*(44), 16.

McClellan, S. (2004, March 15). Hoop dreams. *Broadcasting & Cable, 134*(11), 15.
Media Insight: ESPN *SportsCenter.* (2003, September 22). The America's intelligence wire. Retrieved March 24, 2004, from Infotrac OneFile plus database.
National listings. (2004, June 26). CBS. Retrieved June 25, 2004, from http://cbs.sportsline.com/tvlistings/20040626?national=nopref&AUTO=pref&GOLF=pref&MLB=pref&NBA=pref&SOCCER=pref&WNBA=pref
Nielsen Media Research top 20. (2004, July 5). YahooTV. Retrieved July 7, 2004, from http://tv.yahoo.com/nielsen/.
Packers pervasive. (2003, August 4). *Broadcasting & Cable, 133*(31), 19.
Rich, F. (2004, February 15). My hero, Janet Jackson. *New York Times.* Retrieved February 15, 2004, from http://www.nytimes.com/2004/02/15/arts/15RICH.html?ex=1077869366&ei=1&en=bd2b1d6527b38a4a
Rim shots. (2004, March 29). *Broadcasting & Cable, 134*(13), 19.
Romano, A. (2003a, February 16). Denver teams dump Fox Sports. *Broadcasting & Cable, 133*(7), 28.
Romano, A. (2003b, March 17). NBC cheers for arena football. *Broadcasting & Cable, 133*(11), 10.
Romano, A. (2003c, April 7). As NCAAs end, new net begins. *Broadcasting & Cable, 133*(14), 13.
Romano, A. (2003d, June 30). Plotting NFL's all-year TV season. *Broadcasting & Cable, 133*(26), 8.
Romano, A. (2003e, October 20). ESPN2 hot for its *Cold Pizza. Broadcasting & Cable, 133*(42), 25.
Romano, A. (2003f). New NFL channel needs MSOs to pick up the ball. *Broadcasting & Cable, 133*(43), 9.
Romano. A. (2003g). A hockey channel, eh? *Broadcasting & Cable, 133*(44), 19.
Romano, A. (2003h, November 3). Sports rules cable Nielsens. *Broadcasting & Cable, 133*(44), 19.
Romano, A. (2003i, December 1). How about the fat chance channel? *Broadcasting & Cable, 13*(48), 1, 52.
Romano, A. (2004a, January 5). Cable is keeping it real. *Broadcasting & Cable, 134*(1), 16.
Romano, A. (2004b, January 5). Flat's not so bad for NFL's ratings. *Broadcasting & Cable, 134*(1), 16.
Romano, A. (2004c, January 12). High time for TNT HD. *Broadcasting & Cable, 134*(2), 32.
Romano, A. (2004d, March 1). The sporting life. *Broadcasting & Cable, 134*(9), 20.
Romano, A. (2004e, April 19). Cable's best. *Broadcasting & Cable, 134*(16), 18.
Rudi Johnson, Cincinnati Bengals running back #32, to appear Fox TVs *The Best Damn Sports Show Period.* (2004, March 23). *Business Wire,* 6238.
Sandomir, R. (2003, December 17). The N.F.L. chose Fox, and televised sports were never the same. *New York Times.* Retrieved December 17, 2003, from http://www.nytimes.com/2003/12/17/sports/football/17FOX.html?ex=1072665744&ei=1&en=8354b400e39f4acb
Sandomir, R. (2004a, January 7). Sports media and business: By the numbers, the college game has less action. *New York Times.* Retrieved January 7, 2004, from http://www.nytimes.com/2004/01/07/sports/07TV.html?ex=1074529158&ei=1&en=2377177c6e2808a0
Sandomir, R. (2004b, January 31). Up with much glitzier people. *New York Times.* Retrieved January 31, 2004, from http://www.nytimes.com/ 2004/01/31/sports/football/31SUPE.html?ex=1076644497&ei=1&en=5265dc770c9dc356
Sandomir, R. (2004c, February 5). Citing N.F.L. pressure, ESPN ends *Playmakers. New York Times.* Retrieved February 5, 2004, from http://www.nytimes.com/2004/02/05/sports/football/05ESPN.html?ex=1077073711&ei=1&en=8294c2af2d89e866
Sandomir, R. (2004d, February 19). A channel fades to black, swimming in red ink. *New York Times.* Retrieved February 19, 2004, from http://www.nytimes.com/2004/02/19/sports/football/19TV.html?ex=1078204752&ei=1&en=bb4a83079abe464d
Sandomir, R. (2004e, April 13). Where's the love? Try Augusta for Mickelson. *New York Times.* Retrieved April 13, 2004, from http://www.nytimes.com/2004/04/13/sports/golf/13SAND.html?ex=1083030332&ei=1&en=51bb5d62e1bbc434
Sandomir, R. (2004f, April 20). Broadcasters don't know how to deal with steroid issues. *New York Times.* Retrieved April 20, 2004, from http://www.nytimes.com/2004/04/20/sports/baseball/20TV.html?ex=1083569845&ei=1&en=a6b48934052ae744
Sandomir, R. (2004g, June 8). ESPN looks back, but not at itself. *New York Times.* Retrieved June 15, 2004, from http://www.nytimes.com/2004/06/08/sports/08tv.html?ex=1087703656&ei=1&en=831f3e4d708a30f7
Sandomir, R. (2004h, June 10). Athens Games TV coverage 3 times longer than in 2000. *New York Times.* Retrieved June 15, 2004, from http://www.nytimes.com/2004/06/10/sports/othersports/10olympic.html?ex=1087887728&ei=1&en=c33720895993d0ca
Sandomir, R. (2004i, June 15). ABC bogeyed when it dumped Buick playoff for *America's Funniest. New York Times.* Retrieved June 15, 2004, from http://www.nytimes.com/2004/06/15/sports/golf/15tv.html?ex=1088308403&ei=1&en=fb042090823cf537

Sandomir, R. (2004j, July 13). NBC's trials coverage seems a bit starstruck. *New York Times*. Retrieved July 13, 2004, from http://www.nytimes.com/2004/07/13/sports/othersports/13tv.html?ex=1090714960 &ei=1&en=97d062431349faaa

Smarty helps NBC to high stakes. (2004, June 14). *MediaWeek, 14*(24), 30.

Sokolove, M. (2004, January 18). The lab animal. *New York Times*. Retrieved January 18, 2004, from http://www.nytimes.com/2004/01/18/magazine/18SPORTS.html?ex=1075964001&ei=1&en= 397c996a048d3912

The team player. (2004, April 19). *Broadcasting & Cable, 134*(16), 40.

Television. (2003, September 15). *Autoweek, 53*(37), 51.

Thomaselli, R. (2004, March 15). ESPN vaults tiny H.S. from obscurity to fame; Watersmeet Nimrods get new life without sports. *Advertising Age, 75*(11), 6.

Top 100 television programs for 2003. (2004). *Broadcasting & Cable, 133*(1), 13.

Vecsey, G. (2004, February 3). Sports of the times: Spotlight should have been on the game, not the show. *New York Times*. Retrieved February 3, 2004, from http://www.nytimes.com/2004/02/03/sports/ football/03VECS.html?ex=1076839678&ei=1&en=5c556837c1a370b8

What's hot in cable? (2003, October 27). *Broadcasting & Cable, 133*(43), 14.

Wheel of Fortune loves football. (2003, January 6). *Broadcasting & Cable, 133*(1), 29.

World Series outpacing '02. (2003, October 27). *Broadcasting & Cable, 133*(43), 2.

Yanks top Cablevision. (2004, March 29). *Broadcasting & Cable, 134*(13), 4.

6

The Coverage of Sports in Print Media

Wayne Wanta
University of Missouri

The sports departments at newspapers across the country suffer from identity crises. Newspaper editors often consider sports a necessary evil: Sports sections are among the most read, but sports are not viewed with the same respect as other newspaper staples, such as crime news, politics, and business. Add to this the impression held by many editors that sportswriters do not take themselves seriously and sometimes engage in ethically questionable practices, and it is no wonder that sports departments are often looked upon as the "toy department" of newsrooms—an often-used criticism that originated from an epithet by Howard Cosell (1974) that "Sports is the toy department of life."

Newspaper sports departments, then, lead a schizophrenic life. On the one hand, sports sections are among the most read sections of a newspaper (Miller, 1989). On the other hand, like Rodney Dangerfield, they "don't get no respect." Sports reporters, however, continue to flourish at many newsrooms. As James Michener (1976) pointed out, critics note that the best-written stories in a newspaper are often found in the sports section. Regrettably, the sports section is also where some of the worstwritten stories appear.

What, then, does research tell us about the strange world of the newspaper sports department? Researchers have traditionally ignored sports journalism. Historically, sports journalism has suffered from a news-centered bias: If the research doesn't involve news, it's not important research. In fact, the cumulative index for volumes 1 through 40 of *Journalism Quarterly* does not even have a subhead listing for sports journalism. Meanwhile, from 1924 to 1963, the index does list 231 entries for foreign correspondents. There have been a few exceptions to the lack of research on sports journalism. In addition, sports research has been receiving increased attention from media researchers in recent years.

Overall, sports journalism research can be grouped into three areas: (1) studies of sports news content, or what and how sports get covered; (2) studies of sportswriters, or who produces the sports content; and (3) studies of sports readers, the consumers of sports content.

HISTORICAL PERSPECTIVE

Sports news has a long tradition in American newspapers. Sports stories appeared in newspapers as far back as the 1700s. The *Boston Gazette* published a story on a boxing match between John Faulcomer and Bob Russel in 1733 (Communication Research Trends, 2003). The *New York Herald* in 1832 carried a story of a boxer who died after he lost a 120-round bout.

Because of the fierce competition between several New York newspapers in the late 1800s, several innovations first appeared in New York. The *New York Herald* became the world's largest daily, with a circulation of 77,000 in 1860. In 1862, the *Herald*'s Henry Chadwick became what is commonly considered the country's first baseball writer (Emery, 1972). Also about this time, the *New York World* was taken over by Joseph Pulitzer. To compete in an already flooded New York newspaper market, Pulitzer, in one of his first acts with the *World*, organized a separate sports department (Cozens & Stumpf, 1953). As early as 1896, when visuals in newspapers consisted mostly of woodcuts, the *New York Times* began running sports photographs in a special Sunday picture section. But the biggest innovation came from the *New York Journal*. In 1895, the Journal became the first newspaper in the United States to print an entire section of its newspaper devoted only to sports.

Surprisingly, other cities were slow to jump on the sportssection bandwagon. The *Chicago Tribune* started a Sunday sports section in 1899 but did not have a daily sports section until 1905. Boston, Philadelphia, and Washington began sports sections even later.

In many ways, sports journalism made larger inroads in magazines. Egan's *Life in London* and *Sporting Guide* was published in Great Britain in 1824 (Nugent, 1929). After it was renamed *Bell's Life in London*, it reached a circulation of 75,000 in the mid-1800s. In the United States sports coverage helped the *National Police Gazette* amass a national circulation of 150,000 (Betts, 1974).

By the 1920s, sports coverage was firmly entrenched in the nation's newspapers. The decade saw the emergence of several legendary sports figures—Babe Ruth and Red Grange, to name two. Newspapers battled for scoops about athletes and teams, creating serious concerns about ethical standards of sports reporting. The concerns over ethics became so great that in 1927 a committee appointed by the American Society of Newspaper Editors recommended several changes for sports reporting (Carvalho, 1998). Among the recommendations were committing increased coverage to amateur athletics and ending free publicity for upcoming sporting events.

Ethical concerns persist today, such that some newspapers refuse to allow their sports reporters to attend events without paying to enter the sports venue. Newsroom colleagues also continue to be concerned about sports journalists who befriend athletes and thus do not keep professional distances from sources.

MEDIA COVERAGE: WHAT MAKES IT INTO PRINT

A growing volume of research has examined media coverage of sports. The bulk of the research deals with unequal coverage of men's and women's sports. Research consistently shows that print coverage of women's sports lags behind coverage of men's sports both in quantity and quality. This discrepancy exists despite the fact that 40% of all high school, college, and Olympic athletes are women (Kane, 1996). In fact, 45% of the U.S. athletes at the 2000 Olympics in Sydney were women (Hardin, Chance, Dodd, & Hardin, 2001). Some 21 million American women are active in sport, and 10 times as many women participate in intercollegiate sports than in 1972 (Acosta & Carpenter, 1994).

Quantity of Coverage

According to Lopiano (2000), men have traditionally dominated sports news. In her report on "Modern History of Women in Sports," Lopiano details how 90% of the coverage in newspaper sports sections is devoted to men's sports. Women's sports receive 5%, with horses and dogs receiving 3%. Lopiano notes it was not until 1992 that women's sports surpassed the space allotted to animals.

Several case studies have found similar discrepancies in the amount of coverage afforded to women's and men's sports. For example, Silverstein (1996) compared coverage of the men's and women's NCAA basketball tournaments of 1995 in the *New York Times*. She found that the men's tournament received three times the amount of coverage as the women's tournament. She also noted that the men's tournament appeared on the front page of the sports section 31 times to only 4 times for the women's tournament.

A similar content analysis compared women's coverage in the *New York Times* and the *Indianapolis Star* in 1989 and 1999 (George, 2002). While the coverage of women's sports improved slightly in both papers over the decade, women still received just a fraction of the overall daily sports section. According to George, women's coverage increased in the *Times* from 2.2% in 1989 to 6.7% in 1999. The *Star*'s women's sports coverage rose from 2.7% to 8.6%.

Perhaps the most studied publication in this area is *Sports Illustrated*. Lumpkin and Williams (1991), for example, content analyzed feature articles run from 1954 to 1987. Of these features, 90.8% focused on men, and 91.8% were written by male writers. Men's features also were an average of 10 column inches longer than women's features.

Sports photographic coverage also is dominated by male athletes. Duncan, Messner, Williams, Jensen, and Wilson (1994), in an examination of four of the top-10 sports sections in the country, found that photographs of male athletes outnumbered photographs of female athletes by a 13:1 ratio. Stories about male athletes outnumbered those of female athletes by an even larger margin—23:1.

The lack of coverage, of course, can have far-reaching effects. With sports sections giving such little space to female athletes, readers can get the impression that women's sports are trivial. Gaye Tuchman (1981) noted the same problem with coverage of women in news. She argued that ignoring women in news stories amounts to "symbolic annihilation." Kinnick (1998) echoes this point, noting that when women are underrepresented on the sports pages, the impression is that female athletes either do not exist or do not have any accomplishments that are newsworthy.

Quality of Coverage

While researchers have roundly criticized *Sports Illustrated* for its lack of overall coverage of women's sports, researchers have also been critical of the type of coverage it provides for readers. Critics argue that *Sports Illustrated* emphasizes traditional feminine roles and traditionally "acceptable" women's sports such as gymnastics, tennis, swimming, and diving.

Lumpkin and Williams (1991) contend that *Sports Illustrated*, by limiting the types of women's sports it covers and by focusing on physical appearance instead of physical abilities, reinforces traditional feminine roles. Female athletes are often described in terms of domestic roles. For example, after Chris Evert retired from tennis, *Sports Illustrated* featured her on the cover with a tagline that read: "I'm going to be a full time wife" (August 28, 1989).

Besides covering female athletes in traditional roles, *Sports Illustrated* has also been criticized for portraying women as victims. Between the 1993 and the 1994 swimsuit issues, only three women appeared on the cover of *Sports Illustrated*. The women were Monica Seles, who had been stabbed; Mary Pierce, whose father was abusive; and Nancy Kerrigan, who had been clubbed in her leg.

Another study noting differences in coverage of men and women in *Sports Illustrated* involved a content analysis of three tennis tournaments. Kane and Parks (1992) found that stories often focused on emotions of female athletes, including mentions of women crying. Coverage also included more descriptions of women's clothing choices and more discussion of how women's personal lives negatively impacted their professional lives, including mentions of breakups with boyfriends or problems with domineering parents.

Earlier studies (Boutilier and SanGiovanni, 1983; Salwen and Wood, 1994) found similar patterns of coverage in *Sports Illustrated*. These same patterns were also found in other sports magazines such as *Runner's World, Sport,* and *Tennis* (Bryant, 1980) and *SI for Kids* (Cuneen & Sidwell, 1998; Duncan & Sayoavong, 1990; Rintala & Birrell, 1984). Hardin, Lynn, Walsdorf, and Hardin (2002) examined photographs in *SI for Kids* across a three-year period. They found that gender inequity was widening rather than narrowing and that gender stereotypes were persisting. They suggested several possible reasons for this trend, such as concerns over possible backlash from the magazine's male readers and editors' reluctance to change.

Besides sportswriters, sports photographers have also been criticized for their coverage of women's sports. Wanta and Leggett (1989) compared Associated Press wirephotos from the 1987 Wimbledon tennis tournament and photos used by eight large metropolitan newspapers. Contrary to predictions, male tennis players were depicted showing emotion more often than female players in AP photos, while newspaper photographs showed no difference between genders on emotion. Newspaper photos, male players were shown dominating opponents, while female players were shown being dominated in newspaper photos. AP photos did not differ. Finally, again contrary to expectations, both AP and newspapers concentrated on male players' bodies and female players' faces.

Although the study produced a mixed bag of results, the findings could have been affected by the athletes involved in the tournament. The top male player, Ivan Lendl, was often noted for showing a lack of emotion on the court. When he did show emotion on rare occasions, photographers thought it newsworthy enough to capture the image.

Duncan (1990), on the other hand, reached different conclusions. She found that sports photographs do tend to emphasize women's physical appearance. Women are photographed most often if they resemble the "ideal" femininity. Female athletes are often captured in poses that focus on certain body parts or in submissive positions. Female athletes also are shown in emotional displays and in nonaction pictures more often than men.

While gender inequities on sports pages have received a great deal of attention from researchers, differential coverage of race has been an important area of research as well. Bush (1999) examined coverage of Mark McGuire and Sammy Sosa during their chase for the home run record in 1998. Bush concluded that both McGuire, who is White, and Sosa, who is Black, received positive coverage from the press. McGuire, however, was the focus of significantly more coverage than Sosa, which Bush argues was mainly because of race.

Another content analysis compared mainstream newspapers with the Black press on their coverage of the signing of Jackie Robinson as major league baseball's first Black player in 1945. Kelley (1976) found that the Black press reported the signing as historically significant, while the mainstream newspapers treated it as relatively unimportant.

Other Coverage

As sports have changed through the years, coverage of different aspects of sports has changed as well. Increasingly important is coverage of the business of sports. A case study by Boyle, Dinan, and Morrow (2003) examined Celtic, a highly successful soccer team from Glasgow, Scotland. The authors argue that much of the business side of sports is not covered because of the complexity involved. Sports journalists, who are seldom trained or comfortable in covering business news, instead rely on celebrity sources for their stories.

Sports can also be examined in a political context. Maguire (2001), argues that sportswriters play a significant role in constructing and representing national identity. Through a content analysis of the European soccer championships in 1996, he found that both the British and German press used the championships to "reassert national identity" (p. 85) in opposition to further European integration.

Language of Sports

Several studies have examined the language involved in sports coverage. A classic study (Tannenbaum & Noah, 1959) examined verbs used in sports stories to determine if terms such as "annihilated" and "shaded" accurately communicated the final score of sporting events. Using 84 verbs taken from newspaper stories on high school basketball games in Illinois and Missouri, Tannenbaum and Noah asked 18 sportswriters, 68 regular sports readers, and 28 nonregular sports readers to estimate the margin of victory. They found correlations of actual margin of victory and estimated margin of victory of .86 for regular sports readers, .81 for sportswriters, and .33 for nonregular readers. They conclude that the verbs that sportswriters use do accurately communicate game information to readers.

Language was also at issue when *The Oregonian* in Portland decided to ban the use of sports nicknames that some readers would find offensive. Most of these involved Native American nicknames such as the Indians, Redskins, Redmen, and Braves. Jensen (1994) examined the ethical and political arguments made both by *The Oregonian* in defending its decision and its critics who claimed that *The Oregonian* had abandoned the journalistic principles of objectivity and neutrality.

SPORTS JOURNALISTS IN THE NEWSROOM

Sportswriters have traditionally occupied an odd place in the newsroom. Weischenberg (1978,) as cited in Communication Research Trends, 2003 notes that sports journalists are considered outsiders in the newsroom. This isolation from the other newsroom departments stems in part from the long-time popularity of sports among lower classes, or the lower education level of sports journalists when compared to other newsroom employees—though this has changed recently.

Added to this isolation, sports journalists rarely change departments, possibly because the qualifications for being a sportswriter were different from qualifications needed for news reporters. Many sportswriters also have more contact with writers from other newspapers than they do with the colleagues in other departments at their home paper.

Sports journalists, however, seem to be more accepted in the newsrooms today. Recent studies have shown that sports journalists are now better educated than in the past and consider their work to be more prestigious. And sports journalists and their newsroom colleagues now hold very similar attitudes on newsroom policies.

Vannatta (1981), on the other hand, suggested that sportswriters were fundamentally different from news reporters. She examined newsroom personnel on two physiological types, in which the left hemisphere of the brain is based on logic and analysis, linguistic activity, and thinking language; and the right hemisphere is based on abstract thinking and the appreciation for artistic talent. Hard news writing and business reporting were left-brain activities. Sportswriting, photography, and feature writing, however, were right-brain activities. Vannatta concluded that newspapers should test job applicants for brain dominance and recommended training for newsroom hires who had not already developed techniques that would help them in their new jobs.

Regardless of which brain hemisphere is dominant, sportswriters face several psychological problems with their jobs. Policinski (1998) reported that a survey by Women, Men and Media, a media watchdog organization, interviewed athletes about their relations with the media. One result is especially noteworthy: Almost half of the athletes interviewed reported that they had dealt with reporters who appeared uncomfortable with women's sporting accomplishments.

Bias among sports reporters also has been investigated. Anderson (2001), for instance, examined whether sportswriters had changed from a pro-owner bias to a pro-player bias. He analyzed baseball coverage during labor–management conflicts in 1890 and 1975 to 1976. Findings show that some sportswriters supported the owners' points while others were critical of management in both time periods. Anderson argues that one reason for the similarities in the coverage in the two time periods is that baseball owners used identical arguments in the labor disputes: Players were greedy and selfish, only the owners could preserve baseball, players' demands would lead to financial ruin, and players were overpaid for playing a game.

A study of a Canadian newspaper's sports department examined the routines of a sportswriter's job. Lowes (1999) found that commercial forces are at work in the newsroom that produce an overemphasis on professional sports. This relegates amateur sports to the far back pages of the sports section, if they receive any coverage at all.

McCleneghan (1997) surveyed 131 sports columnists (considered a paper's star writer) at large metropolitan newspapers. He found the typical columnist to be in his mid-50s and with a yearly salary of more than $90,000. He had been a columnist for 15 years and wrote three or four columns per week. Other findings are:

- The best ideas for columns come from intuitive feelings or sporting events. The worst come from sports agents or television talk shows.
- 90% of the columnists said that television has produced millionaire athletes who no longer care about newspaper reporters.
- 85% said the on-the-job pressure that they face is always self-imposed.

Wanta and Kunz (1997) also noted the importance of sports coverage to a newspaper. They surveyed newspaper editors regarding their newspapers' reactions to the 1994 baseball strike. Very few newspapers cut back on the normal newshole allotted to the sports section. Instead, most newspapers devoted expanded coverage to other sports. The baseball strike caused the biggest problems for newspapers in the large circulation category—the category of newspapers that would be most likely to cover baseball extensively.

SPORTS READERS

Many studies of newspaper readership note that the sports section is one of the most popular sections in the newspaper. One such study (Weaver & Mauro, 1978) examined the percentage of time readers spent with specific content in the daily newspaper. They found that 40% of the respondents' reading activity time was spent with "hard news." The next highest category was sports, with 17% of the activity time. This percentage was similar for male and female readers. Sports reading time was higher than entertainment and comics (10%) and business listings, obits, and weather (6%).

The sports section is especially important to younger readers, a demographic that traditionally has not yet developed a newspaper reading habit. A survey conducted by the Richmond papers showed that teens read several sections more than adults, including sports coverage, high school roundups, college roundups, and motor sports reports.

Cobb-Walgren (1990) also found a high level of interest in sports news among young readers. She found that teens typically turned to newspapers for local news and sports. In addition, Thurlow and Milo (1993) found that 35% of students read the sports page of their college newspaper. Interest in sports reporting has increased among young readers through the years (Stone & Boudreau, 1995).

A study by the American Society of Newspaper Editors (ASNE, 2000) found that the sports sections of newspapers nationwide were not only well-read, but also readers were highly satisfied with several aspects of sports coverage. Among male readers, professional sports news was more highly read than other sections such as business news, opinions and analyses, entertainment news, and television listings. The difference between male and female readers, however, was substantial: Whereas 50% of male readers rated professional sports coverage as important, only 31% of women did so.

Satisfaction with coverage of sports, meanwhile, ranked at the top of the survey. The newspaper content that respondents said they were most satisfied with was sports scores and statistics, in which 74% of all respondents said they were satisfied. Professional sports coverage (with 71% satisfied) ranked third, just behind crime news (72%). College sports and high school sports (both with 67%) were not far behind. Overall, then, it appears that readers often read sports and are very satisfied with what they read.

Several newspapers have conducted their own surveys to examine demographics of their readers. The *Seattle Times*, for example, in 2003 found that the typical sports reader was male with an average age of 48.1 years old and an income of $72,600. Sports readers also tended to own their home and have a white-collar job (Seattle Times, 2003).

According to Stempel and Hargrove (1996), men and women differ in their sports preferences. Their survey found that 30% of male respondents reported track as their favorite Olympic sport to only 13% of female respondents. Gymnastics was the choice of 30% of women, but only 7% of men. More women preferred swimming than men by 26 to 13%. Stempel and Hargrove recommend that increasing coverage of gymnastics and swimming may be one way to reach female readers.

The importance of sports media coverage also can be seen by the large number of people who identify themselves as sports fans. Frank (2000) found that 67% of the respondents in his national survey were fans of the National Football League, 54% were fans of the National Basketball Association, and 50% were fans of college basketball.

Effects on Audiences

Sports coverage can have a powerful impact on individuals, especially young readers. Lines (2001) argues that young individuals are susceptible to imitating inappropriate on-and off-field problems of their favorite sports stars.

Attention to sports also may be related to attitudes toward women's sports. Weidman (1997) hypothesized that the more attention individuals paid to sports coverage, the more negative they would view women's sports. Results from her phone survey found that the two variables (attention to sports news and attitudes toward women's sports) were negatively related, though only one of her tests reached statistical significance. She argues that the findings support the assumptions of her study because one of the attitude items tested (the view that women's sports are not exciting) was statistically significant and the relationships between attention to sports media and attitudes toward women's sports was negative as predicted.

FUTURE DIRECTIONS

The increased use of the Internet as a source of sports information offers several opportunities for research. An especially important topic is whether individuals who publish only on the Internet are indeed journalists. This question opens the door to other questions dealing with intellectual property and the distribution of press credentials at sporting events (Dyson, 2001). This area remains unresolved. For example, Rivals.com, a website focused mainly on high school athletes being recruited by universities, has a large network of reporters who routinely scoop local newspapers. In fact, Rivals.com is often cited in newspaper articles reporting on athletes signing letters of intent to play for universities. Do reporters for Rivals.com merit credentials to cover sporting events involving these athletes?

Internet content also could reduce newspaper readership. A survey by the Associated Press Managing Editors (Pitts, 2004), for instance, found that 20% of their respondents read blogs at least sometimes. Individuals, then, could be using blogs as a replacement for traditional news media.

Mass communication researchers have often considered themselves to be watchdogs of the watchdogs—keeping track of the amount and types of coverage the news media devote to certain areas. This is certainly the case with research in sports journalism. A wealth of research has examined gender inequities on the nation's sports pages. While women's sports appear to be making some inroads in coverage, sports sections continue to be dominated by men's sports. This trend should be examined in the future. Even with the volume of research on women, race and sports media, further research should continue to track the discrepancies in coverage. Certainly, this is an extremely important area.

Much more research needs to be done on the sports newsroom. Clearly, attitudes toward the sports department have improved over the years. While scandals have rocked the news departments at several papers, sports departments have remained relatively free of troubles. Several former sports editors have been promoted to other editorial management positions. How these and other factors relate to the higher prestige of the sports department is worthy of investigation. Survey research methods, long employed by mass communication researchers, have not been utilized as frequently by sports researchers.

Economic factors related to sports departments also should be examined. Sports departments have sizable budgets at newspapers. Is the cost of sending several reporters to cover the Olympics in Greece, for example, worth the benefit of increased readership? Is there a good journalist-to-circulation ratio for how big a sports department should be?

Finally, the effects of print coverage of sports offer especially fruitful areas for future research. Researchers have produced a long tradition of research on the effects of violent television programming. Sports television coverage has been one small slice of the research in this area. But sports newspaper coverage certainly could have profound effects on readers. Perhaps the lack of coverage of women's sports on the nation's sports pages is cultivating readers into thinking that women's sports are not important or nonexistent, similar to the theoretical framework of Weidman (1997).

The effects of sports photographs also deserve more research. The content analyses showing women stereotyped as emotional and in traditional roles could be leading to overall negative attitudes toward female athletes.

Interest in sports is at an all-time high. Sports journalism, then, is ripe for exploration.

REFERENCES

Acosta, R. V., & Carpenter, L. J. (1994). The status of women in intercollegiate athletics. In S. Birrell & C. L. Cole (Eds.), *Women, sport, and culture* (pp. 111–118). Champaign, IL: Human Kinetics.

Anderson, W. B. (2001). Does the cheerleading ever stop? Major league baseball and sports journalism. *Journalism & Mass Communication Quarterly, 78,* 355–382.

ASNE (2000, January 12). *Newspaper readership, interests, needs and reader evaluation among men and women*. American Society of Newspaper Editors report. Reston, VA: Author.

Betts, J. R. (1974). *America's sporting heritage: 1850–1950*. Reading, MA.: Addison-Wesley.

Boutilier, M., & SanGiovanni, L. (1983). *The sporting woman*. Champaign: Human Kinetics.

Boyle, R., Dinan, W., & Morrow, S. (2003). Doing the business? Newspaper reporting of the business of football. *Journalism, 3,* 161–181.

Bryant J. (1980, May) A two-year selective investigation of the female in sport as reported in the paper media. *Arena Review, 4*(2), 32–44.

Bush, M. (1999, August). *The great home run race of 1998 in black and white*. Paper presented at the annual convention of the Association for Education in Journalism and Mass Communication, New Orleans, LA.

Carvalho, J. (1998, August). *World Series coverage before and after the depression*. Paper presented at the annual convention for the Association for Education in Journalism and Mass Communication, Baltimore, MD.

Cobb-Walgren, C. J. (1990). Why teenagers do not "Read all about it." *Journalism Quarterly, 67*(2), 340–347.

Communication Research Trends. (2003). *22*(4).

Cosell, H. (1974). *Cosell*. New York: Pocket Books.

Cozens, F. W., & Stumpf, F. S. (1953). *Sports in American life*. Chicago: University of Chicago Press.

Cuneen, J., & Sidwell, M. J. (1998). Gender portrayals in *Sports Illustrated for Kids* advertisements: A content analysis of prominent and supporting models. *Journal of Sport Management. 12,* 39–50.

Duncan, M. C., Messner, M. A., Williams, L., Jensen, K., & Wilson, W. (1994). Gender stereotyping in televised sports. In S. Birrell & C. L. Cole (Eds.), *Women, sport, and culture* (pp. 249–272). Champaign: Human Kinetics.

Duncan, M. C. (1990). Sports photographs and sexual difference: Images of women and men in the 1984 and 1988 Olympic Games. *Sociology of Sport Journal, 7,* 22–43.

Duncan, M. C., & Sayaovong, A. (1990). Photographic images and gender in *Sports Illustrated for Kids*. *Play & Culture, 3,* 91–116.

Dyson, C. (2001, April 6). Online journalists have major-league issues over sports credentials. *ASNE Reporter*. Retrieved from http://www.asne.org/2001reportes/friday/sports 6.html

Emery, E. (1972). *The press and America*. New York: Prentice Hall.

Frank, M. (2000). Fan interest rebounds sharply. *Street & Smith's sports Business Journal, 3*(18), 41, 47.

George, J. J. (2002). Lack of news coverage for women's athletics: A questionable practice of newspapers priorities. Retrieved from http://www.womenssportsfoundation.org

Hardin, M., Lynn, S. Walsdorf, K., & Hardin, B. (2002). *Mass Communication & Society, 5,* 341–360.

Hardin, M., Chance, J., Dodd, J. E., & Hardin, B. (2001, August). *Seeking gender equity on the sports pages: An analysis of newspaper photos from the 2000 Olympics*. Paper presented at the annual convention of the Association for Education in Journalism and Mass Communication, Washington, DC.

Jensen, R. (1994). Banning Redskins from the sports page: The ethics and politics of Native American nicknames. *Journal of Mass Media Ethics, 9,* 16–25.

Kane, M. J. (1996). Media coverage of the post Title IX female athlete: A feminist analysis of sport, gender and power. Duke Journal of Gender Law & Policy, *3*(1), 95–127.

Kane, M. J., & Parks, J. (1992). The social construction of gender difference and hierarchy in sport journalism: Few new twists on very old themes. *Women in Sport and Physical Activity Journal,1,* 49–83.

Kelley, W. B. (1976). Jackie Robinson and the press. *Journalism Quarterly, 53,* 137–139.

Kinnick, K. N. (1998). Gender bias in newspaper profiles of 1996 Olympic athletes: A content analysis of five major dailies. *Women's Studies in Communication, 21*(2), 212–237.

Lines, G. (2001). Media sport audiences – Young people and the summer of sport '96: Revisiting frameworks for analysis. *Media Culture & Society, 22,* 669–680.

Lopiano, D. A. (2000). Modern history of women in sports. Twenty-five years of Title IX. *Clin Sports Med 19*(2), 163–73, vii.

Lowes, M. D. (1999). *Inside the sports pages: Work routines, professional ideologies, and the manufacture of sports news*. Toronto: University of Toronto Press.

Lumpkin, A., & Williams, L. (1991). An analysis of *Sports Illustrated* feature articles, 1954–1987. *Sociology of Sport Journal, 8,* 16–32.

Maguire, J. (2001). The war of the words: Identity politics in Anglo-German press coverage of Euro 96. *European Journal of Communication, 14,* 61–89.

McCleneghan, J. S. (1997). The myth makers and wreckers: Syndicated and non- syndicated sports columnists at 103 metro newspapers. *Social Science Journal, 34,* 337–349.

Michener, J. A. (1976). *Sports in America.* New York: Random House.

Miller, S. (1989, April). Sports sections responding to audience interest and needs. Scripps-Howard Editors' Newsletter, 13.

Nugent, W. H. (1929). The sports section. *The American Mercury, 16,* 336.

Pitts, R. (2004, October 13). APME survey: Newspaper readers use blogs cautiously. PoynterOnline. Retrieved from http://www.poynter.org/content/content_view.asp?id=72453

Policinski, G. (1998, November 13). Study finds media still fail in quality, quantity of women's sports coverage. Report for the Freedom Forum. Retrieved from http://www.freedomforum.org/templates/document.asp?document ID=7597

Rintala, J., & Birrell, S. (1984). Fair treatment for the active female: A content analysis of *Young Athlete* magazine. *Sociology of Sport, 1,* 231–250.

Salwen, M., & Wood, N. (1994). Depictions of female athletes on *Sports Illustrated* covers, 1957–1989. *Journal of Sport Behavior, 17*(2), 98–108. Seattle Times sports readership profile. (2003). Retrieved May 5, 2005, from http://www.seattletimescompany.com/marketingops/sectionprofiles/WeekdaySports/

Silverstein, L. (1996, August). *Full-court press?* The New York Times' *coverage of the 1995 Women's NCAA Basketball Tournament.* Paper presented at the annual convention of the Association for Education in Journalism and Mass Communication, Anaheim, CA.

Stempel, G., III, & Hargrove, T. (1996, November 28). Gaining women, balance on the sports pages. *ASNE News* Retrieved January 11, 2005, from http://www.asne.org/kiosk/editor/september/stempel.html

Stone, G., & Boudreau, T. (1995). Comparison of reader content preferences. *Newspaper Research Journal, 16*(4),13–28.

Tannenbaum, P. H., & Noah, J. E. (1959). Sportugese: A study of sports page communication. *Journalism Quarterly, 36,* 163–170.

Thurlow, G. L., & Milo, K. L. (1993). Newspaper readership: Can the bleeding be stopped or do we have the wrong patient? *Newspaper Research Journal, 14*(3–4), 34–44.

Tuchman, G. (1981). The symbolic annihilation of women by the mass media. In S. Cohen and J. Young (Eds.), The manufacture of news: Deviance, social problems and the mass media (pp. 169–185). Beverly Hills, CA: Sage.

Vannatta, B. A. (1981). Hemisphericity and journalism - How do journalists think? *Newspaper Research Journal, 3,* 9–15.

Wanta, W., & Kunz, W. M. (1997). The impact of the baseball strike on newspapers. *Journalism & Mass Communication Quarterly, 74,* 184–194.

Wanta, W., & Leggett, D. (1989). Gender stereotypes in wire service sports photos. *Newspaper Research Journal, 10,* 105–114.

Weaver, D. H., & Mauro, J. B. (1978). Newspaper readership patterns. *Journalism Quarterly, 55,* 84–91, 134.

Weidman, L. M. (1997, August). *Of sports pages and bad attitudes: An investigation of the relationship between attention to sports media and attitudes toward women's sports.* Paper presented at the annual convention of the Association for Education in Journalism and Mass Communication, Chicago, IL.

Weischenberg, S. (1978). Die Aussenseiter der Redaktion, Struktur, Funktion and Bedingungen des Sportsjournalismus. Theorie and Analyse im Rahmen eines allgemeinen Konzepts komplexer Kommunikatorforschung. Bochum: Brockmeyer. Cited in *Communication Research Trends* (2003). *22*(4).

7

The Coverage of Sports on Radio

John W. Owens
University of Cincinnati

In this era of digital technology, broadband Internet access, and 500-channel television service, it is easy to see how an "old" technology, like radio, can become viewed as ordinary. And when one discusses the media and sports, it might be easy to sidestep our mature broadcast companion in favor of the "fresh" communication technologies that deliver us multimedia highlights of our favorite athletes and/or teams. However, sports fans understand that despite the limitation of providing only audio coverage of a sporting event, radio encourages its listeners to produce their own highlights with an unlimited palette of images supplied by the human mind. Gorman and Calhoun (1994) quoted famous sportscaster Marty Glickman, as he commented on the delivery of legendary CBS announcer Ted Husing: "You could see the rustling of the leaves, you could feel the wind howling through the stadium" (p. 90).

Having been around in an organized fashion since the 1920s, radio has the advantage of being ubiquitous. With nearly six radios in 99% of American households (Tankel & Williams, 1993), radio accompanies us on our daily journeys from the moment we brew our morning coffee until we drift away to sleep at night. And sports, as an important programming element for the medium, has benefited greatly from its relationship with this ever-present media platform. However, there was a time when radios were a possession of society's elite, and the coverage of sports on the airwaves was true experimentation.

SPORT AND EARLY RADIO

While many inventors have laid claim to the title of "father of radio," there is little question about the individual who moved wireless out of the laboratory and into the marketplace. Guglielmo Marconi expanded on the work of Heinrich Hertz and created a device that transmitted Morse code using radio waves. Marconi, frustrated by the lack of foresight by his native Italian government, obtained a patent for his invention in England and in 1897 established the Marconi Wireless Telegraph Company (Gross, 2003). At this time the technology was primarily viewed as a means to improve ship-to-ship and ship-to-shore communication and had not yet included the transmission of human speech.

It took only one year for Marconi and his technology to become involved in the coverage of sports. In 1898, Marconi used his wireless telegraph to send an account of the 1898 Kingstown Regatta to the Dublin Daily Express (Smith, 2001). By 1899, Marconi expanded his enterprise to the United States with the establishment of American Marconi. Word of his successful coverage of the Kingstown Regatta soon found the opportunistic ears of New York newspaper publisher James Gordon Bennett, Jr. Bennett's *New York Herald* was locked in heated circulation wars with rival papers owned by William Randolph Hearst (*New York Journal*) and Joseph Pulitzer (*New York World*). Bennett offered Marconi $5000 to send wireless telegraph messages from the site of the America's Cup yacht race back to the offices of the *Herald*. He hoped that by receiving the result of this popular race more quickly he could scoop his competitors and sell more papers (Smith, 2001). Marconi accepted the offer, and his fifteen-mile wireless transmissions from the coast of New Jersey were successful.

Reginald Fessenden, a professor at Western University of Pennsylvania (now the University of Pittsburgh), pioneered the transmission of voice over wireless. On Christmas Eve of 1906 he successfully transmitted violin music and his own speech to ships off the shore of Massachusetts. Voice reproduction was advanced by the work of Lee DeForrest and his invention, the audion tube. This device, patented in 1907, could detect and amplify radio waves, and it served as a prototype for future engineers in their progress towards a more reliable means of radio transmission (Keith, 2004).

It is not surprising that university laboratories were key nodes for experimentation with radio. In 1912, F. W. Springer and H. M. Turner created an experimental radio station at the University of Minnesota (Smith, 2001). As a part of their experiments, Springer and Turner broadcast accounts of the university's football games. According to Smith (2001), "The efforts at the University of Minnesota preceded the first commercial station in the country, KDKA of Pittsburgh, by broadcasting a football game nearly a decade before the 'first station in the nation' was founded" (p. 15). In addition, these broadcasts at the University of Minnesota "...predated what is generally considered and, incorrectly, recognized as the first wireless broadcast of a football game, that of a 1920 game at College Station between Texas A&M and Texas" (Smith, 2001, p. 15).

Because of America's entry into World War I and the Navy's subsequent takeover of commercial radio in 1917, individual advancements in radio technology and programming were put on hold. After the war, there was some consideration given to transferring permanent control of this new medium to the Navy. While those efforts failed, the U.S. government was still anxious about a foreign company (American Marconi) controlling radio broadcasting in the United States. Therefore, in 1919 Guglielmo Marconi was forced to transfer his U.S. assets to a new organization formed by General Electric (GE) called the Radio Corporation of America (RCA). Soon GE, AT&T, and Westinghouse purchased stock in this new corporation and agreed to share patents, thus clearing the way for significant progress in radio broadcasting (Gross, 2003).

This new partnership of influential manufacturers did not deter the experimentation of amateur broadcasters, like Dr. Frank Conrad. Conrad, from the garage of his Pittsburgh home, broadcast music and talked to whomever could receive it in his community. So popular were his transmissions that a local department store began marketing radio receivers by emphasizing their ability to capture Conrad's "programming." Conrad's employer, Westinghouse, asked him to construct a more powerful facility for them with the hopes that their radios would fly off the shelves if enough programming was available on a consistent basis. After applying for a transmitter's license from the Department of Commerce in 1920, Westinghouse put KDKA on the air (Gross, 2003). The nation now had its first radio station offering a noncoded program schedule available to all with a receiver. The early economic model for the radio industry was now in place, but what was needed was the development of interesting programming. It didn't take long for broadcasters to realize that capturing the drama of sport, and transporting that to the ears of the masses outside of the arena or stadium, would be the perfect incentive for adoption of this new technology.

The 1920s are often referred to as the *Golden Age* of American sports. Great athletes like Babe Ruth, Jack Dempsey, and Red Grange dominated the sports sections of newspapers, the most important mass medium at the time. In fact, many historians point to the 1920s as the golden age of sportswriters as well. According to Rader (1983), "nothing before or since—not even the cool waves of television—created quite the same hot romance between sport and the public as the newspapers in the 1920s" (p. 199). Important writers like Grantland Rice, Paul Gallico, and Damon Runyan were viewed as celebrities in their own right. Municipalities and universities invested heavily in new stadium construction in the '20s, exemplified by a tripling of seating capacity at the top-65 college football programs of the day (McChesney, 1989). America was infatuated with sports, and early broadcasting took advantage.

Although early radio stations like KDKA and WEAF (New York) were providing consistent program schedules, the programming of sports was presented in an ad-hoc, event-oriented manner at the time. One sport that was at the zenith of its popularity at the time fit perfectly into this style of presentation—boxing. Boxing, like radio, experienced a boost after World War I. Prior to the war many states had outlawed the sport because of legislators' belief that it posed a threat to important social morals of society. But the army used boxing as a method of training soldiers, and with the return of America's fighting men came legitimacy for the "sweet science" (Rader, 2004). Attendance figures and gate receipts for boxing matches in the 1920s have never been rivaled.

The first presentation of boxing on radio took place on April 21, 1921, when Johnny Ray and Johnny Dundee fought in the Smoky's City Motor Square Garden (Betts, 1974). The match, transmitted by KDKA, was the first of many boxing events on radio that displayed the power of this new medium. Later that year, RCA, led by Chairman David Sarnoff, built a temporary transmitting facility for the transmission of the Jack Dempsey–Georges Carpentier fight. In addition, Sarnoff linked this transmission with WJY of Hoboken to expand the audience for the fight (Betts, 1974). Indeed, the establishment of such broadcast *chains* helped lead to the creation of radio networks that has brought the entertainment programming into the living rooms of millions (Keith, 2004).

The broadcast of boxing was certainly a hit as evidenced by the estimated listening audience of 2 million for the Louis Firpo–Jess Willard fight in 1923. And, as predicted, sports programming helped move radio receivers from store shelves to home living rooms. According to Betts (1974), "When the Dempsey–Tunney championship bout was broadcast in 1927, it was estimated that it generated sales of over $90,000 worth of radio receivers in one New York department store alone" (p. 59).

Another sport that helped develop the popularity of radio broadcasting was collegiate football. As mentioned earlier, universities were making significant investments in infrastructure for their football programs and the crowds were responding. There were over 100,000 ticket requests for the 1922 Princeton–University of Chicago contest, which was a rematch of a highly publicized game the year prior. Chicago's coach, the legendary Amos Alonzo Stagg, referred to the 1922 match up as the "greatest game of the century" (Smith, 2001, p.16). WEAF, an AT&T-owned station, decided to provide coverage of the game for fans in New York City by sending the signal through their long distance lines. Listeners on the East Coast listened to the 21–18 Princeton victory both by tuning in to WEAF and listening to a special public-address setup in New York's Park Row (Smith, 2001). According to Smith (2001),

> The Princeton–Chicago broadcast was the first of a number of interregional games that were used to promote college football and bring financial rewards to radio stations and networks ... radio had made itself an integral part of the nationalization of football by making interregional competition immediately available to masses through the airwaves. (p. 17)

As the decade of the 1920s progressed, Americans began to embrace radio broadcasting. In 1922, only 1 in 400 homes owned radio receivers. By the end of the decade, radio had penetrated 1 in 3 households (McChesney, 1989). The ad-hoc, interregional broadcasts of the early 1920s gave way to the formal creation of powerful radio networks. The National Broadcasting Corporation (NBC) was the first to arrive in 1926. The Columbia Broadcasting System (CBS) in 1928 and the Mutual Broadcasting System in 1934 followed NBC in the radio network business (Keith, 2004). The ability for nationwide transmission of sports soon followed. This advancement helped develop national fan bases for collegiate and professional teams, but it also served as an important diversion for millions of families who were hurting during the nation's financial crisis. According to Betts (1974), "in the depths of the great depression for the first time a nation could listen to on-the-spot reporting of the great sporting events of the day" (p. 272).

As the decade ended, listeners were enjoying more regularly scheduled sports programming. While single-event coverage, like thoroughbred racing matches, was still common, it was apparent that radio had an excellent sports partner with which to grow—baseball.

BASEBALL

On August 5, 1921, KDKA aired the first baseball game on radio when the Pittsburgh Pirates hosted the Philadelphia Phillies in Pittsburgh's Forbes Field. Harold Arlin, the announcer for that game, didn't think much of that initial broadcast. According to Smith (1987), Arlin stated, "Our guys at KDKA didn't even think that baseball would last on radio. I did it sort of as a one-shot project, kind of addendum to the events we'd already done" (p. 7). Needless to say, the marriage between America's pastime and radio has evolved into much more than a one night stand. As Halberstam (1999) explained, "Like a happy partner still madly in love with his spouse, there was still passion for baseball on the radio at the end of the 20th century" (p. 138).

While not the first baseball game transmitted over the air, the 1922 World Series contest between New York's Yankees and Giants represented one of the most important milestones in the coverage of sports on radio. WJZ, only a year old at the time, was scheduled to cover the event. In order to fully capitalize on this unique broadcast, WJZ collaborated with the *New York Tribune* in promoting the event. The *Tribune* also provided legendary writer Grantland Rice as the play-by-play announcer for the series. According to Halberstam (1999), in order to maximize coverage, "no station went on the air while the World Series was being run on WJZ. This assured the broadcast of being available within an 800-mile radius" (p. 140). The estimated listening audience for the contests was 1 million, but it may be impossible to obtain an accurate accounting of the broadcast's reach. Stories spread about crowds of hundreds huddled around loudspeakers all over New York and New Jersey (Halberstam, 1999).

The World Series became an extremely important programming element for early radio, particularly for the developing radio networks. The 1923 World Series attracted even more listeners than the year before with the addition of AT&T's WEAF as a second broadcaster. AT&T fed WEAF's coverage of the Yankees–Giants rematch via their long distance lines to stations as far north as Massachusetts and as far south as Washington, D.C. (Halberstam, 1999). This chain broadcasting model would be replicated in 1927 by NBC to present the first true coast-to-coast sports broadcast—the Stanford–Alabama Rose Bowl (Smith, 2001).

The presentation of the World Series also helped advance the regular coverage of baseball by hometown radio stations. By the mid-1920s, clubs like the Chicago Cubs and Philadelphia Phillies had radio coverage of their games for their fans in their local communities. However, many team owners were unwilling to put their clubs on the airwaves because they believed the free coverage would reduce gate receipts. In fact, in the early 1930s all three New York teams banned radio coverage of their games (Gorman & Calhoun, 1994). How ironic that the city and teams that hosted those early World Series contests that helped showcase baseball on radio were now turning their back on the medium. That resistance soon faded as the teams realized that the broadcasters were starting to make money from baseball broadcasts with the insertion of advertising. The revenue from advertising allowed the broadcasters to offer the teams cash in exchange for the right to carry their club's games. In 1934, Mobil Oil sponsored the Detroit Tigers' games, and in that same year baseball Commissioner Kennesaw Mountain Landis signed a four-year World Series sponsorship deal with the Ford Motor Company for $400,000 (Gorman & Calhoun, 1994). By late 1930s the New York Yankees eliminated their ban on radio and parlayed their rights into $100,000 from three sponsors (McChesney, 1989). As radio audiences have grown over the years for major league baseball, so too have the radio broadcast rights fees. For example, in 2001 the New York Yankees reached a five-year agreement with WCBS-AM worth $48.75 million (Sandomir, 2001).

As a part of broadcast contracts, both in the past and today, the teams often select their own announcers for the games. Just as with their brethren in the newspaper business before them, early radio announcers rose to celebrity status and established powerful, long-lasting bonds with their audience. Graham McNamee was certainly the first star of radio sports announcing. McNamee was hired by WEAF in 1923 and soon put his baritone voice to covering boxing from New York's Polo Grounds. McNamee's fame truly began after his play-by-play announcing of the 1923 World Series. Listeners enjoyed not only his vivid description of the action, but his filling of the significant dead space between pitches with colorful discussion of the athlete's movements and the reactions of spectators. Smith (1987) quoted famous sportswriter Haywood Broun, who said of McNamee, "A machine amounts to nothing unless a man can ride. Graham McNamee has been able to take a new medium of expression and through it transmit himself—to give it vividly a sense of movement and of feeling. Of such is the kingdom of art" (p. 12).

McNamee's work during the 1925 World Series so moved his audience that WEAF received nearly 50,000 letters of appreciation.

The strong relationship between baseball radio announcers and the fans has not diminished in the years since McNamee's era. In fact, in the small world of baseball broadcasting, the tradition of connecting with the listener was passed down from generation to generation. Walter "Red" Barber grew up idolizing Graham McNamee and then had the honor of broadcasting the first World Series that McNamee didn't work since he started in 1923 (Halberstam, 1999). He went on to have a 38-year career announcing games for the Cincinnati Reds, Brooklyn Dodgers, and New York Yankees. Barber teamed with the "Voice of the Yankees," and fellow southerner, Mel Allen for 13 years as these radio giants brought the sounds of Yankee stadium to life for millions of fans. In 1979, Barber and Allen were the first recipients of the Ford C. Frick Award, presented by the National Baseball Hall of Fame (Halberstam, 1999). Ernie Harwell filled in for an ailing Red Barber in the Brooklyn Dodgers announcers' booth in 1948, and it took 54 years to get him out from behind the microphone. Harwell spent 43 of those years announcing Detroit Tigers' games and, according to Noden (1990), "For millions of fans, Harwell is Tiger baseball" (p. 19). Vin Scully replaced Harwell as the announcer of the Brooklyn Dodgers in 1950 and went on to have the longest consecutive service of any current major league broadcaster for one team. Rushin (2002) stated, "He (Scully) could make Ray Charles see. His broadcasts are a series of deft descriptions, apt allusions and joyful noises, seamlessly strung together like charms on a charm bracelet" (p. 17).

NEW COMPETITION

When the technological changes of the 1940s and '50s brought television into American homes, radio held its own with the help of baseball. According to Rader (2004), "when the number of local AM radio stations doubled between 1945 and 1950, the quantity of big-league games aired on radio ballooned astronomically" (p. 124). An example of this growth was the Mutual Broadcasting "Game of the Day," which was carried by nearly 500 radio stations nationwide. Early television coverage of sports was limited by the cumbersome nature of equipment and the inability to respond easily to the action of sports. In fact, the two most popular sports on television in the 1950s were professional wrestling and roller derby. McChesney (1989) explained that these sports "were ideally suited to low-budget television: a single camera could focus on one or two people at a time. Both sports consisted of staged violence" (p. 60).

However, by the early 1960s television coverage of sports began to explode. McChesney (1989) stated that many factors contributed to the rise of sports on television at the time. First, television had penetrated a large majority of American homes. Second, the technology improved significantly. Third, the passage of the Sports Broadcasting Act of 1961 allowed professional sports franchises to negotiate as a single unit for the broadcast coverage of their sports. And finally, advertisers were more willing to support this new medium and its coverage of sports. An excellent example of television's rapid expansion is exemplified in the case of the National Football League. After receiving limited coverage in the late 1950s and early 1960s, the NFL became America's leading spectator sport in about a decade with the help of television.

By the 1970s the radio industry had changed as well. FM radio was beginning to take audience away from the older AM band. The higher fidelity signal offered by FM led to the continued growth of music-formatted radio stations. Ultimately this meant that sports coverage, dominated by talk, was primarily limited to an older and less popular platform. According to Eastman and Ferguson (2002), "By the late 1970s, radio listeners, especially younger listeners, perceived FM stations as superior, as a part of their new generation" (p. 396). Fortunately, many fans had developed strong emotional ties to their sports teams by listening to "old fashioned" AM radio, so sports on radio remained. In fact, the technological limitations of the AM band forced radio executives to think creatively for ways to build listenership. Jeff Smulyan was one of those creative thinkers, and he just happened to be a huge baseball fan.

ALL-SPORTS RADIO

In 1987, Indianapolis-based Emmis Broadcasting acquired New York's WHN for around $26 million (Jeffery, 1992). Jeff Smulyan, the chairman of Emmis, decided to make a change from the station's existing country format—a big change. The station's call letters were changed to WFAN and with that Emmis brought 24-hour, all-sports radio to the Big Apple.

WFAN was not, however, the first all-sports station in the United States. That distinction goes to KMVP in Denver, which lasted only two years (Gorman & Calhoun, 1994). The introduction of WFAN was a risk for Smulyan, and not everyone was sure he knew what he was doing. "All my friends in the industry thought I was an idiot. People thought it was too narrow—that nobody would listen to sports all day" (Ghosh, 1999, p. 55). WFAN's original format included former ABC Sports personality Jim Lampley as a morning host, sports updates every 15 minutes, live coverage of sports press conferences, and tons of calls from listeners. In fact, John Chanin, WFAN's first programming director, thought early on that the station included too many calls and moved to limit the calls to 12 minutes per hour (Bishop, 1987).

Jeff Smulyan expanded his sports holdings in 1989 when he became the majority shareholder of the Seattle Mariners, a post he held for 3 years. Meanwhile, WFAN showed steady improvement in the Arbitron ratings in the first few years of its existence. In addition, more and more advertisers were supporting this new experiment. Sponsors were attracted to the loyal nature of the all-sports audience and the fact that a majority of listeners represented the ever-elusive male demographic. Not only is the ability to reach men an attractant to advertisers, but also the typical audience member is quite affluent. According to a Radio Advertising Bureau report, about 26% of sports radio listeners have a household income above $50,000. This compares to the 19.6% of all adult households with an income in that range (Radio Advertising Bureau, 2003). Ron Barr, the founder of the syndicated sports program *SportsByLine USA*, explained the attraction of sports programming on radio by stating, "We can relate to sports because sports is a reflection of life itself. We all compete every day; sports is that release" (Brown, 1998, p. 50).

In five short years the station was so successful that Emmis Broadcasting was able to nearly triple its original investment by selling the station to Infinity Broadcasting for $70 million—the richest deal for an AM radio station in history at the time (Jeffery, 1992). By 1996, WFAN had risen to become the nation's top-billing radio station with gross revenues exceeding $45 million ("WFAN," 1997). In 1999, the station was estimated to be worth $300 million (Ghosh, 1999).

But WFAN contributed much more to sports radio than increased advertising dollars. Hundreds of new all-sports stations popped up all across the country, rising to over 429 by 2003 (*Radio Marketing Guide*, 2003). The format was also credited with reviving a quickly declining AM band. Stark (1994) cited a Banner Radio study that concluded, "The decline in AM listening, which had occurred steadily from 1970 on, ended in the late '80s . . . All-sports radio was a major factor in halting AM's erosion" (p. 123). On the heels of WFAN's success came the creation of sports radio networks supplying talk and play-by-play for hundreds of stations all across the United States. In 1992, ESPN rolled out ESPN Radio, which provided 170 affiliates with commentary during drive time ("ESPN Radio," 2004). Today, ESPN Radio provides some level of talk and play-by-play coverage for more than 700 affiliates including exclusive national broadcast radio rights to Major League Baseball, the World Series, the college football Bowl Championship Series, and the WNBA ("ESPN Radio," 2004). The Sporting News Radio boasts over 425 affiliates reaching around 13 million listeners per day ("The Sporting News Radio," 2004). Formerly known as "One on One Sports," The Sporting News Radio benefits from its connection to the nation's oldest sports publication—*The Sporting News*. Writers and columnists from the print publication regularly contribute to the radio programming, therefore providing highly credible and informed guests.

NONTRADITIONAL RADIO COVERAGE

Radio still plays an important role in the coverage of sports in the twenty-first century. While one will still find radio covering the sports that the medium itself grew up with (professional baseball, football, and basketball, high school and collegiate sports, etc.), one will also find it in some fairly new venues. Starting in 1970, the Motor Racing Network (MRN) began its coverage of NASCAR. Many credit the creation and growth of this radio coverage with assisting the astounding growth of the Winston/Nextel Cup series. Today, MRN provides coverage for about 80 racing events, including the NASCAR Busch Series, Grand National Division, and NASCAR Craftsman Truck Series, for nearly 650 stations ("MRN Radio," 2004).

Westwood One Radio Network continues to supply a wide variety of sports programming to its affiliates, including coverage of golf. Since 1981 the Infinity-managed network has enjoyed the rights to United States Golf Association events, which include the U.S. Open, U.S. Women's and Senior Open, U.S. Amateur, and U.S. Women's Amateur (Torpey-Kemph, 2001). Sports are also finding their way within the programming of satellite radio providers. In 2003, Sirius Satellite Radio signed an agreement to distribute the regular season and postseason games for the National Basketball Association ("Sirius Provides Complete Coverage," 2003). The following year Sirius inked a seven-year pact with the NFL to become its official satellite radio partner ("Sirius and National Football League," 2004). XM Satellite Radio offers coverage of Major League Baseball through its partner ESPN Radio, and they created NASCAR Radio, the first 24-hour resource devoted to America's most popular spectator sport ("XM Satellite Radio," 2004).

RESEARCH

While the coverage of sports has made a tremendous impact in our society, very little scholarly research has been published with this topic as its focus. It appears that researchers, like many sports fans, have been captivated by the medium of television. A rich literature base is available examining that combination, but articles exploring radio and sports are primarily limited to the critical analyses of sports talk radio.

Haag (1996) examined the programming of New York's WFAN while acknowledging the importance of sports in her life and her interest in sports talk radio. In general, Haag describes sports talk radio as an important democratizing element in today's detached information age. She states, "sports talk demonstrates an older function of communication, that of concretizing social rather than economic communities" (p. 466). While Haag admits that sports talk radio is primarily "narrowcast" to a White male demographic, she admires its ethic of fairness and the bolstering of regional allegiances. "It is prefeminist, to be sure, yet rooted in a good-humored playfulness toward women...based on a liking for people and a fondness for a listening audience who became a community through sports" (p. 462). According to Haag, sports talk radio represents a rarity in today's public discourse—passionate expression checked by an expectation of civility.

Goldberg (1998) disagreed significantly with Haag's view of sports talk radio as a community-building enterprise. Indeed, Goldberg stated that sports talk radio programs are "...one more indication of democracy's demise than of its regeneration" (p. 212). He viewed these programs as building uniformity in opinion rather than fostering the expression of diverse viewpoints of which democracies boast. "Supporting one's team has taken the place of what it was like supporting one's country, right or wrong. Sports talk radio is the propaganda machine of the new fan-aticism" (Goldberg, p. 216). Rather than encouraging a variety of viewpoints and emphasizing civility, as Haag suggested, Goldberg saw sports talk radio as sustaining "the licensed arrogance of self-opinionated expression where anything goes as long as one is heard to say it forcefully and angrily enough" (p. 217). In addition, Goldberg believes that sports talk radio's stance of racial neutrality (i.e., sport-related discourse should be colorblind) ignores historical, political, and moral reality.

Mariscal (1999), Tremblay and Tremblay (2001), and Nylund (2004) all examined the work of one of talk radio's most popular personalities—Jim Rome. The flamboyant host of "The Jungle" gained popularity while working at XTRA in San Diego and is now syndicated nationwide through the Premiere Radio Networks. Mariscal described Rome as liberal early in his career in comparison to his talk and sports talk colleagues: "Rome urged his listeners to be critical of ownership, to understand the right to collective bargaining and to support union politics" (p. 112). Moreover, according to Mariscal, Rome was very supportive of African-American athletes, callers, and fellow sportscasters. But Mariscal accused Rome of being selective in his rebuking of racially insensitive comments, particularly after his program was syndicated. This is evident, according to Mariscal, in reviewing Rome's comments about Chicanos and Latinos, groups that "have been the easiest targets for the racial projects that constitute contemporary U.S. society" (p. 114). Mariscal highlighted Rome's disdain for soccer, the most popular sport in Latin America, by referencing quotations from his program in which he described the sport as "un-American." According to Mariscal, "Rome's admirable stance against racism directed at African Americans is diminished by his willingness to recycle stereotypes about Latinos, a practice that in the end does damage to all poor communities and people of color" (p. 116).

Tremblay and Tremblay (2001) viewed the *Jim Rome Show*'s popularity as a reflection of its ability to engage male listeners in discussions that reinforce their masculinity. The authors believed this serves an important role in today's society, where "there is a lack of clear role models for men to emulate" (p. 273). Tremblay and Tremblay refered to this as a "speech community" (p. 271) and they posited that *The Jim Rome Show* has replaced the sports bar or corner pub for many men as a place where they can reaffirm their sense of manhood. The researchers observed that the unique structure of the program, where Rome either approves ("rack it") or disapproves ("get run") of caller's ("clones") comments ("takes"), serves as a unique, "unifying force for the enactment of male camaraderie" (p. 279). More specifically, the *Jim Rome Show* "...has become a substitution for the real physical experience formerly acquired in the tangible arenas—the wilderness, the playing and battlefields—for testing manhood and achieving masculinity" (p. 287).

Nylund (2004) conducted a textual and audience analysis of the *Jim Rome Show* with a focus on its presentation of traditional masculine themes and its coverage of homosexuality in sports. In analyzing 390 hours of programming and interviewing 18 Rome fans in sports bars, Nylund came to view this program as a complex example of male-centered speech. On one hand, the program appears to be a classic example of hypermasculine discourse that "contains themes of misogyny, violence, and heterosexual dominance including themes that reinforce sexism and lesbian baiting" (Nylund, p. 145). However, Nylund identified several examples of Rome taking a public stand against homophobia in sports. In fact, several of the Nylund's interview participants praised Rome for this pronouncement. While Nylund identified Rome's unwillingness to put homophobia into its proper historical, social, or political context, he praised him for bucking traditional hegemonic masculinity and "potentially spurring a rethinking of masculinity and sports" (p. 154).

Ferguson (1983) and Reaser (2003) presented examinations of the linguistic characteristics of sports announcing talk (SAT). Both studies relied on the concept of *register*, the identifying characteristics of language structure and use that distinguish different types of communication from one another. Both studies intended to examine the language of sportscasting, with Ferguson selecting a qualitative assessment whereas Reaser implemented a quantitative inquiry.

Ferguson (1983) first attempted to identify the register, thereby labeling the unique, "situational or functional features that seem to characterize" (p. 155) sportscasting. He settled on a three-step approximation that described SAT as

1. the oral reporting of an activity, including background information and interpretation.
2. a monolog or dialog directed at an unseen, unknown, and heterogeneous mass audience who choose to listen and provide no feedback to the speakers.
3. a variety of discourse that varies in level of arousal or excitement.

From there Ferguson carefully identified specific syntactic techniques used during coverage of baseball and football games. These techniques included simplification ("Boone in close at third"), inversions ("On deck is Jim Hill"), result expressions ("Barry throws to first for the out"), heavy modifiers ("The tall Texan Van Poppel is on the mound today"), tense usage ("There is a penalty on the play and they're bringing this one back") and routines (the term *count* is used only one way in baseball coverage).

Reaser (2003) utilized a quantitative content analysis technique to investigate SAT. More specifically, Reaser examined radio and television coverage of the same college basketball game to determine if the SAT differed enough to qualify them as separate subregisters. He transcribed the first 10 minutes and 17 seconds of a North Carolina State basketball game covered by both local radio and television. Reaser then coded every recognizable utterance into four of the feature categories identified previously by Ferguson. His findings showed that radio broadcasts contained 20% more utterances than television, with a much larger percentage of them devoted to action description. Television coverage, on the other hand, provided much more discussion of strategy, player backgrounds, and evaluation of performance and let the pictures describe more of the action. Reaser (2003) concluded that quantitative evaluation of registers is a useful complement to qualitative assessment because of its ability to "capture the diversity that exists within the register" (p. 318).

Zhang, Pease, and Smith (1998) explored the economic importance of radio sports coverage in their examination of the relationship between broadcasting and attendance as sporting events. As mentioned earlier, many baseball owners in the 1920s opposed radio coverage of their games for fear that it would harm gate receipts. Zhang et al. (1998) set out to test this theory by surveying attendees of minor league hockey about their exposure to various media presentations of this hockey franchise and their current and future attendance at the arena. In general, they concluded that media coverage of minor league hockey was positively related to game attendance. Radio coverage of the game was positively related to anticipated attendance the following season, but not strongly related to current attendance. The researchers determined that media coverage of minor league hockey explained a total of 6 to 11% of attendance variance and concluded that radio broadcasts were probably most influential in building team loyalty.

Given the broad appeal of sports on radio, it is surprising to see that the research literature on this topic is somewhat limited. Moreover, nearly all of the research cited here is published in nonmedia-related journals. It appears that media scholars are either not interested in exploring the topic of sports and radio, they find that communication journals are unreceptive to the subject, or both.

CONCLUSION

The rich tradition of sports coverage on radio lives on today and deserves increased attention from media scholars. The impact of new technologies, like satellite radio and enhanced cell phones, on sports coverage would be particularly relevant in our present digital revolution. Just as we have witnessed the movement of sports programming from broadcast television to cable television, might radio listeners be forced to pay a subscription fee to listen to their favorite team over the airwaves? The social, economic, and public policy implications of this type of transition could be significant.

While many authors have commented on the personal and emotional bonds established between radio listeners and play-by-play announcers, no formal research has investigated the essential elements of this relationship or the needs that this material satisfies for audience members. For example, no scholarly research exists examining the bonds between today's young sports fans and the sports announcers on radio. Are television announcers now considered the voice of the team for this new generation? Additionally, exploring the long tradition of high school sports coverage in rural America could expand the concept of community building beyond the domain of White male sports talk listeners.

Sports talk radio calls out for further investigation, but scholars must reach beyond Jim Rome as a subject for analysis. Are other popular commentators promoting hypermasculinity, or are they challenging the sports-bar ethic? What rhetorical devices are these personalities implementing that help them build such loyal followings?

Certainly radio has played an important role in our nation's love affair with sports. There is evidence to indicate that this symbiotic relationship will continue as radio reshapes itself through the advancement of alternative delivery methods. An audio-only presentation of sports is more simplistic than video, easily archived in digital form and completely portable. Combine these characteristics with skilled announcers, loyal fans and the brain's ability to paint unrivaled images and one has a formula for cost effective programming that will continue for the foreseeable future.

REFERENCES

Betts, J. R. (1974). *America's sporting heritage: 1850–1950*. Reading, MA: Addison-Wesley.

Bishop, M. (1987, July 27). Sports around the clock. *Sports Illustrated, 67*, 91.

Brown, S. (1998, July 20). Sports radio: It pays to play. *Broadcasting & Cable, 128*, 50.

Eastman, S. T., & Ferguson, D. A. (2002). *Broadcast/cable/web programming: Strategies and practices*. Belmont, CA: Wadsworth/Thomson Learning.

ESPN Radio (2004). Retrieved May 24, 2004, from http://espnradio.espn.go.com/espnradio/story?storyId= 1457975

Ferguson, C. A. (1983). Sports announcer talk: Syntactic aspects of register variation. *Language in Society, 12*(2), 153–172.

Ghosh, C. (1999, February 22). A guy thing: Radio sports talk shows. *Forbes, 163*, 55.

Goldberg, D. T. (1998). Call and response: Sports, talk radio and the death of democracy. *Journal of Sport and Social Issues, 22*(2), 212–223.

Gorman, J., & Calhoun, K. (1994). *The name of the game: The business of sports*. New York, NY: Wiley.

Gross, L. S. (2003). *Telecommunications: Radio, television and movies in the digital age* (8th ed.). New York: McGraw Hill.

Haag, P. (1996). The 50,000-watt sports bar: Talk radio and the ethic of the fan. *The South Atlantic Quarterly, 9*(2), 453–470.

Halberstam, D. J. (1999). *Sports on New York radio: A play-by-play history*. Lincolnwood, IL: Masters Press.

Jeffery, D. (1992, January 4). Infinity sporting $70 mil for WFAN-AM purchase. *Billboard, 104*, 59.

Keith, M. (2004). The radio station (6th ed.). Burlington, MA: Elsevier/Focal Press.

Mariscal, J. (1999). Chicanos and latinos in the jungle of sports talk radio. *Journal of Sport and Social Issues, 23*(1), 111–117.

McChesney, R. W. (1989). Media made sport: A history of sports coverage in the United States. In L. Wenner (Ed.), *Media, sports, and society* (pp. 49–69). Newbury Park, CA: Sage Publications.

MRN Radio (2004). Retrieved May 24, 2004, from http://dbserver.iscmotorsports.com/MRNRadio/index. cfm

Noden, M. (1990, December 31). Bo and Ernie. *Sports Illustrated, 73*, 19.

Nylund, D. (2004). When in Rome: Heterosexism, homophobia and sports talk radio. *Journal of Sport and Social Issues, 28*(2), 136–168.

Rader, B. (1983). *American sports.* Englewood Cliffs, NJ: Prentice-Hall.

Rader, B. (2004). *American sports: From the age of folk games to the age of televised sports* (5th ed.). Upper Saddle River, NJ: Prentice Hall.

Radio Advertising Bureau. (2003). All sports format profile. Retrieved May 24, 2004, from http://www.rab.com/rab/saleslink/secure /research/PET/formats/ALL_SPORTS.PDF

Radio Marketing Guide and Fact Book for Advertisers. (2003). New York: Radio Advertising Bureau.

Reaser, J. (2003). A quantitative approach to (sub)registers: The case of sports announcer talk. *Discourse Studies, 5*(3), 303–321.

Rushin, S. (2002, August 19). The most artful Dodger. *Sports Illustrated, 97*, 17.

Sandomir, R. (2001, December 28). WCBS wins the rights to Yanks on the radio. *The New York Times,* p. 3, S5.

Sirius and National Football League execute definitive multi-year broadcast and marketing agreement. (2004, February 4). *PR Newswire.* Retrieved May 24, 2004, from http://www.prnewswire.com

Sirius provides complete coverage of NBA playoffs 2003. (2003, April 21). *PR Newswire.* Retrieved May 24, 2004, from http://www.prnewswire.com

Smith, C. (1987). *Voices of the game: The first full-scale overview of baseball broadcasting, 1921 to the present.* South Bend, IN: Diamond Communications.

Smith, R. A. (2001). *Play by play: Radio, television, and big-time college sport.* Baltimore, MD: Johns Hopkins University Press.

Stark, P. (1994, August 27). All-sports gets credit for AM's revival. *Billboard, 106*, 123.

Tankel, J. D., & Williams, W. (1993). Resource dependence: Radio economics and the shift from AM to FM. In A. Alexander, J. Owers, & R. Carveth (Eds.), *Media economics: Theory and practice* (pp. 157–158). Hillsdale, NJ: Lawrence Erlbaum Associates.

The Sporting News Radio (2004). Retrieved May 24, 2004, from http://radio.sportingnews.com/profile/

Torpey-Kemph, A. (2001, February 19). Westwood tees up USGA broadcast rights. *Mediaweek,* 28.

Tremblay, S., & Tremblay, W. (2001). Mediated masculinity at the millennium: The Jim Rome show as a male bonding speech community. *Journal of Radio Studies, 8*(2), 271–291.

WFAN(AM) New York was ranked the nation's top-billing radio station for 1996. (1997, February 3). *Broadcasting & Cable, 127*, 97.

XM Satellite Radio (2004). Retrieved May 24, 2004, from http://www.xmradio.com/programming/neighborhood.jsp?hood=sports

Zhang, J. J., Pease, D. G., & Smith, D. W. (1998). Relationship between broadcasting media and minor-league hockey game attendance. *Journal of Sport Management, 12*, 103–122.

8

Broadcast Television and the Game of Packaging Sports

David B. Sullivan
University of San Diego

Coverage of sports has enjoyed a privileged place among types of television programming since the inception of broadcast TV in the United States. The unpredictable and inherently conflict-oriented nature of sports contests provides television with immediate, unscripted dramatic events—content that is perfectly suited to the medium and to broadcasting's commercial interests. In this sense, broadcast sport is the original reality television programming. Few other broadcast genres amplify real-world events while bringing audiences so intimately close to live action, and none does so with the regularity of televised sports. These characteristics account, in part, for sports' enduring popularity among viewers and broadcasters, and they perhaps have contributed to attracting the interest of academics of various stripes. Broadcast television sports have generated an extensive body of scholarly attention that is differentiated widely by discipline, method, and theoretical focus.

Taken collectively, this scholarship has cataloged the complex interrelationships among the broadcast industry, corporate sponsors, audiences, athletes, leagues, and teams that underlie television coverage, and it provides a context for assessing the significance of sports coverage. This scholarship, varied as it is, addresses the general issue of whether television coverage transforms sports, audience experiences with sports, and cultural values associated with sports. This chapter focuses on a central quality of sports coverage's potential as an agent of change—the role of broadcast TV, especially the networks, in packaging the conflict generated by sports contests as entertainment. This role is grounded in the symbiotic and mutually amplifying relationship between the sports and broadcasting industries, and so this chapter begins with a summary of the coevolution of this relationship and its consequences for coverage.

SPORTS AND BROADCAST TV INDUSTRY SYMBIOSIS AND MUTUAL AMPLIFICATION

The networks remain dominant in television sports despite a fragmented, highly competitive media environment because they anchor the interdependencies among broadcasters, sports organizations, and corporate sponsors. Television money—most of it from broadcast sources—pays the bills in major pro sports, the Olympics, and Division I college sports, and, in return, the networks and broadcast stations cover sports contests to fill their programming schedules, promote other entertainment fare, garner the big events that differentiate themselves from competing networks and cable channels, and attract audiences with the right demographic appeal to advertisers.

The Rise of the Professional Model

Each surge in the coverage of sport has occurred during a period when media have "sharply increased their penetration into the nooks and crannies of American social life" (McChesney, 1989, p. 49). The surge in television coverage began in 1960, when a majority of U.S. households had television sets and economic trends created permanent interdependencies between the sports and broadcast TV industries (for more see Bryant and Holt, chap. 2, this volume). A decade before, broadcast TV coverage of sports had emerged from its experimental stage and had maintained a regular presence on prime-time network schedules, focusing on boxing and wrestling. In the 1960s, however, major team sports adopted a professional business model and began to package themselves for television to compete more successfully against other forms of entertainment, including TV entertainment (Parente, 1977; Rader, 1984).

Network television came to depend on sports to fill programming schedules, particularly on weekends, and to provide advertisers access to a highly desired audience: 18- to 49-year-old men. The networks used the opportunities sports programs provided to promote their prime-time fare, and, by the end of the decade, sports accounted for an increasingly larger percentage of the networks' advertising revenues (Guttmann, 1986). The playing field had become a natural extension of the marketplace, and sports events came to be staged "before a great blinking billboard of commercials" (Johnson, 1971, p. 62).

The deals the networks struck with the pro leagues revolutionized both the sports industry and broadcast television. In 1960, for example, Gillette's $8.5 million sponsorship allowed ABC to bid on major sports, and ABC's emergence as a network sports competitor changed the business of sports TV (Rader, 1984). ABC used Gillette's money to acquire the Olympics, and its coverage of the Games was a major factor in the network's climb from third to first in prime-time ratings (Rader, 1984). The National Football League was the first to exploit a convergence of production technology, market opportunities, and antitrust exemption law (McChesney, 1989; Rader, 1984). Major League Baseball and other major team sports soon followed the NFL, coming to rely on network TV and local broadcast rights fees for their own financial success.

The professional model of athletics established by the major pro sports leagues and fueled by TV money was adopted by amateur leagues and events, leading to rules changes and TV-friendly event scheduling that would build excitement for TV audiences (Rader, 1984). After the 1984 *Board of Regents of University of Oklahoma v.*

NCAA Supreme Court case recognized the right of member institutions and leagues to negotiate their own TV contracts, most of the individual universities with Division I football and basketball programs, the major Division I leagues, and the NCAA itself benefited from greatly enhanced broadcast TV rights fees (Guttmann, 1988), which stand at about $7 billion from the networks for football and basketball alone (Schaaf, 2004). TV money has reshaped conferences. Several schools, including the University of Texas, joined the Big 12 primarily because ABC pays the conference $17 million annually. Miami, Virginia Tech, and Boston College have fled the Big East for the Atlantic Coast Conference, now a football superconference made desirable because of broadcast TV money (Schaaf, 2004).

Copromotion and Cross-Ownership

NBC's $42 million bid for AFL broadcast rights in 1965 presaged the most important aspect of network coverage in the 1970s: the emergence of the television networks as copromoters of major sports leagues and sports events. In this role, the networks emphasize sports coverage as entertainment programming that expands their market reach. Sports programming hours increased from 787 to 1,356 during the decade (McChesney, 1989), and televised sports appeared regularly in prime time, beginning in 1970 with ABC's *Monday Night Football* (*MNF*). Sport is well suited to prime time because it "embodies almost every aspect of popular entertainment" (Altheide & Snow, 1978, p. 191). *MNF* was foremost about show business and only secondarily about sports (Rader, 1984). *MNF* reached a wider audience than is the case for most regularly televised sports events, and its largely upscale audience included young families with buying power (Gorman & Calhoun, 1994). *MNF* was not merely a boon to sports bars: It drew female viewership of the NFL, and it became an important family ritual (Rader, 1984).

Industry symbiosis also underlies media and sports cross-ownership, which has contributed to wide discrepancies in coverage for teams. CBS' controlling ownership of the New York Yankees might have been a financial and competitive failure in 1964 (Johnson, 1971), but media ownership of sports franchises is commonplace today. Team owners with ties to television include or have included Jack Kent Cooke (NBA and NFL franchises), Ted Turner (the NBA and MLB Atlanta franchises), John Rigas (the NHL's Buffalo franchise), and Miami-area broadcaster Wayne Huizenga (owner of Florida teams in the NFL, NHL, and MLB). More recently, major media corporations have invested heavily in sports properties and directly related media holdings: the Tribune Company owns baseball's Cubs and superstation WGN-TV; Walt Disney Co. owns ABC, ESPN, cable channels, and the NHL's Anaheim Mighty Ducks and holds purchasing control of Anaheim's MLB team; News Corp. owns the Fox network, cable channels, and the Los Angeles Dodgers and has a stake in both the NBA's Knicks and NHL's Rangers; and cable giant Time Warner bought the Atlanta teams from Turner, along with his cable stations (Strauss, 1998; Quirk & Fort, 1999).

The Big-Event Model

If it were not for the huge rights fees that leagues and event owners secure from competitive bidding, sports event coverage would be enormously profitable for the networks. Instead, the networks have either struggled to break even or have lost money (Eastman & Meyer, 1989; "Rethinking the Model," 2003). Rights fees account for between 75% and 80% of the networks' total cost of producing sports (Eastman & Meyer, 1989; Gorman & Calhoun, 1994), with collective broadcast rights fees having escalated dramatically over 20 years—$1.5 billion in 1988 (Eastman & Meyer, 1989), $1.7 billion in 1994 (Strauss, 1998), and $5.8 billion in 2004, which is as much as the networks spend on prime-time scripted programming ("Rethinking the Model," 2003). As a result, the networks have reduced their coverage of regular-season contests in the major sports while abiding by big-event theory. A network pays the big rights fees to secure one or more of the marquee sports events that routinely place among the year's most highly rated programs to generate massive advertising revenues, distinguish itself from the other networks, and raise its status above that of cable competitors in regular-season coverage (Gorman & Calhoun, 1994). CBS, for example, paid $3.5 billion for NFL, MLB, NCAA, and Winter Olympics telecast rights and replicated ABC's feat of moving from third to first in prime-time ratings in the 1991–1992 season.

NBC has profited by adopting a big-event strategy for its Olympics coverage. The network paid the International Olympic Committee $555 million for U.S. rights to the 2002 Winter Olympics, but it sold $720 million in ads and netted $75 million (Barney, Wenn, & Martyn, 2002; Schaaf, 2004). Similarly, NBC made $50 million and $60 million, respectively, in profits on its coverage of the 1996 and 2000 Summer Olympics, and it anticipated similar earnings from coverage of the 2004 Games in Athens ("In U-Turn," 2003).

The Sports Pseudoevent

Industry symbiosis may find its ultimate expression in the sports media event, or what Boorstin (1964) termed the pseudoevent. The presence of network TV, as co-promoter, *creates* sports events. Although examples include so-called trash sports and celebrity events, which began in 1973 with ABC's *Super Sports* (Eitzen & Sage, 1978), big events themselves are earlier and more conspicuous representatives of this genre. The Super Bowl, conceived as a media event in 1967, would not have occurred if not for the promise of network TV exposure (Izenberg, 1968; Johnson, 1971) and has remained true to its pseudoevent roots.

Since the first Super Bowl, the networks have increasingly viewed the organizations they cover as marketing partners (Strauss, 1998), and both the networks and sports leagues have grown savvy in how they manage the message. The NFL, for example, has its own marketing company, its own video and film production company, and its own film archives. Leagues and the networks create a slew of joint promotional opportunities: exhibition and preseason games, draft day, spring training camps, awards ceremonies, and the like are part of daily, year-round sports coverage (Schaaf, 2004). The program-length sports commercial is a logical next step, as has already been demonstrated on cable with *Nike Training Camp*, the first six episodes of which featured tips from college coaches whose employers had inked Nike endorsement deals ("Professional College Sports," 2003).

Industry Symbiosis as a Double-Edged Sword

Industry symbiosis can have either positive or negative effects for each industry's major players. In general, leagues, team owners, and local stations capture most of the profits from TV contracts. In exchange for rights fees, the networks gain credibility as the copromoter of major sports, secure "must-buy" programming for advertisers, and limit competitors' access to big sports events. Arguments in favor of industry symbiosis include other potentially positive outcomes. Network money, for example, may have improved the quality of play in major sports. Pete Rozelle asserted that the network TV deals he made in the 1960s increased the average player pay to make the NFL competitive with any potential white-collar job employer of college graduates (Johnson, 1971). It could also be argued that the 1960s' revolution in sports broadcasting engendered fan loyalty, or what Quirk and Fort (1999) called *fan equity*. Compared to the limited sports lineup available in the 1950s, more extensive television coverage gave fans choices (Klatell & Marcus, 1988). The desire to recoup the money spent on rights fees and production, especially for NFL and Olympics coverage, motivated the networks to develop video and audio technologies to nuance their coverage in ways that maintain viewer attention.

Network affiliate stations, however, are not always satisfied by the network's copromotional role in broadcast sports. Affiliates in many markets often can make more money by airing movies on weekend afternoons than broadcasting the networks' sports feeds; the alternative, usually syndicated programming, achieves higher ratings on average and the affiliate does not have to yield most of each hour's advertising minutes to the networks (Klatell & Marcus, 1988). Further, affiliates claim that the networks poison their relationship by asking the locals to help pay sports rights fees. CBS has sought $15 million in such reverse compensation from its affiliate stations; NBC has made a similar request of its affiliates to offset Olympics rights fees; and both Fox and ABC have used reverse compensation to help cover NFL costs ("Sports on the Rocks," 2003).

Industry symbiosis has had other tangible adverse affects. Local stations enter into copromotional relationships with pro sports franchises, sometimes with mixed results—mostly for the franchises. Broadcast rights fees have contributed to competitive imbalance in some pro sports leagues, with teams boasting bigger pockets receiving more extensive coverage. Although network revenues are shared equally among league members, big-market teams in all pro sports except the NFL generally earn higher local broadcast incomes than do small-market teams (Quirk & Fort, 1999). A low local TV broadcast rights fee bid can make or break a franchise financially, particularly in small markets (Gorman & Calhoun, 1994).

The Amplification Effect

Broadcast TV coverage has amplified the importance of sports in the United States. Network TV brought the big leagues to the hinterlands, first through exposure, then via new franchises, the number of which doubled in the 1960s (Johnson, 1971). The NFL relied on this exposure to market itself as a national, rather than regional, sport. The escalation in rights fees demonstrates the networks' insistence on retaining their market power, which, combined with the monopoly control of pro sports leagues and player free agency, has generated both new leagues and new events for the networks to cover. The promise of broadcast amplification led to the creation of many more championship events, expanded playoff formats, and entirely new sports.

Each of the major pro sports leagues has grown greatly since the beginning of the television era, and there has been a corresponding tendency for franchises to move to lucrative TV markets (Bellamy, 1989) because network money has driven up franchise prices. Network money has also elevated league earnings and player and coaching salaries (Quirk & Fort, 1999; Shaaf, 1995). At the turn of the twenty-first century, the pro sports industry is the 22nd largest industry in the world (Schaaf, 2004). In 1991, the NFL generated in broadcast revenues two times what it earned in ticket sales, including $783 million from network TV alone (Schaaf, 1995). Five years later, that figure was $1.29 billion. Today, the average NFL *team* makes $73 million in broadcast rights fees (Quirk & Fort, 1999). Similarly, more than one half of MLB's 1990 revenues were from TV broadcast fees; by 1996, local and network TV rights fees for baseball reached $706 million, or $28 million per team—about the average team payroll that year (Quirk & Fort, 1999). The average NBA player salary just prior to free agency in 1975 was $170,000; as of 2002, the NBA's network TV contract alone was $660 million and the average player salary was $4.5 million (Schaaf, 2004). The average major pro sports team athlete made, in salary alone, $41,000 in 1974; that figure was $1.4 million in 2002 (Schaaf, 2004).

Sports Coverage and the Commodification of Athletes

Scholars have noted the potentially negative outcomes of television exposure, arguing, for example, that the spirit of play has eroded while the ethos of work pervades all levels of sports (Rader, 1983) and that television exposure brings star athletes status as celebrities, with a corresponding emphasis placed on covering athletes as personalities (Klatell & Marcus, 1988; Whannel, 2002). Perhaps most significantly, given the commercial goals of both the broadcasting and sports industries, broadcast TV sports coverage appears to be dedicated to "the circulation of commodities (Jhally, 1989, p. 79). The processes of corporate sponsorship, broadcast rights fees, program sponsorship, and cross-ownership have not simply transformed sport, but have transformed a principal commodity that sports sell: individual identity. Athletes themselves try to become a commodity "that they can in turn sell—celebrity" (Jhally, p. 80). TV exposure alters definitions of cultural icons, transforming the star athlete's status from hero to celebrity, such that appearance and personality "become the currency with which fame is purchased" and charisma becomes a marketable commodity that can replace talent (Whannel, 2002, p. 190).

The Intimacy Effect

Broadcast TV exposure amplifies the apparent significance of sports events and the athletes who participate in them. But, at same time, the medium holds an affective bias: Television imitates the interpersonal situation, infusing a sense of intimacy between the viewer and the event being telecast. This bias cuts two ways, heightening the viewer's identification with athletes, teams, and nations, on the one hand, but also fostering a communal feeling among viewers, especially for big events. Perhaps most importantly, television's intimacy reassures viewers even in coverage of unsettling public events.

The regularity of broadcast TV sports confirms for viewers that there is continuity in the events of larger society, thus fostering a sense of reassurance not provided even by news coverage of current events (Stone, 1955). The 1964 Olympics in Tokyo, for example, showed millions of viewers in the United States and around the world that a former enemy had returned "from the ravages of World War II as a full and respected member of the international community" (Barney et al., 2002, p. 81). Unlike other kinds of reality-based programming, televised sport integrates the public and the personal: Team loyalties formed in childhood and continued into adulthood "may serve to remind one . . . that some things have permanence amid the harassing interruptions and discontinuous transitions of daily experience" (Stone, 1955, p. 90). Personal identity for fans is tied at least in part to their identification with teams and performers.

PACKAGING SPORTS AS CONFRONTAINMENT

The social impact of broadcast TV coverage is defined in part by the medium's dual properties of amplification and intimacy; broadcast production, therefore, strives to place sports events within a dramatic framework for audience interpretation. Sports telecasts blend news and entertainment functions, mixing a concern with objective facts and the need to tap into viewers' affective responses to human drama. Like all reality television, sports TV thrives on *confrontainment*, the packaging of confrontation as entertainment. This characteristic underlies both praise and criticism of sports coverage. On the one hand, sports TV takes advantage of the role television plays in viewers' daily lives by presenting "suspense, raw emotion, real anger, unvarnished joy" (Klatell & Marcus, 1988, p. 4), thereby inviting the viewer's vicarious experience. In contrast stand complaints that television dilutes the cultural significance of sports by promoting and presenting sports events primarily as entertaining spectacles (Eitzen & Sage, 1978).

Sports as Entertaining Spectacle

Increases in spectatorship and an expanded market for all forms of entertainment in the 1920s ushered in an era in which fans, not players, "determined the broad contours of American sport" (Rader, 1983, p. 196). Media coverage at the time followed these contours, as did broadcast TV in its early years. Johnson (1971) asserted that broadcast TV exposure in the 1960s transformed national sports (i.e., baseball, football, hockey, and basketball) in at least eight ways, each of them rooted in the sports and media industries' desire to create and sell spectacle. Johnson noted, for example, that the Olympic Games' opening and closing ceremonies became increasingly lavish because of the tremendous growth in TV money over the decade. Mascots, cheerleaders, artificial grass, jumbo scoreboards, stroke play in professional golf, arena music (including theme music for star players), lighting during televised day games, the use of TV replays to arbitrate referees' decisions, the 3-point shot and shot clock in basketball, the branding of athletes' uniforms and equipment, the emergence of the Bowl Championship Series in college, TV timeouts, the NFL's two-minute warning, television-dictated game scheduling, schedule changes in Olympics events for U.S. television—all are examples of sports' willingness to bend to meet TV's demands (Rader, 1984; Guttmann, 1986). More significantly, many sports changed game rules to alter the balance between offense and defense to increase viewer interest (Rader, 1984).

The Transformational Power of Coverage

One might argue that the purpose and means in major team sports, such as football and baseball, are fundamentally the same ever since these games were first commercialized. The difference is that the principal market to exploit has been amplified by television exposure and, indeed, that market is the viewing audience, not in-person attendees. Each game is presented as part of a "total entertainment package, not simply as a contest of skill" (Chandler, 1988, p. 89). Two aspects of broadcast sports' dramatic appeal—its visual intimacy and the importance of commentary in amplifying for the viewer what story is to be gleaned from the events covered—were identified as early as 1939, when baseball, boxing, pro football, pro hockey, college basketball, and track and field had all been on TV. In his *New York Times* review of the first televised boxing match, telecast by W2XBS, Orrin E. Dunlap, Jr., wrote that television projected intimacy into the boxers' performance and that the commentary served to thread the "illustrated" story together (as cited in Johnson, 1971, p. 43).

Although sports, unlike most other forms of entertainment, provides unpredictability and unambiguous resolution to live drama, the networks discovered early on that sports contests could not be covered simply as actualities, with the networks functioning as a mere window on the events. The networks used cameras and narration to transform the signifying material of the live event from sport to entertainment (Gruneau, 1989). The camera lends plot to what is an unpredictable, unscripted story by enhancing the imaginary (Morse, 1983). Commentary contributes to this transformation by identifying and personalizing the contestants as characters and creating a story around their actions on the field of play. Because conflict drives drama, broadcast TV uses camera coverage and commentary as tools to identify, focus on, and interpret key moments of conflict.

The Intimacy of TV Sports Visuals

Sports visuals heighten the viewer's sense that the players are giving their all, sacrificing themselves for team success or national pride, whatever inconsistencies might be occurring off the field, such as salary negotiations, drug-use controversies, or legal battles between cities and franchise owners (Chandler, 1988). Used so routinely, such visual manipulations do not strike viewers as odd or obtrusive, but instead resonate familiarly, as if the camera were a natural extension of the eye.

The huge variety of sports camera shots, the various optical refinements made to provide improved and detailed visuals, and the ubiquitous use of computer graphics and graphic chalkboards convey an insider's point of view. The visual coverage invites the viewer to identify with the performers. The liberal use of instant replay, slow motion, zooms, stop action, reverse angle, hand-held cameras, and mini-cam coverage places the viewer amid the action; blimp shots, split-screen shots, insets, the telestrator, fan shots, unidirectional microphones directed at particular athletes, and computer-generated graphics relating team statistics and athlete profiles place events in greater context for interpreting their significance; submersible and trackside cameras capture the precise execution of the breaststroke and the sprinter's split-second winning finish. Sports program directors use text overlays, sideline interviews, taped interviews, and diverse camera angles in varying order to enhance visual variety.

Such visual devices may grab viewer attention at the expense of realism. TV coverage may restrict the spectator's freedom because the production crew literally calls the shots. In compressing time and space with the zoom lens, stretching time via slow motion, and continually displacing the viewer's perspective, TV coverage obliterates the viewer's appraisal of linear time, gravity, and spatial dimensions in relation to the live event (Morse, 1983). The camera tends to reveal either too little or too much in large-field sports such as football, focusing on individuals while butchering the wide geometry of the game (Oriard, 1981). The use of overhead, wide-angle shots lends only a modicum of realism (Morse, 1983). Viewers, on the other hand, see details the in-attendance spectators never witness (Johnson, 1971), and they benefit from sports' value as social currency; not only are sports events and figures themselves often the topics of interpersonal conversation, but also viewers are exposed to a wide range of issues and themes beyond the confines of sports and competition (Klatell & Marcus, 1988).

Perhaps the most important development in broadcast TV coverage wasn't technological at all but instead was Roone Arledge's realization in the 1960s that producing a sports telecast that attracts sponsors means involving viewers emotionally in the live event (Johnson, 1971). Engaging viewer involvement sometimes entails turning the focus of coverage away from the event and placing it on the audience. Seen this way, coverage is not so much about packaging the event as it is about packaging the viewer. The sports event may be real and public, but the TV experience with the sports contest is a simulated and personal experience.

The real setting of televised sports isn't the playing field or the arena; it's the TV screen. The primary event being covered isn't the contest itself, but its immediacy, thereby eliminating, in a sense, the game itself as referent (Sandvoss, 2003). Arledge and ABC covered sports not as breaking news, as ABC and CBS had done, but as human interest stories, packaging human drama to exploit the medium's bias in favor of the intimate and the personal (Powers, 1984). Following ABC's lead, broadcast coverage makes frequent use of close-ups of the participants' faces, airs interviews of players' family members in the stands, and relates details of players' private lives, encouraging viewers not just to identify with players but to place themselves, perceptually, amid a "circle of friends" at the stadium (Chandler, 1988, p. 44). This level of involvement may be stronger for sports telecasts than for other entertainment programming (Gantz, 1981).

Commentary and Dramatic Framing

As gripping as visuals sometimes are in televised sports, they do not, in themselves, convey the story of an event in a way that promotes audience enjoyment and virtual participation. That role falls to commentary. Johnson (1971) noted that, ironically, the image of televised sports most familiar to the public is the one created by the commentator. In mediating the viewer's experience of the sports event, television first sets up an "anteroom, beside which everything is happening," but then makes this anteroom "the arena, the reaction the event, and the commentators the real agents" (Williams, 1970, p. 522).

In narrating sports events, commentators of both types—play-by-play and color—use objective, judgmental, and historical modes to place contests within whatever context of meaning will strike viewers as lending the event importance (Morris & Nydahl, 1983). Play-by-play commentary emphasizes the objective mode by summarizing the action captured by the cameras. This mode may include attention to aesthetic dimensions of athletic performance, overlapping with the role of color commentary in placing events within contexts of meaning that aid viewer appreciation of, for example, athletic grace, power, technique, and talent. Play-by-play commentary is characterized by linguistic choices that are limited to terms viewers may readily index as relevant (Kuiper, 1996). Play-by-play commentary also references events in the present, underscoring the televised game's immediacy.

Color commentary, often tendered by an ex-athlete whose use of jock jargon demonstrates his or her credibility as game expert, tends to reference historical events and moments just passed to provide a wider context for interpreting the significance of game events. Color commentators, more so than play-by-play announcers, are expected to bridge the gaps in action, particularly between pitches in baseball and between plays in football. According to Chandler (1988), more than half of all commentary in football and baseball consists of description and talk that has nothing to do with the game. Characterized by more frequent use of judgmental and historical modes, color commentators voice presumptions about player motivations, coaching strategies, team goals, and ideals in athletic performance. They draw upon statistical and biographical information to place games and their participants into historical perspective and chart an athlete's progress.

All commentary is intended to serve a second function, that of dramatizing sports events. Commentators seek to maximize viewer attention because they work within the promotional tradition of sports as entertainment (Chandler, 1988; McChesney, 1989; Rader, 1984). Dramatic narration sets the stage, emphasizing the emotional elements of sports. Dramatic narration, for example, pays strict attention to aggressive play, the contestants' apparent enmity, and hard physical contact between players, even in traditionally noncontact sports (Bryant, Comisky, & Zillmann, 1977; Bryant & Zillmann, 1983; Sullivan, 1991). Dramatic commentary amplifies the suspense inherent in sports contests by focusing on conflict, the emotional elements of competition, and player aggression (Sullivan, 1991). Dramatic framing builds a rooting interest in the conflict at hand, generates an enthusiasm for the event that is enjoyable even for the casual viewer (Wenner & Gantz, 1989), and intensifies fans' personal and group identification with athletes, teams, and the in-attendance crowd (Morse, 1985).

Even sports broadcast TV's most memorable moments, which seemingly bypass electronic mediation altogether to bring viewers directly to human triumph and tragedy, are given shape and purpose by the commentators' emotional call of them. As often as not, these moments involve major reversals of fortune or against-all-odds stories, with the commentator punctuating the viewer's emotional connection to the events, as when ABC's Al Michaels exclaimed, "Do you believe in miracles" during the final seconds of Team USA's hockey semifinal victory over the Soviet Union in the 1980 Winter Olympics. In such cases, it is easy for both the commentator and viewer to lose sense of their formal relationship to each other: The commentator and viewer become united in the common bond of fanship.

Alternatively, dramatic narration may tilt in the direction of bathos. In constructing overly drawn, one-dimensional protagonists and antagonists who represent contrasting morals, commentary often reframes sports contests as melodrama. Daddario (1998), for example, pointed out that CBS adopted the narrative form of soap opera in covering women's figure skating at the 1994 Winter Games. The story that emerged was less about athletic competition than about how hubris led to Tonya Harding's downfall while virtue rewarded rival Nancy Kerrigan with a silver medal and $11 million in commercial endorsements (Daddario, 1998).

BROADCAST TV COVERAGE AND VALUES IN SPORTS

Perhaps the most telling aspect of CBS' coverage of the Tonya/Nancy saga was the contrast in values the network drew between the athletes. The network aired interviews with Harding's "two dads" and Kerrigan's legally blind mother (Daddario, 1998). At the heart of both individual and collective identity are values. Sports constitute a symbolic dialogue, functioning as idealized forms of social life "which establish identity with a consensual certainty that in social life itself is not always possible" (Ashworth, 1971, p. 40). The principal values amplified by televised sports are those associated with the nature and purpose of competition, such as hard work, open and accessible opportunity to compete, innovation, co-operation and teamwork, individual freedom and self-determination, self-sacrifice, and an emphasis on result over process (Chandler, 1988; Whannel, 1992). *Contest* implies a testing of what is not certain: which team or athlete is faster, stronger, and better skilled. It implies unfettered, competitive, equal-opportunity activity in which the best performer wins, regardless of social class, race, or any other characteristic not relevant to the athletic pursuit at hand.

Whatever else is happening in the stadium, however, the broadcast cameras focus most of the viewer's attention on winners and on individuals, particularly players who score, or who make the spectacular play, or who simply mug for the cameras (Oriard, 1981). Coverage may obscure the reality of competitive sports, particularly at the highest levels: Playing fields are not always level; victory is sometimes secured by the athlete who best bends the rules, not to the most able or to the best-trained athlete; the star isn't necessarily clean; and very few college standouts ever make a living at sport.

Sports Coverage and Images of Success

The influence of live mediation on concepts of sports suggests that concepts of various kinds of social behavior are rooted in representation rather than the experience of participation (Whannel, 2002). TV images of sports stars present powerful icons of success, income, achievement, and competitiveness. The pro athlete becomes part jock and part business professional, or what Johnson (1971) called the entrepreneur-athlete. Athletic stars today are walking corporations, their white-collar status amplified to global proportions (Brookes, 2002) and standing a world apart from that of blue-collar pro athletes prior to television exposure. Given these images, sports participants at all levels are likely to intensify their efforts to achieve what they see the sports stars achieve (Klatell & Marcus, 1988).

Although the very nature of amateurism in U.S. athletics had changed before the arrival of television (Guttmann, 1988), broadcast TV money became the necessary factor in the professionalization of the NCAA in the 1950s (Sack & Staurowsky, 1998). As colleges and universities compete for star players who can produce winning teams, academic standards have been virtually abandoned at some major athletic programs (Sack & Staurowksy, 1998). Claims to the contrary, research supports the argument that those who watch television sports are more likely to participate in sports (Kubey & Csikszentmihalyi, 1990), but this participation has been characterized by increasing attention to athletics as serious competition, an ethic that affects parents and youth league coaches as much as youth athletes themselves, and which affects amateur athletes at all levels. The nutrition and personal coaching industries have evolved to aid the competitive goals of amateurs. For some critics, sports have become more about commercialism and ego gratification than about sportsmanship and personal development (Gerdy, 2002).

Sports Coverage's Mixed Messages of Inclusion

Broadcast sports TV coverage might provide viewers an informal multicultural education (Klatell & Marcus, 1988): Diversity is represented, often absent a political framing, and coverage of international competitions may foster an appreciation for diverse customs and challenge ethnocentric attitudes. Positive images for non-Whites and women, however, exist for a highly visible few, both on the field and on air, and executive positions in both industries continue to be dominated by White males. Coverage often is politicized or placed within an ethnographic frame (Daddario, 1998; Whannel, 1992). Chinese international Yao Ming, for example, was often featured in 2003–2004 network NBA coverage as a potential superstar, even while commentators made references to the "Ming Dynasty" and to Yao as the Chinese "threat."

Klatell and Marcus (1988) provided a revealing example of such mixed messages: The NBA and NFL coproduce public service announcements to air during network game coverage in which stars speak out against drug and alcohol use and urge kids to stay in school—and yet more and more star draftees don't stay in school, athletes' use of both recreational and performance-enhancing drugs is widespread, and beer companies remain among the foremost sponsors of televised sports. The fact that the networks air such PSAs reveals their own confusion about whether broadcast sports merely reflect or influence cultural values. The PSAs suggest that the networks assume some responsibility to represent the public interest.

Attention as a Sports Coverage Value

Yet, as copromoter of pro leagues and de facto copromoter of high-level amateur sports, broadcast television tends not to take an adversarial approach to lapses in integrity by leagues, teams, and players (Whannel, 1992; Williams, 1987). Viewers do not seem to want sports TV anchors and reporters asking hard questions, and the public has demanded little in the way of news from sports broadcasting (Klatell & Marcus, 1988; Strauss, 1998). Even when network sportscasters do attempt adversarial reporting, the results are often limpid, at best, when compared to some cable sports news programs (Strauss, 1998) and when assessed from normative standards of journalism, such as those advocated by the Society of Professional Journalists. Network coverage of sports is compelled by the bottom line and the networks' copromotional interest in the events at hand, creating a journalistic conflict of interest. Broadcast rights contracts pose a chilling effect on adversarial reporting because the networks tend to avoid offending their marketing partners for fear of losing out the next time the contract comes up to bid (Strauss, 1998).

What matters most is attention, and nothing draws attention better than entertaining pictures that demonstrate a seemingly clear-cut difference between good versus bad, us versus them, truth versus hypocrisy. Broadcast sports news and event coverage take on dimensions of celebrity culture: One cannot always tell the difference between a sports news event and a sports stunt staged for maximum exposure (Williams, 1987). "Good" network sports journalism often consists simply of putting a target on air and hoping that figure will say something foolish, substituting the immediacy of the moment for content, as was the case in Jim Gray's interview with Pete Rose broadcast live and on-field before Game 2 of the 1999 World Series. Gray's conduct was deemed controversial, and hence newsworthy, because Gray put the potential Hall-of-Famer on the spot during what was for some fans an emotional moment: Rose, banned from MLB for betting on baseball, had just stood among some of the sport's greats in being named to an All-Century team promoted by one of NBC's major sponsors.

Sports Coverage as Dramatic Life-World

Television coverage of sports may, at times, provide viewers with an escape from everyday reality and, at other times, mirror biases that do exist both in sports and in society. Being inserted into the sports context, however, highlights the values of the larger society, which may explain, for example, why high-identifying fans found the use of sports–war analogies, common in sportscasts, to be appropriate in sports coverage following the terrorist attacks of September 11, 2001 (End, Kretschmar, Campbell, Mueller, & Dietz-Uhler, 2003). Broadcast TV represents sports as a dramatic life-world (Lipsyte, 1975; Lipsky, 1981), functioning as a form of celebration of the dominant order. Such coverage propagates national norms and society's central value systems (Real, 1975) while minimizing cultural differences (Johnson, 1971); it offers emotional gratification and moral affirmation as compensatory fulfillment for a loss of fair play (Jhally, 1989); and it presents intuitively pleasing images of individual and collective identification that make such social constructions appear to be naturally occurring and inevitable (Lipsky, 1981; Whannel, 1992).

The appeal to audience desires accounts in part for imbalanced coverage in one aspect of this life-world—gender (for more see Duncan, chap. 14, this volume). Many of the values associated with both sports participation and sports spectatorship—such as self-discipline, aggressiveness, strength, and leadership—are deeply ingrained in the culture as masculine traits. In their study of TV sports audiences, Gantz and Wenner (1991) found that these gendered assumptions translated into frequent differences between men and women in ways they "approached, observed, and responded to televised sports" (p. 241). In short, men are more likely than women to behave like fans: They pay more attention to the game, they are more likely to tune in early to watch every minute of coverage, and they are, more than women, emotionally involved in the contest (Gantz & Wenner, 1991). The fact that sports programs, compared to other TV genres, attract a higher proportion of 18- to 49-year-old male viewers explains, in part, why women's sports receive scant coverage compared to men's sports in both news reporting and game coverage (Duncan & Messner, 1994; Tuggle, 1997).

Analyses of NCAA Division I Championship basketball game telecasts also reveal subtle differences in coverage between women's and men's games. Women's games received more negative sportscaster comments than men's games in 1986, suggesting that coverage trivializes female athletes' efforts (Duncan & Hasbrook, 1988). CBS' coverage between 1991 and 1995 used longer full-court shots and focused less attention to on-court action in the women's games than in men's games (Hallmark & Armstrong, 1999). Olympic Games telecasts, in contrast, demonstrate a decided bias toward female viewers. A commercial interest in women's increased participation in sports is evident in NBC's coverage of both the Summer and Winter Olympics since 1996. More than half of Olympics viewers for the 1996 Summer Games were women, and the network represents the Games with the female viewer in mind (Daddario, 1998).

CONCLUSION

Whatever its faults, and whatever the validity of the criticisms of it, broadcast TV remains at the center of major team and big-event sports, both economically and culturally, continuing to wield enormous influence over nearly every facet of contemporary athletics in the United States. Broadcast TV coverage has greatly expanded spectator access to sports contests, strengthened the market reach of leagues and fan base of teams, magnified the perceived importance of athletics in American life, and elevated and transformed the status of athletes. Sports coverage also has helped the networks to enhance their status as national media. Viewers, especially fans, perhaps benefit most from broadcast TV attention to sports: The coverage is free, it validates the viewer's choice to tune in, and it can enhance the individual's national pride and sense of belonging to an ethnic or status group.

A point Johnson (1969) made during TV coverage's initial surge is still relevant today: Ask any fan whether TV changed sports and whether those changes have benefited, on balance, the fan most of all. Whether broadcast TV creates the audience segments that sponsors want to reach, or whether preexisting audience motivations shape TV content, broadcast sports coverage taps into viewers' desires, as well as prevailing social myths and assumptions, in an effort to attract and maintain that audience. Ultimately, this viewing interest is rooted in the enduring fascination with sports (Edmonds, 1982), which the networks and their promotional partners have cultivated while fiercely protecting their stake in it.

REFERENCES

Altheide, D. L., & Snow, R. P. (1978). Sports versus the mass media. *Urban Life*, 7, 189–204.

Ashworth, C. E. (1971). Sport as symbolic dialogue. In E. Dunning (Ed.), *Sport: Readings from a sociological perspective* (pp. 40–46). London: Cass.

Barney, R. K., Wenn, S. R., & Martyn, S. G. (2002). *Selling the five rings: The International Olympic Committee and the rise of Olympic commercialism*. Salt Lake City: University of Utah Press.

Bellamy, R. V. (1989). Professional sports organizations: Media strategies. In L. A. Wenner (Ed.), *Media, sports, and society* (pp. 120–133). Newbury Park, CA: Sage.

Boorstin, D. (1964). *The image: A guide to pseudo events in America*. New York: Harper and Row.

Brookes, R. (2002). *Representing sport*. New York: Oxford University Press.

Bryant, J., Comisky, P., & Zillmann, D. (1977). Drama in sports commentary. *Journal of Communication*, 27(3), 140–149.

Bryant, J., & Zillmann, D. (1983). Sports violence and the media. In J. H. Goldstein (Ed.), *Sports violence* (pp. 195–211). New York: Springer-Verlag.

Chandler, J. M. (1988). *Television and national sport*. Urbana: University of Illinois Press.

Daddario, G. (1998). *Women's sport and spectacle: Gendered television coverage and the Olympic Games*. Westport, CT: Praeger.

Duncan, M. C., & Hasbrook, C. A. (1988). Denial of power in televised women's sports. *Sociology of Sport Journal*, 5(1), 1–21.

Duncan, M., & Messner, M. (1994). *Gender stereotyping in televised sports: A follow-up to the 1989 study*. Los Angeles: Amateur Athletic Foundation.

Eastman, S. T., & Meyer, T. P. (1989). Sports programming: Scheduling, costs, and competition. In L. A. Wenner (Ed.), *Media, sports, and society* (pp. 97–119). Newbury Park, CA: Sage.

Edmonds, A. O. (1982). Sports, ritual, and myth. In D. W. Hoover & J. T. A. Koumoulides (Eds.), *Conspectus of history: Sports and society* (vol. 1, no. 8, pp. 27–42). Muncie, IN: Department of History, Ball State University.

Eitzen, D. S., & Sage, G. H. (1978). *Sociology of North American sport*. Dubuque, IA: William C. Brown.

End, C. M., Kretschmar, J., Campbell, J., Mueller, D. G., & Dietz-Uhler, B. (2003). Sport fans' attitudes toward war analogies as descriptors for sport. *Journal of Sport Behavior*, 26, 356–367.

Gantz, W. (1981). An exploration of viewing motives and behaviors associated with television sports. *Journal of Broadcasting*, 25, 263–275.

Gantz, W., & Wenner, L. A. (1991). Men, women, and sports: Audience experiences and effects. *Journal of Broadcasting & Electronic Media*, 35, 233–243.

Gerdy, J. R. (2002). *Sports: The all-American addiction*. Jackson: University Press of Mississippi.

Gorman, J., & Calhoun, K. (1994). *The name of the game: The business of sports*. New York: John Wiley.

Gruneau, R. (1989). Making spectacle: A case study in television sports production. In L. A. Wenner (Ed.), *Media, sports, and society* (pp. 134–154). Newbury Park, CA: Sage.

Guttmann, A. (1986). *Sports spectators.* New York: Columbia University Press.

Guttmann, A. (1988). *A whole new ball game: An interpretation of American sports.* Chapel Hill: The University of North Carolina Press.

Hallmark, J. R., & Armstrong, R. N. (1999). Gender equity in televised sports: A comparative analysis of men's and women's NCAA Division I basketball championship broadcasts, 1991–1995. *Journal of Broadcasting & Electronic Media, 43,* 222–235.

In U-turn, NBC weighs return to pro sports. (2003, September 1). *Advertising Age,* p. 1.

Izenberg, J. (1968). *The rivals.* New York: Holt, Rinehart, and Winston.

Jhally, S. (1989). Cultural studies and the sports/media complex. In L. A. Wenner (Ed.), *Media, sports, and society* (pp. 70–93). Newbury Park, CA: Sage.

Johnson, W. (1969, December 22). TV made it all a new game. *Sports Illustrated,* pp. 86–102.

Johnson, W. O. (1971). *Super spectator and the electric Lilliputians.* Boston: Little, Brown.

Klatell, D. A., & Marcus, N. (1988). *Sports for sale: Television, money, and the fans.* New York: Oxford University Press.

Kubey, R., & Csikszentmihalyi, M. (1990). *Television and the quality of life: How viewing shapes everyday experience.* Hillsdale, NJ: Lawrence Erlbaum Associates.

Kuiper, K. (1996). *Smooth talkers: The linguistic performance of auctioneers and sportscasters.* Mahwah, NJ: Lawrence Erlbaum Associates.

Lipsky, R. (1981). *How we play the game: Why sports dominate American life.* Boston: Beacon.

Lipsyte, R. (1975). *SportsWorld: An American dreamland.* New York: Quadrangle.

McChesney, R. W. (1989). Media made sport: A history of sports coverage in the United States. In L. A. Wenner (Ed.), *Media, sports, and society* (pp. 49–69). Newbury Park, CA: Sage.

Morris, B. S., & Nydahl, J. (1983). Toward analysis of live television broadcasts. *Central States Speech Journal, 34,* 195–202.

Morse, M. (1983). Sport on television: Replay and display. In E. A. Kaplan (Ed.), *Regarding television: Critical approaches, an anthology* (pp. 44–66). Frederick, MD: University Publications of America.

Morse, M. (1985). *Talk, talk, talk.* Screen, *26*(2), 2–15.

Oriard, M. (1981). Professional football as cultural myth. *Journal of American Culture, 4,* 27–41.

Parente, D. E. (1977). The interdependence of sports and television. *Journal of Communication, 27*(3), 128–132.

Powers, R. (1984). *Supertube: The rise of television sports.* New York: Coward-McCann.

Professional college sports. (2003, November). *St. Louis Journalism Review, 33,* 6–7.

Quirk, J., & Fort, R. (1999). *Hard ball: The abuse of power in pro team sports.* Princeton, NJ: Princeton University Press.

Rader, B. G. (1983). *American sports.* Englewood Cliffs, NJ: Prentice-Hall.

Rader, B. G. (1984). *In its own image.* New York: The Free Press.

Real, M. R. (1975). Super Bowl: Mythic spectacle. *Journal of Communication, 25*(1), 31–43.

Rethinking the model. (2003, September 8). *Television Week,* p. 11.

Sack, A. L., & Staurowsky, E. J. (1998). *College athletes for hire: The evolution and legacy of the NCAA's amateur myth.* Westport, CT: Praeger.

Sandvoss, C. (2003). *A game of two halves: Football, television and globalization.* New York: Routledge.

Schaaf, P. (1995). *Sports marketing: It's not just a game anymore.* New York: Prometheus.

Schaaf, P. (2004). *Sports, Inc.: 100 years of sports business.* New York: Prometheus.

Sports on the rocks. (2003, November 3). *Broadcasting & Cable,* p. 35.

Stone, G. P. (1955). American sports: Play and dis-play. *Chicago Review, 9,* 83–100.

Strauss, L. (1998, September/October). Does money tilt the playing field? *Columbia Journalism Review,* pp. 16–17.

Sullivan, D. B. (1991). Commentary and viewer perception of player hostility: Adding punch to televised sports. *Journal of Broadcasting & Electronic Media, 35,* 487–504.

Tuggle, C. A. (1997). Differences in television sports reporting of men's and women's athletics: ESPN *SportsCenter* and CNN *Sports Tonight. Journal of Broadcasting & Electronic Media, 41,* 14–24.

Wenner, L. A., & Gantz, W. (1989). The audience experience with sports on television. In L. A. Wenner (Ed.), *Media, sports, and society* (pp. 241–269). Newbury Park, CA: Sage.

Whannel, G. (1992). *Fields in vision: Television sport and cultural transformation.* New York: Routledge.

Whannel, G. (2002). *Media sports stars: Masculinities and moralities.* New York: Routledge.

Williams, R. (1970, April 16). There's always the sport. *The Listener,* pp. 522–523.

Williams, H. (1987, Fall). The news in network TV sports. *Gannett Center Journal, 1*(2), 25–38.

Zillmann, D., Bryant, J., & Sapolsky, B. S. (1979). The enjoyment of watching sport contests. In J. H. Goldstein, (Ed.), *Sports, games, and play* (pp. 297–335). Hillsdale, NJ: Lawrence Erlbaum Associates.

9

The Coverage of Sports on Cable TV

Chris Wood
University of Georgia and JWA

Vince Benigni
College of Charleston

INTRODUCTION: CABLE TV AND SPORTS: ACTIVE, CONSUMER-DRIVEN SUCCESS

Has it been 25 years? Hard to believe that 2004 marked the 25th anniversary of the Entertainment and Sports Programming Network (ESPN), the Disney subsidiary that has revolutionized sports coverage on cable and satellite television. With this anniversary comes the realization by the industry, the academy, and the consumer that the landscape of sports and cable television has changed drastically in the past few decades. What's most noticeable is what's at stake today: the corporate revenues and business deals that dictate the people's access to, and enjoyment of, televised sports coverage and programming.

Just look at the cable networks that have formed to compete for the growing audience tuning into this type of entertainment fare. Since ESPN (which hails itself as the "Worldwide Leader in Sports") formed to provide the "ultimate source of sports programming" that includes professional and college sports, sports news, and information, several other program providers have followed suit.

Within the ESPN family, there is ESPN2, which bills itself as a differentiated 24-hour sports network that features live and/or original sports programming targeting young and light to moderate sports viewers, while appealing to all sports fans in some way. ESPN News, ESPN Classic, and ESPN U round out the five major networks of this industry leader of national sporting news and information, as well as event and nonevent sports programming. ESPN continues to expand the brand across cultural lines, with offerings such as ESPN Deportes, a 24/7 Spanish-language network.

The top contender to contest ESPN ratings dominance is Fox Sports Net. Recently branded as FSN, the regional sports network combines live, local event programming, framed by regionally and customized pre- and postgame sports news. Fox Sports South, for example, provides the southeastern region of U.S. sports fans with a complete sports package, while banking on the popular notion that "all news is local."

While events targeted on regional sports networks tend to gain better ratings than "national" offerings (Reynolds, 2005), the niche philosophy is not universally profitable. For example, Carolinas Sports Entertainment Television (C-SET), launched in Fall 2004 by BET founder and Charlotte Bobcats' (NBA) owner Robert Johnson, ceased operations after just 10 months.

Other cable networks, although not entirely dedicated to sports programming, have grown the amount of sports coverage in their respective programming lineups. The USA Network provides live and tape-delayed coverage of sporting events to complement its original pictures and series, special movie presentations, network sitcoms, and children's programming.

From the Turner/AOL Time Warner family of networks, TNT includes sports programming among the products aired on this complete entertainment network. Turner South is a regional cable station that showcases the "Southern way of life" with original, exclusive programming selected and developed for the interests of Southern viewers. Southerners love their sports, too, and Turner South accommodates them with sports-related programs such as *The College Show, WCW Classics*, as well as televised Atlanta Braves (MLB), Hawks (NBA), and Thrashers (NHL) contests.

Also within the AOL Time Warner family are CNN and CNN Headline News, which include sports news coverage among their ongoing, 24-hour comprehensive telecasts of live and late-breaking national and global news events. Although CNN/SI was a failed attempt to establish a national sports cable network to rival ESPN, the corporation remains active investing programming resources in sports coverage on cable.

In fact, Atlanta's WTBS remains a reigning superstation, along with Chicago's WGN, which carry Atlanta Braves and Chicago Cubs games, respectively, among other sports programs to a national audience via cable distributors across the country. It can be argued that the role of the superstation redefined sports programming distribution and strategy when "America's teams" began to draw a nationwide audience.

Atlanta is also home to TV33, which bills itself as Atlanta's hometown television channel, reaching nearly 700,000 households with locally originated programming, including high school and college sports; *Sports Unlimited* and *Mayhem in the PM* provide studio sports talk and commentary in which local viewers can interact.

Although not entirely dedicated to sports programming like their sister cable network, FSN, the Fox properties of FX, Fox News Channel, and Fox Family, include sprinklings of marquee sporting events, such as Major League Baseball, and sports news updates, all within their respective programming schedules.

Still other cable networks, though narrowcasting to nontraditional sports viewers such as women 25 years of age and older, are experimenting with premium sports programming and coverage in an attempt to build audience ratings and share. Lifetime, as an example, provides contemporary, innovative entertainment and informational programming of particular interest to women, such as regular telecasts of WNBA women's professional basketball games.

Non-traditional sports channels such as the Outdoor Life Network (OLN) have made headlines by grabbing high-profile worldwide events such as the Tour de France and the America's Cup, and most recently, the National Hockey League package, which includes exclusive contents for Comcast's high-speed Internet customers (Stump, 2005). This Comcast-owned "Sweat Network" is also pursuing the coveted 18–34 male demographic through other programming such as the *Gravity Games* (Cannella, 2005).

Because the young male demographic is so elusive for television executives, cable networks often turn to sister platforms for positive results. ESPN uses edgy commentators, streaming video, interactive fantasy-league services, and in-house promos that send viewers to the company's other platforms (Lowry, 2005). In fact, sports websites have successfully incorporated broadband, exclusive fantasy services, and Insider columns into subscription services to appease the more ardent fans. This model works on the same premise that made satellite radio, and of course, cable television, compelling alternatives to their respective broadcast network genres.

For the sports coverage on cable television from the perspectives of the established national and regional networks mentioned previously, the common denominator for these providers is that they typically are included on a basic cable television subscription package. In other words, there is still more sports coverage yet to be explored on premium or pay channels.

In fact, when discussing current trends in sports cable television, it's worth noting the gravitation of more networks from basic cable to pay packages, or at least into premium channel tendencies. In addition, pay-per-view (PPV) offerings in sports are increasing through independent agreements with cable and satellite television providers. The Golf Channel, for example, has moved from the basic to premium tiers on some cable and satellite systems in the United States, whereas HBO, Showtime, and some of the other premium cable programming providers are looking into more and more hours dedicated to sports coverage, from live boxing events to originally produced programming.

By 1999, seven cable networks included or dedicated significant time to sports programming—HBO, TNT, USA, TBS, CNN, and Showtime, in addition to ESPN. In fact, these seven were among the top-14 rated television networks at that time. Arguably, half of the top networks in television—including the four broadcast network affiliates—incorporated sports coverage as a part of their overall programming strategy ("Top 25," 1999).

How did sports coverage become so prevalent and dominant in cable television in what is a relatively short time in the history of growth in mass media entertainment? Let's look at some of the cable industry's historical developments, deals, and partnerships that provided the impetus for expanded sports coverage.

HISTORY: THIS IS NO GAME, THE BUSINESS OF THESE GAMES

When considering sports coverage prior to its inclusion in mass media, "the sports messages sent to those absent from the action on the field contained little else of fact other than a score and a winner, and the message reached the receiver a day, week, or month later" (Durand, 2002, p. 431).

ESPN, launched in 1979, was the first all-sports cable network and is considered the gold standard, not just because it's been on the air the longest, but also because it has provided a number of industry innovations in sports programming. Its primary programming cycle includes live events and news, including its signature *SportsCenter*, which provides a collection of highlights and perspectives for viewers. However, ESPN has also branched out into other programming categories, to be discussed at greater length later.

ESPN has also been a model of media convergence, especially with regard to its on-air news talent. *SportsCenter* anchors or analysts also contribute content and commentary regularly to the network's Web site, radio network, and magazine, which provide efficient utilization of their skills and knowledge, while likewise strengthening the brand for a variety of demographics and audiences.

After ESPN broke ground and built success as the first exclusive sports network on cable, others followed, seeking pieces of the mass media ratings pie that had grown to impressive industry numbers. In fact, by 1997, according to Nielsen Media Research, cable ratings were impressively strong, "thanks to the abundance of sports and sports-related programming" (Burgi, 1997a, p. 14).

The cable networks and partnerships that began to materialize in the mid-90s also testified to this swelling audience's demand for additional sports coverage. On November 1, 1996, Fox Sports Net—a joint venture of Liberty Media, seeking to restore its regional Prime Sports networks, and News Corp., parent to the Fox FX cable network—embarked on a journey to assemble a network of regional channels dedicated to sports coverage. Programming of the new national network would include the debut of *Fox Sports News* to compete with *SportsCenter* in providing cable audiences with sports information, highlights, and news coverage (McConville, 1995; Lindemann, 1996). Earlier that year, Turner Corp. and Time Warner Inc.'s periodical *Sports Illustrated* launched CNN/SI, yet another sports news and information network, which was based out of CNN headquarters in Atlanta (Brown, 1996).

Partly in response to the competition posed by CNN/SI bringing additional sports news coverage to cable television viewers, ESPN countered by launching ESPN2 and dedicating more newscasts and related news shows to its programming schedule. News programming on ESPN and ESPN2 combined for 13.5 hours of news coverage each weekday (Burgi, 1996). But ESPN didn't stop there. By November of 1996, ESPN had introduced ESPN News to cable viewers as another first—an exclusive sports-news channel. Ironically, ESPN News sought success with a program schedule and style similar to CNN Headline News, with quick sports updates, concise newscasts, and sports news programming running 24 hours per day.

In another ironic, apparent reversal of sports programming strategy, FSN, which had built a reputation for keeping sports coverage local through its expanding regional network of affiliates, went global in November of 1997 with the airing of Fox Sports World. This channel featured 24 hours of international sports content for cable and satellite viewers (Burgi, 1997b). But a closer look into the strategic programming of the leading sports networks will reveal that FSN continues to build its ratings success with better coverage of regional events and supplemental programs of the hometown teams. FSN presently targets those local viewers or fans who seek additional insight on their favorite teams and players—insight inadequately offered during the few minutes of local sportscasts on network affiliate stations.

Superstations (i.e., WTBS in Atlanta, WGN in Chicago, and WOR in New York) garner strong viewer loyalty among nationwide audiences by airing major professional sporting events. In particular, the Atlanta Braves became known as "America's Team" in Major League Baseball (MLB), whereas the Chicago Cubs became cultural icons, both because of national cable access. Former Braves owner and WTBS President Ted Turner and other visionaries proved that airing live sporting events can be not only lucrative, but also an effective counter-programming strategy to network fare of syndicated first-run or off-network programs utilized by competing stations. In addition, live sporting events, as these superstations proved, serve as effective promotional tools for upcoming entertainment and news programs on the superstation or affiliated channels.

In general, all-sports networks (ESPN, FSN, CNN/SI, etc.) have benefited from the fractionalization of television programming. For nearly four decades, sports fans relied on network offerings such as the game of the week or concept shows such as *Wide World of Sports* to fill their viewers' needs. The shortcomings of broadcast television networks were illuminated as cable provided greater options for live events and expanded coverage of pre- and postevent happenings. Today, ESPN and TNT are significant players in major sports coverage, whereas broadcast network giants such as NBC and Fox have sometimes been relegated to alternative programming, such as Arena League Football, NFL Europe, and the now-defunct XFL, to attract sports fans.

Niche sports cable networks, such as The Golf Channel and ESPN Classic, have proved to be profitable as well, because suitable programming is inexpensive to produce, purchase, and air, while it is more attractive to advertisers seeking niche viewers. In addition, nonsports networks, such as TNT (with NBA coverage), USA (covering tennis *and* golf, while also rekindling the popular "Monday Night Raw" wrestling program), and Lifetime (airing WNBA games), have penetrated into sports programming. In fact, cable stations often promote broadcast network telecasts of the same sport, and vice versa. Instead of being competing parties, sometimes networks and cable stations engage in deals to cross-promote product offerings of their respective brands—a strategy that will garner more discussion during a closer review forthcoming on trends of cable sports coverage.

As a result of the overall success of the ESPN brand of cable networks—which by 1996 included ESPN, ESPN2, and ESPN News, with ESPN Classic and ESPN U on the way—and other mass media properties (ESPN Radio, ESPN's website, *ESPN The Magazine*, and other branded products), *Advertising Age* named the all-sports network the "Cable TV Marketer of the Year." The accolades came as a result of ESPN's corporate ability "to turn an epiphany into a business strategy, to extend its brand into new, revenue-generating arenas with vehicles that further reinforce the core brand, and to package all its inventory for advertisers" (Jensen, 1996, p. 1).

ESPN President George Bodenheimer, who was executive vice president of sales and marketing at ESPN at the time of the *Advertising Age* award in 1996, provided a sound assessment of the state of sports news coverage and programming then, especially from his company's perspective as the industry's giant. "Once upon a time, our company was our network and our network was our company," he said. "Those days are gone. We are selling and creating all the time" (Jensen, 1996, p. 2).

But as the revenues generated from increased sports coverage on cable began to grow in the 90s, so too did the severity and enormity of the competition among sports programmers, cable operators, and anyone else attempting to carve out a share of the market. *Advertising Age* described this battle as "nasty for the eyes and ears of sports junkies" (Jensen, 1997, p. 18). Describing the aftermath of the ESPN News and CNN/SI launches, Jensen (1997) noted,

> Most participants claim there's room for everyone. But the problem is they all want more turf. The jostling of elbows has already produced bruises and lawsuits. It is likely the road to growth (of sports coverage on cable) will be rocky, considering the fierce competition for channel space, ad dollars and programming (Jensen, 1997, p. 18).

That "rocky road" of growth in recent years has expanded to lawsuits and industry arguments beyond those of the rival sports networks. Some cable operators have spiked overall subscription fees in light of these basic cable channels, as carriage of networks such as ESPN have driven them toward including the all-sports channels in premium, tiered packages for subscribers. Advertisers have pressured cable networks to combine more consumers in a package of group network and related product sales. Regulatory agencies, typically more lenient on cable programming in years past, have had more occasions to review the evolving, potentially explicit nature of new programs being developed by the sports networks. The effects of such categories of sports programs and entertainment fare are receiving more attention by the academy as well. A closer analysis of this more recent history of potential industry confrontations appears later in the discussion of current trends of sports coverage on cable television.

But what about the viewing habits of the typical sports viewer through the years? Yes, he (the dominant demographic remains males 18 and older) has a greater variety of offerings on cable. But this cornucopia of sports coverage, which could lead to a *zapping* culture, may prove harmful in regard to advertising recognition, recall, and revenues. Many viewers, aided by the historical advancements of the remote control TiVo, and related (digital) technologies, eschew commercials, especially in high-traffic viewing periods such as evenings and weekends.

In response, many stations have incorporated graphics that include sponsorships, often accompanying game scores and situations, such as base runners in a Major League Baseball telecast or down-and-distance for competing football teams during college or pro football televised games. As another example, advertisements are digitally superimposed on banners placed behind home plate on centerfield camera shots during baseball games. And Web site URLs are listed above basketball backboards for high-angle shots.

Sports tickers (crawling scores and descriptions of news at the bottom of the screen) have embraced the zapping concept of television watchers and have greatly increased viewership on sports networks. In addition, the competition of sports Web sites, providing instant access to scores and scenarios, has spawned the drive to fill the needs of those avid sports fans. They are a group who, according to the uses and gratifications perspective of self-selecting media, seek those media messages that are most beneficial, and entertaining, to them at the time. Past generations had to wait for the next day's newspaper for statistics and breakdowns of salient games. More recently in the history of sports viewership, fans had to labor until the 11 p.m. (Eastern Standard Time) local sports newscast, or the evening airing of *SportsCenter* or *Fox Sports News*, to obtain a rundown of the day's action.

New media are not only supplementing the growing coverage of sports on cable television, but also this content is providing further, more empirical evidence that today's sports viewer can be defined as an active, emotive respondent who makes mass media selections, for the most part, with meaning and purpose. A decade ago, platforms complementing cable television included radio stations and the Internet. Now we have innovations such as podcasts and broadband to accommodate the demand for enhanced viewing experiences by the more involved, program-driven media consumer. The entertainment as effects perspective, and related theoretical approaches that help sharpen our understanding of the behavioral patterns of sports viewers, likewise assists us in better comprehending the past, present, and future coverage of sports on cable.

THEORY:
THE HUNGER OF SPORTS ENTHUSIASTS
AND THE ENTERTAINMENT INSTITUTIONS
THAT FEED THEM

During college football season, a good day in the home of an avid Georgia fan (granted, that's somewhat of a redundancy) is when a Bulldog win is coupled with a Georgia Tech or Florida loss. Making a good day even better would be when the Dawgs win in a blowout, while Tech and the Gators lose in similar fashion. And greatest of all for those decorated in Red and Black is for that blowout win to come at the expense of those hated rivals.

Such is a lay description of a case where sports entertainment, provided in greater volume and with more in-depth coverage on cable television as we have discussed, serve as media effect—primarily some form of viewer enjoyment. There is little doubting the enjoyment of sports coverage on cable television, as ratings and additional research results attest, and there is something multidimensional to the nature of sports when televised. To borrow an expression from the five-star restaurant, "it's all in the presentation." That said, sports coverage on cable certainly pays strong consideration to presentation. Some see viewers of televised sports being fascinated, not just with the actual event, but also with the aesthetic terms and conditions of sports coverage (Raunsbjerg & Sand, 1998).

But what is it that the cable sports television viewer enjoys and why? Help explaining the enjoyment of entertainment, particularly sports coverage, comes from the theoretical perspectives of uses and gratifications research and other behavioral studies such as those focusing on the critical elements of entertainment, or the disposition of viewers, which contribute to enjoyment. Previous research attention on the characteristics and content of entertainment programming, which includes sports coverage, has shifted to include the perspective of a viewer's motives for watching and the resulting behavior from the viewing experience. A better understanding of the enjoyment of sports coverage on cable is also aided by an appreciation for the *selective exposure* perspective of media viewing habits, which proposes that television viewers make programming selections in order to (1) meet certain social-psychological needs or (2) reflect personal preferences for entertainment (Bryant & Thompson, 2002). But this explanation is somewhat limited in addressing enjoyment of sports coverage on cable, because it fails to delineate between passive viewers and active ones, with strong dispositions toward the sports contests and characters they seek.

Bryant and Raney (2000) helped explain critical entertainment dimensions of the enjoyment of televised sports further by comparing mediated experiences with non-mediated experiences. That is, there are pros and cons to watching a game at the stadium versus the living room, but several factors critical to enjoying sports in either setting are universal. Some have even studied crowd behavior within a stadium setting during a sporting event, to confirm that audience activity and interaction contribute to the involvement and subsequent enjoyment of these in-person, entertaining viewing experiences (Hocking, 1982). But for examining sports coverage on cable television, there is no doubting "the enjoyment audiences apparently derive from watching a plethora of sports contests on the screen" (Bryant & Raney, 2000, p. 153).

According to these researchers and others, sports coverage certainly qualifies for categorizing as a classic form of entertainment programming. But the enjoyment of sports is contingent upon several factors, including *drama*, certainly present in suspenseful games; *interesting characters*, who are covered extensively by sports news and programming sources; *conflict*, an inherent component of athletic competition; and *satisfying resolutions*, reflected in winning or losing efforts. Taking these variables into consideration, researchers have applied the disposition model in several settings (Zillmann, 1991; Zillmann, 1980; Zillmann, Bryant, & Sapolsky, 1979; Zillmann & Cantor, 1976), which have helped identify the programming means for assuring viewer enjoyment of televised sports. The disposition model has been advanced "to predict audience enjoyment of drama, humor, and sports" (Bryant & Thompson, 2002, p. 359).

Many things influence the enjoyment of sports on cable television and the subsequent ratings boon and industry competition as a result of this entertainment. But most influential is one's disposition going into, and results coming out of, a sports viewing experience. As Bryant and Miron (2002) attested, nothing seems "to control enjoyment as strongly and as universally as do affective dispositions toward interacting parties, especially parties confronted with problems, conflict, and aversive conditions" (Bryant & Miron, 2002, p. 527).

What parties are more at "conflict under aversive conditions" than competing teams—and their respective sports viewing fans—as in our opening example of a heated rivalry of Southern college football powers? Passions are so high, and feelings so deep, that memorable college football and basketball games are repeated on regional cable outlets as classic television offerings.

Furthermore, enjoyment "depends not so much on conflict as on its resolution and what that resolution means to the parties involved. It depends on how much those who come out on top are liked and loved, and on how much those who come out on the short end are disliked and hated" (Bryant & Miron, 2002, p. 567). Predispositions and dispositions, then, toward personalities, players, teams, and other stimuli in a sporting event, are critical to the viewer's enjoyment of that mediated experience. How does this theoretical perspective of the television viewer advance our current discussion of sports coverage on cable television? Certainly, the ongoing efforts of sports cable television programmers to provide additional coverage, information, and analysis of teams and their cast members contribute to the viewer's development of sentiments toward the very characters portrayed in these growing number of televised contests. The proliferation of college coaches shows on regional cable outlets in the 1980s is one example of this increased analysis.

What a logical explanation of expansive sports coverage on cable! The programmers seek to build or reinforce viewer dispositions, whereas viewers respond most tellingly in their demand for sports coverage, with cable television providing the ideal means to that end. Bryant and Miron (2002) explained further: "Positive and negative affective dispositions toward the agents in drama are vital and must be created if drama is to evoke strong emotions," including enjoyment (Bryant & Miron, 2002, p. 567). Connecting dispositions toward elements of sports programming content with the affective reactions of sports viewers, the authors concluded: "Once an audience has thus placed its sentiments pro and con particular characters, enjoyment of conflict and its resolution in drama depends on the ultimate outcome for the loved and hated parties" (Bryant & Miron, 2002, p. 568).

Because the roles of participants and outcomes of the games are not predetermined—save perhaps a quasi-sporting event such as professional wrestling—the programs televised in great detail and with technological innovations on cable can be easily classified as dramatic fare. In addition, an exhilarating, thrilling contest can create a transfer of excitement from the event to a continual, concentrated sense of enjoyment at game's end. This *excitation transfer* is explained thus: "The intensification of the enjoyment of favorable final outcomes by residual excitation from preceding uncertainty and distress should apply to the appreciation of athletic performances, too" (Bryant & Miron, 2002, p. 571).

Helping explain further the understanding of viewer enjoyment of sports on cable television is the notion that the sports viewer is an active participant in the mediated experience—one who often selects sports programming on cable for meaningful and useful purposes, according to premises of uses and gratifications theory, rather than for arbitrary means or no reasons at all. Although some of the traditional media effects research provides a look at mass communication processes and influences from the perspective of the communicator or channel—for example, the sports cable network and their programming strategists—the uses and gratifications perspective more closely examines the nature of the audience member (Rubin, 2002), especially the sports viewing fan.

At the heart of this idea that media content is consumed to gratify viewers and alter psychological states is the premise that the typical cable television sports viewer is most likely an active, often avid and experienced, participant in the process, although not all consumers are active in the same manner or to the same degree (Rubin, 2002). Indeed, it appears the sports fan most often locates cable television programming with intent, rather than impulsively stumbling onto this entertainment by happenstance, as more spontaneous selective exposure to sports programming would indicate (Bryant & Miron, 2002). No, ratings for sports coverage on cable television today can quantify that such mass audiences are more likely *pursuing* sports entertainment, rather than passively being exposed to it.

Some fans apparently extend active viewership to actual rituals, manifested in superstitions that they feel bring them closer to the action or more involved in the viewing experience. In some instances, this active fan's involvement results, almost comically, in the notion that they think they might actually impact the ultimate outcome of the game (Eastman & Riggs, 1994). And fans active in sports viewing experiences have been influenced by facets of the game that to outsiders might seem trivial, such as sports commentary (Sullivan, 1991). Pessimistic and acerbic *homers* such as the University of Georgia's Larry Munson and the late Boston Celtics announcer Johnny Most have become legends to fans, as have more traditional college basketball voices such as the late University of Kentucky's Caywood Ledford and UNC-Chapel Hill icon Woody Durham. Certainly, fans of these teams and their announcers have confessed to watching regional and national telecasts on mute, with the play-by-play guys offering radio commentary and analysis to enhance the enjoyment of the event.

Rubin (2002) notes that the active viewer seeks out mediated stimuli—entertaining sports programming, for example—as a result of a viewing ritual or a need to obtain relevant information about a salient topic. "Ritualized and instrumental media orientations tell us about the amount and type of media use and about one's media attitudes and expectations" (Rubin, 2002, p. 534). Explaining further, Rubin (2002) defined *instrumental orientation* as a viewer's use and subsequent gratification from "media content for informational purposes. It entails greater exposure to news and informational content and perceiving that content to be realistic. Instrumental use (of media content) is active and purposive. It suggests utility, intention, selectivity, and involvement" (Rubin, 2002, p. 535).

The prevalence of sports coverage on cable television, then, would support the argument that viewers proactively select (use) sports programming with a specific intent or instrumental use in mind, and are highly attentive and involved, greatly affected by the resulting enjoyable (gratifying) viewing experience. Then, we would argue that the need for sports entertainment is strongly predictive of television affinity first, and escapism second. Viewers can be broken down into three distinctive viewer archetypes: medium-oriented viewers, network-oriented viewers, and station-oriented viewers (Adelman & Atkin, 2000).

In addition, entertainment on sports Web sites can be linked to beneficial Web use; sports offer need-based benefits, including entertainment, excitement, and escape. Also, with increased opportunity costs of cable, the Internet might become a more cost-effective alternative for audiences in the future (Perse & Ferguson, 2000). Although new media may turn cable television into old media, current indications are that a symbiotic relationship between cable TV and Web sites exists, and sports viewers are responding favorably.

Demographic differences in audiences—and gratifications sought by sports program providers—drive news media use, which is congruent with the uses and gratifications perspective (Vincent & Basil, 1997). Students' media use and surveillance needs increase with college education, which might help explain the huge push for viewership among the male 18 to 34 demographic. ESPN2, and even ESPN U for example, have been established to reach such a prospective target audience.

Viewers are also providing evidence that the use of cable television for sports programming is becoming preferred, at least in ratings, over broadcast television events. In 2004, ESPN's and TNT's ratings grew by 8 and 17%, respectively, because of NBA telecasts. ABC's NBA telecasts, conversely, fell 8% and became the lowest average in NBA history for a broadcast network. ABC lost 13% of its male 18 to 34 audience (to a 2.0 rating), whereas TNT improved ratings in that demo 18% to a 1.3 rating, and the same growth was documented for ESPN (Consoli & Larson, 2004). Additionally, sports coverage on cable appears to be outperforming even national and global news on rival cable networks as well. In October 2003, ESPN's football and baseball coverage showed a 41% increase over ratings in October 2002, while news cable channels Fox News, CNN, and MSNBC all suffered declines (Romano, 2003a).

The history of cable television, which includes a growing number of sports networks, is characterized by continual discourse between idealists who seek more progressive programming and realists who see an industry based on the bottom line (Mullen, 2002). It would be helpful, then, to look further into the industry trends—those programming and business decisions—that impact sports coverage on cable.

TRENDS:
FROM LOCAL TO GLOBAL TO MERGING
AND CONVERGING

Sports Coverage Impacting the Game, and Cultivating Much More

Sports coverage on cable is not only expanding to include more and more events and other forms of programming, but also sports coverage is beginning to increasingly impact the game as well. Old-school sports enthusiasts lament the ESPNization of highlight packages, where dunks and home runs take precedence over jump shots and moving up runners. Many blame the lack of fundamentals in young athletes to the emphasis of flashy, one-on-one play over teamwork. Sharpies, imaginary cell phones, and fire-extinguished track shoes have become *SportsCenter* lore in recent years. Next-day water cooler discussions often bypass game strategy or soundness of play, instead focusing on gamesmanship and self-promotion.

Major League Baseball (MLB), as another example, has been making moves of late to improve its brand and attract more consumers, with the help of sponsors and cable/TV networks, among others. Certainly, this stands out as no industry trend—a professional sports league seeking to increase its market share and expand its product to new audiences. But what is interesting is how those influencing professional sports such as MLB are stacking up in priority to the league.

Cable television networks and programming sources have more power in the industry today than ever before. Evidence comes in the form of Fox, ESPN, and the other corporate partners of the league (MLB) spending $170 million—in the form of programming rights, media buys, and promotional dollars—over the course of the 2002 season alone.

Fox, which also carries a number of regional MLB games via its FSN cable affiliates, committed $2.5 billion to MLB for its network deal through the year 2006. In doing so, the network "quietly pushed for the possible new format of the All-Star Game, in which the game gains added significance by having the winning league earn home-field advantage in that year's World Series" (Thomaselli, 2003a, p.3).

Fox certainly has the right to pay what the market demands for sports coverage on its broadcasting and cable networks, but what about its influence on the game? Furthermore, what of the Major League Baseball teams who are establishing their own cable operations or seeking broadcast and cable exclusive partnerships to carry local games (McAvoy, 2003)? Is there no conflict of interest in a baseball team extending its influence in local business and entertainment by providing its own sports coverage?

It appears that coverage dictates content when cable and broadcasting networks influence, for example, the time of day a game is played. Furthermore, the line between content and coverage is continually blurred when professional teams venture beyond the boundaries of media partnership and into the realm of media ownership, and vice versa—when media properties invest or retain ownership in sports teams.

Obviously, cable coverage of sporting events such as MLB games has facilitated industry trends that are reflective of the growth in popularity of sports entertainment.

Business Deals, Broadcast/Cable Partnerships and Mergers Are on the Rise

Cable has changed the nature of coverage in sports, especially narrowcasted events such as professional golf tournaments. Today, all four rounds of PGA majors and other big tournaments are covered—the weekday rounds on cable outlets such as ESPN, USA, or TNT, and the weekend final rounds on ABC, NBC, or CBS. These broadcast and cable network partnerships are indicative of what business arrangements are being made for other sports coverage as well.

Furthermore, cable stations and networks have seen a dramatic drop in golf ratings (potential revenues), coinciding with Tiger Woods' relative slump in 2003 and 2004 (Foust, 2005). This downturn has resulted into a scheduling change that mirrors Nascar's "Quest for the Cup", a season-ending set of races to determine the

Nextel points champion. The proposed FedEx Cup—like its Nascar equivalent—would be determined by a point system built into a season-ending series of championship events.

Although both are Disney properties, ABC Sports and ESPN talked in 1998 about using the latter's cable network name (ESPN) to market some of the broadcast network's (ABC) sports programs. In addition, the two networks have had mutual interest in combining advertising sales forces as well (Cooper, 1998a).

Fox Sports and FSN have had a long and lucrative relationship with MLB, among other sports. In 2000, the network was the leading local-rights holder for cable and was gaining ground on local rights for broadcast television as well (McAvoy, 2000). That same year, cable networks carried more than 2,300 baseball games, whereas broadcast television accounted for just 1,550. The good news for Fox continued the next year when, in 2001, Fox Sports increased its ratings for baseball, while its FSN regional cable channels showed strong gains during that time as well (Schlosser & Tedesco, 2001). Cable continues to air more baseball games than broadcast television because of the growth in national telecasts by ESPN, but more so because of the wealth of regional games available across the country on FSN affiliates (McAvoy, 2000).

Baseball broadcast and cable partnerships—and the trend of more games siphoning from broadcast to cable—also extend to the Turner network of sports outlets. In 2000, Atlanta's WUPA-TV lost 30 Braves games to Turner South, who joined Fox Sports South as cable stations carrying Braves games locally. WTBS, the Braves' flagship station and Turner's superstation, held on to its 90-game schedule that same year. Counting WTBS's availability as a cable superstation, sports coverage of MLB by cable networks is dominant, almost exclusive, in the Atlanta market (McAvoy, 2000).

Basic Cable Sports Channels Taking on Premium Channel Tendencies

Basic cable began to take on pay cable tendencies at least 15 years ago, when networks were unable to pass on rising programming costs to the cable franchises. At that time, pay-per-view programming provided an out (Moshavi, 1991). Today, the line between inclusion and exclusion of sports programming on a basic cable tier is becoming more and more difficult to distinguish.

ESPN has built into most of its contracts with cable operators a provision for regular rate increases. The network justifies these rate hikes by claiming that the additional revenues from distribution are necessary to keep the sports programming network competitive against the Big Four broadcast networks when bidding for the rights to major professional and college sporting events, which have become increasingly expensive through the years (Higgins, 2001).

But the cable operators are beginning to balk, saying the fees they have to pass on to subscribers are making the cost for access to basic sports cable channels, such as ESPN, look more like pay channels. When Cablevision Systems refused to carry the Yankees Entertainment & Sports (YES) regional network, the operator argued that the $2 per subscriber demand by YES forced it into "offering to sell YES as a pay service" (Romano, 2002a, p. 22). The brawl has even been labeled as "nasty" when referring to Cox Communications' opposition (Higgins, 2003, p. 8). ESPN, of course, wants to retain its basic cable status, so it may continue to reap the lucrative benefits of independent advertising sales from its sports coverage.

"ESPN wants to avoid becoming a tiered cable station because that makes it more difficult to sell advertising. Less ad revenue could mean even higher monthly cable bills" (Thomaselli, 2003b, p. 4).

Because ESPN has invested heavily into previously network-dominated domains—most notably the $1.1 billion annual package for *Monday Night Football* beginning in 2006 and a hefty renewal of its Major League Baseball package through 2013—it is investing heavily into Nielsen tracking services to measure the impact of sponsorships and sales activity (Deeken, 2005a). This includes online platforms such as podcasts, underwritten by Verizon, which include sponsored audio tags at the beginning and end of the 5–10 minute spots. Turner Sports announced an integrated marketing sponsorship with Orbitz, an online airline travel service company, for TBS's college football games and TNT's coverage of the PGA Grand Slam of Golf. The new NFL Network, a tiered, subscription-based channel, has tabbed Sprint for its wireless platforms, while TiVo has partnered its digital video recorder (DVR) platform with CSTV.

Sports executives and networks have cited DVR technology as a reason for facilitating the historically discouraging trend of viewers skipping out on paid advertisements. Many DVR-related ads play during the contests. However, recent studies show that "commercial avoidance" is insignificant, especially with regard to live programming such as sports and news (Kerschbaumer, 2005).

In fact, some cable networks are embracing technology that may take viewers away from their television sets. In 2005, the broadband Web property ESPN360 aired more than two dozen live college shows, with plans to offer users on-demand game highlights, analysis, and extended SportsCenter interviews with players and coaches.

Basic cable sports coverage has begun to take the look of pay cable recently in programming ideas as well. Station owners and managers continue to crave the elusive demographic of 18 to 34-year-old males. Sports cable offerings such as Fox Sports Net's *Best Damn Sports Show, Period* push the envelope. "Broadcast and cable executives harbor some jealousy toward [pay cable stations such as] HBO, which does not have to answer to advertisers. So they are delicately trying programming that can create similar audience interest, while still [getting the buy-in of] advertisers" (Goetzl, 2002, p. 63).

Sports Media, Technology, and Product Innovations Are Converging

As new technologies and innovations continually converge with every advancement and refinement of the digital age, sports coverage on cable is no doubt impacted. One of the primary technological advancements changing the ways of sports coverage and viewership is high-definition television (HDTV). The broadcasting and cable industry participants agree that the programming offered in high definition will likely spur consumers into upgrading their cable subscriptions to high-definition packages, as well as prompt them into obtaining high-definition television capabilities. But even with a high-definition television and a cable system capable of reception, 70% of cable subscribers were not able to view this type of programming. That's because the cable networks and cable operators continue to haggle over the price of the new HD programming (Consoli, 2003).

The HDTV *early adopters* may be classified as the more fanatical sports viewer, more emotionally and financially vested in the games as fans. There is evidence at least that awareness and potential adoption of HD technology is positively associated (more likely) among those individuals who have, obviously, an appreciation for picture sharpness and size, in addition to individuals who attend movies regularly, own other home entertainment products, are younger, and have higher incomes. And most telling of the importance of sports coverage on cable was the finding that the likely adopters of HDTVs are also those more often engaged in sports viewing (Dupagne, 1999).

In 2002, ESPN began assembling a team to design a new digital facility at its Bristol, Connecticut, headquarters (Kerschbaumer, 2002). President George Bodenheimer also confirmed that ESPN would "offer a wide range of media brand extensions and . . . grow them further as the digital landscape expands" (Romano, 2002b, p. 32). Cable executives, including programmers and operators, also proclaimed during a recent industry conference that it is "important to be ready for the eventual boom of HDTV. Cable operators are increasingly ready to deliver high-def to subscribers, and programmers such as ESPN (and others) are stepping up with content" (Romano, 2003b, p. 3).

In 2005, the network launched a contest to give away 100 HDTVs through a partnership with Philips; the promotion involved multiple platforms (its networks, radio station and Web site). In essence, the promotion "forced" viewers to watch commercials during "HDTV-compatible" game telecasts to access a code word, allowing viewers to enter the contest through the Web site. Winners were announced the following morning on ESPN Radio and ESPN News.

In addition to feeling the impact of HDTV, sports coverage has been affected by other technologies, tie-ins, product offers, promotions, and ventures, all indicative of convergence. ESPN joined Nokia Corp. and Castrol Asia-Pacific recently to offer interactive contests and special promotions for cable viewers of English Premier League soccer (Shuk Wa, 2003). However, ESPN's foray into brand extensions dates back more than a decade. Video games have been inspired by ESPN programming, and the network has spawned other media as well, including *ESPN The Magazine*, ESPN Radio, ESPN.com, and their other cable networks, not to mention ESPN Zone restaurants in markets across the country (Burgi, 1994; Jensen, 1994; Berniker, 1994).

High-speed Internet access has greatly supplemented, rather than supplanted, sports coverage on cable to date. The industry has seen a blurring of the traditional boundaries of what constitutes broadcast, cable, satellite, and even new media programming as a result (Lindemann, 2001). "Partnerships that are built around the concept of content owners and distributors could be fractured as the Internet provides content owners (including cable sports networks) a way to reach the television sets of viewers without the help of traditional distribution methods" (Lindemann, 2001, p. 42). In short, if sports leagues such as MLB or the NFL are viewed as product wholesalers, who's to say these parties won't deal directly to the consumer via the Internet and potentially bypass the distribution channel currently provided by broadcasting and cable television networks? Content, and the public's demand for it, will ultimately determine how the media and message convergence in sports eventually plays out.

Still, research shows that web users are more autonomous than television viewers, and that the Web is supposed to be the antithesis of scheduled programming— it's there when you want it (Pulser, 2005). According to McGrail and Roberts (2005), technology innovation, with regard to broadband cable television, is not (yet) a significant factor to a company's overall competitive position.

As for the commercialism of our games, product placement by regional and national advertisers is not limited to movies or TV drama. Sports coverage on cable has also featured additional sightings of strategic product placements, though subtle and appropriate thus far (Romano, 2003c). The trend of the growing number of product placements in sports programming is simply indicative of cable programmers' attempt to create a more attractive product package for advertisers, who are continually seeking an easier, more effective means for building their brands among targeted audiences. "Turner, ESPN, and others are selling packages across most of their (programming) services with that strategy in mind" (Cooper, 1999, p. 62).

Local to National to Global and Back Again

Technology pioneer Paul Allen (Microsoft cofounder and owner of the NBA's Portland Trail Blazers) launched the Action Sports Cable Network in 2001, showing Trail Blazers, Seattle Seahawks, and Portland Fire WNBA games, as well as coaches' shows. This was a landmark breakthrough—the airing of HD sports in a regional market. That's because the biggest impediment to HDTV sports production, especially in local and regional market coverage, is a lack of HD-compatible production trucks and the additional expenses that come from doing two individual productions for the same event (Prikios, 2001). With that in mind, HD television is no doubt worth it. So, too, is the sports coverage trend that is seeing more dollars—and technology—being invested in local and/or regional programming.

In 2004, Fox Sports Net aired more than 200 contests on HDTV across its regional sports networks, at the behest of Time Warner Cable. According to Fox Sports Net President Bob Thompson, a key to cable success is the power of "localism," which this tactic addresses by targeting regional networks (Stump, 2004).

Although ESPN has become the standard bearer for sports coverage on cable nationally, even through coverage via high-definition technology, FSN has carved into those ratings by following an age-old programming trend that "all news is local." The local angle, even when viewed as a traditional news value for determining the newsworthiness of events, has served Fox well in terms of its sports news and event programming strategy. Rather than expand its depth of national and world sporting news coverage like rival ESPN, FSN has been more involved in building its national presence by assembling a host of regional sports channels that focus more on local coverage. In an attempt to simplify its brand among local consumers and retain an image recognizable across all regional markets, Fox Sports Net has even begun to transform its name into FSN (Linnett & Kerwin, 2004).

FSN has been focused on local sports programming for some time. As early as 1998, the network "reconfigured its regional sports networks... in a bid to bite into sports rival ESPN's revenues" (Cooper, 1998b, p. 9). The revised FSN at that time began to link local networks together, providing local programming relevant to each regional cable channel, while likewise complementing a national programming block. FSN eventually cancelled its evening *National Sports Report* to focus even more resources on its *Regional Sports Reports* and the local news covered on those programs (Frutkin, Larson, & Mundy, 2002).

As a result, the industry has experienced a trend of declining ratings for sports on broadcast and national cable, "while regional sports networks are growing" (Romano, 2001, p. 28). In response, ESPN has tried to launch its own regional sports networks. Ventures such as ESPN West, a regional cable outlet targeting programming and viewers of Southern California, Hawaii, and Nevada, did not do well from the start (Burgi, 1997c). The fall of this regional network just a year later, ironically, came at a time when regional coverage of marquee events such as baseball began to rise. Of the 27 regional sports channels owned or operated by FSN in 1998, 17 showed ratings increases from the past year (Freeman & Cooper, 1998).

In an attempt to deliver the best in programming for a collection of regional audiences, FSN has worked hard to partner with major college conferences, where teams compete regionally, to provide sports coverage of these league games. One of the first regional cable and athletic conference deals came in 1994, when Raycom and Jefferson-Pilot formed ACC Properties to distribute and sell the telecasts of ACC games. More recently, the PAC-10 Conference struck a deal with FSN to provide similar programming and sports coverage on the cable network, under the direction of their joint PAC-10 Properties (Consoli, 2004).

Finally, FSN set an industry precedent by assembling a national advisory board to help generate ideas on how FSN could better support local high school sports programs. Among the novelties suggested was a ranking of the "Fox Fab 50" top high school football teams, a high school football bowl game featuring these ranked teams, as well as an *Inside High School Sports* weekly cable news magazine show (Torpey-Kemph, 1999). This concept is a more comprehensive local offshoot of the long-running ESPN weekly show *Scholastic Sports America.*

High schools—inherently the most localized of developing sources of live programming—equate to high stakes in today's cable sports market. In the past few years, we have seen live telecasts of prep basketball phenoms such as LeBron James and Sebastian Telfair, as well as significant coverage of high-school dunk contests and all-star games, sponsored by popular brands such as McDonald's. FSN airs national and regional recruiting shows, and oftentimes, networks air live press conferences announcing where a marquee player is heading to college. The "reality" of high-school sports is showcased on several shows as well, including ESPN's *Bound for Glory* (2005), which featured NFL Hall of Famer Dick Butkus as a "hired gun" to coach a struggling Western Pennsylvania football team.

PROGRAMMING:
FROM NEWS COVERAGE TO LIVE COVERAGE
TO NO COVERAGE AT ALL

Although television or cable coverage might insinuate news coverage in most discussions, coverage of sports on cable extends to so many other programming categories. The growth of sports coverage on cable to include new and innovative programming is driven in part by the successful cross-promotion of shows within respective sports networks. In their examination of sports promotion, Eastman and Billings (2000) found ratings improved, or at least held pat, as a result of sports marketing and media, promotion of sports within sports programs, as well as promotion of prime time shows within sports programs.

Sports coverage, sports programming, or sports entertainment, would all be appropriate categories for sports news. ESPN is still the gold standard for both event/game programming and studio newscasts. They adhere to traditional news-gathering protocol (confirming multiple sources before airing a story, allocating considerable resources and time for investigative pieces, etc.). They employ top names in various fields, including attorney Roger Cossack (formerly of Court TV and CNN) for commentary on high profile cases, such as the Kobe Bryant sexual assault trial and the Jayson Williams manslaughter trial. Bob Ley, one of two original ESPN anchors from 1979 (along with Chris Berman, perhaps the network's most visible anchor in addition to Dan Patrick), hosts the investigative sports/news magazine *Outside the Lines*. Sharp-tongued NBA analyst Stephen A. Smith rose to prominence on ESPN's *NBA Shootaround*, and in 2005 landed an edgy talk show titled *Quite Frankly*, set in front of an *Arsenio*-like studio audience.

Embracing its role as "The Worldwide Leader," the network hired respected *Washington Post* sports editor/columnist George Solomon in July 2005 to become one of the industry's first ombudsmen. He regularly writes columns for ESPN.com and other platforms to objectively critique the work of his company's reporters and anchors. Other original programming has become listener staples—shows such as *Pardon the Interruption* and *The Sports Reporters* on ESPN, as well as *Sports Century* on ESPN Classic.

In 1998, FSN launched the news shows *Goin' Deep* and *The Last Word* for national audiences ("Fox Sports," 1997). These programs, as well as FSN's *National Sports Report*, suffered from the popularity of *SportsCenter* and ESPN's related news programs, which have helped to propel that network to the top of audience rankings. Cable networks are also willing to revive once-popular or struggling programs that originally aired on national networks. In 2005, ESPN picked up NBC castoffs *The Contender* (a boxing reality show) and coverage of The Breeders Cup. One bout on *The Contender* drew a 2.2 rating in the coveted male 18–34 category, the highest boxing score in that demo in more than a decade (Deeken, 2005b).

Several cable networks have successfully utilized the documentary genre. FSN's *Beyond the Glory* provides a type of a hard-hitting, first-person style program to mirror the previous success of ESPN's Peabody and Emmy-winning *Sports Century*. Cable networks appear more willing (than broadcast networks) to tell complex stories with themes central to social commentary as race and heroism, and one's ability to overcome obstacles to success (Paige, 2005).

Generally, FSN has struggled with ESPN's megabrands such as *SportsCenter* for national news coverage. However, FSN has made headway with a revamped localized news strategy to improve the content and delivery of news on its *Regional Sports Reports*. And the strategy worked. As FSN President Tracy Dolgin noted, the network tried unsuccessfully to create its own *SportsCenter*. The increased investment FSN placed in its *Regional Sports Reports*, then, reflected the network's overall strategy "to become more of an entertainment sports network with a strong regional focus" (Larson, 2002a, p. 5). Thus, the differences in the networks and subsequent programming strategies between FSN and ESPN are highlighted in their respective approaches to sports news coverage (Schlosser, 1998).

While FSN goes local and ESPN reaches global with their respective news content, they are not the only heavy hitters in sports news coverage on cable. In 1995, HBO Sports launched its successful *Real Sports* with Bryant Gumbel (Burgi, 1995a). The cable programmer has followed the success of *Real Sports* with the airing of a similar news magazine program format featuring sports broadcasting notable Bob Costas.

Aside from Gumbel's long-running success, the HBO sports brand includes venerable hits such as *Inside the NFL*, *Arli$$* (featuring a wisecracking sports agent), and high-profile boxing packages. Showtime has been a major player in boxing, a sport that has traditionally been a pay-per-view spectacle, which works well within the pay-channel concept. More recently, ESPN has tried to directly link sports and entertainment news and events with its *ESPN Hollywood*, which airs to a format similar to long-running news magazine shows such as *Entertainment Tonight* and *Inside Edition*, featuring primarily investigative journalism and exposes (gossip) on sports and entertainment stars.

A decade ago, talk shows did well on cable and were a mainstay of the network programming lineup (McClellan, 1994). ESPN has fared well with the talk format. In addition to its award-winning *Outside the Lines*, which brings a number of timely news topics to the forefront of public debate, related news/talk formats have included ESPN's long-running *The Sports Reporters*, as well as the more recent, often irreverent offerings *Pardon the Interruption, Around the Horn*, and *Cold Pizza*.

ESPN is also notable for its repetition and repurposing of popular programs. The latest edition of *Sports Center* is repeated throughout the following morning on the parent network, and programs ranging from the *World Series of Poker* to *NFL Films Presents* are typical "filler fare" on a variety of time slots. ESPN's understanding of media symbiosis and repurposing is evidenced through such programming strategies as simulcasts of radio shows on ESPN News (such as *Mike and Mike in the Morning*, done in a similar fashion to MSNBC's *Imus in the Morning*), ESPN's *Instant Classics* (reruns of top games, aired on ESPN Classic), and the morning talk show *Cold Pizza* (shaved down to a shorter *First and 10* in the afternoon).

As if news and talk weren't enough, ESPN is treating the promos for its newscasts as another form of programming in its own right. Because of their humorous and entertaining content, the advertisements for "This is SportsCenter" have created a significant buzz in the industry and among viewers. Collectively, this promotional campaign can even be viewed in its entirety on ESPN's Web site (Friedman, 2000). The network has gone "retro" with its NBA promos, with funky music and psychedelic fonts and colors to appeal to the "old school 'ballers" (Janoff, 2005).

Although sports news coverage is a critically important facet of the overall programming strategy of sports cable networks, the bell cow of all coverage continues to be the gamut of major sporting events these networks pay enormous fees for the rights to carry live, and usually with great fanfare. In addition to the aforementioned ESPN football and baseball blockbuster deals, Fox Sports inked a $2.5-billion deal in 2001 to carry the entire postseason and a majority of the regular season telecasts of MLB games through 2006. In addition, FSN tacked on another 2,000-plus games to its regional cable channels across the country after it secured the local cable rights for 26 of the 30 MLB franchises (Schlosser, 2001). It would be reasonable to argue that America's pastime, as a major television programming event, put Fox and FSN on the map.

In essence, baseball, as a televised event, has done for FSN what professional football did for its competitor, ESPN, a decade earlier. In 1992, ESPN acquired select rights to air NFL regular season and postseason games, the Super Bowl and Pro Bowl, as well as related sports programs ("Worldwide NFL," 1992). Its influence on professional and college football coverage on cable grew from there. Today, ESPN is known for not only innovative game day coverage, but also its own *Game Day* (college football), *Prime Time* (NFL), and other programs (i.e., gavel-to-gavel coverage of pseudoevents such as the NFL draft) featuring in-depth analysis of the sport. The NFL also jumped on the opportunity to secure sponsors for what are referred to as *shoulder* television programs, which air on broadcast and cable networks in conjunction with coverage of the league's football games (Jensen, 1998).

Sports coverage on cable has also expanded to include nonevents or niche programs. One of the recent programming battles between ESPN and FSN was in the area of classic sports, that is, the airing of memorable historic contests that resonated with nostalgic buffs. By 1997, ESPN had acquired Classic Sports Network for an estimated $150 to 175 million, while FSN countered with controlling interest in American Sports Classic (Burgi, 1997d). ESPN has also popularized the awards show the *ESPYs,* which highlights outstanding individual performances in all sports, as well as other categories, in an Oscar type of special event gala televised each year.

In an ironic twist, ESPN has gone full circle a quarter century after debuting in a tiny operation in remote Bristol, Connecticut. Early programming was primarily syndicated showings of sports such as Australian Rules Football. Now, nontraditional games/sports have regained cult followings. ESPN's tape-delayed packages of the *World Series of Poker* event have garnered solid ratings and have spawned copycat programs on other cable networks such as The Travel Channel (*World Poker Tour*) and Bravo (*Celebrity Poker Showdown*). A-list celebrities such as Ben Affleck have appeared on such programs, and Affleck joined buddy Matt Damon and Tobey Maguire as contestants for the 2004 *World Series of Poker.*

Another non-traditional sports hook is the recent bass fishing craze. In 2005, ESPN bagged strong ratings for the *Bassmaster Classic,* using 35 cameras and Pixar-type animation. That year, ESPN showed 29 different fishing shows, including a four-hour block on Saturday mornings. FSN counters with its weekly *FLW Outdoor Tour,* which employed underwater "snorklecams," and OLN, which has lured several major sponsors to angle for viewership (Ressner, 2005).

In the spring of 2004, FSN (angler) aired at least four nonevent programs within its weekly lineup, including *Saturday Night Poker,* as well as *Fox Sports Across America, Sports List,* and *I Max,* a talk show featuring Max Kellerman, the former host of ESPN's *Around the Horn* and analyst of professional boxing for ESPN2 (Larson, 2004).

At the same time FSN was announcing its nonevent program lineup for 2004, the newly formed College Sports Television (CSTV) was creating an instructional show titled *CSTV U,* which would feature 100 new shows for student-athletes, aimed at instruction, demonstration, and motivation. The new shows complement existing programs on the network, such as *Nike Training Camp* and *Coach* ("News of the Market," 2004, p. 40). CSTV has since partnered with similar platforms, including the Pax ("i") network in 2005.

In an attempt to reach younger demographics and appeal to the advertisers of this generation-x target audience, cable programmers began to produce programs best categorized as alternative. In 1995, ESPN and ESPN2 (established originally with programming for younger audiences in mind) announced plans to sponsor the first annual *Extreme Games.* At the time, industry insiders were skeptical of the potential for these *X-Games,* noting that Ted Turner's attempt to host the Goodwill Games as an Olympic alternative failed to succeed for the cable sports mogul (Burgi, 1995b). Nonetheless, the *X-Games* have gained a popular following through the years, even expanding its current coverage on cable to include winter and summer games.

As a result of the *X-Games* phenomena, Music Television (MTV) experimented with a weekly MTV Sports program entitled *Sandblast,* which highlighted performances in extreme water sports (Fitzgerald, 1996). Fox Sports Net got in on the action in 1999, with its *G-Force Rush Hour* extreme sports program, and NBC aired its first *Gravity Games* that same year (Larson, 1999).

If not extreme games, how about game shows? Traditionally, game shows have not fared well when included in sports coverage on cable. Chris Berman's *Boardwalk and Baseball* experienced modest success in the 1980s. ESPN also experimented with the *2-Minute Drill* to provide challenges for contestants well versed in sports trivia, and a more recent version, *Stump the Schwab*, that debuted in 2005. *Beg, Borrow, and Deal* offered a format featuring a real-world challenge among contestants (Consoli, 2001). Fox Sports Net established its own brand of game show in 2000, with the airing of *Sports Geniuses*, according to a similar format as that of the popular game show *Jeopardy*, yet with an emphasis on names and dates of historical sports figures and events (Schlosser, 2000).

The Golf Channel launched *The Big Break*, along with several successful sequels; the program pits amateurs against each other for lucrative prizes, and has even embraced Ryder Cup-style formats to globalize the show.

Reality TV has also had an impact on sports coverage on cable as well. ESPN's *D-League* was coproduced with the NBA to provide an insight into the real lives of minor-league players struggling to make it professionally (Consoli, 2001). The *And 1 Basketball Diaries*, and *Mixed Tape Tour*, promoting a more free-flowing, hip-hop style, has garnered a strong niche audience as well. ESPN's *Dream Job* (the first winner, Mike Hall, was immediately tapped to become the signature anchor for its new ESPNU network), built in the mold of NBC's hit show *The Apprentice*, has been added to its reality television programming lineup. An earlier attempt at reality television by ESPN was *I'd Do Anything*, in which a friend or relative endures four days of excruciating tasks to help a loved one realize a dream encounter with a star athlete or favorite team.

One of the more recent household games to impact sports coverage on cable is the apparent craze for fantasy sports. As sports fans, family, friends, and office pools, conduct mock drafts and chart player performances in respective professional sports throughout the year (primarily baseball and football), cable sports networks are providing more in-depth stats and analysis according to the rules and standings of the fantasy games. Although countless statistics and correlating point totals for players are critical to fantasy sports success, it appears the Internet is the ideal media tool to accommodate this never-ending search for information by the fantasy sports participant. As a result, sports cable networks, such as ESPN, have also incorporated fantasy sports coverage on the network's Web site, where regular updates and standings can be posted and accessed easily by fantasy league combatants (Tedesco, 1999).

The fantasy notion sometimes spreads outside the boundaries of media and sports to include traditionally overused advertising attention-grabbing techniques, such as ESPN's cheesecake ads of scantily-clad beauties touting the network's fantasy football Web site (Janoff, 2005).

Finally, the time has come for sports cable networks to extend their coverage to incorporate original programming, which to date has included both the feature film and the dramatic series. In 2002, ESPN aired its first television movie—the panned *A Season on the Brink* (from John Feinstein's best-seller about then Indiana University head basketball coach Bob Knight)—and followed that up with the critically acclaimed *The Junction Boys* (adapted from the Jim Dent book about then Texas A&M football coach Paul "Bear" Bryant), with plans to air as many as five original movies per year. In 2005, ESPN debuted *Four Minutes*, a retrospective of Sir Roger Bannister breaking this iconic standard for the mile run. While ESPN remains dedicated to events and sporting news, the sports programming network has experimented with original programming because it "can no longer grow on sports rights alone" (Larson, 2002b, p. 4).

ESPN's Mark Shapiro, senior vice president and general manager of programming and acquisitions, said the network is "captive to seasonal events, but there is so much competition that we need programming to supplement our games"

(Larson, 2002b, p. 4). ESPN has a rich history in airing nonevents and even included some feature films in its programming lineup years ago, prior to moving such entertainment to the regular programming schedule on its ESPN Classic network (Larson, 2002b).

But ESPN didn't stop there. The original programming experiment of the sports cable network has extended into the realm of the dramatic series. *Playmakers* began airing in the summer of 2003, and drew significant ratings in prime time (Frutkin, 2003). However, outcries from NFL brass followed, criticizing the program's producers for brazenly exaggerating the use of drugs and performance enhancements, as well as the extent of sexual conduct and infidelity, by the professional football players portrayed in the show.

CONCLUSIONS AND FUTURE AREAS OF INTEREST

Sports coverage on cable, like any other medium, must heed the dilemma of audience siphoning. Newspapers, often grudgingly, provide some of their content free of charge on their Internet sites. Although studies show that about 10% of newspaper readers eschew the hard copy for the free cyber version, the Internet does provide immediacy of stories and an outlet for younger audiences. For now, cable continues to siphon broadcast network viewership, and, for the first time, total cable viewing has eclipsed broadcast network television. One reason, obviously, is the narrowcasting capability of cable. In addition, cable is relatively lacking in editorial and governmental constraints.

So the question for future research and industry analysis is "What will siphon sports viewers from cable?" From this perspective, where is sports coverage, and likewise viewership, headed?

Fortunately, sports programming is one of the few genres generally immune from the timeshifting phenomenon that began in the 1970s with VCRs and has continued with sophisticated multimedia devices such as TiVo. Because most sporting events and studio shows are broadcast live, viewers are generally unlikely if not loath to tape a game and watch it at their convenience. The excitement that builds during dramatic sporting events, aided by the disposition and curiosity of the viewer, greatly affects the enjoyment of sports coverage on cable according to the outcome of the contests, as we have discussed. As long as there is quality sports coverage on cable television, fans will be tuned in. But will the plethora of additional coverage on new media aid or detract from the enjoyment of the cable TV sports viewing experience?

REFERENCES

Adelman, R., & Atkin, D. (2000). What children watch when they watch TV: Putting theory into practice. *Journal of Broadcasting & Electronic Media, 44*(1), 143.

Berniker, M. (1994). ESPN gets into interactive game. *Broadcasting & Cable, 124*(21), 61–62.

Brown, R. (1996). Turner, Sports Illustrated plan sports network. *Broadcasting & Cable, 126*(8), 12.

Bryant, J., & Miron, D. (2002). Entertainment as media effect. In J. Bryant & D. Zillmann (Eds.), *Media effects: Advances in theory and research* (549–582). Mahwah, NJ: Lawrence Erlbaum Associates.

Bryant, J., & Raney, A. (2000). Sports on the screen. In D. Zillmann & P. Vorderer (Eds.), *Media entertainment: the psychology of its appeal* (153–174). Mahwah, NJ: Lawrence Erlbaum Associates.

Bryant, J., & Thompson, S. (2002). *Fundamentals of media effects*. New York: McGraw-Hill.

Burgi, M. (1994). Cable TV. *Media Week, 4*(38), 10.

Burgi, M. (1995a). Cable TV. *Media Week, 5*(7), 9.

Burgi, M. (1995b). Don't try this at home. *Media Week, 5*(24), 24.

Burgi, M. (1996). Cable TV. *Media Week, 6*(10), 14.

Burgi, M. (1997a). Cable TV. *Media Week, 7*(24), 14.

Burgi, M. (1997b). Cable TV. *Media Week, 7*(38), 12–13.

Burgi, M. (1997c). Cable TV. *Media Week, 7*(47), 9.

Burgi, M. (1997d). Classic sports: First and 10. *Media Week, 7*(33), 9.

Cannella, S. (2005). Cable Ready: OLN—once the Outdoor Life Network—wants to woo viewers from the glitzy "Worldwide Leader" with a macho lineup that looks a lot like...the original ESPN. *Sports Illustrated, 103*(8), 16.

Consoli, J. (2001). ESPN expanding to movies, reality and game shows. *Media Week, 11*(28), 6.

Consoli, J. (2003). Delay of game. *Media Week, 13*(22), 22.

Consoli, J. (2004). PAC 10 mentality. *Media Week, 14*(4), 22.

Consoli, J., & Larson, M. (2004). NBA passes to cable. *Media Week, 14*(16), 6.

Cooper, J. (1998a). Narrower world of sports. *Media Week, 8*(9), 6.

Cooper, J. (1998b). FSN unveils its holy grail. *Media Week, 8*(5), 9.

Cooper, J. (1999). Building the brand. *Media Week, 9*(22), 62–63.

Deeken, A. (2005a). Nielsen to measure sponsorships on ESPN. *Media Week, 15*(11), 34.

Deeken, A. (2005b). Contender punches up ESPN ratings. *Media Week, 15*(38), 29.

Dupagne, M. (1999). Exploring the characteristics of potential high-definition television adopters. *Journal of Media Economics, 12*(1), 35–50.

Durand, C. (2002). Game, set and message: The growing importance of sport as communication product. *Communication Abstracts, 25*(4), 431–586.

Eastman, S. T., & Billings, A. C. (2000). Promotion in and about sports programming. In S. T. Eastman (Ed.), *Research in media promotion* (pp. 203–220). Mahwah, NJ: Lawrence Erlbaum Associates.

Eastman, S. T., & Riggs, K. E. (1994). Televised sports and ritual—fan experiences. *Sociology of Sport Journal, 11*(3), 249–274.

Fitzgerald, K. (1996). Extreme-ly hot. *Advertising Age, 67*(26), 44–45.

Foust, D. (2005). The PGA Tour: sand trap ahead; as it negotiates new TV deals, the Tour finds itself in a weakened position. *Business Week,* 3957, 88.

Fox sports to add shows with news edge. (1997). *Media Week, 7*(47), 3.

Freeman, M., & Cooper, J. (1998). Regionals round second. *Media Week, 8*(29), 8.

Friedman, W. (2000). ESPN treats promos as programming. *Advertising Age, 71*(47), 8.

Frutkin, A. J. (2003). ESPN hikes football drama. *Media Week, 13*(29), 6.

Frutkin, A. J., Larson, M., & Mundy, A. (2002). Media Wire. *Media Week, 12*(3), 4–5.

Goetzl, D. (2002). Taking cue from cable, gingerly. *Advertising Age, 73*(11), 63.

Higgins, J. M. (2001). ESPN hikes rates. *Broadcasting & Cable, 131*(20), 30.

Higgins, J. M. (2003). Cox, ESPN brawl gets nasty. *Broadcasting & Cable, 133*(23), 8.

Hocking, J. E. (1982). Sports and spectators: Intra-audience effects. *Journal of Communication, 32*(1), 100–108.

Janoff, B. (2005a). ESPN points to NBA virtues; sharp electronics is on the ball. *Brandweek, 46*(36), 10.

Janoff, B. (2005b). Chicks dig fantasy football. *Brandweek, 46*(29), 26.

Jensen, J. (1994). ESPN plays games to pump up brand. *Advertising Age, 65*(22), 32.

Jensen, J. (1996). Cable TV marketer of the year. *Advertising Age, 67*(50), 1–2.

Jensen, J. (1997). Battle gets nasty for eyes and ears of sports junkies. *Advertising Age, 68*(15), 18–19.

Jensen, J. (1998). Coke, Direct TV to support NFL "shoulder" TV shows. *Advertising Age, 69*(27), 26.

Kerschbaumer, K. (2002). NTC gets into the game. *Broadcasting & Cable, 132*(46), 23.

Kerschbaumer, K. (2005). DVRs not so hot? ESPN study shows they aren't for everybody. *Broadcasting & Cable, 135*(24), 26.

Larson, M. (1999). Taking it to the extreme. *Media Week, 9*(7), 14.

Larson, M. (2002a). Local news draws fans. *Media Week, 12*(27), 5.

Larson, M. (2002b). ESPN calls up sports dramas. *Media Week, 12*(7), 4–5.

Larson, M. (2004). FSN tries to avoid the squeeze play. *Media Week, 14*(8), 4–5.

Lindemann, C. (1996). Fox Sports Net debuts Nov. 1. *Broadcasting & Cable, 126*(44), 48.

Lindemann, C. (2001). Stream 2. *Broadcasting & Cable, 131*(26), 42–44.

Linnett, R., & Kerwin, A. M. (2004). FSN to be the new face of Fox Sports. *Advertising Age, 75*(10), 45.

Lowry, T. (2005). Espn.com: guys and dollars; with plenty of sports on the Net, espn.com lures more male viewers 18 to 34 than any of its competitors. *Business Week,* 3955, 74.

McAvoy, K. (2000). Batting clean-up. *Broadcasting & Cable, 130*(13), 32–34.

McAvoy, K. (2003). Baseball seeks key for the Fox TV lock. *Broadcasting & Cable, 133*(13), 31.

McClellan, S. (1994). Talk, talk, talk: Cable can't get enough. *Broadcasting & Cable, 124*(8), 42–43.

McConville, J. (1995). Fox, Liberty going global with sports. *Broadcasting & Cable, 125*(45), 8–9.

McGrail, M. & Roberts, B. (2005). Strategies in the broadband cable TV industry: the challenges for management and technology innovation. *Info, 7*(1), 53–65.

Moshavi, S. D. (1991). Basic cable turning to PPV. *Broadcasting, 121*(25), 39–40.

Mullen, M. (2002). The fall and rise of cable narrowcasting. *Convergence, 8*(1), 62–83.

News of the Market. (2004). *Media Week, 14*(16), 40.

Paige, T. (2005). Golden age is now for sports documentaries: genre gains popularity among programmers. *Multichannel News, 26*(33), 16.

Perse, E. M., & Ferguson, D. A. (2000). The benefits and costs of web surfing. *Communication Quarterly, 48*(4), 343–359.

Prikios, K. A. (2001). The perfect marriage needs some help (Action Sports Cable Network, launched by Paul Allen). *Broadcasting & Cable, 131*(27), 32.

Pulser, B. (2005). TV news meets cyberspace: will freewheeling Internet users watch online shows? *American Journalism Review, 27*(4), 74.

Raunsbjerg, P., & Sand, H. (1998). TV sport and rhetoric: The mediated event. *Communication Abstracts, 21*(1), 159–174.

Ressner, J. (2005). Cable TV's big fish fight: will Disney outfox the competition in its bass battle? *Time, 166*(15), A28.

Reynolds, M. (2005). OLN still filling NHL roster. *Multichannel News, 26*(43), 18.

Romano, A. (2001). Some like it local. *Broadcasting & Cable, 131*(25), 28–30.

Romano, A. (2002a). Ganging up on sports fees. *Broadcasting & Cable, 132*(20), 22–23.

Romano, A. (2002b). ESPN sees gold in digital. *Broadcasting & Cable, 132*(51), 32.

Romano, A. (2003a). Sports rules cable Nielsens. *Broadcasting & Cable, 133*(44), 19.

Romano, A. (2003b). Cable ops, programmers ready for high-definition. *Broadcasting & Cable, 133*(24), 3.

Romano, A. (2003c). Cable takes to product tie-ins. *Broadcasting & Cable, 133*(4), 14.

Rubin, A. M. (2002). The uses-and-gratifications perspective of media effects. In J. Bryant & D. Zillmann (Eds.), *Media effects: Advances in theory and research* (pp. 525–548). Mahwah, NJ: Lawrence Erlbaum Associates.

Schlosser, J. (1998). Game of Fox and mouse heats up. *Broadcasting & Cable, 128*(47), 6–7.

Schlosser, J. (2000). The game show of champions. *Broadcasting & Cable, 130*(13), 52.

Schlosser, J. (2001). Fox: View from the hill. *Broadcasting & Cable, 131*(14), 27.

Schlosser, J., & Tedesco, R. (2001). Fox scores with baseball. *Broadcasting & Cable, 131*(44), 25.

Shuk Wa, T. (2003). Nokia and Castrol tap EPL interactive appeal. *Media Asia, 14.*

Stump, M. (2004). HD sports coverage goes local: Fox Sports Net, Time Warner Cable roll out regionalized games. *Multichannel News, 25*(13), 34.

Stump, M. (2005). Comcast's ice age begins: NHL drops the puck on streaming of live games. *Multichannel News, 26*(42), 31.

Sullivan, D. B. (1991). Commentary and viewer perception of player hostility: Adding punch to televised sports. *Journal of Broadcasting & Electronic Media, 35*(4), 487–504.

Tedesco, R. (1999). ESPN fantasies sell. *Broadcasting & Cable, 129*(5), 54.

Thomaselli, R. (2003a). Baseball tries makeover. *Advertising Age, 74*(5), 3–4.

Thomaselli, R. (2003b). ESPN launches blitz against Cox. *Advertising Age, 74*(47), 4–5.

Top 25 television networks (1999). *Broadcasting & Cable, 129*(51), 31–36.

Torpey-Kemph, A. (1999). Inside media. *Media Week, 9*(44), 38–39.

Vincent, R. C., & Basil, M. D. (1997). College students' news gratifications, media use, and current events knowledge. *Journal of Broadcasting & Electronic Media, 41*(3), 380–392.

Worldwide NFL. (1992). *Broadcasting, 122*(19), 48.

Zillmann, D. (1980). Anatomy of suspense. In P. H. Tannenbaum (Ed.), *The entertainment functions of television* (pp. 133–163). Hillsdale, NJ: Lawrence Erlbaum Associates.

Zillmann, D. (1991). Empathy: Affect from bearing witness to the emotions of others. In J. Bryant & D. Zillmann (Eds.), *Responding to the screen: Reception and reaction processes* (pp. 135–167). Hillsdale, NJ: Lawrence Erlbaum Associates.

Zillmann, D., Bryant, J., & Sapolsky, B. S. (1979). The enjoyment of watching sport contests. In J. H. Goldstein (Ed.), *Sports, games, and play: Social and psychological viewpoints* (pp. 297–335). Hillsdale, NJ: Lawrence Erlbaum Associates.

Zillmann, D. & Cantor, J. R. (1976). A disposition theory of humour and mirth. In A. J. Chapman & H. C. Foot (Eds.), *Humour and laughter: Theory, research, and applications* (pp. 93–115). London: Wiley.

10

Sports Online: The Newest Player in Mediasport

Michael Real
Royal Roads University

From its explosive development in the last decade of the twentieth century, the World Wide Web has become an ideal medium for the dedicated sports fanatic and a useful resource for even the casual fan. Its accessibility, interactivity, speed, and multimedia content are triggering a fundamental change in the delivery of mediated sports, a change for which no one can yet predict the outcome. Like an unanticipated child, the newest member of the sports media family has disrupted everything. Family roles, once clearly established, are shifting as the older siblings—newspapers, magazines, radio, television, VCRs, and even computers—adjust to this new invasive presence.

The global technology network of the online Internet, nicknamed "the Web," is not so much a new and separate medium for sports use as it is a new combination of previous media. It offers the textual information and data that have made newspaper sports pages valuable for more than a century. It offers the speed and sound of the live radio broadcast that has produced programs and stars in sports since the Roaring Twenties. The Web can bring to the fan the sights, sounds, and immediacy of the family's previous star sibling, the sports of live-action and prerecorded television, offerings whose presence was vastly multiplied by satellite and cable. The Web even evokes the on-demand control of computers and video games. And, by having all these talents, this mixture of angel and demon offers more than any of the previous media from which it has emerged. Still young and unfocused, the Web is the gifted younger sibling whose promise generates both excitement and threat for all members of the family

Research on the Internet is understandably yet at an early stage. Internet use for political and social purposes—travel, political campaigns, issue advocacy, dating, pornography—are important and under examination in journals and books. Sports as an interest group, or *genre*, of Internet use offers the opportunity to explore in depth the leisure uses and social dimensions of the Internet. An early study looked at the Web's use for sports history (Cox & Salter, 1998). A look at gender in ABC's online Olympic coverage in 2000 found the same reduction and stereotyping of female athletes as has been found in other media (Jones, 2004). A more comprehensive look (Beck & Bosshart, 2003) briefly distinguished the Web's role as a sports encyclopedia, an interactive medium for self-publishing, a publicity vehicle for teams and athletes, a betting site, an outlet for neglected sports, and a site of struggle between independent website designers/bloggers and the megamedia conglomerates already dominating sports and media.

From the few studies and from the real world of online sports, many questions emerge. What is the combination of technologies and applications that comprises the world of sports online? What are the real and projected scales and economies of sports on the Web? Who are emerging as the dominant players, the winners and losers, in this complex? What conflicts and controversies have marked the first decade of the growing availability of sports over the Internet? What do answers to these questions tell us of the nature of the Internet? Of sports today? Of media theory? This analysis seeks answers to these questions through a mixture of methods: interviews with producers of Web sports and a focus group of fans, an examination of sports Web history and industry reports, a survey of Internet use by media/sport researchers, and comparisons to traditional theories of media. The picture that emerges from this has some of the blurriness and jumpiness of most online video, but the action on-screen is, in its own way, as exciting as any major sporting event.

HISTORY AND SCALE: SPORTS SCORE BIG ONLINE

Noting the popularity and new economic profitability of sports online, the technology editor of *BusinessWeekOnline*, Salkever titled his 2003 report simply "Sports Score Big Online." By that time, annual income from advertising on sports-themed Web sites was expected to approach $2.4 billion, and sports-related electronic commerce was estimated to bring in $4.7 billion. Featuring play-by-play audio plus real-time data, Major League Baseball was charging $14.95 per month to its 300,000 subscribers and netting a profit of nearly $6 million on an income of $80 to 90 million from its 31 Web sites (Holt, 2004). At the same time, 150,000 Nascar.com subscribers were paying $19.95 to receive live audio of the races, along with such extras as telemetry feeds of technical and performance information (brake, throttle, GSP location) of cars on the track and the two-way radio conversations between drivers and pit crews (Salkever, 2003). In a surprisingly short time, sports Web sites had matured from unprofitable labors of love by fanatics to supplemental loss-leaders for leagues, teams, and media corporations to directly profitable enterprises with huge growth potential. Sports fantasy league members were willing to pay $20 or more merely to participate, creating one of many revenue sources for sports Web sites.

By the first decade of the twenty-first century, the biggest sports Web sites were ESPN.com, Yahoo! Sports, AOL Sports, SI.com, and Sportsline.com, each recording more than a million unique visitors each week (Databank Sports, 2001). The success of these sites did not happen overnight or without struggle. The pioneers saw their utopian visions of the 1990s give way a few years later to the dot.com recession. As on the playing field, from this unanticipated challenge the strongest competitors emerged in more dominant positions, but the process had been longer and more arduous than the competitors might have wished.

Sports Web sites have evolved with the Web itself. As Beck and Bosshart (2003) noted, the transmission rates of data over the web and the limited memories of personal computers made the early Internet a very limited resource. It took patience for early adopters to log on, find their way to useful information, and receive it. Transmission of anything other than small blocs of text was impractical. No more. As a result, both production and content have expanded exponentially.

The history of ESPN.com,[1] the leader in the field, indicates the erratic if successful trajectory of the development of the Internet and Web sports. In 1995 ESPN signed a two-year contract with Starwave, a start-up operated by the former partner of Bill Gates at Microsoft, Paul Allen, to develop and operate a Web site for ESPN, the 24-hour sports network that had begun amid great skepticism in 1979 and came to dominate the field. Even the Web site's name was unstable in the early years. After toying with the label "Satchel.com," the first address became "ESPN-net.sportszone.com," but that was reduced a few years later to "ESPNnet.com" and finally to "ESPN.com." A handful of Starwave's employees operated the ESPN site first from Belleville, Washington, and then from Seattle. Beginning in 1999, ESPN.com was moved in stages to the central ESPN complex in Bristol, Connecticut, where, still in its first decade, it employed more than 100 editorial staff and perhaps twice that many technical staff, all in addition to its marketing staff in New York. Before it reached such success, there were more than a few times when its ownership seemed at a loss as to what ESPN.com might be. When the Walt Disney Company bought ABC and ESPN, Disney sold ESPN.com's operating company, Starwave, to Infoseek in Sunnyvale, California. But, rethinking its strategy, Disney then bought Starwave back and incorporated it into its new division, the Walt Disney Internet Group, known as "w.dig." During ESPN.com's rocky evolution, there were conflicts between east and west employee groups, between editorial and advertising interests, and between ESPN.com and ESPN's television and magazine operations.

Sports Web site content was also evolving significantly during this first decade, as changes at ESPN.com reflected. In the early years, ESPN.com featured little more than regularly updated scores and related information from the NFL, MLB, the NBA, and their college counterparts. This information was simply transferred from wire services such as the Scripps Howard News Service, which did not cover all sports; the Associated Press, whose information was available only to ESPN.com premium subscribers; and other sports tickers and services. Gradually the site began to incorporate information on soccer, golf, tennis, and other less dominant sports. The staff labored to include a short nightly feature, "In the Zone," but the site was close to pure data information. Finally, by 2004, the site was offering 10,000 pages of sports items updated continuously.

Even after the move to Bristol, the Web site was not integral to ESPN's larger purposes. ESPN.com was confined to conducting polls in conjunction with television events and offering chat rooms for NFL fans and similar groups. By 2003 this had changed to the point where ESPN.com was named one of the company's six priority areas and was one of the principles in the nightly production meetings of ESPN. ESPN.com also joined the television and magazine components of ESPN in

---

[1]The history of ESPN.com is based on an extensive interview with Kevin Jackson (April 19, 2004, Athens, OH), who has been with the site since its beginning and is now chief desk editor for ESPN.com. Industry trade publications extended and confirmed many of his details.

jointly creating and operating an "Enterprise Reporting Team." This investigative unit could manage each outlet for maximum effect in releasing its work. For example, when they were preparing to break the story of association between Ohio State football player Maurice Clarett and a known gambler, they chose to release the story first on the Web site, then on *SportsCenter* that night, and eventually in the magazine. Using the Web site first enabled ESPN to explain the story and its background in sufficient detail so that its release on television that night would be less likely to generate erroneous or misleading pickup by other media. The magazine's two-week production schedule made it impractical for releasing the Clarett story first in the magazine.

ESPN.com added two features in 2004, one providing television clips and the other encouraging personalizing of individual access to ESPN.com. "ESPN Motion" during the night sends several minutes of full-motion video to a subscriber's hard drive, where a single click during the day will bring up a highlight reel with the highest quality video currently available on the Internet. Dunks, touchdowns, and home runs are shown interspersed with 30-second commercials, utilizing a technology developed in-house by ESPN. The second feature, "My ESPN," enables a subscriber to customize his (92% of ESPN.com subscribers are male) or her homepage to highlight teams, sports, and players of most personal interest. Information that might have been three or four menus and clicks away is immediately featured.

AUDIENCE SIZE AND CHARACTERISTICS: TAKE ME OUT TO THE WEBCAST

The growth of the number of persons accessing sports sites on the World Wide Web has grown in a manner parallel to the growth of Web production and content, perhaps at even a faster rate. When compared to television numbers, the subscription numbers to leading sports Web sites seem small, but they have been expanding rapidly.

MLB.com's Web sites were making a profit less than two years after the league planned them in 2000, according to a report by Holt (2004). At that time, the baseball owners voted to centralize baseball's Internet operations with one site for the major leagues and one site for each of thirty teams. Bob Bowman, the CEO of MLB.com, a wholly owned subsidiary of Major League Baseball, projected 25,000 subscribers for the first full year of service in 2003. Against the backdrop of Web surfers expecting everything to be available free, MLB.com was asking $79.95 for the season or $14.95 per month. Yet, in its first few weeks, the service achieved its target number and within the year was claiming 300,000 subscribers. In addition to paying that fee for live audio of all games, subscribers could also download the video of "Baseball's Best," the more than 50 games deemed most historic, dating back to the 1936 World Series. MLB.com reported that 2 to 3 million fans each day visited major league sites during the six-month season, and 65 million visitors accessed a total of 560 million page hits on the sites during the 26 days of the playoffs (Holt, 2004).

The 2003 Super Bowl on ABC-TV was viewed in 43.4 million homes in the United States, while only 1,028,000 visitors accessed the official Super Bowl Web site. But that Web number was nearly triple the number from two years earlier. In 2001 only 359,000 persons had accessed the Web site. The numbers are small but the growth is rapid. The same 2003 Super Bowl saw more than 1.4 million unique visitors on the ESPN.com Web site. With both ABC and ESPN owned by Disney, the telecast and Web site could be effectively coordinated.

Like sports on television, the demographics of those accessing sports Web sites are desirable to many commercial sponsors. A majority of ESPN.com users are in the 18 to 34 male demographic. They average 9 minutes per page, while the global average according to Nielsen (2004b) is 45 seconds per Web page. The second- and third-page usage on ESPN.com, where the fan has found what he is most seeking, averages an amazingly sustained 13 minutes. The majority of users are college educated or in college. They are affluent, white-collar types.

Certain sports events are irresistible to the Web sports fan. March Madness features 64 NCAA college teams engaged in basketball games in the same two-day period on a Thursday and Friday. The sheer number of teams and games drives fans to the Internet. Nielsen//NetRatings reports 20 million unique visitors to sports Web sites for those games. Nielsen analyst Ryan explains: "Online tournament brackets, real-time game results, and up-to-the-minute commentary make the Web a huge attraction for March Madness fans" (Nielsen, 2004a, para 3). ESPN.com's audience during the first week of March Madness in 2004 was 4.493 million; Yahoo Sports had 2.396 million; and AOL Sports, SI.com, and Sportsline.com all had more than 1 million unique visitors. Total Web sport site users increased by 13% for that week.

When we expand the picture of Web sports to the world, as in the Olympics, the scale and duration of the attentive, purposeful audience is striking. Nielsen (2004b) reported that the average global user of the Internet engages in 24 to 29 sessions per month, visits 58 domains, and accesses 1,014 pages, each for an average of 45 seconds. The sessions average 48 minutes, totaling more than 23 hours per month. Given what advertisers are willing to pay for access to the viewers of television, it is not surprising that they are beginning to develop successful methods to reach the global Web audience. And Nielsen (2004b) reported that three of every four Americans have access to the Internet, with more than half having broadband access. The two fastest growing sites in the United States in August, 2004, were NBCOlympics.com, the Web site of the television network carrying the Games, and Athens2004.com, the official Web site of the Games. Their number of unique visitors was up more than 12%, making NBC's total more than 2.2 million unique visitors. Nielsen analyst Gotta (Nielsen, 2004c, para 7) noted, "Due to the time zone differences between Athens and the United States, this year's Olympics on the Web has turned out to play a significant role for American fans." With time differences of six hours or more from Athens, Web surfers in the United States, as in many parts of the world, could seek the factual information during the day and watch the television replays in the evening.

TELEVISION AND THE WEB: ENEMIES OR ALLIES—WHO IS UNDERMINING WHOM?

The emergence of the Web has triggered debates on whether the hard-copy daily newspaper will disappear and how soon, whether video rentals and video games will migrate to Web delivery systems, whether television networks will be reduced to just another lane on the information superhighway, and whether countries and cultures will blend into the long-anticipated Global Village. But for the Web, most potential rivalries have turned into partnerships, somewhat akin to when an international soccer club entices rival stars onto its roster. The playing field of Web sports is still an open one—there are many independent Web sites—but the trend has clearly been toward consolidation of ownership and convergence with other major media entities.

By 1999, warning shots were being fired about how the Web may destroy television's lucrative world. Burton (1999), a sports marketing expert, warned in *Advertising Age* that the Web could bring about the demise of TV as we know it. Under the inflammatory headline "The Internet Stands Ready to Undermine TV's Costly Sports Empire," Burton noted Nielsen's report that online homes watch 13% less television, about one hour less per day. Sports were the "killer application" that drove the success of radio and television, in Burton's analysis, and will do the same for the Internet (para 5). The huge television contracts of major sport leagues ($17.6 billion for eight years for the NFL) could be threatened by the overly cluttered sports telecasting world and its failure to deliver efficiently the 12- to 24-year-old computer-friendly male target. For Burton, the old broadcasting model faced the new multicasting model. He saw television networks offering sports Web sites as a potentially self-destructive move, one which would contribute to greater Internet usage and undercut television sports rights fees. He cautioned, "The sports circus may cause young males to move from the slow-paced world of TV Town to the infinitely more exciting lure of Digital Depot. That could mean the TV joins the radio in the attic (para 20)."

In 2000, Jordan (2000) continued the argument in *Nieman Reports* by charging that "The Web Pulled Viewers Away From the Olympic Games." His question was "How much longer will exclusive broadcast rights hold sway over the way that viewers take in these events?" His argument was made through the 56 million and 46 million page views, respectively, recorded by the official Olympics Web site and Sports Yahoo during the duration of the Sydney Games. NBC's television ratings were down but its Web site had 66 million page views, an average of more than 4 million daily. In 1996, he noted, NBC had two full-time staff on its Web site for the Atlanta Olympics but had 40 full-time and 100 part-time in Sydney for its Web site. On the television side, the network paid $705 million in rights fees for the lowest rated television Olympics since Mexico City in 1968. It required NBC to pay advertiser buy-backs, but the network still projected profits in the tens of millions of dollars. While television declined at the 2000 Games, the Internet was on the rise. One third of Internet users reported watching less television as a result. Jordan wonders whether a nation of computer-outfitted households will again be content to turn to television for events that ended hours before.

Even as Burton and Jordan were making their nightmare arguments about the future of television, Web sites were successfully exploring webcasting and seeking out partnerships with television networks. Seeing the successful synergy of ESPN and its Web site and CBS and its Web site, SportsLine, the venerable sports publication *The Sporting News* spent years working up a partnership for its Web site, an effort which resulted in its joining forces with Fox television. The benefits shared between Sporting News Online, *Sporting News Magazine*, and Fox Sports included major cross-promotions of each other's offerings and a sharing of columnists/commentators and celebrity features.

At the same time, streaming video technology had forged another bridge uniting television and the Web by making the transmission of television over the Web practical (Krikke, 2004) without the need to download large files before playback. Also, access-on-demand could be coupled with new miniaturized wireless devices for access anywhere. The move from online to television and back became more seamless, and television and computer screens began to be more interchangeable. Consoli (2003) reported that a traditional online corporation, AOL, capitalized on the synergy by advertising in the 2003 Super Bowl that it offered the Super Bowl ads on its Web site. It drew 5.5 million people within 36 hours. AOL also airs video clips from NBA, MLB, and Nascar, and four-minute highlight clips from each NFL game on Sunday nights. A potentially long legal battle emerged between a television recording/playback system and the NFL when the FCC (Cannella & Bechtel, 2004) cleared TiVoGo to allow its users to disseminate programs to remote television sets, thus opening a means to circumvent the NFL's regional and blackout rules. Clearly, television and the Web could be made synergistic allies as easily as blood enemies.

As six major transnational media conglomerates came to own and dominate a large part of the world of media by the early twenty-first century (McChesney, 2004; "Who Owns What," 2004), cross-ownership and operating agreements were erasing the distinctions between previously competing media like television and the Web or newspapers and radio. The high profile Web sites for sports were merely one member of the diverse media family being employed by megacorporations to maximize the publicity and control of media products and information channels. The once unruly youngster, the Web, had been made to line up alongside his siblings in formal family photos and forget former loyalties or antagonisms in the new family unity of commercialism-above-all.

SPORTS GAMBLING AND THE WEB: YOU CAN BET ON IT

Gambling and sports have an uneasy relationship at best, from the Chicago "Black Sox" World Series scandal of 1919 to Pete Rose's various acknowledgements and denials. The Internet has the potential to multiply the problem. Web-based gambling is available to anyone anytime, night or day, dressed or not. While illegal in the United States due to the inclusion of the Web under the 1961 Federal Wire Act prohibition of betting over the phone (Angwin, 2004), offshore online sites can be readily accessed by casual betters, children, gambling addicts, and even athletes.

Like sports on the Web, gambling online has grown rapidly, most of it centered on sports. Between 1997 and 2003, the number of gambling Web sites grew from 25 to 1,800 (Weir, 2003). During that time, Internet gambling losses grew from an estimated $300 million to somewhere between $3 billion and $6 billion. Internet gambling addiction increased by 25% over two years and was the number-one gambling problem among college students. A study by the Division on Addictions of the Harvard University Medical School ("The Motivated Scholar," 2002) reported that 5.6% of U.S. college age and young people are pathological in their betting—gambling to recoup losses, spending money they don't have, unable to stop—almost three times the rate among the general adult population. Having it available so effortlessly has made the Internet the primary source for college student betting and sports gambling. White, college-educated males with sports participation backgrounds are the majority among sports gambling addicts. Even prominent athletes have become its victims. Washington Capitals hockey star Jaromir Jagr admitted to running up a $500,000 debt betting through a Belize-based offshore Web site. Cross and Vollano (1999) found 35% of student athletes had gambled on sports and

5% of males had bet on their own games, accepted bribes to play poorly, or provided insider tips for gamblers. A 2000 University of Cincinnati study found 25.5% of Division I basketball and football players gambled on college sports and 3.7% on their own games (Weir, 2003). An NCAA report (2004) found that 6% of male student athletes gambled on the Internet and 21% gambled on college sport; 2% of female athletes gambled on the Web and 6% on college sports. Access to Web gambling exacerbates the problems of both student and student-athlete gambling.

Australia, New Zealand, and the United Kingdom have legalized online wagering, bringing regulation and taxation to the industry. The U.S. approach has resisted legalizing it and has worked with credit card companies to try to prevent it. The MGM Mirage casino operated an offshore gambling Web site until congressional opposition forced it to close. With the gambling industry lobbying for its legalization and gambling counselors and critics opposing it, online gambling is a site for struggle over whether to let anyone be his or her own bookie or to further oppose the industry that dares not meet in the country of its best customers (Richtel, 2004).

THE ACTIVE FAN: WEB SITES, BLOGGING, AND FANTASY LEAGUES

The shift in media research and theory away from the passive couch potato of bullet theory to the active user seeking information and gratification finds an ultimate expression and qualifier in the Web sports fan. The qualifying condition is that the Web sports fan is NOT the participating athlete actually playing the game. The average fan still receives and absorbs messages and media, is outside the action, and does not score the dramatic winning touchdown, hit the late-inning home run, or sink the game-clinching long jumper as time runs out. But, given that qualification, the fan today through the Web can be strikingly active, taking a step beyond even the success of sports radio talk shows in the 1980s and 1990s.

Fantasy leagues are now huge businesses in which a fan pays up to $100 to play by selecting players and then working the team through the season. When other Web sites go from free use to a fee charge, subscriptions dry up. But fantasy-league Web sites have performed impressively by achieving better than a 20% successful conversion rate, according to John Bruel, a sports marketing consultant. By 2003 Yahoo Sports claimed 10 million players in its fantasy football league and a growth rate of 40% per year (Salkever, 2003). Other major sports sites have similar fantasy leagues and membership rates. The quantity and depth of information available on the Web enables a fantasy league player to be the well-informed general manager of a complex, seemingly realistic virtual team. Subscribing to specialized Web sites and information sources, constantly exchanging opinions and insights with other fans, tracking down rumors and trivia, developing personnel and game strategies, the diehard player in an online fantasy league is exercising a new option first anticipated in British newspapers for soccer fans, an engrossing, time-consuming chance to "play" with and against the best. And, like gambling or sports channel obsessions, it can be addictive.

The active fan is also present in the creation of the endless number of sports-oriented Web sites and the success of specialized Web services. Most sports teams, leagues, school athletic departments, and other institutional presences in sports have dedicated Web sites. But these tend to be islands of safe, noncontroversial items: schedules, statistics, game stories, personal features. These sites are surrounded by dozens of fan-generated Web sites that express and feed the insatiable appetite of fans for connections to their favorite team or competitor. These scattered sites have, in turn, given rise to large and complex organizations feeding the hunger for team and region information. Layden (2003) found that Rivals.com, for example, from its base in Tennessee, by 2003 had 83 Web sites devoted to college sports and operated by local experts, whether sports journalist or avid fan. TheInsiders.com ran 87 such sites from its base in Seattle, and countless others did likewise. One of Rival.com's sites was Volquest.com. It claimed 2,000 University of Tennessee fans who paid up to $10 per month, accessed 250,000 pages per day, and flooded the site on national football signing day in February with more than one million visits.

Fan Web sites have expanded the traditional watchdog function of the press by having eyes and ears everywhere. In 2003, Iowa State basketball coach Larry Eustachy lost his position because of pictures and stories of him drinking and partying with students after a game in Missouri. The damaging photos were first posted on tigerboard.com three months before they were published by the *Des Moines Register.* Also in 2003, newly appointed Alabama football coach Mike Price was first charged on a rival fan's message board, autigers.com, with throwing money and scandal around at a strip club in Pensacola, Florida. In a few days the story went to the mainstream press and Price was fired (Layden, 2003). While fan Web sites are normally preoccupied with coaching strategy and player recruitment, they actually serve many uses and provide a variety of gratifications. Rivals.com Web sites have a network of analysts that cover each major market in the United States and offer photos, audio and video highlights, message boards, a recruiting database, and more (Clark, 2003).

Sports Web sites have also expanded on the quantity of reporting on sports, even offering real-time running Web logs, or *blogs*, of sporting events while they happen. The Web-based fan can listen to the play-by-play audio of many sports in far-flung places, watch video of some, and read details of each stage of the action both as reported, the news function, and as analyzed, the editorial function. Apropos of this latter function, beginning in 1998 a sports columnist for the *St. Paul Pioneer Press* was providing a play-by-play written commentary on play selection and performance in real-time during Minnesota Vikings games. He was dubbed the "laptop quarterback" (Gray, 2000). Neighborhood blogs on local sports, schools, and politics capitalize on the Web's potential for ultralocal community services by providing localized people-power content (Palser, 2004).

THE DEATH OF DISTANCE IN SPORTS FANDOM

As Kevin Jackson (personal communication, April 19, 2004) of ESPN.com put it, "There are no displaced sports fans anymore." Extending a process that began with cable and satellite television featuring teams by subscription from afar, the Web can now make a fan feel local even when hundreds or thousands of miles away. Walker (2003, para 8) reported that 55% of Major League Baseball fans do not live near their favorite team; he dubs them "the long-distance fan." Each morning, a geographically distant fan can read the local press coverage of his team, shop in the team store, satisfy his hunger for debate on the team through message boards, and follow the game action as it happens—all on the Web. He can watch premium-television sports packages, get score updates on his cell phone, and feel as engaged with his team as if he were in that city (Walker, 2003). Also, the one-sport fans can find on the Web just what they want and only that, wherever it may be, whether snowboarding, cheerleading, or the NBA, as our student panel reported (Focus Group, 2004). The internationalism of the Web creates exotic opportunities. Soccer fans in South Africa follow European teams closely, Japanese fans track the careers of their heroes performing in American baseball, franchises buy Chinese players to get access to that huge market, media moguls buy teams and leagues to provide content for their global satellites—and distance disappears.[2]

The stadium-without-walls parallels the online university-without-walls[3] and other institutions that provide access and connection to previously excluded publics. Mass communication first brought accounts of sports events to those not present through the next day's newspaper; then through same-day broadcasts; and now through instantaneous, globally available versions of both, and more.

SPECIALIZED WEB SPORTS USAGE: ACADEMICS IN CYBERSPACE

How do specialized groups use the Internet for sports? A survey of one group——international academic researchers specializing in sports and media—suggests some patterns (Real & Beeson, 2004). The convenience sample of 22 researchers from 11 countries included 7 females and 15 males. Fifteen of them use the Internet daily to access sports information, three weekly, three monthly, one rarely, but none never. Respondents most sought out information on scores and results, followed closely by events and teams. But they also sought information on athletes, features, chats, and research. All 22 had been obtaining online sports information since at least 2001, 10 from 1997 or earlier. The effect of Web usage on other media usage was spread relatively evenly. It led to reduced newspaper use for five, television for four, radio for three, magazines for three, and personal sources for four. Eighteen of the 22 have sports Web sites bookmarked as favorite sites. The sites varied from country to country and included general sports Web sites; sport-specific Web sites; university sports Web sites; and, in one case, a local hockey team Web site.

---

[2]This deterritorialization of sport has been explored by Cornel Sandvoss (2003) in *A Game of Two Halves: Football, Television, and Globalization* (London: Routledge). I have experienced this also in my own life as a fan. In 1971, when I moved from the Midwest to Southern California, I could no longer follow my lifelong team, the Chicago Cubs. Within a decade, I discovered to my surprise that I had, instead, become a San Diego Padres fan; because of local media coverage, when the Cubs visited San Diego, I knew none of the Cubs and all of the Padres. By 2000, when I moved back to the Midwest, this had changed dramatically. I could still follow my San Diego Chargers closely through the NFL Sunday Package on satellite and Web sports sources. If you know the Chargers' record in that period you know what a mixed blessing this was.

[3]In 2004, I joined the faculty of an innovative Canadian campus, Royal Roads University. Offering undergraduate and graduate degrees through online instruction and annual three-week residencies, this institution illustrates the new institution-without-walls capabilities available for sports, education, and other sectors.

The Web serves useful purposes for researchers, but most add notes of caution. Among the comments were[4] "Very, very useful.... Mostly, helpful and accurate.... Good access to material through official sports clubs websites, e.g., financial data.... A wonderful source of information for facts and figures, some discussion rooms are very helpful.... Economic information (e.g., ownership) outdates so rapidly that the Internet can be a useful way of updating." Frustrations include "Long search for in-depth information.... Methodologically difficult.... One difficulty of web studies still is the lack of a standard technique for studying the web, so each study has to develop its own methodological framework." The accuracy of Web information is a common concern of researchers: "It is a fine resource if used appropriately and not relied on exclusively.... You can use it for information, but always have a second source.... Be sure to double check information to ensure accuracy.... Check very carefully every source." One respondent explained, "As is the case with everything Internet related, be careful. General/background information (i.e., Olympic medal winners) is no big deal, and legitimate sources, such as a major newspaper, are fine. But I refuse to consider anything from any source that I am not familiar with. And there are far too many of those out there!" Another respondent was concerned with escalating expectations: "It just keeps getting better although there is an increased expectation in terms of the amount of information one should be able to get and process."

The future of the Web offers both steps and jumps forward in the view of survey respondents:

Faster, smoother and much more reliable.... Ticket booking will become more common on the Web. Live streaming will grow.... More audio and video streaming. Soon you will be able to access any sporting event from the Web.... Convergence is the way we are going; we'll be able to see more and more—and better quality—pictures on the web.... Streams of highlights, more in-depth information, a special site with resources for researchers on sports and mediasport.

One respondent suggested some details:

Broadband access will increase even further and the IOC will eventually feature online Olympic sports once they get their territorial issues sorted out, to name one example. Also, enhanced digital technology will make our typical current technology categories—such as the web vs. analog TV/radio sets—obsolete, as there will be a fusion of both, particularly via wireless technologies.

THEORETICAL IMPLICATIONS: HOW DIFFERENT IS THE WEB?

The emergence of strong centralized Web sites—ESPN.com, Sportsline, Nascar.com, cnnsi.com, MLB.com—confirms the importance of the editorial function of media, that is, the ability to coordinate information and make sense of it. Impossible

---

[4]Quotations cited here are from the original responses of survey participants. The elisions in these quotations indicate separate statements from *different* respondents.

amounts of information are available somewhere on the Web, but coordinating them into a meaningful, accessible assemblage is the service that makes possible Web *usage* as opposed to random Web wandering. The public looks to Web sites for gatekeeping of information and even agenda setting of its relative importance, although search engines like Google make Web agenda setting more audience-driven than in traditional media. Search engines and user-friendly Web site organization are crucial. Mere access to information means little in the age of information overload.

On the other side, access to *producing* information for the medium sets the Web apart from many traditional media where only professionals could produce newspapers or television and the public could only receive them. This open system recalls the emancipatory structuring of media called for by radical theorists such as Enzensberger (1974). This open structure, however, is constricted as major-media Web sites gain predominance over the quirky individual Web sites left over from the Web's first generation.

Media theories of political economy and globalization are clearly central to gaining an intellectual grasp of the world of Web sports. Globalizing trends are unmistakably evident in the Web itself, the ownership structure of media, and increasingly in the world of sport franchises and leagues. These parallel forces are exploited by the large corporations, many of which own both sports and media properties, including dominant Web sites ("Who Owns What," 2004). For example, the Walt Disney Company had revenues of $25 billion in 2000 from its holdings, which included the professional hockey team, The Mighty Ducks of Anaheim, as well as ABC sports; the nine cable television channels of ESPN; and all or part of ESPN.com, Soccernet.com, NBA.com, NFL.com, and Nascar.com. By 2004, the Time Warner Corporation owned the Atlanta Braves (MLB), Hawks (NBA), and Thrashers (NHL) alongside *Sports Illustrated* and 12 other leading sports magazines, TBS Superstation, Turner Network Television (TNT), and cnnsi.com. Rupert Murdoch, however, has taken this media—sport merger trend the furthest. His News Corporation and News Limited are large in the United States, owning the Fox network, 34 television stations, and the DirecTV satellite service. His News Corporation, in addition, owns 18 Fox Sports regional networks, Madison Square Garden Network, and Fox Sports Radio Network. It owns all or part of the American professional sports franchises the Los Angeles Dodgers, New York Rangers, New York Knicks, Los Angeles Kings, and Los Angeles Lakers. Still, Murdoch's *international* combination of sports and media ownership is more extensive yet. He owns major newspapers in London, New York, and Australia; major international satellites; and the television rights to major sports in many parts of the world. It is no surprise that *The Sporting News* placed Murdoch at the top of its list of the 100 most powerful people in sport for two consecutive years, the first person to repeat (Rowe & McKay, 1999).

Given these trends toward convergence and consolidation of ownership, the likelihood of a Spiral of Silence emerges, one in which fringe, minority voices get less hearing and are gradually brought into conformity. Similarly, as dominance of the Web reverts, as seems to be happening, toward the media monopolies, the hegemony of the privileged over Web content and values will marginalize less powerful groups as it has in other media. The *volume* of a distinct opinion, as in the adamancy of sports and political radio callers, should not be mistaken for *differentness*. As Herbert Schiller (1991) warned, abundance is not the same as diversity. Nations and global forces bent on conformity will find ways to enforce it even with the Web, however much more difficult and imperfect that enforcement may be on the Web compared to earlier centrally controlled media.

McLuhan (1964) remarked that the content of a new dominant medium is the previous dominant medium. The content of the novel was its predecessor, the epic poem. The content of film was the novel, the medium that preceded it historically. The content of television was both radio and film. Projecting in this manner, will the content of the Web turn out to be television, its predecessor as the dominant public medium? That, like so many fascinating questions concerning the Web, will be answered only by time.

REFERENCES

Angwin, J. (2004). Could U.S. bid to curb gambling on the web go way of prohibition? *Wall Street Journal— Eastern Edition, 244*(22), B1. Retrieved August 23, 2004, from EBSCOhost Web site: http://epnet.com

Beck, D., & Bosshart, L. (2003). Sports and the Internet. *Communication Research Trends, 22*(4), 14.

Burton, R. (1999). A world wide web of sports. *Advertising Age, 70*(46), 66. Retrieved August 23, 2004, from EBSCOhost Web site: http://epnet.com

Cannella, S., & Bechtel, M. (2004). Under review. *Sports Illustrated, 101*(6), 26. Retrieved August 23, 2004, from EBSCOhost Web site: http://epnet.com

Clark, E. (2003). Rivals.com keeps online sports fans in real time. *Network Magazine, 18*(6), 50. Retrieved August 23, 2004, from EBSCOhost Web site: http://epnet.com

Consoli, J. (2003). AOL rushing for more TV yardage. *Media Week, 13*(34), 4. Retrieved August 23, 2004, from EBSCOhost Web site: http://epnet.com

Cox, W., & Salter, M. (1998). The IT revolution and the practice of sports history: An overview and reflection on Internet research and teaching resources. *Journal of Sports History, 25*(2), 283–302.

Cross, M. E., & Vollano, A. G. (1999). *The extent and nature of gambling among college student athletes.* Ann Arbor, MI: University of Michigan Athletics Department. Retrieved August 23, 2004, from EBSCOhost Web site: http://epnet.com

Databank Sports. (2001). *Advertising Age, 72*(30), 25. Retrieved August 23, 2004, from EBSCOhost Web site: http://epnet.com

Enzensberger, H. (1974). *The consciousness industry.* New York: Seabury Press.

Focus Group. (2004, May 25). [Author conducted group interview with ten Ohio University students.] Athens, Ohio: unpublished data.

Gray, R. (2000). Laptop quarterback. *American Journalism Review, 22*(1), 16. Retrieved August 23, 2004, from EBSCOhost Web site: http://epnet.com

Holt, C. (2004). Major League Video. *Video Systems, 30*(4), 58. Retrieved August 23, 2004, from EBSCOhost Web site: http://epnet.com

Jones, D. (2004). Half the story? Olympic women on ABC news online. *Media International Australia - Incorporating Culture & Policy*, 15. Retrieved August 23, 2004, from EBSCOhost Web site: http://epnet.com

Jordan, G. B. (2000). Web pulled viewers away from the Olympic games: From Sydney, it was a tale of two technologies, yesterday's and tomorrow's. *Nieman Reports, 54*(4), 43. Retrieved August 23, 2004, from EBSCOhost Web site: http://epnet.com

Krikke, J. (2004). "Streaming video transforms the media industry." *IEEE Computer Graphics and Applications. 24*(4), 6. Retrieved August 23, 2004, from EBSCOhost Web site: http://epnet.com

Layden, T. (2003). Caught in the net. *Sports Illustrated, 98*(20), 46. Retrieved August 23, 2004, from EBSCOhost Web site: http://epnet.com

McChesney, R. (2004). *The problem of the media: U.S. communication politics in the 21st century.* New York: Monthly Review Press.

McLuhan, M. (1964). *Understanding media: The extensions of man.* New York: McGraw-Hill.

The motivated scholar: Gambling in college. (2002, December 11). *The Wager. 7*(50). Retrieved August 12, 2004, from http://www.thewager.org/Backindex/vol7pdf/wager750.pdf.

NCAA. (2004, May 12). *Executive summary for the National study on collegiate sports wagering and associated health risks.* Retrieved May 26, 2004, from http://www.ncaa.org/gambling/2003NationalStudy/slideShow

Nielsen//NetRatings. (2004a, March 19). March madness draws college hoops fans online. Retrieved August 24, 2004, from http://www.nielsen-netratings.com/pr/pr_040319_2.pdf

Nielsen//NetRatings. (2004b, August 18). U.S. broadband connections reach critical mass, crossing 50 percent mark for web surfers. Retrieved August 24, 2004, from http://www.nielsen-netratings.com/pr/pr_040818.pdf

Nielsen//NetRatings. (2004c, August 24). The Olympic Games sweep fastest growing sites last week. Retrieved August 24, 2004, from http://www.nielsen-netratings.com/pr/pr_040824.pdf

Palser, B. (2004). The difference a year makes. *American Journalism Review, 26*(1), 58. Retrieved August 23, 2004, from EBSCOhost Web site: http://epnet.com

Real, M., & Beeson, D. (2004, May 29). *Sports and the Internet: A preliminary examination of a new medium.* Paper presented at the International Communication Association, New Orleans.

Richtel, M. (2004). An industry that dares not meet in the country of its best customers. *New York Times, 153*(52852), C4. Retrieved August 23, 2004, from EBSCOhost Web site: http://epnet.com

Rowe, D., & McKay, J. (1999). Field of soaps: Rupert v. Kerry as masculine melodrama. In R. Martin & T. Miller (Eds.), *SportCult* (pp.191–210). Minneapolis: University of Minnesota Press.

Salkever, A. (2003, April 15). Sports score big online. *Business Week Online.* Retrieved August 23, 2004, from EBSCOhost Web site: http://epnet.com

Schiller, H. (1991). *Culture inc: The corporate takeover of public expression.* New York: Oxford University Press.

Walker, S. (2003). The long distance fan. *Wall Street Journal – Eastern Edition, 242*(13), W1. Retrieved August 23, 2004, from EBSCOhost Web site: http://epnet.com

Weir, T. (2003, August 22). Online sports betting spins out of control. *USA Today.* Retrieved August 23, 2004, from EBSCOhost Web site: http://epnet.com

"Who owns what." (2004). *Columbia Journalism Review.* Retrieved March 8–15, 2004, from http://www.cjr.org/tools/owners/

11

Sports Fiction: Critical and Empirical Perspectives

R. Glenn Cummins
Kennesaw State University

In the fall of 2003, ESPN premiered its first entry in the realm of scripted, fictional television programming, *Playmakers*. The program chronicled, often with explicit detail, the trials and tribulations of a fictional pro football team, the Cougars. Dubbed a "macho soap opera" (Flynn, 2004, p. 68), plot lines revolved around everything from murder, to drug abuse, to domestic violence, to homosexuality, to abortion. The aging veteran, the raw rookie, the greedy owner—characters on the program embodied just about every conceivable sports stereotype.

Playmakers was the product of the network's newly formed Original Entertainment division, created as part of ESPN's new strategy to expand beyond its core audience of young male viewers by developing original movies and other types of specialty programming (Umstead, 2003). The strategy worked. *Playmakers* was a hit, consistently drawing viewers from the highly coveted 18- to 34-year-old male demographic (Romano, 2003). The program also succeeded in attracting more female viewers to the network, ten times the number that ESPN was drawing in the same time slot just one year earlier, to be exact (Umstead, 2003). Furthermore, the program also drew support from some unlikely sources such as the gay community for spotlighting the turmoil one closeted homosexual player faced after coming out to his teammates and team owners (Page, 2003; Rowe, 2003). *Sports Illustrated* even branded *Playmakers* its "Show of the Year" (Deitsch, 2003).

Any celebration caused by these accolades was short lived, for as much praise as *Playmakers* received, it drew an equal amount of scorn. NFL Commissioner Paul Tagliabue repeatedly voiced his objections to the program, calling it a "gross mischaracterization" of the sport ("Tagliabue knocks," 2003, p. 4). Some real-life players were also angered, and the NFL Players Association complained to ESPN, asking the network not to air the program (Fryer, 2003).

Throughout these protests, the network's response remained the same, that the program was for entertainment only, a work of pure fiction. However, many observers questioned this defense, noting that the origins of some characters and storylines on the program could easily be found in contemporary newspaper headlines. In fact, several writers argued that one had to look no further than the NFL's Carolina Panthers to find a number of scandals every bit as salacious as those depicted on *Playmakers* (Czaban, 2003; Pells, 2004). Moreover, at the same time that Commissioner Tagliabue was trying to combat the negative image being generated by the program, former NFL linebacker Lawrence Taylor was hitting the talk show circuit, actively publicizing his autobiography that recounted in graphic detail "a life far more drug-addled and pornographic than any presented on the TV series" (Elliott, 2003, p. Z6).

Although the abundance of criticism may not have cost the program its viewers, it did cost one high-profile sponsor. Gatorade pulled its advertisements from the season finale of the series, citing concerns over the program's content (Lowry, 2003). Despite the ratings gains produced by the show, the cumulative effect of all the negative attention forced ESPN to cancel *Playmakers* after only one season (Betchel, 2003; Sandomir, 2004).

All of this controversy is recounted only to provide context for one small fact, which the creators of *Playmakers* were quite clear about from the program's inception—the show was not really about football. As ESPN Vice President Mark Shapiro said, "Sports is just a backdrop for this series" (Tierney, 2003, p. 2C). One critic noted in her review that *Playmakers* "is a show about football that shows almost no football" (Stanley, 2003, p. E1). This revelation is nothing new. It shows only that the network has learned what novelists, playwrights, and Hollywood film and television producers have known for years, that sports serves as an ideal backdrop for telling other stories. In his thorough examination of baseball films, Good (1997) wrote that "baseball films are only marginally about baseball. They are more about the human condition" (p. 7). Berman (1981) expressed a similar sentiment: "Sports fiction is always about reality; only the metaphor the fictional work utilizes to describe reality varies" (p. 10). Indeed, no other observation about sports in fiction receives as much unanimous support as the notion that sports is a "dynamic metaphor for reality" (p. 4) and that books and films about sports serve as an efficient means for examining other aspects of life. Racism, sexism, social inequality, the splintering of the American family—all of these issues have been addressed in countless fictional narratives that revolve around sports.

THE POPULARITY OF SPORTS FICTION

Fictional narratives involving sports have become a popular staple of the modern entertainment landscape. One admittedly limited bibliography chronicling American sports fiction of the twentieth century lists 631 literary works about sports (Burns, 1987). And despite some claims that sports films are "box-office poison" (Sayre, 1977, p. 182), sports films continue to be a popular draw in theaters. Cable network ESPN Classic features the program *Reel Classics*, where a different sports film is screened every week. Moreover, an Internet search for "sports films" yields an abundance of "top 10" lists, providing more evidence that the genre has an extremely loyal following eager to discuss at great length the various qualities that make certain sports films great. The sports film genre is as prolific as it is popular.

Zucker and Babich's (1987) index of every sports film ever made enumerated approximately 2,000 sports films made before 1985. The sports film genre dates back to the origins of the medium, and, in fact, films about baseball actually predate the World Series (Good, 1997)! The trend continues with two more entries into the genre in early 2004—*Miracle*, which depicts the victory by the U.S. ice hockey team over the Soviet team in the 1980 Winter Olympic Games, and *Against the Ropes*, a film about a female boxing promoter struggling to succeed in a male-dominated business. Although television programs about fictitious sports teams are less common and frequently short-lived, they nonetheless continue to surface on network schedules every few years, from *The White Shadow* in 1978 to the most recent entry into the genre, the aforementioned *Playmakers* in 2003.

Despite the long history of sports in literature and in the cinema, some scholars argue that relatively little research exists examining sports fiction, and only recently have those within the academic community begun to realize the potential value for new insights and knowledge that sports fiction represents. Dickerson (1991) noted in his analysis of 60 years of baseball films that sports have become more than mere entertainment and that organized athletics have become "politically, economically, socially, and legally intertwined with our nation's infrastructure" (p. 4). Moreover, he uses this argument as evidence to support the need for focusing greater attention on depictions of sports in film. Nonetheless, to date, Dickerson's findings remain true: "The sports film seems to have been overlooked as a major film genre" (p. 5).

Novels and other written works about sports have likewise been "denigrated as a subject for serious literature" (Oriard, 1982, p. 8). Oriard blamed this lack of serious scholarly attention on the genre's roots within early dime novels and juvenile fiction such as Burt L. Standish's countless stories about Frank Merriwell, "America's preeminent fictional sports hero" (p. 308). Although he acknowledged the genre's long history within youth fiction, he and other critics (e.g., Berman, 1981) rightly noted that many of America's literary giants such as Ernest Hemmingway and William Faulkner also invoked sports during their careers.

SPORTS FICTION: THE NON-GENRE

The assertion that sports fiction is simply drama or comedy that happens to involve sports leads to the question of whether sports fiction actually constitutes a distinct genre of entertainment. Most analyses of films and literature within the genre bypass this vexing question in favor of more clear-cut areas of inquiry. After all, addressing this question forces a number of somewhat arbitrary decisions regarding the definition of genre, as well as what elements are required to merit inclusion within any given genre.

Virtually every scholar who has attempted to define sports fiction has been faced with a myriad of highly problematic questions (e.g., Burns, 1987; Dickerson, 1991; Oriard, 1982; Zucker & Babich, 1987). For example, is the mere presence of sports in a narrative enough to justify inclusion as sports fiction, or must sports be central to the storyline? To that end, how large a role must sports play in a narrative before it is considered a central element? In addition, should all forms of athletic competition be included, or only organized sports? For example, in their rather exhaustive reference guide to the early history of the sports film genre, Zucker and Babich (1987) made some rather arbitrary decisions about what constitutes a sports film, stating that sports must play "an integral part in the film, even if it's not basically about sports" (p. 3). However, the definition of what constitutes an "integral part" is clearly open to interpretation and is sure to result in numerous discrepancies among scholars and critics. The problem is no less vexing for critics examining written works about sports. Oriard (1982) defined a sports novel "simply as one in which sport plays a dominant role or in which the sport milieu is the dominant setting" (p. 6). In addition, Burns (1987) arbitrarily eliminated countless literary works about sports from his critical bibliography of the genre, including juvenile fiction and stories about motor sports.

In one enlightening critical and cultural analysis of baseball films, Good (1997) pondered whether baseball films constitute a valid and distinct genre of entertainment. Although he did not examine the larger body of work that falls within the broader domain of sports films in general, the discussion begins to answer some of the fundamental questions regarding the nature of genre(s) from a conceptual level. Good noted that "Film scholars have borrowed the concept of genre from their literary colleagues, but have applied it far less systematically and precisely" and later added that "the definition of genre in film studies remains curiously unfixed" (p. 10). He resisted applying the term genre to baseball films, largely because of the blended nature of most baseball films (e.g. baseball biopics, baseball-romance stories, baseball comedies, baseball musicals, etc.). Instead, Good preferred the use of "type" or "category" to describe the films he examined. Unfortunately, the author concluded the discussion by remarking that the debate regarding the nature of film genres is a matter best left to film scholars. Likewise, the present discussion does little to clarify whether sports films exist as a distinct genre.

THEMES AND CLICHÉS IN SPORTS FICTION

Few other scholars have sought to question whether sports films constitute a distinct genre of entertainment. Instead, they have proceeded under the assumption that sports films are indeed a coherent genre of entertainment and have focused on the various conventions or dominant themes that characterize the genre. Zucker and Babich (1987) argued that sports films as a whole display an astonishing lack of thematic diversity and that every sports film ever made utilized one of only three repetitive themes: "the triumph of the underdog, the fall (and sometimes resurrection) of the mighty, and the sporting event as a pretext" (p. 1). To support their argument, the authors cited example after example of films that fall within one or more of these categories. Although a few scholars take issue with this highly reductionistic view of the various themes utilized within sports films (e.g., Erickson, 1992), dissenting voices are rare.

In addition, most critics examining fictional narratives about sports have repeatedly noted their heavy reliance on clichés. Early in his analysis of baseball films, Good (1997) profiled the numerous clichés that populate such films—the mythical status of the ballpark; the fatherly team manager; the presence of dual contrasting female leads, one pure, one tempting. As he argued, in contemporary baseball films characters are "raw rookies and worn-out veterans" (p. 22). Movies about baseball are hardly the only sports fictions guilty of utilizing these stereotypical characters, as those same stereotypes can be found in narratives depicting other sports, including the aforementioned television series *Playmakers*, as well as *Slapshot, Any Given Sunday*, and others. In addition, a host of other cinematic clichés can be found in virtually all sports fiction. For example, a review of the recent boxing film *Against the Ropes* complimented the film for its successful use of several conventions of the sports film genre, most notably the "slow clap" and the "big fight" at the climax of the film (Ebert, 2004).

THE MEANING OF SPORTS FICTION: CRITICAL PERSPECTIVES

Critics who have turned their attention toward sports fiction have taken a number of different approaches in examining this body of work. A number of scholars have examined literary works about sports to explore the conflict between play (cf. Huizinga, 1955) and sport (e.g., Berman, 1981; Messenger, 1990; Oriard, 1991). For example, Berman (1981) argued that the sports fiction of the 1970s explored the tension between true play, which is possible through sport, and contemporary culture, which is "actively hostile to any manifestation of freedom, any play" (p. 8). In general, analyses of literary works involving sports are vastly more complex (and esoteric) than their cinematic counterparts, possibly due to the level of depth afforded by the printed word not possible in the span of a 120-minute film. Likewise, critics examining sports literature have a much older body of work upon which to draw.

Other scholars have approached the topic from a historical perspective, tracing the ebb and flow of the popularity of sports films through the decades, while also examining the dominant cultural ideology reflected in these stories. For example, based on the argument that "the products of Hollywood do mirror the changes of the culture that gives birth to the films" (Dickerson, 1991, p. 153), Dickerson performed a rigorous sociocultural analysis of baseball films from 1929 to 1989, dividing the 60-year history of baseball films into a number of distinct eras and methodically examining each period chronologically.

However, the majority of analyses of sports in narrative fiction have examined the works along thematic lines, exploring how the many fictional films and novels about sports have addressed a myriad of relevant topics. A global review of these assorted critiques reveals a surprising amount of consistency both in regard to the topics addressed as well as in the various critical interpretations of these themes. As Oriard (1982) stated, literary works of sports fiction display "amazing unanimity in their major interests . . . because they portray issues fictionally that are essential to the nature of sport in America" (p. 21). Nonetheless, because analyses of this nature are subject to an almost infinite number of competing interpretations, only a few of the more dominant and consistent findings are presented here for discussion. In this respect, this chapter is in part a summary of literally thousands of pages of critical analyses and cannot fully explore all the meaning implicit in the many texts referenced. Those seeking to explore these themes more fully are advised to consult the various works cited herein.

Gender and Sexuality

Perhaps no other element of sports fiction has received as much attention as how these films and television programs address elements of gender, sexuality, and dominant ideology. The traditionally highly gendered nature of athletic competition makes fictional representations of sports inherently reflective of gender issues in society at large. Thus, "to some degree every sports film is about gender" (Baker, 2003, p. 3).

Organized sports have typically been dominated by men, especially prior to Title IX. Therefore, it should be no surprise that sports fiction, like most other forms of fictional entertainment, are dominated by male characters. Perhaps the dominant ideology regarding masculinity in fictional narratives is the dramatic depiction of an individual struggling against great odds to achieve success. "This heroic individual overcomes obstacles and achieves success through determination, self-reliance, and hard work" (Baker, 2003, p. 49). Oriard (1982) termed this ideological male the "athlete-hero" and traced the origin of this figure back to the roots of sports fiction in juvenile literature of the early twentieth century. The author argued that the prototype of this character in sports fiction can be found in the immensely popular works of Horatio Alger and the action-oriented dime novels popular at the turn of the twentieth century, noting that "a single strain runs consistently through all three literary types—the concept of the self-made man" (p. 47). Although these youth-oriented novels taught youngsters lessons about morality and fair play and espoused the benefits of athletic competition, they also implicitly taught readers this dominant ideology.

Although examples can be found throughout the history of sports fiction, one recent example is the character of Billy Chapel in the film *For Love of the Game*. The story takes place over the course of one game, where the aging pitcher throws a no-hitter in his final appearance on the mound. As one sportscaster says in the film, "He's pitching against time, he's pitching against the future, against age, against ending." Through flashbacks, the viewer is witness to the challenges that Chapel has faced on and off the mound in coming to this pivotal moment in his career, particularly to Chapel's rehabilitation after a potentially career-ending injury. In the end, he overcomes these obstacles to finish his long career on a high note.

Such depictions of athletes struggling to overcome great obstacles are most often found in sports biopics, "sports soap operas" (Berman, 1981, p. 3) that depict the lives of famous athletes in rather dramatic fashion. Although sports biopics are grounded in reality, these "fictionalized biographies" (Sayre, 1977, p. 183) often exaggerate the events of the athletes' lives for dramatic license and elevate the subjects of the films to mythical status. Good (1997) argued that sports biopics are a blend of both history and fiction, and he noted how some films make use of numerous cinematic devices to add historical credibility to biopics and mask their fictionalized nature. For example, the author cited the use of newsreel footage to add a documentary-like feel to such films, as well as the casting of real-life sports heroes in early sports biographies such as *The Pride of the Yankees*. Because sports biopics are so closely aligned with fictional narratives, these films and the ideology they reflect merit inclusion as sports fiction.

Good (1997) argued, "No other film genre so celebrates the traditional American belief that any person can achieve success through dint of his own efforts. The belief seems especially pronounced in baseball biopics, whose heroes played what is, after all, 'the national game'" (p. 55). Perhaps the most prolific era of sports biopics was from the early 1940s to the mid 1950s (Dickerson, 1991; Good, 1997). Numerous films of this variety were produced during this period, including baseball biopics *The Pride of the Yankees*, *The Babe Ruth Story*, *The Stratton Story*, *The Jackie Robinson Story*, as well as films about heroes from other sports such as *Jim Thorpe— All American* and *Knute Rockne—All American*. In virtually all of these films, the main character battles some tremendous obstacle(s) on his path to athletic stardom. For

Lou Gehrig, it was debilitating illness. Monty Stratton returned to the game after losing a limb. And Jackie Robinson and Jim Thorpe battled prejudice and racism to break the color barrier in their respective sports.

Numerous authors have argued that the abundance of such films during this period was in response to America's ideological needs of the post-World War II era. Dickerson (1991) wrote that *Pride of the Yankees* "embodies the moral standards, ethics, and popular values that Hollywood creators and the Roosevelt administration sought to exemplify and reinforce for the American audiences during this period of world strife" (p. 43). Sports biopics experienced a renaissance during the 1980s and 1990s with films such as *The Natural, Eight Men Out, The Babe,* and *Rudy.* Dickerson called this period a "return to mythbuilding" (p. 119). Much like the postwar era that produced the first round of sports biopics, these films were produced in response to cultural changes in society (Dickerson, 1991; Good, 1997). For example, Dickerson (1991) argued that films like *The Natural,* which closely resembles sports biopics from earlier decades, served to fulfill America's yearning for traditional values following the turbulent decades of the 1960s and 1970s.

Explorations of male sexuality are relatively rare in sports fiction, and overt depictions of homosexuality are rare. Baker (2003) conducted one of the more thorough analyses of the depiction of male sexuality in sports fiction, tracing the changing image of ideal masculinity in sports films. The author asserted that sports films help define ideal masculinity throughout the decades and noted, "Sports films provide an interesting site for [the analysis of masculinity] because they often foreground dominant masculinity, yet they also show how it has been refigured over time" (p. 49). For example, Baker chronicled how some of the earliest sports films helped define new notions regarding ideal male masculinity in the 1920s through the 1950s. The author then traced the changes in depictions of masculinity throughout the history of sports fiction to present day films such as *The Replacements* and *Any Given Sunday.* Regarding these more recent films, Baker wrote that "the presentation of ideal masculinity in such postmodern sports films has had to include variations on dominant masculinity that present greater inclusiveness and new forms of appeal" (p. 53). Indeed, such variations can also be found on the previously discussed television football drama, *Playmakers,* where one of the many subplots on the program focused on a closeted homosexual player struggling to conceal his sexuality from his teammates and coaches, the team owner, and the media. In addition, *The Greg Louganis Story,* a made-for-TV film about the Olympic swimmer, is another example of how new modern notions of masculinity have been reconciled with classic Hollywood ideology.

Women in Sports Fiction

Women, when depicted in sports fiction at all, have traditionally been relegated to a limited number of roles, most of which are secondary to their male counterparts. By and large, this tradition continues today in films such as *Hoosiers,* where women are relegated to the traditional roles of "mother, spectator, cheerleader, booster" (Tudor, 1997, p. 94). Like many other themes present in contemporary sports fiction, Oriard (1982) noted that this tradition springs from juvenile literature that depicted women only as mothers or as one-dimensional, overwhelmingly supportive girlfriends. Good (1997) echoed the assertion that women occupy a limited number of roles in sports films, noting that in baseball films women serve either as supportive nurturers or as temptresses. As evidence the author cited examples from the earliest baseball films of the Depression era, through biographical films like *The Pride of the Yankees* and *The Stratton Story* in the 1940s, to more contemporary baseball films such as *The Natural, Bull Durham*, and *Field of Dreams*.

Despite changes in culture and society, these stereotypes continue to permeate contemporary sports fiction. However, as one author noted, "When women characters occupy a more central position in the narrative, increasingly complex articulations of gender occur" (Tudor, 1997, p. 102). Nowhere is this more evident than in *Bull Durham*, where Annie Savoy takes the dominant role in her relationship with rookie pitcher Ebby Calvin "Nuke" LaLoosh, teaching her younger partner about the ways of baseball, life, and love. Likewise, *The Natural* also contains a somewhat unusual portrayal of a woman with the depiction of a single mother living alone in the big city. Nonetheless, "beneath the feminist trappings . . . they fill essentially the same role as the women in the earlier films. They exist to help men" (Good, 1997, p. 153).

Depictions of women as athletes are rare, and, even then, critics argue that women are still ultimately portrayed as subservient to men (Sayre, 1977). *Pat and Mike* was perhaps one of the earliest feature films to revolve around a female athlete, and, although the film does depict a female as a successful athlete, Baker (2003) noted that such success in athletic competition is only possible for a woman "provided she has the guidance of a good man" (p. 79). Baker employed the somewhat contradictory phrase "female masculinity" to describe the nature of women athletes in sports films. The author argued that although women are portrayed as adopting masculine traits on the field, they are forced to retain their feminine qualities off the field. "Women can compete in athletics, but only to the degree that it doesn't impede, and better yet supports, conservative ideas of femininity and thus the greater importance of male control" (p. 80).

The role of women in sports fiction has not changed significantly over the years, despite advances in women's rights and governmental actions, such as Title IX (Pearson, 2000; Tudor, 1997). One of the few, if not the only, empirical examinations of the role of women in sports films utilized content analysis to assess the role of women in sports films from 1930 to 1998. Although the results showed that in terms of sheer numbers women were depicted as heroes in sports films more after the implementation of Title IX, "many of the films, like their predecessors, trivialized women's athletic prowess as a result of their comedic nature and emphasis on heterosexual attractiveness" (Pearson, 2000, p. A-102).

Nonetheless, some critics have cited films like *The Bad News Bears* as evidence for the changing role of women in society (Dickerson, 1991). Although women still occupy a limited number of roles in that film, the characters they play represent a distinct break from previous sports films. The character who most notably embodies this difference is Amanda, the young girl recruited as pitcher for the team. Her character is a "reflection of the contemporary liberated female, able to compete with her male counterparts on any level" (p. 112). Likewise, some cite films such as *A League of Their Own* as further proof for the gains made by women on the field of competition. However, Good (1997) argued that *A League of Their Own* only superficially challenges traditional depictions of women in sports fiction. Although women take center stage as the athletes in that film, their strength and independence is undermined as they ultimately serve only to support their manager and inspire him to "stop drinking and start caring" (p. 159). Furthermore, the team's star player ultimately abandons her sports career to return home and support her husband (Baker, 2003). A similar theme can be found in the more recent film *Bend It*

Like Beckham, where two of the star players fall for their coach. However, because of his success in coaching the women's team, he is later called upon to "advance" to coaching a men's team. Interestingly, both *A League of Their Own* and *Bend It Like Beckham* were directed by women.

In actuality, the women's rights movement of the 1960s and 1970s may have affected sports films in a negative way. Numerous films from recent decades such as *Slap Shot, Major League*, and *Any Given Sunday* have vilified females by depicting them as greedy owners who are at odds with the male protagonists of the films. For example, the team owner in *Major League* is portrayed as a "wicked stepmother" (Good, 1997, p. 118) who sets out to doom the team so that she can relocate it for personal gain. Likewise, the female team owner in *Any Given Sunday* is portrayed as a meddling nuisance, threatening to undermine the coach's authority as leader of the team. Furthermore, some argue that a backlash against the social change that characterized the 1960s and 1970s fueled a return to the more traditional role of women as supporters and nurturers in the sports films of the 1980s, such as *Hoosiers* and *The Natural* (Dickerson, 1991; Tudor, 1997).

Race and Minorities

Much like women, minorities have frequently been mistreated in fictional narratives about sports. Most critics who have written on the depiction of ethnic minorities in sports films have largely observed that many films serve to propagate negative stereotypes. For example, in his examination of minorities in baseball films, Good noted that such films "often mistreat the player by giving him certain childish or uncivilized traits" (1997, p. 140). The author offered *The Bingo Long Traveling All-Stars & Motor Kings* as evidence to support this thesis, arguing that the film reinforced negative stereotypes by depicting the characters as clownish rather than emphasizing their skill and athletic prowess. The author also cited more recent films such as *Major League*, where a Cuban-born Black player "shaves his head clean with a hunting knife and communicates mostly by grunting and glaring" (p. 151) as further evidence that Hollywood continues to portray ethnic minorities in a negative light. "Whatever noble ideals the films mean to express, what emerges is the dominant culture's contempt for minority cultures" (p. 152).

Baker (2003) noted that most early depictions of Black athletes in films relegated them to supporting roles or depicted them as challenges for White athletes to face and overcome. Although some would argue that the increase in films where Blacks play a more central role represents a positive step in the depiction of minorities on the big screen, most critics argue that even in films where the central protagonist is Black the narrative operates to reinforce White superiority. For example, *The Joe Louis Story* was narrated by a White male voice (Baker, 2003). In addition, Good's (1997) critical analysis of *The Jackie Robinson Story* emphasized the paternal, authoritative role of team owner Branch Rickey in guiding Robinson through the treacherous waters of the integration of organized athletics. In that relationship, "Rickey just naturally assumes the role of master, Robinson that of servant" (p. 143). Baker's (2003) thoughtful analysis of Black athletes in mainstream Hollywood cinema pondered the meaning behind more recent basketball films such as *White Men Can't Jump, The Air up There*, and *Above the Rim*. The author argued that all three films emphasize the importance of interracial relationships and represent a "raceless utopia wished for by a white audience" (p. 35). Numerous other examples, give additional credence to this argument such as *Cool Runnings, The*

Legend of Bagger Vance, or the *Rocky* films. These films portray more positive relationships between Black and White characters and could be viewed as a positive step in the depiction of minorities in sports fiction. However, Baker (2003) concluded his analysis by stating that these films "avoid careful engagement with the moral and social complexities that confront working-class African-American men" (p. 40).

Youth and Aging

Other critics have noted that one theme that permeates sports films is the coming of age or transition from one stage of life to another of one or more of the characters in the films. Sports fiction may be particularly adept at exploring this tension because "the polarity of youth and age is sharply focused in the sports world" (Oriard, 1982, p. 126). Oriard also argued that this recurrent theme is the product of a culture fascinated with youth, and the author cited the larger-than-life figure of *"Babe"* Ruth as evidence (p. 128). An additional reason that sports fiction may serve as an ideal vehicle for exploring the transition from one stage of life to another is the natural conflict between work and play embodied in professional sports, where grown men make their living playing children's games (Tudor, 1997).

Although numerous scholars have discussed this recurrent theme within sports films, Good (1997) provided the most thorough analysis, in which he argued that the transition from childhood into adulthood is best embodied in films that focus on the relationship between pitchers and catchers. Good began the discussion by noting the virtually universal phenomenon of adolescent initiation into adult society. These rites of passage require "the intervention of the older men, who remove the boys from their previous environment and prepare them for the full range of adult experiences and duties" (p. 94). Because contemporary culture has abandoned many of the rituals that are a part of this transition into adulthood, American males are "left mostly to their own devices to learn manly behavior" (p. 95). Therefore, to find examples of what it means to be a man, many adolescents look to athletes and sports stars as role models. Good claimed that sports represent the closest thing to an initiation ritual in contemporary society, and "probably nowhere is this more obvious than in the relationship between pitchers and catchers" (p. 95).

Good (1997) developed the analogy between initiation ritual and athletic competition by describing the typical roles taken by pitchers and catchers in sports narratives. He noted that the catcher is usually an older, more experienced athlete, nearing the end of his athletic career. "But as old as he is, he won't psychologically be a grown-up until he relinquishes the merry masculine priorities of drinking beer, chasing women, and playing ball" (p. 97). The catcher serves as a mentor for his younger counterpart, the pitcher. The pitcher in sports films is often wild and inexperienced, both on and off the diamond. As evidence, Good cited the nickname "Wild Thing" for the character of Rick Vaughn in *Major League*. A more colorful description of a pitcher's wild, uncontrolled nature was offered in *Bull Durham*, where Millie describes rookie pitcher Ebby Calvin "Nuke" LaLoosh: "Well, he fucks like he pitches—sorta all over the place."

In this onscreen relationship between pitchers and catchers, the catcher's job is to teach his young teammate about the game of baseball, mirroring the initiation of adolescents into adulthood. Good (1997) argued that pitchers assert their manliness through their physical abilities on the field, whereas catchers are wiser and more developed psychologically. However, neither character is able to advance to the next stage of human development until they are tested in the "big game." Once the pitcher prevails over his opponent in this game, he is given full status as an accepted, even celebrated member of the team. Likewise, the catcher is able to give up the game and move to a more adult role, for example as husband, parent, or even coach. Oriard (1982) echoed this analogy, noting that this passing of authority from veteran to rookie serves to "re-enact ancient ritual deaths" (p. 126).

Although Good argued that this transition from one stage of life to another is most evident in the pitcher/catcher relationship, it can also be found in other fictitious relationships. In his analysis of the youth versus aging theme, Oriard (1982) stated that the roots of this familiar narrative can be found in Jack London's "A Piece of Steak," a short story about a once-successful aging boxer pitted against a younger foe. Ultimately, the elder fighter loses and the younger boxer emerges victorious, thus completing the transition for the characters. The author later cited *The Hundred-Yard War,* by Gary Cartwright, as a variation on this theme. That novel explores the trials that a rookie must endure to gain acceptance from his teammates. Tudor (1997) argued in his analysis of the cinematic adaptation of *The Natural* that Roy Hobbs is "lost in a perpetual adolescence" (p. 99), despite his age. In the story, Hobbs is guided into adulthood by the team's manager, aptly named "Pop." The transition into adulthood occurs at the climax of the film in the big game, where "it is time for Roy to become the father and leave his infancy and childhood behind" (p. 101). Hobbs succeeds in doing so, hitting the game-winning home run and rounding the bases in slow-motion. Fittingly, the film concluded by offering evidence demonstrating Hobbs' progression into adulthood—the final scene depicts him back home in his rural origins, throwing the baseball with his son.

The recent film *For Love of the Game* serves as another example of this transition into adulthood depicted in sports fiction. In addition to struggling against age and injury to win his final game, veteran pitcher Billy Chapel is struggling with the transition into the role of husband and father. Chapel is romantically involved with a single mother, and the film chronicles how the character slowly adapts to the role of husband and father until he suffers the injury to his pitching hand. The injury is not only a setback to his athletic career, but it also represents a setback on his journey into adulthood. Only after Chapel wins his final game is he able to leave baseball behind and devote himself to marriage and family.

Religion

Virtually every critic who has examined sports fiction has noted that works within this genre are heavily laden with religious references and symbolism. No doubt, this is the byproduct of the intricate relationship between sports and religion. Numerous authors have explored the parallels between modern religion and sports— stadia as places of worship, the highly ritualistic nature of both sports spectatorship and religious observances, and how athletes are often elevated to god-like status (e.g., Higgs, 1995; Magdalinski & Chandler, 2002; Price, 2000). These parallels are not limited solely to contemporary Judeo-Christian religious practices. Oriard (1982) noted that in college football, many bowl games "honor various crops (roses, cotton, oranges, sugar, peaches, tangerines)" (p. 227), harkening back to more ancient religious rituals and ceremonies. It is only fitting that in a society where sport and religion share so much common ground that fictional works about sports reflect this curious relationship.

Although some critics argue that this is a more recent phenomenon (e.g., Dickerson, 1991), sports fiction has long endowed athletes with supernatural (or Christ-like) powers. For example, in *The Babe Ruth Story*, "Ruth actually heals the sick on several occasions by his words and deeds" (Tudor, 1997, p. 52). Good (1997) also cited the original *Angels in the Outfield* as another early sports film that employed a supernatural theme. Likewise, novels about baseball, as well as their cinematic adaptations produced during the renaissance of the genre in the late 1980s, such as *The Natural* and *Field of Dreams*, were ripe with symbolism or statements about religion.

In writing about the character of Roy Hobbs in the novel and film versions of *The Natural*, both Tudor (1997) and Oriard (1982) drew a number of parallels between Hobbs and tales from Greek and Norse mythologies. Similarly, Good (1997) argued that the film "weaves together Biblical allusions, Greek myths, Arthurian legends and baseball folklore" (p. 27). For example, Good noted the supernatural aura that surrounds Hobbs' homemade bat "Wonderboy," forged from a tree struck by lightening. Furthermore, the author argued that the wound in Hobbs' side was Christ-like. Bergesen (2000) likewise noted the abundance of religious symbolism present in the film adaptation of *Field of Dreams*. The author draws parallels between the baseball diamond that the protagonist builds in the middle of an Iowa cornfield to the Garden of Eden. Likewise, Bergesen also compared Ray Kinsella's mandate to build the baseball diamond to Noah's instruction to build an arc. The analogy fits remarkably well, as both individuals become the object of ridicule for undertaking such seemingly bizarre tasks.

The analogy made in *Bull Durham* is qualitatively different from those made in the prior two films. Unlike other sports films where athletes are given religious qualities or elements are reminiscent of Biblical events, *Bull Durham* advances the notion of sport as religion. This is most clearly articulated in a monologue by Annie Savoy: "I believe in the Church of Baseball. I've tried all the major religions, and most of the minor ones. I've worshipped Buddha, Allah, Brahma, Vishnu, Siva, trees, mushrooms, and Isadora Duncan. I know things. For instance, there are 108 beads in a Catholic rosary and there are 108 stitches in a baseball. When I heard that, I gave Jesus a chance."

Additional examples of religious or supernatural elements in sports fiction are seemingly endless. Dickerson (1991) noted that the character of Pedro Cerrano in *Major League* worships a voodoo god who he believes controls his fate on the baseball diamond. The author stressed the contrast played out in the film between that character and a teammate who is a born-again Christian. Others have noted that sports films "have invested the ballpark with a supernatural aura" (Good, 1997, p. 46). *For Love of the Game* offers another example of religious references in sports films, in which the main character is (not-so) coincidentally named Billy Chapel. One play-by-play announcer in the film makes the reference more explicit when he says, "The cathedral that is Yankee Stadium belongs to a Chapel." Religious imagery can also be found in films depicting other sports, such as *The Legend of Bagger Vance*. In *Field of Dreams,* a baseball diamond is heaven; however, in *The Legend of Bagger Vance,* a golf course is where the film's narrator will spend his afterlife. In addition, the ghost of a dead basketball player helps his former teammates win in the basketball comedy *The Sixth Man*.

Analysis of the implicit meaning underlying sports fiction could continue ad infinitum. Various authors have written extensively on the depiction of a wide range of topics in sports fiction, including the nature of class in narratives about boxing (e.g., Baker, 2003; Berman, 1981; Oriard, 1982), changes in culture and society (e.g., Dickerson, 1991), and so forth. However, the preceding summary chronicles some of the dominant themes in sports fiction that have received attention and provides a sufficient encapsulation of the vast critical literature examining depictions of sports in narrative fiction.

THE ENJOYMENT OF SPORTS FICTION: EMPIRICAL PERSPECTIVES

Critical analyses of sports fiction do little to explain the popularity of such films or why audiences enjoy them. Relatively few critics pause to consider such questions, although occasionally authors have tendered somewhat tentative explanations. Good (1997) considered the question of why viewers enjoy films about baseball but did little to answer the question. The author noted only that it is not solely because viewers are fans of the game, for the simple reason that films about baseball and baseball games are qualitatively different entities. Although not explicitly offered as a theory of enjoyment, Dickerson (1991) argued that the values depicted in fictional narratives about baseball resonate with audiences. Berman (1981) more thoroughly explicated this argument, stating that sport "speaks very directly to the experience of contemporary America" (p. 12), adding, "We simply do not identify with scientists or painters in the way we identify with athletes" (p. 13). Sayre (1977) also noted the importance of identification and character development in the enjoyment of sports fiction: "If our emotions are to be involved in winning or losing, we need to give a hoot about the individual who's sweating glycerin and gnawing his lip and panting like the athlete he isn't" (pp. 183–184).

Unfortunately, none of these critical explanations for the appeal of sports films possess the rigor necessary to withstand a more thorough empirical or theoretical examination. However, social scientists operating primarily under the general domain of media psychology have generated a considerable body of research that seeks to answer questions regarding how and why viewers enjoy a wide variety of media entertainment. These extant theories exploring other genres of entertainment may be useful in understanding why viewers passionately root for characters like Rocky Balboa or Roy Hobbs.

Parallels Between Sport and Fictional Entertainment

As long as people have gathered together to be entertained, either by athletes doing battle on the field of competition or by actors performing on a stage, philosophers, psychologists, and scholars have tried to understand the appeal of entertainment (Zillmann, 2000). Only relatively recently has the nature of the entertainment phenomenon become the subject of serious empirical study. A review of recent literature within the burgeoning domain of media psychology finds numerous theories to explain the appeal of both fictional entertainment such as dramas and comedies (e.g., Vorderer & Knobloch, 2000; Zillmann, 2000) and the appeal of sports spectatorship (e.g., Bryant & Raney, 2000; Bryant, Zillmann, & Raney, 1998; Giles, 2003). Interestingly, most attempts to explain the appeal of these seemingly distinct areas of media entertainment rely on the same theories. A brief review of these theories finds a tremendous amount of conceptual common ground for the enjoyment of both sports spectatorship and fictional entertainment, both of which are embodied within sports fiction.

Catharsis

Perhaps one of the oldest and most popular theories explaining why individuals seek out various forms of entertainment is the catharsis doctrine. It has been examined as an explanation for the appeal of violent sports (e.g., Goldstein, 1998; Bryant & Raney, 2000; Bryant, et al., 1998; Guttmann, 1998), as well as for dramas (e.g., Vorderer & Knobloch, 2000). Put simply, the catharsis argument rests on the notion that individuals are able to release pent-up frustrations, hostilities, and desires vicariously through viewing others. The catharsis doctrine was first presented in Aristotle's *Poetics* (350 B.C./1951) as a way of explaining the appeal of tragedy, whereby "exposure to it may in fact evoke undesirable experiences. But these experiences, nevertheless, help to diminish such negative emotions in the real life of the observers" (Vorderer & Knobloch, 2000, p. 66).

Obviously, no large leap in logic is required to extend this argument to the enjoyment of sports fiction. According to the catharsis doctrine, viewers watching violent sports films such as *Gladiator* or *Rocky* should hypothetically purge any pent-up bloodlust, and thus, exposure to fictional sports violence should result in decreased hostility on the part of the viewer. However, precious little empirical evidence exists to support this theory. Zillmann (1991, 1998) argued that catharsis is fraught with numerous conceptual difficulties, and, in fact, an abundance of evidence exists to contradict the doctrine (e.g., Baron & Richardson, 1994; Geen & Quanty, 1977). Moreover, the overwhelming majority of empirical research has demonstrated that exposure to violent entertainment is positively correlated with increased aggression, contrary to the prediction one would expect based on the catharsis doctrine (Paik & Comstock, 1994). Despite this contradictory evidence, the catharsis argument continues to have a wide following. However, its utility to explain the continued appeal of sports fiction has yet to be explored.

Disposition Theory

Scholars have long sought to understand how and why entertainment content can so effectively elicit impassioned responses from viewers. Why do we experience such great euphoria when Roy Hobbs hits the game-winning home run in his final at bat in *The Natural*, or why do we wish to see the ragamuffin team of little leaguers known as *The Bad News Bears* win, despite a demonstrated lack of athletic prowess? Those who support the catharsis doctrine would argue that viewers are vicariously participating in this fictitious event, and as a result they share in the characters' jubilation (or sadness) at the climax of the film. However, an alternative and more parsimonious explanation to catharsis is offered by disposition theory (Zillmann, 1994, 1996). According to disposition theory, viewers form opinions about characters depicted in fictional narratives as they process media messages. The viewer hopes for positive outcomes for characters with whom a favorable disposition has been formed (i.e., the good guy), and negative outcomes for those with whom an unfavorable disposition has been formed (i.e., the bad guy). Thus, as the story unfolds the viewer experiences either positive or negative emotions, depending on the fate of the characters and the outcome of the narrative. This theory has been employed to explain the appeal of both comedies (e.g., Zillmann, 2000) and dramas (e.g., Vorderer & Knobloch, 2000). Likewise, scholars have also employed disposition theory to explain why sports fans experience the highest euphoria when their team wins as well as the depths of despair when their team loses (e.g., Zillmann, Bryant, & Sapolsky, 1989).

The previously discussed comments regarding the need for caring about characters suggests the potential for the application of disposition theory in the investigation of the appeal of sports fiction. By utilizing an example from the world of sports fiction, Bryant and Zillmann (1983) briefly alluded to this potential. They argued that presumably, sports fans would not wish to see a liked protagonist injured in athletic competition. "It is likely that only under unusual conditions in which the spectators fear or hate the victim or potential victim—such as depicted in the 'redneck' stock car race spectators' hatred for the 'nigger' Wendell Scott, portrayed by Richard Pryor in the movie *Greased Lightning*—will people really enjoy seeing the destruction of the sports contestant" (p. 200). Although this argument has not been formally tested, it suggests numerous opportunities for the exploration of the role of affective disposition in the enjoyment of sports fiction.

Because audiences are witness to the events that unfold throughout the narrative structure of sports fiction, they are able to form dispositions with the characters depicted in the story. To again call upon the recent film *For Love of the Game*, viewers follow the career of pitcher Billy Chapel leading up to his final appearance on the mound. They are witness to the many events that have transpired in his life and career, and because of this, they root all the more strongly for him and experience great euphoria as he finishes his career with a perfect game. Although this argument displays a tremendous amount of face validity, it remains for scholars to thoroughly explore the power of affective disposition in the enjoyment of sports fiction.

Suspense and Arousal

One of the most nebulous concepts in the understanding of media entertainment is that of suspense. Numerous scholars representing a variety of research traditions and methodologies have attempted to understand and conceptualize suspense and its role in the enjoyment of media (e.g., Vorderer, Wulff, & Friedrichsen, 1996). Despite the lack of unity in how suspense is conceptualized, virtually all those who have examined the phenomenon agree that suspense plays a central role in the enjoyment of media content.

Carroll (1996) and Zillmann (1996) offered two similar but competing conceptualizations of suspense. Carroll (1996) stressed the role of uncertainty in the generation of suspense. The author argued that the viewer forms ideas about a preferred outcome to a fictional narrative, and suspense is experienced as the viewer hopes for that desired outcome and fears an undesirable outcome. However, Zillmann (1996) took a slightly contrary viewpoint, stressing that suspense is felt by viewers certain of an undesirable outcome. Thus, the greater the perceived certainty of this undesirable outcome, the greater the degree of suspense felt by the viewer. Scholars who have explored the enjoyment of sports spectatorship have also stressed the role of suspense in viewing athletic competition, as spectators anxiously hope to see their favorite team emerge victorious in any given game (e.g., Bryant, et al., 1998; Bryant & Raney, 2000).

Without question, suspense plays a critical role in the enjoyment of sports fiction. However, the concept remains somewhat problematic when applied to sports fiction. As previously stated, the genre relies heavily on a somewhat limited number of narrative conventions, and, perhaps more than any other genre, sports films are notorious for recycling the same stories over and over again in different guises (Zucker & Babich, 1987). What then is the role of suspense in the enjoyment of these somewhat predictable films? After all, is there any doubt that the underdog basketball squad from Hickory High will beat the odds and win the state championship in *Hoosiers*? Precious few examples, such as the original *Rocky* and *The Bad News Bears*, exist to contradict these cinematic conventions (although it is interesting to note that the sequels to both these movies do return to the convention of the sports film genre where the protagonist does win in the end). To date, few scholars have tackled the problem of suspense when the viewer is relatively certain about the outcome of an event depicted on screen (e.g., Brewer, 1996). Thus, the only conclusion that can be offered at present is that more research is needed to explicate the role of suspense in the enjoyment of sports fiction.

The role of arousal in enhancing the level of suspense experienced during the consumption of sports fiction cannot be understated. Guttmann (1998) argued that one of the central appeals of violent sports is its potential for arousing viewers and that witnessing athletic competition is an effective way for spectators to alleviate boredom. Sports films in particular may be uniquely effective in altering a viewer's mood state through the combination of elements from both drama and sports, as well as because of the higher degree of graphicness possible with audiovisual media (e.g., Zillmann, 1991). As previously stated, the stories portrayed in sports films are not altogether different from those of traditional dramas or comedies. Thus, the mechanisms for generating suspense present in these genres of entertainment are likewise present in sports fiction. However, perhaps the sole distinguishing characteristic of these films is their reliance on athletic competition to advance and often provide a climax to the narrative. Thus, the arousal generated by the inclusion of athletic competition serves to increase the suspense experienced by the viewer as the story reaches its climax. After all, each film in the *Rocky* series culminates with a final showdown between our hero and his latest nemesis. Blow by blow, the viewer eagerly watches the films' main characters slug it out until the protagonist wins the fight and the credits roll. Unfortunately, no empirical evidence exists to test the generation of arousal or suspense during the consumption of sports fiction. This unique combination of narrative conventions and athletic competition embodied in sports films provides a wealth of opportunities for social scientists seeking to develop theories of enjoyment for sports fiction.

Sports-Specific Theories

In addition to the previously discussed theoretical explanations for the appeal of both fiction and sports spectatorship, a number of unique theoretical explanations have been offered to further explain why individuals find sports viewing so enjoyable. Guttmann (1998) suggested that spectators' fascination with some types of athletic competition satisfies a sadomasochistic desire within the viewer. For example, fans of NASCAR and other forms of auto racing will freely admit to tuning in to watch every week in the hopes of witnessing a wreck occur. Likewise, crowds annually pack the streets of Pamplona, Spain, to witness the running of the bulls, where numerous participants yearly receive major and sometimes life-threatening injuries. Arguments regarding the sadomasochistic appeal of sports date back as far as Roman times, where thousands of spectators gathered to witness sporting events that routinely ended in severe injury and death (Zillmann, 2000). Sports films have the ability to graphically depict all manner of harm and injury through the use of close-ups and other formal features of the medium (e.g., Potter & Smith, 2000). As such, they may be adept at satisfying some masochistic urges within viewers. Although this argument may hold some validity, formal explorations for why viewers enjoy witnessing the specter of death and serious injury are still vastly underdeveloped. Moreover, despite visual media's capacity for graphically depicting injury and harm, viewers remain aware on some level that the events they are witnesses are fictitious, further complicating the application of this theory to sports fiction.

Bryant and Raney (2000) suggested that another factor that enhances viewer enjoyment of sports is the degree to which the play being viewed is perceived as particularly novel, risky, or effective. The authors cited empirical evidence that supports the claim that spectators appreciate these factors when viewing televised sports (Zillmann, et al., 1989). In his critical analysis of portrayals of race in sports films, Baker (2003) noted the improvisational style of play frequently identified with African-American characters. This characteristic is embodied in films like *White Men Can't Jump*, which starkly contrasts the improvisational style of African-American players with a more textbook approach taken by White characters in the film. Numerous other critics have noted the parallel between basketball and creative play (e.g., Berman, 1981; Oriard, 1982). The degree to which audiences are able to perceive and appreciate novel play in sports fiction is analogous to the degree to which similar play enhances enjoyment in real-life athletic competition. As such, this represents another area ripe for exploration utilizing empirical research methods.

One final theory posited to explain the enjoyment of sports spectatorship is that "humans are constantly motivated to enhance their own power and self-esteem by *asserting dominance* over others" (Bryant, et al., 1998, p. 259). This need is most clearly fulfilled through actual head-to-head athletic competition. However, through alignment or identification with a team or athletic hero, a sports spectator is also able to fulfill this need whenever his or her favorite team or athlete wins a competition. Although rooted in the examination of the enjoyment of sports spectatorship, the argument could also be invoked to understand the appeal (for viewers in the United States at least) of such films as *Miracle* or *Rocky IV*, both films where the American protagonists emerge victorious over foes from the Soviet Union. Again, empirical research testing such a theory is to date nonexistent.

CONCLUSION

This review has explored the nature of sports films from a number of rival perspectives. Critical/cultural scholars who have explored the depths of latent meaning behind sports fiction assert that these narratives are on the whole powerful statements about gender and sexuality, the role of men and women in society, race, changes in culture and society, and countless other topics. On the other hand, social scientists have investigated the appeal of entertainment by exploring the psychological processes that viewers engage in while consuming such fare. What, if any, common ground can be found among all these different approaches to understand and explain the continued popularity of this genre of entertainment? An answer to this vexing question is problematic. On a broad conceptual level, both approaches to sports fiction examine how the viewer makes meaning of any given text. Scholars writing from a critical perspective examine the meaning generated by sports fictions with the implied assumption that viewers will recognize this meaning on some level of consciousness. Thus, the crux of their work is the analysis of the messages that viewers will absorb in the process. Whereas critical scholars focus largely on the meaning contained within the various films and television programs that constitute the genre of sports fiction, scholars within the domain of media psychology study the reception processes in which viewers engage in the consumption of these media messages. Thus, to borrow a phrase from Messenger (1990), scholars within both areas of inquiry are exploring the area "between the author's text and the reader's experience" (p. 424). As a brief summary of these two research traditions, it is hoped that this chapter will encourage scholars representing both methodological research traditions to seek common ground between their differing approaches and validate the knowledge generated by those within rival research traditions.

Regardless of what connections will be made between these distinct areas of research, what is clear is that audiences will continue to watch fictionalized depictions of athletic competition on screens both big and small, and authors will continue to mine the depths of contemporary culture through the metaphor of sports. Again, this is not because sports fiction represents some wholly unique genre of entertainment. Instead, these creative works operate like virtually all other genres by making us laugh, cry, and sit on the edge of our seats hoping to see our heroes beat the buzzer and sink the winning basket, hit the home run, or make the winning touchdown and bring a happy ending to these fictional stories.

REFERENCES

Aristotle. (1951). The poetics. In S. H. Butcher (Trans.), *Aristotle's theory of poetry and fine art* (pp. 7–111). New York: Dover Publications. (Original work written 350 B.C.)

Baker, A. (2003). *Contesting identities: Sports in American film*. Urbana, IL: University of Illinois Press.

Baron, R. A., & Richardson, D. R. (1994). *Human aggression* (2nd ed.). New York: Plenum Press.

Bergesen, A. (2000). Is this heaven? No, it's Iowa. In A. J. Bergesen & A. M. Greeley (Eds.), *God in the movies* (pp. 55–70). New Brunswick, NJ: Transaction Publishers.

Berman, N. D. (1981). *Playful fictions and fictional players: Game, sport, and survival in contemporary American fiction*. Port Washington, NY: Kennikat Press.

Betchel, M. (2003, November 24). One and done: Has the NFL sacked the controversial Playmakers' second season? *Sports Illustrated, 99*(20), 24.

Brewer, W. F. (1996). The nature of narrative suspense and the problem of rereading. In P. Vorderer, H. J. Wulff, & M. Friedrichsen (Eds.), *Suspense: Conceptualizations, theoretical analyses, and empirical explorations* (pp. 107–128). Mahwah, NJ: Lawrence Erlbaum Associates.

Bryant, J., & Raney, A. A. (2000). Sports on the screen. In D. Zillmann & P. Vorderer (Eds.), *Media entertainment: The psychology of its appeal* (pp. 153–174). Mahwah, NJ: Lawrence Erlbaum Associates.

Bryant, J., & Zillmann, D. (1983). Sports violence and the media. In J. H. Goldstein (Ed.), *Sports violence* (pp. 195–212). New York: Springer-Verlag.

Bryant, J., Zillmann, D., & Raney, A. A. (1998). Violence and the enjoyment of media sports. In L. A. Wenner (Ed.), *MediaSport* (pp. 252–265). London: Routledge.

Burns, G. (1987). *The sports pages: A critical bibliography of twentieth-century American novels and stories featuring baseball, basketball, football, and other athletic pursuits*. Metuchen, NJ: Scarecrow Press.

Carroll, N. (1996). The paradox of suspense. In P. Vorderer, H. J. Wulff, & M. Friedrichsen (Eds.), *Suspense: Conceptualizations, theoretical analyses, and empirical explorations* (pp. 71–91). Mahwah, NJ: Lawrence Erlbaum Associates.

Czaban, S. (2003, October 1). ESPN's "Playmakers" not realistic enough. Retrieved January 27, 2004, from http://www.onmilwaukee.com/articles/playmakers.html

Deitsch, R. (2003, December 29). Under review. *Sports Illustrated, 99*(25), 38.

Dickerson, G. E. (1991). *The cinema of baseball: Images of America, 1929–1989*. Westport, CT: Meckler.

Ebert, R. (2004, February 20). 'Ropes' floats like a butterfly but stings like a flea [Review of the motion picture *Against the Ropes*]. *Chicago Sun-Times*, Weekend Plus, p. 29.

Elliott, J. (2003, December 15). Giant confessions: The NFL hall of famer writes about sex, drugs, and his suicidal thoughts. *Sports Illustrated, 99*(23), Scorecard Extra, p. Z6.

Erickson, H. (1992). *Baseball in the movies: A comprehensive reference, 1915–1991*. Jefferson, NC: McFarland & Company.

Flynn, G. (2004, June 18). Playmakers: The complete series. [Review of the television series *Playmakers*]. *Entertainment Weekly, 770*, 68.

Fryer, J. (2003, September 12). 'Playmakers' drawing ire across the NFL. *AP Sportswire*, p. 1.

Geen, R. G., & Quanty, M. B. (1977). The catharsis of aggression: An evaluation of a hypothesis. In L. Berkowitz (Ed.), *Advances in experimental social psychology* (Vol. 10, pp. 1–37). New York: Academic Press.

Giles, D. (2003). *Media Psychology*. Mahwah, NJ: Lawrence Erlbaum Associates.

Goldstein, J. (Ed.). (1998). *Why we watch: The attractions of violent entertainment*. New York: Oxford University Press.

Good, H. (1997). *Diamonds in the dark: America, baseball, and the movies*. Lanham, MD: Scarecrow Press.

Guttmann, A. (1998). The appeal of violent sports. In J. Goldstein (Ed.), *Why we watch: The attractions of violent entertainment* (pp. 7–26). New York: Oxford University Press.

Higgs, R. J. (1995). *God in the stadium: Sports and religion in America*. Lexington, KY: University of Kentucky Press.

Huizinga, J. (1955). *Homo ludens: A study of the play element in culture*. Boston: Beacon Press.

Lowry, T. (2003, November 7). Gatorade sacks ESPN's *Playmakers*. Retrieved January 27, 2004, from http://www.businessweek.com:/print/bwdaily/dnflash/nov2003/nf2003117_2616_db016.html

Magdalinski, T., & Chandler, T. J. L. (Eds.). (2002). *With God on their side: Sport in the service of religion*. London: Routledge.

Messenger, C. K. (1990). *Sport and the spirit of play in contemporary American fiction*. New York: Columbia University Press.

Oriard, M. (1982). *Dreaming of heroes: American sports fiction, 1868–1980*. Chicago: Nelson Hall.

Oriard, M. (1991). *Sporting with the gods: The rhetoric of game and play in American culture*. Cambridge, England: Cambridge University Press.

Page, J. (2003, November 3). ESPN gets it mostly right. Retrieved January 27, 2004, from http://www.outsports.com/columns/page/20031103playmakers.html

Paik, H., & Comstock, G. (1994). The effects of television violence on antisocial behavior: A meta-analysis. *Communication Research, 21*, 516–546.

Pearson, D. W. (2000). The depiction and characterization of women in sport theme feature films after Title IX. *Research Quarterly for Exercise and Sport, 71*(1), A-102.

Pells, E. (2004, January 24). Controversial show puts NFL, EPSN in awkward positions. *AP Sportswire*, p. 1.

Potter, W. J., & Smith, S. (2000). The context of graphic portrayals of television violence. *Journal of Broadcasting & Electronic Media, 44*, 301–323.

Price, J. L. (Ed.). (2000). *From season to season: Sports as American religion*. Macon, GA: Mercer University Press.

Romano, A. (2003, November 24). Is Playmakers off to the showers? Football drama is a hit on ESPN but not with the NFL. *Broadcasting & Cable, 133*(47), 30.

Rowe, M. (2003, October 14). The incredible hunk: Daniel Petronijevic stars as a pro football player coming out of the closet on ESPN's Playmakers. *The Advocate*, p. 74.

Sandomir, R. (2004, February 5). Citing NFL, ESPN cancels 'Playmakers.' *The New York Times*, p. D1.

Sayre, N. (1977). Winning the weepstakes: The problems of American sports movies. In B. K. Grant (Ed.), *Film Genre: Theory and Criticism* (pp. 182–194). Metuchen, NJ: The Scarecrow Press.

Stanley, A. (2003, August 26). Psyching out football in an ESPN drama. *The New York Times*, p. E1.

Tagliabue knocks ESPN's Playmakers. (2003, September 8). *Broadcasting & Cable, 133*(36), 4.

Television Critics Association. (2004, January 12). *Mediaweek, 14*(2), 3.

Tierney, M. (2003, August 26). Pigskin drama a hard hit. *The Atlanta Journal-Constitution*, p. 2C.

Tudor, D. V. (1997). *Hollywood's vision of team sports: Heroes, race, and gender*. New York: Garland Publishing.

Umstead, R. T. (2003, October 27). ESPN's 'Playmakers' playing to women. *Multichannel News, 24*(43), 14.

Vorderer, P., & Knobloch, S. (2000). Conflict and suspense in drama. In D. Zillmann & P. Vorderer (Eds.), *Media entertainment: The psychology of its appeal* (pp. 59–72). Mahwah, NJ: Lawrence Erlbaum Associates.

Vorderer, P., Wulff, H. J., & Friedrichsen, M. (Eds.). (1996). *Suspense: Conceptualizations, theoretical analyses, and empirical explorations*. Mahwah, NJ: Lawrence Erlbaum Associates.

Zillmann, D. (1991). Empathy: Affect from bearing witness to the emotion of others. In J. Bryant & D. Zillmann (Eds.), *Responding to the screen: Reception and reaction processes* (pp. 135–167). Hillsdale, NJ: Lawrence Erlbaum Associates.

Zillmann, D. (1994). Mechanism of emotional involvement with drama. *Poetics, 23*, 33–51.

Zillmann, D. (1996). The psychology of suspense in dramatic exposition. In P. Vorderer, H. J. Wulff, & M. Friedrichsen (Eds.), *Suspense: Conceptualizations, theoretical analyses, and empirical explorations* (pp. 199–231). Mahwah, NJ: Lawrence Erlbaum Associates.

Zillmann, D. (1998). The psychology of the appeal of portrayals of violence. In J. H. Goldstein (Ed.), *Why we watch: The attractions of violent entertainment* (pp. 179–211). New York: Oxford University Press.

Zillmann, D. (2000). The coming of media entertainment. In D. Zillmann & P. Vorderer (Eds.), *Media entertainment: The psychology of its appeal* (pp. 1–20). Mahwah, NJ: Lawrence Erlbaum Associates.

Zillmann, D., Bryant, J., & Sapolsky, B. S. (1989). Enjoyment from sports specatorship. In J. H. Goldstein (Ed.), *Sports, games, and play: Social and psychological viewpoints* (2nd ed., pp. 241–278). Hillsdale, NJ: Lawrence Erlbaum Associates.

Zucker, H. M., & Babich, L. J. (1987). *Sports films: A complete reference*. Jefferson, NC: McFarland & Company.

12

Alternative Media versus the Olympic Industry

Helen Jefferson Lenskyj
University of Toronto

This chapter begins by analyzing the general role of the mainstream media in relation to the Olympic industry and the specific coverage of Olympic-related issues in the period leading up to the Sydney 2000 Olympic Games. I then investigate the development of alternative media, specifically independent media centers and other activist web sites organized by anti-Olympic and Olympic watchdog groups.

INTRODUCTION

The modern Olympic Games had their beginnings in 1896, but it has been only in recent decades that they have gained a reputation as a media spectacle and an economic bonanza. In contrast to the current cutthroat competition between bidding cities every two years for the right to host Summer or Winter Games, there were periods in the 1960s and 1970s when the International Olympic Committee (IOC) faced declining international interest in hosting the Olympics. The 1984 Games in Los Angeles marked a turning point: This was the only city willing to organize the event and the first to claim that it had generated a profit by doing so. At the same time, the Olympics promised unprecedented profits for corporate sponsors, television networks, and other mass media outlets.

Given their vested interests in the Olympic industry, the mass media were unlikely to expend much energy on investigative journalism, and it wasn't until 1998 that two decades of bribery and corruption in the bid process finally came to light (Lenskyj, 2000). Furthermore, as Olympic critic Burstyn (2000) observed, "Because of what has amounted to a de facto mainstream media blackout of organized anti-Olympic struggles, most people know little about the efforts and concerns of hundreds of citizens' groups . . . for more than twenty years" (p. xii).

The most obvious links between the mass media and the Olympic Games involve commercial television coverage of the actual sporting events—most notably NBC's multibillion dollar investment since 1988—and these connections have attracted considerable scholarly attention (e.g., Burstyn, 1999; Jackson, 1989; MacNeill, 1995, 1996; Rothenbuhler, 1995; Wenner, 1994, 1998). Equally important, but seriously under-researched, are the ways in which social activists use the media, both mainstream and alternative, to direct public attention to negative Olympic impacts on vulnerable populations and environments and to uncover the links between the Olympic industry and global capitalism.

It is disturbing, but not surprising, to see how the mainstream media trivialize or ignore anti-Olympic activists, but widespread neglect on the part of academic researchers is more difficult to explain. Many Olympic studies specialists—sport historians and sport sociologists—are affiliated with university centers for Olympic studies that derive some of their funding from national Olympic committees or from the IOC. While in theory this does not interfere with their academic freedom, they may believe that it is prudent to avoid appearing to legitimize anti-Olympic activists and their critiques (Lenskyj, 2002). Alternatively, as I've suggested elsewhere (Lenskyj, 2000), the vicarious excitement generated by unofficial membership in the so-called Olympic Family and the goose-bumps effect of rubbing shoulders with Olympic athletes and VIPs may lead some researchers to see the Olympic industry through a less-than-critical lens. Furthermore, as Olympic critics MacAloon (1984) and Booth (2004) proposed, the official televised version of the Olympics, with its emphasis on sporting stars and hierarchies, limits researchers' historical focus and leads them to ignore alternative perspectives and narratives.

On the related issue of alternative media, even the progressive fields of media studies and cultural studies have, until recently, paid relatively little attention to community-based activists who are using their information technology expertise to organize for social change (Atton & Couldry, 2003). However, a second edition of John Downing's classic book, *Radical Media*, in 2001 and a special issue of *Media, Culture and Society* in 2003 reflect growing interest in the topic. Insights from these areas of inquiry provide a useful starting point for the following analysis of the communication struggles of grassroots anti-Olympic and Olympic watchdog organizations in the face of the Olympic industry's media machine.

ALTERNATIVE MEDIA AND CITIZENSHIP

As media critics have demonstrated, the issue of citizenship underlies all alternative media practices. Atton and Couldry (2003) posed the cogent questions: "What are the conditions under which citizens in the 21st century can expect to be engaged in politics, on whatever scale, and what do the resources of media production and media consumption contribute to these conditions?" (p. 580). As they go on to explain, the Internet has increasingly become a key means of communication within grassroots political movements. Alternative media practitioners are concerned with both the medium and the message; they have something to say, theoretically and empirically, about democracy, global development, media and communications, and social justice (Atton & Couldry, 2003). Community groups in cities involved in recent Olympic bids or preparations share these concerns at both local and global levels; the citizenship issues that they raise include housing and homelessness, poverty, threats to civil liberties, global capitalism, exploitation of workers, and degradation of the natural environment (Lenskyj, 2000, 2002, 2004a, 2004b).

In this context, *alternative* generally denotes liberal or leftwing, although there are, in addition, countless conservative and reactionary groups that rely on Web sites and other electronic communication modes. Given the considerable financial disparities between the two sides, it is not surprising that the latter mount larger and more elaborate Web sites (Downey & Fenton, 2003). The IOC is a pertinent example of an information-heavy mainstream Web site that is unlikely to be matched by those of anti-Olympic and Olympic watchdog groups, operating as they do on shoestring budgets. However, there are some examples of successful David-and-Goliath encounters on the Internet. The huge McSpotlight Web site, established in 1996 in support of two UK activists whom McDonalds (fast food company) had charged with libel, has been maintained by volunteers from 22 countries ever since (Downey & Fenton, 2003).

THE OLYMPIC INDUSTRY AND THE MEDIA

The 1998 to 1999 exposure of widespread bribery and corruption in the IOC and the global Olympic industry marked a new era in mainstream media treatment of all things Olympic. The five rings, as the media were fond of saying, were now tarnished. Most mainstream journalists, however, focused on individuals rather than on systemic problems. It was easier to demonize specific IOC members—and the western media were expert at doing so when the members under suspicion came from Africa or South America—than to engage in serious investigative journalism. Few reporters examined a system that crossed national boundaries and normalized dishonesty at all levels, from the IOC, national Olympic committees, and bid and organizing committees to coaches and administrators who espoused so-called Olympic values. In reality, as Olympic critics have argued, winning at all costs by whatever means necessary appears to be the most salient value of Olympic sporting competition. "You don't win a silver medal, you lose gold"—the advertisement that Nike ran during the 1996 Games—captured this ethos (Lenskyj, 2000, 2002).

In their treatment of the IOC scandal, mainstream media generally adopted the bad-apples approach, while clinging to an idealistic view of Olympic sport, which they erroneously separated, as *pure*, from the explicitly commercial and political components. And so they continued to dismiss or ignore the cogent critiques that anti-Olympic and Olympic watchdog groups had been developing since the late 1980s. In fact, these groups' early efforts foreshadowed later whistle-blowing initiatives, most notably Swiss IOC member Marc Hodler's 1998 allegations—eventually substantiated by various commissions of inquiry—of vote-buying during site selection for the preceding four Olympics, in Atlanta 1996, Nagano 1998, Sydney 2000, and Salt Lake City 2002. In this climate, activist groups relied heavily on alternative media to counter Olympic industry and government propaganda, to organize protests, and to provide a forum for community debate, particularly on issues that Olympic organizers attempted to keep hidden from public scrutiny.

SYDNEY 2000: "SHARE THE SPIRIT"

In Australia, the Olympic industry successfully harnessed the mainstream media in its relentless promotion of the Sydney 2000 Olympic project, not only as a magic moment in Australian nationhood and Australians' personal histories, but also as an unprecedented opportunity to boost the economy through tourism, employment, and private sector investment. With the slogan "Share the Spirit," the Sydney Olympics were touted as a once-in-a-lifetime experience for Australians. The country was saturated with ad campaigns urging everyone to buy tickets and to volunteer their time at the Games.

Well-grounded concerns about the objectivity of the Australian mass media surfaced in the early 1990s when Sydney began organizing its bid for the 2000 Olympics. Newspapers, in particular, adopted the role of bid boosters, and articles by *Sydney Morning Herald* reporter Sam North were so positive that they served as unpaid advertising for the bid committee. There was disturbing evidence, too, that freelance journalists who tried to expose problems with the Olympic budget could not get their articles published in major newspapers (Bacon, 1993). Murray Hogarth, the *Herald*'s environment editor in the mid-1990s, viewed the paper's earlier boosterism as atypical and considered its tougher approach after 1998 as evidence that it had not abandoned its usually uncompromising editorial stance. For example, the *Herald* published Hogarth's numerous exposés of dioxin contamination at the Homebush Bay Olympic site, along with his critiques of government and bid committee attempts to conceal the full extent of the problem (M. Hogarth, personal communication, April 22, 1999; Lenskyj, 2000).

In 1997, for the first time in Olympic sponsorship history, it was announced that Australia's two major newspaper companies, Fairfax and News Limited, would share Olympic sponsorship status. The marketing and promotion of Olympic properties were divided, with the torch relay and the ticket sales allocated to News Limited, and volunteer recruitment, the arts festival, and the school newspaper to Fairfax. The arrangement, instead of dampening longstanding rivalries, appeared to promote even greater competition between the two newspaper giants. One of the many subsequent controversies concerned News Limited's announcement of the Olympic torch design, a story that the organizing committee's head, Michael Knight, claimed was Olympic promotion, and not Olympic news. A journalist for News Limited subsequently asserted that, regardless of the distribution of various Olympic properties, Olympic organizers had no influence over the editorial perspective that a news story took (King, 1998, 11). There was, however, a clear financial disincentive to "bite the (Olympic) hand that feeds you."

EMERGING CRITIQUES
IN THE MAINSTREAM MEDIA

In the aftermath of the IOC bribery scandal, Sydney 2000 organizers could no longer rely on the mainstream press to treat Olympic issues uncritically. Once the floodgates were opened, experienced journalists, including *Sydney Morning Herald* Olympic editor Matthew Moore and reporters Jacqueline Magnay and Michael Evans, regularly uncovered new Olympic controversies at home as well as abroad. These included scandals over ticket sales, budget blowouts, broken environmental promises, and, overall, the excessive level of secrecy surrounding Olympic-related projects. The organizing committee's policies and practices were not conducive to information flow, and journalists were particularly frustrated when, in March 2000, press conferences were replaced by "background briefings" and no television cameras or radio microphones were allowed (Peatling, 2000).

Moore resorted to Freedom of Information requests in his numerous attempts to uncover the full story behind Olympic controversies and led the way in critical investigative journalism. In his former roles as head of the staff union and political reporter, he had been active in the campaign to establish editorial independence at the *Herald*—an especially valued ethos in light of that paper's reputation as Sydney's more intelligent newspaper. He reported that, by the mid-1990s, he and his colleagues could publish stories that were critical of the government and Olympic organizers, as long as they were "accurate and balanced" (M. Moore, personal communication, May 16, 2000). The *Herald*, too, was arguably the only paper to provide a semblance of balance in its coverage of Indigenous, environmental, antipoverty, and human rights protest groups, with Debra Jopson, in particular, providing insightful discussion of complex Indigenous political issues (Jopson, 1999, 2000a, 2000b, 2000c, 2000d). The *Herald* also provided a public forum for a few respected church, social services, and indigenous leaders who served on the organizing committee's Social Impact Advisory Committee, but the more radical leaders of grassroots activist organizations were less likely to be given a voice in this newspaper.

ALTERNATIVE MEDIA AS RESISTANCE

Australian anti-Olympic and Olympic watchdog organizations had some notable successes in putting social, economic, environmental, human rights, and Aboriginal issues on the public agenda, internationally as well as locally, through their own Web sites, news releases, and newsletters and through independent media centers established for that purpose. They were also newsmakers themselves, as they mounted numerous protest rallies, marches, direct actions, and civil disobedience, most of which were dismissed as the actions of *ratbags* (fringe elements) by the mainstream media in Australia.

In 1999, Greenpeace launched a global campaign targeting Coca-Cola, through the Web site cokespotlight.com. Thousands of supporters around the world joined in demanding that the company improve its environmental practices in relation to refrigeration. The campaign had some successes: In June 2000, Coca-Cola agreed to phase out hydrofluorocarbons (HFCs) in its cooling equipment by the 2004 Athens Olympics, to expand its research into refrigeration alternatives, and to require suppliers to install HFC-free refrigerants in all new equipment by the 2004 Olympics.

With the Melbourne meeting of the World Economic Forum scheduled for September 2000, just before the Sydney Games, global social justice protesters established one of Australia's first independent media centers (IMC), melbourne.indymedia.org, earlier that year, while sydney.indymedia.org began operating in mid-June. IMCs were interactive Web sites and physical spaces modeled on the Seattle site, seattle.indymedia.org. The automatic publishing software used in Seattle had been developed by a team of media activists that included Matthew Arnison, a member of the Sydney community activist technology collective, Cat@lyst. Like its counterparts in other countries, the Sydney IMC operated on the principle that "Everyone is a witness. Everyone is a journalist." By 2004, there were about 140 independent media centers on five continents, in seven languages.

However, more than 50% were based in English-speaking countries and only 13 were operating in Asia and Africa.

The dual functions of the Sydney IMC were to communicate *unfiltered* Olympic-related news and views and to provide "a permanent record of our experience of protesting the many social injustices highlighted and/or exacerbated by the Olympics, an alternative, activist record of events and experiences." Organizers explained, "As activists we are weary of having our actions trivialized and our views marginalized by the mainstream corporate-owned press" (Home page, Sydney IMC, 2000). With the two major Australian newspaper companies sharing joint Olympic sponsorship rights, and despite official assurances that editorial content would not be affected by these sponsorship deals, anti-Olympic activists were justly concerned about bias in the print media.

Other environmental, anti-Olympic, and Olympic watchdog organizations based in Australia made effective use of the Internet before and during the Sydney Olympics. Rentwatchers, Greenpeace, Green Games Watch 2000, Bondi Beach Watch, and PISSOFF (People Ingeniously Subverting the Olympic Farce Forever) were among the numerous groups that organized Web sites, electronic notice boards, and mailing lists. In 2000, these and other community groups formed a coalition called the Anti-Olympic Alliance (AOA). Web sites had links to their international counterparts such as Toronto's Bread Not Circuses Coalition, which successfully challenged that city's bids for the 1996 and the 2008 Olympics. Some alternative Web sites were also set up specifically to critique the Olympics using Australia's unique brand of humor and satire: for example, realgames.org.au, Unolympics.com, sillyolympics.com, and the olympisc.org (deliberately misspelled). And, in another independent media initiative, the Sydney Alternative Media Center (SAMC), staffed by media professionals, provided international journalists with a progressive alternative to the official information sources like the Sydney organizing committee and government trade and tourism agencies. SAMC covered nonsport topics including Australia's environmental record and the history and culture of Australian Aboriginals.

Committed to democratic principles, interactive Web sites like IMCs featured a simple self-publishing process, with no screening of materials. Inappropriate or offensive postings from Olympic supporters and, occasionally, from Olympic critics, were not censored. The Sydney IMC guidelines explained that the collective would only correct obvious mistakes and delete postings that were outside the purpose of the site. As a consequence of the nonscreening principle, a large number of Olympic supporters flooded the AOA interactive page, and the AOA e-list was spammed so frequently than most people unsubscribed themselves in the weeks before the Games. However, the Sydney IMC was undoubtedly an alternative media success. By September, it featured hundreds of articles and dozens of photos, sound recordings, and videos, mostly on Olympic-related social, political, and environmental issues—all linked to the broader sociocultural context of a city, state, and country plagued with problems of race relations, poverty, homelessness, and unemployment.

In 2000, the National Infrastructure Protection Center identified the AOA as a potential security threat and predicted that anti-Olympic hackers (*hactivists*) like the IMC collective would attempt to down official Olympic sites. In reality, both these groups, like the other anti-Olympic and Olympic watchdog organizations listed above, were organized for completely legal and legitimate purposes: nonviolent protest and free expression of views critical of the Olympics. Ray Jackson, an

Indigenous activist, aptly described the FBI report as "capitalist/corporate paranoia" (Jackson, 2001, p.6).

The Olympic industry, for its part, was more concerned with financial threats and the protection of sponsors' interests. In August 2000, the IOC hired software experts to search the Internet for unauthorized domain names using the magic "O" word—primarily commercial sites—and for unauthorized Internet media that planned to stream live coverage. About 20 internet sites were ordered to remove Olympic-related audio and video clips, while 15 pornography and 43 gambling Web sites were named in an IOC lawsuit (Barkham, 2000; IOC, 2000). Anti-Olympic groups did not, however, escape scrutiny, and Unolympics.com was warned of legal action for unauthorized use of the Olympic rings and the Sydney 2000 logo. After the group explained that the symbols were deliberately distorted and obviously different from the official logo and Web site, IOC lawyers withdrew the threat (Unolympics.com, 2000).

VANCOUVER/WHISTLER ACTIVISTS FIGHT BACK

In 2001, Vancouver and Whistler, in British Columbia, Canada, entered the race for the 2010 Winter Olympics. Several Olympic watchdog groups were subsequently organized to raise issues of social, economic, and environmental impacts. These included Impact of the Olympics on Community Coalition (IOCC), Association of Whistler Area Residents for the Environment (AWARE), No Games 2010 Coalition, and Oust the Olympics. All these groups set up Web sites that provided organizing information and critiques of Olympic industry propaganda, as well as opportunities for discussion. Web sites of longer standing, like vancouver.indymedia.org and publicspace.ca/vancouver regularly included Olympic protest groups' news and critiques, while creativeresistance.ca introduced a Web page called Olympic Watch.

Early in 2002, two Whistler activists, Van Powel and Troy Assaly, set up the interactive Web site olympicinfo.org. A few months later, residents heard that the Whistler Council had been secretly negotiating with the World Economic Forum (WEF) to host its 2004 meeting. Powel and Assaly established a second site, whistlerinfo.net, to publicize the WEF's plans and Whistler Council's undemocratic decision-making process. Faced with a petition signed by 1,300 residents, the council passed a set of stringent conditions, thereby ensuring that the WEF would not find Whistler an attractive site. However, social activists' struggle to keep the Winter Games out of Vancouver/Whistler was lost.

RESISTANCE IN SALT LAKE CITY

Utahns for Responsible Public Spending, Citizen Activist Network, and Salt Lake Impact 2002 were among the many watchdog groups organized in Salt Lake City in the late 1990s as that city prepared to host the 2002 Winter Olympics. The Salt Lake Impact Web site included report cards on the organizing committee's treatment of low-income tenants and homeless people and its promises of affordable housing as an Olympic legacy (Salt Lake Impact, 2002). Documentation of the ACLU's eventually successful struggles in 2001 and 2002 to protect free-speech zones for protesters during the Games was available on their Web site aclu.org. The grassroots public radio show *Democracy Now* also included coverage of protests and critiques of corporate profiteering from the Salt Lake Olympics on its Web site democracynow.org.

CONFRONTING THE SPORTING GOODS GIANTS

The Olympic industry's links with global sporting goods companies that rely on sweatshop labor have long been subject to critique. In 2000, the Australian Nike activist group Fairwear, which had been launched in 1996, embarked on a major campaign to draw public attention to Nike's labor practices domestically and internationally. In September, another group—Nikewatch—released a new Oxfam report on conditions in Indonesian Nike factories, with documentation of previously unreported human rights abuses. Both of these groups made extensive use of the Internet for organizing and educational purposes.

At the time of the 2002 Olympics, Sweatshop Watch groups in Amsterdam held an alternative opening ceremony in protest against Salt Lake City's purchase of Burmese sportswear for Olympic torchbearers. Two years later, an international protest known as the Play Fair Campaign was mounted by Oxfam International and the European Clean Clothes Campaign, in collaboration with national and local labor organizations in several countries. These groups were protesting the brutal exploitation of workers employed by the global sportswear industry to make Olympic merchandise. Through its Web site oxfam.ca, Oxfam Canada organized an online e-mail petition, with letters of protest sent to heads of the Canadian Olympic Committee, the Vancouver 2010 Organizing Committee, and Roots Canada, the official supplier of the Canadian Olympic team. A full report of working conditions in the sportswear industry and detailed recommendations for companies, suppliers, governments, the "Olympic movement," and the public were available on fairolympics.org.

Although these efforts were to be commended, their approach revealed a somewhat naïve reliance on Olympic industry rhetoric. For example, the Play Fair recommendations referred to the "Olympic movement" uncritically (as if it were purely a humanitarian enterprise), and the Play Fair press release endorsed Olympic industry rhetoric by asserting that "The Olympics is all about fair play." (www.fairolympics.org). In the same vein, the Australian Nikewatch campaign four years earlier had organized a public debate on the question "Do conditions in Nike factories meet the Olympic ideal of respect for human dignity?"—thereby treating this so-called ideal as a reality.

In fact, Sydney Olympic organizers and New South Wales politicians had a mixed record on the issue of human dignity and were responsible for draconian policies and legislation that criminalized homelessness and curtailed freedom of assembly (see Lenskyj, 2002). In 2002, when the World Trade Organization held talks in a hotel on the former Olympic site, protesters were effectively suppressed not only by the sheer numbers of police officers, police horses, attack dogs, and helicopters, but also by the still-operative Olympic security legislation, which included $5000 fines for distributing political leaflets ("WTO in Sydney," 2002).

ATHENS, GREECE

In the lead-up to the 2004 Olympics in Athens, local Olympic watchdog and anti-Olympic groups made use of athens.indymedia.org, anti2004.net, and other Web sites to publish critiques and document protest actions.[1] In one action in April 2004, Athens protesters with the slogan "The Olympics' culture isn't ours" identified commercialization, environmental destruction, repression, and workplace accidents in their list of negative Olympic impacts. Earlier protest marches by anarchists and others had drawn public attention to the number of workplace accidents on Olympic construction sites—about 20 deaths, compared to only one death during the Sydney 2000 Olympic construction—and had blamed companies for low safety standards. As one alternative Web site posting went on to explain, the modern Olympics "are all about money, steroids and 'security', meaning more cops and cameras on the streets" ("The Greek Bosses," 2002; "Workers Labor News," 2003). During a February 20 protest march, police had used tear gas to disperse about 1,000 anarchists ("Anarchists," 2004).

As had been the case in Sydney in the 1990s, housing and homelessness issues were exacerbated by Olympic preparations in Athens, and housing and antipoverty advocates used the Internet to publicize abuses by landlords and state authorities. Urban squatters and other "undesirable" Athens residents became the frequent targets of state intervention in the years prior to the Olympics. The *Global Survey on Forced Evictions* (2003, p. 60) reported that Roma communities in and around Athens had been evicted from their settlements by municipal authorities in 2001 and 2002. Several incidents were documented, with more than ten Roma homes and their contents bulldozed or burned to the ground. No eviction orders had been served on the families, and Greek authorities and the IOC had remained silent on the issue.

Following the pattern of many European cities, there were numerous squatted buildings in and around Athens when Olympic preparations began. In 2002, independent media sources reported that residents in a squat established in 1988, Lelas Karayanni 37, were threatened with violent eviction, and water and electricity were cut off. Squatters in a university students' house were also ordered to vacate it so that journalists could be accommodated there during the Olympics ("Occupied student homes," 2002).

Alternative media centers reported on the aftermath of the Olympics in another European city—Barcelona—which was facing a second "clean-up" in preparation for the six-month-long European Union Forum beginning in May 2004. As some Olympics critics had predicted in the early 1990s (Montalban, 1992), the gentrification trend had dire consequences for Barcelona's poor:

> The cityscape itself is transformed into a consumer playground that is much too expensive for "normal" people to continue to live there ... Barcelona can scarcely afford to tolerate poverty and immigration, much less squats and squatted centers ... there have been harsh attacks against the 100+ squatted buildings in and around the city, including evictions, demolitions, prosecution, and threats of evictions. ... (IMC Philly, 2003)

CONCLUSION

The examples presented here show how anti-Olympic and Olympic watchdog groups have effectively reaped the benefits of instant and relatively inexpensive

---

[1]In this discussion I am commenting only on English language postings. As the reference list shows, some of these appeared on Athens-based sites, and others were posted on indymedia sites in the UK, Australia, and elsewhere.

electronic communication offered by the Internet to form international networks in solidarity with other local and global social justice organizations. Through these methods, they have had some successes in raising public awareness about the negative social and environmental impacts that result from hosting Summer or Winter Olympics. Admittedly, confronting the powerful Olympic industry puts these groups in a David-and-Goliath situation. However, as an activist involved with the Bread Not Circuses Coalition in Toronto since 1998, the AOA in Sydney in 2000, and various Vancouver/Whistler groups in 2001, I can say with certainty that members of these groups are continuing their efforts with commitment and energy. In addition to their community activism, some are working in local government or running for political office in order to bring about social change from within the system, while others continue to do their advocacy work from the outside. Developments in the alternative media over the last decade have undoubtedly facilitated their efforts in the cause of global social justice.

REFERENCES

Anarchists against the Athens 2004 Olympic Games. (2004, February 20). IMC Athens. Retrieved March 15, 2004, from http://www.athens.indymedia.org

Atton, C., & Couldry, N. (2003). Introduction to special issue. *Media, Culture and Society, 25*(5), 579–586.

Bacon, W. (1993). Atlanta's watchdog. *Reportage.* Retrieved September 6, 2004, from http://journalism.uts.edu.au/archive/ olympics/atlanta.html

Barkham, P. (2000, September 25). Special report: the Sydney Olympics. *The Guardian.* Retrieved September 26, 2000, from http://www.guardianunlimited.co.uk

Booth, D. (2004). Post-olympism? Questioning olympic historiography. In J. Bale & M. Christensen (Eds.), *Post Olympism? Questioning sport in the twenty-first century* (pp. 13–32). London: Berg.

Burstyn, V. (1999). *The rites of men.* Toronto: University of Toronto Press.

Burstyn, V. (2000). Forward. In H. Lenskyj, *Inside the Olympic industry: Power, politics and activism.* Albany, NY: SUNY Press.

Downey, J., & Fenton, N. (2003). New media, counter publicity and the public sphere. *New Media and Society, 5*(2), 185–202.

Downing, J. (2001). *Radical Media.* Thousand Islands, CA: Sage.

Global Survey on Forced Evictions No. 9. (2003, June). Center on Housing Rights and Evictions. Retrieved March 15, 2004, from www.cohre.org

The Greek bosses open a full scale attack against society. (2002, November 16). Retrieved March 15, 2004, from http://www.adelaide.indymedia.org.au/front.php3? article_id=3701andgroup=webcast

IMC Philly (Trans.). (2003, October 5). International demonstration against the governmental commercialization of living spaces. Retrieved March 15, 2004, from http://www.barcelona.indymedia.org/newswire/display/55557/index.php

IOC (2000, July 13). Media release: IOC, USOC, and SLOC jointly file groundbreaking lawsuit against cybersquatters. Retrieved July 20, 2000, from http://www.olympic.org

Jackson, R. (Ed.). (1989). *The Olympic movement and the mass media.* Calgary: Hurfurd Enterprises.

Jackson, R. (2001, April). SOCOG 3: and you're out. *Djadi-Dugarang, 3*(2), 1–6.

Jopson, D. (1999, August 9). Aborigines to push Games of shame. *Sydney Morning Herald.* Retrieved August 9, 1999, from www.smh.com.au

Jopson, D. (2000a, March 28). Protesters told: Say what you like, but don't say it on Olympic grounds. *Sydney Morning Herald.* Retrieved March 28, 2000, from http://www.smh.com.au

Jopson, D. (2000b, May 27). In harmony they lament: Why is sorry so hard? *Sydney Morning Herald.* Retrieved May 27, 2000, from http://www.smh.com.au

Jopson, D. (2000c, July 26). Council pegs back Aboriginal tent embassy. *Sydney Morning Herald.* Retrieved July 26, 2000, from http://www.smh.com.au

Jopson, D. (2000d, August 7). Enough is enough. *Sydney Morning Herald.* Retrieved August 7, 2000, from http://www.smh.com.au

King, M. (1998, April 23). Problems in reporting the build up to the Sydney 2000 Olympics. *The Media Report*, ABC Radio National. Retrieved January 26, 2001, from http://www. abc.net.au

Lenskyj, H. (2000). *Inside the Olympic industry: Power, politics and activism.* Albany, NY: SUNY Press.

Lenskyj, H. (2002). *The best ever Olympics: Social impacts of Sydney 2000.* Albany, NY: SUNY Press.

Lenskyj, H. (2004a). Making the world safe for global capital: The Sydney 2000 Olympics and beyond. In J. Bale & M. Christensen (Eds.), *Post Olympism? Questioning sport in the twenty-first century* (pp. 135–45). London: Berg Publishers.

Lenskyj, H. (2004b). The Olympic industry and civil liberties: The threat to free speech and freedom of assembly. *Sport in Society, 7*(3), 370–384.

MacAloon, J. (1984). Olympic Games and the theory of spectacle in modern societies. In J. MacAloon (Ed.), *Rite, drama, festival, spectacle.* Philadelphia, PA: Institute of Human Issues.

MacNeill, M. (1995). Olympic power plays. *Journal of International Communication, 2*(1), 42–65.

MacNeill, M. (1996). Networks: Producing Olympic ice hockey for a national television audience. *Sociology of Sport Journal, 13*, 103–124.

Montalban, M. (1992). *Barcelonas* (A. Robinson, Trans.). London: Verso.

Occupied student homes and Lelas Karayanni 37 squat under repression. (2002, September 19). Retrieved March 15, 2004, from http://www.indymedia.org.uk/en/regions/world/topics/culture

Peatling, S. (2000, March 28). Freedom of information. *Sydney Morning Herald.* Retrieved March 28, 2000, from http://www.smh.com.au

Play Fair at the Olympics. (2004, March 8). Retrieved May 13, 2004, from http://www.fairolympics.org/en/report/olympicreporteng.pdf

Rothenbuhler, E. (1995). The social distribution of participation in the broadcast Olympic Games. *Journal of International Communication, 2*(1), 66–79.

Salt Lake Impact 2002 (2002, February). Report card for the Salt Lake Organizing Committee and the City of Salt Lake. Retrieved March 7, 2002, from http://www.xmission.com/~xrdsurb/ReportCard.pdf

Sydney Independent Media Center Website. (2002). http://www.sydney.indymedia.org

Unolympics.com (2000, September 29). IOC backs away from legal action. Sydney IMC. Retrieved September 30, 2000, from http://www.sydney.indymedia.org

Wenner, L. (1994). The dream team, communicative dirt, and the marketing of synergy. *Journal of Sport and Social Issues, 18*(3), 282–92.

Wenner, L. (Ed.). (1998). *MediaSport.* London: Routledge.

Workers' Labor News. (2003, September 19). Retrieved March 15, 2004, from http://www.workers.labor.net.au

WTO in Sydney. (2002, November 15). Retrieved November 15, 2002, from http://www.moz.net.nz/activism/nowto/

13

World Cup Worlds: Media Coverage of the Soccer World Cup 1974 to 2002

Andrew Tudor
University of York

In 1974 Ed Buscombe, publications editor at the British Film Institute, persuaded a group of us to research and analyze British television coverage of that year's World Cup finals. It seemed an appropriate moment. The 1970 World Cup had witnessed considerable expansion in British television coverage (not least because England had won the competition in 1966), and ITV, then the sole British commercial channel, had introduced a much publicized panel of expert football worthies whose function was to frame and interpret both individual games and the competition as a whole. Even more coverage was promised in 1974 in spite of the fact that England (though not Scotland) had failed to qualify for the 1974 finals, and the experimental format of four years earlier had now emerged as a fully-fledged program template.

But such pragmatic considerations were not the only precipitants of the research. In the late 1960s and early 1970s, cultural and media studies in the UK had undergone something of a revolution in both scale and perspective. Television was now attracting much interest from those hitherto more concerned with film, and ideas begged, borrowed, or stolen from structuralism and semiology appeared to offer an exciting and innovative theoretical focus. United in our belief that television constructed the worlds on which it purported simply to report, rather than merely reflecting them, we set out to uncover some of the conceptual and representational building blocks, the *codes*, involved in that process. The scene setting offered by the two major schedule-listing magazines, *Radio Times* and *TV Times*; the framing provided by title sequences; and the different emphases of visual style, of commentaries, and of panel discussions formed our focus. The collection of essays that we produced (Buscombe, 1975a) was published as the fourth in the British Film Institute's new series of *Television Monographs*.

It may not have been a lengthy volume, but it attracted a good deal of interest. It was, after all, the first systematic, qualitative attempt to study media coverage of one of the two great international sporting events (the Olympics and the World Cup), and it served to open up a whole series of issues about television soccer coverage which would be revisited, amended, and superseded by other researchers for every subsequent World Cup. During those years, of course, television coverage increased as the competition expanded. In 1974, 16 teams competed in the finals—the survivors from a starting group of 92 countries. By 2002, the group of finalists had doubled to 32 drawn from 195 starters, a sporting megaevent (Horne & Manzenreiter, 2004) that now exceeds all others in scale and international popularity.

Yet all this grew from small beginnings. The idea of a soccer world cup was first voiced in 1904 but began to develop fully only in 1930 when 13 teams competed (much of Europe did not) and a crowd of 80,000 watched Uruguay beat Argentina in the final. Two more competitions followed in the 1930s, and the finals returned in 1950 after the hiatus occasioned by World War II. By then, of course, the world was experiencing major expansion of television, and the 1954 competition in Switzerland was the first to see the opening ceremony and opening match televised. The scale of the enterprise has increased steadily since then, with concomitant growth in television coverage. According to the organizing body FIFA, who commissioned a TV audience analysis of the 2002 finals, coverage that year went to 213 countries and involved over 41,100 hours of dedicated viewing time, a new record for a single sporting event. Over the 25 days of the finals it is estimated that the world-wide home TV audience summed to 28.8 billion viewers, a figure which does not include the many millions more who watched on big public screens or in bars and cafes the world over. Given this remarkable scale, then, it is hardly surprising that World Cup TV coverage and reporting has continued to attract the attention of media researchers since the 1974 study.

Here I examine this accumulated body of research analytically and historically, with a view to tracing the fate of the main issues raised in that first study and identifying the additional themes that have engaged the attention of the subfield over the last 30 years. I do so under two main headings. Under the first, "systems of discourse," I consider the kinds of general methodological and theoretical frameworks that have been employed and summarize, albeit schematically and very briefly, the range of topics that researchers have addressed. Under the second, "stereotyping and national identity," I pay much closer attention to what is by far the most extensively researched aspect of the World Cup and other international football coverage. It is this work, more than anything else, that reflects the central concerns of 30 years of World Cup media research.

SYSTEMS OF DISCOURSE

The single most frequently employed concept in this body of literature is *discourse*. This is hardly surprising given the research program's ancestry in the qualitative tradition of media and cultural studies wherein *discourse analysis* is a widely accepted perspective—there is only one piece of World Cup media research that adopts an unalloyed, quantitative content analysis approach (Billings & Tambosi, 2004). What is not so clear is precisely what analyzing discourses involves, and the frequency with which the term itself is used is matched only by the infrequency with which it is defined. That is not necessarily a serious problem, of course, for although conceptual clarity is generally desirable, there are some concepts that are useful precisely because of the range of their coverage and the concomitant diffuseness of their definition. The concept of culture, for example, is one such, and it seems likely that *discourse* is constructively ambiguous in similar ways. But at a general level the term's import is clear enough: it serves to focus attention on the structuring systems that render communication possible and, in so doing, construct them as naturalized modes of communication. Embedded in the concept of discourse, then, is a strong sense of systematicity and taken-for-grantedness. Discursive systems are assumed to provide spectators with the cultural materials out of which they construct and reconstruct their sense of a coherent and intelligible social setting. Systems of discourse, that is, organize the terms in which we organize the world.

Within that broad consensus, however, there remains a good deal of room for maneuver, both in identifying the mechanisms by which such discourses function and establishing the kinds of theories and methods best suited to their elucidation. Even the most cursory examination of the World Cup and international football literature reveals a considerable variety of strategies for discourse analysis even though there appears to be general agreement on the centrality of the focus upon discourse itself. O'Donnell (1994), for example, reflecting on the theoretical resources with which the discourse of national sporting stereotypes might best be analyzed, noted "clear areas of overlap with social identity theory" (pp. 346–347), viewing national stereotypes as cognitive constructs which always have to be understood in their sociological and historical context. Maguire, Poulton, and Passamai (1999) were similarly concerned with historically and socially contextualizing stereotyping processes in their account of media coverage of the England–Germany match in the 1996 European Football Championships, though they prefer to utilize the concept of *national habitus* as that has been elaborated by Norbert Elias. Elsewhere one finds researchers invoking *framing theory* (Delgado, 2003) in analyzing the ways in which different and sometimes conflicting discourses may be marshaled in media coverage; *media event theory* (Alabarces, Tomlinson, & Young, 2001) in exploring how the sporting event generates social and cultural meanings far beyond the world of sport; the use of metaphor (Dauncey & Hare, 2000) in examining the significance of the 1998 World Cup in France; and *discursive upgrading* as a key process in constructing and reconstructing coherent narratives of national character in the television coverage of Italia '90 (Tudor, 1992).

What these diverse theoretical strategies have in common is a desire to elucidate the various means through which media accounts of international football draw upon an array of preestablished systems of discourse in making sporting events intelligible to viewers, readers, and, indeed, media functionaries themselves. As yet, clearly, there is no consensus on precisely which analytic resources are best suited to this task, nor is it to be expected that any one theoretical or methodological strategy will meet all such requirements. The sheer variety of discourses implicated in World Cup coverage makes that all but impossible. Nor is it any more than an assumption (though a plausible one) that the discourses do indeed perform the world-constructing functions identified, since most World Cup media research has focused only on the media texts themselves. But inasmuch as the mutual interrelation among discursive systems is a contingent accomplishment of their actual use by agents in specific social situations, there is now a pressing need to examine the ways in which readers and viewers actually engage with the discourses promulgated to them by the media. As has happened more generally in cultural and media studies, the active reader must be propelled to the fore.

As yet, of course, that move has not been made, so we must be satisfied here with an outline examination of the modes of media discourse as researchers have revealed them in analysis of media texts: newspapers, television commentary, panel discussions, and so forth. In the main, researchers have focused upon two primary modes of discourse implicated directly in media coverage and three secondary or metadiscourses, which are drawn upon as and when they are required. The primary modes are those of linguistic discourse (whether spoken or written) and audiovisual discourse, and of the two it is the linguistic mode, that has received the lion's share of research attention. The major secondary modes are articulated through the two primary modes and derive from the more general social discourses of national identity, expertise, and narrativity.

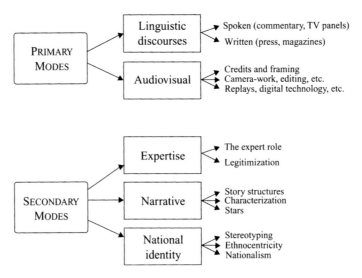

FIG. 13.1.   Areas of World Cup media research.

Using this rough classification, it is possible to summarize schematically (see Fig. 13.1) the main topics on which World Cup media research has focused. I use these headings to organize the account of the field that follows, beginning with some general observations on the prominence of linguistic discourses in research, then moving on to a brief consideration of two of the secondary discourses that find expression through that linguistic channel—those of expertise and narrativity. Then, after noting the striking absence of attention paid to audiovisual discourses, I turn to a consideration of national identity. This last topic has been especially prominent in the literature, for which reason I devote the entire second part of this paper to its examination.

Linguistic Discourses

As already observed, linguistic discourse has been the most common source of data for World Cup media researchers. Given the prominence of television coverage in the literature, it might seem somewhat surprising that there has not been more attention paid to the visual dimension. However, a moment's reflection will confirm that linguistic discourse in the form of commentary, preview and postmatch analysis, background reporting, and news reporting is the predominant channel through which coverage is constituted as meaningful. Accordingly, much research effort has gone into exploring the ways in which the World Cup is framed for viewers and readers by those commenting upon it in spoken or written form. It has long been recognized, of course, that sports commentary plays a crucial role in mediating the cognitive and emotional apprehension of a sporting event (Bryant, Comisky, & Zillmann, 1977; Bryant, Brown, Comisky, & Zillmann, 1982; Comisky, Bryant, & Zillmann 1977). The World Cup offers, in addition to commentary, a sustained and temporally focused exercise of framing in a whole variety of televisual and journalistic contexts. What commentators, experts, journalists, and participants actually say or write, therefore, has been the basic data for most researchers.

The specific character of that linguistic discourse itself, however, has not often been the focus for research. True, there has been some discussion of the use of metaphoric language resources and the variable application of particular tropes—for example, the tendency to use military metaphors in framing specific matches or teams. Writing of the 1990 World Cup in Italy, for example, Blain, Boyle, and O'Donnell (1993) noted that "throughout European journalism on the World Cup there runs a subterranean current of football as a 'substitute war.' However, the military metaphors are applied above all to the German team" (p. 77). This was a specially notable feature of press coverage of the Euro '96 tournament where England met Germany in the semifinal (Garland & Rowe, 1999; Maguire, et al., 1999), perhaps most dramatically summed up by the well known *Daily Mirror* headline "ACHTUNG SURRENDER" accompanied by the subhead "For You Fritz, Ze Euro 96 Championship is Over" (Maguire, et al., 1999, p. 442). Though this example is extreme, less dramatic use of military metaphors is commonplace in tabloid press coverage of international football, often linked (as above) to specific historical contexts. As Alabarces et al. (2001) suggested, "the use of military terminology to articulate a discourse of football captures perfectly the essence of Englishness in the 20th century: a sense of superiority based on victories in World Wars" (p. 557). In these respects the notorious British tabloid press leads the way, but there is also evidence to suggest "an increasing trend toward the penetration of television by the tabloid press's style of treatment of sport" (Blain, et al., 1993, p. 50). Since that was written there is no doubt that, in Britain at least, the tabloidisation of television has become increasingly apparent. The characteristic language and framing devices common to the popular press now inform much of television's football talk, and systematic research into this particular form of linguistic intertextuality is urgently required.

Secondary Discourses: Expertise

In the main, however, speech or writing has been treated by World Cup media researchers as a relatively transparent medium of communication through which to access other discursive systems. For example, the discourse by which expertise is constructed and legitimized was a topic addressed in the first study of the 1974 World Cup (McArthur, 1975/1981; Tudor, 1975/1981) where it is noted that television performs a self-legitimizing function in relation to those it presents as experts. Whatever their actual qualifications for the role, tele-experts take on the patina of minor celebrity and, thereby, credibility from their constant television exposure. So, in World Cup coverage and football coverage more generally, "we are presented with the seemingly unitary world of televised football, with its familiar faces, and agreed rules on what constitutes a football 'expert'" (Blain, et al., 1993, pp. 43–44). To be an expert is to have the right to guide the rest of us to a proper understanding of the televised events.

Secondary Discourses: Narrative

This legitimization of tele-experts by repeated exposure then provides the grounds for effective operation of another of the secondary discourses continuously drawn upon in World Cup coverage: the discourse of narrativity. Television panelists and newspaper journalists tell us stories. They render events intelligible by mapping them into preestablished narrative templates in which actions are understood to interrelate in specified ways and "characters" are constructed who display distinctive attributes and intentions (Tudor, 1992). Television, in particular, dramatizes events using narrative conventions borrowed from fictional television, the cinema, and so on, to constitute an acceptable "sporting narrative" (Goldlust, 1987, pp. 87–106). In this context a whole star system develops whereby leading protagonists are afforded distinctive sets of character traits, a *persona*, which in the limiting case—for example, Maradona or Gascoigne at Italia '90 (Blain & O'Donnell, 1994, p. 255; Tudor, 1992, pp. 397–398; Whannel, 1992, pp.147–148)—can attract quite remarkable attention right across the media system. Such sports stars may be expected to perform near miracles on the field of play, as both Gascoigne and Maradona were more than once described as doing, but it is when they are "narrativized" (Whannel, 1992, pp. 140–148; 1999, p. 258) that they become central to media representations of sport—to the telling of plausible stories crystallized out from the flux of events. As with their Hollywood progenitors, furthermore, their narrativization feeds the commercial interests involved. Transformed into potent signifiers, televised sport stars are fictional creations caught at the confluence of a whole series of increasingly globalized discourses and interests.

Audiovisual Discourses

This marshalling of the discourses of expertise and narrative is achieved primarily through words. That is to say, natural language is the medium in which televised events are routinely glossed and interpreted. Nevertheless, the World Cup is now a specifically televisual event of giant proportions. According to Hare (1999) there was a cumulative television audience of some 40 billion for the France '98 tournament, with "the Final watched by 1.7 billion viewers world-wide, the biggest shared experience in human history" (p. 124). So the visual discourses of television itself—especially in broadcast matches where all national TV networks receive the same feed—significantly form the ways in which all those billions actually *see* the games. Unfortunately, since the pioneering study of the 1974 World Cup there has been relatively little attempt to research the audiovisual coding of television coverage. In that volume Buscombe (1975b) examined the coding of the credit sequences for the two main channel's preview programs, while Barr (1975) and Ryall (1975) explored aspects of visual style in two broadcast matches. This kind of sustained analysis of visual material has not been replicated for later tournaments, although changing technology and the globalization of television technique would make examination well worthwhile. Such innovations as action replays, extension of the range of camera setups, multiple angles, and the arrival of digital technology have strikingly enhanced the possibilities for stylistic elaboration in television coverage. For the most part, however, these developments have been noted in passing rather than afforded systematic attention (Geraghty, Simpson, & Whannel, 1986; McKeever, 1999). The distinctive audiovisual discourses of World Cup television remain sadly neglected.

In marked contrast to that neglect, however, the complex interaction between ethnic stereotyping, ethnocentricity, ideology, and the multiple discourses of national identity has attracted the most consistent attention from researchers. It is to the history and analytic presuppositions of this, the single most prominent topic in the World Cup media literature, that I now turn.

STEREOTYPING AND NATIONAL IDENTITY

To begin with, this research was largely focused on documenting the range of stereotypes utilized by journalists, experts and others in the course of reporting and commentating upon events. The essays in the original *Football on Television* collection by McArthur (1975/1981), on the scene-setting coverage in the listing magazines, and by Tudor (1975/1981), and on TV panel discussions and commentary, examined the ways in which players, teams, and, by implication, whole societies were rendered intelligible in stereotypical terms. In the main this was a descriptive enterprise, reporting on the specific content of stereotypes and their occasions of use, but not especially seeking to locate them in a larger social, political, or, indeed, theoretical context.

The stereotyping processes themselves exhibited both an individual and a collective dimension. Particular players were constructed (and, in changing circumstances, reconstructed) by reporters as bearing certain attributes, while teams were accorded distinctive stylistic traits presumed to derive from their histories and their national character. As McArthur (1975/1981) observed, "Where 'hard' information was lacking on any team the coverage fell back on more general racist, national and ideological stereotypes" (p. 11). The primary division in 1974 was to be found in the repeated contrast made between teams who were said to exhibit "Latin temperament"—those of Latin America and Southern Europe— and those of Northern Europe, a categorical system which, as O'Donnell (1994) has subsequently shown, had long been established in European sports reporting. These apparently cultural distinctions, Tudor (1975/1981) suggested, were in fact often "ethnic masquerading as cultural. Though explicit terminology is not commonly racial in its reference, its underlying assumptions may well be: many distinctions prevalent in sports coverage would reduce quite easily to interpretations based upon race" (p. 60). This feature was to become more prominent in subsequent World Cups when the arrival of substantial numbers of teams from new footballing nations in Africa and Asia would set reporters, commentators, and experts acute problems in deploying what were more overtly racist stereotypes.

I return to that topic later. For the present, however, it is sufficient to note that, while in this first research into the World Cup coverage's reservoir of national stereotypes there was much evidence of their frequent use—stereotyping was *the* constitutive feature of the broadcasters' discursive repertoire—there was as yet no real attempt by researchers to analyze the observed patterns within a broader framework. However, given the intellectual concerns of British cultural and media studies at that time—Carey (1989) would later characterize the field as "ideological studies" (p. 97)—the obvious move, already implied in aspects of the 1974 research, was to locate stereotyping in its political and ideological context. Thus, when Nowell-Smith (1979/1981) examined national stereotyping in the 1978 World Cup coverage, he drew the oppositions of its "signifying map" somewhat more elaborately (Nordic/Latin, European/South American, Spanish South America/Brazil, and so on) as well as attending much more closely to the political dimension of national characterizations. This was particularly apposite in 1978, of course, when the tournament took place in an Argentina whose military dictators were much concerned to utilize sport in the cause of nationalism. In this context, therefore, the football was overtly politicized (Alabarces, 1999; Alabarces, et al., 2001; Archetti, 1994; Duke & Crolley, 1996) in an attempt to manipulate both domestic populace and international opinion. But, as Nowell-Smith (1979/1981) made clear, ideological representation of nations is never simple: "A national concept is always both overdetermined in its production and polyvalent in its availability and its effects" (p. 169). It is this polyvalence of the links between ideology and sports media coverage which was then to come increasingly to the fore, and with it a growing concern with themes of national identity.

That is hardly surprising. In a competition, which was fundamentally structured in terms of nation-states, and in relation to a sport that had long been associated with local and regional identities in its domestic organization, the ideologies of nation and nationalism come naturally. Except, of course, there is nothing natural about it. The articulation of national interests in sport is only possible "because of a major ideological construction of the activities of particular athletes and teams as the representatives or bearers of national prestige" (Clarke & Clarke, 1982, p. 65). To examine the various modes of application of national stereotyping, then, is to see in action the sometimes ambiguous, often flexible, but always ideological discourses of reporting, discourses which are not unidimensional and which interrelate in a variety of ways. It is this growing recognition that World Cup coverage was more varied in its deployment of stereotyping than the somewhat reductive terms of the 1974 research suggested which was foregrounded in Wren-Lewis and Clarke's (1983) reflections on the 1982 tournament.

The 1982 World Cup, held in Spain, posed special problems for British television and press. As the tournament opened, Britain was conducting a military campaign in the South Atlantic against Argentina, whose national team were the current World Cup holders, and during the tournament's first week came the news that the British forces had been victorious. Unsurprisingly, then, overt nationalist discourses were prominent in the initial coverage of the England team, with very little attention paid to Argentina. However, as the tournament developed (and as the England team faltered and was eliminated) this overt nationalism also went into retreat. Wren-Lewis and Clarke argue that this was a case of what they call the "dominant football discourse" (p. 128) constituting the primary framework within which other forms of discourse are then variably employed. When the England team failed in footballing terms, "the conflation of sport and politics inspired by 'the Falklands factor' proved short lived—*because it depended upon a footballing narrative that was no longer capable of sustaining it*" (Wren-Lewis & Clarke, 1983, p. 128). Most generally, then, their argument is that discourses specific to the world of football (shared by players, ex-players, coaches, commentators, journalists, etc.) have considerable autonomy and cannot adequately be rendered in terms of reductive stereotypes. Although this language—"a well developed form of the lexicon of competition familiar to all sports commentators" (Wren-Lewis & Clarke, p. 131)—is indeed open to influence from other discourses, this is not simply a one-way imposition of non-footballing, crudely nationalistic conceptions.

It can be argued that Wren-Lewis and Clarke overstate the autonomy of the footballing language. Certainly later studies suggest as much, especially as the distinctively jingoistic tone of the British tabloid press becomes increasingly influential in football coverage, whether in print or on television. Theoretically, however, their point is well made that World Cup coverage involves complex and contingent interactions among a variety of discourses, and this is an assumption which informs most subsequent research in one form or another. As well as this awareness of discursive complexity, however, there is also a second thread of argument which comes to the fore in the 1980s. The publication of Benedict Anderson's influential *Imagined Communities* in 1982 had helped to crystallize concern more generally in media and cultural studies with the role of communications in the formation of national identity. If our national *imagined communities* were indeed constructed and reconstructed out of materials supplied through modes of mass communication, then popular media coverage of international sport was a prime candidate to be examined from this perspective.

Accordingly, World Cup media research in the later 1980s and 1990s became both more sophisticated in its understanding of stereotyping processes and much concerned with their often complex relation to national identity conceptions. It was increasingly recognized that, as Tomlinson & Whannel (1986) put it in their volume on the 1986 competition, "any understanding of the significance of the World Cup and of the forms of nationalism expressed in and through it must recognize the complexities and tensions within the development of different national identities" (p. 2). Nor was national identity simply to be conflated with nationalism, even though there are occasions when the two are merged in World Cup coverage— notably when the discourse of national identity, with its fundamental distinction between "us" and "them," is infused with partisan national ardor. In this context Blain & O'Donnell (1994) in search of greater conceptual clarity, adduced a whole series of nation-related modes of expression that feature in the media discourses routinely applied to international sport. Their comparative framework (encompassing both international media and different sports; see also Blain, et al., 1993) allowed them to explore communalities and differences in, for example, the stereotypes deployed to conceptualize the English and the Germans in relation to football at Italia '90 and tennis at Wimbledon '91. Thus, they suggested, "Germanness" is similarly characterized across the sports presses of Italy, England, Spain, and Russia: "a militaristic, aggressive, highly disciplined nation which either blasted or steamrollered its opponents out of existence" (Blain & O'Donnell, 1994, pp. 260–261). Treatment of the English, however, proved more varied, in spite of the fact that for Italia '90 it was the expected violent behavior of English fans that dominated pretournament coverage. Where Italia '90 coverage did prove particularly distinctive, however, was in the necessity to find a language and framing structure within which to conceptualize teams from Africa (and their national styles and characters) who were largely unfamiliar to sports journalists and commentators. Tudor (1992) argued that forms of inferential racism were constantly apparent in this coverage, relying on variably deployed stereotypes of naivety, innocence, excitability, and primitivism combined in an essentially patronizing discourse. In the event, the progress of the Cameroon team to the quarterfinals of the competition (when they lost to England) necessitated some revision of these stereotypes in British coverage, and this was perhaps the last World Cup in which such a blatantly racist discourse was to be found. Nevertheless, racism remains an important issue in both national and international sports coverage (Garland & Rowe, 2001; Tudor, 1998).

For the 1994 World Cup, however, researchers found topics other than ethnocentricity and national identity rather more pressing. For the first time the tournament was scheduled to take place in the United States, where soccer (in U.S. coverage afforded this, its "proper" name, to distinguish it from American football) had very little following compared to baseball, basketball, American football, and ice hockey. Concern about the likely adverse impact of this "American exceptionalism" (Markovits & Hellerman, 2001) on the success of the tournament exercised media across the world prior to the event itself, though, as it turned out, with no great foundation in fact. And although 1994 provided the occasion for further reflections on issues of national identity and World Cup football in 11 different national contexts (Sugden & Tomlinson, 1994), that work was produced prior to the event itself and did not relate specifically to media coverage. It is notable therefore that, although Markovits and Hellerman (2001) provided an extensive and informative account of U.S. media coverage in both 1994 and 1998, questions of national identity hardly feature. In some part that is no doubt an empirical consequence of American exceptionalism—major sporting interest in the U.S. media is primarily domestic, not as consistently oriented to *international* competition as their European or Latin American counterparts—and it also reflects the authors' primary concern with the precarious status of football in what they call the American "sports space." Thus, even the much anticipated confrontation of the U.S. and Iranian teams at France '98 did not lead to quite the kinds of nationalistic coverage in the American media that could have been expected elsewhere, for, as Markovitz and Hellerman (2001) themselves observed, "even a game against a nation led by a regime as hated as Iran's theocracy failed to put soccer on the radar screen of most American sports fans, let alone the public at large" (p. 251). So, while the American press clearly did frame the match in political terms, in the end this had more to do with "notions of American liberalism and openness to the nation, government, and people of Iran" (Delgado, 2003, p. 302) than with the kind of assertive nationalism and national stereotyping customarily found elsewhere in World Cup coverage.

Although American exceptionalism molded much of the 1994 research, by the 1998 and 2002 tournaments media researchers outside the United States were returning to the familiar questions of national identity and national styles. Consider, for example, the analysis of media treatment of England versus Argentina in the 1998 tournament by Alabarces et al. (2001). Their main concern was with the Argentina–England game as an occasion for "expression of national identity" (p. 549), to which end they offer a historical account of the established myths of footballing style of the two countries, both in general and as they have been played out in previous football encounters between the teams. In this context Alabarces et al. explored media treatment of the game itself and its aftermath in both countries, arguing that in the wake of defeat there was an "attempted rearticulation of Englishness" (p. 559) in the British press, revolving around a villain/hero contrast established between two players (Beckham and Owen) in which the latter was represented as incarnating the proper values of the English style. Meanwhile the Argentinean media continued to sustain the central mythology of the Argentinean style in a discourse where "the dominant tone was a combination of overflowing chauvinism and exalted emotion, framed by the national flag as dominant symbol" (Alabarces, p. 559). Embedded in these typifications, of course, are the familiar and longstanding Latin and Northern European stereotypes—unpredictable and temperamental creativity versus commitment and hard work—which, as Alabarces et al. (2001, p. 563) echoing O'Donnell (1994) observed, manifest "an astonishing uniformity . . . within and across national boundaries."

Where Alabarces et al. traversed familiar terrain, albeit with more contextual and comparative detail than many earlier such studies, Marks (1999) and Dauncey and Hare (2000) took a somewhat different tack, examining the generalized metaphorical role of international football and its media coverage in relation to 1990s France.

It seems that international football in the 1990s in France has increasingly taken on an analogous role to sport in Victorian Britain. That is to say, quite simply, sport becomes a metaphor for life. This contrasts to the situation in the British press, where sport is infused with metaphors from other areas of life. (Marks, 1999, p. 54)

The key issue, as Marks suggested and on which Dauncey and Hare expanded, is the problem of (ethnic) integration in modern France. Borrowing a distinction between types of identity construction from Castells (1997), Dauncey and Hare argued that in the course of the 1998 World Cup (won by France) the outstanding French player Zinedine Zidane (the son of North African immigrants) came to represent a "resistance identity" relating to the integration issued, which was balanced by a "legitimizing identity" in the form of the French coach, Aimé Jacquet, whose success was seen to represent traditional values. The French victory, then, was constructed by the media as simultaneously reflecting both a modernizing impulse towards French racial integration *and* a reassertion of traditional French values. Thus was an apparent contradiction of national identity overcome, if temporarily, through the discourses surrounding France's World Cup victory. Had they not been victorious, of course, then no sense of common purpose might have emerged in the contingent intersection of the two forms of identity construction, and as Dauncey and Hare (2000) noted, "whether this common purpose can survive the contradictory social and cultural directions inherent in the two metaphorical versions of France 98 is another matter" (p. 345).

What this analysis underlines, of course, is the complex relations of contradiction and complementarity of group identity which may be, and often are, articulated within media World Cup discourses. That is not to suggest that the direct stereotyping apparent in the initial 1974 research has disappeared with growing media sophistication and/or changing attitudes to ethnicity. Garland (2004), for example, recently noted the "xenophobic and sometimes racist nature of the coverage of the Nigerian, Argentinean and French teams during the [2002] World Cup" (p. 89) in the British tabloid press. What *has* changed, however, are the concepts with which researchers address representations of identity in World Cup coverage. Although simple stereotyping is still common enough in coverage, and likely to remain so, research into successive World Cups over the past 30 years has led to an increasing sensitivity to the multiform operation of media discourses in constituting, reforming, and rearticulating the terms within which (national) identity is formulated.

CONCLUSION

What, then, is to be said of the World Cup world as it is constituted by the media? That it is deeply imbued with variable conceptions of group and national identity, certainly, and that those conceptions—some of them overtly racist and xenophobic—exercise a powerful influence upon the discourses of television and the press. It is understandable, therefore, that so much of the research since 1974 has continued to focus on this particular aspect of coverage. However, a price has been paid for that. In the 30 years since its publication, one might have expected rather more development of some of the other topics initially explored in *Football on Television*. Particularly striking is the minimal research effort that has been devoted to detailed analysis of the audiovisual discourses of TV coverage. Though of less immediately dramatic social and political significance than ethnic stereotyping and "them and us" identity formulations, the codes of camera work, editing, framing, and so on are a constitutive element in the ways in which viewers experience the World Cup. There is surely an urgent need to further examine this aspect of coverage—all the more so given the remarkable technological innovations which have been impacting the global television system in recent years. After all, it is only in the interaction between the audiovisual, linguistic, and narrative discourses that we can come more fully understand the systematic media construction of the World Cup world.

Perhaps even more significant than this bypassing of the audiovisual dimension is the absence of any systematic attempt to incorporate the spectator into analysis. The founding moment of World Cup media research in the 1970s ensured that it was marked by a commitment to analyzing the dynamics of the cultural text itself as a route to understanding the deeper ideological regularities it revealed. Spectators, it was presumed, were positioned by the discourses deployed, and that process could be adequately conceptualized without reference to any agency that they might exercise. Since then it has been recognized that this "top-down" model is deficient in various respects, and "active readership," variously understood, has become an essential reference point in cultural and media research (Tudor, 1999, p. 165–194). This changing emphasis has yet to find its way into World Cup media research, where the cultural text itself still has priority. While it would be foolish to recommend attending to the reader/viewer at the expense of attending to the text—as we have seen, some excellent work has been done by analyzing the discursive formations apparent in TV and press coverage—it would be equally foolish to continue to ignore the human agency of spectators. After all, discourses do not do their job of organizing, selecting, filtering, and constructing our understanding of the media-constituted World Cup world by themselves. They are made to do so by social agents. Understanding that process has to be a priority if World Cup media research is to progress yet further beyond the terms laid down thirty years ago.

REFERENCES

Alabarces, P. (1999). Post-modern times: Identities and violence in Argentine football. In G. Armstrong & R. Giulianotti (Eds.), *Football cultures and identities* (pp. 77–85). London: Macmillan.

Alabarces, P., Tomlinson, A., & Young, C. (2001). Argentina versus England at the France '98 World Cup: Narratives of nation and the mythologizing of the popular. *Media, Culture and Society, 23*(5), 547–566.

Anderson, B. (1991). *Imagined communities: Reflections on the origin and spread of nationalism.* London: Verso.

Archetti, E. (1994). Argentina and the World Cup: In search of national identity. In J. Sugden & A. Tomlinson (Eds.), *Hosts and champions: Soccer cultures, national identities and the USA World Cup* (pp. 37–63). Aldershot: Arena.

Barr, C. (1975). Comparing styles: England v West Germany. In E. Buscombe (Ed.), *Football on television* (pp. 47–53). London: British Film Institute.

Billings, A. C., & Tambosi, F. (2004). Portraying the United States vs portraying a champion. *International Review for the Sociology of Sport, 39*(2), 157–165.

Blain, N., & O'Donnell, H. (1994). The stars and the flags: Individuality, collective identities and the national dimension in Italia '90 and Wimbledon '91 and '92. In R. Giulianotti & J. Williams (Eds.), *Game without frontiers: Football, identity and modernity* (pp. 245–269). Aldershot: Ashgate Publishing.

Blain, N., Boyle, R., & O'Donnell, H. (1993). *Sport and national identity in the European media.* Leicester: Leicester University Press.

Bryant, J., Brown, D., Comisky, P., & Zillmann, D. (1982). Sports and spectators: Commentary and appreciation. *Journal of Communication, 32*(4), 109–119.

Bryant, J., Comisky, P., & Zillmann, D. (1977). Drama in sports commentary. *Journal of Communication. 27*(3), 140–149.

Buscombe, E. (Ed.). (1975a). *Football on television.* London: British Film Institute.

Buscombe, E. (1975b). Cultural and televisual codes in two title sequences. In E. Buscombe (Ed.), *Football on television* (pp. 16–34). London: British Film Institute.

Carey, J. W. (1989). *Communication as culture: Essays on media and society.* Boston: Unwin Human.

Castells, M. (1997). *The power of identity.* Oxford: Blackwell.

Clarke, A., & Clarke, J. (1982). "Highlights and action replays" - ideology, sport and the media. In J. Hargreaves (Ed.), *Sport, culture and ideology* (pp. 62–87). London: Routledge and Kegan Paul.

Comisky, P., Bryant, J., & Zillmann, D. (1977). Commentary as a substitute for action. *Journal of Communication, 27*(3), 150–153.

Dauncey, H., & Hare, G. (2000). World Cup France '98: Metaphors, meanings and values. *International Review for the Sociology of Sport, 35*(3), 331–347.

Delgado, F. (2003). The fusing of sport and politics: Media constructions of U.S. versus Iran at France '98. *Journal of Sport and Social Issues, 27*(3), 293–307.

Duke, V., & Crolley, L. (1996). *Football, nationality and the state.* London: Addison Wesley Longman.

Garland, J. (2004). The same old story? Englishness, the tabloid press and the 2002 football World Cup. *Leisure Studies, 23*(1), 79–92.

Garland, J., & Rowe, M. (1999). War minus the shooting: Jingoism, the English press and Euro '96. *Journal of Sport and Social Issues, 23*(1), 80–95.

Garland, J., & Rowe, M. (2001). *Racism and anti-racism in football.* Basingstoke: Palgrave.

Geraghty, C., Simpson, P., & Whannel, G. (1986). Tunnel vision: Television's World Cup. In A. Tomlinson & G. Whannel (Eds.), *Off the ball: The football World Cup* (pp. 20–35). London: Pluto Press.

Goldlust, J. (1987). *Playing for keeps: Sport, the media and society.* Melbourne: Longman Cheshire.

Hare, G. (1999). Buying and selling the World Cup. In H. Dauncey & G. Hare (Eds.), *France and the 1998 World Cup: The national impact of a world sporting event* (pp. 121–144). London: Frank Cass.

Horne, J. D., & Manzenreiter, W. (2004). Accounting for mega-events. *International Review for the Sociology of Sport, 39*(2), 187–203.

Maguire, J., Poulton, E., & Possamai, C. (1999). Weltkrieg III? Media coverage of England versus Germany in Euro 96. *Journal of Sport and Social Issues, 23*(4), 439–454.

Markovits, A. S., & Hellerman, S. L. (2001). *Offside: Soccer and American exceptionalism.* Princeton & Oxford: Princeton University Press.

Marks, J. (1999). The French national team and national identity: "Cette France d'un 'bleu métis." In H. Dauncey & G. Hare (Eds.), *France and the 1998 World Cup: The national impact of a world sporting event* (pp. 41–57). London: Frank Cass.

McArthur, C. (1981). Setting the scene: *Radio times* and *TV times*. In T. Bennett, S. Boyd-Bowman, C. Mercer, & J. Woollacott (Eds.), *Popular television and film* (pp. 144–149). London: British Film Institute/ Open University Press. (Reprinted in abridged form from *Football on television*, pp. 8–15, by E. Buscombe, Ed., 1975, London: British Film Institute.)

McKeever, L. (1999). Reporting the World Cup: Old and new media. In H. Dauncey & G. Hare (Eds.), *France and the 1998 World Cup: The national impact of a world sporting event* (pp. 161–183). London: Frank Cass.

Nowell-Smith, G. (1981). Television—football—the world. In T. Bennett, S. Boyd-Bowman, C. Mercer, & J. Woollacott (Eds.), *Popular television and film* (pp. 159–170). London: British Film Institute/Open University Press. (Reprinted in abridged form from *Screen*, 1979, *19*(4), 45–59.)

O'Donnell, H. (1994). Mapping the mythical: A geopolitics of national sporting stereotypes. *Discourse and Society, 5,* 345–380.

Ryall, T. (1975). Visual style in "Scotland v Yugoslavia." In E. Buscombe (Ed.), *Football on television* (pp. 35–46). London: British Film Institute.

Sugden, J., & Tomlinson, A. (Eds.). (1994). *Hosts and champions: Soccer cultures, national identities and the USA World Cup.* Aldershot: Arena.

Tomlinson, A., & Whannel, G. (Eds.). (1986). *Off the ball: The football World Cup.* London: Pluto Press.

Tudor, A. (1981). The panels. In T. Bennett, S. Boyd-Bowman, C. Mercer, & J. Woollcott (Eds.), *Popular television and film* (pp. 150–158). London: British Film Institute/Open University Press. (Reprinted in abridged form from *Football on television.* (pp. 54–65, by E. Buscombe, Ed., 1975, London: British Film Institute.)

Tudor, A. (1992). Them and us: Story and stereotype in TV World Cup coverage. *European Journal of Communication, 7,* 391–413.

Tudor, A. (1998). Sports reporting: Race, difference and identity. In K. Brants, J. Hermes, & L. V. Zoonen (Eds.), *The media in question: Popular cultures and public interests* (pp. 147–156). London, Thousand Oaks, New Delhi: Sage.

Tudor, A. (1999). *Decoding culture: Theory and method in cultural studies*. London Sage.

Whannel, G. (1992). *Fields in vision: Television sport and cultural transformation*. London: Routledge.

Whannel, G. (1999). Sports stars, narrativization and masculinities. *Leisure Studies, 18*(3), 249–265.

Wren-Lewis, J., & Clarke, A. (1983). The World Cup—A political football. *Theory, Culture and Society, 1*(3), 123–132.

14

Gender Warriors in Sport: Women and the Media

Margaret Carlisle Duncan

University of Wisconsin–Milwaukee

"Femininity always demands more. It must constantly reassure its audience by a willing demonstration of difference, even when one does not exist in nature..." (Brownmiller, 1984, p. 15)

To talk about women in sport is to describe a paradox, for sport is a province that is deemed most properly male. What it takes to be successful in sport, at least according to conventional wisdom, is the very ideal of a man: superiority, mental and physical toughness, competitiveness, initiative, strength, power, aggression, and confidence. As children, we learn that men and women are not only different; they are actually opposites. Whatever men are, we know that women must be the very antithesis. How does one describe a woman? Inferiority, weakness, incompetence, cooperation, passivity, timidity, and vulnerability. Sport is, according to our commonsense understanding of the world, a celebration of manhood. How, then, can a woman be a successful athlete?

Because of our society's oppositional view of gender, when a woman succeeds in sport, she can be seen as a challenge to the established gender order and an unwelcome intruder into the world of sports. The media, like sport and all our social institutions, are bearers of masculine hegemony, an ideology or set of beliefs about the world that privileges men and disadvantages women. For this reason, media accounts of women's sports are often ambivalent or derogatory. As readers will see, hegemonic masculinity is particularly problematic when it comes to fairly representing the skills of sportswomen.

Nonetheless, it seems impossible to ignore the accomplishments of women athletes in the last decade. The advent of professional women's basketball; the proliferation of Web sites and magazines dedicated to women's sports and fitness; the stunning victories of American sportswomen at the 1994 Winter Olympics; the so-called

"Olympics of the Women" (the 1996 Atlanta Summer Games); the growing popularity of women's tennis; the emergence of successful women's team sports, such as the 1999 Women's World Cup Soccer Championship that generated unprecedented fan support—shouldn't we be optimistic? All of these events seem to suggest that women's sport occupies an increasingly significant place in our sociocultural world. Logically, then, one might assume that women's sports would receive a correspondingly significant increase in the quantity and quality of sports coverage. Much of the research on mediated portrayals of female athletes in the last decade has been motivated by the possibility that improvements in reporting women's sports may have occurred. Whether this is, in fact, the case is the subject of this chapter.

In recent years, studies on sports media portrayals have grown exponentially, making it a daunting task to track and organize this literature. My strategy, therefore, is to use as a touchstone the research findings with which I am most familiar, the 2000 Amateur Athletic Foundation of Los Angeles Report (hereafter referred to as the AAF Report). This report, *Gender in Televised Sports: 1989, 1993, and 1999*, is based on the research of coinvestigators, Michael Messner and I, with the help of our research assistants, Cheryl Cooky and Kerry Jensen. Although this series of studies focuses on televised sports, many of its major themes mirror those found in other forms of media such as newspapers and magazines. To supplement this discussion, I explore media studies that focus on images of women in a broader range of media, including magazines, newspapers, books, and in-house literatures.

An important consideration is to include the most recent research findings on mediated portrayals of female athletes. The AAF Report was published in 2000, based on 1999 data. In the intervening five years, numerous media studies have contributed valuable insights to our body of literature. I rely on these recent scholarly articles, as well as some classic articles in the field, to enrich the thinking on media representations and to provide the most comprehensive review.

Although the AAF Report noted some ways in which race inflects gender, many other media studies do not explicitly consider how the social factors of race, class, sexuality, nationality, and ability/disability might intersect with gender to produce qualitatively different representations of women athletes. Certainly, trying to understand the total social context is a much more complex project than analyzing one social factor in isolation. Many researchers are unaccustomed to thinking about the multiple identities that simultaneously shape a woman's experience. My chapter reflects the scholarship in the field only in proportion to its depth and complexity of study. The dearth of more sophisticated scholarship that frames images of women in the context of social relationships such as race, class, and sexuality will be explored at the end of the chapter, and articles that present a more nuanced model for future studies will be discussed and recommended.

My project is to focus on women, rather than gender per se; however, it is next to impossible to analyze portrayals of women's sports/female athletes without making some reference to men's sports/male athletes. This is true because gender ideology is based on the oppositional binary described earlier. What is feminine must necessarily take its meaning from what is masculine.

THE AMATEUR ATHLETIC FOUNDATION STUDIES

The AAF study published in 2000 incorporates the data of three specific time periods: 1989, 1993, and 1999. In each case both quantitative data (amount of coverage) and qualitative data (nature of coverage) relating to women's and men's sports were examined. The 2000 study was intentionally designed to replicate and, to some extent, elaborate on the previous studies. We chose particular sporting events with an eye to a comparative analysis; in other words, we wanted to focus on events that were gender parallel, that is, those with both women's and men's competitions. Therefore, we selected the NCAA Basketball Final Four, the U.S. Open Tennis Tournament, the WNBA and NBA (included for the first time in 1999), ESPN *SportsCenter* (also included for the first time in 1999), and nightly televised sports news.

This chapter starts with a discussion of the production of mediated sport, comprising three sections: the quantity of coverage of women's sports, the technical quality of that coverage, and the strategies used to build audiences for women's sports. The second part of the chapter focuses on the discourse of mediated women's sports; this is the category into which most of the qualitative studies on women's sports and female athletes fall. The third section provides a summary and conclusion and ends with recommendations for future research on media portrayals of women's sports.

PRODUCTION OF MEDIATED SPORT

Quantity of Women's Sports Coverage

The AAF Report showed very little change in the quantity of television coverage given to women's sports. As in 1989 and 1993, the proportion of airtime given to women during televised sports news, though marginally larger than in previous years, amounted to what Tuchman has termed "symbolic annihilation" (Tuchman, Daniels, & Benet, 1978). In 1989 women's sport received 5% of the local sport news coverage. In 1993, women's sport received 5.10% of the coverage. In 1999, women's sport received 8.70% of the coverage. Compared to men's sport, which garnered 92% of the coverage in 1989, 93.8% of the coverage in 1993, and 88.20% of the coverage in 1999, the quantity of reporting on women's sports and female athletes has not increased significantly.

The presentation of sport news is necessarily limited because a nightly broadcast must include other kinds of news. What about a show completely devoted to sport coverage? One might reasonably surmise that such a show would provide significantly more coverage of women's sports and female athletes. In fact, the 1999 AAF study revealed that the very opposite was true. ESPN's *SportsCenter* devoted a dismal 2.2% of the broadcast to women's sports, while lavishing 96.7% of the airtime upon men's sports, the remaining 1.1% being both or neutral. Regardless of what measure was used—number of minutes, number of news stories, number of lead stories—women's sports went seriously underreported.

As the reader will see, this underreporting of women's sports was a consistent theme in other sports media studies, irrespective of medium. However, for the sake of analytical convenience, I organize the following research findings by the medium analyzed.

Television Studies

Perhaps because the 1996 Olympics were marketed as "The Olympics of the Woman," several different TV studies focused on NBC's coverage of the Summer Games. Three of these studies (Andrews, 1998; Eastman & Billings, 1999; Tuggle & Owen, 1999) concluded that the quantity of coverage—which on the surface appeared to represent gains in women's events—was nevertheless compromised by the network's disproportionate reporting of women's individual events compared to women's team events/strength events: "Men's team competitions received substantially more coverage than did women's team events, and women in sports that involved power or hard physical contact between athletes received almost no attention" (Tuggle & Owen, 1999, p. 171). Eastman and Billings (1999) and Andrews (1998) argued that although the network conspicuously hyped the women's events (primarily motivated by marketing strategy), no real improvements in coverage occurred. The fourth study (Higgs, Weiller, & Martin, 2003) arrived at a different conclusion, most likely because the researchers examined a random sample of on-air segments (60 out of 150 hours) rather than the total broadcast time: "Women's sport coverage increased in 6 out of the 11 sports analyzed; men's sport coverage declined in 4 out of 11 sports analyzed" (p. 54).

Cable television stations revealed more extreme quantitative disparities in the presentation of women's sports. In a cross-media comparison study of 177.5 hours, Eastman and Billings (2000) found that ESPN's *SportsCenter* devoted a meager 4% of its coverage to women's sports, while CNN's *Sports Tonight* devoted only 6% of its coverage to women's sports, both findings holding true despite the day or week (i.e., including those days on which important women's sports tournaments or championships were held). Another investigation of ESPN showed a similar skew in a television special dedicated to the top athletes of the twentieth century. Of the 50 half-hour segments given to the top-50 athletes, only 4 segments (8%) profiled female athletes (Billings, 2000).

Likewise, research on Swedish televised sport broadcasts revealed the comparatively small amount of coverage given to women's sports in 1995 to 1996 and again in 1998 (Koivula, 1999). During both periods the percentage of time given to women's sports was significantly less than that given to men's sports. According to the 1995 and 1996 data, 86.7% of the coverage featured men's sports, 11.7% featured women's sports, and 1.7% involved both or neutral. The 1998 data revealed a similar imbalance.

Sport Magazines

Several quantitative studies analyzed *Sports Illustrated* (*SI*) and *Sports Illustrated for Kids* (*SIK*). In a classic study, Davis (1997) exposed the *SI* swimsuit issue as a bastion of masculine hegemony. Davis (1997) argued that "the cultural significance of the swimsuit issue derives from the fact that it contributes to a larger project that celebrates a politically reactionary form of contemporary masculinity" (p. 8). It is therefore not surprising that the regular issues of *SI* are underpinned by the same hegemonic logic, which gives the men's sports the lion's share of coverage, while largely neglecting or giving token attention to women's sports. Bishop (2003) analyzed *SI* for the total number of articles per issue, gender of the athlete featured, number of pages per article, and number of photographs accompanying each article. He found "no significant increase since 1979 in feature coverage of women's sports" (p. 192) and a marked decrease in the percentage of photos portraying women.

Three studies analyzed *SIK*, two for the photographs and one for the advertisements. The underlying premise in all of the *SIK* research was that visual images are particularly persuasive to younger children who may not have developed strong written literacy skills and rely on the pictures to a greater extent than older children and adults. Younger children are also less likely to be media literate, that is, to understand that certain forms of media are politically or commercially motivated. Duncan and Sayaovong (1990) and a later replication of that study conducted by Hardin, Walsdorf, Walsdorf, and Hardin (2002) found that photos of female athletes were consistently outnumbered by those of male athletes, especially in cover photographs and those photos featuring athletes in action (rather than posed or passive shots). The later study concluded that the results were "especially significant when current interscholastic participation rates are considered. Girls comprise about 37% of all high school athletes" (p. 353).

Cuneen and Sidwell (1998) studied advertisements in *SIK*, reasoning that commercial images communicate gender ideals to children by showing males and females in their so-called socially "appropriate" roles. Using the same protocol as Duncan and Sayaovong's (1990) research, they found that images of women and girls were vastly outnumbered by those of men and boys (by a one to twelve ratio). Compounding this discrepancy was the fact that the ads showed women as athletes only one-sixth of the time that they depicted men as athletes (in active player positions).

In a combined study, Fink and Kensicki (2002) examined both *SI* and *Sports Illustrated for Women* (*SIW*) for coverage of women in sports, using the same set of standards for each magazine. The now defunct *SIW* described its mission as "[giving] voice and vision to the stories of women in sports" (Fink & Kensicki, p. 322). Yet in a content analysis spanning 1997 to 1999, the researchers found that, despite the victories of women in the 1996 Olympics and the ensuing optimism about women finally having proven their mettle, women and girl athletes "continued to be underrepresented, portrayed in traditionally feminine sports, or shown in nonsport-related scenery in both media outlets" (p. 317). It seems likely that the underrepresentation of sportswomen in the magazine accounted at least in part for the demise of *SIW*.

Newspapers and Miscellanea

Regardless of the type of newspaper, the quantitative findings confirmed and extended the results of both television and magazine analyses. Eastman and Billings' (2000) cross-media study examined *The New York Times* (*NYT*) and *USA Today* (*UT*) and concluded that both publications seriously underreported women's sports in proportions that reflect the findings of television studies. For example, "the NYT included a total of 641 photographs on its sports pages, of which men got 86%, women 11%, and non-gendered other 3%. The newspaper carried a total of 951 articles on its sports pages, of which men got 85%, women 11%, and other 4%" (p. 199). *UT*, even though it has explicitly targeted women as readers, offered only negligibly better coverage of women's sports.

Research on European and Canadian newspapers yielded comparable findings. Analyzing two popular British tabloids, Harris and Clayton (2002) described even more lopsided coverage over a period of 22 days during the Wimbledon 2000 Tennis Championship, wherein women received 5.9% of the newspaper coverage and men received 85.8% of the coverage. One of the article's major findings was "the invisibility of women athletes" (p. 399). Similarly, a longitudinal analysis of *The Globe and Mail*, a popular Canadian newspaper, on portrayals of athletes in the Winter Olympic Games from 1924 to 1992 found that sportswomen were consistently underrepresented (Urquhart & Crossmann, 1999); predictably, articles featuring sportswomen appeared at one fourth of the rate of articles featuring sportsmen.

Pirinen (1997a) analyzed portrayals of women and sport in a Finnish daily newspaper (*Helsingin Sanomat*) with the largest circulation in the country. She restricted her study to representations of female athletes in a variety of so-called "masculine" sports in which women were relative newcomers: boxing, ski jumping, hammer throwing, triple jump, and pole vault. In fact, she discovered that there were relatively few articles about women's participation in these sports, and those she found tended to be brief accounts of records established by the winners.

Perhaps most telling are studies of in-house newspapers and media guides. In the case of the former, the argument that media are constrained by advertisers (or market decisions) is irrelevant, as is the argument that people aren't interested in women's sports, and the media are simply giving people what they want (read: men's sports). For example, Shifflett and Revelle (1994) studied eight issues of NCAA news, a medium that is mainly produced as a service to its constituents, individuals associated with both women's and men's teams. Nevertheless, female athletes were featured considerably less often than male athletes, and the fall issues devoted less than 10% of their coverage to women's sports in both photographs and articles.

Wann, Schrader, Allison, and McGeorge (1998) examined university-sponsored newspapers at three schools of different sizes; in each case the female athletes received far less coverage than the male athletes in the college newspapers, even when student enrollment data and the number of varsity sports open to women and men were taken into consideration. In addition, only a handful of sport stories (3%) were written by women, with the far greater share (97%) authored by men; this imbalance may have suggested to readers that sports reporting and sports in general were not an appropriate domain for women.

Whether television, magazine, or newspaper, media accounts of sports competitions consistently underreported female athletes and women's sports, while highlighting male athletes and men's sports. The dearth of coverage marginalized women's participation in sport, rendering men's sports authentic sports, and women's, a pale imitation.

Technical Quality of Women's Sport Media

The technical quality of a sportscast includes, but is not limited to, camera work, editing, graphics, and sound. Even the framing of the sporting event and the expertise of the commentators shape the quality of technical production. Often the opening of the game, the halftime show, and the conclusion of the game are segments that reveal the extent to which the network is invested in presenting an exciting, colorful, professional spectacle. All three AAF studies (1990, 1994, and 2000) found lower production values in the coverage of women's sports, compared to men's sports. However, the disparity has lessened somewhat over the past 15 years.

The greatest contrast in technical production was found in the 1990 report where the women's NCAA basketball production lagged far behind the men's. The lower quality production, camera work, editing, and sound were obvious when compared to the men's games; for instance, the women's broadcasts were less likely to feature slow-motion replays, interesting camera angles, frequent appearances of the shot clock, relevant statistics (visual and verbal), clever computer graphics, and sophisticated framing. Instead of presenting the women's games dramatically with the fanfare accorded to most men's games, the opening framings of the women's games were given all the flash and allure of neighborhood pickup games. Since then, the technical quality has improved incrementally. In 1999 one main difference appeared in the postgame shows, where the women's were significantly shorter and contained less sophisticated analysis and fewer replays of game highlights. A second difference occurred in the use of statistics. In 1999 women's games featured statistics less than half as often as men's.

In the 2000 AAF study the technical production of the WNBA and NBA games appearing on NBC showed few major differences. However, the one WNBA game broadcast on the Lifetime Channel seemed to lack the professional polish that typified the NBC games. The pregame and halftime shows, the poor sound quality, and the mawkish framing of that contest all contributed to lower production values.

Of recent studies only a few have considered the technical production of women's sport contests. Koivula's research on Swedish televised sports (1999) mentioned the lower technical quality (fewer camera angles, fewer game highlights, and missing statistics) of women's games compared to men's games.

Audience-Building

One of the findings of the 2000 and 1994 AAF Reports concerned the deliberate strategies used by networks to build audiences for upcoming sporting events. These strategies are ways of ensuring that viewers will tune in to future sport spectacles and are so common as to go largely unnoticed by the audience. For example, using television previews as teasers, hyping upcoming games during halftime shows, and interviewing athletes and coaches about future sports contests are all ways to capture viewers' interest and build anticipation for approaching games. The extent to which audience-building strategies are employed tells us the extent to which the network values the competition and believes it to be important. When there are few previews, few mentions of the upcoming contest, or little attention directed to its key players, potential viewers may conclude the game is not worth watching, especially if the technical production turns out to be substandard and shoddy. And when this occurs in women's sports, producers sometimes argue that they tried broadcasting women's games but, because of the lack of viewer interest, they no longer do so. In short, they say that they are simply responding to market forces. But certainly it is possible that the network's lack of investment in promoting and producing a quality show is what renders that event uninteresting to many viewers.

The 2000 AAF study found some significant differences in the use of audience-building strategies for women's and men's sports. One typical strategy was the use of previews (sometimes called *teasers*). Previews usually contain exciting footage and game highlights from a segment that is coming up. Oftentimes a well-known athlete or team is identified during the teaser. This practice piques viewers' interest and keeps them watching. It also signifies the importance of a particular event, at least in the eyes of the producers.

The AAF study analyzed footage of three television network affiliates and *Sports-Center*. We found many fewer previews for women's sports than we did for men's sports. *SportsCenter* was the worst offender, as only 2% of their previews were devoted to women's sports, compared to 98% for men's sports. The network affiliates showed slightly more women's sports previews, but the affiliate with the largest percentage (KABC at 14.8%) included many previews of gag features, where a woman was featured as a sex object (a scantily clad pro wrestler) or the butt of a joke (a nude bungee jumper). Lead stories—another measure of importance—almost never focused on female athletes (an average of 2.9% among the three networks and *SportsCenter*), and *SportsCenter* presented no lead stories *at all* about women's sports.

Very little research has explored the way audience building occurs in mediated sports events. In addition to an article based on the AAF data (Messner, Duncan, & Cooky, 2003), only one other media study seems to have addressed this issue, and that in an oblique way. Hardin et al. (2002) concluded their study on *SIK* by arguing that even when a medium can clearly reap financial benefits from audience building for women or girls' sports, producers fail to do so. In this case, the authors pointed out that editorial photos in *SIK* were overwhelmingly dominated by men and boys. The publishers might argue that they just responded to the market, since *SIK*'s readership is largely male (71% boys, 29% girls). Yet given the huge increase in girls' and young women's sports participation since the passage of Title IX, it would be profitable for the publishers to aggressively target this new market. Neglecting this niche suggests that something other than market forces influences the producers' decisions.

To sum, audience building has to do with the way producers intentionally build interest for particular sporting events or athletes. Although producers employ these strategies to promote men's sports—with much success—they are far less likely to employ them to advance women's sports, even when it would be to their advantage to do so.

THE DISCOURSE OF MEDIATED SPORT

The majority of the media studies published in the last decade focus on qualitative data: the discourse of mediated sport. This discourse was verbal (on-air commentary), written (newspaper or magazine print), visual (TV footage, photographs, on-screen graphics), or some combination thereof. The AAF studies revealed that there are many ways for discourse to frame a game or an athlete's performance. This framing is rarely, if ever, unambiguous. I do not want to imply that viewers perceive and interpret the frame exactly as the producer intended. But I do want to point out that what viewers make of sports media messages has not been thoroughly examined in our field. I revisit this issue at the end of this chapter.

Perhaps the most common feature of the discourse studied by researchers in the past ten years was the insistence on *sexual difference* (Duncan & Sayaovong, 1990; Feder-Kane, 2000). Journalists and commentators culturally construct differences between females and males and address readers/viewers as though these gender differences are natural and real. Since the masculine is the default position in our society, the feminine is seen as *the Other*. This is the logical extension of the oppositional gender binary discussed at the very beginning of this chapter. In this section, I describe ten categories of discourse about female athletes and women's sports. For the sake of analytical convenience, I present these categories as though they are separate. Keep in mind, however, that in actual sports reporting, these categories are often overlapping and do not operate in isolation of one another. In fact, journalists and commentators tend to use several discursive strategies at the same time.

The following categories comprise sexual humor, sexuality, sexual orientation, infantilization, emotions and attitudes, beauty and grace, gender-specific sports, noncompetitive roles, attributions/agency, and gender marking.

Sexual Humor

The AAF research found asymmetries in the qualitative coverage of female athletes and women's sports. In some cases these differences decreased over the decade; in other cases, they remained at the same level or actually increased. One persistent theme in the sports discourse on women—whether athletes or not—was sexual humor. Men were occasionally depicted in humorous ways, but the large quantity of men's serious sport coverage diluted the effects of the gag features. Since women received only a tiny amount of the coverage that men received, the effects of sexual objectification and sarcasm were that much more powerful. Viewers were left with the impression that women in sports were laughable and that they belonged in the bedroom, not on the playing field. For example, one segment focused on Brandi Chastain's now legendary act of yanking off her jersey at a triumphant moment (AAF, 2000). Another featured a nude female bungee jumper, who painted her body with a giant shamrock in honor of St. Patrick's Day (AAF, 2000). A third example was a gag interview with Sable, a female pro wrestler, primarily because she had appeared in a *Playboy* spread (AAF, 2000).

For the most part, gag features involving women were limited to nightly news broadcasts and some of the ESPN *SportsCenter* reporting. A few commentators could always be counted on to inflect the sports segments with sexualized portrayals of women. Others, if not consistently respectful, were more likely to deliver serious, straightforward reports on women's sports. Unfortunately, those in the former group tended to receive the better ratings, perhaps because the commentators were known for providing entertaining segments at the expense of women (AAF, 2000).

Apart from the article (Messner, et al., 2003) based on the AAF 1999 research, only a few other studies discussed the humorous put-downs of women. This might be due to the fact that most researchers chose to analyze commentary from specific competitions such as the Olympics, rather than to look at nightly news sportscasting or *SportsCenter*-format types of programs. Researchers have argued that "daily sportscasting differs in tone and approach from special coverage such as in the Olympics and other major events" (Eastman & Billings, 2000, p. 210).

Similar to the findings of the AAF study, Eastman and Billings' (2000) study of ESPN's *SportsCenter* revealed that the sportscasters "disparaged women's sports by means of more comic . . . coverage" (p. 210). Eastman and Billings also mentioned the "predominantly sarcastic tone used on ESPN" (p. 210).

In a study on Finnish newspaper coverage, Pirinen (1997a) identified the sarcasm of several journalists in describing female athletes entering sports that had previously been considered men's sports. For example, women's boxing was described as "peaceful dancing around" and "disco-dancing" (p. 244). Research on British tabloids' reporting of Euro '96 football (soccer) revealed that puns were used that simultaneously mocked and sexualized women through phrases such as "Ger yet kits out for the lads" (p. 102), a play on the familiar football chant, "Get your tits out for the lads" (p. 103), and "England expects every man to do his beauty [duty]" (p. 103).

Sexuality

The category "sexuality" covers a multitude of concepts. In common parlance, "sexuality" is broadly used to mean almost anything relating to sexual practices, sexual behaviors, sex roles, gender stereotypes, and other gender concerns. In this chapter, I use the term specifically to mean the eroticized female body, heterosexuality, and homosexuality (particularly, the implied "threat" of lesbianism) in women's sports. Virtually every study turned up evidence of the eroticization of the female body. This was expressed in numerous ways. Journalists and photographers sometimes called attention to signifiers of sexual difference and female sexuality, such as breasts and hips. In the AAF (2000) study, a typical example was the media's preoccupation with Brandi Chastain's chest or, more specifically, her black sports bra. Other segments contained footage of comely female sport spectators, often clad in revealing clothing such as tank tops or bikinis. Usually these images were accompanied by sniggering commentary.

In a study on newspaper coverage of the 1999 Women's World Cup Soccer Championship (Christopherson, Janning, & McConnell, 2002), researchers found that references to the sexuality, body, or appearance of the female athletes (or spectators) were made in almost one third of the articles; in addition, they argued that sex appeal "was frequently used to explain why the women's team was popular" (p. 179). Researchers on English tabloid coverage of tennis player Anna Kournikova found that 67% of the articles about her focused on non-tennis-related issues, primarily Kournikova's desirability as a woman; perhaps even more significant, over half of the tabloid stories on Wimbledon 2000 featured Kournikova, despite the fact that she has never won a singles title (Harris & Clayton, 2002). Similarly, Stevenson's (2002) print and television study of the 1999 Australian Tennis Open found that television coverage made much of Anna Kournikova (her body shape and sexiness) and her male fans' worshipful behavior. Harris (1999) examined tabloid representation of Euro 96 (soccer championships) in which barebreasted "Page 3 Girls" were used to promote the competition. Even in magazines directed at children (*SIK*), women and girls were frequently shown in sexually suggestive poses, such as in advertisements for designer clothes (Cuneen & Sidwell, 1998).

Numerous other studies remarked on the media's construction of *hyperfemininity*, or emphasized femininity, when reporting on women. Eroticized female bodies were a key component of this coverage (e.g., Bernstein, 2002; Jamieson, 2000; McDonald, 2002; Spencer, 2003; Stevenson, 2002; Wright & Clarke, 1999).

Sexual Orientation

Portrayals of women as hyperfeminine imply that heterosexuality is normative behavior. Writers such as Andrea Dworkin (1987) and Simone de Beauvoir (1953/1989) have characterized heterosexuality as a social institution that shores up masculine hegemony. The logic is clear; if women believe they need to please men to survive, then they are more likely to support the exercise of men's power. If women believe they need *not* please men, then they are more likely to exercise their own power, which could radically undermine the system of patriarchy. Therefore, lesbianism, as a social institution that supports women's independence from men, may be perceived as a threat to straight men (and women), and discursive strategies in sports journalism must manage this "threat," especially when sportswomen exhibit so-called masculine qualities, such as strength and athleticism.

One way to avert the threat of lesbianism is to call attention to the alleged feminine characteristics of women in sport. This was clearly demonstrated in the preceding section where journalists and commentators insisted upon the sexualization of the female body. When women steal into manly sports or appear to have mannish qualities, the threat of lesbianism is greater, so heterosexuality must be defended that much more vigorously. Long perorations about women athletes' dating habits, marriages, and pregnancies are not uncommon. Wright and Clarke (1999) studied the women's rugby union, a combative contact sport, and found that the print media constructed "a view of the women and their game which foreground[ed] their skill, their camaraderie, their human (and generally heterosexual) qualities.... What was *not* emphasized, particularly in relation to individual women, [were] the specifically masculine attributes associated with the brutality and violence of the rugby game" (p. 238). If the players could not establish their heterosexual credentials, then they were ignored completely, another form of symbolic annihilation. Even when the "lesbian question" was explicitly raised (very seldom), it was instantly dismissed, denied, or labeled irrelevant (p. 240). One journalist reported the words of a player: "Another myth is that [rugby is] a game for lesbians...that's not true. It's a game for rugby players. That's the only thing that matters" (p. 240).

McDonald (2002), analyzing the discourse surrounding WNBA athletes, and Jamieson (2000), analyzing the discourse on Nancy Lopez, pointed to similar journalistic strategies wherein threats to both Whiteness and heterosexuality were effectively neutralized. In these studies frequent mentions of the athletes' maternal, nurturing side and references to husbands and children ensured that the specter of lesbianism was put to rest. As long as the athletes of color behaved like good girls, they became honorary White women. Pirinen (1997a) and Feder-Kane (2000) described compulsory heterosexuality as a strategy that hid lesbianism, even as its threat was never far from the surface.

Interestingly, several authors described an uneasy alliance in which femininity and masculinity were allowed to coexist in women athletes, as long as the stereotypically female qualities were always in the foreground. In a study by Christopherson et al. (2002) of the 1999 Women's World Cup Soccer Championship, the researchers found that the discursive explanation for the U.S. women's team victory was based on their stereotypically masculine qualities (e.g., toughness, strength, athleticism). Their win was then proudly declared evidence of women's empowerment in United States, thus enhancing our national status as a democratic country. At the same time, newspaper discourse insisted that these soccer players exhibited traditionally feminine and heterosexual qualities as well, thereby casting them as positive role models for young girls. Here the discourse did the ideological work of both compulsory heterosexuality and ethnocentrism. Stevenson (2002) and Spencer (2003) described similar discursive strategies in which feminine and masculine were juxtaposed, resulting in a reaffirmation of heterosexuality and national pride.

Infantilization

The narratives surrounding women's sports and female athletes are often rife with female stereotyping. One of the lingering stereotypes associated with women is their childishness. The 1990 AAF study explicitly referred to a strategy that renders grown women childlike; we called this the infantilization of female athletes. Since then many researchers have found media discourse describing women infantilizing. A typical example of such stereotyping was mentioned in Spencer's (2003) analysis of the Evert/Navratilova rivalry. Evert was recurrently framed as "America's Sweetheart," the stereotype of the youthful, innocent girl next door (p. 18). Similarly Daddario (1994) argued that female athletes were frequently constructed "according to an adolescent ideal" (p. 275), wherein sportswomen, some in their mid- and late twenties, were again characterized in primarily childlike terms: "Little sister," "favorite girl next door," "pixie," and "Tinkerbell" (p. 275). Koivula (1999) found that female athletes were occasionally called "girls," although men were never called "boys," but instead "men" or "guys" (p. 596).

A second infantilizing strategy comprised a "hierarchy of naming." This practice, first identified in the AAF studies, described first name/last name usage by commentators and journalists. Naming is important because it conveys status and prestige. Dominants, that is, people in powerful positions, may reinforce their power by first-naming subordinates, people in less powerful positions. For example, bosses may call their secretaries by their first names only—"Barbara," "Patti," or "Mike"— while the secretaries may be expected to call their bosses "Mr. Smith," "Ms. Jones," or "Mr. Trump." Adults often call other people's children by their first names only, while the children are expected to use the grownups' titles, such as Mr. Martin. In contrast, referring to individuals by both their first and last names or last-name-only suggests that the relationship between two people is more egalitarian.

In 1989 and 1993, we found that commentators were more likely to first name female athletes—"Martina," for example—than they were to male athletes. Commentators were less likely to use both first and last names and less likely to use last-names-only when referring to women. This usage symbolically reduced women to a subordinate status, one that suggested they were childlike and powerless. Although the naming hierarchy has diminished over the last 15 years, in 1999, we discovered this practice still operated in televised tennis competitions.

Koivula (1999) reported that the typical naming practice was to use both first and last names for women and men athletes, an improvement over the practices described by the early AAF studies. Even so, first-name-only use was greater for women than for men, and women were called by their last names one-half the number of times that men were. In the earlier study by Halbert and Latimar (1994), who analyzed the television version of the so-called "Battle of the Champions," the researchers reported that Martina Navratilova's full name was employed only half the number of times that Jimmy Connors' full name was used. This naming practice implied that Navratilova was the subordinate, while Jimmy Connors was the dominant.

Emotions and Attitudes

In the section called "The Gender of Emotion," the 2000 AAF study pointed up discursive differences in the way emotions were attributed to women and men. Commentators tended to see emotions as significant to the players and the outcome of the game. Women's emotions, however, were framed differently than men's emotions. Women's emotions (mainly stemming from losses, such as the death of a relative) turned them into serious, moral people and made them more cooperative and team- or community-minded. Emotions were resources, but resources for good works, in addition to a higher level of play. Men's emotions (rarely prompted by losses) were also resources, but in their case, these resources propelled them towards successful performances in which they exhibited intensity, aggression, or passion for the game (p. 27) and became more fully developed as athletes. While women's emotions united the team, men's emotions individuated them (AAF, 2000). In short, commentators focused on women's grief (an emotion that made them seem weak) as what inspired them to better performance, while they highlighted men's heart or fire (an emotion that made them seem strong) as what inspired them to better performance.

The desire for harmony was another emotion/attitude deemed feminine. Numerous researchers remarked upon sports discourse that emphasized sportswomen's cooperation rather than their competitive zeal (Daddario, 1994; Kennedy, 2000; McDonald, 2002; Wright & Clarke, 1999). Commentators' paeans to women's moral, self-sacrificing nature were not infrequent. Cooperation became a code word for femininity, which included selflessness, high moral standards, and modesty (Christopherson, et al., 2002), not bad qualities in general, but seldom leading to athletic success.

Some kinds of emotion were seen to operate to the detriment of female athletes. Journalists' discourse suggested women were particularly susceptible to stress, and under competitive pressure they might collapse because of their emotional instability (Kane & Disch, 1993; Harris & Clayton, 2002; Mayeda, 2001). For instance, Halbert and Latimer (1994) noted that commentators frequently described Martina Navratilova's emotions as rendering her vulnerable in "The Battle of the Champions" telecast, while the emotions of her opponent, Jimmy Connors, were rarely mentioned.

Beauty and Grace

To focus on a female athlete's beauty is to introduce a non sequitur: It is a discursive strategy that trivializes a sportswoman's accomplishments because her appearance has nothing to do with her athletic performance. It is also a way to sexualize a woman and thus objectify her, as discussed earlier. The AAF studies did not explicitly deal with beauty and grace discourse except in the context of sexuality. However, numerous other researchers have written about the media's obsession with female athletes' looks, their clothing, and their graceful movements. Commentators sometimes rhapsodized over female athletes' fashion choices (their tennis dresses, for example), their shoes, their jewelry, and other adornments. Jones, Murrell, and Jackson (1999) expressed it quite succinctly in the title of their research study, "*Pretty versus powerful* in the sports pages: Print media coverage of the US Women's Olympic gold medal winning teams" [my italics]. Likewise, the title of Knight and Giuliano's (2001/2002) study is instructive: "He's a Laker; she's a "looker...." Numerous other researchers have attested to the media's inappropriate preoccupation with female athletes' appearance (Bernstein, 2002; Dworkin & Messner, 2002; Eastman & Billings, 2000; Eskes, Duncan, & Miller, 1998; Fink & Kensicki, 2002; Harris and Clayton, 2002; Mayeda, 2001; Stevenson, 2002).

A good example comes from the televised media treatment of Marion Jones in the 2000 Olympics: "According to NBC's lead track and field analyst, Tom Hammond, Jones's 'Drive for Five' was largely a concern about beauty, about whether or not Jones could sustain her smile throughout her drive for five gold medals" (Mayeda, 2001, p. 167).

The obsession with an athlete's beauty diverts attention from the potential threat that a sportswoman poses to hegemonic masculinity and reaffirms sexual difference by playing up her feminine appearance. John Berger's (1972) insights are as applicable today as when he first argued, "Men act and women appear. Men look at women. Women watch themselves being looked at" (p. 47).

Similarly, during the infrequent times when the sports media do take women seriously, it is often in those sports that are considered beautiful—movement forms that are aesthetically pleasing, lyrical, and dance-like such as figure skating, gymnastics, rhythmic gymnastics, and synchronized swimming. Many researchers have noted the media's emphasis on graceful movements and the elegance of the athlete when a woman is participating in a feminine sport (e.g., Bishop, 2003; Feder-Kane, 2000). The framing of figure skater Nancy Kerrigan was a case in point. As Feder-Kane (2000) argued, "the narrative surrounding Nancy Kerrigan in 1992 always emphasized her beauty and elegance; she could not step onto the ice without the commentators, male or female, remarking how 'lovely-elegant-angelic-sophisticated' she was" (p. 214). This discussion of beauty leads naturally into the next category.

Gender-Specific Sports

The AAF studies did not specifically examine differences in media coverage according to whether a sport was deemed feminine and therefore socially acceptable for women or masculine and therefore socially unacceptable for women. The issue of sex typing is nonetheless important, as research has shown.

Several discursive strategies work to keep women in their (feminine) place and to prevent them from poaching on masculine territory. As mentioned above, any sport that has a graceful, aesthetically pleasing character is deemed appropriate for women, and female athletes who participate in these sports are generally portrayed positively. Men may also participate (such as in figure skating), but because the sport is so closely aligned with women, men's participation often places their masculinity and heterosexuality at issue.

Individual sports are seen as most properly feminine, and media discourse tends to be approving when women participate in individual events. Women are supposed to engage in competition only if it places them at some distance from their competitors. This allows them to avoid getting roughed up, hurt, or dirty, all conditions that would call their femininity into question (Kane & Snyder, 1989; Metheny, 1965). Team sports, which feature head-to-head competition, especially those that require body contact and aggression, are perceived as most properly masculine (Kane & Snyder, 1989; Metheny, 1965).

Many researchers noted the differences in the coverage of women when they were portrayed in aesthetically pleasing, individual (feminine) sports compared to the coverage when women were depicted in combative, team (masculine) sports. Bishop (2003), Harris and Clayton (2002), Higgs et al. (2003), Koivula (1999), and Urquhart and Crossmann (1999) all found that a disproportionate amount of coverage was given to female athletes participating in "feminine" sports, especially when compared to the coverage of female athletes competing in "masculine" sports. For example, Bishop (2003) found that one fifth of all (35) stories on women in *SI* featured figure skating, while only three stories described women's achievements in more traditionally male sports (soccer and college basketball). Tuggle and Owen (1999) discovered that the 1996 Olympic Games gave about twice as much television coverage to women in individual sports as they did to women in team sports, and "the disparity was even greater when gymnastics was removed from the team category" (p. 175).

Christopherson et al. (2002) studied the media discourse on the 1999 Women's World Cup Soccer Champions, a good test case, since soccer is an aggressive, contact team game, in short, a "masculine" sport. They found that although sport discourses appeared illogical or contrary, they also relieved a perceived public challenge to masculinity presented by women's athleticism. For instance, women athletes who "did femininity" well disarmed the widespread perception that women soccer players had to become masculine to succeed. Even when female athletes were strong and aggressive, these qualities were seen merely to emphasize their independence rather than to undermine their femininity. However, in neither case was the basic inequality of women and men challenged.

Ultimately, the authors concluded:

> the consistent presentation of the games as a new era for women's empowerment was packaged to resonate with and appeal to women. Part of the real contradiction of the games, however, may be that the Women's World Cup was also packaged to resonate and appeal to men. . . . This representation appeals to the hopes of women, while perhaps reassuring the men that nothing has really changed. (Christophserson et al., 2002, p. 184)

Here the authors suggested that, in trying to please both female and male viewers, the producers had to present conflicting narratives. Unfortunately, the empowerment narrative was undermined by the masculine hegemony narrative. Duncan and Hasbrook (1988, p. 8) labeled this strategy, wherein a blend of positive and negative commentary coexist, "ambivalence," discourse that generally functions to undercut the accomplishments of female athletes.

Two European media studies revealed similar patterns. Von der Lippe's (2002) study analyzed the discourse surrounding female handball athletes in five European countries. She argued that media representations of sportswomen in this sport were not predictably stereotypical, but conflicting. Pirinen (1997a), who studied newspaper coverage of women in five traditionally masculine sports (boxing, ski jumping, hammer throwing, triple jump, and pole vault), also revealed contradictory themes, one of which was potentially empowering (the equality theme) alongside one that was predictably derogatory and trivializing (the women-as-second-rate-athletes theme). Overall, however, she concluded that "women's participation in new sports were portrayed as 'less than' and 'other than' their male counterparts" (p. 247). In both of the previous studies, it seems likely that these contradictory themes could again be considered a form of ambivalence. Other researchers, too, have identified similar conflicts in the tension between femininity and athleticism (Banet-Weiser, 1999; Dworkin & Messner, 2002; Fink & Kensicki, 2002; Wearden & Creedon, 2002).

In sum, commentary surrounding women in "masculine" sports tended to be rife with contradictions, probably because women were encroaching on male turf. On the other hand, the "containment" (Kane & Snyder, 1989, pp. 79, 90) of women in feminine sports was less likely to produce conflicting narratives, perhaps because female-appropriate sports are seen as watered-down versions of real sports (that is, men's sports) and because feminine sports point up women's sexual difference from men.

Noncompetitive Roles

In the 2000 AAF study, we noted that, in the minimal coverage given to female athletes, there were some gag features that introduced nonathlete women, occasionally nubile spectators in the stands, but sometimes women who could only be described as random—having little relevance to the sport itself. For example, during one nightly news segment, one commentator cut to footage of a group of referees clustered around an instant-replay monitor. The viewing audience was shown what the referees were allegedly watching: a Victoria's Secret ad with models in various states of undress.

In a similar way, other researchers have shown that commentators and journalists sometimes introduced facts that had very little to do with sportswomen's performances. Typical examples included discussions of female athletes' dating habits, their family roles as daughters or mothers, and their interest in domestic tasks (Daddario, 1994; Eastman & Billings, 2000; Harris & Clayton, 2002; Kennedy, 2001; McDonald, 2002). Sometimes non-athlete women would be brought into the mix when male athletes were discussed; in that context, they were cast as cheerleaders, supporters, girlfriends, and wives, but rarely in leadership roles or as individuals in their own right (Bishop, 2003; Cuneen & Sidwell, 1998; Hardin, et al., 2002; Harris & Clayton, 2002). Clearly this kind of discursive strategy—providing extraneous information that is gender coded—does perform an important function; it reaffirms the femininity of women, whether athletes or not, and magnifies sexual difference.

Attributions/Agency

The 1989 and 1993 AAF reports found gender differences in the ways weakness and strength were attributed to athletes. Weakness descriptors such as frustrated, jittery, panicked, vulnerable, shaky, and dejected were more likely to be attributed to female athletes than to male athletes. Strength descriptors such as powerful, strong, confident, dominant, and aggressive were less likely to be attributed to female than to male athletes. These asymmetries gave the viewer the sense that female athletes are passive reactors with little control over their fate, while male athletes are active agents controlling the outcomes of their acts. The 2000 study, however, revealed a more symmetrical distribution of strength and weakness descriptors; we reported that some progress had occurred in the way that commentators characterize female athletes' performances.

The findings of other researchers seem to confirm this trend toward more balanced attributions. Pirinen (1997b) discovered that the framing of female athletes in Finnish women's magazines was quite positive; writers emphasized the successes of sportswomen and commented on the athletes' failures only when they served as a goad to larger accomplishments. In their study of sportscasting and sports reporting, Eastman and Billings (2000) reported no dramatic gender differentials when analyzing written and televised attributions of athletic successes and failures. In an earlier (1999) study, the same authors researched television coverage of the 1996 Olympics, and similarly concluded that the producers and commentators "were careful to attribute women's success and failures to the same characteristics as men's success and failures" (p. 165), although other evidence of gender bias was abundant.

Gender Marking

Gender marking is a linguistic practice identified in all three of the AAF studies (1990, 1994, and 2000). It consists of labeling women's sports as the *Women's* NCAA Final Four (rather than the NCAA Final Four, which is the locution typically used for the men's competition) or labeling female athletes (the *women's* world record holder, rather than the world record holder). In the parallel men's competitions or in descriptions of male athletes, no such gender marking occurs. What makes this linguistic practice significant is the assumption that men's events and male athletes have primacy and therefore need no qualification, unlike the women's events and women. Because of the differential linguistic usage, any event or athlete marked as "women's" or "woman" sounds derivative, a poor cousin to the real deal, which is, of course, men's.

Only a few other researchers have analyzed gender marking in sports: Koivula (1999), who examined television coverage of Swedish sports in 1995 to 1996 and 1998, and Halbert and Latimar (1994), who studied the televised "Battle of the Champions," featuring a tennis match between Martina Navratilova and Jimmy Connors. Both authors turned up asymmetries, wherein women's events and women were gender marked many more times than men's events and men.

SUMMARY AND CONCLUSIONS

At the beginning of this chapter, I posed a key question: Given the increased popularity (and success) of women's sports and female athletes, has there been a correspondingly significant improvement in women's sports coverage? I revisit that question now and offer some answers.

One important measure of improvement is quantity. Has there been a measurable increase in the amount of coverage given to women's sports and female athletes? From 1989 to 1993 the coverage of local sports news on women's sports increased by 0.10%, from 5.00% to 5.10%. From 1993 to 1999 the coverage of women's sports increased 3.60%, from 5.10% to 8.70%. Strictly speaking, this is an improvement, although a small one. We should also keep in mind that some of that increased coverage involved the humorous sexualization of women (e.g., footage of a celebrity volleyball game in which nuns in their habits played alongside sexy bikini-clad women; AAF, 1994).

What about the quantity of sports reporting in formats other than nightly sportscasts? Sporting events such as ESPN's *SportsCenter* and its television special on the top 100 athletes of the twentieth century fell into this category, yet the quantity of reporting on women's sport, compared to men's, was equally skewed. Even when the numbers seemed to suggest that coverage had become more equitable (Higgs, et al., 2003), more sophisticated analyses of the same events (Andrews, 1998; Eastman & Billings, 1999) showed that, despite parity on some measures, reporting on women's sports and female athletes still lacked salience, as Eastman and Billings (1999) argued:

> Although the network carefully balanced its prime-time promos by gender, just as it balanced the number of minutes given to women's and men's sports, and its hosts and on-site reports were careful to attribute women's successes and failures to the same characteristics as men's success and failures, the network's preproduced profiles continued to strongly favor men, discourse about men athletes and men's sports dominated talk of women, and what can be labeled unfortunate stereotyping crept into the appearance descriptors. (p. 165)

Typically, producers of sport media justify the underreporting of women's sports by arguing that they are merely responding to market forces. "Look what happens when we do cover women's games—viewers don't watch because they are simply not interested," they declare. But is that genuinely the case, or is it that production values in women's sports coverage are inferior to those of men's sports because producers don't commit nearly the resources to women's games that they do to men's? Whether women or men, few viewers are likely to watch games in which there are unsophisticated or missing graphics, poorly informed commentators, incoherent or overly sentimental narratives, few replays, and muffled sound. Few women readers will subscribe to magazines in which female athletes are mocked, sexualized, or trivialized. In addition, without intentional audience-building strategies such as promos and previews, the audience for women's sports is not likely to grow. Rather than blaming the market, producers should take a harder look at their own production practices and the ideologies that underpin them.

Qualitative coverage revealed few dramatic improvements. Overall, the discourse on women's sport and female athletes included humorous sexualization, compulsory heterosexuality, as well as veiled references to the "threat" of lesbianism, infantilization, gender-coded emotions, sports sex typing, suggestions of sexual difference, ambivalence, abundant stereotyping. There is, however, one area in which television commentators appear to have made progress. They are becoming less likely to attribute failures to women's lack of talent and more likely to attribute successes to women's skill and strength—in short, to their agency—in proportions that match the attributions of men's failures and successes.

Some researchers have argued that although sexism in sports reporting is not so blatant as it once was, more sophisticated strategies of marginalization are at work. What makes these strategies insidious is the *appearance* of equity in sport journalism and commentary (Eastman & Billings, 1999; Lenskyj, 1998). For example, Eastman and Billings (1999) contended that although NBC hyped the 1996 Summer Games in Atlanta as the "Olympics of the Women" and a "watershed event for women's sports" (p. 141), this was primarily a marketing strategy to promote the Games to female viewers. There were few *substantive* changes in coverage that would back up NBC's claim. For this reason, the authors concluded that this framing of the Olympics failed to make the women's events more salient, if one defines salience as "prominence coming from equal quantity and *equally positive quality* of network discourse about women's sports, teams, and athletes in Olympic coverage in comparison to men's sports, teams, and athletes" (italics added, p. 146).

The answer to our critical question? It seems that despite the advances made in women's sports, despite the competitive triumphs, the new women's professional sport leagues, the burgeoning popularity of women's soccer and other team sports, the proliferation of Web sites and magazines dedicated to sportswomen, it is still reasonable for Curry, Arriagada, and Cornwell (2002) to conclude, "Sports images primarily serve to reinforce the existing gender order" (p. 409).

RECOMMENDATIONS FOR FUTURE RESEARCH

My recommendations for future research flow out of what I see as issues in the most recent round of sport media studies. As mentioned earlier, the number of sport media studies that focus on textual analysis is increasing exponentially. Many, however, simply replicate previous studies or apply already validated coding schemes to this year's sporting events. What changes is frequently *not* the theorizing but merely the texts being analyzed. At this point, I'm not sure we need more of the same. The themes of sexualization, emphasized femininity, infantilization, ambivalence, and so on have become so commonplace as to yield very little new data. Unless and until real change occurs on the broader social front, sport analysts need to focus on other areas.

Overall, what we do need is *more nuanced* studies. Here I am using the term *nuanced* to mean several different qualities. The first sense in which nuance applies is research that strikes a balance between theorizing and data. Studies that offer much data and little theorizing tend to be unenlightening. Without a guide to interpretation—what these data mean and why they are important—research rarely advances. Studies that provide much theorizing and little data tend to be vague. How do these abstractions play out in the material world? How are they anchored to our everyday social experience? Without answers to these questions, research lacks vitality.

A model that avoids both extremes is Mary Jo Kane's (1998) "Fictional Denials of Female Empowerment: A Feminist Analysis of Young Adult Sports Fiction." This article tackled two areas that were previously un- or underexplored: adolescent girls and young adult sport novels. Kane added to our theoretical understanding by identifying and exploring a new genre of sport fiction: lone girl stories. Her careful empirical research into lone girl novels yielded rich data. This data enabled Kane to characterize lone girl fiction as narratives that ultimately end in denials of female empowerment. In good articles like these, the theory and data work together symbiotically.

The second sense in which I am using nuance relates to research that takes into consideration the intersections of social relationships such as race, ethnicity, gender, sexuality, class, ability, and so on. Exemplars of this type of research—emerging in the last few years—bear our careful study. Several of the studies already cited in this chapter could illustrate this idea, for example, McDonald's (2002) "Queering Whiteness: The Peculiar Case of the Women's National Basketball Association," Stevenson's (2002) Women, Sport, and Globalization: Competing Discourses of Sexuality and Nation," and Jamieson's (2000) "Reading Nancy Lopez: Decoding Representations of Race, Class, and Sexuality."

I am also using the term *nuanced studies* to refer to underdeveloped lines of research. Although textual analyses of sport media discourse abound, there are few genuine reception studies, that is, research that contextualizes the effects of media discourse on viewers and readers. While writers in other disciplines have examined audience responses to media, only a handful of authors in sports studies, especially in sociology of physical activity, have done so. Toni Bruce's 1998 research "Audience Frustration and Pleasure: Women Viewers Confront Televised Women's Basketball" exemplified this kind of research, along with Knight and Guiliano's (2001/2) "He's a Laker; She's a 'Looker': The Consequences of Gender-Stereotypical Portrayals of Male and Female Athletes by the Print Media," and Duncan and Brummett's (1993) "Liberal and Radical Sources of Female Empowerment in Sport Media."

Another underdeveloped line of research is production studies. The "isms" (sexism, racism, heterosexism, classism, ageism, and so on) are not limited to individual acts of prejudice, but are part and parcel of institutional structures that operate in taken-for-granted ways. As Nancy Theberge and Alan Cronk's classic (1986) study, "Work Routines in Newspaper Sports Departments and the Coverage of Women's Sports," demonstrated, customary ways of doing things (in this case sportswriters' methods of uncovering newsworthy stories) may have unintended consequences that result in the disadvantaging of some social groups and the privileging of others.

More research is needed on work routines, those of editors of sport magazines and newspapers, sport photographers and writers, and producers and commentators of network or cable sportscasts.

Finally, other underinvestigated areas include physical activity and disability, working class studies, regional (e.g., southern and southwestern) studies, and Web-based studies of sport and physical activity culture. Perhaps most intriguing, we lack a fully nuanced account of sport media as social movement. If, as Alain Touraine (2000) famously remarked, sociology is the study of social movements, can we ask to see real change in sport media if we do not promote an agenda that lends itself to change—sport media research as social action? Sport media are images in motion; let them move us, too.

ACKNOWLEDGMENTS

I wish to thank the Amateur Athletic Foundation of Los Angeles for their support in funding the three AAF studies cited in the chapter. I also thank Michael A. Messmer for his contribution of research expertise to the same studies.

REFERENCES

Andrews, D. L. (1998). Feminizing Olympic reality: Preliminary dispatches from Baudrillard's Atlanta. *International Review for the Sociology of Sport, 33,* 5–18.

Banet-Weiser, S. (1999). Hoop dreams: Professional basketball and the politics of race and gender. *Journal of Sport and Social Issues, 23,* 403–420.

Beauvoir, S. de (1989). *The second sex* (Reissued ed.). NY: Vintage Books (Original work published 1953).

Berger, J. (1972). *Ways of seeing.* London: BBC/Penguin.

Bernstein, A. (2002). Is it time for a victory lap? Changes in the media coverage of women in sport. *International Review for the Sociology of Sport, 37,* 415–428.

Billings, A. C. (2000). In search of women athletes: *ESPN's* list of the top 100 athletes of the century. *Journal of Sport and Social Issues, 24,* 415–421.

Bishop, R. (2003). Missing in action: Feature coverage of women's sports in *Sports Illustrated. Journal of Sport and Social Issues, 27,* 184–194.

Brownmiller, S. (1984). *Femininity.* NY: Fawcett Columbine.

Bruce, T. (1998). Audience frustration and pleasure: Women viewers confront televised women's basketball. *Journal of Sport and Social Issues, 22,* 373–397.

Christopherson, N., Janning, M., & McConnell, E. D. (2002). Two kicks forward, one kick back: A content analysis of media discourses on the 1999 Women's World Cup Soccer Championship. *Sociology of Sport Journal, 19,* 170–188.

Cuneen, J., & Sidwell, M. J. (1998). Gender portrayals in *Sports Illustrated for Kids* advertisements: A content analysis of prominent and supporting models. *Journal of Sport Management, 12,* 39–50.

Curry, T. J., Arriagada, A., & Cornwell, B. (2002). Images of sport in popular nonsport magazines: Power and performance versus pleasure and participation. *Sociological Perspectives, 45,* 397–413.

Daddario, G. (1994). Chilly scenes of the 1992 Winter Games: The mass media and the marginalization of female athletes. *Sociology of Sport Journal, 11,* 275–288.

Davis, L. R. (1997). *The swimsuit issue and sport: Hegemonic masculinity in* Sports Illustrated. NY: State University of New York Press.

Duncan, M. C., & Brummett, B. (1993). Liberal and radical sources of female empowerment in sport media. *Sociology of Sport Journal, 10,* 57–72.

Duncan, M. C., & Hasbrook, C. A. (1988). Denial of power in televised women's sports, *Sociology of Sport Journal, 5*(1), 1–21.

Duncan, M. C., Messner, M. A., Willms, N. *Gender in televised sports: 1989, 1993 and 1999.* Retrieved November 4, 2005, from http://www.aafla.org/9arr/ResearchReports/tv2000.pdf

Duncan, M. C., & Sayaovong, A. (1990). Photographic images and gender in *Sports Illustrated for Kids. Play & Culture, 3,* 91–116.

Dworkin, A. (1987). *Intercourse.* NY: The Free Press/Macmillan.

Dworkin, S. L., & Messner, M. A. (2002). Introduction to special issue on gender relations and sport. *Sociological Perspectives, 45*, 347–352.

Eastman, S. T., & Billings, A. C. (1999). Gender parity in the Olympics: Hyping women athletes, favoring men athletes. *Journal of Sport and Social Issues, 23*, 140–170.

Eastman, S. T., & Billings, A. C. (2000). Sportscasting and sports reporting: The power of gender bias. *Journal of Sport and Social Issues, 24*, 192–213.

Eskes, T. B., Duncan, M. C., & Miller, B. M. (1998). The discourse of empowerment: Foucault, Marcuse, and women's fitness texts. *Journal of Sport and Social Issues, 22*(3), 317–344.

Feder-Kane, A. M. (2000). A radiant smile from the lovely lady: Overdetermined femininity in "ladies" figure skating. In S. Birrell and M. G. McDonald (Eds.), *Reading sport: Critical essays on power and representation* (pp. 206–233). Boston: Northeastern University.

Fink, J. S., & Kensicki, L. J. (2002). An imperceptible difference: Visual and textual constructions of femininity in *Sports Illustrated* and *Sports Illustrated for Kids*. *Mass Communication & Society, 5*(3), 317–339.

Halbert, C., & Latimar, M. (1994). Battling gendered language: An analysis of the language used by sports commentators in a televised coed tennis championship. *Sociology of Sport Journal, 11*, 298–308.

Hardin, M., Walsdorf, S. L., Walsdorf, K., & Hardin, B. (2002). The framing of sexual difference in *Sports Illustrated for Kids* editorial photos. *Mass Communication & Society, 5*(3), 341–359.

Harris, J. (1999). Lie back and think of England: The women of Euro '96. *Journal of Sport and Social Issues, 23*, 96–110.

Harris, J., & Clayton, B. (2002). Femininity, masculinity, physicality and the English Tabloid press: The case of Anna Kournikova. *International Review for the Sociology of Sport, 37*, 397–413.

Higgs, C. T., Weiller, K. H., & Martin, S. B. (2003). Gender bias in the 1996 Olympic Games: A comparative analysis. *Journal of Sport and Social Issues, 27*, 52–64.

Jamieson, K. M. (2000). Nancy Lopez: Decoding representations of race, class, and sexuality. In S. Birrell and M. G. McDonald (Eds.), *Reading sport: Critical essays on power and representation* (pp. 144–165). Boston: Northeastern University.

Jones, R., Murrell, A. J., & Jackson, J. (1999). Pretty versus powerful in the sports pages: Print media coverage of U.S. Women's Olympic gold medal winning teams. *Journal of Sport and Social Issues, 23*, 183–192.

Kane, M. J. (1998). Fictional denials of female empowerment: A feminist analysis of young adult sports fiction. *Sociology of Sport Journal, 15*, 231–262.

Kane, M. J., & Disch, L. J. (1993). Sexual violence and the reproduction of male power in the locker room: The "Lisa Olson Incident." *Sociology of Sport Journal, 10*, 331–352.

Kane, M. J., & Snyder, E. (1989). Sport typing: The social "containment" of women. *Arena Review, 13*, 77–96.

Kennedy, E. (2000). Bad boys and gentlemen: Gendered narrative in televised sport. *International Review for the Sociology of Sport, 35*, 59–73.

Kennedy, E. (2001). She wants to be a sledgehammer? Tennis femininities in British television. *Journal of Sports and Social Issues, 25*, 56–72.

Knight, J. L, & Giuliano, T. A. (2001/2). He's a Laker; she's a "looker": The consequences of gender-stereotypical portrayals of male and female athletes by the print media. *Sex Roles, 45*(3/4), 217–229.

Koivula, N. (1999). Gender stereotyping in televised media sport coverage. *Sex Roles, 41*(7/8), 589–604.

Lenskyj, H. J. (1998). "Inside Sport" or "On the Margins"? Australian women and the sport media. *International Review for the Sociology of Sport, 33*, 19–32.

Mayeda, D. (2001). Characterizing gender and race in the 2000 Summer Olympics: NBC's coverage of Maurice Greene, Michael Johnson, Marion Jones, and Cathy Freeman. *Social Thought and Research, 24*(1/2), 145–186.

McDonald, M. G. (2002). Queering whiteness: The peculiar case of the Women's National Basketball Association. *Sociological Perspectives, 45*, 379–396.

Messner, M. A., Duncan, M. C., & Cooky, C. (2003). Silence, sports bras, and wrestling porn: Women in televised sports news and highlight shows. *Journal of Sport and Social Issues, 27*, 38–51.

Metheny, E. (Ed.). (1965). *Connotations of movement in sport and dance*. Dubuque, IA: William C. Brown.

Pirinen, R. M. (1997a). Catching up with men? Finnish newspaper coverage of women's entry into traditionally male sports. *International Review for the Sociology of Sport, 32*(3), 239–249.

Pirinen, R. M. (1997b). The construction of women's positions in sport: A textual analysis of articles on female athletes in Finnish woman's magazines. *Sociology of Sport Journal, 14*, 290–301.

Shifflett, B., & Revelle, R. (1994). Gender equity in sports media coverage: A review of the NCAA news. *Journal of Sport and Social Issues, 18*, 144–150.

Spencer, N. E. (2003). "America's Sweetheart" and "Czech-Mate": A discursive analysis of the Evert-Navratilova rivalry. *Journal of Sport and Social Issues, 27,* 18–37.

Stevenson, D. (2002). Women, sport, and globalization: Competing discourses of sexuality and nation. *Journal of Sport and Social Issues, 26,* 209–225.

Theberge, N., & Cronk, A. (1986). Work routines in newspaper sports departments and coverage of women's sports. *Sociology of Sport Journal, 3,* 195–203.

Touraine, A. (2000). *Sociologie de l'Action.* Paris: LGF.

Tuchman, G. (1978). The symbolic annihilation of women by the mass media. In G. Tuchman, A. K. Daniels, & J. Benet (Eds.), *Hearth and home: Images of women in the mass media* (pp. 3–38). NY: Oxford University Press.

Tuchman, G., Daniels, A. K., & Benet, J. W. (1978). *Hearth and home: Images of women in the mass media.* London: Oxford University Press.

Tuggle, C. A., & Owen, A. (1999). A descriptive analysis of NBC's coverage of the Centennial Olympic Games: The "games of the woman"? *Journal of Sport and Social Issues, 23,* 171–182.

Urquhart, J., & Crossmann, J. (1999). *The Globe and Mail* coverage of the winter Olympic Games: A cold place for women athletes. *Journal of Sport and Social Issues, 23,* 193–202.

Von der Lippe, G. (2002). Media image: Sport, gender and national identities in Five European countries. *International Review for the Sociology of Sport, 37,* 371–395.

Wann, D. L., Schrader, M. P., Allison, J. A., & McGeorge, K. K. (1998). The inequitable newspaper coverage of men's and women's athletics at small, medium, and large universities. *Journal of Sport and Social Issues, 22,* 79–87.

Wearden, S. T., & Creedon, P. J. (2002). "We got next": Images of women in television commercials during the inaugural WNBA season. *Culture, Sport, Society, 5,* 189–210.

Wright, J., & Clarke, G. (1999). Sport, the media and the construction of compulsory heterosexuality: A case study of women's Rugby Union. *International Review for the Sociology of Sport, 33/34,* 227–243.

Utilizing Televised Sport
to Benefit Prime-Time Lineups:
Examining the Effectiveness
of Sports Promotion

Andrew C. Billings
Clemson University

Given the plummeting ratings of basic network television (Umstead, 2004), the elasticity of the sports broadcast market is particularly remarkable. While sports such as the NHL and NBA have experienced decreased ratings, a proportionally equal number, such as NASCAR and the NFL, have enjoyed ratings surges. Indeed, at a time in which cable ratings are now larger than the ratings of the seven broadcast networks (Reynolds, 2003), sports programming has provided some of the surest bets in the industry, with ratings for events such as the Super Bowl and Olympics often ranking among the top telecasts in history (Barron, 2004).

Still, networks rarely break even on sports broadcast contracts (Friedman, 2004); instead, networks enter into long-term sports deals for four primary reasons. First, there is a prestige factor to being the home of a certain sport. For instance, NBC's logo incorporates the five Olympic rings because NBC executives want viewers to associate their nonsport programming with pinnacle megasports such as the Olympics. Similarly, TNT touts itself as a "home" of the NBA, and the USA network links its programming with the opening rounds of PGA Golf tournaments. In sum, televised sports are considered the crown jewels of network broadcasting.

Second, networks telecast sporting events because they attract much-desired demographics for advertisers. James (2003) reported that events such as the World Series continue to draw increasing numbers of viewers in the 18 to 49 age bracket, and Ault (2002) reported that Olympic coverage draws both men and women viewers ages 25 to 54 in record numbers. Advertisers must pay higher ad rates because sportscasts have proven reliable in garnering the demographics they crave, with events such as the Super Bowl now yielding over $2 million for a 30-second advertisement (Reinan, 2004).

Third, fledgling cable networks sign sports broadcasting contracts because cable and satellite providers could add their network to their list of channel offerings if demand is high for the sport they now have the rights to air. The classic example was the fourth-network status of Fox, which was only seven years old and had no sports division when it purchased the rights to broadcast NFL games in 1994. Fox was not then available in many key markets, but after the network secured the NFL deal, all major markets soon had Fox affiliates. Not only did Fox gain a greater coverage area, Ennis (2003) reported that Fox moved from fourth to second in the coveted adult 18 to 49 demographic for all its programming. Smaller but significant cases also occurred with cable programming when ESPN received the rights to cover the first round of the NCAA tournament in the 1980s and when TNT purchased a Sunday night NFL contract in the 1990s.

Fourth—and perhaps most important—networks eagerly purchase sports contracts because of the promotional value sporting events have in yielding higher ratings for a prime-time lineup. Eastman, Newton, and Pack (1996) argued that networks used sporting events as vehicles for attracting much-desired demographics to sitcoms, dramas, movies, and more. Billings, Eastman, and Newton (1998) reported that megasporting events are purchased in no small part because of their timing in relation to sweeps months and their potential springboard effects on prime-time ratings. For instance, the 2004 Summer Olympics in Athens, Greece, took place in August; NBC believed so strongly in the ability of the Olympics to jumpstart its fall season that chief executive Jeff Zucker began new fall programming a month early to take full advantage of the promotional power of the Olympic telecast. Indeed, Zucker was right to make such a decision based on past precedent; in the last decade the Olympics has typically provided 17 consecutive nights of top ratings, meaning that 55 consecutive prime-time hours were dominated by the same host network. In comparison, an entire season of first-run episodes of CBS stalwart *CSI* and NBC's megahit *Friends* would yield a total of only 31 hours of top ratings combined. Without question, megasporting events provide a unique venue for promoting other programs in ways that no other telecast can accomplish.

Because of the long-held network belief that promotion can significantly impact ratings, it is important to ascertain (a) whether sportscasts actually continue to provide ideal opportunities for promotion of prime-time lineups, (b) which variables most influence Nielsen ratings, and (c) what approaches to sports promotion future sportscasts should adopt.

THE ROLE OF PROMOTION WITHIN SPORTS COMMUNICATION

The breadth and depth of sport communication research has become significant over the course of the past three decades as scholars (Real, 1989; Wenner, 1998) particularly focused upon the impact that mediated sport has on mainstream society. With regard to packaging megasporting events as media commodities, Real and Mechikoff (1992, p. 323) analyzed what they termed the "deep fan" as exemplar of the profound impact sports culture has on highly involved individuals; McAllister (1998) identified ways in which college bowl television sponsorship deals affect amateur athletes; and scholars such as Moragas Spa, Rivenburgh, and Larson (1995) studied the role of the Olympic telecast on societal attitudes. In all cases, researchers found that sport plays a critical role in millions of lives and that many people who may not even play sports are significantly affected as avid fans of myriad sports.

Outlining a model of sport structuration, Halone (2003) identified the critical role that media and spectator play in the sport communication process, arguing that there are two agencies in play (human and mediated) and these agencies ultimately result in reacting to the sporting event and enacting the sporting event, respectively. Halone's contention is that media drives fan behavior and that the role of athlete and spectator are indelibly linked. In sum, perhaps the largest connecting theme within sports communication is that mediated sport usually has a profound impact on societal behaviors. As such, it is crucial for the sport communication scholar to ascertain how to measure behavior. In the case of sport promotion, behaviors have been measured using Nielsen ratings—not only in the rating of the sport program, but also in the subsequent rating of the promoted program. In doing so, impact can be determined through the crude yet accurate counting of number of eyeballs that tune to a promoted program after viewing promotion within televised sport.

PROMOTION SALIENCE: THEORY AND ANALYSIS

Salience theory, as first postulated by Eastman and Newton (1998, 1999), contends that certain structural characteristics of on-air promotion result in increased program ratings. Grounded in the Elaboration Likelihood Model (Petty & Cacioppo, 1986), salience theory argues that on-air messages with salient features are more likely to be processed centrally and stored in long-term memory. In sum, salience theory has caused promotion to be added to inherited viewing, competition, and scheduling as one of the four primary factors that determine program ratings (Webster & Phalen, 1997; Eastman & Meyer, 1989; Eastman & Newton, 1999). Consequently, choices such as cuts, edits, and sound effects can cause viewers to process and remember promotions with more salient features, including orienting responses (Lang, 1990). Scholars such as Eastman, Newton, and Pack (1996) have long argued that promotion is actually the second-largest factor (after inheritance) in determining what viewers will watch. Inheritance (the rating of the lead-in program) has long influenced the rating of the proceeding program, with scholars arguing that 50% of all rating variance can be attributed to this single factor.

In sum, myriad studies of promotion (Billings, Eastman, & Newton et al., 1996; Eastman & Billings, 2000, 2004; Eastman & Newton, 1998, 1999; Eastman, Newton, & Pack et al., 1996; Eastman & Otteson, 1994; Walker, 1993; Walker & Eastman, 2003) have resulted in 15 variables that can be tested to measure the salience of on-air promotion within televised sportscasts. The following list identifies and defines these characteristics:

1. Reach (rating of carriage program),
2. Construction (number of programs promoted in a given promotional spot/i.e., promoting one game vs. promoting a triple-header),
3. Frequency (number of promos for a given program within a sportscast),
4. Clutter (number of elements [defined by number of ads plus promos plus network news spots] in a commercial break),
5. Location (whether the promotion occurs within a sportscast or between a sportscast and an other program),

6.   Position (placement within the commercial break; first or last position is most salient),
7.   Distance (number of hours/days/weeks between when the promotion airs and when the promoted program will air),
8.   Length (timed duration of a promo in seconds [15-, 30-, 60-second spots most common),
9.   Design (whether a promo is for a specific program or a generic promo for the series as a whole [i.e., the difference between a promo for what will happen on the next *Survivor* and a promo that advertises *Survivor* in general for all future airings]),
10.   Familiarity (whether the promo is for a new program/movie or for a continuing program with which the viewer might already be familiar),
11.   Goal (the proportion of promos with an acquisitive purpose to those with a retentive purpose),
12.   Compatibility of audience (whether the age/gender demographics of the carriage program closely match the age/gender demographics of the promoted program),
13.   Compatibility of genre (match between carriage program genre and promoted program genre),
14.   Night bunching (whether promos are crowding toward the beginning or ending of a sportscast), and
15.   Event bunching (whether promos are crowded toward the last day(s) of a multiple-day event, [i.e., Olympics or World Series]).

In sum, much work has been conducted that has resulted in some understanding as to how and why promotion does or does not work within on-air sportscasts. While many types of sporting events have not yet been analyzed, work regarding megasporting events has yielded directions for future research regarding the application of salience theory to sportscasts.

METHODS OF DETERMINING PROMOTION'S EFFECTIVENESS

Two ways of measuring promotion effectiveness within televised sport have been articulated by scholars: ratings gain/loss comparisons and regression analysis of salience variables. The former method indicates the extents to which programs that were promoted within a sporting event experienced ratings losses or gains when they aired after the sporting event. The latter method identifies the percentage of program rating changes that can be attributed to the presence or lack of salience variables in a promo.

Ratings gains and losses for programs promoted within sports have been measured for over a decade since Eastman and Otteson's (1994) initial analysis of promos within the 1992 Winter and Summer Olympics. This study compared the ratings of programs for the three weeks prior to the Olympics to the ratings three weeks immediately after the Olympics. For new programs, ratings of the time slot were used for comparative purposes. This three-week comparative process was then repeated for the 1996 Atlanta Summer Olympics (Billings, et al., 1996). However, scholars noted a key limitation to this method—primarily that there are good and bad parts of the ratings season and that conclusions may have been drawn from faulty comparisons. For instance, when CBS aired the 1998 Nagano Games, the two of the three weeks prior to the Olympic Games contained many reruns of popular programs, whereas CBS aired virtually all first-run series in the three weeks after the Olympic Games, especially because the February sweeps month had not yet ended. Thus, any comparison of ratings from reruns compared to first-run programs would necessarily yield increased ratings.

As a result, Eastman and Billings (2004) implemented three comparative frames for their examination of the promotion aired by NBC in the 2000 Summer Olympics in Sydney, Australia. Because of seasonal differences for the Northern and Southern Hemispheres, the Sydney Games aired in late September, meaning that—more than ever—NBC could use the Games as a promotional springboard for its new fall lineup because the premiere episodes would air immediately after the closing ceremonies. Researchers felt it was important to compare the new ratings (October 2000) to three different time frames: (a) three weeks in October 1999, which would indicate how these same programs/time slots fared at the same point in the calendar year of the previous season, (b) three weeks in May 2000, the last time these programs aired first-run episodes, and (c) three weeks in late August and early September 2000, the time immediately prior to the Games—the method that had been utilized in the past. The researchers still found potential flaws in the method—such as the new practice of airing popular programs multiple times in the same week, often labeling them *encore* presentations—but also indicated that the three-frame analysis was a much more advanced way of addressing questions of promotion effectiveness than a single frame consisting of findings with less power and reliability.

The second method that has frequently been discussed to evaluate promo effectiveness involved regression analysis of salient variables in each individual promo. Eastman, Newton, & Pack et al. (1996) were the first to use this process within televised sport when they examined 245 hours and 51 games and events of coverage on multiple networks. The researchers coded for whether or not (and to what degree) each promotion contained salient features. For instance, the *distance* variable was measured by coding for the number of days between the airing of the promo and the airing of the promoted program, with the shortest distance (same night or next night) being more salient than the longer distances (next week or more than two weeks); similarly, the *goal* variable was measured by identifying whether the promo mentioned a specific episode/date/time (more salient) or if the promo mentioned the program only generically (less salient). The initial 1996 model first accounted for lead-in share (inheritance) and then combined it with salience variables such as distance, genre, construction, format, and goal. Future models (Eastman & Billings, 2000, 2004) included additional variables such as clutter, position, carriage program rating, frequency, location, placement, and program status (new or continuing).

Regression models have consistently found inheritance to contribute approximately 50% of the variance, with salience variables in promotion contributing anywhere from 3 to 10% of additional variance. The analysis of the 1998 Nagano Games produced the highest percentage of total variance attributable to inheritance and promotion with 65%. Concurrent and subsequent nonsport-related promotion studies have recognized the importance of identifying structural elements of promos as being either effective or ineffective in garnering increased ratings (Eastman &

Bolls, 2000; Eastman, Newton, & Bolls, 2003), examining new issues such as humor and presentation as vital avenues for evaluating on-air promotion.

SPORTS PROMOTION: A SURVEY OF CRITICAL STUDIES

One commonality within all sport communication research is that the Olympic telecast is perceived to be the pinnacle of sport studies (Billings & Eastman, 2002, 2003; Eastman, Brown, & Kovatch, 1996). The first analysis of promotion within televised sport occurred when Eastman and Otteson (1994) analyzed promotion effectiveness for prime-time programming in the 1992 Winter (CBS) and Summer (NBC) Olympics. Surprisingly, the researchers found promotion within both Olympic telecasts to be highly ineffective. Using comparisons of the average ratings/shares three weeks before the Olympics to three weeks after the Olympic telecasts indicated that the majority of the continuing CBS programs had even lower ratings and shares after the Olympics than they did before the Games aired. Even more startling, all of the new CBS programs yielded lower ratings relative to their time slots. The 1992 Summer Olympic telecasts on NBC did marginally better but still failed to support the long-held industry claim that megasporting events such as the Olympics were ideal vehicles for promoting prime-time shows. In sum, only 6% (three programs) of the promoted programs in both of the Olympics experienced significant ratings gains, leading Eastman and Otteson (1994) to argue that the high costs of securing the television rights to the Olympics—now standing at $700 million for the 2004 Athens Games (Abrahamson, 2001)—may be much higher than they should be.

Using this information, Eastman, Newton, & Pack et al. (1996) selected a wider array of megasporting events to analyze and determine whether the trends Eastman and Otteson (1994) found were true within this larger sample. The 245-hour database included (a) the 1993 World Series, (b) the 1993 All-Star Game, (c) seven major bowl games from the 1993 to 1994 college football season, (d) the 1993 and 1994 Super Bowls, (e) the 1994 AFC and NFC Championship games, (f) the 1994 Pro Bowl, (g) the last seven games of the 1994 NCAA basketball tournament, (h) the 1994 NBA Finals, (i) the 1994 NBA All-Star Game, (j) the 1994 World Cup soccer championship game, (k) the three 1994 Triple Crown horse racing events, (l) the Daytona and Indy 500s, (m) the men's and women's tennis finals from the French Open and Wimbledon, (n) the weekend rounds of the 1994 Golf Grand Slam tournaments, and (o) 90 hours of 1994 Winter Olympic coverage. Within this wider net, 677 on-air promos for ABC, CBS, and NBC were analyzed. The results offered a complete reversal of the findings from Eastman and Otteson (1994), as promotion was highly effective in garnering higher ratings for prime-time programs. One third of program shares went up in the three-week period after the promo(s) aired and another one fourth stayed flat. The researchers noted that the 1994 Olympic Games yielded much higher ratings than the 1992 Olympic telecasts (as it was the year of the Nancy Kerrigan–Tonya Harding controversy) and that increased ratings/shares for the carriage programs likely resulted in increased promotional effectiveness for other prime-time programs.

Two research studies on promotion in the 1996 Atlanta Olympic Games were published by Billings et al. (1998) and Billings and Eastman (1998). The former study examined the effectiveness of on-air promotion for NBC's fall prime-time lineup; the latter addressed the extent to which NBC was able to promote future Olympic events within the Olympics itself.

First, Billings et al. (1998) analyzed 183 promotions for prime-time programs within the Atlanta Games, finding that—contrary to the 1992 Olympic promotion studies—the Olympics served as an ideal platform for promotion. Beyond the time-tested correlation between inheritance and increased ratings (Webster, 1985), the study lent support for the belief that promotion within sportscasts was more effective for continuing programs rather than new programs—most likely because continuing programs aired directly after the Olympic telecasts whereas NBC's new programs did not debut until six weeks after the Atlanta Games ended. Surprisingly, the study also found that NBC was much more likely to employ more generic than specific promos—again, most likely because new programs would air so far in the future that spots for specific episodes would prove futile. Overall, the authors concluded that the importance of these primarily positive findings was that even small ratings gains can have large effects as "one new hit show might swing an entire evening to one network…and success can be worth millions of dollars in advertising revenue and brand prestige" (Billings, et al., 1998, p. 75).

Second, Billings and Eastman (1998) addressed on-air promotion within the 1996 Olympics from a different point of view by analyzing the ways in which NBC promoted future Olympic events within the Olympics itself. They identified 303 promos in commercial pods and broke down promos into groups depending on whether the night was highly rated, moderately rated, or relatively low rated compared to the rest of the Olympic telecast. Results indicated that promos for highly rated nights focused more on women athletes (55%) than the promos for low-rated nights (34%). Thus, the researchers concluded that "nights with high ratings attracted both men and women viewers, whereas the lowest rated nights seemed to have an unbalanced gender appeal in favor of men" (Billings & Eastman, 1998, p. 82). Such findings lent credence to studies such as Eastman and Billings' (1999), which indicated that viewership for women is elastic, while viewership for men is static—meaning that men will watch sports no matter what, but women need more of a reason to tune in to the Olympics. Consequently, NBC chooses to air and promote more female-targeted sports (such as gymnastics or figure skating), opting not to air and promote more male-oriented sports (such as boxing or wrestling).

The next study pertinent to the area of promotion in televised sport was when Eastman and Billings (2000) reported an analysis of the 1998 Nagano Winter Olympics. Utilizing a database of 267 promos for prime-time programs aired during CBS' coverage of the Games, several positive findings were illuminated. In terms of change scores, 92% of all promoted programs either gained points or stayed flat, which was a far better result than the 1992 and 1996 Olympic studies showed. Additionally, regression analysis indicated that 9% of the impact on ratings was attributable to salience variables, including promotion frequency, carriage program rating, position, and clutter. This, when coupled with the 56% of variance attributed to inheritance (lead-in ratings), meant that nearly two thirds of all variance was accounted for in the study.

Finally, the most recently published study of sport promotion was conducted by Eastman and Billings (2004) and analyzed promo effectiveness for the 2000 Sydney Olympics telecast by NBC. The nightly telecasts created a new dilemma for this line of research as NBC opted to begin the telecast two hours before prime time and frequently continued to air Olympic events until midnight EST. Still, for consistency purposes, the investigators included only promotion within prime-time hours as these hours still garnered the largest audiences. In all, NBC aired 178 promos, significantly less than in Atlanta (215 promos) and Nagano (216 promos).

The analysis of the salience variables in the 2000 Olympics yielded four key findings. First, NBC chose to focus their promotion on a set number of programs. In fact, the top three programs represented nearly 30% of the database. Second, NBC implemented bunching techniques, with more promos airing in the final hour of prime-time coverage than in any other programming hour. Third—and in a similar vein—NBC utilized event bunching strategies, with 40% of the promos occurring in the first ten days of the telecast and 60% occurring in the final week. Fourth, NBC used shorter promo lengths (15 seconds). Given that the average promo length in the Atlanta telecast was 30 seconds, NBC actually spent less than half of the total clock-time on promotions in Sydney than it did in Atlanta—likely a function of NBC

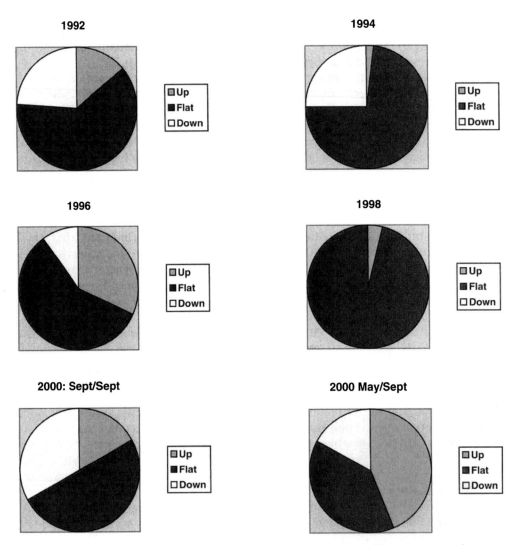

*Up/down/flat ratings determined by comparing two-week pre-Olympic ratings of program (or time slot for new programs) with two-week post-Olympic ratings.

FIG. 15.1.   Olympic promotion effectiveness (1992–2000)*.

being required to air "make-good" ads for companies advertising during the Games after the ratings came in lower than expected.

In regard to difference scores, using comparisons between September 1999 times-lot ratings and September 2000 program ratings, results indicated that twice as many programs experienced ratings decreases (33% of all promoted programs) as ratings increases (17% of all promoted programs). Such a stark difference to the 1996 and 1998 studies indicates that perhaps NBC's decisions to air significantly fewer and shorter promos backfired, as they did not opt to fully utilize the promotional platform that the Olympics tends to offer.

In sum, analyses of the effectiveness of prime-time promotion in sports events has largely been relegated to Olympic telecasts, with these analyses offering diverse results that often depend on external factors such as (a) whether the Games are held in the United States, (b) when on the programming calendar the Games is scheduled, and (c) whether results of events were already aired on news programs before NBC showed taped events at night. Factors such as the Internet (which can offer immediate results before taped events air) and the diminished ratings of network television in the advent of increased cable and satellite offerings could yield even more different results in future sports promotion studies. Figure 15.1 indicates the differing results that Olympic promotion studies have provided, ranging from meager effects (such as in 1994) to strong effects (such as in 1998). As shown in the figure, promotional effectiveness has varied widely, from having no programs with ratings decreases (as was the case in 1998; Eastman & Billings, 2000) to having one third of the programs experiencing ratings decreases (as was the case in the 2000 September to September comparison; Eastman & Billings, 2004). Such diverse findings indicate that external factors may be crucial to understanding the extent to which sports promotion is worth the investment many networks provide.

FUTURE DIRECTIONS FOR SPORT PROMOTION RESEARCH

Myriad advances in the study of sport promotion has lent to more sophisticated analyses over the past decade. Still, many future avenues for sport promotion research remain ideal for communication scholarship in the twenty-first century. First—and perhaps most notably—the venues for future research must be expanded. In terms of the televised sports that have been examined, almost all of the research has been relegated to the Olympic telecasts, which, while being the preeminent example of using a sportscast as a promotional vehicle, still do not incorporate the thousands of other sportscasts that utilize promotion on a daily basis. In terms of the promos themselves, all previous sport studies have examined promotion only for prime-time programming, leaving daytime and late-night promotion ripe for examination. Given that previous scholars have examined venues as diverse as soap opera promotion (Billings, 2001) and made-for-TV movies (Eastman, Schwartz, & Cai, 2002), addressing promotional impact in other venues seems a next logical step.

A second avenue for future research involves the examination of non-U.S. programming. Eastman (2003) examined such practices in South Africa, but even this study did not confine itself to the realm of sport. The importance of measuring salient variables in other countries would be invaluable, as different cultures may respond to promotion in markedly different ways. Such future studies could add depth and breadth to the work that has already been completed in North America.

Third, future sport research should implement findings in other promotion research (Eastman & Neal-Lunsford, 1993; Eastman, Neal-Lunsford, & Riggs, 1995; Eastman & Newton, 1995) regarding the growing problem of measuring promotion effectiveness with variables such as remote control use and grazing. Indeed, researchers are now finding that just because NBC may air several hundred promos for prime-time programs within the 2004 Athens Olympics does not mean even the avid Olympic watcher will view these commercials rather than opting to channel surf during commercial breaks.

REFERENCES

Abrahamson, A. (2001, November 25). NBC aiming to play to nation's mood; Olympics: Network sees coverage of Salt Lake Games as potential for "patriotic catharsis." *Los Angeles Times*, p. 1.

Ault, S. (2002, April 1). L.A.'s KNBC feathers nest with Olympic coverage. *Daily Variety*, p. 2.

Barron, D. (2004, Feb. 3). Houston Super Bowl draws record viewership; more than 140 million see at least some of CBS' coverage. *Houston Chronicle*, p. 5.

Billings, A. C. (2001). Promoting the daily occurrence: An analysis of television soap opera promotion. *Carolinas Communication Annual, 17,* 1–12.

Billings, A. C., & Eastman, S. T. (1998). Marketing the Olympics within the Olympics. *Ecquid Novi, 19*(2), 74–87.

Billings, A. C., & Eastman, S. T. (2002). Selective representation of gender, ethnicity, and nationalism in American television: Coverage of the 2000 Summer Olympics. *International Review for the Sociology of Sport, 37*(314), 351–370.

Billings, A. C., & Eastman, S. T. (2003). Framing identities: Gender, ethnic, and national parity in network announcing of the 2002 Winter Olympics. *Journal of Communication, 53*(4), 369–386.

Billings, A. C., Eastman, S. T., & Newton, G. D. (1998). Atlanta revisited: Prime-time promotion in the 1996 Summer Olympics. *Journal of Sport & Social Issues, 22*(1), 65–78.

Eastman, S. T. (2003). Programming television and radio in South Africa. *Ecquid Novi, 24*(1), 70–83.

Eastman, S. T., & Billings, A. C. (1999). Gender parity in the Olympics: Hyping Women athletes, favoring men athletes. *Journal of Sport and Social Issues, 23*(2), 140–170.

Eastman, S. T., & Billings, A. C. (2000). Promotion in and about sports programming. In S. T. Eastman (Ed.), *Research in media promotion* (pp. 203–230). Mahwah, NJ: Lawrence Erlbaum Associates.

Eastman, S. T., & Billings, A. C. (2004). Promotion's limited impact in the 2000 Sydney Olympics. *Television and New Media, 5*(1), 339–358.

Eastman, S. T., & Bolls, P. D. (2000). Structure and content in promotion research. In S. T. Eastman (Ed.), *Research in media promotion* (pp. 55–100). Mahwah, NJ: Lawrence Erlbaum Associates.

Eastman, S. T., Brown, R. S., & Kovatch, K. J. (1996). The Olympics that got real? Television's story of Sarajevo. *Journal of Sport & Social Issues, 24,* 366–391.

Eastman, S. T., & Meyer, T. P. (1989). Sports programming: Economics and scheduling. In L. A. Wenner (Ed.), *Media, sports, and society* (pp. 97–119). Newbury Park, CA: Sage.

Eastman, S. T., & Neal-Lunsford, J. (1993). The RCD's impact on programming and promotion. In J. Walker & R. Bellamy, Jr. (Eds.), *The remote control device in the new age of television* (pp. 189–209). Westport, CN: Praeger.

Eastman, S. T., Neal-Lunsford, J., & Riggs, K. E. (1995). Coping with grazing: Prime-time strategies for accelerated program transitions. *Journal of Broadcasting & Electronic Media, 39,* 92–108.

Eastman, S. T., & Newton, G. D. (1995). Delineating grazing: Observations of remote control use. *Journal of Communication, 45*(1), 77–95.

Eastman, S. T., & Newton, G. D. (1998). The impact of structural salience within on-air promotion. *Journal of Broadcasting & Electronic Media, 42,* 50–79.

Eastman, S. T., & Newton, G. D. (1999). Hitting promotion hard: A network response to channel surfing and new competition. *Journal of Applied Communication Research, 27*(1), 73–85.

Eastman, S. T., Newton, G. D., & Bolls, P. (2003). How promotional content changes ratings: The impact of appeals, humor, and presentation. *Journal of Applied Communication Research, 31*(3), 238–259.

Eastman, S. T., Newton, G. D., & Pack, L. (1996). Promoting prime-time programs in megasporting events. *Journal of Broadcasting & Electronic Media, 40,* 366–388.

Eastman, S. T., & Otteson, J. L. (1994). Promotion increases ratings, doesn't it? The impact of program promotion in the 1992 Olympics. *Journal of Broadcasting & Electronic Media, 38,* 307–322.

Eastman, S. T., Schwartz, N. C., & Cai, X. (2002). Children and promoted television movies: Unwanted and inescapable content. *Communication, 28*(1), 3–15.

Ennis, C. (2003, December 12). Fox celebrates 10-year anniversary of first NFL contract. *AP Newswire,* BC cycle.

Friedman, W. (2004, February 16). Tourney rebounds for CBS with solid sales. *Television Week,* p. 27.

Halone, K. K. (2003). *The structuration of sports broadcast commentary: Implicating the system and structure of mediated athletic performance.* Paper presented at the meeting of the Southern States Communication Association, Birmingham, AL.

James, M. (2003, October 28). World Series ratings up 8%, boosting Fox. *Los Angeles Times,* p. C3.

Lang, A. (1990). Involuntary attention and physiological arousal evoked by structural features and emotional content in TV commercials. *Communication Research, 17,* 275–299.

McAllister, M. P. (1998). College bowl sponsorship and the increased commercialization of amateur sports. *Critical Studies in Mass Communication, 15*(4), 357–381.

Moragas Spa, M., Rivenburgh, N. K., & Larson, J. F. (1995). *Television in the Olympics.* London: John Libby.

Petty, R. E., & Cacioppo, J. T. (1986). *Communication and persuasion: Central and peripheral routes to attitude change.* New York: Springer-Verlag.

Real, M. R. (1989). *Super media: A cultural studies approach.* Newbury Park, CA: Sage.

Real, M. R., & Mechikoff, R. A. (1992). Deep fan: Mythic identification, technology, and advertising in spectator sports. *Sociology of Sport Journal, 9,* 323–339.

Reinan, M. (2004, January 31). A 30-second Super Bowl spot costs $2.25 million, so the pressure is on to create a standout ad. *Minneapolis Star-Tribune,* p. 1D.

Reynolds, M. (2003, November 17). Cable sweeps up during week one. *Multichannel News,* p. 12.

Umstead, R. T. (2004, February 2). Cable nets January jump on broadcast. *Multichannel News,* p. 8.

Walker, J. R. (1993). Catchy, yes, but does it work? The impact of broadcast network promotion frequency and type on program success. *Journal of Broadcasting & Electronic Media, 47*(3), 615–634.

Walker, J. R., & Eastman, S. T. (2003). On-air promotion's effectiveness for programs of different genres, familiarity, and audience demographics. *Journal of Broadcasting & Electronic Media, 47,* 618–637.

Webster, J. G. (1985). Program audience duplication: A study of television inheritance effects. *Journal of Broadcasting & Electronic Media, 37,* 197–207.

Webster, J. G., & Phalen, P. F. (1997). *The mass audience: Rediscovering the dominant model.* Mahwah, NJ: Lawrence Erlbaum Associates.

Wenner, L. A. (1998). *MediaSport.* New York: Routledge.

16

60 Seconds to Air: Television Sports Production Basics and Research Review

Marc A. Krein
Sheree Martin
Oklahoma State University

As other chapters in this volume attest, the electronic media have relied on sports as a significant source of programming since the earliest days of broadcast radio. Sporting events were among the content chosen for the first public delivery of television signals. For example, as early as 1937, live coverage of tennis at Wimbledon was shown on the BBC, while sporting events, both real and staged, were included in early on-air tests of television in the United States (Berkman, 1988; Neal-Lunsford, 1992). As the technology improved, interest in and demand for mediated sports grew accordingly. During the late 1940s, increased sales of television sets were directly associated with television's live broadcast of specific sports events such as the 1947 World Series and the Army–Navy football game on NBC (Neal-Lunsford, 1992; Baran, 2004). In light of the limited production capabilities during the first two decades of television, boxing was a mainstay on television from 1946 through the mid-1960s (Neal-Lunsford, 1992). By the 1960s, rules of the game, once believed sacrosanct, were being changed to make the various sports more telegenic, while sporting events themselves were being conceived of and contrived specifically for television. This chapter begins with a brief summary of the rather limited body of published research that has considered the actual production techniques used in creating a sports telecast. The remainder of this chapter describes the elements of a modern, live television sports production.

SPORTS-RELATED TELEVISION PRODUCTION RESEARCH

There is relatively little published academic research that specifically focuses on the use of broadcast technology in sports production. Media history scholars typically describe technological changes that are reflected in the televised sports event. But these historical accounts rarely, if ever, attempt to empirically measure the effects of such technological evolution on the media product of interest here—the sports telecast. Most of the published research that does take into account the role of media technology does so in the context of the commodification and commercialization of sports (See, for example, Wenner, 1998; Jhally, 1989).

Real's (1975) analysis of the "one-sided and boring" (p. 32) Super Bowl VIII appears to be the earliest published academic study to incorporate consideration of production techniques as part of the overall study design. Real's approach, myth analysis, focused on the finished product (the telecast), but his discussion provides some insight into the production techniques being used at the time to "package" football for drama and entertainment (p. 41). According to Real,

> The 1974 telecast opened with a pregame half-hour show featuring Bart Starr's analysis of filmed strengths, weaknesses, and strategies of each team, and it concluded with a panel of 15 CBS sportcasters interviewing heroes of the day's game. In between, there were the striking multicolor visuals with rapid, dramatic score opening each section of the telecast, the grandiose adjectives and historical allusions by announcers, the endless reciting or superimposing on screen of statistics and records, the pre-game pageantry, the halftime extravaganzas and "Playbook," and, of course, the 52 advertisements. (p. 41)

One of the few published studies to concentrate solely on the production techniques used in televised sporting events is Williams' (1977) content analysis to determine the structural components and degree of mediation in football telecasts.[1] For example, Williams characterized the "live play-action . . . coverage throughout the telecasts" as "a kaleidoscopic, dynamic mode of presentation" (p. 136). Williams then provided support for this characterization through his careful and specific descriptions of production techniques including shot construction and selection, camera positioning, and the use of graphics and sound sources. Despite being extremely dated in terms of production capabilities and stylistic norms, Williams' study provides a useful framework and foundation for evaluating more modern live sports telecasts, especially college and professional American-style football productions. Williams' work also provides a basis for identifying specific changes in production style that may or may not be attributed to newer technology.

Gruneau (1989) conducted a case study of the Canadian Broadcast Corporation's on-location coverage of the 1986 Whistler World Cup downhill ski event. Gruneau's attendance at production meetings, access to production facilities, and interviews with the telecast director and members of the production crew, before and during the ski competition, enabled him to deliver a rare, detailed account of sports television production practices from the standpoint of a scholarly researcher. The coverage consisted of live-to-tape commentary of competition footage taped earlier in the day. The telecast itself gave the appearance that the commentary was occurring simultaneously with the actual ski races, rather than after the results were already known. The nature of this particular sports telecast makes Gruneau's analysis valuable because he was able to identify specific ways in which production

---

[1]Williams (1977) cited an earlier, similar study of soccer broadcasts published in 1975 by the British Film Institute.

values and techniques used in creating a sports telecast shape, or at least guide, the viewer's experience.[2]

Although most live sports telecasts don't present the technical challenges of covering sailboats on the open sea, Boshier (2004) delivered a nice description of the technology used in Television New Zealand's 2002 and 2003 coverage of two major sailing regattas, the Louis Vuitton and the America's Cup:

> These days' helicopters carry cameras capable of zooming in on a hand turning a winch.... There were numerous microphones on the boats and three layers of commentary. There are photo-boats such as *Northstar* or the $900,000 power cat *Into The Blue* on all parts of the course. Cameras on the bow and stern are worth $1.03 million each, can move through 360 degrees and have powerful zoom lenses. Attached to titanium tubes, they look like a giant eyeball. Dennis Harvey, TVNZ Head of Sports, called it "probably the most technically difficult of any sports coverage in the world... you don't have a defined field of play, it's shifting constantly and there's nothing connected to the camera." (Boshier, para. 9.3)

Since the early 1980s, a sizable body of academic research has addressed the relationship between media and sports—particularly that of television and sports—and the effect this relationship has on the audience/spectator, the sport itself, and on society in general. Much of this published research is the work of scholars within the cultural and critical perspectives. As Gruneau (1989) pointed out, much of this research has focused on the capitalist values inherent within the production system and how these values are promulgated and perpetuated in the content of televised sports. Gruneau also identified one of the main weaknesses of the textual analysis method utilized by these scholars—the lack of meaningful consideration of the actual production techniques and practices that are the foundation upon which a sports telecast is created. As a consequence of this missing link, doubts can be raised about the legitimacy of the meanings ascribed to texts when such studies have, as Gruneau put it, "all but ignored analysis of the actual technical and professional practices—the labor process—involved in producing sports for television" (p. 135). As a result, Gruneau continued, "assessments of relationships between television sports 'texts' and their 'contexts' of production have been speculative at best" (p. 135).

In a case study of Canada's The Sports Network (TSN), Sparks (1992) apparently considered the cable network's production techniques during data collection. However, other than a detailed breakdown of the quantitative difference in programming devoted to men's versus women's sports, Sparks presented no data or description of the network's production practices in support of the following statement: "Off-air sampling and live viewing of TSN's programming between 1988–1992 demonstrate that TSN's presentation and narrative standards have been conceived to give the network a distinctly 'high tech' and masculine image and appeal" (p. 7). The absence of any description or support for this interpretation does not mean Sparks'

---

[2]Professor Gruneau served as dissertation adviser for MacNeill's (1994) similar study of the CTV's 1988 Winter Olympic Ice Hockey competition. MacNeill's work encompassed an ethnographic study of "elements of production" that included, among other things, the "social-aesthetic use of broadcast technology, the conventional employment of sporting codes of commentary and visual codes of television mediation."

conclusions were not valid, but such an omission presents challenges for other researchers who seek to build upon prior studies.

Announcer commentary during televised sporting events is the focus of another body of research. Sports commentary research can be further categorized, with some studies emphasizing the effect of commentary on audience enjoyment, particularly with regard to perceptions of drama, conflict, competitiveness, and violence or hostility. Sullivan (1991); Bryant, Comisky, and Zillmann (1977); and Comisky, Bryant, and Zillmann (1977) are but three such examples. Other studies consider a variety of social and cultural ramifications associated with announcer commentary, including gender and racial stereotyping. Bruce (2004), Billings (2003), Vande Berg and Projansky (2003), Koivula (1999), and Tuggle (1997) are examples of the many studies that analyze commentary in the context of gender, race, and other cultural issues.

TELEVISION SPORTS PRODUCTION BASICS

Television sports production continues to evolve in both the look and transmission. TV sports production is expensive, but it delivers a highly desired target audience that regular programming cannot deliver. While the technology is constantly changing, the template for most productions has remained fairly consistent over the years: Hook the audience by building the drama of the event; set up the players; review the history of the rivalry; let 'em play; add features throughout the show; get the reactions of the outcome of the event and other controversies; and constantly promote other programming.

It would be impossible to explain in a few pages all the intricacies and variables involved in the live telecasting of a sporting event. Obviously, each is different in scale, venue, and technical requirements. What works for a college basketball game is far less complicated than a NASCAR race. Entire books have been written that detail the function of each piece of the technical puzzle for nearly each type of event. But there is a common thread that each event follows: obtaining rights, selecting a unit manager/technical manager, contracting a production truck, hiring a crew, setting up for transmission, securing sponsorship, and performing a postproduction assessment.

The balance of this chapter relays a likely scenario of the major elements involved in producing a nationally televised college event such as a football or basketball event.

The Fight for Rights

Obtaining the rights to produce and air an event is the programming management version of poker: The more money you have and larger the target audience you can deliver, the more likely you are to win the purse.

In the high stakes game of professional sports, multiyear rights contracts are determined years in advance. Obtaining rights to college events can be a little more complicated because in many cases different networks will buy the rights to the entire conferences. In the case of the NCAA tournaments, rights must be obtained through the NCAA or the network that bought the rights to the tournament (which may be sold by the network). Many networks will bid on the rights for entire conferences with the option to sell some of their rights of individual events. During the football season, the bidding may result in one network obtaining the rights to the "A" game in a specific conference, while another network or regional station may obtain rights to the "B" and "C" games, and other regional networks or area stations may obtain the rights to other remaining games (NCAA, 2004). The difficulty is that the best game may not be determined until a few days in advance, which makes scheduling technical and assigning the crew quite a challenge.

This is an admittedly brief glossing of the rights obtaining process. The important information here is that you must have obtained the official rights to an event before any other process may begin.

Who's Going to Coordinate All the Technical Stuff?

Once an event's rights have been confirmed and the network has scheduled a specific event to be aired, the next step is to hire a tech manager (also referred to as a unit manager or technical producer). The tech manager has an incredibly long to-do list and must be extremely organized to make sure some critical elements are not overlooked. Many of the networks have a template known as "The Book" that details all of the elements needed to produce a show, and the tech manager is the main person responsible for making sure everything is in place well in advance of the production truck's arrival. The tech manager's Book will include the following items.

- Event information: date(s), venue, teams/type of event, air times, "park & power" time with venue contacts,[3] and call times.
- Facility information (referring to the truck): truck owner, crewer, EIC[4] maintenance, driver, equipment available and requested for show (number of cameras, EVS[5]-VTRs, audio, graphics, switcher, DVE, other), and rented and/or owned equipment that will need to be installed (Super Slo-Mo, Clock & Score).
- Show contacts: producer, director, assistant director, tech manager, and talent.
- Parking: where the truck will park and where crew will be allowed to park.
- Power requirements.
- Uplink and transmission.
- Facility contacts: director of operations/facilities at the venue, sports information director, and catering.
- Vendor contacts (if using rented equipment).
- Camera placement and assignments: game, tight Iso (i.e., isolated camera on one person), handheld, slash, midcourt, supermo,[6] and jib (i.e., the camera attached to a portable boom system).
- Monitor assignments (PL[7]): determining where extra monitors inside the venue need to be located.

---

[3]"Park & power" refers to making sure that, once the truck arrives, a certified and venue-approved electrician is available to hook up the power cable to the truck through venue power supplies or a rented generator. Many venues have pre-cabled their facility for power, audio, and video, which they will charge the network a fee to utilize.

[4]The EIC (or engineer in charge) is the lead engineer responsible for all engineering and equipment setup in the truck.

[5]The Electronic Video System (EVS) is a computer-based digital video system that allows the operator to play back and record at the same time. EVS operators are referred to as "Elvis." Most of the video elements used during a show (features, opens, in-bumps, billboards, promos, in-game packages, roll-out, and replays) will come from Elvis.

[6]Supermo is a digital super slow-motion video replay device manufactured by EVS.

[7]Private line or production line. The channel(s) selected for communication to the various crew members.

10:00 am	Park & power
11:00 am	Crew call
11:30 am	Uplink on site to park & power
2:30 pm	Full FAX[8]
3:00 pm	Tape and camera meeting[9]
3:30 pm	Meal break (60 min)
4:45 pm	Transmission test w/ audio sync tape
5:10 pm	Live cut in w/ studio
5:20 pm	Record JIPS[10]
5:30 pm	Show talent tape and graphic elements; rehearse
6:00 pm	Live to air
9:00 pm	Strike[11] and melt[12]

FIG. 16.1.   Typical television production schedule for a 6:00 pm sporting event.

- Communication assignments: determining which PL channel each crew member is assigned to monitor and use, scheduling to have phone lines run to the truck for communication to master control, and establishing a backup audio feed over the phone line in the event of a transmission problem.
- Lighting: what lighting is necessary to light the talent.
- Tape: what each tape machine will be called[13] and which camera(s) will be going into specified video recording devices.
- Audio requirements: number of talent announce headset mics, number of stick mics, number of shot gun mics, announce table PL headset needed (for A2, stage manager, talent stat person), scoring table PL headsets needed (for official statistician, time-out coordinator), number of RF stick mics (roving reporter), IFB[14] assignments, mix-minus (i.e., the ability for the talent to communicate with the talent back in the main studio), and RF info (i.e., the exact frequency on which the wireless microphones are transmitting).
- Schedule of operations: the times when things are supposed to happen. Figure 16.1 details a typical schedule for a 6:00 pm event.

---

[8]FAX is the term used to make sure all audio and video units are working correctly.

[9]The director explains the story line of today's event; he/she will go over what is expected from each position and possibly human interest shots to look for.

[10]Joined in Progress. The main talent will record a series of JIPS for games that will be replayed at another time slot but edited for time constraints. "You're watching ... Due to time constraints we will move to further action in the third quarter ... ").

[11]Strike means to tear down all equipment, roll up cables, and pack the truck.

[12]Melt means to get all the best highlights and color shots from each tape machine to a single tape that the producer will leave behind for future use.

[13]Traditionally the tape machines are referred to as A, B, X, Y, and Green. EVS is typically Red and Blue. Super Slo-mo is typically Mo and L. There is not a standard for the naming of playback machines, but these seem to be the most traditional name assignments.

[14]Internal foldback. This allows the producer to talk directly into the headset or earpiece of the on-air talent.

- Credential request and crew list: provides the sports information director (SID) with crew names (if required in advance). Also provides the tech manager with specific names, the crew function, and their contact information.
- Network traffic work order: provides the uplink truck and network master control with specific information relative to satellite transmission coordinates and the phone numbers of all those who need to be in the transmission loop.
- Remote emergency escape locations: rarely used but nice to know about. Outside crewmembers can be the farthest away from an escape location when a severe storm hits.
- Hotel information.
- Directions: from the airport to the hotel and from the hotel to the venue.
- Rental information: additional equipment required that is not available in the truck, such as a gator utility vehicle, aerial, or whatever the needs are; contact information for vendors and shippers are also typically included.

Contracting a Truck

Depending on the budget and technical needs of an MU (i.e., Mobile Unit), there are trucks available all over the world. The costs vary depending on the amount of equipment the client plans to use, how much travel is planned for the truck, the number of additional engineering personnel, and length of use. Production trucks can range from a single wide (typically $10,000 to $20,000 per day) to an expando (typically 30 to 40% more). HDTV trucks will be double to nearly triple that amount. These figures assume six cameras, EVS, four tape machines, graphics, and most of the other equipment required to produce a six-camera event with replay and playback. Additional equipment will obviously increase the charges, typically $1,000 for each add-on of a camera or video replay/recording device.

Hiring the Crew

There can be many levels of obtaining and assigning crew for a specific event (Owens, 2003). At the network level, a network-employed crewing team will assign a staff or subcontract a producer, a director, a tech manager, and the announce talent. Some of the more prominent positions may also be subcontracted through the network crewer (also known as the core crew and including such positions as the technical director, A1, graphics, and EVS ops).[15] Some crews are assembled early in the year to be available for the entire season and will work together each week.

For much of the crew, a regional crewer will be contracted to provide camera operators, A2s,[16] tape operators, utilities, runners, parab operators, stats, stage managers, bug operators, 1st & 10 coordinators,[17] and possibly uplink trucks. By contracting with a local crew, the networks save thousands of dollars in airline tickets, travel day pay, hotel costs, mileage, and per diem. Local crews are often familiar with the venue facilities and home team, which are both of great value to

---

[15]The A1 is the lead audio person, and the EVS operator is the lead videotape person.

[16]A2s are the secondary audio personnel.

[17]The 1st & 10 is the superimposed line showing where the first down should be in football games.

the technical setup and aesthetics of the show. Regional crewers are paid either a prenegotiated fee for each position they fill or a flat rate for filling all the requested positions.

Crewers are a small club and many of them know each other nationwide. However, they are also in competition with each other to fill positions and get paid for filling those positions. The reality of last-minute scheduling of an event will often mean that there is an intense scramble to fill positions. In these situations, crewers will rely on their private network of freelancers. However, often these freelancers may already be booked for another event. In desperation, crewers will depend on other crewers for possible available freelancers. Many crewers, however, are reluctant to give out information about potential freelancers because they receive no financial gain from having someone else hire their usual freelancer, and, more importantly, the needy crewer will have a new freelancer on his or her list to contact for future events. Crewers are very protective of their freelancers. The positions and responsibilities of crewed freelancers are outlined in Fig. 16.2.

Each freelancer either negotiates a day rate or, more often, is told what the day rate will be. A day rate is based on a 10-hour workday from the beginning of crew call until the truck is packed up and ready to go. Overtime is typically based on time-and-a-half of the hourly amount of the day rate. Should a crewmember not be allowed a meal break, he/she will receive an additional overtime hour added to his/her check. If a freelancer will drive to an event from more than 50 miles, the he/she typically receives additional pay for mileage and a food per diem.[18]

Fire Up the Bird

The majority of events are transmitted via satellite from an uplink truck back to the master control studio, where the signal is sent back up to another satellite and received for rebroadcast by local stations, cable head-ends, and other dish network operators. The time lag in this process can be anywhere from one to ten seconds. This is why it is difficult to listen to a radio station call of the event and watch the television feed at the same time.[19]

After "park & power," the uplink truck runs program audio and video lines from the production truck back to the uplink truck. Once that signal is secured, the uplink operator will dial in the coordinates of the satellite (often referred to as *The Bird*) that has been contracted for use in this show. The satellite contract typically allows for satellite usage one hour before the event. If the event is basketball, typically only three more hours of satellite time are contracted (allowing for overtime and postgame programming). Most other events will require an extra hour. When events extend far longer than expected or if an event is delayed, there must be a quick renegotiation of the contract to allow the network to remain on the air.

Securing Sponsorship

Yes, somebody must pay the bills. Just about everything that can be sold during an event will be sold: shot clock, replays, plays of the game, scoreboard, the bug,

---

[18]Mileage and per diem rates vary from each network and crewer. Both are typically higher than what a state government rate would be.

[19]Most radio is sent via phone lines and has a much quicker rebroadcast cycle.

Position	Responsibilities
Camera operators	build the cameras, run the cables, and run cameras during event
Video shader	sets up CCUs (camera control units) so that all cameras are correctly color balanced with each other, shades the iris during the event so that cameras are not too dark or too bright, and is the lead person for the proper setup and operation of all cameras used during the telecast
Technical director	sets up switcher and switches the event
Assistant director	keeps track of spots break and counts down the truck as to when the crew is back on the air, assists with traffic of elements to be replayed during the game
Graphics[20]	set up all graphics, call up graphics, and update and retrieve game graphics current during event
A1	sets up audio board, patches all audio and communications, and runs the board during the event
A2	sets up booth audio and all other audio/mics inside the venue
Tape	sets up tape decks, and performs editing & playback, replay, and melt
EVS	works with producer to build elements that will be used during the event such as playback, replays, in-game packages, and rollouts
Bug operator[21]	sets up equipment and operates it during the event
Stage manager	assists producer by working with talent to hand them promos and sponsorship reads
Time-out coordinator (TOC)	notifies officials when the show is back live and they may resume play
Utility	works with camera ops to run cable, shadows handheld cams to keep cables from interfering with game play, and strikes
Runner	assists producer, tech manager, and other truck personnel with running errands

FIG. 16.2. Freelance position and responsibilities for broadcast TV sports productions.

readers during the game, and whatever else the sales division decides is sponsorable (for more on sponsorship, see Kinney, chap. 18, this volume).

Spot advertising breaks are different for each event, but they are predetermined and must be adhered to by the producer. Most shows have the spots played back from master control, but some productions will have a break-reel that must be played from the truck tape room. A certain amount of spot time is allocated to pregame, in-game, overtime/sudden death, and postgame events. A fairly standard template for a basketball game would include 22 minutes of planned spot advertising at the following positions: pregame (two breaks at 2 minutes each); the first half

---

[20]Often referred to as the Infinit! or the Duet (both graphic systems are manufactured by Chyron) and the Deko (TilteDEKO is manufactured by Pinnacle).

[21]Also know as the FOX Box and Clock & Score, the bug is typically the score and clock information that is constantly updated during the event.

(1 minute and 30 second breaks at under-16:00 remaining, under-12:00 remaining, under-8:00 remaining, and under-4:00 remaining marks); halftime (three breaks at 2 minutes each); and the second half (1 minute and 30 second breaks at the same four time intervals as the first half).

Should an event go beyond the regular playing time, bonus breaks are usually available but not sold in advance. Spot rates are determined by the potential size of the target audience. At each event the time-out coordinator (located within eyesight of the officials/umpires) relays break-related information from the producer as to when a commercial time-out is to be taken and to hold up play until the production is back on the air.

How Did the Production Go?

Early in the week (typically Monday morning), the major parties involved in the production meet via a conference call to assess the production. The conversations range from technical miscues and wrong graphics to new items implemented into the production that did not work and petty personnel conflicts. One of the main points of discussion during the conference call will center on consistency of telecasts when it comes to use of effects, graphics, in-bumps/out-bumps, promos, talent, and animation. After discussion of the prior week, the meeting will focus on the upcoming week.

THE FUTURE OF BROADCASTING SPORTS

As equipment evolves, so will the look of televised sporting events. Prior to each season, the networks develop their look for the season based on style and technology. While player introductions and promotions have been a part of sports telecasts from the beginning, the way they are delivered is constantly evolving.

The main technological advancement taking place is the transition to high-definition television (or HDTV), which has a video resolution of 720 or 1080 lines compared to the 525 lines in the United States (and 625 lines in Europe) currently viewed. HD broadcasts and reception on an HD set make the viewer feel as if he or she were at the event. Better still for advertisers, this means that the sponsor logos are clearer and larger.

Superimposing certain sponsors' logos and other game-related details (e.g., 1st & 10 line in football, country flags of competitors in racing lanes) will become more prominent and clever. The technology will become so subtle that viewers will not be able to decipher the difference between actual banners at the event and one generated by the production crew computers that has been carefully embedded into the program. This technology will also likely create controversy between venues (who promote and sell to sponsors the opportunity to get their messages on the air via cameras) and the networks (who obviously are selling to additional sponsors). Venues are already claiming that they own the rights to the pictures that come out of the event, while the networks feel that since they have paid for the rights to the event they may be allowed to sell sponsorships at their discretion.

Sports packages via cable, dish networks, and the Internet also promise to become more fan-friendly. The prices for receiving events are likely to continue to rise, but the fan will have more choices and be able to buy more individual events (rather than the current model of buying entire packages). That is, the high-tech sporting business will likely follow the strategy employed by the recording industry to combat the illegal downloading of MP3s: If consumers do not want to pay for an entire package, then they will create a way to sell them just the one item they prefer. With bandwidth technology constantly improving, consumers will likely increase their viewing of events over the Internet. Furthermore, networks will continue to move toward convergence in their own telecasts, implementing various ways that the fan can interact with the action.

However, as the technology continues to change the way sporting events are presented, many argue that one thing will never change: Rivalries sell television. The reality soap opera surrounding a sporting event is the "sell," not the production. As the traditional target audiences for sporting telecasts continue to evolve, expect more features, packages, drama, and, of course, special effects. Televised sporting events are a major capital generator and are targeted toward a highly desired audience. Expect to see more sports on television.

ACKNOWLEDGMENTS

The authors acknowledge and thank the following people for their assistance in the writing of this chapter: Tim Cushing, Manager, Operations/Productions, Oklahoma State University; Michael H. Moore, Executive Coordinating Producer, ESPN Regional Television; and Paula Boyce, Crewing Coordinator, ESPN Regional Television.

REFERENCES

Baran, S. J. (2004). *Sports and television.* The Museum of Broadcast Communications. Retrieved on April 21, 2004, from http://www.museum.tv/archives/etv/S/htmlS/sportsandte/sportsandte.htm

Berkman, D. (1988). Long before Arledge . . . sports & tv: The earliest years: 1937–1947—as seen by the contemporary press. *Journal of Popular Culture, 22*(2), 49–62.

Billings, A. C. (2003). Dueling genders: Announcer bias in the 1999 U.S. Open tennis tournament. In R. S. Brown & D. J. O'Rourke, III (Eds.), *Case studies in sport communication* (pp. 51–62). Westport, CT: Praeger Publishers.

Boshier, R. (2004). Using globalization technology for localization: How Schnack-Net reconstructed the America's Cup. *Sociology of Sport Online, 6*(2). Retrieved February 24, 2005, from http://physed. otago.ac.nz.argo.library.okstate.edu/sosol/v6i2_2.html

Bruce, T. (2004, November). Marking the boundaries of the 'normal' in televised sports: The play-by-play of race. *Media, Culture & Society, 26*(6), 861–875.

Bryant, J., Brown, D., Comisky, P. W., & Zillmann, D. (1982). Sports and spectators: Commentary and appreciation. *Journal of Communication, 32*(1), 2109–2120.

Bryant, J., Comisky, P., & Zillmann, D. (1977). Drama in sports commentary. *Journal of Communication, 27*(3), 140–149.

Bryant, J., & Raney, A. A. (2000). Sports on the screen. In D. Zillmann & P. Vorderer (Eds.), *Media entertainment: The psychology of its appeal.* (pp. 153–174). Mahwah, NJ: Lawrence Erlbaum Associates.

Comisky, P., Bryant, J., & Zillmann, D. (1977). Commentary as a substitute for action. *Journal of Communication, 27*(3), 150–153.

Gruneau, R. (1989). Making spectacle: A case study in television sports production. In L. A. Wenner (Ed.), *Media, sports, & society* (pp. 134–154). Newbury Park, CA: Sage.

Jhally, S. (1989). Cultural studies and the sports/media complex. In L. A. Wenner (Ed.), *Media, sports, & society* (pp. 70–93). Newbury Park, CA: Sage.

Koivula, N. (1999). Gender stereotyping in televised media sport coverage. *Sex Roles, 41*(7/8), 589–604.

MacNeill, M. E. (1994). Olympic power plays: A social analysis of CTV's production of the 1988 Winter Olympic ice hockey tournament. *Dissertation Abstracts International, 56*(11), 4192A. Retrieved

March 28, 2005, from http://proquest.umi.com.argo.library.okstate.edu/pqdweb?did=741436371&Fmt=2&clientid=4653&RQT=309&Vname=PQD

NCAA. (2003–2004). *NCAA broadcast manual championship guidelines*. Retrieved May 12, 2004, from http://www1.ncaa.org/eprise/main/Public/mlp/broadcast_services/broadcast_media_index.html

Neal-Lunsford, J. (1992). Sport in the land of television: The use of sport in network prime-time schedules in 1946–50. *Journal of Sport History, 19*(1), 56–76. Retrieved December 15, 2004, from http://www.aafla.org/SportsLibrary/JSH/JSH1992/JSH1901/jsh1901d.pdf

Owens, J. (2003). *Television sports production*. Salt Lake City: International Sports Broadcasting.

Real, M. R. (1975). Super Bowl: Mythic spectacle. *Journal of Communication, 25*(1), 31–43.

Sparks, R. (1992). "Delivering the male": Sports, Canadian television, and the making of TSN. *Canadian Journal of Communications, 17*(3). Retrieved December 15, 2004, from http://www.cjc-online.ca/viewarticle.php?id=101&layout=html

Sullivan, D. B. (1991). Commentary and viewer perception of player hostility: Adding punch to televised sports. *Journal of Broadcasting & Electronic Media, 35*(4), 487–504.

Tuggle, C. A. (1997). Differences in television sports reporting of men's and women's athletics: ESPN *SportsCenter* and CNN *Sports Tonight*. *Journal of Broadcasting & Electronic Media, 41*(1), 14–24.

Vande Berg, L. R., & Projansky, S. (2003). Hoop games: A narrative analysis of television coverage of women's and men's professional basketball. In R. S. Brown & D. J. O'Rourke, III (Eds.) *Case studies in sport communication* (pp. 27–49). Westport, CT: Praeger Publishers.

Wenner, L. A. (1998). *MediaSport*. London: Routledge.

Williams, B. R. (1977). The structure of televised football. *Journal of Communication, 27*(3), 133–139.

17

Sports Economics and the Media

Michael Mondello
The Florida State University

As the sports industry continues to grow in terms of participants, spectators, and overall industry size, the economics associated with sport media coverage have escalated accordingly. As networks continue to encounter technological changes in an effort to maintain financial viability, the role of televised sporting events will undoubtedly be a major factor. Soaring rights fees paid for major sporting events and advertising broadcast revenues are two examples of the economic influences of television on sport–media relationships. In fact, the most expensive sports rights today have reached levels that seemed unimaginable only a few years ago. For example, the rights fees for the 1948 Summer Olympics in London were sold for $1,500, whereas the 2000 Sydney Olympic Games commanded $1.3 billion (Solberg, 2002).

Theoretically, if media firms with increasing demands are to flourish among their competition, economic concepts must be strategically integrated to operate a financially solvent operation. In his seminal work on economics, Samuelson (1976) defined economics as "The study of how people and society end up choosing, with or without the use of money, to employ scarce productive resources that could have alternative uses, to produce various commodities and distribute them for consumption, now or in the future, among various persons and groups in society" (p. 3). Consequently, economics is primarily concerned with *what* is produced, the technology and organization of *how* it is produced, and for *whom* it is produced (Owers, Carveth, & Alexander, 2004).

Historically, networks appear to disburse substantial broadcast fees to televise sporting events and moreover tolerate significant financial losses because they view sport as a means of validating their position within the industry (Cuneen & Branch, 2003). This raises the question of why television networks would financially guarantee large sums of money to broadcast various sporting events if the end result is not financially sensible. Industry analysts hypothesize that money and prestige account for a large percentage of these decisions. For example, Fox gained instant credibility as a major player in the network industry after obtaining the rights for National Football League (NFL) games in 1993 for $100 million. Prior to this landmark deal, Fox historically struggled to obtain a competitive viewing audience compared to the established original networks including ABC, CBS, and NBC (Nichols, Moynahan, Hall, & Taylor, 2002).

The evolution of the television network combined with the growth of the cable industry altered the economic power structure. By the late 1980s, the Big Three networks were consistently losing audiences to cable services and the new Fox network. Sport programming provided one of the better examples of this change in demographics as cable subscribers were categorized as a more efficient match demographically for advertisers. Moreover, the cable industry's dual revenue stream of advertising and subscriber fees gave cable companies the opportunity to develop services concentrating on sports programming (Bellamy, 2002).

Television coverage of high profile sport possesses a rare capacity for attracting high concentrations of the 18- to 34-year-old male consumers representing the prized demographic viewership to corporate advertisers. Sales of broadcast rights helped alleviate other financial concerns exacerbated by declining gate receipts and escalating player costs impacting professional sport organizations. Similarly, rights fees represented a guaranteed revenue stream that was to a certain extent isolated from changes in fan preferences, economic downturns, and corporate sponsorship decisions. Furthermore, once television contracts are signed, future revenue streams are independent of poor weather, injuries to key players, and changes in ticket demand preferences significantly impacting on-site revenue streams. Finally, television has the ability to include literally billions of global viewers (Coakley, 2004).

Media buyers assert that sports programming benefits from a loyal, core audience creating ratings more predictable than other types of programming (Grossman, 2004). Included in Table 17.1 are the sports advertising revenues generated by programming type. Generally, sports programming conforms to the economic tenets of supply and demand. Specifically, if there is excess demand for available time, then costs will increase. Comparatively, if inventory increases, then prices fall proportionately (Grossman, 2004). The dollar amount of advertising paid by the various sports networks in 2003 is included in Table 17.2.

While much of the media focus includes professional sports, the economic growth in collegiate television contracts has increased substantially as well. For example, when the National Collegiate Athletic Association (NCAA) renewed an eleven-year basketball television contract with CBS for 6.2 billion in 1999, this was the largest television deal in amateur sports (Cuneen & Branch, 2003). Following this landmark agreement, the NFL signed a $17.6 billion television deal in 1998 with multiple networks including ABC, CBS, ESPN, and Fox (Solberg, 2002).

Major professional sport leagues and a growing number of college athletic programs have become reliant on the revenue streams from networks, cable services, and local stations. Because audiences are bought and sold, they must also be measured. Fundamentally, the commercial broadcasting system links audience size and revenue, as networks attempt to secure programming appealing to larger, more valuable audiences. The relationship between a sport organization and a television station can survive and furthermore prosper only if both parties are satisfied they are receiving a fair return in the form of profits or in long-term gains such as

TABLE 17.1
Sports Advertising Revenue by Programming Type

Program Type	2003 Ad Revenue ($)	2002 Ad Revenue ($)	Percent Change	2003 Networks
Professional football[a]	2,000,487,690	1,881,121,210	6.3	ABC, CBS, ESPN, ESPN2, ESPN Classic, Fox, NBC
Professional basketball[a]	579,405,080	769,352,460	−24.7	ABC, ESPN, ESPN2, ESPN Classic, Oxygen, TBS, TNT
Golf	578,834,990	525,678,000	10.1	ABC, CBS, CNBC, ESPN, ESPN2, ESPN Classic, Golf Channel, NBC, Nickelodeon, Outdoor Life Network, TNT, USA
College basketball[a]	521,737,330	497,998,340	4.8	ABC, CBS, ESPN, ESPN2, ESPN Classic
Auto racing	472,624,370	441,813,330	7.0	ABC, CBS, ESPN, ESPN2, ESPN Classic, Fox, FX, NBC, Outdoor Life Network, Speed Channel, Spike TV, TNT, Travel Channel
College football[a]	449,534,380	423,857,390	6.1	ABC, BET, CBS, ESPN, ESPN2, ESPN Classic, Fox, NBC, TBS
Sportscast	444,863,300	355,798,850	25.0	CBS, ESPN, ESPN2, ESPN Classic, Speed Channel
Professional baseball[a]	438,522,490	409,543,890	7.1	ESPN, ESPN2, ESPN Classic, Fox, FX, TBS
General sports show	361,562,110	302,381,580	19.6	BET, Bravo, CNBC, Comedy Central, Discovery Channel, ESPN, ESPN2, ESPN Classic, FX, Galavision, Golf Channel, Learning Channel, MTV, Outdoor Life Network, Speed Channel, Spike TV, TNT, Travel Channel
Tennis	156,073,540	150,792,790	3.5	ABC, CBS, ESPN, ESPN2, ESPN Classic, NBC, Oxygen, USA
Hockey	127,116,210	99,831,290	27.3	ABC, ESPN, ESPN2, ESPN Classic
Sports magazine	60,916,660	53,369,930	14.1	ABC, CBS, CNBC, ESPN, ESPN2, ESPN Classic, Fox, Golf Channel, MTV, NBC, Outdoor Life Network, Speed Channel, Spike TV, TNT
Horse racing	26,295,810	22,247,310	18.2	CBS, CNBC, ESPN, ESPN2, ESPN Classic, NBC, Outdoor Life Network
Sports entertainment	24,361,330	32,749,650	−25.6	ABC, CBS, ESPN, ESPN2, ESPN Classic, Fox, FX, Galavision, Golf Channel, NBC, Outdoor Life Network, Speed Channel, Spike TV
Soccer	21,533,150	44,283,590	−51.4	ABC, ESPN, ESPN2, ESPN Classic, Galavision, Pax
Rodeo show	11,368,350	5,447,080	108.7	CBS, ESPN, ESPN2, NBC, Outdoor Life Network

(Continued)

TABLE 17.1
(*continued*)

Program Type	2003 Ad Revenue ($)	2002 Ad Revenue ($)	Percent Change	2003 Networks
Nonprofessional baseball[a]	10,435,600	9,673,350	7.9	ABC, ESPN, ESPN2, ESPN Classic, Fox
Nonprofessional basketball[a]	7,110,180	6,099,310	16.6	ABC, ESPN, ESPN2, ESPN Classic
Nonprofessional football	6,603,240	5,990,530	10.2	ESPN, ESPN2, ESPN Classic
Boxing	5,308,720	5,899,020	−10.0	ESPN, ESPN2, ESPN Classic, Galavision, NBC
Bowling	4,722,010	1,839,450	156.7	ESPN, ESPN2
Track and field	3,282,040	969,800	238.4	ABC, CBS, ESPN, ESPN2, NBC
College baseball	1,758,430	1,123,800	56.5	ESPN, ESPN2
Children's sports	117,200	378,200	−69.0	CBS

Note: From Street & Smith's Sports Business Journal. TNS Media Intelligence/CMR.
[a]Includes pregame and/or postgame programming.

promotion, competitive advantage, or improved public image (Ashwell & Hums, 2004).

Although sport organizations are constantly examining different methods to increase their revenues, sometimes a decision is made to leave money on the negotiating table to ensure greater exposure. For example, when the NCAA signed their original broadcast deal with CBS, they mandated that CBS televise a number of games from the women's basketball tournament as well as other low profile sports (Ashwell & Hums, 2004).

Theoretically, with its high degree of fixed costs and relatively low degree of variable costs, television broadcasting includes several unique financial advantages. For example, although the initial production and transmission of television programs require considerable capital outlay, businesses affording the entrance costs have an opportunity to generate significant revenue. Moreover, because the cost of a television program is unaffected by the number of viewers watching, the marginal cost of transmitting a program to one more additional viewer within any broadcasting market is literally zero (Solberg, 2002).

Sports are unique forms of entertainment, requiring the media to provide a combination of coverage and news. People can attend plays and concerts and furthermore engage in many leisure activities without requiring regular media coverage to enhance enjoyment. However, media coverage is extremely important with sports and creates a mechanism for fans to discuss upcoming games, review others, and critique the on-the-field decisions made by players and coaches. Collectively, the media represent important vehicles for these discussions (Coakley, 2004).

In the 1950s, televised Major League Baseball (MLB) games were considered instrumental in reducing attendance at both MLB and minor league events, and similar sentiments were voiced in other sports. For example, in an effort to increase attendance, the NCAA limited the number of televised broadcasts for college football games (Downward & Dawson, 2000).

TABLE 17.2
Dialing in Dollars: 2003 Advertising Revenue

Networks[a]	Sports Revenue ($)	% Change From 2002	Non-Sports Revenue ($)	% Change From 2002	Total Ad Revenue 2003 ($)	% of Ad Revenue From Sports Programming
CBS	1,435,634,000	8.7	4,392,038,300	7.5	5,827,672,300	24.6
ABC	1,330,153,000	49.2	3,797,174,600	5.6	5,127,327,600	25.9
Fox	1,176,177,800	−9.0	1,824,795,600	9.5	3,000,973,400	39.2
ESPN	1,163,533,880	26.4	NA[b]	NA	1,163,533,880	100.0
NBC	472,256,200	−73.9	5,103,742,400	11.0	5,575,998,600	8.5
TNT	221,566,320	43.6	508,502,740	7.0	730,069,060	30.3
ESPN2	219,222,140	34.5	NA	NA	219,222,140	100.0
The Golf Channel	88,371,360	30.7	NA	NA	88,371,360	100.0
Speed Channel	62,938,780	64.0	NA	NA	62,938,780	100.0
USA	44,290,150	112.2	522,739,750	29.3	567,029,900	7.8
FX	43,511,230	20.5	230,748,430	21.8	274,259,660	15.9
TBS	34,382,140	−36.2	718,502,600	17.1	752,884,740	4.6
Outdoor Life Network	34,121,990	75.5	16,275,860	74.8	50,397,850	67.7
ESPN Classic	19,823,430	27.8	NA	NA	19,823,430	100.0
Galavision	19,566,040	145.2	60,927,180	148.7	80,493,220	24.3
Spike TV	14,077,470	−30.2	275,754,710	14.3	289,832,180	4.9
MTV	7,521,030	178.3	828,000,120	12.7	835,521,150	0.9
CNBC	6,708,400	−70.4	416,216,420	−14.2	422,924,820	1.6
BET	4,742,350	141.6	257,008,780	46.2	261,751,130	1.8
Discovery Channel	4,235,720	77.6	408,583,550	4.5	412,819,270	1.0
Pax	1,206,600	−67.5	161,006,900	−26.9	162,213,500	0.7
TLC	1,146,890	29.7	347,932,470	19.1	349,079,360	0.3
Travel Channel	825,220	NA	73,768,500	11.4	74,593,720	1.1
Oxygen	729,310	106.7	64,985,230	47.2	65,714,540	1.1
Comedy Central	110,070	−88.1	388,735,830	15.5	388,845,900	0.0
Nickelodeon	29,940	−74.8	844,059,080	12.9	844,089,020	0.0
Bravo	2,010	NA	91,284,690	28.7	91,286,700	0.0

Note: From Street & Smith's SportsBusiness Journal. TNS Media Intelligence/CMR.
[a]Networks listed by dollar amount of advertising on sports-related programming.
[b]NA: Not applicable.

Television contributed to the nationalization of sports by making the prosperity of sports dependent on the creation of a broad-based national constituency (Lee & Chun, 2002). For example, when NBC first televised live coverage of the World Series in 1949, fewer than 12% of U.S. households possessed television sets. In addition, networks generated most of their revenues from comedies, westerns, and popular dramas. Consequently, because sports were not considered a major revenue producer for television networks, they did not consider sports programming critical to their overall success. However, this would eventually change in the 1960s when ABC invested significant financial resources in an attempt to provide their network with greater visibility, establish additional local affiliates, and improve audience ratings for all shows (Lee & Chun, 2002).

With so many viewing options now available, sports broadcast networks have been significantly impacted by fragmentation. Specifically, with multiple

TABLE 17.3
Profit/Losses of Select TV Network Contracts

Year	2001–02	2002–03	2003–04
NFL	(378)[a]	(274)	(270)
NHL	(70)	(74)	(77)
MLB	(325)	(346)	(370)
NBA	(282)	(250)	(246)
NASCAR	(158)	(163)	(106)
Olympics	78	0	10
College football	24	31	43
College basketball	7	(54)	(55)
Total	(1,103)	(1,129)	(1,070)

Note: From "Teams Face Low-Scaring TV Deals," by J. M. Higgins, 2003, *Broadcasting & Cable, 31.* Retrieved October 22, 2003, from http://www.broadcastingcable.com/atrticle/CA314858.html?display=Special+Report.
[a]($Million).

programming options besides the over-the-air choices, viewers are in a position to favor one network program over another. Moreover, some networks must rely on evenly matched championship series lasting the entire scheduled duration just to have an opportunity to turn a profit (Battin, 2003). According to estimates, financial losses on sports broadcasting contracts from 2001 to 2006 could exceed $6 billion (Higgins, 2003). This is illustrated in Table 17.3.

Another challenge facing over-the-air sports broadcasting is the continual threat of pay TV establishing a larger market share. Historically, sporting events have served as catalysts to unite nations around their televisions. For example, one in three Australians watched the closing ceremonies of the 2000 Olympics; nearly 40% of France watched their team triumph in the 1998 World Cup; over 11 million people in the United Kingdom watched Tim Henman in the 2003 Wimbledon finals; and 130 million Americans annually watch the Super Bowl (Field, 2003).

Despite this competition between free and pay networks, the Disney Corporation has successfully utilized both ABC and ESPN to cover the National Basketball Association (NBA). Under this agreement, ABC televises up to 27 regular and post-season season games while ESPN carries 99 games. This flexibility allows ABC to access games needed for Sunday viewings while maintaining a more flexible schedule for ESPN. Collectively, the Disney corporation committed more than $13 million in various broadcast rights to major sporting events for their two networks (Field, 2003).

One of the most important economic characteristics of audiovisual media products is their strong public-good element. Specifically, a public good is defined as a good or service where one's consumption does not reduce the amount of the good or service available for consumption by others (Gaustad, 2000). For televised sport, the value to the viewer is particularly dependent upon factors such as the quality of players, outcome uncertainty, and the quality of the coverage. For example, some viewers will watch a game regardless of score but others will lose interest once the game's outcome is secure.

One of the more recent trends concerning broadcast rights involves the situation where a news organization purchases a sport franchise. In these scenarios, the media providers believe it is more profitable to own the team rather than purchase residual broadcast rights. However, Fort (2003) identified several mitigating concerns with media-provider ownership. Media providers could potentially start bidding up the price of sports teams if teams are worth more to media-providers than to individual owners. Consequently, if this trend continues, media-provider ownership could lead to two problems. First, if teams are indeed more valuable as a division of media-providers, then revenues will be higher for those teams, thus exacerbating the revenue disparity between teams. This could potentially lead to competitive balance issues and decreasing fan interest. Second, if the move of media-provider ownership is the front end of a trend, current owners would face an interesting dichotomy. For example, while franchise values will increase and franchise owners will become wealthier, they could have an abbreviated career in the sports business because, to actually accrue this additional wealth, media owners would have to sell their respective teams.

An ongoing issue involves the notion of how much sport organizations are willing to pay for advertisements. Essentially, if the revenue earned from the additional sales generated by advertisements exceeds the additional costs, then financially the broadcast rights prove to be a worthwhile investment. As previously noted, the sports division of a media provider may actually be willing to lose money because obtaining broadcast rights potentially provides an ancillary benefit. Specifically, marginal revenue of broadcast rights extends beyond the value of marketing windows sold to advertisers (Fort, 2003). The contribution to revenue associated with an additional unit of input is called its marginal revenue product (MRP).

Although several revenue streams for sport organizations are relatively inelastic such as stadium seating and to a lesser degree ticket prices, broadcast revenues have infinite growth potential, which may explain their tremendous popularity over the past 20 years. In fact, while the Internet is becoming more influential, electronic media constitutes the financial foundation of the sport industry.

Economically, broadcasters and sport managers must consider the total return generated by sporting events, not just the bottom line. For example, several nonpecuniary benefits may also accrue from television exposure including an increased fan base, promotion of upcoming games, and additional licensed merchandise sales (Ashwell & Hums, 2004). Broadcast rights can vary according to the specific sport property involved with the network. The broadcast rights to various sports properties are included in Table 17.4.

Media critics questioned the business decision of Fox to bid $1.58 billion to broadcast National Football Conference (NFC) games. However, Fox immediately developed a presence in several key markets—including Detroit, Dallas, and Atlanta—allowing established stations an opportunity to gain access to these games. In addition, Fox promoted other shows to audiences that had previously been unaware of its programming (Ashwell & Hums, 2004).

PROFESSIONAL SPORTS

The television broadcast rights for each of the four major sport leagues including the NBA, NFL, National Hockey League (NHL), and MLB are listed in Table 17.5.

TABLE 17.4
Broadcast Rights to Major Sports properties

Rights holder(s)	Property	Length	Total Value	Final Season of Contract
Fox				
	NFL	8	4.4 billion[a]	2005
	MLB	6	2.5 billion	2006
	NASCAR	8	2.4 billion[b]	2008
ABC				
	NFL	8	4.4 billion[a]	2005
	NBA	6	4.6 billion	2007–08
	NHL	5	600 million	2003–04
	MLS	5	[d]	2006
	PGA[c]	4	850 million	2006
	IRL	5	60–65 million	2004
	NCAA Bowl Championship Series	4	400 million	2005-06
	U.S. Figure Skating Championships	8	96 million	2006
CBS				
	NFL	8	4 billion[a]	2005
	PGA[c]	4	850 million	2006
	NCAA Men's Basketball Tournament	11	6 billion	2012-13
	CART	4	[e]	2004
	USTA U.S. Open	4	38 million/year	2004
	The Masters	1	[f]	Year-to-year
NBC				
	Olympics	Winter and Summer Games	[g]	2012
	PGA[c]	4	850 million	2006
	NASCAR	6	2.4 billion[b]	2008
	Arena Football League	NA[h]	[i]	NA
	Triple Crown	5	51.5 million	2005
	Wimbledon	4	52 million	2006
	Notre Dame football	5	45 million	2004

Note: ABC contracts may share cable rights with ESPN channels; NBC contracts may share cable rights with TBS/TNT. CBS shares USTA cable rights with USA Network. *Source.* From Street & Smith's SportsBusiness Journal research.

[a]Portion of total $17.6 billion deal assigned to the specific rights holder.

[b]Represents a six-year, $2.4 billion deal, plus two additional years for Fox.

[c]The PGA contract took effect in 2003 and gives CBS the annual rights to air 15 events, ABC 14 and NBC 5.

[d]MLS in February 2002 extended a previous four-year deal with ABC. In conjunction with that extension, MLS paid more than $40 million to Kirch Group, the worldwide rights holder to the FIFA World Cup. That payment called for ABC and cable partners ESPN and ESPN2 to broadcast World Cup matches in 2002 and 2006, with MLS responsible for all ad sales and production costs.

[e]Deal calls for CART to pay CBS an estimated $235,000 per hour for air time, according to CART. The races will be produced by Fox Cable Networks, which will share in ad sales proceeds generated by CART for the broadcasts after CART first allocates money to recoup its costs.

[f]CBS and the Augusta National Golf Club reportedly have agreed to split production costs for the event's broadcast, estimated at $1.5 million to $2 million, in conjunction with the club's decision to have the event aired without commercials.

[g]NBC secured the 2004, 2006 and 2008 Games with a total $2.3 billion bid. In July 2003, NBC landed the 2010 and 2012 Games with a $2.001 billion bid.

[h]NA: Not available.

[i]Deal provides NBC with an equity stake in the league.

TABLE 17.5
Broadcast Rights of the Four Major Sport Leagues

Contract Period	Rights Holder(s)	Total Rights Fee ($)	Avg. Annual Value/ League ($)
NFL			
1994–1997	ABC, Fox, NBC, ESPN/TNT	4.3 billion	1.1 billion
1998–2005	ABC, Fox, CBS, ESPN	17.6 billion	2.2 billion
MLB			
1996–2000	Fox, NBC, ESPN	1.7 billion	340 million
2000–2005ᵃ	ESPN	851 million	141.8 million
2001–2006	Fox	2.5 billion	416.7 million
NBA			
1994–1998	NBC, TNT	1.1 billion	275 million
1998–2002	NBC, TNT/TBS	2.64 billion	660 million
2002–2008	ABC/ESPN, AOL Time Warner	4.6 billion	766.7 million
NHL			
1994–1999	Fox	155 million	31 million
1999–2004	ABC/ESPN	600 million	120 million

Note: From Street & Smith's SportsBusiness Journal research.
[a]Terms of the deal replaced the terms of the previous MLB deal for ESPN for the 2000 season.
[b]Represents a six-year, $2.4 billion deal, plus two additional years for Fox. Under the terms of NASCAR's previous television contract, individual tracks made their own TV deals and Winston Cup races were spread across CBS, ABC, ESPN, TNN, TBS and NBC for about $100 million in total rights fees paid.

Domestically, professional sport programs generate significant amounts of advertising revenue as advertisers have successfully leveraged sports broadcasting for the efficient promotion of products. The NFL's Super Bowl has epitomized this advertising relationship, illustrated by the 30-second commercial slots cost that $2.3 million in 2004. Financially, advertisers would be hesitant to spend such large sums of money without achieving their desired goal of promoting brand awareness.

Major League Baseball

On both national and local levels, MLB possesses a tenuous relationship with television. Specifically, many of the economic issues associated with baseball and, more specifically, the league's perceived competitive balance issue can be largely attributed to the revenue disparity among teams' local television revenues. Furthermore, the inequality in local television revenue created by the vast difference in the size of the media markets defines large and small market teams in baseball much more than actual city size. For example, from 1987 to 1991 the Minnesota Twins drew approximately the same number of fans as the New York Yankees, but the Twins were never regarded as a large-market team (Leeds & von Allmen, 2002).

The importance of television to MLB is difficult to overstate as television was cited for exposing MLB to a much larger audience, generating a financial windfall for owners, increasing franchise values, and combined with the development of cable, shaping the way Americans followed the game (Bellamy & Walker, 2001). However, baseball has traditionally been considered a poor television sport due to the large number of regular season games, the length of the games, the pace of play, and the unaccommodating size of the playing field for television.

Although portrayed as "America's pastime," MLB has increasingly trailed the NFL in both national interest and television appeal. While baseball appeared on national television networks in the 1950s, the initial contract blacked out games in cities where the home teams' games were broadcast on local television. Moreover, local stations had already been broadcasting games for over a decade, establishing the foundation for intense fan loyalties. Consequently, MLB struggled to overcome these local enthusiasts and still suffers in growing a national fan base similar to the NFL. For example, despite the best year ever in their short history of broadcasting MLB postseason games and increasing the price for a 30-second World Series commercial by 8% to $325,000, Fox anticipated losing money in 2003 (Isidore, 2003).

Historically, television audiences for baseball broadcasts trailed those of football. Yet, in 1975 ABC challenged NBC's long-term stranglehold on MLB's television rights. The league awarded ABC the lucrative *Monday Night Baseball* telecasts plus additional alternating rights to the playoffs and the World Series. Although NBC was discontented with the new deal leaving the network with the less desirable Saturday afternoon package, MLB proved to be an overall winner. Specifically, the league garnered $92.8 million over four years from the two networks, representing $20 million more than NBC paid independently (Rader, 1984).

The turf battles between ABC and NBC over MLB rights continued to escalate in the ensuing years and intensified in 1983. In an effort to monopolize baseball broadcast rights, NBC upped their ante to a staggering $550 million for approximately half of the rights package, leaving ABC vulnerable to potentially losing baseball if they refused to pick up the other half. Essentially, this power move had two distinct intentions. First, if ABC refused to pick up the remaining package, NBC expressed an interest in doing so for an unprecedented $1 billion, forcing ABC to come up with an equivalent sum or drop out of the baseball broadcasting race entirely. Second, by opening with a substantial financial bid, NBC anticipated financially draining ABC to the extent that the network would be unable to realistically compete for the broadcast rights to the upcoming 1988 Seoul Olympics. Despite NBC's motives, ABC agreed to pay the remaining balance for its share of the big-league television package. The aftermath of the battle parlayed the total amount baseball received to $1.1 billion, more than three times the previous contract and generating revenue of $4 million annually per organization (Rader, 1984).

In addition to sharing national media rights, baseball teams differentiate themselves from each other with their local television contracts. Because baseball was the lone established sport when commercial broadcasting emerged in the 1920s, MLB's initial contracts were secured with local broadcasters. In fact, the emphasis on local broadcasts prevented national *Game of the Week* broadcasts until 1965. Traditionally, MLB franchises have relied heavily on local revenues that contributed approximately half of all broadcast revenue. Since this money is not shared, the variances in the revenues generated contribute substantially to overall revenue disparity and impact competitive balance. For example, in comparing the large-market New York Yankees to the small-market Pittsburgh Pirates reveals an approximately ten to one disparity in local and regional rights fees (Bellamy & Walker, 2001).

Historically, philosophical differences among team owners influenced the role of local television rights. For example, for Chicago Cubs owner Phil Wrigley local television became a means of promoting his team and expanding their local audience in the 1950s and 1960s. In 1963, Wrigley sold the Cubs' television rights for only $500,000 because he justified that a growing fan base would help recuperate the lost revenue. In fact, Cubs broadcast rights for both television and radio were sold for only $500,000, which represented half of the fees earned by franchises in New York and Los Angeles and $350,000 less than the cross-town rival White Sox (Bellamy & Walker, 2001).

Capitalizing on the technological advances, approximately 1,000 MLB games were broadcast via the Internet in 2003, marking the first time a major sports league offered Internet viewing for the entire season (*Play Ball*, 2003). Also, with the recent influx of international players and in particular Japanese players, Japanese advertising mogul Dentsu and MLB reached a landmark six-year $275 million deal for the right to broadcast games in Japan effective for the 2004 season, which executives recognized as the most lucrative international deal reached between a U.S. league for distribution in a single country (King, 2003).

National Basketball Association

The NBA has been considered a pioneer and trendsetter of several innovative marketing strategies targeted at both domestic and international audiences. Consequently, these efforts have positioned the league as one of the largest beneficiaries of the increasing globalization of the television industry (Bellamy, 2002). Historically, the NBA struggled to land a lucrative television contract as initial contracts with the DuMont network (1952–1953) and later with NBC (1953–1962) produced only nominal revenues (Rader, 1984). Even with the additional playoff games matching hall of famers Wilt Chamberlain and Bill Russell, NBA basketball failed to develop an identity on network television evidenced by NBC's decision to drop its coverage of regular season games altogether in 1962.

Under the direction of new commissioner Walter Kennedy, a new broadcast deal was struck with ABC for the Sunday afternoon television rights. However, NBA ratings lagged behind the ratings posted by the more popular college and professional football games, leading the NBA to divorce their relationship with ABC and sign a contract with competitor CBS in 1973. Despite a new network, ratings further declined, demonstrated by a humiliating low in 1980 when the NBA championship games were broadcast on tape delay starting at 11:30 pm eastern time (Rader, 1984).

Despite the poor television ratings, one of the most lucrative television broadcast contracts in all of sports materialized in professional basketball during the mid-1970s. Specifically, despite the fact their former team the St. Louis Spirits never played in the NBA, Ozzie and Dan Silna have collected approximately $100 million from the league since 1976 (Rovell, 2003). When the American Basketball Association (ABA) merged with the NBA, only four ABA teams were allowed to join the NBA with an agreement the remaining two teams (St. Louis and Kentucky) would be compensated according to ABA bylaws. The Kentucky owner, John Brown, accepted a $3 million buyout, which provided the initial financing to purchase the Boston Celtics in future years. Comparatively, as part of his buyout compensation, Silna negotiated and convinced the other franchise representatives to agree to share one seventh of their national television revenues with him. As a result, Silna has collected over $98 million in broadcast revenues and, with a new television deal under negotiations, this figure will surpass $100 million by next year (Rovell, 2003).

After the league agreed to a $4.6-billion television deal with TNT and newcomer ESPN/ABC beginning with the 2002 to 2003 season, the NBA has been predominantly televised on cable. Citing losses of $300 million over four years, longtime NBA broadcaster NBC offered only $325 million, $75 million less than ESPN's $400 million offer (Martzke, 2003).

National Football League

Thanks in large part to the limited number of games, which enhances the overall value of each contest, the NFL has traditionally been regarded as the preeminent television sports league. In addition to their limited schedule, the NFL was instrumental in the passing of the Sports Broadcasting Act of 1961 which essentially allowed all professional sports franchise owners to share national television revenues equally (Bellamy, 2002).

Although the NFL is widely regarded as the healthiest professional sports league when compared to the other three leagues in terms of television appeal, fan base, and sales of licensed merchandise, much of this success can be attributed to the groundwork paved by former commissioner Pete Rozelle. Regarded as a respected and experienced negotiator, Rozelle successfully leveraged the NFL's appeal by taking advantage of the bidding competition between the networks. By the late 1970s, all three networks regarded pro football television rights as absolute essential in retaining the loyalties of their affiliates (Rader, 1984). Moreover, to survive the volatile battles with their competitors, networks understood the importance of sharing NFL television rights.

In 1951, the DuMont network paid the NFL $75,000 to nationally televise the first league championship game. In 1977, Rozelle engineered an impressive $656-million four-year package that provided nearly $6 million annually to each franchise, representing a sixfold increase from the previous 1964 contract. Consequently, television revenue exceeded gate receipts for the first time in league history as a source of team income (Rader, 1984).

As financially impressive as the previous television contract was, Rozelle successfully negotiated and landed an improved contract in 1982, as the networks collectively agreed to pay the NFL $2 billion over five years (Rader, 1984). This represented the single richest television contract in show business history. As a result of this deal, each of the then 28 franchises witnessed their respective compensation balloon from $5.8 million to $14.2 million annually. To place the deal in perspective, the annual television share of the Washington Redskins exceeded the team's gross revenues from the previous year (Rader, 1984).

In November 2004, the NFL agreed to an $8-billion contract extension of their current television deals with Fox and CBS to televise Sunday afternoon games for an additional six years. In addition, the new provision allows these networks the opportunity to modify their schedules late in the season to allow games with greater playoff implications the opportunity to be televised in prime time (Hiestand, 2004).

National Hockey League

Historically, the NHL has struggled to gain an identity in the United States both from a participant/spectator perspective and by generating a sustained television audience. Specifically, low-scoring games were unappealing to fans, and the lack of commercial opportunities due to continuous play was unattractive to advertisers (Leeds & von Allmen, 2002). Confined primarily to Canadian and northern U.S. cities, the league operated without a broadcast contract throughout the 1970s, 1980s, and early 1990s (Bellamy, 2002). In an effort to create additional fan interest and help with the overall marketing of the league, the NHL hired Commissioner Gary Bettman from the NBA. Ironically, Bettman was directly responsible for orchestrating the NBA's salary cap but has yet to construct a similar deal to help alleviate the financial problems of the NHL. Currently, the league is completing the final year of a five-year, $600-million deal with ABC/ESPN (Thomaselli, 2003).

Other Professional Sports

The television market for tennis has been particularly challenged the past two years as broadcasting deals with the French Open and Wimbledon were renewed for essentially flat rights fees for broadcast television and suffered decreased revenues on cable (Bernstein, 2003). Despite these financial challenges, CBS signed a four-year, $120-million extension to televise the U.S. Open through 2008. The 2004 U.S. Open tournament was expected to generate $55 million in domestic television revenue, making it the richest annual sporting event in North America not affiliated with a sports league (Bernstein, 2003).

Bolstered by the popularity of Tiger Woods, the Professional Golf Association (PGA) renewed its most recent television contract for an additional four years through 2007 and will receive $900 million collectively from three network (ABC, CBS, and NBC) and cable (ESPN, USA, and the Golf Channel) companies (Martzke, 2001). Comparatively, the Ladies Professional Golf Association (LPGA) has purchased television time for most tournaments.

In 1999, the National Association of Stock Car Racing (NASCAR), which oversees the Winston Cup and Busch Grand National races, reached a six-year television agreement worth 2.8 billion with FOX, NBC, and TBS, marking the first time NASCAR successfully sold rights to all of its races. Moreover, the new agreement represented a 400% increase in rights fees from the previous contract (Ashwell & Hums, 2004). The motorsports industry had over 900 sponsors committed to their involvement because NASCAR's brand loyalty is widely regarded as the highest among sport consumers (Horrow, 2002).

In just a decade's time, the X Games have become one of the most valuable enterprises in television sports and a favorite platform for marketers attempting to reach what has traditionally been an elusive audience: 12 to 19 year olds. An anomaly in this era of pampered, overpriced athletes, the X-Games TV ratings for the winter and summer competitions have increased 88% and 150% since 2000 (Burke, 2004).

International Sport

Price escalation of sports rights domestically started in the early 1970s, while the European fees were quite moderate until the 1990s (Solberg, 2002). However, discussions involving broadcast rights and fees associated with the Summer Olympic Games must also include differences in population sizes. For example, while the U.S. population was 276 million in 1999, the European population was 690 million (Solberg, 2002). Consequently, when evaluating the Olympic broadcast fees and

TABLE 17.6
Television Rights Per Capita (US $)

Year League	NFL	English Premier
1990	3.3	0.4
1994	4.0	1.1
1998	8.0	4.1
2000	8.0	11.0

Note: From "The Economics of Television Sports Rights:
Europe and the US—A Comparative Analysis," by H. A. Solberg,
2002, *Norsk Medietidsskrift, 9*(2), p. 57–80.

how much more expensive they are in the United States compared to Europe, the nominal price gap per viewer is further revealed when populations are accounted for.

The Olympics is reportedly one of the few sport properties generating television profits. For example, NBC's deal with the International Olympic Committee through 2008 estimates the network will realize a $65-million profit for the 2004 Summer games in Athens, although the 2008 games in Beijing are projected to lose $72 million (*Global Business*, 2003). In 2003, NBC extended its broadcast contract for the 2010 and 2012 games for $2.201 billion. Under the agreement, NBC will pay $12 million for the rights to the Olympic trials and an additional $10 million for the development of a digital TV library and archiving system. Collectively, this deal represents a 32.6% price increase over what NBC paid for the 2006 Winter Games and 2008 Summer Olympics (Associated Press, 2003).

Historically, in terms of both ratings and rights fees, soccer has been the dominant televised sport in Europe. In fact, soccer rights comprised 51% of the sports rights in the United Kingdom and Spain, 64% in Italy, and 41% in Germany (Solberg, 2002). Furthermore, while the Olympic Games are still the most expensive in the United States, a different representation emerges regarding team sports. The television rights per capita between the NFL and English Premier League (EPL) in U.S. dollars are included in Table 17.6. Comparatively, the current EPL contract is more expensive when adjusted for population differences and has escalated 3000% from 1990 to 2002 (Solberg, 2002).

In terms of assessing European television contracts, one must consider that Europe is not a homogenous market, as the prices of sports rights vary substantially from one nation to another even when adjusted for differences in population size (Solberg, 2002). For example, domestic soccer rights are significantly more expensive in the five big nations (Britain, France, Germany, Italy, and Spain) compared to the rest of Europe.

COLLEGIATE SPORTS

Major college athletic departments are now creating innovative revenue streams to help meet the growing financial demands. Because the antitrust provisions of the Sports Broadcasting Act do not apply to all games, the NCAA owns rights to only its championship events. Consequently, each university and individual conference has the authority to negotiate its own broadcast contracts (Ashwell & Hums, 2004).

DuMont television was considered a maverick in the broadcast industry because the company is the only network that did not emerge from radio broadcasting in the 1930s and in 1940 it was the first licensed American television network, predating CBS, NBC, and ABC. Initially, DuMont began broadcasting New York Yankee baseball games in 1946 and three years later, in 1949, successfully challenged CBS, NBC, ABC, and Chicago-based WGN for the broadcast rights to televise Notre Dame football games. A year later, DuMont again survived intense competition for the Notre Dame rights, but this changed the following year after the NCAA took control by limiting the number of football telecasts for each institution (Smith, 2001).

The NCAA continued to rule over broadcast rights for the next three decades, contracting with NBC, ABC, and CBS. However, there were various discrepancies among conferences and individual institutions as to how broadcast rights should be awarded. To broadcast the *Game of the Week* in 1956, NBC paid $1.25 million for the rights fees. After a financially disastrous one-year attempt to broadcast college football, ABC reentered the NCAA bidding war at the start of the next decade. Trailing CBS and NBC in the ratings, ABC bid just over $3 million and became the network of the NCAA in 1960 (Smith, 2001). A year later, ABC would forever establish itself as a legitimate player in the sports broadcasting arena. However, a review of the proceeding events ultimately shaping ABC's legacy is warranted.

As detailed in Smith (2001),

> Meeting with the NCAA in New York City, NBC's Tom Gallery brought with him two, or possibly three, contract bids in separate envelopes. If Gallery felt there were no other serious bids, he planned on submitting the lower bid. As CBS was strongly involved in telecasting NFL games, Gallery sensed that CBS would not be a player in the college contract. He looked around the room and saw no one from ABC or CBS, leading him to believe that his lower bid would surely win. Yet ABC's Scherick knew of Gallery's traditional tactics and had sent into the meeting an unknown and innocuous-looking employee from ABC's business department, Stan Frankle. Acting the part of an espionage agent and looking as inconspicuous as he could, Frankle waited for Gallery to submit NBC's bid. Gallery looked around and seeing no competitor, deposited his low bid with the NCAA. Frankle then walked up to the NCAA's chief TV negotiator, Asa Bushnell, and submitted the lowest of two ABC bids. ABC won with a two-year, $6,251,114 bid, projecting that NBC would offer only its usual 10 percent over the previous contract. The $1,114 was added to the $6.25 million bid "to give the bid character," according to Scherick. This shrewd move began ABC's rise in becoming the world's leading sports network. (p. 104)

During the growth phase of televised sports in the 1970s, with the exception of professional football, the most attractive television package for the networks included college football games. In 1977, CBS sought to dissolve ABC's monopoly, which dated back to 1966. However, Roone Arledge solidified another four-year deal bolstered by an impressive sum of $120 million over four years to retain ABC's exclusive rights. While CBS initially failed to lure away the broadcast rights to college football in 1977, this would eventually change four years later in 1981. The NCAA reached an agreement with ABC and CBS to share broadcast rights to traditional Saturday afternoon games while incumbent Turner Broadcasting System

(TBS) handled select evening telecasts (Rader, 1984). Consequently, the new packages produced a sharp increase in revenues as conferences received $74.3 million annually from television rights, representing twice the money received just two years earlier.

Enhanced by a national appeal, the University of Notre Dame successfully reached a broadcast agreement in selling the rights to all home football games to NBC in 1991. Despite a 5–7 record and an unremarkable 2.4 television rating in 2003, NBC extended their annual $9-million contract an additional five years, securing the rights to all Irish home games through the 2010 season. Although other networks expressed interest in Notre Dame's games, including ABC/ESPN and CBS, under NBC's current agreement other networks are prohibited from negotiating with Notre Dame (Martzke, 2003).

Understanding these challenging financial times and realizing that individual broadcast deals similar to the one garnered by Notre Dame are unrealistic for most college athletic departments, the University of Hawaii (UH) agreed to televise its football games via pay-per-view (PPV) by agreeing to a five-year, $6.2-million deal guaranteeing UH $2.1 million over three years with an opportunity to earn additional revenues based on PPV sales. In addition to the $700,000 rights fees, UH will receive 70% of the initial $1 million in PPV revenue with distributor Oceanic Cable receiving the remaining 30%. Revenue exceeding the $1-million benchmark is equally divided among the university, Oceanic, and the station KFVE (Schechter, 2002).

The University of Florida joined approximately a dozen other institutions by initiating video streaming and allowing Internet users the opportunity to watch various sports events via their computers for a nominal fee. Essentially, this pay-per-view feature allows fans to purchase the rights to individual events or a season package of games. Individual games either live or archived can be purchased for $8 and $6, respectively, while the all-sports package sells for $99.95 (Dirocco, 2004).

In 1999, the NCAA agreed to a landmark television agreement with CBS by signing an 11-year, $6-billion contract. Collectively, the deal included Internet rights, worldwide television, radio, licensing, and publishing (Horrow, 2004). While this deal has generated significant media coverage, some analysts predict the network will lose over $600 million during the life of the contract. The NCAA benefited in their negotiations with CBS deu to the strong public interest publicized by Disney's ABC/ESPN in obtaining the basketball rights. However, CBS easily retained its exclusive rights by virtue of a bid that an analyst valued was approximately a $1 billion more than any competitive offer (Flint, 2004).

Revenue generated by the current NCAA men's basketball tournament accounts for 98% of the NCAA's overall income. However, this tournament has undergone several developments leading to the lucrative financial deal existing today. The initial five-year contract reached in 1963 designated television rights totaling $140,000. Next, NBC paid $547,500 for the broadcast rights in 1969 as the tournament's net income exceeded the million-dollar benchmark for the first time. Four years later, NBC renewed their contract for $1,165,755, and the championship game was shown in prime time for the first time. In 1982, CBS was awarded the tournament for the first time, and in 1991, the network began a seven-year contract for $1 billion allowing live coverage of all sessions of the championship. Next, in 1995 CBS replaced the existing contract with another seven-year deal worth $1.725 billion.

An interesting dilemma emerged in 1989 when CBS negotiated its contract with the NCAA to carry the broadcast rights for the men's basketball tournament. As part of the initial contract, the NCAA mandated CBS also broadcast several of the women's tournament games as well as championships in other low-profile competition including baseball, track, and swimming. Executives at CBS actually offered the NCAA a higher fee provided they did not have to broadcast the aforementioned telecasts, but the NCAA rejected this offer, sacrificing the additional revenue for the added exposure (Ashwell & Hums, 2004). Comparatively, ESPN paid $163 million for an 11-year television deal to broadcast the women's NCAA basketball tournament.

As part of its current agreement with CBS, the NCAA has successfully bundled several other facets in an unprecedented manner including increased exposure for all of its championships, a more extensive platform of television networks, and an opportunity to capitalize on revenues accrued through the Internet. Conceptually, the NCAA is leveraging its most valuable commodity to augment the value of the rest of its assets. In addition to the aforementioned benefits, the bundle provides more. Specifically, radio broadcasts, opportunities enabling CBS and ESPN to cross-promote their NCAA events on the other's airtime, and close to 200 promotional messages airing annually on CBS (Brown, 2002).

In 2004, the Big 12 Conference extended one of the most lucrative cable deals by adding four years to its existing broadcast agreement with Fox Sports Networks for $19.5 million annually, pushing the deal through the 2011–2012 academic year. Overall, Fox retains the rights to all football games not carried by ABC and all other sports with the exception of men's basketball (Bernstein, 2004). In 2003, College Sports Television (CSTV) unveiled a 24-hour network devoted exclusively to college sports. Due to other contractual agreements, the network will not carry men's Division I basketball or football, the two most attractive packages for viewers. However, CSTV offers inexpensive programming to cable and satellite operators. For example, whereas ESPN is paid $2 monthly for each subscriber by the cable operators, CSTV earns only 7 cents as it has significantly lower costs than other networks because colleges clanor for additional exposure (Burke, 2003). As the sports industry grows and expands with the addition of more teams and league, Stakeholder involved with the media can expect the economic landscape to change accordingly.

REFERENCES

Associated Press (2003). $2.201 billion bid beats competitors.

Ashwell, T., & Hums, M. (2004). Sale of broadcast rights. In *Financing sport* (2nd ed., pp. 387–412). Morgantown, WV: Fitness Information Technology.

Battin, P. (2003). *Television sports rights 2003.* Retrieved October 30, 2003, from http://gouldmedia.com/nv_rpt_tsr03.php

Bellamy, R. (2002). The evolving television sports marketplace. In L.Wenner (Ed.), *Mediasport* (pp. 73–87). London, England: Routledge.

Bellamy, R., & Walker, J. (2001). Baseball and television origins: The case of the Cubs. *Nine, 10,* 31–48.

Bernstein, A. (2003). CBS keeps Open, buys into new series. *SportsBusiness Journal.* Retrieved November 10, 2003, from http://sportsbusinessjournal.com/index.cfm? fuseaction=search.show_article& articleId=34858&keyword=bernstein

Bernstein, A. (2004, February 16). Big 12, Fox add 4 years to deal at increased rate of $19.5M a year. *SportsBusiness Journal.* Retrieved March 1, 2004, from http://sportsbusinessjournal.com/index.cfm? fuseaction=search.show_article&articleId=36837&keyword=bernstein

Brown, G. I. (2002, March 18). The $6 billion plan. *The NCAA News.* Retrieved March 1, 2004, from www.ncaa.org/news/2002/20020318/active/3906n35.html

Burke, M. (2003, March 17). For the love of the game. *Forbes.* Retrieved November 23, 2003, from www.forbes.com/forbes/2003/0317/058_print.html

Burke, M. (2004, February 9). X-treme economics. *Forbes*. Retrieved may 30, 2004 from www.forbes.com/business/global/2004/0209/058.htm

Coakley, J. (2004). *Sports in society: Issues and controversies* (8th ed.). New York, NY: Mcgraw-Hill Publishers.

Cuneen, J., & Branch, D. (2003). TV and sport's mutually beneficial partnership: 20th century summary and 21st century potential. *International Journal of Sport Management, 4*, 243–260.

Dirocco, M. (2004, February 13). Gators pull fans into Web. *Florida Times-Union*. Retrieved February 13, 2004, from http://www.jacksonville.com/tu-online/stories/021304/ col_14807746.shtml

Downward, P., & Dawson, A. (2000). *The economics of professional sports teams*. New York, NY: Routledge.

Field, W. (2003). Free for all? *Sportsbusiness International, 85*, 24–25.

Flint, J. (2004, March 15). NCAA basketball tournament; Air ball? CBS was determined to win the men's tournament's TV contract; be careful what you wish for. *Wall Street Journal*, p. R10.

Fort, R. D. (2003). *Sports economics*. Upper Saddle River, NJ: Prentice Hall Press.

Gaustad, T. (2000). The economics of sports programming. *Nordicom Review, 21*(2), 101–113.

Global Business of Sports Television. (2003, March). Retrieved October 30, 2003, from http://www.gii.co.jp/english/scr12920_sports_television.html

Grossman, A. (2004, May 3). Advertisers make their pick. *SportsBusiness Journal*, pp. 19–24.

Hiestand, M. (2004, November 9). NFL signs multibillion TV deal with CBS, Fox. *USA Today*. Retrieved November 9, 2004, from http://www.usatoday.com/sports/ football/nfl/2004-11-08-tv-deal_x.htm

Horrow, R. (2002, July 2). *NASCAR looks to ride TV deals, new sponsors to long-term success*. Retrieved March 31, 2004, from http://cbs.sportsline.com

Horrow, R. (2004). *The business of college basketball*. Retrieved from http://www.sportsline.com/columns/writers/horrow

Higgins, J. M. (2003). Teams face low-scoring TV deals. *Broadcasting & Cable, 31*. Retrieved October 22, 2003, from http://www.broadcastingcable.com

Isidore, C. (2003, October 17). Fox sure loser in series. *Money*. Retrieved November 23, 2003, from http://cnnmoney.com/2003/10/16/news/companies/fox_baseball/index.htm

King, B. (2003). MLB's Japenese TV deal a record. *Sports Business Journal*. Retrieved November 11, 2003, from http://www.sportsbusinessjournal.com/index.cfm

Lee, S., & Chun, H. (2002). Economic values of professional sports franchises in the United States. *The Sport Journal*. Retrieved May 13, 2004, from http://www.thesportjournal.org/2002Journal/Vol5-No3/econimic-values.asp

Leeds, M., & von Allmen, P. (2002). *The economics of sports*. Boston, MA: Adison Wesley.

Martzke, R. (2001, July 5). PGA tour TV deals to soar by 50% *USA Today*. Retrieved March 29, 2004, from www.usatoday.com/sports/golf/pga/2001-07-04-tv.htm

Martzke, R. (2002, January 22). NBA finalizes TV deals: Goodbye NBC. *USA Today*. Retrieved October 30, 2003, from www.usatoday.com/money/media/2002-01-22-nba.htm

Martzke, R. (2003, December 18). NBC, Notre Dame stretch grid deal through 2010. *USA Today*. Retrieved December 19, 2003, from http://www.usatoday.com/sports/college/football/independents/2003-12-18-nbc-notre-dame_x.htm

Nichols, W., Moynahan, P., Hall, A., & Taylor, J. (2002). *Media relations in sport*. Morgantown, WV: Fitness Information Technology.

Owers, J., Carveth, R., & Alexander, A. (2004). An introduction to media economics theory and practice. In A. Alexander (Ed.), *Media economics: Theory and practice* (pp. 3–47). Hillsdale, NJ: Lawrence Erlbaum Associates.

Play ball! Baseball to webcast games. (2003, March 12). Retrieved January 17, 2004, from www.cnn.com/2003/TECH/internet/03/12/baseball.net.ap.

Rader, B. (1984). *In its own image: How television has transformed sports*. New York, NY: The Free Press.

Rovell, D. (2003). *Spirit of NBA deal lives on for Silna brothers*. Retrieved October 12, 2003, from http://sports.espn.go.com/espn/sportsbusiness/index.

Samuelson, P. (1976). *Economics*. New York, NY: McGraw-Hill.

Schechter, B. (2002, August 19). Pay TV might work for Hawaii, but others have little to show. *SportsBusiness Journal*. Retrieved March 5, 2004, from http://sportsbusinessjournal.com/index.cfm?fuseaction=search.show_article&articleId=24068&keyword=schechter

Smith, R. (2001). *Play-by-play: Radio, television, and big-time college sport*. Baltimore, MD: Johns Hopkins University Press.

Solberg, H. A. (2002). The economics of television sports rights: Europe and the US—a comparative analysis. *Norsk Medietidsskrift, 9*(2), 57–80.

Thomaselli, R. (2003, September 2). NBC again eyes pro sports. *AdAge.com* Retrieved October 27, 2004, from http://www.adage.com/news.cms?newsId=38618

18

Sports Sponsorship

Lance Kinney
University of Alabama

While sports event viewing and attendance are well-established entertainment and leisure activities, viewing, attending, or listening to a contemporary sports event may feel more like a shopping spree. Many branded products and services have raced to sports events as a means of meeting sales, corporate, and communication objectives. Some product categories, such as beer and shaving cream, have traditionally been linked with sports. And athletes have historically been among the most highly sought celebrities for brand endorsement. What has changed about the use of sports events as marketing platforms is the variety of brands and services seeking to associate with sports, increasingly sophisticated marketing programs built around sports, and expanding budgets dedicated to sponsoring and supporting sports-based marketing efforts. Some brands now use sports event sponsorship as the brand's primary marketing communication strategy. Cornwell described this intense reliance on sponsorship as sponsorship-linked marketing (Cornwell, 1995).

Sponsoring sports events or individual athletes can be traced to ancient cultures. Events were staged as public spectacle, while athletes were embodiments of the civic pride of the sponsoring town or region (Arthur, Scott, & Woods, 1997). The rebirth of the modern Olympiad in 1896 also included sponsors' brands, including Kodak (Shani & Sandler, 1998). Sports and brand associations were reported in the United Kingdom in 1898 (Marshall & Cook, 1992). Coca-Cola supplied soft drinks for the 1928 U.S. Olympic team (Sandler & Shani, 1993). But the bellwether event for modern sports sponsorship may well be the 1984 Olympic Games in Los Angeles, California (Lough & Irwin, 2001; Shani & Sandler, 1998). Under the leadership of Peter Ueberroth, sponsorship was used to stage the Games with minimal public funds. In fact, the Games actually returned a profit (Shani & Sandler, 1998).

As noted in Chart 18.1, sports event sponsorship spending growth continues to outpace other marketing communication activities, including advertising.

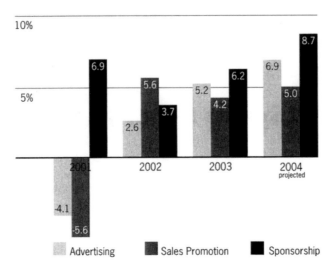

Chart. 18.1.   Annual Growth of Advertising, Sales Promotion And Sponsorship.

Sponsorship spending for North American companies across all types of events and activities is expected to reach $11.14 billion in 2004, with the largest share, 69%, dedicated to sports events ("Sponsorship spending," 2003). When considered as a single marketing communication activity, sponsorship approximates the estimated $11 billion spent in consumer magazines by American advertisers in 2003. Sponsorship expenditures exceed spending for out-of-home media, the Internet, and business publications ("US ad spending," 2004). Chart 18.2 illustrates which events brands prefer to sponsor. Sponsor dollars overwhelmingly gravitate to sports events. Lesa Ukman of International Event Group (IEG) noted the allure of sports for marketers: "The advantage sponsorship has over all other media is that it is the only medium that gives brands the opportunity to create, enrich and facilitate engaging experiences, emotions and ideas" ("Assertions," 2003, p. 2).

Just as marketers have embraced sports events, the events have welcomed marketers. Producing sports events can be expensive, even at the local level. Selling sponsorship rights helps fund events, provides income to meet the ever-increasing salary demands of professional athletes, and underwrites the costs of building and operating sports venues (Coleman, Kelkar, & Goodof, 2001). New sports leagues are forming in an effort to attract sponsor dollars. Recent football

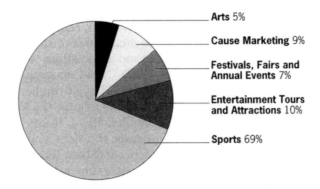

Chart. 18.2.   Projected 2004 North American Sponsorship Spending By Property Type.

entries include the Arena Football League and the National Women's Football Association (Fitzgerald, 2003).

In the following sections of this chapter, sports sponsorship is formally defined, followed by a consideration of the objectives brands seek to meet by partnering with sports events. Special consideration is given to brand marketing communication objectives along with event selection and evaluation strategies. Also included here is a review of research into sports sponsorship's effects on consumers. The chapter concludes with a review of the controversies associated with sports event sponsorship, including unofficial or ambush sponsors, as well as sponsorship by tobacco brands.

MANAGERIAL CONSIDERATIONS

Defining Sport Sponsorship

Sponsorship is often defined as "a cash or in-kind fee paid to a property in return for access to the exploitable commercial potential associated with that property" (Ukman, 1995, p. 1). Commercial interest distinguishes sponsorship from charity and patronage, as brands engaged in the latter activities may not necessarily expect any commercial return (Cornwell, 1995; Meenaghan, 1991). Sports events can be extremely localized, such as a high school team or a civic sports league, or worldwide events, such as the Olympic Games and World Cup Soccer. Sport sponsorship might also include sponsoring sporting federations, such as the National Football League. Sponsorship should be considered distinct from more general sports-related advertising. Many brands may advertise during the broadcast of a sports event; however, these brands need not be formally associated with the event. Often, sponsor brands will have an advertising presence during the event's broadcast, as well as in other media, to establish the crucial link between the sponsoring brand and the event (Crimmins & Horn, 1996). Sponsorship need not be confined to sports events. Brands may sponsor other types of civic or arts events. Sports events may be more appealing because of the drama and health associations of sports. Sports are also noted to be character building and may make the brand appear competitive and aggressive by association (Abratt, Clayton, & Pitt, 1987; Arthur, Scott, Woods, & Booker, 1998; Witcher, Craigen, Culligan, & Harvey, 1991).

Brands have turned to sports event marketing for a variety of reasons, including a fuller consideration of what constitutes brand marketing communication. Sophisticated brands now manage all potential exchanges between the brand and the consumer to deliver brand-building messages. Consumers do not differentiate between direct mail, public relations, advertising, product placement, or other brand communication activities. Rather, consumers perceive all of these as advertising. Schultz, Tannenbaum, and Lauterborn (1994) call these brand contacts. Also, as advertising clutter has increased in other media, finding unique vehicles to deliver brand messages becomes increasingly difficult. Properly leveraged sports events that are likely to receive repeated coverage while driving strong emotional connections between viewers and attendees offer brands fresh opportunities to reach consumers. However, sports sponsorship's growth has produced its own clutter. Overlapping sports seasons produced more than 200 professional and collegiate events in October 2000 (Petrecca, 2000). Sports sponsorship can also be justified in terms of contemporary consumer behavior theories. Keller (1993) theorized that customer-based brand equity is the result of unique awareness and image associations for a brand relative to its competitors. Sports event sponsorship can serve new brands in both areas while helping established brands strengthen or develop brand awareness and image among new target consumers. Nextel® uses its NASCAR sponsorship to meet brand awareness and brand image objectives (Thomaselli, 2003b, 2004b). Some product categories, such as alcohol and tobacco, may use sports events to obtain the media visibility that advertising regulators deny these brands (Cornwell, 1997; Meenaghan, 1991). International sports events can offer brands with true global presence, such as Coca-Cola®, an efficient marketing communication platform independent of cultural or language barriers (O'Sullivan & Murphy, 1998).

Sponsor Brand Objectives

Brands use sports events to meet a number of corporate and consumer objectives. While a number of specific objectives are noted in the literature, Lee, Sandler, and Shani (1997) classified objectives into three major categories: corporate objectives, marketing objectives, and media objectives. Corporate objectives are designed to improve company or brand image among important targets, including consumers, regulatory personnel, corporate clients, members of the distribution channel, or even the firm's own employees. The importance of these objectives is noted in a number of research reports (Farrelly, Quester, & Burton, 1997; Grimes & Meenaghan, 1998; Ludwig & Karabetsos, 1999; Mack, 1999; Marshall & Cook, 1992; Meenaghan, 1991; Morris & Irwin, 1996; Pope & Voges, 1994; Scott & Suchard, 1992; Witcher, et al., 1991). Marketing objectives are based on communication variables likely to result in sales, such as brand awareness, on-site sampling or merchandise sales, as well as brand image or position (Lough & Irwin, 2001; Meenaghan, 1991; Nicholls, Roslow, & Laskey, 1994; Scott & Suchard, 1992; Witcher, et al., 1991). Press exposure or media coverage provides media presence without advertising expenditure. For example, title sponsoring an event, such as the FedEx® Orange Bowl, guarantees that the brand name will be mentioned each time the event is referenced in mass media reports. Brands can also issue press releases or sponsor press-related events touting the brand's sponsorship. These efforts can generate mass media coverage apart from the competition, thereby enhancing media presence (Farrelly, et al., 1997; Marshall & Cook, 1992; Scott & Suchard, 1992; Witcher, et al., 1991).

While research is available on the nature of preferred objectives as well as discussions of general objectives, very little research investigates how firms rank objectives in terms of importance. Lough and Irwin (2001) noted that public service and image-based objectives might be more important for brands considering sponsoring women's sports to reach female consumers. Witcher et al. (1991) reviewed objectives for sponsoring firms in the United Kingdom and reported that corporate image is paramount. Brand awareness and market share objectives appear to be more important in Australia (Pope & Voges, 1994; Scott & Suchard, 1992). Small business owners are more likely to be concerned with supporting the local communities in which they operate (Mack, 1999).

Sports Event Selection

Brand managers considering sports sponsorship strategies may select events that serve multiple objectives simultaneously. Major sponsor brands may receive as many as 1000 event proposals each year (Arthur, et al., 1997). As part of a sponsorship selection strategy, Irwin and Asimakopoulos (1992) suggested a variety of objectives for brands considering sports event sponsorship. Their six-step selection model identifies a number of variables and allows decision makers to apply subjective, quantitative weighting criteria to justify event selection.

The most likely reason for a brand to select a specific sports event is that the participants or the likely audience coincides with the brand's target market (Arthur, et al., 1998; Barr, 1993; Farrelly, et al., 1997; Marshall & Cook, 1992). Morris and Irwin (1996) suggested that event properties should approach potential sponsors with demographic and behavior profiles for viewers and participants. Meenaghan (1991) also suggested investigating events in demographic, lifestyle, and geographic terms to assess the probability of meeting brand objectives. The best events will serve the brand in each of these areas. If image development or positioning is a primary objective, brands should seek events where the brand/event images are congruent (Barr, 1993; Ferrand & Pages, 1996; Gwinner & Eaton, 1999; Marshall & Cook, 1992; Martin, 1994; Meenaghan, 2001a). For example, an auto race sponsorship might imply speed and excitement, while an upscale golf or tennis tournament might develop brand images associated with prestige or exclusivity. Cornwell, Pruitt, and Van Ness (2001) defined functional congruence between the brand and the event. In this relationship, the brand may be used as part of the competition, such as a motor oil or tire sponsoring an auto race. Arthur et al.'s (1998) sport sponsorship acquisition model suggests that once objectives and other variables are specified, selecting and contracting with sports events should be undertaken as a formal organizational buying process similar to other firm expenditures. Other considerations for brand managers include the professionalism of the event and its managers (Farrelly, et al., 1997), the gender of the event (Martin, 1994), and competitive pressures (Heffler, 1994). Fahy, Farelly, and Quester (2000) cautioned that brands should not enter sponsorships if the firm does not have the personnel or expertise to manage the sponsorship for maximum competitive advantage.

Some brands wishing to sponsor sports events may face budget constraints. Sponsorship rights fees have escalated to the point that some brands are forgoing established sponsorships (Elkin, 2000; Fatsis, 1998). The United States Postal Service questioned the value of its estimated $9 million sponsorship of cyclist Lance Armstrong and the U.S. Pro Cycling Team (Teinowitz & Thomaselli, 2004.) As significant as rights fees can be, they are just a portion of what brands must spend to establish a link between the brand and the sponsor. Other promotion activities, including package tie-ins, merchandise, advertising, publicity, and public relations, could run several million dollars more. Coca-Cola® spent an estimated $500 million to support its 1996 Olympic Games sponsorship (Ludwig & Karabetsos, 1999). Delpy (1996) offered capsule reviews of the leveraging efforts used by sponsors of the 1996 Olympic Games in Atlanta, Georgia. A number of sports sponsorship strategists stress the importance of the affordability of all sponsorship-related activities (Arthur, et al., 1998; Barr, 1993; Delpy, 1996; Farrelly, et al., 1997; Heffler, 1994; Meenaghan, 1991; Witcher, et al., 1991). If the brand cannot afford support in addition to rights fees, managers may consider alternative promotion strategies or more affordable sponsorship opportunities. "If the brand cannot afford to spend to communicate its sponsorship, then the brand cannot afford sponsorship at all" (Crimmins & Horn, 1996, p. 16).

Evaluation Strategies

As with many mass-mediated marketing communication strategies, it is difficult to link sports sponsorship efforts directly to sales response (Marshall & Cook, 1992; Meenaghan, 1991). Therefore, sponsorships are often evaluated in terms of intervening *cognitive effects variables*, such as brand recall, recognition, and awareness, or *affective variables*, such as brand preference, image, or brand position. If a corporation sponsors an event, rather than a specific brand, many of these same assessments may still be used. Research indicates that many sponsors do not place as much emphasis on evaluation relative to selecting the event or managing the sponsorship (Marshall & Cook, 1992; Witcher, et al., 1991). Barr (1993) and Heffler (1994) listed questions and evaluation strategies to help sponsor brands determine the contribution made by sponsorship. Using a case study, Furst (1994) comprehensively detailed how one brand selected, managed, and evaluated its involvement with figure skating. Komoroski and Biemond (1996) reported how a sports property demonstrated tactical value to its sponsoring partners.

The media audit is a relatively simple evaluation that is often recommended and often used (Abratt & Grobler, 1989; Ludwig & Karabetsos, 1999; Meenaghan, 1991; Pope & Voges, 1994). With this method, the sponsor monitors media coverage of the event, then determines the value of similar visibility. For example, a sponsorship investment of $5 million that produces $10 million of media coverage may be considered successful. While this type of evaluation is simple and economical, it has several problems, most notably its inability to assess impact and unsuitability for examining some types of objectives. If the sponsor's brand objective was to improve brand image or increase brand awareness, the media audit will not indicate if the objective was met. A second difficulty is assessing the value of coverage. The brand must set a multiplier and determine relative value. Is a 30-second event recap on a sports show really as valuable as 30 seconds of paid advertising? Is a newspaper report of the event with two brand name mentions equal to the advertising expenditure required to obtain the same number of column inches? Is on-field or arena signage as valuable as television advertising? Pokrywczynski (1994) reported that recall levels for conventional advertising were four to ten times higher than for arena signage. Similarly, Lardinoit and Derbaix (2001) observed better recall scores for television references when compared to on-field signage. Clearly, the media audit has some fundamental deficiencies. As with other types of marketing communication research, sponsor brands should budget funds for postevent assessment. Sponsor brands should also use research strategies, such as consumer surveys, that allow for more sophisticated evaluation of the sponsorship's effectiveness. Developing better evaluation metrics is key to sustaining sponsorship's rapid growth (Friedman, 1999).

Consumer Attitudes

Consumers seem to accept sponsor brands and associated advertising as part of the contemporary sports landscape. At the very least, consumers offer few strong objections to brands associating with sports events. Cuneen and Hannan's (1993) survey of golf event attendees demonstrated that attendees were not distracted by or opposed to signage at the event. Kinney and McDaniel (2004) reported American survey results that indicate consumers are somewhat more supportive for sponsorship of professional sports, as compared to collegiate events. These respondents did not believe that ticket prices were reduced, nor did they perceive sponsor brands to be better than nonsponsor competitors. Support increased as the respondent's general sports interest increased. However, older subjects were somewhat less supportive (Kinney & McDaniel, 2001). Focus group research conducted by Meenaghan (2001b) documented a "halo of goodwill" (p. 209), with sponsorship viewed as less obtrusive, more subtle, and less selfish than traditional advertising. Sponsoring brands were also perceived as more prominent and socially supportive than nonsponsoring brands. Roy and Graeff (2003) suggested females hold more goodwill for sponsoring brands than males. Tobacco and alcohol brands as sports sponsors are viewed as areas of concern. Smokers and alcohol beverage drinkers are more likely to support these brands, especially for professional sports events (Kinney & McDaniel, 2004). Generally, females are less supportive than males. Kropp, Lavack, Holden, and Dalakas (1999) and Danylchuk (2000) also found support among drinkers and smokers, while nondrinkers and nonsmokers showed more opposition.

SPORTS SPONSORSHIPS EFFECTS RESEARCH

Published research on sports sponsorship encompasses a variety of research methods across many academic domains, including psychology, sociology, marketing, advertising, and mass communication. Research is available on all types of sports at local, national, and international levels. Therefore, it is difficult to make conclusive, definitive statements about sports sponsorship effects. Sponsor brands and sports event properties may also conduct research; however, some of this research may be proprietary and unavailable for scholarly review. It is also noted that sound theoretical bases are uncommon (Cornwell & Maignan, 1998; Cunningham & Taylor, 1995; Lee, et al., 1997; Meenaghan, 1999). In this section, some of the available research is presented, with an emphasis on research investigating consumer cognitive, affective, and behavioral effects.

Conceptual Models

As of this writing, there is no predominant sport sponsorship model or effects theory, although several researchers have proposed models. Crimmins and Horn (1996) proposed a model grounded in consumer data obtained from tracking surveys. Consumers feel gratitude toward sponsor brands, which in turn impacts consumer brand perception. However, they described no formal theory to explain this effect. The model proposed by Lee et al. (1997) is also based on consumer survey data. They described consumer attitudes toward sponsorship based on three constructs: attitudes toward the event, attitudes toward commercialization, and attitudes toward behavioral intent. Gwinner (1997) suggested a model incorporating elaboration likelihood and transfer of cultural meaning. Gwinner offered a number of testable, image-based effects propositions, including the influence of the consumer's prior brand experience, event size, and event frequency. Meenaghan's (2001a) model hypothesized that sponsorship effects, be they goodwill, image, or purchase intention, are processed through a series of generic, category, and individual activity processing filters. These filters lead to a hierarchy of effects beginning with awareness and culminating with brand purchase. Effects in this hierarchy may be more pronounced based on the individual differences variables of contingent goodwill and fan involvement with the event. Pracejus (2004) outlined seven potential influential mechanisms that could produce effects, including simple awareness (recall and recognition), affect transfer of event attitude to the brand, and event image transfer to sponsor brands. Other frameworks for investigating sports sponsorship effects include advertising schemas; associative memory networks; brand prominence or category dominance; and ability, motivation, and opportunity to process advertising information.

Cognitive Effects

Cognitive sponsorship effects refer to the consumer's ability to recognize, recall, or otherwise associate official sponsor brands with sports events. McDaniel and Kinney (1999) investigated the ability of consumers to link sponsor brands with the 1996 Olympic Games two weeks after the event concluded. Respondent sex, patriotism, and general sports interests influenced viewing time, with males spending more time viewing the Games. These variables significantly affected a viewer's ability to link sponsor brands with the Games. Higher education levels also predicted accurate recall, while older consumers were less likely to recall sponsor brands. Pham (1992) experimented with varying levels of consumer involvement with a soccer telecast and observed a curvilinear (inverted-U) relationship. At extremely low and high involvement levels, the subject's ability to recognize a brand featured in the program segment was impaired. High self-reported levels of arousal inhibited sponsor brand recognition, while viewing pleasure did not significantly impact recognition levels.

Pham and Johar (2001) conducted an intriguing experiment that helps explain how consumers may misidentify sponsor brands. They hypothesized that consumers make intuitive links between brands and sponsored events. If asked to identify official sponsors, consumers search their memories for brands that they think are most likely to sponsor the event. Often, these are the dominant market share brands in their respective categories. Pham and Johar call this heuristic the "market prominence bias" (p. 124). Since the largest brands are often more readily accessible in memory, they are more likely to be identified or misidentified as event sponsors; "Consumers appear to consciously infer from the brand's prominence that it must be the sponsor" (p. 137). This is not an automatic process, though. Consumers will consider how related the brand and the event are to one another. If consumers are asked to identify a golf tournament sponsor, for example, they are likely to consider brands they think might be related to golf, such as sports apparel and golf club brands. From this evoked set, consumers are more likely to select what they consider to be the most prominent brand. This effect is more pronounced when consumers have difficulty learning the link between the brand and the event. When learning the correct link is easy, consumers are more likely to identify the correct sponsor brand, even if that brand is not the most prominent in its category. Such consumer confusion regarding event sponsorship is not uncommon. Stotlar (1993) reported that subjects were unable to distinguish between different Olympics sponsorship categories. In fact, several competing brands fared as well or better than official sponsor brands in recall tests. Similar confusion is noted by Sandler and Shani (1993). Brands with no competitive sponsor presence during the Olympics broadcast fared better.

Affective Effects

Affective effects include brand or corporate image and position, as well as attitudinal measures regarding the brand and the event. Perhaps one of the most noted attitudinal effects of sports sponsorship is a halo or gratitude effect. Several researchers have noted that brands sponsoring sports events are perceived as more socially minded. Sponsor brands' participation is appreciated by these consumers (Crimmins & Horn, 1996; Dean, 2002; Meenaghan, 2001b; Pope, 1998; Roy & Graeff, 2003; Stipp & Schiavone, 1996). Levin, Joiner, and Cameron (2001) investigated how brands sponsoring NASCAR races are perceived by television viewers. The most positive brand attitudes were noted for brands that appeared on vehicles as brand logos combined with conventional televised advertising presence during the event telecast. It appears that involvement with the races, an individual differences variable, amplified this effect. Levin et al. ascribed their results to the accessibility of the brand in memory due to its prominent position during the race and the telecast.

Enhancing brand or corporate image was noted earlier as a key objective for brand managers; however, research indicates that image effects may be subject to a number of conditions. Javalgi, Traylor, Gross, and Lampman (1994) suggested that corporate image is a multiple-factor construct. While event sponsorship may change or improve some image components, it may not necessarily impact the variables that influence consumer perceptions. If the brand has a negative image prior to the sponsorship, cynical consumers may perceive the sponsorship as a manipulative effort to rehabilitate a poor public image (Dean, 2002). Similarly, Till and Shimp (1998) observed that negative associations for one partner could transfer and undermine the image of the other partner. Gwinner and Eaton (1999) demonstrated how images are transferred from sports events to brands under function- and image-based congruency conditions. A stronger effect is noted for image congruent brand–event pairings. Turco (1994) investigated brand perceptions of the title sponsor of an international hot air balloon rally, concluding that image may be bolstered with sponsorship if the consumer is already a brand user. Stipp and Schiavone (1996) noted stronger image effects for Olympics sponsors if the supporting advertising is engaging and memorable and appears with enough frequency for viewers to learn the link between the brand and the event. Crimmins and Horn (1996) pointed out that brand managers should not assume that consumers make the link between the brand and the event. Brands that make the link clearly and explicitly are more likely to reap image-based benefits. The brand's contribution to the event must be made clear in all other communication activities used to support the sponsorship.

In the same experiment that established market prominence bias, Pham and Johar (2001) concluded that brands correctly or incorrectly identified as sponsors are likely to receive enhanced image effects. Prominent sponsor brands are perceived as more energetic relative to less prominent brands in the same product category. McDaniel and Kinney (1999) established some individual differences that impact linking a brand to an event, noting that the ability to make this link impacts subsequent brand image. If consumers cannot make the link, postevent brand image is not significantly different from preevent brand image. They also reported more noticeable image effects among females, whereas males demonstrated more cognitive effects. Females have also been observed to report a significantly higher attitude toward the ad for sponsor brands (McDaniel, 1999). The same experiment also suggested a small but significant effect for media vehicle selection for sponsorship support advertising.

Behavioral Effects

The research reviewed for this chapter uncovered no definitive reports of brand sales response to sports sponsorship. Sales response data are much more likely to be proprietary and closely guarded by sponsor brands. However, some research using experiments or surveys does use self-reported purchase intention as a proxy for behavioral data. Turco (1994) reported that corporate image was enhanced for brands sponsoring a hot air balloon rally and resulted in higher self-reported purchase intention for sponsor brands. Similarly, Pope and Voges (2000) also observed a significant relationship between a sponsor's corporate image and purchase intention. Stotlar's (1993) consumer survey detailed that 66% of respondents reported favorable purchase intention for Olympics sponsor brands. McCarville, Flood, and Froats (1998) conducted an experiment allowing subjects to sample a sponsor's pizza brand. Subjects receiving the sample reported a significantly higher intention to purchase the brand. McDaniel's (1999) experiment found a significantly higher sponsor brand purchase intention for females under some circumstances. Working within a social identity theory framework, Madrigal (2000, 2004) determined that individuals strongly identified with a sports team report significantly more purchase intention for sponsor brands. Despite these positive purchase intention studies, there is survey and experimental research suggesting that consumers are no more likely to seek sponsor brands when compared to nonsponsor brands (Kinney & McDaniel, 2004, 1996; McDaniel & Kinney, 1996; Pope, 1998; Sandler & Shani, 1993).

SPORTS SPONSORSHIP CONTROVERSIES

Ambush Marketing

Ambush marketing is an attempt by nonsponsor brands to be associated with an event without paying the sponsorship rights fees (Sandler & Shani, 1993; Shani & Sandler, 1998). Ambush brands engage in "unauthorized association... of their names, brands, products or services with a sports event or competition through any one or more of a wide range of marketing activities" (Townley, Harrington, & Couchman, 1998, p. 333). Some ambush methods, such as purchasing advertising during an event's broadcast, arena signage, and hospitality or other place-based activities near, but not in conjunction with, the event are perfectly legal (Meenaghan, 1994). Other activities are clearly illegal, such as appropriating an event's logo or deliberately misleading consumers into false impressions concerning the brand's status. Townley et al. (1998) presented a review of legal and illegal ambush activities, along with suggestions for defeating both types. Meenaghan (1994) and Payne (1998) both recognized the difference between illegal and immoral ambushing. Many ambushers break no laws, even if the general morality of ambushing is questionable. Event producers that do not offer sponsor brands some protection are likely to see the credibility of the sponsorship compromised, which ultimately devalues sponsorship. Questions about an event's ability to deliver brand value for its sponsors may eventually place the event itself in jeopardy (Meenaghan, 1994). The International Olympic Committee manages its own extensive sponsor protection program, including educating the public about the contribution official sponsors make toward staging the Olympics (Payne, 1998).

There is evidence suggesting that ambush brands can confuse consumers enough to undermine sponsor brands. McDaniel and Kinney (1996) demonstrated that even if consumers could correctly identify official sponsors, the same consumers could question or even change their conclusion after seeing advertising from an ambusher. Brands using the Olympics rings logo or stating sponsor status in the copy fared better, but even these creative tactics were not complete protection. Similarly, Kinney and McDaniel (1996) noted that official sponsors fared no better than ambushers in terms of attitude toward the ad, attitude toward the brand, and purchase intention. Females reported significantly higher scores than males on some attitudinal variables regarding official sponsors and ambush brands (McDaniel & Kinney, 1998).

Meenaghan (1998), in a review of ambush strategies and responses, described how consumer fan involvement with the event and knowledge of the official sponsor's contributions to the event protect official sponsors from ambushers. Of particular note is the finding that once ambush brands are identified, consumers express anger at the ambush brand. Consumers do not like feeling misled or manipulated. Similar findings are noted in other research (Payne, 1998). Shani and Sandler's (1998) attitudes research is somewhat more equivocal; their subjects reported ambush strategies as acceptable business practices in a highly competitive marketplace. They also suggested that the Olympics created confusion among official sponsor ranks by offering sponsorship opportunities in too many categories. Lyberger and McCarthy (2001) reported similar consumer ambivalence. An obvious ambusher need not be present to misidentify official sponsor brands. Consumers may be confused as to which brand officially sponsors an event independent of ambush efforts. Consumers may infer official sponsor status from brand prominence or congruence between the brand and the event (Johar & Pham, 1999; Pham & Johar, 2001). Ludwig and Karabetsos (1999) considered ambushing from an official sponsor's point of view. Their respondents indicated little concern about ambushing, as the event's organizers were aggressive about protecting official sponsors.

Alcohol and Tobacco Brand Sponsorship

Alcohol and tobacco brands have long associations with sports. Many fans also consume alcohol and tobacco brands as part of their sports viewing behavior. Tobacco is the third largest category of sports event sponsor brands, directly behind automobiles and alcohol (Turco, 1999). Both categories have been controversial as critics note that drinking and smoking are incompatible with high levels of sporting success. Brands in both categories have been accused of exploiting the sponsorship loophole (Cornwell & Maignan, 1998) that allows incidental coverage of tobacco and alcohol brands in areas where advertising these products would be prohibited. Incidental coverage could include arena signage, automobile decoration, logos on sporting apparel, and so forth. Some alcohol and tobacco brands may be title sponsors of an event that receives significant coverage. Critics also contend that sports and alcohol associations target underage consumers, provide mixed messages about health concerns, and make these brands appear glamorous (Cornwell, 1997; Hoek, Gendall, and Stockdale, 1993; Lough & Irwin, 2001). Of the two product categories, tobacco brands have generated the most research and criticism. A fuller discussion of the history and regulation of tobacco and alcohol brands relative to sports is available in McDaniel, Mason, and Kinney (2004).

Hoek et al. (1993) demonstrated that young people might perceive sports activities as mitigating the harmful effects of smoking. They also noted that a single advertising exposure in a sporting context could reinforce current smoking behavior or influence the approval of smoking as an acceptable behavior, as well as increase brand awareness and brand preference. Turco (1999) describes the current relationship between American sports and tobacco brands relative to the tobacco industry's settlement with 40 states' attorneys general. Under this settlement, various forms of advertising are eliminated or curtailed, such as outdoor billboards and promotional paraphernalia. Both of these restrictions could limit tobacco brand visibility at sporting venues. Most notable, though, "Tobacco companies will no longer be able to use brands to sponsor any sports event..." (p. 36). These terms are in accordance with U.S. statutes and may not apply internationally. Other countries may address tobacco and alcohol brands within the bounds of their national codes. Kropp et al. (1999) noted that sweeping bans could imperil existing events or even entire sports leagues. Should sports events be destabilized, Kropp suggests a period of public funding allowing events to continue until new sponsorships can be negotiated. Future sports industry professionals may be asked to market events to tobacco and alcohol brands. Their willingness to do this may depend on how prepared they feel to address these issues, as well as their age (McDaniel, Kinney, & Chalip, 2001).

Other Sponsorship Controversies

While tobacco and alcohol brands receive most of the attention, sports sponsorship is also embroiled in other controversies. Critics note the increasingly commercial nature of the sports experience, which suggests corporate interests may debase sports and compromise competition (McAllister, 1998). Covell (2001) argued that financial interests might undermine educational interests at the collegiate level. Advertising clutter may increase, along with ambushers, as virtual signage technology allows broadcasters to insert ever more advertising into the viewing frame (Mendez, 1999). Ethical questions are arising across all areas of sports marketing, including the escalating price of attending sports events; public cynicism about the motives of owners, athletes, and marketers; as well as the content of some sports-related advertising (Jackson & Andrews, 2004; Laczniak, Burton, & Murphy, 1999). Broader social concerns are creeping into sports, including criminal behavior (Thomaselli, 2003a). The recent protest of the Masters golf tournament by women's groups brought class and sex distinctions to bear on sports sponsorship. The Masters responded by dismissing its sponsors and lowering the price for television rights (Thomaselli, 2004a). Sports events must introduce new levels of scrutiny and consider the perceptions of any potential sponsor partner. Corporate financial scandals and athletic scandals may taint events and devalue sponsorship as a marketing communication tactic (Ruth & Simonin, 2003; Till & Shimp, 1998).

Future Research Areas

Much research and development remains to be done in the sports sponsorship area. The field will not benefit from more research into corporate objectives or the prevalence of sports sponsorship. Consumer attitude studies and corporate case studies also seem superfluous. Sponsorship research must mature and begin considering more sophisticated, challenging questions. Of most importance is theory and model building, and several attempts are noted in other sections. Researchers proposing theories and models must begin empirically and test the reliability and validity of their models with firm hypotheses and rigorous methods. Of particular interest would be continuing research on image transfer and building associations between brands and events. The review conducted to prepare this chapter did not locate any sports sponsorship studies using physiological research theories or methods.

Sponsorship research would also benefit from research investigating the impact of cross-promotion strategies. For example, how do advertising, sales promotion, and special packaging interact to produce results? Additionally, sponsor brands could also make a contribution by allowing comprehensive review of actual data obtained from the marketplace. Publishing authors could protect the sponsoring company's identity and confidentiality. Response theories could then be checked against real-world data, or grounded theory could be developed working back from ecologically valid observations. Lastly, nearly all the research reviewed here focuses on consumers. As noted in an earlier section, many sponsorship objectives, such as corporate hospitality, are not rooted in consumer response. Research on the effectiveness of sports sponsorship in meeting these and other corporate objectives would be a welcome addition to the literature.

REFERENCES

Abratt, R., Clayton, B. C., & Pitt, L. F. (1987). Corporate objectives in sponsorship. *International Journal of Advertising, 6*(4), 299–311.

Abratt, R., & Grobler, P. S. (1989). The evaluation of sports sponsorships. *International Journal of Advertising, 8*(4), 351–362.

Arthur, D., Scott, D., & Woods, T. (1997). A conceptual model of the corporate decision-making process of sport sponsorship acquisition. *Journal of Sport Management, 11*(3), 223–233.

Arthur, D., Scott, D., Woods, T., & Booker, R. (1998). Sport sponsorship should . . . A process model for the effective implementation and management of sport sponsorship programs. *Sport Marketing Quarterly, 7*(4), 49–60.

Assertions (2003, December 22). *IEG Sponsorship Report*, p. 2.

Barr, J. M. (1993). Maximizing the value of sports sponsorships. *The Public Relations Journal, 49*(4), 30–31.

Coleman, L. J., Kelkar, M., & Goodof, D. A. (2001). Contemporary sports marketing: Issues, challenges and opportunities. *Journal of Promotion Management, 7*(1/2), 195–213.

Cornwell, T. B. (1995). Sponsorship-linked marketing development. *Sport Marketing Quarterly, 4*(4), 13–24.

Cornwell, T. B. (1997). The use of sponsorship-linked marketing by tobacco firms: International public policy issues. *The Journal of Consumer Affairs, 31*(2), 238–254.

Cornwell, T. B., & Maignan, I. (1998). An international review of sponsorship research. *Journal of Advertising, 27*(1), 1–22.

Cornwell, T. B., Pruitt, S. W., & Van Ness, R. (2001). The value of winning in motorsports: Sponsorship-linked marketing. *Journal of Advertising Research, 41*(1), 17–31.

Covell, D. (2001). The role of corporate sponsorships in intercollegiate athletics. *Sport Marketing Quarterly, 10*(2), 245–247.

Crimmins, J., & Horn, M. (1996). Sponsorship: From management ego trip to marketing success. *Journal of Advertising Research, 36*(4), 11–21.

Cuneen, J., & Hannan, M. J. (1993). Intermediate measures and recognition testing of sponsorship advertising at an LPGA event. *Sport Marketing Quarterly, 2*(1), 47–56.

Cunningham, M. H., & Taylor, S. F. (1995). Event marketing: State of the industry and research agenda. *Festival Management and Event Tourism, 2*(3/4), 123–137.

Danylchuk, K. E. (2000). Tobacco sponsorship: Spectator perceptions at an LPGA event. *Sport Marketing Quarterly, 9*(2), 103–111.

Dean, D. H. (2002). Associating the corporation with a charitable event through sponsorship: Measuring the effects on corporate community relations. *Journal of Advertising, 31*(4) 77–87.

Delpy, L. (1996). Marketing notes: The 1996 Olympic Games. *Sport Marketing Quarterly, 5*(2), 43–44.

Elkin, L. (2000, September 11). IBM farewell offers tribute to unknowns. *Advertising Age*, pp. 72–73.

Fahy, J., Farrelly, F., & Quester, P. (2000, June). A resource-based perspective of sponsorship management and implementation. Paper presented at the Marketing in a Global Economy, International Marketing Educators' Conference, American Marketing Association, Buenos Aries, Argentina.

Farrelly, F. J., Quester, P., & Burton, R. (1997). Integrating sports sponsorship into the corporate marketing function: An international comparative study. *International Marketing Review, 14*(3), 170–182.

Fatsis, S. (1998, October 19). Coke doesn't swing at Yankees' first pitch to remain team's official soft drink. *Wall Street Journal*, p. B12.

Ferrand, A., & Pages, M. (1996). Image sponsoring: A methodology to match event and sponsor. *Journal of Sport Management, 1*(3), 278–291.

Fitzgerald, K. (2003, October 27). Newer leagues gird for grid action. *Advertising Age*, S-2.

Friedman, A. (1999). The question remains: Are sponsorships selling the product? *Street and Smith's Sports Business Journal, 2*(1), 14.

Furst, A. S. (1994). A case study of how one company uses sports sponsorship to reach a female audience. *Sport Marketing Quarterly, 3*(2), 35–42.

Grimes, E., & Meenaghan, T. (1998). Focusing commercial sponsorship on the internal corporate audience. *International Journal of Advertising, 17*(1), 51–74.

Gwinner, K. (1997). A model of image creation and image transfer in event sponsorship. *International Marketing Review, 14*(3), 145–158.

Gwinner, K. P., & Eaton, J. (1999). Building brand image through event sponsorship: The role of image transfer. *Journal of Advertising, 28*(4), 47–57.

Heffler, M. (1994, May 16). Making sure sponsorships meet all the parameters. *Brandweek*, p. 16.

Hoek, J., Gendall, P., & Stockdale, M. (1993). Some effects of tobacco sponsorship advertisements on young males. *International Journal of Advertising, 12*(1), 171–176.

Irwin, R. L., & Asimakopoulos, M. K. (1992). An approach to the evaluation and selection of sport sponsorship proposals. *Sport Marketing Quarterly, 1*(2), 43–51.

Jackson, S. J., & Andrews, D. L. (2004). Aggressive marketing: Interrogating the use of violence in sport-related advertising. In L. R. Kahle & C. Riley (Eds.), *Sports marketing and the psychology of marketing communication* (pp. 307–327). Mahwah, NJ: Lawrence Erlbaum Associates.

Javalgi, R. G., Traylor, M. B., Gross, A. C., & Lampman, E. (1994). Awareness of sponsorship and corporate image: An empirical investigation. *Journal of Advertising, 23*(4), 47–58.

Johar, G. V., & Pham, M. T. (1999). Relatedness, prominence and constructive sponsor identification. *Journal of Marketing Research, 36*(3), 299–312.

Keller, K. L. (1993). Conceptualizing, measuring and managing customer-based brand equity. *Journal of Marketing, 57*(1), 1–22.

Kinney, L., & McDaniel, S. R. (1996). Strategic implications of attitude toward the ad in leveraging event sponsorships. *Journal of Sport Management, 10*(3), 250–261.

Kinney, L., & McDaniel, S. R. (2001). An exploratory investigation of demographic variables as predictors of attitudes toward sports sponsorship. In C. R. Taylor (Ed.), *The Proceedings of the 2001 Conference of the American Academy of Advertising* (pp. 136–143). Villanova, PA: Villanova University.

Kinney, L., & McDaniel, S. R. (2004). American consumer attitudes toward corporate sponsorship of sporting events. In L. R. Kahle & C. Riley (Eds.), *Sports marketing and the psychology of marketing communication* (pp. 211–222). Mahwah, NJ: Lawrence Erlbaum Associates.

Komoroski, L., & Biemond, H. (1996). Sponsor accountability: Designing and utilizing an evaluation system. *Sport Marketing Quarterly, 5*(2), 35–39.

Kropp, F., Lavack, A. M., Holden, S. J. S., & Dalakas, V. (1999). Attitudes toward beer and tobacco sports sponsorships. *Sport Marketing Quarterly, 8*(3), 49–58.

Laczniak, G., Burton, R., & Murphy, P. (1999). Sports marketing ethics in today's marketplace. *Sport Marketing Quarterly, 8*(4), 43–53.

Lardinoit, T., & Derbaix, C. (2001). Sponsorship and recall of sponsors. *Psychology & Marketing, 18*(2), 167–190.

Lee, M., Sandler, D. M., & Shani, D. (1997). Attitudinal constructs towards sports sponsorship. *International Marketing Review, 14*(3), 159–169.

Levin, A. M., Joiner, C., & Cameron, G. (2001). The impact of sports sponsorship on consumers' brand attitudes and recall: The case of NASCAR fans. *Journal of Current Issues and Research in Advertising 23*(2), 23–31.

Lough, N. L., & Irwin, R. L. (2001). A comparative analysis of sponsorship objectives for U.S. women's sport and traditional sport sponsorship. *Sport Marketing Quarterly, 10*(4), 202–211.

Ludwig, S. M., & Karabetsos, J. D. (1999). Objectives and evaluation processes utilized by sponsors of the 1999 Olympic Games. *Sport Marketing Quarterly, 8*(1), 11–19.

Lyberger, M. R., & McCarthy, L. (2001). An assessment of consumer knowledge of, interest in, and perceptions of ambush marketing strategies. *Sport Marketing Quarterly, 10*(2), 130–137.

Mack, R. W. (1999). Event sponsorship: An exploratory study of small business objectives, practices and perceptions. *Journal of Small Business Management, 37*(3), 25–30.

Madrigal, R. (2000). The influence of social alliances with sports teams on intentions to purchase corporate sponsors' products. *Journal of Advertising, 29*(4), 13–24.

Madrigal, R. (2004). A review of team identification and its influence on consumers' responses toward corporate sponsors. In L. R. Kahle & C. Riley (Eds.), *Sports marketing and the psychology of marketing communication* (pp. 241–255). Mahwah, NJ: Lawrence Erlbaum Associates.

Marshall, D. W., & Cook, G. (1992). The corporate (sports) sponsor. *International Journal of Advertising, 11*(4), 307–324.

Martin, J. H. (1994). Using a perceptual map of the consumer's sport schema to help make sponsorship decisions. *Sport Marketing Quarterly, 3*(3), 27–33.

McAllister, M. (1998). College bowl sponsorship and the increased commercialization of amateur sports. *Critical Studies in Mass Communication, 15*(4), 357–381.

McCarville, R. E., Flood, C. M., & Froats, T. A. (1998). The effectiveness of selected promotions on spectators' assessments of a nonprofit sporting event sponsor. *Journal of Sport Management, 12*(1), 51–62.

McDaniel, S. R. (1999). An investigation of match-up effects in sport sponsorship advertising: The implications of consumer advertising schemas. *Psychology & Marketing, 16*(2), 163–184.

McDaniel, S. R., & Kinney, L. (1996). Ambush marketing revisited: An experimental study of perceived sponsorship effects on brand awareness, attitude toward the brand and purchase intention. *Journal of Promotion Management, 3*(1/2), 141–167.

McDaniel, S. R., & Kinney, L. (1998). The implications of recency and gender effects in consumer response to ambush marketing. *Psychology & Marketing, 15*(4), 385–403.

McDaniel, S. R., & Kinney, L. (1999). Audience characteristics and event sponsorship response: The potential influence of demographics, personal interests and values on brand awareness and brand image. *International Journal of Sports Marketing and Sponsorship, 1*(2), 125–145.

McDaniel, S. R., Kinney, L., & Chalip, L. (2001). A cross-cultural investigation of the ethical dimensions of alcohol and tobacco sports sponsorships. *Teaching Business Ethics, 5*(3), 307–330.

McDaniel, S. R., Mason, D., & Kinney, L. (2004). Strange bedfellows: Sports sponsorships that promote alcohol, tobacco and lotteries. In T. Slack (Ed.), *The Commercialization of sport* (pp. 287–306). London: Routledge.

Meenaghan, T. (1991). The role of sponsorship in the marketing communications mix. *International Journal of Advertising, 10*(1), 35–47.

Meenaghan, T. (1994). Point of view: Ambush marketing: Immoral or imaginative practice? *Journal of Advertising Research 34*(5), 77–88.

Meenaghan, T. (1998). Ambush marketing: Corporate strategy and consumer reaction. *Psychology & Marketing, 15*(4), 305–322.

Meenaghan, T. (1999). Current developments and future directions in sponsorship. *International Journal of Advertising, 17*(3), 3–28.

Meenaghan, T. (2001a). Understanding sponsorship effects. *Psychology & Marketing, 18*(2), 95–122.

Meenaghan, T. (2001b). Sponsorship and advertising: A comparison of consumer perceptions. *Psychology & Marketing, 18*(2), 191–215.

Mendez, H. Y. (1999). Virtual signage: The pitfalls of "now you see it, now you don't." *Sport Marketing Quarterly, 8*(4), 15–21.

Morris, D., & Irwin, R. L. (1996). The data-driven approach to sponsorship acquisition. *Sport Marketing Quarterly, 5*(2), 7–10.

Nicholls, J., Roslow, A. F., & Laskey, H. (1994). Sports event sponsorship for brand promotion. *Journal of Applied Business Research, 10*(4), 35–40.

O'Sullivan, P., & Murphy, P. (1998). Ambush marketing: The ethical issues. *Psychology & Marketing, 15*(4), 349–366.

Payne, M. (1998). Ambush marketing: The undeserved advantage. *Psychology & Marketing, 15*(4), 323–331.

Petrecca, L. (2000, October 9). How much is too much? *Advertising Age*, pp. 38–41.

Pham, M. T. (1992). Effects of involvement, arousal and pleasure on the recognition of sponsorship stimuli. In J. F. Sherry & B. Sternthal (Eds.), *Advances in Consumer Research* (vol. 19, pp. 85–93). Provo, UT: Association for Consumer Research.

Pham, M. T., & Johar, G. V. (2001). Market prominence biases in sponsor identification: Processes and consequentiality. *Psychology & Marketing, 18*(2), 123–143.

Pokrywczynski, J. (1994). The differential impact of televised exposure to sports arena displays vs. commercials. In K. W. King (Ed.), *Proceedings of the 1994 Conference of the American Academy of Advertising* (p. 147). Athens, GA: Henry W. Grady College of Journalism and Mass Communication.

Pope, N. K. (1998). Consumption values, sponsorship awareness, brand and product use. *Journal of Product & Brand Management, 7*(2), 124–136.

Pope, N. K., & Voges, K. E. (1994). Sponsorship evaluation: Does it match the motivation and mechanism? *Sport Marketing Quarterly, 3*(4), 37–45.

Pope, N. K., & Voges, K. E. (2000). The impact of sport sponsorship activities, corporate image and prior use on consumer purchase intention. *Sport Marketing Quarterly, 9*(2), 96–102.

Pracejus, J. W. (2004). Seven psychological mechanisms through which sponsorship can influence consumers. In L. R. Kahle & C. Riley (Eds.), *Sports marketing and the psychology of marketing communication* (pp. 175–190). Mahwah, NJ: Lawrence Erlbaum Associates.

Roy, D. P., & Graeff, T. R. (2003). Consumer attitudes toward cause-related marketing activities in professional sports. *Sport Marketing Quarterly, 12*(3), 163–172.

Ruth, J. A., & Simonin, B. L. (2003). Brought to you by brand A and brand B: Investigating multiple sponsors' influence on consumers' attitudes toward sponsored events. *Journal of Advertising, 32*(3), 19–30.

Sandler, D. M., & Shani, D. (1993). Sponsorship and the Olympic Games: The consumer perspective. *Sport Marketing Quarterly, 2*(3), 38–43.

Schultz, D. A., Tannenbaum, S. I., & Lauterborn, R. F. (1994). Integrated marketing communication: Pulling it together and making it work. New York: McGraw-Hill.

Scott, D. R., & Suchard, H. T. (1992). Motivations for Australian expenditure on sponsorship. *International Journal of Advertising, 11*(4), 325–332.

Shani, D., & Sandler, D. M. (1998). Ambush marketing: Is confusion to blame for the flickering of the flame? *Psychology & Marketing, 15*(4), 367–383.

Sponsorship spending to increase 8.7 percent in 2004 (2003, December). *IEG Sponsorship Report 22*(4), 1, 4.

Stipp, H., & Schiavone, N. P. (1996). Modeling the impact of Olympic sponsorship on corporate image. *Journal of Advertising Research, 36*(4), 22–28.

Stotlar, D. K. (1993). Sponsorship and the Olympic Winter Games. *Sport Marketing Quarterly, 2*(1), 35–43.

Teinowitz, I., & Thomaselli, R. (2004, March 22). Post Office won't deliver for Lance Armstrong. *Advertising Age*, p. 32.

Thomaselli, R. (2003a, December 1). Sponsors cry foul on college sports. *Advertising Age*, pp. 1, 36.

Thomaselli, R. (2003b, October 27). Nextel link takes NASCAR to new level. *Advertising Age*, p. S-7.

Thomaselli, R. (2004a, March 29). Can sponsor-free Masters survive? *Advertising Age*, p. 23.

Thomaselli, R. (2004b, February 9). Nextel antes up $70 million to leverage NASCAR alliance. *Advertising Age*, p. 8.

Till, B. D., & Shimp, T. A. (1998). Endorsers in advertising: The case of negative celebrity information. *Journal of Advertising, 27*(1), 67–82.

Townley, S., Harrington, D., & Couchman, N. (1998). The legal and practical prevention of ambush marketing in sports. *Psychology & Marketing, 15*(4), 333–348.

Turco, D. M. (1994). Event sponsorship: Effects on consumer brand loyalty and consumption. *Sport Marketing Quarterly, 3*(3), 35–37.

Turco, D. M. (1999). The state of tobacco sponsorship in sport. *Sport Marketing Quarterly, 8*(1), 35–38.

Ukman, L. (1995). *The IEG's complete guide to sponsorship: Everything you need to know about sports, arts, event, entertainment and cause marketing.* Chicago: IEG, Inc.

US ad spending totals by media (2004, March 8). *Advertising Age*, p. 15.

Witcher, B., Craigen, J. G., Culligan, D., & Harvey, A. (1991). The links between objectives and function in organizational sponsorship. *International Journal of Advertising, 10*(1), 13–33.

SPORTS MEDIA AUDIENCES

19

Why We Watch and Enjoy Mediated Sports

Arthur A. Raney
Florida State University

The importance of mediated sports in contemporary global society is undeniable. Teams and players unify and divide communities and nations. They generate billions of dollars in advertising revenue and merchandising sales. And they arouse feelings of euphoria and despair among their loyal fans. Therefore, it may come as little surprise that the formal academic study of mediated sports boasts a rich tradition; in fact, this volume is a testament to that tradition. The current chapter seeks to illuminate a small portion of that research tradition by discussing factors that motivate the use and viewing of mediated sports. While a fair amount of descriptive work has been conducted in this area, few have attempted to connect these motives to the various theoretical perspectives from media–entertainment research. These perspectives provide a nice framework from which to begin my discussion.

In the mid-1950s, media researchers began to conceptualize the audience member less as a single unit in a passive, homogeneous mass and more as an active member of a diverse, heterogeneous subset. Work in balance theory (Heider, 1958) and cognitive dissonance (Festinger, 1957) helped us understand that people consistently seek information that is consistent with their prevailing attitudes, beliefs, and thoughts. Likewise, people tend to avoid information that they know will contradict existing attitude and belief structures. Theories of cognitive dissonance further propose that when people encounter information incongruent with their existing beliefs they experience psychological and cognitive distress, which leads them to seek out means to alleviate the dissonance and distress.

Given this psychological reality, it is reasonable to assume that individuals attempt to avoid cognitive dissonance—or pursue balance, according to Heider—by seeking out information that is congruent with their existing attitudes, and/or avoiding information that would produce such dissonance. With regard to media content, we refer to this behavioral process as selective exposure (for a complete summary, see Zillmann & Bryant, 1985). In other words, individuals tend to intentionally choose media content that is presumed to be, by and large, consistent with their existing attitudes, beliefs, and thoughts. Support for selective exposure to a variety of content genres is widespread (e.g., Klapper, 1960; Sweeny & Gruber, 1984; Vidmar & Rokeach, 1974).

For entertainment theorists, selective exposure naturally extends to include media content that not only is congruous with prevailing attitudes, but that also presumably brings pleasure to the viewer. So, it follows that fans of certain genres of programming seek out those contents because of their presumed cognitive—and affective, as I soon discuss—benefits. Sports fans are no different. We would expect, and selective-exposure and ratings research has confirmed, that those who find pleasure in consuming mediated sports seek them out in heavy doses.

Another perspective that informs this discussion is the uses and gratifications approach to media effects (for a recent overview, see Rubin, 2002). Blumler and Katz (1974) outlined the basics of the approach: Individuals have social and psychological needs, which they presume certain media content can meet. As a result, people seek out different media contents at different times depending on those needs, with the expectation that their needs will be gratified through media consumption. Application of and support for the uses and gratification approach with a variety of media content and media channels is widespread (e.g., Johnson, 1995; Perse, 1986; Turow, 1974; Vincent & Basil, 1997).

The approach assumes that people are motivated to view (and avoid) particular media content at different times. As I show, one content that is sought after is sports programming. Furthermore, I also show that the needs supporting the various motivations for viewing mediated sports are quite varied.

Studies consistently demonstrate that media content can alter or enhance a viewer's mood. It is assumed that viewers are familiar with this phenomenon (whether they completely understand it or not). Therefore, supported by selective exposure and uses and gratifications research, mood-management theory posits that viewers utilize specific media content to minimize the life and intensity of bad moods and maximize the life and intensity of good moods (see a recent summary in Zillmann, 2000). The principles of mood-management theory are generally supported in the literature (e.g., Biswas, Riffe, & Zillmann, 1994; Christ & Medoff, 1984; Knobloch & Zillmann, 2002). While few studies have investigated the relationship between sports viewing and mood (e.g., Depalma & Raney, 2003), the connection between the two is obvious, especially given the reported motivations and behaviors-while-watching literature that is discussed below.

Admittedly, this is a cursory introduction to these media theories.[1] For my purposes, though, this should suffice. In summary, it is assumed that individuals experience psychological and sociological needs in their daily lives that they expect media content to address and fulfill. These needs certainly vary between individuals of different ages, gender, and stages in life, among other factors, as well as within individuals given situational factors such as mood, time of day, and stress. With this in mind, it should not be surprising that many individuals turn to sports programming to meet the various needs they experience. In fact, media consumers have reported three broad types of motivations for their sports viewing in

---

[1]For more detailed information on these and other media theories, the reader is referred to Bryant and Zillmann's (2002) *Media Effects: Advances in Theory and Research.*

previous research, which presumably give us insight into those underlying needs. In the most general terms, sports media consumers report being motivated by emotional, cognitive, and behavioral or social needs when they view mediated sports.

EMOTIONAL MOTIVATIONS FOR MEDIATED SPORTS CONSUMPTION

Overwhelmingly, media consumers report that they view mediated sports because of the emotional rewards they receive from doing so. As I discuss later, the resulting emotional reactions are not always positive in nature, though positive outcomes (specifically in terms of a win for the favored individual or team[2]) are surely hoped for and thus lead to viewing. In fact, some acknowledge that the emotional highs and lows that occur during the course of a game or match are part of the appeal. But I am getting ahead of myself. In general terms, people view mediated sports because they expect positive emotional impacts from their viewing. These emotional reactions to sports programming are assumed to be dependent upon and governed by the affiliations—or affective dispositions—that viewers hold toward one (or both) of the competing teams. Many scholars actually contend that these affiliations are at the very heart of fanship.[3]

Entertainment Motivation

A rich tradition of scholarship explores how people are socialized as sports fans in the first place, with family (primarily fathers and brothers), peers, school attendance, and community playing the largest roles (cf. Wann, Melnick, Russell, & Pease, 2001). Similarly, people form allegiances toward specific teams for various reasons, such as geography, allegiances held by respected family members and friends, team colors, specific players, styles and strategies of play, and perceived popularity among the masses (or so-called bandwagon effects). A thorough discussion of sports fan socialization and disposition formation is beyond the scope of the current project, but suffice it to say, the process through which people form emotional allegiances with sports teams is quite complex. Regardless, most sports viewers can (and will) readily tell you about their favorite teams and players. In fact, with some fans you need not ask the question; the names of their favored clubs are proudly displayed on shirt sleeves, jackets, hats, scarves, and car bumpers. These team allegiances are at the core of the first motivation for sports viewing on television: entertainment (Gantz, 1981; Gantz & Wenner, 1991, 1995; Krohn, Clarke, Preston, McDonald, & Preston, 1998; Smith, 1988; Wann, 1995; Wann, Schrader, & Wilson, 1999; Wann et al., 2001; Wenner & Gantz, 1998).

---

[2] I acknowledge that particular sports can be either individual- or team-based and that fans often root for a team primarily because of one or two specific players. However, for the sake of simplicity throughout the remainder of the manuscript, when I refer to the participants in a sporting event the term *team* will be used.

[3] To use the term *fanship* in this manner is not to deny the affiliation and appreciation that many individuals hold toward a specific sport (e.g., basketball fans). In fact, sports fanship (as opposed to team fanship) certainly motivates sports viewing quite often. However, the extant literature overwhelmingly discusses the fanship toward a team as a motivation for viewing. As a result, I will primarily focus on team fanship in the current discussion.

More than any other reason, sports media consumers report tuning in to contests involving their favored teams with high expectations of being entertained, experiencing enjoyment, or, as Gantz noted, "to thrill in victory" (Gantz, 1981, p. 268). Simply stated, the most important motivational factor behind viewing mediated sports is for the enjoyment and emotional satisfaction that comes from cheering on a favored team as it follows an undetermined (yet hoped for) path to victory. The disposition theory of sports spectatorship (for a comprehensive summary, see Raney, 2003) explains how enjoyment is derived from viewing a favored team compete in a sports contest.

The disposition theory of sports spectatorship (Bryant & Raney, 2000; Zillmann, Bryant, & Sapolsky, 1989; Zillmann & Paulus, 1993) posits that a fan's affiliation with a team can be described along a continuum of affect (from intense liking through indifference to intense disliking). Ultimately, the enjoyment of viewing a sporting event is a function of the outcome of the game in relation to the strength and valence of the dispositions held toward the competitors. Specifically, enjoyment is thought to increase the more the winning team is favored by the viewer and/or the more the losing team is disliked by the viewer. Conversely, enjoyment is thought to decrease the more the winning team is disliked by the viewer and/or the more the losing team is favored by the viewer. Given this formula, some researchers have suggested that maximum enjoyment from viewing sports should be experienced when an intensely liked team defeats an intensely disliked team. Conversely, maximum disappointment or *negative enjoyment* should be experienced when a loved team is defeated by a hated one (Zillmann & Paulus, 1993).

Many studies yield support for the disposition theory of sports spectatorship with both individual and team contests. Zillmann et al. (1989) detail the majority of these studies. For the sake of brevity, only two studies are noted here. First, the researchers examined how the dispositions held toward two professional American football teams would impact enjoyment of viewing a televised game between the two teams. Fanship toward the two teams was measured, with each participant being categorized as having either a positive, neutral, or negative disposition toward each team. Participants then viewed a live-broadcasted contest between the two teams. The researchers measured enjoyment of every play in the game, as well as of the overall contest. The researchers predicted that those with a positive disposition toward the victorious team would enjoy the game more than those who disliked the team and more than those who liked the defeated one. In fact, it was predicted that enjoyment of the contest would be the greatest for those viewers who really liked the winning team and really disliked the losing team. It was also predicted that enjoyment would be least for those viewers who liked the losing team and disliked the winning team. All of these expectations were met in the study, thus lending support to the disposition theory of sports spectatorship.

Additional support for disposition theory was found in a study of Olympic basketball also reported by Zillmann and his colleagues. College students at a major university in the United States viewed a portion of the 1976 men's gold medal game between the United States and Yugoslavia. Again, the respondents rated their enjoyment of each play in the game. As expected, the American students reported increased enjoyment on plays in which the United States scored. They also reported decreased enjoyment when Yugoslavia scored. These findings lend support to the disposition theory of sports spectatorship. But the researchers found additional support for the theory when they isolated responses to plays involving two select members of the U.S. team who has previously played amateur basketball at the university where the research was conducted. Respondents reported the highest enjoyment of scoring plays involving those two players than for any other U.S. players. The researchers concluded that the participants held even more positive dispositions toward the two former students than the other players on the U.S. squad; therefore, enjoyment was highest on plays in which they scored.

Eustress Motivation

As noted above, the intensity of team fanship and the anticipation about the contest's outcome are a large part of the entertainment motive for sports viewing. These factors also contribute to a second emotional motivation for viewing sports. Several studies report that fans tune into mediated sports because they like the positive emotions coming from the increased arousal and excitement experienced during viewing—the thrill of victory. Some contend that this so-called *eustress motivation* is theoretically driven by the chronic understimulation experienced by many individuals in their daily lives (Gantz, 1981; Gantz & Wenner, 1991, 1995; Krohn, et al., 1998; Smith, 1988; Wann, 1995; Wann, et al., 1999, 2001; Wenner & Gantz, 1998). A similar explanation has been offered for the appeal of sports participation, sports betting, and sports video game usage.

Studies have demonstrated that sports viewing can in fact lead to increased arousal (Bernhardt, Dabbs, Fielden, & Lutter, 1998). Similarly, viewers consistently describe viewing sports as exciting (e.g., Krohn, et al., 1998), arousing (e.g., Wann, et al., 2001), and able to "get me psyched up" (e.g., Gantz, 1981) or "pumped up" (e.g., Wann, 1995). Perhaps the primary source of the excitement and arousal is the suspenseful nature—which Zillmann (1991) theoretically equates with uncertainty—of sports competition. Surprisingly, only a few studies have specifically examined how uncertainty and suspense about a game's outcome affected enjoyment. In one such study, Depalma and Raney (2003) reported higher levels of enjoyment and suspense among viewers of unscripted sports (i.e., professional boxing) and scripted sports (i.e., professional wrestling) action. Bryant, Rockwell, and Owens (1994) found that the commentary accompanying the action can add to the level of suspense and subsequent enjoyment experienced by the viewer. Similarly, Gan and her colleagues had participants rate their enjoyment of one of eight collegiate basketball tournament games (Gan, Tuggle, Mitrook, Coussement, & Zillmann, 1997). To investigate the relationship between enjoyment and suspense, the researchers assumed that the closer the final score, the more suspenseful the game was considered to be. Games were subsequently categorized as minimally (more than a 15-point difference), moderately (10–14 points), substantially (5–9 points), or extremely (less than 5 points) suspenseful. Enjoyment for male participants increased as the final score became closer. The same pattern was observed with females only through the "substantial" category. The researchers hypothesized that the close scores in the "extremely suspenseful" category led to distress among female viewers. Corresponding to the distress, irritation likely increased, which presumably led to a decrease in enjoyment. So while many fans report viewing sports for arousal and stimulation, doing so may mean that they willfully expose themselves to possible displeasure. Specifically, uncomfortably close games may lead to stress (or distress) among some (particularly female) viewers.

Another source of the thrill experienced when consuming mediated sports seems to be the perceived violence contained in the action. For example, Bryant, Comisky, and Zillmann (1981) directly compared the appeal of violent and nonviolent sports. The researchers selected a number of plays from professional American football games, classifying them as either low, intermediate, or high in violence. Research participants then rated their enjoyment of the plays. As predicted, enjoyment increased with the degree of violence in the play. While this general pattern was observed, the relationship was statistically significant only for male viewers. In a related study, DeNeui and Sachau (1996) found that the number of penalty minutes assessed during an amateur hockey game—not how competitive the game was or even which team won—correlated most strongly with reported enjoyment. The increased arousal experienced by fans during the highly violent (and thus highly penalized) games presumably led to the increased enjoyment.

Also, Bryant, Brown, Comisky, and Zillmann (1982) created three versions of a tennis match in which the players were described either as best friends, bitter enemies, or neither friends nor enemies. Participants viewing the players-as-enemies version of the match described the action as significantly more enjoyable, exciting, involving, and interesting than participants viewing the other two versions. Participants also perceived the players to be more hostile, tense, and competitive in the players-as-enemies condition. Thus, the way the violent elements of the game are perceived further impacts the level of excitement and enjoyment experienced during viewing.

As mentioned previously, some researchers have noted that the arousal and excitement experienced by sports viewers can be compounded by the commentary accompanying televised sports. One such study sought to measure the effects of sports commentary on perceptions and enjoyment of hockey matches (Comisky, Bryant, & Zillmann, 1977). Groups of respondents viewed either normal or unusually rough hockey action, presented either with or without commentary about the action. Viewers of the normal play with accompanying commentary that focused on the conflict between the two teams perceived the action to be more intense and violent than those who saw the same action without commentary. The viewers of the normal play with conflict-centered commentary also rated the action as more intense and violent than viewers of the rougher play with and without (nonconflict) commentary. Furthermore, the viewers of the normal play with dramatic commentary had the highest ratings of enjoyment of the four conditions. Sullivan (1991) reported similar findings in a study of televised basketball.

While the eustress motivation is widely reported, some differences have been identified among viewers. Generally speaking, studies consistently report that eustress is more of a motivator for men to view sports than for women (Gantz & Wenner, 1991; Wann, 1995; Wann, et al., 1999). Furthermore, the eustress motivation is negatively correlated with education level, but positively correlated with a preference to view team sports (Wann, 1995; Wann, et al., 1999).

Self-Esteem Motivation

A third emotional motivation for consuming mediated sports is actualized only after the viewing experience is completed. Many report viewing sporting events because the events provide an opportunity for the viewers to increase their self-esteem (Wann, 1995; Wann, et al., 1999; Wenner & Gantz, 1998). In other words, viewers may tune into sporting events because they think the viewing will help them feel better about themselves. Research indicates that this can in fact be the case.

More specifically, watching a favored team win has been associated with more self-esteem and increased confidence in one's abilities and talents. In contrast, watching a favored team lose has been associated with diminished self-confidence and esteem. For example, Hirt and his colleagues demonstrated that viewers of a winning performance by a favored basketball team expected the team to perform better in the future, and likewise estimated their own ability to perform various social, mental, and motor tasks to be greater than their counterparts who viewed a losing performance by a favored team (Hirt, Zillmann, Erickson, & Kennedy, 1992). The researchers further demonstrated that the differences appeared to result from shifts in current levels of self-esteem rather than mood. Madrigal (1995) and Owens and Bryant (1998) also reported similar findings.

A related line of research investigates the emotional utility in being (or being perceived as) a fan. One group of scholars argued that a byproduct of being aligned with a winning team is the opportunity to "bask in the reflected glory" (BIRG) of the team's success (Cialdini, et al., 1976). This alignment can ultimately result in an improved perception of one's own public image. In other words, according to the BIRGing literature, some sports fans think that being readily identified with a winning team will result in being perceived more like a winning person.

Cialdini and his associates demonstrated support for the proposed BIRGing phenomenon among fans of collegiate American football. During one field experiment, the researchers observed a higher percentage of college students wearing apparel identifying their university on Mondays following a football victory than following a defeat. Similarly, students asked to describe the outcome of the game used the pronoun *we* when referring to the team significantly more after a victory than after a defeat. Additional studies lend further support to the BIRGing phenomenon (Cialdini & Richardson, 1980; Snyder, Higgins, & Stucky, 1983).

Therefore, the increased self-confidence that comes from being associated with a winning sports team can serve as another emotional motivation for viewing sports on television. However, this motivation seems to be more prevalent with certain viewers. In particular, men consistently report higher self-esteem motivation for viewing than women. Furthermore, some research indicates that self-esteem becomes less of a motivation for viewing as education level increases (Wann, 1995).

Escape Motivation

To this point, three emotional motivations for viewing sports on television have been discussed: entertainment, eustress, and self-esteem. With each, dispositions toward competing teams and game outcomes play a large role in motivating viewing. That is, as informed by the disposition literature, the extent to which a viewer is emotionally involved with or allegiant to a team involved in a contest, the more likely his/her viewing is motivated by a need to be entertained, to experience eustress, or to enhance self-esteem. However, a final emotional motivation that I discuss is less dependent upon fanship and outcome. Some viewers report that they regularly tune into sports to escape the stress of daily life (Gantz, 1981; Gantz & Wenner, 1991, 1995; Krohn, et al., 1998; Smith, 1988; Wann, 1995; Wann, et al., 1999, 2001; Wenner & Gantz, 1998).

Few would argue that we live in increasingly stressful times. From geopolitical tensions to ever-lengthening workweeks, we all experience pressures from a limitless number of sources. For decades, persons of all ages have reported seeking out media content to help escape from the stress of daily living. Sports fans are no different. As Smith (1988) noted, "While engrossed in the sporting event a fan's mood may fluctuate, but any pain is temporary and minor compared to the relief of gaining a respite from a wearisome existence" (p. 58). While this filler or escape motivation may be more prevalent during time of personal stress or problems (Wann, 1997), it has also been discussed in relation to boredom. For example, Krohn et al. (1998) noted that viewers often tune in to "take a break from a repetitive job schedule" (p. 282). Research supports this claim. Specifically, Wann and Rochelle (1999) found that nearly two in five sports fans report regularly tune in to sports on television to escape boredom.

Males tend to report higher escape motivation for viewing sports on television than women. Similarly, individuals who prefer team sports also report high escape motivation. Contrary to what some have posited, however, escape motivation for viewing is not correlated with enjoyment of violent sports (Wann, et al., 2001).

COGNITIVE MOTIVATIONS FOR MEDIATED SPORTS CONSUMPTION

Viewing of sports on television is not merely an emotional activity. Many sports fans indicate that they tune in for cognitive stimulation as well.

Learning Motivation

One of the most common cognitive motivations for viewing sports on television is learning about players and teams (Gantz, 1981; Gantz & Wenner, 1995; Wenner & Gantz, 1998). Granted, much of the learning seems to be about a viewer's favorite teams or players. However, several scholars have noted how sports fans take pride in being walking encyclopedias of sports knowledge and trivia. Because most sports telecasts are filled with statistical information about players and teams, it appears that fans also tune in to remain current with their facts.

As I will discuss later, this information serves an important social role for fans by providing conversational fodder between friends and strangers. Melnick (1993) noted that "sociability among sports strangers is likely to occur because the possibility of sharing and trading useful information is great" (p. 50). The universal language communicated through sports contests and shared by fans of teams and sports enthusiasts in general arguably transcends social status, education, and occupation (Lever, 1983). In fact, as opposed to politics or religion, sports discussions seemingly offer the welcomed opportunity for friendly disagreements with friends and strangers (Karp & Yoels, 1990). Much of the training for these conversations occurs during televised sporting events, on which endless commentary and countless statistical, historical, and trivial sports facts are communicated.

To a lesser extent, viewers report tuning in to televised sports to learn about sports themselves. Those reporting such motivations tend to be females and non-sports fans. However, the utility of learning such information is similar to that discussed previously: Individuals motivated in this way report a desire to become more knowledgeable of sports so that they can enjoy sports viewing with a loved one. This strategy can be met with differential responses by the sports fan. Some view such attempts as noble, encouraging and facilitating such learning among their loved ones. Others, however, take an elitist position and view such attempts with skepticism and contempt.

Aesthetic Motivation

Research indicates that some viewers are also motivated to watch sports on television because of the aesthetic qualities of the competition (Krohn, et al., 1998; Smith, 1988; Wann, 1995; Wann, et al., 1999, 2001; Wann & Wilson, 1999). Smith (1988) argued that "a splendid athletic performance rivals any great work of art" (p. 58). Others have compared the improvisational aspects of many sports with a jazz performance. When describing this aesthetic attraction, viewers tend to point to both the artistic or stylistic beauty found in sports movements and the novelty, riskiness, and unexpectedness of the play (Zillmann, et al., 1989). While we characterize this motivation as primarily cognitive given its evaluative nature, we should note that the resulting aesthetic appreciation for sports is often experienced as increased positive affect.

Viewers have consistently reported attraction to the beauty or dance of sports. Some scholars have suggested that this aesthetic appeal of sports is essentially erotic (Duncan & Brummett, 1989; Guttmann, 1996; Hargreaves, 1993). This may well be the case, but the point is somewhat tangential to this discussion. Few dispute that certain sports contain more aesthetic elements than others. For example, gymnastics, figure skating, diving, freestyle skiing, and skateboarding competitions are largely evaluated on standardized, aesthetic criteria alone. The more fluid the athletes' motions, the higher their scores. Given this, it should not be surprising that viewers of these sporting events report high aesthetic motivation (Sargent, Zillmann, & Weaver, 1998).

However, fans of other, nonstylistic sports also express appreciation for the beauty and style of the play. This likewise should not be unexpected: The grace of a Michael Jordan layup, a Pele bicycle kick, or an Ichiro diving catch in the outfield are quite apparent. However, one should not assume that fans who tune in for the grace and beauty of sports are also repulsed by the halting ugliness of sports violence. In fact, fans with high aesthetic motivation for viewing are equally likely to enjoy violent and nonviolent sports (Wann & Wilson, 1999).

Some gender differences, though, have been found with regard to aesthetics and sports. Sargent et al. (1998) had participants describe 25 regularly televised sports using a variety of terms, including violence, elegance, and danger. Females tended to report greater enjoyment for stylistic sports (e.g., gymnastics, figure skating, and tennis), while males reported greater enjoyment for combative sports (e.g., football, soccer, and boxing). More specifically, women tended to enjoy sports that they saw as elegant more than those that were seen as violent or dangerous. For men, enjoyment increased the more violent, active, and dangerous they perceived the sport to be. Zillmann (1995) and Bryant et al. (1981) reported similar findings.

Beyond the appeal of the grace and beauty of sports, fans also report being motivated to view by the aesthetics of novelty and high risk. Sports promoters often capitalize on this appeal by highlighting the novelty and unpredictability of a coach's game plan or a player's behavior when promoting an event. Moreover, during the telecasts themselves, novel, unexpected, and highly risky plays and moves are often reshown numerous times in super-slow motion accompanied by dramatic commentary. Of course, successful novel and unexpected plays often prove quite influential on the outcome of the contest as they catch unsuspecting defenses off guard. Other seemingly superhuman efforts on otherwise typical plays often serve similar purposes. Viewers consistently report being motivated to view certain contests because of the increased, yet uncertain, likelihood of seeing such plays.

Zillmann et al. (1989) argued that uncertainty rationales could be applied to sports play in a couple of ways in relation to enjoyment. First, uncommon plays are less expected by and are thus more surprising to viewers. Therefore, these plays should be more enjoyable than more common ones. Similarly, plays entailing a high risk of failure are unexpected and surprising to viewers. When these plays prove to be successful, enjoyment should be high. The researchers then explored the relationship between novel and risky plays, play effectiveness, and enjoyment in a study of American football. As expected, the enjoyment of certain successful plays was predicted with considerable accuracy by the risk of failure they entailed. Sargent et al. (1998) report similar findings concerning riskiness of play.

While researchers understand a bit about people who report high aesthetic motivation for viewing, we have little understanding of the actual mechanisms underlying aesthetic motivation. As Zillmann and Paulus (1993) noted,

> Despite much discussion of flow, harmony, and grace in the locomotion of athletes, and despite likening athletic motions to ballet and declaring athletic performances artistic, sports aesthetics is a poorly understood phenomenon, and the contribution of the aesthetic component of athletic performances to enjoyment remains to be determined. (p. 608)

BEHAVIORAL AND SOCIAL MOTIVATIONS FOR MEDIATED SPORTS CONSUMPTION

Release

As mentioned above, watching your favorite team win can produce boundless joy and exuberance. This fact keeps many viewers coming back time and again. Many fans, though, report that—win or lose—the unfolding drama of sports competition provides them the opportunity to release emotions. It is reasonable to assume that the viewer brings some pent-up emotions to the viewing experience. Furthermore, it is reasonable to assume that emotions are produced or further enhanced through viewing the actual competition. Whatever the source, the expectation of experiencing emotional release drives viewers to sports programming (Gantz, 1981; Gantz & Wenner, 1991, 1995; Krohn, et al., 1998; Wenner & Gantz, 1998).

While one might attempt to equate the release motivation with traditional notions of catharsis, it should be noted that the purging of emotions in the case of sports viewership comes not merely through viewing but through performing various behaviors while viewing. Of particular note, fans high in release motivation report watching "to let loose," "to have a few beers or drinks," "to let off steam," and "to get psyched up" (Gantz, 1981; Gantz & Wenner, 1991). Others explain that enjoyable sports viewing involves applauding and shouting in pleasure, yelling in displeasure and anger, verbally disputing the tactics of the coaches and players and the calls of officials, and pacing the floor in nervousness and anticipation (Gantz,

1981). While the complete set of behaviors that enable viewers "to let loose" or "to let off steam" is currently unknown, the motivation is nonetheless powerful. A necessary condition, however, appears to be the presence of friends.

Companionship

Given the social component of the release motivation, it may be of little surprise that another common motivation for consuming mediated sports is companionship (Dietz-Uhler, Harrick, End, & Jacquemotte, 2000; Gantz, 1981; Gantz & Wenner, 1991, 1995; Krohn, et al., 1998; Melnick, 1993; Smith, 1988; Wann, 1995; Wann, et al., 1999; Wann, et al., 2001; Wenner & Gantz, 1998). Research suggests that sports programming allows for more communicative behaviors between viewers than most television content (Wenner & Gantz, 1998). Whether at home with friends or at a sports bar with complete strangers (Eastman & Land, 1997), sports programming provides people the opportunity to interact on a common ground. Fans consistently report enjoying sports programming during which they talk with friends about the action (Gantz, 1981).

Melnick (1993) highlighted the unique communicative experience between strangers he called the "sports encounter" (p. 49). The author suggested that sports viewing, like air travel, provides strangers interesting and legitimate opportunities to interact. However, unlike airplane conversations, sports encounters carry a set of assumptions: an assumed level of knowledge, an assumed set of shared behaviors and motivations, an assumed commitment to and enthusiasm about the game, and an assumed understanding of time boundaries during which a conversation can take place (e.g., time-out, halftime, during commercials, but not during the actual play). All of these assumptions create a setting that is conducive to conversation. However, as Melnick noted, participants in legitimate sports encounters understand that the conversational topic will be restricted to the current game, the teams, the sport, or perhaps sports in general. To stray from this accepted set of topics is to violate the implicit terms of the social arrangement. However, as long as these assumptions are met, sports encounters may actually be one of the few types of public discourse that allow for friendly disagreements. Understandably, then, viewers find solace and enjoyment in the companionship afforded through sports viewing.

Group Affiliation

Beyond the temporal companionship that sports viewing provides, many fans also report being motivated by a larger sense of group affiliation. Particularly, ardent fans of specific teams note a sense of belonging that is shared by them and other supporters of the team (Krohn, et al., 1998; Smith, 1988; Wann, 1995; Wann, et al., 1999, 2001). Depending on the situation, this sense of belonging and community can be felt on various levels. In fact, Smith (1988) suggested that sports can promote the integration of schools, communities, cities, and even nations. For instance, popular texts like *Friday Night Lights* (Bissinger, 1990) and *Futbol* (Bellos, 2002) have chronicled the power of sports to bring communities and nations together around high school American football and soccer, respectively. Furthermore, global competitions like the Olympics and the World Cup that pit nations against one another can generate increased national pride at least for a short period of time.

For example, the motion picture *Miracle* (2004) recounts the national fervor that erupted in the United States during the 1980 U.S. hockey team's improbable journey to Olympic gold.

Generally speaking, the group-affiliation motivation for sports television viewing is more prominent among younger sports fans and among individuals at higher levels of income. (Wann, 1995)

Family

A related motivation for viewing sports on television is to spend time or to have something to do with family members (Dietz-Uhler, et al., 2000; Gantz, 1981; Gantz & Wenner, 1991, 1995; Wann, 1995; Wann, et al., 1999, 2001; Wenner & Gantz, 1998). For example, a common New Year's Day tradition in the United States is for families to gather around the television to view the Tournament of Roses Parade, followed by the Rose Bowl football game matching two of the nation's top college teams. In fact, sports programming perhaps represents one of the only remaining family co-viewing television experiences. As one might expect, then, the family motivation for sports television viewing is more likely to be reported by married individuals and/or those with children (Wann, et al., 2001). It comes as little surprise that some researchers find that family motivation is positively correlated with age (Wann, 1995). Some research indicates that those with higher family motivation might prefer nonaggresive sports more than aggressive ones (Wann, 1995), though more recent studies have brought this finding into question (see Wann, et al., 2001, for a summary).

Furthermore, research consistently reports that females are significantly more likely to be motivated to view sports on television for family reasons (Dietz-Uhler, et al., 2000; Gantz & Wenner, 1991; Wann, et al., 1999, 2001), a finding that remains even when level of interest in sports is held constant. In other words, all things being equal, females tend to be more motivated to view sports for family-related reasons than males.

Gantz and Wenner (1991) noted that females tend to be less involved in actual viewing than their male counterparts, often completing household tasks during the course of the game. Many possible explanations for this gender difference have been forwarded. One possibility is that, in general, males are socialized to be competitive and aggressive (characteristics that are surely perpetuated through male involvement in sports), while females generally are socialized to be noncompetitive and submissive. As a result, males often take a dominant (and often domineering) role in the male–female relationship. One way that this dynamic is expressed is in the control of the television remote control. Thus, because males tend to view more sports than females, a natural consequence of the socialization process is that females acquiesce to and join in sports viewing with their male family members. Similarly, some have suggested that females, typically strapped with more household responsibilities, utilize the sports viewing situation to both spend time with family and to catch up on mounting chores (Gantz & Wenner, 1991).

Despite different approaches to viewing, research indicates that sports television leads to relatively few conflicts between married couples. Females, more so than males, actually report that sports viewing plays as positive role in the marriage relationship (Gantz, Wanner, Carrico, & Knorr, 1995). Curiously, males are more likely to think that their sports viewing is an irritant to their spouse. Some researchers have suggested that the lack of actual conflicts or resentment within marriages may result from careful negotiations about television viewing in general (but particularly sports) during the first few years of a marital relationship. Others credit the growing number of multiple-television households.

Economics

Finally, some individuals are motivated to view sports on television because of financial investment (Eastman & Land, 1997; Gantz, 1981; Gantz & Wenner, 1995; Wann, 1995; Wann, et al., 1999, 2001). Every day, persons across the globe wager various sums of money on teams and individuals to win (or lose). Odds on sporting events are published daily in newspaper sports sections across the United States and updated every minute on a variety of Web sites. The National Gaming Board of South Africa reported nearly 5.3 million ZA Rand (more than $US 700,000) wagered on horseracing alone in 2002 and 2003. More than $81 million were wagered on the 2004 NFL Super Bowl in Las Vegas alone. In fact, according to industry reports (e.g., Christiansen Capital Advisors, LLC), Americans gambled more than $4 billion on sporting events (including horseracing, greyhound racing, and jai alai) through official bookmakers in 2000; this does not include the reported $2.2 billion in Internet betting.

Sports gambling has destroyed the lives of sports stars like baseball great Pete Rose and ended the promising careers of amateur athletes like former college football quarterbacks Art Schlichter and Adrian McPherson before they even began. Further, gambling experts testifying before the U.S. House Judiciary Committee estimated that up to 4% of adult Americans currently suffer from a gambling addiction, with a large proportion coming from the college-aged population.

Some researchers speculate that sports gambling may be more about "profits than standings" (Wann, 1995, p. 378). In fact, Wann reported that the economic motivation for sports viewing was virtually unrelated to self-reported levels of sports fanship, identification as a sports fan, and overall sports involvement. Furthermore, high economic motivation (in comparison to other motivations) was only weakly related to the enjoyment of watching various sports typically associated with gambling (e.g., football, horse racing, boxing). In other words, individuals primarily motivated to view sports for economic reasons often do not qualify as sports fans at all.

Generally speaking, the economic motivation for sports television viewing is more prominent among males, among viewers who prefer violent sports, and among individuals at higher levels of income (Wann, 1995; Wann, et al., 1999).

SUMMARY

As previously noted, quite a few studies have been conducted to determine the reasons why so many watch and enjoy mediated sports. The findings of those studies have been reported above. In conclusion, though I think it is appropriate to identify tensions or themes that emerge from the research, I encourage the reader to consider the following three observations.

1. *The motivations for and responses to viewing sports on television are primarily functions of affect, but they contain distinctly cognitive and social aspects as well.* Especially with ardent fans, sports are visceral. They are felt. Teams are loved; others are hated. As Jim McKay once proclaimed at the opening of ABC's *Wide*

World of Sports, viewers knowingly and willingly set themselves up to experience "the thrill of victory and the agony of defeat." Games often end with tears of joy on one sideline, and tears of sorrow on the other.

But, sports are more than feelings. Sports involve thinking. Whether it is the recounting of endless statistics from bygone seasons or the intricate dissection of an upcoming opponent's defensive strategy, sports viewing can be a cerebral activity. Again, many sports fans pride themselves on their knowledge of players, teams, sports, and trivia. While support for the dumb-jock stereotype might be readily available, no equivalent dumb-jock fan model exists. Furthermore, sports are social events, serving tremendous social functions in the lives of fans and nonfans alike. As argued, sports provide an opportunity for strangers to cheer together in common love or hatred of a team, to engage in lengthy debates over drinks, or to join hands in silent reverence as an injured competitor is carried from the field. Sports metaphors are often used to discuss the geopolitical environment, not necessarily because sports are inherently contentious, but because sports demonstrate how we can all come together civilly to resolve our differences.

2. *Viewing sports on television is more often than not an intentional action by an active audience member. However, at times, the activity can be spontaneous and/or passive.* As discussed at the beginning of this chapter, several media-related theories help us in our understanding of the appeal of sports television. Most of those perspectives acknowledge an active audience member who is purposive in his or her television viewing habits. As the research record indicates, this is surely the case with most sports viewers. Television schedules are often announced months in advance, allowing sports fans to set up their viewing schedules. Blocks of time are reserved. Parties are planned. Interruptions are not allowed.

However, sometimes fans come across sports serendipitously. Perhaps it is the replay of a game played years ago. Perhaps it is simply the highlights of last night's contest. Perhaps it is the middle-of-the-night, insomnia-inspired viewing of a curling match. Competition of any kind can provide sports fans with a reminder of the joy from viewing his or her favorite team compete. Sports share a common language, a common mood, a common spirit. Merely tapping into that feeling is often all that a sports fan needs.

Furthermore, some fans tune in to sports in order to tune out from everything else. Like the soothing melodies of music, sports can provide the calming background noise needed at the end of a busy day. Like a familiar film or book, sports can be picked up when a fan needs comfort, relaxation, or release.

3. *Watching mediated sports can be an all-consuming passion, but mostly it is experienced within a more holistic perspective on the human condition.* Sports spectatorship as a personal pursuit has been disparaged for decades. In fact, Zillmann and his colleagues argued that the literature reveals "nearly a universal condemnation of sports spectatorship" (Zillmann, Bryant, & Sapolsky, 1979, p. 302). Smith (1988) summarized the major criticism of sports viewing: Some argue that sports function as an opiate for viewers, narcotizing individuals who might otherwise be agents of social change and reform. Others claim that sports transmit distorted values to viewers, such as the acceptability (and in some cases, the glorification) of violence, leisure, banality, racism, and sexism.

While some sports viewers are no doubt addicted to the action, most others have struck a balance between sport and the rest of life. Yes, sports fans paint their faces to display their team loyalty. They brave freezing temperatures to support their team. They refuse sleep in favor of watching their national team play live half way around the world. They schedule their weekends around the next game. They discuss sports trivia and debate standings at home, around the water cooler, and at their place of worship with apparently the same passion with which they discuss the births of their children, their latest promotion, and their faith. Indeed, sports spectatorship taps into the most basic human emotions of joy and sorrow. But, those same sports fans still fulfill their roles as mothers and fathers. They still show up for work. And they still practice their faith. Furthermore, sports fans coach in youth leagues. They are more likely than nonfans to remain physically fit themselves. They embrace the joys and sorrows inherent in sports competition, and in doing so, learn to embrace the joys and sorrows of life. While I may stop short in joining Smith in his praise of the "noble sports fan," I will join him in celebrating mediated sports viewing as more than an ignoble, and potentially as a beneficial, human pursuit.

AUTHOR NOTE

An earlier version of this manuscript appeared in Holger Schramm (Ed.), *Sport Communication, Part III: Reception of Sport in the Media*, Collogne, Germany: Herbert von Halem Publishing, 2004.

REFERENCES

Bellos, A. (2002). *Futebol: Soccer the Brazilian way*. New York: Bloomsbury.

Bernhardt, P. C., Dabbs, J. M., Fielden, J. A., & Lutter, C. D. (1998). Testosterone changes during vicarious experiences of winning and losing among fans at sporting events. *Physiology and Behaviors, 18,* 263–268.

Bissinger, F. G. (1990). *Friday night lights: A town, a team, and a dream*. Reading, MA: Addison-Wesley.

Biswas, R., Riffe, D., & Zillmann, D. (1994). Mood influence on the appeal of bad news. *Journalism Quarterly, 71,* 689–696.

Blumler, J. G., & Katz, E. (Eds.). (1974). *The uses of mass communication: Current perspectives on gratifications research*. Beverley Hills, CA: Sage.

Bryant, J., Brown, D., Comisky, P. W., & Zillmann, D. (1982). Sports and spectators: Commentary and appreciation. *Journal of Communication, 32,* 109–119.

Bryant, J., Comisky, P. W., & Zillmann, D. (1981). The appeal of rough-and-tumble play in televised professional football. *Communication Quarterly, 29,* 256–262.

Bryant, J., & Raney, A. A. (2000). Sports on the screen. In D. Zillmann & P. Vorderer (Eds.), *Media entertainment: The psychology of its appeal* (pp. 153–174). Mahwah, NJ: Lawrence Erlbaum Associates.

Bryant, J., Rockwell, S. C., & Owens, J. W. (1994). "Buzzer beaters" and "barn burners": The effects on enjoyment of watching the game go "down to the wire." *Journal of Sport & Social Issues, 18,* 326–339.

Bryant, J., & Zillmann, D. (Eds). (2002). *Media effects: Advances in theory and research*. Mahwah, NJ: Lawrence Erlbaum Associates.

Christ, W. C., & Medoff, N. J. (1984). Affective state and selective exposure to and use of television. *Journal of Broadcasting, 28,* 51–63.

Cialdini, R. B., Borden, R. J., Thorne, A., Walker, M. R., Freeman, S., & Sloan, L. R. (1976). Basking in reflected glory: Three (football) field studies. *Journal of Personality and Social Psychology, 34,* 366–375.

Cialdini, R. B., & Richardson, K. D. (1980). Two indirect tactics of image management: Basking and blasting. *Journal of Personality and Social Psychology, 39,* 406–415.

Comisky, P., Bryant, J., & Zillmann, D. (1977). Commentary as a substitute for action. *Journal of Communication, 27,* 150–153.

DeNeui, D. L., & Sachau, D. A. (1996). Spectator enjoyment of aggression in intercollegiate hockey games. *Journal of Sport & Social Issues, 21,* 69–77.

Depalma, A., & Raney, A. A. (2003, May). *The effect of viewing varying levels of aggressive sports programming on enjoyment, mood, and perceived violence.* Paper presented at the annual meeting of the International Communication Association, San Diego, CA.

Dietz-Uhler, B., Harrick, E. A., End, C., & Jacquemotte, L. (2000). Sex differences in sport fan behavior and reasons for being a sport fan. *Journal of Sport Behavior, 23,* 219–231.

Duncan, M. C., & Brummett, B. (1989). Types and sources of spectating pleasure in televised sports. *Sociology of Sport Journal, 6,* 195–211.

Eastman, S. T., & Land, A. M. (1997). The best of both worlds: Sports fans find good seats at the bar. *Journal of Sport & Social Issues, 21,* 156–178.

Festinger, L. (1957). *A theory of cognitive dissonance.* Evanston, IL: Row, Peterson.

Gan, S-L., Tuggle, C. A., Mitrook, M. A., Coussement, S. H., & Zillmann, D. (1997). The thrill of a close game: Who enjoys it and who doesn't? *Journal of Sport & Social Issues, 21,* 53–64.

Gantz, W. (1981). An exploration of viewing motives and behaviors associated with television sports. *Journal of Broadcasting, 25,* 263–275.

Gantz, W., & Wenner, L. A. (1991). Men, women, and sports: Audience experiences and effects. *Journal of Broadcasting & Electronic Media, 35,* 233–243.

Gantz, W., & Wenner, L. A. (1995). Fanship and the television sports viewing experience. *Sociology of Sport Journal, 12,* 56–74.

Gantz, W., Wenner, L. A., Carrico, C., & Knorr, M. (1995). Televised sports and marital relationships. *Sociology of Sport Journal, 12,* 306–323.

Guttmann, A. (1996). *The erotic in sports.* New York: Columbia University Press.

Hargreaves, J. (1993). Bodies matter! Images of sport and female sexualization. In C. Brakenridge (Ed.), *Body matters: Leisure images and lifestyles* (pp. 60–66). Eastbourne, UK: Leisure Studies Association.

Heider, F. (1958). *The psychology of interpersonal relations.* New York: Wiley.

Hirt, E. R., Zillmann, D., Erickson, G. A., & Kennedy, C. (1992). Costs and benefits of allegiance: Changes in fans' self-ascribed competencies after team victory versus defeat. *Journal of Personality and Social Psychology, 63,* 724–738.

Johnson, D. D. (1995). Adolescents' motivations for viewing graphic horror. *Human Communication Research, 21,* 522–552.

Karp, D. A., & Yoels, W. C. (1990). Sport and urban life. *Journal of Sport & Social Issues, 14,* 77–102.

Klapper, J. T. (1960). *The effects of mass communication.* New York: Free Press.

Knobloch, S., & Zillmann, D. (2002). Mood management via the digital jukebox. *Journal of Communication, 52,* 351–366.

Krohn, F. B., Clarke, M., Preston, E., McDonald, M., & Preston, B. (1998). Psychological and sociological influences on attendance at small college sporting events. *College Student Journal, 32,* 277–288.

Lever, J. (1983). *Soccer madness.* Chicago: University of Chicago Press.

Madrigal, R. (1995). Cognitive and affective determinants of fan satisfaction with sporting event attendance. *Journal of Leisure Research, 27,* 205–227.

Melnick, M. J. (1993). Searching for sociability in the stands: A theory of sports spectating. *Journal of Sport Management, 7,* 44–60.

Owens, J. W., & Bryant, J. (1998, July). *The effects of a hometown ("Homer") announcer and color commentator on audience perspectives and enjoyment of a sports contest.* Paper presented at the annual meeting of the International Communication Association, Jerusalem, Israel.

Perse, E. M. (1986). Soap opera viewing patterns of college students and cultivation. *Journal of Broadcasting & Electronic Media, 30,* 175–193.

Raney, A. A. (2003). The enjoyment of sports spectatorship. In J. Bryant, J. Cantor, & D. Roskos-Ewoldsen (Eds.), *Communication and emotion: Essays in honor of Dolf Zillmann* (pp. 397–416). Mahwah, NJ: Lawrence Erlbaum Associates.

Rubin, A. M. (2002). The uses-and-gratification perspective of media effects. In J. Bryant & D. Zillmann (Eds.), *Media effects: Advances in theory and research* (pp. 525–548). Mahwah, NJ: Lawrence Erlbaum Associates.

Sargent, S. L., Zillmann, D., & Weaver, J. B. (1998). The gender gap in the enjoyment of televised sports. *Journal of Sport & Social Issues, 22,* 46–64.

Smith, G. J. (1988). The noble sports fan. *Journal of Sport & Social Issues, 12,* 54–65.

Snyder, C. R., Higgins, R. L., & Stucky, R. J. (1983). *Excuses: Masquerades in search of grace.* New York: Wiley-Interscience.

Sullivan, D. B. (1991). Commentary and viewer perception of player hostility: Adding punch to televised sport. *Journal of Broadcasting & Electronic Media, 35*(4), 487–504.

Sweeny, P. D., & Gruber, K. L. (1984). Selective exposure: Voter information preferences and the Watergate affair. *Journal of Personality and Social Psychology, 46*, 1208–1221.

Turow, J. (1974). Talk-show radio as interpersonal communication. *Journal of Broadcasting, 18*, 171–179.

Vidmar, N., & Rokeach, M. (1974). Archie Bunker's bigotry: A study in selective perception and exposure. *Journal of Communication, 24*, 36–47.

Vincent, R. C., & Basil, M. D. (1997). College students' news gratification, media use and current events knowledge. *Journal of Broadcasting & Electronic Media, 41*, 380–392.

Wann, D. L. (1995). Preliminary validation of the Sports Fan Motivational Scale. *Journal of Sport & Social Issues, 19*, 377–396.

Wann, D. L. (1997). *Sport psychology.* Upper Saddle River, NJ: Prentice Hall.

Wann, D. L., Melnick, M. J., Russell, G. W., & Pease, D. G. (2001). *Sports fans: The psychology and social impact of spectators.* New York: Routledge.

Wann, D. L., & Rochelle, A. R. (1999). *Using sports fandom as an escape: Searching for relief from under-stimulation and over-stimulation.* Unpublished manuscript.

Wann, D. L., Schrader, M. P., & Wilson, A. M. (1999). Sports fan motivation: Questionnaire validation, comparison by sport, and relationship to athletic motivation. *Journal of Sport Behavior, 22*, 114–139.

Wann, D. L., & Wilson, A. M. (1999). The relationship between aesthetic fan motivation and preferences for aggressive and nonaggressive sports. *Perceptual and Motor Skills, 89*, 931–934.

Wenner, L. A., & Gantz, W. (1998). Watching sports on television: Audience experience, gender, fanship, and marriage. In L. A. Wenner (Ed.), *MediaSport* (pp. 233–251). London: Routledge.

Zillmann, D. (1991). Television viewing and physiological arousal. In J. Bryant & D. Zillmann (Eds.), *Responding to the screen: Reception and reaction processes* (pp. 103–133). Hillsdale, NJ: Lawrence Erlbaum Associates.

Zillmann, D. (1995). Sports and the media. In J. Mester (Ed.), *Images of sport in the world* (pp. 423–444). Cologne: German Sports University.

Zillmann, D. (2000). Mood management in the context of selective exposure theory. In M. E. Roloff (Ed.), *Communication Yearbook 23* (pp. 103–123). Thousand Oaks, CA: Sage.

Zillmann, D., & Bryant, J. (Eds.) (1985). *Selective exposure to communication.* Hillsdale, NJ: Lawrence Erlbaum Associates.

Zillmann, D., Bryant, J., & Sapolsky, B. (1979). The enjoyment of watching sports contests. In J. H. Goldstein (Ed.), *Sports, games, and play: Social and psychological viewpoints* (pp. 297–335). Hillsdale, NJ: Lawrence Erlbaum Associates.

Zillmann, D., Bryant, J., & Sapolsky, B. (1989). Enjoyment from sports spectatorship. In J. H. Goldstein (Ed.), *Sports, games, and play: Social and psychological viewpoints* (2nd ed., pp. 241–278). Hillsdale, NJ: Lawrence Erlbaum Associates.

Zillmann, D., & Paulus, P. B. (1993). Spectators: Reactions to sports events and effects on athletic performance. In R. N. Singer, M. Murphey, & L. K. Tennant (Eds.), *Handbook of research on sports psychology* (pp. 600–619). New York: Macmillan.

20

The Causes and Consequences of Sport Team Identification

Daniel L. Wann
Murray State University

At most social gatherings, the attendees behave in a highly similar manner. For instance, the actions of those attending church, movies, club meetings, and even college classes are usually hard to differentiate. However, this is not the case with spectators attending sporting events. Rather, for anyone who has attended such an event, one fact becomes readily apparent—some of the attendees are more interested in the game than others. Some fans seem to pay no attention to the event. Others sit quietly, calmly watching the contest while casually carrying on conversations with their friends. And others seem to be captivated in the game. They are dressed (and perhaps painted) in their team's colors and logo, cheer and/or boo loudly throughout the contest, and appear as though their entire existence is hinging on every play. These drastic differences in the behaviors of sport spectators highlight the importance of and can be attributed to variations in team identification.

In this chapter, I examine team identification and its impact on sport fandom. My examination consists of four sections. The first section provides a general introduction to the area of team identification and includes sections on defining and measuring team identification and the stability of this construct. The second section is devoted to potential causes of team identification. This presentation focuses on three different causes: psychological, environmental, and team-related. The third portion of this chapter examines consequences of team identification. Here I review three responses that are impacted by level of team identification: behavioral (e.g., fan aggression), affective (e.g., emotional responses to the team's performance), and psychological (e.g., the impact of team performance on the fan's psychological well-being). A final section offers directions for future research in the area of team identification.

AN INTRODUCTION TO SPORT TEAM IDENTIFICATION

The purpose of this section is to provide the reader with a general understanding of team identification. I begin by clearly defining team identification and then move into discussions of the measurement and stability of the construct.

Defining Team Identification

The concept of an individual's identification with a group has a long history of interest from social scientists, including early psychologists such as Freud (1949), Tolman (1943), Sanford (1955), and Mowrer (1950). In a summary of the early work on group identification (i.e., pre-1960), Kagan (1958) concluded that identification is best defined as "an acquired, cognitive response within a person (S)" and that "some of the attributes, motives, characteristics, and affective states of a model (M) are part of the S's psychological organization" (p. 298). Kagan suggested further that one consequence of the identification is that the individual may "react to events occurring to the M as if they occurred to him" (p. 298). Although this definition is almost half a century old, it is a good starting point for developing a working definition of sport team identification because much of Kagan's conceptualization of group identification relates to sport fandom. For instance, fans identify strongly with their favorite team and respond with an emotional intensity rivaling that of the players.

More recently, the concept of sport team identification has been influenced by the social identity and self-categorizations theories popularized by European social psychologists in the 1980s (e.g., Tajfel, 1981; Turner, 1984). In general, these approaches view group identification as the extent to which a social category is relevant and important to an individual (see Spears, Doosje, & Ellemers, 1999). That is, individuals will have a high level of group identification when the actions of the group are a central component of their social identity and when categorization as a member of this group is important and relevant. Further, according to this approach, one does not have to be an active participant in group activities to feel connected to the group (e.g., spectators do not have to be team members to identify with the team; see Ashforth & Mael, 1989).

Social identity theory influenced many recent definitions of sport team identification.[1] For instance, borrowing from the social identity perspective, Wann and his colleagues (Wann & Branscombe, 1993; Wann, Melnick, Russell, & Pease, 2001) defined team identification as the extent to which a fan feels a psychological connection to a team and the team's performances are viewed as self-relevant. Because

---

[1]Other terms have been used to describe the construct labeled here as *team identification* (see Funk & James, 2001). The most common additional terms include *commitment* (e.g., Allen & Meyer, 1990; Mahony, Madrigal, & Howard, 2000) which is popular in the organizational psychology literature, and *loyalty* (e.g., Backman & Crompton, 1991; Park & Kim, 2000; Wakefield & Sloan, 1995), which is common among sport marketing professionals. Although subtle differences between the terms may exist (Mael & Ashforth, 2001), they will be viewed as interchangeable in this chapter. This is supported by research indicating that measures of team identification and team commitment are highly similar (Wann & Pierce, 2003) and by the fact that operational definitions of these constructs often overlap [e.g., Wann, Melnick, Russell, & Pease (2001) defined team identification as "the extent to which a fan feels psychologically connected to a team" (p. 3) while James, Kolbe, & Trail (2002) argue that team loyalty "involves an individual forming a psychological connection to a team" (p. 216)].

of its acceptance within the sport science community (e.g., Madrigal, 2000), Wann's conceptualization serves as the working definition of team identification for this chapter. Such a perspective is consistent with the aforementioned early work on group identification and the European social identity approach, as well as other recent sport-based operationalizations (e.g., Fisher, 1998; Shamir, 1992; Underwood, Bond, & Baer, 2001).

Measuring Team Identification

Although the first step in the examination of a psychological phenomenon is to operationally define the construct, a second and equally important step is the construction of an instrument designed to accurately assess the topic of interest. Within the realm of team identification, three measures have received substantial use. Two of these scales, the Psychological Commitment to Team (PCT) Scale developed by Mahony, Madrigal, and Howard (2000) and the Connection to Team Scale (CTS) developed by Trail and James (2001; see also James, Kolbe, & Trail, 2002) have received attention primarily from sport marketing and management professionals. The PCT Scale contains 14 Likert-scale items designed for use "in segmenting sport consumers based on loyalty" (p. 15). The authors provided evidence that the PCT Scale is internally consistent and has predictive validity. However, further research by Kwon and Trail (2003) indicated that additional refinements to the PCT Scale may be needed to acquire a more psychometrically sound instrument. The CTS contains three items and is particularly useful when examining the identification of newly formed teams (e.g., Major League Baseball expansion teams).

A third and even more extensively used scale (especially in sport psychology settings) is the Sport Spectator Identification Scale (SSIS) developed by Wann and Branscombe (1993). The SSIS, which contains seven Likert-scale items, has documented internal consistency, test–retest reliability, and validity. The SSIS has been successfully used in dozens of studies of spectator behavior (see Wann, Melnick et al., 2001) and has been translated into several languages including Dutch, German, and Japanese. Although the aforementioned scales have received the most extensive coverage and have the most well-established psychometric qualities, other measures of identification have been used (e.g., Fisher, 1998; Fisher & Wakefield, 1998; Gladden & Funk, 2002; Gwinner & Swanson, 2003; Kwon & Armstrong, 2002; Kwon & Trail, 2001).

Stability of Team Identification

A final general issue concerning team identification warranting discussion concerns the stability of an individual's level of identification with a particular team. Several studies found that team identification is relatively stable across time (Wann & Branscombe, 1993; Wann, Dolan, McGeorge, & Allison, 1994; Wann & Schrader, 1996). When levels of identification were tracked across a sport season, few changes in identification were found. For example, in his analysis of successful and unsuccessful university basketball and football teams, Wann (1996; 2000) found only one consistent change in level of identification throughout the season—fans' identification tended to decline as the season progressed. Other potential factors, such as outcome or location of the previous game, were not consistently related to increases or decreases in identification. Further, when significant changes were found, the effect size was quite small. For instance, although Wann (1996) found that levels of identification for a historically successful collegiate basketball team were higher after a win than a loss, the means were still very similar (e.g., 3.65 and 3.58 on a 1.00 to 8.00 scale). However, although it is safe to conclude that team identification is a stable construct, it is inappropriate to suggest that it is impervious to change (see Spears, et al., 1999). Rather, it is the possibility that levels of team identification might be modifiable that leads sport marketers to develop strategies designed to increase identification, as I discuss later.

CAUSES AND ANTECEDENTS TO SPORT TEAM IDENTIFICATION

One line of inquiry that has interested a number of sport scientists concerns factors encouraging an individual to identify with a particular team. My examination of the causes of team identification focuses on three types of antecedents: psychological, environmental, and team-related. However, before proceeding into a discussion of the causes of team identification, a few general points deserve mention. First, research on the causes of sport team identification can be difficult because there are so many different potential antecedents. An anecdotal example of this fact can be seen in my own development as a Chicago Cubs baseball fan. As a young child, my older brother's favorite team was the St. Louis Cardinals. Due to sibling rivalry, I decided to follow a team that was a rival of the Cardinals, hence my decision to become a Cubs fan. Another anecdotal example was discussed by Farred (2002), who recounted how he became a childhood fan of Liverpool's soccer team simply because he liked the way "Liverpool" sounded. Empirical evidence of the vast number of potential antecedents to team identification can be found in the work of Wann, Tucker, and Schrader (1996). These authors asked almost 100 sports fans to state the reasons they originally began to identify with their favorite team. The fans listed dozens of reasons that were grouped into 42 distinct categories. What is important to note here is that the vast majority of reasons (i.e., over 90%) were listed by fewer than 10% of the participants. There was little overlap in the antecedents reported. Second, my examination of the causes of identification is not limited to empirical or theoretical investigations of sport team identification. Rather, related work from other areas of group psychology (i.e., nonsport) is also included. Though not directly focused on fans, this literature is valuable because many of the suggested causes of group identification are found in spectating environments.

Psychological Causes of Team Identification

Researchers have discussed three psychological factors that can facilitate identification with a sport team. One factor concerns an individual's need for belonging and affiliation, that is, his or her desire to feel unity and cohesion with others (Gwinner & Swanson, 2003; Underwood, et al., 2001). In their discussion of antecedents to team identification, Sutton, McDonald, Milne, and Cimperman (1997) argued that "Community affiliation is the most significant correlate of fan identification" (p. 18). Indeed, in their work on the origin of team identification, Wann et al. (1996) found that the opportunity for affiliation with others was a common antecedent among persons in their sample. This may be a particularly powerful force when identifying with a new team (i.e., a team that has yet to begin play, such as an expansion team; see James, et al., 2002) because, in these situations, other potential factors are not yet in place (e.g., environmental causes such as a unique stadium and team-related causes such as successful performance).

A second psychological antecedent of sport team identification involves our desire to feel part of distinctive groups. Research in social identity reveals that persons are often motivated to view their ingroup as distinct (i.e., different) from outgroups (Ashforth & Mael, 1989; Branscombe, Ellemers, Spears, & Doosje, 1999; Jetten, Spears, & Manstead, 1999) and that our desire for group distinctiveness can, in some instances, be more powerful than our desire for a positive group image (Mlicki & Ellemers, 1996). With respect to sports fans, this cause reflects the fan's desire to become associated with something special or unique (e.g., fans often suggest that followers of their team are categorically different from followers of rival teams; e.g., Wann & Branscombe, 1995a).

A final psychological cause of identification involves the impact of death salience. According to terror management theory (Solomon, Greenberg, & Pyszczynski, 1991), a positive self-image serves as a buffer against the anxiety associated with one's awareness of one's mortality. Applied to sport fandom, terror management theory would predict that identification with a sport team can assist in the maintenance of a positive image and, consequently, assist in one's attempt to deal with one's mortality (Dechesne, Greenberg, Arndt, & Schimel, 2000). When the salience of one's mortality is increased, one's identification for a sport team should also increase because, under such an environment, the protective properties of the identification should be most valuable. However, mortality salience should lead to an increase in identification only with successful teams because increasing bonds with failing teams would likely not provide the image boost needed for use as a buffer against mortality-based anxiety. Dechesne et al.'s (2000) research with university basketball and football fans provides strong support for this pattern of effects.

Environmental Causes of Team Identification

In some instances, the antecedents of team identification lie in the environment surrounding the spectator. One such environmental cause involves the socialization process. A number of authors have suggested that team identification can be fostered through interactions with socialization agents such as exposure to the sport (Gwinner & Swanson, 2003), friends and other fans of the team (Crawford, 2003; Kolbe & James, 2003), and the fan's parents and family (Funk & James, 2001; Greenwood, 2001; Wann, et al., 1996). Research by James (2001) indicated that fathers have a particularly powerful effect as a socialization agent and that parents can influence the team identification of children as young as five. Repeated exposure to the team via the media and Internet also serves as a powerful agent of socialization (Mahony, Nakazawa, Funk, James, & Gladden, 2002; Sutton, et al., 1997), which may help explain the large fan bases for teams with superstations such as the Chicago Cubs and Atlanta Braves. It should be mentioned that socialization agents such as these are not required for identification to develop. Rather, in some instances, sports fans appear to be self-socialized to support a particular team (i.e., they adopt a team in the absence of any socialization agents; see Farred, 2002). Because socialization is such a powerful force, it is not surprising that living in or growing up near a team is an important factor in the origination of a person's team identification (e.g., Greenwood, 2001; Jones, 1997; Uemukai, Takenouchi, Okuda, Matsumoto, & Yamanaka, 1995; Wann, et al., 1996). Living in close geographical proximity to the team leads to increased opportunities for socialization to occur (and, pertinent to my earlier discussion, it provides a greater opportunity to develop a sense of unity with other fans).

Other environmental factors have also gained the attention of researchers. For instance, Kagan (1958) argued that identification increases when the individual has direct contact with a model. This implies that team identification is facilitated by fan-to-player contact, such as during autograph sessions or photo-day opportunities. Ashforth and Mael (1989) argued that the salience of an outgroup can lead to an increased level of identification with the ingroup. Thus, sports fans should report greater levels of identification when rival teams are made salient (e.g., greater media coverage of the New York Yankees invariably leads to greater levels of interest and identification among Boston Red Sox fans). A third additional environmental force concerns the team's stadium (Underwood et al., 2001). Stadiums that are unique or have a long history (e.g., Fenway Park in Boston or Madison Square Garden in New York City) allow fans to feel a sense of pride in their team's arena and provide them with a tangible component of their identification. Finally, Pargament (2002) noted that religious identification often increases during times of stress (thus, the basis for the old adage that there are no atheists in fox holes). It seems reasonable that such a phenomenon may also occur in sport fandom with levels of identification increasing during times of stress. This may be true for nonsport-related stress (such as the anxiety of mortality salience detailed above) and sport-related stress such as when a team is in a championship series (e.g., there are no casual fans during the seventh game of the World Series).

Team-Related Causes of Team Identification

The final set of antecedents to team identification concerns team-related factors. Team related causes can be categorized into three types: organizational characteristics, team performance, and player attributes. Organizational characteristics are those causes that "encompass the 'off-field' image of ownership, decision making, and tradition of the franchise" (Sutton, et al., 1997, p. 15) and include team history and rituals (Underwood, et al., 2001). Sport organizations may be able to increase the identification of their fan base by maintaining a clean reputation (e.g., avoiding NCAA scandal) and by reminding fans of the rich tradition and history of the team (e.g., the New York Yankees often remind fans of their storied past and the fact that they have won the most championships).

With respect to team success, research on group dynamics reveals that increased group status (or prestige) can facilitate identification (Ashforth & Mael, 1989; Ellemers, Van Knippenberg, De Vries, & Wilke, 1988). Consistent with this body of literature, researchers have detected a positive relationship between sport team success and level of identification (Sutton, et al., 1997; Wann, et al., 1996). However, research by Fisher and Wakefield (1998) suggested that team success will have differential effects on the identification of fans supporting historically successful and unsuccessful teams (see also Spears, et al., 1999). In their model, perceived group performance is predicted to impact only the identification of fans following successful teams. Other factors (e.g., player attractiveness) are believed to facilitate identification for fans of poorly performing teams. Fisher and Wakefield's research on professional hockey fans confirmed the hypothesized pattern of effects.

As for player attributes, research indicates that the specific traits of a team's players can be an important cause of team identification (Greenwood, 2001; Wann, et al., 1996). Two player characteristics have received considerable attention: player attractiveness (Kelman, 1961; Fisher & Wakefield, 1998) and player similarity to the fan (Ashforth & Mael, 1989; Kagan, 1958). Fisher (1998) recently examined which trait, attractiveness or similarity, was a better predictor of team identification. This author asked participants to complete a questionnaire assessing their level of identification with their favorite team, team attractiveness (e.g., the extent to which the group was popular), and team member similarity (e.g., "I have a lot in common with the members of this team."). Regression analyses revealed that similarity was a significantly better predictor of identification than attractiveness, leading Fisher to conclude that "sport marketers may benefit from emphasizing the similarities between the fans and their team rather than the attractiveness of the team's players" (p. 286). Fisher also noted that the specific dimensions of similarity (e.g., demographic, geographic, personality) most critical for fostering identification are unknown at this point.

CONSEQUENCES OF SPORT TEAM IDENTIFICATION

In the following sections, I examine several consequences of team identification. Specifically, I review how team identification is related to affective responses, behavioral responses, and psychological well-being. In general, this research indicates that responses of highly identified fans are more intense than those of less identified persons. The concept of *team follower* is more central to the social identity of highly identified fans (Wann, Melnick et al., 2001; Wann, Royalty, & Roberts, 2000). Consequently, the on-field and off-field actions of the team have strong implications for the fan's sense of self-worth, and hence, their reactions to the team's actions are intensified. In fact, the team's performances and image are so important to highly identified fans that some persons report that they would be willing to illegally assist their team in gaining a competitive advantage, such as bribing an official or stealing the opposition's playbook (Wann, Hunter, Ryan, & Wright, 2001).

Team Identification and Affective Responses

A number of researchers have found that spectators report intense affective responses to competitions involving their teams (e.g., Gantz & Wenner, 1995; Kimble & Cooper, 1992; Sloan, 1989). Not surprisingly, this literature indicates that fans report positive emotional responses to their team's successes and negative affect subsequent to their team's failures. However, an examination of sport spectators also reveals that they differ in the intensity of their affective responses. Research suggests that this differential level of intensity is often due to team identification. For instance, Wann et al. (1994) assessed the identification of college basketball fans prior to their attending a contest involving their college's team. The fans witnessed either a difficult win or loss by the home team and then completed an instrument assessing their postcompetition affect state. Highly identified fans reported strong negative reactions to the loss and intense positive responses to the win. Fans with low levels of identification did not report differences in emotion as a function of game outcome. Subsequent research has replicated this pattern of effects (Bizman & Yinon, 2002; Madrigal, 2003).

The relationships among team identification, competition outcome, and spectator affect are perhaps best understood within the framework of the disposition theory of sport spectatorship (Bryant, 1989; Mahony & Moorman, 2000; Sapolsky, 1980; Zillmann, Bryant, & Sapolsy, 1989). This approach argues that fans gain enjoyment (i.e., experience positive affect) from witnessing two types of sporting events: watching their team perform well and watching a rival team perform poorly. The greatest amount of enjoyment is expected to occur when a favored team defeats a despised rival. Disposition theory argues further that a fan's disposition (i.e., identification; see Bryant & Raney, 2000) toward a favorite team and that team's rivals will impact the intensity of affect felt subsequent to a competitive event. Enjoyment from watching one's favorite team perform well should increase with positive sentiments toward the team while enjoyment from watching a rival team lose is expected to increase as sentiments toward that team decrease.

A related line of research has examined the impact of team identification on the anxiety and physiological arousal experienced by fans. If high levels of team identification are associated with greater intensity of affective expression, it stands to reason that identification may also be related to the spectators' anxiety and arousal. With respect to anxiety, research by Wann, Schrader, and Adamson (1998) found that the pattern of anxiety reported by highly identified fans was similar to reports given by athletes. Specifically, highly identified fans expressed increased levels of anxiety as an important game approached, with anxiety peaking at halftime. A second study by Wann and his colleagues indicated that spectators are well aware of their heightened level of anxiety and that fans can accurately recall their anxiety level one week after a competition. Similar findings have been found for fans' levels of physiological arousal as highly identified fans exhibit particularly high levels of arousal when exposed to team-related stimuli (Branscombe & Wann, 1992a; Hillman, et al., 2000).

Team Identification and Behavioral Responses

Quite possibly, the most frequently studied facet of sport team identification concerns the impact of identification on the behaviors of fans. I examine how identification impacts two types of fan behavior: sport consumption and spectator aggression.

Team Identification and Consumption

Our understanding of the relationship between sport team identification and consumption draws largely from research in the areas of sport marketing and management. Sport consumption can be divided into three general categories: game, team-related, and sponsorship. Game consumption involves direct consumption in the form of attendance at sporting events and indirect consumption by following sport via media outlets (e.g., radio, television, and the Internet). Team merchandise consumption concerns the extent to which fans purchase team-related products and appeal (e.g., team posters and hats). Finally, sponsorship consumption concerns fans' perceptions and patronage of sponsors' products.

Research on direct game consumption indicates that there are many factors that influence a fan's decision to attend a sporting event, such as the presence of a star player or a special promotion (see Wann, Melnick et al., 2001; Zhang, Pease, Hui, & Michaud, 1995). However, numerous investigations have found that not only is level of team identification a significant independent predictor of game attendance, it may well be the most powerful factor (Fisher & Wakefield, 1998; Greenwood, 2001; Hill & Green, 2000; Mahony, et al., 2002; Wakefield & Sloan, 1995; Wann & Branscombe, 1993; Wann, Roberts, & Tindall, 1999; Williamson, Zhang, Pease, & Gaa, 2003). The impact of identification on direct consumption remains significant even after controlling for other factors, such as stadium amenities and motivation. Consequently, sport scientists often include identification in their theoretical models of direct sport consumption (e.g., Laverie & Arnett, 2000; Trail, Anderson, & Fink, 2000). Team identification also impacts indirect game consumption as highly identified fans are more likely to consume sport via the media (Fisher, 1998).

Similarly, it is less than surprising to learn that there is a strong relationship between team identification and purchase of team merchandise. Although being a fan of a team is not a prerequisite to purchasing that team's merchandise (e.g., some persons purchase team apparel because they like the look of the product rather than the team), investigators such as Fisher and Wakefield (1998) have found a positive correlation between team identification and purchases of team merchandise. Kwon and Armstrong (2002) asked college students to complete a questionnaire assessing their tendency to exhibit impulse buying of team merchandise for their university's sport teams and four potential predictors of purchasing intentions: identification with the university's sport teams, shopping enjoyment, time availability, and money availability. Regression analyses revealed that team identification was the only significant predictor of impulse merchandise purchasing.

As for perceptions and patronage of sponsors' products, organizations invest a great deal of money to have their name and product linked with a sporting event, player, team, or venue. Their hope, of course, is that fans will associate the sponsor with their team and subsequently acquire a more positive attitude toward the product (thereby increasing consumption of the sponsor's product). Several studies that have investigated the assumed relationship between sponsorship and product consumption suggest that sponsors do reap tangible benefits from their investment. However, it appears as though sponsors are more likely to have successful outcomes when fans have high levels of identification (Madrigal, 2000, 2004). For instance, consider the work of Gwinner and Swanson (2003). These researchers assessed identification with a university football team and several domains related to team sponsorship. Results indicated significant positive relationships between identification and sponsorship recognition (i.e., the ability to accurately identify the team's sponsors), positive attitudes toward team sponsors, satisfaction with team sponsors, and patronage of team sponsors.

Team Identification and Aggression

If one were to examine all of the theoretical and empirical work targeting sports fans, it is likely that the majority will have had a focus on sport fan aggression. Indeed, because so much time has been invested in furthering our understanding of fan aggression, we likely know as much about this topic as any single area of sport fandom. This research suggests that a number of factors can serve as significant contributors to fan aggression including (but not limited to) heat (Dewar, 1979), modeling (Russell, 1981), and alcohol (Wann, Melnick et al., 2001). Team identification is one such variable and, in some instances, identification has been found to be the key factor in facilitating fan aggression.[2] Research reveals that four

---

[2]Although the following sections detail the facilitating role played by team identification in fan aggression, it warrants mention that this does not imply that highly identified fans are more violent than less identified fans, per se. In fact, research indicates that high and low identified fans do not significantly differ in their levels of trait aggression (Wann, 1994; Wann et al., 1999). Rather, events occurring within the context of the sporting event lead highly identified fans to express higher levels of state aggression because, for these persons, a valued social identity is at stake.

types of fan aggression are impacted by high levels of identification: hostile aggression, instrumental aggression, rioting, and parental violence at youth sporting events.

Hostile (or affective) aggression refers to attempts to harm someone simply to cause this person pain and suffering (Buss, 1961). A useful framework for understanding the factors underlying hostile aggression was recently developed by Anderson (1997; Anderson, Anderson, & Deuser, 1996). Anderson's model, termed the General Affect Aggression Model, suggests that situational and personal input variables impact three critical psychophysiological states: affect, arousal, and cognition. These states, in turn, serve as antecedents to hostile aggression. Situational input variables include environmental factors such as temperature and crowding. Personal input variables include traits such as gender and, most relevant to the current discussion, team identification. According to the model, personal variables such as identification directly impact the individual's affect, arousal, and cognition. Support for two of these relationships was described previously as highly identified fans are more likely to experience intense affect and heightened physiological arousal while watching their team compete (e.g., Branscombe & Wann, 1992a; Wann, et al., 1994). To date, research has yet to directly examine the influence of identification on fans' cognitive processing in an aggressive environment. However, we do know that sports fans are often primed to behave aggressively (Wann & Branscombe, 1990a) and that cognition, team identification, and aggression are likely related (Branscombe & Wann, 1992b). Thus, there is tentative support for this component of the model as well. Based on predictions derived from the General Affect Aggression Model, we would expect highly identified fans to act more aggressively than lowly identified fans due to their intense affect state, elevated levels of arousal, and perhaps their cognitive processing. Consistent with this reasoning, a number of research endeavors have found a positive relationship between team identification and hostile aggression (Lanter, 2003; Wann, Carlson, & Schrader, 1999). Highly identified fans also report a greater willingness to anonymously injure opposing players and coaches (Wann, Culver, et al., in press; Wann, Haynes, McLean, & Pullen, 2003).

Instrumental aggression involves situations in which aggression is viewed as a means to an end (Buss, 1961). Unlike hostile aggression in which the ultimate goal is the suffering of the target, the goal of an instrumentally aggressive act is something beyond the pain experienced by the victim. An example from the world of sports is the verbal aggression exhibited by fans in their attempt to disrupt the opponent or intimidate the officials. In these instances, the goal of the spectators is not to injure the target per se but, rather, to help their team gain a competitive advantage. Research has found these aggressive attempts to assist a team are more prevalent among highly identified fans (Lanter, 2003; Wann, Carlson et al., 1999; Wann, Peterson, Cothran, & Dykes, 1999).

However, not all instances of instrumental aggression among highly identified fans are designed to assist the team. In some cases, the reward for the aggression is not team success but rather a restoration of psychological health. Wann's (1993) self-esteem maintenance model, developed out of the social identity literature (Tajfel, 1981; Turner, 1984), is designed to explain how and why highly identified fans use aggression to gain a sense of well-being. According to Wann, highly and lowly identified fans have different reactions to poor team performance. Fans low in team identification tend to distance themselves from the team, thereby protecting their mental health (see the discussion of cutting off reflected failure discussed later). Highly identified fans are not able to dissociate from the team because the role of team follower is too central to their identity. As a result, their collective (i.e., group or social) self-esteem is lowered, resulting in an unpleasant psychological state. These fans will then resort to derogation and aggression toward others (e.g., opposing players and fans, officials) in an attempt to restore their lost self-esteem. Thus, aggression in this instance would be classified as instrumental because the goal of such actions is to regain a sense of self-worth. Research has supported Wann's hypothesized pattern of effects (Branscombe & Wann, 1994).

Team identification has also been found to play a role in sport riots. Certainly, some individuals who participate in sport riots are simply opportunists who have little, if any, connection to the sporting event or the teams involved. These persons are simply interested in trying to "destroy what's not valuable and steal what is" (Wann, Melnick, et al., 2001, p. 138). However, others involved in sport riots are expressing their affective response to a sport competition, whether it be anger following a loss or euphoria after a win. Work by Lanter (2000) revealed that, for these persons, identification is a key facilitator. Immediately following a celebration riot occurring at the University of Maryland (the school's basketball team had defeated Duke University), Lanter asked Maryland students to complete a survey assessing their level of team identification and their involvement in the riot. As expected, the results revealed significant positive relationships between level of team identification and the number of riotous behaviors engaged in by the participant in the current event and their likelihood of future participation in a similar event.

A final form of spectator violence in which team identification is a key contributor involves the abusive and violent actions exhibited by spectators at youth sporting events. These instances of aggression are far from rare. In fact, a recent survey found that 84% of parents had witnessed a violent action from another spectator, and almost 80% had been the target of a violent or abusive action (Pallerino, 2003). Parents often have extremely high levels of identification with their children (Kagan, 1958), and this identification call spill over into the child's athletic endeavors. As adult fans become increasingly more disgruntled by the attitudes and actions of professional and college athletes, they may shift their focus to their child's athletic career (Engh, 1999). These high levels of identification for the child athlete and his or her team, coupled with an overemphasis on winning and performance, lead many adults to act in an abusive and violent manner at youth sporting events (Wann, 2001).

Team Identification and Psychological Responses

The previous sections described how spectators' emotional and behavioral responses are often related to their level of identification with a given team. However, group associations can have consequences for one's psychological health as well. There appear to be two distinct routes to enhanced psychological well-being through group memberships. The first route involves the self-esteem boost that typically accompanies identifying with a successful group (Mael & Ashforth, 2001). This process, termed *basking in reflected glory*, occurs when fans increase their psychological connection with a successful team, thereby gaining a sense of accomplishment and a boost to their self-identity (Cialdini, et al., 1976). This phenomenon is well documented in the sport science literature (Bizman & Yinon, 2002; Boen, Vanbeselaere, & Feys, 2002; Kimble & Cooper, 1992; McHoul, 1997). In fact, research suggests that fans choose to follow certain teams in part because the team will likely experience future success and, consequently, the fan can then bask in the team's glory (End, Dietz-Uhler, Harrick, & Jacquemotte, 2002).

The second route to gaining psychological benefits through team identification does not involve the team's performances. Rather, this route concerns benefits associated with the sense of belonging individuals feel when they associate with others (Mael & Ashforth, 2001). A number of approaches to group behavior, including social identity theory, have argued that membership in valued social groups can lead to positive psychological outcomes, such as lower levels of alienation and loneliness and higher levels of self-esteem (e.g., Cohen & Wills, 1985; Hogg & Abrams, 1990; Rowe & Kahn, 1998). Sport scientists have suggested that similar benefits can be gained through associations with sport teams (Curtis, Loy, & Karnilowicz, 1986; Eastman & Land, 1997; Kelley & Tian, 2004; Melnick, 1993; Smith, 1988, 1989; Zillmann, et al., 1989). However, because it is the connection to society accompanying the act of fandom, and not fandom per se, that is predicted to result in psychological benefits, one would not expect all forms of fandom to result in well-being. Certainly, identifying with a local team should be associated with psychological health because the social connections resulting from the identification should be readily available and salient (i.e., other fans of the team). However, identifying with distant teams and mere sport fandom should be less likely to be associated with psychological health because these activities are less inclined to result in salient connections to others. Research by Wann and his colleagues (Branscombe & Wann, 1991; Wann, 1994a; Wann, Dimmock, & Grove, in press; Wann, Dunham, Byrd, & Keenan, in press; Wann, Inman, Ensor, Gates, & Caldwell, 1999) has found strong support for each of the aforementioned patterns (i.e., psychological health was positively associated with level of identification with a local team but not related to identification with a distant team or sport fandom). This literature indicates that high levels of identification with a local team are related to a variety of psychological health indicators including lower levels of depression, loneliness, alienation, and stress and higher levels of self-esteem, positive affect, and vigor. Furthermore, longitudinal research utilizing structural equation modeling and path analyses suggests a casual pattern in which team identification has a direct effect on well-being (Wann, 2004).

Although the aforementioned research substantiates the positive relationship between team identification and mental well-being, highly identified fans also experience negative psychological consequences when identifying with a team that is performing poorly. The nature of athletic competition guarantees that roughly half of the fans will be disappointed in the outcome of an event. As a result, many highly identified fans report depression, anger, and disappointment (with the game and life in general) after watching their team lose (Bernhardt, Dabbs, Fielden, & Lutter, 1998; Eastman & Riggs, 1994; Hirt, Zillmann, Erickson, & Kennedy, 1992; Schwarz, Strack, Kommer, & Wagner, 1987; Schweitzer, Zillmann, Weaver, & Luttrell, 1992; Wann, et al., 1994). Thus, we are left with a bit of a paradox. On one hand, several studies have found significant positive relationships between identification with a local sport team and various indices of psychological health. On the other hand, an equally impressive list of studies indicates that highly identified fans report poor mental health after watching their team lose. The answer to resolving the paradox lies in the ability of highly identified fans to develop and utilize coping strategies that assist them in dealing with their team's failures and return them to a state of positive mental health. Prior to discussing the specific coping strategies, two points warrant mention. First, the use of these strategies is not prominent among low-identified fans. Because the identity of these fans is not in jeopardy when the team competes, they tend not to experience negative emotional consequences of poor team performance. As a result, they have little need to cope with a loss. Second, research indicates that use of these strategies is not futile. Rather, coping mechanisms often accomplish their purpose of assisting in the maintenance of psychological well-being (Diener, Suh, Lucas, & Smith, 1999), including the well-being of sport fans (Bizman & Yinon, 2002).

One such coping strategy is the tendency of fans to utilize the self-serving bias. The self-serving bias is an attributional pattern in which the individual internalizes successes while externalizing failures (Miller & Ross, 1975). A large number of studies (e.g., Hastorf & Cantril, 1954; Lau & Russell, 1980; Mann, 1974) found that fans tend to form internal attributions to explain their team's successes (e.g., success is attributed to athletic ability or effort on the part of the favored team) and external attributions to account for their team's failures (e.g., failure is attributed to poor officiating or blamed on a curse, such as with Boston Red Sox and Chicago Cubs fans). However, as one would expect, highly identified fans are particularly motivated to determine and understand the causes of sporting events (Wann & Wilson, 2001), and they are especially likely to cope using self-serving attributions (Branscombe, N'gbala, Kobrynowicz, & Wann, 1997; Wann & Dolan, 1994a; Wann & Schrader, 2000).

A second coping strategy commonly employed by highly identified sport fans involves their biased predictions and recollections of team performance. One way to ease the pain of a recent loss is to remember past victories and/or focus on potential future triumphs. Sport fans are well known for their ability to both remember the glory years and to shout, "Wait until next year!" Referred to as the *allegiance bias* (Markman & Hirt, 2002), the tendency for highly identified fans to be overly optimistic about their team's future endeavors is well documented in the sport science literature. For instance, highly identified fans report particularly favorable evaluations of current team performance (Dietz-Uhler & Murrell, 1999), predict better futures for their team in general (Funk & James, 2001; Wann, 1994b, 1996; Wann & Branscombe, 1993; Wann & Dolan, 1994b), and expect greater success for individual team members (Murrell & Dietz, 1992). Interestingly, highly identified fans are able to employ the allegiance bias even after providing rational explanations for potential victory by their team's upcoming opponent (Markman & Hirt, 2002).

With respect to recollections of past team efforts, research indicates that highly identified fans report overly positive memories of their team's performances. For instance, Wann and Dolan (1994b) asked fans high and low in identification with their university's men's basketball team to recall the number of victories the team had achieved in the previous season. Although the actual number of victories was 17, highly identified fans reported that the team had won 20.4 contests. Low-identified fans were more accurate than their highly identified counterpoints, recalling that the team had won 18.7 games, a significantly lower estimate. This finding is intriguing in light of the fact that, as one would expect, highly identified fans are more knowledgeable about the team (Wann & Branscombe, 1995a; Wann, et al., 1997). Thus, we are once again are seemingly left with a paradox. If highly identified fans are indeed more knowledgeable, how are they are able to recall inaccurately positive memories of their team's records? Wann, Morris-Shirkey, Peters, and Suggs (2002) suggested that the answer to this question resides in the type of information in question. These authors distinguished between performance-relevant team information (e.g., the number of championships a team has won) and performance-irrelevant team information (e.g., the name of the team's mascot). The authors reported data indicating that highly identified fans will be biased in their reports of performance-relevant information, thus assisting in their ability to cope. When the information in question is performance-irrelevant, highly identified fans will be highly accurate, thus satisfying their desire to show off their knowledge of team-related information.

A third coping strategy detected by researchers concerns fans' biased evaluations of fellow fans of their team and rival fans of opposing teams. This coping strategy involves the ingroup bias (Brewer, 1979; Howard & Rothbart, 1980) in which fans believe that, although their team may have been inferior on the playing field, their fans are better behaved in the stands (Franco & Maass, 1996; Madrigal, 2004; Sabo, Jansen, Tate, Duncan, & Leggett, 1996). In fact, the ingroup bias is so strong among fans that they are more willing to give charitable contributions to fellow fans than to rival fans (Platow, et al., 1999). Not surprisingly, recent work reveals that this bias is much more prominent among highly identified fans than those lower in identification (Wann & Branscombe, 1995a, 1995b). For example, Wann and Dolan (1994c) asked college students either high or low in identification with their university's men's basketball team to read a scenario describing the abusive actions of a fan attending a university game (the fan's actions were in response to a referee's call). The fan was described as either a fellow fan of the participant's team or a fan of a rival school. Although all subjects read the same scenario, highly identified fans reading about a fellow fan reported that the behavior was more appropriate and were less inclined to recommend a reprimand for the fan than were highly identified fans reading about a rival fan or low identified fans reading about either individual. Although the target fan's behavior was objectionable, highly identified sports fans were able to look beyond the negative behaviors of the fellow fan and maintain a positive impression of him (see Ashforth & Mael, 1989).

Yet another set of coping strategies involves fans' manipulation of their association with a team. Four such strategies have been identified, two of which involve responses to successful team performance and two of which relate to team failure. With respect to team success, one common strategy involves the previously discussed tendency for fans to bask in the reflected glory of their team's success (Cialdini et al., 1976). By increasing their association with a winning team, fans have the opportunity to boost their social identity. Of course, because the identity of team follower is central only to fans with high levels of team identification, these persons are particularly likely to bask in the team's success (Bizman & Yinon, 2002; Wann & Branscombe, 1990b). In some instances, fans may be reluctant to boast of the team's accomplishments due to the possibility that the team may perform poorly in the future. For instance, baseball fans may be hesitant to brag about a victory in the first game of a doubleheader because their social identity will again be at risk during the second game. This tendency to cope by refraining from basking in a team's victory because of one's concern over future performances is termed *cutting off future failure* and is more prevalent among higher identified persons (Wann, Hamlet, Wilson, & Hodges, 1995).

There are also two strategies used to cope with poor team performance. The first strategy, *cutting off reflected failure* (CORF), involves decreasing one's association with an unsuccessful team (Snyder, Lassegard, & Ford, 1986). By lowering their psychological connection to struggling teams, fans are able to protect their social identity. However, research indicates that this coping strategy is less available to persons with high levels of team identification (Gibson, Willming, & Holdnak, 2002; Hirt, et al., 1992; Wann & Branscombe, 1990b). Although these persons may attempt to dissociate themselves from their team immediately subsequent to a loss (Bizman & Yinon, 2002), they reestablish their team association shortly thereafter. Because they maintain their association with the team even during trying times (i.e., they choose not to CORF), highly identified persons must look to a different coping strategy to restore their positive social identity. As noted in our earlier discussion of the self-esteem maintenance model of aggression, this strategy (commonly referred to as *blasting*) often involves the derogation of outgroups such as rival fans and officials (Cialdini & Richardson, 1980; Wann, 1993). By acting in such a manner, highly identified persons are able to regain the lost sense of self-worth due to their team's failure (Branscombe & Wann, 1994).

A few additional coping strategies deserve brief mention. First, most fans actively follow and support more than one team (i.e., they follow their favorite baseball team during baseball season and their favorite football team during football season). One way for highly identified fans to cope with a team's loss, particularly a season-ending defeat, is to shift their focus from the losing team to another team (see Roccas & Brewer, 2002). For instance, fans of a college basketball team that has just been eliminated from the NCAA Tournament could cope by shifting their focus from the basketball team to their favorite Major League Baseball team. Second, fans may be able to cope with their team's performances through pessimism. Two such strategies are available to fans: proactive (i.e., defensive) pessimism and retroactive pessimism. Proactive pessimism occurs when individuals become increasingly less optimistic as an evaluative situation approaches (Shepperd, Ouellette, & Fernandez, 1996). Retroactive pessimism is utilized subsequent to an event by persons who report that, in retrospect, they believe their chances for success were slight (Tykocinski, 2001; Tykocinski, Pick, & Kedmi, 2002). Recent research has found that both of these strategies are utilized by highly identified fans. That is, these persons sometimes report lowered optimism about an upcoming game as the contest draws near (proactive pessimism), and they retroactively state that "we never really had a chance," subsequent to their team's defeat (Wann & Greive, 2003, 2004). And third, it is important to note that humans having an amazing ability to naturally adapt to highly stressful environments (Diener, et al., 1999). Thus, it is also likely that, give a sufficient amount of time, the pain of a tough loss by one's favorite team will subside even without the use of the aforementioned coping mechanisms. The mechanisms may expedite the process of social identity recovery, but they are not necessarily mandatory.

SUGGESTIONS FOR FUTURE RESEARCH

Taken as a whole, the preceding sections reveal that we have acquired an understanding of many causes and consequences of sport team identification. Although research on sport spectators was rare prior to the 1990s (Wann & Hamlet, 1995), the combined efforts of persons from social science backgrounds with individuals from sport management and marketing have greatly advanced our knowledge. However, there is still much to be learned. Perhaps first and foremost, researchers should critically consider and evaluate their operational definitions of sport team identification (Williamson, et al., 2003). Historically, both sport scientists and sport marketing professionals have assessed identification as a unidimensional construct (see the preceding discussion of measurement). However, it is likely that team identification is multidimensional, i.e., that there are many components of identification. Such a conclusion can be drawn from the organizational commitment literature (Meyer & Allen, 1991), predictions derived from social identity theory (Henry, Arrow, & Carini, 1999), as well as work on athletes and sport administrators (Cuskelly, McIntyre, & Boag, 1998; Park & Kim, 2000). In addition, future research on the measurement of identification may want to examine fans' identification with multiple targets. For instance, not only can fans feel psychologically connected to their team, they may also identify with specific players, the organization as a whole, and the sport in question (Basil & Brown, 2004; Hill & Green, 2000; Mahony, et al., 2002; Trail, Robinson, Dick, & Gillentine, 2003; Van Leeuwen, Quick, & Daniel, 2002).

Three other areas of future research are needed. First, with respect to the relationship between team identification and psychological well being, research on other social groups indicates that there may be moderating factors influencing the relationship between group membership and mental health (Diener, et al., 1999; Joiner, Perez, & Walker, 2002; Malka & Chatman, 2003). Future endeavors may want to investigate potential moderators of the team identification–psychological health relationship, such as attendance or team success. Second, investigators from the social sciences and those with interests in marketing and management should combine forces and engage in a greater level of information sharing. Although these two areas are interested in similar phenomena as they relate to identification, in some instances there is a lack of awareness of what persons in the other discipline are doing. And finally, researchers in all areas interested in sport team identification need to engage in greater levels of theory development. Research on the causes and consequences of team identification has progressed to the point where we have an understanding of many of the pieces of the puzzle. However, we now need theoretical models that better explain how the pieces fit together.

REFERENCES

Allen, N. J., & Meyer, J. P. (1990). The measurement and antecedents of affective, continuance, and normative commitment to the organization. *Journal of Occupational Psychology, 63*, 1–18.

Anderson, C. A. (1997). Effects of violent movies and trait hostility on hostile feelings and aggressive thoughts. *Aggressive Behavior, 23*, 161–178.

Anderson, C. A., Anderson, K. B., & Deuser, W. E. (1996). Examining an affective aggression framework: Weapon and temperature affects on aggressive thoughts, affect, and attitudes. *Personality and Social Psychology Bulletin, 22*, 366–376.

Ashforth, B. E., & Mael, F. (1989). Social identity theory and the organization. *Academy of Management Review, 14*, 20–39.

Backman, S. J., & Crompton, J. L. (1991). Using a loyalty matrix to differentiate between high, spurious, latent, and low participants in leisure activities. *Journal of Park and Recreation Administration, 9*, 117–128.

Basil, M. D., & Brown, W. J. (2004). Magic Johnson and Mark McGwire: The power of identification with sports celebrities. In L. R. Kahle & C. Riley (Eds.), *Sports marketing and the psychology of marketing communication* (pp. 159–171). Mahwah, NJ: Lawrence Erlbaum Associates.

Bernhardt, P. C., Dabbs, J. M., Fielden, J. A., & Lutter, C. D. (1998). Testosterone changes during vicarious experiences of winning and losing among fans at sporting events. *Physiology and Behavior, 65*, 59–62.

Bizman, A., & Yinon, Y. (2002). Engaging in distancing tactics among sports fans: Effects on self-esteem and emotional responses. *The Journal of Social Psychology, 142*, 381–392.

Boen, F., Vanbeselaere, N., & Feys, J. (2002). Behavioral consequences of fluctuating group success: An Internet study of soccer-team fans. *The Journal of Social Psychology, 142*, 769–781.

Branscombe, N. R., Ellemers, N., Spears, R., & Doosje, B. (1999). The context and content of social identity threat. In N. Ellemers, R. Spears, & B. Doosje (Eds.), *Social identity* (pp. 35–58). Oxford, UK: Blackwell.

Branscombe, N. R., N'gbala, A., Kobrynowicz, D., & Wann, D. L. (1997). Self and group protection concerns influence attributions but they are not determinants of counterfactual mutations focus. *British Journal of Social Psychology, 36*, 387–404.

Branscombe, N. R., & Wann, D. L. (1991). The positive social and self-concept consequences of sport team identification. *Journal of Sport & Social Issues, 15*, 115–127.

Branscombe, N. R., & Wann, D. L. (1992a). Physiological arousal and reactions to outgroup members that implicate an important social identity. *Aggressive Behavior, 18*, 85–93.

Branscombe, N. R., & Wann, D. L. (1992b). Role of identification with a group, arousal, categorization processes, and self-esteem in sports spectator aggression. *Human Relations, 45*, 1013–1033.

Branscombe, N. R., & Wann, D. L. (1994). Collective self-esteem consequences of outgroup derogation when a valued social identity is on trial. *European Journal of Social Psychology, 24*, 641–657.

Brewer, M. B. (1979). In-group bias in the minimal group situation: A cognitive motivational analysis. *Psychological Bulletin, 86*, 307–324.

Bryant, J. (1989). Viewers' enjoyment of televised sports violence. In. L. A. Wenner (Ed.), *Media, sports, and society* (pp. 270–289). Newbury Park, CA: Sage.

Bryant, J., & Raney, A. A. (2000). Sport on the screen. In D. Zillmann & P. Vorderer (Eds.), *Media entertainment: The psychology of its appeal* (pp. 153–174). New York: Lawrence Erlbaum Associates.

Buss, A. H. (1961). *The psychology of aggression.* New York: Wiley.

Cialdini, R. B., Borden, R. J., Thorne, A., Walker, M. R., Freeman, S., & Sloan, L. R. (1976). Basking in reflected glory: Three (football) field studies. *Journal of Personality and Social Psychology, 34*, 366–375.

Cialdini, R. B., & Richardson, K. D. (1980). Two indirect tactics of image management: Basking and blasting. *Journal of Personality and Social Psychology, 39*, 406–415.

Cohen, S., & Wills, T. A. (1985). Stress, social support, and the buffering hypothesis. *Psychological Bulletin, 98*, 310–357.

Crawford, G. (2003). The career of the sport supporter: The case of the Manchester Storm. *Sociology, 37*, 219–237.

Curtis, J., Loy, J., & Karnilowicz, W. (1986). A comparison of suicide-dip effects of major sports events and civil holidays. *Sociology of Sport Journal, 3*, 1–14.

Cuskelly, G., McIntyre, N., & Boag, A. (1998). A longitudinal study of the development of organizational commitment amongst volunteer sport administrators. *Journal of Sport Management, 12*, 181–202.

Dechesne, M., Greenberg, J., Arndt, J., & Schimel, J. (2000). Terror management of the vicissitudes of sports fan affiliation: The effects of mortality salience on optimism and fan identification. *European Journal of Social Psychology, 30*, 813–835.

Dewar, C. K. (1979). Spectator fights at professional baseball games. *Review of Sport & Leisure, 4*, 14–25.

Diener, E., Suh, E. M., Lucas, R. E., & Smith, H. L. (1999). Subjective well-being: Three decades of progress. *Psychological Bulletin, 125*, 276–302.

Dietz-Uhler, B., & Murrell, A. (1999). Examining fan reactions to game outcomes: A longitudinal study of social identity. *Journal of Sport Behavior, 22*, 15–27.

Eastman, S. T., & Land, A. M. (1997). The best of both worlds: Sports fans find good seats at the bar. *Journal of Sport & Social Issues, 21*, 156–178.

Eastman, S. T., & Riggs, K. E. (1994). Televised sports and ritual: Fan experiences. *Sociology of Sport Journal, 11*, 149–174.

Ellemers, N., Van Knippenberg, A., De Vries, N., & Wilke, H. (1988). Social identification and permeability of group boundaries. *European Journal of Social Psychology, 18*, 497–513.

End, C. M., Dietz-Uhler, B., Harrick, E. A., & Jacquemotte, L. (2002). Identifying with winners: A reexamination of sport fans' tendency to BIRG. *Journal of Applied Social Psychology, 32*, 1017–1030.

Engh, F. (1999). *Why Johnny hates sports.* Garden City Park, NY: Avery.

Farred, G. (2002). Long distance love: Growing up a Liverpool football club fan. *Journal of Sport & Social Issues, 26*, 6–24.

Fisher, R. J. (1998). Group-derived consumption: The role of similarity and attractiveness in identification with a favorite sports team. *Advances in Consumer Research, 25*, 283–288.

Fisher, R. J., & Wakefield, K. (1998). Factors leading to group identification: A field study of winners and losers. *Psychology & Marketing, 15*, 23–40.

Franco, F. M., & Maass, A. (1996). Implicit versus explicit strategies of out-group discrimination: The role of intentional control in biased language use and reward allocation. *Journal of Language and Social Psychology, 15*, 335–359.

Freud, S. (1949). *Group psychology and the analysis of the ego.* London: Hogarth.

Funk, D. C., & James, J. (2001). The psychological continuum model: A conceptual framework for understanding an individual's psychological connection to sport. *Sport Management Review, 4*, 119–150.

Gantz, W., & Wenner, L. A. (1995). Fanship and the television sports viewing experience. *Sociology of Sport Journal, 12*, 56–74.

Gibson, H., Willming, C., & Holdnak, A. (2002). "We're Gators...not just Gator fans": Serious leisure and University of Florida football. *Journal of Leisure Research, 34*, 397–425.

Gladden, J. M., & Funk, D. C. (2002). Developing an understanding of brand associations in team sports: Empirical evidence from consumers of professional sport. *Journal of Sport Management, 16*, 54–81.

Greenwood, P. B. (2001). *Sport fan team identification in a professional expansion setting.* Unpublished master's thesis, North Carolina State University, Raleigh, NC.

Gwinner, K., & Swanson, S. R. (2003). A model of fan identification: Antecedents and sponsorship outcomes. *Journal of Services Marketing, 17*, 275–294.

Hastorf, A. H., & Cantril, H. (1954). They saw a game: A case study. *Journal of Abnormal and Social Psychology, 49,* 129–134.

Henry, K. B., Arrow, H., & Carini, B. (1999). A tripartite model of group identification: Theory and measurement. *Small Group Research, 30*, 558–581.

Hill, B., & Green, B. C. (2000). Repeat attendance as a function of involvement, loyalty, and the sportscape across three football contexts. *Sport Management Review, 3*, 145–162.

Hillman, C. H., Cuthbert, B. N., Cauraugh, J., Schupp, H. T., Bradley, M. M., & Lang, P. J. (2000). Psychophysiological responses of sport fans. *Motivation and Emotion, 24*, 13–28.

Hirt, E. R., Zillmann, D., Erickson, G. A., & Kennedy, C. (1992). Costs and benefits of allegiance: Changes in fans' self-ascribed competencies after team victory versus defeat. *Journal of Personality and Social Psychology, 63*, 724–738.

Hogg, M. A., & Abrams, D. (1990). Social motivation, self-esteem, and social identity. In D. Abrams & M. Hogg (Eds.), *Social identity theory: Constructive and critical advances* (pp. 28–47). New York: Springer-Verlag.

Howard, J. W., & Rothbart, M. (1980). Social categorization and memory for in-group and out-group behavior. *Journal of Personality and Social Psychology, 38*, 301–310.

James, J. D. (2001). The role of cognitive development of socialization in the initial development of team loyalty. *Leisure Sciences, 23*, 233–261.

James, J. D., Kolbe, R. H., & Trail, G. T. (2002). Psychological connection to a new sport team: Building or maintaining the consumer base? *Sport Marketing Quarterly, 11*, 215–225.

Jetten, J., Spears, R., & Manstead, A. S. R. (1999). Group distinctiveness and intergroup discrimination. In N. Ellemers, R. Spears, & B. Doosje (Eds.), *Social identity* (pp. 107–127). Oxford, UK: Blackwell.

Joiner, T. E., Jr., Perez, M., & Walker, R. L. (2002). Playing devil's advocate: Why not conclude that the relation of religiosity to mental health reduces to mundane mediators? *Psychological Inquiry, 13,* 214–216.

Jones, I. (1997). A further examination of the factors influencing current identification with a sports team, a response to Wann et al. (1996). *Perceptual and Motor Skills, 85*, 257–258.

Kagan, J. (1958). The concept of identification. *Psychological Review, 65*, 296–305.

Kelley, S. W., & Tian, K. (2004). Fanatical consumption: An investigation of the behavior of sports fans through textual data. In L. R. Kahle & C. Riley (Eds.), *Sports marketing and the psychology of marketing communication* (pp. 27–65). Mahwah, NJ: Lawrence Erlbaum Associates.

Kelman, H. C. (1961). Process of opinion change. *Public Opinion Quarterly, 25*, 57–78.

Kimble, C. E., & Cooper, B. P. (1992). Association and dissociation by football fans. *Perceptual and Motor Skills, 75*, 303–309.

Kolbe, R. H., & James, J. D. (2003). The internalization process among team followers: Implications for team loyalty. *International Journal of Sport Management, 4*, 25–43.

Kwon, H. H., & Armstrong, K. L. (2002). Factors influencing impulse buying of sport team licensed merchandise. *Sport Marketing Quarterly, 11*, 151–163.

Kwon, H. H., & Trail, G. T. (2001). Sport fan motivation: A comparison of American students and international students. *Sport Marketing Quarterly, 10*, 147–155.

Kwon, H. H., & Trail, G. T. (2003). A reexamination of the construct and concurrent validity of the Psychological Commitment to Team Scale. *Sport Marketing Quarterly, 12*, 88–93.

Lanter, J. R. (2000, November). *Sport spectator identification and involvement in a spontaneous sport victory celebration.* Paper presented at the meeting of the North American Society for the Sociology of Sport, Colorado Springs, CO.

Lanter, J. R. (2003, October). *Aggression and moral reasoning in the highly-identified sport spectator.* Poster session presented at the meeting of the Association for the Advancement of Applied Sport Psychology, Philadelphia.

Lau, R. R., & Russell, D. (1980). Attributions in the sports pages. *Journal of Personality and Social Psychology, 39*, 29–38.

Laverie, D. A., & Arnett, D. B. (2000). Factors influencing fan attendance: The influence of identity salience and satisfaction. *Journal of Leisure Research, 32,* 225–246.

Madrigal, R. (2000). The influence of social alliances with sports teams on intentions to purchase corporate sponsors' products. *Journal of Advertising, 29,* 13–27.

Madrigal, R. (2003). Investigating an evolving leisure experience: Antecedents and consequences of spectator affect during a live sporting event. *Journal of Leisure Research, 35,* 23–48.

Madrigal, R. (2004). A review of team identification and its influence on consumers' responses toward corporate sponsors. In L. R. Kahle & C. Riley (Eds.), *Sports marketing and the psychology of marketing communication* (pp. 241–255). Mahwah, NJ: Lawrence Erlbaum Associates.

Mael, F. A., & Ashforth, B. E. (2001). Identification in work, war, sports, and religion: Contrasting the benefits and risks. *Journal for the Theory of Social Behavior, 31,* 198–222.

Mahony, D. F., Madrigal, R., & Howard, D. (2000). Using the psychological Commitment to Team (PCT) Scale to segment sport consumers based on loyalty. *Sport Marketing Quarterly, 9,* 15–25.

Mahony, D. F., & Moorman, A. M. (2000). The relationship between the attitudes of professional sport fans and their intentions to watch televised games. *Sport Marketing Quarterly, 9,* 131–139.

Mahony, D. F., Nakazawa, M., Funk, D. C., James, J. D., & Gladden, J. M. (2002). Motivational factors influencing the behaviour of J. League spectators. *Sport Management Review, 5,* 1–24.

Malka, A., & Chatman, J. A. (2003). Intrinsic and extrinsic work orientations as moderators of the effect of annual income on subjective well-being: A longitudinal study. *Personality and Social Psychology Bulletin, 29,* 737–746.

Mann, L. (1974). On being a sore loser: How fans react to their team's failure. *Australian Journal of Psychology, 26,* 37–47.

Markman, K. D., & Hirt, E. R. (2002). Social prediction and the "allegiance bias." *Social Cognition, 20,* 58–86.

McHoul, A. (1997). On doing "we's": Where sport leaks into everyday life. *Journal of Sport & Social Issues, 21,* 315–320.

Melnick, M. J. (1993). Searching for sociability in the stands: A theory of sports spectating. *Journal of Sport Management, 7,* 44–60.

Meyer, J. P., & Allen, N. J. (1991). A three-component conceptualization of organizational commitment. *Human Resources Management Review, 1,* 61–89.

Miller, D. T., & Ross, M. (1975). Self-serving biases in the attribution of causality: Fact or fiction? *Psychological Bulletin, 82,* 213–225.

Mlicki, P., & Ellemers, N. (1996). Being different or being better? National stereotypes and identifications of Polish and Dutch students. *European Journal of Social Psychology, 26,* 97–114.

Mowrer, O. H. (1950). *Learning theory and personality dynamics.* New York: Ronald.

Murrell, A. J., & Dietz, B. (1992). Fan support of sports teams: The effect of a common group identity. *Journal of Sport and Exercise Psychology, 14,* 28–39.

Pallerino, M. (2003, March/April). Survey says: End the madness-now. *Sporting Kid,* 13–14.

Pargament, K. I. (2002). The bitter and the sweet: An evaluation of the costs and benefits of religiousness. *Psychological Inquiry, 13,* 168–181.

Park, S.-H., & Kim, Y.-M. (2000). Conceptualizing and measuring the attitudinal loyalty construct in recreational sport contexts. *Journal of Sport Management, 14,* 197–207.

Platow, M. J., Durante, M., Williams, N., Garrett, M., Walshe, J., Cincotta, S., et al. (1999). The contribution of sport fan social identity to the production of prosocial behavior. *Group Dynamics, 3,* 161–169.

Roccas, S., & Brewer, M. B. (2002). Social identity complexity. *Personality and Social Psychology Review, 6,* 88–106.

Rowe, J. W., & Kahn, R. L. (1998). *Successful aging.* New York: Dell.

Russell, G. W. (1981). Spectator moods at an aggressive sports event. *Journal of Sport Psychology, 3,* 217–227.

Sabo, D., Jansen, S. C., Tate, D., Duncan, M. C., & Leggett, S. (1996). Televising international sport: Race, ethnicity, and nationalistic bias. *Journal of Sport & Social Issues, 21,* 7–21.

Sanford, R. N. (1955). The dynamics of identification. *Psychological Review, 62,* 106–118.

Sapolsky, B. S. (1980). The effect of spectator disposition and suspense on the enjoyment of sport contests. *International Journal of Sport Psychology, 11,* 1–10.

Schwarz, N., Strack, F., Kommer, D., & Wagner, D. (1987). Soccer, rooms, and the quality of your life: Mood effects on judgments of satisfaction with life in general and with specific domains. *European Journal of Social Psychology, 17,* 69–79.

Schweitzer, K., Zillmann, D., Weaver, J. B., & Luttrell, E. S. (1992). Perception of threatening events in the emotional aftermath of a televised college football game. *Journal of Broadcasting & Electronic Media, 36,* 75–82.

Shamir, B. (1992). Some correlates of leisure identity salience: Three exploratory studies. *Journal of Leisure Research, 24,* 301–323.

Shepperd, J. A., Ouellette, J. A., & Fernandez, J. K. (1996). Abandoning unrealistic optimism: Performance estimates and the temporal proximity of self-relevant feedback. *Journal of Personality and Social Psychology, 70,* 844–855.

Sloan, L. R. (1989). The motives of sports fans. In J. H. Goldstein (Ed.), *Sports, games, and play: Social and psychological viewpoints* (2nd ed., pp. 175–240). Hillsdale, NJ: Lawrence Erlbaum Associates.

Smith, G. J. (1988). The noble sports fan. *Journal of Sport & Social Issues, 12,* 54–65.

Smith, G. J. (1989). The noble sports redux. *Journal of Sport & Social Issues, 13,* 121–130.

Snyder, C. R., Lassegard, M., & Ford, C. E. (1986). Distancing after group success and failure: Basking in reflected glory and cutting off reflected failure. *Journal of Personality and Social Psychology, 51,* 382–388.

Solomon, S., Greenberg, J., & Pyszczynski, T. (1991). A terror management theory of social behavior: The psychological function of self-esteem and cultural worldviews. In M. Zanna (Ed.), *Advances in experimental social psychology* (Vol. 24, pp. 91–159). San Diego: Academic Press.

Spears, R., Doosje, B., & Ellemers, N. (1999). Commitment and the context of social perception. In N. Ellemers, R. Spears, & B. Doosje (Eds.), *Social identity* (pp. 59–83). Oxford, UK: Blackwell.

Sutton, W. A., McDonald, M. A., Milne, G. R., & Cimperman, J. (1997). Creating and fostering fan identification in professional sports. *Sport Marketing Quarterly, 6,* 15–22.

Tajfel, H. (1981). *Human groups and social categories.* Cambridge, UK: Cambridge University Press.

Tolman, E. C. (1943). Identification and the post-war world. *Journal of Abnormal and Social Psychology, 38,* 141–148.

Trail, G., Anderson, D. F., & Fink, J. (2000). A theoretical model of sport spectator consumption behavior. *International Journal of Sport Management, 1,* 154–180.

Trail, G. T., & James, J. D. (2001). An analysis of the sport fan motivation scale. *Journal of Sport Behavior, 24,* 107–127.

Trail, G. T., Robinson, M. J., Dick, R. J., & Gillentine, A. J. (2003). Motives and points of attachment: Fans versus spectators in intercollegiate athletics. *Sport Marketing Quarterly, 12,* 217–227.

Turner, J. C. (1984). Social identification and psychological group formation. In H. Tajfel (Ed.), *The social dimension: European developments on social psychology* (Vol. 2, pp. 518–538). Cambridge, England: Cambridge University Press.

Tykocinski, O. E. (2001). I never had a chance: Using hindsight tactics to mitigate disappointments. *Personality and Social Psychology Bulletin, 27,* 376–382.

Tykocinski, O. E., Pick, D., & Kedmi, D. (2002). Retroactive pessimism: A different kind of hindsight bias. *European Journal of Social Psychology, 32,* 577–588.

Uemukai, K., Takenouchi, T., Okuda, E., Matsumoto, M., & Yamanaka, K. (1995). Analysis of the factors affecting spectators' identification with professional football teams in Japan. *Journal of Sport Sciences, 13,* 522.

Underwood, R., Bond, E., & Baer, R. (2001). Building service brands via social identity: Lessons from the sports marketplace. *Journal of Marketing Theory and Practice, 9,* 1–13.

Van Leeuwen, L., Quick, S., & Daniel, K. (2002). The Sport Spectator Satisfaction Model: A conceptual framework for understanding the satisfaction of spectators. *Sport Management Review, 5,* 99–128.

Wakefield, K. L., & Sloan, H. J. (1995). The effects of team loyalty and selected stadium factors on spectator attendance. *Journal of Sport Management, 9,* 153–172.

Wann, D. L. (1993). Aggression among highly identified spectators as a function of their need to maintain a positive social identity. *Journal of Sport & Social Issues, 17,* 134–143.

Wann, D. L. (1994a). The "noble" sports fan: The relationships between team identification, self-esteem, and aggression. *Perceptual and Motor Skills, 78,* 864–866.

Wann, D. L. (1994b). Biased evaluations of highly identified sport spectators: A response to Hirt and Ryalls. *Perceptual and Motor Skills, 79,* 105–106.

Wann, D. L. (1996). Seasonal changes in spectators' identification and involvement with and evaluations of college basketball and football teams. *The Psychological Record, 46,* 201–215.

Wann, D. L. (2000). Further exploration of seasonal changes in sport fan identification: Investigating the importance of fan expectations. *International Sport Journal, 4,* 119–123.

Wann, D. L. (2001, June). *Encouraging positive adult behavior at youth sporting events: Changing to a culture of FUN.* Invited address presented at the National Alliance for Youth Sport Summit, Chicago.

Wann, D. L. (2004). *The causal relationship between sport team identification and psychological well-being: Testing the Team Identification – Psychological Health Model.* Manuscript submitted for publication.

Wann, D. L., & Branscombe, N. R. (1990a). Person perception when aggressive or non-aggressive sports are primed. *Aggressive Behavior, 16,* 27–32.

Wann, D. L., & Branscombe, N. R. (1990b). Die-hard and fair-weather fans: Effects of identification on BIRGing and CORFing tendencies. *Journal of Sport & Social Issues, 14,* 103–117.

Wann, D. L., & Branscombe, N. R. (1993). Sports fans: Measuring degree of identification with the team. *International Journal of Sport Psychology, 24*, 1–17.

Wann, D. L., & Branscombe, N. R. (1995a). Influence of identification with a sports team on objective knowledge and subjective beliefs. *International Journal of Sport Psychology, 26*, 551–567.

Wann, D. L., & Branscombe, N. R. (1995b). Influence of level of identification with a group and physiological arousal on perceived intergroup complexity. *British Journal of Social Psychology, 34*, 223–235.

Wann, D. L., Carlson, J. D., & Schrader, M. P. (1999). The impact of team identification on the hostile and instrumental verbal aggression of sport spectators. *Journal of Social Behavior and Personality, 14*, 279–286.

Wann, D. L., Culver, Z., Akanda, R., Daglar, M., De Divitiis, C., & Smith, A. (in press). The effects of team identification and game outcome on willingness to consider anonymous acts of hostile aggression. *Journal of Sport Behavior.*

Wann, D. L., Dimmock, J. A., & Grove, J. R. (in press). Generalizing the team identification – Psychological health model to a different sport and culture: The case of Australian Rules Football. *Group Dynamics: Theory, Research, and Practice.*

Wann, D. L., & Dolan, T. J. (1994a). Attributions of highly identified sport spectators. *The Journal of Social Psychology, 134*, 783–792.

Wann, D. L., & Dolan, T. J. (1994b). Influence of spectators' identification on evaluation of the past, present, and future performance of a sports team. *Perceptual and Motor Skills, 78*, 547–552.

Wann, D. L., & Dolan, T. J. (1994c). Spectators' evaluations of rival and fellow fans. *The Psychological Record, 44*, 351–358.

Wann, D. L., Dolan, T. J., McGeorge, K. K., & Allison, J. A. (1994). Relationships between spectator identification and spectators' perceptions of influence, spectators' emotions, and competition outcome. *Journal of Sport and Exercise Psychology, 16*, 347–364.

Wann, D. L., Dunham, M. D., Byrd, M. L., & Keenan, B. L. (in press). The five-factor model of personality and the psychological health of highly identified sport fans. *International Sports Journal.*

Wann, D. L., & Grieve, F. (2003, October). *The impact of team identification on spectators' use of defense coping: The case of retroactive pessimism.* Poster session presented at the meeting of the Association for the Advancement of Applied Sport Psychology, Philadelphia.

Wann, D. L., & Grieve, F. (2004, September). *Proactive pessimism as a coping strategy for highly identified sport fans.* Poster session submitted for presentation at the meeting of the Association for the Advancement of Applied Sport Psychology, Minneapolis.

Wann, D. L., & Hamlet, M. A. (1995). Author and subject gender in sports research. *International Journal of Sport Psychology, 26*, 225–232.

Wann, D. L., Hamlet, M. A., Wilson, T., & Hodges, J. A., (1995). Basking in reflected glory, cutting off reflected failure, and cutting off future failure: The importance of identification with a group. *Social Behavior and Personality: An International Journal, 23*, 377–388.

Wann, D. L., Haynes, G., McLean, B., & Pullen, P. (2003). Sport team identification and willingness to consider anonymous acts of hostile aggression. *Aggressive Behavior, 29*, 406–413.

Wann, D. L., Hunter, J. L., Ryan, J. A., & Wright, L. A. (2001). The relationship between team identification and willingness of sport fans to illegally assist their team. *Social Behavior and Personality: An International Journal, 29*, 531–536.

Wann, D. L., Inman, S., Ensor, C. L., Gates, R. D., & Caldwell, D. S. (1999). Assessing the psychological well-being of sport fans using the Profile of Mood States: The importance of team identification. *International Sports Journal, 3*, 81–90.

Wann, D. L., Melnick, M. J., Russell, G. W., & Pease, D. G. (2001). *Sport fans: The psychology and social impact of spectators.* New York: Routledge Press.

Wann, D. L., Metcalf, L. A., Adcock, M. L., Choi, C. C., Dallas, M. B., & Slaton, E. (1997). Language of sport fans: Sportugese revisited. *Perceptual and Motor Skills, 85*, 1107–1110.

Wann, D. L., Morris-Shirkey, P. A., Peters, E. J., & Suggs, W. L. (2002). Highly identified sport fans and their conflict between expression of sport knowledge and biased assessments of team performance. *International Sports Journal, 6*, 153–159.

Wann, D. L., Peterson, R. R., Cothran, C., & Dykes, M. (1999). Sport fan aggression and anonymity: The importance of team identification. *Social Behavior and Personality: An International Journal, 27*, 597–602.

Wann, D. L., & Pierce, S. (2003). Measuring sport team identification and commitment: An empirical comparison of the Sport Spectator Identification Scale and the Psychological Commitment to Team Scale. *North American Journal of Psychology, 5*, 365–372.

Wann, D. L., Roberts, A., & Tindall, J. (1999). The role of team performance, team identification, and self-esteem in sport spectators' game preferences. *Perceptual and Motor Skills, 89*, 945–950.

Wann, D. L., Royalty, J., & Roberts, A. (2000). The self-presentation of sport fans: Investigating the importance of team identification and self-esteem. *Journal of Sport Behavior, 23,* 198–206.

Wann, D. L., & Schrader, M. P. (1996). An analysis of the stability of sport team identification. *Perceptual and Motor Skills, 82,* 322.

Wann, D. L., & Schrader, M. P. (2000). Controllability and stability in the self-serving attributions of sport spectators. *Journal of Social Psychology, 140,* 160–168.

Wann, D. L., Schrader, M. P., & Adamson, D. R. (1998). The cognitive and somatic anxiety of sport spectators. *Journal of Sport Behavior, 21,* 322–337.

Wann, D. L., Tucker, K., B., & Schrader, M. P. (1996). An exploratory examination of the factors influencing the origination, continuation, and cessation of identification with sport teams. *Perceptual and Motor Skills, 82,* 995–1001.

Wann, D. L., & Wilson, A. M. (2001). The relationship between the sport team identification of basketball spectators and the number of attributions generated to explain a team's performance. *International Sports Journal, 5,* 43–50.

Williamson, D. P., Zhang, J. J., Pease, D. G., & Gaa, J. P. (2003). Dimensions of spectator identification associated with women's professional basketball game attendance. *International Journal of Sport Management, 4,* 59–91.

Zhang, J. J., Pease, D. G., Hui, S. C., & Michaud, T. J. (1995). Variables affecting the spectator decision to attend NBA games. *Sport Marketing Quarterly, 4*(4), 29–39.

Zillmann, D., Bryant, J., & Sapolsky, B. S. (1989). Enjoyment from sports spectatorship. In J. H. Goldstein (Ed.), *Sports, games, and play: Social and psychological viewpoints* (2nd ed., pp. 241–278). Hillsdale, NJ: Lawrence Erlbaum Associates.

Sport, Violence, and the Media

Barrie Gunter
University of Leicester

ORIGINS OF SPORTS VIOLENCE

Violence has been an integral part of much sporting activity. Most sports comprise a form of competition, much of which intrinsically involves conflict. Sports violence can be traced back through the ages to the earliest examples of competitive games (Guttman, 1998). The violence in sport derives not just from the actions of competitors but is also present in behavior of excitable fans and aroused observers in the crowds or audiences for sports contests. Some sports, such as boxing or wrestling, are inherently violent. Others, such as football and hockey, are vigorously contested, and overenthusiastic competitiveness sometimes erupts into aggressive altercations between contestants on the field of play. Some sports, such as soccer, are associated with violent fan subcultures whose identities are defined not just by the teams they support, but also by their reputation for fighting with supporters of rival football clubs. Indeed, for many such football hooligans, their involvement with a violent fan base is tribal-like in nature and may be the only source of personal identity they value in themselves (Dunning, Murphy, & Williams, 1988).

We should not be surprised therefore to find that sports are a significant contributor to violence in the media. In this chapter, I examine the extent to which there is sports-related violence in the media, the appeal of sports violence, and its impact upon the audience. Before all this, however, it is worth considering the history of sports violence.

The association between sport and violence has a long history. The ancient Greeks prized athletic prowess and held Olympianstyle sports contests that were attended by large crowds of spectators. The Romans also held sports contests that had a different complexion. While the Greeks enjoyed games, the Romans worshipped exercise and fitness. There was more discipline associated with Roman sports. The one ingredient that both Greek and Roman sports had in common was violence.

The Romans, in particular, are best remembered for their gladiatorial games and chariot races. At these events, attended by large and boisterous crowds, contestants were frequently seriously injured or killed. The violence also spilled over into the crowds, with drink often a contributory factor. Thus, the alcohol-fueled crowd troubles at modern soccer matches represent a phenomenon with a 2000-year history.

Gladiators were mostly criminals or slaves. Thus, while they were highly trained and could, when successful in competitive combat, achieve celebrity status with the crowds, they had low social status. Although as gladiatorial games grew in popularity, some free men voluntarily participated as well.

The violence of combat games was a big draw for the crowds. While the skillful use of weapons may have been appreciated by some, the attraction of gladiatorial contests for most spectators was the prospect of witnessing bloody death firsthand. Crowds were also titillated by the emergence of near-naked female gladiators. With gladiatorial games, the violence was usually restricted to the field of play. With relatively less violent chariot races, however, spectator violence was not unusual.

In the next millennium, medieval jousting tournaments also excited crowds with the same fervor as Roman and Greek games. Again, spectators were presented with the prospect of exciting staged aggression in which contestants could be seriously hurt or even killed. Many of the early tournaments, dating back to the twelfth century, contained simulated battles in which opposing teams of knights would fight, take captives, and demand ransoms for the release of prisoners. As the crowds for these medieval tournaments grew, so crowd control became a more serious problem. Violence in these sporting contests often spilled over into crowd trouble, involving fights between rival groups of fans. Indeed, spectator violence became so serious that rules had to be introduced to control it. Spectators would, for instance, be required to carry no lethal weapons such as swords, knives or daggers, or clubbing implements.

Moving ahead to the early twentieth century, prizefights drew large numbers of spectators to watch contained violence. This violence occasionally spilled over into the spectators. Crowd disturbances were particularly likely at bouts featuring Black versus White fighters and were racially motivated (Guttman, 1998).

Soccer is another sport that has witnessed some violence on the field of play, but even more serious disturbances among spectators. Crowd violence at football matches is a worldwide phenomenon. Football hooliganism is often orchestrated by well-organized gangs who have their own colours and plan fights with rival fans well in advance of key games. Some social scientists believe that such violence represents a channelling of resentment against society on the part of individuals who are young, are often unemployed, and feel alienated from and aggrieved with their position in life (Dunning et al., 1988).

REPRESENTATION OF SPORTS VIOLENCE IN THE MEDIA

The growth of mass media, and especially broadcasting, opened new channels through which sports contests could reach vast numbers of people beyond the stadiums in which these competitions were held. Television coverage has enabled millions of people to witness major sporting events they might otherwise never get to see. Viewers at home can follow their favorite football team without ever having to leave their armchairs.

Live coverage means that home viewers get to see everything that happens as it happens, including violent altercations that sometimes take place on the field of play. Aggression may be displayed even in noncontact sports that are normally regarded as civilized in the way players conduct themselves, such as tennis. Television sports coverage is accompanied by commentary. This can add to the excitement of events by putting a certain spin on the way contests are perceived by the audience. Violent contact sports such as boxing and wrestling have become especially popular with television audiences.

Before considering how audiences respond to sports violence in the media, it may be useful to examine the extent to which it is represented. A great deal of research has examined the representation of violence on television, though relatively few such studies have included an analysis of sports violence. A number of content-analysis studies of television in Britain since the mid-1980s have included sports broadcasts in their program samples. These studies have consistently shown that televised boxing and wrestling significantly inflate the total violence found on mainstream television channels. In the mid-1980s, for example, when the violence coded in such broadcasts was discounted, the overall amount of violence, expressed as a proportion of total program running time occupied by violence, fell from 1.1% to 0.6% (Cumberbatch, Lee, Hardy, & Jones, 1987).

Ten years later, further research was conducted on an even larger scale in Britain, covering up to ten major terrestrial and satellite television channels. In an analysis of four weeks' program output from eight channels during 1994 and 1995, there were three boxing matches televised in the weeks examined, two on the main commercial channel (ITV) and one on BBC1 (Gunter & Harrison, 1998), a major terrcotrial television channel. The two ITV broadcasts contained 88.4 minutes of violence, which accounted for 31.3% of all violence on ITV during the two weeks those transmissions occurred (and 20% of all violence on this channel over the full four weeks of analysis in this study). The single BBC1 televised boxing match contained 15.5 minutes of violence, which accounted for 37.3% of violence on that channel during the week of that transmission (and 9.2% of all violence on that channel over the four-week study period).

On the satellite channel Sky One, 16 wrestling broadcasts were coded during the study period — four per weekend. Together, these programs contained 277.3 minutes of violence, representing 44.8% of all minutes of violence recorded on that channel during the four weeks of output monitored. All these wrestling bouts comprised American productions of the World Wrestling Entertainment (WWE) contests.

Over all channels monitored, violence accounted for 1.07% of all program running time (television output was monitored for 24 hours per day, seven days per week, for four distinct weeks). With the above boxing and wrestling transmission taken out, this figure reduced to 0.94%. On BBC1, the percentage of total program running time occupied by violence during the week of the boxing match was 0.50%. This figure was reduced to 0.31% with the contribution of violence in the boxing match removed (a 38% reduction). On ITV, for the two weeks that included boxing coverage, the respective figures were 1.41% with boxing and 0.97% without boxing (a 31% reduction). On Sky One, the percentage of total program running time occupied by violence with wrestling bouts included was 1.74%, and this reduced to 0.96 % with wrestling bouts removed (a 45% reduction).

A follow-up study that analyzed ten television channels over 28 days sampled from 28 different weeks over a period spanning almost 12 months also examined the contribution to total television violence made by boxing and wrestling matches (Gunter, Harrison, & Wykes, 2003). Once again, this analysis revealed that the general level of violence on British television was disproportionately inflated by a small number of programs containing exceptionally large quantities of violence. These broadcasts tended to be sports broadcasts – boxing or wrestling.

On Sky Sports, a major subscription sports channel, the percentage of total program running time occupied by violence when wrestling and boxing matches were included was 3.8%. This figure fell to 0.56% upon removal of boxing and wrestling. On BBC1, three boxing broadcasts occurred during the 28 monitored days. These broadcasts accounted for 15% of all violence-occupied time on the channel.

The ten most violent programs over all the channels monitored, in terms of amount of program running time filled with violence, were boxing and wrestling bouts. All ten were televised on Sky Sports. Together they contained an aggregated total of 10.8 hours of violence, averaging 65.1 minutes of violence per program. These ten programs represented just 0.1% (one in 1000) of all programs monitored but contributed 12.5% of all program running time occupied by violence.

Sports broadcasts have been found to represent a major source of violence on television. In fact, their contribution to overall levels of violence on television is vastly disproportionate to the amount of total broadcast time these programs occupy. Contact sports broadcasts such as boxing or wrestling are the major contributors. By removing these programs from the analysis, research in Britain reported significant reductions in overall amounts of violence on television for those weeks in which such broadcasts occurred.

VIOLENCE AND SPORTS APPEAL

Is violence in sport an essential ingredient that underpins its appeal to spectators? Does violence affect audience appreciation of mediated sports contests? Clearly, combative sports such as boxing and wrestling are very popular. When televised, they can draw large audiences. Subscription television channels have found that significant numbers of people are prepared to pay extra for the privilege of being able to watch such events live. Other sports, such as soccer, rugby, American football, ice hockey, and basketball are not intrinsically violent in the same sense as combat sports, but they do comprise certain aggressive aspects in the ways they are played. Does violence, when it occurs, enhance the entertainment value of these sports?

According to some writers, sports fans enjoy watching violent sports events. Violence works alongside action, pace of play, and the level of skills displayed as key factors in the appeal of televised sports events (Zillmann, 1995). This aspect of the enjoyment that these sports provide spectators is not restricted to obviously violent sports such as boxing or wrestling but also applies to other popular sports such as football and hockey where violence can occur during play or may be emphasised by commentators (Bryant, 1989). Indeed, it has been suggested that, with contact sports, spectators turn up hoping to see players get hurt or injured (Zillmann & Paulus, 1993).

A number of explanations have been offered as to why violence may enhance the entertainment value of sports. One hypothesis is that violent sports enable spectators to purge themselves of pent-up hostilities. This release of aggressive impulses is pleasurable (Lorenz, 1963). In other words, viewing sports is a cathartic experience. If this is true, it might predict a direct correlation between the audience's enjoyment and the amount of violence in a sport's contest. The more arousing the contest, the greater the amount of pent-up aggressive energy it creates in the viewer. While the catharsis idea presents an interesting explanation, empirically it has received little support (Geen & Quanty, 1977; Zillmann, 1979, 1996).

Another viewpoint is that sports violence represents a display of power. Sports fans may identify with sporting heroes who are dominant and powerful. Through associating themselves with successful sports stars or teams, this may help fans to feel superior and powerful themselves. Once again, though, proof of this explanation has not been forthcoming (Zillmann, 1991, 1996).

A further idea is that sport is competition, and competition produces drama. The conflict and tension that are intrinsic components of dramatic entertainment cause excitement in audiences. They can also create the thought that there is a lot at stake. The entertainment value derives from the uncertainty of outcomes and having that uncertainty and the tension it creates resolved (Bryant, Zillmann, & Raney, 1998).

These theoretical models have attempted to identify factors in mediated sports that may explain the role of violence in relation to entertainment value. What empirical evidence is there that violence is an ingredient that affects audience enjoyment? Studies have comprised experiments in which the violence in mediated sports was manipulated and surveys in which post hoc data on violence levels in sports contests was linked to self-reported spectator enjoyment.

Bryant, Comisky, and Zillmann (1981) recorded television broadcasts of American football games. These telecasts were coded for the levels of violence they displayed. Play extracts were then edited into a random sequence and shown to college student participants. These viewers rated each extract for enjoyment level. The findings indicated that violent and rough play was associated with higher enjoyment scores. While this pattern occurred across the sample in general, it was more strongly apparent for males than females.

In a similar approach, DeNeui and Sachau (1996) studied male and female spectators at hockey games. These researchers measured enjoyment levels at 16 different games. Other game statistics were collected, such as how close the game was, whether the home team won or lost, and the aggressiveness of play. Only aggressiveness of play significantly predicted spectator enjoyment.

One significant element of televised sports contests is commentary. This is a special feature of mediated sports that is missing for spectators who attend live sports events. The commentary provides background information about the contestants and the sport and describes the action on the field of play, but it can also inject a degree of emotionality by emphasising certain features of play (e.g., violence). As such, commentary can play an important part in influencing the overall enjoyment of the event for those in the audience. Several studies have examined the role and impact of commentary on the reactions of audiences to mediated sports.

Bryant, Comisky, and Zillmann (1977) compared audience reactions to rough play and normal play from a professional ice hockey game. The experimental design also manipulated the nature of the commentary. In a factorial design, experimental participants were randomly assigned to conditions in which they saw either rough or normal play on screen coupled either with commentary that emphasized or did not comment upon the roughness of play. The commentary was found to be capable of influencing viewers' perceptions of play. Commentary that emphasised rough play made even normal play seem rougher than it was, while commentary that ignored rough play made sequences of rough play seem less rough.

A later study by the same authors demonstrated how commentary in televised sports contests can make even an essentially nonviolent sport appear more aggressive. In this case, commentators at a televised tennis match indicated the nature of the feelings the players held about each other. Under various conditions, opponents were described as hating each other, liking each other, or feeling neutral towards each other. Descriptions of the players as bitter rivals made the play seem tenser and even more hostile than in the other commentary conditions. More significantly, these descriptions also made the game more exciting and enjoyable for viewers (Bryant, Brown, Comisky, & Zillmann, 1982).

In another study in this vein, Sullivan (1991) got viewers to rate a televised university basketball game under various commentary conditions. Viewers were presented either with no commentary, neutral commentary, or commentary that emphasized rough play on the part of one of the two sides. The latter condition significantly influenced viewers' perceptions of the aggressiveness of play, but it also increased overall enjoyment of the match, especially among men.

Further insights into the way viewers react to violent sports on television have been gleaned from qualitative research. Focus group and individual depth interviews have been used to explore viewers' thoughts and feelings about televised wrestling. Research in this vein was conducted in Britain by a media industry consortium that comprised the British Board of Film Classification, Broadcasting Standards Commission, and Independent Television Commission (Cragg, Taylor, & Gilbert, 2001). There was an interest in the way children reacted to American productions of WWE (World Wrestling Entertainment) contests. Interviews were conducted with children aged 8 to 12 as well as with respondents aged 16 and over, including parents of the children. Respondents were also differentiated in terms of whether they had a dedicated or casual interest in wrestling.

Televised wrestling, and especially the WWE brand, was popular with boys, who often described watching it with their fathers. Older male participants could recall the British professional wrestling that was televised in the 1960s and 1970s. It was regarded as amusing buffoonery. Modern (U.S.) wrestling was seen in much the same way, but with higher production values. For young fans, American wrestling had become fashionable. While participants admired the skills of wrestlers, most viewers interviewed in this study did not perceive it as a genuine sport (except some young children). Most believed that bouts and their outcomes were predetermined and the event fully scripted in advance.

When asked to name their reasons for liking televised wrestling, the most common remarks included that it was amusing and generated an exciting atmosphere, that the wrestlers were highly skilled performers, that there was tension and drama, and that it was rewarding for its storytelling qualities. Young boys up to the age of 12 enjoyed televised wrestling because of the action. They enjoyed seeing wrestlers throw each other around. More casual viewers enjoyed the storylines, dialogue, and overall atmosphere. Wrestling had a sexual interest for women viewers. They enjoyed watching well-muscled men grappling with each other. Attractive female wrestlers had a similar appeal for older male viewers.

For most of the interviewees in this investigation, the violence in wrestling was not perceived as real. The action was believed to be faked. A wrestler may appear to have taken a severe beating but then triumphs and walks away apparently unscathed. There was also a view that bouts are tightly controlled and the participants are so highly skilled that no one is allowed to get seriously hurt. That is not to say that contestants always escape without injury; accidents can happen even with the most tightly scripted bouts. The costume and running story elements were frequently referred to as important ingredients. Viewers would suspend reality to enter into the fantasy of wrestling to enjoy it more. While the apparent pain and suffering of some contestants that is displayed in bouts added to their appeal, it was necessary for viewers to suspend belief temporarily to be able to enjoy this sort of spectacle as a piece of fantasy entertainment. The researchers sensed, however, that some interviewees spoke about the significance of narrative elements and the humor in wrestling to make their enjoyment of it somehow more respectable and highbrow. In other words, some viewers may have attempted to suggest a deep level of enjoyment that is more sophisticated than liking purely the raw action in which large men throw each other around.

IMPACT OF MEDIATED SPORTS

While violence in mediated sports contests has emerged as a factor underpinning their entertainment value for audiences, can it have more lasting effects on viewers? Sports sociologists have theorized that sports events invite spectators to express the kinds of hostile impulses that are normally socially inhibited anywhere else. Thus, sports events present fans with opportunities to reach a fever-pitched level of excitement that could then become manifest as aggression. Fans take pleasure in violent contact sports but obtain certain physically pleasurable gratifications themselves by getting actively involved in violent altercations (Elias & Dunning, 1986). Identification and empathy with the athletes on the part of spectators is part of this process. Other writers have been less persuaded by the idea that empathy is an important factor in this context (Guttmann, 1988). However, if spectators do believe that their favorite sports contestants or teams represent them personally, while rivals have the same relationship with opposing contestants or teams, an atmosphere might be created in which the rivalry between competing players and teams extends to their respective groups of fans.

Interest in sports violence on television has stemmed from the wider concern about the potentially harmful effects of screen violence. This is a subject that has been publicly debated and empirically investigated over many decades. In examining the appeal of mediated sports and the role of violence, the notion of catharsis was invoked as an explanation of audience enjoyment. The catharsis hypothesis has also been invoked to explain the postviewing effects of screen violence (Feshbach, 1963; Feshbach & Singer, 1971).

So far, however, there has been limited evidence of a catharsis effect following exposure to mediated violence (Gunter, 1980; Wells, 1973). No evidence has emerged either to demonstrate that cathartic experiences follow exposure to violent sports events. Sports that contain violence can excite the audience and enhance enjoyment but do not reduce aggressive feelings (Goldstein & Arms, 1971). Psychological tests distributed to spectators at wrestling, ice hockey, and swimming events, before and after each type of contest, revealed no evidence of aggression reduction as a function of violent sports exposure (Arms, Russell, & Sandilands, 1979).

Most research on the effects of exposure to media violence has indicated an aggression-enhancing rather than aggression-reducing outcome for viewers. This pattern of behavior can be found specifically in relation to studies of effects of watching violent sports. One of the principal early hypotheses invoked to explain aggression enhancement effects of mediated violence suggested that watching violence could act as a trigger to aggression in the viewer, provided other aggression-eliciting circumstances prevailed. On-screen violence could offer justification for the use of violence in real life. As such, it could act to reduce socially conditioned inhibitions against behaving violently. This disinhibition hypothesis was empirically studied in a series of experimental investigations conducted during the 1960s and 1970s by psychologist Leonard Berkowitz and his students. While this body of research is commonly discussed in the general literature on media violence, it is significant in the current context because one of the key stimulus materials used throughout this work was a film sequence of a fictional boxing match.

These studies were usually carried out with college students who were randomly allocated to viewing conditions in which they saw either the boxing match sequence or a nonviolent clip from a travel documentary. In a separate manipulation, some experimental participants were irritated or angered by an experimental accomplice prior to watching a film clip, while others were not. After viewing a film clip, the participants were placed again with the accomplice and given an opportunity to behave in an aggressive manner towards that person. Broadly, results showed that exposure to a violent clip (of a boxing match) rendered participants more likely to behave aggressively subsequently as compared with those shown a travel clip. This effect was especially likely to occur among participants who had been angered prior to viewing (Berkowitz, 1964, 1965; Berkowitz & Alioto, 1973; Berkowitz & Geen, 1966; Berkowitz & Rawlings, 1963; Geen & Berkowitz, 1966a, 1966b; Geen & O'Neal, 1969).

Later writers challenged the veracity of this methodology. In particular, it was argued that the Berkowitz procedure gave angry respondents only one type of response opportunity in relation to the person who had previously angered them and that this was an aggressive response. In an experimental demonstration of what might happen if a nonaggressive response was also offered, Fisher and Grenier (1994) found that the latter response would be preferred by most participants. It should be noted, however, that this study did not use violent sports sequences as stimulus material.

Another major explanation of mediated violence effects has been the suggestion that social learning occurs through imitation of on-screen depictions. This theory was promulgated by Bandura, who provided a number of empirical demonstrations throughout the 1960s and 1970s (Bandura, 1965, 1977; Bandura, Ross, & Ross, 1963; Bandura & Walters, 1963). Much of this work was conducted among children who were believed to be the most susceptible to such media influences. An imitation type of effect was invoked later in a series of studies that examined links between mediated or highly publicized violent events and subsequent levels of social violence for selected forms of aggressive behavior. In some of these studies, the mediated events were violent sports such as championship boxing matches (Phillips, 1983; Phillips & Hensley, 1984).

One study examined patterns of 140,000 U.S. homicides after media coverage of major prizefights, murder acquittals, life sentences, death sentences, and executions. Statistical analyses indicated that the numbers of homicides significantly increased on the third day after coverage of a major boxing match (Phillips & Hensley, 1984). Further analysis indicated that real-life murder victims during these homicide peaks tended to be from the same racial group as the defeated fighters.

This research has not been universally accepted. The authors made a variety of assumptions in order to draw causal inferences (Bollen & Phillips, 1982). These assumptions have been called into question by other writers (Baron & Reiss, 1985; Freedman, 1984; Kessler & Stipp, 1984). One alternative analysis of Phillips' data noted that many of the cases, including boxing match broadcasts, took place shortly (i.e., three or four days) before key holiday periods when homicide levels peak anyway. The findings may therefore be more artifactual than real (Baron & Reiss, 1985).

TOWARDS A BETTER UNDERSTANDING OF IMPACT

Much of the early research into the impact of mediated violence made blanket assumptions about the nature of audience effects and the universality of those effects. Increasingly such views have been replaced by more sophisticated multivariate models of media engagement by audiences and by the realization that not all members of the audience have the same psychological makeup. Such conceptualizations can also be applied to the study of impact of mediated sports.

Although violent media content may play a part in the conditioning of behavioral dispositions over time or the short-term triggering of aggressive responses among members of the audience, most people learn to suppress their aggressive impulses so that antisocial behavior is not manifest. Nonetheless, there is mounting evidence that there may be internal changes experienced by audience members contingent upon exposure to violent media content. These can take the form of angry or hostile thoughts or mood states (Berkowitz, 1984; Bushman, 1995; Bushman & Geen, 1990).

Individuals who experience these cognitive or mood changes may try to keep them in check or to change them. If this mood management process takes place during the viewing of violent television content, for instance, it requires cognitive effort that can have other side effects. One of these is that memory for adjacent advertising can be impaired (Bushman, 1998a, 1998b; Bushman & Bonacci, 2002; Gunter, Furnham & Pappa, Gunter, Tohala, & Furnham, 2001; in press). This effect has been explained in terms of the interference to cognitive processing that arises from the generation of hostile thoughts and the investment of mental effort to contain those thoughts (Bushman, 1998a).

Aggression mood enhancement has been observed among spectators watching sports tinged with violence (Arms, et al., 1979). Exposure to professional wrestling has been found to give rise to negative mood states in viewers (Depalma & Raney, 2003). Together these findings provide a body of evidence that invites the possibility that violent mediated sports could have significant knock-on effects for sponsors and advertisers whose commercial messages are situated in close proximity to televised sports contests.

The nature of audience reactions to violent sports can vary with the personality of the spectator or viewer. Research with young viewers has indicated that those with disruptive behavior disorders (DBDs) often exhibit different psychophysiological reactions to media violence than same-age peers with nondisturbed psychological profiles. Persons with DBDs may be more attracted to violent displays than non-disturbed individuals (Compas, Connor, Saltzman, Thomsen, & Wadsworth, 2001). When watching movie violence, DBDs have been found to display low levels of excitement and fear arousal, though still to display greater anger levels than individuals with nondisturbed behavioral profiles. Persons with DBDs tend to be characterized by chronic anger that is (genetically and developmentally) preformed and not specifically contingent on their history of media violence exposure. This disposition nevertheless results in a reaction to screen violence that is more "emotionally cold" than that exhibited by other individuals (Grimes, Bergen, Nichols, Vernberg, & Fonagy, 2004). The observation that aggressive personality types enjoy violent sports more than nonaggressive types fits with the above evidence (Bryant, 1989).

SUMMARY AND CONCLUSIONS

Sport and media have become intimately entwined over the past century. The media have fed off sports for news and entertainment, and sports increasingly depend on media exposure and contracts with television for their income. As sports depend more on television and the television environment becomes more competitive, pressures arise to ensure that sports coverage takes the right steps to attract audiences. One consequence of this arrangement is that sports must accommodate to the requirements of television. Conformity to the need to become more and more entertaining may lead to a greater appetite within the media for sports that offer drama. Drama often arises out of conflict, and violent conflict has historically often been associated with higher entertainment value (Diener & DeFour, 1978).

Sport and violence have always gone together. The original crowd-pulling sports of ancient times were characterized by violence on the field of play and among spectators. Sports violence can be found enjoyable by spectators at live contests and audiences for televised contests. This phenomenon has a long history (Guttmann, 1998). Equally though, sports violence can generate negative mood states and for some sectors of the population, already predisposed to behave disruptively, could further feed chronic anger conditions. It must be hoped therefore that the economic needs of television executives operating in increasingly competitive media environments can be tempered by recognition of their social responsibilities to audiences in the context of mediated sports.

The growing mutual dependence of major sports and television, and the increasingly competitive media marketplace in which broadcasters must vie for audiences, places greater pressure on both parties to encourage more dramatic forms of sporting entertainment to emerge. This often means a stronger temptation to facilitate conflict and animosity among contestants, or at least the perception of such antagonism on the part of spectators and audiences. Production practices may also dwell on these ingredients of sports contests with the intention of whipping up high levels of audience excitement. The television entertainment imperative caters to the best interests of television but not necessarily of the sports that are televised or the people who watch them. Future research could therefore play an important role in tracking these developments and their impact upon sports spectators, the wider public, and the sports themselves.

REFERENCES

Arms, R. L., Russell, G. W., & Sandilands, M. L. (1979). Effects of viewing aggressive sports on the hostility of spectators. *Social Psychology Quarterly, 42,* 275–279.

Bandura, A. (1965). Influence of models' reinforcement contingencies on the acquisition of imitative responses. *Journal of Personality and Social Psychology, 1,* 585–595.

Bandura, A. (1977). *Social learning theory.* Englewood Cliffs, NJ: Prentice-Hall.

Bandura, A., Ross, D., & Ross, S. A. (1963). Imitation of film-mediated aggressive models. *Journal of Abnormal and Social Psychology, 66,* 3–11.

Bandura, A., & Walters, R. H. (1963). *Social learning and personality development.* New York: Holt, Rinehart & Winston.

Baron, J. N., & Reiss, P. C. (1985). Same time, next year: Aggregate analyses of the mass media and violent behavior. *American Sociological Review, 50,* 347–363.

Berkowitz, L. (1964). Aggressive cues in aggressive behavior and hostility catharsis. *Psychological Review, 71,* 104–122.

Berkowitz, L. (1965). Some aspects of observed aggression. *Journal of Personality and Social Psychology, 2,* 359–369.

Berkowitz, L (1984). Some effects of thoughts on anti- and pro-social influences of media effects: A cognitive-neoassociation analysis. *Psychological Bulletin, 95,* 410–427.

Berkowitz, L., & Alioto, J. T. (1973). The meaning of an observed event as a determinant of its aggressive consequences. *Journal of Personality and Social Psychology, 28,* 206–217.

Berkowitz, L., & Geen, R. G. (1966). Film violence and the cue properties of available targets. *Journal of Personality and Social Psychology, 3,* 525–530.

Berkowitz, L., & Rawlings, E. (1963). Effects of film violence on inhibitions against subsequent aggression. *Journal of Abnormal and Social Psychology, 66,* 405–412.

Bollen, K. A., & Phillips, D. P. (1982). Imitative suicides: A national study of the effects of television news stories. *American Sociological Review, 47,* 802–809.

Bushman, B. J. (1995). Moderating role of trait aggressiveness in the effects of violent media on aggression. *Journal of Personality and Social Psychology, 69,* 950–960.

Bushman, B. J. (1998a). Effects of television violence on memory for commercial messages. *Journal of Experimental Psychology: Applied, 4*(4), 291–307.

Bushman, B. J. (1998b). Priming effects of media violence in the accessibility of aggressive constructs in memory. *Personality and Social Psychology Bulletin, 24*(5), 537–545.

Bushman, B. J., & Geen, R. G. (1990). Role of cognitive-emotional mediators and individual differences in the effects of media violence on aggression. *Journal of Personality and Social Psychology, 58,* 156–163.

Bryant, J. (1989). Viewers' enjoyment of televised sports violence. In L. A. Wenner (Ed.), *Media, sports and society* (pp. 270–289). London: Sage.

Bryant, J., Brown, D., Comisky, P. W., & Zillmann, D. (1982). Sports and spectators: Commentary and appreciation. *Journal of Communication, 32*(1), 109–119.

Bryant, J., Comisky, P. W., & Zillmann, D. (1977). Drama in sports commentary. *Journal of Communication, 27*(3), 140–149.

Bryant, J., Comisky, P. W., & Zillmann, D. (1981). The appeal of rough-and-tumble play in televised professional football. *Communication Quarterly, 29,* 256–262.

Bryant, J., Zillmann, D., & Raney, A. A. (1998). Violence and the enjoyment of mediated sport. In L. A. Wenner (Ed.), *MediaSport* (pp. 252–265). London: Routledge.

Bushman, B. J., & Bonacci, A. M. (2002). Violence and sex impair memory for television ads. *Journal of Applied Psychology, 87,* 557–564.

Compas, B. E., Connor, J. K., Saltzman, H., Thomsen, A. H., & Wadsworth, M. E. (2001). Coping with stress during childhood and adolescence: Problems, progress, and potential in theory and research. *Psychological Bulletin, 127,* 87–127.

Cragg, A., Taylor, C., & Gilbert, R. (2001, March). *Wrestling: How do audiences perceive TV and video wrestling?* Research report. London: British Board of Film Classification, Independent Television Commission and Broadcasting Standards Commission.

Cumberbatch, G., Lee, M., Hardy, G., & Jones, I. (1987). *The portrayal of violence on British television: A content analysis.* Report prepared for the British Broadcasting Corporation. Aston, UK: Applied Psychology Division, Aston University.

DeNeui, D. L., & Sachau, D. A. (1996). Spectator enjoyment of aggression in intercollegiate hockey games. *Journal of Sport and Social Issues, 20,* 69–77.

Depalma, A. J., & Raney, A. A. (2003). *The effect of viewing varying levels of aggressive sports programming on enjoyment, mood and perceived violence.* Paper presented at the 53rd annual convention of the International Communication Association, San Diego, CA.

Diener, E., & DeFour, D. (1978). Does television violence enhance program popularity? *Journal of Personality and Social Psychology, 36,* 333–341.

Dunning, E., Murphy, P., & Williams, J. (1988). *The roots of football hooliganism*. London: Routledge & Kegan Paul.

Elias, N., & Dunning, E. (1986). *Quest for Excitement*. Oxford, UK: Blackwell.

Feshbach, S. (1963). The stimulating versus cathartic effects of a vicarious aggressive activity. *Journal of Abnormal and Social Psychology, 63*, 381–385.

Feshbach, S., & Singer, J. (1971). *Television and Aggression*. San Francisco, CA: Jossey-Bass.

Fisher, W. A., & Grenier, G. (1994). Violent pornography, antiwomen thoughts, and antiwomen acts: In search of reliable effects. *Journal of Sex Research, 31*(1), 23–38.

Freedman, J. L. (1984). Effect of television violence on aggressiveness. *Psychological Bulletin, 96*, 227–246.

Geen, R. G., & Berkowitz, L. (1966a). Name-mediated aggressive cue properties. *Journal of Personality, 34*, 456–465.

Geen, R. G., & Berkowitz, L. (1966b). Some conditions facilitating the occurrence of aggression after the observation of violence. *Journal of Personality, 35*, 666–676.

Geen, R. G., & O'Neal, E. C. (1969). Activation of cue-elicited aggression by general arousal. *Journal of Personality and Social Psychology, 11*, 289–292.

Geen, R. G., & Quanty, M. B. (1977). The catharsis of aggression: An evaluation of a hypothesis. In L. Berkowitz (Ed.), *Advances in experimental social psychology* Vol. 10, pp. 1–37). New York: Academic Press.

Goldstein, J. H., & Arms, R. L. (1971). Effects of observing athletic contests on hostility. *Sociometry, 34*, 83–90.

Grimes, T., Bergen, L., Nichols, K., Vernberg, E., & Fonagy, P. (2004). Is psychopathology the key to understanding why some children become aggressive when they are exposed to violent television programming. *Human Communication Research, 30*(2), 153–181.

Gunter, B. (1980). The cathartic potential of television drama. *Bulletin of the British Psychological Society, 33*, 448–450.

Gunter, B., Furnham, A., & Pappa, E. (in press). Effects of TV violence on memory for violent and non-violent advertising. *Journal of Applied Social Psychology*.

Gunter, B., & Harrison, J. (1998). *Violence on television: An analysis of amount, nature, location and origin of violence in British programmes*. London, UK: Routledge.

Gunter, B., Harrison, J., & Wykes, M. (2003). *Violence on television: Distribution, form, context and themes*. Mahwah, NJ: Lawrence Erlbaum Associates.

Gunter, B., Tohala, T., & Furnham, A. (2001). Television violence and memory for TV advertisements. *Communications, 26*(2), 109–127.

Guttmann, A. (1988). The modern Olympics: A sociopsychological interpretation. In J. O. Segrave & D. Chu (Eds.), *The Olympic Games in transition*. Champaign, IL: Human Kinetics Press.

Guttmann, A. (1998). The appeal of violent sports. In J. H. Goldstein (Ed.) *Why we watch: The attractions of violent entertainment* (pp. 7–26). Oxford, UK: Oxford University Press.

Kessler, R. C., & Stipp, H. (1984). The impact of fictional television suicide stories on US fatalities: A replication. *American Journal of Sociology, 90*, 151–167.

Lorenz, K. (1963). Das sogenannte Bose: Zur Naturgeschichte der Aggression. Wien: Boratha-Schaelar.

Marsh, P., Rosser, E., & Harre, R. (1978). *Rules of disorder*. London: Routledge & Kegan Paul.

Phillips, D. P. (1983). The impact of mass media violence on US homicides. *American Sociological Review, 48*, 560–568.

Phillips, D. P., & Hensley, J. E. (1984). When violence is rewarded or punished: The impact of mass media stories on homicide. *Journal of Communication, 34*, 101–116.

Sullivan, D. B. (1991). Commentary and viewer perception of player hostility; Adding punch to televised sport. *Journal of Broadcasting and Electronic Media, 35*(4), 487–504.

Wells, W. D. (1973). *Television and aggression: Replication of an experimental field study*. Unpublished manuscript. Zillmann, D. (1979). *Hostility and Aggression*. Hillsdale, NJ: Lawrence Erlbaum Associates.

Zillmann, D. (1991). Empathy: Affect from bearing witness to the emotion of others. In J. Bryant and D. Zillmann (Eds.), *Responding to the screen: Reception and reaction processes*, (pp.135–167). Hillsdale, NJ: Lawrence Erlbaum Associates.

Zillmann, D. (1995, November). *Sports and the media*. Keynote address presented at the International Congress on Images of Sports in the World. Cologne, Germany.

Zillmann, D. (1996). The psychology of the appeal of portrayals of violence. In J. H. Goldstein (Eds.), *Attraction of violence*. New York: Oxford University Press.

Zillmann, D., & Paulus, P. B. (1993). Spectators: Reactions to sports events and effects on athletic performance. In R. N. Singer, M. Murphey, & L. K. Tennant (Eds.), Handbook of research on sports psychology (pp. 600–619). New York: Macmillan.

22

Televised NFL Games, the Family, and Domestic Violence

Walter Gantz
Zheng Wang
Indiana University, Bloomington

Samuel D. Bradley
Ohio State University, Columbia

There can be no mistaking the prominent role that television plays in contemporary American family life. Three of four American households have at least two television sets. The average household has the television on about eight hours per day; the average adult watches more than four hours per day. Television viewing dominates leisure activities and, because of its near ubiquity in contemporary households, television is part, either in the foreground or background, of most in-home activity (Television Bureau of Advertising, 2004).

Television viewing, either alone or with others, generally is a pleasurable experience. Spouses report that they deem television as an opportunity to spend time with one another (Gantz, 1985), and shared viewing is rated as more pleasant than solo viewing (Kubey, 1990). Overall, spouses characterize co-viewing as a valued activity that has few disruptive effects (Gantz, 1985). Yet, within the context of household and family life, television can be a source of conflict. Family members might disagree about when the set should be on and off, the amount of time spent watching television, the programs preferred and viewed, use of the remote control, and the activities that get displaced by television viewing. Accordingly, discrepancies in TV program preferences between husbands and wives have been linked with lower marital satisfaction scores (Gantz, 1985; Gantz, Wenner, Carrico, & Knorr, 1995).

Program preference discrepancies between husbands and wives are greatest for televised sports (Gantz, 1985). Consequently, men outnumber women among televised sports audience (e.g., Frank & Greenberg, 1980; National Association of Broadcasters, 1987). This differential is important because televised sports are now available 24 hours per day, with professional and collegiate sports routinely televised during leisure time (i.e., evenings and weekends) when both spouses are more likely to be home.

In addition to simply outnumbering women in the audience, men appear to experience televised sports differently (Gantz & Wenner, 1991). Men are more likely to experience and react to televised sports as fans. "[Men] are more likely to look forward to TV sports, to be motivated because of interest in the game itself, and to be involved and emotionally responsive while watching. Women are more likely to watch TV sports for social purposes, often watching in order to join friends and family who watch because they are interested in the game itself" (Gantz, et al., 1995, p. 308). For fans, television viewing is an active experience. Fans exuberantly engage the viewing experience, orchestrating previewing, concomitant, and postviewing behaviors around the sports viewing (Gantz & Wenner, 1995). Although men are more likely to be fans, when male and female fans are compared, more similarities than differences are seen. Rather than dividing along sharp gender lines, female and male fans of sports share the same joys, passions, and frustrations (Gantz & Wenner, 1995). Nonfans approach sports differently, and female nonfans are especially different in their approach (Gantz & Wenner, 1995). When both spouses are fans, televised sports offer meaningful co-viewing. However, greater fanship among males guarantees an inequality and sets the stage for disagreement and potential conflict.

Conflicts about televised sports appear to be infrequent and generally low key. Gantz et al. (1995) found that only 1 in 20 married respondents said they would watch their favorite sport even if it meant having an argument with their spouse. More typically, accommodations were made when either the spouse had scheduled some other activity concurrent with televised sports or when the spouse wanted to watch something else. However, some participants did report resentment over sports viewing. In accordance with the fanship trends, women were more likely to report being resentful—a trend that the men seemed to notice, as men were more likely to report that their spouses resented their viewing. Overall, however, the notion of televised sports as an irritant appears small. When asked to label the role of televised sports in their marriage, only one in nine described it as negative.

For years, the popular press has written about football widows and families abandoned for televised sports. These depictions appear somewhat overblown—certainly greater than the perhaps conservative estimates offered by Gantz et al. (1995). Nonetheless, because men are more likely to be sports fans and because sports fans and nonfans experience pregame activities, viewing, and postgame activities so differently, the potential for conflict exists. Conflict here could range from slightly bruised egos to domestic violence.

The relationship between televised football games and domestic violence has concerned the general public, health practitioners, and the scholarly community for some time. The potential linkage of televised football and domestic violence gained a national stage in 1993 when broadcast network NBC agreed to air an anti-domestic violence public service announcement during its Super Bowl coverage (Hohler, 1993). The issue has been simmering ever since. This chapter reports an original study designed to examine the relationship between televised football games and domestic violence.

VIOLENCE IN THE HOUSEHOLD

Domestic violence is a pattern of violent and coercive behavior committed by those in intimate relationships. These behaviors include physical, sexual, and psychological assaults on one's partner as well as attacks on household pets and property. Far more often than not, men are the perpetrators of domestic violence, females the victims. Between 1 million and 4 million American women are victimized by domestic violence each year (American Psychology Association, 1996; Bureau of Justice Statistics, 1995). Incidents vary on the basis of a host of factors including geography, population density, season, climate and weather, day of the week, and time within any day as well as individual factors such as alcohol and drug consumption, communication skills, and stress. Southern and western states have the highest rates of domestic partner homicides. The rate of such homicides is also greater in metropolitan areas of over 250,000 people (Center for Disease Control and Prevention, 2001). Domestic violence most frequently occurs between 6 pm and midnight and often is committed by those under the influence of alcohol or drugs (Bureau of Justice Statistics, 1998; Hutchison, 2003). Nonetheless, domestic violence cuts across social, economic, and geographic divides, affecting people all across the country (and in other nations as well).

Although alcohol has been linked to assault, simple drinking frequency is not a significant predictor of assault when personality trait variables are included in multivariate analysis (Zhang, Wieczorek, & Welte, 1997). Instead, level of drinking interacts with deviant thoughts, aggression and hostility, and impulsivity to predict assault (Zhang, et al., 1997). When batterers and nonbatterers are compared on intelligence, there is no overall difference in intelligence; however, batterers exhibit reduced verbal abilities and show weaker performance on measures of executive function (Cohen, et al., 2003). This reduced verbal ability and impaired executive function could reasonably be expected to suffer further under the influence of alcohol. Further, batterers exhibited greater problems with response inhibition and impulsivity (Cohen, et al., 2003).

THE SPORTS EXPERIENCE

Longstanding interest in the relationship between televised football and domestic violence is related to the popularity and violent nature of the sport. NFL games draw a large and predominantly male audience whose viewing motivations include following their favorite players and teams, enjoying the excitement and tension associated with the action, relaxing and unwinding, and, perhaps conversely, getting psyched up (Gantz & Wenner, 1995; Wenner & Gantz, 1998). The games feature (generally) controlled aggression, with video replays of most plays, including bone-jarring tackles (sports network ESPN replays the hardest noninjury tackles of the week in a feature titled "Jacked Up"). Suspense and violence associated with the games are linked with viewer satisfaction (Bryant & Raney, 2000); among those prone to aggression, sports violence is associated with maximum viewing enjoyment (Bryant, 1989). Televised football abounds with violent clashes, and prolonged exposure to nonsports-based media violence has been shown to initiate hostile behavior in unprovoked individuals—and this effect was greater for men than for women (Zillmann & Weaver, 1999).

There is experimental evidence to suggest that viewers respond to the closeness of a game. Gan, Tuggle, Mitrook, Coussement, and Zillmann (1997) had participants watch various games of the NCAA basketball tournament live. For male participants, enjoyment increased as games became closer. Females, however, showed a different pattern. Their enjoyment increased to a moderate level of closeness (i.e.,

5–9-point spread between teams), but their enjoyment fell off dramatically as games became extremely close. Thus, a situation arises where males and females have disparate responses and leave the game with different moods, levels of satisfaction, and expectations of postgame interaction. An experiment involving psychophysiological responses to sports photographs differentiated individuals who had high fan identification compared to those who had either moderate or low fan identification (Hillman, et al., 2000). Team-relevant sport pictures led to greater reported arousal and pleasantness compared to team-irrelevant pictures only for highly identified fans. Highly identified fans also showed greater heart-rate deceleration (indicative of greater controlled attention) for team-relevant sports pictures, which did not occur for the other two groups. For these highly identified fans then, team-relevant sports may be an entirely different emotional and physiological experience than for moderate and nonfans.

This increased intensity for fans may be most apparent during the Super Bowl. In the United States, the Super Bowl regularly ranks as the most widely watched single program of the year, drawing more than 100 million Americans (National Football League, 2003). The 2001 Super Bowl matching the New York Giants and the Baltimore Ravens, for example, delivered a 40.4 rating, by far the most viewed program of the 2000 to 2001 television season (Nielsen, 2002). For many, the game highlights a day of celebration and partying. Perhaps because of its unique visibility and the disruption it causes in the daily lives of so many, Super Bowl Sunday has been scrutinized by fans, writers, scholars, and those concerned about the adverse consequences of televised sports. Indeed, on January 18, 1993, Fairness and Accuracy in Reporting, a media watchdog group, released a statement that Super Bowl Sunday was one of the worst days of the year for domestic violence against women. A short time later, the then-head of the California Women's Law Center noted that 40 percent more women would be battered on Super Bowl Sunday than on a normal Sunday. Although these allegations were hotly contested in the press (Cadwallader, 1993; Cobb, 1993; Gorov, 1993; Hohler, 1993; Ringle, 1993; Sommers, 1994; Tuohy, 1993), no definitive picture emerged. As noted several years earlier, the public had "black and blue answers" but lacked "hard data" to substantiate them (Ruffini, 1991).

Some hard data from the academic community speak to the issue at hand. Using a lab experiment, Goldstein & Arms (1971) found that observing football games increased spectators' hostility, regardless of whether the spectators' preferred team won or lost. However, generalization from within the laboratory to outside contains substantial risk (Freedman, 1984; Phillips, 1982, 1983). A handful of studies concerning football game violence employed real-life data (Drake & Pandey, 1996; Hettich, 2001; Miller, Heath, Molcan, & Dugoni, 1990; Phillips, 1983; Sachs & Chu, 2000; White, 1989; White, Katz, & Scarborough, 1992). One focused directly on football games and domestic violence.

Sachs and Chu (2000) performed an ecological time trend analysis of the Los Angeles Sheriff Department's data from 1993 to 1995 but failed to find a statistically significant association between domestic violence police dispatches and professional football games. Dispatches increased marginally during the 1993 to 1994 football season and somewhat more dramatically during playoff and Super Bowl weeks. During the following football season, though, dispatches did not increase above baseline levels. Instead, dispatches decreased during the season, including playoff and Super Bowl weeks, although the observed declines were not statistically significant. Super Bowl Sunday was never the biggest day for domestic violence dispatches.

Other studies looked at football's link with homicides (Miller et al., 1990; Phillips, 1983; White, 1989), emergency room admissions (White, et al., 1992), child abuse (Drake & Pandey, 1996), and negative marital interactions (Hettich, 2001). White (1989) examined the effect of NFL football playoff games on the relative incidence of homicides in standard metropolitan statistical areas (SMSAs) with and without participating teams. SMSAs in which home teams lost experienced significantly more homicides over the six days following a game. White argued the result supported the gambling hypothesis (losing money leads to violence) and frustration-aggression theory (frustration leads to violence). However, White et al. (1992) found that the frequency of hospital emergency room admissions of women who were traumatically hurt increased (albeit not significantly) when the football team in their city won a game. Here, the authors concluded that winning could stimulate assaults: "Having a favorite team win may act as a trigger for assault in some males [since] the successful use of violent acts may give the identifying fan a sense of license to dominate his surroundings" (p. 157).

Neither Phillips (1983) nor Hettich (2001) found a significant association between football games and homicides or negative marital interactions. If anything, Phillips felt the Super Bowl was linked with a decline rather than rise in homicide rates. Drake and Pandey (1996) found no association between any sport—including football—and male-perpetrated child abuse cases.

Phillips (1983) also observed an interesting and curious phenomenon he called the "third day peak" effect (p. 562). With the effect, Phillips posits there is a three-day lag between the exposure to televised violence and the strongest real-life violent response. That is, the most significant effect of media information on violent behavior or fatalities appeared on the third day after the media message was on air. California and Detroit auto fatalities peaked on the third day after publicized suicide stories (Bollen & Phillips, 1982; Phillips, 1979), as did U.S. noncommercial airplane crashes after publicized suicide stories (Phillips, 1978, 1980) and homicides after heavyweight championship prizefights (Phillips, 1983). Other scholars (Baron & Reiss, 1985a, 1985b; Miller, et al., 1990) have scrutinized the effect. Baron and Reiss (1985a) suggested the effect may result from the occurrence of holidays or weekends near prizefights or fluctuations in unemployment rates. Adding day of week and employment data as control variables, Miller et al. reanalyzed Phillips's prizefight data and found the effect spread over the third and fourth days but only on Saturdays following those fights. However, in White's study of SMSAs with losing and winning teams, the largest increase of homicides in losing SMSAs was observed on the sixth day (1989). To date, then, occurrence and significance of the third-day peak effect remains unresolved.

Because domestic violence occurs so frequently and has been linked, at least in the popular press, with coverage of professional football games, and past research shows that televised sports have the potential to create conflict within the family, this study examines the relationship between professional football and incidence rates of domestic violence. Although the study is guided by a simple research question—Is there a relationship between professional football and domestic violence?—it would be naive to suspect that all professional football games would affect domestic violence uniformly. Instead, we expect the relationship, if found, to be complex and a product of a host of factors likely to come into play. These include structural variables such as month of the year, day of the week, and time of day when the games are on; competitive variables such as team win–loss records and place in the standings; and dispositional variables such as expected outcomes (which can be measured by point spreads for those who gamble) and actual outcomes (i.e., closeness of the final score and the degree to which the score was consistent with expectations).

METHOD

In order to collect data for this analysis, the authors contacted the police department in every city with an NFL franchise throughout the years 1996 to 2002. Because the Titans/Oilers franchise moved twice during the study period, no data were sought from Houston, Memphis, or Nashville. An attempt was made to determine which police official had the authority to grant the records request for domestic violence dispatches by days. When the proper official was identified, a letter was sent requesting a daily total of domestic violence emergency dispatches by day from January 1, 1996, until the most recent data available. When data were not available for the entire study period, police officials were asked to send as much data as possible. Approximately two weeks after the letters were sent, a follow-up phone call was made to the official. Six weeks after the phone call, a reminder phone call was made. Finally, approximately eight weeks after the reminder call, a second written request was made referencing the respective state freedom of information laws. Data were received from 15 NFL cities: Baltimore, Chicago, Cincinnati, Cleveland, Dallas, Denver, Green Bay, Kansas City, Miami, Oakland, Phoenix, Pittsburgh, San Diego, Seattle, and Tampa Bay. Two additional cities (Atlanta, New Orleans) requested reimbursement for data photocopying and preparation that was cost preventative for this study. One city (Indianapolis) responded that they did not keep such records. The data reported here are based on 26,192 days of domestic violence data from the 15 cities. The number of domestic violence incidents for each city was converted into standardized z-scores because of the great variation among city populations (i.e., the reporting cities range from three top-ten markets to Green Bay, WI).

Predictor Variables

We employed three models to examine the relationship between professional football and domestic violence. These models allowed us to control variance associated with known seasonal, weekly, holiday, and annual trends. After this variance was removed, we were able to examine the statistical relationship between football games and domestic violence. The first model looked at the effect of proximal football games on any given day. Thus, we looked at whether any given day's domestic violence dispatches were influenced by having an NFL football game (in that market) the same day, the day before, two days before, and so forth. This would allow us to see any delayed effect due to a lag in reporting or perhaps an argument that begins during football viewing and festers for some time period before ultimately resulting in domestic violence. In this model, the day is the unit of analysis. The second model allowed us to more closely look at game-related variables. Here each local game is a unit of analysis. This allowed us to examine whether variables related to a game affect domestic violence. This model included variables meant to capture the importance and intensity of the game. In the second model, we looked at whether the game was played at home, whether the game was against a division rival, whether it was a playoff game, whether the game was a win, how many weeks remained in the season, how close the team was to the top of its division (important in playoff considerations), a term that multiplied the number of weeks remaining and how close the team was to the top of the division (thought to capture must-win games), how close the game was predicted to be, and how close the game actually was. It only makes sense that some games are more important than others. This model is designed to capture that varying importance. The third model more closely resembles the first and is used to specifically examine the Super Bowl. This model considers all days and examines whether the Super Bowl falling on a given day causes that day's (or subsequent days') domestic violence incidents.

Weekday

Domestic violence occurrences are heavily influenced by weekly, seasonal, and holiday variations. Because the vast majority of NFL games are played on Sundays, it was important to control for this fluctuation. Accordingly, a dummy code (i.e., 0 or 1) was created for each day of the week except Wednesday because no games occurred on Wednesdays in this sample and midweek days had the fewest incidents. Thus, Wednesday was the baseline weekday to which other days were compared. By using a separate variable for each weekday, this allowed us to remove both linear and nonlinear weekly variations.

Month

Domestic violence peaks during the summer months and decreases steadily throughout the NFL season. To control for this negative, downward trend, dummy codes were also created for each month except March because no games occurred in March and domestic violence dispatches are less frequent during winter months.

Year

A dummy variable was also included to capture fluctuation among years in the data sample because not all cities could provide data for all years. If one year had a particularly high rate of domestic violence, this might be overrepresented in the sample if not controlled. Because some games did occur in all years in this sample, 2002 was arbitrarily selected as the reference year for the first two models. For the Super Bowl model, 2003 was the reference year because the final Super Bowl in this sample occurred in 2003 (i.e., the Super Bowl culminating the 2002 season).

Holidays

Holidays are also known to witness an increase in domestic violence. Three major holidays occur during the NFL season: Thanksgiving, Christmas, and New Year's Day. In addition, for the first and third models, dummy variables were created for Valentine's Day, Memorial Day, Fourth of July, Labor Day, Halloween, and New Year's Eve. Accordingly, a dummy code was created for each holiday.

NFL Game

Using the same method as Phillips (1983), a dummy code was created for days before an NFL game, game days, the day after, two days after, three days after, four days after, and five days after.

Home

NFL games that do not sell out their home stadiums are often blacked out from television viewing. This might lead to a decrease in city residents closely following the game. Accordingly, a dummy code was created for home games.

Division

Each team plays each team in its division twice each season. These games have an especially prominent effect on the playoff race and are often against bitter rivals. Quality of opponent has shown to play a role in fan satisfaction (Madrigal, 1995). Accordingly, a dummy code was created for division games versus nondivision games.

Playoff

Several of the cities that complied with the data request featured playoff teams, including three Super Bowl contenders. Accordingly, it was speculated that these games might create an especially great level of arousal among viewers. Likewise, much of the media speculation on the relationship between domestic violence and professional football centers on the Super Bowl. Out of 26,192 days worth of data, 4 days were Super Bowl days for a *specific* team in the sample. In total, there were 48 playoff days among the sample. Accordingly, all playoff days were coded as 1, and nonplayoff days were coded as 0.

Super Bowl

Because of the large degree of speculation surrounding the Super Bowl, the media hype it generates, and the past study examining Super Bowl and domestic violence, a generic effect of the Super Bowl on domestic violence incidents separate from interest in a specific team was assessed. Accordingly, every day in the dataset ($N = 70$) that fell on a Super Bowl was dummy coded as 1. All other days were coded as a 0.

Win

Both wins and losses could be theorized to elicit high arousal among viewers. Accordingly, a dummy code was created that would capture this contrast. Wins were coded as 1, and losses were coded as 0. The reverse would have had the same effect, except for reversing the coefficient (slope) computed using Type III sums of squares.

Weeks Remaining in Season

It was of interest to capture game-relevant variables that could increase arousal among fans. Especially for playoff contenders, games take on an increasing importance as the season winds down. This was a ratio-level variable coded for the exact number of weeks remaining in the season. Playoff games were coded as 0.

Games Back

The number of games behind the division leader was calculated for each game. The formula was [(leader wins − team wins) + (team losses − leader losses)] / 2.

As teams were closer to the division lead, or in the lead, the games should have taken on an increasing importance.

Games Back × Weeks Remaining

This interaction was computed to capture any effects that being close to the division leader is especially important toward the end of the season.

Published Spread

Because much work on effects of mediated violence suggests that arousal is a driving factor, it was of critical importance to be able to quantify what viewers would expect from the games. Reports of fans show that fans do enter games with certain expectations, and game enjoyment varies as the games depart from preexisting expectations (Madrigal, 1995). In order to have an objective standard that has some scientific merit to what was expected, the authors turned to published game spreads. These spreads are to some degree based on financial interests and should have some homeostatic pressure. Furthermore, the spreads are influenced by betting trends nationwide, so they should in some way reflect the collective consciousness. Accordingly, the published game spread was used as our operationalization of expectations. As was the case with actual spread, it was thought to be more likely that published spreads would have a quadratic effect on viewer arousal rather than a straight linear effect. That is, although potentially frustrating, games that are expected to be blowouts on either end should not be especially engaging or arousing. For mood management purposes, viewers may not engage if their team is expected to win big or be blown out. Accordingly, predicted spread was entered as both a linear and a quadratic predictor.

Actual Spread

Research suggests that close games are more intensely enjoyed (Gan, et al., 1997). This was a simple computation of the difference between the two teams' scores (team score − opponent score). Closer games were thought to increase viewer arousal. Trend analysis in regression suggests that a predictor can have both linear and higher-order (e.g., quadratic and cubic) effects. Because viewer arousal might increase as games get closer and decrease as teams are blown out, actual spread was entered into the model as both a linear and quadratic (i.e., curvilinear) predictor.

Criterion Variables

Individual Days

The raw number of domestic violence incidents was standardized by city using z-scores. This put each market on the same scale and prevented the top-ten markets from swamping the smaller cities. For each market, each day had a z-score computed for the day before, the day itself, and each of the following five days. The game-day z-score and the following five days were calculated to determine any lingering effects of NFL football, akin to what has been shown by Phillips (1983). The z-score for the day before was calculated as a control variable as a check on external validity. That is, the presence of a football game should not increase the previous day's reports. Any variable that predicted domestic violence for the *preceding* day is more likely to be spurious.

Summary Values

For each city, incidents were summed over three different periods: game day plus the next day, game day plus the next two days, and game day plus the next three days. These variables are used to test any carry-over effects.

Statistical Analyses

All analyses were conducted using hierarchical regressions (Type I sums of squares). This method allows one to control for all seasonal variables before testing the variables of interest. Data were analyzed using the general linear model (GLM) procedure of SPSS 12.0 for Windows.

RESULTS

The first regression sought to examine the effect of a game itself after controlling for month, weekday, year, and holiday status. This test was run before the individual game variables were considered. Coefficients (i.e., betas) are not reported here because they are calculated using unique (i.e., Type III) sums of squares. Accordingly, the betas would be especially high for football variables because the games are played on Sundays, when incidents are especially frequent. Beta values would ignore the independent effect of the day of the week. Accordingly, F tests are reported for the inclusion of the factor to the model containing *every variable that came before it.*

There was a modest but significant effect of having an NFL game on that day's domestic violence dispatches, $F(1,25351) = 4.60$, $p = .032$, $\Delta R^2 = .00018$. The results suggest that the presence of an NFL game does slightly increase the number of domestic violence reports. Unlike the Phillips (1983) data, there was no increase on the third day, $F(1, 25351) = .60$, $p = .438$. As can be seen in Table 22.1, no succeeding day approaches significance. Applying this relationship to Chicago (our largest city) the modest relationship would lead to approximately 3.5 additional domestic violence dispatches in a city-proper population of almost 3 million. For the victims, this is a real effect, but the one-in-a-million impact is negligible from an epidemiological perspective.

The second analysis for this study concentrated on the data for the actual 1,155 NFL games collected. In addition to the control variables used in the first hierarchical regression, this analysis included all of the game-related variables discussed above. It is important to note that this analysis was a strictly hierarchical regression, and a step-wise analysis was not conducted. If a rank ordering of effects had been the intent, several of the significance levels reported below would have had lower p values.

Separate regressions were run using the same model for the week surrounding each game (i.e., individual days and each of the summary values). The results are reported in Table 22.2. For the actual game day itself, two predictor variables reached significance. First, even after controlling for seasonal variation, there were still more incidents of domestic violence expected early in the season than late in the season, $F(1,1071) = 11.47$, $p = .001$. This result may be an artifact of the

TABLE 22.1
Hierarchical Effects of Football Games on Standardized Domestic Violence
Rates

Predictor	Mean Square	Df	F	B
Intercept	.02	1	.03	−.45
Saturday	2002.69	1	2990.08***	1.07
Sunday	3357.64	1	5013.07***	1.14
Monday	27.92	1	41.69***	.12
Tuesday	1.92	1	2.86+	.04
Thursday	16.17	1	24.14***	.01
Friday	97.95	1	146.25***	.22
January	116.01	1	173.21***	−.25
February	116.70	1	174.24***	−.16
April	.32	1	.48	.10
May	144.43	1	215.64***	.30
June	144.36	1	215.53***	.30
July	249.08	1	371.88***	.30
August	168.15	1	251.06***	.22
September	91.08	1	135.98***	.03
October	3.18	1	4.75*	−.13
November	13.59	1	20.29***	−.27
December	52.41	1	78.25***	.31
1996	133.35	1	199.10***	.27
1997	246.47	1	367.99***	.29
1998	340.18	1	507.90***	.24
1999	50.72	1	75.73***	.00
2000	66.64	1	99.49***	−.21
2001	4.80	1	7.17**	−.07
New Year	474.57	1	708.54***	2.74
Valentine's	.00	1	.01	.01
Memorial Day	34.90	1	52.11***	.75
July 4th	68.87	1	102.82***	1.01
Labor Day	113.19	1	169.00***	1.30
Halloween	1.82	1	2.71+	.16
Thanksgiving	42.32	1	63.19***	.80
Christmas	110.29	1	164.67***	1.37
New Year Eve	11.82	1	17.65***	.43
Game − 1	.24	1	.36	.01
Game Day	3.08	1	4.60*	.08
Game + 1	1.51	1	2.25	.06
Game + 2	1.79	1	2.67	.05
Game + 3	.40	1	.60	−.01
Game + 4	.42	1	.62	.03
Game + 5	.07	1	.10	.01
Error	.67	25351		

Note. Results shown in the order entered into hierarchical regression
(Type I Sums of Squares). Coefficients shown are computed using Type III
(unique) sums of squares and are not indicative of the model tested. Model
$R^2 = .33$; Adjusted $R^2 = .33$.
*$p < .05$. **$p < .01$. ***$p < .001$. +$p < .10$.

TABLE 22.2
Hierarchical Effects (*F* values) of Seasonal and Football Game-Related Variables on Standardized
Domestic Violence Rates

Predictor	Game Day	T + 1	T + 2	T + 3	T0 + 1	T0 + 123
Intercept	397.06***	257.12***	368.13***	692.00***	17.30***	214.90***
Saturday	1.49	10.20**	.55	.01	1.24	.17
Sunday	86.97***	1.18	.19	5.49*	32.45***	7.81**
Monday	.00	1.99	11.70**	23.07***	.62	15.08***
Tuesday	3.34+	1.12	6.35*	2.60	3.89*	9.51**
Thursday	.05	10.14**	.06	3.68+	4.01*	.29
January	.91	.00	2.41	.16	.55	2.07
August	10.24***	39.44***	1.97	4.37**	35.56***	27.46***
September	34.50***	38.04***	18.91***	8.79**	58.68***	64.36***
October	19.72***	2.76	1.14	2.10	15.60*	13.11**
November	2.03	.17	9.66**	.60	.50	1.51
1996	2.37	.36	.54	6.78**	1.91	4.19*
1997	21.11***	18.56***	6.84**	28.86***	31.50***	43.60***
1998	29.68***	2.98	4.97*	6.64**	21.90***	22.37***
1999	.94	4.71*	5.18*	.13	.46	3.40+
2000	.98	1.26	13.10***	4.18*	.01	4.81*
2001	.14	2.09	3.81	.91	.31	.37
2002	.52	1.37	.51	.05	1.49	.27
Labor Day	15.58***	.20	.26	.11	5.11*	.14
Halloween	3.68+	.00	3.19+	1.68	1.27	.67
Thanksgiving	6.22*	2.92+	3.59+	.65	7.21**	8.00**
Christmas	2.01	2.95+	3.01+	.31	.00	.65
New Year Eve	.71	33.42***	.64	1.07	15.63***	7.18**
Home Game	1.45	.10	2.53	1.70	1.08	2.85+
Division	.88	.27	1.00	.08	.34	1.11
Playoff	1.76	2.58	.02	.47	.03	.12
Win	1.16	1.15	.02	.86	1.76	.23
Weeks Left	11.47***	6.78**	2.87+	.37	14.36***	2.21
Games Back	.55	2.06	1.81	.24	.05	.86
WkLft × GmBk	.02	6.25+	.72	2.56	2.55	1.54
Pr. Spread	6.88**	3.32	.20	1.20	6.93**	3.36+
Pr. Spread^2	.65	1.51	.03	5.35	1.76	2.39
Ac. Spread	.01	.16	.70	1.14	.09	.00
Ac. Spread^2	1.01	.56	.01	.91	.07	.00
Adj.Model R^2	.18***	.13***	.06***	.07***	.18***	.17***

Note. Results shown in the order entered into hierarchical regression (Type III sums of squares).
*$p < .05$. **$p < .01$. ***$p < .001$. +$p < .10$.

analysis and reflect additional seasonal variation that month of the year did not capture. Second, the standardized domestic violence dispatches were inversely proportional to the spread. That is, the more the team was expected to lose, the greater the number of domestic violence dispatches on that game day, $F(1,1071) = 6.88$, $p = .009$. Because many NFL games are not completed until late afternoon, a domestic violence incident might not be reported until after midnight, falling on the next day's reports in police record keeping. Looking at the regression analyzing the sum of the same day *and* the next day, the linear effect of the published spread is again significant, $F(1,1070) = 6.92$, $p = .009$.

In the design of this study, it was anticipated that predicted spread might exhibit a quadratic effect on domestic violence incidents. That is, games that were expected to be close would lead to greater anxiety and subsequent activation of the sympathetic nervous system (i.e., arousal). As can be seen in Table 22.2, there was no such effect for the game day itself. However, the published spread did correlate with exactly the expected pattern for the third day after the game, $F(1,1063) = 5.35$, $p = .021$. Had it been any other day, the value would have been considered spurious and a likely result of Type I error. Instead, it fell on the third day, the same day for which Phillips (1983) found an increase in homicides after heavyweight prizefights, and the same day single-car automobile fatalities have been shown to increase after heavily publicized suicide stories. Furthermore, in his study of prizefights, Phillips (1983) also examined the effect of Super Bowls on homicides. No F value exceeded 1, except for the third day, which was above 2 and marginally significant. If there is a role between football and domestic violence, it appears that its effect may be immediate (i.e., same day) and delayed (i.e., three days later). Furthermore, these data suggest a pattern that makes sense: The quadratic trend suggests that when local, personally relevant games are expected to be close, there is a systematic increase in the number of domestic violence dispatches. When the game is supposed to be a blowout, anxiety should be lesser, and, not surprisingly, no third-day effect is seen.

There is also a small, interesting linear relationship of the term combining games remaining in the season and how close the team is to the division lead, $F(1,1063) = 2.56$, $p = .110$, such that domestic violence is less when either many weeks remain in the season *or* the team is out of contention. Conversely, when games matter the most—when few weeks remain *and* the team is in contention—significantly more domestic violence is reported on the third day. See Table 22.2.

The significant third-day effect for predicted spread squared as well as game importance might be dismissed as Type I error. Yet, these patterns are consistent: When games matter and when they are expected to be close, domestic violence systematically increases. When games matter less, no relationship with domestic violence is seen.

Finally, it remained to test whether the presence of a Super Bowl game on a given day would have an effect on domestic violence independent of city. Again, a hierarchical regression was run controlling for weekday, month, and major holidays before testing for the effect of the Super Bowl. Offering support to the many media reports linking domestic violence and the Super Bowl regardless of whether one's team is playing, these data suggest a significant positive relationship between a Super Bowl and domestic violence even after controls, $F(1,25416) = 7.34$, $p = .007$. As was expected, each holiday event was a significant positive predictor of domestic violence. In total, this model successfully predicted 33 percent of that variance in domestic violence data (adjusted $R^2 = .329$). Although the presence of a Super Bowl was a significant predictor of domestic violence, the overall effect was small. In sum, the data collected here report 1,366,518 domestic violence dispatches from the 15 cities. The above model suggests that 272 of those total incidents throughout the year, or .0199 %, were attributable directly to a Super Bowl falling on a given day. However, those 272 incidents reported on a Super Bowl day represent 6.5% of the incidents ($N = 4,179$) for that day. For comparison, approximately 1,238 incidents were attributable to Christmas in addition to what would have been expected for that day. Looked at across the year, the Super Bowl effect adds a very small number of incidents of domestic violence. For the day itself, there is a noticeable increase.

The Super Bowl also occurs later in the day, and, accordingly, its effect is also seen on the combined measure looking at incidents over two days, $F(1, 25396) = 4.77$, $p = .029$. The other holidays also exhibit this pattern. Interestingly, there is no third-day effect, as was seen with the local, higher personal relevance games, $F(1,25371) = .18$, $p = .670$.

To examine whether this was just a unique effect of Sundays in January (i.e., an interaction) due to the large numbers of degrees of freedom, the model included a control variable dummy code indicating every Sunday in January. That test was not significant, $F(1,25416) = .00$, $p = .99$. Thus, it appears there is indeed a unique contribution made by the presence of a Super Bowl game.

DISCUSSION

This study examined the linkage between professional football and domestic violence, relying on 26,102 days of domestic violence reports collected in 15 cities and 1,155 professional football games. By itself, the presence of a football game only marginally affected domestic violence rates. Given the multitude of factors that influence domestic violence, this is not entirely surprising. Any relationship between professional football and domestic violence is likely to be quite complex and, even with police data, not easy to precisely calculate.

Three analyses reported in this study point to a systematic relationship between domestic violence and football. The first analysis suggests a tentative link between the occurrence of a professional football game and an increase in domestic violence. After controlling for daily, monthly, yearly, and holiday variation, there was a marginal link between a football game for the local team and an increase in domestic violence incidents in that city.

The second analysis suggests a complicated relationship between games likely to increase viewer anxiety and involvement (i.e., games expected to be close and/or meaningful) and domestic violence dispatches peaking on the third day. Although this third-day phenomenon has been documented to affect violence in response to professional boxing and single-car fatalities after heavily publicized suicide stories, the psychological mechanisms remain largely beyond explanation. At least one post hoc explanation merits consideration. Unlike baseball, basketball, and hockey, football fans are forced to live with the results of a bad game for a week. The slate cannot be washed clean as quickly as it would be for those other major televised sports. Combined with midweek frustration, maximal distance from weekends, simmering resentments (and, for some, lost bets), this frustration may need several days after the game to finally boil over. Along those lines, those who bet on football need a week to recoup weekend losses. By midweek, those losses may rankle, particularly if one's spouse is aware of the wagering and annoyed with the activity itself or its outcome.

Little research has been conducted into any possible time lags in domestic violence occurrence and reporting. We do know that when police are called, officers respond more than half of the time within 10 minutes (Bachman & Coker, 1995). Data obtained from battered women indicate that victims are battered far more often than they call police and that male drunkenness plays a significant role in the decision to call police (Hutchison, 2003). Furthermore, substance use was not reported in a majority of battering incidents but may have played a role in which incidents led to a call for police (Hutchison, 2003). In a study of women in a domestic violence shelter, approximately 41 percent of the women had not called police (Coulter, Kuehnle, Byers, & Alfonso, 1999). Female victims of violence (both domestic and otherwise) are more likely to call police following first-time assaults and assaults that lead to injury (Jasinski, 2003). When police were called in response to physical violence, arrests were reported being made less than one fourth of the time (Coulter, et al., 1999). Other reasons given for failure to call police include lack of physical evidence, fear of or past negative experience with police, and fear of repercussion (Wolf, Ly, Hobart, & Kernic, 2003). Thus, we know that these domestic violence calls here are but a fraction of the incidents that occurred. Along with a host of other contributing factors, NFL football may trigger more domestic violence than we report. Unfortunately, we do not know and cannot estimate the proportion of the dispatches included in our dataset that were a day or more after the incidents actually occurred.

The third analysis provides a link between the Super Bowl itself and domestic violence, resulting in an average of 244 additional cases of domestic violence across the 15 cities studied. Since all holidays tested in the study except Valentine's Day and Halloween were significant predictors of domestic violence, the Super Bowl effect reported here may be less of a football effect than that normally encountered with holidays. That is, the Super Bowl is a major event in many American households with all of the fanfare, planning, and preparation of any other holiday. As with Thanksgiving, Memorial Day, and Labor Day, many households prepare special meals around the Super Bowl. As with these other holidays, too, alcohol is often consumed. Viewed from this perspective, it appears that the Super Bowl has all of the elements to spark holiday-related domestic violence: increased expectations, close domestic interaction, and alcohol consumption. And unlike the other three major sports in America, this one game is for all the marbles, raising the stakes for those who care about the outcome. Although it goes against the hopes associated with any holiday, it appears that when one throws together a mix of people, expectations, anxiety, and alcohol—and in many locales, in close quarters under wintry conditions—a same and next day spike in violence is the result. Having said that, we also can account for the comparatively mild spike associated with the Super Bowl. Although the game is the last of the season and, among fans, is of tremendous import for that reason, only a small proportion of those who watch really care for the two teams in the game. Unlike most games that are televised regionally, where fans for each team are likely to make up a sizeable segment of the audience, this game is watched by fans across the country who, earlier in the season, would be rooting for their home team *against* these teams. Super Bowl viewers are likely to take sides, but the passion they bring to the team they root for is likely to be far less intense than what they have for their favorite team. Indeed, they may end up rooting for the team they dislike the least. This sort of identification is not likely to stimulate significant arousal and, if their team loses, much pent-up frustration.

Although our data suggest a pattern between professional football and domestic violence, that is, the pattern holds across years and cities, the data also suggest that the relationship is complex and nonlinear. Those seeking a stimulus–response type link between football and domestic violence will not find unequivocal support in these data. These data suggest that, as games become especially important and are likely to elicit anxiety, domestic violence increases, with notable immediate and delayed effects. This may be a football effect or, more broadly, an effect in accord with the linkage between high-impact media violence portrayals and subsequent real-world violence following a three-day lag.

More broadly, our study contributes to the literature on televised sports and marital (as well as other nonsanctioned long-standing) relationships. On occasion, televised sports can trigger an ugly and violent confrontation between spouses, one that quickly and clearly threatens the relationship itself. Such confrontations represent the end point on a continuum of effects associated with televised sports. We do not know the proportion of these confrontations that result in divorce, much as we do not know the cumulative impact of simmering resentments associated with unequal commitment to televised sports. Domestic violence as well as simmering resentments are far from the norm. Fortunately for all involved, domestic violence triggered by televised football (or, for that matter, other sports) appears to be rare.

REFERENCES

American Psychology Association. (1996). *Violence and the family: Report of the American Psychological Association Presidential Task Force on Violence and the Family*. Washington, DC: Author.

Bachman, R., & Coker, A. L. (1995). Police involvement in domestic violence: The interactive effects of victim injury, offender's history of violence, and race. *Violence and Victims, 10*, 91–106.

Baron, J. N., & Reiss, P. C. (1985a). Same time, next year: Aggregate analyses of the mass media and violent behavior. *American Sociological Review, 50*, 347–363.

Baron, J. N., & Reiss, P. C. (1985b). Reply to Phillips and Bollen. *American Sociological Review, 50*, 372–376.

Bollen, K. A., & Phillips, D. P. (1982). Imitative suicides: A national study of the effects of television news stories. *American Sociological Review, 47*, 802–809.

Bryant, J. (1989). Viewers' enjoyment of televised sports violence. In L. A. Wenner (Ed.), *Media, sports, & society* (pp. 270–289). Newbury Park, CA: Sage.

Bryant, J., & Raney, A. A. (2000). Sports on the screen. In D. Zillmann & P. Vorderer (Eds.), *Media entertainment: The psychology of its appeal* (pp. 153–175). Mahwah, NJ: Lawrence Erlbaum Associates.

Bureau of Justice Statistics. (1995). *Special report: Violence against women: Estimates from the redesigned survey (NCJ-154348)*. Retrieved October 31, 2003, from http://www.ojp.usdoj.gov/bjs/abstract/femvied.htm

Bureau of Justice Statistics. (1998). *Violence by intimates (NCJ-167237)*. Retrieved October 31, 2003, from http://www.ojp.usdoj.gov/bjs/abstract/vi.htm

Cadwallader, B. (1993, February 2). Super bowl battering didn't happen. *The Columbus Dispatch*, P.C1.

Center for Disease Control and Prevention. (2001). *Southern and western states log highest rates of intimate partner homicide*. Retrieved October 31, 2003, from http://www.cdc.gov/od/oc/media/pressrel/r011011.htm

Cobb, J. (1993, May). A super bowl—Battered women link? *American Journalism Review*, 33–38.

Cohen, R. A., Brumm, V., Zawacki, T. M., Paul, R., Sweet, L., Rosenbaum, A. (2003). Impulsivity and verbal deficits associated with domestic violence. *Journal of the International Neuropsychological Society, 9*, 760–770.

Coulter, M. L., Kuehnle, K., Byers, R., & Alfonso, M. (1999). Police-reporting behavior and victim-police interactions as described by women in a domestic violence shelter. *Journal of Interpersonal Violence, 14*, 1290–1298.

Drake, B., & Pandey, S. (1996). Do child abuse rates increase on those days on which professional sporting events are held? *Journal of Family Violence, 11*, 205–218.

Frank, R. E., & Greenberg, M. G. (1980). *The public's use of television*. Beverly Hills, CA: Sage.

Freedman, J. L. (1984). Effect of television violence on aggressiveness. *Psychological Bulletin, 96*, 227–246.

Gan, S., Tuggle, C. A., Mitrook, M. A., Coussement, S. H., & Zillmann, D. (1997). The thrill of the close game: Who enjoys it and who doesn't? *Journal of Sport and Social Issues, 21*, 53–64.

Gantz, W. (1985). Exploring the role of television in married life. *Journal of Broadcasting & Electronic Media, 29*, 263–275.

Gantz, W., & Wenner, L. A. (1991). Men, women, and sports: Audience experiences and effects. *Journal of Broadcasting & Electronic Media, 35*, 233–243.

Gantz, W., & Wenner, L. A. (1995). Fanship and the television sports viewing experience. *Sociology of Sport Journal, 12*, 56–74.

Gantz, W., Wenner, L. A., Carrico, C., & Knorr, M. (1995). Televised sports and marital relationships. *Sociology of Sport Journal, 12*, 306–323.

Goldstein, J. H., & Arms, R. L. (1971). Effects of observing athletic contests on hostility. *Sociometry, 35,* 83–90.

Gorov, L. (1993, January 29). Activists: Abused women at risk on super Sunday. *The Boston Globe,* p. 13.

Hettich, R. R. (2001). The relationship between viewing violent sports on television and negative marital interactions. *Dissertation Abstracts International, 62*(4), 2059(B).

Hillman, C. H., Cuthbert, B. N., Cauraugh, J., Schupp, H. T., Bradley, M. M., & Lang, P. J. (2000). Psychophysiological responses of sports fans. *Motivation and Emotion, 24,* 13–28.

Hohler, B. (1993, February 2). Super Bowl Gaffe. *The Boston Globe,* p. 1.

Hutchison, I. W. (2003). Substance use and abused women's utilization of the police. *Journal of Family Violence, 18,* 93–106.

Jasinski, J. L. (2003). Police involvement in incidents of physical assault: Analysis of the redesigned National Crime Victimization Survey. *Journal of Family Violence, 18,* 143–150.

Kubey, R. (1990). Television and the quality of life. *Communication Quarterly, 38,* 312–324.

Madrigal, R. (1995). Cognitive and affective determinants of fan satisfaction with sporting event attendance. *Journal of Leisure Research, 27,* 205–227.

Miller, T. Q., Heath, L., Molcan, J. R., & Dugoni, B. L. (1990). Imitative violence in the real world: A reanalysis of homicide rates following championship prize fights. *Aggressive Behavior, 17,* 121–134.

National Association of Broadcasters. (1987). *Who watches television sports?* [Information pack]. Washington, DC: Author.

National Football League (2003). *Shania Twain to perform live at SB XXXVII.* Retrieved October 31, 2003, from http://www.superbowl.com/ entertainment/story/6107472

Nielsen (2002). TV, Internet and Advertising Trends Surrounding the Super Bowl. Retrieved October 31, 2003, from http://www.nielsen media.com/newsreleases/2002/2002% pre-super % 20 Bowl.htm

Phillips, D. P. (1978). Airplane accident fatalities increase just after stories about murder and suicide. *Science, 201,* 148–150.

Phillips, D. P. (1979). Suicide, motor vehicle fatalities, and the mass media: Evidence toward a theory of suggestion. *American Journal of Sociology, 84,* 1150–1174.

Phillips, D. P. (1980). Airplane accidents, murder, and the mass media: Towards a theory of imitation and suggestion. *Social Forces, 58,* 1001–1024.

Phillips, D. P. (1982). The behavioral impact of violence in the mass media: A review of the evidence from laboratory and nonlaboratory investigations. *Sociology and Social Research, 66,* 387–398.

Phillips, D. P. (1983). The impact of mass media violence on U.S. homicides. *American Sociological Review, 48,* 560–568.

Ringle, K. (1993, January 31). Debunking the "day of dread" for women. *The Washington Post,* p. A1.

Ruffini, G. (1991). The super bowl's real score. *Ms., 2*(3), 93.

Sachs, C. J., & Chu, L. D. (2000). The association between professional football games and domestic violence in Los Angeles County. *Journal of International Violence, 15*(11), 1192–1201.

Sommers, C. H. (1994). *Who stole feminism? How women have betrayed women* (pp. 188–192). New York: Simon & Schuster.

Television Bureau of Advertising. (2004). *Media trends track: TV basics.* Retrieved January 5, 2005, from http://www.tvb.org/nav/build_frameset.asp?url=/rcentral/index.asp

Tuohy, L. (1993, February 2). No increases in domestic violence reported for Super Bowl. *The Hartford Courant,* p. A3.

Wenner, L. A., & Gantz, W. (1998). Watching sports on television: Audience experience, gender, fanship, and marriage. In L. A. Wenner (Ed.), *Mediasport* (pp. 233–251). London: Routledge.

White, G. F. (1989). Media and violence: The case of professional championship games. *Aggressive Behavior, 15,* 423–433.

White, G. F., Katz, J., & Scarborough, K. E. (1992). The impact of professional football games on battering. *Violence and Victims, 7,* 157–171.

Wolf, M. E., Ly, U., Hobart, M. A., & Kernic, M. A. (2003). Barriers to seeking police help for intimate partner violence. *Journal of Family Violence, 18,* 121–129.

Zhang, L., Wieczorek, W. F., & Welte, J. W. (1997). The nexus between alcohol and violent crime. *Alcoholism: Clinical and Experimental Research, 21,* 1264–1271.

Zillmann, D., & Weaver, J. B., III. (1999). Effects of prolonged exposure to gratuitous media violence on provoked and unprovoked hostile behavior. *Journal of Applied Social Psychology, 29,* 145–165.

23

Fantasy Sports: History, Game Types, and Research

Richard G. Lomax
University of Alabama

As fan is short for fanatic, sports fans have always looked for ways to sustain their sports interests beyond the actual games themselves. This should be obvious from some of the chapters in this volume. Increasingly in recent years, sports fans have attempted to create or recreate interest in their favorite sport, team, and/or player in some format other than reality. This area has become known as fantasy sports.

For example, how would the 1927 New York Yankees do against the 1969 New York Mets? If we replayed the 2003 to 2004 National Basketball Association season, would the Detroit Pistons still win the championship? If we created our own heavyweight professional boxer with specific ability and strategy characteristics, how would he/she perform? If general managers drafted current National Hockey League players onto their own fantasy team (e.g., the Erlbaum Earlybirds), what sort of team should be assembled in order to compete for the Stanley Cup? These are all forms of fantasy sports where sports fanatics can be involved with their favorite sport, team, and/or player 24 hours per day, seven days per week, even when their sport is not in season, and even when they have never actually played the sport.

The purpose of this chapter is to provide an overview of fantasy sports. More specifically, the first section of this chapter is a description of the history of fantasy sports. Next, the different types of fantasy games available are discussed, as well as the sports represented in those games. The third section is a review of the limited available research on fantasy sports. Finally, suggestions are offered for possible areas of future inquiry in fantasy sports.

HISTORY OF FANTASY SPORTS

Fantasy sports have been in existence for over 50 years. Prior to the advent of the microcomputer and the Internet, fantasy sports were played with basic equipment such as game boards, player cards, dice, and/or markers and according to explicit rules. These are known as board games and were initially developed by sports fans. Later some of these board games were commercially marketed, the biggest manufacturers being APBA (Their initial games were baseball, appearing in 1951, and football, in 1958, both developed by Dick Seitz.) and Strat-O-Matic (Baseball was their first game, developed by Hal Richman in 1962.).

Thus, sports board games began as a cottage industry with little or no fanfare, marketing, or media attention. For example, in a baseball board game, each team selects a starting lineup of player cards for each position. Dice are rolled for each batter against the opposing pitcher to determine the outcome of each at-bat. Defensive player cards are placed on the game board, and plastic markers are used for base runners. Score sheets are then filled out and used to compile standings and statistics, all by hand. The completion of an entire season is certainly a major accomplishment. Other sports have similar structures in their board game format.

Beyond board games, consider the early years of fantasy football and baseball games, which traditionally have been the most popular fantasy sports. The roots of fantasy football can be traced back to the fall of 1962 (Esser, 1994). Fantasy football was developed by Bill Winkenbach (from his earlier experiences with baseball and golf games), who was a limited partner of the AFL Oakland Raiders, along with two writers of the *Oakland Tribune*, Scotty Stirling and George Ross. The initial development occurred during an East Coast road trip with the Raiders in a New York hotel. Upon their return home, they created the world's first fantasy football league, the Greater Oakland Professional Pigskin Prognosticators League (GOPPPL). The game itself and other early football leagues were also called GOPPPL until fantasy football became the accepted term.

The roots of fantasy baseball stem from the development of rotisserie baseball (Colston, 1996). The term rotisserie comes from the name of a restaurant in Manhattan (La Rotisserie Francaise) where the idea for rotisserie baseball was first developed by Daniel Okrent, Glen Waggoner, and colleagues in 1980. The charter members were in the publishing industry, which initially helped expose fantasy baseball to the rest of the world (e.g., early press in the *New York Times*, *CBS Morning News*, and *Inside Sports*, which was then followed by how-to guides published by Bantam Books). Okrent also discovered soon-to-be baseball statistics guru Bill James, whose numerous books have generated great interest in the quantitative side of fantasy baseball.

With the development of the microcomputer, the first computerized entry into fantasy sports involved the conversion of board games into computer games. These early computer games had minimal graphics; most were text-based versions of the original board games. These types of games are still available today and are still quite popular, particularly among fantasy sports purists. Over time new computer fantasy games were developed; these games incorporated more sophisticated computer features as they became possible to implement. For example, game graphics were incorporated as computer graphics became more advanced. In addition, the computer could generate standings, schedules, statistics, and player ratings (e.g., you can generate your own fantasy players rather than actual players who come with the game), and automatic or quick play also became possible. A wide variety of computerized fantasy sports games are available today for microcomputers and gaming systems (e.g., EA Sports, ESPN, *Madden NFL, Gretzky NHL, and NBA Live*).

The next historical event was the Internet exploding onto the fantasy sports scene. This enabled one to advertise electronically and find league participants around the globe rather than relying on friends in a local neighborhood or workplace. Most leagues have their own Web sites, and many Web sites include just about every type of information imaginable (e.g., team information; player information such as ratings, contracts, and statistics; league standings; league statistics; transactions between teams; newsletters; and e-zines). In fact, what has happened over time is that most features that actual general managers and teams have available to them have become incorporated into fantasy sports (e.g., sports agents, salary caps, trade deadlines, salary demands, and free agency). The obvious reasoning is to make the fantasy as realistic as possible. As one would expect, the more realistic the game, due to the incorporation of more realistic features, the more time it consumes of the participant.

As an aside, the Fantasy Sports Trade Association (FSTA) was established in 1999 to represent the interests of fantasy sports participants. The FSTA hosts an informative Web site (http://fsta.org/index.shtml), including articles, a message board, history and mission statements, committees, awards, a hall of fame, FAQ, and advocacy news. In addition, the FSTA hosts two annual national conferences; the tenth was held September 2004.

TYPES OF FANTASY SPORTS

Just about every sport imaginable is available in a fantasy gaming platform. As one would expect, there are the major sports (baseball, basketball, football, and hockey), as well as most other sports (e.g., bowling, boxing, cricket, cycling, fishing, golf, gymnastics, outdoor sports, racing, rugby, skiing, soccer, sumo wrestling, tennis, and wrestling). So, whatever sport is of interest, there are probably leagues to be found out there in cyberspace.

Next, consider how these fantasy leagues typically work. First, an individual decides to form his or her own league and becomes commissioner. He or she asks his or her friends and colleagues if they are interested in joining as general managers (or coaches) and might even advertise the openings on the Internet. Rules are decided upon for each of the features that the league chooses to implement, sometimes solely by the commissioner, other times in consultation with some or all of the participants. Typically either individual players or entire teams are drafted onto fantasy teams, making the initial draft a very important activity in the life of a league.

Over time, most leagues become more and more sophisticated in terms of features, as they strive for more realistic play. Thus, a league might eventually implement features such as free agency, contract lengths and salaries, team salary caps, player agents, drafting of new players, and trades. Games can be played by the commissioner, or in head-to-head play over the Internet (the two opposing participants compete directly against one another by making real-time decisions as the game progresses), or by the home team on their own computers. Results are posted by the commissioner to the league Web site, through email, or in an e-zine. From these results, statistics and standings are then generated, as well as whatever other features the league has decided to implement. For individual sports, as opposed to team sports, participants draft, or even create, individuals such as race car drivers, horses, golfers, or boxers.

There are several different types of games out there in the fantasy sports world, some more true to the original board games and others more technology oriented. What follows is a brief description of the major types of fantasy games. The first type of fantasy game is known as board games (e.g., APBA, Strat-O-Matic), as previously discussed. These are still available, both in their traditional board form as well as in computerized versions.

A second type of fantasy game is known as simulation games, where a computer software program simulates actual game play. For example, APBA and Strat-O-Matic are available for many sports; there are also sport-specific simulation games (e.g., in hockey the most popular are FHL and HLS2). The simulator utilizes a rating system of the important characteristics for each player (e.g., speed, agility, passing, 3-point shooting, blocking, defense), and then uses these to play out an entire game. This enables the simulator to generate a wide variety of game information, such as play-by-play, standings, team statistics, individual statistics, and so forth. In theory, the better the rating system and the better the simulator, the more accurate the results should be as compared to actual play (although no research has yet been conducted in this area). In other words, the intent is for players to perform in the fantasy domain as closely as possible to their actual performance.

Each of the major sports has several different simulators currently available. Typically the simulators are utilized with actual players from the most recently completed actual season. However, there are two notable exceptions. First, some simulators allow the participants to create their own players. For example, one could create his or her own boxer with specific physical characteristics (e.g., height, weight class) and performance characteristics (e.g., power puncher with strong left hook). Second, historical leagues allow one to recreate past seasons. For example, Brad's Old Time Hockey League (BOTHL) began with the 1960 to 1961 NHL season and gradually moved forward. It should also be noted that simulation league participants often assist the commissioner in developing the rules and in running the league.

Internet-based leagues constitute a third form of fantasy sports and are run by companies or sports Web sites (e.g., ESPN, CBS Sports Line, Yahoo!). Internet leagues can be free, although some of them charge a nominal fee to join a league (typically in the $20 to 50 range), depending on the features available. Some leagues even offer prizes, from trophies to shirts to cash (anywhere from $50 to $3,000). There are even Internet leagues that involve gambling, although sports gambling is described in a separate chapter of this volume. Internet-based leagues can handle unlimited numbers of participants. As a result, Internet participants generally are not involved in developing the rules or in running the league. The major Internet leagues have extensive Web sites including free content (e.g., player rankings, statistics, tips on strategy) and commissioner services (e.g., drafting tools, league software, statistic generation).

A fourth type of fantasy sports are rotisserie and pool leagues whose results are based on current actual play. Players are drafted by general managers to each team. Teams compete against one another based on the statistics actually generated by the players during a week or so of real play. For example, in baseball the typical statistical categories include batting average, home runs, runs batted in, stolen bases, earned run average, wins, saves, and a composite ratio. The winner of each statistical category is given one victory. So if the players on Team X actually hit more home runs last week than the players on Team Y, then Team X is credited with one victory and Team Y with one loss. As another example, in football points can be generated through statistical categories such as scoring plays (touchdown, extra point, field goal, etc.), total yardage gained, or defensive play.

Prior to the availability of personal computers and the Internet, rotisserie and pool participants had to wait for the arrival of their local daily newspaper for the most basic statistics and results, and even longer for the arrival of weekly newspapers, such as *The Sporting News*, for more detailed information. A calculator was the only tool available for compiling league statistics. With current Internet capabilities, real-time scores and statistics are generated online, and computer software can quickly be used to update league statistics. Thus, running rotisserie and pool leagues has never been easier.

A fifth form of fantasy sports differentiates single-season leagues from continuing leagues. Some leagues retain their teams and rosters for only a single season. Thus, each season involves new teams, new players, and new participants. Other leagues retain their teams and rosters over many seasons, and are known as keeper leagues. A keeper league can create a community of participants who are in constant communication via e-mail, discussion lists, and/or instant messaging (IM, ICQ, IRC).

Personal experience with several leagues in several different sports has taught me that a league can range from being quite impersonal (usually the single-season leagues) to being quite engaging and interactive (usually the keeper leagues). It is the latter that tend to survive and flourish over many seasons. For example, over the past decade I have become close friends with many general managers in a keeper hockey league involving participants from three countries; others have made the same claim (Esser, 1994; Indiana University, 2000).

Finally, it should be noted that a league can consist of combinations of several of these categories. Thus, there might be a simulation league that is historical and is a keeper league. For example, you might begin with the 1960 to 1961 Chicago Blackhawks hockey team, have a computer program simulate the games, and maintain the same teams and participants for many seasons.

LITERATURE ON FANTASY SPORTS

To assist in determining the published literature on fantasy sports, 15 different databases were searched in the following disciplines: sports, media and communications, education, physical education, social and behavioral sciences, business, and statistics. While there are quite a few publications in the popular press (e.g., annual guides to fantasy sports and articles in magazines such as *Sports Illustrated* and on the Internet), there is little scholarly research on fantasy sports. This is interesting given that a recent Internet search on the topic of fantasy sports yielded over 3 million hits. Clearly there is tremendous activity and interest in fantasy sports, with more data and statistics than could ever be examined, but little systematic research.

What follows are the most commonly addressed themes presented in the popular press (for a nice early discussion of online sports, including fantasy sports, see Intille, 1996). First, there are numerous articles on the increasing popularity of fantasy sports, literally exploding over the past 20 years (Berlin, 1996; Muellner, 2000; Yahoo!, 2003). For example, a Harris Interactive poll was conducted on fantasy sports in December 1999, sponsored by fanball.com. The poll indicated that (a) there were 29.6 million participants aged 18 and older, (b) 85% of the participants used the Internet in some fashion, and (c) fantasy sports generated over $100 million in revenue.

A survey conducted by the Ipsos-Reid Group (Isidore, 2003) for the Major League Baseball Players Association indicated that football is the most popular fantasy sport (65% of those surveyed), followed by baseball (27%), basketball (24%), hockey (11%), NASCAR (9%), and golf (3%). It is speculated that football is the most popular sport because fewer games are played; thus, fewer statistics and results need to be generated, leading to somewhat less participation time. Other sports such as baseball, basketball, and hockey involve more games and tend to be much more time consuming for participants.

A second popular topic, probably as a result of the unexpected growth of fantasy sports, deals with the business and economic side of the venture. According to *CNN Money* (Isidore, 2003), in 2002 CBS SportsLine.com had more than 80,000 leagues, over 1 million participants, and over $14.2 million in subscription and premium products revenue, up from $4.3 million in 2001. Yahoo! (2003) reported that CBS SportsLine.com generated over $1 million in revenue on services alone in 2002.

In terms of profitable products and services, one can subscribe to Internet pay sites for articles (e.g., participant strategy, how to play fantasy sports, how to start a league, a cheat sheet of rankings for the draft), statistical information, player ratings, draft information, as well as published magazines and guides. According to Greg Ambrosius, president of the FSTA, while Internet services for fantasy sports were largely free in the 1990s, many of those moved into the fee category as the industry began to realize a giant revenue, and thus many of those sites now earn large profits. In the same Yahoo! article (2003), Ross Levinsohn of FoxSports.com stated that "Fantasy is the killer app online for sports sites... as it's built perfectly for the Web." Muellner (2000) mentioned that fantasy sports will experience continued growth as technology improves, while Banks (2002) further described the business value and role of fantasy sports in society.

A comprehensive survey was conducted by the Sports and Entertainment Academy (Indiana University, 2000) of students and executives in the sports and entertainment industry. Some of the more notable results were as follows: (a) football was more popular than any other sport by a 2 to 1 ratio; (b) 90% of fantasy sports participants cited friendship as a reason for joining, mostly their top reason; (c) fun was cited by 60% of participants as the second most important reason, followed by the thrill of competition and the challenge; (d) prizes provided little incentive; (e) participants were mostly male, with less than 10% female (although this could have been skewed by the nature of the sample); and (f) most participants spent between one and four hours per week in fantasy sports.

Thus, nearly all of the literature on fantasy sports deals with either news, information, or basic survey research, as previously noted. Given this immense popularity, it is interesting to speculate as to why there is so little serious inquiry in the area of fantasy sports. One reason is that until recently sports-related research has not been given as much respect as other areas of inquiry. This has begun to change in the following ways: (a) the American Statistical Association (ASA) has had a section on Statistics in Sports for over ten years, part of which involves the presentation of papers at the annual joint meetings; (b) the *Chance* journal, published by ASA for over 15 years, regularly includes a column on sports statistics ("A Statistician Reads the Sports Pages"), as well as sport-related research articles; (c) the *STATS* magazine, published by ASA for students, includes a regular column titled "The Statistical Sports Fan"; and (d) research on the pedagogy of sport has been popular in scholarly journals for more than a decade.

Unfortunately, while some areas of sports-related research have become more mainstream in the academic literature, research on fantasy sports has made few inroads in academic publication circles. What follows are three notable exceptions located as a result of the literature search.

A survey study involving more sophisticated quantitative methods was conducted by Wirakartakusumah (2002). Sports Web sites hosting fantasy sports (FS; $n = 75$) and sports Web sites not hosting fantasy sports (NFS; $n = 75$) completed an online survey. The main purpose of the survey was to assess the impact hosting fantasy sports had on the profitability of sports Web sites. While both types of sites had similar marketing strategies and generated substantial revenue, the groups differed on revenue and pricing models used for banner advertisements. The amount of money spent was very highly correlated with revenue generated for the FS group ($r = .91$) but was uncorrelated for the NFS group ($r = .04$). The FS group generated significantly more revenue and profit than the NSF group ($p < .05$), although the groups did not significantly differ on the amount of money spent. Despite there being a nonsignificant correlation between the number of fantasy sports offered and profit ($r = .03$), the FS group expressed a desire to add more sports and services. Thus, while fantasy sports profits are attainable, inadequate business strategies have kept them from reaching their true potential.

A rather innovative qualitative study was conducted by Hiltner and Walker (1996) on the effects of depriving fantasy sports participants of their Prodigy rotisserie baseball game. On Sunday, May 31, 1992, the Prodigy service had a technical breakdown such that participants could not access the system to play their games for 19 hours. Hundreds of participants contributed to the system's electronic bulletin board to discuss their frustration, generating around 250 pages of single-spaced text. This allowed the researchers to examine fantasy sports media deprivation, how an electronic community formed as a result of the breakdown, as well as literary aspects of the text.

Consider a few of the more interesting results. Three easily identifiable groups of participants emerged: whiners, philosophers, and fans. The whiners and philosophers had a linguistic competition, replacing the baseball competition. The whiners complained about the breakdown, placed blame on the system and the commissioner, and posed threats (e.g., refunds, lawsuits). The philosophers philosophized that all systems breakdown and were sympathetic to the system and the commissioner. The fans did not engage in the linguistic competition but merely commented on their play. The rhetoric of each group was quite distinct. Theories about the disruption ranged from a carefully plotted conspiracy (trust being quite important in running fantasy sports leagues) to technical issues. Other themes dealt with the use of appropriate language; the discussion being more fun than the Prodigy game itself; lessons learned from the experience; the diversity and complexity of the community; and the amount of time spent in fantasy sports (with some significant others grateful for the respite).

In a contrasting study from a methodological perspective, Lomax (2001) quantitatively examined fantasy hockey player categories. The research question posed was whether the traditional categories used to describe realistic hockey players would also apply to fantasy hockey players. In real hockey, general managers, coaches, the media, and other hockey experts classify players into categories such as skilled players, grinders, enforcers, offensive and defensive defensemen, and penalty killers. Thus, the purpose of the study was to determine whether these same categories could be derived from fantasy hockey.

Fantasy player ratings (e.g., skating, passing, speed, puck stopping, checking) and fantasy player statistics (e.g., goals, assists, penalty minutes, save percentage, hits) were gathered over a two-season period from a particular simulation hockey league using the APBA simulator. Cluster analysis was performed on these rating and statistical variables to group or cluster players together who were most similar for the entire set of variables. When the contract of an actual player expires, this is precisely what general managers and player agents do, in a much less rigorous way, when negotiating with a player on a new contract. The cluster analysis was performed separately for forwards, defensemen, and goalies, as these positions require different categories.

The results largely substantiated the subjective categories commonly held by actual hockey experts. Some example clusters included power forwards, defensive forwards, marginal players, skilled players, defensive defensemen, and elite goalies. In other words, actual hockey players who are commonly placed in certain categories were similarly categorized in this analysis of fantasy hockey players. Consider these two example categories. Commonly known skilled players, such as Pavel Bure and Peter Bondra, were placed into the same category based on their fantasy results. Players recognized for their fighting and hard hitting skills, such as Tie Domi and Matthew Barnaby, were placed together into a different category. Because these fantasy-based results mirrored the commonly held impressions of actual hockey players, this study provides some validity for the ratings and statistics generated by one particular hockey simulator.

AREAS FOR FUTURE INQUIRY IN FANTASY SPORTS

What follows are several suggested areas for future inquiry in fantasy sports that would be particularly welcome to both the user and academic communities. However, because there is little scholarly work in fantasy sports, literally the sky is the limit. Presented here briefly are six areas in which research questions could easily be posed and answered in a scholarly fashion.

First, many sports have several competing simulation software programs. Questions to ask in this area could certainly include (a) how a simulator should be evaluated (e.g., subjective or statistical criteria, which might include measures of accuracy, realism, and enjoyment), and (b) which simulator is most accurate or realistic (i.e., a direct comparison of the different simulators in the same sport with the same season, teams, and players). Opening up the black box of these simulators could also lead to more realistic play, as well as ways of marketing fantasy sports products (e.g., an award for the "Most Accurate Baseball Simulator of 2005").

A second question to pose is determining the keys to success for a fantasy sports team. For example, it would be interesting to determine the optimal mix of players to have for a baseball team to be successful (e.g., how many infielders, outfielders, starting pitchers, relievers, power hitters, etc.). Alternatively, in order for a hockey team to win a championship, what strategies should the general manager use? For example, how much playing time should individual players have, how much offensive versus defensive play should there be, when should the goalie be pulled, and which players should defend against the opposing team's top players? Should the same strategies be used that real general managers or coaches use? When should golfers play it safe— when they are up by two strokes with two holes to play or in some other situation? In football, when a team scores a touchdown, when should it go for one point versus two points? Many of these types of strategy questions are also relevant in actual sports, as simulation seems to be the quickest method for playing multiple seasons under multiple conditions.

A third area to address is the development of player ratings. Typically player ratings are developed each season by a committee of commissioners and general managers. What is the most accurate system to use and which mix of characteristics should be included (e.g., skating ability, dribbling, speed on the bases, punching power, putting)? Other questions to ask might include (a) which characteristics are most important, (b) whether the characteristics should be equally weighted, (c) what an optimal rating scale for each characteristic is (e.g., 5 point scale, 9-point scale, 100-point scale), and (d) exactly what information these ratings should be based on (e.g., actual game statistics, actual ratings of coaches or scouts, subjective ratings of fantasy sports experts).

A fourth potential research question deals with satisfaction of the participants, particularly as concerned with the products and services utilized. Examples to address might include the following: (a) the needs and wants of users, (b) the satisfaction of participants with their league and software, (c) areas in most need of improvement, (d) services that are most useful or most cost efficient, and (e) making a league successful (e.g., some leagues have existed for over 20 years, while others fail to last a single season). These are all questions that marketing researchers (and others) might pose.

A fifth general area deals with communication and education. For example, what are the best methods for communicating information, predictions, and/or results? Are we better off with Web sites, e-zines, newsletters, magazines, discussion forums, e-mail, instant messaging, and/or some other device? A related topic deals with the public perception of fantasy sports. For instance, what do people in different walks of life think of fantasy sports? Is it merely a form of entertainment, or is there some educational value? Do fantasy sports deserve a place in the curriculum somewhere? If large numbers of students are already involved in fantasy sports (as some classrooms are), then it would be a natural to incorporate lessons that deal with math, statistics, writing, communication, and/or history. Why not use an area that already possesses high student interest and take advantage of that interest pedagogically?

A final area of inquiry deals with championships. For example, in NCAA Division I collegiate basketball, 65 men's and 65 women's teams compete for national championships. Basketball simulators could be used to compare the actual champions with the fantasy champions over multiple replays of the same season. For example, what is the probability of a simulator generating the actual Final Four of 2004? Or, was an actual game truly an upset when the same game is simulated many times? Similar questions could be posed for any tournament or playoff competition, such as the World Cup of international soccer, the World Championships of ice hockey, the Olympics, the BCS bowls of NCAA Division I football, and the NBA playoffs. Another question often posed is to determine the best team of all time in a particular sport. Which was the best major league baseball team, the 1927 New York Yankees, the Oakland Athletics of the early 1970s, or the Yankee dynasty of recent years? Which Montreal Canadians team was the best? Could anyone have beaten the Boston Celtics of the 1960s? Or was Martina Navratilova the best woman's tennis player of all time? Being able to simulate sports events many times will give us empirical answers to these types of questions.

SUMMARY

In conclusion, fantasy sports have literally exploded onto the sports scene. Their growth, both in terms of participation and revenue, seems unlimited for the foreseeable future. From their humble beginnings 50 years ago on kitchen tables, fantasy sports have made a huge footprint on the Internet as well. This chapter began with a brief discussion of the history of fantasy sports, moving on to the types of fantasy games and sports available. While much is known through surveys of the popularity and demographics of fantasy sports, very little research has been conducted. Thus, the chapter concluded with some scholarly questions that might be posed by researchers interested in fantasy sports.

REFERENCES

Banks, B. (2002). He shoots, he scores. Digger Turnbull is a sports junkie and his obsession pays. *Canadian Business, 75*(8), 77–78.

Berlin, E. (1996). Just a fantasy. Feel the thrill of victory and the agony of defeat, virtually, by playing a bevy of fantasy sports and games on the Internet. *Internet World, 7*(7), 102, 104.

Colston, C. (1996). Revisiting Roto's roots. *USA Today Baseball Weekly.* Retrieved June 2, 2004, from http://www.usatoday.com/sports/baseball/bbw/v96/bbw9605.htm

Esser, L. (1994). The birth of fantasy football. *Fantasy Football Index.* Retrieved April 7, 2004, Reprinted in http://www.fantasyindex.com/Birth.html

Hiltner, J. R., and Walker, J. R. (1996). Super frustration Sunday: The day *Prodigy's* fantasy baseball died; An analysis of the dynamics of electronic communication. *Journal of Popular Culture, 30*, 103–117.

Indiana University, Sports and Entertainment Academy, Kelley School of Business. (2000). *It's football, friends and fun, but few women interested in sports fantasy leagues, study finds* [Press release]. Retrieved March 3, 2004, from http://www.iuinfo.indiana.edu/ocm/releases/fantasy.htm

Intille, S. S. (1996). Sport online. Retrieved March 3, 2004, from http://www.media.mit.edu/~intille/st/sp.html

Isidore, C. (2003, September 2). The ultimate fantasy – profits. *CNN Money.* Retrieved June 2, 2004, from http://money.cnn.com/2003/08/29/commentary/column_sportsbiz/index.htm

Lomax, R. G. (2001). Using statistical methods to evaluate hockey players. *The Hockey Research Journal, 5*, 43–45.

Muellner, A. (2000). Fantasy games big leaders. *Street & Smith's Sports Business Journal, 3*(27), 36–37.

Wirakartakusumah, D. N. (2002). *Prospects of fantasy sports as a profitable sport marketing media.* Eugene, OR: University of Oregon, Kinesiology Publications. [M.S. thesis completed at the University of Wisconsin, La Crosse]

Yahoo. (2003, September 16). Fantasy football scores synergy touchdown. Retrieved March 3, 2004, from http://tv.yahoo.com/news/va/20030916/106370561600.html

24

An Untapped Field: Exploring the World of Virtual Sports Gaming

David Leonard
Washington State University

At 20, Jeremy Deberry surely is the best football player at Central Piedmont Community College in Charlotte, N.C. He practices six days a week, plays both ways and is generally regarded by his peers as among the nation's elite performers, having earned the moniker the Champ. Few address the sophomore as anything but. (2004, p. 17)

These accolades were not directed at a high school all-American or even a finalist for the John Wodden award, but a video game player. Jeremy Deberry is one of many talented virtual athletes cashing in on hand–eye success with fame and fortune. Donning jerseys, talking trash, and working from excessive levels of testosterone, virtual playing fields, and the surrounding competitive performances are a ripe source of critical inquiry.

Despite the immense popularity of sports games, academic discourses perpetually ignore and resist critical inquiry into virtual athletic fields. With only a few titles examining the genre of sports games, and a vast majority uncritically celebrating this part of the industry, the field of sports games studies represents a barren wasteland of knowledge. As of yet, there has been little work examining the centrality of race or gender, representation of sport, notions of realism, or the related competitions.

This chapter accepts the task of examining the limited discourse and literature surrounding sports games, paying particular attention to the nature of the sports game industry, the literary contributions, the gapping lapses, and possible future directions. This chapter argues that the genre of sports video games represents a powerful medium within both the worlds of sports and video games, requiring extensive research to provide both greater understanding and the basis for future scholarship and discussions on virtual sports reality.

The sports gaming industry is the crown jewel of the video games world. Sports games account for more than 30% of all video games sales. While *Tony Hawk* and other extreme sports games, which deploy race (Whiteness) in particular ways, are growing increasingly popular, the most popular games remain those of sports dominated by Black athletes. Since 1989, over 19 million units of John Madden football have been sold. In 2002 alone, EA Sports sold 4.5 million units (Ratliff, 2003). In total, the video games sports industry represents a $1-billion industry. "Today's gaming resides squarely in mainstream America, and for them fantasy means Tigers and Kobes" (Ratliff, 2003, p. 96).

Despite the economic and cultural popularity of sports video games, very little, if any, work has been undertaken to explore the social, cultural, and economic meaning of these games. This chapter provides insight into the world of sports games through an examination of both the academic and popular literature. As of yet, the literature tends to embrace noncritical celebrations of the sports gaming industry, offering insight into the technological and economic advancements within this genre of games. Equally present are discussions of the relationship between sports video games and other media, in the form of professional/college sports, film, music, and sports magazines. For example, the literature contains a few articles that explore the growing relationship between sports video games and the hip-hop industry. Moreover, there is an increasing presence of video games within sports magazines, which necessitates discussion. As such, this chapter explores the literature for both its themes of discussion and the severe absences in the literature. The absence of critique, especially concerning the ways race and gender are constructed, employed, and deployed within sports games is especially troubling. This chapter documents the discourse surrounding sports video games, providing a discussion of the games themselves, an analysis of the superficial literary engagement, and, most importantly, illustrate the numerous possibilities for future research.

VIRTUAL PLAYING FIELDS: AMERICA'S BIG FOUR

At the center of the video games industry are those games that attempt to recreate and tap into the popularity of America's top four sports: basketball, football, baseball, and hockey. Soccer' global popularity should also be acknowledged. See Table 24.1 for examples. Although the literature, given its scarcity, provides only scant understanding of the issues of the sports gaming industry, it is crucial to explore the nature of these games (my focus is be on games of the last couple of years). Rather than summarizing each game, it is instructive to talk about the issues raised by these games as both defining themes and the basis of future inquiry.

Following my recent review of *Major League 2004*, an executive at Sony sent me a nasty e-mail concerning my criticism of the game. As a San Francisco Giants fan, I was disappointed by the absence of Barry Bonds from the game (his decision to break from the Players Association contributed to this fact). This Sony executive reminded me that they go to every length to create games that reflect reality. With this in mind, the following discussion focuses on the ways that sports games attempt to blur the lines between the ballpark and the virtual stadium, the athlete and the virtual athlete.

The growth in the sports game industry, in fact, is very much connected to the technological transformations that allow for almost identical recreations of sports games. For example, the graphic details of each stadium and the fans in attendance are quite remarkable within *Major League Baseball 2005*. Playing *MLB 2005* is, thus,

TABLE 24.1
"Big Five:" Team Sport Games

Basketball	Football	Baseball	Hockey	Soccer
NBA Live 2005	Madden NFL 2005	Major League Baseball 2005	NHL 2004	World Soccer Tour 05
NCAA 2004	NCAA Football 2005	MVP Baseball 2004 All Star Baseball 2005	ESPN NHL Hockey	FIFA Soccer 2005
ESPN NBA Basketball	ESPN NFL Football	ESPN Baseball	NHL Hitz	UEFA Euro 2004
	NFL Blitz	High Heat Major League Baseball 2004		World Soccer
	NFL Fever 2004			Winning Seven Eleven International Sega Soccer Slam

like taking a tour of America's classic parks, such as Fenway and Wrigley, as well as its newest shrines—Pac Bell, Minute Maid Park (Houston), and Comerica Park. No detail is ignored, with vivid images of the Yankee Hall of Fame and the play areas of Bank One Ball Park. From the privacy of my living room, *MLB 2005* enables its players to take a vacation across America, experiencing a virtual tour of every ballpark in America. Whether through a public address calling for parents to meet their lost child, hot dog vendors, game time raffles, or Sammy Sosa's homerun trot, *MLB 2005* brings its players into the contemporary world of major league baseball, with all the excitement of America's national pastime. In *NCAA 2004*, players experience Dick Vitale's play-by-play right alongside of team mascots leading the student section in cheers. Regardless of the specific game, the level of realism and the dedication to replicate every detail of the sports world is a defining element of the sports genre.

Another key element of the big-five sports games is their reliance on recreating the entire sporting experience. Whereas games of the past focused exclusively on a single athletic contest, today's games are invested in providing the entire experience from scouting and drafting to marketing and business decisions. Success on the court, as in the real world, is connected to off-court decisions, providing a much more holistic experience. For example, in *NCAA: 2004*, the franchise option opens its players up to a world of recruitment and scouting so that each year players add and lose talent as if it were a real college program. In *MLB: 2005*, the franchise option enables players to conduct a draft, go into spring training, develop players, or otherwise improve the team through free agents or trades. A game player's responsibilities within the franchise mode move beyond team management toward franchise management. Players must oversee stadium facilities, which includes seating additions, parking rates, and the hiring/firing of vendors. Players are also responsible for guaranteeing player health and satisfaction with maintenance of rehabilitation facilities and transportation amenities. The game, in effect, monitors the progress of a franchise at the playing, financial, and marketing levels. Players can borrow money to upgrade the team's field or pay for advertising. In fact, marketing, with its emphasis on building a fan base, is a key element of the game. Whether buying media time or having bobble-head nights, *MLB: 2005* provides entry into the entire baseball experience. Players are simultaneously owner, general manager, manager, and team members. The attention to realism and the expansive nature of virtual sports truly defines today's sports gaming industry. Because games are grounded in the hope of mirroring reality, there is much less creativity in that the players, teams, stadiums, and basic organization are readily determined from year to year. The ability to expand beyond the playing field will continue to define this genre of sports game.

VIRTUAL PLAYING FIELDS: INDIVIDUAL SPORTS

Games based on individual sports reflect a second type of sports video gaming. As with the big five, those games based on individual sports (golf, boxing, tennis) are very much invested in realism and holistic experiences. The games are not purely about virtual athletic field challenges, but also include the challenges of sports participation in the twenty-first century. For example, in *Top Spin* players compete on the court and then spend game playing time on the practice court, at the airport (flying around the globe to play), at the offices of various sponsors (where they compete for commercials and endorsements), in sports shops, in salons (image is everything), and, of course, at the coach's house. In *NASCAR Thunder 2004*, players not only drive the cars around virtual tracks, but also participate in the construction of the cars, negotiate sponsorship deals, and orchestrate rivalries with other drivers. As with *Top Spin*, *Tiger Woods PGA Tour 2004* also offers a tour mode in which virtual golfers travel on virtual planes from virtual city to virtual city, while stopping in between events at pro shops to buy the newest glasses, watches, or clubs.

At a certain level, these games are more invested in offering an alternative reality because the attractiveness of these games lies in the ability to play Pebble Beach or battle at Wimbledon. The tourist or colonization aspects of virtual reality are at the center of this genre of sports game.

Another element to consider about these games, beyond available courses and playing surfaces for the virtual golfer or tennis player, are which virtual athletes are accessible. Within team sports games it is rare that a player is not available on the game, yet it is common not to have every golfer or tennis player. The realities of capitalism preclude signing every athlete; therefore, most individualized sports games offer only a select few players . For example, EA Sports relies on the popularity of Tiger Woods, surrounding him with a number of less popular golfers. This game gives little attention or importance to the numerous other American golfers and almost no exposure to international stars like Vijay Singh or Ernie Els. Within *Top Spin*, many of the top performers of today—Venus and Serena Williams, Justin Henin, Andre Agassi, and Andy Roddick – are absent from virtual reality. Therefore, although there is an equal investment in providing the consumer with a real experience, these games face obstacles and structural limitations that affect their efforts to provide a window into the sporting world.

ONTO THE EXTREME: AMERICA'S VIRTUAL LOVE AFFAIR WITH EXTREME SPORTS

Another significant market within the video games industry is extreme sports. As with the real sports world, the desire to court White suburban males has led to a proliferation of these games. Specifically, the video game industry offers several

TABLE 24.2
Extreme Sports Games

Skateboarding	Surfing	Snowboarding	Motor Cross
Tony Hawk Underground II Punk	Kelly Slater's Pro Surfer Sony Garcia Surfing	SSX SSX Tricky	Jeremy McGrath Supercross World MX 2002 Featuring Ricky Carmichael
Tony Hawk Underground	Transworld Surf	ESPN Winter X-Games Snowboarding 2	
Tony Hawk's Skater 4	Amped	Salt Lake 2002	
ESPN X Games: Skateboarding	Cool Boarders 4	EvolutionSnowboarding	
Evolution Skateboarding	Biking		
Aggressive Inline	MattHoffman's Pro BMX Dave Mira Freestyle BMX 2 BMX XXX		

Individual Sports Games	Sports Games as Cartoons	Street Games
Tiger Words PGA Tour 2004	Black and Bruised	NBA Street
Mike Tyson Heavyweight Boxing	Ready to Rumble	Street Hopes
Knockout Kings 2002	Outlaw Golf	NFL Street
Top Spin; Tennis 2K	Dead or Alive Extreme Beach Volleyball	NBA Ballers
WTA Tennis Tour; Smash Court Tennis II	Backyard Basketball	
Agassi Tennis Generation	Backyard Football	
ESPN International Track and Field	Backyard Baseball	
Sydney Olympics 2000	Backyard Hockey	
NASCAR Thunder 2004	Backyard Soccer	
NASCAR Racing Season 2003		
AMF Bowling 2004		
World Championship Pool		

games within the realm of extreme sports. Although skateboarding games remain the most popular type of extreme sports games, there is an abundance of alternative games that challenge players to master this space with creativity, manipulation, and innovation: surfing, biking, snowboarding, and motor cross (see Table 24.2). Each, as with the entire genre of sports games, are invested in realism, but games in this category are simultaneously more grounded in the creativity and transgressive nature of extreme sports. Whether in its inscription of sexualized images of women (all games), its erasure of people of color (all games), or its glorification of illegal activities (*Tony Hawk: Under Ground*), extreme sports video games take their cues from extreme sports in terms of themes and values. The descriptor for *Tony Hawk* is emblematic here: "You own the underground. This time it's your journey. Break the rules. Beat the odds. Become a star." As a space of Whiteness, rule and law breaking such as Graffiti or defying orders of police officers, are celebrated within extreme sports games.

One of the many extreme sports games is *Sony Garcia Surfing*. It, like so many of the extreme sports games, emphasizes individual mastery and creativity. The game takes place in Hawaii, and players have the opportunity to enter into a series of surf competitions. As with other games, the focus is mastery over a series of moves in hopes of securing more points than the opponents. The ability to transport oneself to Hawaii, to accept the challenges of Hawaii's biggest waves, as well as to attempt flips or 360s off waves reflect the excitement of the game. As with other extreme sports games, it is about virtual adrenaline, pushing oneself to limit and the celebration of Whiteness in the absence of virtual athletes of, color—in this instance there is one surfer of color in this game.

AN UNREAL REALITY: SPORTS GAMES AS CARTOONS

A all sports games are not necessarily invested in replicating reality. There are series of games that do not pretend to be grounded in the real sports world or invested in blurring the lines between the virtual and reality. These games, like *Black and Bruised*, *Ready to Rumble*, or *Alive Extreme Beach Volleyball*, rather, use sports as a point of departure. Using cartoonish figures, emphasizing the extreme, and embracing more comedic aspects of game culture, these games are marketed (geared) toward younger children. Both the image and the virtual ease of these games demonstrate this fact.

Of additional importance is the racial (and gendered) content of these games in their deployment of racial stereotypes. Although those sports games invested in realism certainly offer racist imagery, these cartoonish games offer grotesque racialized images. For example, *Ready to Rumble*, a boxing game, includes racialized stereotypes of virtually every community of color. The most popular character in the game is Afro Thunder, a gigantic, Afro-wearing boxer, who is more adept at talking trash than fighting. The game additionally features a Hawaiian sumo wrestler, who of course is fat, speaks poor English, and has slanty eyes; a heavily accented Croatian immigrant; and a Mexican boxer named Angel "Raging" Rivera. *Black and Bruised* may actually be worse, with the scowling Black pimp-like, stereotypical African American; the proverbial Irish boxer in green with a tattoo of a four-leaf clover; several big-breasted women (all of whom are White); and of course, the all-American blonde American in red, white, and blue trunks. *Dead or Alive Extreme Beach Volleyball* seeks to bring together sports and fighting games yet merely serves as a platform for male objectification of women. As noted in the game's description, this game offers its players the opportunity to "spend the day playing volleyball, gambling in the casino, shopping for swimsuits and accessories, lounging around the island, or trying to befriend the other girls on the island." Better said, it offers its players the opportunity to enjoy almost-naked women with extreme breast sizes and impossibly small waistlines. These games offer anything but subtlety in their deployment of stereotypical images of race and gender.

IT'S A GHETTO THANG: A VIRTUAL SPORTS INVASION OF "URBAN AMERICA"

One of the more popular types of sports game is the street game, as evident with *NBA Street*, *Street Hopes*, *NFL Street*, and *NBA Ballers*. Playing on the popularity of urban life and the fetishization of hip-hop, these games are not invested in realism but in grotesque images and exaggerated play features. Players can jump twenty feet in the air or run through a brick wall. More importantly, the emphasis of these games is the imagined culture of street life, rather than the sports themselves. For example, while players may play basketball on *NBA Ballers*, the allure and focus of the game resides with the ability to live out "the fantasy lifestyle of an NBA superstar.... Bask in all the bling success can bring: cribs, chromed-out cars, jets and much more."

The problematic nature of these games lies in their acceptance and promotion of stereotypes that emphasize the athletic power of black bodies. The ubiquitous focus on street basketball and the glorification of deindustrialized spaces of poverty contribute to commonly held misconceptions of inner city communities and the predominance of play within the Black community. For example, *NFL Street* takes traditional football gaming into both the streets and realm of hip-hop. As players start against the NFC and AFC West, the initial street battles take place on the EA Sports campus, a pristine field with a few trashcans littered about, a brick wall for out-of-bounds, and the beaches of the Pacific Ocean, with its waves proving to be the only obstacles to a touchdown. Upon defeat of all eight teams, players are able to unlock the other conferences and battle on the dangerous streets of Detroit or on New York rooftops. Interestingly, and not surprisingly given its namesake, the goal of the game is to be able to play on the streets, within America's ghettos, rather than on a sports field.

The popularity of these games has little to do with their playability but with their emphasis on an imagined street (Black) culture. Whether in the never-ending hip-hop soundtracks, the constant shots of graffiti art, or the emphasis on bling-bling, these games play to America's love affair with urban America, particularly that which is imagined as Black. As these games glamorize inner city spaces, commodifying them as seedy and dangerous places, what sorts of social commentaries emanate from these cultural products?

ODD ABSENCES

As the discussions about sports games are extremely limited in scope, depth, and number, it is important to garner an understanding of the larger discourse surrounding video games. The failure to interrogate virtual athletic fields is not unique given that the bulk of the already limited literature celebrates games for their expansive and colonizing possibilities.

Present conversations about video games are largely uncritical celebrations. Whereas one might expect popular pieces to celebrate video games and academics to offer substantive critique, celebrations emanate from both circles. Henry Jenkins (1998b), director of Comparative Media Studies at MIT, encapsulated the celebratory side of the emerging field of game studies through his deployment of historically racialized and problematic language: "Now that we've colonized physical space, the need to have new frontiers is deeply in the games. [Video Games] expand the universe." As the literature connects the popularity of video games to fantasy, "exploration and discovery," and colonization and penetrating "the virtual frontier" as if each were raceless projects, it is important to link games and the surrounding discourse to historical projects of white supremacy, based on the power of becoming and occupying the other (Gee, 2003; Jenkins, 1998b). Jenkins, a revered scholar of video games, demonstrated the massive shortcomings of the present literature. With celebrations erasing critique and thoughtful analysis, the future of game studies appears to be questionable at best. This is especially the case with sports games because the literature is bare of any sort of analysis concerning this genre.

While rare, more intellectual and scholarly accounts of video games have engaged a number of issues. The literature reveals a significant amount in terms of technological improvements within the industry and the expansive economic opportunities within virtual reality (Berger, 2002; Hertz, 1997; Kent, 2001; King, 2002; Kushner, 2003; Poole, 2000); the power and centrality of fantasy (Bernstein, 1991; Jenkins, 1998a; Jenkins, 1998b; Jones, 2002; Poole, 2000; Stallabras, 1993; Turkle, 1984/2003); the effects of violence on children (Anderson, 2000; Berger, 2002; Funk, Buchman, Jenks, & Bechtolt, 2002; Jenkins, 1998b; Jones, 2002); video games' impact on learning and children (Berger, 2002; Gee, 2003; Funk, et al., 2002; Jenkins, 1998b; Jones, 2002; Turkle, 1984/2003); the deployment or construction of time and space (Jenkins, 1998a; Stallabras, 1993; Turkle, 1984/2003; Wolf, 2001); the idea of video games as a distinct medium (Berger, 2002; Gee, 2003; Poole, 2000; Turkle, 1984/2003; Wolf, 2002); the emerging field of games studies (Wolf, 2002); the gender politics and presence of female-based stereotypes (Berger, 2002; Jenkins, 1998a; Jenkins, 1998b); and ideology offered through games (Berger, 2002; Gee, 2003; Stallabras, 1993). As provocative as these popular and intellectual readings tend to be, serious scholarly or critical examinations of video games to date have omitted several key areas of concern (race, power), remained at the surface (gender representation, games as tourism, ideologies), and ignored several genres of game play (sports, war). With this in mind, this chapter seeks to highlight the significance of games, illustrating the pathetic nature of its literature and the immense research possibilities within the field of virtual sports studies.

A FEW CONTRIBUTIONS

While the literature offers few examinations of sports games, celebrations or critiques, future work can build from a few bright lights. One of those studies is *Fair Play? Violence, Gender and Race in Video Games*, a study conducted by Children Now (2002), a child advocacy group based in Oakland, California. While limited in analysis and scope, this study provides ample quantitative scholarship that is vital to any study of video games. Specific to sports games, the authors of *Fair Play* concluded that 70% of male video game characters are competitors, whereas less than 40% of female characters took on roles as competitors. In terms of racial breakdowns, the study found that Latinos make up only 2% of game characters and appear only in sports games. Each of 32 Latino characters studied was from a sports game, particularly baseball. Similar circumstances face Black male characters, with 83% cast in sport-oriented games (Black female characters are mostly props and bystanders). Visibility is not the only concern, with 61% of African-American sports competitors emotionally unaffected by violence and a mere 15% exhibiting any levels of pain (compared to 43% and 23% of White characters). Moreover, the study found the African-American virtual athletes habitually engaged in aggressive behaviors, with almost 80% displaying physical and verbal aggression (compared to only 57% of White virtual athletes). This study represents a massive step forward in terms of the seriousness it places on the subjects, quantitative documentation, and the emphasis on race and gender representation. Yet, given its constituency and orientation toward description over analysis, of surface over depth, the limitations are obvious. Situated within all scholarly studies of video games, the work of *Fair Play* exists as a profound research of sports game studies.

A significant contribution to the literature has been the work of Andy Miah and Simon Easson (2002). While covering a spectrum of issues related to technology and sport, Miah and Esson's collection contains several pieces that advance a discourse on sport video games. As one of the few texts that critically interrogate sports video games in a scholarly fashion, this work is crucial toward the continued examination of virtual athletic fields.

Clarke, McBride, and Reece (2002) chronicled the patterns of virtual consumption within military and athletic circles. Using the military as an example of visionary forethought, the authors celebrated those coaches and athletic programs that have begun to see the value of virtual training. "In the near future the true value of simulation of sports training should be realized. The skills of high-level athletes cluster tightly and simulation-based training can provide the small, but crucial winning edge" (Clarke et al., p. 223). This article touches on one of the central themes of the existing literature in terms of both the connections between the real and virtual as well as the practical uses of sports video games. The authors equally hunted for the commercial possibilities of a growing sports video game industry given their increasing use within college and professional athletic programs. Just as the development of symbiotic relationships between the military, universities, and video game producers has resulted in a major shift in the industry toward the production of both training and commercial war video games, Clarke et al. saw a bright future in the construction of virtual athletic fields.

Andy Miah (2002) offered greater focus on virtual athletics. Miah entered into a discourse "of virtual realities [that have] omitted to consider their affect upon the way in which spectators or athletes engage with sports" (p. 225). As noted, the little engagement of sports through literature has been limited to the ways in which simulation or virtual reality has been used for training purposes, thereby erasing the virtual spectator. Miah persuasively, while superficially, argued that "the spectator's experience tends increasingly towards being more integrated with the sport event" (p. 226). He "considers how virtual reality can allow the spectator to be, virtually, placed within the activity and become an athlete as well. It is not simply a case of the spectator becoming more interactive. Rather, the spectator becomes located virtually, in the sporting event, through virtual reality" (p. 226).

In other words, Miah postulated how the relationship between the watched and the watcher, between spectator and athletes, has forever been altered by virtual sports games. Additionally, Miah concluded that the lines between the virtual and real athletic fields have become so blurred, given the amazing technological advancements and the skills required for mastery over these, that it is sometimes difficult to distinguish between athletes and virtual athletes. Building on the larger discourse which argues that technology challenges the limits imposed on the body and creates an imagined community through the provision of the virtual, Miah celebrated the possibilities of virtual playing fields, ignoring the racialized, gendered, and unreal dimensions of virtual reality.

A final piece from this collection that reflects specifically on virtual games comes from N. Ben Fairweather (2002). Fairweather, like the two previous authors, celebrated the possibilities of virtual sports games to benefit not just professional athletes, but the casual sports fan/weekend athlete as well. In his estimation, it is about access and opportunity:

> By contrast [to real sports], virtual sport offers, for example, the chance to experience a simulation of skiing where mountainsides remain unaffected by erosion, a simulation of participation in sports stadiums without need for a stadium, a simulation of motor sports without the air pollution and all without the need to travel and the adverse environmental effects of that travel. Virtual sport can offer efficiencies: skiing without the need to spend time on ski lifts, or team sports without the need to travel to the same point as the rest of the team. (p. 237)

Fairweather (2002) maintained this line of celebration in praising virtual sport games for the promotion of equality (providing the experience of competition to isolated individuals), minimalization of danger, and training possibilities. "Virtual sport offers a sporting experience without many of the negative environmental effects of much of conventional sport" (p. 246). What defines this literature more than its celebration is the absence of a sustained critique. Fairweather, like the others, never went beyond the surface and was determined to claim the environmental and competitive possibilities of virtual athletic fields. Although each of the authors reflected on the ethic or moral acceptability of virtual gaming, few provided a hint of analysis concerning the colonization of virtual sports spaces, the problems associated with blurring the real and the virtual, the pedagogy (ideological function) of games, and, most importantly, the racialized, gendered, and sexualized content (and context) of sports video games.

The increasing popularity of video games has also elicited commentaries from popular sources on how games affect children's attitudes toward violence, hand–eye coordination development, child obesity, and gender identity (Jensen, 2002; Kushner, 2003; Marriott, 2003; Ratliff, 2003; Salter, 2002; Sellers, 2002). The popular literature is particularly concerned with morality and violence (Costikyan, 1999; Freidenberg, 2003; Harmon, 2003; Napoli, 2003). As with movies, television, and music, cultural critics continually interrogate the moral consequences of this economic boom within the video game industry. Yet, despite the popularity of sports and sport video games, there has been very little attention paid to this genre of virtual reality. Moreover, the random articles within popular discourses are no more critical in their analysis of sport games than the rest of the literature. Beyond the weekly reviews in *Rolling Stone*, *Maxim*, *ESPN: The Magazine*, and a host of other mainstream publications that merely celebrate the growth of sports gaming, the literature is a barren wasteland of nonengagement.

Two articles that have stood out in terms of their elaborate celebrations are in the work of Salter (2002) and Ratliff (2003). As both articles were published within business journals (*Fast Company* and *Wired*), each focuses on the business aspects of sports video games, emphasizing the vast markets and success of EA Sports, Sega, and 989 Sports. Ratliff chronicled specifically "how sports came to rule the 9-billion dollar video game industry" (p. 96). Offering a plethora of financial statistics, Ratliff's work, while celebratory, surfaced, and uncritical, provided additional ground to stand on in terms of the popularity of sports games and the business aspects. Salter offered similar background information, focusing his attention on the rise and power of EA Sports. In both cases, numbers and organizational histories are key, leaving future scholars with raw material in need of analysis.

Another significant space of discursive engagement with sports games is the Internet. While there are a number of sites dedicated to game studies (most of which situate sports games at the periphery) and many more emphasizing strategy toward game mastery, the ESPN Gamer site is a powerful commentator on sport games. With a popular orientation and often little critical commentary on games, it sits at the center of the sports gaming world. The fact that ESPN, the "leader in sports news," would dedicate a significant part of its Web site to game culture is revealing. The focus, extensive coverage, and tone contribute to a blurring process, where the real and the virtual once again become indistinguishable. The fact that articles contain reports on games as if they were real athletic contests and numerous stories chronicling the gaming habits of professional athletes situates this site as a valuable resource for sports gaming. Whether searching for information on technological advancements, the relationship between professional sports (and athletes) and sports games, or merely information on the direction of the industry, this is a great resource.

FUTURE DIRECTIONS: SO MUCH WORK TO BE DONE

As evident, the future directions of the study of sports games are limitless. The literature does not merely contain gaps requiring exploration; rather, the extent of the discourse itself is a major gap in the larger video games literature (Miah, 2002). Even the discourse surrounding video games is superficial and limited. Without a sufficient level of literary engagement, future research is needed in a number of different directions. Beyond sheer volume to establish a foundation for future scholarship and debate, there are specific areas demanding critical inquiry.

The limited literature available offers no attempt to theorize or discuss the racialized content of, and discourse surrounding, video games. Given the centrality of race within the deployment, organization, and consumption of sports, it seems crucial to explore the manner in which race operates on virtual playing fields. Such research is even more necessary given the constructed nature of this form of popular culture. Despite claims of realism, racial stereotypes saturate sports games, from the subtle over emphasis on black muscularity to the grotesque images of street and boxing games.

Beyond the need for textual analysis particular to real meanings and subtext, there is an equal need to examine race in the context of both production and consumption. In terms of production there needs to be scholarship that explores the racial and gendered demographics of companies like EA Sports or 189 Sports to provide more expansive histories addressing the racialized/gendered production of games. We must move beyond institutional narratives that celebrate the rise of EA Sports to interrogate critically who is behind the scenes to provide a more expanded racial context for the sports game industry. In constructing organizational histories, with particular attention paid to race and gender, researchers should begin to investigate a series of related questions: Does it matter that a majority of sports game production is overseen and designed by twenty-something White suburban males? Do the demographics affect content, and how? Does the industry of sports video games, like other sports industries, exploit Black bodies for white financial gain? These questions, and the larger question of ownership and production, need to be included within future scholarship addressing race, gender, and game production as well.

Of equal importance is research concerning consumption and race—who buys and plays these games? Without numbers, it is difficult to talk about players and race. Needing to move beyond pure numbers, there exists a need to do qualitative research or oral histories to understand sports game players. Having written theoretically on the links between minstrelsy and sports games, in that virtual playing fields offer a primarily White suburban game-playing population the opportunities to become Black athletes in virtual space, my scholarship contains gaps; there is neither quantitative nor qualitative research on players' racial or gender demographics. In general, greater attention is needed on players and their stories, thereby offering insight to race, gender, and the connected pleasures generated through virtual athletic play.

Just as there is a serious need for scholarship exploring race on the virtual athletic field, there is equal need for exploration of genders within this medium. There are several possible research opportunities within this large potential discourse, ranging from the erasure of women within most sports games to the sexualized representation offered to the few virtual female athletes. In terms of representation, there has been a decent amount of scholarship on gender within video games (Berger, 2002; Children Now, 2002; Jenkins, 1998a; Jenkins, 1998b), yet very little specifically addressing gender representation within sports games. Using scholarship on how sports reduces women to sex objects, cheerleaders, and the source of advertisement or mere sexual commodities, it is crucial to examine the ways in which video games replicate these images, roles, and ideologies. For example, each victory in *BMX XXX* results in the reward of a woman stripping. In *SSX*, male competitors wear traditional snowboarding clothes: baggy pants and shirts. Yet Elise, a female whom the game describes as 5'11" and 120, dons a very tight one-piece snowsuit that accentuates her large breasts. As the announcer calls her name in preparation for her snowboard run, she seductively slides her hands up and down her sides, rubbing herself in a provocative way.

Additional research is needed on games that exclude or erase female participation. For example, there is no WNBA game, nor is there a women's option for *NCAA: 2004*. Despite the increasing popularity of Cheryl Swoops, Diana Taurasi, and Lisa Leslie, there is no option to play virtual basketball with them. Tiger Woods is a star of virtual video games, but Michelle Wie is not even available. Nor are the Williams sisters, even though women's tennis is part of *Top Spin*, a game for X-Box. Not surprisingly, almost all of the women tennis players found in sports video games are highly sexualized as the most attractive women on the tour. Within all of the extreme sports games there are virtually no women, except as eye candy. The potential research lies beyond discussions of representation (or lack thereof) within sports games and resides with potential debates surrounding the gendered impact of these games. What are the effects of such erasure on young girls and their sport participation? What is the relationship between claims of realism and the failure to construct virtual playing fields available for women? Such questions should form the basis of future research. Moreover, scholarship is needed that examines the intersections of race and gender, documenting what Black and male means within virtual reality, compared to Black and female or White and female. Beyond the need to explore the lack of application of Title IX within virtual reality, research is needed on the playing habits of both boys and girls.

In addition to quantitative numbers and studies exploring gender representation and its effects, it is crucial to have scholarship on the ways that young males, especially within collective settings, perform masculinity through sports playing on virtual athletic fields. The potential avenues of research are endless, given the representation of the gendered content of games, the gendered nature of play, and its overwhelming male constituency.

As previously mentioned, there is a tremendous opportunity to conduct qualitative research or oral histories on the production and consumption of sports video games. There has been no work on the experiences of game producers and even less on the players themselves. Researchers have dismissed sports video games as kid's play and given little attention to game spectators (players), so much so that they are rendered as insignificant manipulators of toys. Done through interviews or participant observations, research documenting the sense of pleasure; visions of race, gender, and sexuality; motivation; and the relationship between players, games, and realism is crucial toward a larger understanding of sports game culture. Is the popularity of sports games connected to White adoration of Blackness, particularly Black athletes? Do sports games represent a form of racialized tourism in which White males get to become someone else or play in otherwise inaccessible spaces? Future research needs to begin to answer these questions.

WHERE DO WE GO FROM HERE?

It has become commonplace in the world of sports to blur reality with the virtual through the deployment of video games. Whether on TNT's *NBA Tonight* or ESPN's *College Game Day*, sports programs increasingly rely on video games technology as a tool of imagination and fantasy. Bypassing actual game footage, media outlets are now able to force Yao to battle Shaq, even if the big Aristotle is injured, or see a pass play despite the coach's decision to run at the end of the game. Whether on ESPN.com or within sports telecasts, the last five years have thus witnessed a merging of the virtual and the real within the sport world.

Beyond the fantastical desires of spectators, sporting video games increasingly serve as a tool of prognostication. If you are curious about the outcome of a game or are planning to make a wager, video games exist as a pedantic source of information. This was no truer than during the pregame festivities for the 2004 Super Bowl. As the teams prepared in the locker room, the CBS pregame show provided viewers with a preview using virtual technology—EA Sports football. To further obfuscate the divide between the virtual and real, their homage to video games allowed not just representations of games and players, but a virtual reincarnation of the announcers as well. Upon completion of the simulated scenarios that might present themselves after kickoff, the coverage fluidly shifted from the virtual conversations of Jim Nantz, Boomer Esaison, Dan Marino, and Deion Sanders to their actual bodies, leaving Primetime speechless. Without hesitation, Sanders lamented the absence of realism in their virtual treatment, exclaiming, "It looks nothing like me. It looks like something from the planet of the apes." Pulling out his cell phone, Primetime continues telling his silent White peers, "I am calling Johnny Cochran to get this straightened out." As one researches sporting video games, it is clear that the racialized representation of Deion Sanders reflects the guiding ideologies and image of the virtual sports world given the preponderance of gorilla-like images and jungle settings. Yet, in this one example there are countless possibilities for research in the absence of a significant discourse or sufficient literature.

The need for qualitative research is especially necessary, given the rise of sports games competitions. At homes, in tournaments, and within EA Sports stadiums, video game players will now battle each other in *Madden* or *NCAA 2004* for the ultimate crown of cyberathletes (and sometimes lots of cash). These competitions are ripe for research picking, given the competitive elements and the ubiquitous deployment of racialized and gendered identities. Whether they are viewed from the position of researcher or participant observer, virtual athletic competitions represent a crucial site of potential research.

The potential future research concerning sports video games is limitless, reflecting an untapped dimension of popular culture. The importance of video games and sports necessitates greater attention from scholars. Whether we examine games as texts; for the relationship between games and hip-hop cultures; or for the connection between racial, gendered, and sexualized meanings within a virtual athletic context (i.e., the ways in which ideologies of race, gender, and sexuality are constructed, disseminated, and consumed through games); or whether we write about the national championships for sports games, our understanding of not just video games but sports, race, gender, popular culture, and virtual reality will come only with additional scholarship on sports video games.

REFERENCES

Anderson, C. (2000). Video games and aggressive thoughts, feelings, and behavior in the laboratory and in life. *Journal of Personality and Social Psychology*, Vol. 78,N. 4, pp. 772–790.

Berger, A. (2002). *Video games: A popular culture phenomenon*. New York: Transaction Publishers.

Bernstein, C. (1991). Play it again, Pac-Man. *Postmodern Culture*. Retrieved July 8, 2003, from http://jefferson.village.virginia.edu/pmc/text-only/issue.991/pop-cult.991

Children Now. (2002). *Fair play? Violence, gender, and race in video games*. Oakland: Children Now.

Clark, T. L., McBride, D. K., & Reece D. (2002). All but war is simulation. In A. Miah & S. Eassom (Eds.), *Sports technology: History, philosophy and policy* (pp. 215–224). Amsterdam: JAI.

Costikyan, G. (1999). Games don't kill people – Do they? *Salon.com*. Retrieved July 8, 2003, from http://www.salon.com/tech/feature/1999/06/21/game_violence/print.html

Fairweather, N. B. (2002). Disembodied sport: Ethical issues of virtual sport, electronic games, and virtual leisure. In A. Miah & S. Eassom (Eds.),*Sports technology: History, philosophy and policy* (pp. 235–252). Amsterdam: JAI.

Freidenberg, M. (2003). War video games popular as real battles rage. *The Digital Collegian*. Retrieved July 8, 2003, from http://www.collegian.psu.edu/archive/2003/04/04-03-03tdc/04-03-03dnews-01.asp

Funk, J., Buchman, D., Jenks, J., & Bechtoldt, H. (2002). An evidence-based approach to examining the impact of playing video and computer games. *Simile*. Retrieved July 9, 2003, from http://www.utpjournals.com/jour.ihtml?1p=simile/issue/funkfulltext.html

Gee, J. P. (2003). *What video games have to teach us about learning and literacy*. New York: Palgrave Macmillan.

Harmon, A. (2003). More than just a game, but how close to reality? *The New York Times*. Retrieved July 8, 2003, from http://query.nytimes.com/gst/abstract.html?res=F40612F9345D0C708CDDA D0894DB-404482

Hertz, J. C. (1997). *Joystick nation: How video games ate our quarters, won our hearts and rewired our minds*. New York: Little Brown.

Jenkins, H. (1998a). Voices from the combat zone: Game grrlz talk back. In J. Cassell & H. Jenkins (Eds.), *Barbie to mortal Kombat: Gender and computer games*. Cambridge: MIT Press. Retrieved July 8, 2003, from http://web.mit.edu/21fms/www/faculty/henry3/gamegrrlz.html

Jenkins, H. (1998b). Complete freedom of movement: Video games as gendered play spaces. In J. Cassell & H. Jenkins (Eds.), *From Barbie to mortal kombat: Gender and computer games*. Cambridge:

MIT Press. Retrieved July 8, 2003, from http://web.mit.edu/ 21fms/www/faculty/henry3/ gamegr-rlz/pub/complete.html

Jensen, J. (2002, December). Video game nation. *Entertainment Weekly*, pp. 20–41.

Jones, G. (2002). *Killing monsters: Why children need fantasy, super heroes, and make-believe violence.* New York: Basic Books.

Kent, S. (2001). *The ultimate history of video games: From Pong to Pokemon – The story behind the craze that touched our lives and changed the world.* New York: Prima.

King, L. (2002). *Game on.* New York: Universe, 2002.

Kushner, D. (2003). *Masters of doom: How two guys created an empire and transformed pop culture.* New York: Random House.

Marriott, M. (2003, May 15). Fighting women enter the arena, no holds barred. *New York Times.* Retrieved July 8, 2003, from http://query.nytimes.com/gst/abstract.html?res=F30C1EF6345B0 C768DDDAC0894-DB404482

Miah, A. (2002). Immersion and abstraction in virtual sport. In A. Miah & S. Easson (Eds.), *Sports technology: History, philosophy and policy* (pp. 225–234). Amsterdam: JAI.

Miah, A., & Easson, S. (2002). *Sports technology: History, philosophy and policy* Amsterdam: JAI.

Napoli, L. (2003, March 27). War by other means. *New York Times.* Retrieved July 8, 2003, from http://query.nytimes.com/gst/abstract.html?res=F30716FD35540C748EDDAA0894DB404482

Poole, S. (2000). *Trigger happy: Video games and the entertainment revolution.* New York: Arcade Publishing.

Ratliff, E. (2003, January). Sports rule. *Wired*, pp. 94–101.

Salter, C. (2002, December). Playing to win. *Fast Company*, pp. 80–91.

Sellers, J. (2002, December). Gaming: 2002: A road map to the tiles guaranteed to get your motor running. *Spin*, pp. 111–116.

Sellers, J.(2004, February 5). *Sports Illustrated on Campus*, pp. 17–18.

Stallabras, J. (1993). Just gaming. *New Left Review.* Retrieved July 8, 2003, from http://www.rochester. edu/College/FS/ Publications/ Stallabras.html

Turkle, S. (2003). Video games and computer holding power. In N. Wardrip-Fruin & N. Montfort (Eds.), *The new media reader* (pp. 449–514). Cambridge, MA: MIT Press. (Original work published 1984)

Wolf, Mark J. P., and Ralph B. (2002). *The Medium of the Video Games.* Austin: University of Texas Press.

The New Online Arena: Sport, Marketing, and Media Converge in Cyberspace

Joseph E. Mahan, III
Stephen R. McDaniel
University of Maryland

The tremendous growth of the Internet has been argued to have altered the way in which business is conducted across many sectors of industry, including sport and media (Boyle & Haynes, 2002; Chan-Olmstead & Ha, 2003; McDaniel & Sullivan, 1998). The Internet, or World Wide Web (Web), offers a global multimedia platform with the potential for interactivity and personalization that is highly appealing to its users, whether they be commercial or noncommercial entities. As was the case with the diffusion of traditional media, the Web has essentially changed the ways in which sport media is produced, distributed, and consumed (McDaniel & Sullivan, 1998). In exploring the nature of the sport media supply chain, prior to the time that the Web was in common use, Wenner (1989) posited a *transactional model* that involved the mass mediation of content produced by sports organizations and packaged by sports journalists and media organizations, the latter of which subsequently delivered it to the sports audience for consumption. Throughout the evolution of media technology in the twentieth century, Wenner's model was fairly representative of the flow of communication between members of what he termed the *mediated sports production complex* (sports organizations, journalists, and media organizations) and consumers (the audience).

For example, in the early days of television in the United States, sports entertainment like professional wrestling and boxing enjoyed success because the narrow scope of action suited the limitations of single-camera broadcast technology at that time (McChesney, 1989). Likewise, the television networks benefited because wrestling charged little or nothing for broadcast rights (McChesney, 1989). In years since, professional wrestling and boxing have migrated to cable, satellite, and pay-per-view channels, and team sports like football, baseball, and basketball have come to dominate sports programming characterized by multiple camera angles and instant replays. Thus, the content of mass mediated sport (and the audience's experience of it) has always been impacted by a confluence of techno-logical and/or economic factors, along with the related gatekeeping function of the mediated sports production complex (Bellamy, 1998; Jhally, 1989; Whitson, 1998).

Although the mediated sports production complex expanded its reach and earn-ing potential as broadcast technologies continued to evolve and diffuse (Andrews, 2003), certain aspects of the Wenner (1989) paradigm remained constant before the commercial growth of the Web. For example, television and print media still had relatively finite boundaries, in terms of time and/or space, which often lim-ited the breadth, depth, and immediacy of sports coverage (Singer, 2001). These constrictions can been seen as a combination of technological, commercial, and regulatory factors, due to the effects of media programming (broadcast) or for-matting (print), audience size, related advertising revenues, as well as contractual arrangements between networks and sports properties or government regulation of broadcast media (e.g., the FCC in the United States). One of the biggest impli-cations of the finite (and increasingly commercialized) nature of traditional sport media in the United States was that it tended to constrain the focus and availability of sports coverage to telegenic events or athletes that would capture the largest audiences, which also limited coverage to sports entities with the largest regional and/or national appeal (Whitson, 1998). Until the arrival of satellite television (and sports bars), many displaced fans were typically not able to follow their favorite teams or sporting events. And even with availability of sport on satellite TV, the coverage and availability of certain sports still had a decided class and gender bias (Creedon, 1998; Whitson, 1998). The control that media organizations have had over sport content impacted not only audiences but sport organizations as well, as the popularity and subsequent revenues of the latter have typically been driven by (positive) publicity in the mass media (Wenner, 1989; Whitson, 1998). Although sport and media have historically enjoyed a symbiotic business relationship much of the time (McChesney, 1989), this has not meant that sport organizations and athletes have always been portrayed in a positive light (Donohew, Helm, & Haas, 1989; MacNeill, 1998).

Another characteristic of the mediated sports production complex, prior to the Internet of the early 1990s, was the one-way nature of communication between sport media producers and distributors and their audience. While the fans could experience sport via mass media, they were relatively disconnected from the sport and media entities involved in their production and delivery. Outside of local sports call-in shows, the audiences' ability to communicate with media and sports figures was typically limited to the parasocial variety (e.g., yelling at athletes or coaches during an event broadcast) and fanmail or letters to the editor.

As we discuss herein, the Internet has changed the communication and business dynamic in the mediated sports production complex, as originally conceived by Wenner (1989). While the members of the sport media supply chain have remained the same, their role in the production, distribution, and consumption of sport media has changed, along with the arrival of an interactive and multimedia platform for the global delivery of sport content.

CYBERBRANDING AND THE MEDIATED SPORTS PRODUCTION COMPLEX

Similar to other forms of media, (sport-related) content on the Internet represents the continued blurring of the boundaries between marketing and entertainment

(Shrum, 2004). As such, it is readily apparent that sport and media have come to be seen as branded commodities that are shrewdly managed in a global marketplace (Andrews, 2003; Bellamy, 1998; Burton, 2004; McDaniel, 2004; McDowell & Sutherland, 2000). As with other sectors in today's economy, brand management has become an important business strategy in the mediated sport production complex. Many argue that the Internet is a vital tool in promotion (and extension) of media and sport brands (Bergstrom, 2000; Burton, 2004; Chan-Olmstead & Ha, 2003). It is a strategy Bergstrom (2000) referred to as "cyberbranding" (p. 11). Building on the notion of cyberbranding, this chapter examines how Internet technology has changed the nature of communication (and commerce) in Wenner's (1989) mediated sports production complex. We illustrate that established sport and media organizations have extended their brands into cyberspace, which has subsequently helped them to foster stronger relationships with existing consumers and to gain access to new markets. The Web has allowed traditional media organizations not only to distribute sports content but to become outlets for goods, like licensed sports apparel, from the teams they cover (and tacitly promote). Sports organizations, which once only produced sport, have also developed the power to distribute their wares, as they have been empowered by online media technology. Likewise, new brands (and noncommercial voices) have emerged as a result of computer-mediated sport, which also has implications to their consumption (i.e., audience experience).

Sport Organizations in Cyberspace

As Wenner (1989) noted, there have traditionally been layers of organizational control in both amateur and professional sports that have influenced the mediated sport product. This section examines the hierarchical structure of sport organizations in terms of how the Internet has altered the business and communication dynamic from governing bodies all the way down to individual athletes. We demonstrate that the Web in many ways has changed the nature of the mediated sports production complex to allow those who traditionally produced the sports product to have more control over the promotion and distribution of their brand(s) online. This has helped them to strengthen relationships with their various publics and in some cases helped them to garner additional streams of revenue through brand extensions (i.e., new products or services) and/or penetrate new markets.

Sport Governing Bodies

In Wenner's (1989) sport media paradigm, the governing body's role was typically limited to negotiating media rights deals on behalf of its membership. Once those rights were sold, members were greatly dependent upon media organizations for the distribution and promotion of their sport products. With the use of the Internet, sports governing bodies have a media presence which provides them a forum to communicate with their various constituencies (i.e., members and fans). Aside from negotiating media rights, other functions of a governing body include legislation of policies and rules that help to standardize the sport product, oversight of membership (teams and/or athletes), and archiving of historical information. The Internet has revolutionized the way in which these sport organizations perform such functions.

The Web site of the arguably most pervasive governing body in sport, the International Olympic Committee (IOC; http://www.olympic.org), serves as a portal through which one can access information about past, current, and future Olympics. It serves as an example of how the Internet has impacted the global promotion of one of the oldest and most established brands in all of sport. For example, the IOC site contains pages featuring athletes, statistics, and other historical facts dating back to the first modern Games. With this, individuals can access a wealth of information through their computers—from how many medals were won by the U.S. team in the 1896 Olympics in Athens (20) to the winner of the fencing gold medal at the 1948 London Games (Aladar Gerevich of Hungary). Under the old model of sport and mass media, finding such disparate information at any given time would have been nearly impossible. The seemingly limitless nature of the Web, however, allows the IOC to provide its wired fans across the world with instantaneous access to voluminous amounts of archived information on the organization and it storied past.

One of the unique aspects of online sport in this instance is that it allows a sporting brand (the IOC) that stages events on a four-year cycle (Summer and Winter Games) to maintain a constant global media presence. Moreover, the site not only allows the Olympic brand to maintain its visibility but also offers a promotional platform for its corporate sponsors, such as Coca Cola and McDonald's, who pay millions of dollars to the IOC to associate their brands with the Olympic movement. It not only gives a history of the quasiphilanthropic relationships between such brands and IOC events but also provides links to the corporate Web sites of the former entities (e.g., http://www.coke.com). Unlike many other sports organizations, the Olympic Games do not allow sponsors to maintain visible signage at their events, which would otherwise afford them brand exposure during television coverage. Consequently, the Web has given the IOC a new approach to help promote their corporate partners 365 days per year, year in and year out, without the reliance on traditional media.

The Internet has also given rise to an innovative extension of the IOC brand, Olympic Games Knowledge Services (OGKS). OGKS (http://www.ogks.com) provides an online gateway through which organizers of future Games—as well as those wishing to organize other large-scale sporting events—can access solutions to logistical, security, or organizational problems associated with mega–sports events. In essence, OGKS is an online template for complete sport event management from the bid process to event operations. Through an online presence, this IOC consulting service can provide detailed guidance without being bound by geographical limitations typical of the old technology model. Registered event organizers have over twelve gigabytes of examples from past Olympic and Commonwealth Games at their disposal (M. Kimmerly, personal communication, February 15, 2005).

While the Internet has provided a global sports organization like the IOC a means to bridge time and distance, it is also utilized by national governing bodies in much the same way. In the United States, the National Collegiate Athletic Administration (NCAA) oversees more than 1,200 member colleges and universities that compete nationally in 23 sports. As a governing body, the NCAA serves a variety of publics with which it must maintain lines of communication. Each of these groups—including student athletes, coaches, athletic administrators, marketing departments, and university presidents—has vastly different needs and priorities that must be met. Through its comprehensive Web site (http://www.ncaa.org), the NCAA is able to target its various constituencies more effectively with distinct pages designed for their respective needs. Consistent with online branding strategies, the look of each page remains constant throughout; however, topics and links differ to reflect information relevant to a particular group (Rowley, 2004). For example, the pages for student athletes (and parents) emphasize eligibility and academic information whereas the pages for administration and compliance officers have a focus on NCAA bylaws and recent legislation.

The manner in which the NCAA delivers college sports news content has also been changed by the Internet. One NCAA site (http://www.ncaasports.com) is designed to provide sports news, statistics, and scores in an easy-to-read format targeting fans of college sports. This site is run through a partnership between the NCAA and CBSSportsline.com and offers content about a variety of NCAA sports, a search engine for the name and division of an NCAA member institution, a ticket-purchase feature for upcoming NCAA championship events, as well as the official NCAAsports.com online store. Unlike many sports media outlets, this site provides the NCAA with the ability to deliver interested fans instant access to all NCAA sports—not just basketball and football. Thus, those sports that are not typically covered by traditional media (e.g., Division III women's swimming) now have a media presence on the Web. The Internet has supplied the NCAA an efficient conduit for organizational and marketing communication that was otherwise not possible with traditional media.

Professional Sports Leagues

Just as the Internet has influenced the governance and promotion of amateur sports like the IOC or the NCAA, it has also influenced the way in which professional sports leagues promote their brands and extend them into new markets. For example, the National Football League (NFL) has employed the Internet in an effort to cultivate a fan base for American professional football in China (Lai, 2004). The special site (http://www.nflchina.com) allows users in China to register for sport discussions and utilizes streaming video of football plays in an effort to help educate Chinese people about a sport that is uniquely American. The NFL's cyberbranding foray into China can aid in its future exportation of NFL coverage and licensed merchandise to a huge, heretofore untapped foreign market. Similarly, the Major League Baseball (MLB) Web site (http://www.mlb.com) offers a variety of information, photos, games, and ticket and merchandise sales as well as the opportunity to purchase live streaming audio and video of MLB games. Links to an online shop with merchandise from all thirty MLB teams as well as an auction site containing memorabilia, trading cards, and baseball experiences allow MLB to extend another American sporting brand into the global entertainment marketplace (as the success of such players as Ichiro Suzuki and Hee Seop Choi have helped increase the popularity of the MLB brand in countries like Japan and Korea).

According to Brown (2003), the incorporation of e-commerce into sites is vital to the survival of sport organizations in the Internet era. This is an area in which MLB has made significant strides. For example, the Baltimore Orioles (http://www.baltimore.orioles.mlb.com) provide information about their team, ticket sales, and an online store containing Orioles merchandise. Not only are tickets made available for online purchase, but there is also an interactive map of Oriole Park at Camden Yards that shows a view of the field from a particular seating section. Prior to the Internet, teams could offer purchase of tickets only via telephone or in person—and the only view of the field was in the form of a two-dimensional picture of the stadium. Another feature is that each team's site is connected to that of any other MLB team via the drop-down menu. This interconnectivity, along with the uniformity of team sites within the MLB domain, allows for simultaneous communication with consumers and fans of all thirty major league clubs.

An important facet of the new mediated sports production complex is the decreased reliance of sport organizations on traditional sports media outlets to deliver content and coverage. Internet technology (i.e., streaming audio and video) has given MLB the ability to go beyond traditional media distribution channels. Through its Web site, MLB offers purchase of streaming audio or video content of all MLB games for a particular season. Streaming (audio or video) content is available from home (or work) computers in return for a flat rate. Whereas television contracts often preclude viewing of games in certain cities (i.e., blackouts), streaming MLB content is not bound by contracts or viewing restrictions. The producer (MLB) owns both the content (the game) as well as the distribution channel (MLB.com), and the Internet provides the means for bringing the product directly to the consumer. Likewise, the MLB domain also links to the domain for Minor League Baseball (http://www.minorleaguebaseball.com), a sport that, despite no television coverage, has experienced a renaissance in the past decade, even though it was almost destroyed by the advent of televised sports over 40 years ago (McChesney, 1989; Reason, 2002).

Incorporation of Web technology into communication strategies is not restricted to professional sports leagues in the United States. For example, the Australian Rugby Union (ARU) employs a comprehensive site (http://www.rugby.com.au) that combines several approaches in disseminating rugby coverage to consumers. In addition to bringing extensive statistics, news stories, and scores to a worldwide audience, the ARU site features downloads of rugby laws (rules) as well as a search tool for those interested in becoming a player, coach, or official. Thus, ARU can extend the reach of its brand throughout Australia—and around the world—by transmitting information via the Web. Another approach taken by ARU is the EdRugby portion of its site. This type of grassroots marketing initiative functions as a means to target and cultivate a broader cross-section of consumers (i.e., youth) that might otherwise be untapped by traditional media. The EdRugby pages contain a combination of educational and sport-related content in addition to information for implementing rugby into school curricula. This mix of approaches in distributing mediated rugby content allows ARU to maintain its relationship with existing fans and to grow a new fan base through experiential marketing (e.g., getting more kids to play the sport).

Collegiate Athletic Programs

Historically, college and university athletic programs were completely reliant on traditional media to distribute sports content (and on the NCAA and its member conferences to negotiate their media rights). Over the years, collegiate athletic departments have gained more control over their television and radio broadcast rights and the subsequent ability to disseminate information to their alumni and fans. The Internet has afforded these programs the added luxury of controlling when and how information about their brands can be delivered online. Along with professional sport organizations, college athletic organizations have played a central role in the development of the Web itself (Kahle & Meeske, 1999). This has been done through the emergence of college- and university-owned Web sites which post scores, statistics, and team information, as well as provide merchandise sales and stream content of sporting events (e.g., University of Illinois;

http://www.fightingillini.com). Traditional media typically cater to coverage of major college programs and so-called revenue-generating sports such as football and basketball. However, athletics at smaller schools and a greater variety of sports are gaining a newfound voice online (Kahle & Meeske, 1999). Internet technology, along with the ability to outsource the building and maintenance of athletic Web sites (which is discussed in greater detail later), has allowed collegiate athletic programs of all sizes to deliver sports content to fans without reliance on traditional media. Thus, a small brand, such as an NCAA Division III school in the American Northeast like Endicott College (http://www.ecgulls.com), which received little or no regional or national coverage in traditional media, now has the opportunity to transmit information across the United States or abroad in a similar manner as national powers Stanford University (http://www.gostanford.com) or Notre Dame (http://www.und.com).

The constant state of change in Internet technology does present some challenges for sport organizations, such as collegiate athletic programs. For example, many of these programs are limited in terms of the financial and human capital they can allocate to the design and maintenance of Web sites. To solve this problem, colleges and universities have turned to a new trend of the industry: outsourcing the design, hosting, and maintenance of athletic department Web sites. Companies like College Sports Online, Inc. (CSO), which is owned by College Sports Television (CSTV), serve as a hybrid of Web site service provider and media organization. The nature of such Web services is quite different than that of traditional mass media, where content is more subject to the gatekeeping function of the press (Singer, 2001). A company like CSO exists to provide varying levels of service so that college sport organizations can obtain an attractive, user-friendly site while still maintaining direct control over how their brand is promoted. In addition to Web pages that contain information such as scores and statistics, the service offers pages specifically designed to operate as additional streams of revenue, including those for selling merchandise, tickets, and subscription-based streaming audio and video. Thus, similar to the cyberbranding strategies of an MLB franchise, those athletic department Web sites utilizing the services of CSO will have uniformity of design that is consistent with their branding objectives. However, because each institution regulates content, the athletic program has more control over its brand image in communicating with its fans, alumni, and recruits than is possible with traditional media coverage.

The CSO Web domain provides sports information for all colleges and universities in the United States as well as some in Canada. Athletic departments that partner with CSO can have their pages directly accessed via a links page from a central site (http://www.cstv.com). Additionally, this site provides live in-game statistics for a variety of sports events (e.g., a women's ice hockey contest between Colgate and Harvard) that are not covered by television or radio, and for which information or results are not disseminated outside the campuses involved in the contest. Collegiate sports at all levels—from football programs at major universities to nonrevenue sports at small schools that receive little or no coverage in traditional media—appear to have benefited from the way the Web has helped transform the mediated sports production complex.

Similar to the outsourcing of athletic Web sites, another recent trend in online sports media involves what has been termed a *private label Internet TV site* that further blurs the lines between journalism, publicity, and product placement. Fridgetv. com (http://www.fridgetv.com)—named after current University of Maryland head football coach Ralph Friedgen—offers access to expanded video content on players, coaches, games, and events that cannot be seen via traditional media. This site appeals to highly identified (or die-hard) fans of Terrapin football as it includes lengthy streaming video clips (some up to ten minutes) of game, practice, and press conference footage for the current season as well as an archive of past seasons' play. The depth and breadth of content represents a departure from coverage offered by broadcast media, constrained by previously noted time and space limitations. The clearest differentiation from the offerings of traditional media is perhaps the inclusion of streaming video that gives behind-the-scenes coverage of off-season conditioning practices and pregame and halftime locker room speeches by the head coach (which are often off-limits to reporters). Sites like Fridgetv.com, and a similar venture called the All Coach Network (http://www.allcoachnetwork.com), have helped coaches, like Friedgen and University of Arizona Basketball coach Lute Olson, enhance their recruiting efforts and earning potential in sports and media through their increased publicity and subsequent endorsement potential.

Created by a former sports anchorman and Maryland football player, the quasi-journalistic tone of Fridgetv.com serves as a unique recruiting tool for the school's football program, while giving the coach and the Terrapin football brand a distinct position in the college football market. Whereas NCAA rules limit the number of campus visits a recruit can make, the Fridgetv.com site allows the University of Maryland to provide a prospective recruit with an around-the-clock inside look into its football program. The virtually limitless storage potential and instantaneous nature of updated content aids in making Fridgetv.com a unique source of coverage for college football fans. Thus, through its partnership with the creators of the above site, Maryland football can gain a potential advantage vis-à-vis its regional and national competitors that was otherwise unattainable through the old sport media model. Further, Fridgetv.com is characteristic of the marriage of marketing and entertainment media, as noted by Shrum (2004). The site features sports apparel manufacturer Under Armour as the major sponsor, including a link to its site (http://www.underarmour.com). In addition, it provides a valuable product placement opportunity for the above brand in the form of Maryland athletes shown wearing the company's uniforms and gear via the site's streaming video content.

Professional Athletes

Under the old sport–mass media model, access to information about athletes was typically limited by the sports organizations they represented or by that which was reported by traditional media outlets. As we previously illustrated regarding coaches, the Internet has also afforded individual athletes more control in communicating with fans and the ability to commercially leverage their celebrity status. Sites that are maintained on behalf of professional athletes allow them to communicate more directly with their fan base and to do it on a more personal level than with traditional media. This type of site serves not only to provide sports information (i.e., statistics) but also operates as a public relations venture for the individual athlete. While many of these sites include features similar to those of teams and leagues—such as chat rooms, message boards, and online stores—some also provide personalized content like online journals that give a more personal look into the life of an athlete. Age-specific content, such as fan clubs, contests, and other activities serve to attract younger fans, who are more Internet-savvy and are more likely to surf for information on their favorite sports stars. As in the past, the use of new communication technology often creates subsequent legal issues, as is sometimes the case with athletes' use of the Internet. For example, according to Boyle and Haynes (2002), sport organizations now face a challenge in negotiating contracts with athletes in terms of whether the organization or the athlete has control over the rights to the latter's online presence.

A prime example of an American professional athlete who has established an identity on the Web is National Basketball Association (NBA) star LeBron James. His site (http://www.lebronjames.com) utilizes a multimedia platform to reach his fans. In the days of the old media–sport model, professional athletes relied on professional gatekeepers for publicity—usually disseminated in feature stories or biographies. As is demonstrated in the daily journal portion of James' site, professional athletes are now producers in the media–sport production complex and have the ability to continually update personal, behind-the-scenes content that is not available through organizational (e.g., NBA) Web sites. It also helps athletes, like James, leverage their celebrity status as product endorsers by featuring links to the brands they represent, such as Nike (http://www.nike.com).

As previously noted, the commercialized nature of the mediated sport production complex often resulted in coverage that was biased in terms of gender (Creedon, 1998; Whitson, 1998). Given the disparity in coverage, female athletes have typically failed to receive the same amounts of coverage given their male counterparts, which also impacted their marketability as celebrity endorsers. Thus, the Internet represents a departure from traditional media in terms of empowering female athletes to maintain a media presence and reach their fans. The case of Cathy Freeman, an Australian track and field athlete who was a gold medalist at the 2000 Olympics, provides one example of the Internet helping extend an athlete's media presence on a global scale. Whereas traditional media coverage of the Olympics is sufficient during the Games, an athlete's notoriety subsequently fades. However, the Web has provided an opportunity for those athletes to enjoy an extended shelf life. Freeman's site (http://www.cathyfreeman.com.au) archives her records, awards, and race results; posts pictures from her travels and races; and chronicles her career from its beginnings to the current day. In utilizing another feature that is unique to these Web sites, Freeman also includes a newsletter sent in the form of regular e-mails to registered users. This cyber fan club involves the production and distribution of custom content to specifically targeted individuals while simultaneously building a database of user profiles. The continuing evolution of Internet technology continues to improve the communication capabilities of professional athletes across the globe. In addition to bringing the athletes closer to fans, these sites serve as a public relations tool in maintaining a positive image because athletes have much less control over what kind of information is reported in traditional media.

Sports Media in Cyberspace

Despite the diffusion of new media technologies, no traditional medium has become completely obsolete. Rather, each has continued to survive due to its own distinctive qualities (Turner, 1999). For example, the newfound power of sport organizations to have greater control over the distribution of their content via pay-per-view, cable and satellite television, and radio poses a potential threat to the role of traditional media (Bellamy, 1998). In addition, the Web has provided another information and entertainment alternative for consumers, which has helped to further fragment media audiences (Dimmick, Chen, & Li, 2004). Thus, in order to keep pace in the changing global media economy, traditional sports media have had to alter their business practices and promotion tactics. As was noted earlier in this chapter about sport organizations and their members, media organizations have also extended their brands into cyberspace. In doing so, they have incorporated Web technology into existing communication strategies, along with the development of sites whose identities have become distinct from the original (i.e., television, radio, or print) brand (Boyle & Haynes, 2002). Likewise, new brands of sport media providers have also developed as a result of a new delivery platform.

Sports Television

Broadcast, cable, and satellite television have provided around-the-clock sports content for many years now. However, televised sports are still marked by certain limitations such as a finite number of program slots, the demand for local or regional coverage of teams, or so-called blackouts due to contractual agreements. For example, television coverage of international events such as the Olympics have often been constrained by the communication abilities of the (American) networks that carry them. According to Turner (1999), the convergence of television and Internet technologies can help television networks conquer some of these problems. One notable issue in coverage of events such as the Olympics has been the ability to effectively deliver live broadcasts, as these events often take place across the globe (e.g., Athens, Greece) in different time zones (outside the key prime-time viewing hours in the United States). In the traditional commercial network television model, ratings and subsequent ad sales tend to drive prime-time programming choices; this has subsequently translated into covering events that have the potential to draw the largest audiences, even if this means airing tape-delayed content. Thus, these traditional electronic media organizations have had to adopt new communication strategies to stay competitive in the Internet age.

According to Ha and Chan-Olmstead (2004), the television industry has come to view the Web as a way to provide "enhanced television," (p. 620) a practice which can improve the audience's viewing experience. According to ABC's site (http://heavy.etv.go.com/etvHome/) more than 40 million homes in the United States have a computer network connection and a television in the same room; thus, viewers are encouraged to surf the Web while tuned into their programs. In fact, the vast majority of ABC's programming in this area is related to their sports coverage: *Monday Night Football*, the Bowl Championship Series, college football, the PGA Tour, and the Super Bowl. This Internet strategy can also provide added value for cable subscribers when brands, such as ESPN, get fans involved in online polls, promotional games or trivia contests, and e-mail correspondence with on-air personalities.

Another example of the above approach applied to sports took place during the 2004 Games in Athens, Greece. The American network (NBC) that covered the Games provided more than 1,200 hours of content across its family of networks, but a significant portion of that coverage was not live (McKee, 2004). In the age of 24-hour cable sports (ESPN) and the Internet, audiences have an expectation of up-to-the-minute results and highlights. NBC sought to meet this need with a combination of television coverage and an online presence through a comprehensive Web site (http://www.nbcolympics.com). They created an online network—using their national site (http://www.nbc.com) along with those of local NBC affiliates across the United States—where access of any NBC-related Web site resulted in instant connection to the central Olympic site containing all Olympics-related content (McClellan, 2003). The Web allowed NBC to deliver real-time content instead of providing it in the form of tape-delayed television programming. Thus, television and cable networks, like NBC and ESPN, have developed a synergy with their Web sites that allows them to compliment and cross-promote their different media offerings and delivery platforms (Ha & Chan-Olmstead, 2004).

An illustration of a new niche brand of televised sports that has developed in the age of digital media is the aforementioned College Sports Television (CSTV). At the time of this writing, CSTV offers coverage of college sports through certain cable and satellite providers. In addition, it has also ventured into on-demand Webcasting by offering streaming audio and/or video for more than 5,000 college sporting events per year (Kerschbaumer, 2005). For instance, it provided college basketball fans the opportunity to order out-of-market games during the 2005 NCAA men's basketball tournament. Unlike most households in the United States, college campuses are generally wired with broadband technology that has the capacity to handle the large amounts of visual data required to transmit and view a video Webcast in real time (Kerschbaumer, 2005). It remains to be seen how CSTV will fare in an increasingly competitive sport media marketplace, however, given that Disney-owned ESPN has launched a rival service, ESPNU, which will also offer college sports coverage via cable and the Internet (Kerschbaumer, 2005). The company can deliver ESPNU's offerings to Web audiences via one of its many brand extensions, ESPN360.com, which is an online platform that allows fans to view or listen to other events and offline cable products (such as *SportsCenter*), while working at their computers.

Sports Radio

Despite the regionalized, ad-driven nature of broadcast radio, the medium has remained viable for the delivery of sports content. This viability, however, has been threatened by digital technology as employed by satellite radio and the Internet. New technology offers satellite radio providers in the United States (e.g., XM and Sirius) the ability to deliver commercial-free programming on a national scale. Further, these providers are utilizing sports content as a foundation upon which to extend their brand. XM and Sirius, for example, sought contractual agreements with sports properties like NASCAR and the NFL in order to follow a model similar to that of satellite television (Cassidy, 2005).

Research has suggested that the Internet, while not rendering other forms of media obsolete, is superior in meeting consumers' needs (Dimmick, Chen, & Li, 2004). Thus, though a relationship with the NFL has created new branding opportunities, providers such as Sirius (http://www.sirius.com) and XM (http://www.xmradio.com) rely on Web sites for the promotion of their products and services. The Sirius Web site offers access to channel descriptions and programming information as well as the capacity to purchase and activate satellite service. XM, on the other hand, provides a portal through which subscribers can manage their account, thus enhancing the provider's ability to meet the needs of consumers. Therefore, digital and traditional media technologies alike have come to utilize the vast offerings of the Web in extending the reach of their brands.

As was the case with television, the Internet appears poised to have a larger impact than satellite on the delivery of sports content on the radio (McBride,

2004). Two distinct models have emerged that have affected the ability of radio organizations to maintain a presence on the mediated sports landscape. The first model entails traditional radio broadcasters' production of online simulcasts of their on-air programming (McBride, 2004). This method enables a local radio station to reach local listeners at work (or otherwise not near a radio) as well as listeners on a national (or global) scale who live outside of broadcast range. One example of this model is 2KY 1017AM in Sydney, Australia. Through its Web site (http://www.2ky.com.au), this station offers live horse racing simulcasts in addition to sports talk radio programming on an international scale. Thus, this local station has the ability to leverage its brand beyond the geographical limitations of traditional radio technology. The Web further provides for distribution of streaming radio content via portal sites that catalog sports talk radio stations. These sites, such as RadioTower.com (http://www.radiotower.com) and Talk Radio/Radio Talk (http://www.radiotalk.org/sportstalk.htm), extend the reach of traditional radio, creating a new global cyberbrand.

The second model that has emerged on the sports radio landscape involves Internet-only broadcasting (McBride, 2004). In the production and distribution of sports content via traditional radio, established stations—usually corporate-owned—controlled the market. Because the Internet grants individuals the ability to produce sports content, personal radio stations have come into being. Sites like Live365.com (http://www.live365.com) provide Webhosting services for new entrants into the Internet radio business. Through streaming audio technology, these stations can compete with traditional radio stations for a share of the Internet radio market. As noted by Kahle and Meeske (1999), the Web has made the obscure accessible to many. This premise is exemplified by one sports talk show found on Live365.com. Fred Johnson and the eponymous *The Fred Johnson Show* (http://www.geocities.com/radiocuts/) transmit content through Live365.com without the expense and equipment necessary to broadcast via traditional radio. As a result, sports fans are transformed into producers in the less commercially constrained Internet media environment.

Sports Journalism

Since the early nineteenth century, print media have been an important provider of sports content (McChesney, 1989). Newspapers and magazines relied heavily on their sports journalists to provide accurate—and vivid—depictions of events for their readers. Yet, as has been noted with other types of mass media, print outlets have had to alter the way in which they conduct business with the advent of the Internet (Singer, 2001). It could be argued that newspapers have perhaps experienced the most changes due to the multimedia potential of Web technology. However, the initial forays of daily newspapers onto the Internet often represented a mere redundancy of that day's print version, or what Singer (2001) terms after-market "shovelware" (p. 67). Boyle and Haynes (2002) noted, however, that many of these sites have evolved over time to differentiate from the off-line print brands. For example, Singer (2001) found that the two daily papers in Denver featured a greater sports-to-news ratio in their online offerings than was the case with their print versions, as a function of the demand for sports information on the Web.

Changed, too, is the speed with which a print outlet can update content (Singer, 2001). Online editions of newspapers allow for the constant update of news items, which the traditional print delivery of content does not allow. Similarly, a national daily paper such as *USA Today*, which does not run print versions on the weekends, could not compete for readers with papers that offered Saturday and Sunday editions (prime days for many major sporting events). However, a fan interested in the latest sports scores and statistics over the weekend can now access *USA Today* on the Web by logging onto http://www.usatoday.com. Thus, the media organization can still maintain a brand presence with sports fans throughout the week by providing them information via the Internet. In addition to time constraints, space limitations dictated by production costs versus the revenues garnered by readership and advertising have also presented barriers to the amount of coverage newspapers could devote to sports. The relatively unbounded nature of the Internet means that online newspaper sites have the ability to earn ad revenue without necessarily affecting the amount of content that can be delivered. However, existing research in this area suggests that Web staffing costs could be a factor currently limiting the amount of online coverage featured by daily newspapers compared to the total number of stories in their print offerings (Singer, 2001).

According to Wenner (1989), sport magazines, which like their newspaper counterparts have finite amounts of space, typically do not suffer the same time-related constraints. For example, a weekly publication such as *Sports Illustrated (SI)* features content that is often retrospective in nature (e.g., sports news that has occurred in the past week or month.) Thus, magazine articles are written in such a way that content would have a somewhat longer shelf life than those in newspapers. However, in keeping pace with rival brands of sports periodicals that have gone online, *SI* has also developed a Web presence called SI.com (http://sportsillustrated.cnn.com/). The site involves a variation on the cobranding strategies previously mentioned in this chapter, by cross-promoting a cable news channel (i.e., CNN) and a sports magazine, both owned by media conglomerate Time Warner. While featuring some of the same content and columnists as the print version, SI.com is differentiated from the print brand in that it offers up-to-the-minute scores (which members can also have emailed to them), fantasy leagues and relevant coverage, searchable archives of its front cover dating back to its inception in 1954, as well as a link to photos of its Swimsuit Issue models that are not available off-line. The site also provides a marketing platform for *SI* and its brand extensions, as it allows visitors to subscribe to magazines (*SI* or *SI Kids* and includes an online customer service portal for current subscribers).

In a media environment where technology is constantly changing and business strategies evolving, sport media organizations that have best incorporated the benefits of the Web into their communication strategies are the brands that are likely to remain the most viable (Ha & Chan-Olmsted, 2004). As these organizations move forward in the twenty-first century, their role with respect to the other entities in the mediated sports production complex will no doubt continue to change as well.

New Members of the Mediated Sports Production Complex

Whereas the Web has altered the business and communication dynamic for corporate entities in the mediated sports production complex, it has also created opportunities for less commercial organizations to be heard. As we illustrate in this section, the Internet has provided a new forum for groups to challenge the status quo that many argue has been fostered by the economic and political forces in the mediated sports production complex (Jhally, 1989; Wenner, 1989).

Fan Advocacy Groups and Nonprofit Sport Organizations

Given the highly commercialized nature of sports media and subsequent control over content, critics of the sports entertainment industry were rarely afforded a platform to voice their discontent or to lobby for changes. The Sports Fans of America Association (SFAA), a group that has mobilized through the Web and purports to represent the interests of sports fans across the globe, is one such example. Furthermore, grassroots initiatives related to issues like gender and sport participation (e.g., the Women's Sports Foundation) have not been allowed much of a media presence. The Web has subsequently increased the reach and exposure of such organizations, allowing them a global platform to voice their concerns.

Despite the sport industry's reliance on ticket and merchandise revenues, the sports audience played a much more passive role in the old mediated sport production complex. Accordingly, advocacy groups that could provide a catalyst for changes in potentially unfair business practices by sports organizations were seldom recognized in a system where sport and media organizations enjoyed a symbiotic business relationship (McChesney, 1989). Using the Web as a means to organize and communicate, the SFAA has positioned itself as an advocate for sports fans. For example, the SFAA Web site (http://www.sportsfansofamerica.com) contains a "Sports Fans Bill of Rights" that stresses nine principles (e.g., "The right to attend games at reasonably affordable prices") by which the organization operates. With this bill of rights as its foundation, the structure of the SFAA seeks to empower sports fans to be treated more fairly as consumers. Additionally, the SFAA site has links to different chapters of the organization in various cities in the United States and across the world. Existing as virtual local chapters in cyberspace, these subgroups of SFAA can serve the singular interests of a particular location (e.g., fans in Chicago) while remaining simultaneously connected to the entire SFAA network. Through communication tools such as chat rooms, message boards, and blogs, the SFAA creates a more cohesive worldwide community of sports fans.

Similar to the SFAA, another fan advocacy group, the League of Fans, uses the Web as a platform for the advancement of fan-relevant issues (e.g., unfair business practices by sport organizations) in the United States. This organization, started by Ralph Nader, uses its site (http://www.leagueoffans.org) to alert fans to particular happenings in the sports world as well as to encourage their participation in supporting the League's causes. While demonstration and protest have existed for ages, the Web opens an alternative channel of communication for organizing similar efforts on behalf of sports enthusiasts. The League of Fans, using various subject threads on a message board, campaigns for fan involvement in such activities as signing online petitions and e-mailing Congress to spur change to the status quo in various areas of the sport industry. For example, in a recent posting to its site, the group spoke out against the cancellation of the NHL's 2004–2005 season, accusing the league of mismanagement (and taking fans for granted) and calling for state and local governments to no longer use public money to subsidize arenas for professional hockey teams.

In addition to sites devoted to fan advocacy groups, the Web also has given nonprofit organizations, such as those that exist to promote participation in sport, an expanded role as part of the mediated sports production complex.

For example, women's sports have traditionally been marginalized by the male-dominated institutions of sport and mass media (Creedon, 1998). Organizations such as the Women's Sports Foundation (WSF), through the use of their Web site (http://www.womenssportsfoundation.org), have been able to expand their reach by utilizing new technology. This comes at a time when a recent study found an increasing number of young women (ages 9–18) are using the Internet to access sports-related content (Gardyn, 2001). In 2005, the WSF posted an online petition in an effort to help stop the Bush administration from amending Title IX legislation, which the group felt would hinder equal opportunities for women in sport. While advocacy groups and nonprofit organizations like the WSF have typically not had the same public presence as large sport and media organizations, the Internet has provided them an effective platform to organize and mobilize the public to voice their concerns about sport (business) and related public policy.

E-Commerce and Sports Consumers

The sole function of sport manufacturers and brick-and-mortar retailers, prior to the Web, was to provide revenue in the ad-driven mediated sports production complex. The Internet, however, has provided these organizations with a new means of marketing communication and distribution which allows them to play different roles in the new paradigm. For instance, these organizations have experienced a shift in how they promote their products. As early as 2001, online advertising revenue had reached the billions of dollars (Brown, 2003). The multimedia capabilities of the Web allow these companies to utilize *advotainment* (i.e., entertainment that functions as advertising) as part of the promotions mix. Not only does the new medium change the way retailers can promote their products, but also it grants the retailers an opportunity to employ a clicks-and-mortar business model to sell goods and services online, in addition to their traditional retail operations. Furthermore, manufacturers and retailers that sponsor sporting events or related organizations can receive direct links from the Web sites of the properties they sponsor, thus increasing traffic to their own sites and creating increased brand exposure and potential online sales opportunities.

An example of a relatively new company that leveraged the marketing potential of the Web to its advantage is Under Armour (UA), a performance sportswear manufacturer. According to Kahle and Meeske (1999), the Internet has enabled small businesses like UA to better compete with the larger, more established brands in that sector. As a new entrant into the performance apparel category, UA was faced with challenging more established brands (e.g., Nike and Reebok), which have a greater brand presence in the media and in retail outlets. Through the use of their Web site (http://www.underarmour.com), UA has been able to utilize Internet technology to help establish its brand image and increase its distribution. For example, form-fitting UA products appear on its site as 3-D interactive images. Thus, it functions like an interactive virtual catalog. Visitors to the site can select different products and colors from its various lines and view images of them as they might look when worn. In addition, the site uses streaming video and audio so users can watch UA's television ads as well as longer spots (i.e., 90 seconds) that highlight various products and sponsorship deals with sport organizations. The UA site also operates as a point of distribution, allowing consumers to purchase apparel directly from the site. UA, as with many manufacturers, also combines this new channel of distribution with more traditional ones as the site lists retail outlets that sell its products. Site visitors can use the interactive map of the United States or Canada to find brick-and-mortar stores at which to purchase UA products. These new abilities afforded sporting goods manufacturers by the Web have changed the roles that they play in traditional media, allowing them to become media producers and online retailers by extending their brands into cyberspace.

The Web has also given rise to so-called e-tailers, those retailers that do not operate stores but sell sports merchandise exclusively online, such as Fogdog.com. As traditional media supported the product promotion needs of retail stores, Internet technology provides for the existence of this unique type of business to serve sport participants. The continued evolution of the Internet as a mass medium should contribute to the prevalence of this type of retailer, as industry projections suggest online sales of sporting goods will be over $8 billion by 2010. However, as noted by Brown (2003), further expansion of online commerce will rely on the resolution of Web-related issues such as information security and consumer privacy.

Perhaps the most distinctive aspect of sports e-commerce is that of online auctions for trading cards, tickets, memorabilia, and sporting goods. eBay (http://www.ebay.com) is the largest of these sites, with control of over 85% of the online auction market and 86 million registered users (Vizcaino, Mason, & McDaniel, 2005; Krauss, 2003). Sites like eBay bring about buying and selling of sports trading cards and memorabilia on a global scale. Additionally, large quantities of sporting goods (new and used) and tickets to sporting events are also bought and sold. Thus, there is an online auction subculture in which buyers and sellers can transcend distance to buy and sell their wares. However, the online auction dynamic can create a phenomenon known as information asymmetry, where sellers place items on the site (and therefore have exclusive access to product information, such as the quality of a trading card) and buyers must bid on items based purely on product information provided on the eBay auction site by the seller and access to reviews of the seller's business reputation (or posted feedback ratings) based on other buyers' experiences with that individual in previous auction transactions (Vizcaino, Mason, & McDaniel, 2005).

THE AUDIENCE EXPERIENCE WITH ONLINE SPORTS MEDIA

One of the key departures from Wenner's (1989) model is that the audience experience has changed from mere media consumption to include production as well. This holds true with fans as well as sports participants. Sports fans have gone digital to communities across the world equipped with the means to produce their own online content. The Web has also changed fans' media consumption patterns, with the availability of split-second retrieval of large amounts of information about their favorite sports teams, athletes, or coaches, along with the ability to celebrate or commiserate with fellow fans across the globe. All of this occurs across the chasm of time and space that—until now— has rendered sports fans a relatively anonymous and disjointed population. Furthermore, the Internet dynamic has transformed the manner in which individuals can access sports content. For example, the Web now provides content on demand, through interactive and multimedia platforms (e.g., streaming video/audio) and via wireless technology (e.g., laptops, PDAs, and cell phones). Thus, sports fans can access sports information in ways not possible with traditional media. Likewise, sports participants also have a burgeoning

Internet presence, with sites created by groups, organizations, and individuals for connecting to those with similar sports interests. Amateur athletes now have increased access to participation opportunities, as registration processes for sports events (e.g., road races) have been digitally enhanced with Web technology. In addition, they can go online to purchase athletic equipment, apparel, nutritional supplements, and other services (e.g., online personal trainers) that relate to their individual interests in sporting activities.

The Digital Fan Experience

A significant issue in the success of the relationship between sport spectators and the Internet has been one of supply and demand. It has been posited that sports fans demand highly specific information in an instant, and the Internet has shown a greater capacity to meet this need than traditional mass media (Jones, Bee, Burton, & Kahle, 2004). Evidence of this dynamic can be found in the vast amount of sport content on the Web that is produced by individuals—including sports fans—rather than corporate (i.e., sport or media) gatekeepers. The content of sites maintained by sports fans ranges from sycophantic to disparaging in nature, thus pointing to the relatively unregulated nature of the Internet as a communication medium. One example of an unofficial fan site is produced by a supporter of the NFL's Oakland Raiders (http://www.silverandblackattack.com). Because its content is not controlled by the traditional mediated sport production complex, this site can offer otherwise unorthodox content such as a glossary of Raiderisms (i.e., common terms used by Raider fans) as well as multimedia content (e.g., music downloads and interactive games). Visitors to noncommercial fan sites like the above have the ability to share information instantly with other users of similar interests.

Prior to the Internet, fans who wished to express their displeasure with a particular sports personality or entity were relegated to radio call-in programs or letters to the editor. Now these individuals can publish Web pages of their own and provide a forum in which other fans can participate. American college football fans have particularly taken to this approach, as shown in the case of a site devoted to former University of Florida head football coach Ron Zook in the early 2000s. Within twenty-four hours of his promotion to head coach, a fan had created a site in his "honor": FireRonZook.com (Kennedy & Deitsch, 2002). During Zook's embattled tenure as coach, this site remained as a vehicle by which Gator fans could vent their frustrations by posting messages about their team and coach (and they could purchase T-shirts and other merchandise related to their cause). The site, which remained up after Zook lost his job in 2004, later touted the hiring of his replacement (Coach Urban Myer) early in 2005. The use of the Internet as an outlet to express pride, camaraderie, or anger permits sports fans to participate more fully in an exchange of information that is not typically available via traditional media.

Another form of online opportunity for sports fans is Internet-mediated communities (IMCs). IMCs, which include message boards and chat rooms, have been defined as "groups of people who share interests and, during some time, make use of the same Internet tools to exchange information with each other regarding shared interests" (Bellini & Vargas, 2003, p. 5). Fans of the MLB's Boston Red Sox have such an outlet in the Sons of Sam Horn Web site (http://www.sonsofsamhorn.com). Multiple message boards are made available on this site, which allow for simultaneous participation in more than one discussion. These discussions are separated into threads under which users can post replies and engage in asynchronous dialogue (Weiser, 2001). The IMC requires that each user select a screen name, an alias that prevents one's real identity from being revealed. The anonymity afforded by the screen name has given rise to the creation of a different persona than if the interaction took place in a face-to-face setting (Weiser, 2001).

The interactivity of the IMC outdistances fan participation opportunities in traditional media, such as sports talk radio. Call-in shows of sports talk radio have long allowed fans a voice on popular topics of the time. However, limits of the medium (e.g., program length and format) have prevented radio from truly becoming an interactive medium for sports fans. Several aspects of the IMC have combined to create a new atmosphere for fans. For example, a message board on the Fridgetv.com site featured more than 700 different threads in the first two years of its existence—some of which do not even discuss football. Unlike the call-in format found on sports talk radio, registered users have the option of posting replies to a current thread or beginning their own, even if it is unrelated. In contrast, the limited time frame of radio call-in shows usually requires that callers keep to one topic. Further, message boards allow users to participate regardless of login time or geographical location, a feature that allows for worldwide participation.

Two closely related types of IMCs—the chat room and live chat—are similar to radio call-in shows in terms of their time constraints. In order to participate in a chat room, an individual (using a screen name) must be logged on at the same time as other users. Likewise, a live chat session with a sports figure or member of the media is limited by the amount of time reserved for the online interview. They both differ, however, in that there are an infinite number of users who may participate in a session. In addition, whereas each individual is limited to one contribution per radio program, participants in a chat room or live chat may submit multiple questions or comments. In serving as a surrogate for in-person interaction, IMCs play an important role in meeting the real-time demands of many sports fans.

Fantasy sports are also one of the fastest growing aspects of online sports content (Umstead, 1999; also see Lomax, chap. 23, this volume). While participation in fantasy sports leagues and games has existed for years, the Internet has allowed participants to become more heavily involved and has made it easier for those unfamiliar with fantasy sports to join ("Fantasy sports," 2003). As a result, the association's figures showed that more than 15 million American adults played fantasy sports during 2002. Besides the increase in participant numbers, the variety of fantasy offerings has also skyrocketed. Currently, there are 16 unique fantasy sports games available on Yahoo.com, 17 on ESPN.com, and 7 on Sportsline.com, including leagues that allow players, to act as virtual commissioner, draft a team of former major league baseball players, (ESPN's *Classic Fantasy Baseball*) as well as participate in fantasy auto racing and fishing. Fantasy sports also represent an emerging revenue stream for the organizations that host the games, as they accounted for 75% of the $50 million in paid online sports content in 2003 (Elliot, 2003).

Although it can be argued that the interactivity of the Internet has contributed to a complete transformation of the sports audience experience, some parallels may still be drawn to the consumption of sport content with traditional media. Market segmentation research by Shoham and Kahle (1996) revealed that sports spectators could be categorized into communities characterized by patterns of consumption or communication. Communication communities (i.e., sports spectators, sports viewers, and sports readers) were defined as groups of sports consumers who used similar forms of media (Shoham & Kahle, 1996). Although Shohan and Kahle's analysis included only traditional media (i.e., television and print), some aspects of their typology could be extrapolated to the audience experience in cyberspace.

One example of sports viewers on the Internet might be those individuals who watch or listen to a Webcast that involves either streaming video or audio of a live sporting event. MLB offers single-game and season packages of such content on their official site. In addition, the streaming video and audio content offered via collegiate athletic Web sites extends the community to include those fans who live beyond the reaches of certain sports broadcasts. Another example of a sports viewing opportunity that is unique to the age of the Internet is the real-time scoring feature found on sites like CBSsportsline.com (http://www.cbssportsline.com). This technology provides (depending on the speed of the Internet connection) instant updates of scores, individual and team statistics, and even in-game happenings such as injuries or weather delays for live sporting events. Thus, the audience without access to streaming audio and video can follow a sporting event as it happens. Due to the technological advances of the Internet, the community of sports viewers now has the ability to follow live sporting events without being restricted by program offerings of broadcast or cable networks.

Using the definition provided by Shoham and Kahle (1996), sports readers on the Internet could be recognized as the community of individuals who use the medium as a vehicle for seeking sports news and information (such as scores, schedules, or statistics). For example, a search performed on the Google search tool for the term *baseball statistics* returned more than 6 million Web documents. The depth of offerings allows fans of all interest levels to access a variety of information with ease. Additionally, media organizations—either sports-specific (e.g., ESPN and *Sports Illustrated*) or general news (e.g., CBS and *USAToday*)—sponsor Web sites containing information such as recent scores for the casual fan and pages upon pages of in-depth statistics for the more involved fan (and/or fantasy league enthusiasts). The proliferation of sources on the Web for sports information has infinitely increased the opportunities for sports readers over those available via traditional print or electronic media.

Given that Shoham and Kahle's (1996) analysis did not include the Internet, one could argue that the evolution of the sport–mass media relationship has given rise to a fourth communication community. Distinct from the sports readers or sports viewers who use the Internet in ways similar to traditional media (i.e., one-way communication), there exists a group of consumers who take advantage of the more interactive aspects of the new medium. These consumers are characterized by their use of two-way forms of communication found on the Web including both synchronous (e.g., chat rooms, online polls) and asynchronous (e.g., e-mail, message boards) technologies. Further, the advent of portable technology (i.e., wireless laptops, PDAs, and Web-enabled cell phones) permits these consumers to stay connected regardless of location, which affords them the same degree of portability as traditional print media, with the ability to access more current information. It is the above audience that highlights the breadth of sports offerings in cyberspace.

Sport Participants in Cyberspace

Sports spectators are not the only segment of the industry whose needs are met by the Internet. Sport participants, like their spectator counterparts, have sites with chat rooms, bulletin boards, and other IMCs in which to share their experiences and passion for a particular sport. A vast number of amateur sports clubs, groups, and organizations have Web sites that provide specific information to current and potential participants alike. A search performed using the Google search tool and entering the term *amateur sports* returned 3.8 million documents. Sites range from broad, such as the Amateur Athletic Union (AAU, http://www.aausports.org); to narrow, as in the National Fastpitch (softball) Coaches Association (http://nfca.org); to international, with the Japan Amateur Sports Association (http://www.japan-sports.or.jp). Participants are afforded seemingly unlimited opportunities to seek out others with similar sporting interests. Accordingly, new or obscure sports not afforded publicity and coverage via traditional media have the ability to reach a wide range of enthusiasts. Complementing this growth are Web sites of sport governing bodies on which sport-specific rules are made available. The National Collegiate Athletic Administration (NCAA), for example, provides the rule books for many of their sports in a format suitable for downloading. Other sites, such as Everyrule.com (http://www.everyrule.com/framesets/sportsframes.htm) and Rulescentral.com (http://www.rulescentral.com/sports/sports.html), serve as a catalog for accessing official rules of a multitude of sports from baseball to windsurfing. Photos, diagrams, and, in some cases, video clips are used to convey information formerly restricted to in-person coaching or instructional videotapes or DVDs. The Internet has also made registration for sports much easier for event organizers and participants. Signmeupsports.com is a portal to "help organizations automate registration, payment, communication and data management" (https://www.signmeupsports.com, para. 1) in outdoor competitive sports such as running, cycling, and triathlons, as well as a variety of other participant sports. This dynamic offers expanded reach for local or regional events and can minimize time- and labor-intensive registration methods like mail-in or race-day registration, while also making it easier for participants to find and register for such competitions.

While sports participation remains unchanged in the Internet age, technology has advanced the manner in which participants communicate. Using Shoham and Kahle's (1996) notion of consumption communities—that is, groups formed by consumers based on the type of sport activity—one can identify how the Web has benefited these groups. In particular, the limitless nature of cyberspace allows for a wealth of sites and pages dedicated to fans of a particular sport or participants in certain sports activities. Further, enthusiasts of a particular sport are brought closer together by the Internet, given the increased accessibility via e-mail, messages boards, and chat rooms. This increased connectivity has resulted in a shift in the dynamic of the communities formed by participants. Consumption communities that were once disjointed by the limits of time and space are now more unified by their Web presence.

SUMMARY AND CONCLUSION

The arrival of the Internet has had a profound effect on the production, distribution, and consumption of mediated sport content (McDaniel & Sullivan, 1998). Prior to the time the Web was commonly used, Wenner's (1989) mediated sports production complex—sports organizations, journalists, and media organizations—had control over the production and distribution of most sport media. Time and space constraints of traditional media technologies (e.g., television, radio, and print) led to content that was narrow in focus and included only established sport organizations that had far-reaching appeal (Whitson, 1998). Internet technology has granted sport organizations the ability to control how, where, and when content is distributed, thus bypassing many of the traditional gatekeeping functions of mass media. Traditional media organizations have responded by extending their brands into cyberspace and reasserting their existence as part of the mediated sports production complex. These traditional sport and media organizations have had to revolutionize their communication strategies in order to remain viable in the digital age.

A lack of limits and boundaries on the Web has resulted in an influx of new brands and players in the production and delivery of mediated sport. For example, athletes and coaches are now able to leverage their own brands through Web sites, thus increasing their celebrity status on the mediated sports landscape. Additionally, those sport organizations (e.g., grassroots initiatives) not allowed a voice as a result of the commercialized nature of the traditional mediated sports production complex now have the ability to be heard on a global scale. The result is a more significant role for these organizations in shaping sport media. Further, the birth of e-commerce technology has greatly enhanced the communication abilities of sports retailers and manufacturers. The Internet has given rise to new business models such as clicks-and-mortar, e-tailing, and online auctions that have allowed retailers and manufacturers to move beyond their traditional and limited role as media advertisers. Likewise, traditional sport media organizations have been transformed from conduits for sports content and advertising to the role of online merchants, selling products like licensed merchandise from the teams they cover.

As the mediated sports production complex has been forever altered by the new digital medium, so too has the role of the sports audience. Sports fans and participants alike are afforded the opportunity to produce their own sport content and distribute it in the form of pages and sites on the Web. The Web is populated with sports sites ranging from devotional to disparaging to instructional that provide fans and participants with an accessible and limitless communication vehicle through which many can promote their own personal brand of sport media. Thus, individuals now have a place next to traditional producers of sport content (i.e., sport and media organizations) on the digital sports landscape.

The Internet has altered the consumption patterns and abilities of the audience as well. Instant access to sports information, sports organizations, sports reporters, and other fans are benefits now realized by wired sports enthusiasts, none of which was typically possible with traditional media. Technology such as IMCs—that highlights the interactivity of this new medium—draws spectator sports fans closer together across the gap of time and space. Whereas sports fans were a largely disorganized populace in Wenner's (1989) model, Web technology has afforded them the ability to instantly communicate with each other and members of the mediated sports production complex regardless of where they are located.

Research suggests that the Internet has had considerable impact on the sport–mass media relationship (Boyle & Haynes, 2002). Ever-evolving Web technologies—including streaming audio and video, message boards, and broadband—cause difficulty in estimating the exact impact the Internet will have on this dyad. Cyberbranding (Bergstrom, 2000) is one strategy in which the Internet has been utilized by sport and media organizations as a means of creating and extending brands while transitioning into the digital age. It is quite plausible that some of the sport and media brands referenced herein will not be successful in their online endeavors and will be replaced by new brands or new business models as online technology and usage continues to evolve. Given the importance of sport to commercial media organizations and the diffusion of new technology, like the Internet, it will be important to follow the continuing developments in online sport media.

REFERENCES

Andrews, D. L. (2003). Sport and the transnationalizing media corporation. *Journal of Media Economics, 16,* 235–251.

Bellamy, R. V. (1998). The evolving television sports marketplace. In L. A. Wenner (Ed.), *MediaSport* (pp. 73–87). London: Routledge.

Bellini, C. G. P., & Vargas, L. M. (2003). Rationale for Internet-mediated communities. *CyberPsychology & Behavior, 6,* 3–14.

Bergstrom, A. (2000). Cyberbranding: Leveraging your brand on the Internet. *Strategy & Leadership, 28,* 10–26.

Boyle, R., & Haynes, R. (2002). New media sport. *Culture, Sport, Society, 5,* 95–114.

Brown, M. T. (2003). An analysis of online marketing in the sport industry: User activity, communication objectives, and perceived benefits. *Sport Marketing Quarterly, 12,* 48–55.

Burton, R. (2004). Teams as brands: A review of the sports licensing concept. In L. Kahle & C. Riley (Eds.), *Sports marketing and the psychology of marketing communication* (pp. 259–269). Mahwah, NJ: Lawrence Erlbaum Associates.

Cassidy, H. (2005, January). Sending fans a clear signal. *Brandweek, 46,* 20–24.

Chan-Olmstead, S. M., & Ha, L. (2003). Internet business models for broadcasters: How television stations perceive and integrate the Internet. *Journal of Broadcasting and Electronic Media, 47,* 597–617.

Creedon, P. J. (1998). Women, sport, and media institutions: Issues in sports journalism and marketing. In L. A. Wenner (Ed.), *MediaSport* (pp. 88–99). London: Routledge.

Dimmick, J., Chen, Y., & Li, Z. (2004). Competition between the Internet and traditional news media: The gratification-opportunities niche dimension. *Journal of Media Economics, 17,* 19–33.

Donohew, L., Helm, D., & Haas, J. (1989). Drugs and (len) bias on the sports page. In L. A. Wenner (Ed.), *Media, Sports, & Society* (pp. 225–240). Newbury Park, CA: Sage.

Elliot, N. (2003). Fantasy sports online. Jupiter Research [On-line]. Retrieved April 26, 2005, from http://www.jup.com

Fantasy sports participation on the rise, association says. (2003, August 14). [Electronic version]. *St. Louis Business Journal.* Retrieved April 26, 2005, from http://stlouis.bizjournals.com/stlouis/stories/2003/08/11/daily62.html

Gardyn, R. (2001). A league of their own. *American Demographics, 23,* 12–13.

Ha, L., & Chan-Olmstead, S. M. (2004). Cross-media use in electronic media: The role of cable television Web sites in cable television network branding and viewership. *Journal of Broadcasting and Electronic Media, 48,* 620–645.

Jhally, S. (1989). Cultural studies and the sports/media complex. In L. A. Wenner (Ed.), *Media, Sports, & Society* (pp. 70–96). Newbury Park, CA: Sage.

Jones, S., Bee, C., Burton, R., & Kahle, L. (2004). Marketing through sports entertainment: A functional approach. In L. J. Shrum (Ed.), *Blurring the lines between entertainment and persuasion: The psychology of entertainment media* (pp. 309–322). Mahwah, NJ: Lawrence Erlbaum Associates.

Kahle, L., & Meeske, C. (1999). Sports marketing and the Internet: It's a whole new ball game. *Sport Marketing Quarterly, 8,* 9–12.

Kennedy, K., & Deitsch, R. (2002, November). On-line coach bashing. *Sports Illustrated, 97,* 19.

Kerschbaumer, K. (2005). Battle for college sports fans. *Broadcasting & Cable, 135,* 23.

Krauss, M. (2003). EBay 'bids' on small-biz firms to sustain growth. *Marketing News, 37,* 6.

Lai, H. (2004, October 8). NFL hits web for China loyalty bid. *Media,* p. 17.

MacNeill, M. (1998). Sports journalism, ethics, and Olympic athletes' rights. In L. A. Wenner (Ed.), *MediaSport* (pp. 100–118). London: Routledge.

McBride, S. (2004, December 13). Technology (A special report); Where the listeners are: What's the biggest competitor to regular radio? No, guess again. *Wall Street Journal,* p. R4.

McChesney, R. W. (1989). Media made sport: A history of sports coverage in the United States. In L. A. Wenner (Ed.), *Media, Sports, & Society* (pp. 49–69). Newbury Park, CA: Sage.

McClellan, S. (2003). NBC's Olympics Web site will integrate network and affiliate sites. *Broadcasting & Cable, 133,* 38.

McDaniel, S. R. (2004). Sensation seeking and the consumption of televised sports. In L. J. Shrum (Ed.), *Blurring the lines between entertainment and persuasion: The psychology of entertainment media* (pp. 323–335). Mahwah, NJ: Lawrence Erlbaum Associates.

McDaniel, S. R., & Sullivan, C. B. (1998). Extending the sports experience: Mediations in cyberspace. In L. A. Wenner (Ed.), *MediaSport* (pp. 266–281). London: Routledge.

McDowell, W., & Sutherland, J. (2000). Choice versus chance: Using brand equity theory to explore TV audience lead-in effects, a case study. *Journal of Media Economics, 13,* 233–247.

McKee, S. (2004, August 13). Summer Olympics—television: It'll be deja view on NBC. *Wall Street Journal,* p. A10.

Reason, T. (2002, April 1). Diamonds in the rough. *CFO, 18,* 54–58.

Rowley, J. (2004). Online branding. *Online information review, 28,* 131–138.

Shoham, A., & Kahle, L. (1996). Spectators, viewers, readers: Communication and consumption communities in sport marketing. *Sport Marketing Quarterly, 5,* 11–19.

Shrum, L. J. (2004). What's so special about entertainment media and why do we need a psychology for it?: An introduction to the psychology of entertainment media. In L. J. Shrum (Ed.), *Blurring the lines between entertainment and persuasion: The psychology of entertainment media* (pp. 1–9). Mahwah, NJ: Lawrence Erlbaum Associates.

Singer, J. B. (2001). The metro wide Web: Changes in newspapers' gatekeeping role online. *Journalism and Mass Communication Quarterly, 78,* 65–80.

Turner, P. (1999). Television and Internet convergence: Implications for sport broadcasting. *Sport Marketing Quarterly, 8,* 43–49.

Umstead, R. T. (1999). Fantasy sports are said to be one of the fastest-growing segments of the Internet and provide sports-oriented Web sites a tool for generating revenue and increasing brand awareness. RDS [On-line]. Retrieved April 26, 2005, from http://rdsweb2.rdsinc.com/texis/rds/suite/+IomMnewxwwwwwFqz6XX6Xxv68xFqm1M.html

Vizcaino, S. A., Mason, D. S., & McDaniel, S. R. (2005). Online auctions of sports trading cards: How do card characteristics and seller reputations affect final bid prices? *International Journal of Sport Managment, 6,* 99–121.

Weiser, E. B. (2001). The functions of Internet use and their social and psychological consequences. *CyberPsychology & Behavior, 4,* 723–743.

Wenner, L. A. (1989). Media, sports, and society: The research agenda. In L. A. Wenner (Ed.), *Media, Sports, & Society* (pp. 13–48). Newbury Park, CA: Sage.

Whitson, D. (1998). Circuits of promotion: Media, marketing, and the globalization of sport. In L. A. Wenner (Ed.), *MediaSport* (pp. 57–72). London: Routledge.

CRITICAL PERSPECTIVES ON SPORTS MEDIA: CASES AND ISSUES

Sport and Globalization: Key Issues, Phases, and Trends

Joseph Maguire

Loughborough University

Over the course of three centuries, achievement sport diffused out of its Anglo-European birthplace to all parts of the globe. This long-term development was, and continues to be, bound up in globalization processes. These processes have had a significant impact on people's lives, cultures, and environments. Questions emerge as to the causes and consequences, costs and benefits, and winners and losers involved in globalization in general, and global achievement sport in particular. It is in this context that questions concerning homogeneity or heterogeneity and sustainability arise. What can be concluded about the current global state of play? Judging by the evidence to hand, it can be argued that achievement sport is the dominant ludic body culture; that folk game traditions survive, albeit in residual forms; and that new body cultures continue to emerge, challenging the hegemonic position of achievement sport. There is, then, evidence for both homogeneity and heterogeneity. To put this another way, as I have argued elsewhere, ludic body cultures are marked by *both* diminishing contrasts and increasing varieties (Maguire, 1999). Such observations raise several questions. What are the main dynamics and key power struggles involved? What are the major implications flowing from these processes?

In order to address these questions, it is necessary to tackle the analysis in several steps. First, consideration is given to some key issues regarding general processes of globalization. Second, the main features of a figurational perspective on both globalization *and* sport are outlined. Third, several key structured processes that have permeated global sport over the past three centuries are highlighted. On this basis it is possible to address not only why ludic diversity is being threatened, and why such alternative body cultures need to be maintained, but also why it is necessary that sustainable body (sport) cultures be developed. These questions are, or should be, of major significance to physical educators and social scientists as we grapple with the problems of living in this so-called postmodern age.

GLOBALIZATION: KEY ISSUES AND DEBATES

The concept of globalization is subject to intense political, ideological, and social scientific debate. Surveying these debates, it can be concluded that globalization refers to the growing network of interdependencies—political, economic, cultural, and social—that bind human beings together, for better and for worse. Globalization processes are not of recent origin. Nor have they occurred evenly across all areas of the globe. They involve an increasing intensification of global interconnectedness and are very long-term in nature. Nevertheless, the more recent history of globalization would suggest that the rate of change is gathering momentum. Despite the unevenness of these processes, it is becoming increasingly difficult to understand local or national experiences without reference to these global flows. The flow of leisure styles, customs, and practices from one part of the world to another, such as the Olympic games, is an example of globalization at work.

People's living conditions, beliefs, knowledge, and actions are intertwined with globalization. The emergence of a global economy, a transnational cosmopolitan culture and a range of international social movements, a multitude of transnational or global economic and technological exchanges, communication networks, and migratory patterns characterize these interconnected world processes. As a result people are experiencing spatial and temporal dimensions differently. There has been both a speeding up of time and a shrinking of space. Modern technologies enable people, images, ideas, and money to crisscross the globe with great rapidity. This leads not only to a greater degree of interdependence, but also to an increased awareness of the notion of *one world*. People become more attuned to the notion that their lives and place of living are part of a single social space—the globe. As I note in discussing issues of diversity and sustainability in ludic cultures, this awareness has implications for issues of environmentalism.

Globalization, then, can be seen to involve a flexible network of multidirectional movements of people, practices, customs, and ideas. This network forms an interdependent figurational field of established and outsider positions, which are shaped and contoured by time–space geometry, traditions, and power struggles. This interdependent network has seemingly paradoxical dimensions. One side of the coin highlights elements that are planned, are predictable, follow specific paths, and form clear trajectories. Inspection of the other side of the coin reveals nonisomorphic patterns: a blind, unplanned dimension. The network has a relative autonomy from the intentions of specific groups and is bound up in multiple disjunctures. Thus, a more adequate analysis has to probe both dimensions—and do so using varying measures of time and space.

The sport and leisure-wear industry can be used to highlight how consumption of cultural goods is bound up with globalization. As a fashion item, the wearing of sports footwear has become an integral feature of consumer culture. One premier brand is Nike. The purchase and display of this footwear are but the final stages in a dynamic network involving designers, producers, suppliers, distributors, and the parent or broker company, in this case, Nike. Though its headquarters are located in Oregon, the range of subcontractors involved straddles the globe. Its suppliers and production companies are located in different Southeast Asian countries: Thailand, Singapore, Korea, and China. Its designers attempt to provide shoes with a worldwide demand that will also appeal to local tastes. Local franchise operations ensure appropriate distribution backed by global marketing strategies. Here again, Nike uses the media–sport production complex by endorsing sports stars and sports events. In addition, Nike advertises within the television schedules that carry these sports and other appropriate programs. This much is clear: Cultures communicate, compete, contrast, and conflict with each other in a more interdependent manner than was previously the case. This intermingling of, and status competition between, cultures occurs on a global scale and is patterned along a series of global flows that are marked by power balances, disjunctures, and civilizational struggles.

Five global flows bear highlighting. The international movement of people such as tourists, migrants, exiles, and guest workers constitutes the flow of *people*. The *technology* flow is reflected in the transfer between countries of the machinery and equipment produced by transnational (TNCs) corporations and government agencies. The *economic* flow centers on the rapid exchange of money and its equivalents around the world. The *media* flow entails the movement of images and information between countries, produced and distributed by newspapers, magazines, radio, film, television, and video. Finally, the *ideological* flow is linked to the transmission of ideas centrally associated with state or counterstate ideologies and movements. All five flows can be detected in early twenty-first century leisure and sports development. Thus, the global migration of professional sports personnel and artistic performers has been a pronounced feature of recent decades. This appears likely to continue in the future. The flow across the globe of goods, equipment, and landscapes such sports complexes and golf courses has grown to the state of a multibillion-dollar business in recent years. As such, it represents a transnational technological development in the sports sphere. Regarding economic issues, clearly the flow of finance in the global sports arena has come to center not only on the international trade in personnel, prize money, and endorsements, but on the marketing of sport as well. For example, the transformation of American and North American sports—such as basketball, baseball, ice hockey, and American football—into global sports is part of this development.

Closely connected to these flows has been a development at the level of the media. The media–sport complex projects images of individual sports labor migrants, leisure forms, and specific cultural messages to global audiences. The marketing of the American basketball player Michael Jordan or the Russian tennis player Anna Kournikova are examples of these processes at work. The pervasiveness of the media–sport nexus has forced a range of leisure practices, in local places, to align with this global model. Failure to do so would place in question their ability to survive in the global media marketplace. At the level of ideas, global sports festivals such as the Olympics have come to serve as vehicles for the expression of ideologies that are transnational in character and, at times, lie outside the scope of the state. Yet, the state continues to play a powerful role in the governance of global sport. A complex and shifting balance of power exists between several groups—the representatives of the state, transnational formations such as the European Union (EU), nongovernmental organizations, sport associations, and multinational corporations. Tracing these global sport flows is one task; another is to explain the patterns they form.

GLOBALIZATION AND SPORTIZATION:
A FIGURATIONAL PERSPECTIVE

From a figurational perspective it is evident that over time, in global terms, *Western* societies have become the equivalent of the established groups within particular European nations (Elias, 1939/1982). The spread of civilized (i.e., Western) patterns of conduct occurred through the settlement of occidentals or through their assimilation by the upper strata of other nations. Crucially, the same double-bind tendencies that marked the upper classes' colonization of outsiders within the West were and remain evident in the West's dealings with outsider (non-Western) nations and peoples. With this spread came the dominant, if contested, view of civilization and of humanity as a whole. The members of Western societies were acting as an established group on a global level (Elias, 1939/1982). Their tastes and conduct, including their sports, had similar effects as those of elite cultural activities within Western societies themselves, acting as signs of distinction, prestige, and power. Yet, just as the established groups within Western societies found that their distinguishing conduct flowed, intentionally or unintentionally, across social strata, so the occidentals of the colonies also discovered that a similar process occurred in their dealings with their colonial social inferiors. Indeed, in the context of this cultural interchange, non-Western codes and customs began to permeate into Western societies.

It is important to note, however, that the rise of the West was contested and its triumph was not inevitable. Furthermore, Western culture had long been permeated by non-Western cultural forms, people, technologies, and knowledge. Put succinctly, these cultural interchanges stretch back to long before the West became more dominant in cultural interchange. In addition, Western culture was not exactly homogeneous. Considerable variations existed within it. These cross-cultural processes were characterized by a combination of intentional and unintentional features. The manner and form of commingling were dependent on several factors, including the form of colonization; the position of the area in the network of political, economic, and military interdependencies; and the particular region's history and structure. Processes of commingling were, and are, characterized by unequal power relations. One means by which the established Western elites maintained their status and distinction was through the exercise of specific forms of conduct such as their status-enhancing sporting practices, which reinforced their culture, habitus, and identity.

Determining the course of these civilizing offensives is an empirical question. The precise patterns experienced in specific countries or regions, and indeed in globalization, depend on the balance of diminishing contrasts and increasing varieties, that is, of homogenizing and differentiating tendencies. At different stages the relative balance may incline in favor of one end of the continuum or another. In a specific phase, in a particular region, the dominant feature may favor a decrease in contrasts. This may be particularly the case where a form of colonization is taking place. Clearly the dynamics of these processes are closely connected to the prevailing balance of power between established and outsider groups.

Tracing this development over the long term, it is clear that the social barriers built between established Westerners and the native outsiders have proved semipermeable. The contrast between Western and non-Western societies has indeed begun to diminish, and we may already be living in a period that could be characterized as the waning of the West. However, the extent to which Western values have spread through specific regions reflects the history and structure of the areas in question. This also applies in the diffusion of non-Western conduct back to specific Western nations. Established and outsider groups were and are active in the interpretation of Western and non-western forms of conduct and culture. This recognition points to the possibility that existing varieties of civilized conduct could survive and new ones emerge.

The figurational approach rejects the idea that the spread or diffusion of styles of behavior depended solely on the activities of established groups. Established groups deploy semipermeable barriers to maintain their distinctiveness, power, and prestige. However, a two-way process of cultural interaction characterizes these semipermeable boundaries. The more they become interconnected with outsider groups, the more they depend on them for social tasks. In so doing, the contrasts between the established culture and outsiders diminish. The power ratio between these groups moves in an equalizing direction. Concomitantly, new styles of conduct emerge (Elias, 1939/1982). As civilized forms of conduct spread across both the rising lower classes of Western society and the different classes of the colonies, an amalgamation of the western and the indigenous patterns occurs. Over time there is an interpenetration of conduct—of the upper class and of the rising groups. People placed within this situation attempt to reconcile and fuse the pattern of "occidentally civilized societies with the habits and traditions of their own society," and in this they achieve "higher or lesser degree(s) of success" (Elias, 1939/1982, pp. 309–310). Concepts such as diminishing contrasts, increasing varieties, established culture and outsiders, I/we and they/them balances, and interdependent commingling can assist in this task of making sense of a global world.

What implications are there for the sociological study of global sport? Elias and Dunning did not use all of these concepts to assist their analyses of sport. Nevertheless, they were aware of the global reach of sports. Examining the growing seriousness of sport, Dunning (1986) concluded:

> It remains necessary to spell out precisely what the connections were between, on the one hand, the growing seriousness of sports participation and, on the other, state-formation, functional democratization and the civilizing process. It also remains to show how this trend was connected with the international spread of sport. (p. 214)

Commenting on the diffusion of English pastimes to continental Europe and beyond, Elias addressed the connection between sportization and civilizing processes. Noting the reigning in of violence, the development of tighter standardizing sets of rules, the development of governing bodies, and the shift in body habitus, Elias (1986) observed that "the sportization of pastimes, if I may use this expression as shorthand for their transformation in English society into sports and the export of some of them on an almost global scale, is another example of a civilizing spurt" (pp. 21–22).

Sportization did not merely involve the multilayered flow of sports, personnel, technologies, and landscapes—important though it is to explore the interconnected patterns these flows form (Maguire, 1999). Studies of sportization can also be understood "as contributions to knowledge of changes in the social habitus of people and of the societies they form with each other" (Elias, 1986, p. 23). More important than simply the global movement of cultural wares, this shift towards the competitive, regularized, rationalized, and gendered bodily exertions of achievement sport involves changes at the level of personality, body deportment, and social interaction. This rationalized male body habitus has come to affect people and groups in different societies across the globe in fairly fundamental ways.

Though Elias did not fully develop his analysis of the export of the sportization of pastimes, he did point to the significance of the relative autonomy of these sport forms for their adoption outside of England. Questions of this type lie at the core of an analysis of the links between sportization and globalization. Note that it is male achievement sport, emerging out of England, that is the dominant mode. Though European rivals existed, in the form of German and Swedish gymnastics and the Czech Sokol movement in particular, and although some older folk pastimes also survived, it was male achievement sport that was to affect people's body habitus on a global scale. That is not to suggest that there occurred no resistance to, reinterpretation of—indeed recycling of—this body culture. Here, too, evidence of the interweaving of the local and the global is evident.

The spread of high status English sport forms to continental Europe during the nineteenth century prompted various reactions. In Nordic countries, English sport appears to have been readily embraced, and also restyled, in the light of local body culture and tradition. In Germany, sections of society resisted this diffusion. English sport forms were regarded as threats to German national culture and identity. Viewing the body culture of the Turner gymnastics movement as superior, nationalists viewed English sport forms as socially inferior. The Germans were not alone. Great Britain's other main European rival, France, also had citizens who advocated resistance. For example, Pascal Grousset, who founded the Ligue Nationale de l'Education Physique in the late 1880s, condemned the importation of English games and values and argued that the French people would do better to seek their models in antiquity rather than from across *la manche*. Ancient games of football were promoted and medieval competitive pageants revived, but to no avail. Those, like Baron de Coubertin, who were advocates of English games and public school values but also of Greek antiquity won the day. By 1892, de Coubertin felt able to declare, "Let us export our oarsmen, our fencers, our runners into other lands. That is the true free trade of the future; and the day it is introduced into Europe the cause of Peace will have received a new and strong ally" (Maguire, 1999, p. 11).

Closely connected to the late-nineteenth century reinvention of tradition and the intensification of interstate tensions, achievement sports came "to serve as symbolic representations of competition between states" and "as a status symbol of nations" (Elias, 1986, p. 23). Considering achievement sport development during the twentieth century, Elias (1986) went on to argue that

> The achievement sport culminating today in the Olympic Games provides telling examples. There the struggle for world records has given the development of sport a different direction. In the form of achievement sport the playful mimetic tensions of leisure sport become dominated and patterned by global tensions and rivalries between different states. (pp. 43–44)

What Elias did not fully appreciate and acknowledge, however, is that while male achievement sport culture developed in and diffused out of an English context, aspects of it were more fully developed in a later phase of sportization in the context of North America and, in particular, the United States. In England, achievement sport was shackled to an amateur ethos that emphasized fair play and downplayed seriousness. Yet, during the third sportization phase (1870–1920), along with the achievement sport body cultures, the notion of fair play did diffuse to continental Europe and to both the formal and informal British Empire. While such a notion might have been viewed as a sign of distinction and a cultural marker of English gentlemen, sport advocates in other societies chose to practice their sports differently and more seriously. By the fourth sportization phase (1920s to mid-1960s), it was an American version of the achievement sport ethos that had gained relative ascendancy.

The third sportization phase then entailed the differential diffusion of English sport forms. The remarks made by one historian, Ensor, highlight the British perception of this diffusion. In commenting on "the development of organized games," Ensor (1936) observed that this "may rank among England's leading contributions to world culture" (p. 164). Whatever the merits of this evaluation, this diffusion was closely connected to two interrelated processes: the emergence of intense forms of nationalism and an intensification in globalization. During this period we see the intensification of national sentiment, the emergence of ethnic nation-states, and the invention of traditions. This was to be the seedbed of what Elias noted as a feature of twentieth-century sport, namely, the "self-escalating pressure of interstate competition in sport and its role as a status symbol of nations" (Elias, 1986, p. 23).

In seeking to understand global sport, it is necessary then to grasp how sportization is bound up in intercivilizational exchanges. It is possible to conclude that those sports which initially appeared in the West do appear to have some universal significance and value, whatever that might be, but it is also clear that these sports have indigenized, acquiring local and particular meanings. In stressing the connection with intercivilizational exchanges, a related point needs to be made. A very long-term perspective in exploring globalization is required. Although some sociologists may mistakenly retreat to the present in exploring global processes, in examining the making of modern sports a long-term intercivilizational analysis is much more fruitful. Here questions concerning what constitutes modern sport need to be addressed.

In examining the initial sportization phase, it is important to stress that the longer-term links of both mainland European and non-Occidental ancient civilizations with the making of modern sport should not be overlooked. Though England was the cradle of modern sport, other European societies, Germany included, played a part in its formation, and indeed, in sportization more generally. Fellow Europeans were also at play before the emergence of modern sport! Acknowledgment of this issue needs to be developed to refer to an assessment of how, if at all, Islam and the Orient influenced European folk games and royal pastimes.

This observation applies both to an understanding of the early phase of sportization and to more recent developments. The interdependency chains that tie more recent developments within the West to non-Occidental cultures require consideration. In emphasizing these points, my analysis seeks to steer clear of an overly Western interpretation of global sport processes. Yet, this is not to overlook that representatives of some cultural traditions have proved more powerful in the development of global sport. Issues of power—economic, political, and cultural—have to be central to the analysis. While the development of modern sport can be clearly associated with the West, it is important to both probe the interconnections with preexisting non-Occidental body cultures and assess the degree to which contemporary sport has been permeated by Asian forms and values. At this stage of our knowledge development, it is only possible to point to the direction which the analysis must take. Issues of this kind lie at the heart of the debate concerning globalization, intercivilizational analysis, and the role and meaning sport plays within global processes.

It is also necessary to grasp that local cultures are never hermetically sealed off from other cultures. There is no past folk game or sporting *Gemeinschaft*, English or mainland European, waiting to be discovered. The local was always semipermeable. What is needed is an understanding of the competing centrifugal and centripetal forces that characterize geographical arenas—old and new. A further observation that guides this figurational account of sport and globalization needs to be stressed. The balance of forces at work in intercultural exchanges is marked by a series of power networks; elimination struggles; and a mutual contest of cultural sameness, difference, and commingling between competing groups (Elias, 1939/1982). In this regard, the stratified nature of these processes, which include but are not exhausted by gender, ethnicity, class, and age-based divisions, requires careful unraveling. Intercivilizational analyses provide some important guidelines by which to conduct this task.

While allowing for non-Occidental linkages, resistance, and indigenization, an account has also to be given of the rise and relative dominance of the West. To argue this does not mean slipping into a Western-centric view of global development. Such an intercivilizational analysis must avoid the pursuit of monocausal explanations, the use of dichotomous thinking, and the tendency to view global processes as governed by either the intended or the unintended actions of established or outsider groups of people. Analyses that emphasize the multifaceted, multidirectional, and complex sets of power balances are better placed to probe and trace the dynamics of global sport. Yet, as noted, the stratified nature of these processes needs careful exploration. We need to view these divisions as interdependent features of individual identities, identity politics, and the structured processes that characterize human relations.

TOWARDS A MODEL OF GLOBAL SPORT: KEY STRUCTURED PROCESSES

There are a number of competing explanations for the making of modern sport (Elias & Dunning, 1986; Gruneau, 1988). Guttmann (1978) provided a coherent account based on a Weberian analysis. Guttmann insightfully identified seven characteristics of the shift from "ritual to record." These characteristics were secularism, equality of opportunity, specialization, rationalization, bureaucratic organization, quantification, and a quest for records. His more recent work (Guttmann, 1994), drawing on a more cultural hegemonic approach, but also a figurational analysis drawn from Maguire, dealt with the diffusion of modern sporting forms. Van Bottenburg's work (2001), while largely descriptive and removed from globalization and sport research, does tend to reinforce the figurational approach. Rojek's early work (1985) also drew on this approach, and he identified four main characteristics of modern sporting practice: privatization, individuation, commercialization, and pacification. Again, there is much of value in these analyses. Here, I want to build on the type of thinking provided by Guttmann and Rojek and thus identify a series of features that have permeated the emergence, diffusion, and current practice of global sport. This requires some elaboration.

Based on a developmental account of the making of modern sport, it is clear that, over the course of three centuries, a series of structured processes that characterize global achievement sport have emerged and grown in intensity (Maguire, 1999; see also Roudometof & Robertson, 1995; Therborn, 2000, for a discussion of globalization in general). They permeate the sportization phases that have framed the development of global sport and flow from a complex blend of intended and unintended social actions. It is also important to add that while the reach and spread of each of these structured processes has varied over time and across space, they now form an interlocking fabric—that of modern achievement sport—that provides the context within which people experience global sport. Furthermore, its pattern and development also reflects and reinforces the prevailing established culture-outsider relations and power geometry within specific societies. Let me briefly highlight the central elements involved:

1. The emergence and diffusion of achievement sport has witnessed the decline of both Western and non-Occidental folk body cultures. Irrespective of time period or society, the impact of modern achievement sport has been to marginalize indigenous games. While such practices have not disappeared and may, in some societies, be undergoing some revival, the overall trend is for folk games to become residual features of body cultures (Renson, 1997).

2. Given that modern sport was devised by and for men, we should not be surprised that global sport reflects, through to the present day, a gendered ideology and content. In addition to this, the corridors of power—at FIFA and at the IOC—remain the preserve of men. Global sport then is a "male preserve" whose levers of power are still handled by men (Hargreaves, 1994).

3. Concomitant with the globalization of modern achievement sport, we have seen the development of a set of body practices that involve schooling the body. Here it is possible to trace the shifts from nineteenth and twentieth century forms of drill, European forms of gymnastics and dance, physical training, and physical education through to late twentieth century changes such as human movement studies, sport science, and kinesiological studies (Kirk, 1998). The state, through its compulsory schooling policies, has thus played an active role in the reinforcement of global sport.

4. From its inception through to its high-tech manifestations of the present day, modern achievement sport has reflected and reinforced the medicalization, scientization, and rationalization of human expressiveness. The athlete has increasingly been seen as an enhanced, efficient machine, adhering to a sport ethic associated with the ultimate performance. The logic at work may well be leading the athlete towards genetic modification and a cyborg coexistence (Berryman & Park, 1992; Hoberman, 1992).

5. The impact of global sport has been not only on the habitus of people of different societies, but also on the habitats in which they live. Over the long term, as sport practices moved from small to large scale, from low intensity to high intensity forms, and from natural materials to synthetics, the athlete, spectator, viewer, and employers became consumers of scarce resources and threats to the environment. The need to proclaim the Sydney Olympic Games as a *green games* highlights the very issues that confront us now and—if the present trends are maintained—will continue to plague us in the future (Maguire, Jarvie, Mansfield, & Bradley, 2002).

6.   Not only does the global diffusion of sport reflect the ongoing balance of power within and between nations, but also, by the present day, the sport power elite have both maintained their grip on power and have been joined by a range of representatives from big business. These include media moguls, marketing personnel, and the representatives of TNCs (Miller, Lawrence, McKay, & Rowe, 2001). Demands for democratic control, transparency, and accountability in decision making remain unfulfilled, while academic stakeholders are frozen out of the sport policy process.

7.   In both the making and ongoing formation of global sport, we have witnessed the reinforcement and enhancement of global inequalities within the West and between the West and non-Occidental societies. Here, questions of cultural power and civilizational struggles are at the fore (Maguire, 1999).

These, then, are some of the structured processes through which people experience global sport. They also provide the seedbed on which future global sport processes will unfold. As has been noted, all are characterized by issues of power, culture, and control; they remain contested terrain.

CONCLUSION

What is the global state of play? what chance is there to maintain and cherish a diverse range of body cultures and develop some notion of sustainable sport? With the seven structured processes that have permeated the sportization phases highlighted here as benchmarks, there does not seem that much room for optimism. In making this assessment let me try to connect the broader global condition with the position within the world of sport. In environmental terms the planet faces the loss or diminution of habitat diversity. Species face extinction—due either to environmental degradation, climate change, or the introduction of new species. What was once dominant becomes residual. In order to combat these trends the Green movement has highlighted the need for new ethics—for the celebration of diversity, sustainability, and a challenge to the activities of TNCs.

In similar fashion TNCs are linked to a sporting goods industry nexus and media–sport complex that pollute the environment, exploit indigenous workers, and market homogeneity. Across the planet ways of life, folk cultures, and body movement traditions are threatened with degradation, depletion, and extinction. The tentacles of modern achievement sport, either through the Olympic movement or school based physical education programs, ensure that it is elite sport that counts. And yet, as with the environment, what is desperately needed is the preservation and promotion of a diverse range of body habitus and the development of a sustainable sport process. Notions of *green* sport, though still in their infancy, need to be based on three key tenets.

First, there is a need to respect the diversity and richness of local cultures. Second, it must be recognized how different body (sport) traditions have potential meaning and significance not just to the local, but to humankind as a whole. Third, there must emerge an acceptance that the practice of sport be based on principles of environmental sustainability. Here, then, questions of habitat and habitus, diversity and sustainability, interweave. A green sport ethics is needed so that we may confront the version of global sport provided by the media, sport, and sporting goods nexus. In this regard we must develop both a sense of stewardship of the planet (and thus the sporting environment) and an awareness of the rich cultural heritage that still exists in the habitus traditions of different civilizations.

The most recent phase of sport globalization (mid-1960s to the present day) contains, as noted, elements that reinforce both diminishing contrasts between, and increasing varieties of, body cultures. A set of twin processes are at work: There is both the consolidation of global, mediated, commodified sport and challenges to modern achievement sport. Commodified sport products are embedded in a complex political economy that reflects the interests of the West in general and TNCs in particular. The fan is a consumer, the athlete a worker, the club a brand, and the sport a commodity. Yet, this remains contested terrain. This is evident in several ways. The West is being challenged on and off the field of play. TNCs are increasingly subject to the glare and boycott of activists and environmental groups. New varieties of body cultures have and continue to emerge as counterhegemonic practices—here we witness resistance, reinvention, adaptation, and indigenization. In addition, folk traditions have, like endangered species, an ability to adapt, survive, be recycled, and be rer.ewed.

Those involved in physical education programs must decide whose body (sport) culture counts. Modern achievement sport can continue to be promoted in our universities and schools as the dominant, exclusive form of body culture. Sport education replaces physical education, coaches replace teachers, and talent identification schemes channel young people's early experiences of movement along narrow, prescribed lines. Alternatively, degree programs could be informed by a model of human development rather than human performance (Maguire, 1991). In addition, a *desportization* of the curriculum can be promoted. Diversity can be promoted and the richness of different habitus or body cultures recognized. Through the development of sustainable sport and the teaching of environmental ethics, a sense of stewardship of both habitat and habitus would be encouraged. These changes would be one part of the attempt to move global sport in the direction of being more democratic, with its decision making more transparent and its decision makers more accountable.

REFERENCES

Berryman, J. W., & Park J. (Eds.). (1992). *Sport and exercise science: Essays in the history of sport medicine.* Urbana, IL: University of Illinois Press.

Dunning, E. (1986). The dynamics of modern sport: Notes on achievement — Striving and the social significance of sport. In N. Elias & E. Dunning (Eds.), *Quest for excitement: Sport and leisure in the civilizing process* (pp. 205–223). Oxford: Blackwell.

Elias, N. (1982). *The civilizing process: State formation and civilization.* Oxford: Blackwell. (Original work published 1939).

Elias, N. (1986). Introduction. In N. Elias & E. Dunning (Eds.), *Quest for excitement: Sport and leisure in the civilizing process* (pp. 19–62). Oxford: Blackwell.

Elias, N., & Dunning, E. (1986). *Quest for excitement: Sport and leisure in the civilizing process.* Oxford: Blackwell.

Ensor, R. C. K. (1936). *England 1870–1914. The Oxford history of England.* Oxford: Oxford University Press.

Gruneau, R. (1988). Modernization or hegemony: Two views on sport and social development. In J. Harvey & H. Cantelon (Eds.), *Not just a game. Essays in Canadian sport sociology* (pp. 9–32). Ottawa: University of Ottawa Press.

Guttmann, A. (1978). *From ritual to record. The nature of modern sports.* New York: Columbia University Press.

Guttmann, A. (1994). *Games and empires: Modern sports and cultural imperialism.* New York: Columbia University Press.

Hargreaves, J. (1994). *Sporting females: Critical issues in the history and sociology of women's sports.* London: Routledge.

Hoberman, J. (1992). *Mortal engines. The science of performance and the dehumanization of sport.* New York: Free Press.

Kirk, D. (1998). *Schooling bodies: School practice and public discourse 1880–1950.* London: Leicester University Press.

Maguire, J. (1991). Human sciences, sports sciences and the need to study people 'in the round'. *Quest, 2*, 190–206.

Maguire, J. (1999). *Global sport: Identities, societies, civilizations.* Cambridge: Polity Press.

Maguire, J., Jarvie, G., Mansfield, L., & Bradley, J. (2002). *Sport worlds: A sociological perspective.* Champaign: Human Kinetics.

Miller, T., Lawrence, G., McKay, J., & Rowe, D. (2001). *Globalisation and sport.* London: Sage.

Renson, R. (1997). The reinvention of tradition in sport and games. In G. Doll-Tepper & D. Scoretz (Eds.), *Ancient traditions and current trends in physical activity and sport* (pp. 8–13). Berlin: ICSSPE.

Rojek, C. (1985). *Capitalism and leisure theory.* London: Tavistock.

Roudometof, V., & Robertson, R. (1995). Globalization, world-system theory, and the comparative study of civilizations: Issues of theoretical logic in world-historical sociology. In S. K. Sanderson (Ed.), *Civilization and world systems: Studying world-historical change* (pp. 273–300). London: AltaMira.

Therborn, G. (2000). Globalisations: Dimensions, historical waves, regional effects, normative governance. *International Sociology, 15*, 151–170.

Van Bottenburg, M. (2001). Global games. Chicago: University of Chicago Press.

27

Sport, the Media, and the Construction of Race

Andrew Grainger
Joshua I. Newman
David L. Andrews
University of Maryland

Race has been one of the most productive, and indeed important, areas of inquiry for those interested in the critical analyses of the relationship between sport and the mass media (Birrell & McDonald, 2000; Bruce, 2004; Davis & Harris, 1998; McDonald & Birrell, 1999). Given that, as a major public arena, sport, and *mediasport* (Wenner, 1998) in particular, is a key site of contemporary corporeal display and consequently racial signification, this is perhaps hardly surprising. Indeed, Denzin (1996) argued that mediated sport is perhaps "the most significant feature" (p. 319) of a contemporary racial order in which race is increasingly understood through media representation. Its cultural import therefore means that the politics of racial presence and absence, as played out in the realm of the sport media, have wider implications for the reproduction and reinforcement of racial hierarchies and the patterns of identification this may generate. That is, mass-mediated sport is a site where ideologies of race (and racism) are both constructed and negotiated and thus acts as an important "signifier for wider questions about identity within racially demarcated societies" (Carrington, 2001/2002, p. 94). Further, the central role of mediated sports within the mass-media entertainment complex means that athletes, and athletes of color in particular, are increasingly important actors in the construction and reproduction of racial or ethnic identity. How athletes of color are represented in the sports media, or whether they are even represented at all, and the power of the sport media "in confirming and reconstructing images that are congruent with hegemonic discourses about social group relations" (van Sterkenburg & Knoppers, 2004, p. 302), would thus seem to wholly justify the critical scholarly attention that the race–media–sport nexus has garnered.

In this chapter, we provide an overview of such research on the construction and representation of race in sport media texts. Obviously, given the scale, scope—in subject and academic discipline—and, of course, vibrancy of this literature, our summary herein is by no means exhaustive. Our aim instead is to present a critical review of what could be termed a *representative literature* that provides some indication of the nature and variety of research examining the intersections of race, sport, and the media. One further caveat is that our focus is primarily on the United States and, in particular, African-American (male) athletes. This is in many ways a reflection of a general research trend: The vast majority of studies of race and ethnicity in the sports media have focused on African-American athletes, whether because of the extensive media coverage they receive or the limited coverage afforded to other athletes of color (see also the earlier review by Davis & Harris, 1998). In doing so we do not wish to deny an expanding literature on media coverage of Native-American (for example, see Banks, 1993; Davis, 1993; King & Springwood, 2001a, 2001b; King, Staurowsky, Baca, Davis, & Pewewardy, 2002), Latino/a(-American) (see Hoose, 1989; Jamieson, 2000; Klein, 2000; Rodriguez, 2002; Sabo, Jansen, Tate, Duncan, & Leggett, 1996), and Asian(-American) (see Sabo, et al., 1996) athletes nor devalue the important contributions of scholars critically analyzing the interconnections of race, sport, and the media in contexts outside the United States. Rather, and especially given the limits of space and the aims of this collection, it is to suggest that the representation of African Americans in the sports media provides an extensive and important body of research in and of itself.

REPRESENTING RACE: COVERAGE, CONTENT, AND STEREOTYPING

In this chapter, our primary focus is the issue of how athletes of color are, and have historically been, represented in the media. Certainly, we concur with Carrington (2001/2002) in his view that the process of representation should be seen as a "primary site for the construction and constitution of identities, collective and individual, rather than merely being a secondary reflection of already formed social identities" (p. 92), something well reflected in the fact that the vast majority of research on race, sport, and the media has been concerned with matters of representation and, in particular, the continuities and articulations of racial ideologies as manifest within the sports media. Notably, however, many early studies of race and ethnicity in the sports media were actually concerned with the *extent*, rather than *content*, of coverage.

In particular, several studies have suggested that black athletes have historically been underrepresented in the sports media. For instance, in their study of feature articles in *Sports Illustrated*, Lumpkin and Williams (1991) concluded that coverage of African-American male athletes was not proportional to their participation (see also Condor & Anderson, 1984). Similarly, Francis' (1990) analysis of *Sports Illustrated*'s coverage of men's Division I basketball between 1954 and 1986 found that, despite their increasing participation, Black players nonetheless "received far fewer articles than their contribution to the sport seems to warrant" (as cited in Davis & Harris, 1998, p. 155). The limited coverage afforded Black athletes has also appeared across gender, with studies such as Williams' (1994)—who noted only five African-American women donning the cover of *Sports Illustrated* during a span of 1,835 issues—and Corbett's (1988)—who found limited coverage of African-American women across 14 different magazines—suggesting African-American women athletes are also underrepresented in the print media (see also Douglas, 2002; Green, 1993; Oglesby, 1981; Scraton, 2001). Though feature articles about Black athletes in magazines and newspapers have undoubtedly increased since these analyses were conducted—arguably as a result of the increasing number of African-American play-ers as opposed to a decline in media bias (Davis & Harris, 1998)—nevertheless, it would still appear that coverage in the print media is still well short of reflecting elevated rates of Black athletic participation.

Sport on television has been historically been characterized by similar trends of African-American underrepresentation. Though scholars such as Sabo et al. (1996) argued that race is not always a factor in determining the amount of coverage, there is nonetheless some evidence to suggest that African-American athletes have also been underrepresented in the televisual media (Davis & Harris, 1998; Sailes, 1993; Smith, 1995). For instance, in a study of the National Broadcasting Corporation's (NBC) coverage of the 1992 Olympics, Hilliard (as cited in Davis & Harris, 1998) noted that there were no features on Native Americans or Asian Americans and found that features on European-American men were more in-depth than features on African-American athletes. This could perhaps be reflective of a more general bias in the televisual media where researchers have shown African Americans "to be underrepresented (or nonexistent) in all areas of television programming" (Wilson & Sparks, 1996, p. 407).

Of course, though they may have historically been underrepresented in the tele-visual media, undoubtedly African-American athletes are now receiving increasing media coverage—in newspapers, on television, and in advertising. In fact, it could even be argued that, as Carrington (2001/2002) suggested, far from being marginal-ized, African-American athletes are now hyper-visible in the contemporary sport media. Such coverage afforded Black athletes could perhaps be seen as indicative of an end to discrimination, bias, and racism in the sport media. However, it more likely reflects the African-American dominance of professional sport in America. Even if overt racism—by way of exclusion and underreporting—may not be a fea-ture of the contemporary sport media, mass-mediated sport is still nonetheless a key site for the construction and reinforcement of racist ideologies. Studies of the sport media have suggested that these ideologies include reproduction of the myth of natural African-American athletic superiority (Davis, 1990; Denham, Billings, & Halone, 2002; Sailes, 1993; Simons, 2003; Smith, 1990; Wonsek, 1992)—something which, by association, both essentializes and naturalizes categories of Black and White (Davis, 1990) as well as relies on the dissemination of stereotypical dumb jock (Sailes, 1993) representations of Black athletes; the demonization of male Black ath-letes by way of their articulation to stereotypical associations of African-American males with crime, deviance, and sexual promiscuity (Andrews, 1996b; Boyd, 1997b; Carrington, 2001/2002; Cole, 1996; Cole & King, 1998, 1999; Kellner, 1996; Lule, 1995; Maharaj, 1997); and the reinforcement of racial stereotypes relating to African-American males through the construction of a racial binary of atypical good Blacks and typical bad Blacks (Wenner, 1995; see also Andrews, 1996a, 1996b; Boyd, 1997b, 2000; McDonald, 1996; McDonald & Andrews, 2001; Shropshire, 2000; Wilson, 1997).

STEREOTYPING THE BLACK ATHLETE: THE SPORTING BLACK BODY AND RACIAL IDEOLOGIES

While we elaborate on these ideologies later, it is also important to note how, in addition to visual and narrative representations which reinforce racial stereotypes, the sport media further supports racism by portraying the presence and success of

African-American athletes as evidence of the absence of racism. To some at least, the coverage afforded African-American athletes may seem to symbolize a decline in, or at least delegitimation of, racism not only in the sports media, but also in society more generally. That is, the contemporary dominance of certain sports by African Americans, and Black men in particular, could be used to "reinforce an argument that the US is an open society, and that blacks are improving their economic and social positions" (Wonsek, 1992, p. 457). Given sport's symbolic significance, images of Black athletic success provide a persuasive counterargument to suggestions that the American racial meritocracy is a myth. As Cole (1996) argued, images of Black athletic success, of upward social and economic mobility, are "appealing because they offer faith in America, in the American system, and the American way of life" (p. 389; see also Andrews, 1996a, 1996b; Baker, 2000; Goldman & Papson, 1998; Maharaj, 1997; McDonald, 1996; McDonald & Andrews, 2001; Robbins, 1997; Sandell, 1995).

A number of authors have pointed to the way in which successful African-American athletes are framed within varying media discourses as symbolic validations of the American dream (Andrews, 1996a, 1996b, 2001; Baker, 2000; Cole & King, 1998, 1999; Davis & Harris, 1998; Goldman & Papson, 1998; Maharaj, 1997; McDonald, 1996; McDonald & Andrews, 2001; Robbins, 1997; Sandell, 1995). For instance, Andrews (1996a) noted how the popular and promotional signification of basketball player Michael Jordan, in drawing on and actively mobilizing the discourses of a New Right neoliberal agenda, implied the continued efficacy of the rags-to-riches parable that is the American dream (see also Andrews, 1996b). Boyd (1997b), Cole (1996), Goldman and Papson (1998), McDonald (1996), and McDonald and Andrews (2001) similarly noted how Jordan's mediated identity alluded to, and served to reproduce, the myths of American racial democracy. Likewise, McKay (1995) argued in his analysis of athletic apparel advertising that the commercials often mythologized notions of individualism and meritocracy, "thereby allowing white audiences to deny the existence of institutionalized racism both in sport and American society in general" (Wilson, 1997, p. 178).

Numerous critics have suggested that one area of the media which has been especially powerful in regard to reinforcing this myth of American racial meritocracy has been cinema (Baker, 2000). Basketball films, both fictional and documentary, have been a particular topic of analysis and critique. For instance, Baker argued that movies, like most other media presentations of basketball, "avoid careful engagement with the moral and social complexities that confront working-class African American men" (p. 230) by instead suggesting that "personal initiative and achievement can overcome even the obstacle of racial discrimination" (p. 223). One film which has come under particular critical scrutiny is the 1994 documentary *Hoop Dreams* (see Baker, 2000; Cole, 1996; Cole & King, 1998, 1999; Mosher, 1995; Robbins, 1997; Sandell, 1995; Smith, 1995). Generally, these authors have suggested that while, superficially at least, the documentary appears to be a critique of both racial and class boundaries in the United States and the false promise of sport as a route to wealth and fame for the African-American working classes, it in fact reinforces the upward mobility myth "that it pretends to disapprove of.... [the film fails to] take on the real issues of the inner city" (Robbins, 1997, p. 111). As Sandell (1995) concluded, "In an increasingly conservative climate, *Hoop Dreams* alleviates liberal guilt and reaffirms the belief that minority athletes can succeed at the American Dream *despite* an increase in structural and institutional oppression" (p. 67).

As these analyses suggest, the media frame sport, and the possibility of a professional sports career for African Americans (and African-American male youth in particular), as an escape from poverty and a means to circumvent the racial discrimination in many other occupations. Hence, as symbols of the American dream, successful Black athletes (Michael Jordan in particular; see Andrews, 1996a, 1996b, 2001; Dyson, 1993; McDonald, 1996; McDonald & Andrews, 2001) suggest that African Americans can, and regularly do, achieve both economic success and upward social mobility. As the authors cited previously allude to, the implication is that those who do not can be explained by individual moral inferiority as opposed to structural or systematic racism or racial prejudice (see Andrews, 1996a, 1996b; Baker, 2000; Cole, 1996; Cole & King, 1998, 1999; Davis & Harris, 1998; Goldman & Papson, 1998; Hartmann, 2000; Maharaj, 1997; McDonald, 1996; Robbins, 1997; Sandell, 1995; Soar, 2001). As Wilson and Sparks (1996) explained, the dominant message in nonstereotypical representations of Black athletic, social, and economic success is that the athletes in question "have reached this level of success because they take advantage of opportunities that poor Blacks do not" (p. 407). In displacing social and structural factors, and in emphasizing the efforts and achievements of individual Black athletes, the media imply that poverty is a result of "individual shortcoming" (Baker, 2000, p. 227) and "reinforce the view that the failure of the black underclass is their own" (Wilson, 1997, p. 185). Black athletic success stories thus falsely suggest sport to be a viable space for African-American social and economic advancement and provide African-American—and African-American men in particular—a "stereotypical representational politics that denies and even disavows the complexities of their cultural situation and the pluralistic nature of the subject positions they currently inhabit" (Lafrance & Rail, 2001, p. 41). Hence, although Black athletes often seek "status, respect, empowerment and upward mobility through athletic careers" (Dworkin & Messner, 1999, pp. 4–5) as a means of circumventing racial and class barriers, doing so within the venue of sports may actually reproduce racism and justify a system of racial inequality (Cole, 1996; Hartmann, 2000; Maharaj, 1997; Sandell, 1995; Smith, 1995).

In a similar fashion to the way in which they may serve to validate the myth of an American racial meritocracy, successful Black athletes are also often seen to symbolize American liberal, racial inclusiveness (Andrews, 1996a, 1996b; Andrews & Cole, 2000; Cole & Andrews, 2001; Crenshaw, 1997; Johnson & Roediger, 1997; McKay, 1995; Uchacz, 1998). Several authors have suggested that, implicitly at least, the media portray sport as a space devoid of racial discrimination; the mere presence of African-American athletes is "readily perceived as evidence of integration" (Douglas, 2002, para. 5.3). For instance, golfer Tiger Woods has often been framed within media discourse as the exemplar of a meritocratic, multicultural America (Andrews & Cole, 2000; Cole & Andrews, 2001; Uchacz, 1998). As Andrews and Cole (2000) argued, through various mediated texts, images, and narratives, Woods affirmed the seemingly multicultural nature of late 1990s America and came to symbolize American liberal, racial inclusiveness (see also Cole & Andrews, 2001; Uchacz, 1998). His presence within the elite, and historically racially segregated, space of golf means that Woods has often been used by the core American values and ideologies (i.e., those cultural intermediaries operating within the ratings-driven media and poll-driven centrist politics) as self-evident proof of the existence of an American color-blind meritocracy (Cole & Andrews, 2001). Similarly, McKay (1995) and Wonsek (1992) argued that the use of Black celebrity athletes within contemporary advertising—when the use of African Americans has historically been avoided by advertising agencies (see Edwards, 1969; Greenberg & Brand, 1994; Wonsek, 1992)—could be used by those in the dominant White middle classes as means of denying both individual and societal racism.

Even if the increasing presence of African Americans within American popular and commercial cultures was emblematic of an end to discrimination, the ubiquity of representations that reinforce dominant and highly racialized stereotypes of the Black other is indicative of how racism is still prevalent in the mass media. These racial stereotypes are further accentuated by the fact that African Americans are overrepresented in some areas of media programming, such as comedy, music, and, of course, sport, while they are all but absent in others (see Greenberg & Brand, 1994; Real, 1989; Wonsek, 1992). Of the limited range of media genres and discourses within which African Americans, and especially African-American males, have been represented and described, the dominance of televised elite male sport by Black athletes and their overrepresentation in the "athletic paradigm of advertisements" (Wonsek, 1992, p. 456) are perhaps most problematic. In particular, the media's focus on "Black men as athletes," and the disproportionate coverage given to Black athletic achievement, further obscures "the diversity of everyday successes by African American men" (Wenner, 1995, p. 228). Moreover, and as we alluded to previously, overrepresentation implies that sport is one of the few potential routes of upward mobility for African-American youth. As critics such as Edwards (1969, 1973; see also Cole & King, 1998, 1999; Davis & Harris, 1998; Goldman & Papson, 1998; Smith, 1995) argued, the media and economic successes of Black athletes give African-American youth a false sense of "the very limited career prospects of collegiate and professional sport" (Wilson & Sparks, 1996, p. 399).

SPORT, THE BLACK ATHLETE, AND THE MYTH OF NATURAL PHYSICALITY

Arguably, the media's portrayal of sport as one of only a limited range of opportunities for social and economic mobility for African-American working class youth also serves to reinforce the myth of natural Black athleticism. By effacing socioeconomic environment, cultural modeling, communal norms, and familial expectations in favor of genetic explanations for Black athletic success, the natural athlete myth suggests that African Americans possess innate physiological advantages while conversely lacking the necessary skills and intelligence to succeed in other occupational areas (Bruce, 2004; Davis, 1990; Denham, Billings, & Halone, 2002; Murrell & Curtis, 1994; Sailes, 1993; Smith, 1990). The stereotype further implies that White athletes are "disadvantaged relative to black athletes, who are seen as having superior physiology" (Davis & Harris, 1998, p. 158). Studies such as Andrews' (1996a, 1996b), Davis' (1990), Sailes' (1993), and Smith's (1995) all suggested that televised elite male sport plays an important part in promoting such "stereotypical and divisive, yet common-sense, embodied articulations of race and racial difference" (Andrews, 1996b, p. 132). Indeed, Bruce (2004) argued that "representations of natural black physicality continue to be reproduced in live sports television" (p. 875).

Likewise, numerous other researchers have also found this natural black athlete stereotype to be common in other areas of the sport media (Andrews, 1996b; Davis, 1990; Denham, Billings, & Halone, 2002; Jackson, 1987, 1989; Murrell & Curtis, 1994; Sailes, 1993; Smith, 1990; Staples & Jones, 1985). For instance, Jackson (1989) found that, in comparison to White athletes, the performances of Black athletes are more often attributed to innate physical skill, and he elsewhere also argues that media discourses, both visual and narrative, often portray African Americans as *naturally* athletic (see also Jackson, 1987). Similarly, Staples and Jones (1985) found in their analysis of Black television images that "black excellence on the [sports] field was interpreted as a function of genetically endowed skills" (pp. 13–14), and van Sterkenburg and Knoppers (2004) also suggested that a "natural physicality discourse" is often used by those in the media to "explain the great number of black athletes in certain events and sports" (p. 312).

Such stereotypes are reinforced by the fact that African-American athletes receive the greatest media coverage in sports such as track and field and basketball, as natural athleticism is, as Jackson (1987) noted, most commonly associated with physiological advantages in speed and jumping ability (see also Davis, 1990; Smith 1990). Thus, it is perhaps hardly surprising that, in their analysis of audience responses to dominant discourses about race and ethnicity in sport, van Sterkenburg and Knoppers (2004) reported: "Both black and white respondents used (a natural physicality) discourse to attribute the relative over-representation of black athletes in certain sports/events (sprinting events and basketball) to difference in bodily explosive power" (p. 307).

In contrast to Black athletes, who are frequently framed in terms of their physicality, White athletes are most often depicted as relying on intellectual means to achieve their sporting success (Davis, 1990; Denham, Billings, and Halone, 2002; Murrell & Curtis, 1994; Smith, 1990). Research has suggested that while Black athletes are often praised for being naturally talented, White athletes are often praised for either their hard work or perceived intellect and leadership (Denham, Billings, & Halone, 2002; Eastman & Billings, 2001; Jackson, 1989; Murrell & Curtis, 1994; Wonsek, 1992). As Bruce (2004) suggested, "North American sports commentators and journalists tend to identify male white players as leaders and hard workers and represent male black players as *athletes* with little reference to hard work or intellect" (p. 861). Murrell and Curtis' (1994) analysis of print media coverage of National Football League (NFL) quarterbacks similarly found that the performance of Black quarterbacks was characterized by *innate* ability, whereas the performance of White quarterbacks was attributed to the notion of "intellect." Wonsek (1992) argued that such stereotypes also "seem to operate in relation to the commercial advertisements which are an integral part of the media broadcasts" (p. 460), an observation supported by Dufur (1998), who found in her examination of the representation of Black and White athletes in print media advertising that the Black athletes were more commonly portrayed in terms of their physicality or athleticism as opposed to White athletes, who were characterized in terms of their character or intellect.

A further finding of the study by Murrell and Curtis (1994) was the way in which the success of White quarterbacks was often attributed to effort rather than physical ability. This notion of effort is in many ways typical of the way in which the natural athlete stereotype also reinforces the assumption that White athletes are more hardworking than Black athletes. Indeed, a number of studies have found that the media depict the efforts of White athletes more often than those of Black athletes (Cole & Andrews, 1996; Jackson, 1987, 1989; Murrell & Curtis, 1994; Sailes, 1993; Smith, 1990). In suggesting that White athletes are more hardworking, the sport media devalues the work of Black athletes, implies that black athletes are lazy, and further naturalizes Black athletic skill as being biologically-based (Bruce, 2004; see also Davis, 1990). The stereotype that Black athletes purportedly rely on innate physical advantages also implies that Black athletes lack discipline and application, something further reinforced by the way in which Black athletic success is often attributed to the guidance or skill of a White coach or White authority figure (see Andrews 1996b; Robbins, 1997). Thus, although many elite televised sports may be dominated by Black players, "these images are mitigated and undercut by the overwhelming predominance of white images, some of which represent individuals in positions of authority (coaches and sportscasters). Not only does this place the Black players in a secondary and entertainment role, but it may also serve to reassure the White majority that its dominance is not really being threatened" (Wonsek, 1992, p. 454; see also Thomas, 1996).

CRIME, DRUGS, AND (SEXUAL) DEVIANCE: THE MEDIA CONSTRUCTION OF BLACK SPORTING MASCULINITY

Further to laziness and lack of leadership, intellect, and discipline—attributes embodied by, and implied in, presuppositions of natural athleticism—the sports media also reflect and reproduce a number of wider racialized discourses associated with African Americans, and African-American masculinity in particular. As Andrews (1996b) argued, the representation of Black athletes in the media commonly reflects and reinforces the more general portrayal of African-American males as deviant, unruly, violent, and animalistic—or, as he suggests, generally "threats to society"—in popular cinema, television, literature, and the print media (see also Boyd, 1997a, 1997b; Staples & Jones, 1985). Likewise, Smith (1995) contended that representations of the familial failings, drug usage, and other forms of deviance among Black male athletes is common in both public and media discourse, and Wenner (1995) also noted how portrayals of Black athletes as naturally threatening correspond with the more conventional negative and stereotypical portrayals of Blackness (see also Boyd, 1997a, 1997b; Cole, 1996; Wilson, 1997; Wonsek, 1992). Such depictions are believed to lead some audiences to draw a parallel between deviant African-American male athletes and wider criminality among African-American males in society (see Leonard, chap. 31, this volume, as well as Cole, 1996; Wilson & Sparks, 1996).

Allusions to the supposed off-field criminality of African-American male athletes are particularly common in the sport media. For instance, Cole and Andrews (1996) argued that the re-imaging of the NBA in the 1990s was an attempt to distance the league from the popular public and media associations of its players with drugs, gambling, and criminality (see also Andrews, 1996a, 1996b; Cole & Denny, 1995; Shropshire, 2000). As Cole and Andrews contended, in the late 1970s and early 1980s, the mediation of the NBA reinforced dominant and residual discourses of African-American masculinity. Reflecting the "racist rhetoric" of the American New Right, the NBA was seen as too black and too drug infested to appeal to marketers or ever become a truly popular element of American culture (see Cole & Andrews, 1996; Shropshire, 2000). Though Black players such as Michael Jordan and Magic Johnson undoubtedly helped make the NBA of the mid-1980s and early 1990s accessible to the White middle class consumer (see Andrews, 1996a, 1996b, 2001; Cady, 1979; Cole & Andrews, 1996; Cole & Denny, 1995), Boyd (1997b) argued that the contemporary promotion of the Black NBA basketball player, often through popular narratives of deviance, violence, and laziness, similarly situates the Black sporting celebrity in a discourse of working class, masculine, urban society, or what he terms *nigga culture*—regardless of his economic wealth. Similarly, Boyd and Shropshire (2000) also suggested, "the present generation of NBA stars are depicted as synonymous with greed, arrogance, selfish individualism, and an overall disrespect that has often embarrassed the 'positive image'-driven league" (p. 10).

In many, if not most, cases, the purported failings of the Black community are seen as the explanation for both the purported selfishness or the sexual or criminal deviance of African-American athletes. Supposedly a reflection of African-American culture more generally, the deviance of African-American athletes is often linked to stereotypes of single-parent families, welfare dependency, drugs, and crime (Cole 1996; Cole & King, 1998, 1999; Goldman & Papson, 1998; Hartmann, 2000; Maharaj, 1997; Robbins, 1997). This is perhaps most evident in the way in which African-American male athletes are commonly linked to the discourses and narratives of threatening urban Black masculinity (Boyd, 1997a, 1997b; Cole, 1996; Cole & King, 1998, 1999; Goldman & Papson, 1998; Maharaj, 1997; Robbins, 1997; Shropshire, 2000; Walton, 2001; Wilson, 1997). For instance, in his analysis of media constructions of African-American athletes in Canadian basketball, Wilson (1997) found that "both print and electronic portrayals stereotyped African-Americans as criminal, arrogant, unruly, undisciplined and threatening" and that, "although explicit references to race were not made, there were powerful, subtle associations with the inner-city, gangs and crime on the one hand, and African-American basketball players on the other" (p. 184). Maharaj (1997) similarly noted the discursive link, in advertising and the media more generally, between African-American basketball players and the "street," wherein the "street" is associated with "black male lawlessness, parental irresponsibility, and emasculation" (p. 97).

Interestingly, however, while the links between Black athletes, and particularly Black NBA basketball players, and crime in Black communities may be a common narrative, the media also suggests sport as an alternative to Black deviance (Andrews, 1996a, 1996b, 2001; Cole, 1996; Cole & King, 1998, 1999; Goldman & Papson, 1998; McDonald, 1996; Wenner, 1994). Within this sport–crime binary, sport is positioned as providing poor African-American youth with direction and purpose, "while socializing them into responsible citizens" (Goldman & Papson, 1998, p. 111). As Cole (1996, p.371) argued, the stereotype is often presented in terms of a mediated discourse which positions urban Black youths within an oppositional "sport/gang dyad." According to Cole and King (1999), the media promote two common tropes of Black culture in America: black youths redeemed by following the right path (sport) or, alternatively, the failed black family leading to the wrong path (gangs and drugs) (Cole & King, 1999; see also Cole & King, 1998). Such stereotypes not only offer limited visions of the Black experience in sport, and society more broadly—and especially those associations with violence and criminality—but further serve to reproduce a neoliberal ideology which pathologizes Black communities while failing to address social and systemic inequality (Andrews, 1996a, 1996b; Cole, 1996; Cole & King, 1998, 1999; Hartmann, 2000; Maharaj, 1997, Robbins, 1997; Sandell, 1995). In particular, "the sport/gang dyad, its corresponding somatic reterritorialization, and its exclusions, not only inscribe racialized criminal and threatening masculinity and stabilize fundamental categories embedded in 'America,' but produce desires for policing, punishment, and revenge directed at African American inner city youth" (Cole, 1996, p. 371).

Despite the fact that Black athletes are commonly linked to deviance, violence, and criminality, Berry and Smith (2000) argued that there is no data which supports the notion that African-American sports figures are more likely to be engaged in crime than White sports figures. Just as African Americans are overrepresented in the reporting of crime in the general media, Berry and Smith (2000) instead suggested that the associations between race, sport, and crime are misrepresented in the sports media. In comparing the disproportionate coverage of the crimes of Black professional athletes to the overrepresentation of African Americans in media reporting of crime in general, their findings suggest that the attribution of criminal activity to African-American athletes mirrors that of young Black men more generally.

A further finding of the research by Berry and Smith (2000) was that, of the crimes involving Black athletes reported by the media, the majority were related to either assault and battery or drugs and alcohol. Although this is certainly something supported by other research (Donohew, Helm, & Haas, 1989; Messner & Solomon, 1993; Walton, 2001), public associations of African-American athletes with either assault and drugs have also been reinforced by high-profile criminal trials such as those of boxers Sugar Ray Leonard (see Messner & Solomon, 1993) and Mike Tyson (see Carrington, 2001/2002; Lule, 1995; Sloop, 1997) and football player O. J. Simpson (see Barak, 1996; Crenshaw, 1997; Johnson & Roediger, 1997). The media discourse surrounding these trials was largely characterized by the use of stereotypical associations of drug use, violence, and sexual abuse to Black athletes and Black masculinity. For instance, in their critical examination of the newspaper coverage surrounding the 1990 divorce trial of Sugar Ray Leonard—during which Leonard admitted to using drugs in the three years following his retirement from boxing and to physically abusing his spouse—Messner and Solomon (1993, p. 119) argue that the press formulated their discourse around the "jock-on-drugs" theme which already dominated sports media coverage of Black athletes. Carrington (2001/2002), Lule (1995), Sloop (1997), and Walton (2001) also examined the ways in which the media frame assault and domestic violence among Black athletes. These studies have suggested that the Black (male) body is a significant site through which notions of athleticism and animalism provide the discursive boundaries within which Black subjecthood is framed. In particular, Carrington (2001/2002) contended that the sports media "have played a central role in biologising black performance via their constant use of animalistic similes to describe black athletes" (p. 94; see also Jackson's [1998] analysis of the media coverage of Canadian sprinter Ben Johnson). An example is the media coverage of the 1992 rape trial of former heavyweight boxing champion Mike Tyson, in which Tyson's Blackness often served to position him as a violent, sexual predator (see Carrington, 2001/2002; Lule, 1995; Sloop, 1997). As Sloop (1997) contended, throughout the trial, the media constructed a racialized discourse of Tyson which framed him as a "man-beast-machine," something which "worked to position him as likely to be guilty of rape" (p. 102). Similarly, in his examination of the newspaper coverage of the trial, Lule (1995) found that the media mobilized two common stereotypical tropes of African Americans: the "animal savage" stereotype and the "hapless victim" stereotype (Lule, 1995, p. 177). He suggested that the news coverage during a nine-month span immediately following the launch of a police investigation against Tyson often reinforced pervasive notions of the violent, athletic Black body (Lule, 1995).

As the Tyson case attests, crime, violence, and the Black male athlete are also often connected to sexuality in media discourse. As Rowe, McKay, and Miller (2000) contended, the mediated image of "the black male sporting body, like that of the black male pop star, is a heavily sexualized one" (p. 259). Carrington (2001/2002) argued that questions of race and racism "have from the outset inherently connected with wider issues concerning the social organisation and display of sexuality," and further suggested that "historical colonial fantasies about the excesses of black sexuality continue to exercise a hegemonic role in the representation of blackness" (Carrington, 2001/2002, p. 91). Certainly, Tyson's case is also illustrative in that it reflects many of the traditional discourses of Black masculinity, and particularly those relating to Black male sexual promiscuity. As further example, in her analysis of representations of the Black male athlete within professional basketball, Tucker (2003) concluded that "historical images of Black men as hypersexual criminals inform contemporary responses to, and representations of, Black male basketball players" (p. 307).

The case of basketball player Earvin "Magic" Johnson is also illustrative of the way in which race, sexuality, and media stereotypes may intersect. Studies by both Cole and Denny (1995) and King (1993), for instance, argued that that Johnson's announcement in 1991 that he was HIV positive undermined his status as an embodiment of 1990s American New Right racial ideology: a hard bodied, disciplined, racially understated African American. Subsequently, Johnson was discursively situated within a media discourse which appropriated and reinforced a range of stereotypes about Black sexual promiscuity (Cole & Andrews, 1996; Cole & Denny, 1995; King, 1993). McDonald (1996) argued that images of African American men, and particularly African American male athletes, have historically reproduced and reinforced "racist and sexist meanings that associate African Americans with nature, animality, hypersensuality, and eroticism" (p. 345), and, similarly, the media positioned Johnson as confirmation of the "perceived sexual excesses of black masculinity" (Carrington, 2001/2002, p. 98). In sum, the cases of Tyson and Johnson are testament to Carrington's (2001/2002) contention that sport, and mediated sport in particular, has been perhaps the primary arena in which colonial myths about Black sexuality and power have been most clearly expressed.

SPORT, THE BLACK ATHLETE, AND THE IMPOSSIBILITY OF RACIAL TRANSCENDENCE

Studies of race in the sports media therefore largely suggest that African-American male athletes are most commonly associated with discourses of deviance, sexual promiscuity, and criminality and are often portrayed as selfish, lacking discipline, arrogant, and disrespectful. Further, as Smith (1995) suggested, there has traditionally been little coverage given to African American athletes who contradict these stereotypical norms of Black culture; rather, counternarratives are often neglected in favor of commonplace discourses of Blackness. In some instances, however, African-American athletes have been able to distance themselves from these stereotypes and subsequently achieve wider mainstream, that is, White, appeal. Perhaps the most famous example is basketball player Michael Jordan who, in contrast to traditional stereotypes of the Black athlete, was portrayed throughout much of his career as hardworking and disciplined (see Andrews, 2001; McDonald, 1996; McDonald & Andrews, 2001). In both the popular and sporting media, Jordan's imaged identity was distanced from the racial signifiers which dominated popular representations of African-American males. This was because corporate image makers recognized that, if he was to become an American sporting icon, they could not afford to explicitly associate him with the threatening expressions of Black culture and experience (see Andrews, 1996a, 1996b, 2001; McDonald, 1996; McDonald &

Andrews, 2001). As Baker (2000) contended, this "narrative conflict" was characterized by an "exceptional/pathological, Michael Jordan/gansta character quality that dominates media representation of black basketball in particular and African Americans in general" (2003, p. 38). In advertisements for sponsors such as Nike and in televised coverage of the NBA, Jordan was promoted as the atypical African-American male, stripping him of his Blackness and the negative signifiers of African-American otherness (Andrews, 1996a, 1996b). As Andrews (1996a, 1996b) argued, Jordan's popular appeal was predicated upon the downplaying of his race or racial *Otherness*, achieved primarily through counterposing his mediated image against the more traditional signifiers of Black masculinity (sexual promiscuity, crime, violence); thus, the "phenomenal—and radically *atypical*—success" of Jordan "as an enormously wealthy, black basketball star and media celebrity" can be attributed "at least in part to the successful preclusion of these particular associations" (Soar, 2001, p. 39).

Comparable examples of this downplaying of race are Nike's recent advertisements for golfer Tiger Woods and the reimaging of the NBA in the 1980s discussed in brief previously (see also Houck, chap. 28, this volume). In the case of Woods, Andrews and Cole (2000) noted how Nike attempted to promote a more inclusive, less threatening version of Woods' "otherness" after early commercial failings in which they tried to "African Americanize" (p. 115) him (see also Cole & Andrews, 2001; Uchacz, 1998). In a similar fashion, Cole and Andrews (1996) suggested that the reimaging of the NBA in the 1990s was characterized by marketing campaigns which provided more accommodating images of African-American athletes and promoted more acceptable, racially understated representations of Black America (see also Cole & Denny, 1995; Shropshire, 2000). Notably, Jordan in particular played a crucial role in making the NBA accessible to the White American populace, who had previously been turned off, and turned away, by the game's overtly Black identity and demeanor (see Cady, 1979; Cole & Andrews, 1996; Cole & Denny, 1995; Shropshire, 2000).

Arguably, athletes such as Jordan and Woods are indicative of the way in which "many of the White population are gracious enough to accept, even adulate, African Americans, but only if they do not explicitly assert their Blackness" (Andrews, 1996b, p. 140). As Shropshire (2000) concurred, "those Black performers who have been widely accepted project images that are raceless, colorless, and apolitical" (p. 83). A number of scholars have noted how, in order to garner popular appeal, people of color are encouraged to abdicate their racial or ethnic identities and be seen to assimilate into the practices, values, and ideologies of mainstream white America (Andrews, 1996a, 1996b; Johnson & Roediger, 1997; McDonald, 1996; McDonald & Andrews, 2001; Wenner, 1995; Wilson, 1997). Hence, even though African-American athletes may be accepted within contemporary popular and commercial cultures, Black athletic celebrities are often framed within visual and narrative discourses which are seemingly unconnected to race or are race "neutral" (Goldman & Papson, 1998): "A celebrity athlete—so long as he had a personality, or appeared to have a personality—proved to be a commodity that seemed unconnected to race as a category" (p. 100). Thus, as Johnson and Roediger (1997) contended, the nonthreatening rearticulation of the Black other is perhaps a better reflection of a seemingly progressive marketplace rather than an actual progressive politics.

Furthermore, these atypical African-American celebrities may actually exemplify and reinforce many of the dominant racial meanings associated with typical African-American males (Andrews, 1996a, 1996b). Black athletes such as Tyson, and even other Black basketball players such as Latrell Sprewell (see Walton, 2001) and Dennis Rodman (see Dunbar, 2000; Lafrance & Rail, 2001), are "more often than not, situated contentiously in relation to more disciplined images and cultural roles of other Black male athletes" (Tucker, 2003, p. 321) such as Jordan or Woods. Thus, as Andrews (1996b) argued in the case of Jordan, rather than *transcending* their Blackness, *atypical* African-American athletes may actually act as agents for the *displacement* of stereotypical black signifiers onto the bodies of typical black Others.

Moreover, in the popular media, the supposed racelessness of athletes such as Jordan and Woods is often negotiated, and race can be reinscribed. For instance, Andrews (1996b) suggested that media coverage of Jordan's gambling threatened to undermine his race-neutral status and therefore his appeal to White mainstream audiences. Similarly, Crenshaw (1997), Johnson and Roediger (1997), and Wenner (1995) suggested O. J. Simpson was once been "perhaps America's most raceless black man . . . the triumph of the discursive paradigm of colorblindness" (Crenshaw, 1997, p. 102; see also Barak, 1996). Carefully mediated, Simpson was corporate America's Black ideal, his "seemingly colorless" image a "valuable commodity" (Johnson & Roediger, 1997, p. 199) to appeal to the White middle classes. Yet, both during and following his 1994 double-murder trial, media coverage served to reinscribe and rearticulate Simpson's Blackness: Although the Simpson case was originally framed within the "liberal" narrative structure of "colorblindness" (Crenshaw, 1997, p. 98), it was replaced by polarizing discourses of accountability, criminality, and victimization; "the nefarious consequence of an unjustified departure from colorblindness reduce[d] complex issues of institutional power, racially divergent subjectivities, intersections of race, gender, and class, and a host of other issues all onto one flattened plane of race" (Crenshaw, 1997; see also Barak, 1996; Wenner, 1995).

COMMODIFYING BLACKNESS: SPORT, "THE STREET," AND THE SELLING OF RACE

However, while the race of African-American athletes may have been traditionally downplayed as a means of gaining popular appeal, several authors have argued that more recently there has been a commodification of Blackness, and the Black athletic body in particular, within even mainstream media marketing. It would seem that explicit representations of race are more prevalent within today's cultural economy, and racial difference has been increasingly appropriated as a means to sell to particular markets (Boyd, 1997a, 1997b; Carrington, 2001/2002; Goldman & Papson, 1998; Maharaj, 1997; Sandell, 1995). This is particularly true of the corporate and commercial appropriation of images of the postindustrial, inner city, something which has traditionally been associated with the stereotypes of what Maharaj (1997) referred to as "urban blackness" (p. 100): unemployment, crime, poverty, welfare dependency, and drugs (see also Cole, 1996; Cole & King, 1998, 1999). Several authors have suggested that street culture, and more specifically the culture of Black urban male youth, is often used by the commercial media as a means of denoting an authentic Blackness that appeals to White, middle class consumers (Cole, 1996; Goldman & Papson, 1998; Maharaj, 1997; Sandell, 1995). As Goldman and Papson (1998) noted in their analysis of the relationship between race and class in Nike commercials, advertisers often "[invoke] images of poverty and inner city children in order to turn them into the currency of legitimacy" (p. 116). Likewise, Maharaj (1997) argued that in the mid-1990s advertisers (most notably Nike) attempted to distance themselves from the purported overcommercialization of professional basketball—and, more specifically, spectator's and consumer's resentment of exponentially increasing players' salaries—through commercials which appealed to "the 'purity' of the game's 'roots' as an urban community practice" (p. 104). Thus, the postindustrial city was made economically productive "through its symbolic representation as the locus of racial and sexual difference" (Maharaj, 1997, p. 101; see also Cole, 1996; Cole & King, 1998, 1999).

Arguably, this "selling of the most strident forms of African American discourse" (Boyd, 1997, p. 140) is indicative of the way in which "difference" has become perhaps "*the* commodity" (Maharaj, 1997, p. 101) in postmodern consumer culture. For instance, Maharaj (1997) suggested that attempts to commodify the connection between the street (and the popular racial signifiers encoded therein) and Black sport culture reflects the prevailing late capitalist logic of consumption of, and through, difference (Maharaj, 1997). Similarly, Carrington (2001/2002) and Boyd (1997a, 1997b) both argued that strident Blackness has been an increasingly valued marker of difference and cultural hipness, particularly among young, White, middle-class consumers (see also Maharaj, 1997; Sandell, 1995). Thus, as Boyd (1997b) contended, "no longer off limits, all forms of Black popular culture are fair game for representation within the massive circuit of entertainment" (p. 140). He cited Charles Barkley as an illustration of an African-American athlete who is both demonized and capitalized upon through his recurring Blackness, something apparent in the way in which Nike's presentation of Barkley's Blackness is packaged under the guise of rebellion and sold to mass audiences as authentic nigga (see Boyd, 1997b) culture (see also Boyd, 1997a). The media, and advertising in particular, has therefore reduced difference to a cultural commodity (see Sandell, 1995) and valorized "a particular, mediated notion of urban blackness" (Soar, 2001, p. 51), which connects non-Black, suburban youth to only "the most desirable aspects of urban black male experience and physicality—all from a safe and sanitized distance" (Soar, 2001, p. 53).

As Soar alluded, this contemporary "commodification of blackness" is problematic in that, "through it, black bodies function as racialised symbols of cultural difference, without of course challenging the unequal power relationships that structure this consumption" (Carrington, 2001/2002, pp. 108–109; see also Goldman & Papson, 1998; Sandell, 1995). The fact that otherness is being produced for consumption also means that difference is required to be rendered both acceptable and understandable to mainstream audiences. Within corporate capitalism, "differences based on cultural and social identities are often acceptable only as long as they either assimilate into mainstream culture or remain at a safe distance where they can be consumed as an alternative or exotic cultural experience" (Sandell, 1995, p. 57). Therefore, the commodification of the Black athletic body, and the commercial appropriation and exploitation of Blackness as a means of market differentiation more generally, certainly has implications for the oppositional potential of both multicultural and Black politics. As Sandell (1995) argued, "much of the political import of the critical multicultural agenda" has been undermined by the way in which "hegemonic capitalism" has reduced "difference" and "marginality" "to commodities to be bought and sold in the marketplace" (p. 57). Likewise, Carrington (2001/2002) noted how, despite the "hyper-visibility of blacks within media culture," there has been "no concomitant developments within the public sphere of black political mobilisation" (p. 104). Though the culture industries may make substantial investments in Blackness, taking the visibility—and consumption—of Blackness as emblematic of racial progress and the demise of racial prejudice, this may actually serve to obscure the real social, political, and economic conditions faced by many African Americans (Goldman & Papson, 1998; Maharaj, 1997; Sandell, 1995). Carrington (2001/2002) suggested, furthermore, that the spectacle of the Black athletic body has "simultaneously diminished the space for progressive politics itself. . . . It appears that we have moved from a position of black athletes embodying a politics of social transformation to politics itself being reduced to the bodies of individual athletes" (pp. 104–106). Increasingly, African Americanness is defined though bodies engaged in characteristic activities—usually sexual or sporting—while Blackness has increasingly become a commercially inspired reflection of difference produced for consumption, predominantly by White audiences, which expresses no real oppositional politics. It seems that within the context and logics of capitalism there has been an "emptying out both the possibilities of sport as a transformative sphere, and of black culture as a site of resistance" (Carrington, 2001/2002, pp. 118–119).

This is not to suggest that sport, and in particular mediated sport, does not provide a potential space for the challenging of racist stereotypes and of racism more generally. Indeed, as Messner (1992) argued, certain groups of people have been able to "use sport as a means to resist (at least symbolically) the domination imposed upon them," and thus sport must "be viewed as an institution through which domination is not only imposed, but also contested" (p. 13). However, while the sport media have attempted to address "past criticisms of prejudicial treatment of blacks"—something evident in the "lower use of physical descriptors and negative evaluations with reference to black athletes" (Sabo, et al., 1996, p. 13; see also Bruce, 2004; Messner & Sabo, 1994; Sabo & Jansen, 1994)—as we have argued in this chapter, the increasing visibility of and coverage afforded African-American athletes should not necessarily be seen as indicative of a reduction of racism in the sport media. Moreover, even if there has been a decline in overt forms of racism within the sport media (traditionally exhibited in areas such as underrepresentation, underreporting, and biased commentaries), the media nonetheless supports racist discourses and beliefs through stereotypical portrayals of Black athletes as lazy, lacking discipline, deviant, or naturally athletic.

CONCLUSION: THE CRITICAL ANALYSIS OF MARGINALITY IN THE SPORT MEDIA

Given that these stereotypical, simplistic conceptions of racial otherness and "images of blackness are actively implicated in the reinscription of dominant norms and codes" (Lafrance & Rail, 2001, p. 44), further critical analysis of the discursive boundaries of Blackness, as suggested by the mediated Black athletic body, is therefore required. As cultural representations "operate to sustain specific power relationships between groups and therefore influence lived cultures" (Carrington, 2001/2002), there is a need to trace how the meanings embedded within cultural representation serve to regulate and reproduce themselves as resources or sites for the construction of Black identity. In particular, there is a demand for ethnographic audience research which examines how mediated discourses of race are decoded, or read, by consumers. As Davis and Harris (1998) argued, "it is important to move beyond speculating about media effects and begin real audience study. We need to understand what audience members from different social categories bring to their readings of sport media texts, and how varied social contexts shape meaning" (p. 168). Sport media texts should be seen as sites of negotiation and contestation "which different social groups use to create and sustain discourses about social relations of power" (van Sterkenburg & Knoppers, 2004, p. 303), and thus "audience research is necessary for understanding what audiences do with" these texts (Wilson & Sparks, 1996, p. 400). The relationship between texts and social subjects is dialogic, and the "encoded" message is "not guaranteed to be decoded in accordance with its producer's intentions" (Wilson & Sparks, 1996, p. 402; see also Hall, 1980). Hence, there is a need to examine the processes through which media representations of the African-American athlete are interpreted and assimilated.

As the studies we make reference to in this chapter perhaps suggest, currently, the vast majority of work on race, sport, and the media focused on the encoded and encoding of meanings and the politics of representation within the sport media. The extent to which audiences, particularly those members of specific ethnic groups, "reject, negotiate or may be complicit in maintaining hegemonic discourses has received relatively little attention from researchers" (van Sterkenburg & Knoppers, 2004, p. 305; see also Wilson, 1997; Wilson & Sparks, 1996). The few exceptions include Wilson and Sparks' (1996) study of the interpretation of apparel commercials by both Black and White youth communities in Canada, Armstrong's (1999, 2000) and Bierman's (1990) similar studies of Black youth in the United States, and van Sterkenburg and Knoppers' (2004) analysis of the dominant discourses concerning race and sport used by White and Black students in the Netherlands. If, as numerous scholars have suggested (Radway, 1991; Wilson, 1997; Wilson & Sparks, 1996), meaning is produced in an active negotiation between audiences and texts and "textual interpretations are related to the social locations of readers" (Wilson, 1997, p. 186), then it is necessary to complement textual analysis with further ethnographic studies of this sort (Radway, 1991; Wenner, 1991, 1994; Wilson, 1997; Wilson & Sparks, 1996). As Wilson (1997) argued, "reception studies are also needed in order to discern how different audiences consume messages about race and sport, and which groups should be targeted with initiatives derived from this kind of research (beyond the public accountability issues raised with the media producers)" (p. 186).

Similarly, there is a need for further analysis of the politics and practices of the production of sport media texts and how these serve to reinforce, reproduce, or even challenge the dominant discourses of the Black athlete within media culture. As Bruce (2004) noted, although several authors—"reading off texts" (p. 864)—suggest that the sports media may be more informed about, and have attempted to address, issues of race and racism (see Messner & Sabo, 1994; Sabo & Jansen, 1998), conclusions based on texts alone must be nonetheless considered conjectural "without investigating the practices, conventions and beliefs of those involved in the production of sport media texts" (Bruce, 2004, p. 864). As Soar (2001) argued, we "need a better understanding of the cultural intermediaries and their relationship to the Text" (p. 47) and therefore further ethnographies of production which complement both textual and audiences' analyses of the intersections of sport, race, and the media.

As we suggested previously, although there has been a great deal of research done on race and ethnicity in the sports media, "it has largely focused on black men" (Douglas, 2002, para. 1.6; see also Scraton, 2001). As Davis and Harris (1998) concurred, "Research on racial/ethnic stereotyping in the sports media has focused on the portrayal of African-American athletes to the relative exclusion of other racial/ethnic categories" (p. 164). The few exceptions include studies such as those by Hoose (1989), Jamieson (2000), Klein (2000), Rodriguez (2002), and Sabo et al. (1996) that have examined the portrayal of Latino/a-Americans in the sport media; research such as by Sabo et al. (1996) examining the coverage of Asian-American athletes; and studies examining media representation of Native-American athletes and the issue of Native-American mascots (see, for example, Banks, 1993; Davis, 1993; King & Springwood, 2001a, 2001b; King, et al., 2002). The fact that these studies are so relatively few, especially in relation to those concerned with the Black male athlete, suggests that there is a need for additional research which examines the ways in which other marginalized social categories—and particularly, other ethnic or racial categories such as Native-Americans, Latino/a-Americans, and Asian-Americans—have been trivialized, stereotyped, or excluded by the mainstream sports media.

Further, there is also a need to examine "the intersection of race and gender" (Douglas, 2002, para. 1.6) in the sports media. As Douglas (2002, para. 1.6; see also Green, 1993; Oglesby, 1981; Smith, 1983; Scraton, 2001) noted, "the sport literature contains few analyses in which Black women are subjects of study," while, more broadly, there have been few studies of the interconnectedness of race, class, sexuality, and gender in the sport media. Thus, there is a need for research examining the "racialized construction of gender and sexuality" that frames women of color as the "Other" "in order to reinforce white women as the hegemonic standard" (Douglas, 2002, para. 3.1; see also Green, 1993). This notion of White athletes as the hegemonic standard should also be extended to the construction of Whiteness more generally, as there has been a tendency in the analysis of race and sport in the sport media to "address race as if it is only relevant to those perceived to be raced subjects" (Douglas, 2002, para. 8.1). While studies such as Altimore's (1999), Kusz's (2001a, 2001b, 2001c), and Long and Hylton's (2002) recognized how part of the ideological power of Whiteness is its status as the standard by which difference is identified (see Hall, 1985), there is nonetheless a need for further analysis of the way in which "whiteness" informs dominant racial discourse (Douglas, 2002, para. 8.1).

REFERENCES

Altimore, M. (1999). "Gentleman athlete": Joe DiMaggio and the celebration and submergence of ethnicity. *International Review for the Sociology of Sport, 34*(4), 359–367.

Andrews, D. L. (1996a). Deconstructing Michael Jordan: Reconstructing postindustrial America. *Sociology of Sport Journal, 13*(4), 315–318.

Andrews, D. L. (1996b). The fact(s) of Michael Jordan's Blackness: Excavating a floating racial signifier. *Sociology of Sport Journal, 13*(2), 125–158.

Andrews, D. L. (Ed.). (2001). *Michael Jordan Inc.: Corporate sport, media culture, and late modern America.* Albany, NY: SUNY Press.

Andrews, D. L., & Cole, C. L. (2000). America's new son: Tiger Woods and America's multiculturalism. *Cultural Studies: A Research Annual, 5,* 107–122.

Armstrong, K. L. (1999). Nike's communication with Black audiences: A sociological analysis of advertising effectiveness via symbolic interactionism. *Journal of Sport and Social Issues, 23*(3), 266–286.

Armstrong, K. L. (2000). African-American students' responses to race as a source cue in persuasive sport communications. *Journal of Sport Management, 14*(3), 208–226.

Baker, A. (2000). *Hoop Dreams* in Black and White: Race and basketball movies. In T. Boyd & K. L. Shropshire (Eds.), *Basketball Jones: America above the rim* (pp. 215–239). New York: New York University Press.

Baker, A. (2003). Contesting identifies: Sports in American film. Urbana, IL: University of Illinois Press.

Banks, D. (1993). Tribal names and mascots in sports. *Journal of Sport and Social Issues, 17*(1), 5–8.

Barak, G. (Ed.). (1996). *Representing O. J.: Murder, criminal justice and mass culture.* New York: Harrow and Hurston.

Berry, B., & Smith, E. (2000). Race, sport, and crime: The misrepresentations of African Americans in team sports and crime. *Sociology of Sport Journal, 17,* 171–197.

Bierman, J. A. (1990). The effect of television sports media on Black male youth. *Sociological Inquiry, 60*(4), 413–428.

Birrell, S., & McDonald, M. G. (2000). Reading sport, articulating power lines. In S. Birrell & M. G. McDonald (Eds.), *Reading sport: Critical essays on power and representation* (pp. 3–13). Boston: Northeastern Universtiy Press.

Boyd, T. (1997a). *Am I Black enough for you?: Popular culture from the 'hood and beyond.* Bloomington, IN: Indiana University Press.

Boyd, T. (1997b). The day the niggaz took over: Basketball, commodity culture, and Black masculinity. In A. Baker & T. Boyd (Eds.), *Out of bounds: Sports, media, and the politics of identity* (pp. 123–142). Bloomington, IN: Indiana University Press.

Boyd, T. (2000). Preface: The game is to be sold, not to be told. In T. Boyd & K. L. Shropshire (Eds.), *Basketball Jones: America above the rim* (pp. ix–xii). New York: New York University Press.

Boyd, T., & Shropshire, K. L. (2000). Introduction: Basketball Jones: A new world order? In T. Boyd & K. L. Shropshire (Eds.), *Basketball Jones: America above the rim* (pp. 1–11). New York: New York University Press.

Bruce, T. (2004). Marking the boundaries of the "normal" in televised sports: The play-by-play of race. *Media, Culture and Society, 26*(6), 861–879.

Cady, S. (1979, August 11). Basketball's image crisis. *The New York Times,* p. 15.

Carrington, B. (2001/2002). Fear of a Black athlete: Masculinity, politics and the body. *New Formations, 45,* 91–110.

Cole, C. L. (1996). American Jordan: P.L.A.Y., consensus, and punishment. *Sociology of Sport Journal, 13*(4), 366–397.

Cole, C. L., & Andrews, D. L. (1996). "Look—Its NBA ShowTime!": Visions of race in the popular imaginary. In N. K. Denzin (Ed.), *Cultural studies: A research volume, 1,* 141–181.

Cole, C. L., & Andrews, D. L. (2001). America's new son: Tiger Woods and America's multiculturalism. In D. L. Andrews & S. J. Jackson (Eds.), *Sport stars: The cultural politics of sporting celebrity* (pp. 70–86). London: Routledge.

Cole, C. L., & Denny, H. (1995). Visualizing deviance in post-Reagan America: Magic Johnson, AIDS, and the promiscuous world of professional sport. *Critical Sociology, 20*(3), 123–147.

Cole, C. L., & King, S. (1998). Representing black masculinity and urban possibilities: Racism, realism, and *Hoop Dreams.* In G. Rail (Ed.), *Sport and postmodern times* (pp. 49–86). New York: State University of New York Press.

Cole, C. L., & King, S. (1999). Documenting America: Ethnographies of inner-city basketball and logics of capitalism. In R. R. Sands (Ed.), *Anthropology, sport, and culture* (pp. 147–172). Westport, CT: Bergin and Garvey.

Condor, R., & Anderson, D. F. (1984). Longitudinal analysis of coverage accorded Black and White athletes in feature articles of *Sports Illustrated* (1960–1980). *Journal of Sport Behavior, 7*(1), 39–43.

Corbett, D. R. (1988). The magazine media portrayal of sport women of colour. In F. A. Carre (Ed.), *I.C.P.E.R./C.A.H.P.E.R. world conference: Towards the 21st century* (pp. 190–195). Vancouver, BC: School of Physical Education and Recreation, University of British Columbia.

Crenshaw, K. W. (1997). Color-blind dreams and racial nightmares: Reconfiguring racism in the post-civil rights era. In T. Morrison & C. B. Lacour (Eds.), *Birth of a nation'hood: Gaze, script, and spectacle in the O. J. Simpson case* (pp. 97–168). New York: Pantheon Books.

Davis, L. R. (1990). The articulation of difference: White preoccupation with the question of racially linked genetic differences among athletes. *Sociology of Sport Journal, 7,* 179–187.

Davis, L. R. (1993). Protest against the use of Native American mascots: A challenge to traditional American identity. *Journal of Sport and Social Issues, 17*(1), 9–22.

Davis, L. R., & Harris, O. (1998). Race and ethnicity in US sports media. In L. A. Wenner (Ed.), *MediaSport* (pp. 154–169). London: Routledge.

Denham, B. E., Billings, A. C., & Halone, K. K. (2002). Differential accounts of race in broadcast commentary of the 2000 NCAA Men's and Women's Final Four basketball tournaments. *Sociology of Sport Journal, 19*(3), 315–332.

Denzin, N. K. (1996). More rare air: Michael Jordan on Michael Jordan. *Sociology of Sport Journal, 13,* 319–342.

Donohew, L., Helm, D., & Haas, J. (1989). Drugs and (Len) Bias on the sports page. In L. A. Wenner (Ed.), *Media, sports, and society* (pp. 225–237). Newbury Park, CA: Sage.

Douglas, D. D. (2002). To be young, gifted, Black and female: A meditation on the cultural politics at play in representations of Venus and Serena Williams. *Sociology of Sport Online* [On-line]. Retrieved, April 26, 2005, from http://physed.otago.ac.nz/sosol/v5i2/v5i2_3.html

Dufur, M. (1998). Race logic and "Being like Mike." In G. Sailes (Ed.), *African Americans in sport: Contemporary themes* (pp. 67–81). New Brunswick, NJ: Transaction Publishers.

Dunbar, M. D. (2000). Dennis Rodman—Do you feel feminine yet?: Black masculinity, gender transgression, and reproductive rebellion on MTV. In J. McKay, M. Messner, & D. F. Sabo (Eds.), *Masculinities, gender relations, and sport,* (pp. 263–285). London: Sage.

Dworkin, S. L., & Messner, M. A. (1999). Just do . . . what?: Sport, bodies, gender. In J. Lorber, M. M. Ferree, & B. Hess (Eds.), *Revisioning gender* (pp. 341–364). Thousand Oaks, CA: Sage.

Dyson, M. E. (1993). Be like Mike? Michael Jordan and the pedagogy of desire. *Cultural Studies, 7*(1), 64–72.

Eastman, S. T., & Billings, A. C. (2001). Biased voices of sports: Racial and gender stereotyping in college basketball announcing. *The Howard Journal of Communications, 12,* 183–201.

Edwards, H. (1969). *The revolt of the Black athlete.* New York: Free Press.

Edwards, H. (1973). *The sociology of sport.* Homewood, IL: Dorsey Press.

Francis, M. E. (1990). *Coverage of African American basketball athletes in* Sports Illustrated. Unpublished master's thesis, University of Oregon, Eugene, Oregon.

Goldman, R., & Papson, S. (1998). *Nike culture.* Thousand Oaks, CA: Sage.

Green, T. S. (1993). The future of African-American female athletes. In D. D. Brooks & R. C. Althouse (Eds.), *Racism in college athletics: The African-American athletes' experience* (pp. 205–223). Morgantown, WV: Fitness Information Technology.

Greenberg, B., & Brand, J. (1994). Minorities and the mass media: 1970s to 1990s. In J. Bryant & D. Zillmann (Eds.), *Media effects: Advances in theory and research* (pp. 273–314). Hillsdale, NJ: Lawrence Erlbaum Associates.

Hall, S. (1980). Encoding/decoding. In S. Hall, D. Hobson, A. Lowe, & P. Willis (Eds.), *Culture, media, language: Working papers in cultural studies, 1972–79* (pp. 128–138). London: Hutchison.

Hall, S. (1985). The White of their eyes: Racist ideologies and the media. In G. Dines & J. M. Humez (Eds.), *Gender, race, and class in media* (pp. 18–27). Thousand Oaks, CA: Sage.

Hartmann, D. (2000). Rethinking the relationships between sport and race in American culture: Golden ghettos and contested terrain. *Sociology of Sport Journal, 17,* 229–253.

Hoose, P. M. (1989). *Necessities: Racial barriers in American sports.* New York: Random House.

Jackson, D. Z. (1987, June 14). Stereotyping on the airwaves. *Newsday,* pp. 2–4.

Jackson, D. Z. (1989, January 22). Calling the plays in Black and White. *The Boston Globe,* pp. A30, A33.

Jackson, S. J. (1998). Life in the (mediated) Faust lane: Ben Johnson, national affect and the 1988 crisis of Canadian identity. *International Review for the Sociology of Sport, 33*(3), 227–238.

Jamieson, K. M. (2000). Reading Nancy Lopez: Decoding representations of race, class, and sexuality. In S. Birrell, & M. G. McDonald (Eds.), *Reading sport: Critical essays on power and representation* (pp. 144–165). Boston: Northeastern University Press.

Johnson, L., & Roediger, D. (1997). "Hertz, don't it?" Becoming colorless and staying Black in the crossover of O. J. Simpson. In T. Morrison & C. B. Lacour (Eds.), *Birth of a nation'hood: Gaze, script, and spectacle in the O. J. Simpson case* (pp. 197–239). New York: Pantheon Books.

Kellner, D. (1996). Sports, media culture, and race: Some reflections on Michael Jordan. *Sociology of Sport Journal, 13,* 458–468.

King, C. R., & Springwood, C. F. (2001a). *Beyond the cheers: Race as spectacle in college sport.* Albany, NY: State University of New York Press.

King, C. R., & Springwood, C. F. (2001b). *Team spirits: The Native American mascot controversy.* Lincoln: University of Nebraska Press.

King, C. R., Staurowsky, E. J., Baca, L., Davis, L. R., & Pewewardy, C. (2002). Of polls and race prejudice: *Sports Illustrated*'s errant "Indian Wars." *Journal of Sport and Social Issues, 26*(4), 381–402.

King, S. (1993). The politics of the body and the body politic: Magic Johnson and the ideology of AIDS. *Sociology of Sport Journal, 10,* 270–285.

Klein, A. (2000). Latinizing Fenway Park: A cultural critique of the Boston Red Sox, their fans, and the media. *Sociology of Sport Journal, 17*(4), 403–422.

Kusz, K. W. (2001a). Andre Agassi and Generation X: Reading White masculinity in 1990s America. In D. L. Andrews & S. J. Jackson (Eds.), *Sport stars: The cultural politics of sporting celebrity* (pp. 51–69). London: Routledge.

Kusz, K. W. (2001b). "I want to be the minority": The politics of youthful White masculinities in sport and popular culture in 1990s America. *Journal of Sport and Social Issues, 25*(4), 390–416.

Kusz, K. (2001c). Jerry Maguire: Reading the politics of the White male redemption. *International Review for the Sociology of Sport, 36*(1), 83–89.

Lafrance, M., & Rail, G. (2001). Excursions into otherness: Understanding Dennis Rodman and the limits of subversive action. In D. L. Andrews & S. J. Jackson (Eds.), *Sport stars: The cultural politics of sporting celebrity* (pp. 36–50). London: Routledge.

Long, J., & Hylton, K. (2002). Shades of White: An examination of whiteness in sport. *Leisure Studies, 21*(2), 87–103.

Lule, J. (1995). The rape of Mike Tyson: Race, the press and symbolic types. *Critical Studies in Mass Communication, 12*(2), 176–195.

Lumpkin, A., & Williams, L. D. (1991). An analysis of *Sports Illustrated* feature articles, 1954–1987. *Sociology of Sport Journal, 8*, 16–32.

Maharaj, G. (1997). Talking trash: Late capitalism, Black (re)productivity, and professional basketball. *Social Text, 50*(1), 97–110.

McDonald, M. G. (1996). Michael Jordan's family values: Marketing, meaning, and post-Reagan America. *Sociology of Sport Journal, 13*, 344–365.

McDonald, M. G., & Andrews, D. L. (2001). Michael Jordan: Corporate sport and postmodern celebrity-hood. In D. L. Andrews & S. J. Jackson (Eds.), *Sport stars: The cultural politics of sporting celebrity* (pp. 20–35). New York: Routledge.

McDonald, M. G., & Birrell, S. (1999). Reading sport critically: A methodology for interrogating power. *Sociology of Sport Journal, 16*, 283–300.

McKay, J. (1995). "Just do it": Corporate sports slogans and the political economy of enlightened racism. *Discourse: Studies in the Cultural Politics of Education, 16*(2), 191–201.

Messner, M. A. (1992). *Power at play: Sports and the problem of masculinity.* Boston, MA: Beacon.

Messner, M. A., & Sabo, D. F. (Eds.). (1994). *Sex, violence, and power in sports: Rethinking masculinity.* Freedom, CA: The Crossing Press.

Messner, M. A., & Solomon, W. S. (1993). Outside the frame: Newspaper coverage of the Sugar Ray Leonard wife abuse story. *Sociology of Sport Journal, 10*(2), 119–134.

Mosher, S. D. (1995). Whose dreams? Basketball and celluloid America. *Journal of Sport and Social Issues, 19*(3), 318–322.

Murrell, A. J., & Curtis, E. M. (1994). Causal attributions of performance for Black and White quarterbacks in the NFL: A look at the sports pages. *Journal of Sport and Social Issues, 18*(3), 224–233.

Oglesby, C. A. (1981). Myths and realities of Black women in sport. In T. S. Green, C. A. Oglesby, A. Alexander, & N. Franke (Eds.), *Black women in sport* (pp. 1–13). Reston, VA: American Alliance for Health, Physical Education, Recreation and Dance.

Radway, J. (1991). *Reading the romance: Women, patriarchy, and popular literature.* Chapel Hill, NC: University of North Carolina Press.

Real, M. (1989). *Super media: A cultural studies approach.* Newbury Park, CA: Sage.

Robbins, B. (1997). Head fake: Mentorship and mobility in *Hoop Dreams. Social Text, 50*, 111–120.

Rodriguez, G. S. (2002). Saving face, place, and race: Oscar de la Hoya and the "All-American" dreams of U.S. boxing. In J. Bloom & M. N. Willard (Eds.), *Sports matters: Race, recreation, and culture* (pp. 279–298). New York: New York University Press.

Rowe, D., McKay, J., & Miller, T. (2000). Panic sport and the racialized masculine body. In J. McKay, M. Messner, & D. F. Sabo (Eds.), *Masculinities, gender relations, and sport* (pp. 245–262). London: Sage.

Sabo, D. F., & Jansen, S. C. (1994). Seen but not heard: Images of Black men in sports media. In M. A. Messner, & D. F. Sabo (Eds.), *Sex, violence, and power in sports: Rethinking masculinity* (pp. 150–160). Freedom, CA: The Crossing Press.

Sabo, D. F., & Jansen, S. C. (1998). Prometheus unbound: Constructions of masculinity the sports media. In L. A. Wenner (Ed.), *MediaSport* (pp. 202–217). Newbury Park, CA: Sage.

Sabo, D. F., Jansen, S. C., Tate, D., Duncan, M. C., & Leggett, S. (1996). Televising international sport: Race, ethnicity, and nationalistic bias. *Journal of Sport and Social Issues, 20*(1), 7–21.

Sailes, G. (1993). An investigation of campus stereotypes: The myth of Black athletic superiority and the dumb jock stereotype. *Sociology of Sport Journal, 10*, 88–97.

Sandell, J. (1995). Out of the ghetto and into the marketplace: *Hoop Dreams* and the commodification of marginality. *Socialist Review, 25*(2), 57–82.

Scraton, S. (2001). Reconceptualising race, gender, and sport: The contribution of Black feminism. In B. Carrington & I. McDonald (Eds.), *Race, sport, and British society* (pp. 170–187). London: Routledge.

Shropshire, K. L. (2000). Deconstructing the NBA. In T. Boyd & K. L. Shropshire (Eds.), *Basketball Jones: America above the rim* (pp. 75–89). New York: New York University Press.

Simons, H. D. (2003). Race and penalized sports behaviors. *International Review for the Sociology of Sport, 38*, 5–22.

Sloop, J. M. (1997). Mike Tyson and the perils of discursive constraints: Boxing, race, and the assumption of guilt. In A. Baker & T. Boyd (Eds.), *Out of bounds: Sports, media, and the politics of identity* (pp. 102–122). Bloomington, IN: Indiana University Press.

Smith, B. (Ed.). (1983). *Home girls: A Black feminist anthology.* New York: Kitchen Table Women of Color Press.

Smith, E. (1990). The genetically superior athlete: Myth or reality. In T. Anderson (Ed.), *Black studies: Theory, method, and cultural perspectives* (pp. 120–131). Pullman, WA: Washington State University Press.

Smith, E. (1995). Hope via basketball: The ticket out of the ghetto? *Journal of Sport and Social Issues, 19*(3), 312–317.

Soar, M. (2001). Engines and acolytes of consumption: Black male bodies, advertising, and the laws of thermodynamics. *Body and Society, 7*(4), 37–55.

Staples, R., & Jones, T. (1985). Culture, ideology and Black television images. *The Black Scholar, 16*(3), 10–20.

Thomas, R. (1996). Black faces still rare in the press box. In R. E. Lapchick (Ed.), *Sport in society: Equal opportunity of business as usual?* (pp. 212–233). Thousand Oaks, CA: Sage.

Tucker, L. (2003). Blackballed: Basketball and representations of the black male athlete. *American Behavioral Scientist, 47*(3), 306–328.

Uchacz, C. (1998). Black sports images in transition: The impact of Tiger's roar. In G. Sailes (Ed.), *African Americans in sport: Contemporary themes* (pp. 53–66). New Brunswick, NJ: Transaction Publishers.

van Sterkenburg, J., & Knoppers, A. (2004). Dominant discourses about race/ethnicity and gender in sport practice and performance. *International Review for the Sociology of Sport, 39*(3), 301–321.

Walton, T. (2001). The Sprewell/Carlesimo episode: Unacceptable violence or unacceptable victim? *Sociology of Sport Journal, 18*, 345–357.

Wenner, L. A. (1991). One part alcohol, one part sport, one part dirt, stir gently: Beer commercials and television sports. In L. R. Vande Berg & L. A. Wenner (Eds.), *Television criticism: Approaches and applications* (pp. 388–407). New York: Longman.

Wenner, L. A. (1994). Drugs, sport, and media influence: Can media inspire constructive attitudinal change? *Journal of Sport and Social Issues, 18*(3), 282–292.

Wenner, L. A. (1995). The good, the bad, and the ugly: Race, sport, and the public eye. *Journal of Sport and Social Issues, 19*(3), 227–231.

Wenner, L. A. (Ed.). (1998). *MediaSport.* London: Routledge.

Williams, L. D. (1994). Sportswomen in Black and White: Sports history from an Afro-American perspective. In P. J. Creedon (Ed.), *Women, media, and sport* (pp. 45–66). Thousand Oaks, CA: Sage.

Wilson, B. (1997). "Good blacks" and "bad blacks": Media constructions of African-American athletes in Canadian basketball. *International Review for the Sociology of Sport, 32*(2), 177–189.

Wilson, B., & Sparks, R. (1996). "It's gotta be the shoes": Youth, race, and sneaker commercials. *Sociology of Sport Journal, 13*(4), 398–427.

Wonsek, P. L. (1992). College basketball on television: A study of racism in the media. *Media, Culture and Society, 14*, 449–461.

28

Crouching Tiger, Hidden Blackness: Tiger Woods and the Disappearance of Race

Davis W. Houck

Florida State University

Truth be told, I was supposed to be about 80 miles further north along the California coast. On this beautiful mid-June day, instead of working through dusty stacks of archives at the Hoover Institution on War, Revolution, and Peace at Stanford University, I was taking in the first round of the 2000 U.S. Open golf tournament at Pebble Beach. It wasn't the first time that I'd visited America's most famous seaside golf course; in the early 1990s, a group of us would head south and west to take in the sights at the Bing Crosby Pro-Am, now the AT&T Pro-Am. The tournament was a unique mixture of professional golf and *People Magazine*: Clint Eastwood was a regular attendee; so was Kevin Costner and a host of professional athletes.

But professional golf in the late-Bush, early-Clinton years lacked one important person: Tiger Woods.

Over the past decade, I've followed Woods' career carefully: I watched with curiosity his three consecutive wins at the nation's most elite amateur event, the U.S. Amateur. Against improbable odds, the young Woods would rally first against Tripp Kuehne, then Buddy Marucci, and finally Steve Scott. Nobody had ever won three Amateurs in a row—not even Jack Nicklaus. I soon learned that Woods had also won three straight U.S. Junior Amateur Championships, the most prestigious event for junior golfers. Then it was on to late summer and Tiger's improbable attempt to win his Tour card, which would make him exempt on the Professional Golfers Association (PGA) Tour.[1] Not only did he earn his card, he won two of the first seven professional tournaments that he entered. It was such a stunning and unlikely beginning that the bastion of American sports journalism, *Sports Illustrated*, named

---

[1] Full exemption on the 1997 PGA Tour required Woods to finish in the top 125 money winners on the Tour, an improbable feat given that he had but seven events from which to earn enough money to qualify.

him its 1996 Sportsman of the Year.[2] Then in the spring of 1997, amidst Augusta's Azalea splendor, I was one of the 44 million who witnessed Tiger's record-breaking, 12-shot triumph at the Masters, his first major professional victory.[3] From there I was hooked: I witnessed his dominance of the Tour throughout 1999, after revamping his golf swing in 1998 with coach Butch Harmon. Along the way came the incredible endorsement deals: the $40 million, five-year deal to endorse Nike, the deals with American Express, Wheaties, Rolex, Titleist, and later General Motors—all of whom paid millions to put a golfer on pop culture's center stage. A golfer, of all people!

My interest in Tiger Woods stems from the game we share: Growing up in small-town Ohio, I excelled on the local golf scene. In college, I made several all-conference teams and even a few all-American teams. At one point I'd given serious consideration to a career in professional golf. And so, I'd come to see Tiger Woods at the 2000 U.S. Open, not the splendor of Pebble Beach, nor the tributes to the fallen 1999 champion, Payne Stewart. It was a sort of personal inspection: I wanted to see for myself just how good this kid Woods was. Golf can be watched on television, but it can't be truly appreciated in a two-dimensional medium. Unlike most sports, golf's arena is always changing—even the same course plays very differently from day to day, especially a seaside course like Pebble Beach. It is a game to be watched, felt, experienced in corporeal ways.

A friend and I strategically positioned ourselves close to the 15th teeing area, a fairly short par-4 hole of which Tiger, no doubt, had great memories: Just four months earlier he'd made a dramatic eagle (a score of two on a par four) at the 15th hole on his way to winning his sixth tournament in a row, coming back from a seven-shot deficit in just seven holes. I wanted to see Tiger hit his driver, the club of maximum distance, and the club that has made Tiger famous with golf galleries around the world. As for why we weren't following Tiger around the entire course, the galleries surrounding him are just too large to see many golf swings. Walking the course with Tiger's pairing means that you'll see some great scenery, but you won't see much of him. So we staked out our ground and waited.

Finally, after about an hour of waiting, Tiger arrived at the 15th hole, having made a birdie at the par-five 14th look very routine. He was now leading the tournament already early in the first round; it was a lead he wouldn't relinquish. The gallery was immense; security guards seemed everywhere; writers and photographers and officials recorded his every gesture and movement. His two playing partners—Jose Maria Olazabel and Jesper Parnevik—were just an afterthought. The buzz was for only one person.

I confess to being disappointed. It was all so, well, ordinary. There was Tiger, just a few feet from me. He looked just like I'd seen him a million times on television, all concentration, quiet and serious, looking down the fairway. There were the ubiquitous swooshes that Nike paid him so much to advertise. There were the trademark

---

[2]The article that came out of *Sports Illustrated*'s Sportsman of the Year issue was Gary Smith's now famous "The Chosen One" (Smith, 1996) Many felt that Woods didn't deserve such acclaim; it was the first time, one writer noted, that the award had been given "on spec."

[3]A *major* championship refers to one of four annual tournaments: the Masters, the U.S. Open, the British Open, or the PGA Championship. To win all four is golf's Holy Grail, the grand slam. Sportswriters credited Woods with the "Tiger Slam" when he won four major championships in a row, but not in the same calendar year. To understand the importance of the majors, see John Feinstein's (1999) book by the same name.

black golf shoes, again from Nike. The dark grey slacks and blue shirt, I'd seen before. His caddie, Steve Williams, looked just like I'd pictured him. The golf bag with Buick emblazoned on the side looked identical to the one on television. Even the tee shot he eventually hit—with his driver—didn't stand out from the other golfers whom we'd watched. He was very human.

Upon reflection, it dawned on me that Tiger is just that: flesh, blood, and sinew, just like the rest of us. Perhaps I'd expected a Jesus moment—a miracle that we could all tell our grandchildren about, how the Great Tiger Woods had reconfigured the laws of nature to his own improbable ends—yet again. Perhaps all those mediated images, all the hyperbolic representations, had led me to believe that Tiger was so fundamentally different from other golfers that something transcendent could and would happen whenever he hit a golf ball. Or maybe when he was just standing there waiting to play. And that body of his: It clearly belonged to him. There was nothing remarkable about it. Anyone could inhabit such a form. It wasn't a Herculean body; it wasn't the "Cablinasian" body that Tiger had discussed back in 1997 with Oprah; it certainly didn't glow, gleam, or levitate like a body singled out as The Chosen One might be expected; it didn't even produce any thunder.

Tiger would shoot 65 on this day. He would go on to win professional golf's most demanding tournament by the laughable margin of 15 strokes, the largest margin in the history of major championships. It would also be the first major championship in his string of four in a row, or what has been called the Tiger Slam. No one in golf's long history had ever won four straight major championships, in the same calendar year or not.

Perhaps ironically, the very real, material, embodied Tiger Woods that I'd witnessed and experienced with my own body on the 15th hole at Pebble Beach in the first round of the 2000 U.S. Open seemed to be more fiction than fact, a mysterious, perhaps even hollow, three-dimensional signifier in an age of two-dimensional representation. More than anyone else, he has seen to that. And his dad, too. In this chapter I map the trajectory of mediated representational choices made by Woods and his advisors. Beginning with the much-celebrated "Hello World" advertising campaign in the summer of 1996, and concluding with the gender flap that played out at Augusta National in 2002 and spilled over to Annika Sorrenstam in 2003, Tiger Woods has refashioned himself—from a proponent of racial change and activism to a neutered, nonraced establishment golfer. In charting this trajectory, the motivation behind such representational changes is also considered.

From the beginning, Tiger Woods has been carefully packaged, a meticulously choreographed mediated representation. The first and most important choreographer was his father, Earl Woods. Through his son's phenomenal success, we have come to know something of Tiger's father. But even before Tiger Woods started winning important golf tournaments, Earl Woods was already working feverishly on his son's image and fame. The two-year-old Tiger appeared on national television—*The Mike Douglas Show*—to hit golf balls into a net before an incredulous Bob Hope and Jimmy Stewart. Three years later, Tiger was nationally featured in a spot on *That's Incredible!* By all accounts, Earl Woods loved the attention just as much, if not more, than his son. We're left with several questions: Is it fatherly pride that puts Earl Woods in front of the nation's cameras, to give his son an extended bear hug after winning the Masters—in 1997, in 2001, and yet again in 2002? Why not hug off camera? Is it odd that his son's ability to win golf tournaments has sanctioned

Earl Woods to give parenting advice in several books?[4] What of his failed first marriage? What of his failed second marriage?[5] What of his three other children whom we know nothing about? Even now, Earl Woods gives his son very public advice on women generally and marriage specifically, advice tinged with misogyny. Why not offer the advice in private, away from the media's prying eyes and ears?

In much the same way that Feder (1995) argued that the media often codes, and thereby contains, the success of many female athletes within the context of family, so too with Earl Woods. The only difference is that Tiger's father actively seeks out such publicity; in so doing, Earl Woods often becomes the focal point of media interest. To take but one now infamous example of mediated self-aggrandizement, at the November 1996 Fred Haskins Award dinner to honor the nation's best collegiate golfer, Earl Woods wanted to speak, of course. Here is how he introduced his son before a large crowd, with media present:

> Please forgive me...but sometimes I get very emotional...when I talk about my son...My heart...fills with so...much...joy...when I realize...that this young man...is going to be able...to help so many people.... He will transcend this game...and bring to the world...a humanitarianism...which has never been known before. (Smith, 1996, p. 1)

Heady praise, for sure, but Earl Woods was just rounding into prophetic form:

> The world will be a better place to live in...by virtue of his existence...and his presence...I acknowledge only a small part in that...in that I know that I was personally selected by God himself...to nurture this young man...and bring him to the point where he can make his contribution to humanity...This is my treasure...Please accept it...and use it wisely...Thank you." (p. 1)

This is the voice of a prophet, someone who knows the mind of God, someone who can see into that future. Though his son's birth was not quite the virgin birth, Earl Woods nonetheless manages rhetorically to play the role, if not of Yahweh himself, of at least an important patrilineal player in this God-ordained drama. *Sports Illustrated*, whether being ironic, tragic, or comedic, or perhaps none of the above, titled the lengthy piece where the quotation first appeared "The Chosen One." In the Cosmos-according-to-Earl, many have been left to wonder: Would God knowingly allow his Chosen One to miss the cut at the Canadian Open? This would be the functional equivalent of Christ turning water into, well...water, or raising Lazarus from the dead only to have him vapor lock on his way home. Was Earl Woods claiming that God had given His blessing to the deaths of more than 58,000 Americans and the maiming of a generation so that he could meet his Thai-wife—Kultida (Tida)—during a tour of duty in Vietnam?

Maybe Earl had been drinking during the Haskins. Maybe *SI*'s Gary Smith hadn't heard him aright. And so the press asked Earl Woods if he was serious. As it turns

---

[4]To date Earl Woods has authored three books: *Training a Tiger* (1997), *Playing Through* (1998), and *Start Something* (2000). Perhaps in keeping with the mission of the Tiger Woods Foundation, of which Earl Woods is CEO, much of the self-help emphasis in some of the books is targeted to children and their parents.

[5]While Earl and Kultida Woods have not divorced, it's clear that they are separated and live very separate lives, Kultida in the more posh Tustin while Earl continues to live in Tiger's boyhood home in Cypress, California, 35 miles southeast of Los Angeles (Owen, 2001).

out, no one had been drinking to excess at the Haskins: "Tiger will do more than any other man in history to change the course of humanity. More than any of them [Muhammad Ali and Arthur Ashe], because he is more charismatic, more educated" (Smith, 1996, pp. 2–3). Even more than Gandhi and Nelson Mandela? Earl Woods was asked.

> Yes, because he has a larger forum than any of them. Because he's playing a sport that's international. Because he is qualified through his ethnicity to accomplish miracles. He's the bridge between East and West. There is no limit. I don't know yet exactly what form this will take. But he is the Chosen One. The world is just getting a taste of his power. (p. 3)

Even Tida seems to have bought into her erstwhile husband's hokum: "Tiger has Thai, African, Chinese, American Indian and European blood. He can hold everyone together. He is the Universal Child" (Smith, 1996, p. 7). Over the intervening several years, family Woods hasn't relented in touting their son's off-the-course potential. After meeting then South African president Nelson Mandela, Earl Woods gushed, "It was the first time Tiger met a human being who was equal to him, who was as powerful as Tiger is" (Mariotti, 2001, p. 94).

Sportswriters and critics around the country reacted with predictable cynicism to Earl Woods' comments: This was just the sort of hype that fathers of tennis stars Mary Pierce and Jennifer Capriati and football player Todd Marinovich used to run their cash-cow kids into the ground. And we shouldn't forget that Earl's initial prophesying was made less than four months after his son had turned pro. Said Art Taylor, associate director of the Center for the Study of Sport in Society at Northeastern University, "Thank God he survived his father because I think his father is the worst example of what can happen in sports—the pushy parent" (Morrissey, 1997, p. C18). But Earl Woods wasn't just a pushy parent; his presence, even less than a year into his son's professional career, had become conspicuous. Sports psychologist Bob Rotella (Markon, 1997, p. D1) wondered, "Why does his dad want to take all the credit for Tiger Woods?"

Race has also been important to Earl Woods' choreography of his son's image. The "humanity" to which he refers in a previous quotation is seen by Earl's oracles to mean improving race relations, thus the favorable comparison with Mandela. Race has figured quite prominently in his carefully scripted Tiger Woods Story. For example, Earl let it be known that his own battles with racism prefigured his son's; that is, growing up in Manhatten, Kansas, the youngest of six children, Earl Woods became the first Black baseball player at Kansas State University and in his conference. Traveling with the team was difficult in the Jim Crow United States Earl also played up his role in integrating a lily white, middle-class neighborhood in Cypress, California, where he and Tida would raise Tiger.[6] Similarly, Tiger is also seen overcoming racism, when, as a five-year-old and on the first day of kindergarten, older White schoolboys tied him to a tree while yelling racial epithets. Racism, too, lurks at the local Navy golf course in southern California where young Tiger was prohibited from playing.

And of course with his victory in the 1997 Masters, Tiger Woods was slamming the door on the last bastion of racial privilege in the United States. He was also finally bringing the PGA Tour into twentieth-century race relations, an organization

---

[6]For more on the issue of race and Earl Woods, see Strege (1997).

which until 1961 limited membership to "Professional golfers of the Caucasian race" (Owen, 2001, p. 179). It was very hard to miss race and the 1997 Masters: Not only did Tiger openly link his achievements to the Black golfers who had preceded him along professional golf's segregated trail,[7] but also Fuzzy Zoeller's racially loaded comments, picked up by a television camera, quickly fanned the flames of country club racism around the country.[8] Woods' 12-stroke humiliation of the field was particularly sweet for those wanting to read race into the event: Augusta, in the Old South, had been home to the idea, manifested over nearly 40 years, that Whites played the golf and Blacks carried the bag. The man who ruled the Masters for many decades, Clifford Roberts, was reported to have said to one Black golfer, "As long as I live there will be nothing at the Masters besides black caddies and white golfers" (Grant, 2001, W10). In many ways, Roberts got his wish: Until 1983, White professional golfers were forced to employ Black caddies at Augusta National. Only in 1975, two years before Roberts committed suicide on Augusta National's eighth hole, did a Black man, Lee Elder, first compete in the Masters.[9]

But even before the 1997 Masters, there was Earl Woods, the Greater Milwaukee Open, and "Hello World." In late August 1996, following his unprecedented third U.S. Amateur title, Tiger weighed the options of turning professional or returning for his junior year at Stanford University, where he had dominated college golf the two previous years. Less than a month before classes began for fall term, Tiger opted to turn pro; his professional debut would take place at a most unlikely venue: the Greater Milwaukee Open, a low-level tournament stop on the PGA Tour. ABC Sports suddenly and serendipitously had a major media event on its hands: The phenomenon known as Tiger Woods would officially take up residence on the Tour.

Before even teeing off, Tiger, with his father as advisor, signed a five-year, $40-million endorsement deal with Nike—by far the largest single endorsement deal for a player in the history of golf. Hughes Norton of the International Management Group (IMG) had negotiated the deal with Nike. Norton and IMG had courted the Woods family for years, even putting Earl on the payroll as a talent scout. Nike CEO Phil Knight had also pursued Tiger for years, going so far as to be part of Tiger's gallery at the 1996 U.S. Amateur. Part of the drama outside the ropes at the Greater Milwaukee Open was Nike's ad campaign featuring Tiger Woods. At a press conference earlier that week announcing his decision to turn professional, Woods began somewhat haltingly, "Well, I guess, hello world" (Strege, 1997, p. 192). Shortly thereafter, Nike began an advertising blitz that made some sense of Woods' cosmopolitan but awkward introduction; in the *Wall Street Journal*, a three-page $324,000 spread appeared, featuring "Hello World" and the ubiquitous Nike swoosh; on television, Nike pulled all of its planned weekend advertising so as not to clutter its "Hello World" spot. In the television advertisement, Nike wasn't selling its latest golf line; it was selling part of Earl Woods' vision. Over short video clips of his successful amateur career was this narrative account already familiar to so many golf fans:

Hello world.
I shot in the 70s when I was 8.

---

[7]For a history of African-American professional golfers, see Dawkins and Kinloch (2000).

[8]A camera crew from CNN picked up Zoeller's remarks about a potential Woods victory at the Masters: "The little boy's playing great out there. Just tell him not to serve fried chicken at the (champions) dinner next year. Or collard greens or whatever it is they serve" (see Feinstein, 1998, p. 64).

[9]For an interesting and revealing history of Augusta National and the Masters, see Sampson (1998).

I shot in the 60s when I was 12.
I won the US Junior Amateur when I was 15.
Hello world.
I played in the Nissan Open when I was 16.
Hello world.
I won the US Amateur when I was 18.
I played in the Masters when I was 19.
I am the only man to win three consecutive US Amateur titles.
Hello world.

So far, so good; the story was the standard protégé account that Earl Woods had so carefully packaged through the years. But the ad was not quite finished:

There are still courses in the US I am not allowed to play because of the color of my skin.
I've heard I am not ready for you.
Are you ready for me? (Cole & Andrews, 2001, p. 75)

Set to a haunting, percussive score, the "Hello World" spot had the sports world talking—and not for the rehearsal of Tiger's golfing achievements. As Elliott (1996) noted, "The message leaps from the television screen with the impact of a 3-wood to the forehead" (p. 1). It was racial discrimination that was being foregrounded, not biography; the ad was personal, even confrontational. Tiger was clear about the ad's intentions: "I've been kicked off golf courses for my skin color. I've had death threats, hate mail . . . A lot of people have been denied the privileges of just playing. It's nice to have it [race] in the open. Let's not shy away from the issue any more" (Elliott, 1996, p. 1). The ad, claimed Woods, was simply opaque truth telling: "It's just clips from the past, but I think it's a message that's been long awaited. Being a non-white person, I've lived through this. Nike is just telling the truth" (Weyler, 1996, p. C1).

The agenda was set: Nike, Tiger Woods, and Earl Woods were confronting a worldwide audience with skin color, discrimination, and golf's past/present. Some sportswriters hated the ad; as Custred (1996, p. 27) observed, "few expected the first commercial made by Woods to be quite so provocative." Bob Garfield of Advertising Age (Scarborough, 1996) was more specific: "I hated the Tiger Woods thing because it was phony. It was phony because Tiger Woods was not a victim of racism. And they're exploiting the race issue to sell golf shoes to black people and I think that's cynical" (p. A2).

But many loved it, for one simple reason: In the mediated age of Michael Jordan, where activism and politics took a back seat to the revenue column, here was a preternaturally talented Black athlete willing to take on institutional racism in his very first ad campaign. The fact that Tiger Woods couldn't name a course where he would be barred from playing didn't matter. This was the athlete and the message that so many activists had been waiting for. Whether Earl Woods helped to create the ad isn't known. What is known is that he approved it. Thus would commence the "humanity" of Tiger Woods, the ability to change the world by being a prodigiously talented Black golfer. Three things, though, would happen on the way to World Racial Accord: Michael Jordan/Nike, Oprah, and Charles Pierce.

Before getting to these three things, though, Tiger Woods was able to overcome the very loud buzz over the "Hello World" advertising campaign by showcasing his golfing talents to an incredulous public. Woods made the cut at Milwaukee, but finished far back of the leader, in a tie for 60th place.[10] So much for Woods taking over the game; after all, Scott Verplank had won a tournament even before turning professional, as had Phil Mickelson. Ben Crenshaw actually won his first professional event. Maybe "Hello, Sheboygan" might have been a more apt salutation, some cynics felt. Woods soon proved his already-boisterous critics wrong: He won two of the next six tournaments he entered, at one point finishing in the top five in five consecutive events. He had done the improbable: he had won his Tour card in just a few tournaments, even qualifying for the prestigious Tour Championship by making the Tour's top 30 on the official money list. The naysayers from Milwaukee had been quickly silenced.

The momentum carried over into 1997 at the Mercedes Championship, where only Tour winners from 1996 were invited. Before an elite field not far from where he grew up, Woods birdied the last four holes of his third round to force a final round showdown with the formidable Tom Lehman, the 1996 PGA Player of the Year. A driving rain, though, cancelled the fourth round, sending Woods and Lehman into a one-hole playoff to decide the winner. Lehman hit first. He put his tee shot on the par three into the water. Woods could play safely and win the tournament. Instead he sent a towering seven-iron at the pin; he almost holed the shot, as it ended up less than a foot away. The legend was growing.

The legend became legendary at the 1997 Masters, Tiger Woods' first major championship that he had entered as a professional. In addition to breaking several scoring records with his 18-under par-performance, Tiger was also setting some Nielsen records: The final round during which he was never challenged turned in the highest rating ever recorded for a golf tournament. Keep in mind that the only drama of the last round was by how much Woods would win and whether he would break several scoring records. It's rare to garner an audience for a blowout, but the nation watched intently as Woods conquered Augusta National and a field of the world's best golfers. Even President Bill Clinton watched and later called to congratulate Woods.

While Woods' on-course play dominated golf discussion in the spring of 1997, off the course, Nike was already rethinking Tiger Woods' public image. In late 1996, Nike debuted a second Woods advertising campaign, much different from "Hello World." Shot in black and white, young golfers from across the racial, ethnic, gender, and class spectrum repeat the same four-word mantra, "I am Tiger Woods." Using super slow-motion technology, Woods closes the ad by driving a golf ball towards a distant and imperceptible target. While certainly foregrounding the issue of diversity, "I am Tiger Woods" was seemingly far from confrontational and controversial. Many noticed a striking similarity with that other Nike advertising genius, Michael Jordan. The ontological flip side of the ad was the catchy "Be like Mike" jingle put together by Gatorade. Noted Thill (1997), "Tiger Woods [sic] marketability and skill are so immense that Nike's campaign took the only logical, ontological slogan left over after the Jordan reign: 'I am Tiger Woods'" (para. 13).

Beyond Jordan, though, there was controversy. Commenting on the ad, Holland (1997) noted cynically, "It's all so dramatic, so inspiring. So hypocritical" (p. D1).

---

[10]Most professional golf events have a cut after two days of play or 36 holes. Typically, the field is cut in half, with the bottom half essentially being expelled from the tournament. It should also be noted that, unlike most sports, golf money is typically not guaranteed. Those who miss a cut don't get paid. Amazingly, Woods has missed but one cut in his six years on the Tour.

There was only one problem with the "I am Tiger Woods" spot: It featured a young girl. Woods' instructor, "Butch" Harmon, was the head professional at Lochinvar Golf Club, a male-only golf mecca just north of Houston where Tiger occasionally worked with Harmon. When confronted with the issue of gender discrimination at the golf course, Woods replied, "I can't be a champion of all causes." *USA Today's* Christine Brennan commented, "If it were an issue of race, it would be huge. That little girl who's in that commercial ["I am Tiger Woods"]... cannot walk onto the golf course where Tiger Woods trains with his pro" (Holland, 1997, p. D1). Tiger Woods with a vagina, even a prepubescent one, couldn't be Tiger Woods after all.

Beyond the minicontroversy of the second Nike advertising campaign, it seems clear in hindsight that the Michael Jordanizing of Tiger Woods had already begun. Slowly, subtly, Earl Woods' racial messiah was being replaced by an apolitical, sexually neutered, significantly whitened golfer. Tiger Woods was getting image advice from the most imaged and imagined man on the planet. When their friendship began is unclear, but by the spring of 1997, Tiger gushed at a press conference (T. Woods, 1997):

> He's [Michael Jordan] one of my best friends and is one of—he's a big brother to me, helps me out... off the court he handles himself so well, a true gentleman, and that's what it's all about, and that's one of the reasons I look up to Mike. That's one of the reasons I said I'd like to be the Michael Jordan of golf, not only because of his on-court performances but just the way he conducts himself in general. (p. 15)

If there's anything that sport scholars and journalists agree on, it's that Michael Jordan is no political activist, he of "Republican's buy sneakers, too" fame when asked to support the black Democratic candidate Harvey Gantt in his bid to unseat North Carolina's senatorial racial provocateur, Jesse Helms.[11] Keown (1997), for example, challenged his readers: "Here's a test: Find even the smallest hint of social conscience in anything Michael Jordan has done. Name one time in which he stood up for something that wasn't directly tied to him or his career" (p. B1). Andrews (2000), writing in the semiotic tradition, come to similar, though perhaps less strident, conclusions as Keown. In one of the better scholarly essays on Jordan, Andrews wrote, "Michael Jordan's carefully engineered charismatic appeal which had such an impact on popularizing the NBA to corporate and middle America alike is not an example of racial transcendence. Rather, it is a case of complicitous racial avoidance" (p. 177). Further, Andrews argues, "Jordan's image was coveted by the media primarily because of its reassuring affinity with the affective investments associated with America's white-dominated national popular culture... his identity has been shrewdly severed from any vestiges of African American culture" (p. 177). In sum, for the sake of monetary gain, Michael Jordan self-consciously allowed himself to be whitened. In the eight years since "Hello World," so too with Tiger Woods. That he often seeks out Jordan's counsel suggests that the

---

[11]Over the past ten years, a number of scholars have taken up the Michael Jordan phenomenon, primarily with an eye towards representation and capitalism; most of that work is collected in Andrews' (2001) anthology titled *Michael Jordan, Inc.* Walter LaFeber's (1999) work on Jordan examines Jordan's international influence. As for other excellent contributions, albeit biographical, to the Jordan corpus, see Smith (1992), Halberstam (1999), and Greene (1993, 1995). I would also recommend Henry Louis Gates' (1998) essay titled "Net Worth."

"Jordanizing" of Tiger Woods has had everything to do with representation, money, and image.

To take but one very prominent example, Nike has featured Woods as a carnival sideshow, someone who can bounce a ball on his golf club for nearly 30 seconds, do some cute tricks while not stopping the bouncing, and then hit the ball in midair. The ad was a sensation, so much so that it spawned a sequel. For advanced golfers, the trick isn't difficult. But that's not the point: From racial spokesman to carni-freak, Tiger Woods has become oh-so-safe. His Nike ads have evolved (degenerated?) steadily to the point where they are solely about him and his success and abilities as a golfer. In his recent Nike ads, for example, a black and white (thus deracialized?) Woods challenges the technicians at Nike to continue the fine work on the golf ball and the driver that enabled him to win several recent tournaments. This is about capitalism translating into sporting success—and thus dollars.

A similar depoliticization can be seen in his ads with Buick, who signed Woods late in 1999 to a five-year, $30-million deal. In one ad, he caricatures himself, teaching a group to mimic his behavior and his press conference statements. In another, a horror parody, he ends the ad by asking, "what, you were expecting Igor?" In a third ad, also for the Buick Rendezvous, Woods borrows from the Wizard of Oz fantasy, "Looks like we're not in Kansas anymore." Asked if he was Tiger Woods by a passenger, he shakes his head, "no." Such a denial of self-signification goes to the heart of the "post-Hello World" Woods. Most recently Earl Woods' messiah has been seen changing the world by carrying on inane conversations with his smart-talking orange headcover. Recalling Anfernee "Penny" Hardaway's confabulations with Lil' Penny, a talking tiger sock is getting far more lines than his benefactor.

Even Earl Woods seems to have picked up on Michael's lead, though for clearly different ends. Recently during an interview with *TV Guide*'s Rob Tannenbaum, Earl imagined a dialogue: "A wife can be a deterrent to a good game of golf. Case in point: 'All you do is practice. Why don't you stay home and have some quality time with me?' 'Honey, I'm a professional golfer.' 'Well, I'm your wife.'" Concluded Earl, "He doesn't need that" (Cushman, 2001). Earl told *Sports Illustrated*'s Reilly (2000) much the same. On the subject of balancing his son's golfing life, Earl editorialized, "[Jack] Nicklaus had his wife and kids for balance. Tiger only has me and his mother. Girlfriends don't do it. Girlfriends are here today, gone tomorrow" (p. 96). So much for Joanna Jagoda, with whom Woods had a lengthy relationship at the time.[12]

But quite aside from Nike and Buick, Tiger has had a very direct hand in marketing himself as not-Black—despite what the Hello World campaign might have been saying about his very blackness. Shortly after winning the 1997 Masters, Woods accepted an invitation to appear on Oprah Winfrey's talk show. His father came with him. In many ways, John Hoberman, whose controversial book *Darwin's Athletes* focuses on Black athletes, the media, and the question of racial genetic differences, presciently forecasted what was coming on *Oprah*: "there's going to be a lot of African-Americans out there who are waiting for this guy to sort of declare his color" (as cited in Morrissey, 1997, p. C18). Referring to an earlier radio show that addressed the question of Woods' race, Hoberman noted, "What I picked up

---

[12]Tiger has taken no small flack for dating white women. One columnist recently asked, "Tiger, can a sistah get a break? What does it take for a sistah to get a date with the world's richest, young black athlete[?] Oops, sorry. Scratch that word, black" (as cited in Clay, 2002). After ending his nearly three-year relationship with Joanna Jagoda, Tiger recently courted and married another blonde-haired, blue-eyed woman, Swedish model Elin Nordegren.

was a certain amount of displeasure with his defining himself as a biracial person...a significant number of black people...are going to want this guy to join the team." The controversial self-definition to which Hoberman was alluding was a press release that Woods put out at the 1995 U. S. Open. The release read in part, "The various media have portrayed me as an African-American, sometimes Asian. In fact, I am both...Truthfully, I feel very fortunate and equally proud to be both African-American and Asian" (Poe, 1997, n.p.).

Before a national audience, Oprah asked him the million-dollar question: How would you classify yourself? Tiger responded with the now famous moniker that he had invented when he was a teenager: He called himself "Cablinasian"—"Ca," Caucasian; "bl," Black; "in," Native American or Indian; "asian," Asian.[13] He explicitly denied being African American; in fact, he didn't like to be called African American. It was a distinction that pleased no one, save perhaps its creator. Perhaps most striking about the term is its contradiction: Just two years prior, Woods had baldly called himself "a non-white person." Now, as one Black woman, Gloria Bashir, noted, such a term "puts Caucasian first" (Wilkerson, 1997, p. 99). Wilkerson noted another contradiction: "It [Cablinasian] seemed both a naive plea for a color-blind, colorless America...and a throwback to the quadroon days of old Louisiana, where people measured their bloodlines by the teaspoon" (p. 99). Nonetheless, Woods had missed The point altogether: The term "'Black' was a political statement, a cultural declaration" (Wilkerson, p. 99). Clarence Paige of the *Chicago Tribune* wasn't at all pleased with the term, stating that it was "the last thing we wanted to hear" (Spiers, 1997, p. 33). Kenneth Shropshire (n.d.) also saw the term as troublesome: "Politically, this broader identification option is problematic. As the numbers of those who consider themselves African American decrease, so could the political power of the African American community" (para. 7).

Tiger's *Oprah* appearance and attempt at self-definition were so controversial that she had a follow-up show—without either Woods present—to adjudicate the matter. *Ebony* immediately rushed into print a lengthy article titled "Black America and Tiger's Dilemma," (1997) which responded directly to the *Oprah* flap and the Cablinasian reference. Hugh P. Price, President of the National Urban League, was somewhat ambivalent on the matter: "As to how Black America should respond to Tiger, I think we should be thrilled and should embrace him as one of us because he is one of us, just as he rightly belongs to other ethnic groups as well." Price clearly gets the larger significance of Cablinasian: It implicates a rhetoric of ownership. Actress Salli Richardson, of mixed race herself, advised: "I think he should probably just be saying I'm mixed, I'm Thai and I'm Black and that's who I am, instead of bringing in all of these other things." The Reverend Jesse Jackson began his remarks thus: "I respect Tiger Woods' personal choice to call himself whatever he chooses. I don't think he meant to be offensive. However, I don't think he understands the politics of the issue or how explosive it is." Jackson was quite explicit about what that political dimension was: "the politics of it is that he runs the risk of making Black people feel that he is disassociating himself from Black people and that he is uncomfortable with Black people." And, as with Price, so too with Jackson: "We are so proud of him, you know; we have a sense that he is ours, and we are his." The rhetoric of ownership, redux. Sharon Robinson, the daughter of America's most important athletic racial signifier, Jackie Robinson, was clearly annoyed

---

[13]For an interesting reading of the Cablinasian term in concert with Oprah's show, see Cole and Andrews (2001) and Uchacz (1998).

by Woods' self-definition. Part of her anger might have stemmed from Tiger's often-revisited snub in which he rejected President Clinton's invitation to celebrate the 50th anniversary of Robinson breaking Major League Baseball's color line. In any case, Robinson stated, "His much-publicized comments concerning his race are a concern to me at best, and downright disturbing to me at worst." She specified further, "I have a problem with his apparent decision to choose his Caucasian and Asian ancestry over his Black heritage." Perhaps because "bl" got lexically squeezed into the middle, Robinson viewed the beginning and ending as far more privileged signifiers. Ultimately, the matter didn't redound to the lexical: "he has to realize that, whether he likes it or not, whether he wants to believe it or not, most people see him as a Black golfer" (Black Am. and Tiger's Dilemma, para.). If Tiger didn't understand this, all he needed to do was recall the Fuzzy Zoeller incident: "If Tiger Woods prefers no racial labeling, that is his right. But it was clear to us all that when Fuzzy Zoeller made a wisecrack to Woods about collard greens and fried chicken . . . the reference was to the fact that this African American had invaded a space long dominated by white men" (Shropshire, n.d., para. 7)

Woods' buddy and fellow Nike shill, Charles Barkley, echoes this sentiment: "Tiger likes to be OK with everybody, to appeal to all people. And I tell him 'That's cool, but the race card is here to stay. . . . I tell him that Thai people don't get hate mail, but black people do" (Mariotti, 2001, p. 94).

In sum, the Tiger Woods of "Hello World" is a very different Tiger Woods than even the post-1997 Master's Tiger Woods. Racial eclipse has far transcended racial foregrounding. Like Michael Jordan, Tiger knows almost instinctively by now that "Republicans buy golf products, too." How then does Tiger Woods see the issue of race, several years after the heady days of the Greater Milwaukee Open? Largely in raceless and ethnicless terms: "People like to nitpick on everything. I know that, and I accept the fact you can't please everybody. I get criticized for my 'charities' not being as 'ethnic' as they could be, but I can't get caught up in that either" (Mariotti, 2001, p. 94). Of course Woods can't get involved in the issue precisely because he doesn't want to get enmeshed in it. These days Woods isn't even referring to himself as Cablinasian, let alone Black. By his own choosing, he is racially and ethnically neuter, a dominant and dominating golfer. Period. On the public surface, Blacks have accepted Woods, but as Clay (2002) insightfully notes, "Beneath the surface of platitudes and gratuities lies an element of resentment and anxiety. Many black people seethe when Tiger, 26, won't accede to their wishes regarding his racial nomenclature" (p. 67). Much, indeed, has changed since those racially charged halcyon days of the Greater Milwaukee Open.

But the person who has perhaps influenced Tiger Woods' public persona more than Michael Jordan, Nike, Oprah Winfrey, and, yes, even Earl Woods is a complete stranger to most people. Even among journalists and academics, his name is far from a household one. But Tiger Woods afficionados know his name: Charles P. Pierce. Shortly after Woods' spectacular seven-iron at the Mercedes Championships to defeat Tom Lehman, GQ Magazine sent the seasoned and gifted Pierce to do a feature on The Chosen One. While the article was featured on GQ's April 1997 cover, most in the media didn't begin to cover its sensational contents until after the Masters, after the Fuzzy Zoeller controversy, and after Oprah. The PR folks at IMG are still trying to pretend that the article doesn't exist, nor did it ever exist. So, what was it about the GQ piece that caused Earl Woods, the man who claimed that he taught his son how to "handle" even the most cunning and unscrupulous writers, to state categorically, "Tiger will never trust the media in the same way again" (Lieber, 1997, p. C1)?

Tiger Woods cracked racist and sexist jokes, and used foul language. As any good reporter trying to humanize Woods might, Pierce recorded, and then revealed, the details.

Many American men who've just made it to the legal drinking age might dabble in the occasional off-color joke. But this was Tiger Woods—The Chosen One, the One who had promised to redeem our collective humanity. Would Gandhi crack a joke such as this:

> The Little Rascals are at school. The teacher wants them to use various words in sentences. The first word is *love*. Spanky answers, 'I love dogs.' The second word is *respect*. Alfalfa answers, 'I respect how much Spanky loves dogs.' The third word is *dictate*. There is a pause in the room. Finally, Buckwheat puts up his hand. 'Hey, Darla,' says Buckwheat. 'How my dick ta'te?'" (Pierce, 1998, p. 169)

Would Nelson Mandela query a total stranger with "Why do two lesbians always get where they're going faster than two gay guys? Because the lesbians are always going sixty-nine" (Pierce, 1998, p. 170). Would Martin Luther King, Jr., rub his feet together for the same stranger and ask, "What's this? It's a black guy taking off his condom" (Pierce, 1998, p. 170). Would Jesus Christ wonder aloud, "What I can't figure out is why so many good-looking women hang around baseball and basketball. Is it because, you know, people always say that, like, black guys have big dicks?" (Pierce, 1998, p. 167). And after regaling his audience with this frathouse potpourri, would our Racial Redeemer turn to his attentive listener and command, "Hey, you can't write this"? (Pierce, 1998, p. 171). As Charles Pierce quickly found out, to detail such gory details was indeed to blaspheme. But, who was doing the blaspheming?

Woods initially denied the accuracy of the quotes attributed to him. That didn't work: Among sportswriters, Pierce was an all-star, a frequent contributor to "Best American Sports Writing" anthologies, of which the GQ essay would make the 1998 edition. Next came a press release issued through IMG: "It's no secret that I'm 21 years old and that I'm naive about the motives of certain ambitious writers. The article proves that, and I don't see any reason for anyone to pay $3 to find that out" ("Woods put off," 1997, para. 5). At this point in Tiger's career, he was as naive about sportswriters as Tyra Banks was about push-up bras. Nobody bought it. Then, a third try: His jokes were just an attempt to relax a film crew during a shoot. This was a laugher to the estimable *New York Times'* Lipsyte (2001): "Right. We know how awed those crews are by child golfers" (p. 11). As Jones (2002) later recounted, IMG was so angered by the article—the deal had been negotiated by them in the first place—that they "wanted the writer's hide" (p. E1).

For Earl Woods, the GQ cover story was later interpreted as part of The Plan. In an interview with the *London Times'* Hopkins (1997, p. 29), he explained, "You know all these public relations faux pas he has made and the trouble he has been in with the press? I could have prevented all that, but I wanted him to fumble and bumble his own way so he would learn, grow and mature. And it has worked" (p. 29).

Of course Earl had the supernatural prescience to keep his 21-year-old kid from being 21. Just to prove that Earl's nonintervention intervention was understood and appreciated by Tiger, he continued, "Two weeks ago, he called me and said he had been doing some soul-searching. He thanked me for allowing him to make the mistakes that had made him grow. He was truly grateful" (Hopkins, 1997, p. 29).

And grow he has—into a two-dimensional automaton too involved with his corporate sponsors to say anything of social or political significance. After a round at the 2000 Masters, for example, Woods came to the pressroom. The issue of South Carolina—the site of the PGA Tour's next stop for the MCI Classic at Hilton Head—and the Confederate flag was broached by a reporter. Other Black athletes had boycotted the state, as per recommendations from the NAACP. Asked the reporter, "Are you playing in South Carolina this week at all? Tomorrow?" Woods replied, "No, I'm not." A follow-up question: "Are you familiar with the flag issue?" Woods: "Uh-huh." Reporter: "Have you been contacted by the NAACP, ... and do you have any comment on that?" Woods: "Un-uh." Reporter: "Is that why you're not playing there?" Woods: "No. I'm going home. I've had a good run up to this week, and now it's time for me to take a little break" (Brennan, 2000). Hello World? How about Hello World's Leading Corporate Spokesman? The eloquence of the Greater Milwaukee Open had, in less than four years, become monosyllabic grunts, not the well-spoken Stanford-educated "humanitarian."

For all of his bombast, his self-aggrandizing prophesying, and the Dr. Spock-of-the-links parenting advice, we're left to wonder what Earl Woods thinks about his son's silence. Did he give us a hint back in July 2000, not long after the flag flap? Was this Earl Woods talking? "I'm in awe of Tiger's physical prowess and his mental strength, but his humanity and his compassion need work. They have to counterbalance his striving for superiority.... Without the proper balance, the individual becomes pompous and domineering" (Reilly, 2000, p. 96). Was the "individual" in the last sentence really his son? Was The Chosen One listening this time? Not so for Brennan (2001): "every time he has been presented with a chance to make a social comment, he has turned and walked the other way. Every time he has had an opportunity to make a statement about one of society's ills, he has gone mute. He is ... all about money and corporate acquiescence and playing it safe on the sponsor's dime" (p. C6).

In their analysis of how the media has treated Tiger Woods, Giacobbi and DeSensi concluded (1999), "his presence on the tour and the threat he represents to the established white upper class males in the golf subculture will remain" (p. 416). Five years later, and it's easy to see that this characterization is hopelessly anachronistic in the Age of Woods. The "white upper class males" these days are laughing all the way to the bank, whether they're on any one of several professional golfing tours or at the local segregated country club. In fact, at least one golfer—the fourth-ranked player in the world, Phil Mickelson—reportedly thanks Tiger every time he sees him. And it's obviously not because Tiger keeps kicking Phil's ass at every important championship (save for 2004); it's because Phil's bank account has swelled considerably since the summer of 1996. There simply is no threat to White upper class male hegemony on the golf course. Or, is there? This issue is brought home forcefully even as I close this essay.

In the summer of 2002, a prominent women's organization challenged Augusta National and its chairman, Hootie Johnson, to finally admit a woman as a member before the 2003 Masters. Instead of ignoring the challenge, or downplaying it, Johnson wrote back an incendiary three-page letter, stating emphatically that "There may well come a day when women will be invited to join our membership, but that timetable will be ours, and not at the point of a bayonet" ("Not that simple," 2002, para. 9). Augusta National would not be coerced into making such changes.

Johnson was no doubt speaking the truth, but as a public relations maneuver, the letter and its release to the public started the golf world, even the sporting world, talking. And, as golf's most visible star, the issue descended squarely and rapidly onto Tiger Woods' broad shoulders.

Perhaps not surprisingly, the Jordanized Woods responded in much the same way that he did to the Lochinvar flap. Asked at his press conference before the 2002 British Open about the Augusta National controversy coupled with the fact that the site of this year's British Open championship—Muirfield—didn't even allow women in the clubhouse, Woods replied, "It's one of those things where everyone has ... they're entitled to set up their own rules the way they want them. It would be nice to see everyone have an equal chance to participate if they wanted to, *but there's nothing you can do about it* [italics added]" ("Not that simple," 2002, para. 17).

Asked if he would feel the same way if the issue affected Blacks or Asians, Tiger stated, "It's unfortunate. But's it's just the way it is." When pressed whether he might use his stature as sport's biggest star to influence change, he responded, "It would be nice to see every golf course open to everyone who wanted to participate, but that's just not where society is." (para. 7).

Let history record that on Thursday afternoon of the 2000 U.S. Open, the round was called on account of a dense, blanketing fog. My buddy and I were of course disappointed as we'd hoped to see more golf, see more of Pebble Beach, and maybe even see Tiger Woods hit practice balls at the driving range after his round. Earl Woods, of course, would have seen no mere metaphor in the weather: This was Tiger haze, Tiger-induced funk meant to signal the end of the tournament and the beginning of something otherworldly. Not just a young man playing great golf who happened to have fortunate timing. And Earl might have prophesied if Tiger could change the weather, he could certainly change the world.

And for the better.

And many believed.

And many still do. Amen.

REFERENCES

Andrews, D. L. (2000). Excavating Michael Jordan's Blackness. In S. Birrell & M. McDonald (Eds.), Reading sport: Critical essays on power and representation (pp. 166–205). Boston: Northeastern University Press.

Andrews, D. L. (2001). *Michael Jordan, Inc.* Albany, NY: SUNY Press.

Black America and Tiger's dilemma. (1997, July). *Ebony*, p. 28.

Brennan, C. (2000, April 20). On flag issue, cat's got Tiger's tongue. *USA Today*, p. C3.

Brennan, C. (2001, June 13). Time for Tiger to meet father's expectations. *USA Today*, p. C6.

Clay, G. (2002, March 31). Tiger's love life creates storm. *The Sunday Telegraph* (Sydney), p. 67.

Cole, C. L., & Andrews, D. L. (2001). America's new son: Tiger Woods and American multiculturalism. In D. L. Andrews & S. J. Jackson (Eds.), *Sport stars: The cultural politics of sporting celebrity* (pp. 70–86). London: Routledge.

Cushman, T. (2001, June 10). Tiger's dad makes case that marriage should wait. *The San Diego Union-Tribune*, p. C8.

Custred, J. (October 6, 1996). Swoosh! There it goes. *The Houston Cronicle*, p. 27.

Dawkins, M. P., & Kinloch, G. C. (2000). *African American golfers during the Jim Crow era.* Westport, CT: Praeger.

Elliott, M. (1996, September 10). Tiger helps add color to pro golf. *The Tampa Tribune*, p. 1.

Feder, A. M. (1995). "A radiant smile from the lovely lady": Overdetermined femininity in 'ladies' figure skating. In C. Baughmann (Ed.), *Women on ice: Feminist essays on the Tonya Harding/Nancy Kerrigan spectacle* (pp. 22–46). London: Routledge.

Feinstein, J. (1998). *The first coming. Tiger Woods: Master or martyr?* New York: Ballantine.

Feinstein, J. (1999). *The majors.* New York: Ballantine.

Gates, H. L. (1998 June 1). Net worth. *The New Yorker,* pp. 48–61.

Giacobbi, P. R., Jr., & DeSensi, J. T. (1999). Media portrayals of Tiger Woods: A qualitative deconstructive examination. *Quest, 51,* 408–17.

Grant, T. (2001, April 7). Augusta's hidden past. *Herald Sun,* p. W10.

Greene, B. (1993). *Hang time: Days and dreams with Michael Jordan.* New York: St. Martin's.

Greene, B. (1995). *Rebound: The odyssey of Michael Jordan.* New York: Viking.

Halberstam, D. (1999). *Michael Jordan and the world he made.* New York: Random House.

Holland, E. (1997, July 17). Paper Tiger. *St. Louis Post-Dispatch,* p. D1.

Hopkins, J. (1997, July 14). Turning Tiger into golf's young master. *The Times,* p. 29.

Jones, T. (2002, May 19). Wily Woods wisely reveals little about what makes him tick. *The Columbus Dispatch,* p. E1.

Keown, T. (1997, April 21). Tiger Woods won't fight for a cause. *San Francisco Chronicle,* p. B1.

LaFeber, W. (1999). *Michael Jordan and the new global capitalism.* New York: W. W. Norton.

Lieber, J. (1997, May 8). Giving Tiger Woods direction Earl Woods furnishes son love, lessons. *USA Today,* p. C1.

Lipsyte, R. (2001, April 22). One writer's Tiger Woods problem. *New York Times,* sec. 8, p. 11.

Mariotti, J. (2001, June 15). Too far out of bounds: Tiger's father needs reminder about what his amazing son isn't. *Chicago Sun-Times,* p. 94.

Markon, J. (1997, May 31). "Training a Tiger": Successful blueprint. *The Richmond Times Dispatch,* p. D1.

Morrissey, R. (1997, April 20). . . . and they will follow. *Denver Rocky Mountain News,* p. C18.

"Not that simple." (2002, July 16). Retrieved August 10, 2002, from http://www.sportsillustrated.cnn. golfonline/2002/ british_open/news/

Owen, D. (2001). *The chosen one.* New York: Simon & Schuster.

Pierce, C. P. (1998). The man. Amen. In Bill Littlefield (Ed.), *The best American sports writing 1998* (pp. 165–181). Boston: Houghton Mifflin.

Poe, J. (1997, April 21). Tiger Woods spotlights multiracial identity; golf star sparks pride in heritage. *Chicago Tribune,* n.p. http:// tigertales.com/tiger/pride 042197.html accessed 12/4/01.

Reilly, R. (2000, July 24). An audience with the Earl. *Sports Illustrated,* p. 96.

Sampson, C. (1998). *The Masters: Golf, money, and power in Augusta, Georgia.* New York: Villard.

Scarborough, R. (1996, October 31). Critics hit Nike ads with sneaker suspicion; Woods spots par for the course. *The Washington Times,* p. A2.

Shropshire, K. (n.d.). A Black Thai affair. Retrieved May 4, 2002, from http://www.africana.com

Smith, G. (1996, December 23). The chosen one. *Sports Illustrated.* Retrieved June 6, 2001, from http://sportsillustrated.cnn.com/golf/pga/features/tiger/chosen

Smith, S. (1992). *The Jordan rules.* New York: Simon & Schuster.

Spiers, G. (1997, June 15). The messiah is chosen, and America begins to get lost in the Woods. *Scotland on Sunday,* p. 33.

Strege, J. (1997). *Tiger: A biography of Tiger Woods.* New York: Broadway.

Thill, S. (1997, November). The importance of being Tiger Woods. *Bad Subjects.* Retrieved July 29, 2002, from http://eserver.org/bs/35/thill.html

Uchacz, C. P. (1998). Black sports images in transition: The impact of Tiger Woods. In G. A. Sailes (Ed.), *African Americans in sport* (pp. 53–66). New Brunswick, NJ: Transaction.

Weyler, J. (1996, September 1). Out of it and still favored. *Los Angeles Times,* p. C1.

Wilkerson, I. (1997, November). The all American. *Essence,* p. 99.

Woods put off by off-color quotes, comments on father. (1997, March 23). Retrieved May 8, 2002, from http://www.tigertales.com/tiger/gq032397.html

Woods, E., with McDaniel, P. (1997). *Training a Tiger: A father's guide to raising a winner in both golf and life.* New York: HarperCollins.

Woods, E. (1998). *Playing through: Straight talk on hard work, big dreams, and adventures with Tiger.* New York: HarperCollins.

Woods, E., with Wenk, S. L. (2000). *Start something: Every kid can make a difference.* New York: Simon & Schuster.

Woods, T. (1997, May 28). Press conference, 1997 Memorial Tournament, Dublin, Ohio. Retrieved May 11, 2001, from http://www.asapsports.com/golf/1997/memorial/052897TW.html

29

Women, Team Sports, and the WNBA: Playing Like a Girl

Daniela Baroffio-Bota
Sarah Banet-Weiser
University of Southern California

June 21, 1997, marked the inaugural season of the Women's National Basketball Association (WNBA). Although a century of women's basketball—including some unsuccessful professional leagues—preceded the WNBA, this time promised to be different. The official slogan of the WNBA, "We Got Next," assured basketball fans of not only a televised team sports league during the lagging summer off-season of the National Basketball Association (NBA) but also a future for women's basketball, complete with high-powered demonstrations of athletic skill and competition. In 1999, following the debut of the WNBA, the U.S. media enthusiastically covered the victory of the U.S. women's team in World Cup Soccer, and the Williams sisters, Venus and Serena, made (and continue to make) headlines for both their superior tennis playing and their fashion politics. It is an expected part of middle-class suburban life in the United States for young girls to participate in team sports such as softball and soccer, and the female athletes competing for the United States in the 2004 Olympics had many more victories—both as individuals and on teams—than the male athletes. It is clear that women's sports are no longer a peripheral event but rather an important part of mainstream culture in the United States.

Yet, the politics surrounding female athletes—as well as the coverage of female athletes in the media—are framed within conventional discourses of the sexualized body. The complexities surrounding popular understandings of women's team sports and the behavior of female athletes on the field became clear when champion soccer team member Brandi Chastain caused a media uproar when she ripped off her jersey after scoring the deciding goal in the 1999 USA World Cup series. The action shots of strong, sweaty female bodies, simply by their sheer corporeality, challenge dominant masculine conventions involving sport. This challenge to the clearly male-dominated realm of team sports requires complicated cultural negotiations by both the leagues and its sponsors in order to establish that professional women's team sports such as soccer and basketball are a "legitimate" sport—and that the athletes themselves are "legitimate" women. So for women, team sports have had to also situate themselves within a long and conflicted history about women and sport. Part of this task has been to adopt strategies intended to assuage sponsors and fans that their sport, while professional and athletic, was not overly "masculine," which is to say, not lesbian "occupied." The WNBA, for instance, has strategically represented itself in such a way as to counteract the American public's fears about the players—and thus, by association, the sport—being homosexual. Fans and sponsors are encouraged to see basketball as a sport where not only those women labeled as "deviant" by dominant ideology could play, but as a game played by those who followed normative conventions of heterosexual femininity. On another plane of sexuality, when female athletes' heterosexuality is assumed, they are often critiqued as overtly sexual—especially when depicted in the media in a provocative manner.

While femininity and athleticism are upheld as incompatible by cultural discourses, another dimension linked to the affirmation of female athletes and women's team sport is informed by dominant racial narratives surrounding the Black athletic body. This is most evident in the case of the WNBA. Within the complicated strategies that have worked to establish the WNBA as a legitimate and profitable professional athletic organization, a curious shift in the politics of race and gender that surround sport has occurred. This shift has taken place in the inevitable comparison between the WNBA and the NBA—a comparison that is made ostensibly on the grounds of athletic ability but is really much more about the intersection of race and gender in professional sports. As Michael Dyson, bell hooks, and others have noted (Dyson, 1993; Hoberman, 1997; hooks, 1994;), dominant narratives of race have informed the public understanding of the NBA since its inception, where the Black players of the NBA have often been characterized according to their "natural" athletic prowess, while the White athletes have been publicly understood (and valorized) as the "smarter" and more intellectual players. Because of the focus on race in the NBA, and perhaps because it is a sport that has been professionally all male for most of its history, masculinity has been an obvious, and thus unremarked upon, category. Rather, categorizing players has functioned on the level of what *kind* of men the players were—the cerebral "smart" White players or the incorrigible, athletic Black players.

In the case of basketball, the arrival of the WNBA has shifted this perspective a bit. Concepts of race and gender are now simultaneously employed as explanatory frameworks for figuring out who, and what, professional basketball players are and should be. While it is clear that women participate in athletics and are skilled, their very participation in the cultural realm of sport signifies a challenge to athletic masculinity. Women's professional team sports have thus been defined as cultural arenas that are primarily about *gender*. In other words, in the cultural context of late twentieth-century U.S. society, the question that is consistently asked by the press and the public is: what *kind* of women play professional team sports? On what terms and conditions does the cultural representation of these female players occur? There has been much media hoopla about the way in which the WNBA "transcends" gender, simply because it is a professional arena that *allows* for female athletes. Professional women's basketball, it seems, is now considered "equal" because corporations and advertisers have found that, 27 years after the passing of Title IX, there is a market audience for female basketball players. Since community membership increasingly means good market share, the WNBA is now part of the basketball community. Similarly, the U.S. women's Olympic softball team is part of this community, proving through athletic skill that gender doesn't "matter" in quite the way it once did. However, while there has been a growing presence and perhaps even acceptance of women in sports, much of the rhetoric framing media depictions of female athletes revolves around the relation between the commodification of sport and female empowerment, working to further highlight the gendered dimension around women and sports.

TEAM WORK: THE PROBLEM OF FEMALE TEAM SPORTS

Within the frame of the media, the bodies of female athletes are understood and legitimated first and foremost as being about femininity rather than athleticism. This is visible in some of the current popular controversies around the sexualized depiction of female athletes in popular men's magazines and Web sites. While certainly male athletes are also (increasingly) objectified in the media, the character of that objectification is quite different when it comes to female athletes. For instance, the controversies around three-time Olympic veteran Amanda Beard's choice to pose along with other Olympians on the 2004 cover of *FHM* magazine wearing only a white string bikini, where critics claimed she was denigrating the sport, were about the apparent incompatabilites between the sexualized body and the athletic body. These discourses also frame social understandings of women's team sports around the gendered characteristic of the athletes. In other words, despite the rhetoric of "equality," it is precisely conventional narratives of *femininity* that give women team sports cultural legitimation as all-female team sports. These conventional narratives of femininity work to mediate the tensions between traditional representations of femininity and the cultural ideal that values men's athleticism over that of women's.

This is not to say that women have not been valued as athletes. However, the American public's fascination with female athletes has almost always centered on individual athletes—tennis players, professional golfers, figure skaters, and gymnasts (Chisholm, 1999a; Chisholm, 1999b). These sports demonstrate the agility and elegance "natural" to women and, although athleticism is clearly a major aspect of these sports, the individual stars are known, culturally at least, more for their "feminine" attributes: self-sacrifice, glamour, grace. Indeed, the public recognition of individual female athletes attends much more to their feminine beauty and objectified status as particular kinds of commodities than to their athletic skill. And, if individual women athletes are not naturalized as sexual, feminine beings, it is usually because they are not, in fact, women at all but rather little girls. In the last two decades, sports such as tennis, figure skating, and gymnastics can hardly be called "*women's*" sports: Tara Lipinski won the Olympic gold medal in figure skating when she was fourteen years old, there was not a single individual over the age of twenty on the entire American Olympic team of female gymnasts, and tennis superstars are often still teenagers. In contrast, team sports usually feature *women*—in the WNBA, for instance, the players are required to complete their college eligibility or be twenty-one years old. Hence, they can acquire their status as role models *for* little girls—an important feature of professional team sports in the United States— precisely because, unlike Tara Lipinski or Carly Patterson, they are *not* little girls. In fact, it is the maturity of the players that is often lauded in the press. The focus on maturity accomplishes at least two different things: one, it establishes the players as experienced professionals, not little girls who will, simply because of physical development, grow too large at any moment to be a superstar gymnast or ice skater. Two, it also establishes the WNBA players as different from the NBA players—the maturity of the WNBA is in direct contrast to the "immaturity" of the NBA.

DIFFERENCES FROM MEN'S TEAM SPORTS

Professional sports, and especially professional men's basketball, is often highlighted as a cultural space in which racist practices that formulate American cultural life are transcended—indeed, even obliterated—because it is seen as a "positive" arena for integration (Hoberman, 1997).[1] In fact, it is the idea of the NBA as an "interracial theater" that has allowed for an insidious kind of opening: The focus on the "difference" between Black and White players has helped to reinvigorate biological racism. Within this "interracial theater" of the NBA, many of the fantasies and fears of White audiences about Black men are played out. The NBA exploits and exoticizes the racist stereotypes of the Black menace even as it domesticates this cultural figure.

The media discourse that surrounds professional basketball has often pointed out the basketball arena as a place free of racial tensions, a triumph of post-Civil Rights American culture. This kind of denial about the racial tensions that have always characterized professional sports in the United States makes the racist argument about biological difference between Black and White athletes all the more credible. The fact that Black athletes dominate the NBA easily translates (in current cultural politics) to the "fact" that professional basketball must therefore *not* be a racist organization. Because there are ostensibly no cultural barriers for African Americans to become professional athletes, there needs to be some kind of explanatory framework for the athletic prowess of the Black players. The explanation, therefore, for both skill and bad behavior, must be biology: Those same genetic propensities that allow for the high jumps and superior athletic skill also "cause" uncontrollable and recalcitrant social behavior on the court.[2]

While conventional narratives of *femininity* work to give women's team sports such as the WNBA cultural legitimation as an all-female team sport, the consolidation of the Black male athlete as culturally legitimate, especially in the NBA, derives from the players' ability to manage their raced bodies in the face of a predominantly White organizational culture. The dominant understanding of the bodies of Black athletes works to both commodify and naturalize these bodies. The iconization and image of Michael Jordan, placed on everything from cologne to long distance companies to hamburgers, continues to stand in stark contrast to the image of someone like Ron Artest, involved recently in a physical brawl with fans so violent that the basketball game had to be called. Where Jordan is used to confirm the successful use of the Black athlete as a commodity, Artest both affirms and disrupts

---

[1]This is precisely the reason why Hoberman criticizes Black intellectual scrutiny of the NBA. Hoberman argues that there is little scrutiny because basketball has been seen as a positive arena for self-definition and empowerment for young Black men. While his is a compelling argument, this chapter does not present such a view; rather, we are scrutinizing the media coverage of Black players in the NBA.

[2]We can see that this is clearly about race; we never find the media speculating on what particular *White* gene must be present to explain the skill of, say, hockey players or golfers.

assumptions about the naturalized Black body (Dyson, 1993). In much the same way as the unruly racial politics of the NBA function to solidify the moral status of the gender politics that shape the WNBA, Dennis Rodman, one of the most controversial players in the NBA, notably known for his tie-dyed hair colors, tattoos, and many body piercings, through his defiance, stabilizes the image of Jordan and serves to contain the potential threat of his Black body. This shaping of Black male athletes into objects dilutes the potential threat that they carry simply by *being* Black male bodies. It is clear in the media that more recently other players in the NBA, through their challenge to authority and defiance, have "needed" precisely this kind of domestication. Indeed, the rhetoric of "poor sportsmanship" that shapes the media discourse of the NBA, along with "bad-boy" behavior, the violence and aggression that is increasingly part of the game, and the presence of cultural bodily markings such as tatoos and body piercing signify Blackness and menace. The underlying subtext of the "ego problems" of the NBA players, occasionally young men straight out of high school who are made instant millionaires, is that these are men from the "inner cities" (another code word for race in U.S. cultural politics) and that they are both natural athletes and natural thugs. As such, the cultural arena of the NBA is about normative masculinity, Whiteness, respectability, and, perhaps most importantly, class.

The threat posed by Black players in the NBA is thus understood culturally as one of a lack of respect, an unwillingness—and implicitly, an incapability—of accepting authority. In order to assuage the challenge posed by some NBA players, the marketing and manufacturing networks have worked assiduously to construct the more well-known athletes as commodities. The threat that players such as Artest, Alan Iverson, and others pose is diluted by their commodification, by making them into things that one can buy or observe. However, this kind of marketing is precarious because players such as Sprewell, suspended by the NBA for attacking the Warriors' head coach in 1997, and Rodman are explicitly *needed* by the NBA as particular kinds of commodities—players such as these offer an attractive "edge" for youth marketing. Hence, the threat posed by unruly players must be balanced in a way that maintains the public titillation caused by the defiant Black male body while not disrupting the broad marketability of the league.

Interestingly, the positioning of the Black male athlete as a commodity—and thus as a passive object—is a curious reversal of the way that women's bodies have been traditionally objectified. As bell hooks (1994) commented, "it has taken contemporary commodification of Blackness to teach the world that this perceived threat, whether real or symbolic, can be diffused by a process of fetishization that renders the Black masculine 'menace' feminine through a process of patriarchal objectification" (p. 110).

The cultural fear of the Black male body is diluted by shaping Black male athletes as commodities, even as this fear is legitimated by what is ostensibly seen and experienced on the court. The WNBA occupies a position in stark contrast to the NBA, which is increasingly scrutinized by the press as a group of spoiled, ungrateful, violent Black men invading the minds of innocent White middle-class boys and men. The WNBA, with its "wholesome" players who are grateful that they have a job at all, becomes the respectable—and respectful—player in this particular game. In short, the gendering of the WNBA has functioned culturally to trump the racial politics of the NBA. The media has recently focused on the idea of women's basketball as representing a "purer" form of the game—the WNBA apparently demonstrates the way the game "should" be played. The rhetoric of purity is deeply embedded in a discourse of morality—the female players of the WNBA function as morally superior athletes in comparison to the NBA.

So, ironically, the racist discourse that shapes the media construction of the NBA works to offer a more positive picture of the WNBA. Of course, the same discourses that shape conventions of Black masculinity have also constructed damaging representations of Black women. However, despite the overwhelming African-American presence in the league, at present the WNBA has been characterized more in terms of normative femininity—maternal, moral, collaborative—than according to dominant representations of Black women, which in other arenas have emphasized sexuality and amorality. While it can be argued that the figure of the trash-talking "bad boy" in the NBA has a specific cultural purpose, there is no racialized "bad-girl" equivalent in the WNBA—at least not yet. The racial politics of the NBA that represent the Black male body as naturalized and dangerous also serve as the negative screen against which the WNBA creates its positive gender commodity image.

In an interesting discursive move, the naturalized bodies of the female athletes of the WNBA have been reframed to represent values more often associated with masculinist team sports, allowing talent to reign over glamour. The athletes of the NBA, on the other hand, are increasingly objectified, shaped as individual stars, their bodies transformed into objects through their relentless commodification. The WNBA and the NBA work off each other; the categories of race and gender that are so crucial to the self-definition of the leagues are mutually constituitive. The media portrayals of the NBA represent the Black players as potentially dangerous and menacing, allowing for the WNBA to construct itself in positive opposition to these racial politics. And, in the women's league, dominant conventions of gender function on the surface to threaten the NBA, but these politics implicitly serve to contain the unruly Blackness of the NBA, stabilizing the league by helping to police the "greed" and the bodies of unruly Black men of the NBA. With the racial and gender boundaries tightened and clarified, the safely domesticated Black male bodies can become the symbols that advertisers want, and the female players emerge as appropriate role model spokespersons for the league.

But because the masculinist assumptions of team sports challenge the individualist and moralist ideology that constructs sports such as figure skating and gymnastics, the women athletes in the WNBA have had to manage a contradictory set of cultural images. Strategies are needed to reassure fans that although they are not dancing gracefully over the ice in designer outfits, professional female basketball players are in fact feminine beings. And while for some, the WNBA is a shining example of the transcendence of gender in professional sports, a place where, finally, gender does not "matter," it is just as clear that gender matters tremendously. In much the same way as the NBA is often lauded as being a positive example of integration for precisely the same reasons that it *remains* a racist organization, the WNBA is seen as a positive arena for women to be "equal" to men—even while it is clear that it is the athletes' definition as *women* that legitimates the sport.

FASHIONABLE PLAYERS: FEMALE ATHLETES, SEXUALITY, AND GLAMOUR

The traditional trappings of femininity—fashion, motherhood, beauty, morality—characterize the players of women team sports. For example, on the official Web site of the WNBA, alongside features that list game schedules, highlights from previous games, and new sponsorship partners, there is a section called "WNBA Unveils Uniform." This section claims that the WNBA "injects fresh perspective into the creation of its basketball uniforms," and there is information about the decisions made for the official WNBA uniforms: Should they wear dresses? Tunics over shorts? Unitards? Or "skorts" (skirts/shorts)? There is also detailed information about the materials and colors used for the final choice of uniforms (which, incidentally, was shirts and shorts). Finally, there is a section where fans can vote on their favorite uniform, with pictures of both the home and away uniforms (WNBA Official Web site, 1999). Clearly, this particular section of the Web site contributes to a dominant ideology that women are overly concerned with clothing and fashion. There is no comparable section on the Web site of the NBA, and, while not surprising, the presence of this feature tells us something about the various ways in which the players and the institution of the WNBA function to shore up dominant notions and ideologies about the construction of womanhood.

Most media discourses surrounding coverage of female athletes are shaped around the connection between athletic recognition and legitimate femininity. For instance, the fact that most female tennis players still wear skirts rather than the more comfortable, albeit less feminine, shorts tends to also be discussed in light of this connection. Consider this online column in *Slate Magazine:*

> Tennis's designated sexpot, Anna Kournikova, wore shorts in last year's U.S. Open. But most don't. This is likely because looking cute on the court (and giving a little panty flash now and then) is a way for female athletes to rally fan support, and more importantly, increase the value of their endorsement contracts. (Kournikova doesn't have to worry about increasing her stock as a sex symbol, which is why she can afford to wear shorts. (Truitt, 2001)

In discussing the backless yellow spandex dress worn by tennis player Venus Williams in the 2000 U.S. Open, this same article asked:

> Would Venus Williams have scored a $40 million endorsement contract from Reebok—the highest ever for a female athlete—if she dressed in the baggy shorts of a WNBA or LPGA player? Unlikely. Her earning power depends mainly on winning matches, but looking stunning in a tight yellow dress helps. (Truitt, 2001, para.)

Clearly, given the threat that is posed by paying women to play and perform in sporting events and thus recognizing them as professionals, naturalizing them as "true women" is a predictable strategy.

The fact that some athletes also model is something that is emphasized by reporters. The modeling career of Lisa Leslie, a player for the Los Angeles Sparks, is the consistent focus of the articles that feature her:

> The worlds of hoops and haute couture seem galaxies apart to most people. Not Lisa Leslie. All poise and confidence, the Olympic gold medalist and aspiring supermodel is equally comfortable dribbling down the lane in a sweaty fury and breezing down the runway in four inch heels and an Armani evening gown. (Huntington, 1996, p. 50)

It is clear that it is absolutely crucial for Leslie to be "equally" comfortable in either the athlete or model mode—it is precisely this easy movement between the two that helps legitimate her status as a star athlete. As Leslie herself puts it: "'That's what I call my Wonder Woman Theory'...When I'm playing, I'll sweat and talk trash. However, off the court, I'm lipstick, heels and short skirts. I'm very feminine, mild-mannered, and sensitive.'" The rest of the article is quite bald-faced about this particular strategy, calling the "sudden" fact that "women's hoops are vogue, chic and feminine" as "all part of the plan" (Marks, 1997, p. 46). A similar argument was made by Australian soccer team player Amy Taylor following the release of the infamous "nude Matildas 2000 Calendar" (Matildas is the name given to the Australian all-women soccer team), featuring nude shots of 12 of the players on the team. On the official Matildas Web site the team members justified the nude calendar by saying, "We just find that we're not getting the media attention or the publicity that we deserve and we needed to do something to lift our profile" (Matildas, 2005). Taylor, who was featured on the cover of the calendar, said, "We wanted to prove we're not all butch lesbians. We are attractive, feminine girls who play soccer" (O'Keefe, 2000). As if the calendar was not a strong enough indication of the athletes' femininity, the Matilda's official Web site runs a banner stating, "The Matildas: The New Fashion in Football." These practices are clearly about establishing the players' commitment to being feminine, and they are an explicit argument against the history of female athletes, who were so often criticized for their distinctly unfeminine qualities—such as muscularity and athletic skill (Cahn, 1998; Schulze, 1990).

Indeed, the threat of women participating in the sporting world, explicitly acknowledged by the Matildas, is by no means a new one. Cahn (1998) argued that the stereotype of the mannish, lesbian athlete has worked to shape not only female competitors themselves, but also sports organizations, funding sources, and the overall popularity of women's sports. The most common strategy employed by athletic organizations to overcome this stereotype is to reassure audiences and fans that women involved in sports are indeed "women"—meaning, of course, that they are heterosexual. As Cahn (1998) pointed out, "The lesbian stereotype exert[s] pressure on athletes to demonstrate their femininity and heterosexuality, viewed as one and the same" (p. 76). Not surprisingly, it is in those sports that most resemble masculinized athletics (for example, soccer, softball, or hockey), and those that have the greatest need to attract a paying audience, that the fear of and anxiety over lesbianism are most prominent. Because these sports are culturally defined as masculine, and because there is an easy cultural slippage between "masculine women" and lesbian identity, strategies are needed by the players in order to redefine and recast the sport as feminine or womanly. For example, "sex appeal" is translated as "flex appeal" in the context of female body building, female tennis players are often depicted as "playing for" their love interest in the stands, and female professional basketball and soccer players are shown as fashion models and mothers (Messner, 2002; Schulze, 1990).

Intriguingly, stories about the lesbian following of the WNBA have shaped the media discourse and promotion strategies of the league. As *Newsweek* put it in September of 1997, the first season of the WNBA,

The league also has another, less trumpeted core constituency. Though TV broadcasts pan moms with their kids, plenty of women come on their own. Says Sarah Pettit, editor of *Out* magazine, 'Next to the 'Ellen' episode, this is the biggest news in the lesbian community all year long. If there's one thing lesbians are talking about, it's who's on the bench and who's on the floor. (Leland, Rosenberg, VanBoven, & Gegax, 1997, p. 57)

Not surprisingly, the WNBA does not acknowledge any gay following; Rick Welts, chief marketing officer for both the NBA and the WNBA, replied when asked about a lesbian audience, "I'm not aware of that...We don't take attendance that way. The league does not discriminate" (Leland, et al., 1997, p. 57).

Although Welts uses antidiscriminatory rhetoric as a slick way to deflect questions about the public awareness of a lesbian following of the WNBA, a more successful strategy to reassure fans of the players' heterosexuality has been to focus on maternity. When WNBA star Sheryl Swoopes of the Houston Comets became pregnant the first season of the league, it proved to be a great advantage to her as a player and a golden marketing opportunity for the league. When asked about Swoopes, Welts said, "We embrace maternity" (Leland, et al., 1997, p. 57). Her pregnancy became a press bonanza, with soft news stories about maternity in general, balancing baby with basketball, and the generous sacrifice of Swoopes' husband, Eric Jackson, to stay home with the baby. Rosie O'Donnell, an extremely public WNBA fan, was exuberant in her praise of Swoopes, explicitly because of her maternity:

> People go to NBA games and they can figure out pretty fast that Michael Jordan is the most valuable player because he's the best. WNBA fans don't think that way. Our MVP was Sheryl Swoopes, not because she led the league in scoring or acrobatics, but because she had a baby and six weeks later, she was back on the court playing basketball. (as cited in Whiteside, 1998, p. 3)

She continued, "Sheryl gets ready to go in the game and every mom in the crowd stands up and cheers: 'Hey Sheryl! Go girl! Can you believe how good she looks! She had a baby! Go Sheryl! You still nursing? Sheryl, you look great!'" When Swoopes plays, the camera continually returns to shots of the sideline where the baby and father watch the game.

Although Swoopes may be the most recognizable mother in the WNBA because of the intense scrutiny of her activities, other maternal players receive attention because of their decisions to have children. For example, on the official WNBA Web site, there is a section called "Ask Olympia" that allows visitors to the Web site to write in questions to Utah's Olympia Scott-Richardson. A full three fourth of these questions asked about the player's recent pregnant status, what sex the baby would be, what her name would be, and whether or not Scott-Richardson would take her baby on tour with her (WNBA Official Web site, 1999). This focus on maternity resonates with another dominant cultural assumption about women: that they are, above all, interested in becoming mothers. But unlike the younger female athletes such as 14-year-old golfer Michelle Wie or 16-year-old gymnast Carly Patterson, WNBA players do not merely embody the promise of *future* motherhood—many of them are already mothers, leaving no doubt to their feminine nature. Not only do these kinds of media strategies provide what seems to be ironclad evidence of the players' heterosexuality, they also establish the WNBA as a family-oriented, moral game, or as *Newsweek* put it, the WNBA is "the good apple in the increasingly rotting barrel of professional sports" (Leland, et al., 1997, p. 57).

Establishing the WNBA as a sporting event for the family is an important discursive move. The league is often lauded as a "hoop dream come true for millions of American girls" and is explicitly marketed as a sport the whole family can watch together. Moreover, the long-held dominant ideology that women are "morally superior" to men finds its way to the WNBA in the way that the women athletes are seen as less corrupted, whether by power or money, than NBA athletes. The players of the WNBA often talk about their teams as their "family"; as Cynthia Cooper of the Houston Comets said, "Families are very, very important to me, both my own family and the family that I have on the court, because we did become a family during the season" (Whiteside, 1998, p. 25). Prior to its demise in 2003, the professional soccer league WUSA followed a similar strategy by openly targeting families. In the words of Shaun May, the league's director of public relations, "The so-called soccer mom market is what we're going after" (Drehs, 2001, para.). In the 2003 season the WUSA teamed up with Maytag's "Search for Outstanding Soccer Moms" contest in which four semi finalists would win a trip for four to the WUSA Founders Cup 2003 Championship game, and the National Finalist/Grand Prize winner would receive a 2003 Hyundai Santa Fe Sport Utility Vehicle, as well as a Maytag Appliance Suite, including a washer, gas dryer, dishwasher, Gemini double oven, and refrigerator. Mothers and families were definitely the target of this campaign. Despite having folded in 2003 following three years of playing and a reported $100 million in fiscal losses, the players of the WUSA and of the more successful WNBA embody a different type of sportsmanship. As one columnist put it, "For women's basketball to become a major sport in America, as opposed to a profitable one like arena football, something is going to have to be offered other than just pure skill. That something should be, and in fact will have to be, a different attitude, a purer sense of the sport, than the men deliver" (Kallam, 1999).

This "different attitude" resides in the bodies of the female players, indeed, *is* the bodies of the players, bodies that are more moral, more pure, less likely to succumb to temptation, and less corrupt than male bodies. Simply, the bodies of the WNBA players *are* the "purer sense of the sport." The discourse of the family and maternity play into a dual construction, where the family-oriented players of the WNBA and the former WUSA offer wholesome good fun and healthy competition to their fans, as opposed to the lone mavericks of male teams such as the NBA, seemingly out only for themselves and their own personal glory.

But, while the discourse of family and maternity legitimate women's professional team sports, they also work themselves into arguments for the minimal popularity of all women team sports. In fact, media discourse surrounding the minimal attendance and TV ratings of women's sports compared to men's sports justifies this discrepancy by arguing that it is precisely the gendered aspect of the event that works to alienate potential fans, men and women alike. In an interview published in the online version of the U.S. National Soccer Team Player's Monthly, Kevin McGeehan, Director of Media Relations for the Johnstown Chiefs noted:

> The reason that you have not seen men's supporters groups at women's games, U.S. or WUSA, is simple: women's soccer has never marketed itself as simply "soccer." It has always been about the women's movement, or giving six-year-old girls' soccer role models, or nice, clean family fun. I am not against these things, per se, but I don't really want my sports mixed with feminism or screeching six-year-olds. ("Round not oval," 2003)

It is precisely this denigrating and condescending rhetoric that works to both normalize male sports as "real" sports, dedicated to the game, and women's sports as more of a distraction, one more event among many in a woman's life. In other words, the qualities of femininity so necessary for the cultural legitimation of women's professional team sports become the site on which discourses about sexuality, morality, and respectability converge.

SHOWING SOME RESPECT

Although clearly the feminine body of the WNBA player is naturalized through a variety of discourses and strategies, it is also the case that the players are not objectified in the way that women's bodies have been objectified traditionally. Again, they are constantly referred to in the press as "mature women," and the play itself shapes the bodies of the players as active subjects rather than passive objects, team players rather than prima donnas. Ann Meyers, a former All-American basketball player and currently a coach, has pointed out:

> Basketball is basketball, regardless of gender, race, or age...The women's edge is they do the fundamentals. It's a great game. The men's game has gotten out of hand a little bit. They carry the ball, they travel. They've gotten away from fundamentals. The taunting, the fights, the trash talking. I don't think there's anyplace for it in the game. (as cited in Salter, 1996, p. 110)

This characterizes the NBA as a realm where "taunting" and "trash talking" works to solidify the purity of the WNBA, even as it also functions to construct the NBA implicitly in terms of race politics.

Moreover, the purity of the WNBA is recognized through the gratitude of the players. Before the WNBA and the American Basketball League (ABL) were established, the only place where women could play professional basketball was overseas (Whiteside, 1998).[3] The players of the WNBA are grateful to *have* a professional organization in the United States, and they consistently demonstrate this gratitude to their fans. Traditionally, gratitude, like self-sacrifice, has been a characteristic of femininity. Indeed, the players of the NBA, in contrast, are nonconformist and certainly not grateful, as they heckle fans and attack their coaches. In an ironic twist, the female teams of the WNBA are perhaps organized according to the "old-boys" school of professional sport, where the players have a place, know that place, and are simply grateful that someone has offered them that place. The NBA, on the other hand, is increasingly unable—and the players unwilling—to stabilize this kind of hierarchy.

Despite the gestures toward conformity displayed by WNBA athletes, the league *does* offer new potentials and conditions for shifting dominant understandings of femininity. Journalist Marks (1997) wrote about the WNBA:

> The new-age prototype for Cosmo Woman has (finally!) turned the page from bikini-clad babes with big, er, smiles to women in baggy shorts, ponytails and

---

[3]The ABL folded in 1998 due to financial difficulties. The WNBA players, if they played professional ball at all, would play for teams overseas. See Whiteside (1998) for more discussion of the players' careers overseas.

killer jump shots. Meet the new millennuim of supermodels, led by Lisa Leslie, Rebecca Lobo and Sheryl Swoopes. Hope you're buying, 'cause the WNBA is definitely selling. (p. 46)

This article continues to claim that the WNBA is "attempting to change the public perception of what femininity really is"—a tall order, clearly, but one that an all-female, professional team sports league may have a better shot at than, say, academics or Britney Spears. The play on the word "model" in Marks' statement about the WNBA becoming "the new millenium of supermodels" suggests that the American public is eager for strong, aggressive, competitive female role models. The idea of modeling for girls and young women has been both a lucrative marketing strategy and, it seems, a realistic goal for the WNBA players. For example, a Nike television advertisement shown on Lifetime depicted Cynthia Cooper of the Houston Comets, who simply said to the camera:

We get out in the malls and we're laughing and joking and I actually took a picture with the first person—she hasn't sent it to me yet—with the first little girl that I saw with my jersey. It was awesome. *It was awesome.* I wanted to cry. She came up to me and she said 'would you please sign my autograph?' I said, 'Can I take a picture with you, pleeeaasse?' It was great. It was amazing. (Nike television Advertisement, 1998)

The ad ends with a stylized black and white photograph of Cooper, with the words "I can inspire" merging with the words "I can aspire" (Nike Advertisement, 1998). This ad is typical for Nike, a company that has found role-modeling for young girls to be an emotive and profitable strategy. Indeed, it is promising that girls and young women can witness a public validation of women who do not quite fit normative standards of femininity—that there is, in short, a public role model for young girls who look and act differently from the current Miss America.

But contemporary discourses surrounding female empowerment are constructed primarily in and through commercial culture. Gender representations of women in the media are driven by the commercial market, and revenue is generated through tried and true formulae so that normative conventions of femininity are the surest bet for networks. While both celebrating and producing ideologies of female empowerment is media representations of female empowerment demonstrate contradictions in cultural understandings of femininity. The empowerment is demonstrated in and through the strong, muscular bodies of female athletes, whose very participation in the traditional male sphere of sports imbues their bodies with significant feminist politics. Yet, as with all representations, empowering representations of female athletes are tricky. So, while it is clear that female athletes' participation in dominant conventions of gender is a prerequisite for their legitimation as athletes, these same conventions work to reduce female athletes to a sex object rather than emphasize the way that they embody athletic achievement and skill. Yet this contradiction—between sexual objectification and athleticism—is actually a false one, as both these constructions of femininity reinforce each other in current manifestations of gender. From The Matilda's nude calendar to the Canadian Women's cross-country team producing a "Nordic Nude" calendar in September 2000, many women team sports and individual athletes have responded to low ratings and minimal social and cultural attention by relying on something that has been historically lucrative: the display of the female body. As one article commenting on female U.S. athletes' provocative appearances put it, "While some feminists fumed over the photos, others held them up as proof of how self-assured women have become" (Litke, 2000). Clearly, the easy dismissal of these representations of empowerment ignores the contradictory narratives shaping most media productions of femininity and, furthermore, works to support the normative conventions of femininity through which female athletes have to negotiate their identities as both women and athletes.

FROM MUSCLES TO SEX

Discourses about race, femininity, and empowerment intersect and are mapped onto popular representation of female athletes. If, in the case of the WNBA, the commodification of the Black male body of the NBA assures the legitimation of the female players as symbols of respectable athletic femininity, that respectability is compromised when female athletes are seen as willingly participating in the objectification of their already *sexualized* bodies. Similarly, where the female athletic body as *feminine* works to evade the threat of being labeled a lesbian, this same body, when voluntarily subjected to the objectification of the camera by posing semicovered or entirely nude, is seen as responsible for minimizing athletic achievement and skill. In other words, the very *femininity* that in the case of the WNBA, for instance, works to legitimate women's basketball as wholesome, pure, and about talent becomes, in the case of female athletes showing off their bodies in magazines such as *Maxim, Sports Illustrated,* and others, the site for the constitution of discourses about gender and sexuality. Consider this comment by Wendy Wright of Concerned Women for America in discussing whether female Olympians should pose in magazines:

> It's degrading to all women, but there's an added element here. Now these women have earned their spot on the Olympic team, but more than that, it's an honor to represent the United States of America. So they are role models, and more than that, they're ambassadors of the United States. And at this time when American athletes are being told that in Greece, they shouldn't wave the flag too much, because it might set off violent elements, the violent elements aren't set off by the flag. They're more set off by things like a decadent culture. So I think that what these women have done is incredibly irresponsible. (CNBC's Capital Report, 2004)

Here the female athletic body is invested with discourses about sexuality, empowerment, and objectification in ways that render visible the gendered dimensions of popular understandings of the female athlete and further normalize the masculine athletic body as an unremarked-upon category. Indeed, the implication of Wright that somehow the depiction of Amanda Beard's bikini-clad body might inspire a terrorist act is testimony to the deep entrenchment of these categories. In other words, the same reasons that permit a celebration of the female athlete as about empowerment and progress also confront discourses about the female body as overtly sexualized and as such first and foremost feminine, rather than athletic.

The media uproar surrounding female athletes' revealing poses has been framed around the tensions between female empowerment on the one hand, and female objectification on the other. On the one hand, they are celebrated for not only becoming comfortable with their bodies, but also for successfully adapting these bodies to succeed in an arena traditionally perceived as the province of men. These female athletes are judged by women, men, and other female athletes alike, for apparently emphasizing their femininity over their athletic skills and for having used the cultural capital of their athletic ability to do so. This underlying discourse implies that the argument is that, rather than being grateful for the opportunity of being allowed to participate in the cultural realm of sport, these unappreciative women clearly lack the ability to represent themselves as any thing other than *woman* and sexual. As one article put it, "Because female athletes receive 80–90% less coverage of their athletic achievement in the print and electronic media than their male counterparts, female athletes who use this opportunity for non-sport exposure allow the media to continue to marginalize the achievements of the female athlete" (Women's Sports Foundation, 2000).

Much in the same way that class politics in the NBA normalizes Black men as incapable of negotiating themselves in a social and economic status other than their *natural* street environment, the underlying narrative here is that women really do not know how to manage their *naturally* sexual bodies in what still is the domain of men. Additionally, the political and cultural significance of the realm of sport is changing, representing both female and male bodies as able to participate in contests of endurance and skill. The display of the athletic body offers a different image from the models in magazines or actors in the media. Commenting on this difference, one article argued, "Olympic swimmer Jenny Thompson says her nearly naked pose in *Sports Illustrated* is a welcome alternative to the ubiquitous images of anorexic women that come at us from Hollywood and Madison Avenue" (Tucker, 2000).

Indeed, as *"girl culture"* emerges as an interesting and necessary site for scholarly study, it seems female team sports are a perfect subject of inquiry. Recent scholarship has focused on those icons that have provided young American girls with role models and inspirations: teen magazines, book series such as the American Girl Series and the stalwart Nancy Drew, and, of course, dolls (Inness, 1998).[4] Yet, athletes provide a somewhat different model from these traditional icons. Although Mattel has predictably clued into the popularity of sports and young girls by producing a WNBA Barbie (along with a USA Team Soccer Barbie and others), the dolls are obviously different from the real bodies of the players: big (many of the players are over six feet tall), sweaty, and aggressive. The sheer physicality of the sport—a physicality that is so visually different from the way women's bodies are traditionally imaged and imagined—makes it a place where one can conceptualize new conditions of possibility for definitions of the feminine.

Thus, despite the various ways in which professional sports normalize conventional notions of femininity and the politics of gender that both surround and shape then, sports present an opportunity for a disruption of these conventions. The association of power with girls, whatever the source, deserves at least some critical attention. The major sponsors of the professional women's sports, Nike and Reebok, have adopted explicit liberal feminist rhetoric into their advertisements, and although they obviously use this language as a lucrative avenue for selling products, it nonetheless shapes the dominant construction of women athletes.

---

[4]And the dolls are not just Barbie anymore (although she remains the best-selling toy in history), but also what Inness (1998) calls "anti-Barbies," the American Girl dolls, "dolls that could teach American history, family values, and self-reliance."

What we have attempted to demonstrate in this chapter are the ways in which the media employs particular strategies in the visual representation of sports and athletes. Television in particular provides frameworks of meaning which, in effect, selectively interpret not only the athletic events themselves but also the controversies and problems surrounding the events. In a new media sport such as the WNBA, this is particularly apparent, since discourses and practices of gender and race are palpably on display. Our interest in thinking about these issues as they pertain to sports is not in questioning whether there is a biological difference between male and female athletes. Our interest, rather, lies in how it is that the media interprets this biological difference within a social and cultural set of meanings. As Baker and Boyd (1997), Messner (1998), Cahn (1998), and Heywood and Dworkin (2003) have argued, the task at hand is not to provide evidence that differences exist and to what extent; rather, our goal is to ask why some differences and not others are taken as important and in support of racist and sexist ideologies.

REFERENCES

Baker, A., & Boyd, T. (1997). *Out of bounds: Sports, media, and the politics of identity.* Bloomington, IN: Indiana University Press.

Cahn, S. K. (1998). From the "muscle moll" to the "butch" ballplayer: mannishness, lesbianism, and homophobia in U.S. women's sports. In R. Weitz (Ed.), *The politics of women's bodies: Sexuality, appearance, and behavior* (pp. 67–81). Oxford: Oxford University Press.

Drehs, W. (2001, May). *Other sports not quick to follow WNBA's lead.* Retrieved April 18, 2005, from http://espn.go.com/page2/s/drehs/010524/sidebar.html

Dyson, M. E. (1993). *Reflecting Black: African-American cultural criticism.* Minneapolis: University of Minnesota Press.

Heywood, L., & Dworkin, S. L. (2003). *Built to win: The female athlete as cultural icon.* Minneapolis: University of Minnesota Press.

Hoberman, J. (1997). *Darwin's athletes: How sport has damaged Black America and preserved the myth of race.* New York: Mariner Books.

hooks, b. (1994). Feminism inside: Toward a Black body politic. In T. Golden (Ed.), *Black male: Representations of masculinity in contemporary American art.* New York: Whitney Musuem of American Art.

Inness, S. (1998). "Anti-barbies": The American Girls collection and political ideologies. In S. Inness (Ed.), *Delinquents and debutantes: Twentieth century American girls' cultures.* New York: New York University Press.

Kallam, C. (1999, March). *What's more important? Political correctness or a thriving sport?* Retrieved April 18, 2005, from Full Court Press Web site: http://fullcourt.scout.com/

Leland, J., Rosenberg, D., Van Boven, S., & Gegax, T. T. (1997, September). Up in the air. *Newsweek*, p. 57.

Litke, J. (2000, August). *Women command center stage at summer games.* Retrieved April 18, 2005, from http://www.ottawalynx.com/2000GamesNewsArchives/aug26_wom.html

Marks, R. (1997, July). Supermodels. *Sport*, p. 46.

Matildas, The Australian Women's Soccer Team Official Web site. Retrieved April 18, 2005, from http://www.matildas.org.au

Messner, M. (1988). Sport and male domination: The female athlete as contested ideological terrain. *Sociology of Sport Journal, 5,* 197–211.

Messner, M. (2002). *Taking the field: Women, men and sports.* Minneapolis: University of Minnesota.

Nike Television Advertisement. (1998, August). Lifetime Network.

O'Keefe, M. (2000). Sexploitation or pride? Female Olympians' revealing poses stir debate. *Newhouse News Services.* Retrieved April 18, 2005, from http://www.newhouse.com/archive/story1a091500.html

Round not oval: Supporting WUSA (20003, September). Retrieved April 18, 2005, from http://www.ussoccerplayers.com/rno/discussion092003.html

Salter, D. F. (1996). *Crashing the old boy's network: The tragedies and triumphs of girls and women in sports.* Westport, CT: Praeger.

Schulze, L. (1990). On the muscle. In J. Gaines & C. Herzog (Eds.), *Fabrications: Costume and the female body* (pp. 59–78). New York: Routledge.

Truitt, E. (2001, July). Athletes in Skirts: Why don't women tennis players wear shorts? *Slate Magazine* [Online]. Retreived April 18, 2005, from http://slate.msn.com/id/111580/

Tucker, C. (2000, September). *Female Olympic athletes now command attention*. Retrieved April 18, 2005, from http://www.uexpress.com/asiseeit/?uc_full_date=20000914

Whiteside, K. (1998). *WNBA: A celebration: Commemorating the birth of a league*. New York: HarperCollins.

Women's National Basketball Association Official Web site. Retrieved April 18, 2005, from http://www.wnba.com

Women's Sports Foundation (2000). *Response to Media Queries RE: Nude/Semi-Nude Photos of Athletes in Sports Magazines*. Retrieved from http://www.womenssportsfoundation.org

Thinking Through Power in Sport and Sport Media Scholarship

Mary G. McDonald
Miami University (Oxford, Ohio)

In attempting to theorize the relationships between power and sport, North American sport scholars have applied a wide range of diverse writings including those by Louis Althusser, Gloria Anzaldúa, Jean Baudrillard, Judith Butler, Pierre Bourdieu, bell hooks, Jacques Derrida, Norbert Elias, Frantz Fanon, Michel Foucault, Anthony Giddens, Paul Gilroy, Antonio Gramsci, Elizabeth Grosz, Stuart Hall, C. L. R. James, Jacques Lacan, Karl Marx, C. Wright Mills, Charles Mills, Gayatri Spivak, Max Weber, and Raymond Williams. Close inspection of these applications reveals that specific historical moments give rise to different debates and understandings of power, and indeed particular understandings of power have been ascendant at various times within sport studies scholarship.

In this chapter I address competing understandings and contextual complexities by offering a highly selective and partial mapping of two recent engagements with power that I call *rearticulating power* and *troubling power*. In outlining this discussion of power, I draw upon influential English language debates and writings within the sociology and cultural studies of sport and sport media scholarship, particularly emphasizing the North American and British academic contexts.

Rearticulating power is meant to signify three ways that power has been (re)conceived within post-Marxist sport studies scholarship through the application of hegemony theory to sport and the sport media; the expansion of hegemony theory to include relations of gender and race within the sport and the media; and the promotion of a *contextual cultural studies* of sport. Troubling power recognizes the transformation ushered in by a focus on the microlevel and productive elements of power, especially as expressed via Michel Foucault's writings. This section discusses sport and media scholars' application of key Foucauldian concepts including power/knowledge, panoptic power, normalization, and governmentality while noting affinities with other antifoundational critiques especially as expressed in the writings of Judith Butler. The paper concludes by very briefly discussing emerging theories of power within postcolonial sport studies.

While sociological writings about power can be traced back to the creation of the discipline, my narrative begins in more recent times. In the 1970s and the 1980s, attempts to reformulate understandings of power in sport studies scholarship initially represented attempts to move beyond both popular mainstream misunderstandings of sport as apolitical and doctrinaire interpretations of Marxist concepts. One of the most visible responses by sport scholars, particularly those immersed in debates from the Center for Contemporary Culture Studies (CCCS) at the University of Birmingham, England, is the application of hegemony theory to sport and the sport media as significant sites where power is not merely asserted but contested and struggled over. In this way sport scholars were among a growing group of scholars directing criticisms against both Marxist arguments themselves and the recognition that "the social world has changed" in significant ways "since key ideas were formulated over a century ago" (Barrett, 1991, p. 3). These changes include an increasingly globalizing economy with complex local manifestations including greater diasporic flows of people, the ubiquity of media images and technologies, and the proliferation of social movements (Civil Rights, gay and lesbian, indigenous, women's, etc.). Each of these changes in turn inspire retheorizing and application of power by diverse cultural critics.

More recently emerging poststructuralist and postmodern debates have produced new ways of thinking about power apart from Marxist-inspired scholarship. This new sensibility has not sought to repair the breaks opened up by poststructuralists' critique of such grand theories as Marxism and structural linguistics. Nor has this theorizing attempted to remake traditional class-based analysis in light of various social movements' challenges to the mythological unity of this standpoint. Rather scholars such as Foucault have instead "sought new ways of thinking outside" of Marxist-inspired accounts of power (McHoul & Grace, 1993, p. 3).

Emerging within the past decade, Foucauldian-inspired scholarship on sport and the media is just now emerging as "a growth area" (Andrews, 2000, p. 123). Therefore, this body of writings is not as voluminous as Marxist-inspired writings, nor has it yet been subject to the same sustained internal critique and revision as has been the case within the lengthier legacy of Marxist-inspired sport and media scholarship. And yet, Foucauldian sport and sport media scholarship notably troubles post-Marxist understandings by reconceptualizing power, not as repressive, but as productive, often pleasurable, constituted through a multiplicity of hierarchical domains of knowledge, normative institutions, and bodily practices.

This narrative I have just written about rearticulating power and troubling power suggests that each is the result of discontinuous and deliberate conversations between and among theorists, rather than being discrete and bounded entities. At the risk of homogenizing diverse and nuanced understandings of power, I choose to trace each separately for analytic purposes. I also point briefly toward convergences between the paradigms of articulating power and troubling power. My goal is to clarify conceptualizations of power, to analyze what these conceptualizations have already contributed to understandings of the sport media complex, and, via this analysis, to suggest what happens as power travels across diverse debates and historical contexts.

REARTICULATING POWER

Rearticulating power plays off the multiple meanings of the word *articulate*. One usage of this term means to speak. Another usage suggests a joining together as is the case with an articulation between two joints of the body. To rearticulate thus suggests a type of restating, rejoining, that is, a remaking of a concept, idea, or practice. Thus I specifically deploy *rearticulate* to suggest the complex ways that power has been rethought and reenacted within post-Marxist writings specifically via (a) the use of hegemony theory, originally proposed by the Italian Marxist Antonio Gramsci, as a corrective to the presumed economic determinism of Marxist writings about sport and the media; (b) the expansion of hegemony theory beyond economic and class-based interpretations to include discussions related to gender and race; and (c) the development of a contextual cultural studies of sport, that is, the exploration of particular linkages or specific articulations and rearticulations of hegemonic power within specific temporal conjunctures and spatial locations.

Rearticulating Power: Critical Theorists Respond to Economic Determinism

One of Karl Marx's enduring legacies for contemporary sport sociology, media, and cultural studies is the way subsequent scholars have drawn upon his writings to rethink the labor process within political economic conditions of contemporary capitalist societies and sport (Beamish, 2002). And yet, to this day scholars continue to question long-held Marxist and emerging "beliefs pertaining to the relationship between the economic base of a society, and the cultural institutions and practices of everyday life" (Howell, Andrews, & Jackson, 2002, p. 153). The 1982 publication of *Sport, Culture and Ideology*, edited by Jennifer Hargreaves, serves as a key text in which several scholars reconfigure Marxist sensibilities to argue against economically reductive approaches to British, South African, and Soviet sport while theorizing the specific manifestations of dominance and resistance in sport. Drawing upon a synthesis of ideas from Anthony Giddens' and Raymond Williams' understanding of hegemony, Gruneau's (1983) analysis of class-based struggles within Canadian sport stands with John (J. E.) Hargreaves' (1986) analysis of British sport as among the first extended applications of hegemony theory to sport. In sum, each of these works seeks to expose and rewrite the deterministic tendencies underling early Marxist applications to sport scholarship.

For example, J. E. Hargreaves (1982b) criticized the economic reductionism of such positions as that offered by Brohm (1978), who drew upon Freudian sensibilities and a Marcusian abstraction (Gruneau, 1983) of structural Marxism to suggest that power is all pervasive in reflecting top-down economic interests. From this perspective sport and the sport media serve to reproduce alienating relations as sites where power is exerted ideologically and structurally to the benefit of the wealthy and the state in (over)determining working class' consciousness and human agency.[1]

---

[1]For more detailed discussions of the early critics of sport inspired by Marxist writings, see Beamish (2002). For a discussion of Marxist and neo-Marxist sensibilities within sport and sport media scholarship, see Hargreaves and McDonald (2000) and Rigauer (2002). Cantelon and Ingham (2002) delineate the impact of Max Weber's writings on the sociology of sport.

Brohm's (1978) ultimate aim is economic revolution, and once that is achieved, sport "would disappear in a universal communist society" (p. 52). For under capitalism,

> sport treats the human organism as a machine, in the same way as the worker becomes a mere appendage of the machine in the capitalist system. Sport as an ideology reproduces and strengthens the ideology of alienated labour: work, continuous effort, struggle, the cult of transcending one's own limitations, the cult of suffering, the cult of self-denial, self-sacrifice, etc. Sport is a morality of effort, which conditions people for the oppressive work of the factory. (p. 50)

Although important in pointing to the pervasive influence of corporate capitalism and the conservative values often celebrated in mainstream elite competitive sport and then widely circulated in the sport media, this polemic standpoint is also problematic in reducing conflict to that of coercive and manipulative economic interests (J. E. Hargreaves, 1982b). While Brohm does allow for the possible development of class consciousness, on the whole "for Brohm, capitalism has shaped sport in its own image, and anyone who believes that an interest in sport is any way compatible with the pursuit of class struggle is simply a falsely-conscious dupe" (Gruneau, 1983, p. 38). Brohm's position further assumes capitalism, class, and power as coherent, static, and essential entities.

In contrast to this position, hegemony theory argues for a complex, often imperceptible notion of power that acknowledges both the agency of subordinated classes and the historically specific, fluid character of ideologies that seek to bolster the status of the dominant group. Advocates of hegemony theory within sport studies typically assert that power represents "the capacity of a person or group of persons to employ resources of different types to secure outcomes" (Gruneau, 1988b, p. 22). Power is therefore a "relationship between agents, the outcome of which is determined by agents' access to relevant resources and their use of appropriate strategies in specific conditions of struggles with other agents" (J. E. Hargreaves, 1986, p. 3). Those who advocate for hegemony theory argue for a more unstable, shifting notion of power where leadership is secured and maintained only to the extent that particular ideologies and their materialized and institutionalized signifying practices are made to accommodate at least some oppositional beliefs and activities from shifting sets of alliances of dominant and subordinate groups. Popular cultural forms such as sport and the sport media are thus understood "neither as an unambiguous site for class-based ways of life nor as the ideological support of capitalist relations of production" (Gruneau, 1988b, p. 20). Thus conceived, hegemony theory allows for a "war of positions" that acknowledges both "top-down" and "bottom-up" dialectical understandings where power is owned and exerted but "characterized by conflict and consent, coercion and struggle" (J. E. Hargreaves, 1982a, p. 118). This reformulation emphasizing the dialectic character of agency and constraint counters orthodox economic reductionism and notions of ideological power as uniform, illusionary, and unidirectional (J. E. Hargreaves, 1982a).

While power is conceived of as relationally possessed and grappled over, this struggle is most often engaged under inequitable conditions as some individuals and classes are granted greater access to the important signifying systems like the media to promote a particular worldview. Socially produced resources enable at least three different measures of social power by different groups: "(a) the capacity to structure sport in preferred ways and to institutionalize these preferences in sports rules and organizations; (b) the capacity to establish selective sports traditions; and (c) the capacity to define the range of legitimate practices and meanings associated with dominant sporting practices" (Gruneau, 1988a, p. 22).

Read from this perspective, many of the most visible mainstream sports promoted in the media seek

> to justify and uphold dominant values and ideas. The model of the social order encoded in media practices and assumptions is a pluralist and basically harmonious one, but threatened by deviations from established procedures and the outbreak of conflict. The figure of the judge, referee or umpires symbolizes legitimate authority, whose duty it is to punish infringements of the norms, and whose decisions are beyond challenge. A good game/society is one conducted according to the established rules; a problematic game/society is one where infringements of the established order occur. (J. E. Hargreaves, 1982a, pp. 127–128)

This formulation is the basic framework for Sage's (1998) textbook that interrogates the United States context to analyze how dominant ideologies and resistant practices work within the context of sport and the state, the capitalist economy, professional sport, the sport media, and educational systems while also exploring the way these ideologies seek to promote particular class, gender, and race relations. Sage (1998) also noted specific resistant practices remade through sport, highlighting such divergent events as the residual salience of working class, antirationalist amusements such as cockfighting and dogfighting, the multinational Olympic boycott against South African apartheid most visibly seen in the 1980s, and the contemporary challenge to homophobia offered through the alternative sport form of the Gay Games.

Other applications of hegemony theory explore both the ideological and often emotionally compelling character of both sport and the sport media. For example, Jhally (1989) argued that a symbiotic economic relationship, what he terms *the sport–media complex*, exists between elite competitive professional sport and the media. Here sport produces an audience for advertisers, and the media provides publicity for professional and college sport within this mutually beneficial relationship. And in this era of heightened concentration of ownership, sport content is increasingly becoming an important element of transnational media corporations' television programming and cross-marketing endeavors. Transnational media conglomerates like Rupert Murdock's News Corporation mobilize popular understandings and particular (local) national identifications around sport in the United States, the United Kingdom, and Australia to enhance profits and fashion "a global media entertainment empire" (Andrews, 2003, p. 235).

As an oligarchy, media structures enjoy the upper hand in encoding sporting texts. Television producers of such worldwide media events as the Olympic Games attempt to create spectacles of accumulation and legitimation in an effort to enhance profits and separate their programming from their competitors' (MacNeill, 1996). In doing so sport media producers tend to avoid controversial framings, thus closing "the range of possible meanings" to which a diverse array of viewers must always respond, although these are always contested and not univocal (Jhally, 1989, p. 89). Thus conceived, within this commodity relationship too often the media producers provide highly selective reformulations or reinterpretations of sporting events in ways that seek legitimation for dominant understandings of militarism, nationalism, competition, authority, and consumption (Jhally, 1989).

Advertisers play a key role in this process. For example, Nike's motto of "Just do it" resonates with ideologies of individualism and popular mythologies of both sport and America as meritocracies. Thus, advertisers such as those at Nike who suggest that personal characteristics of "grit, determination, and effort" are prerequisite for both sporting and economic success deflect attention away from multinational capitalism's stratifying effects (Goldman & Papson, 1998, p. 20). And similar romantic depictions of sport as a level playing field are especially powerful given the historical popular pleasures and "structures of feelings" they promote, suggesting that the "passions involved, emotional entanglements with the events that we witness . . . cannot simply be explained under terms such as consciousness and ideology. They are a large part (for many people, heretofore largely male) of how social identity is formed" (Jhally, 1989, p. 73).

Jhally's scholarship suggests an embodied, affective process of negotiation where power is struggled over by certain alliances through the ideological component of common sense that Gramsci characterized as "the conception of the world which is uncritically absorbed by the various social and cultural environments in which the moral individuality of the average person is developed" (Gramsci, 1971, p. 419). Active consent is most convincingly won in hegemonic struggles when particular worldviews appear to be inevitable, natural, and wise and yet actually exist "in conformity with the social and cultural position of those masses whose philosophy it is" (Gramsci, 1971, p. 419). The worldviews subscribed to by those in power thus become the seemingly only acceptable approach, and thus particular interests are mistaken as the interests of all. Important signifying institutions including sport and the media greatly assist in the production of consensus (Hall, 1982).

This theoretical understanding shifts the focus away from orthodox Marxist notions of false consciousness and deterministic understandings of ideology to an emphasis that supplements and at times displaces the centrality of class analysis (classically the proletariat) with a focus on constraint, agency, resistance, accommodation, and consent. This alteration opens up important questions: "Who produces the consensus? In what interests does it function? On what conditions does it depend?" (Hall, 1982, p. 86). These questions are never easily explicable as the hegemonic process is fraught with contradictions and is always shifting, given the continuous process of resistance and the ongoing accommodation of a manageable level of opposition to commonsense ideologies. Just as significant is the notion that any consensus is never complete, but a matter of degree and compromise that has to be continuously rewon.

Rearticulating Power: Feminist and Critical Race Theorists' Use of Hegemony Theory

While a considerable amount of work about common sense has been written in relationship to class relations and sport, the shift in focus to relations of agency and constraint has enabled several feminist scholars (see especially Birrell, 1988; Birrell & Theberge, 1994a, 1994b; Hall, 1996; J. A. Hargreaves, 1994, 2000) to build on the hegemony framework as well, although not without criticism. In total, this work demonstrates that "whatever the appeal of a class-based model of politics and society, it cannot function adequately in any orthodox fashion as the fountainhead of intervention and resistance in sport" (Rowe, 1998, p. 245). Much of this feminist scholarship challenges the presumption of masculinity that too often underlies discussions of power and thus is aligned with those Foucauldian sensibilities that argue the body is a significant site for the enactment of power. A great deal of this feminist sport scholarship is indebted to Willis' (1982) critique of the traditional masculine domain of sport. According to Willis, the gender order is embedded in sport, and gender segregation is constituted as the only fair and reasonable arrangement for sport. The regulation of sporting bodies to the ideological realm of the "natural" and commonsense understandings of biology are an important mechanism in this process. Overlapping achievements between and among men and women are ignored; rather, physical performance differences between the sexes are understood and circulated in popular consciousness, most notably via the media, as the ideological proof of female sporting and social inferiority. While always contested and challenged, sport has become one site to legitimate a larger gender ideology about presumed natural male superiority and the bipolar "nature of the sexes" (Willis, 1982, p. 119).

In 1988 Birrell identified four themes central to this commonsense gendering process, themes that still receive a great deal of scholarly attention well over a decade later (Birrell, 2000): (a) the production of masculine ideologies and power through sport; (b) media practices that assist in legitimating commonsense understandings of female athleticism; (c) ideologies related to physicality, sexuality, and the body as important sites of hegemonic struggle; and (d) the ongoing resistance of women to dominant notions of sport, sexuality, and the body. Messner (1988) weaved together many of the same elements identified by Birrell to argue that bodies of female athletes serve as "contested ideological terrain" (p. 197). Messner argues that throughout the twentieth century "organized sports have come to serve as a primary institutional means for bolstering a challenged and faltering ideology of male superiority" where men of all backgrounds are ideologically encouraged through mediated spectacles like professional football to identify men's sporting excellence with apparent "natural proof" of male sporting and cultural superiority (Messner, 1988, p. 197). In an era when the feminist movement has challenged masculine hegemony, presumably objective and equitable sports reporting nonetheless encourages men to ignore cultural and historical structures of opportunities and framings of sport to understand female athletes as "at a decided advantage, 'fighting biology all the way'" (Messner, 1988 p. 206). Practices such as women's bodybuilding challenge these views about physicality, muscularity, and femininity. And yet too often this resistance is trivialized or outright ignored by the mainstream media, thus further bolstering the commonsense framing of women as inherently unable "to measure up to men," and hence male power is remade through the sport media complex (Messner, 1988, p. 207).

Adding to the influence of this and similar constructions is the pervasive homophobic atmosphere of sport that in turn fuels popular and media obsessions with the sexuality of female athletes (Griffin, 1998; Griffin & Genasci, 1990; Lenskyj, 1991). Griffin and Genasci (1990) suggested that girls and women who transgress ideologies of appropriate "femininity" via serious participation in physically taxing "masculine" sports are frequently discouraged via homophobic taunts and rude questions about their sexual orientation, thus demonstrating that "homophobia is the glue that holds sexism together" (Griffin & Genasci, 1990, pp. 213–214). While the homosocial character of sport has enabled some women to bond in intimate and erotically meaningful ways, homophobia means that many women also fail to fully participate in sport and the many lesbian athletes who do participate are too often forced to live in fear and silence (Griffin, 1998). The media defensively participates in this homophobic process by continuously focusing on the presumed (hetero)sexual attractiveness of iconic female athletes (Birrell & Theberge, 1994a).

The ideological construction of difference via the media is a reoccurring, some might say seeming inexhaustible, theme in contemporary gender analysis of sport ideology. Duncan (1990) explored the construction of sexual difference by examining the content within sport photographs (physical appearance, body poses, emotional expressions, and camera angles) and context of sport photographs (captions, surrounding written text, and visual spacing) from popular North American magazine coverage of the 1984 and 1988 Olympic Games. She provides evidence that demonstrates a continuing obsession with sexual difference as female athletes are frequently portrayed in submissive bodily poses, in ways that emphasize emotional displays, and camera angles repeatedly position athletes such as track star Florence Griffith-Joyner and figure skater Katarina Witt in sexually suggestive poses. Other media portrayals such as those preferred by marketers of the Women's National Basketball Association (WNBA) frequently focus on the maternity and superior morality of the players, a framing that counters the racist stereotype of "exotic others" that too often adheres to African-American women in sport (Banet-Weiser, 1999; McDonald, 2000). The cumulative impact of these seemingly objective framings is that female athletes are frequently constructed ambivalently where female athleticism is downplayed in relationship to such gendered representations as the girls next door, moral maternity, or the positioning of particular stars as the (presumed) object of heterosexual desire. In contrast, the media frequently portrays male athletes as the epitome of hegemonic masculinity as strong, assertive athletes and active agents of heterosexuality.

There is a plethora of writings that document the pervasive influential ways that masculine power is both remade and challenged through sport and the sport media (Messner, 2002). And yet, as the previous examples demonstrate, not all women are similarly positioned nor do all men share equal status within a complex and shifting gender order. For example, the scholarship on the use of Native Americans as mascots in sport has demonstrated the ways in which white appropriation of Native traditions and images serves as fodder for media spectacles that mimic Native people in ahistorical, stereotypical fashion as "noble savages." These framings trivialize the lives of Native men and women while serving to bolster white hegemony and masculine power in sport and the wider culture (King & Springwood, 2001).

Critiquing the Eurocentric bias of much sport scholarship around masculinity, Carrington (1998) traced the various forms of cultural resistance performed by Black men in response to White racism expressed through cricket and wider British culture. In post-colonial contexts where Black men are frequently feminized and terrorized via White-dominated ideologies and cultural practices, the Black cricket club serves as both a resistant radicalized space "providing many of the Black men a sense of ontological security" and a symbolic marker of the Black community.

St. Louis (2004) convincingly demonstrated the ways in which the alleged "natural" athletic superiority of Black athletes, especially Black male athletes, is structured through a simplistic (mis)understanding of genetics, the scientific method, and the mythological assumption that somehow "deep physiological internal characteristics" match "external phenotypical differences" of distinctively separate racial and ethnic groups (p. 34). These claims are made all the more powerful given the mobilization and synthesis of these naive understandings with new narratives produced within what St. Louis calls "corporate managerial horizontalism," that is, a historical shift away from White attempts to promote racial exclusion and hierarchy toward a marketing sensibility that seemingly celebrates diversity, heterogeneity, and the tolerance of different cultures (p. 39). The resulting "multicultural common sense" promoted in popular media including books like Entine's (1999) *Taboo: Why Black Athletes Dominate Sports and Why We're Afraid to Talk About It* is indicative of a new historical block (what Gramsci identifies as a wide array of institutions, social relations, and ideas), where racist biological explanations of Black athletic success now masquerade paradoxically as "facts" of human cultural and biodiversity. St. Louis' analysis elaborates upon Gramsci's understanding of common sense as shifting, "fragmentary" and often "incoherent," while suggesting the need for diligence in both exposing and debating the moral and ethical consequences of taken-for-granted claims promoted in popular mythologies of genetic science (p. 40).

Rearticulating Power Without Guarantees: Contextual Cultural Studies

Emerging from a focus on power as contested and fluid, poststructuralist critiques of grand theory, and the "linguistic turn" within social analysis, several sport scholars articulate a "neo-Gramscian approach" that "keys on the uniqueness of the historical moment or conjuncture in question" (Andrews, 2002, pp. 112–113). Drawing on the writings of Stuart Hall and Lawrence Grossberg, Andrews is among the most persuasive advocates of this contextual cultural studies of sport and the sport media which also aims to delineate strategic principles as a means not just to describe, but as with followers of Gramsci, to intervene in social life by challenging shifting and inequitable relations of power. Within this conceptualization, Grossberg (1991) and Hall (1986, 1991) contended that there is no law which assures in advance that a particular worldview of a class or social group is already and unequivocally given to correspond with the shifting position the group holds in the social and economic relations of late capitalism (Hall, 1991). Thus Hall also advocates another post-Marxist understanding of power, a power "without guarantees," suggesting that there is no necessary correspondence or noncorrespondance between "one level of a social formation and another between the social structure and the human agent, or between a cultural practice such as sport and the varied forces that act within a social structure" (Andrews, 2002, p. 112). Building upon Laclau's (1977) theory of articulation, Hall suggests that the effects and consequences of power are not inherent in any text, identity, or practice; rather, politically salient meanings are produced through the linkage of texts, practices, and contexts (Grossberg, 1991). As Hall stated,

> Thus an articulation is the form of the connection that can make a unity of two different elements, under certain conditions. It is a linkage, which is not necessary, determined, absolute and essential for all time. You have to ask, under what circumstances can a connection be forged or made? So the so-called "unity" of a discourse is really the articulation of different, distinct elements, which can be rearticulated in different ways because they have no necessary "belongingness." (as cited in Grossberg, 1986, p. 53)

The presumption of fluid and historically contingent and complex articulations of power is readily apparent in discussions of health lifestyles (Howell & Ingham, 2001) as well as the representational politics of sport celebrities (Andrews & Jackson, 2001; Birrell & McDonald, 2000; McDonald & Birrell, 1999; Whannel, 2002) including the most celebrated basketball superstar, Michael Jordan (Andrews, 2001). Indeed, Andrews (1995) supplemented Hall's writings with Derridean deconstruction to conceptualize Jordan's mediated persona as a free-floating signifier that links to, at times works against, but ultimately supports many of the regressive racialized politics and images of post-Reagan America. Jordan's all-American persona and reputation as a hardworking African-American athlete who allegedly transcends his race serve to reinforce an image that the American dream is merely a matter of personal determination rather than constrained or enabled by structures of opportunity. Whether engaging the star's on-court exceptionalism, off-the-court gambling activities, or the brutal murder of his father, representations of Jordan "act as markers of an American cultural racism which oscillates between patronizing and demonizing representations of African American Otherness" (Andrews, 1995, p. 153). Ultimately Jordan serves as a free-floating signifier that crystallizes many historically created racist codes at a time when regressive and conservative social ideas and policies downplay racism and economic inequalities to disproportionately blame African Americans and the poor for their plight. Thus, Andrews used Jordan to demonstrate Hall's (1981) assertion that "the meaning of a cultural symbol is given in part by the social field . . . with which it articulates and is made to resonate" (p. 237).

My own work on Michael Jordan (McDonald, 1996) drew upon feminist understandings about the intersectional and fluid character of power and subjectivities to explore the ways that narratives of gender, race, class, and sexuality are articulated through both the texts of Jordan's persona and the contexts of the recent regressive family values climate in the United States. Media images of Jordan encourage viewers to identify with a vision of Black masculinity as a "safe sex symbol" designed to induce desire instead of invoking dread. In this sense Jordan's cultivated image of modest sensuality projected through commercials and mainstream sports reports throughout the 1980s and most of the 1990s challenges a legacy of racist images of Black men as overtly sexual and dangerous. Yet the repeated media framing of Jordan within the nuclear family as a rugged individual, concerned father, and upright citizen are also very similar to the family values character discourses used by American conservatives throughout the same era to promote regressive social policies that mostly favored the wealthy and capitalist expansion while frequently blaming the victim by positioning people of color and especially poor women of color as morally lacking.

Analysis of the global–local media reach of Jordan's media image demonstrate yet another example of how competing contexts give rise to divergent political consequences. The diverse and contradictory reception of Jordan within such differing local spaces as Poland, New Zealand, and across the Black Atlantic suggests Jordan's commodifed influence cannot merely be understood as just another crass example of homogenization through Amercianization. Rather this analysis reveals the contingency of meaning and politics, as the mediated sign of Jordan links with local histories. For many Poles living in a post-Communist nation, for example, Jordan signifies the ideology of the American dream most readily embraced by younger generations who are apparently more comfortable with consumer capitalism. And yet, within the context of New Zealand, Jordan's commercialized persona has paradoxically helped to generate wider interest in all sports, while particularly helping to rejuvenate traditional New Zealand sporting activities. And to others, particularly members of the transnational diasporic community that composes the Black Atlantic, Jordan represents the hopes and possibilities that are imagined through the circulation of media images representing Black achievement, resolve, and pride (Carrington, Andrews, Jackson, & Mizur, 2001).

And finally, analyses of the changing meanings of Canadian track athlete Ben Johnson also reveals that specific historical conjunctures and media events (co)produce diverse and shifting politicized meanings in this case in relationship to the crises of race, ethnicity, and nation. Although once hailed as an upright citizen and emblem of Canadian national unity, Johnson's image and function changed dramatically after his 1988 gold-medal disqualification for a positive drug test during the Seoul Olympics. Johnson was once hailed as an icon of Canadian multiculturalism but after his fall from sporting grace increasingly was referenced in the White-dominated Canadian press as a Jamaican-born immigrant (Jackson, 1998). This framing of Johnson as a now exterior threat to the imagined pride of the (White) Canadian nation articulates to wider cultural anxieties over Canadian identity, vulnerability, and alleged loss of innocence within an increasingly racially diverse nation and globalizing world (Abdel-Shehid, 1999; Jackson, 1998). Years later in the mid-1990s the "absent-but-present" Ben Johnson would serve as the negative foil in media stories celebrating the track successes of Black Canadian Donovan Bailey. The result is a Manichaean comparison where the media narratives represent the two in ways that align with lingering (post)colonial fantasies: Johnson is constructed as representing "bad" Black masculinity and Bailey is projected as "good," thus rearticulating yet another illusory vision of a tolerant, color-blind, multicultural nation (Abdel-Shehid, 1999). This analysis of the shifting meanings of Ben Johnson reveals that the politics of representation are never settled for all time; rather, fresh ideological meanings are constantly being rearticulated according to the needs and interests of particular historical moments.

TROUBLING POWER

The word *troubling* most often suggests something worrisome, even annoying, which frequently induces discomfort as well. *Troubling* also implies a successful subversion. Both definitions of troubling have been attributed to Michael Foucault's conceptualizations of power, for his writings rebel against popular understandings of power as exclusively repressive, a bothersome insurgency to those theorists who hold modernist assumptions of power. This section outlines this troubling movement of power by mapping applications of such Foucauldian concepts as power/knowledge, panoptic power, normalization, and governmentality to sport and the sport media.

Troubling Power: Power/Knowledge, Sport, and the Media

Contrary to the popular belief that power is exclusively repressive and prohibitive, Michel Foucault recognizes modern power as imaginative, mobile, malleable, ascending, and ubiquitous—an entity to be studied on its own terms rather than as a function of group hierarchies or capitalist economy. In this way then, his concept of power is not just incompatible with Marxism, but also with that of most modern social science (Barrett, 1991). In an often-cited passage, Foucault (1979) argued that "we must cease once and for all to describe the effects of power in negative terms: it 'excludes,' it 'represses,' it 'censors,' it abstracts,' it 'masks,' it 'conceals.' In fact, power produces: it produces reality; it produces domains of objects and rituals of truth" (p. 194).

Thus in opposition to persistent popular, sociological, and (neo)Marxist theoretical assumptions, power is not owned by a sovereign power such as a king, or by a particular group or class of people. Rather, power "is exercised rather than possessed; is not attached to agents and interests but is incorporated in numerous practices" (Barrett, 1991, p. 135). Thus power is a strategy that is constantly performed through microlevel, capillary-like networks and hierarchical webs of bodies, knowledges, and institutions.

Increasingly scholars have engaged with Foucault's argument that knowledge is inseparable from relations of power to reverse "the traditional belief that knowledge is power" and instead focused on "how people effect knowledge to intervene in social affairs" (Popkewitz & Brennan, 1998, p. 16). This sensibility has been especially deployed by several authors writing about sport and the body and by those interrogating the politics of knowledge within sport studies scholarship.

Cole (1994) also drew upon Foucault's insights about the human (social) sciences to both engage and extend feminist, Gramscian, and Althusser-inspired accounts in arguing for a new understanding of "sport." Cole notes that poststructuralist, post-Marxist, and feminist cultural studies have not merely analyzed sport but have also destabilized sport as an object of knowledge. Taken to its logical conclusion, this movement opens up new possibilities to view sport as both the subject and object of discourse, "as an ensemble of knowledges and practices" imbued with modern power "that disciplines, conditions, reshapes, and inscribes the body through the terms and needs of a patriarchal, racist capitalism" (Cole, 1994, p. 15). Sport is thus conceived "as an apparatus that organizes and is organized by normalizing practices and strategies of science, technology, and the media; a technology that produces multiple bodies (raced, classed, gendered, heterosexualized, prosthetic, pure, patriotic, etc.) in the context of an image-dominated consumer culture" (Cole, 1996, p. 288).

Thus within this framework the object of interrogation ceases to be "sport per se," and this post-sport sensibility "compels researchers to problematize sport's implicit relation" to modern power (Andrews, 2000) that too often limits our perceptions of alternative, subjugated ways of understanding. Applying Foucault's insights about "the discursive limits of the episteme" forces "us to see the strangeness of our current state of knowledge and to question the way we think, and the conceptual tools" we think with (Mills, 2003, p. 64).[2]

Taken as a whole, applications of Foucault within sport and media studies challenge Marxist and some Gramscian applications that posit ideology as a type of false consciousness meant to stand in virtual opposition to something else which is supposed to count as truth. In this formulation the truth is thought to be a liberating ethos (presumably provided by Marxist science) that somehow stands outside the purview of power. In contrast, for Foucault "effects of truth are produced within

---

[2]See Rail and Harvey (1995), Andrews (2000), and Maguire (2002) regarding the influence of Foucault within sport and sport media scholarship. For a broader discussion regarding the influence of postmodernism and poststructuralism on sport studies, see Rail (1998, 2002).

discourses which in themselves are neither true or false" but are always implicated in power (Foucault, 1980, p. 118). Far from suggesting that there is no truth, Foucault suggests that there are multiple "truths," each with its own rationality. And yet for one "truth" to be established, equally plausible information needs to be discredited.

Given these Foucauldian insights it is clear that scholars of sport and the media are not concerned with offering a general theory of what power is; nor are they attempting to delineate the intentions, aims, motives, and interests of those exerting power. Instead these scholars are concerned with the *how* of power, that is, with delineating the mechanisms, strategies, and technologies that constitute modern power relations (Barrett, 1991). This formulation suggests that it is more important to study the "*effectiveness* of power/knowledge" through such techniques or modes of application as the panopticon and normalization than to seek to produce a timeless, essential "truth" of liberation against power (Hall, 1997, p. 49). Simply stated, careful genealogical analysis makes visible the techniques, practices, and effects of disciplinary power as a means of revising subjugated knowledges to better enhance and enable practices of resistance through sport.

Troubling Power: The Panopticon and Surveillance

Perhaps the most famous symbol connected to Foucault's writings is his use of Jeremy Bentham's panopticon, a prison structure with a visibly imposing guard tower in the center. That Foucault would deploy the metaphor of the panopticon is not surprising because writings about prisons function as key analytic models for his wider theorization of modern disciplinary power. According to Foucault, public displays of torture and executions that demonstrated the king's power were increasingly replaced during the Enlightenment by seemingly more humane practices of incarceration. This movement from public torture to incarceration has more to do with wider shifts in how power operates in modern times, with the mechanisms of modern biopower (the regulation of life and populations) increasingly operating by making individuals both the objects and subjects of power.

The panoptic tower provides a space for guards to observe and police the actions of the prisoners in their cells. Yet, the spatial design of the prison is such that the inmates can never see into the tower and are thus never quite sure when a guard is present. The effect of this design is to "induce in the inmate a state of conscious and permanent visibility that assures the automatic functioning of power" (Foucault, 1979, p. 201) where inmates monitor themselves, irrespective of whether the guard is in the tower or not. This is significant for "he who is subjected to a field of visibility, and who knows it, assumes responsibility for the constraints of power; he makes them play spontaneously upon himself; he inscribes in himself the power relations in which he simultaneously plays both roles; he becomes the principle of his own subjection" (Foucault, 1979, p. 37).

In a feminist application of this metaphor, Duncan (1994) sought to understand the operations of power in regard to the women's body ideals promoted in the media, specifically in the fitness magazine *Shape*. The texts of *Shape* interact within a fitness culture frequently structured to reproduce the male gaze. The result is that female readers and exercisers are encouraged via the pages of *Shape* to become both spectator and spectacle in comparing their bodies to public ideals through self-disciplining practices such as eating low caloric diets and engaging in rigorous exercise routines. And yet, this creation of docile bodies through surveillance and self-policing is not just evident in the prison, media, or the gymnasium but anywhere people "are distributed administratively in order to be watched and trained for optimal performance" (Rail & Harvey, 1995, p. 378).

Two more examples of the disciplinary power of the panopticon from the world of high performance sport were discussed by Shogan (1999). Much like the guard tower system, sport team practices are organized so that the coach has the potential to see each athlete. Knowing that they are subject to the coach's gaze, but never knowing at what exact moment, athletes monitor their own behavior. Athletes adopt the coach's messages so that when they "perform skills incorrectly or without intensity, the movement feels 'wrong' or 'unnatural'" (p. 38). This self-monitoring is not just a means of avoiding punishment, but it also represents the ways athletes have "incorporated both the technologies and values of docility and correct training" (p. 38). In a similar way, random drug testing serves as a panoptic device as athletes internalize the knowledge that they could be tested at any time. And yet, self-surveillance is not always accomplished as the recent debates over the proliferation of steroid use within professional baseball demonstrate. Thus the use of prohibited performance-enhancing drugs by athletes also reveals the continuous and complex play between power and resistance.

Troubling Power: Subject to Normalization

One of Foucault's most provocative theses is the rejection of humanist ontologies, that also ground Marxist and neo-Marxist formulations, whereby people are presumed to possess an essential core entity and intentionally act in rationale ways. Foucault specifically detailed and developed this claim in relationship to sexuality (see especially Foucault, 1990). Within this conceptualization, the categories of homosexuality and heterosexuality are seen as recent discursive inventions, the product of proliferating knowledges imbued with power related to sexuality and not the natural expression of an essential (or repressed) identity. Thus, although there had long been sexual relationships and practices between same sex couples, by the late nineteenth century an individuated "species" appeared, marked with a particular identity thought to be infused with perverse sexuality.

This visible rendition of alleged sexual perversity is part of a wider epistemic shift away from the sanctioning of acts and practices toward the creation, regulation, and criminalization of identities. Like the criminal and other pathological bodies, "the homosexual" was now both the subject of and subject to disciplinary power via sustained inquiry in a wide range of discursive fields and the human sciences including demography, education, law, and medicine (Spargo, 1999). Thus, much as with the criminal, the homosexual body serves as an effect of modern power that creates and contains "'what' and 'who' are threatened and threatening in order to produce and stabilize the norm" (Cole, 1996, p. 284).

And despite attempts at social control in this alleged area of perversity, Foucault also documented what he terms a "reverse" discourse whereby "homosexuality began to speak in its own behalf to demand that its legitimacy or 'naturality' be acknowledged, often in the same vocabulary, using the same categories by which it was medically disqualified" (Foucault, 1990, p. 101). This "reverse" discourse suggests that an individual might also mobilize the category of the "deviant" to question and resist his or her social and political status. Read from this perspective, the category of the deviant also produces knowledge that can be strategically deployed by its subjects, thus further suggesting a dynamic network in which power is asserted, not via repression or force, but rather through a multiplication of knowledges and pleasures (Spargo, 1999).

In their analysis of mainstream media framings of sexuality through representations of HIV-positive athletes, Dworkin and Wachs (1998) built upon Foucault's contention that the construction of deviance and normalcy demonstrates "how power is constitutive" (p. 4) as particular social formations and identifications are conceptualized while others remain unthinkable. Power is additionally infused through multiple sets of "hierarchicalized dualities," through identities fragmented in relationship to race, class, gender, and sexuality (p. 4). For instance, HIV-infected athletes basketball star Magic Johnson, diver Greg Louganis, and boxer Tommie Morrison are narrated to the public in diverse ways. Self-identified heterosexual athletes, Johnson and Morris are framed differently from the openly gay Louganis whose sexuality is conflated with his HIV status. As time goes by, Johnson's linkages to myths of excessive Black sexuality are reframed as he is represented as a (re)dedicated family man who serves as a positive role model to young Black men, and Morrison's working class status is ignored as he is promoted as having gained increased maturity. Thus, both Morrison and Johnson are redeemed and normalized by the media as they constantly celebrate the athletes' commitments to abstinence and heterosexual monogamy. In contrast to this normalized reading of sexuality, Dworkin and Wachs also outlined the diversity and range of sexual pleasures and identities, thus revealing that bodies, desires, and sexual practices are not so inevitably and naturally aligned as the mainstream media suggests.

A considerable focus of Cole's scholarship has been to map the discursive production and subsequent cultural effects of deviant bodies. For example, Cole's (1996) analysis of Magic Johnsons' public persona and early media coverage of the revelation that he had acquired HIV relies upon a cultural logic that produces and distinguishes between unproductive, degenerative bodies and imagined healthy and hard bodies. Although appearing to be descriptive, these identity categories serve as optics that both enable and constrain a sense of morality related to conduct of self and others that are crucial in establishing the cultural common sense regarding AIDS. On the one hand, the bodies of female fans ("groupies") are marked as the carriers of infection. On the other hand, in other narratives, "promiscuous" African-American athletes, including Johnson himself, stand in for the larger Black community as homophobic, contaminated, infected, and sexually excessive. These framings concurrently produce a normative, yet uninterrogated, image that absolves Middle America from any responsibility for poverty, crime, and ill health in the inner city. These mechanisms of containment serve to conceal the Reagan administration's "failure to address AIDS, the racism, sexism, and homophobia of science, and the pharmaceutical industry's interests in AIDS while authorizing defunding strategies and repressive politics" (Cole, 1996, pp. 299–300). Ultimately this focus on the alleged deviancy of particular bodies is infused with relations of power that seek to marginalize competing interpretations while obscuring other paths of action.

Judith Butler builds upon Foucault's ideas about the diffuse, subjectifying effects of power to argue for the performativity of identity and identifications. In doing so Butler also responds to some of the most persistent critiques about the inadequacy of Foucault's conceptualizations of power in relationship to resistance. While his writings acknowledged that "where there is power there is resistance" and his later writings sought to develop transformative notions via "technologies of the self," a portion of Foucault's work seems deterministic by mostly making visible conforming, docile bodies caught in the grip of power relations. The theory of performativity serves to "mediate between individual agents and the network of power relations in which they are caught" in ways that attempt to overcome the limitations of Enlightenment subjectivity (Allen, 1999, p. 57). That is, the theory of performativity attempts to move beyond both the docility underling much Foucauldian scholarship as well as the voluntaristic assumptions that ground both popular wisdom and neo-Marxist conceptualizations of agency.

Performativity represents an unstable repetitive process whereby bodies often cite and thereby apparently legitimate the norm, but because these citations are continuously enacted and performed, it is possible to subvert and alter these norms. For Butler, the most powerful norm is related to heterosexual discursive ideals where woman–feminine–heterosexual is promoted as the authentic, "prediscursive" form for women to embody. Indeed "girling the girl" suggests a regulatory, disciplining process whereby the "girl" is produced through the expectation that she should embody an idealized femininity and thus is "compelled to cite the norm in order to qualify and remain a viable subject" (Butler, 1993, p. 232). Appeals to norms are thus infused with modern power whereby failure to refer back to norms renders particular bodies unintelligible and abject. Thus, gender norms come to serve in two distinctive ways within the heterosexual matrix, first as a set of imaginary, regulatory "ideals by which gendered bodies become recognizable; second, they are ideals which no gendered body fully or exhaustively embodies" (Butler, 1999, p. 109).

The domain of women's sports and the muscular athleticism of notable female athletes vividly demonstrate these "ideals are not static, but constitutive norms or standards that are surpassable and revisable" (Butler, 1999, p. 104). The malleability, instability, contingency, and transformability of gendered norms for female sexed-bodies are evident, for instance, in tennis star Martina Navratalova's movement from a monstrous sporting outsider to a body lauded for strength, power, and musculature as the "very standard of tennis performance" (Butler, 1999, p. 111).

Although most often used to understand the relationship among sex, gender, and desire (sexuality), the performative, unstable, regulatory function of identity and identifications has been applied to such diverse domains as women's football (soccer) (Caudwell, 2003) and sport advertising and the (Canadian) nation (Helstein, 2000). The raced body is also conceived as "performatively constituted by the very 'expressions' that are said to be its results," suggesting that bodies repeat preexisting, culturally intelligible racial styles and norms (Butler, 1990, p. 25). This insight is readily apparent in the popular sport media including sport films such as the 2002 box-office success, Gurinder Chadha's *Bend It like Beckham* (Giardina, 2003). Grossing over $20 million (US) dollars in its first 12 weeks of release, the film focuses on the football (soccer) exploits and romantic entanglements of two teenage girls, one Asian, the other White, who eventually leave their London homes for athletic scholarships in the United States. Written to appeal to liberal feminist notions of empowerment, the internationally distributed film also celebrates normative multicultural understandings of race and nation, especially a conservative image of what it apparently means to embody the liminal position of being "British-Asian" (Giardina, 2003). These continuous liberal citations also seek to infer that race is a natural component of embodiment even though as with the gendered body there is "no ontological status apart from the various acts which constitute its reality" (Butler, 1990, p. 173). This recognition opens up the possibility to mobilize and resignify race in ways not previously imagined or authorized in seeking more progressive ends.

Yet another expansion upon Butler's understanding of performativity is Helstein's (2003) interrogation of the politics of desire in recent Nike advertising campaigns directed toward women. Infusing Lacanian understandings of the symbolic, imaginary, and real, Helstein argued that Nike's promotion of excellence and emancipation as keys to athletic and personal success suggest "that progress, as a result of true and innocent knowledge and effort, will free us to become 'who [we] want to be'" (Helstein, 2003, p. 287). These idealized notions of excellence and emancipation play upon historically contingent unconscious needs, wishes, and fantasies that ultimately serve as "reiterative performative failures" (p. 288). This means that while constantly repeated these terms exist in a constant state of deferral because we will always "believe that we should be more" because the psychic idealization ("who I want to be") produced as the subject of Nike "is the embodiment of desire constructed by fantasy at the level of the signified" (p. 288). Stated differently, although excellence and emancipation interact with the symbolic and imaginary to appear as desirable and highly attractive imaginings, they are in effect unobtainable. Furthermore, while speaking to a desire for progress and emancipation for all women, this Nike discourse is also aligned with similar historically specific neoconservative and postfeminist projects that deny inequitable social conditions while attempting to compel women to embody social and gender norms. This analysis of Nike is significant both in extending social and cultural critique to explore and problematize the psychic elements of power and in making visible the normalizing and policing effects of popular sport and fitness advertising discourses.

Troubling Power: Governmentality and Sport

Although given only scant attention in Foucault's writings in comparison to other concepts and only recently emerging in the scholarship on sport, the concept of governmentality is important to explicate in more detail as it suggests divergent understandings of modern formulas of power by specifically linking both the macro- and microlevels between the State and individual conduct. Thus governmentality suggests that rather than being under the direct control of state institutions, governing occurs in diffuse and multiple sites without "which the State would not be what it is" (Bratich et al., p. 5). Thus a diverse array of "State, quasi-State and private institutions, practices and policies" including such divergent entities as public schools, volunteer associations, public health initiatives, and the pharmaceutical industry all work to elaborate State interests, although not always successfully or without conflict (Bratich et al., 2003, p. 8).

King (2003) revealed the ways the "Susan G. Komen Breast Cancer Race for the Cure" acts as a technology of governmentality in an era of decreased welfare state spending and subsequent emphasis on volunteerism, philanthropy, and attention to personal health. King argued that the event produces morally compelled consumer-citizens who raise donations for cancer treatment (a process that is itself mainly narrated around individual responsibility in seeking prevention via mammography) through participation and commitment to their own good health and fitness. Thus "therapeutic discourse of survivorship together with acts of personal and corporate giving come to be mobilized and deployed as collective, political action even as dissent and criticism of dominant socio-economic relations is marginalized" (King, 2003, p. 312). King concluded by arguing for the need to agitate against the "Race for the Cure's" narrow version of ideal citizenship and limited understanding of morality.

(IN)CONCLUDING THOUGHTS: IMAGINING POWER CONTINUES

This chapter suggested several ways in which power has been imagined within sport and sport media scholarship. Yet, this analyses also reveals shortcomings beyond my own highly selective rendering, most notably that these understandings of power have drawn largely upon Western, predominately European and North American, theoretical discussions. However, a growing body of sport scholarship is now exploring emerging perspectives that transcend geographic borders to embrace, for example, what Pérez (1999) termed the "decolonial imaginary," that is, a nonlinear, nonexclusively Western postcolonial understanding of desire and power. Notable works related to sport include Jamieson's (2003) application of Chicana feminism to the world of college softball whereby Latina college softball players in the United States struggle "with histories, acts of colonization, and desire to engage with power through higher education and elite athletics" and enact resistant practices (p. 11). These actions include resisting attempts by family and teammates to definitively classify their identities and actions in regressively static ways. The differential *mestiza* consciousness deployed throughout this essay explores a "third space" feminism where difference reigns and bodies are seen as multiple, ambiguous, and unstable; infused with power; and sites for reimagining toward more resistant collective aims.

With comparable aspirations, Abdel-Shehid (2005) challenged stagnant concepts of identity and reductive understandings of power evident in the singular focus on the racism facing Black male athletes, often characteristic of sociological writings about Black masculinity, sport, and the media. Instead, Abdel-Shehid incorporates queer postcolonial perspectives to reread the production of Black athletes including Ben Johnson, Donavon Bailey, and former Canadian Football League (CFL) quarterbacks as both art and (exploited) labor. This discussion also reveals that gender, sexuality, hybridity, and diaspora are crucial in understanding Black diasporic identifications as unstable, leaky performances fraught with both limitations and possibilities. As is the case in the scholarship of Perez and Jamieson, by eschewing Enlightenment/colonialist positions that argue for an either/or binary formula, Abded-Shehid's work is important in providing a nonlinear account of time, space, and power. And as with similar postcolonial writings, comparable diverse processes of theorizing will no doubt continue to open up fresh questions and new possibilities for thinking through power, sport, and the media.

REFERENCES

Abdel-Shehid, G. (1999). Can't forget Ben: Representational ambiguities and Canadian nationalism. In M. Reif-Hulser (Ed.), *Borderlands: Negotiating boundaries in post-colonial writing* (pp. 157–173). Amsterdam: Rodopi.

Abdel-Shehid, G. (2005). *Who da man? Black masculinities and sporting cultures.* Toronto: Canadian Scholars.

Allen, A. (1999). *The power of feminist theory: Domination, resistance, solidarity.* Boulder, CO: Westview.

Andrews, D. L. (1995). The facts of Michael Jordan's blackness: Excavating a floating signifier. *Sociology of Sport Journal, 16,* 125–158.

Andrews, D. L. (2000). Posting up: French post-structuralism and the critical analysis of contemporary sporting cultures. In J. Coakley & E. Dunning (Eds.), *Handbook of sports studies* (pp. 106–138). London: Sage.

Andrews, D. L. (Ed.). (2001). *Michael Jordan, Inc.: Corporate sport, media culture, and late modern America.* Albany: State University of New York.

Andrews, D. L. (2002). Coming to terms with cultural studies. *Journal of Sport and Social Issues, 26*(1), 110–117.

Andrews, D. L. (2003). Sport and the transnationalizing media corporation. *The Journal of Media Economics, 16*(4), 235–251.

Andrews, D. L., & Jackson, S. (2001). *Sport stars: The cultural politics of sporting celebrity.* London: Routledge.

Banet-Weiser, S. (1999). Hoop dreams: Professional basketball and the politics of race and gender. *Journal of Sport and Social Issues, 34*(4), 403–420.

Barrett, M. (1991). *The politics of truth: From Marx to Foucault.* Stanford: Stanford University.

Beamish, R. (2002). Karl Marx's enduring legacy for the sociology of sport. In J. Maquire & K. Young (Eds.), *Theory, sport & society* (pp. 25–39). London: JAI.

Birrell, S. (1988). Discourses on the gender/sport relationship: From women in sport to gender relations in sport. *Exercise and Sport Science Reviews, 16,* 459–502.

Birrell, S. (2000). Feminist theories for sport. In J. Coakley & E. Dunning (Eds.), *Handbook of sports studies* (pp. 61–76). London: Sage.

Birrell, S., & McDonald, M. G. (Eds.). (2000). *Reading sport: Critical essays on power and representation.* Boston: Northeastern University.

Birrell, S., & Theberge, N. (1994a). Ideological control of women in sport. In D. M. Costa & S. Gutherie (Eds.), *Women and sport: Interdisciplinary perspectives* (pp. 361–376). Champaign: Human Kinetics.

Birrell, S., & Theberge, N. (1994b). Feminist resistance and transformation of sport. In D. M. Costa & S. Gutherie (Eds.), *Women and sport: Interdisciplinary perspectives* (pp. 361–376). Champaign: Human Kinetics.

Bratich, J., Parker, J., & McCarthy, C. (2003). Governing the present. In J. Bratich, J. Parker, & C. McCarthy (Eds.), *Foucault, cultural studies, and governmentality* (pp. 3–22). New York: State University of New York.

Brohm, J. M. (1978). *Sport: A prison of measured time.* London: Ink Links.

Butler, J. (1990). *Gender trouble: Feminism and the subversion of identity.* New York: Routledge.

Butler, J. (1993). *Bodies that matter: On the discursive limits of sex.* New York: Routledge.

Butler, J. (1999). Athletic genders: Hyperbolic instance and/or the overcoming of sexual binarism. *Stanford Humanities Review, 6,* 103–111.

Cantelon, H., & Ingham, A. (2002). Max Weber and the sociology of sport. In J. Maquire & K. Young (Eds.), *Theory, sport & society* (pp. 63–83). London: JAI.

Carrington, B. (1998). Sport, masculinity, and Black cultural resistance. *Journal of Sport and Social Issues, 22*(3), 275–298.

Carrington, B., Andrews, D., Jackson, S., & Mizur, Z. (2001). The global Jordan. In D. L. Andrews (Ed.), *Michael Jordan, Inc.: Corporate sport, media culture, and late modern America* (pp. 177–216). Albany: State University.

Caudwell, J. C. (2003). Sporting gender: Women's footballing bodies as sites/sights for the rearticulation of sex, gender, and desire. *Sociology of Sport Journal, 20*(4), 371–387.

Cole, C. L. (1994). Resisting the canon: Feminist cultural studies, sport and, technologies of the body. In S. Birrell and C. L. Cole (Eds.), *Women, sport, and culture* (pp. 6–28). Champaign: Human Kinetics.

Cole, C. L. (1996). Containing AIDS: Magic Johnson and Post[Reagan] America. In Seidman, S. (Ed.), *Queer Theory/Sociology* (pp. 280–310). Cambridge, MA: Blackwell.

Duncan, M. C. (1990). Sports photographs and sexual difference: Images of women and men in the 1984 and 1988 Olympic Games. *Sociology of Sport Journal, 7,* 20–40.

Duncan, M. C. (1994). The politics of women's body images and practices: Foucault, the panopticon, and *Shape* magazine. *Journal of Sport and Social Issues 18*(1), 48–65.

Dworkin, S. L., & Wachs, F. L. (1998). Disciplining the body: HIV-positive male athletes, media surveillance and the policing of sexuality. *Sociology of Sport Journal, 15*(1), 1–29.

Entine, J. (1999). Taboo: Why Black athletes dominate sports and why we are afraid to talk about it. New York: Public Affairs.

Foucault, M. (1979). *Discipline and punish: The birth of the prison.* London: Vintage.

Foucault, M. (1980). *Power/knowledge: Selected interviews and other writings, 1972–1977.* New York: Pantheon.

Foucault, M. (1990). *The history of sexuality: Volume I: An introduction.* New York: Vintage.

Giardina, M. (2003). "Bending it like Beckham" in the global popular. *Journal of Sport and Social Issues, 27*(1), 65–82.

Goldman, R., & Papson, S. (1998). *Nike culture.* London: Sage.

Gramsci, A. (1971). *Selections from the prison notebook.* New York: International.

Griffin, P. (1998). *Strong women, deep closets: Lesbians and homophobia in sport.* Champaign: Human Kinetics.

Griffin, P., & Genasci, J. (1990). Addressing homophobia in physical education. In M. Messner & D. Sabo (Eds.), *Sport, men, and the gender order* (pp. 211–221). Champaign: Human Kinetics.

Grossberg, L. (1986). On postmodernism and articulation: An interview with Stuart Hall. *Journal of Communication Inquiry, 10*(2), 45–75.

Grossberg, L. (1991). Strategies of Marxist cultural interpretation. In R. Avery & D. Eason (Eds.), *Critical perspectives on media and society* (pp. 126–162). New York: Guilford.

Gruneau, R. (1983). *Class, sports, and social development.* Amherst: University of Massachusetts.

Gruneau, R. (1988a). Modernization or hegemony: Two views on sport and social development. In J. Harvey & H. Cantelon (Eds.), *Not just a game: Essays in Canadian sport sociology* (pp. 9–32). Ottawa: University of Ottawa.

Gruneau, R. (1988b). Introduction: Notes on popular culture and political practice. In R. Gruneau (Ed.), *Popular culture and political practices* (pp. 11–32). Toronto: Garamond.

Hall, M. A. (1996). *Feminism and sporting bodies: Essays in theory and practice.* Champaign, IL: Human Kinetics.

Hall, S. (1981). Cultural studies: Two paradigms. In T. Bennett, M. Graham, C. Mercer, & J. Wollacott (Eds.), *Culture, ideology, and social process: A reader* (pp. 19–38). Worcester, UK: Billings & Sons.

Hall, S. (1982). The rediscovery of 'ideology': Return of the repressed in media studies. In M. Gurevitch, T. Bennett, J. Curran, & J. Woollacott (Eds.), *Culture, society, and the media* (pp. 55–90). London: Methuen.

Hall, S. (1986). The problems of ideology: Marxism without guarantees. *Journal of Communication Inquiry, 10*(2), 28–44.

Hall, S. (1991). Signification, representation, ideology: Althusser and the post-structuralist debates. In R. Avery & D. Eason (Eds.), *Critical perspectives on media and society* (pp. 88–113). New York: Guilford.

Hall, S. (1997). *Representation: Cultural representations and signifying practices.* London: Sage.

Hargreaves, J. A. (Ed.). (1982). *Sport, culture, and ideology.* London: Routledge & Kegan Paul.

Hargreaves, J. A. (1994). *Sporting females: Critical issues in the history and the sociology of women's sport.* London: Routledge.

Hargreaves, J. A. (2000). *Heroines of sport: The politics of difference and identity.* London: Routledge.

Hargreaves, J. A., & McDonald, I. (2000). Cultural studies and the sociology of sport. In J. Coakley & E. Dunning (Ed.), *Handbook of sports studies* (pp. 48–60). London: Sage.

Hargreaves, J. E. (1982a). Sport and hegemony: Some theoretical problems. In H. Cantelon & R. Gruneau, (Eds.), *Sport, culture, and the modern state* (pp. 104–140). Toronto: University of Toronto.

Hargreaves, J. E. (1982b). Sport, culture, and ideology. In J. A. Hargreaves, (Ed.), *Sport, culture, and ideology* (pp. 30–54). London: Routledge & Kegan Paul.

Hargreaves, J. E. (1986). *Sport, power, and culture.* New York: St. Martin's.

Helstein, M. (2000, May). *Can saying make it so? The protective illusions of "I am Canadian."* Paper presented at the Globalization of Sport and Leisure Conference, University of Alberta, Edmonton, Alberta, Canada.

Helstein, M. (2003). That's who I want to be: The politics and production of desire within Nike advertising to women. *Journal of Sport and Social Issues, 27*(3), 276–292.

Howell, J., & Ingham, A. (2001). From social problem to personal issue: The language of lifestyle. *Cultural Studies, 15*(2), 326–351.

Howell, J., Andrews, D., & Jackson, S. (2002). Cultural studies and sport studies: An interventionist practice. In J. McGuire and K. Young (Eds.), *Theory, sport & society* (pp. 152–177). Boston: JAI.

Jackson, S. (1998). A twist of race: Ben Johnson and the Canadian crises of racial and national identity. *Sociology of Sport Journal, 15*(1), 21–40.

Jamieson, K. (2003). Occupying a middle space: Toward a mestiza sport studies. *Sociology of Sport Journal, 20*(1), 1–16.

Jhally, S. (1989). Cultural studies and the sport/media complex. In L. Wenner (Ed.), *Media, sports & society* (pp. 70–93). Newbury Park: Sage.

King, C. R., & Springwood, C. F. (2001). *Beyond the cheers: Race as spectacle in college sport.* Albany: State University of New York.

King, S. (2003). Doing good by running well: Breast cancer, the race for the cure and the new technologies of ethical citizenship. In J. Bratich, J. Parker, & C. McCarthy (Eds.), *Foucault, cultural studies, and governmentality* (pp. 295–316). New York: State University of New York.

Laclau, E. (1977). *Politics and ideology in Marxist theory*. London: New York Books.

Lenskyj, H. (1991). Combating homophobia in sport and physical education. *Sociology of Sport Journal, 8*(1), 61–69.

MacNeill, M. (1996). Networks: Producing Olympic ice hockey for a national television audience. *Sociology of Sport Journal, 13*(2), 103–124.

Maguire, J. S. (2002). Michel Foucault: Sport, power, technologies and governmentality. In J. Maguire & K. Young (Eds.), *Theory, sport & society* (pp. 293–316). London: JAI.

McDonald, M. G. (1996). Michael Jordan's family values: Marketing, meaning and postReagan America. *Sociology of Sport Journal, 13*(4), 344–365.

McDonald, M. G. (2000). The marketing of the Women's National Basketball Association and the making of postfeminism. *International Review for the Sociology of Sport Journal, 35*(1), 35–48.

McDonald, M. G., & Birrell, S. (1999). Reading sport critically: A methodology for interrogating power. *Sociology of Sport Journal, 13*, 344–365.

McHoul, A., & Grace, W. (1993). *A Foucault primer: Discourse, power and the subject.* New York: New York University.

Messner, M. (1988). Sport and male domination: The female athlete as contested ideological terrain. *Sociology of Sport Journal, 5*, 197–211.

Messner, M. (2002). *Taking the field: Women, men, and sports.* Minneapolis: University of Minnesota.

Mills, S. (2003). *Michel Foucault.* London: Routledge.

Perez, E. (1999). *The decolonial imaginary: Writing Chicanas into history.* Bloomington: Indiana University.

Popkewitz, T., & Brennan, M. (1998). Restructuring a social and political theory in education: Foucault and a social epistemology of school practices. In T. Popkewitz & M. Brennan (Eds.), *Foucault's challenge: Discourse, knowledge, and power in education* (pp. 3–38). New York: Teacher's College.

Rail, G. (1998). Seismography of the postmodern condition: Three theses on the implosion of sport. In G. Rail (Ed.), *Sport and postmodern times* (pp. 143–161). Albany: State University of New York.

Rail, G. (2002). Postmodernism and sport studies. In J. Maguire & K. Young (Eds.), *Theory, sport & society* (pp. 179–210). London: JAI.

Rail, G., & Harvey, J. (1995). Body at work: Michel Foucault and the sociology of sport. *Sociology of Sport Journal, 12*(2), 164–179.

Rigauer, B. (2002). Marxist theories. In J. Coakley & E. Dunning (Ed.), *Handbook of sports studies* (pp. 28–47). London: Sage.

Rowe, D. (1998). Play up: Rethinking power and resistance in sport. *Journal of Sport and Social Issues, 22*(3), 241–251.

Sage, G. (1998). *Power and ideology in American sport* (2nd ed.). Champaign: Human Kinetics.

Shogan, D. (1999). *The making of high-performance athletes: Discipline, diversity, and ethics.* Toronto: University of Toronto.

Spargo, T. (1999). *Foucault and queer theory.* New York: Totem.

St. Louis, B. (2004). Sport and common-sense racial science. *Leisure Studies, 23*(1), 31–46.

Whannel, G. (2002). *Media sport stars: Masculinities and moralities.* London: Routledge.

Willis, P. (1982). Women in sport in ideology. In J. A. Hargreaves (Ed.), *Sport, culture and ideology* (pp. 117–135). London: Routledge & Kegan Paul.

31

A World of Criminals or a Media Construction? Race, Gender, Celebrity, and the Athlete/Criminal Discourse

David Leonard
Washington State University

After four books and countless numbers of articles, it is clear that something might be going on here. *Pros and Cons, The Dark Side of the Game, Athletes and Acquaintance Rape,* and *Public Heroes, Private Felons* all explore the supposed epidemic of crime within American sports. Turn on the TV and Geraldo Rivera is interviewing Kathy Redmond about Kobe Bryant or the Colorado sex scandal. Neither events are seen as aberrations, but as just another incident within a long string of athletes committing crimes. Listen to the radio or turn on the computer and there's an endless array of commentary on the misbehavior of today's athletes. If these were the only sources of information about crime and sports, one would have to conclude that America's athletes are out of control, preying on women while disregarding America's laws, all the while remaining above the fray of accountability and consequences because of celebrity, class, and media power.

Thankfully, there are other voices within this discourse that downplay the existence of a problem specific to the world of sports. Rather than sensationalize crime as an epidemic, these authors interrogate societal commentary about sports and crime, elucidating the manner in which notions of race, gender, class celebrity, crime, and racism play through this discursive field. It is the task of this chapter to analyze each segment of the literature, examining predominant themes and the ways in which defining authors see criminal activity as either a major problem or a sign of dominant white supremacist discourses.

The literature has revealed a significant amount in terms of gambling within the world of sports as well as specific instances of point shaving (Ginsburg, 1995; Millman, 2002; Nathan, 2003; Pellowski, 2003; Savage, 1997; Sperber, 2001; Zimbalist, 2001); the problems of drug use and abuse by athletes (L. Cole, 1989; Harris, 1987; Mottram, 2002; Smith, 1992; Wilson & Derse, 2000); links between organized crime and sports (Friedman, 2000; Moleda, 1995; Mortensen, 1991; Ross, 2003); and the personal testimonies of athletes engaged in criminal misconduct (Howe, 1989; Lucas, 1994; Rose, 2004; Taylor, 2003; Thompson, 1990; Wells, 2003). As provocative as these popular and intellectual readings tend to be, the majority of serious scholarly or critical examinations of criminality and crime in sports tend to focus on contemporary manifestations of crime within the world of sports. Interestingly, the rest of the literature almost decriminalizes crime activity within sports as a problem particular to sports that corrupts its aesthetics, morals, and values. That is, steroids are constructed less as a criminal dimension of the sporting world and more as a challenge to the purity of the game. Gambling is not a violation of the law but a challenge to the integrity of the game. While provocative and deserving of study, the literature that enters into the debate about "street (violent) crimes" committed by athletes is far more powerful as a defining discourse of sports criminality. With this in mind, this chapter provides a space for the examination of the key themes and works on crime within sports, paying particular attention to the way the literature and the surrounding discourse enters into debates about whether violent crime is a severe problem within contemporary sports. Specifically elucidating the ways race, gender, and the criminal justice system are constructed and disseminated, this chapter equally gives voice to the dialectical relationship between discourses on sport and those on crime. In chronicling the larger themes and major contributions to the literature, this chapter demonstrates the varied ways in which commentators interpret the issue of crime within the sport world, as well as the ways in which race, gender, and celebrity penetrate the discursive field.

CRIME AND SPORTS: A MAJOR PROBLEM

This segment of the literature purports itself to be giving voice to the dark side of sports. In an environment of sport idolization and a media more invested in images and ratings, Jeff Benedict, Don Yaeger, Tim Green (1996), Charles Ogletree, and a vast array of investigative reporters seek to provide a forum for the epidemic of athletics committing crimes within sports.

> Those responsible for the mayhem chronicled on these pages are no ordinary criminals. They are perceived as heroes. Rather than being stigmatized like cons, these pros are cheered, idolized, and highly paid because they bring us thrills. And we are not talking about just a few bad apples here. (Benedict & Yaeger, 1998, p. ix)

As evident, this segment of the literature constructs the world of sport as a space overflowing with criminals. Moreover, it depicts criminality within sports as a spectacle, a serious problem worthy of dramatic intervention. While these writers tend to call for legal (criminal justice, league) intervention, they feel their greatest weapon is to out and make public the criminal records of athletes. In their estimation, if the public understood the private lives of their sports heroes, they would probably not support them, sending a message of accountability.

Beyond outing athletes, these authors spend an equal amount of time providing statistical evidence of the problem of crime within the world of American sports. Benedict and Yaeger, in *Pros and Cons*, concluded that 20%, or 1 in 5, of the members of the NFL have been charged with a serious crime. Numbers in hand, Benedict and

Yaeger challenged the NFL and those commentators who deny the existence of a problem. Between the numbers and the array of anecdotal evidence, all of which is sensationalized, Benedict and Yaeger contribute to the hegemonic discourse concerning excessive criminal behavior of American athletes. In actuality, this book and their work elsewhere resides at the center of the literature, in that those who write about this problem habitually cite their statistics and make their conclusions without regard to the severe problems (arrest rates instead of conviction, context, race) with their work.

While this segment of the literature explores the criminal misconduct of athletes, the true focus lies with athletes and crimes against women (Benedict, 2004; Benedict & Yaeger, 1998; Benedict, 1997; Benedict, 1998; Brackenbridge, 2003; Messner & Sabo, 1994; Roberts, 2000; Robinson, 1998; Wenzel, 1998). Given that a majority of these writers are White males talking about Black athletes assaulting White women, this fact provokes a lot of thought. The history of White supremacist surveillance and lynchings in the name of protecting White women must be understood as the context for this level of discourse.

As with the rest of the literature, the preponderance of these works seek to undermine a "distorted perception of athletes" (Benedict, 1997, p. ix). Given the media's refusal to cover sexual violence against women, especially those cases involving athletes; the statistics that demonstrate a common problem; and the stories that elucidate the severity and consequences of the problem, all of this vein of research serves to illustrate the true reality of sports. In *Public Heroes, Private Felons*, Benedict (1997) cited that between 1986 and 1996, over 425 professional and college athletes "were publicly reported for violent crimes against women" (p. ix). In 1995 and 1996 alone, this number reached 199 athletes charged with physical or sexual attacks against women. The great majority, according to Benedict, never faced prosecution, incarceration, negative media coverage, or public scrutiny. The absence of accountability is as much a problem as the disproportionate incidences. "The fact that popular athletes, society's most recognized male role models, routinely escape accountability for domestic violence, rape, gang rape and other crimes has dulled public consciousness of their increasing levels of deviance" (Benedict, 1997, p. ix). As already noted, this portion of the literature, thus, attempts to rectify this blindness through irrefutable statistics and by giving voice to the oft-silent victims. More importantly, the work of Benedict and others tries to explain the reason for excessive violence against women. Beyond lapsed accountability and false media depictions, Benedict focuses on the sports subculture, with all its entitlements, as crucial to understanding why so many athletes commit crimes of sexual violence. From pathologizing male athletes as weak and their status as celebrities, to sports subculture and the sense of entitlement, Benedict sees little surprise in this problem given that the world of sports sanctions, facilitates, and encourages criminal activity, especially against women, all the while shielding them from prosecution or consequences.

At the core of a reactionary literature that sees a crime epidemic within American sports is the idea that society "awards them with special attention and privileges," which "may give them a sense of entitlement and freedom from accountability" (Ogletree, 2000, p. 18). Specifically, these special privileges and status, in conjunction with a promotion of extreme forms of masculinity, manifest themselves through misogyny and sexual violence. "Included in that," argued Alan Klein, "is the view of women as always at one's beck and call. It's a combination of that and never being held accountable for anything" (Ogletree, 2000, p. 18). In their estimation, athletes view women as part of their contract, so male athletes are sanctioned to demand then at any moment. "Professional players perceive access to limitless sex as just another facet of the entitlements that accompany being a professional athlete," argued Benedict (p. 20). "Whereas the sport subculture fosters images of women as sexually compliant, and simultaneously facilitates opportunities for players who may possess proclivities toward sexual abuse to be pursued by women, sport also offers" the means to avoid prosecution and consequences through public relations firms, the best lawyers, and a media that does not care about their misconduct (Benedict, 1998, 21–22). Ogletree (2000) agreed, in "Privileges and Immunities for Basketball Stars and other Sports Heroes," citing the media's focus on stats over criminal records and society's hero worship as explanatory factors for the disproportionate levels of sexual violence among athletes. In his article, Ogletree cited many examples that supposedly demonstrate excessive criminal and immoral activities and the absence of accountability within sports. Yet, Ogletree, as with this segment of the literature, made no distinction between those accused of crimes and those found guilty. Without even researching each case, I found that almost 50% of the athletes used as evidence for the problem of sexual violence were never convicted, with a great majority never having been charged. It seems that "innocent until proven guilty" means little to these authors, especially in the examination of a world dominated by Black males.

Another element of this segment of the literature is the legal privileges experienced by athletes. In other words, a problem exists because athletes do not face consequences, legal or otherwise, when accused, arrested, or convicted of a crime. Worse, in the eyes of people like Ogletree (2000), is that "despite their unflattering records, many star athletes continue to receive respect and admiration and are too often protected from the law's just enforcement" (p. 13). Given the adoration and hero worship associated with America's athletes, Ogletree concluded that "In light of the difference between how the justice system treats great athletes and how it treats their non-athlete counterparts maybe the slogan 'Equal Justice Under Law' should be changed to 'Equal Justice Under Law for Some'" (pp. 22–23). Under an argument of racial erasure that ignores the White supremacist orientation of the criminal justice system (Cole, 2000; Davis, 1998a, 1998b; Mauer, 2001), Ogletree, Benedict and the like posited that celebrity athletes transcend their race, securing elevated status that puts them above the law. To them, athletic skills represent a get-out-of-jail-free card that provides universal immunity, thereby guaranteeing a persistent problem within sports. Whether because of fancy lawyers, above-the-law celebrity status, or a media to downplay the problem, society allows athletes to commit crimes without any fear of repercussions, which, in there writers' eyes, facilitates a continuation of the problem. Although these ideas emanate from books and scholarly articles, this alarmist discourse finds its roots within the sports media, which has a far greater reach into society.

A CONVERGENCE OF THE FRONT
AND BACK PAGES

As with the sensationalized literature, the popular press ubiquitously offers the impression that athletes are committing crimes at disproportionate rates, although the bulk of the coverage centers on the alleged criminal activities of Black athletes (Benedict, 2003; Lapchick, 2003a, 2003b; Vlahos, 2003). The previously mentioned books and numerous Web sites equally focus on the supposed problem of overindulged athletes, who lack discipline and commit crimes without regard for anyone but themselves (Benedict, 1999; Benedict & Yaeger, 1999; Messner & Sabo, 1994; Wenzel, 1998). The Associated Press recently sent out a wire story that merely listed athletes, all but one of whom was Black, accused of various crimes. Not mentioned in the article is that five out of the seven were never charged or were found innocent. Numerous examples, from the coverage of the O. J. Simpson and Rae Carruth murder trials, to the lesser known bar fights and traffic violations, reveal this convergence of the front and back pages. The recent firestorm of media coverage surrounding Kobe Bryant has prompted a series of articles, all of which contextualize the allegations against Bryant within a larger problem of crime-committing athletes. For example, following the arrests of Jayson Williams and Kobe Bryant, there was a rash of articles purporting a crime epidemic among America's athletes. Chris Sheridan, Bill Redeker, and Rob Fernas all used the allegations against Kobe Bryant as a launching pad to address the violent trend facing sports (Fernas, 2003; Redeker, 2003; Sheridan, 2003). In a section entitled "Here Comes Trouble," Redeker (2003) lamented the out-of-control nature of the predominantly Black NBA:

> In recent years, the NBA and trouble seem to have become synonymous. In the past year alone, some of the biggest names in basketball—Jerry Stackhouse, Marcus Fizer, Darrell Armstrong, Allen Iverson and Glenn Robinson—have all had run-ins with the law. (para 7)

> So many members of the Portland Trail Blazers have had problems with the law in recent years, sneering sports commentators have begun calling them the "Jail Blazers." (para 8)

> Some players have been charged with spousal abuse, others have been caught carrying guns, while still others have gotten into brawls with police. (para 9)

Playing on a blind nostalgia for a time when sports was isolated from violence, when American athletics had values and an overwhelmingly White playing population, all three writers situate accusations against both Jayson Williams and Kobe Bryant as the most celebrated and visible incidents in a wave of problems. Yet, despite claims of a system-wide problem, none of the articles provides evidence that does not come through a series of Black bodies. All of the articles use Black athletes (Michael Pittman, Damon Stoudamire, Jerry Stackhouse, Darrell Armstrong, and Glenn Robinson) as evidence of the problem. Ignoring the fact that most of their examples are of athletes accused of crimes, yet never charged, these articles reflect a larger tendency in much of the literature to conflate arrest with criminal activity. Moreover, each represents the widespread practice of deploying color-blind frames and codes in that each speaks about a problem of the sports world, yet they confine examples and explanations to clearly render the problem as one of Black bodies and influences on sports. Blaming ghetto culture, hip-hop, gangster identities (given Kobe's difficulties with hip-hop credibility and his suburban upbringing, such projects of essentialization are powerful), and overindulged and pampered upbringing, each author solidifies racialized arguments as the explanation for the wave of crimes committed by (Black) athletes.

NEW MEDIA, SAME OLD GAME

While we usually define the literature in terms of written work, whether books, articles, or popular media, a broader definition is needed concerning a criminal–athlete discourse. With the expansion of new media, it is crucial to explore the ways in which the Web engages the questions about crime within sports. In addition to Web sites like ESPN.com or fan-based sites, both of which quickly disseminate information about athletes accused of crime, there has been a proliferation in Web sites dedicated to crime and sports. For example, fuckedsports.com and badjocks.com are both sites that exclusively report on criminal accusations against athletes. Deploying rhetoric about out-of-control athletes and the declining values of sports, these Web sites comfortably talk about crime in sports through Black bodies. One Web site even contains a sports hall of shame, proffering a list of events of the worst sports has to offer fans. Like the rest of the literature, these sensationalized Web sites give the impression that professional and collegiate athletes commit an inordinate number of crimes, especially crimes of sexual violence. This subsequently leads us to conclude that Black men commit inordinate amounts of crime compared to the rest of society, which follows its rules without exception. The White supremacist orientation of these Web sites, and the literature on the whole, is exceptionally transparent within White nationalist Web sites, which are almost obsessed with sports and crime.

At Newnation.org, a site dedicated to "minority and migrant crime," skinheads situate the epidemic of athletes committing crimes within the context of an epidemic of Black-on-White crime. With statistics on Black men raping White women and anecdotes about the alleged criminal activities of Black athletes, this site identifies athletes as a major threat to White values and women. In covering the Kobe Bryant trial, editors of the Web site wrote about the charges against Kobe as anything but surprising, given the epidemic problem of "black on white rape." The headline for its sports section read as "just another n*gg*r rapist," with pictures of eight Black athletes who had been accused of sexual violence. Making clear that the Kobe case was not an isolated incident, this site situates his attack within a long-standing problem of Black sexuality vis-à-vis White female purity. In its tips on how to avoid rape, the site calls upon its readers not to "date blacks or Mexicans," "avoid traveling through Black and Mexican neighborhoods," and "acquire a handgun, and learn how to use it" (http://www.newnation.org/NNN-news-crime.html).

The level of critical engagement with this portion of the literature leaves a lot to be desired. Its failure to contextualize the problem of athletes committing (oftentimes, allegedly) crimes against women and society, within larger discourses on race and criminality or within the history of U.S. domestic state violence (James, 1996), reflect its limitations. Beyond this, its replication of White supremacist ideologies, including nostalgia for an imagined period when athletes did not commit crimes (before integration), its deployment of ideologies demonizing Black male bodies, and its elevation of feminist discourses over those oriented toward antiracism, reveal its reactionary and sensationalized nature. Given its hegemonic location within both the popular media and imagination, the rest of the literature merely works in opposition to these very powerful voices.

INSERTING RACE, A LITERATURE OF OPPOSITION

Despite the hegemony of a literature grounded more in sensationalism than sustained scholarly inquiry, a few scholars' studies interrogate the issues of sexual violence and athletics. As a whole, these commentators and scholars challenge the dominant mythology on the propensity of athletes to engage in sexual violence, citing widespread acceptance of racial stereotypes, media hype, and fear based on myths as the basis of widespread misinformation.

Sawyer (2002), in "Rape Myth Acceptance among Intercollegiate Student Athletes: A Preliminary Examination," challenged the absence of available research on sexual violence on college campuses as well as the tendency to base assumptions on mythology in absence of facts. Despite widespread belief that student athletes are more likely to engage in sexual violence, her research reveals the statistical problematics of these assumptions. Although fraternity members represent only 25% of male student populations, this constituency accounts for 63% of reported sexual assaults on college campuses; almost 25% of sexual assaults occur at fraternities. Yet the media and commentators like Jeff Benedict have, through their sensationalized coverage, reduced the issue to a problem of overindulged student athletes. In providing this statistical data, Sawyer seeks to undermine the media-driven myths that confine the societal problem of rape in a safe, explainable space. While ignoring race, she denounced the media for its promulgation of the athlete-rapist myth. Another significant absence is a sustained discussion of the problems or complexities with the existing literature concerning rape and student athletes. She concluded that student athletes account for only 2% of the male student population but represent 23% of those accused of sexual violence. Yet she fails to interrogate the meanings imbued with these statistics in terms of race, celebrity, or visibility. In fact, the literature surrounding criminality among athletes often falls into this trap, accepting statistical data without any reservation or explanation. To casually accept rates of accusation against a primarily Black population, given the history of racism within the criminal justice system, especially within the context of Black men and White women, limits the usefulness of this study, and much of the literature. While lacking a sustained analysis, the work of Sawyer offers a framework for additional qualitative and quantitative analysis concerning sexual violence committed by student athletes.

In wake of the Kobe Bryant case, accusations against the Colorado football program, and reports about sex recruiting parties at universities across the nation, there was an outpouring of articles, reports, and commentaries on the epidemic of sexual violence within sports. "Nobody can tell me that there is not a problem with athlete violence," said Kathy Redmond, founder of the National Coalition Against Violent Athletes in Littleton, Colorado. "These types of cases happen all the time." Citing an incident involving Duane Carswell of the Denver Broncos, Redmond spoke about the absence of legal or societal accountability. "He still hasn't missed any playing time," Redmond said. "There are people walking around who should be in jail. They gain so much from a system that protects them. We need to start treating athletes like human beings, not gods" (Fernas, 2003, para 19). Redmond, Benedict, Crosset (1999) and others have sought to document the problem while blaming a permissive sports culture for this widespread phenomenon. Yet Lapchick (2002) sees the problem of rape, sexual violence, and misogyny not in sports, but as an unfortunate dimension of society. "I really don't believe that athletes are disproportionately involved. They're part of a huge problem in our country" (Pratt, 2004, para 13).

Lapchick (2003a, 2003b) persistently argued that, despite the presumed "facts that athletes are guilty of violence and mistreatment of women at a higher rate than the general population," which plays on racial stereotypes and stereo- types of athletes, statistics undermine claims of an epidemic within the world of sports (Lapchick, 2003a, 2003b). Lapchick, almost in direct response to Benedict, Redmond, and the mainstream media, revealed that athletes commit roughly two sexual assaults per week; since 1998, an average of 100 cases have been reported per year involving basketball and football players accused of battery or sexual vi- olence. Yet the unfortunate fact is that sexual assault in the sports world is not unique, but rather reflects a larger societal problem. In the United States, a rape occurs every eighteen seconds. An estimated 3% of American men are guilty of battery. American men batter more than 8,200 women and rape over 2,345 women per day. In a single year, America sees 3 million cases of battery and over 1 mil- lion incidents of rape (Lapchick, 2003a). Given these startling numbers, it should be clear that violence against women takes place outside of the sports arena with great regularity. Even with the 100 arrests per year involving athletes and numer- ous other rapes that go unreported (estimates put a ratio at ten incidents unre- ported for every one reported), it is clear that athletes who commit sexual crimes account for a mere fraction of the millions of violent crimes committed against women.

The public discourse that plays on racist stereotypes, as Lapchick noted is evi- dent with the media's coverage of the Kobe Bryant trial, erases the stubborn facts of sexual violence, leading America to continue to be "afraid of the wrong things" (Glassner, 1999, p. ix). Together, this element of the literature questions not just the veracity of the hyperfocus on sexual violence by athletes, but also its problematic consequences as it leads popular opinion to see it as a problem of the sports world rather than a problem of America.

ERASING RACIAL ERASURE: GIVING VOICE TO RACIAL DISCOURSE

Whereas Sawyer erased race from a discourse of crime and athletes, Lapchick (Lapchick, 2002, 2003a) centered race within his discussion of the issue of crimi- nality and athletics. While there has been little substantive work that interrogates the construction and dissemination of racial stereotypes within both media cover- age and academic discourses surrounding crime and athletes, there are a couple of lone souls. Lapchick, King, Springwood, Andrews, C. L. Cole, and Boyd each demon- strate the racialized nature of this discourse, revealing its problems and connection to larger discourses of White supremacy. All insert race into an otherwise color- blind literature that pretends that race does not matter either in the sports world or in those author's engagement with that reality. Lapchick (2002), in *Smashing Bar- riers*, argued that the discourse surrounding athletes and crimes "provides whites with the chance to talk about athletes in a way that reinforces these [black as more violent, prone to drug use, and inclined toward violence against women] stereo- types" (p. 265). He noted how the hyperfocus on crime among athletes is limited to football and basketball (not hockey or baseball), which Not surprisingly are those sports dominated by Black athletes. This issue, thus, is not so much related to crime and sports, but to crime and those sports dominated by Black bodies. Race is at the center of any discussion of sports and criminality.

> I believe that at least part of the systematic coupling of athletes and crime revolves around racial stereotyping. The media has persistently and consistently suggested that basketball and football players, who happen to be overwhelmingly African-American, are more violent than athletes in other sports and people in society in general. The result is that nearly everyone, including the police, women, fans, the media, sport administrators, and the athletes themselves, believe that certain athletes, especially basketball or football players, are more inclined to be violent in general and violent against women in particular. (Lapchick, 2002, p. 266)

Lapchick focused much of his attention on the media, ostensibly blaming them for playing to sensationalism and fear, often ignoring facts. Lapchick challenged Benedict, the leading voice on "pros and cons," as to the veracity of his statistical claims. He sees no significance in claims that 21% of NFL players have a criminal record, because 35 to 46% of adult males under 30 have arrest records as well. Yet, the media continues to harp on alleged crimes committed by athletes. Lapchick (2002) argued that this reflects the overwhelmingly white media establishment. Although he ignored structural inequalities, he argued that racialized stereotypes, connected to crime and sports, are a result of "fans who are mostly white, observing sport through a media filter that is created by an overwhelming number of white men" (p. 268).

These oppositional voices do not limit their attention to rape mythology, exploring the interplay between White supremacy and discourse surrounding athletes and the consequences of this process of racialization inside and outside of sports. With their larger examination of college sports as a racial spectacle, King and Springwood (2001) examined the interplay between race, sports, and criminality. Touching on the predominant themes of the more critical elements of the literature, their work represents a significant contribution. Specifically, they explored the ways in which "criminality indelibly marks the African American athlete," and the manner in which "public perceptions and media representations transform minor infractions into moral dramas and major transgressions into scandals often of national import" (p. 116). While King and Springwood argued that illicit activities and accusations of criminal activities against athletes, regardless of race, receive "unprecedented importance," they situated race at the center of this discourse. "The particular history of blackness and peculiar return of race in sociopolitical discourse imprint all African Americans as deviant, not simply those who break the law" (King & Springwood, 2001, pp. 116–117).

Although the literary discourse positing a major criminal problem in sports does so through a self-proclaimed color-blind lens, King and Springwood illustrated the impossibility of comprehending the discourse of crime and athletes outside the American paradigm of race. The evidence for the racialized nature of this discursive field exists within material reality as well. King and Springwood cited the differentiated coverage of two Nebraska football players as clear evidence of the ways race infects and affects societal coverage and reception of accusations of crime against athletes. When Christian Peter, a White all-American defense lineman, was convicted of assaulting a former Miss Nebraska, his case received little media attention outside of Lincoln, Nebraska. When Lawrence Phillips, on the other hand, who is Black and an all-American running back, was charged with beating his girl-friend, the incident generated national coverage and OUTRAGE. "Although both athletes have extensive records and have committed offenses certain to evoke public contempt—violence against women—the scrutiny they were subjected to differed immensely" (King & Springwood, 2001, p. 117). Compared to Peter, who received little media or public construction Philips faced a suspension, a firestorm of criticism, and national media attention. Given the similarity of circumstances, "the over-determining feature undoubtedly was race and the interracial relationship" (King & Springwood, 2001, p. 117). Similar examples can be found with the varied reactions and coverage of Mike Tyson and Mark Chamura, as well as Kobe Bryant and Mike Danton. In her study on the media and rape, Moorti (2002) elucidated the disperate ways the media covered the Mike Tyson and William Kennedy Smith rape trials. Whereas the media declared the innocence of Kennedy Smith through stories that revealed his humanity and how he was incapable of such a crime, it constructed Tyson as a pathological animal (Moorti, 2002; O'Connor, 2002; Sloop, 1997).

Similar to others (Berry & Smith, 2000; Crenshaw, 1997; Leonard, 2004; Moorti, 2002; Williams, 2001), King and Springwood situated the cases of Phillips and Peter within a larger history of Black student athletes and White supremacy. Philips, like so many Black student athletes, faced public, media, and legal criminalization because he violated the collegiate and societal taboo of dating a White woman. The panic over Black rapists and criminal athletes can never be understood outside this context, outside the discourse of White fear of Black male sexual bodies and White male protectionism of White females (King & Springwood, 2001; Miller, 2002; Moorti, 2002; Williams, 2001).

Another defining element of the more critically engaged, theoretical aspects of literature is that of criminalization. Focusing on the ways sports (and the criminal justice system) criminalizes Black bodies and the impact of White supremacist discourses on Black athletes accused of crimes, the literature (Andrews, 2001; Berry & Smith; 2000; Boyd, 2003; Cole & Andrews, 1996; Hoberman, 1997; King & Springwood, 2001; Lapchick, 2002; Leonard, 2004) provides a thorough examination of the ways in which Black athletes embody and deploy notions of Black criminality.

Throughout history, Black male bodies have come to represent that which is deviant, criminal, and threatening. Gray (1995) argued, "The black other occupies a complex site, a place where fears, desires, and repressed dreams are lodged. The black other is a site of spectacle, in which whites imagine blackness as a potential measure of evil and menace" (p. 165). Blackness within dominant society and within the world of sports represents a sign of decay, disorder, and danger (Andrews, 2001, p. 117). Color-blind racism, with its cultural and biological components, assumes that "these innately physical males (black athletes) would be misbehaving" without sports (Andrews, 2000, p. 182). Giroux (1994) further clarified the centrality of Black criminality discourses within White supremacy when he wrote, "In this racism, the other's identity warrants its very annihilation because it is seen as impure, evil, and inferior. Moreover, whiteness represents itself as a universal marker for being civilized and in doing so posits the Other within the language of pathology, fear, madness, and degeneration" (p. 75). From the political pulpit to the constant articles about the epidemic of crime within sports, the White imagination locates crime within Black bodies, leading to a fear of the Black male population, while simultaneously exonerating Whiteness of all societal transgressions.

Criminalization reflects the process of extending criminal meaning to a previously legally unclassified social practice, body, or group. Similar to the process of constructing racialized bodies, criminalization is a historically specific, ideological process that mediates competing political projects. Angela Davis (1998b), writing on the prison industrial complex, notes that the "fear of crime has attained a status that bears a sinister similarity to the fear of communism . . . during the 1950s and 1960s" (p. 271). The ideological project naturalizing Black men as criminals saturates a number of American institutions, obfuscating the deleterious effects of structural racism and late twentieth-century capitalism. It is crucial to understand this context in that the proliferation of media coverage and interest in criminality of athletes parallels this political, cultural, and ideological shift. The criminalization of Black youth through both the criminal justice system and popular culture has relegated an entire generation of Black youth as criminals within the White popular imagination. The lurking Black male represents the ideologized body that lays the foundation and evidence for greater state power and surveillance (C. L. Cole, 2001, Mauer, 2001).

Hoberman, with *Darwin's Athletes*, provided additional insight as to the criminalization of Black athletes and the function of Black athletes within larger discourses of criminalized Black bodies. Although his conclusions fall short, his discursive analysis elucidates the centrality of racialized body politics within the larger societal debate about crime and sports. He aptly noted the limits of differentiation between the criminal and the athlete within the White popular imagination. "The black male style has become incarnated in the fusion of black athletes, rappers, and criminals into a single menacing figure who disgusts and offends many blacks as well as whites," wrote Hoberman in *Darwin's Athletes* (1997, p. xix). In recent years, popular culture has merged the "athlete, the gangster rapper, and the criminal into a single black male persona that the sports industry, the music industry, and the advertising industry have made into the predominant image of black masculinity" (Hoberman, 1997, p. xviii). A dialectical relationship, then, exists between images of Black athletes and Black criminals, as equally "pathologically deficient individuals," as interchangeable (Andrews, 2000, p. 184). The construction of Black athletes as criminals provides evidence to the criminal nature of all Black men. If Black men, who have money, prestige, and everything to lose, are still committing crimes, imagine what those who have nothing to lose will do to you. Sports and deployment of images of Black athletes as criminal "reinscribes the pathologizing line drawn between the 'good' and 'bad'; the normal and the deviant, the cerebral and the physical, the controlled and the violent, the healthy and the diseased, the white and the black" (Andrews, 2001, p. 111; Gillman, 1985). Through the discursive field and the harsh drug policies within the NBA (as compared to the MLB), society not only learns about the cultural and biological reality of a criminalized Black male body, but also simultaneously justifies the necessity of surveillance and policing (Andrews, 2001; D. Cole, 2000; Foucault, 1995; Grossberg, 1988). Whether on the court or in the street, Black male bodies require containment and control.

IRON MIKE TYSON AND O. J. SIMPSON: TWO SHORT CASE STUDIES

Although there are a few texts dedicated exclusively to the exploration of the criminal–athlete discourse, there are a number of key works that collectively define the scope of inquiry. As with the previously mentioned texts, the literature as a whole explores the interplay between race, gender, sport, and criminality.

Paying particular attention to cases involving sexual violence, given the transparency of race, gender, and sexuality, the literature offers significant insight into intersectionality (Moorti, 2002; O'Connor, 2002; Sloop, 1997). For example, in exploring the coverage and trial of Mike Tyson, Sloop (1997) elucidates how both his athleticism and Blackness served as the basis of explaining why he raped Desiree Washington. "The Mike Tyson that emerges from this axis works to create and/or reinforce the assumption that Tyson's behavior, based on race, class and career, is likely to lead to dangerous and violent relations" (p. 108). In the media's coverage and the prosecution's case, Mike Tyson was guilty of his Blackness and because he was "trained to be a pit-bull," who if left uncontrolled would likely transgress social and cultural boundaries as well as legal mandates. A second defining element that is evident within the work of Sloop and Andrews (2000), among others, is the connection between the frame or trope of athlete as criminal and larger discourses of White supremacy. Sports, thus, represent a powerful venue to construct ideologies that demonize Blackness as predatorial, dangerous, and hypersexual. Describing both media coverage and the statements of the prosecutors, Sloop (1997) argued: "Tied together with the image of inarticulate predator, Tyson fits comfortably in the cultural stereotype of the sexually insatiable black with an appetite that demands attention at any cost" (p. 111). In other words, Black plus boxer (overindulged athlete) equals rapist and criminal. Sloop, King, and Andrews all locate this discourse within both classical White supremacist ideologies and those of new racism.

> The new cultural racism was prefigured on the virulent assumption that these innately physical males would be misbehaving were it not for the involvement of their natural physical attributes in the disciplinary mores and stringencies imposed by the dominant (sporting) culture. According to the spurious logic, within sporting activity African American males have found salvation (if only temporary, i.e., Mike Tyson and O. J. Simpson) from themselves (Andrews, 2000, p. 182).

In other words, you can take the Black athlete out of crime/ghetto, but you can't take the criminal/ghetto out of the athlete. In fact, this idea sits at the core of this segment of the literature on the spectacle of athletes committing crimes at alarming rates.

A final defining characteristic is the widespread discussion of the media. Whether through analyzing the ways in which mass media constructs African-American males as pathologically deficient, or the reduction of a hip-hop sports culture to a thug life that not only perverts sports, but also threatens America's moral fabric, the critical elements of the literature excoriate the media for its dissemination and deployment of classical and new racist discourses.

The nature of the literature is no more evident than with the engagement with the O. J. Simpson trial. With its share of work that both sensationalizes the trial (Bugliosi, 1996; Lange, 1996; Thaler, 1997) and links it to larger trends of criminality within the world of sports (Cose, 1997; Gibbs, 1996; Morrison, 1997; Williams, 2001), it is more aptly defined by a series of texts that examine the discursive articulations, constructions, and dissemination of racial meanings during the Simpson trial and its aftermath. Given the racialized nature of both the case and its reception, it is not surprising that an overwhelming amount of focus lies with race. Specifically, the literature explores six distinct themes, all of which define the larger literature:

addressing crime, sports & media construction (1) color blindness and the race card, (2) racialization, (3) O. J. and the media, (4) the impact of the case on American race relations, (5) the intersections of race and gender, and (6) the unfortunate competition between antiracist and feminist agendas. Although it is impossible to explore the literature's treatment of each theme within this space, it is important to understand the ways in which the literature on O. J. reflects the larger themes of the discourse on criminality and athletes. For example, Crenshaw (1997) and Johnson and Roediger (1997) demonstratd the ways in which color blindness and the race card frame attempts to decenter race from the O. J. discourse, pointing to a larger theme within the literature. Just as the media racialized O. J. through its language, or by darkening his photo on the cover of *Time* magazine, much of the literature either reaffirms or challenges the process of racialization associated with the coverage of athletes accused of committing crimes. In fact, the literature surrounding O. J. reveals a tremendous amount about the current discourse, especially in terms of the unfortunate conflicts between those who give voice to sexual violence (e.g., the feminist agenda) and those who challenge the persistence of racism in the persecution of Black males.

> The task at hand is to develop political discourses that reject the reductive either/or framing that surrounds the Simpson trial and other controversies involving such vexed categories as race, gender, and class. Such cases call for an intersectional politics that merges feminist and antiracist critiques of institutional racism and sexism. While both feminists and civil rights activists have developed useful critiques of the issues played out in the Simpson case, there was no readily accessible framework that allowed critiques to be aligned in a complementary rather than implicitly oppositional fashion. (Crenshaw, 1997, pp. 158–159)

More than her analysis about athletics, crime, race, gender, and the media, Crenshaw's challenge to construct a framework that recognizes both sexual violence and White supremacy represents the most important contribution of the literature. Future efforts need to begin to eschew the reductive elements of the literature (e.g., Benedict) and build on the insight of Crenshaw, Williams CL Cole, Andrews, King, and Springwood, all of whom demonstrate the potential, possibility, and necessity of antiracist, feminist scholarship concerning crime in sports.

THE END OF THE GOLDEN AGE

One final element that finds its way into some of the literature, albeit occasionally at a superficial level, is the consequences of the athlete–criminal discourse (Edwards, 1998; Edwards & Leonard, 2000). A large segment focuses on the discursive impact within the sports world, as to how NBA packages Allen Iverson or how these discourses permeate through the media (Berry & Smith, 2000; Boyd, 1997; King & Springwood, 2001). Edwards (1998) argued that the rise of the prison industrial complex and an increased focus on law and order has ushered in an end of the golden age of Black athletics. Concluding that we were burying, disqualifying, and otherwise alienating the future crop of athletes, Edwards challenged sports intellectuals, commentators, and fans alike to envision a future without Black athletes. Whether by the increasing rates of incarceration of Black men because of the war on drugs, or because of the corresponding decline in educational budgets, Edwards sees a bleak future for Black athletes. "In the face of such discouraging circumstances, many black youths have opted to go with the flow, exchanging team colors for gang colors, or simply dropping out of everything and chillin" (Edwards, 1998, p. 20). The United States spends roughly $40 billion annually maintaining its prisons, and close to $100 billion each year to support the entire criminal justice system. Between 1971 and 1992, government spending on prisons increased from $2.3 billion to $31.2 billion. In 1995 alone, money allocated for university construction dropped by $954 million, while expenditures for prison construction jumped by $926 million (Davis, 1998a). Within such an environment, in which excess money is funneled away from social services to institutions of social control, and where notions of criminality are linked to racial signs, Black youth have suffered significantly. Between 1970 (200,000) and 2000 (2,000,000), America's prison population has increased by 500%, as opposed to a mere 45% increase in the overall population. In the 1990s alone, nearly 2 million people were imprisoned. As we account for race, it becomes even clearer how both deindustrialization and the connected growth in state power have systematically jailed the potential "black athletes, right along with our potential black doctors, black lawyers and so forth" (Edwards & Leonard, 2000). At the brink of the twenty-first century, close to 3,500 Black men for every 1,000,000 were behind bars (Beck & Harrison, 2000). In 1990, the Washington D.C.-based Sentencing Project concluded that on a given day within the United States, one out of four Black men between the ages of 20 and 29 was either in jail, in prison, or on probation or parole (Miller, 1996, p. 7). In 1992, the National Center on Institutions and Alternatives released a study on African Americans in Washington D.C. It concluded that on any day in 1991, 42% (four in ten) of all Black males 18 to 35 living in the District of Columbia were in jail, in prison, on probation or parole, out on bond, or facing an arrest warrant. Similar numbers were found in Baltimore (and throughout the nation), where 56% of young Black men were in prison or otherwise connected to the criminal justice system (Miller, 1996). Specifically, Edwards (1998) argued that mass incarceration has so depleted the pool that has historically fed the athletic ranks that the five Black athleters are no longer there. He concludes that the systematic incarceration of primarily young Black males has slowly eroded the pool of potential athletes, while at the same time eroding the basis of America's support for the Black athlete. Edwards plants an important seed for interrogating the dramatic impact of the prison industrial complex on the world of sports, providing encouragement as to how to build bridges between critical studies on the criminal justice system and the sports arena.

A FUTURE OF POTENTIAL: UNSETTLING SENSATIONALISM

While there is a fair amount of literary engagement with the issues related to crime and athletics (athletes), there are sizable gaps in terms of both theoretical and critical analysis. Beyond the tendency toward sensationalism and pure descriptive narratives, there are many possibilities. The absence of a thorough interrogation of the interplay between athletes, race, and crime, as well as the relationship between a discourse of criminal athletes and that of law and order, truly undermines our comprehension of the issues. For example, what sort of contexts and consequences are evident in the convergence of the front and back pages? This sort of question is absent from the literature. In addition to greater literary emphasis on how sports discourses around criminality contribute to the process of criminalizing Black men, there are two concrete areas of needed inquiry.

First, as the scholarship addressing the ways race operates within the discourse of criminal as athlete is at best surface-level, there are significant issues that face erasure. The literature requires studies that examine the ways in which the media depicts athletes accused of crime particular to race differences. In both scope and content, there needs to be studies that document the ways in which the media differentiates reporting on criminal accusations against Black and White athletes. As with the case of Mark Chamura compared to that of Kobe Bryant, or even the incidents involving Latrell Sprewell and Kevin Greene (King & Springwood, 2001), it is clear that accusations of criminal misconduct warrant varied reactions and levels of coverage depending on the race of that athlete. Yet very little attention has been afforded to this issue, not just in terms of the amount of coverage, but in the codes and frames employed to chronicle these events. For example, the arrest and trial of Kobe Bryant provoked twenty-four hour, multiple-channel coverage that not only documented the alleged rape and the legal maneuvering, but also situated the accusation within Kobe Bryant's life story. The rape allegations, thus, have given impetus for stories and articles about his sometimes selfish on-the-court behavior, his idiosyncrasies, and his tendency to disengage with teammates as somehow providing a cue as to why he may have committed this heinous crime. These explanatory factors serve not to explain the accusation, but to pathologize Kobe Bryant as another ungrateful (Black) athlete. Worse, the media habitually contextualizes the alleged criminal acts of Black athletes as part of a larger pattern of misbehavior. Kobe bespeaks of a larger problem, whereas charges against Mark Chamura and Mike Danton are merely isolated incidents. This discourse necessitates critical interrogation, especially in light of the kid-glove treatment of White athletes accused of crimes. Whether talking about Steve Howe or Christian Peter, it is important to develop research that explores the ways in which their criminal pasts are consumed and treated by the media, their respective leagues, and the public through comparative analysis.

Mike Danton represents another example that proves the necessity of scholarship on criminalized athletes, race, and the media. In 2004, the police arrested Danton, a member of the St. Louis Blues, on charges of conspiracy to commit murder after he allegedly sought a murder for hire to kill his agent. What followed was not a series of damaging articles or a string of commentary on the wave of criminal misconduct of professional hockey players, but rather a barrage of sympathetic coverage. From ESPN to local newspapers, reports portrayed Danton as depressed, mentally unbalanced, and having a dysfunctional upbringing to explain why this White athlete would commit this crime. The focus was less on the alleged crime and more on the history of manipulation done by his agent—another source of explanation for his crime. Whereas the media and commentators sought small details in explaining the alleged misdoings of Kobe and Jayson Williams (after all, they are overindulged Black male athletes), many commentators provided elaborate reasons for why Danton, a White hockey player, could potentially hire a hit man to kill his agent. This example reveals a clear rupture in the literature, necessitating scholarship that explores the interplay between race, criminality, media coverage, celebrity status, and league reaction. At both a theoretical level and through examples of case studies, scholarship is needed that examines the dialectical relationship between race, sport, and criminality.

Another significant literary gap lies with the tendency to analyze criminality in terms of exceptionalism. Whether in reference to the subculture of sports, the hypermasculinity promoted through sports participation, or the presumed coddling of athletes, the majority of the literature sees the uniqueness of sports as reason for why there is a disproportionate level of criminal activity committed by athletes. As such, we need scholarship that examines the arguments of exceptionalism, providing comparative analysis to like institutions. To compare crime rates of athletes with the general population, given issues of visibility, celebrity, race, class, and power, represents a major flaw in the literature. To explore why athletes have high crimes rates, compared to "average Joes," is just bad research. What is needed is research that takes into account the problems in the statistical data, or, better yet, seeks comparative data from similar fields or institutions (crime rates among CEOs). In the end, scholarship is needed that answers the question of whether or not athletes commit more crimes, and if so, why? As of yet, despite the claims of many, no such research exists, as the bulk of it relies on faulty data that erases race, class, and celebrity. Moreover, the societal erasure of criminal activities within less visible or prestigious arenas, compared to the focus on sports, necessitates action if we are to use scholarship to elucidate the problems of sexual violence and crime.

Given recent events, there is an ongoing need for active, in-the-moment scholarship that critically engages the intersections of sport and criminality. More importantly, increased studies need to treat these issues within larger contexts and discourses, including racism, media growth, and celebrity. For example, little work is out there on the trials of Rae Carruth, Jayson Williams, or Kobe Bryant. There is almost nothing, academic or popular, addressing the racial contexts of each case, nor the media's coverage. Equally absent is scholarship or even popular accounts on Michael Danton, nor the Colorado sex recruiting scandal, beyond sensationalized or feel-good stories. The relative silence concerning these cases, especially given the Whiteness of those involved, requires inquiry and intervention into how, why, and by what means race impacts the criminal discourse of America's athletic arena.

Race sits at the center of the organization and of our understanding of both the world of sports and the criminal justice system. Recognizing this fact, and the place of gender, sexuality, and celebrity, is central to the success or failure of current scholarship on the discourse of crime and athletes, as well as future research. Boyd (1999) acknowledged this fact as he argued:

> America loves their Black entertainers when they behave "properly" and stay in their place. These entertainers are socialized at an early age live under a microscope, and are constantly held to the expectations of a mainstream society that has no understanding for the fact that not everyone shares the same world view. When the players realize their value, their significance to the game, and try to capitalize on this, they are held guilty in the highest court of contempt. (para 8)

Berry and Smith (2000) concur, noting how "there seems to be limitations to what African American athletes can get away with," especially concerning crime (p. 191). As evident in the failures of Benedict and others, along with the successes of Lapchick, King, Hoberman, Andrews, and CL Cole, the discourse replicates dominant mythology about African-American males, reifying hegemonic notions of criminality. "The truth about African American athletes' representation in crime may parallel the pattern of distorted representation of African American non-athletes in crime" (Berry & Smith, 2000, p. 191). The literature must not, in the name of antiracism and challenging dominant stereotypes of Blackness, replicate patriarchal views as to sexual violence. In recognizing racism, we cannot avoid gender; in interrogating the criminal justice system and the history of racism, we must not erase sexual and domestic violence as a problem within and without sports. The failures of the existing literature reside in the unwillingness to examine complexity, to interrogate context, multiple meanings, or intersectionality. As such, the strength lies with those works that have, and will continue to examine, the complex meanings of sport and criminality within a multiple of contexts, elucidating the messiness of the discourse and the interplay between texts, theories, ideologies, and histories.

REFERENCES

Andrews, D. (2000). Excavating Michael Jordan's blackness. In S. Birrell & M. McDonald (Eds.), *Reading sport* (pp. 166–205). Boston: Northeastern University Press.

Andrews, D. (2001). The fact(s) of Michael Jordan's blackness: Excavating a floating racial signifier. In D. L. Andrews (Ed.), *Michael Jordan, Inc.* (pp. 107–151). Albany: State University of New York Press.

Beck, A., & Harrison, P. (2000). *Prisoners in 2000* (p. 11, table 15).United States Department of Justice, Bureau of Justice Statistics.

Benedict, J. (1997). *Public heroes, private felons: Athletes and crimes against women.* Evanston: Northwestern University Press.

Benedict, J. (1998). *Sage series on violence against women.* Vol. 8. *Athletes and acquaintance rape,* Thousand Oaks, CA: Sage Publishers.

Benedict, J. (2003, August 5). Athletes and allegations. *New York Times.* Retrieved July 27, 2004, from http://www.ncava.org/articles/nytimeskobe.html

Benedict, J. (2004). *Out of bounds: Inside the NBA's culture of rape, violence, and crime.* New York: Harper Collins.

Benedict, J., & Yaeger, D. (1998). *Pros and cons: The criminals who play the NFL.* New York: Warner Books.

Berry, B., & Smith, E. (2000). Race, sport, and crime: The misrepresentation of African Americans in team sports and crime. *Sociology of Sport Journal, 17*(2), 171–197.

Boyd, T. (1997). *Am I Black enough for you: Popular culture from the 'hood and beyond.* Bloomington: Indiana University Press.

Boyd, T. (1999, June 11). "Amerikkka's most hated." *Sports Jones.* Retrieved July 23, 2003, from http://www.sportsjones.com/sj/185.shtml

Boyd, T. (2003). *Young, Black, rich and famous: The rise of the NBA, the hip hop invasion and the transformation of American culture.* New York: Doubleday.

Brackenbridge, C. (2003). *Sexual harassment and abuse in sport: International research and policy perspectives.* New York: Whiting & Birch.

Bugliosi, V. (1996) *Outrage: The five reasons why O. J. Simpson got away with murder.* New York: W.W. Norton & Company.

Cole, C. L. (2001). Nike's America/America's Michael Jordan. In D. L. Andrews (Ed.), *Michael Jordan, Inc.* (pp. 65–103). Albany: State University of New York Press.

Cole, C. L., & Andrews, D. (1996). Look—It's NBA show time!: Visions of race in popular imaginary. In N. Denzin (Ed.), *Cultural studies: A research volume* (pp. 141–181). New York: Routledge.

Cole, D. (2000). *No equal justice: Race and class in the American criminal justice system.* New York: New Press.

Cole, L. (1989). *Never too young to die: The death of Len Bias.* New York: Pantheon Press.

Cose, E. (Ed). (1997). *The Darden dilemma: 12 Black writers on justice, race, and conflicting loyalties.* New York: Harper Collins.

Crenshaw, K. W. (1997). Color-blind dreams and racial nightmares: reconfiguring racism in the post-Civil Rights Era. In T. Morrison (Ed.), *Birth of a nation hood* (pp. 97–168). New York: Pantheon Books.

Crosset, T. (1999). Male athletes' violence against women: A critical assessment of the athletic affiliation, violence against women debate. *Quest,* 244–257.

Davis, A. (1998a). Masked racism: Reflections on the prison industrial complex. *Colorlines.* Retrieved July 23, 2003, from http://www.arc.org/C_Lines/CLArchive/story1_2_01.html

Davis, A. (1998b). Race and criminalization: Black Americans and the punishment industry. In W. Lubiana (Ed.), *The house that race built* (pp. 264–279). New York: Vintage Books.

Edwards, H. (1998). An end of the golden age of Black participation in sport? *Civil Rights Journal,* 19–24.

Edwards, H., & Leonard, D. (2000). The decline of the black athlete. *Colorlines.* Retrieved July 23, 2003, from http://www.arc.org/C_Lines/CLArchive/story3_1_03.html

Fernas, R. (2003, July 19). Athletes part of violent trend. *Los Angeles Times.* Retrieved July 23, 2003, from http://www.latimes.com/sports/la-sp-crime19jul19002426,1,5915255.story

Foucault, M. (1995). *Discipline and punish: The birth of the prison.* New York: Vintage Books.

Friedman, R. (2000). *Red mafiya: How the Russian mob has invaded America.* New York: Little, Brown and Company.

Gibbs, J. T. (1996). *Race and justice: Rodney King and O. J. Simpson in a house divided.* New York: Jossey-Bass.

Gillman, S. (1985). *Differences and pathology: Stereotypes of sexuality, race and madness.* Ithaca: Cornell University Press.

Ginsburg, D. (1995). *The fix is in: A history of baseball gambling and game fixing scandals.* New York: Macfarland and Company.

Giroux, H. (1994). *Disturbing pleasures: Learning popular culture.* New York: Routledge.

Glassner, B. (1999). *The culture of fear: Why Americans are afraid of the wrong things.* New York: Basic Books.

Gray, H. (1995). *Watching race: Television and the struggle for blackness.* Minneapolis: University of Minnesota Press.

Green, T. (1996). *The dark side of the game: My life in the NFL.* New York: Warner Books.

Grossberg, L. (1988). *We gotta get out of this place: Popular conservatism and postmodern culture.* New York: Routledge.

Harris, J. (1987). *Drugged athletes: The crisis in American sports.* New York: Simon & Schuster.

Hoberman, J. (1997). *Darwin's athletes: How sport has damaged Black America and preserved the myth of race.* Boston: Houghton Mifflin.

Howe, S. (1989). *Between the lines: One athlete's struggle to escape the nightmare of addiction.* New York: Masters Press.

James, J. (1996). *Resisting state violence: Radicalism, gender, and race in U.S. culture.* Minneapolis: University of Minnesota Press.

Johnson, L., & Roediger, D. (1997). Hertz don't it? Becoming colorless and staying black in the crossover. In T. Morrison (Ed.), *Birth of a Nation'hood* (pp. 197–240). New York: Pantheon Books.

King, C. R., & Springwood, C. F. (2001). *Beyond the cheers: Race as spectacle in college sport.* Albany: State University of New York.

Lange, T. (1996). *Evidence dismissed: The inside story of the police investigation of O. J. Simpson.* New York: Pocket Books.

Lapchick, R. (2002). *Smashing barriers.* New York: Madison Books.

Lapchick, R. (2003a). The Kobe Bryant case: Athletes, violence, stereotypes and the games we play. *Sports Business Journal.* Retrieved July 23, 2003, from http://www.sportinsociety.org/rel-article34.html

Lapchick, R. (2003b). Race, athletes, and crime. *The Sports Business Journal.* Retrieved July 23, 2003, from http://www.sportinsociety.org/rel-article13.pdf

Leonard, D. (2004). The next MJ or the next OJ? Kobe Bryant, race and the absurdity of colorblind rhetoric. *Journal of Sport and Social Issues., 28*(3), 284–313.

Lucas, J. (1994). *Luke's way.* New York: Hazelden Press.

Mauer, M. (2001). *Race to incarcerate.* New York: New Press.

Messner, M., & Sabo, D. (1994). *Sex, violence & power in sports: Rethinking masculinity.* New York: Ten Speed Press.

Miller, J. G. (1996). *Search and destroy: African American males in the criminal justice system.* New York: Cambridge University Press.

Miller, T. (2002). *Sportsex.* Philadelphia: Temple University Press.

Millman, C. (2002). *The odds: One season, three gamblers, and the death of their Las Vegas.* New York: De Capo Press.

Moleda, D. (1995). *Interference: How organized crime influences professional football.* New York: Harper Collins.

Moorti, S. (2002). *Color of rape: Gender and race in television's public sphere.* Albany: State University of New York Press.

Morrison, T. (1997). *Birth of a Nation'hood: Gaze, script, and spectacle in the O.J. Simpson Case.* New York: Pantheon Books.

Mortensen, C. (1991). *Playing for keeps: How one man kept the mob from sinking its hooks into pro football*. New York: Simon & Schuster.

Mottram, D. (Ed.). (2002). *Drugs in sport*. New York: Routledge.

Nathan, D. (2003). *Saying it's so: A cultural history of the Black Sox scandal*. Urbana: University of Illinois Press.

———(2004). *New Nation News*. Retrieved July 23, 2003, http://www.newnation.org/NNN-news-crime. html

O'Connor, D. (Ed.). (2002). *Iron Mike: A Mike Tyson reader*. New York: Thunder's Mouth Press.

Ogletree, C. (2000). Privileges and immunities for basketball stars and other sports heroes. In T. Boyd & K. Shropshire (Eds.), *Basketball Jones* (pp. 12–26). New York: New York University Press.

Pellowski, M. (2003). *The Chicago "Black Sox" baseball scandal: A headline court case*. New York: Enslow Publishers.

Pratt, M. B. (2004, March 4). Sexism & sports: The playing field of profit. *Workers World News Paper*. Retrieved July 23, 2003, from http://216.239.57.104/search?q=cache:wKy0uFYq9N0J:www.mail-archive. com/wwnews%40wwpublish.com/msg03161.html++Minnie+Pratt+and+richard+lapchick&hl=en

Redeker, B. (2003, July 30). NBA bad boys: Do basketball players get in trouble more often than other athletes. *ABCnews.com*. Retrieved July 23, 2003, from http://abcnews.go.com/sections/wnt/US/ nba030730_badboys.html

Roberts, R. (2000). *Heavy justice: The trial of Mike Tyson*. Fayetteville: University of Arkansas Press.

Robinson, L. (1998). *Crossing the line: Violence and sexual assault in Canada's national sport*. New York: McClelland & Stewart.

Rose, P. (2004). *My prison without bars*. New York: Rodale Books.

Ross, R. (2003). *Bummy Davis vs. Murder, Inc.: The rise and fall of the Jewish Mafia and an ill-fated prizefighter*. New York: St. Martins Press.

Rowe, D. (1999). *Sport, culture and media*. Philadelphia: Open University Press.

Savage, J. (1997). *A sure thing?: Sports and gambling*. New York: Lerner Publications.

Sawyer, R., Thompson, E., & ChirCorelli, A. M. (2002). Rape myth acceptance among intercollegiate student athletes: A preliminary examination. *American Journal of Health Studies*. Retrieved July 23, 2003, from http://articles.findarticles.com/p/articles/mi_m0CTG/is_1_18/ai_96267469Books, Vol 18, ISS 1, pp. 19–25

Sheridan, C. (2003, August 4). Kobe's true lesson. *SouthCoastToday.com*. Retrieved July 23, 2003, from http://www.southcoasttoday.com/daily/08-03/08-03-03/e10sp176.htm

Sloop, J. M. (1997). Mike Tyson and the perils of discursive constraints: Boxing, race and the assumption of guilt. In A. Baker & T. Boyd (Eds.), *Out of bounds* (pp. 102–122). Bloomington: University of Indiana Press.

Smith, C. F. (1992). *Lenny, lefty, and the chancellor: The Len Bias tragedy and the search for reform in big-time college basketball*. New York: Bancroft Press.

Sperber, M. (2001). *Beer and circus: How big-time college sports is crippling undergraduate education*. New York: Owl Books.

Stewart, G. (1998). *Drugs and sport*. New York: Greenhaven Press.

Taylor, L. (2003). *LT: Over the edge: Tackling quarterbacks, drugs, and a world beyond football*. New York: Harper Collins Publishers.

Thaler, P. (1997). *The spectacle: media and the making of the O. J. Simpson story*. New York: Praeger Publishers.

Thompson, C. (1990). *Down and dirty: The life and crimes of Oklahoma football*. New York: Carol Graf and Company.

Vlahos, K. B. (2003) Kobe Case Draws Attention to Athlete Allegations, *Foxnews.com*. Retrieved June 15, 2004, November 17, http://www.foxnews.com/story/0,2933,103248,00.html

Wells, D. (2003). *Perfect I'm not: Boomer on beer, brawls, backaches, and baseball*. New York: William Morrow and Company.

Wenzel, L. (1998). *Athletes and domestic violence, a position paper*. Retrieved July 23, 2003, from http://www.unc.edu/depts/ppps/position/violence.htm

Williams, L. (2001). *Playing the race card: Melodramas of black and white from Uncle Tom to O. J. Simpson*. Princeton: Princeton University Press.

Wilson, W., & Derse, E. (2000). *Doping in elite sport: The politics of drugs in the Olympic movement*. New York: Human Kinetics Publishers.

Zimbalist, A. (2001). *Unpaid professionals: Commercialism and conflict in big-time college sports*. Princeton: Princeton University Press.

Sporting Bodies

Davis W. Houck

Florida State University

The Thriller in Manilla

How many times must you try to explain?
Those last few rounds with Joe were like death.
Your head pounding away from the heat, the noise,
   And the lights; your arms and legs aching
      Beyond the limits of pain: There were
      White-hot fires raging inside every muscle.
         You tried to tell them.
You wanted to make them understand
   How a man's body can scream in silent agony,
   How this fight could make his very heart conspire
      With death.
How fruitless to describe weariness that goes through the body
   And into the soul!
Pain is far more real than the impoverished syllables to
      Name it.
Those who have never fought before or within any hot gates,
   How could they ever hope to understand a pain
      So all-consuming?
It is not "borderline death." Could it be "borderline,"
   When you have crossed the silent boundaries
      And come back
In the midst of a leather barrage of crackling lefts and
      Rights?
You tell the reporters simply, "It was like death."
They soon file out of the dressing room thinking,
   "A great fighter, but not too bright or articulate."

—Raymond Fleming (1979, p. 5)

In a chapter about sport and bodies, it seems appropriate that Muhammad Ali, Cassius Clay, the Louisville Lip, gets pride of place. Even though Fleming never names the boxer weaving between the liminal spheres of living and dying, the title gives it away: If nothing else, Don King had a thing for marketing and rhymes (and memorably bad hair). This was Ali at his greatest—after the unlikely knockout of Sonny Liston in Miami and his "ain't got no quarrel with them Vietcong," but before the punch-drunk caricature of Spinks–Holmes–Berbick. It was an athlete pushed beyond anything previously experienced into an inarticulate and mute place. Sadly, that is the space where Ali now resides. The impassive face and the tremors function as nostalgic reminders of the loquacious poet, "float like a butterfly, sting like a bee."[1] But to those of us who grew up watching The Champ (and Howard Cosell), today's visage of Ali functions also as an indictment: Who was consuming the spectacle? Who was putting Ali back in the ring when he should've been counting his millions? Why do we wince when we look at Ali? Are we catching a reflection?

Beyond Muhammad Ali, Fleming's prose poem speaks directly to sport and the body—how athletic expenditure is bound up with the limits of existence. One of the most obvious examples of this relationship occurs annually at the Ironman/woman competition, whose events, if not distances, are becoming commonplace around the world. I'll return to the topic of sport and mortality later, but for now it's enough to note the obvious: Sport is bound up with the body. As Duncan (1994) noted, "the body is the ground for any investigation of sport or physical activity" (p. 48). Loy, Andrews, and Rinehart (1993) said much the same thing: "the human body comprises the chief corporeal component of sporting practices" (p. 69). Neither sport nor the body, however, are unproblematic categories, things that can be safely taken for granted. Both exist at the complex intersection of economics, politics, nationality, race, gender, sexuality, science, and technology. I can't (and won't) do that complexity justice in this chapter; rather, I will proceed topically, moving across issues of race, gender, nationality, and violence. And rather than focus on a specific sport, I discuss pivotal moments across several sports for what they say about the complex and evolving relationship between sport and the body.

Critical theory has clearly been at the leading edge of the revitilization of studies of sport; more specifically, the work of French historian and philosopher Michel Foucault has provided a conceptual foundation easily transferable from the history of the human sciences to contemporary sport and its practices. That foundation, perhaps not surprisingly, analyzes the body—particularly the surveilled and disciplined body (Foucault, 1979). For Foucault, knowledge and power, via discursive channels, traverse complex networks, but they manifest themselves in the same place: on the individual.[2] Power, as such, is less repressive and state-controlled than fluid, strategic, multiple, potentially positive, and put into circulation by a host of institutional sites (government, education, science). It functions most perniciously

---

[1]Surprisingly, cultural critics have not done much work on arguably the twentieth century's most important athlete. Gorn's (1995) anthology is a good place to begin "reading" Ali; see also Saeed (2003), Farred (2003), and Lemert (2003). For the third of the Ali–Frazier bouts, I highly recommend Kram's (2001) *Ghosts of Manila*. For the much-anticipated fight between George Foreman and Ali, Mailer's (1997) *The Fight* is without peer. The so-called "Rumble in the Jungle" in Mobutu's Zaire is also the basis for the Academy Award-winning documentary *When We Were Kings*. Two other Ali-related books provide an important cultural backdrop to his rise to fame: Remnick's (1998) *King of the World* and Marquesee's (1999) *Redemption Song*.

[2]Foucault's most accessible treatment of power is *Power/Knowledge* (1981). The opening chapter of *Discipline and Punish* (1979) is also excellent. For a detailed account of his archaeological method, see Foucault (1972).

when rendered invisible and natural. Perhaps not surprisingly, sport critics have made extensive and revelatory use of Foucault in "places" such as gyms, spas, and other workout facilities where the body is carefully watched and monitored.[3] These are public spaces where the body is disciplined to take on a very specific form.

The Foucauldian point, and the point of many others working in critical sport studies, is that bodies aren't merely biological entities; far more than nature is at work when bodies meet on athletic fields. Cole (1993) put the point well:

> Sport has been and remains a particularly powerful ideological mechanism because it is dominated by the body, a site of ideological condensation whose manifest meaning is intimately bound to the biological. The biologistic knowledges (Foucault's truth-effects) and their appeal to the natural (the body-narratives) work to dissolve the traces of cultural and productive labor on and the training of the body and its movement. (p. 86)

The moment of critical intervention is precisely to reconstruct that dissolution and to map the contours of the culture's training of the body. Common racial wisdom, for example, has it that Black bodies are inherently more athletic than White bodies.[4] Moreover, that racial atavism gets coded rhetorically in myriad outlets that serve only to reify the Black body/White mind stereotypes. The seemingly harmless born-to-dunk label is not so harmless when it functions to naturalize athletic (Black) difference (Andrews, 1996).

Growing up a Boston Celtics fan, the tension between Black athleticism and White mental smarts was never far from the surface. Larry Bird was the avatar of this particular tension. A common theme among sportswriters and scholars is that Bird (with Magic Johnson) saved the league once he arrived in 1979. Here was a slow, gravity-bound White guy from a working-class Indiana background—the so-called "Hick from French Lick"—whose indefatigable practice sessions were legendary—he was later dubbed Larry Legend—and whose unique strength was his fundamentals (viz., passing, shooting, and being a smart team player). He was slow to speak, self-effacing, didn't wear gold chains, and dove after every loose ball. Not surprisingly, both the Boston media and the national media loved him; he was the antidote to the athletic but undisciplined, lazy, and overly stylized Black athlete with a taste for cocaine.[5]

The professional basketball player who perhaps best embodied all that Bird had redeemed was Marvin Barnes of the American Basketball Association (ABA) St. Louis Spirits and several National Basketball League (NBA) teams. Nicknamed "Bad News," by players and sportswriters for beating a college teammate with a tire iron, the "News" as he liked to refer to himself, typically showed up minutes before the

---

[3]See for example the work of Cole (1993), Markula (2001), Aycock (1992), and Duncan (1994). For Foucault's more global applications in the critical study of sport, see Hargreaves (1986), Andrews (1993), Rail and Harvey (1995), and Loy et al. (1993).

[4]For an extended cultural, political, and scientific discussion of the subject see Hoberman (1997) and Entine (2000).

[5]Ironically, in the 1986 NBA draft, the Celtics chose University of Maryland senior Len Bias with the second overall pick. Two days later he was dead from a cocaine overdose. He was the player who was finally supposed to give Bird some much-needed rest during the regular season. In his autobiography, Bird (1989) noted, "I was so excited when we drafted him. I thought, 'Oh boy, here we go. We're on a roll now. We've finally gotten a player who can give me a break" (p. 153). For the only book-length account of the Bias death and its aftermath at the University of Maryland, see Cole (1989). For a Foucaultian analysis of the death of Len Bias, see Houck (1991).

game in a Rolls, usually sporting a full-length mink coat, two Dobermans, multiple women, and a hangover. The African-American Barnes would then often bust his opponent for 30 points and 20 rebounds (Pluto, 1990). Barnes also did a stint with the pre-Bird Celtics, where he admitted snorting cocaine on the Celtics' bench. The point isn't so much Barnes' excesses as what he represented to White America: the overstylized, oversexed, criminal (but natural) Black athlete who didn't need to practice and who had little use for teammates.[6]

Isiah Thomas was nobody's fool when it came to representation, race, and Larry Bird. The diminutive Thomas, long-time point guard for the Detroit Pistons and most recently President of Basketball Operations for the New York Knicks, was the lineal NBA descendent of the "News." Following a particularly contentious playoff series loss to Bird's Celtics in the 1987 Eastern Conference Finals, Thomas' frustrations about race boiled over in front of several sportswriters. Commenting on pre-gender bender and be-boa'd teammate Dennis Rodman's complaints that Bird was overrated because of his race, Thomas chimed in, "If Bird was black, he'd be just another good guy." Thomas' comments were less about Bird and more about discursive representation: Bird was favored by a predominantly White media because he was a White star.[7] Thomas explained himself days later to the *New York Times*' Ira Berkow: "Magic (Johnson) and Michael Jordan and me, we're playing on God-given talent, like we're animals, lions and tigers who run wild in the jungle, while Larry's success is due to intelligence and hard work." Thomas continued, it's as if "all we do is run and jump. We never practice or give a thought to how we play. It's like I came dribbling out of my mother's womb" (as cited in Brazell, 2000).

Isiah Thomas probably doesn't know Michel Foucault from Michelle Kwan. Nor might he care. But his comments speak rather directly to the French historian: Sporting bodies are bound up in complex networks of knowledge, power, and discourse wherein talents and abilities are often normalized (thus disciplined) along racial lines. Disentangle that network and we find that economics and politics are also implicated. Without an economy of sporting consumption, the Bird–Isiah contretemps don't matter; nor do they even exist. The latter point is hard to overstate: Discourse has a materiality that puts into circulation what can and cannot be said.[8] And as Andrews (1993) noted, when sport becomes an object of discourse, the "discursive formations that surround sport define and create individual subjectivities based on such diverse classifications as gender, age, ethnicity, class, and nationality" (p. 162). In other words, the discourse of sport, precisely because it is always partial and interested, functions to include and exclude, punish and reward; in the interstices of its many valences do we define who we are or might be.

Those possibilities of being have been explored with particular interest by many feminist sport scholars. A different Foucauldian theoretical apparatus, though, underwrites such studies—that of panopticism. In his study of prisons, hospitals,

---

[6]There are two iconic images of the ABA: the red, white, and blue basketball and the near Beavis-altitude afros sported by many players, but most memorably by Virginia Squires star Julius "Dr. J" Erving. For the best book on the brief life of the ABA, see Pluto (1990).

[7]Bird (1989) was nonplussed at the media's response to Thomas' comments: "I was astonished when this thing became the biggest nonplaying sports issue in the country. All over the country, writers and broadcasters were taking sides. *Rodman's a jerk. Rodman's not a jerk. Isiah's a racist. Isiah's not a racist. Bird's overrated. Bird's not overrated.* Sociologists and political columnists were jumping into it. It was completely crazy" (p. 165). More than one sportswriter, 16 years later, reads Bird's firing of Thomas as head coach of the Indiana Pacers in the summer of 2003 within the context of this racial incident.

[8]For a brilliant explication and application of this theoretical point, see Sloop (1997).

barracks, and schools, Foucault (1979) theorized that a culture of bodily discipline is intimately related to visible bodies. What better and more efficient way to engender good behavior than to render subjects constantly visible? "He who is subjected to a field of visibility, and who knows it, assumes responsibility for the constraints of power; he makes them play spontaneously upon himself; he inscribes in himself the power relation in which he simultaneously plays both roles; he becomes the principle of his own subjection" (pp. 202–203).

Foucault (1979) continued, the apparatus of visibility always wins: "By this very fact, the external power may throw off its physical weight; it tends to the noncorporal; and, the more it approaches this limit, the more constant, profound and permanent are its effects: it is a perpetual victory that avoids any physical confrontation and which is always decided in advance" (pp. 203).

Profound indeed. When a generation of young women come of age under body image distortion (BID) and young men under body dysmorphia (Bigorexia), we have indeed become all too willing to regiment our bodies—sometimes to death (Markula, 2001; Pope, Phillips, & Olivardia, 2000). The visual logic is comparative: What sorts of public and commodified bodies showcase health, success, physical desirability, and relational bliss? Almost without exception they are athletic bodies—toned, fit, in control, and active. Perhaps we might even call it a masculinized hard body; for if muscles are coded masculine, even swimsuit and lingerie models aren't fully feminine anymore. Cheryl Tiegs is no Veronica Varekova: In a short period of 25 years *Sports Illustrated*'s celebrated cover girls have gone from shapely soft bodies to taut, improbably breasted, and airbrushed cyborgs who today tend to pose with their bikinis or have them painted on rather than actually wear them.[9] Is it any wonder, then, that *SI* has begun featuring prominent female athletes in its vaunted end-of-winter swimsuit sale? And while we might applaud *SI* for including Serena with Anna, the commodified body exists to be consumed, thus emulated.

To be sure, a muscular female body, as Cole noted (1993) "is always already a suspicious body" (p. 90). As top-flight female athletes have won timed events that just a few years prior would have beaten all the men, suspicions have arisen as to the true femininity of female competitors. Thus did the International Olympics Committee, until Sydney in 2000, hew to gender verification tests. Originally such tests involved appearing nude before a panel of judges or undergoing a gynecological exam. More recently, a procedure known as a buccal smear was used to test an athlete's chromosomal structure.[10] More commonly, though, the manly female athlete is less a threat to the XY universe than to the sometimes fragile heteronormative world of the highly commodified sport spectacle. At the 1999 Australian Open, for example, Martina Hingis reportedly told German sportswriters that French player Amelie Mauresmo was "half a man" (Atkin, 1999). Similarly did American star Lindsay Davenport state, after being trounced by Mauresmo in the semis, "I thought I was playing a guy." (Atkin, 1999) Hingis' and Davenport's comments speak less to the need for gender verification surveillance and more perhaps to the threat posed by mannish (re: lesbian) players—a threat not lost on American television networks or women's athletic associations. We like our female athletes muscled and competitive—but also safely heterosexual.

---

[9]For an interesting, if sometimes underread, analysis of the *Sports Illustrated* swimsuit issue, see Davis (1997).

[10]For an interesting exploration of the transgendered athlete and mediated representations therein, see Birrell and Cole (1990/2000).

The specter of lesbianism extends far beyond women's professional tennis. That it haunts the Ladies Professional Golf Association (LPGA) and its marketability was illustrated by its commissioner Ty Votaw. In March 2002, Votaw encouraged players to shape up for the good of the tour. Part of that shaping involved showing more skin and being far more attentive to fashion and appearance. Sixty players reportedly consulted for a full-day seminar with New York make-up and hair experts brought in by Votaw. Said the commissioner after the seminar: "I was proud of our players for wanting to learn about things that could help them present themselves to the public. I think it's one of the high points of the year. It's no different from any other entertainer who is concerned that they present themselves in the most favorable light" (Isidore, 2002, para. 7).

With male spectatorship of the PGA Tour surging—and thus prize money—the LPGA is actively looking for, as well as cultivating, the next Laura Baugh or Jan Stephenson.[11] Without a Tiger Woods to spike television ratings in highly profitable and predictable ways, Votaw and many players are banking on the notion that an exposed, stylish, and heteronormative golfer might pique male spectatorship.[12]

The context of the LPGA Tour's deliberate (hetero)sexual investment shouldn't be overlooked. The Women's Tennis Association (WTA), which actively promotes the sexuality of its top players, appeals to good tennis and good looks—most notably in Serena Williams and Anna Kournikova. Women's figure skating is made to order for the heteronormative male gaze: Sequined tiny outfits with simulated nudity and the specter of a Katarina Witt bursting a strap in mid-axel titillate—and generate enormous television audiences.[13] The sultry and coquettish former East German also knows something about generating huge audiences in another domain: Her *Playboy* pictorial was rumored to be the highest-selling issue of Heff's slick. Witt and Tonya Harding aren't the only figure skaters to go from the kiss-and-cry to the bedroom. The most recent figure skater to cash in on the sport's erotic allure is Canadian Jamie Sale, who, with partner David Peltier, won a contested gold medal in pairs figure skating at the 2002 Winter Olympics. In a January 2004 spread in *FHM* (*For Him Magazine*), Sale posed in a white bikini—with the top conspicuously absent in several poses. Women's beach volleyball, and its near thong-ification on the sands of Southern California, has also made a concerted pitch for the male viewer. It's star Gabriella Reece, à la Witt, did a much-heralded 2001 spread for *Playboy*. Nor should we forget pseudosports such as wrestling, where oiled-up, Speedo-wearing behemoths in face paint desperately need to be surrounded by centerfolds and lingerie models lest their masculinity be impugned.[14] In other words, it seems that the double standard is alive and well; more importantly perhaps, many female athletes

---

[11]I am aware of only one critical analysis of a female golfer; see Jamieson (2000) for an analysis of mediated representations of Nancy Lopez. For an ethnographic account of the LPGA Tour, see Crossett (1995).

[12]Much the same dynamics were in play especially during the inaugural season of the Women's National Basketball Association; see Banet-Weiser (1999). She notes that the "traditional trappings of femininity—fashion, motherhood, beauty, morality—characterize the players of the WNBA" (p. 412). See also Miller (2001).

[13]For an interesting, if variable, collection of critical essays on figure skating, see Baughman (1995). Of all the essays I've read on figure skating, the work of Feder-Kane (1995) stands alone. For a more popular, but very insightful, look at figure skating, see Brennan (1997, 1999).

[14]For an insightful ethnographic treatment of professional wrestling, see Mazer (1998). Regarding the overdetermined masculinity of the professional wrestling spectacle, see Oppliger (2004).

seem to be actively embracing their sexualization, even as competition heats up for the heterosexual male viewer.[15]

The sexualization and commercialization of the female athletic body certainly isn't anything new; the ubiquity is, but not the idea. What is new, and I think quite dangerous for female athletes and the future of female athletic leagues, is intergender competition. When Swedish golf star Annika Sorenstam competed against Professional Golfers Association (PGA) regulars at the 2003 Colonial Invitational, most of the debate and interest surrounded whether she should have been granted a sponsor's exemption and/or how she would fare. Given that she performed quite well—though missing the cut—and given the phenomenal achievement several months later of 14-year-old amateur prodigy Michelle Wie—who missed the cut at a 2004 PGA event in her home state of Hawaii by a mere one stroke and beat scores of professional men twice her age—we can already glimpse the future definition of success: Can a woman measure up to the men?[16] Sorenstam's and Wie's (and Suzy Whaley's) successes notwithstanding, their invasion of male sporting turf can certainly be read as a grab for publicity and dollars. Far more consequential, though, is the logical extension of their achievements: Women aren't really much good until they compete against—and beat—the men. Thus does success become a benchmark for future failure, while simultaneously undermining the concept of intrafemale competition and its commercial viability.

Golf isn't the only game in which cross-gendered competition is a reality. In a 2004 dunk contest at the McDonald's All-American game, high school senior Candace Parker beat five male competitors to win a title that features such luminaries as Vince Carter and LeBron James. To dunk, and dunk hard, is the pinnacle of individual basketball accomplishment, thus solidifying Parker's claim to this masculine preserve.[17] These days it isn't a "battle of the sexes" in which an elite athlete (Billie Jean King) beats a misogynist geezer (Bobbie Riggs) in need of publicity. Nor is it lowering the rim or hitting from the ladies tees. It's equal to equal, and female victory today, I fear, augurs the backlash tomorrow. And, if not the backlash, certainly the expectations have been ratcheted up.

Male athletic bodies have been sexualized and commodified as well. This isn't an altogether recent occurrence, as Bordo (1999) among others documented. While I was growing up, my mom commented more than once on Jim Palmer and his rather sparse Jockey briefs. But male athletic bodies still labor under one constraint, even in our supposed post-civil rights era, that women don't: a Black man cannot exhibit sexual agency with a White woman. As Dyson (1993) noted, "Fear of black male sexuality is often at root a fear of miscegenation" (p. 169). America's sad and long history of lynching testifies to that fear.[18] Two fairly recent ad campaigns testify to

---

[15]In the September 4, 2000, issue of *Sports Illustrated*, Rick Reilly addressed the uproar caused by Olympic swimmer Jenny Thompson's topless (though covered) pictures published in the magazine the week prior. His view was not different from many male journalists: "Jenny Thompson's topless portrait sends young girls a terrific message: Fit is sexy. Muscles are sexy. Sport is sexy" (p. 99) Reilly's daughter or wife have yet to pose topless.

[16]Whereas Sorenstam and Wie both were granted invitations to the PGA events, Suzy Whaley actually earned her spot in the Greater Hartford Open by winning the 2003 Connecticut Section PGA Championship. She would miss the cut at the GHO.

[17]For a rhetorico-cultural reading of dunking, see Houck (2000).

[18]There are several excellent books that document interracial sexual contact between Black men and White women as the cause for lynching in both the North and South; see Whitfield (1988) Dray (2002), For a graphic and haunting photographic exploration of lynching, see Allen (2000).

the power (and longevity) of the nation's interracial fears. They involve arguably the two most prominent athletes and endorsers in the world, Tiger Woods and Michael Jordan. Buick has managed to hawk cars by peddling Tiger Woods' sex appeal; the ad in question is for Buick's hybrid vehicle, the Rendezvous. A dark-haired, provocatively dressed woman does her alchemical best to mix parts of several cars to arrive at the Rendezvous. Her last part of the potion is a Nike golf ball (Jordan's cross-marketing strategy, in spades) and a golf glove. Magically, Tiger Woods arrives in the Rendezvous to take the beautiful (White) enchantress to parts unknown. Tiger exclaims, "I love this town." Importantly, Tiger Woods is the sex object, not the sexual subject seeking to satisfy his libidinal urges.[19]

Buick (and Woods) had a good teacher in Jordan, whose sex appeal is a given— even while muted. For example, Jordan shills for Hanes underwear. How do you sell Jordan and Hanes while not tapping into the racist, but powerful, myth? Hanes' solution initially was to feature Michael with his now late father, James Jordan. And rather than wearing the underwear in question, à la Palmer, they simply examined the boxers and briefs under the auspices of a Christmas present from Michael's mom, Deloris. A second ad was equally muted. Instead of confining Jordan's incip-ient sexuality to a parental domestic sphere, he becomes the object of the female gaze as he walks by two White women speculating aloud on whether the passersby are wearing "boxers or briefs." Attuned to their game, Jordan responds, "Hanes and let's just leave it at that." Michael's a brand, not a buck; a star, not a stud. As McDonald (2001) summarized, "Jordan thus exposes the women's game without being exposed" (p. 166). The advertisement thus functions rhetorically to diffuse "lingering impressions of masculine force, black hypersexuality, and deviance" (p. 160).[20]

Just as female athletic muscles have grown more prominent, so too for the men. The growth of the male body—muscles, penis, and hair—is also a multibillion dollar industry, fueled by what Pope et al. (2000) called the *Adonis complex*. In an age of bigger is better, high school boys and college-aged men are bulking up on pricey supplements and illegal steroids. And we know too that bigger has tangible material effects on the athletic field as well as the bedroom; after all, the secret is out: "chicks dig the long ball." Effete pitchers like Tom Glavine and Greg Maddox who resemble Prada fashion models after a weekend bender got the message: Baseball's economic resurrection had more to do with Mark McGwire and Sammy Sosa blasting tape-measure home runs rather than control pitchers working the corners. McGwire also let us in on his little secret: Androstenedione made other parts of his body hard; "Big Mac" indeed.

But that bigness has come with some consequences: whereas heavily muscled female bodies invoke the threat of lesbianism, male (and increasingly female) ath-letes labor under suspicions of steroid use. Even as the Summer Olympics in Athens neared, track's megastar Marion Jones and boyfriend and 100-meter world-record holder Tim Montgomery faced serious accusations of steroid use. Former

---

[19]Of course the irony of Tiger Woods' lack of sexual agency is that he's married to a White woman, Swedish nanny-cum-fashion model Elin Nordegren. For critical work on Tiger Woods, see Cole (2002), Cole and Andrews (2001), Giacobbi and DeSensi (1999), Uchacz (1998), Yu (2002), and Polumbaum and Wieting (1999). I would also recommend Owen's (2001) *The Chosen One* and Pierce (1998).

[20]David L. Andrews' (2001) fine anthology *Michael Jordan, Inc.*, is an excellent place to begin critical exploration of the megastar. I would also recommend LaFeber (1999) and Andrews (1996). For more popular accounts of Jordan and his immense fame, I recommend Greene (1993, 1995) and Halberstam (1999).

world-champion sprinter Kelli White is only the first of what will likely be many athletes to be sanctioned and suspended for doping. Professional baseball's Barry Bonds is also under investigation for his rather conspicuous bodily transformation. Bonds is just the latest in a line of male athletes whose record-setting performances—in Bonds' case, 73 home runs in 2002 and his pursuit of Hank Aaron's home run record—are tinged by suspicions of illegal drug use. Ever since Canadian Ben Johnson shattered the world record in the 100-meter dash at the 1988 Summer Olympics and had his gold medal stripped by a positive drug test, the male athletic body has come under increased scrutiny.[21] The surveillance and suspicions have only intensified with players coming forward—notably Ken Caminiti (now deceased from a drug overdose) in professional baseball—and leadoff hitters like the former Baltimore Oriole Brady Anderson hitting 52 home runs. It doesn't help Bonds' case that his trainer at BALCO has made important confessions, nor that twinned images of his body are now frequently used in before and after shots long a staple of the muscle magazines.

Far more interesting than Barry Bonds' recent walnuts-in-a-condom body is President George W. Bush's choice to put the topic of steroids and steroid abuse in his 2004 State of the Union address—a choice that prompted a great deal of critical commentary. For a nation at war on several fronts, steroid use among professional athletes seemed rather tangential. But Bush, once a part owner of the Texas Rangers and a big baseball fan, served notice to the nation that professional sporting bodies were under his administration's watchful eye. "To help children make right choices, they need good examples. Athletics play such an important role in our society, but, unfortunately, some in professional sports are not setting much of an example," Bush stated:

> The use of performance-enhancing drugs like steroids in baseball, football, and other sports is dangerous, and it sends the wrong message—that there are shortcuts to accomplishment, and that performance is more important than character. So tonight I call on team owners, union representatives, coaches, and players to take the lead, to send the right signal, to get tough, and to get rid of steroids now. (Bush, 2004, para. 58)

The assumption, of course, is that President Bush thinks there is a problem and he understands its extent, but the begged question remains: how? Which drug tests is he privy to that a scandal-thirsty media isn't? Has Bush been watching too much *SportsCenter*? Additionally, in our postmodern age of the commodified spectacle, Bush misses the obvious: Performance is character. Athletic heroes are heroic, so the calculus goes, precisely because of what they do on the athletic field and when they do it, not by a mythic and pastoral private sphere redolent of *The Natural* or *Field of Dreams*.

Growing up as an avid baseball and football card collector in the 1970s, I studied statistics and bodies. I can still remember my amazement at then Houson Oiler rookie John Matuszak's size: At 6'8" and 285 pounds, the defensive tackle was as big as they came in professional football. Nowadays "The Tooz" would be an undersized

---

[21]For a critical examination of Ben Johnson, see Jackson, Andrews, and Cole (1998). I would argue that suspicions, and ultimately access, of/to the sporting body generally and the Black (male) sporting body specifically are tied less to Johnson and much more to Len Bias. It was in the wake of Bias' 1986 cocaine overdose (and also Cleveland Browns safety, Don Rogers') that Congress passed and President Reagan signed into law punitive antidrug legislation; see Houck (1991) and Reeves & Campbell (1994).

lineman on either side of the ball. With many linemen now tipping the scales at more than 350 pounds, the massive and precipitate growth of the male athletic body is both suspicious and frightening: If the growth is due to steroids or unregulated supplements, what are the long-term consequences for a player's health? Perhaps we might be wiser to focus on the short term. How many more Korey Stringers might there be waiting for their internal organs to melt in the summer heat of conditioning drills? The Minnesota Vikings' 335-pound all-pro guard died on August 1, 2001, 15 hours after struggling through morning drills; his body temperature as he entered the hospital neared 109°F.

William "the Refrigerator" Perry was far luckier than Stringer. It will be recalled that the massive Chicago Bears' nose guard—barely six feet and nearly 350 pounds—capitalized on his bulk, starring in McDonald's ads and music videos during the 1986 and 1987 seasons. These days, the Fridge's body is still an object of fascination and commodification: The nearly 400-pound Perry, who supposedly lays bricks with his father-in-law, recently fought the 7'7" former professional basketball player Manute Bol in Fox's *Celebrity Boxing*. Whereas Perry's body was once useful in clogging the middle, these days his body is pure spectacle, a human freak show whose obese Black body participates in the racialized discourse of the lazy, unproductive Black male out to score a quick hustle.

Whereas White America might have read the Fridge as a gap-toothed and cartoonish, if likeable, football player-cum-pitchman in the mid-1980s, today his massive body portends its own self-indulged demise. We don't need Foucault to remind us that visible and overweight bodies are some of the most disciplined and discussed objects in contemporary culture.[22] In our increasingly health- and diet-crazed culture, public fat is always overdetermined, especially when gendered and raced. If Monica Lewinski didn't have a complex pre-cigar and pizza delivery girl, she certainly had one following her affair with then-President Bill Clinton. Late night comics in particular regularly skewered the former intern for the shape and size of her body. Lewinski would no doubt get sympathy from many women, whose publicly exposed bodies, even when suitably hard, serve as lightning rods of judgment, comment, and comparison. How many "which female athlete/sportscaster/sportswriter/referee would you most like to see naked" lists will *Playboy* publish? The frequent polls function as a cultural barometer of heterosexual male desire in a commodified spectacle that loves to twin sport and sex (Guttmann, 1996; Miller, 2001). If there is a recent iconic moment that embodies the sexualization of sport, it's the photograph of Brandi Chastain, baring her hard torso for all to see at the 1999 World Cup. A common gesture of soccer exultation was transformed into a ubiquitous centerfold in one penalty kick and shutter flash. A hard, hetero, and suitably attractive "soccer babe" revealed to the world that a sporting male could indeed have it all. Whither Briana?

If you're going to read Foucault's key text on the body, *Discipline and Punish*, do so on an empty stomach. A frequent lament of my undergraduates is "You didn't tell us the book begins like that." In extensively quoted prose, Foucault tells the story of Damiens the Regicide, an eighteenth-century French prisoner condemned

---

[22]In his fascinating and suggestive chapter on "docile bodies," Foucault (1979) details the punitive properties of "the table": "In the eighteenth century, the table was both a technique of power and a procedure of knowledge.... It allows both the characterization of the individual as individual and the ordering of a given multiplicity. It is the first condition for the control and use of an ensemble of distinct elements: the base for a micro-physics of what might be called a 'cellular' power" (pp. 148–149). These days, height and weight tables indeed often exert a tyrannizing power of the norm.

to a grim (and very public) death, the *amende honorable*. Red-hot pinschers are first used to tear away his flesh; molten lead and sulphur are then poured on his gaping wounds. He is next drawn and quartered by a team of horses, legs and arms being literally pulled from the torso. The severed appendages are then thrown, along with the lifeless torso, onto a pyre. It is a rather horrific spectacle, certainly a memorable opening to a memorable book. Foucault's point is really quite simple: A painful and public death would dissuade any would-be regicides that the king's sovereign power wasn't to be challenged—public spectacle as surplus power.

The revulsion/attraction to bodily gore certainly isn't new. Whether fact or fiction, county road or movie theater, imperiled bodies exert a palpable allure. Relatively new televisual technologies also enable us to encounter exploding sporting bodies in the comfort of our Barcaloungers. A royal isn't engaged in a rhetoric of deterrence; rather, producers are showing us (rather graphically) that sport can be a dangerous game, one played, lest we forget, by very fragile and mortal bodies even while doing amazing things. Slow motion, in particular, is used so frequently in televising sporting events that its use functions as a dead metaphor; in an age of optic innovation and short attention spans, it lengthens the collective gaze. And it has myriad uses, claimed Fiske (1989): "Slow motion is used . . . to celebrate and display the male body in action, to produce a sense of awe by making the physical performance appear beautiful" (p. 219). "The male body in televised sport does not consist merely of brutish muscularity, but is aestheticized." I would agree with Fiske, especially when super slow motion captures an extraordinary athlete like Michael Jordan dunking at impossible angles, seemingly suspended in the air, ballet in high tops. But this is only one function. Perhaps a more common function of the technology is to provide Damiens-like intimacy to bodies literally being opened up and/or torn apart—not by a team of horses but by opponents, missteps, and even deranged fans.

The Mt. Everest of exploding sporting bodies, the Ur-text of televisual carnage, remains the Joe Theismann/Lawrence Taylor *danse macabre* which occurred during a nationally televised *Monday Night Football* game between the New York Giants and the Washington Redskins on November 18, 1985. Captured at several angles in slow motion, Taylor's hit snapped the quarterback's lower leg, resulting in multiple compound fractures and ending the all-pro Theismann's career. Even the National Football League's (NFL) ultimate tough guy, LT, won't watch the hit to this day. Among football fans, the hit is something of a canonical moment in televised sporting gore; it frequently makes top-10 lists—Letterman for the strong stomached—of best (worst?) hits. The hit also doubles as a frequent Internet joke: A sarcastic television digest has ESPN2 filling its 9 o'clock hour with "60 minutes of Joe Theismann's leg snapping."

I was a college freshman watching the game live when it happened. And, without more than one replay, I would have missed the gruesome moment; from the regular perpendicular camera angle, viewers could see only a tackle, not a disfigurement. For the next several minutes, as Theismann writhed on the ground in agony, ABC replayed the hit in pornographic detail; it was a money shot that network producers giddily rewound. For those not watching prime-time professional football at the time, the moment was replayed countless times over the next several days. Major League Baseball (MLB) writer Klayman (2002) speaks for many:

> Every time a player suffers a grotesque injury, the automatic comparison to Lawrence Taylor breaking Joe Theismann's leg in 1985 comes up. It's one of those moments that every single sports fan actually remembers watching.

And almost everyone will agree that nothing was as gross as watching the Redskin quarterback's career end. (para. 10)

With the rise of 24-hour cable sports stations like ESPN, there's been a Theismann-ification of programming, the Internet joke notwithstanding. In a July 2001 episode of ESPN's *Outside the Lines*, for example, host Bob Ley explored the rather gratuitous subject of "Comebackers," major league pitchers who've been hit in the face by line drives off the bats of opposing hitters. Viewers are repeatedly treated to vicious shots off the faces of Bryce Florie, Billy Wagner, and Mike Mussina. Although the program attempted to psychologize the on-field violence, and thus situate it within the context of pitchers overcoming their fears to get back on the mound, the visuals are pure gore: pitchers prostrate and bleeding, recounting what the moment of impact felt like and looked like later. The show, in brief, is pure commodification of sporting gore.[23]

MLB had its own Joe Theismann-like moment back in 1999 when then Pittsburgh Pirate catcher Jason Kendall suffered a compound fracture of his ankle as he hit the first base bag awkwardly while trying to beat out an infield hit. The carnage, compared in frequent mediated accounts to Theismann, quickly went mainstream: The injury was repeatedly aired during the next several days on cable and broadcast news segments and highlight shows. Slow motion technology was employed to slow down and pinpoint the moment of dislocation in excruciating detail. Foucault claims that discipline often takes the form of an anatomy of detail, and although he means something quite different from sports' rupturing bodies caught on videotape, the effect can be similar: bodily training to gain efficiencies and to prevent such painful injuries.

Sports injuries and their commodification and consumption don't always take place within the context of players trying to win a game. Network executives could at least claim that the injuries to Theismann, the pitchers, and Kendall occurred while competing; as such, it wasn't gratuitous to replay them. One such event hovers over the NBA, one that the league and its players would like to forget. On December 9, 1977, in a game between the Houston Rockets and the Los Angeles Lakers, Kevin Kunnert and Kermit Washington got into a tussle. Washington swung blindly at a sprinting Rudy Tomjanovich, whom he saw fast approaching out of the corner of his eye. When the Rockets forward finally came to, he wondered if the scoreboard in the Forum had fallen on him. A proximate Kareem Abdul-Jabbar said the impact sounded like a watermelon hitting the pavement. Lakers assistant coach Jack McCloskey called it "the hardest punch in the history of mankind." (Van Vliet, 2002) Doctors compared the trauma to Tomjanovich's face to a person hitting a windshield at 50 mph. The bone structure of his face was loosened from his skull. Spinal fluid was leaking into his nose. More than one person feared for Tomjanovich's life. "The Punch," as it's now simply known and remembered, was even the subject of an entire book by noted sports author Feinstein (2003).

The raw power of the punch and its devastating impact on Tomjanovich's body, and the fact that it was captured on videotape, has become the archetypal moment whenever the subject of the NBA and violence comes up—as invariably it does each year. Neither player has quite overcome the punch: Washington blames it for his disappointing career and inability to find a coaching position; Tomjanovich, while

---

[23]For an online transcript of the program, see http://sports.espn.go.com/page2/tvlistings/show67 transcript.html.

a fine NBA coach, has never escaped being on the receiving end of the most devastating punch ever thrown—in or out of a boxing ring. The punch, in other words, is inseparable from either man; it defines Washington and haunts Tomjanovich. Taken out of context—the manner in which the videotape is typically presented—the punch serves only to heighten racial antagonism and warrant racial fears in a sporting world where outsized Black bodies visit violence upon smaller, unsuspecting White bodies. That Kermit Washington would be blackballed is hardly surprising given the acontextual framing of the event. It doesn't much matter that he was an Academic All-American, or earned a degree in psychology, or funded charities out of his own pocket. A Black man nearly killed a White man on a basketball court. Enough said; enough seen.

Whereas race often frames the punch, nationality frames the events of April 30, 1993, in Hamburg, Germany. During a changeover in a match against Magdalena Maleeva, a deranged German fan, Gunther Parche, stabbed Monica Seles in the back. His reason? He wanted fellow German Steffi Graf to reclaim the number-one ranking. Just weeks later, he got his wish. Moreover, even though the injury was not career-threatening, Seles took 27 months to come back to tennis. She would never regain her place atop the women's rankings. Nor would she testify against Parche, who never served a day of jail time for the televised attack.

While the knife attack on Seles is rarely shown, fan proximity to athletes can be harrowing. I can vividly recall following Tiger Woods at the 2000 U.S. Open. What struck me most about Woods wasn't his play; it was the enormous size of his gallery and the fact that any calculating person could do serious bodily harm to the world's most popular athlete. Golf is somewhat unique in that fans have fairly immediate access to players, but in an age of shrapnel-wielding and hopeless 18-year-olds looking to earn their way into the company of lascivious and paradisical virgins, why not the crowded athletic field and the crowded outdoor café? Parche's sadism was radically individual. What of international nihilism in an age of live television and cheap camcorders? Do the video executions of Nicholas Berg and Daniel Pearl suggest that sport for the Jihadists, like the Taliban, is executing infidels? If the Twin Towers, why not the twin towers? And still we giggle at the sight of gelatinous Brits streaking across the prim grounds of the All England Club.

Certain sports, of course, are more prone to creating the violent spectacle: football, hockey, auto racing, and boxing aren't golf, synchronized swimming, the hammer throw, or curling. Perhaps it's not surprising that spectatorship for extreme sports such as the triathlon and K2 boxing, among many others, has multiplied exponentially in just the past few years. One important manifestation of that demand is the Extreme Sports Channel, which debuted in Europe in 1999 and presently reaches more than 50 countries with 24-7 coverage of skateboarding, surfing, BMX, and other extreme sports. ESPN continues to score big with the X Games—a riff on Generation X—which it created in 1995 to appeal to younger viewers for whom baseball is the national bedtime and golf is bad pants with monotone British accents. The updated and decidedly hip Olympics continue to gain viewers even as the line between recognized and alternative sports continues to evolve.

One of the many ironies of imperiled sporting bodies seemingly endlessly looped for a rubbernecking public is that our appetite for such "real" images does not extend to other theaters. The most recent Gulf War, eagerly broadcast by U.S. networks, was almost totally devoid of bleeding bodies—Iraqi or American. To see the war's casualties, viewers would need to tune their satellites to Al-Jazeera; there they could find civilians and soldiers maimed, dying, and dead (see Houck

& Davenport, 2004). The only bleeding American soldier to whom viewers were granted access was the heroic Jessica Lynch—and that access was very partial, even as we celebrated her homecoming to West Virginia. The Pentagon, in fact, cried foul when photographs of flag-draped American coffins made their way to the Internet and then to television. Whereas the vernacular of warfare underwrites the violence of professional sports—the metaphors, again, are dead—war's victims remain largely off-screen and therefore out of the nation's consciousness. Seeing, after all, is believing.

The ultimate bodily expenditure—death—does occur in televised athletic competition. This brings us full circle, back to Ali in Manila, back to sport's demands on the body. The sight of Loyola Marymount basketball starter Hank Gathers collapsing near mid-court following an alley-oop dunk; the death of NASCAR legend Dale Earnhardt at Daytona; boxer Ray Mancini's sanctioned brutalization of South Korean Duk Koo Kim that resulted in death—each reminds us that sporting bodies are very material, mortal things. We don't much care for that reminder. Or do we? American culture reminds us daily, perhaps hourly, that we should be forever young. In an age of Dick Clark, Botox, the double helix, and the Raelians, the discourse of death is everywhere absent. By loudly lauding the youthful athletic body, death lurks in the representational shadows. Who are we running from when we put in those three hard miles? What are we climbing toward as we gasp on the StairMaster? What distant land are we rowing toward on the rowing machine? And to where are we pedaling on the stationary bike?

Perhaps baseball great Ted Williams is the perfect metaphor, one who best embodies our hopes even as we snicker at the seeming absurdity of an 83-year-old corpse hanging upside down in a stainless steel sarcophagus, head removed, entombed in liquid nitrogen. Despite the legal wrangling among his surviving children, it seems that the Splendid Splinter, baseball's greatest hitter, got his last wish. Here death is but a temporary sleep, the body the ultimate palimpsest. As in his baseball career, Williams is ahead of his times, waiting for the inevitable to play itself out and redeem our last .400 hitter. For a man whose hand–eye coordination remains without rival, why not wager on science? Need we even mention that this isn't Simon and Garfunkel's generation? Our nation's "lonely eyes" are affixed less on aging stars to whom we look for direction and more on two-dimensional static bodies to whom we look for looking. But sporting bodies are alive and ready for the next game. Sporting bodies whose promise lies eternally present in bone, muscle, and sinew. Coo coo cachoo.

REFERENCES

Allen, J. (2000). *Without sanctuary: Lynching photography in America*. Santa Fe, NM: Twin Palms.

Andrews, D. L. (1993). Desperately seeking Michel: Foucault's genealogy, the body, and critical sport sociology. *Sociology of Sport Journal, 10*, 148–167.

Andrews, D. L. (1996). The fact(s) of Michael Jordan's blackness: Excavating a floating racial signifier. *Sociology of Sport Journal, 13*, 125–158.

Andrews, D. L. (2001). *Michael Jordan, Inc.* Albany, NY: SUNY Press.

Atkin, R. (1999, Jan. 31). Hingis uses mind to beat muscle. The Independent (London), p. 14.

Aycock, A. (1992). The confession of the flesh: Disciplinary gaze in casual bodybuilding. *Play & Culture, 5*, 338–357.

Banet-Weiser, S. (1999). Hoop dreams: Professional basketball and the politics of race and gender. *Journal of Sport & Social Issues, 23*, 403–420.

Baughman, C. (1995). Women on Ice: Feminist Responses to the Tanya Harding/Nancy Kerligan Spectacle. London: Routledge.

Bird, L., with Ryan, B. (1989). *Drive: The story of my life.* New York: Doubleday.

Birrell, S., & Cole, C. L. (2000). Double fault: Renee Richards and the construction and naturalization of difference. In S. Birrell & M. G. McDonald (Eds.), *Reading sport: Critical essays on power and representation* (pp. 279–309). Boston: Northeastern University Press. (Original work published 1990)

Bordo, S. (1999). *The male body: A new look at men in public and in private.* New York: Farrar, Straus and Giroux.

Brazell, B. (2000, July 23). *Race and NBC sports.* Retrieved May 18, 2004, from http://www.theguycode.com/stories/index.php?id=117

Brennan, C. (1997). *Inside edge: A revealing journey into the secret world of figure skating.* New York: Penguin.

Brennan, C. (1999). *Edge of glory: The inside story of the quest for figure skating's Olympic gold medals.* New York: Penguin.

Bush, G. W. (2004, January 20). *State of the Union address.* Retrieved May 18, 2004, from http://www.whitehouse.gov/news/releases/2004/01/20040120-7.html

Cole, C. L. (1993). Resisting the canon: Feminist cultural studies, sport, and technologies of the body. *Journal of Sport & Social Issues, 17,* 77–97.

Cole, C. L. (2002). The place of golf in U.S. imperialism. *Journal of Sport & Social Issues, 26,* 331–336.

Cole, C. L., & Andrews, D. L. (2001). America's new son: Tiger Woods and American multiculturalism. In D. L. Andrews & S. J. Jackson (Eds.), *Sport stars: The cultural politics of sporting celebrity* (pp. 70–86). London: Routledge.

Cole, L. (1989). *Never too young to die: The death of Len Bias.* New York: Pantheon.

Crossett, T. (1995). *Outsiders in the clubhouse: The world of women's professional golf.* Albany, NY: SUNY Press.

Davis, L. R. (1997). *The swimsuit issue and sport: Hegemonic masculinity in Sports Illustrated.* Albany, NY: SUNY Press.

Dray, P. (2002). *At the hands of persons unknown: The lynching of Black America.* New York: Random House.

Duncan, M. C. (1994). The politics of women's body images and practices: Foucault, the panopticon, and *Shape* magazine. *Journal of Sport & Social Issues, 18,* 48–65.

Dyson, M. E. (1993). *Reflecting Black: African-American cultural criticism.* Minneapolis: University of Minnesota Press.

Entine, J. (2000). *Taboo: Why Black athletes dominate sports and why we are afraid to talk about it.* New York: Public Affairs.

Farred, G. (2003). *What's my name? Black vernacular intellectuals.* Minneapolis: University of Minnesota Press.

Feder-Kane, A. M. (1995). "A radiant smile from the lovely lady': Overdetermined femininity in 'ladies' figure skating. In C. Baughmann (Ed.), *Women on ice: Feminist essays on the Tonya Harding/Nancy Kerrigan spectacle* (pp. 22–46). London: Routledge.

Feinstein, J. (2003). *The punch: One night, two lives, and the fight that changed basketball forever.* Boston: Back Bay.

Fiske, J. (1989). *Television culture.* New York: Routledge.

Fleming, R. (1979). *Ice & honey.* Ardmore, PA: Dorrance.

Foucault, M. (1972). *The archaeology of knowledge & the discourse on language* (A. M. Sheridan Smith, Trans.). New York: Pantheon.

Foucault, M. (1979). *Discipline and punish: The birth of the prison* (A. Sheridan, Trans.). New York: Vintage.

Foucault, M. (1981). *Power/knowledge: Selected interviews and other writings, 1972–1977* (C. Gordon, Trans.). New York: Pantheon.

Giacobbi, P. R., Jr., & DeSensi, J. T. (1999). Media portrayals of Tiger Woods: A qualitative deconstructive examination. *Quest, 51,* 408–417.

Gorn, E. J. (1995). *Muhammad Ali: The people's champ.* Urbana, IL: University of Illinois Press.

Greene, B. (1993). *Hang time: Days and dreams with Michael Jordan.* New York: St. Martin's.

Greene, B. (1995). *Rebound: The odyssey of Michael Jordan.* New York: Viking.

Guttmann, A. (1996). *The erotic in sports.* New York: Columbia University Press.

Halberstam, D. (1999). *Michael Jordan and the world he made.* New York: Random House.

Hargreaves, J. (1986). *Sport, power and culture: A social and historical analysis of popular sports in Britain.* Cambridge, UK: Polity.

Hoberman, J. (1997). *Darwin's athletes: How sport has damaged Black America and preserved the myth of race.* Boston: Houghton Mifflin.

Houck, D. W. (1991). The death and rebirth of Len Bias: An archaeological analysis. *Hayward Conference on Rhetorical Criticism, 24,* 1–24.

Houck, D. W. (2000). Attacking the rim: The cultural politics of dunking. In T. Boyd & K. L. Shropshire (Eds.), *Basketball Jones: America above the rim* (pp. 151–169). New York: New York University Press.

Houck, D. W., & Davenport, J. (2004). Redeeming 9-11. *The Long Term View, 6,* 122–130.

Isidore, C. (2002, August 23). *Sex in play in women's sports.* Retrieved May 18, 2004, from http://money.cnn.com/2002/08/23/commentary/column_sportbiz/women_sex/

Jackson, S. J., Andrews, D. L., & Cole, C. (1998). Race, nation, and authenticity of identity: Interrogating the 'everywhere' man (Michael Jordan) and the 'nowhere' man (Ben Johnson). *Journal of Immigrants and Minorities, 17,* 82–102.

Jamieson, K. M. (2000). Reading Nancy Lopez: Decoding representations of race, class, and sexuality. In S. Birrell & M. G. McDonald (Eds.), *Reading sport: Critical essays on power and representation* (pp. 144–165). Boston: Northeastern University Press.

Klayman, G. (2002, June 19). *Klayman's katastrophes.* Retrieved May 20, 2004, from http://www.mlb.com/NASApp/mlb/mlb/fantasy/mlb_fantasy_columns.jsp?story=klayman0619

Kram, M. (2001). *Ghosts of Manila: The fateful blood feud between Muhammad Ali and Joe Frazier.* New York: HarperCollins.

LaFeber, W. (1999). *Michael Jordan and the new global capitalism.* New York: W. W. Norton.

Lemert, C. (2003). *Muhammad Ali: A trickster in the house of irony.* Cambridge, UK: Polity.

Loy, J. W., Andrews, D. L., & Rinehart, R. E. (1993). The body in culture and sport. *Sport Science Review, 2,* 69–91.

Mailer, N. (1997). *The fight.* New York: Vintage (Original work published 1975).

Markula, P. (2001). Beyond the perfect body: Women's Body Image Distortion in fitness magazine discourse. *Journal of Sport & Social Issues, 25,* 158–179.

Marqusee, M. (1999). *Redemption song: Muhammad Ali and the spirit of the sixties.* London: Verso.

Mazer, S. (1998). *Professional wrestling: Sport and spectacle.* Jackson, MS: University Press of Mississippi.

McDonald, M. G. (2001). Safe sex symbol? Michael Jordan and the politics of representation. In D. L. Andrews (Ed.), *Michael Jordan, Inc.* (pp. 153–174). Albany, NY: SUNY Press.

Miller, T. (2001). *Sportsex.* Philadelphia: Temple University Press.

Oppliger, P. A. (2004). *Wrestling and hypermasculinity.* Jefferson, NC: McFarland.

Owen, D. (2001). *The chosen one.* New York: Simon & Schuster.

Pierce, C. P. (1998). The man. Amen. In B. Littlefield (Ed.), *The best American sports writing 1998* (pp. 165–181). Boston: Houghton Mifflin.

Pluto, T. (1990). *Loose balls: The short, wild life of the American Basketball Association.* New York: Simon and Schuster.

Polumbaum, J., & Wieting, S. G. (1999). Stories of sport and the moral order: Unraveling the cultural construction of Tiger Woods. *Journalism & Communication Monographs, 1,* 69–118.

Pope, H. G., Phillips, K. A., & Olivardia, R. (2000). *The Adonis complex: The secret crisis of male body obsession.* New York: Free Press.

Rail, G., & Harvey, J. (1995). Body at work: Michel Foucault and the sociology of sport. *Sociology of Sport Journal, 12,* 164–179.

Reeves, J. L., & Campbell, R. (1994). *Cracked coverage: Television news, the anti-cocaine crusade, and the Reagan legacy.* Durham, NC: Duke University Press.

Reilly, R. (2000, September 4). Bare in mind. *Sports Illustrated,* p. 99.

Remnick, D. (1998). *King of the world.* New York: Random House.

Saeed, A. (2003). What's in a name? Muhammad Ali and the politics of cultural identity. In A. Bernstein & N. Blain (Eds.), *Sport, media, culture: Global and local dimensions.* Portland, OR: Cass.

Sloop, J. (1997). Mike Tyson and the perils of discursive constraints: Boxing, rape, and the assumption of guilt. In A. Baker & T. Boyd (Eds.), *Out of bounds: Sports, media, and the politics of identity* (pp. 102–122). Bloomington, IN: Indiana University Press.

Uchacz, C. P. (1998). Black sports images in transition: The impact of Tiger Woods. In G. A. Sailes (Ed.), *African Americans in sport* (pp. 53–66). New Brunswick, NJ: Transaction.

Van Vliet, J. (2002, Jan. 27). It's been 25 years since Kermit Washington's devastating blow crushed the face of Rudy Tomjanovich. *Sacramen to Bee,* pg. C1.

Whitfield, S. J. (1988). *A death in the delta: The story of Emmett Till.* New York: Free Press.

Yu, H. (2002). Tiger Woods at the center of history: Looking back at the twentieth century through the lenses of race, sports, and mass consumption. In J. Bloom & M. N. Willard (Eds.), *Sports matters: Race, recreation, and culture* (pp. 320–353). New York: New York University Press.

33

Sports Mascots and the Media

C. Richard King
Washington State University

Laurel Davis-Delano
Springfield College

Ellen Staurowsky
Ithaca College

Lawrence Baca
Alexandria, Virginia

This chapter critically assesses the relationships between sports mascots and the media. While sexist team names and Confederate symbols have attracted limited attention (Eitzen & Zinn, 1989, 1993; King & Springwood, 2001a; Vanderford, 1996), the use of (pseudo)Indian imagery in sports has dominated media coverage, scholarly inquiry, and political debates. Consequently, this chapter centers exclusively on Native American mascots in the media.

The chapter begins with a review of the scholarly literature, identifying its key preoccupations and central themes. On this foundation, it presents a theoretically informed consideration of the relationships between media production, texts, consumption, and social context. Against this background, in turn, it examines the relationships between media coverage and public opinion. A discussion of future directions for research closes the paper.

THE LITERATURE

Although American Indian political leaders and students first criticized mascots in the late 1960s, scholars did not begin to examine them until the early 1990s. Over the past decade, increasingly sophisticated studies traced the history and significance of Native American mascots (Connolly, 2000; Davis, 1993; Fryberg, 2002, 2004; King, 2004; King & Springwood, 2001b; Nuessel, 1994; Pewewardy, 1991; Rodriguez, 1998; Spindel, 2000).

Mascots stereotype American Indians. Not surprisingly, stereotyping has become one of the central preoccupations of the literature on Native American mascots in sports. Scholars have cataloged the ways in which sports teams and educational institutions tend to take clichéd elements associated with Indians and

Indianness (often borrowed without permission or, worse, copied directly from Hollywood westerns) to rearticulate values important to them, such as pride, valor, aggression, strength, and tradition, and have found that they recycle misleading, flat, and fictional renderings of Native Americans for pleasure and profit.

Native American mascots do more than stereotype; they also reveal much about the unequal position of American Indians in the contemporary United States. Indeed, Strong (2004) argued that (pseudo)Indian imagery in sports reflects and contributes to the denial of cultural citizenship for Native Americans. The acceptance of misleading and hurtful images, such as Chief Wahoo, she contended, make it impossible for American Indians to be recognized as fully human social actors and to exercise the rights and protections accorded them under the law. Unfortunately, this compromised and constricted space often sets the terms on which Native Americans can enter into broader fields of social and political action. Indeed, several studies have found that for American Indians to be recognized as Indians and heard as meaningful actors they must contort themselves to fit White stereotypes (Davis & Rau, 2001; King, 2001; King & Springwood, 2000; Springwood, 2001). Worse, as Fryberg (2002, 2004) showed, Native American mascots negatively impact American Indian youth. Such imagery hurts them, affecting most adversely those individuals who do have a problem with it.

Importantly, while marginalizing indigenous peoples, Native American mascots empower EuroAmericans, clearing a space in which to fashion identities, histories, and communities. A number of studies demonstrated the ways in which Indianness lays the foundation for the construction of intimate networks, powerful spaces, and meaningful traditions (Eckert, 2001; Fisher, 2001; Landreth, 2001; LeBeau, 2001; Prochaska, 2001; Spindel, 2000). Indianness, ascribed to a collective or to an individual, is perceived as authorizing legitimate taking of land, religion, symbols, and stories from native nations (Prochaska, 2001; Springwood & King, 2000; Staurowsky, 1998, 2000, 2001). Indianness is not simply defined in White terms, but through individualism that presumes that individuals can choose who they are, fashion their own identities, and opt to choose or reject stereotypical imagery and the identities that come with it (Fryberg, 2004). These forms of racialized power, as Straurowsky (2004) suggested, derives from and reproduces White privilege.

(Pseudo)Indian imagery in sports not only captures Indianness and secures Whiteness, it also contributes to more complex articulations of nationalism, gender, and social hierarchy. Davis (1993) understood early on that Native American mascots reflect core ideas of what it means to be traditionally American, White, and male. Prochaska (2001) and Springwood and King (2000) expanded on this argument, more fully explicating the connections between national identity and imperial endeavors. The racial dimensions of Native American mascots, of course, are more complex than the binary of Indian/White. King (2002) detailed the estrangements between Native Americans and African Americans around the issue of sports mascots. More importantly, as King and Springwood (2000, 2001a) contended, Native American mascots are better conceived in a broader, even comparative, framework that connects Whiteness, Indianness, and Blackness. Such a perspective encourages the recognition of how racial meanings articulate to fashion racialized ideologies and social hierarchies in sporting worlds and everyday life. Finally, Davis (1993) and King (in press) highlighted the importance of gender to the formulation of racialized identities.

Numerous studies have stressed the centrality of educational institutions to the perpetuation of racial imagery, identities, and inequities through Native American mascots. Many scholars have underscored the ways in which schools using Native American mascots contribute to the stereotyping and mistreatment of American Indians. At root, they argued, Native American mascots miseducate (Davis, 2002; Pewewardy, 1991, 1998, 2001; Staurowsky, 1999), transforming schools and stadiums into hostile environments for indigenous peoples (Baca, 2004). Others directed attention to the social aspects of educational institutions with Native American mascots. Connolly (2000) examined the importance of booster culture to the retention of (pseudo)Indian imagery at colleges and universities. King (2002), in turn, outlined the ways in which educational institutions seek to retain controversial school symbols. Most recently, McEwan and Belfield (2004) studied the economic impact of retiring Native American mascots. They found that the 34 schools that have stopped using Indian imagery have seen alumni giving drop slightly, buttressing in small measure arguments advanced by some supporters that retaining an Indian mascot is good for the fiscal health of educational institutions.

Perhaps because of their centrality to miseducation and the maintenance of problematic ideas about race, history, and nation, (pseudo)Indian imagery increasingly has become the site of social struggle. Several studies detailed efforts to challenge Native American mascots (Davis & Rau, 2001; Harjo, 2001; Machamer, 2001); others explored the complexities and contradictions of opposition to mascots (King, 2001; Springwood, 2001) or the rhetoric deployed to challenge (pseudo)Indian imagery in sports (King, 2004). Of equal importance, critical attention has been directed at the strategies employed to defend Native American mascots (Davis, 1993; Farnell, 2004; King, 2002, 2003; Springwood, 2004). And, the legal aspects of Native American mascots have fostered much debate (Baca, 2004; Clarkson, 2003; Claussen, 1996; Clegg, 2002; Kelber, 1994; Likourezos, 1996; Pace, 1994; Staurowsky, 2004; Trainor, 1995).

MEDIA THEORY AND THE MASCOT ISSUE

Although there is considerable scholarship on the topic of Native American mascots, and much of this scholarship mentions the media, few pieces of scholarship focus primarily on the relationship between the media and the mascot issue. There are two exceptions: Rosenstein (2001) described media coverage of the mascot issue and King, Staurowsky, Baca, Davis, and Pewewardy (2002) analyzed a particular *Sports Illustrated* (*SI*) article about the mascots. Neither of these articles devoted much attention to media theory.

In this section of the chapter, we discuss how some aspects of media theory relate to the issue of Native American mascots. The most essential aspect of media theory is the interaction of four social realms: media production, media texts, media consumption, and social context. Mediated meaning is created through the interaction of media production, media texts, and media consumption, all of which are influenced by social context. The first three realms are interrelated in this cyclical way: production influences texts, texts influence consumption, consumption influences production, production influences consumption, consumption influences texts, and texts influence production. Various aspects of the wider social context, such as the economy, government, education, religion, peers, and families, influence all three of these realms. For example, media producers are influenced by their economic context (i.e., being embedded in for-profit media corporations), the structures and subcultures of media production, and their prior socialization experiences. Audience members' consumption choices and interpretations of media texts are influenced by media texts that they have consumed in the past and by their other life experiences (e.g., their family, education, etc.). In what follows, we use this general theoretical framework to discuss the relationship of Native American mascots and the mass media.

Media Texts

When considering media and mascots, there are two types of media texts one must recognize. First, there is the name and logo of the teams. Sport logos are pictorial representations that appear in various locations throughout society, including on buildings, billboards, and clothing. Second, there is media coverage of the teams that are affiliated with such logos.

The overwhelming majority of media texts that represent Native American mascots simply feature repetitive depiction of the team logos and names. For example, a picture might include a football helmet with an "Indian head" on it, or written text will say, "The Indians trounced the Blue Jays by a score of 8 to 2." Simply by repetitively representing the mascot names and logos, the media affirm the normalcy of such depictions, implying that there is nothing problematic about such names or logos and reinforcing to some degree that such names and logos are positive in nature. Yet, as many scholars have pointed out, these mascots are problematic because they depict and reinforce stereotypes of Native Americans. There are a few noteworthy exceptions to the practice of representing these names and logos, as the *Portland Oregonian*, *Lincoln Star Journal* (Nebraska), *St. Cloud Times* (Minnesota), and *Telegraph Forum* (Bucyrus, Ohio) refuse to print some names and/or logos.

Media coverage of Native American mascots sometimes veers off the path of simply representing the names and logos, to more directly furthering the already existent stereotypes inherent to the mascots. For example, texts include phrases like "Red Sox scalp the Indians" and "Chiefs are on the Warpath." *SI*'s poll and article "The Indian Wars" was a blatant case of legitimating such stereotypes in sport (King, et al., 2002).

Media coverage of Native American mascots rarely includes either critique of the mascots or discussion of the social context that gives rise to or supports such mascots. When critique of these mascots is covered, usually in the form of news coverage of protests, the discussion is often simplistic (Native American Journalists Association, 2003). For example, writers mention the issue of stereotyping but provide few details to help the reader understand the nature or sources of such stereotyping. Texts often highlight diversity of opinion among Native Americans about the mascot issue, implying that the mascots are not problematic unless all Native Americans oppose them and ignoring the facts that there is no racial group with consensus about issues and many Native Americans have been socialized to accept stereotypes of their own racial category. The critique which is evident in the small amount of in-depth coverage of the mascot issue is likely muted and muffled by saturation of uncritical representation of these mascots in the media.

In any regard, antimascot advocates are at a distinct disadvantage in regard to media coverage, as Rosenstein (2001) described:

American Indians [who oppose the mascots] will always have to be part of a newsworthy event, such as a protest . . . in order to have their point of view included in the media. But the Washington nickname Redskins and Cleveland's

Chief Wahoo can be propagated in the media almost daily, since they are considered acceptable parts of the sports world. (p. 254)

Media Production

There are several aspects of media production that scholars should consider relative to the mascot issue. First, there is the fact that for-profit corporations generate most mass media texts in the United States. Some of these corporations even own professional sport teams; for instance, the Atlanta Braves are owned by Time Warner. Of course, when a media corporation covers its own team, it is doubtful that such coverage will be anything less than positive. But, even when media corporations do not own individual teams, media corporations have an interest in promoting teams to draw (particular) consumers and thus enhance their profits from advertising dollars. Because media producers depend on sport, these producers work to develop and maintain affable relationships with people who control the sport industry. As Rosenstein (2001) explicated:

The bottom line is that...the networks and leagues are basically business partners. And, just as it is in any business, it is rarely in one's best interest to criticize a partner...[S]portswriters depend on access to players and coaches in order to gather enough material to fill [their sports] sections. A media outlet that is critical of a team might find itself getting less access than others, putting it at a great competitive disadvantage...[R]eporters can easily save themselves—and their employers—a lot of money and grief simply by ignoring controversial issues and sticking to stories about the games...Especially in smaller communities, the media see themselves as part of the hometown community, and that usually means being fans of the local team...[T]he rules that govern news and sports are very different. Sports reporters are not held to the same standards of fairness, balance, and objectivity as news reporters...[I]t is completely acceptable—and, in fact, expected—for sports reporters to cheer for and support the local team. (pp. 244–246)

Thus, the for-profit nature of media companies facilitates the production of media texts that simply represent mascot names and logos, while discouraging any critical coverage of the mascot issue. On the other hand, the fact that media producers often use controversy to attract audience members might prompt greater coverage of the mascot issue. Yet, this issue might not be a fruitful draw, because one side challenges the identities and racial ideologies to which many (potential) audience members are wedded. Of course, the sport industry is also dependent on the media to enhance its profits, directly (e.g., money from television contracts) and indirectly (e.g., the publicity that increases merchandise sales).

Although (regular) news coverage often highlights social issues (although usually without much depth), media coverage of sport, much like media coverage of consumer products (e.g., fashion, automobiles, and home furnishings), seems to more often ignore social issues (Rosenstein, 2001). Sport coverage most often involves description of what happened on the field, court, and so forth, supplemented by occasional focus on scandals regarding particular sport figures (who are portrayed as deviants rather than representatives of widespread social patterns). Although coverage of social issues in sport does exist, coverage of such issues (e.g., gender bias, public subsidization of stadiums, and the subculture of violence) seems relatively rare. Thus, it seems natural that sport producers ignore the mascot issue, much like they usually ignore other social issues in sport.

One aspect of the media subculture that actually encourages media producers to support the antimascot position is the norm that discourages the representation of words or images that are perceived as offensive to consumers. Thus, the mainstream media rarely represents explicit sexual acts, words like *nigger*, and extremely overt stereotypes (e.g., the depiction of Blacks as monkey-like). Of course, producers' concerns about loss of audience members, and thus decrease in profits, is a primary reason why this norm exists. Given that many are offended by Native American mascots, one would think that the media might hesitate to depict them. Yet, as Sigelman (1998) pointed out, the number of people who find such mascots offensive is quite limited. Thus, profits built on the backs of average sport media consumers trump concerns about the numerical minority who find such mascots problematic. Additionally, most media producers, like the majority of people in United States' society, are unaware of the nature of contemporary stereotyping of Native Americans. And thus, the subcultural norm of trying not to offend does not seem relevant. Yet, it was this very norm that led the *Portland Oregonian*, *St. Cloud Times*, and *Lincoln Star Journal* newspapers to their decisions to avoid depicting Native American team names and logos (Native American Journalists Association, 2003).

Media Consumption

Individual interpretations of media texts are influenced by both the nature of the texts themselves and the past and present social contexts that affect(ed) these individuals. Thus, among other things, interpretations are influenced by written symbols in the text, pictorial symbols in the text, the larger text within which the specific words or images are embedded (e.g., the magazine where an image appears), the site of consumption (e.g., a bedroom, a bar, or an airplane flight), the culture of the consumer (e.g., United States, Pakistan, or Brazil), the consumer's membership in a subculture (e.g., environmentalism, religious right, or gay), and the prior experiences of the consumer (e.g., child abuse, international travel, or experience with particular media genres). Thus, all media texts are open to many different interpretations. This can be easily illustrated in regard to Native American mascots, where a variety of interpretations exist, including: "These mascots honor Native Americans," "These mascots are problematic because they stereotype," and "The term 'redskins' should be banned but not other Native American mascots." And, people who live in an area of the world where images of Native Americans are (almost) nonexistent would not even recognize signifiers designed to depict Native Americans.

One important distinction to make when considering audience interpretations is the analytical difference between denotative and connotative levels of meaning: "'Denotation' is nothing more than a useful rule for distinguishing, in any particular instance or operation, those connotations which have become naturalized and those which, not being so fixed, provide the opportunity for more extensive ideological representations" (Heck, 1984, p. 126).

Encodings and decodings have an "achieved equivalence" at the denotative level (Hall, 1984, p. 132). Some correspondence between encoded and decoded meanings is required for effective communication (Condit, 1989; Hall, 1984). In other words, within a single society, common cultural knowledge often leads to similar interpretations of denotative-level meaning, while connotative-level meaning remains contested. Thus, unlike those who live in an area of the world where images of Native Americans are (virtually) nonexistent, most people from the United States are familiar with the stereotypical signifiers that media producers use to convey Native Americans. Most people in the United States, regardless of their opinion on the mascot issue, interpret the Cleveland Indian and Kansas City Chiefs logos as representing Native Americans. On the other hand, there is much struggle over meaning at the connotative level (Condit, 1989; Hall, 1984). As Condit (1989) described the situation, often "the audience members share understandings of the denotations of a text but disagree about the valuation of these denotations to such a degree that they produce notably different interpretations" (p. 106).

Thus, although most people in the United States agree that the mascots represent Native Americans, they have different interpretations of the mascot imagery (e.g., "These images honor Native Americans" versus "These images represent problematic stereotypes of Native Americans"). Sigelman (1998) shows that only a small percentage of people in the United States views Native American mascots as problematic. Davis (2002) argues that this lack of enlightenment is due to thorough socialization of stereotypes of Native Americans (from the media and other sources) and lack of comprehension that stereotypes can (appear to) be positive (e.g., the stereotype that Native Americans are brave). Given widespread acceptance of many stereotypes of Native Americans, it is not surprising that most media consumers do not perceive the mascots or media coverage of the mascots as representing stereotypes and thus as problematic. On the other hand, consumers who have different socialization experiences (e.g., accurate education about contemporary Native American issues) likely view the mascots and media coverage in a different light. In this case, mainstream media coverage of mascots is seen as creating a hostile environment.

The Social Context

By now it should be clear that various aspects of the social world impact both media production and consumption. We have already discussed the way that production of media texts representing the mascots is embedded in, and thus influenced by, the capitalist economic system. Cultural stereotypes are also a central part of the relevant context.

During the colonial period, colonists created stereotypes of Native Americans to justify murder, the acquisition of land, political control, and cultural assimilation (Berkhofer, 1978; Bird, 1996). Such stereotypes are still prevalent, yet they have been modified and extended. Now, the stereotype of Native Americans as physically aggressive is seen (at least on the surface) as positive rather than negative. Whereas once the stereotype of Native Americans as close to nature was seen negatively as an indication of lack of civilization, it is now considered, from a romantic perspective, as an ideal characteristic. The present day cultural milieu represents and reinforces stereotypes of Native Americans through mediums such as television, film, novels, consumer products (e.g., Land O'Lakes butter, Argo corn starch, and Crazy Horse beer), tourist sites, and sport. Most often, the education system simply reinforces these stereotypes by including biased versions of history and excluding information about contemporary Native Americans. This historical and present day cultural environment of stereotypes is what frames production and retention of the mascots in sport and unquestioning representation of these mascots by media producers. Additionally, this cultural milieu is the main source of unquestioning consumption of media coverage of these mascots and consumer claims that these representations honor Native Americans. This cultural environment has also facilitated acceptance of such stereotypes by some Native Americans. Some Native Americans, perhaps especially those facing stark economic opportunities, even draw upon this milieu of stereotypes to sell their "Indianness" to non-Natives for money.

PUBLIC OPINION, MEDIA, AND MASCOTS

The media have had a profound impact on public understandings of Native American mascots and ongoing struggles to retire them. The media normalize Native American mascots, making them appear acceptable, appropriate, and even natural. Indeed, as one of the more influential forms of popular pedagogy, the media socialize consumers to not think about mascots as social objects with complex meaning, history, or effects, but rather to embrace them as consumable and pleasurable signs emptied of power, social significance, and controversy. Media coverage, moreover, recycles stereotypical images of indigenous peoples that injure American-Indian individuals and communities and perpetuate racial hierarchy. Consequently, most media portrayals of Native Americans foster misrecognition of Native Americans, their histories and identities, and the issues that matter to them. The media support Native American mascots to enhance popularity and profitability of their programming and products. In short, the media play a powerful role in articulating common-sense ideas about Native Americans, and Native American mascots, shaping the terms of public opinion and political debate.

In this section, we turn our attention to public opinion polls to clarify the ways in which media simultaneously report and shape what people think about Native American mascots. In particular, we are interested in what polls can tell us about the struggle over the use of Indian imagery in sports, and moreover about the impact of the media on how people think about this issue. We contend, following Splichal (1999), that "The fundamental significance of the mass media for the processes of (public) opinion formation and expression largely arises from the fact that they help to determine and demonstrate the *limits of legitimate public* discussion in society" (p. 274). In essence, what the public thinks and feels about issues like the use of Indian imagery in sports emerges from what Gawiser and Witt (1994) called the "opinion triangle" (p. 5). The opinion triangle works like this: "Polls measure what the public thinks. And what the public thinks on many issues, is shaped, in part, by what people learn from news reports" (p. 5). Furthermore, according to Gawiser and Witt (1994), "polls have an accuracy that is quite seductive for journalists. It is too easy to report the poll numbers as truth without taking the time and trouble to see if the poll was done well and if the results are really what the sponsor says" (p. 6). We are suggesting that it may be inappropriate for media organizations, which greatly influence opinions, to sponsor polls, and that when the media does cover poll results that specially trained journalists should discuss the potential biases and limitations of such polls.

Surveying Surveys

A number of polls have examined how Native Americans, Euro-Americans, sports fans, students, and/or citizens in general feel about the continued use of Indian symbols in sports. Here, we summarize the results of the most prominent public opinion surveys.

In July 1997, *USA Weekend* (1997) asked its readers "What is your opinion about changing a sports team's mascot because it offends Native Americans?" Visitors could vote in support of changing or keeping such mascots and submit a reaction to the ongoing controversy. Of those who went to the newspaper's Web site, 2,419 participated in the "quick poll" with 42% voting to change and 58% voting to retain such mascots (see King, 2003).

Analyzing two surveys of public opinion, Sigelman (1998) found an even more dramatic divide. He compared a national poll of 810 individuals and a local poll of 1,244 Washington, D.C., residents, both of which sought to assess whether the Washington area football team should change its team name and mascot. Sigelman found that whereas 7.4% of national and 16.2% of local respondents supported such a change, 88% of national and 80.6% of local respondents were opposed to such a change.

In stark contrast, the National Spectator Association (1999), an organization serving sports fans, found that 80% of respondents believed that the Cleveland Indians team name should be changed because it is offensive.

Fenelon (1999) found that Native Americans and Euro-Americans exhibited pronounced differences of opinions about the Cleveland mascot, Chief Wahoo, with most Whites favoring retention under all circumstances and the majority of Native Americans opposing the mascot.

As reported by Stapleton (2001), the United States Patent and Trademark Board obtained a similar finding about the name of Washington's professional football team that showed 46% of the general public ($n = 301$) and 37% of American Indians ($n = 358$) viewed *Redskin* as an offensive term. Independently, Stapleton (2001) also studied the opinions of fans ($n = 28$) and Native Americans ($n = 32$) with Web sites: Whereas 96% of the fans opposed changing the team name, 72% of indigenous peoples favored the name change.

In March 2001, Kolb (2001) reported the findings of a Gallup poll of 458 Native Americans. The results showed 25% felt honored, 21% were not offended, 18% were partially offended, 6% were very offended, and 23% did not care; in turn 11% found Native American mascots to be very harmful, 27% thought they were partially harmful, 51% believed they were not harmful, and 10% did not care.

Later the same year, *Indian Country Today* (*ICT*) (American Indian Opinion Leaders, 2001) published results of its survey of its American Indian Opinion Leaders, a group of self-selected Native Americans who offer feedback to the newspaper on issues of importance. Respondents overwhelmingly held critical views of mascots and their implications: 81% found them to be "offensive and deeply disparaging"; 10% thought names and mascots were respectful; 73% believed they fostered a hostile environment; 75% agreed that they were a violation of antidiscrimination laws; and 69% indicated that funds should be withheld from schools with Native American mascots.

Perhaps with the greatest fanfare, *SI* included a survey of 351 Native Americans and 743 sport fans in its sensational article "Indian Wars" (King, et al., 2002; Price, 2002). The poll, conducted by the Peter Harris Research Group, indicated that 83% of Native Americans and 79% of sports fans endorsed the continued use of Indian names, symbols, and mascots and that only 12% of sports fans and 23% of Native Americans believed these uses of Indianness contributed to discrimination against American Indians.

Some results from a survey of alumni, faculty and staff, and students at the University of North Dakota (2000) contradict the *SI* poll. The survey of 3,169 people (601 alumni, 1,158 employees, 603 students, and 447 minorities, of whom 53% were self-identified American Indians or Alaska Natives) revealed sharp differences. Whereas the vast majority of Whites agreed that the Fighting Sioux mascot honored UND (87% of alumni and 91% of students), only 54% of non-Whites concurred. And moreover, while most Euro-Americans (82% of alumni and 79% of students) felt the mascot honored the Sioux, only 39% of minorities agreed. Most non-Whites (61%) wanted the mascot to be changed, compared with 25% of alumni and 30% of students. Finally, a plurality of minorities (43%) believed that the Fighting Sioux perpetuates discrimination against Native Americans; in contrast, only 9% of students and 27% of employees agreed.

Although these polls exhibit great variation, a few things are apparent. First, Euro-Americans are more likely than Native Americans to support Native American mascots. Second, the (overwhelming) majority of Euro-Americans endorse the use of Indian symbols and mascots. Third, Native Americans, like Euro-Americans, do not (nor should not be expected to) agree about mascots. Fourth, while many Native Americans disapprove of Native American mascots, other Native Americans are untroubled or even support them. Finally, population, techniques, questions asked, and so on have a profound impact on the findings. With this in mind, we turn our attention to "The Indian Wars" to more fully explore a particular case of the relationship between media and public opinion.

Influence of the "Indian Wars"

Undoubtedly, the most influential poll to date has been that conducted by the Peter Harris Research Group and featured prominently in *SI*. The survey not only reinforced dominant views, but also has reframed the debate over mascots from a concern over racism to another example of oversensitive political correctness. Central to these shifts is the supposed unbiased quality of survey research. The perception of poll objectivity does create an aspect of seductiveness for both journalists and the reading public alike because "Numbers are solid, reliable, and real. They don't have caveats or bias or hidden agendas. Or so some journalists think" (Gawiser & Witt, 1994, p. 1). In the aftermath of the survey's publication in *SI*, the reported results have fueled pro mascot viewpoints among individuals and organizations as well. An exemplary instance of this pattern occurred when King County (Washington) Executive Ron Simms (2002) asked his constituents their opinion of Native American mascots. One suggested, "This is America. It's a democracy . . . LISTEN to the majority of Native Americans. If the independent Peter Harris Research Group poll that was published in *SI* is correct (it claims a 4% margin of Error), and 81% of Natives want to keep the names, leave them alone. Majority rule" (para. 20).

Beyond individual opinion and political debates, the survey has also impacted institutional and policy reform at a national level. Most notably, it has altered the work that the Minority Opportunities and Interests Committee (MOIC) of the National Collegiate Athletic Association was doing on American-Indian nicknames. Writer Pickle (2002) noted that ". . . the research has added an interesting dimension to the NCAA's ongoing study of the issue" and that the then chair of the committee described the research as "provocative" (para. 7).

Beyond the affects that the poll conveys because of its perceived basis in fact is the almost total lack of consideration for the racialized context that shapes the poll results, with *SI* as the commissioner of the poll and the Peter Harris Research Group as the organization willing to conduct the study. The history of the (mis)treatment of Native Americans in the United States argues for an awareness that there is an ingrained bias against Native Americans within American culture. Stereotypes of Native Americans abound in U.S. popular culture, including the media (e.g., Bird, 1996; Coombe, 1999; Deloria, 1998; Green, 1988). A study by Clarkson (2003) demonstrated that cultural bias favoring the mascots can be assumed, as the top nine mascots used by high schools in the United States "were either carnivorous animals or Indians" (p. 396) and of the Indian mascots identified, 94% are racial in nature (as compared to tribal references). These patterns are replicated in mass media, as most media outlets simply reproduce the names and images of these mascots. Notably, the position of the Native American Journalists Association calling for the elimination of mascot references was not mentioned in the *SI* article and is rarely acknowledged anywhere on the sports pages, least of all at the *Minneapolis Star Tribune*, where their editorial policy of not reporting derogatory or negative sport team nicknames and mascots was reversed in the summer of 2003 in favor of what they described as "accuracy" in reporting.

Within the context of the *SI* survey, a superficial attempt to discern nuance by examining apparently different populations (sports fans and Native-Americans both on and off the reservation) is seen as producing a monolithic outcome, as expressed in the conclusion that the majority of people do not find Native American mascots offensive. The attempt on the part of *SI* to create an impression of equity by polling sports fans and Native Americans obscures the fact that no matter what Native Americans do, they will be responding from a minority position, being 1% of the population within the United States, while sports fans, most of whom represent the clientele of *SI,* possess the power of the majority.

Defending "Our" Indians

Whereas *SI*'s poll results merely demonstrated once again that there is widespread ignorance of Native American stereotypes and that people disagree on the issue of Native American mascots, *SI* missed the opportunity to examine in greater detail the nature of the arguments for retention of these images. The intriguing question to consider is not whether people, Native American and non-Native American alike, disagree on mascots but why, after all this time, so much resistance continues to surface when recommendations are made to eliminate them. The consistency in the responses of those who oppose the move by Native Americans and their supporters to rid the American landscape of these images truly is remarkable.

Whether it is in supposed neutral polls like the one commissioned by *SI*, the editorial pages of newspapers and magazines, or radio call-in talk shows, three rhetorical tools are used by mascot supporters to defend their position. To summarize, supporters of these mascots frequently assert that Native-Americans who oppose the mascots are wrong using three specific lines of logic: honor, trivialization, and claiming Indianness (see also Davis, 1993; King, 2003).

According to those who wish to retain Native American mascots, claims of honoring Native Americans are to be accepted regardless of whether Native Americans wish to be honored or feel honored. Within this construction, Native Americans are wrong to be insulted, regardless of how objectionable the image may be to them. The mascot supporters who use this argument take the position that if they explain their belief that the images are indeed honoring Indians often enough, then any offended Indian will see it differently. The Washington NFL franchise has put forward perhaps the classic in this strain of logic. In the face of strong evidence that the word *redskin* is a pejorative and a negative racial reference to American Indians, the club owners argue that they have used the name in a positive non-racialized manner for so long that the term now has taken on a new and positive meaning. The franchise did not, however, put forward any examples of the use of the term *redskin* that were positive other than the references to their team. If, in fact, the word had taken on a positive meaning, there would be within literature, the press, and movies or television examples where the term was used in the positive manner. No examples were presented because they don't exist. Second only to this absurdity would be the University if Illinois, the home of Chief Illiniwek, where fans purport to honor the Illinois Indians by dressing up in another tribe's regalia and performing a faux Indian dance. It is simply beyond credulity that one honors any nation of Indians by taking on the regalia of another and performing a dance of neither. One pundit at a conference, in defense of the "it honors you" position, stated that people don't pick things they don't like for mascots—yet the Miami Hurricanes come to mind. He failed to recognize the juxtaposition of mascots for three Florida universities (an animal, a weather formation, and a human). Indian people often point out that the Indian race is treated on the same level as animals (Clarkson, 2003)—when the University of Florida plays Florida State, one team's mascot is an alligator and the other is a human being.

Those who wish to retain Native American mascots often attempt to make Indian's concerns seem ridiculous by associating them with what the speaker believes are even more ridiculous concerns. Think about the straw arguments that are often thrown up. "Should we ban the Giants because tall people are offended?" (even though no group of tall people has ever protested at a game) or the "I'm Irish and I don't think the Fighting Irish of Notre Dame is offensive." This is always from individuals who are trying to bolster their challenge to Native American's concerns about racial stereotypes. They invent their own theoretical concern or point to imagined concerns that they would find equally ridiculous. They do not identify any protest they have made at a stadium or to officials at the offending school. Indeed they can't because they haven't. No group of Scandinavians has stood outside the Vikings' stadium alleging that they feel demeaned. No group of cowboys have held signs in Dallas saying, "I am a human not a mascot." The Indian response is simple—no one's race should be stereotyped and mocked. Show up at the protest and Indians will be with you. The simple reality is that those protestors simply don't exist.

Another offensive retort is from those who have never professed any Indian heritage until they need to ratify their position that Indian mascots are a good thing by claiming that they are Indian. Indians are not a monolithic group that thinks one way about anything. There are in fact some Indian people who like the name of the Cleveland baseball team or the imagery of the Washington football team. But many Indian people are seriously skeptical of those who defend Native American mascots and then state an Indian heritage that they possess although they can't name the tribes their ancestors are from.

Ultimately, the fact that Native American mascots, and other stereotypes of Native Americans, *are* so prevalent contributes to the public opinion that they must be acceptable. At a fundamental level, to challenge Native American mascots is to raise the spectre that the society is overtly racist. Many people from the United States believe that racism has been essentially eliminated and thus the mascots are either not a stereotype or are somehow acceptable. In the alternative, one is left to wonder if public advocacy for keeping these mascots provides a convenient means of saying what societal prohibitions deter people from saying out loud, namely, that real Indian people should go away and be quiet.

IMPLICATIONS

Given the symbiotic relationship between the media and sport, it is not acceptable to simply locate the mascot problem in sport and let the media off the hook. Before the rise of contemporary sport, the media created, expanded, and spread stereotypes of Native Americans. No doubt, the media was the primary inspiration for the creation of Native American mascots. Today, the media both shape, and benefit from, commercial sport. For these reasons, the media must play a role in modifying sport so that socially harmful phenomena, such as stereotypes, are minimized. The media has substantial power to affect sport because commercial sport depends on the mass media to generate (substantial) profit.

The interactive nature of social contexts, media production, media texts, and media consumption demonstrates the need for multipronged approaches to social change. Efforts for change must target media producers, media consumers, and the larger social context.

Obviously, education that contributes to greater understanding of Native American stereotypes and realities is absolutely necessary. Educating the public, including future sports fans, media producers, and media consumers, is a monumental and complicated task. The school system is key to such education. Information about Native Americans in history classes needs to be both expanded in quantity and focus, and modified to reduce bias and simplicity. More importantly, information about contemporary Native American lives and issues needs to be brought into the social studies curriculum. Education of the public via the mass media is also necessary. Media producers need to generate realistic fictional and nonfictional stories about contemporary Native American lives and issues.

Changes within the mass media are obviously essential. Sensitivity training for media producers about Native American stereotypes is required. Some media producers have initiated sensitivity training for sport commentators in regard to stereotypes of African Americans, and some scholars think that this training reduced biased commentary about African American athletes (Sabo, Jansen, Tate, Duncan, & Leggett, 1996). Banning the representation of Native American mascots, as (partially) undertaken by the *Portland Oregonian*, *St. Cloud Times*, and *Lincoln Star Journal*, is appropriate. A report by the Native American Journalists Association (2003) provides excellent rationale and advice for media producers in this regard. Reframing the nature of sport coverage, so that it includes coverage of social issues, would be beneficial. It is clear that the profit motive, and the structure and subculture of media production, limit media producers' desire and ability to implement changes in coverage. Thus, government regulations that restrain the power of the profit motive, and encourage social justice, are required.

Activists rightly target stereotypical representations of Native Americans in the media, sport, consumer products, and the like. As a result of such activism, many teams have eliminated their Native American mascots and some companies have modified the logos associated with their products.

Native American mascots, as a nexus of race, sport, and media, invite further action and inquiry. They promise to prompt additional study, media attention, and calls for change. To date, journalists, pundits, and (to a lesser extent) scholars have asked, what do people think about mascots? This, we trust our analysis has demonstrated, is the wrong question. To better understand Native American mascots, the media, sport, and anti-Indian racism, we hope, following Fryberg (2004), that scholars, journalists, and school administrators increasingly will ask: What are the affects of Native American mascots? How do they impact American Indian youth? How do such deformed images harm indigenous peoples, manifested in high suicide and dropout rates, no less than antisovereignty movements? In turn, how do the media shape public opinion, retarding justice, while contributing to prejudice and discrimination? Not only does posing such questions encourage more complex assessments of the relationships between race, media, and sports, but also grappling with the issues raised by this reframing assures the dissolution of what Davis and Rau (2001) dubbed "the tyranny of the majority" around issues of racial justice and indigenous sovereignty.

REFERENCES

American Indian opinion leaders. (2001). American Indian mascots: Respectful gesture or negative stereotype? *Indian Country Today, 21*(8), A5.

Baca, L. (2004). Native images in schools and the racially hostile environment. *Journal of Sport and Social Issues, 28*, 71–78.

Berkhofer, R. F. (1978). *The White man's Indian: Images of the American Indian from Columbus to present.* New York: Vintage/Random House.

Bird, S. E. (Ed.). (1996). *Dressing in feathers: The construction of the Indian in American popular culture.* Boulder: Westview.

Clarkson, G. (2003). Racial imagery and Native Americans: A first look at empirical evidence behind the Indian mascot controversy. *Cardozo Journal of International and Comparative Law, 11*, 393–407.

Claussen, C. L. (1996). Ethnic team names and logos: Is there a legal solution? *Marquette Sports Law Journal, 6*, 409–421.

Clegg, R. (2002). American Indian nicknames and mascots for team sports: Law, policy, and attitude. *Virginia Sports and Entertainment Law Journal, 1*, 393–405.

Condit, C. M. (1989). The rhetorical limits of polysemy. *Critical Studies in Mass Communication, 6*, 103–122.

Connolly, M. R. (2000). What in a name? A historical look at Native American related nicknames and symbols at three U.S. universities. *Journal of Higher Education, 71*, 515–547.

Coombe, R. J. (1999). Sports trademarks and somatic politics: Locating the law in critical cultural studies. In R. Martin & T. Miller (Eds.), *SportCult* (pp. 262–288). Minneapolis: University of Minnesota Press.

Davis, L. R. (1993). Protest against the use of Native American mascots: A challenge to traditional, American identity. *Journal of Sport and Social Issues, 17*, 9–22.

Davis, L. R. (2002). The problems with Native American mascots. *Multicultural Education, 9*, 11–14.

Davis, L. R., & Rau, M. (2001). Escaping the tyranny of the majority. In C. R. King & C. F. Springwood (Eds.), *Team spirits: Essays on the history and significance of Native American mascots* (pp. 304–327). Lincoln: University of Nebraska Press.

Deloria, P. (1998). *Playing Indian.* New Haven: Yale University Press.

Eckert, R. C. (2001). Wennebojo meets the mascot: A Trickster's view of the Central Michigan University mascot/logo. In C. R. King & C. F. Springwood (Eds.), *Team spirits: Essays on the history and significance of Native American mascots* (pp. 64–81). Lincoln: University of Nebraska Press.

Eitzen, D. S., & Zinn, M. B. (1989). The de-athleticization of women: The naming and gender marking of college sport teams. *Sociology of Sport Journal, 7*, 362–369.

Eitzen, D. S., & Zinn, M. B. (1993). The sexist naming of collegiate athletic teams and resistance to change. *Journal of Sport and Social Issues, 17*, 34–41.

Farnell, B. (2004). The fancy dance of racializing discourse. *Journal of Sport and Social Issues, 28*, 30–55.

Fenelon, J. V. (1999). Indian icons in the world series of racism: Institutionalization of the racial symbols of wahoos and Indians. *Research in Politics and Society, 6*, 25–45.

Fisher, D. M. (2001). Chief Bill Orange and the Saltine Warrior: A cultural history of Indian symbols and imagery at Syracuse University. In C. R. King & C. F. Springwood (Eds.), *Team spirits: Essays on the history and significance of Native American mascots* (pp. 25–45). Lincoln: University of Nebraska Press.

Fryberg, S. (2002). *Representations of American Indians in the media: Do they influence how American Indian students negotiate their identities in mainstream contexts?* Unpublished doctoral dissertation, Stanford University.

Fryberg, S. (2004, November 4). *"We're honoring you, dude": The impact of using American Indian mascots.* Paper presented at the Annual Meetings of the North American Society for the Sociology of Sport, Tucson, AZ.

Gawiser, S. R., & Witt, G. E. (1994). *A journalist's guide to public opinion polls.* Westport, CT: Praeger Press.

Green, R. (1988). The tribe called wannabee: Playing Indian in America and Europe. *American Journal of Folklore, 99,* 30–55.

Hall, S. (1984). Encoding/Decoding. In S. Hall, D. Hobson, A. Lowe, & P. Willis (Eds.), *Culture, media, language: Working papers in cultural studies, 1972–79* (pp. 128–138). London: Hutchinson & The Centre for Contemporary Cultural Studies, University of Birmingham.

Harjo, S. S. (2001). Fighting name calling: Challenging "Redskins" in court. In C. R. King & C. F. Springwood (Eds.), *Team spirits: Essays on the history and significance of Native American mascots* (pp. 189–207). Lincoln: University of Nebraska Press.

Heck, M. C. (1984). The ideological dimension of media messages. In S. Hall, D. Hobson, A. Lowe, & P. Willis (Eds.), *Culture, media, language: Working papers in cultural studies, 1972–79* (pp. 122–127). London: Hutchinson & The Centre for Contemporary Cultural Studies, University of Birmingham.

Kelber, B. C. (1994). "Scalping the Redskins": Can trademark law start athletic teams bearing Native American nicknames and images on the road to reform? *Hamline Law Review, 17,* 533–588.

King, C. R. (2001). Uneasy Indians: Creating and contesting Native American mascots at Marquette University. In C. R. King & C. F. Springwood (Eds.), *Team spirits: Essays on the history and significance of Native American mascots* (pp. 281–303). Lincoln: University of Nebraska Press.

King, C. R. (2002). Defensive dialogues: Native American mascots, anti-Indianism, and educational institutions. *Studies in Media & Information Literacy Education, 2*(1), Article 16. Retrieved 7 Oct. 2005, from http://www.utpjournals.com/jour.ihtml?lp=simile/issues/King1.html

King, C. R. (2003). Arguing over images: Native American mascots and race. In R. A. Lind (Ed.), *Race/ Gender/Media: Considering diversity across audiences, content, and producers* (pp. 68–76). Boston: AB-Longman.

King, C. R. (2004). Borrowing power: Racial metaphors and pseudo-Indian mascots. *CR: The New Centennial Review, 4,* 189–209.

King, C. R. (in press). Being a warrior: Race, gender, and Native American mascots. *International Journal of the History of Sport, 23*(2). New York: Palgrave.

King, C. R., & Springwood, C. F. (2000). Choreographing colonialism: Athletic mascots, (dis)embodied Indians, and EuroAmerican subjectivities. *Cultural Studies: A Research Annual, 5,* 191–221.

King, C. R., & Springwood, C. F. (2001a). *Beyond the cheers: Race as spectacle in college sports.* Albany: State University of New York Press.

King, C. R., & Springwood, C. F. (Eds.). (2001b). *Team spirits: Essays on the history and significance of Native American mascots.* Lincoln: University of Nebraska.

King, C. R., Staurowsky, E. J., Baca, L., Davis, L. R., & Pewewardy, C. (2002). Of polls and race prejudice: *Sports Illustrated*'s errant "Indian Wars." *Journal of Sport and Social Issues, 26,* 382–403.

Kolb, J. J. (2001). Indian mascots: Activists say change needs to begin at home. *American Indian Report, 11,* 24–25.

Landreth, M. (2001). Becoming the Indians: Fashioning Arkansas State University Indians. In C. R. King & C. F. Springwood (Eds.), *Team spirits: Essays on the history and significance of Native American mascots* (pp. 46–63). Lincoln: University of Nebraska Press.

LeBeau, P. R. (2001). The fighting braves of Michigamua: Adapting vestiges of American Indian warriors in the halls of academia. In C. R. King & C. F. Springwood (Eds.), *Team spirits: Essays on the history and significance of Native American mascots.* Lincoln: University of Nebraska Press.

Likourezos, G. (1996). A case of first impression: American Indians seek cancellation of the trademarked term 'Redskins'." *Journal of the Patent and Trademark Office Society, 78,* 275–290.

Machamer, A. M. (2001). Last of the Mohicans, braves, and warriors: The end of American Indian mascots in Los Angeles public schools. In C. R. King & C. F. Springwood (Eds.), *Team spirits: Essays on the history and significance of Native American mascots* (pp. 208–220). Lincoln: University of Nebraska Press.

McEwan, P. J., & Belfield, C. (2004). *What happens when schools stop playing Indian?* Retrieved May 5, 2004, from http://www.wellesley.edu/Economics/mcewan/Papers/playing.pdf

National Spectator Association. (1999). *Fan poll.* Retrieved January 15, 2000, http://www.nsa.com/Poll1. cfm?Poll_ID=260

Native American Journalists Association. (2003). *Reading red report 2003: A call for the news media to recognize racism in sport team nicknames and mascots.* Retrieved February 22, 2004, http://www.naja. com/docs/2003ReadingRed.pdf

Nuessel, F. (1994). Objectionable sports team designations. *Names: A Journal of Onomastics, 42,* 101–119.

Pace, K. A. (1994). The Washington Redskins and the doctrine of disparagement. *Pepperdine Law Review, 22,* 7–57.

Peter Harris Research Group. (2002). *Methodology for* Sports Illustrated *survey on the use of Indian nicknames, mascots, etc.* Unpublished manuscript.

Pewewardy, C. D. (1991). Native American mascots and imagery: The struggle of unlearning Indian stereotypes. *Journal of Navaho Education, 9,* 19–23.

Pewewardy, C. D. (1998). Fluff and Feathers: Treatment of American Indians in the literature and the classroom. *Equity and Excellence in Education, 31,* 69–76.

Pewewardy, C. D. (2001). Educators and mascots: Challenging contradictions. In C. R. King & C. F. Springwood (Eds.), *Team spirits: Essays on the history and significance of Native American mascots* (pp. 257–279). Lincoln: University of Nebraska Press.

Pickle, D. (2002). Members to be queried on Indian mascot issue. *The NCAA News.* Retrieved November 4, 2002, from http://www.ncaa.org/news/2002/20020401/active/3907n02.html

Price, S. L. (2002, March 4). The Indian wars. *Sports Illustrated, 96*(10), 66–72.

Prochaska, D. (2001). At home in Illinois: Presence of Chief Illinwek, absence of Native Americans. In C. R. King & C. F. Springwood (Eds.), *Team spirits: Essays on the history and significance of Native American mascots* (pp. 157–188). Lincoln: University of Nebraska Press.

Rodriquez, R. (1998). Plotting the assassination of Little Red Sambo: Psychologists join war against racist campus mascots. *Black Issues in Higher Education, 15*(8), 20–24.

Rosenstein, J. (2001). "In whose honor?" Mascots, and the media. In C. R. King & C. F. Springwood (Eds.), *Team spirits: Essays on the history and significance of Native American mascots* (pp. 241–256). Lincoln: University of Nebraska Press.

Sabo, D., Jansen, S. C., Tate, D., Duncan, M. C., & Leggett, S. (1996). Televising international sport: race, ethnicity, and nationalistic bias. *Journal of Sport & Social Issues, 2,* 7–21.

Sigelman, L. (1998). Hail to the Redskins? Public reactions to a racially insensitive team name. *Sociology of Sport Journal, 15,* 317–325.

Simms, R. (2002, June 13). Do you favor or oppose keeping Native American mascots for high school, college, or professional sport teams. *King County Weekly Poll.* Retrieved November 4, 2002, from http://www.metrokc.gov/exec/survey/feedback mascots.html

Spindel, C. (2000). Dancing at halftime: Sports and the controversy over American Indian mascots. New York: New York University Press.

Splichal, S. (1999). *Public opinion: Developments and controversies in the Twentieth century.* Lanham, MD: Rowman & Littlefield.

Springwood, C. F. (2001). Playing Indian and fighting (for) mascots: Reading the complications of Native American and EuroAmerican alliances. In C. R. King & C. F. Springwood (Eds.), *Team spirits: Essays on the history and significance of Native American mascots.* Lincoln: University of Nebraska Press.

Springwood, C. F. (2004). "I'm Indian too!": Claiming Native American identity, crafting authority in mascot debates. *Journal of Sport and Social Issues, 28,* 56–70.

Springwood, C. F., & King, C. R. (2000). Race, power, and representation in contemporary American sport. In P. Kivisto & G. Rundblad (Eds.), *The color line at the dawn of the 21st century* (pp. 161–174). Thousand Oaks, CA: Pine Valley Press.

Stapleton, B. (2001). *Redskins: Racial slur or symbol of success?* San Jose, CA: Writers Club Press.

Staurowsky, E. J. (1998). An act of honor or exploitation? The Cleveland Indians' use of the Louis Francis Sockalexis story. *Sociology of Sport Journal, 15,* 299–316.

Staurowsky, E. J. (1999). American Indian imagery and the miseducation of America. *Quest, 51,* 382–392.

Staurowsky, E. J. (2000). The Cleveland Indians: A case study in cultural dispossession. *Sociology of Sport Journal, 17,* 307—330.

Staurowsky, E. J. (2001). Sockalexis and the making of the myth at the core of the Cleveland "Indians" imagery. In C. R. King & C. F. Springwood (Eds.), *Team spirits: Essays on the history and significance of Native American mascots* (pp. 82–107). Lincoln: University of Nebraska Press.

Staurowsky, E. J. (2004). Privilege at play: On the legal and social fictions that sustain American Indian sport imagery. *Journal of Sport and Social Issues, 28,* 11–29.

Strong, P. T. (2004). The mascot slot: Cultural citizenship, political correctness, and pseudo-Indian sports symbols. *Journal of Sport and Social Issues, 28,* 79–87.

Trainor, D. J. (1995). Native American mascots, schools and the Title VI hostile environment analysis. *University of Illinois Law Review, 5,* 971–997.

University of North Dakota. (2000). *Name commission poll.* Retrieved March 3, 2001, from http://www.und.edu/namecommission/index.html

USA Weekend. (1997). *Chief Wahoo Poll.* Retrieved December 12, 1997, from http://www.usaweekend.com/quick/results/chief_wahoo_qp_results.html

Vanderford, H. (1996). What's in a name? Heritage or hatred: The school mascot controversy. *Journal of Law and Education, 25,* 381–388.

34

Disability and Sport: (Non)Coverage of an Athletic Paradox

Marie Hardin

Pennsylvania State University

In sit volleyball, the players pivot and lunge, dive and spike, many of them with legless torsos supported by strong, agile arms. There's also wheelchair rugby, which sounds like a contradiction in terms until you see it. It's the down-and-dirty wheelchair sport, the roughest and most aggressive of them all. The players—all quadriplegics—crash and smash it up in the rugby tradition, though the game is played in a gym. Think rugby by way of bumper cars.

—Sportsjones.com (2001, August 24, para. 1)

Under the glare of an international media spotlight, thousands of able-bodied athletes from all over the globe vied for gold and glory during the August 2004 Olympic Games in Athens, Greece. When they left, they cleared the way for another elite sporting competition—second in size only to the Olympics—just days later at the same venue.

The biggest difference between the two events was not in the intensity of sport, the level of competition, the degree of nationalist pride, or even the occurrence of scandal (Golden, 2002; Nash, 2001). Instead the marker lay in awareness and publicity for the events. NBC, which owned exclusive broadcast rights to the Olympic Games in the United States, provided coverage 24 hours per day on its various networks. The network provided not even 1% of that level of coverage to the Paralympics, which followed in September and showcased 4,000 athletes from 140 countries (Paralympics, 2004). Americans interested in the Paralympics were forced to follow the Games on the Web, using mostly foreign media sites.

The blackout of Paralympic coverage continues an American media tradition that stretches back to the beginning of televised sports coverage. Even when the Paralympics take place in the United States, American journalists do a far poorer job of covering them than do foreign journalists (Golden, 2002). Witness the 2002 Games in Salt Lake City: Although NBC paid hundreds of millions of dollars for the rights to air the Olympics in prime time each night during the Games, the Paralympic Games garnered one hour of coverage by NBC: the opening ceremonies—two days after they occurred. For eight days, A&E aired a one-hour segment that highlighted the day's events; there was no comment from A&E on the money involved. National Public Radio did a segment prior to the Paralympic Games and interviewed the president of the International Paralympic Committee, Phillip Craven. Meanwhile, the nation's major newspapers (including *USA Today, The New York Times,* and *The Washington Post*) each ran hundreds of articles about the Olympics but a collective total of 13 about the Paralympics (Golden, 2002; Hardin & Hardin, 2003).

Noncoverage of the Paralympics is typical of the treatment afforded elite disabled athletes in general; it is as difficult to find serious mainstream coverage of disability sport as it is to find a hair on ESPN commentator Dick Vitale's head (Wasenius, 2003). Although participation by disabled athletes in elite competition is growing, mainstream media have persisted in their usual approach of exclusion and stereotyping (DePauw & Gavron, 1995; DePauw, 1997). For instance, marathoner Jean Driscoll's seventh win in the Boston Marathon's wheelchair division was framed as a social event in a 1996 edition of *Runner's World*; CBS aired six of seven events at the 1997 "World's Fastest Man" competition, opting not to air the race for the world's fastest amputee athletes (DePauw, 1997). It is easier to find a poker or billiards game on ESPN than to find coverage of disability sporting competition.

Organizers and promoters of disability sports events are constantly challenged to prove their legitimacy and must struggle to get coverage (Botelho, 2000). "The biggest challenge is the whole credibility and legitimacy issue. The reality is that the disabled sports movement is 15 years behind women's sports," said consultant and Paralympian Eli Wolff (Botelho, 2000, para. 9).

THE PARADOX PRESENTED BY DISABLED SPORT

In light of the lack of coverage, it is not surprising that many people who consider themselves die-hard sports fans are not aware of disability athletics. The thought of an athlete with a disability competing in mainstream sports may seem unimaginable—even ludicrous—to sports fans accustomed to the ideal body standard so prized in U.S. culture (DePauw, 1997). "Disability sport has not been viewed as legitimate sport, but rather as something less . . . Opportunities, rewards, public recognition and the like have not been afforded athletes with disabilities" (DePauw & Gavron, 1995, p. 10). Because of cultural norms regarding the body and athleticism in U.S. culture, the notion of *disabled sport* may be likened to the ideological paradox also presented by the notion of *lesbian mother* (Cherney, 2003; DePauw & Gavron, 1995; Golden, 2002; Hardin, Lynn, & Walsdorf, 2003; Thompson, 2002).

Because of an overwhelming emphasis on physicality in sport, athletes with disabilities are an especially marginalized group, and among the most recent (along with gay and lesbian athletes) to begin fighting for front-gate entrance to athletic halls and fields (Hardin & Hardin, 2003). Many individuals with disabilities do not view their bodies as entirely weak, frail, and imperfect, perhaps explaining the increase in their sports participation and the development of a national, thriving network for disabled sport (DePauw, 1997; Hoffer, 1995). A number of organizations in the United States, including Disabled Sports USA, Wheelchair Sports USA, and the National Disability Sports Alliance, support competitive disabled athletes who compete in adapted versions of virtually every sport. Another nod to athletes with disabilities came in 2002, when the ESPY Awards added that category to its roster of annual honors for athletes. Visually impaired climber Erik Weihenmayer won the first ESPY award for a disabled athlete. Another boost to disability sport in the United States came when the U.S. Olympic Committee created the U.S. Paralympics division in May 2001 to focus efforts on enhancing programs, funding, and opportunities for people with physical disabilities to participate in Paralympic sport.

Sports Illustrated writer Hoffer (1995), in one of the few mainstream sports articles written on the disability sports movement, acknowledged the "explosion" in participation and the competitive legitimacy: "Really, the distinction between wheelchair racers and the Olympians is fading at these high levels" (p. 65). A look at the records for able-bodied and disability sports clarifies his point. Donovan Bailey's Olympic record in the men's 100 meters is 9.84 seconds; the Paralympic record, set by Nigerian arm amputee Adjibola Adeoye, is 10.72 seconds. In four powerlifting categories, Paralympic records exceed world records for able-bodied competitors (Sports, 2004). Participation in sport "demonstrates that individuals with disabilities are more able and similar to their non-disabled peers than stereotypes suggest" (Taub, Blinde, & Greer, 1999, p. 1469).

SPORT, THE BODY, AND U.S. CULTURAL HEGEMONY

Yet scholars argue that athletes with disabilities are perceived as weak and dependent, thus not valid in terms of sport. Disabled athletes report high levels of stigmatization—being stared at or having their entire identities construed in terms of their disabilities (Ashton-Shaeffer, Gibson, Autry, & Hanson, 2001).

In many ways, people with disabilities who participate in the world of sport provide prima facie contradictions to accepted societal norms regarding disability (Hardin & Hardin, 2003). Those who dare enter the realm of sport are, in a sense, participating in resistance to cultural hegemony by the very act of picking up a ball or a barbell. Their active participation in sport appears as a contradiction, because sport (like life in U.S. culture) has been constructed as an able-bodied activity (DePauw, 1997).

U.S. Cultural Hegemony, Media, and Sport

The theory of cultural hegemony, rooted in the writings of Antonio Gramsci, may help explain cultural resistance to disability sport in the United States. Hegemony may be defined as the perpetuation of ideological norms that serve the most powerful groups in a culture; in other words, ideas presented in the culture as common sense serve some groups while oppressing others (Altheide, 1984; Condit, 1994; Croteau & Hoynes, 2000; Holtzman, 2000). Social structures and relationships that help some but disadvantage others are presented as natural. Social relations and political policy are framed within a worldview that serves the powerful but has gained passive acceptance ("that's the way it is") from other groups oppressed by it.

Mass media are crucial to the function of cultural hegemony in the United States (Croteau & Hoynes, 2000; Herman & Chomsky, 1988; Holtzman, 2000). Media inculcate individuals with values essential to institutional structures in society by adopting dominant assumptions and framing content within them (Croteau & Hoynes, 2000). Hegemonic ideas are presented as universally valid, and alternative views are appropriated into the dominant frame (Artz & Murphy, 2000; Condit, 1994).

Sport is also considered by scholars to be a powerful hegemonic institution in the United States (DePauw, 1997). Sport reflects the dominant values, norms, and standards of the culture in which it operates; the inequity in sport is reproduced in the form of social inequalities, and vice versa (Hardin & Hardin, 2003).

Moral Order of the Body

Sport media are ideal sites to reinforce American cultural values, such as respect for authority, individualism, sacrificing for the team, and hard work. American culture glorifies tales of the rugged individualist by rejecting interdependence as weak and undesirable (Barr, 2000). Autonomy and physical fitness are valued, and physical dependence is generally viewed with disdain (Ashton-Shaeffer, et al., 2001). The sport–media complex reinforces this dominant ideology as common sense through its obsession with the ideal body, one that is fit and able to contribute to economic production (Hahn, 1988; Hargreaves, 1994). Sports deemed most popular in U.S. culture are those that reinforce male hegemony through emphasis on strength, power, height, and weight (Sage, 1990). Bodies deemed most valuable (male, able-bodied) are placed at the top of a "moral order" of the body; gender/sexuality, race, and able-bodiedness are factors in what is deemed the *norm* versus the *deviant* (Hahn, 1988; Hall, 1996, 1997).

Disability, perhaps more than any other difference from the standard, is considered deviant (Hahn, 1988). The link between hegemonically defined sport and the ideal body reflects emphasis on a normalized body in the larger culture.

Because they fall outside the norm—what is culturally desirable—people with disabilities are rendered invisible. The ideal body is one that fits an environment constructed for the majority; people with disabilities are a liability for their inability to navigate that environment (Davis, 1999). This is especially true in sport, where the ideal body is idolized and anything less is viewed with disdain. Murphy wrote (1995), "[W]e are subverters of an American Ideal, just as the poor betray the American Dream. And to the extent that we depart from the ideal, we become ugly and repulsive to the able-bodied" (p. 143).

Perhaps the most literal case of disability as liability in sport during recent years has been in coverage of Casey Martin, a PGA golfer who appealed to the U.S. Supreme Court for the right to use a golf cart. Casey was sometimes vilified by media columnists and commentators who believed he should not have received accommodation from the PGA (Jenkins, 2001).

COVERAGE OF DISABILITY SPORT

Despite the continuing progress in technology, legal rights, and sports participation, athletes with disabilities continue to be stigmatized because their bodies do not reflect the socially constructed norm (Shapiro, 1993; Taub, et al., 1999). People with disabilities have historically been excluded from the sport–media complex because of their failure to meet hegemonically prescribed ideals of physicality (DePauw, 1997).

Thus, noncoverage of athletes with disabilities is the norm for American media. Research on visual representations of people with disabilities and sport shows a pattern of almost complete exclusion. A study by Maas and Hasbrook (2001) examined photos in golf magazines and found no representation of golfers with visible disabilities. Studies of women's sports magazines in 1999 and in 2003 found the same results: Female athletes with disabilities were shut out (Hardin, et al., 2003; Schell, 1999). A study of the only major children's sports magazine in the United States, *Sports Illustrated for Kids*, found that children with disabilities are virtually invisible in that magazine, reinforcing to young readers the hegemonic notion that sport is a realm for the able bodied (Hardin, Hardin, Lynn, & Walsdorf, 2001).

Coverage of the Paralympic Games, which officially began in 1960 with 400 athletes from 23 countries, has historically been sparse (History, 2004). Coverage of the Salt Lake City Paralympics in 2002, which drew disabled athletes from all over the globe, was virtually nonexistent in U.S. media except for coverage by the A&E Network (Golden, 2002). Golden, who interviewed sports reporters at the Olympics and the Paralympics, found that many American journalists did not view disabled sports as valid because the journalists believed the disabled athletes could not be competitive. Golden (2002) quoted an American broadcast reporter who said about disabled athletes and the Paralympics: "They can't compete on the same level as the Olympic athletes, so it's a bone they throw to them to make them feel better. It's not a real competition, and I, for one, don't see why I should have to cover it" (p. 13).

Another reporter, from a large-circulation newspaper, said he didn't see the Olympics and Paralympics as equitable: "It [the Paralympics] is not a real competition. You wouldn't hold a high school tournament in Yankee Stadium. You wouldn't hold an amateur competition at Madison Square Garden" (Golden, 2002, p. 13).

Golden (2002) found that major American newspapers published from zero to five articles apiece on the 2002 Paralympics, compared with hundreds of stories during the Olympics. Although newspapers in other countries, such as Britain, Germany, and France, publish more articles covering the Paralympics, scholars say the coverage reflects emphasis on an able-bodied ideal for Paralympic athletes (Thomas & Smith, 2003) or an undue emphasis on national success and medal rankings (Schantz & Gilbert, 2001).

Disabled athletes who train and compete at the highest levels express frustration at their systematic exclusion. One athlete, a wheelchair basketball player who often calls in game scores to a local newspaper, said he is shut out by sports editors: "They put in pages of high school sports, and yet they refuse to put [us] in … That's so stupid! We're athletes … One thing people probably don't realize is that there's 53 million disabled people out there. We're probably the largest single group in the country" (Hardin & Hardin, 2003, p. 255).

The "Supercrip"

Over the past decade, coverage of disability sports has increased ever so slightly (Schantz & Gilbert, 2001). However, authors of the most recent studies acknowledge that the type of coverage has not improved. Reporters still focus primarily on the "disabled" instead of the "athlete"; when athletes with disabilities are covered, they are usually covered as feature stories instead of sports stories (Schantz & Gilbert, 2001; Shapiro, 1993).

This de-emphasizes the athlete's sporting accomplishments. One wheelchair basketball player, ranked as a top player in the world during the 1990s, said he'd rather not see coverage of disabled athletics if it is "going to make the general public say, 'Ah, wow, the poor pitiful soul'":

> Talk about that person's athletic abilities or the team's athletic accomplishments, and it's OK to mention a disability, because that's what makes the person who he or she is, but you don't focus in. The interest should not be that person's disability.... Maybe the people in the media need to have an in-service or a memo that says, 'These guys would rather be treated as athletes when you're dealing with a sporting event, so let's put the emphasis there' (Hardin & Hardin, 2004).

When athletes with disabilities do break into mainstream sports pages, it is either in a story of the "supercrip" mold or a story involving controversy over the disabled athlete (Schantz & Gilbert, 2001; Schell & Rodriguez, 2001; Stone, 2001). The supercrip model, which emphasizes the person with a disability as overcoming a disability to lead a normal life (Clogston, 1991; Shapiro, 1993), is common. The supercrip model supports cultural hegemony in that it rests on the common-sense assumption that disability is an individual condition, one for which the larger society has no obligation for accommodation. Thus, media use of the supercrip model assumes that people with disabilities are pitiful (and useless), until they overcome their disabilities through rugged individualism and pull off a feat considered heroic by the mainstream (Iwakuma, 1997; Schell & Rodriguez, 2001; Shapiro, 1993). Perhaps the feat is climbing Mt. Everest as a blind person or playing basketball in a wheelchair (Hardin & Hardin, 2003).

Erik Weihenmayer, a 32-year-old blind mountain climber who conquered Everest in 2001, was framed as a supercrip in extensive media coverage (Hardin & Hardin, 2004; Kahn, 2001). He was hailed as a hero in media accounts and compared to blind pioneers like Helen Keller. "His Everest trip has that historic feel to it," read a story in *The Boston Globe* (Ingold, 2001, p. B2).

Although the attention to Weihenmayer was praised, it was also criticized by disability advocates. Kathi Wolfe, a blind journalist who often writes about disability issues, wrote that after Weihenmayer's climb, she was approached by well-meaning people and asked when she, too, would climb Everest (Wolfe, 2001). She wrote:

> One of us bursts onto the cultural radar screen as a superhero, and all of us are expected to perform amazing feats... Supercrips are everywhere in the media. The person with no use of her arms who paints masterpieces with her feet, the guy with Tourette's syndrome who becomes a radio announcer. Stephen Hawking explaining the universe from his wheelchair. And, of course, that blind mountain climber... The supercrip exacerbates the already difficult challenges that people with disabilities face. If we hear enough such stories we may feel defeated by comparison. (p. B4)

More progressive media models recognize the social construction of disability, the rights of people with disabilities, and the roles of people with disabilities as multifaceted and unlimited (Haller, 2000). Proponents of fair and equitable coverage of disability sports prefer progressive coverage, as have disabled athletes through self-framing during media interviews (DePauw, 1997; Hardin & Hardin, 2004; Schell & Rodriguez, 2001).

However, athletes who attempt to cast themselves away from the supercrip mold find resistance. Researchers who analyzed coverage of 1996 Paralympian Hope Lewellen found distinct use of the supercrip model by CBS as an overlay to Lewellen's own attempt to frame herself as an athlete who was part of a larger, culturally diverse sport world (Schell & Rodriguez, 2001). CBS insisted on attempting to frame Lewellen as a supercrip who overcame the odds to emerge as a model of disability, instead of as a genuine athlete. Analysis of CBS' overall coverage of the 1996 Paralympics revealed the same pattern; commentators "often dramatized the enormously difficult challenges and obstacles faced by athletes with disabilities," and the network featured "supercrip par excellence" Christopher Reeve (Schell & Duncan, 1999, p. 43). Similar research on print sport media finds the same kinds of results. The focus of articles is on how athletes cope with their conditions, instead of on the performances of these athletes in their sports (Schantz & Gilbert, 2001).

THE FUTURE: RECASTING DISABILITY SPORTS COVERAGE

Although disability sports continue to thrive in the United States, their growth is limited unless they receive adequate media coverage. Without fair and accurate coverage, athletes are denied financial opportunities (through media exposure and sponsorships) afforded to able-bodied athletes. As Hoffer (1995), wrote, disabled athletes "have been condemned to sport's netherworld, where most of the attention they do get is unflattering and maddening" (p. 64).

American sports media producers who dare cover competitive disability events, such as the Paralympics, know the potential of such sports coverage as exciting and entertaining, in the same spirit as able-bodied competition. Ian Furness, a commentator with the A&E Network during the 2002 Paralympics in Salt Lake City, told an interviewer: "Just because these athletes face some challenges physically doesn't mean they're not competitive... For somebody to say that these guys aren't competitive—that's wrong, because they are. When they say that, they [the Olympic reporters] have never seen a [Paralympic] event" (Golden, 2002, p. 19).

Furness points to the need for media producers to become educated about disability sports; many, for instance, still confuse the Paralympics with the Special Olympics, a national program of sporting events for individuals with cognitive disabilities (The Paralympic Games, 1996). However, changes in the U.S. media approach to disability sport will not take place until normative ideology about sport, competition, and the ideal body is expanded in such a way as to address the unfair, hegemonic power relations in sport and society. Coverage of disability athletics by the U.S. sport–media complex should reflect acceptance and accommodation of sporting bodies that deviate from the norm in a culture that overtly prides itself on democratic, egalitarian values.

Such a revisioning of competitive sport would open doors to a richer, more diverse array of media offerings. Further, it would help level the playing field for one of the most disenfranchised minority groups in U.S. culture. As DePauw (2003) wrote, perhaps soon "we will be better able to see individuals with a disability as they often view themselves—not as 'deviant,' nor their bodies as weak or frail, or even imperfect" (p. 361).

REFERENCES

Altheide, D. L. (1984). Media hegemony: A failure of perspective. *Public Opinion Quarterly, 48*, 476–490.

Artz, L., & Murphy, B. O. (2000). *Cultural hegemony in the United States.* Thousand Oaks: Sage.

Ashton-Shaeffer, C., Gibson, H. J., Autry, C. E., & Hanson, C. (2001). Meaning of sport to adults with physical disabilities: A disability sports camp experience. *Sociology of Sport Journal, 18*, 95–114.

Barr, G. W. (2000). Out of sight, out of mind. *America, 183*(19), 15–16.

Botelho, G. (2000, Oct. 23). Paralympics making great strides. *CNNfyi.com.* Retrieved April 4, 2004, from http://wwww.cnn.com/2000/fyi/news/10/23/paralympics

Cherney, J. (2003). *Sport as ableist institution: "Body is Able," Casey Martin, and the PGA Tour, Inc.* Unpublished manuscript.

Clogston, J. S. (1991). Reporters' attitudes toward and newspaper coverage of persons with disabilities. (Doctoral dissertation, Michigan State University). *Dissertation Abstracts International, 53*, 230.

Condit, C. (1994). Hegemony in a mass-mediated society: Concordance about reproductive technologies. *Critical Studies in Media Communication, 11*(3), 205–223.

Croteau, D., & Hoynes, W. (2000). *Media/Society* (2nd ed.). Thousand Oaks, CA: Pine Forge Press.

Davis, L. J. (1999). J'Accuse! Cultural imperialism-ableist style. *Social Alternatives, 18*(1), 1–5.

DePauw, K. (1997). The (in)visibility of disability: Cultural contexts and 'sporting bodies.' *Quest, 49*, 416–430.

DePauw, K. (2003). Social-cultural context of disability. In S. Eitzen & G. Sage (Eds.), *Sociology of North Americans sport* (p. 361). Boston: McGraw-Hill.

DePauw, K., & Gavron, S. (1995). *Disability and sport.* Champaign, IL: Human Kinetics.

Golden, A. (2002, August). *An analysis of the dissimilar coverage of the 2002 Olympics and Paralympics: Frenzied pack journalism versus the empty press room.* Paper presented at the Association for Education in Journalism and Mass Communication Annual Meeting, Miami, FL.

Hahn, H. (1988). Advertising the acceptably employable image: Disability and capitalism,' *Policy Studies Journal, 15*(3), 551–570.

Hall, M. A. (1996). *Feminism & sporting bodies.* Champaign, IL: Human Kinetics.

Hall, S. (1997). The spectacle of the "other." In W. H. Hall (Ed.), *Representation: Cultural representations and signifying practices* (pp. 350–365). Thousand Oaks: Sage.

Haller, B. (2000). If they limp, they lead? News representations and the hierarchy of disability images. In D. Braithwaite & T. Thompson (Eds.), *Handbook of communication and people with disabilities* (pp. 273–288). Mahwah, NJ: Lawrence Erlbaum Associates.

Hardin, B., & Hardin, M. (2003). Conformity and conflict: Wheelchair athletes discuss sport media. *Adapted Physical Education Quarterly, 20*(3), 246–259.

Hardin, B., & Hardin, M. (2004). The 'Supercrip' in sport media: Wheelchair athletes discuss hegemony's disabled hero. *Sociology of Sport Online, 7*(1). Retrieved May 14, 2004 from http://physed.otago.ac.nz/sosol/v7i1/v7i1.html

Hardin, B., Hardin, M., Lynn, S., & Walsdorf, K. (2001). Missing in action? Images of disability in *Sports Illustrated for Kids. Disability Studies Quarterly, 2*(2), 21–32. Retrieved May 14, 2004 from http://www.cds.hawaii.edu/dsq

Hardin, M., Lynn, S., & Walsdorf, K. (2003, August). *Depicting the sporting body: The intersection of disability with gender and race in women's sport/fitness magazines.* Paper presented to the Disability Issues Caucus of the National Communication Association, Miami, FL.

Hargreaves, J. (1994). *Sporting females.* London: Routledge.

Herman, E., & Chomsky, N. (1988). *Manufacturing consent.* New York: Pantheon Books.

History (2004). *Athens 2004 Paralympic Games.* Retrieved May 14, 2004, from http://www.athens2004/page/legacy?

Hoffer, R. (1995, August 14). Ready, willing and able. *Sports Illustrated, 83*(7), 64–74.

Holtzman, L. (2000). *Media messages.* Armonk, NY: M. E. Sharpe.

Ingold, J. (2001, June 14). Blind climber at the peak of fame. *The Denver Post*, p. B2.

Iwakuma, M. (1997, August). *From pity to pride: People with disabilities, the media, and an emerging disability culture.* Paper presented at the Association for Education in Journalism and Mass Communication Annual Meeting, Chicago.

Jenkins, S. (2001, May 30). A good walk is truly spoiled. *The Washington Post*, p. D1.

Kahn, J. (2001, June 27). Touching the sky: Having conquered Everest, blind climber Erik Weihenmayer is still looking up. *The Boston Globe*, p. F1.

Maas, K. W., & Hasbrook, C. A. (2001). Media promotion of the paradigm citizen/golfer: An analysis of golf magazines' representations of disability, gender, and age. *Sociology of Sport Journal, 18*, 21–36.

Murphy, R. (1995). Encounters: The body silent in America. *Disability and culture.* Berkeley, CA: University of California Press.

Nash, E. (2001, July 22). We are not the champions. *The (London) Independent*, p. 18–22.

The Paralympic Games and Special Olympics: What are the differences? (1996, August 16). *PR Newswire*. Retrieved June 1, 2004, from http://www.prnewswire.co.uk/cgi/news/release?id=25141

The Paralympics paradox (2001, August 24). *Sportsjones.com*. Retrieved May 31, 2004, from http://www.sportsjones.com/sj/147-6.shtml

Paralympics 2004: The independent guide to the 2004 Paralympic Games from Athens. Retrieved May 14, 2004, from http://www.paralympics.com/index.htm

Sage, G. (1990). *Power and ideology in American sport*. Champaign, IL: Human Kinetics.

Schantz, O., & Gilbert, K. (2001). An ideal misconstrued: Newspaper coverage of the Atlanta Paralympic Games in France and Germany. *Sociology of Sport Journal, 18*, 69–94.

Schell, B., & Rodriguez, S. (2001). Subverting bodies/ambivalent representations: media analysis of Paralympian, Hope Lewellen. *Sociology of Sport Journal, 18*, 127–135.

Schell, L. A. (1999). Socially constructing the female athlete: A monolithic media representation of active women. (Doctoral dissertation, Texas Women's University, Denton). *Dissertation Abstracts International, 61*, 397.

Schell, L. A. & Duncan, M. D., (1999). A content analysis of CBS' coverage of the 1996 Paralympic Games. *Adapted Physical Activity Quarterly 16*, 27–47.

Shapiro, J. (1993). *No pity: People with disabilities forging a new civil rights movement*. New York: Times Books.

Sports. (2004). *Athens 2004 Paralympic Games*. Retrieved May 14, 2004, from http://www.athens2004.com/athens2004

Stone, E. (2001). Disability, sport, and the body in China. *Sociology of Sport Journal, 18*, 51–68.

Taub, D., Blinde, E., & Greer, K. (1999). Stigma management through participation in sport and physical activity: Experiences of male college students with physical disabilities. *Human Relations, 52*(11), 1469.

Thomas, N., & Smith, A. (2003). Preoccupied with able-bodiedness? An analysis of British media coverage of the 2000 Paralympic Games. *Adapted Physical Activity Quarterly 20*(2), 166–182.

Thompson, J. (2002). *Mommy queerest: Contemporary rhetorics of lesbian maternal identity*. Amherst: University of Massachusetts Press.

Wasenius, B. (2003, July 2). Former MLC center reflects on All-American career. *Fremont Tribune*, Section B, p. 1.

Wolfe, K. (2001, July 1). He's your inspiration, not mine. *The Washington Post*, p. B4.

Author Index

Subject Index